Dear Student,

You are about to begin a journey, perhaps with enthusiasm, or maybe because your study path requires a course in economics. Let's think about this journey as a trip down Economics Road. Because I've been down that road before, I can tell you a little about what you can expect.

You are going to read about the basics of economics. The basics constitute the nuts and bolts of economics – topics such as supply and demand, price elasticity of demand, market structures, competition, gross domestic product, unemployment, inflation, interest rates, economic policy, and more.

Not only will the basics provide you with various new ideas to learn about, but the basics will also provide you with certain economic tools – tools that will be used throughout your study of economics to analyze different settings.

Continuing on down the road, you are also going to learn how to apply some of the economic tools you acquire, and why applying these tools matters to you, whether you will go on to continue studying economics or not. You know the old saying, "Give a man a fish and you feed him for a day, but teach a man to fish, and you feed him for life." We don't want you to learn economics the way some people learn foreign languages: They get A's on all the tests, but in the end they can't speak the language. We want you to learn the language of economics, and then we want you to be able to use it – to analyze the world in which you live. Many real-life applications in this book will help you to do this.

Finally, a major pit stop along Economics Road will be at a place called "Thinking Like an Economist." It is not enough to learn the basics of economics, and it's not enough to know how to use some of the analytical tools; we also need to know something about how economists think.

To some degree, we learn how economists think by applying the tools of economics in various settings. In other words, sometimes we learn how economists think by doing what economists do.

But often more is needed. Sometimes it is incumbent upon economists to step back from their analysis, and tell their audience about the perspective they are using to get answers to their questions. We do that regularly in this book. For those of you who want a bigger dose of learning how to think like an economist, I have written a small book, **How to Think Like an Economist,** that seeks to show you, through various examples, how economists view the world and how they solve problems and answer questions.

Is it worthwhile to travel down Economics Road? Many people think so. For many students, just a short 10 to 15 weeks of studying economics leaves them understanding so much more about the world in which they live and work. They read an economics article in a magazine and understand it; they see an economic report on television and know more about what is going on; they begin to use economic analysis to understand their own, everyday world better.

One last point: a warning of sorts. As you proceed down Economics Road, don't think an economics textbook (like this one) can be read the same way a popular novel can be. When reading a popular novel, the reading is usually easy, and understanding often comes quickly. Rarely do people go back to reread passages. That is not how an economics textbook reads. We have done our best to make this economics textbook readable – but no matter what we do, it will never be as easy and quick a read as a popular novel will be. Sometimes you will have to read a passage more than once, often you will have to reread a section. It takes sustained effort – and some dedicated patience – to learn economics. But, as we said this journey is well worth it. You might even think of your journey down Economics Road as a mapping expedition that will continue to help guide you on future journeys in your academic, professional, and personal pursuits.

The best of luck as you begin your study of economics.

Roger A. Arnold

Roger A. Arnold
California State University San Marcos

economics

8e

economics

8e

Roger A. Arnold

California State University San Marcos

THOMSON
™
SOUTH-WESTERN

Australia · Brazil · Canada · Mexico · Singapore · Spain · United Kingdom · United States

THOMSON
★
SOUTH-WESTERN
™

Economics, **8th edition**
Roger A. Arnold

VP/Editorial Director:
Jack W. Calhoun

VP/Editor-in-Chief:
Alex von Rosenberg

Sr. Acquisitions Editor:
Michael W. Worls

Sr. Developmental Editor:
Jennifer E. Baker

Sr. Marketing Manager:
Brian Joyner

Content Project Manager:
Jennifer A. Ziegler

Technology Project Manager:
Dana Cowden

Sr. Manufacturing Coordinator:
Sandee Milewski

Production House:
Lachina Publishing Services

Printer:
Quebecor World
Taunton, MA

Art Director:
Michelle Kunkler

Cover and Internal Designer:
c miller design

Cover Images:
© Illustration Works/Michael Bishop

Photography Manager:
Deanna Ettinger

Photography Researchers:
Terri Miller

Library of Congress Control Number:
2006938030

For more information about our
products, contact us at:
Thomson Learning Academic
Resource Center
1-800-423-0563

Thomson Higher Education
5191 Natorp Boulevard
Mason, OH 45040
USA

To
Sheila, Daniel,
and David

Contents

MACROECONOMICS

Part 2 Macroeconomic Fundamentals

Part 3 Macroeconomic Stability, Instability, and Fiscal Policy

chapter

7

Aggregate Demand and Aggregate Supply 152

chapter

8

The Self-Regulating Economy 177

Part 4 Money, the Economy, and Monetary Policy

Part 5 Expectations and Growth

MICROECONOMICS

Part 6 Microeconomic Fundamentals

Behavioral Economics 388

Are People Willing to Reduce Others' Incomes? 388   Is $1 Always $1? 389   Coffee Mugs and the Endowment Effect 390   Does the Endowment Effect Hold Only for New Traders? 391

A Reader Asks 392

Analyzing the Scene 393

Chapter Summary 393

Key Terms and Concepts 394

Questions and Problems 394

Working with Numbers and Graphs 395

Appendix C: Budget Constraint and Indifference Curve Analysis 396

The Budget Constraint 396

Slope of the Budget Constraint 396   What Will Change the Budget Constraint? 397

Indifference Curves 397

Constructing an Indifference Curve 398

Characteristics of Indifference Curves 398

The Indifference Map and the Budget Constraint Come Together 401

From Indifference Curves to a Demand Curve 402

Appendix Summary 403

Questions and Problems 404

chapter

19

Production and Costs 405

Why Firms Exist 406

The Market and the Firm: Invisible Hand Versus Visible Hand 406   The Alchian and Demsetz Answer 406   Shirking in a Team 406   Ronald Coase on Why Firms Exist 407   Markets: Outside and Inside the Firm 408

The Firm's Objective: Maximizing Profit 408

Accounting Profit Versus Economic Profit 410   Zero Economic Profit Is Not as Bad as It Sounds 411

features

economics *24/7*

Do Secretaries Who
Work for Investment Banks
Earn More Than Secretaries
Who Work for Hotels?
409

High School Students,
Staying Out Late, and More
417

What Matters to Global
Competitiveness?
421

"I Have to Become an
Accountant"
424

Production 411

Production in the Short Run 412   Marginal Physical Product and Marginal Cost 414   Average Productivity 416

Costs of Production: Total, Average, Marginal 417

The AVC and ATC Curves in Relation to the MC Curve 419   Tying Short-Run Production to Costs 422   One More Cost Concept: Sunk Cost 422

Production and Costs in the Long Run 426

Long-Run Average Total Cost Curve 426   Economies of Scale, Diseconomies of Scale, and Constant Returns to Scale 427   Why Economies of Scale? 428   Why Diseconomies of Scale? 428   Minimum Efficient Scale and Number of Firms in an Industry 428

Shifts in Cost Curves 429

Taxes 429 Input Prices 429 Technology 429

Part 7 Product Markets and Policies

Part 8 Factor Markets and Related Isues

chapter

29

features
economics *24/7*

THE GLOBAL ECONOMY

Part 10 International Economics and Globalization

chapter

30

PRACTICAL ECONOMICS

Part 11 Financial Matters

features

economics *24/7*

Is There Genius When It Comes to Picking Stocks?
721

Are Some Economists Poor Investors?
724

$1.3 Quadrillion
727

ECONOMICS, 8E

Arnold continues to set the standard for clear, balanced, and thorough coverage of principles of economics that truly engages students. With four new chapters, easy customization, and fully integrated digital and course management options, *Economics, 8e* is the perfect solution for your classroom. Packed with intriguing pop culture examples to which students relate, the text bolsters student interest in economics by describing the unexpected places economics occurs, illustrating how economic forces link events around the world to their lives, and demonstrating how economics can be used as a tool in understanding the world. In addition, the eighth edition is integrated with such powerful resources as ThomsonNOW™, Aplia™, and the Tomlinson Videos.

NEW Macro & Micro Themes: A new organizing feature in the 8th edition is the use of Macro and Micro themes to help students understand the big questions that macro- and microeconomists seek to answer. Framing the content through these major themes helps readers to see how the themes and policies are interconnected. Macroeconomics is organized into understanding price level and GDP, economics stability vs. instability, and policy efficacy. Microeconomics themes are objectives of the individual or firm, constraints on the individual or firm, and choices made given the objectives and constraints.

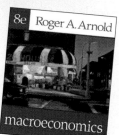

NEW Chapters: Arnold continues to set the standard for clear, current, and topical economic coverage. All-new chapters on globalization and financial markets cover two areas of increasing importance to readers as they try to understand the implications of news stories they hear and see on these issues. In addition, innovative online chapters cover agriculture and international impacts of macroeconomics, giving instructors flexibility in tailoring courses to topics they want to cover.

Economics 24/7: Illustrating the practical relevance of economic concepts, this intriguing feature explores anything and everything that can be better explained through economic analysis. For example, why is Fox's series *24* so suspenseful? Why are airlines so often overbooked? How does supply and demand work on the highway? Economics 24/7 trains readers to look for economic forces at work everywhere around them— and understand the principles behind them.

ThomsonNOW™ Teaching Tools: Part of the text's fully integrated course management system, this time-saving suite of online tools offers unrivaled course planning and management tools, enabling instructors to pinpoint how well students master key concepts. Instructors can assign personalized study plans (a pre- and post-assessment of student knowledge with resources to reinforce concepts), view results in their gradebook, and then gear lectures around student needs. With its proven ease of use and efficient paths to success, it delivers the results instructors want—NOW. ThomsonNOW™ can be integrated with WebCT® and Blackboard®.

Personalizing Your *Economics*, 8e... with Custom and Tomlinson

Thomson Custom Solutions develops personalized solutions to meet your economics education needs. Match your learning materials to your syllabus and create the perfect learning solution. Consider the following when looking at your customization options for any Thomson Economics texts:

- Remove chapters you do not cover, or rearrange their order to create a streamlined and efficient text that students will appreciate.
- Add your own material to cover new topics or information, saving you time and providing students a fully integrated course resource.
- Include contemporary economic issues from our Economic Issues Collection, found on our custom website. Many of these issues are brief and applied, ideally suited for the introductory Principles of Economics course.

Thomson Custom Solutions offers the fastest and easiest way to create unique customized learning materials delivered the way you want. Our custom solutions also include: accessing on-demand cases from leading business case providers such as *Harvard Business School Publishing, Ivey, Darden* and *NACRA,* building a tailored text online with www.textchoice2.com, and publishing your original materials. For more information about custom publishing options, visit www.thomsoncustom.com or contact your local Thomson representative.

Thomson South-Western is excited to announce three new video lecture products featuring award-winning teacher and professional communicator Steven Tomlinson (Ph.D, Stanford). These new web-based lecture videos—*Economics with Steven Tomlinson, Economic JumpStart®,* and *Economic LearningPath®*—are sure to engage your students, while reinforcing the economic concepts they need to know.

Visit www.thomsonedu.com/economics for more details about this new video series!

ThomsonNOW™

Designed by the instructor for the instructor, ThomsonNOW™ is the most reliable, flexible, and easy-to-use online suite of services and resources. ThomsonNOW™ for *Economics,* 8e takes the best of current technology tools including online homework management; a fully customizable test bank; and course support materials such as online quizzing, videos, and tutorials to support your course goals and save you significant preparation and grading time!

This powerful, fully integrated online teaching and learning system provides you with the ultimate in flexibility, ease of use, and efficient paths to success to deliver the results you want—NOW!

- **Plan** student assignments with easy online homework management.
- **Manage** your grade book with ease.
- **Teach** today's student using valuable course support materials.
- **Reinforce** student comprehension with personalized learning paths.
- **Test** with a customizable test bank.
- **Grade** automatically for seamless, immediate results.

Find Out More!

We are confident that you will find that ThomsonNOW™ for Economics is the most reliable, easy-to-use, online suite of services and resources ever developed. For more information, visit **www.thomsonedu.com/thomsonnow** or contact your local Thomson South-Western representative today!

Thomson is proud to continue our partnership with Aplia™ Inc.! Created by Paul Romer, one of the nation's leading economists, Aplia enhances teaching and learning by providing online interactive tools and experiments that help economics students become "active learners." Our partnership allows a tight content correlation between *Economics,* 8e and Aplia's online tools.

Students Come to Class Prepared

It is a proven fact that students do better in their course work if they come to class prepared. Aplia's activities are engaging and based on discovery learning, requiring students to take an active role in the learning process. When assigned online homework, students are more apt to read the text, come to class better prepared to participate in discussions, and are more able to relate to the economic concepts and theories presented. Learning by doing helps students feel involved, gain confidence in the materials, and see important concepts come to life.

Assign Homework in an Effective and Efficient Way

Now you can assign homework without increasing your workload! Together, *Economics* and Aplia provide the best text and technology resources to give you multiple teaching and learning solutions. Through Aplia, you can assign problem sets and online activities that automatically give feedback and are tracked and graded, all without requiring additional effort. Since Aplia's assignments are closely integrated with *Economics,* 8e, your students are applying what they have learned from the text to their homework.

Contact your local Thomson South-Western Representative to find out how you can incorporate this exciting technology into your course. **www.aplia.com/thomson**.

This book could not have been written and published without the generous expert assistance of many people. A deep debt of gratitude is owed to the reviewers of the first through seventh editions and to the reviewers of this edition, the eighth.

First Edition Reviewers

Jack Adams
University of Arkansas, Little Rock

William Askwig
University of Southern Colorado

Michael Babcock
Kansas State University

Dan Barszcz
College of DuPage, Illinois

Robert Berry
Miami University, Ohio

George Bohler
Florida Junior College

Tom Bonsor
Eastern Washington University

Michael D. Brendler
Louisiana State University

Baird Brock
Central Missouri State University

Kathleen Bromley
Monroe Community College, New York

Douglas Brown
Georgetown University

Ernest Buchholz
Santa Monica Community College, California

Gary Burbridge
Grand Rapids Junior College, Michigan

Maureen Burton
California Polytechnic University, Pomona

Carol Carnes
Kansas State University

Paul Coomes
University of Louisville, Kentucky

Eleanor Craig
University of Delaware

Wilford Cummings
Grosmont College, California

Diane Cunningham
Glendale Community College, California

Douglas C. Darran
University of South Carolina

Edward Day
University of Southern Florida

Johan Deprez
University of Tennessee

James Dietz
California State University, Fullerton

Stuart Dorsey
University of West Virginia

Natalia Drury
Northern Virginia Community College

Lu Ann Duffus
California State University, Hayward

John Eckalbar
California State University, Chico

John Elliot
University of Southern California

Charles Fischer
Pittsburg State University, Kansas

John Gemello
San Francisco State University

Carl Guelzo
Cantonsville Community College, Maryland

Jan Hansen
University of Wisconsin, Eau Claire

John Henderson
Georgia State University

Ken Howard
East Texas Baptist University

Mark Karscig
Central Missouri State University

Stanley Keil
Ball State University, Indiana

Richard Kieffer
State University of New York, Buffalo

Gene Kimmett
William Rainey Harper College, Illinois

Luther Lawson
University of North Carolina

Frank Leori
College of San Mateo, California

Kenneth Long
New River Community College, Virginia

Michael Magura
University of Toledo, Ohio

Bruce McCrea
Lansing Community College, Michigan

Gerald McDougall
Wichita State University, Kansas

Kevin McGee
University of Wisconsin, Oshkosh

Francois Melese
Auburn University, Alabama

Herbert Miliken
American River College, California

Richard Miller
Pennsylvania State University

Ernest Moser
Northeast Louisiana University

Farhang Niroomand
University of Southern Mississippi

Eliot Orton
New Mexico State University

Marty Perline
Wichita State University, Kansas

Harold Petersen
Boston College

Douglas Poe
University of Texas, Austin

Joseph Rezney
St. Louis Community College, Missouri

Terry Ridgway
University of Nevada, Las Vegas

Thomas Romans
State University of New York, Buffalo

Robert Ross
Bloomsburg State College, Pennsylvania

Keith A. Rowley
Baylor University, Texas

Anandi Sahu
Oakland University, Michigan

Richard Scoggins
California State University, Long Beach

Paul Seidenstat
Temple University, Pennsylvania

Shahram Shafiee
North Harris County College, Texas

Alan Sleeman
Western Washington University

John Sondey
University of Idaho

Robert W. Thomas
Iowa State University

Richard L. Tontz
California State University, Northridge

Roger Trenary
Kansas State University

Bruce Vanderporten
Loyola University, Illinois

Thomas Weiss
University of Kansas

Richard O. Welch
University of Texas at San Antonio

Donald A. Wells
University of Arizona

John Wight
University of Richmond, Virginia

Thomas Wyrick
Southwest Missouri State University

Second Edition Reviewers

Scott Bloom
North Dakota State University

Thomas Carroll
University of Nevada, Las Vegas

Larry Cox
Southwest Missouri State University

Diane Cunningham
Los Angeles Valley College

Emit Deal
Macon College

Michael Fabritius
University of Mary Hardin Baylor

Frederick Fagal
Marywood College

Ralph Fowler
Diablo Valley College

Bob Gilette
Texas A&M University

Lynn Gillette
Indiana University, Indianapolis

Simon Hakim
Temple University

Lewis Karstensson
University of Nevada, Las Vegas

Abraham Kidane
California State University, Dominguez Hills

W. Barbara Killen
University of Minnesota

J. David Lages
Southwest Missouri State University

Anthony Lee
Austin Community College

Marjory Mabery
Delaware County Community College

Bernard Malamud
University of Nevada, Las Vegas

Michael Marlow
California Polytechnic State University, San Luis Obispo

Phil J. McLewin
Ramapo College of New Jersey

Tina Quinn
Arkansas State University

Terry Ridgway
University of Nevada, Las Vegas

Paul Snoonian
University of Lowell

Paul Taube
Pan American University

Roger Trenary
Kansas State University

Charles Van Eaton
Hillsdale College

Mark Wheeler
Bowling Green State University

Thomas Wyrick
Southwest Missouri State University

Third Edition Reviewers

Carlos Aguilar
University of Texas, El Paso

Rebecca Ann Benakis
New Mexico State University

Scott Bloom
North Dakota State University

Howard Erdman
Southwest Texas Junior College

Arthur Friedberg
Mohawk Valley Community College

Nancy A. Jianakoplos
Colorado State University

Lewis Karstensson
University of Nevada, Las Vegas

Rose Kilburn
Modesto Junior College

Ruby P. Kishan
Southeastern Community College

Duane Kline
Southeastern Community College

Charles A. Roberts
Western Kentucky University

Bill Robinson
University of Nevada, Las Vegas

Susan C. Stephenson
Drake University

Charles Van Eaton
Hillsdale College

Richard O. Welch
The University of Texas at San Antonio

Calla Wiemer
University of Hawaii at Manoa

Fourth Edition Reviewers

Uzo Agulefo
North Lake College

Kari Battaglia
University of North Texas

Scott Bloom
North Dakota State University

Harry Ellis, Jr.
University of North Texas

Mary Ann Hendryson
Western Washington University

Eugene Jones
Ohio State University

Ki Hoon Him
Central Connecticut State University

James McBrearty
University of Arizona

John A. Panagakis
Onondaga Community College

Bill Robinson
University of Nevada, Las Vegas

George E. Samuels
Sam Houston State University

Ed Scahill
University of Scranton

Charles Van Eaton
Hillsdale College

Thomas Wyrick
Southwest Missouri State University

Fifth Edition Reviewers

Kari Battaglia
University of North Texas

Douglas A. Conway
Mesa Community College

Lee A. Craig
North Carolina State University

Harry Ellis, Jr.
University of North Texas

Joe W. Essuman
University of Wisconsin, Waukesha

Dipak Ghosh
Emporia State University

Shirley J. Gideon
The University of Vermont

Mary Ann Hendryson
Western Washington University

Calvin A. Hoerneman
Delta College

George H. Jones
University of Wisconsin, Rock County

Donald R. Morgan
Monterey Peninsula College

John A. Panagakis
Onondaga Community College

Bill Robinson
University of Nevada, Las Vegas

Steve Robinson
The University of North Carolina at Wilmington

David W. Yoskowitz
Texas Tech University

Sixth Edition Reviewers

Hendrikus J.E.M. Brand
Albion College

Curtis Clarke
Dallas County Community College

Andrea Gorospe
Kent State University, Trumbull

Mehrdad Madresehee
Lycoming College

L. Wayne Plumly
Valdosta State University

Craig Rogers
Canisius College

Uri Simonsohn
Carnegie Mellon University

Philip Sprunger
Lycoming College

Lea Templer
College of the Canyons

Soumya Tohamy
Berry College

Lee Van Scyoc
University of Wisconsin, Oshkosh

Seventh Edition Reviewers

Pam Coates
San Diego Mesa College

Peggy F. Crane
Southwestern College

Richard Croxdale
Austin Community College

Harry Ellis, Jr.
University of North Texas

Craig Gallet
California State University, Sacramento

Kelly George
Embry-Riddle Aeronautical University

Anne-Marie Gilliam
Central Piedmont Community College

Richard C. Schiming
Minnesota State University, Mankato

Lea Templer
College of the Canyons

Jennifer VanGilder
California State University, Bakersfield

William W. Wilkes
Athens State University

Janice Yee
Wartburg College

Eighth Edition Reviewers

Dr. Clive R. Belfied
Queens College, City University of New York

Barry Bomboy
J. Sargeant Reynolds Community College

James Bryan
North Harris Montgomery Community College

Peggy F. Crane
Southwestern College

Richard Croxdale
Austin Community College

Harry Ellis, Jr.
University of North Texas

Kelly George
Embry Riddle Aeronautical University

Alan Kessler
Providence College

Denny Myers
Oklahoma City Community College

Charles Newton
Houston Community College

Ahmad Saranjam
Northeastern University

Jennifer VanGilder, PhD
*California State University
Bakersfield*

Janice Yee
Wartburg College

I would like to thank Peggy Crane of Southwestern College, who revised the Test Bank, and Jane Himarios of the University of Texas at Arlington, who revised the Instructor's Manual. I owe a deep debt of gratitude to all the fine and creative people I worked with at Thomson South-Western. These persons include Jack Calhoun, Alex von Rosenberg, Mike Roche, Mike Worls, Senior Acquisitions Editor; Jennifer "RIP Mr. Eko" Baker, Senior Developmental Editor; Jennifer Ziegler, Content Project Manager, Brian Joyner, Executive Marketing Manager for Economics; Michelle Kunkler, Senior Art Director; and Sandee Milewski, Senior Frontlist Buyer.

My deepest debt of gratitude goes to my wife, Sheila, and to my two sons, David, sixteen years old, and Daniel, nineteen years old. They continue to make all my days happy ones.

Roger A. Arnold

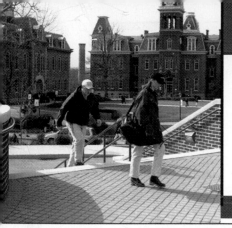

What Economics Is About

Setting the Scene Jackie and Stephanie share an apartment about a mile from West Virginia University. Both are juniors at the university; Jackie is a history major, and Stephanie is an economics major. The following events occurred one day not too long ago.

7:15 A.M.

Jackie's alarm clock buzzes. She reaches over to the small table next to her bed and turns it off. As she pulls the covers back up, Jackie thinks about her 8:30 American history class. Should she go to class today or sleep a little longer? She worked late last night and really hasn't had enough sleep. Besides, she's fairly sure her professor will be discussing a subject she already knows well. Maybe it would be okay to miss class today.

11:37 A.M.

Stephanie is in the campus bookstore browsing through two economics books. She ends up buying both books. As she leaves the bookstore, she glances over at a blue jacket with the West Virginia University emblem on it. She knows that her brother, who is a junior in high school, would like to have a WVU jacket. Stephanie tells herself that she might buy him the jacket for his birthday next month.

1:27 P.M.

Jackie, who did skip her 8:30 American history class, is in her European history professor's office talking to him about obtaining a master's degree in history. Getting a master's degree is something that mildly interests her, but she's not sure whether she wants it enough or not.

9:00 P.M.

Stephanie has been studying for the past three hours for tomorrow's midterm exam in her International Economics course. She says to herself, I don't think more studying will do very much good. So she quits studying and turns on the television to watch a rerun of one of her favorite movies, *Sleepless in Seattle.*

? Here are some questions to keep in mind as you read this chapter:

- *Is Jackie more likely to miss some classes than she is to miss other classes? What determines which classes Jackie will attend and which classes she won't attend?*

- *What does a basic economic fact have to do with Stephanie's buying two books at her campus bookstore?*

- *Does whether or not Jackie will go on to get a master's degree have anything to do with economics?*

- *Stephanie stopped studying at 9:00 P.M. Would she have been better off if she had studied 30 more minutes?*

See analyzing the scene at the end of this chapter for answers to these questions.

A Definition of Economics

In this section, we discuss a few key economic concepts; then we incorporate knowledge of these concepts into a definition of economics.

Goods and Bads

Economists talk about *goods* and *bads*. A **good** is anything that gives a person **utility** or satisfaction. A good can be tangible or intangible. If a computer gives you utility or satisfaction, then it is a good. If friendship gives you utility or satisfaction, then it is a good. (A computer is a tangible good, and friendship is an intangible good.)

A **bad** is something that gives a person **disutility** or dissatisfaction. If the flu gives you disutility or dissatisfaction, then it is a bad. If the constant nagging of an acquaintance is something that gives you disutility or dissatisfaction, then it is a bad.

People want goods and they do not want bads. In fact, they will pay to get goods ("Here is $1,000 for the computer"), and they will pay to get rid of bads they currently have ("I'd be willing to pay you, doctor, if you can prescribe something that will shorten the time I have the flu").

Resources

Goods do not just appear before us when we snap our fingers. It takes resources to produce goods. (Sometimes *resources* are referred to as *inputs* or *factors of production*.)

Generally, economists divide resources into four broad categories: *land, labor, capital,* and *entrepreneurship*. **Land** includes natural resources, such as minerals, forests, water, and unimproved land. For example, oil, wood, and animals fall into this category. (Sometimes economists refer to this category simply as *natural resources*.)

Labor consists of the physical and mental talents people contribute to the production process. For example, a person building a house is using his or her own labor.

Capital consists of produced goods that can be used as inputs for further production. Factories, machinery, tools, computers, and buildings are examples of capital. One country might have more capital than another. This means that it has more factories, machinery, tools, and so on.

Entrepreneurship refers to the particular talent that some people have for organizing the resources of land, labor, and capital to produce goods, seek new business opportunities, and develop new ways of doing things.

Scarcity and a Definition of Economics

We are now ready to define a key concept in economics: *scarcity*. **Scarcity** is the condition in which our wants (for goods) are greater than the limited resources (land, labor, capital, and entrepreneurship) available to satisfy those wants. In other words, we want goods, but there are just not enough resources available to provide us with all the goods we want.

Look at it this way: Our wants (for goods) are infinite, but our resources (which we need to produce the goods) are finite. Scarcity is our infinite wants hitting up against finite resources.

Many economists say that if scarcity didn't exist, neither would economics. In other words, if our wants weren't greater than the limited resources available to satisfy them, there would be no field of study called economics. This is similar to saying that if matter and

Good
Anything from which individuals receive utility or satisfaction.
Utility
The satisfaction one receives from a good.
Bad
Anything from which individuals receive disutility or dissatisfaction.
Disutility
The dissatisfaction one receives from a bad.
Land
All natural resources, such as minerals, forests, water, and unimproved land.
Labor
The physical and mental talents people contribute to the production process.
Capital
Produced goods that can be used as inputs for further production, such as factories, machinery, tools, computers, and buildings.
Entrepreneurship
The particular talent that some people have for organizing the resources of land, labor, and capital to produce goods, seek new business opportunities, and develop new ways of doing things.
Scarcity
The condition in which our wants are greater than the limited resources available to satisfy those wants.

Thinking like **AN ECONOMIST** *The economist says that everyone in the world—no matter how rich—has to face scarcity. But what about Bill Gates, the cofounder of Microsoft and a billionaire? He may be able to satisfy more of his wants for tangible goods (houses, cars) than most people, but this doesn't mean he has the resources to satisfy all his wants. His wants might include more time with his children, more friendship, no disease in the world, peace on earth, and a hundred other things that he does not have the resources to "produce."*

economics 24/7

24

You are going to tell me what I want to know, it's just a matter of how much you want to hurt.

—Jack Bauer

The FOX show *24* is said to be one of the more suspenseful shows on television. The main character of the show, Jack Bauer (Kiefer Sutherland), is a CTU (Counter Terrorism Unit) field agent. His job is to stop whatever impending doom is hanging over the country—such things as nerve gas, a deadly virus being released on the American public, or a nuclear warhead directed at a major American city.

What is it that makes *24* as suspenseful as it is? The answer, we think, has a lot to do with "utility" and "disutility" and the chance of moving from one to the other. Essentially what the writers of *24* do, early in the series, is set up two different worlds for the viewers. The one world is the world of the status quo; it is the world that exists; it is the world where people are receiving utility in their daily lives. The second world—the world that "could be"—is the world where something awful happens, pushing hundreds of thousands, if not millions, of people into disutility. It is the world where the nerve gas has killed hundreds of thousands of people; it is the world where the nuclear warhead kills millions of people in a major American city; it is the world where millions die an excruciatingly painful death as the result of a fatal virus.

Then, after the writers of *24* have shown the audience the two worlds—the good (high-utility) world and the bad (high-disutility) world—they essentially tell the viewer that just one tiny slip-up can be the difference between living in the high-utility world and living in the high-disutility world. Sometimes, it is just a matter of Jack Bauer doing something five seconds earlier (instead of later) that makes the difference between which world we end up living in.

The same kind of suspense holds for things other than TV shows, of course. People who are avid sports fans, for example, will feel very nervous watching their favorite team. That's because who wins the game can mean the difference between utility and disutility for them. If their team wins—utility; if their team loses—disutility. And of course, the closer the two teams are in ability, the greater the suspense is. That's because the closer the two teams are in ability, the smaller the slip-up can be in deciding who wins and who loses.

Will the writers of *24* ever change the basic formula of the show? Probably not. It will most likely always be the same: Good (high-utility) world can turn into bad (high-disutility) world if just the tiniest mistake is made. Thankfully, Jack Bauer is never going to make that tiniest of mistakes.

---

motion didn't exist, neither would physics, or that if living things didn't exist, neither would biology. For this reason, we define **economics** in this text as the science of scarcity. More completely, economics is the science of how individuals and societies deal with the fact that wants are greater than the limited resources available to satisfy those wants.

THINKING IN TERMS OF SCARCITY'S EFFECTS Scarcity has effects. Here are three: (1) the need to make choices, (2) the need for a rationing device, and (3) competition. We describe each.

Choices People have to make choices because of scarcity. Because our unlimited wants are greater than our limited resources, some wants must go unsatisfied. We must choose which wants we will satisfy and which we will not. Jeremy asks: Do I go to Hawaii or do I pay off my car loan earlier? Ellen asks: Do I buy the new sweater or two new shirts?

Economics

The science of scarcity; the science of how individuals and societies deal with the fact that wants are greater than the limited resources available to satisfy those wants.

Rationing Device

A means for deciding who gets what of available resources and goods.

Need for a Rationing Device A **rationing device** is a means of deciding who gets what. Scarcity implies the need for a rationing device. If people have infinite wants for goods and there are only limited resources to produce the goods, then a rationing device must be used to decide who gets the available quantity of goods. Dollar price is a rationing device. For example, there are 100 cars on the lot and everyone wants a new car. How do we decide who gets what quantity of the new cars? The answer is "use the rationing device dollar price." Those people who pay the dollar price for the new car end up with a new car.

Is dollar price a fair rationing device? Doesn't it discriminate against the poor? After all, the poor have fewer dollars than the rich, so the rich can get more of what they want than can the poor. True, dollar price does discriminate against the poor. But then, as the economist knows, every rationing device discriminates against someone.

Suppose that dollar price could not be used as a rationing device tomorrow. Some rationing device would still be necessary because scarcity would still exist. How would we ration gas at the gasoline station, food in the grocery store, or tickets for the Super Bowl? Let's consider some alternatives to dollar price as a rationing device.

Suppose first come, first served is the rationing device. For example, suppose there are only 40,000 Super Bowl tickets. If you are one of the first 40,000 in line for a Super Bowl ticket, then you get a ticket. If you are the 40,001st person in line, you don't. Such a method discriminates against those who can't get in line quickly. What about slow walkers or people with a disability? What about people without cars who can't drive to where the tickets are distributed?

Or suppose brute force is the rationing device. For example, if there are 40,000 Super Bowl tickets, then as long as you can take a ticket away from someone who has a ticket, the ticket is yours. Who does this rationing method discriminate against? Obviously, it discriminates against the weak.

Or suppose beauty is the rationing device. The more beautiful you are, the better your chance of getting a Super Bowl ticket. Again, the rationing device discriminates against someone.

These and many other alternatives to dollar price could be used as a rationing device. However, each discriminates against someone, and none is clearly superior to dollar price.

In addition, if first come, first served, brute force, beauty, or another alternative to dollar price is the rationing device, what incentive would the producer of a good have to produce the good? With dollar price as a rationing device, a person produces computers and sells them for money. He then takes the money and buys what he wants. But if the rationing device were, say, brute force, he would not have an incentive to produce. Why produce anything when someone will end up taking it away from you? In short, in a world where dollar price isn't the rationing device, people are likely to produce much less than in a world where dollar price is the rationing device.

Scarcity and Competition Do you see much competition in the world today? Are people competing for jobs? Are states and cities competing for businesses? Are students competing for grades? The answer to all these questions is yes. The economist wants to know why this competition exists and what form it takes. First, the economist concludes, *competition exists because of scarcity.* If there were enough resources to satisfy all our seemingly unlimited wants, people would not have to compete for the available but limited resources.

Second, the economist sees that competition takes the form of people trying to get more of the rationing device. If dollar price is the rationing device, people will compete to earn dollars. Look at your own case. You are a college student working for a degree. One reason (but perhaps not the only reason) you are attending college is to earn a higher income after graduation. But why do you want a higher income? You want it because it will allow you to satisfy more of your wants.

Suppose muscular strength (measured by lifting weights) were the rationing device instead of dollar price. People with more muscular strength would receive more resources and goods than people with less muscular strength would receive. In this situation, people would compete for muscular strength. (Would they spend more time at the gym lifting weights?) The lesson is simple: *Whatever the rationing device, people will compete for it.*

SELF-TEST

(Answers to Self-Test questions are in the Self-Test Appendix.)

1. Scarcity is the condition of finite resources. True or false? Explain your answer.

2. How does competition arise out of scarcity?

3. How does choice arise out of scarcity?

Key Concepts in Economics

There are numerous key concepts in economics—concepts that define the field. We discuss a few of these concepts next.

Opportunity Cost

As noted earlier, people must make choices because scarcity exists. Because our seemingly unlimited wants push up against limited resources, some wants must go unsatisfied. We must therefore *choose* which wants we will satisfy and which we will not. The most highly valued opportunity or alternative forfeited when a choice is made is known as **opportunity cost**. Every time you make a choice, you incur an opportunity cost. For example, you have chosen to read this chapter. In making this choice, you denied yourself the benefits of doing something else. You could have watched television, e-mailed a friend, taken a nap, eaten a few slices of pizza, read a novel, shopped for a new computer, and so on. Whatever you *would have chosen* to do had you decided not to read this chapter is the opportunity cost of your reading this chapter. For example, if you would have watched television had you chosen not to read this chapter—if this was your next best alternative—then the opportunity cost of reading this chapter is watching television.

OPPORTUNITY COST AND BEHAVIOR Economists believe that a change in opportunity cost will change a person's behavior. For example, consider Bill, who is a sophomore at the University of Kansas. He attends classes Monday through Thursday of every week. Every time he chooses to go to class, he gives up the opportunity to do something else, such as the opportunity to earn $8 an hour working at a job. The opportunity cost of Bill spending an hour in class is $8.

Now let's raise the opportunity cost of attending class. On Tuesday, we offer Bill $70 to skip his economics class. He knows that if he attends his economics class, he will forfeit $70. What will Bill do? An economist would predict that as the opportunity cost of attending class increases relative to the benefits of attending class, Bill is less likely to attend class.

Opportunity Cost
The most highly valued opportunity or alternative forfeited when a choice is made.

Thinking like
AN ECONOMIST *Economists are fond of saying that there is no such thing as a free lunch. This catchy phrase expresses the idea that opportunity costs are incurred when choices are made. Perhaps this is an obvious point, but consider how often people mistakenly assume there is a free lunch. For example, some parents think education is free because they do not pay tuition for their children to attend public elementary school. Sorry, but there is no such thing as a free lunch. Free implies no sacrifice, no opportunities forfeited, which is not true in regard to elementary school education. Resources that could be used for other things are used to provide elementary school education.*

Consider the people who speak about free medical care, free housing, free bridges ("there is no charge to cross it"), and free parks. None of these is actually free. The resources that provide medical care, housing, bridges, and parks could have been used in other ways.

economics 24/7

WHY LEBRON JAMES ISN'T IN COLLEGE

LeBron James was born on December 30, 1984. So, he is currently the age of many people attending college. But LeBron James is not attending college. He went directly from high school into the NBA. He is currently playing professional basketball.

Why isn't LeBron James in college? It's not because he cannot afford the tuition charged at most colleges. Also, it's not because he wouldn't be admitted to any college. LeBron James is not in college because it is more expensive for him than it is for most 18- to 25-year-olds to attend college.

To understand, think of what it costs you to attend college. If you pay $1,000 tuition a semester for eight semesters, the full tuition amounts to $8,000. However, $8,000 is not the full cost of your attending college because if you were not a student, you could be earning income working at a job. For example, you could be working at a full-time job earning $25,000 annually. Certainly, this $25,000, or at least part of it if you are currently working part time, is forfeited because you attend college. It is part of the cost of your attending college.

Thus, the *tuition cost* may be the same for everyone who attends your college, but the *opportunity cost* is not. Some people have higher opportunity costs for attending college

than others do. LeBron James has extremely high opportunity costs for attending college. He would have to give up the millions of dollars he earns playing professional basketball and endorsing products if he were to attend college on a full-time basis.

This discussion illustrates two related points made in this chapter. First, *the higher the opportunity cost of doing something, the less likely it will be done.* The opportunity cost of attending college is higher for LeBron than it (probably) is for you, and that is why you are in college and LeBron James is not.

Second, according to economists, *individuals think and act in terms of costs and benefits and only undertake actions if they expect the benefits to outweigh the costs.* LeBron James is likely to see certain benefits to attending college—just as you see certain benefits to attending college. However, those benefits are insufficient for him to attend college because benefits are not all that matter. Costs matter too. For LeBron James, the costs of attending college are much higher than the benefits, and so he chooses not to attend college. In your case, the benefits are higher than the costs, and so you have decided to attend college.

This is how economists think about behavior, whether it is Bill's or your own. *The higher the opportunity cost of doing something, the less likely it will be done.* This is part of the economic way of thinking.

Before you continue, look at Exhibit 1, which summarizes some of the things about scarcity, choice, and opportunity cost up to this point.

Benefits and Costs

If it were possible to eliminate air pollution completely, should all air pollution be eliminated? If your answer is yes, then you are probably focusing on the *benefits* of eliminating air pollution. For example, one benefit might be healthier individuals. Certainly, individuals who do not breathe polluted air have fewer lung disorders than people who do breathe polluted air.

But benefits rarely come without costs. The economist reminds us that while there are benefits to eliminating pollution, there are costs too. To illustrate, one way to eliminate all car pollution tomorrow is to pass a law stating that anyone caught driving a car

economics 24/7

THE COSTS AND BENEFITS OF ATTENDING CLASS

Do you attend every single class in college? Probably, there are some days when you do not. For example, you might be sick one day and thus choose not to attend class. But are there days when you are well and could attend class but choose not to? If so, do you pick these days to be absent from class randomly? We think not. We think it has to do with the costs and benefits of attending class.

In southern California, some students choose not to attend class when the surf is particularly good. In other words, the benefits of going to class that day may be just as high as going any other day, but the costs—the opportunity costs—on that particular day are higher. That's because it is a particularly good day for surfing. In other words, the opportunity cost of going to class when the surf is good might be much higher for a surfing enthusiast on this particular day. If the opportunity costs are high enough on this day, they may just be greater than the benefits of going to class, and so the student chooses not to go to class but to surf instead.

Think of costs and benefits in dollar terms for the surfer. Usually, the surfer sees the benefits of going to class as equal to $40 and the costs as equal to $30. In other words, there is a net benefit of going to class, or benefits are greater than costs, and so he goes to class. But when the surf is good, the cost rises from $30 to $55. Now the costs of going to class are greater than the benefits—there is a net cost to attending class—and so he chooses to not attend class.

will go to prison for 40 years. With such a law in place, and enforced, very few people would drive cars, and all car pollution would be a thing of the past. Presto! Cleaner air! However, many people would think that the cost of obtaining that cleaner air is too high. Someone might say, "I want cleaner air, but not if I have to completely give up driving my car. How will I get to work?"

What distinguishes the economist from the noneconomist is that the economist thinks in terms of *both* costs *and* benefits. Often, the noneconomist thinks in terms of one or the other. There are benefits from studying, but there are costs too. There are benefits from coming to class, but there are costs too. There are costs to getting up early each morning and exercising, but let's not forget that there are benefits too.

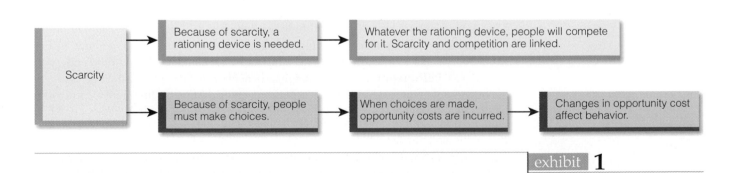

exhibit **1**

Scarcity and Related Concepts

Decisions Made at the Margin

It is late at night and you have already studied three hours for your biology test tomorrow. You look at the clock and wonder if you should study another hour. How would you summarize your thinking process? What question or questions do you ask yourself to decide whether or not to study another hour?

Perhaps without knowing it, you think in terms of the costs and benefits of further study. You probably realize that there are certain benefits from studying an additional hour (you may be able to raise your grade a few points), but there are costs too (you will get less sleep or have less time to watch television or talk on the phone with a friend). Thinking in terms of costs and benefits, though, doesn't tell us *how* you think in terms of costs and benefits. For example, when deciding what to do, do you look at the total costs and total benefits of the proposed action, or do you look at something less than the total costs and benefits? According to economists, for most decisions, you think in terms of *additional,* or *marginal,* costs and benefits, not *total* costs and benefits. That's because most decisions deal with making a small, or additional, change.

To illustrate, suppose you just finished eating a hamburger and drinking a soda for lunch. You are still a little hungry and are considering whether or not to order another hamburger. An economist would say that in deciding whether or not to order another hamburger, you will compare the additional benefits of the additional hamburger to the additional costs of the additional hamburger. In economics, the word *marginal* is a synonym for *additional.* So we say that you will compare the **marginal benefits** of the (next) hamburger to the **marginal costs** of the (next) hamburger. If the marginal benefits are greater than the marginal costs, you obviously expect a net benefit to ordering the next hamburger, and therefore, you order the next hamburger. If, however, the marginal costs of the hamburger are greater than the marginal benefits, you obviously expect a net cost to ordering the next hamburger, and therefore, you do not order the next hamburger.

What you don't consider when making this decision are the total benefits and total costs of hamburgers. That's because the benefits and costs connected with the first hamburger (the one you have already eaten) are no longer relevant to the current decision. You are not deciding between eating two hamburgers and eating no hamburgers; your decision is whether to eat a second hamburger after you have already eaten a first hamburger.

According to economists, when individuals make decisions by comparing marginal benefits to marginal costs, they are making **decisions at the margin**. The president of the United States makes a decision at the margin when deciding whether or not to talk another 10 minutes with the speaker of the House of Representatives, the employee makes a decision at the margin when deciding whether or not to work two hours overtime, and the college professor makes a decision at the margin when deciding whether or not to put an additional question on the final exam.

Efficiency

What is the right amount of time to study for a test? In economics, the "right amount" of anything is the "optimal" or "efficient" amount, and the efficient amount is the amount for which the marginal benefits equal the marginal costs. Stated differently, you have achieved **efficiency** when the marginal benefits equal the marginal costs.

Suppose you are studying for an economics test, and for the first hour of studying, the marginal benefits *(MB)* are greater than the marginal costs *(MC):*

$$MB \text{ studying first hour} > MC \text{ studying first hour}$$

Given this condition, you will certainly study for the first hour. After all, it is worthwhile: The additional benefits are greater than the additional costs, so there is a net benefit to studying.

Marginal Benefits

Additional benefits. The benefits connected to consuming an additional unit of a good or undertaking one more unit of an activity.

Marginal Costs

Additional costs. The costs connected to consuming an additional unit of a good or undertaking one more unit of an activity.

Decisions at the Margin

Decision making characterized by weighing the additional (marginal) benefits of a change against the additional (marginal) costs of a change with respect to current conditions.

Efficiency

Exists when marginal benefits equal marginal costs.

Suppose for the second hour of studying, the marginal benefits are still greater than the marginal costs:

MB studying second hour > *MC* studying second hour

You will study for the second hour because the additional benefits are still greater than the additional costs. In other words, it is worthwhile studying the second hour. In fact, you will continue to study as long as the marginal benefits are greater than the marginal costs. Exhibit 2 graphically illustrates this discussion.

The marginal benefit *(MB)* curve of studying is downward sloping because we have assumed that the benefits of studying for the first hour are greater than the benefits of studying for the second hour and so on. The marginal cost *(MC)* curve of studying is upward sloping because we assume that it costs a person more (in terms of goods forfeited) to study the second hour than the first, more to study the third than the second, and so on. (If we assume the additional costs of studying are constant over time, the *MC* curve is horizontal.)

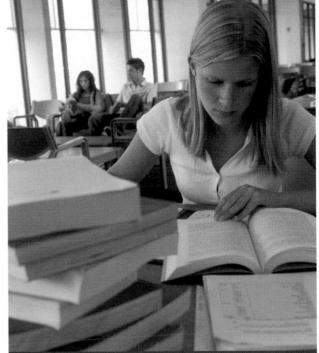

© PIXLAND/JUPITER IMAGES

In the exhibit, the marginal benefits of studying equal the marginal costs at three hours. So three hours is the efficient length of time to study in this situation. At fewer than three hours, the marginal benefits of studying are greater than the marginal costs; thus, at all these hours, there are net benefits from studying. At more than three hours, the marginal costs of studying are greater than the marginal benefits, and so it wouldn't be worthwhile to study beyond three hours.

MAXIMIZING NET BENEFITS Take another look at Exhibit 2. Suppose you had stopped studying after the first hour (or after the 60th minute). Would you have given up anything? Yes, you would have given up the net benefits of studying longer. To illustrate, notice that between the first and the second hour, the marginal benefits curve (blue curve) lies above the marginal costs curve (red curve). This means there are net benefits to studying the second hour. But if you hadn't studied that second hour—if you had

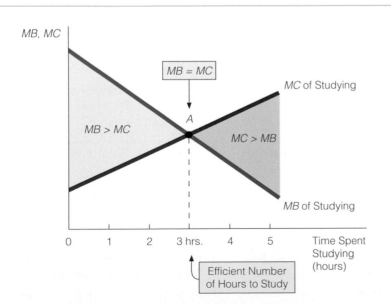

Efficiency

MB = marginal benefits and *MC* = marginal costs. In the exhibit, the *MB* curve of studying is downward sloping and the *MC* curve of studying is upward sloping. As long as *MB* > *MC*, the person will study. The person stops studying when *MB* = *MC*. This is where efficiency is achieved.

Does a person have to know about marginal costs and marginal benefits before he or she can achieve efficiency?

There may be people who do not know the definition of marginal cost and marginal benefit, but this doesn't prevent them from achieving efficiency in much the same way that a person who doesn't know much about how a car works can still drive a car. All the person has to "sense" is whether or not doing more of something comes with greater benefits than costs. As long as a person can do this—and there is plenty of evidence that people do this as naturally as they breathe air or walk—then efficiency can be achieved.

stopped after the first hour—then you would have given up the opportunity to collect those net benefits. (That's like leaving a $10 bill on the sidewalk.) The same analysis holds for the third hour. We conclude that by studying three hours (but not one minute longer), you have maximized net benefits. In short, efficiency (which is consistent with $MB = MC$) is also consistent with maximizing net benefits.

Unintended Effects

Has anything turned out differently from what you intended? No doubt, you can provide numerous examples. Economists think in terms of unintended effects. Consider an example. Andres, 16 years old, currently works after school at a grocery store. He earns $6.50 an hour. Suppose the state legislature passes a law specifying that the minimum dollar wage a person can be paid to do a job is $8.50 an hour. The legislators' intention in passing the law is to help people like Andres earn more income.

Will the $8.50 an hour legislation have the intended effect? Perhaps not. The manager of the grocery store may not find it worthwhile to continue employing Andres if she has to pay him $8.50 an hour. In other words, Andres may have a job at $6.50 an hour but not at $8.50 an hour. If the law specifies that no one will earn less than $8.50 an hour and the manager of the grocery store decides to fire Andres rather than pay this amount, then an unintended effect of the $8.50 an hour legislation is Andres' losing his job.

As another example, let's analyze mandatory seatbelt laws to see if they have any unintended effects. Many states have laws that require drivers to wear seatbelts. The intended effect is to reduce the number of car fatalities by making it more likely drivers will survive an accident.

Could these laws have an unintended effect? Some economists think so. They look at accident fatalities in terms of this equation:

Total number of fatalities = Number of accidents × Fatalities per accident

For example, if there are 200,000 accidents and 0.10 fatalities per accident, the total number of fatalities is 20,000.

The objective of a mandatory seatbelt program is to reduce the total number of fatalities by reducing the fatalities per accident. Many studies have found that wearing seatbelts does just this. If you are in an accident, you have a better chance of not being killed if you are wearing a seatbelt.

Let's assume that with seatbelts, there are 0.08 instead of 0.10 fatalities per accident. If there are still 200,000 accidents, this means that the total number of fatalities falls from 20,000 to 16,000. Thus, there is a drop in the total number of fatalities if fatalities per accident are reduced and the number of accidents is constant.

Number of Accidents	Fatalities per Accident	Total Number of Fatalities
200,000	0.10	20,000
200,000	0.08	16,000

However, some economists wonder if the number of accidents stays constant. Specifically, they suggest that seatbelts may have an unintended effect: *The number of accidents may increase.* This happens because wearing seatbelts may make drivers feel safer. Feeling safer may cause them to take chances that they wouldn't ordinarily take—such as driving faster or more aggressively, or concentrating less on their driving and more on

economics 24/7

WHY DID THE BRITISH SOLDIERS WEAR RED UNIFORMS?

When George Washington and the colonists fought the British, the colonists were dressed in rags, while the British troops were clad in fine bright red uniforms. Commenting on this difference, people often say, "The British were foolish to have worn bright red uniforms. You could see them coming for miles."

Economists would not be so quick to label the British as foolish. Instead, they would ask why the British troops wore bright red. For instance, David Friedman, an economist, thinks it is odd that the British, who at the time were the greatest fighting force in the world, would make such a seemingly obvious mistake. He has an alternative explanation, an economic explanation.

Friedman reasons that the British generals did not want their men to break ranks and desert because winning the

war would be hard, if not impossible, if a lot of men deserted. Thus, the generals had to think up a way to make the opportunity cost of desertion high for their soldiers. The generals reasoned that the higher the cost of desertion, the fewer deserters there would be. The British generals effectively told their soldiers that if they deserted, they would have to forfeit their freedom or their lives.

Of course, the problem is that a stiff penalty is not effective if deserters cannot be found. Therefore, the generals had to make it easy to find deserters, which they did by dressing them in bright red uniforms. Certainly, it was possible for a deserter to throw off his uniform and walk through the countryside in his underwear alone, but in the harsh winters of New England, doing so would guarantee death. He had almost no choice but to wear the bright red uniform.

---

the music on the radio. For example, if the number of accidents rises to 250,000, then the total number of fatalities is 20,000.

Number of Accidents	Fatalities per Accident	Total Number of Fatalities
200,000	0.10	20,000
250,000	0.08	20,000

We conclude the following: If a mandatory seatbelt law reduces the number of fatalities (intended effect) but increases the number of accidents (unintended effect), it may, contrary to popular belief, not reduce the total number of fatalities. In fact, some economic studies show just this.

What does all this mean for you? You may be safer if you know that this unintended effect exists and you adjust accordingly. To be specific, when you wear your seatbelt, your chances of getting hurt in a car accident are less than if you don't wear your seatbelt. But if this added sense of protection causes you to drive less carefully than you would otherwise, then you could unintentionally offset the measure of protection your seatbelt provides. To reduce the probability of hurting yourself and others in a car accident, *the best policy is to wear a seatbelt and to drive as carefully as you would if you weren't wearing a seatbelt.* Knowing about the unintended effect of wearing your seatbelt could save your life

Exchange

Exchange or **trade** is the process of giving up one thing for something else. Economics is sometimes called the "science of exchange" because so much that is discussed in economics has to do with exchange.

Exchange (Trade)
The process of giving up one thing for another.

We start with a basic question: Why do people enter into exchanges? The answer is that they do so to make themselves better off. When a person voluntarily trades $100 for a jacket, she is saying, "I prefer to have the jacket instead of the $100." And of course, when the seller of the jacket voluntarily sells the jacket for $100, he is saying, "I prefer to have the $100 instead of the jacket." In short, through trade or exchange, each person gives up something he or she values less for something he or she values more.

You can think of trade in terms of utility or satisfaction. Imagine a utility scale that goes from 1 to 10, with 10 being the highest utility you can achieve. Now suppose you currently have $40 in your wallet and you are at 7 on the utility scale. A few minutes later, you are in a store looking at some new CDs. The price of each is $10. You end up buying four CDs for $40.

Before you made the trade, you were at 7 on the utility scale. Are you still at 7 on the utility scale after you traded your $40 for the four CDs? The likely answer is no. If you expected to have the same utility after the trade as you did before, it is unlikely you would have traded your $40 for the four CDs. The only reason you entered into the trade is that you *expected* to be better off after the trade than you were before the trade. In other words, you thought trading your $40 for the four CDs would move you up the utility scale from 7 to, say, 8.

SELF-TEST

1.   Give an example to illustrate how a change in opportunity cost can affect behavior.

2.   There are both costs and benefits of studying. If you continue to study (say, for a test) as long as the marginal benefits of studying are greater than the marginal costs and stop studying when the two are equal, will your action be consistent with having maximized the net benefits of studying? Explain your answer.

3.   You stay up an added hour to study for a test. The intended effect is to raise your test grade. What might be an unintended effect of staying up an added hour to study for the test?

Economic Categories

Economics is sometimes broken down into different categories according to the type of questions economists ask. Four common economic categories are positive economics, normative economics, microeconomics, and macroeconomics.

Positive and Normative Economics

Positive Economics
The study of "what is" in economic matters.

Normative Economics
The study of "what should be" in economic matters.

Positive economics attempts to determine *what is*. **Normative economics** addresses *what should be*. Essentially, positive economics deals with cause-effect relationships that can be tested. Normative economics deals with value judgments and opinions that cannot be tested.

Many topics in economics can be discussed within both a positive framework and a normative framework. Consider a proposed cut in federal income taxes. An economist practicing positive economics would want to know the *effect* of a cut in income taxes. For example, she may want to know how a tax cut will affect the unemployment rate, economic growth, inflation, and so on. An economist practicing normative economics would address issues that directly or indirectly relate to whether the federal income tax *should* be cut. For example, she may say that federal income taxes should be cut because the income tax burden on many taxpayers is currently high.

This book mainly deals with positive economics. For the most part, we discuss the economic world as it is, not the way someone might think it should be. Keep in mind, too, that no matter what your normative objectives are, positive economics can shed some light on how they might be accomplished. For example, suppose you believe that absolute poverty should be eliminated and the unemployment rate should be lowered. No doubt you have ideas as to how these goals can be accomplished. But will your ideas work? For example, will a greater redistribution of income eliminate absolute poverty? Will lowering taxes lower the unemployment rate? There is no guarantee that the means you think will bring about certain ends will do so. This is where sound positive economics can help. It helps us see what is. As someone once said, "It is not enough to want to do good; it is important also to know how to do good."

Microeconomics and Macroeconomics

It has been said that the tools of microeconomics are microscopes, and the tools of macroeconomics are telescopes. Macroeconomics stands back from the trees to see the forest. Microeconomics gets up close and examines the tree itself, its bark, its limbs, and its roots. **Microeconomics** is the branch of economics that deals with human behavior and choices as they relate to relatively small units—an individual, a firm, an industry, a

Microeconomics
The branch of economics that deals with human behavior and choices as they relate to relatively small units—an individual, a firm, an industry, a single market.

A Reader Asks...

What's in Store for an Economics Major?

This is my first course in economics. The material is interesting, and I have given some thought to majoring in economics. Please tell me something about the major and about job prospects for an economics graduate. What courses do economics majors take? What is the starting salary of economics graduates? Do the people who run large companies think highly of people who have majored in economics?

If you major in economics, you will certainly not be alone. Economics is one of the top three majors at Harvard, Brown, Yale, the University of California at Berkeley, Princeton, Columbia, Cornell, Dartmouth, and Stanford. U.S. colleges and universities awarded 16,141 degrees to economics majors in the 2003–2004 academic year, which was up nearly 40 percent from five years earlier. The popularity of economics is probably based on two major reasons. First, many people find economics an interesting course of study. Second, what you learn in an economics course is relevant and applicable to the real world.

Do executives who run successful companies think highly of economics majors? Well, a *BusinessWeek* survey found that economics was the second favorite undergraduate major of chief executive officers (CEOs)

of major corporations. Engineering was their favorite undergraduate major.

An economics major usually takes a wide variety of economics courses, starting with introductory courses—principles of microeconomics and principles of macroeconomics—and then studying intermediate microeconomics and intermediate macroeconomics. Upper division electives usually include such courses as public finance, international economics, law and economics, managerial economics, labor economics, health economics, money and banking, environmental economics, and more.

According to the National Association of Colleges and Employers Salary Survey in Spring 2004, the average starting salary for a college graduate in economics was $43,000. For a college graduate in business administration, the average starting salary was $36,515, and for a college graduate in computer science, the average starting salary was $46,536. Also, according to the Economics and Statistics Administration of the U.S. Department of Justice, economics undergraduates have relatively higher average annual salaries than students who have majored in other fields. Specifically, of 14 different majors, economics majors ranked third. Only persons with bachelor's degrees in engineering or agriculture/forestry had higher average annual salaries.

Macroeconomics

The branch of economics that deals with human behavior and choices as they relate to highly aggregate markets (e.g., the goods and services market) or the entire economy.

single market. **Macroeconomics** is the branch of economics that deals with human behavior and choices as they relate to an entire economy. In microeconomics, economists discuss a single price; in macroeconomics, they discuss the price level. Microeconomics deals with the demand for a particular good or service; macroeconomics deals with aggregate, or total, demand for goods and services. Microeconomics examines how a tax change affects a single firm's output; macroeconomics looks at how a tax change affects an entire economy's output.

Microeconomists and macroeconomists ask different types of questions. A microeconomist might be interested in answering such questions as:

- How does a market work?
- What level of output does a firm produce?
- What price does a firm charge for the good it produces?
- How does a consumer determine how much of a good he or she will buy?
- Can government policy affect business behavior?
- Can government policy affect consumer behavior?

On the other hand, a macroeconomist might be interested in answering such questions as:

- How does the economy work?
- Why is the unemployment rate sometimes high and sometimes low?
- What causes inflation?
- Why do some national economies grow faster than other national economies?
- What might cause interest rates to be low one year and high the next?
- How do changes in the money supply affect the economy?
- How do changes in government spending and taxes affect the economy?

! analyzing the scene

Is Jackie more likely to miss some classes than she is to miss other classes? What determines which classes Jackie will attend and which classes she won't attend?

The lower the cost of not attending class, the more likely Jackie will not attend. On this particular day, Jackie is fairly sure that "her professor will be discussing a subject she already knows well." Therefore, the cost of missing this class is probably lower than missing, say, a class where the professor will be discussing an unfamiliar subject or a class in which a midterm exam will be given. Not all classes are alike for Jackie because the cost of attending each class isn't the same.

What does a basic economic fact have to do with Stephanie's buying two books at her campus bookstore?

Stephanie uses money to buy the two books. She pays the dollar price of each book. But what is dollar price? It is a rationing device. And why do we need rationing devices in

society? Because scarcity—a basic economic fact—exists. Both Stephanie *and* the long shadow of scarcity are together in the campus bookstore.

Does whether or not Jackie will go on to get a master's degree have anything to do with economics?

Jackie is undecided about whether or not she will pursue a master's degree. When she says she is not sure she wants it enough, she is really thinking about the costs and benefits of getting a master's degree. The benefits of getting the degree relate to (1) how much higher her annual income will be with a master's degree than without it, (2) how much she enjoys studying history, and so on. The costs relate to (1) the income she will lose while she is at graduate school working on a master's degree, (2) the less leisure time she will enjoy during the time she is studying, writing papers, and attending classes, (3) the tuition costs of the program, and so on. Are the benefits greater than the costs, or are the costs greater than the benefits? Jackie is thinking through an economic calculation, although she may know nothing about economics.

Stephanie stopped studying at 9:00 P.M. Would she have been better off if she had studied 30 more minutes?

Stephanie stopped studying after three hours. Studying for 30 more minutes might have provided some benefits for Stephanie, but she also would have incurred some costs.

Remember, Stephanie considers both the benefits *and* the costs of studying for 30 more minutes. If the costs are greater than the benefits, Stephanie is better off *not* studying for 30 more minutes. Stephanie likely believes she has studied the efficient amount of time—the amount of time at which the marginal benefits of studying equal the marginal costs of studying. It is possible to study too much ($MC > MB$), too little ($MB > MC$), or just the right amount ($MB = MC$).

chapter summary

Goods, Bads, and Resources

- A good is anything that gives a person utility or satisfaction.
- A bad is anything that gives a person disutility or dissatisfaction.
- Economists divide resources into four categories: land, labor, capital, and entrepreneurship.
- Land includes natural resources, such as minerals, forests, water, and unimproved land.
- Labor refers to the physical and mental talents that people contribute to the production process.
- Capital consists of produced goods that can be used as inputs for further production, such as machinery, tools, computers, trucks, buildings, and factories.
- Entrepreneurship refers to the particular talent that some people have for organizing the resources of land, labor, and capital to produce goods, seek new business opportunities, and develop new ways of doing things.

Scarcity

- Scarcity is the condition in which our wants are greater than the limited resources available to satisfy them.
- Scarcity implies choice. In a world of limited resources, we must choose which wants will be satisfied and which will go unsatisfied.
- Because of scarcity, there is a need for a rationing device. A rationing device is a means of deciding who gets what quantities of the available resources and goods.
- Scarcity implies competition. If there were enough resources to satisfy all our seemingly unlimited wants, people would not have to compete for the available but limited resources.

Opportunity Cost

- Every time a person makes a choice, he or she incurs an opportunity cost. Opportunity cost is the most highly valued opportunity or alternative forfeited when a choice is made. The higher the opportunity cost of doing something, the less likely it will be done.

Costs and Benefits

- What distinguishes the economist from the noneconomist is that the economist thinks in terms of *both* costs and benefits. Asked what the benefits of taking a walk may be, an economist will also mention the costs of taking a walk. Asked what the costs of studying are, an economist will also point out the benefits of studying.

Decisions Made at the Margin

- Marginal benefits and costs are not the same as total benefits and costs. When deciding whether to talk on the phone one more minute, an individual would not consider the total benefits and total costs of speaking on the phone. Instead, the individual would compare only the marginal benefits (additional benefits) of talking on the phone one more minute to the marginal costs (additional costs) of talking on the phone one more minute.

Efficiency

- As long as the marginal benefits of an activity are greater than its marginal costs, a person gains by continuing to do the activity—whether the activity is studying, running, eating, or watching television. The net benefits of an activity are maximized when the marginal benefits of the activity equal its marginal costs. Efficiency exists at this point.

Unintended Effects

- Economists often think in terms of causes and effects. Effects may include both intended effects and unintended effects. Economists want to denote both types of effects when speaking of effects in general.

Exchange

- Exchange or trade is the process of giving up one thing for something else. People enter into exchanges to make themselves better off.

Economic Categories

- Positive economics attempts to determine what is; normative economics addresses what should be.

- Microeconomics deals with human behavior and choices as they relate to relatively small units—an individual, a firm, an industry, a single market. Macroeconomics deals with human behavior and choices as they relate to an entire economy.

key terms and concepts

Good

Utility

Bad

Disutility

Land

Labor

Capital

Entrepreneurship

Scarcity

Economics

Rationing Device

Opportunity Cost

Marginal Benefits

Marginal Costs

Decisions at the Margin

Efficiency

Exchange (Trade)

Positive Economics

Normative Economics

Microeconomics

Macroeconomics

questions and problems

1   The United States is considered a rich country because Americans can choose from an abundance of goods and services. How can there be scarcity in a land of abundance?

2   Give two examples for each of the following: (a) an intangible good, (b) a tangible good, (c) a bad.

3   What is the difference between the resource labor and the resource entrepreneurship?

4   Explain the link between scarcity and each of the following: (a) choice, (b) opportunity cost, (c) the need for a rationing device, (d) competition.

5   Is it possible for a person to incur an opportunity cost without spending any money? Explain.

6   Discuss the opportunity costs of attending college for four years. Is college more or less costly than you thought it was? Explain.

7   Explain the relationship between changes in opportunity cost and changes in behavior.

8   Smith says that we should eliminate all pollution in the world. Jones disagrees. Who is more likely to be an economist, Smith or Jones? Explain your answer.

9   A layperson says that a proposed government project simply costs too much and therefore shouldn't be undertaken. How might an economist's evaluation be different?

10 Economists say that individuals make decisions at the margin. What does this mean?

11 How would an economist define the efficient amount of time spent playing tennis?

12 A change in X will lead to a change in Y; the predicted change is desirable, so we should change X. Do you agree or disagree? Explain.

13 Why do people enter into exchanges?

14 What is the difference between positive economics and normative economics? between microeconomics and macroeconomics?

Working with Diagrams

A picture is worth a thousand words. With this familiar saying in mind, economists construct their diagrams or graphs. With a few lines and a few points, much can be conveyed.

Two-Variable Diagrams

Most of the diagrams in this book represent the relationship between two variables. Economists compare two variables to see how a change in one variable affects the other variable.

Suppose our two variables of interest are *consumption* and *income*. We want to show how consumption changes as income changes. Suppose we collect the data in Table 1. By simply looking at the data in the first two columns, we can see that as income rises (column 1), consumption rises (column 2). Suppose we want to show the relationship between income and consumption on a graph. We could place *income* on the horizontal axis, as in Exhibit 1, and *consumption* on the vertical axis. Point *A* represents income of $0 and consumption of $60, point *B* represents income of $100 and consumption of $120, and so on. If we draw a straight line through the various points we have plotted, we have a picture of the relationship between income and consumption, based on the data we collected.

Notice that our line in Exhibit 1 slopes upward from left to right. Thus, as income rises, so does consumption. For example, as you move from point *A* to point *B*, income rises from $0 to $100 and consumption rises from $60 to $120. The line in Exhibit 1 also shows that as income falls, so does consumption. For example, as you move from point *C* to point *B*, income falls from $200 to $100 and consumption falls from $180 to $120. When two variables—such as consumption and income—change in the same way, they are said to be **directly related**.

Now let's take a look at the data in Table 2. Our two variables are *price of compact discs (CDs)* and *quantity demanded of CDs*. By simply looking at the data in the first two columns, we see that as price falls (column 1), quantity demanded rises (column 2). Suppose we want to plot these data. We could place *price* (of CDs) on the vertical axis, as in

exhibit 1

A Two-Variable Diagram Representing a Direct Relationship

In this exhibit, we have plotted the data in Table 1 and then connected the points with a straight line. The data represent a direct relationship: as one variable (say, income) rises, the other variable (consumption) rises too.

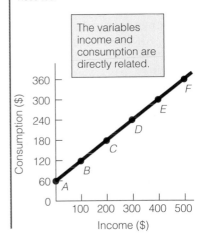

The variables income and consumption are directly related.

Directly Related

Two variables are directly related if they change in the same way.

table 1

(1) When Income Is:	(2) Consumption Is:	(3) Point
$ 0	$ 60	A
100	120	B
200	180	C
300	240	D
400	300	E
500	360	F

table 2	(1) When Price of CDs Is:	(2) Quanity Demanded of CDs Is:	(3) Point
	$20	100	A
	18	120	B
	16	140	C
	14	160	D
	12	180	E

Exhibit 2, and *quantity demanded* (of CDs) on the horizontal axis. Point *A* represents a price of $20 and a quantity demanded of 100, point *B* represents a price of $18 and a quantity demanded of 120, and so on. If we draw a straight line through the various points we have plotted, we have a picture of the relationship between price and quantity demanded, based on the data in Table 2.

Notice that as price falls, quantity demanded rises. For example, as price falls from $20 to $18, quantity demanded rises from 100 to 120. Also as price rises, quantity demanded falls. For example, when price rises from $12 to $14, quantity demanded falls from 180 to 160.

When two variables—such as price and quantity demanded—change in opposite ways, they are said to be **inversely related**.

As you have seen so far, variables may be directly related (when one increases, the other also increases), or they may be inversely related (when one increases, the other decreases). Variables can also be **independent** of each other. This condition exists if as one variable changes, the other does not.

In Exhibit 3(a), as the *X* variable rises, the *Y* variable remains the same (at 20). Obviously, the *X* and *Y* variables are independent of each other: as one changes, the other does not.

In Exhibit 3(b), as the *Y* variable rises, the *X* variable remains the same (at 30). Again, we conclude that the *X* and *Y* variables are independent of each other: as one changes, the other does not.

Inversely Related

Two variables are inversely related if they change in opposite ways.

Independent

Two variables are independent if as one changes, the other does not.

Slope

The ratio of the change in the variable on the vertical axis to the change in the variable on the horizontal axis.

Slope of a Line

It is often important not only to know *how* two variables are related but also to know *how much* one variable changes as the other variable changes. To find out, we need only calculate the slope of the line. The **slope** is the ratio of the change in the variable on the vertical axis to the change in the variable on the horizontal axis. For example, if *Y* is on the vertical axis and *X* on the horizontal axis, the slope is equal to $\Delta Y/\Delta X$. (The symbol "Δ" means "change in.")

$$\text{Slope} = \frac{\Delta Y}{\Delta X}$$

Exhibit 4 shows four lines. In each case, we have calculated the slope. After studying (a)–(d), see if you can calculate the slope in each case.

Slope of a Line Is Constant

Look again at the line in Exhibit 4(a). We computed the slope between points *A* and *B* and found it to be −1. Suppose that instead of computing the slope between points *A* and *B*, we had computed the slope between points *B* and *C* or between points *C* and *D*.

exhibit 2

A Two-Variable Diagram Representing an Inverse Relationship

In this exhibit, we have plotted the data in Table 2 and then connected the points with a straight line. The data represent an inverse relationship: as one variable (price) falls, the other variable (quantity demanded) rises.

The variables price and quantity demanded are inversely related.

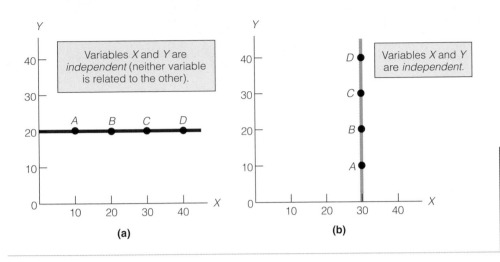

exhibit **3**

Two Diagrams Representing Independence Between Two Variables

In (a) and (b), the variables X and Y are independent: as one changes, the other does not.

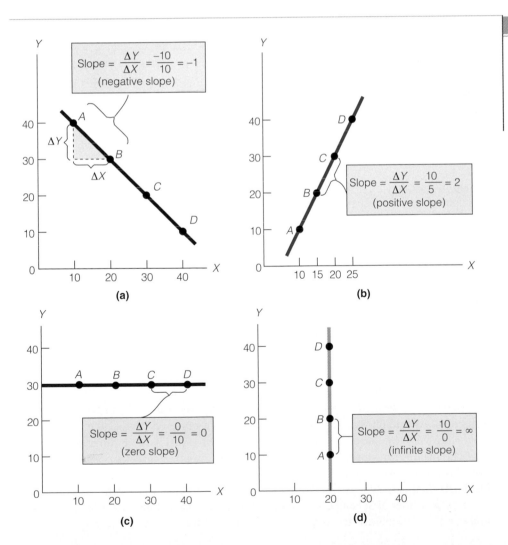

exhibit **4**

Calculating Slopes

The slope of a line is the ratio of the change in the variable on the vertical axis to the change in the variable on the horizontal axis. In (a)–(d), we have calculated the slope.

exhibit 5

Calculating the Slope of a Curve at a Particular Point

The slope of the curve at point A is 0.67. This is calculated by drawing a line tangent to the curve at point A and then determining the slope of the line.

Would the slope still be −1? Let's compute the slope between points B and C. Moving from point B to point C, the change in Y is −10 and the change in X is +10. So, the slope is −1, which is what the slope was between points A and B.

Now let's compute the slope between points A and D. Moving from point A to point D, the change in Y is −30 and the change in X is +30. Again the slope is =1.

Our conclusion is that the slope between any two points on a (straight) line is always the same as the slope between any other two points. To see this for yourself, compute the slope between points A and B and between points A and C using the line in Exhibit 4(b).

Slope of a Curve

Economic graphs use both straight lines and curves. The slope of a curve is not constant throughout as it is for a straight line. The slope of a curve varies from one point to another.

Calculating the slope of a curve at a given point requires two steps, as illustrated for point A in Exhibit 5. First, draw a line tangent to the curve at the point (a tangent line is one that just touches the curve but does not cross it). Second, pick any two points on the tangent line and determine the slope. In Exhibit 5 the slope of the line between points B and C is 0.67. It follows that the slope of the curve at point A (and only at point A) is 0.67.

The 45° Line

Economists sometimes use a *45° line* to represent data. This is a straight line that bisects the right angle formed by the intersection of the vertical and horizontal axes (see Exhibit 6). As a result, the 45° line divides the space enclosed by the two axes into *two equal parts*. We have illustrated this by shading the two equal parts in different colors.

The major characteristic of the 45° line is that any point that lies on it is equidistant from both the horizontal and vertical axes. For example, point A is exactly as far from the horizontal axis as it is from the vertical axis. It follows that point A represents as much X as it does Y. Specifically, in the exhibit, point A represents 20 units of X and 20 units of Y.

exhibit 6

The 45° Line

Any point on the 45° line is equidistant from both axis. For example, point A is the same distance from the vertical axis as it is from the horizontal axis.

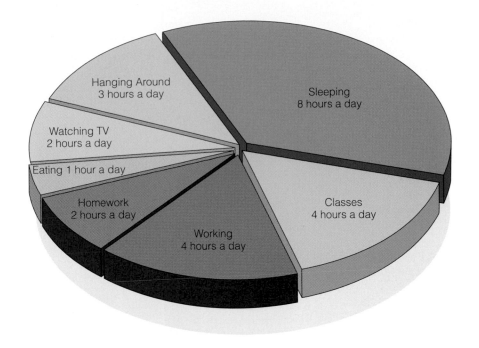

exhibit 7

A Pie Chart

The breakdown of activities for Charles Myers during a typical 24-hour weekday is represented in pie chart form.

Pie Charts

In numerous places in this text, you will come across a *pie chart*. A pie chart is a convenient way to represent the different parts of something that when added together equal the whole.

Let's consider a typical 24-hour weekday for Charles Myers. On a typical weekday, Charles spends 8 hours sleeping, 4 hours taking classes at the university, 4 hours working at his part-time job, 2 hours doing homework, 1 hour eating, 2 hours watching television, and 3 hours doing nothing in particular (we'll call it "hanging around"). Exhibit 7 shows the breakdown of a typical weekday for Charles in pie chart form.

Pie charts give a quick visual message as to rough percentage breakdowns and relative relationships. For example, it is easy to see in Exhibit 7 that Charles spends twice as much time working as doing homework.

Bar Graphs

The *bar graph* is another visual aid that economists use to convey relative relationships. Suppose we wanted to represent the gross domestic product for the United States in different years. The **gross domestic product (GDP)** is the value of the entire output produced annually within a country's borders. A bar graph can show the actual GDP for each year and can also provide a quick picture of the relative relationships between the GDP in different years. For example, it is easy to see in Exhibit 8 that the GDP in 1990 was more than double what it was in 1980.

Gross Domestic Product (GDP)

The value of the entire output produced annually within a country's borders.

Line Graphs

Sometimes information is best and most easily displayed in a *line graph*. Line graphs are particularly useful for illustrating changes in a variable over some time period.

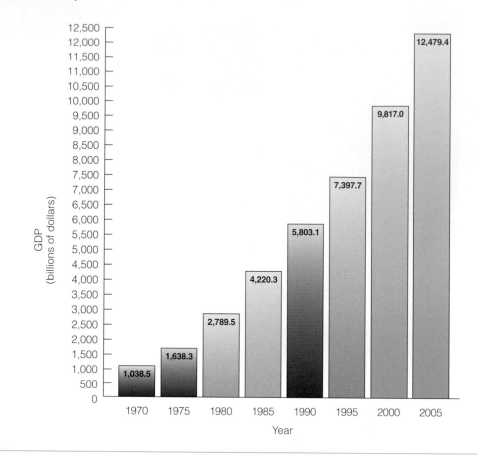

exhibit 8

A Bar Graph

U.S. gross domestic product for different years is illustrated in bar graph form

Source: Bureau of Economic Analysis

Suppose we want to illustrate the variations in average points per game for a college basketball team in different years. As you can see from Exhibit 9(a), the basketball team has been on a roller coaster during the years 1994–2007. Perhaps the message transmitted here is that the team's performance has not been consistent from one year to the next.

Suppose we plot the data in Exhibit 9(a) again, except this time we use a different measurement scale on the vertical axis. As you can see in (b), the variation in the performance of the basketball team appears much less pronounced than in (a). In fact, we could choose some scale such that if we were to plot the data, we would end up with close to a straight line. Our point is simple: Data plotted in line graph form may convey different messages depending on the measurement scale used.

Sometimes economists show two line graphs on the same axes. Usually, they do this to draw attention to either (1) the *relationship* between the two variables or (2) the *difference* between the two variables. In Exhibit 10, the line graphs show the variation and trend in federal government expenditures and tax receipts for the years 1996–2007 and draw attention to what has been happening to the "gap" between the two.

(a)

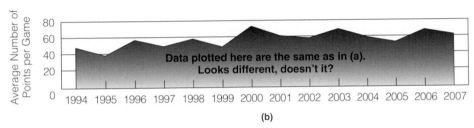

(b)

exhibit 9

The Two Line Graphs Plot the Same Data

In (a) we plotted the average number of points per game for a college basketball team in different years. The variation between the years is pronounced. In (b) we plotted the same data as in (a), but the variation in the performance of the team appears much less pronounced than in (a).

Year	Average Number of Points per Game
1994	50
1995	40
1996	59
1997	51
1998	60
1999	50
2000	75
2001	63
2002	60
2003	71
2004	61
2005	55
2006	70
2007	64

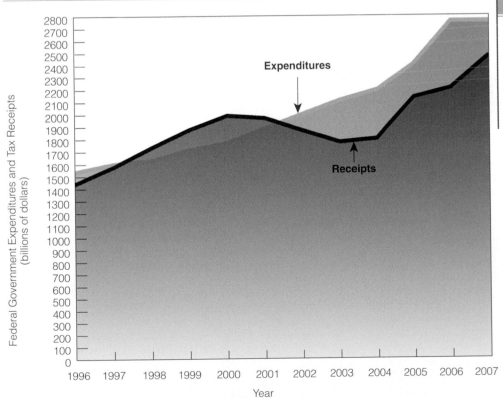

exhibit 10

Federal Government Expenditures and Tax Receipts, 1996–2007

Federal government expenditures and tax receipts are shown in line graph form for the period 1996–2007. The data for 2006 and 2007 are estimates.

Source: Bureau of Economic Analysis

appendix summary

- Two variables are directly related if one variable rises as the other rises.
- An upward-sloping line (left to right) represents two variables that are directly related.
- Two variables are inversely related if one variable rises as the other falls.
- A downward-sloping line (left to right) represents two variables that are inversely related.
- Two variables are independent if one variable rises as the other remains constant.
- The slope of a line is the ratio of the change in the variable on the vertical axis to the change in the variable on the horizontal axis. The slope of a (straight) line is the same between every two points on the line.

- To determine the slope of a curve at a point, draw a line tangent to the curve at the point and then determine the slope of the tangent line.
- Any point on a 45° line is equidistant from the two axes.
- A pie chart is a convenient way to represent the different parts of something that when added together equal the whole. A pie chart visually shows rough percentage breakdowns and relative relationships.
- A bar graph is a convenient way to represent relative relationships.
- Line graphs are particularly useful for illustrating changes in a variable over some time period.

questions and problems

1   What type of relationship would you expect between the following: (a) sales of hot dogs and sales of hot dog buns, (b) the price of winter coats and sales of winter coats, (c) the price of personal computers and the production of personal computers, (d) sales of toothbrushes and sales of cat food, (e) the number of children in a family and the number of toys in a family.

2   Represent the following data in bar graph form.

Year	U.S. Money Supply (billions of dollars)
2001	1,182
2002	1,219
2003	1,304
2004	1,372
2005	1,369

3   Plot the following data and specify the type of relationship between the two variables. (Place "price" on the vertical axis and "quantity demanded" on the horizontal axis.)

Price of Apples ($)	Quantity Demanded of Apples
0.25	1,000
0.50	800
0.70	700
0.95	500
1.00	400
1.10	350

4   In Exhibit 4(a), determine the slope between points C and D.

5   In Exhibit 4(b), determine the slope between points A and D.

6   What is the special characteristic of a 45° line?

7   What is the slope of a 45° line?

8   When would it be preferable to illustrate data using a pie chart instead of a bar graph?

9   Plot the following data and specify the type of relationship between the two variables. (Place "price" on the vertical axis and "quantity supplied" on the horizontal axis.)

Price of Apples ($)	Quantity Supplied of Apples
0.25	350
0.50	400
0.70	500
0.95	700
1.00	800
1.10	1,000

Should You Major in Economics?   b

You are probably reading this textbook as part of your first college course in economics. You may be taking this course because you need it to satisfy the requirements in your major. Economics courses are sometimes required for students who plan to major in business, history, liberal studies, social science, or computer science. Of course, you may also be taking this course because you plan to major in economics.

If you are like many college students, you may complain that not enough information is available to students about the various majors at your college or university. For example, students who major in business sometimes say they are not quite certain what a business major is all about, but then they go on to add that majoring in business is a safe bet. "After all," they comment, "you are pretty sure of getting a job if you have a business degree. That's not always the case with other degrees."

Many college students choose their majors based on their high school courses. History majors sometimes say that they decided to major in history because they "liked history in high school." Similarly, chemistry, biology, and math majors say they chose chemistry, biology, or math as a college major because they liked studying chemistry, biology, or math in high school. In addition, if a student had a hard time with chemistry in high school and found it boring, then he doesn't usually want to major in chemistry in college. If a student found both math and economics easy and interesting in high school, then she is likely to major in math or economics.

Students also often look to the dollars at the end of the college degree. A student may enjoy history and want to learn more history in college but tell herself that she will earn a higher starting salary after graduation if she majors in computer science or engineering.

Thus, when choosing a major, students often consider (1) how much they enjoy studying a particular subject, (2) what they would like to see themselves doing in the future, and (3) income prospects.

Different people may weight these three factors differently. But no matter what weights you put on each of the factors, it is always better to have more information than less information, *ceteris paribus*. (We note *"ceteris paribus"* because it is not necessarily better having more information than less information if you have to pay more for the additional information than the additional information is worth. Who wants to pay $10 for a piece of information that only provides $1 in benefits?)

We believe this appendix is a fairly low-cost way of providing you with more information about an economics major than you currently have. We start by dispelling some of the misinformation you might possess about an economics major. Stated bluntly, some things that people think about an economics major and about a career in economics are just not true. For example, some people think that economics majors almost never study social relationships; instead, they only study such things as inflation, interest rates, and unemployment. Not true. Economics majors study some of the same things that sociologists, historians, psychologists, and political scientists study. We also provide you with some information about the major that you may not have.

Next, we tell you the specifics of the economics major—what courses you study if you are an economics major, how many courses you are likely to have to take, and more.

Finally, we tell you something about a career in economics. Okay, so you have opted to become an economics major. But the day will come when you have your degree in hand. What's next? What is your starting salary likely to be? What will you be doing? Are you going to be happy doing what economists do? (If you never thought economics was about happiness, you already have some misinformation about economics. Contrary to what most laypeople think, economics is not just about money. It is about happiness too.)

Five Myths About Economics and an Economics Major

MYTH 1: ECONOMICS IS ALL MATHEMATICS AND STATISTICS. Some students choose not to major in economics because they think economics is all mathematics and statistics. Math and statistics are used in economics, but at the undergraduate degree level, the math and statistics are certainly not overwhelming. Economics majors are usually required to take one statistics course and one math course (usually an introductory calculus course). Even students who say, "Math isn't my subject" are sometimes happy with the amount of math they need in economics. Fact is, at the undergraduate level at many colleges and universities, economics is not a very math-intensive course of study. There are many diagrams in economics, but there is not a large amount of math.

A proviso: The amount of math in the economics curriculum varies across colleges and universities. Some economics departments do not require their students to learn much math or statistics, but others do. Speaking for the majority of departments, we still hold to our original point that there isn't really that much math or statistics in economics at the undergraduate level. The graduate level is a different story.

MYTH 2: ECONOMICS IS ONLY ABOUT INFLATION, INTEREST RATES, UNEMPLOYMENT, AND OTHER SUCH THINGS. If you study economics at college and then go on to become a practicing economist, no doubt people will ask you certain questions when they learn your chosen profession. Here are some of the questions they ask:

- Do you think the economy is going to pick up?
- Do you think the economy is going to slow down?
- What stocks would you recommend?
- Do you think interest rates are going to fall?
- Do you think interest rates are going to rise?
- What do you think about buying bonds right now? Is it a good idea?

People ask these kinds of questions because most people believe that economists only study stocks, bonds, interest rates, inflation, unemployment, and so on. Well, economists do study these things. But these topics are only a tiny part of what economists study. It is not hard to find many economists today, both inside and outside academia, who spend most of their time studying anything but inflation, unemployment, stocks, bonds, and so on.

As we hinted earlier, much of what economists study may surprise you. There are economists who use their economic tools and methods to study crime, marriage, divorce, sex, obesity, addiction, sports, voting behavior, bureaucracies, presidential elections, and much more. In short, today's economics is not your grandfather's economics. Many more topics are studied today in economics than were studied in your grandfather's time.

MYTH 3: PEOPLE BECOME ECONOMISTS ONLY IF THEY WANT TO "MAKE MONEY." Awhile back we asked a few well-respected and well-known economists what got them interested in economics. Here is what some of them had to say:[1]

Gary Becker, the 1992 winner of the Nobel Prize in Economics, said: "I got interested [in economics] when I was an undergraduate in college. I came into college with a strong interest in mathematics, and at the same time with a strong commitment to do something to help society. I learned in the first economics course I took that economics could deal rigorously, à la mathematics, with social problems. That stimulated me because in economics I saw that I could combine both the mathematics and my desire to do something to help society."

Vernon Smith, the 2002 winner of the Nobel Prize in Economics, said: "My father's influence started me in science and engineering at Cal Tech, but my mother, who was active in socialist politics, probably accounts for the great interest I found in economics when I took my first introductory course."

Alice Rivlin, an economist and former member of the Federal Reserve Board, said: "My interest in economics grew out of concern for improving public policy, both domestic and international. I was a teenager in the tremendously idealistic period after World War II when it seemed terribly important to get nations working together to solve the world's problems peacefully."

Allan Meltzer said: "Economics is a social science. At its best it is concerned with ways (1) to improve well being by allowing individuals the freedom to achieve their personal aims or goals and (2) to harmonize their individual interests. I find working on such issues challenging, and progress is personally rewarding."

Robert Solow, the 1987 winner of the Nobel Prize in Economics, said: "I grew up in the 1930s and it was very hard not to be interested in economics. If you were a high school student in the 1930s, you were conscious of the fact that our economy was in deep trouble and no one knew what to do about it."

Charles Plosser said: "I was an engineer as an undergraduate with little knowledge of economics. I went to the University of Chicago Graduate School of Business to get an MBA and there became fascinated with economics. I was impressed with the seriousness with which economics was viewed as a way of organizing one's thoughts about the world to address interesting questions and problems."

Walter Williams said: "I was a major in sociology in 1963 and I concluded that it was not very rigorous. Over the summer I was reading a book by W.E.B. DuBois, *Black Reconstruction,* and somewhere in the book it said something along the lines that blacks could not melt into the mainstream of American society until they understood economics, and that was something that got me interested in economics."

Murray Weidenbaum said: "A specific professor got me interested in economics. He was very prescient: He correctly noted that while lawyers dominated the policy-making process up until then (the 1940s), in the future economics would be an important tool for developing public policy. And he was right."

Irma Adelman said: "I hesitate to say because it sounds arrogant. My reason [for getting into economics] was that I wanted to benefit humanity. And my perception at the time was that economic problems were the most important problems that humanity has to face. That is what got me into economics and into economic development."

Lester Thurow said: "[I got interested in economics because of] the belief, some would see it as naïve belief, that economics was a profession where it would be possible to help make the world better."

---

[1]See various interviews in Roger A. Arnold, *Economics, 2d edition* (St. Paul, Minnesota: West Publishing Company, 1992).

MYTH 4: ECONOMICS WASN'T VERY INTERESTING IN HIGH SCHOOL, SO IT'S NOT GOING TO BE VERY INTERESTING IN COLLEGE. A typical high school economics course emphasizes consumer economics and spends much time discussing this topic. Students learn about credit cards, mortgage loans, budgets, buying insurance, renting an apartment, and other such things. These are important topics because not knowing the "ins and outs" of such things can make your life much harder. Still, many students come away from a high school economics course thinking that economics is always and everywhere about consumer topics.

However, a high school economics course and a college economics course are usually as different as day and night. Simply leaf through this book and look at the variety of topics covered compared to the topics you might have covered in your high school economics course. Go on to look at texts used in other economics courses—courses that range from law and economics to history of economic thought to international economics to sports economics—and you will see what we mean.

MYTH 5: ECONOMICS IS A LOT LIKE BUSINESS, BUT BUSINESS IS MORE MARKETABLE. Although business and economics have some common topics, much that one learns in economics is not taught in business and much that one learns in business is not taught in economics. The area of intersection between business and economics is not large.

Still, many people think otherwise. And so thinking that business and economics are "pretty much the same thing," they often choose to major in the subject they believe has greater marketability—which they believe is business.

Well, consider the following:

1. A few years ago *BusinessWeek* magazine asked the chief executive officers (CEOs) of major companies what they thought was the best undergraduate degree. Their first choice was engineering. Their second choice was economics. Economics scored higher than business administration.

2. The National Association of Colleges and Employers undertook a survey in the summer of 2005 in which they identified the starting salary offers in different disciplines. The starting salary in economics/finance was $42,928. The starting salary in business administration was 7.8 percent lower.

What Awaits You as an Economics Major?

If you become an economics major, what courses will you take? What are you going to study?

At the lower-division level, economics majors must take both the principles of macroeconomics course and the principles of microeconomics course. They usually also take a statistics course and a math course (usually calculus).

At the upper-division level, they must take intermediate microeconomics and intermediate macroeconomics, along with a certain number of electives. Some of the elective courses include: (1) money and banking, (2) law and economics, (3) history of economic thought, (4) public finance, (5) labor economics, (6) international economics, (7) antitrust and regulation, (8) health economics, (9) economics of development, (10) urban and regional economics, (11) econometrics, (12) mathematical economics, (13) environmental economics, (14) public choice, (15) global managerial economics, (16) economic approach to politics and sociology, (17) sports economics, and many more courses. Most economics majors take between 12 and 15 economics courses.

One of the attractive things about studying economics is that you will acquire many of the skills employers highly value. First, you will have the quantitative skills that are important in many business and government positions. Second, you will acquire the writing skills necessary in almost all lines of work. Third, and perhaps most importantly, you will develop the thinking skills that almost all employers agree are critical to success.

A study published in the 1998 edition of the *Journal of Economic Education* ranked economics majors as having the highest average scores on the Law School Admission Test (LSAT). Also, consider the words of the Royal Economic Society: "One of the things that makes economics graduates so employable is that the subject teaches you to think in a careful and precise way. The fundamental economic issue is how society decides to allocate its resources: how the costs and benefits of a course of action can be evaluated and compared, and how appropriate choices can be made. A degree in economics gives a training in decision making principles, providing a skill applicable in a very wide range of careers."

Keep in mind, too, that economics is one of the most popular majors at some of the most respected universities in the country. As of this writing, economics is the top major at Harvard, Princeton, Columbia, Stanford, University of Pennsylvania, and University of Chicago. It is the second most popular major at Brown, Yale, and the University of California at Berkeley. It is the third most popular major at Cornell and Dartmouth.

What Do Economists Do?

Employment for economists is projected to grow between 21 and 35 percent between 2000 and 2010. According to the *Occupational Outlook Handbook*:

Opportunities for economists should be best in private industry, especially in research, testing, and consulting firms, as more companies contract out for economic research services. The growing complexity of the global economy, competition, and increased reliance on quantitative methods for analyzing the current value of future funds, business trends, sales, and purchasing should spur demand for economists. The growing need for economic analyses in virtually every industry should result in additional jobs for economists.

Today, economists work in many varied fields. Here are some of the fields and some of the positions economists hold in those fields:

Education
College Professor
Researcher
High School Teacher

Journalism
Researcher
Industry Analyst
Economic Analyst

Accounting
Analyst
Auditor
Researcher
Consultant

General Business
Chief Executive Officer
Business Analyst
Marketing Analyst
Business Forecaster
Competitive Analyst

Government
Researcher
Analyst
Speechwriter
Forecaster

Financial Services
Business Journalist
International Analyst

Newsletter Editor
Broker
Investment Banker

Banking
Credit Analyst
Loan Officer
Investment Analyst
Financial Manager

Other
Business Consultant
Independent Forecaster
Freelance Analyst
Think Tank Analyst
Entrepreneur

Economists do a myriad of things. For example, in business, economists often analyze economic conditions, make forecasts, offer strategic planning initiatives, collect and analyze data, predict exchange rate movements, and review regulatory policies, among other things. In government, economists collect and analyze data, analyze international economic situations, research monetary conditions, advise on policy, and much more. As private consultants, economists work with accountants, business executives, government officials, educators, financial firms, labor unions, state and local governments, and others.

Median annual earnings of economists were $68,550 in 2002. The middle 50 percent earned between $50,560 and $90,710. The lowest 10 percent earned less than $38,690, and the highest 10 percent earned more than $120,440.

Places to Find More Information

If you are interested in an economics major and perhaps a career in economics, here are some places where you can go and some people you can speak with to acquire more information:

- To learn about the economics curriculum, we urge you to speak with the economics professors at your college or university. Ask them what courses you would have to take as an economics major. Ask them what elective courses are available. In addition, ask them why they chose to study economics. What is it about economics that interested them?
- For more information about salaries and what economists do, you may want to visit the *Occupational Outlook Handbook* Web site at http://www.bls.gov/oco/.
- For starting salary information, you may want to visit the National Association of Colleges and Employers Web site at http://www.naceweb.org/.
- To see a list of famous people who have majored in economics, go to http://www.marietta .edu/~ema/econ/famous.html.

Concluding Remarks

Choosing a major is a big decision and therefore should not be made too quickly and without much thought. In this short appendix, we have provided you with some information about an economics major and a career in economics. Economics may not be for everyone (in fact, economists would say that if it were, many of the benefits of specialization would be lost), but it may be right for you. Economics is a major where many of today's most marketable skills are acquired—the skills of good writing, quantitative analysis, and thinking. It is a major in which professors and students daily ask and answer some very interesting and relevant questions. It is a major that is highly regarded by employers. It may just be the right major for you. Give it some thought.

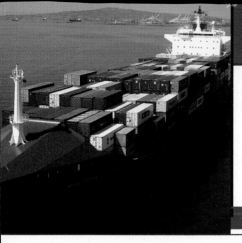

Economic Activities: Producing and Trading

2

Setting the Scene   The following events happened on a day in March.

8:25 A.M.

Two presidential advisors are in the West Wing of the White House discussing what Eduard Shevardnadze said in 1990. Shevardnadze had been the Soviet foreign minister before the collapse of the Soviet Union. He had said the Soviet Union collapsed because of the conflict between the Kremlin and the people. The Kremlin wanted "more guns," and the people wanted "more butter," but it was impossible to get more of both. Something had to give, and so it did: The Soviet Union imploded.

10:13 A.M.

Bob and Jim are roommates and students at the University of Missouri Kansas City. Bob says, "I have two final exams tomorrow—biology at 9 and calculus at 2. I think it's come down to choosing where I want to get an A. I don't have enough study time tonight to get As in both courses." Jim comments, "If we could

only produce 'more time' the same way people produce more watches or more cars. I bet we could sell *that* for a pretty penny."

5:55 P.M.

Karen and Larry have been married for eleven years. They have two children: a boy, James, nine years old, and a girl, Caroline, six years old. Every night, Karen cooks the dinner and Larry washes the dishes. Fact is, when Karen and Larry first got married, they decided to split the households tasks "right down the middle." To them, this meant that Karen and Larry would each do half of everything: Karen would do half the cooking, and Larry would do half the cooking; Karen would do half the cleaning, and Larry would do half the cleaning. It hasn't turned out that way, though. Each does 100 percent of certain tasks. In a way, each has specialized in performing certain tasks around the house.

6:25 P.M.

Jayant says to Helena. "What eBay did really wasn't that hard." Helena replies, "I just wish I had done it."

?   Here are some questions to keep in mind as you read this chapter:

- *What does a point on a production possibilities frontier have to do with the collapse of the Soviet Union?*

- *Why can't Bob get As in both biology and calculus, and what does Jim's desire to produce "more time" tell us about life?*

- *What led Karen and Larry to specialize in doing certain tasks?*

- *What did eBay do that really wasn't that hard?*

See   analyzing the scene   at the end of this chapter for answers to these questions.

The Production Possibilities Frontier

This section discusses the production possibilities frontier (PPF) and numerous economic concepts that can be illustrated by it.

The Straight-Line PPF: Constant Opportunity Costs

Assume the following:

1. Only two goods can be produced in an economy: computers and television sets.

2. The opportunity cost of 1 television set is 1 computer.

3. As more of one good is produced, the opportunity cost between television sets and computers is *constant*.

Production Possibilities Frontier (PPF)

Represents the possible combinations of two goods that can be produced in a certain period of time under the conditions of a given state of technology and fully employed resources.

In Exhibit 1(a), we have identified six combinations of computers and television sets that can be produced in our economy. For example, combination A is 50,000 computers and 0 television sets, combination B is 40,000 computers and 10,000 television sets, and so on. We plotted these six combinations of computers and television sets in Exhibit 1(b). Each combination represents a different point in Exhibit 1(b). For example, the combination of 50,000 computers and 0 television sets is represented by point A. The line that connects points A–F is the production possibilities frontier. A **production possibilities frontier (PPF)** represents the combination of two goods that can be produced in a certain period of time under the conditions of a given state of technology and fully employed resources.

The production possibilities frontier is a *straight line* in this instance because the opportunity cost of producing computers and television sets is *constant*.

Straight-line PPF = Constant opportunity costs

For example, if the economy were to move from point A to point B, from B to C, and so on, the opportunity cost of each good would remain *constant* at 1 for 1. To illustrate, at point A, 50,000 computers and 0 television sets are produced. At point B, 40,000 computers and 10,000 television sets are produced.

Point A: 50,000 computers, 0 television sets
Point B: 40,000 computers, 10,000 television sets

Production Possibilities Frontier (Constant Opportunity Costs)

The economy can produce any of the six combinations of computers and television sets in part (a). We have plotted these combinations in part (b). The production possibilities frontier in part (b) is a straight line because the opportunity cost of producing either good is constant: for *every* 1 computer not produced, 1 television set is produced.

Combination	Computers	Television Sets	Point in Part (b)
A	50,000	0	A
B	40,000	10,000	B
C	30,000	20,000	C
D	20,000	30,000	D
E	10,000	40,000	E
F	0	50,000	F

(a)

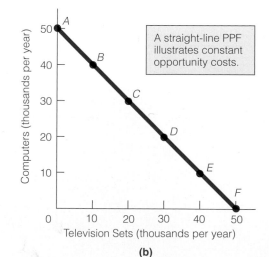

A straight-line PPF illustrates constant opportunity costs.

(b)

We conclude that for every 10,000 computers not produced, 10,000 television sets are produced—a ratio of 1 to 1. The opportunity cost—1 computer for 1 television set—that exists between points *A* and *B* also exists between points *B* and *C*, *C* and *D*, *D* and *E*, and *E* and *F*. In other words, opportunity cost is constant at 1 computer for 1 television set.

The Bowed-Outward (Concave-Downward) PPF: Increasing Opportunity Costs

Assume two things:

1. Only two goods can be produced in an economy: computers and television sets.

2. As more of one good is produced, the opportunity cost between computers and television sets *changes.*

In Exhibit 2(a), we have identified four combinations of computers and television sets that can be produced in our economy. For example, combination *A* is 50,000 computers and 0 television sets, combination *B* is 40,000 computers and 20,000 television sets, and so on. We plotted these four combinations of computers and television sets in Exhibit 2(b). Each combination represents a different point. The curved line that connects points *A–D* is the production possibilities frontier.

In this case, the production possibilities frontier is *bowed outward* (concave downward) because the opportunity cost of television sets *increases* as more sets are produced.

Bowed-outward PPF = Increasing opportunity costs

To illustrate, let's start at point *A*, where the economy is producing 50,000 computers and 0 television sets, and move to point *B*, where the economy is producing 40,000 computers and 20,000 television sets.

Point *A*: 50,000 computers, 0 television sets
Point *B*: 40,000 computers, 20,000 television sets

Q&A   *Opportunity cost and PPF seem like two economic concepts that are linked together somehow. Are they?*

Yes. When we move *from one point on the PPF to another point on the PPF, we automatically incur an opportunity cost. To illustrate, suppose we move from point* C *in Exhibit 1(b) to point* D. *Notice what happens: We get more television sets but fewer computers. What we have to "give up" to get more television sets is the opportunity cost of those additional television sets.*

exhibit **2**

Production Possibilities Frontier (Increasing Opportunity Costs)

The economy can produce any of the four combinations of computers and televisions sets in part (a). We have plotted these combinations in part (b). The production possibilities frontier in part (b) is bowed outward because the opportunity cost of producing television sets increases as more television sets are produced.

Combination	Computers	Television Sets	Point in Part (b)
A	50,000	0	A
B	40,000	20,000	B
C	25,000	40,000	C
D	0	60,000	D

(a)

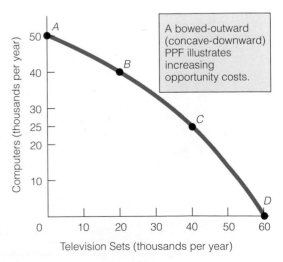

A bowed-outward (concave-downward) PPF illustrates increasing opportunity costs.

(b)

What is the opportunity cost of a television set over this range? We see that 20,000 more television sets are produced by moving from point *A* to point *B but at the cost of only 10,000 computers.* This means for every 1 television set produced, 1/2 computer is forfeited. Thus, the opportunity cost of 1 television set is 1/2 computer.

Now let's move from point *B*, where the economy is producing 40,000 computers and 20,000 television sets, to point *C*, where the economy is producing 25,000 computers and 40,000 television sets.

> Point *B:* 40,000 computers, 20,000 television sets
> Point *C:* 25,000 computers, 40,000 television sets

What is the opportunity cost of a television set over this range? In this case, 20,000 more television sets are produced by moving from point *B* to point *C but at the cost of 15,000 computers.* This means for every 1 television set produced, 3/4 computer is forfeited. Thus, the opportunity cost of 1 television set is 3/4 of a computer.

Law of Increasing Opportunity Costs

As more of a good is produced, the opportunity costs of producing that good increase.

What statement can we make about the opportunity costs of producing television sets? Obviously, as the economy produces more television sets, the opportunity cost of producing television sets increases. This gives us the bowed-outward production possibilities frontier in Exhibit 2(b).

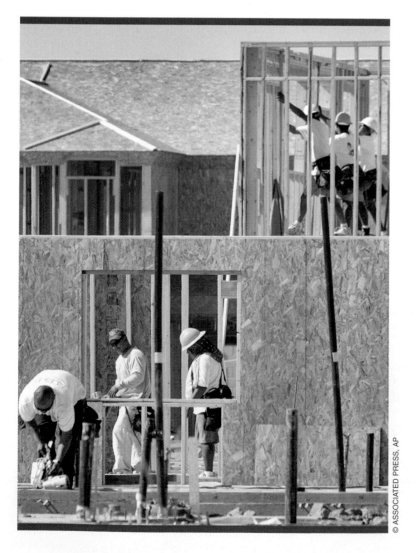

© ASSOCIATED PRESS, AP

Law of Increasing Opportunity Costs

We know that the shape of the production possibilities frontier depends on whether opportunity costs (1) are constant or (2) increase as more of a good is produced. In Exhibit 1(b), the production possibilities frontier is a straight line; in Exhibit 2(b), it is bowed outward (curved). In the real world, most production possibilities frontiers are bowed outward. This means that for most goods, the opportunity costs increase as more of the good is produced. This is referred to as the **law of increasing opportunity costs**.

But why (for most goods) do the opportunity costs increase as more of the good is produced? The answer is because people have varying abilities. For example, some people are better suited to building houses than other people are. When a construction company first starts building houses, it employs the people who are most skilled at house building. The most skilled persons can build houses at lower opportunity costs than others can. But as the construction company builds more houses, it finds that it has already employed the most skilled builders, so it must employ those who are less skilled at house building. These (less skilled) people build houses at higher opportunity costs. Where three skilled house builders could build a house in a month, as many as seven unskilled builders may be required to build it in the same length of time. Exhibit 3 summarizes the points in this section.

exhibit **3**

A CLOSER LOOK

A Summary Statement About Increasing Opportunity Costs and a Production Possibilities Frontier That Is Bowed Outward (Concave Downward)

Many of the points about increasing opportunity costs and a production possibilities frontier that is bowed outward are summarized here.

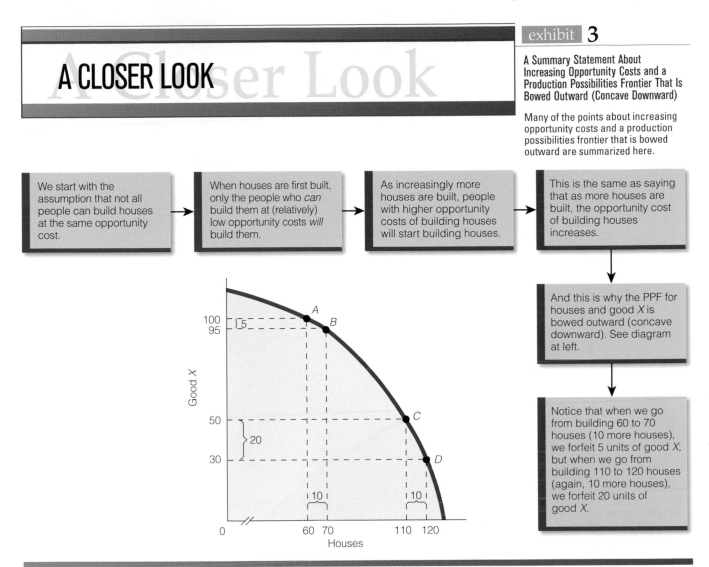

We start with the assumption that not all people can build houses at the same opportunity cost.

When houses are first built, only the people who *can* build them at (relatively) low opportunity costs *will* build them.

As increasingly more houses are built, people with higher opportunity costs of building houses will start building houses.

This is the same as saying that as more houses are built, the opportunity cost of building houses increases.

And this is why the PPF for houses and good *X* is bowed outward (concave downward). See diagram at left.

Notice that when we go from building 60 to 70 houses (10 more houses), we forfeit 5 units of good *X*; but when we go from building 110 to 120 houses (again, 10 more houses), we forfeit 20 units of good *X*.

Economic Concepts within a PPF Framework

The PPF framework is useful for illustrating and working with economic concepts. This section discusses seven economic concepts in terms of the PPF framework (see Exhibit 4).

SCARCITY Recall that scarcity is the condition where wants (for goods) are greater than the resources available to satisfy those wants. The finiteness of resources is graphically portrayed by the PPF in Exhibit 5. The frontier (itself) tells us: "At this point in time, that's as far as you can go. You cannot go any farther. You are limited to choosing any combination of the two goods on the frontier or below it."

The PPF separates the production possibilities of an economy into two regions: (1) an *attainable region*, which consists of the points on the PPF itself and all points below it (this region includes points *A–F*) and (2) an *unattainable region*, which consists of the points above and beyond the PPF (such as point *G*). Recall that scarcity implies that some things are attainable and others are unattainable. Point *A* on the PPF is attainable, as is point *F*; point *G* is not.

exhibit **4**

The PPF Economic Framework

exhibit **5**

The PPF and Various Economic Concepts

The PPF can illustrate various economic concepts: (1) Scarcity is illustrated by the frontier itself. Implicit in the concept of scarcity is the idea that we can have some things but not all things. The PPF separates an attainable region from an unattainable region. (2) Choice is represented by our having to decide among the many attainable combinations of the two goods. For example, will we choose the combination of goods represented by point *A* or by point *B*? (3) Opportunity cost is most easily seen as movement from one point to another, such as movement from point *A* to point *B*. More cars are available at point *B* than at point *A*, but fewer television sets are available. In short, the opportunity cost of more cars is fewer television sets. (4) Productive efficiency is represented by the points on the PPF (such as *A–E*), while productive inefficiency is represented by any point below the PPF (such as *F*). (5) Unemployment (in terms of resources being unemployed) exists at any productive inefficient point (such as *F*), whereas resources are fully employed at any productive efficient point (such as *A–E*).

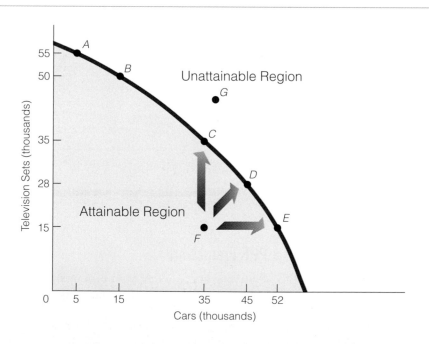

Choice and opportunity cost are also shown in Exhibit 5. Note that within the attainable region, individuals must choose the combination of the two goods they want to produce. Obviously, hundreds of different combinations exist, but let's consider only two, represented by points *A* and *B*. Which of the two will individuals choose? They can't be at both points; they must make a choice.

Opportunity cost is illustrated as we move from one point to another on the PPF in Exhibit 5. Suppose we are at point *A* and choose to move to point *B*. At *A*, we have

economics 24/7

CAN TECHNOLOGY ON THE FARM AFFECT THE NUMBER OF LAWYERS IN THE CITY?

There is no doubt that an advance in technology affects the industry in which it is developed and used. For example, a technological advance in the car industry will increase the output of cars; a technological advance in the house-building industry will increase the output of houses.

But can a technological advance in one industry have ripple effects beyond the industry in which it is developed and used? With this question in mind, let's start with some facts about farming. The United States had 32.1 million farmers in 1910, 30.5 million farmers in 1940, 9.7 million farmers in 1970, and about 4.8 million farmers in 2000. Farmers accounted for 34.9 percent of the U.S. population in 1910, 23.2 percent in 1940, 4.8 percent in 1970, and only 1.9 percent in 2005. Where did all the farmers go, and why did they leave farming?

Many farmers left farming because farming experienced major technological advances during the 20th century. Where farmers once farmed with minimal capital equipment, today they use computers, tractors, pesticides, cellular phones, and much more. As a result, more food can be produced with fewer farmers.

Because fewer farmers were needed to produce food, many farmers left the farms and entered the manufacturing and service industries. In other words, people who were once farmers (or whose parents and grandparents were farmers) began to produce cars, airplanes, television sets, and computers. They became attorneys, accountants, and police officers.

What should we learn from this? First, a technological advance in one sector of the economy may make it possible to produce goods in another sector of the economy. Technological advances in agriculture made it possible for fewer farmers to produce more food, thus releasing some farmers to produce other things. In other words, there may be more services in the world in part because of agriculture's technological advances.

Second, technological advances may affect the composition of employment. The technological advances in agriculture resulted in (1) a smaller percentage of people working in rural areas on farms and (2) a larger percentage of people working in manufacturing and services in the cities and suburbs. (Is the growth of the suburbs in the last 50 years due in part to technological advances on farms?)

55,000 television sets and 5,000 cars, and at point *B*, we have 50,000 television sets and 15,000 cars. What is the opportunity cost of a car? Because 10,000 *more* cars come at a cost of 5,000 *fewer* television sets, the opportunity cost of 1 car is 1/2 television set.

PRODUCTIVE EFFICIENCY Economists often say that an economy is **productive efficient** if it is producing the maximum output with given resources and technology. In Exhibit 5, points *A*, *B*, *C*, *D*, and *E* are all productive efficient points. Notice that all these points lie *on* the production possibilities frontier. In other words, we are getting the most (in terms of output) from what we have (in terms of available resources and technology).

It follows that an economy is **productive inefficient** if it is producing less than the maximum output with given resources and technology. In Exhibit 5, point *F* is a productive inefficient point. It lies *below* the production possibilities frontier; it is below the outer limit of what is possible. In other words, we could produce more goods with the resources we have available to us. Or we can get more of one good without getting less of another good.

Productive Efficiency
The condition where the maximum output is produced with given resources and technology.

Productive Inefficiency
The condition where less than the maximum output is produced with given resources and technology. Productive inefficiency implies that more of one good can be produced without any less of another good being produced.

exhibit 6

Economic Growth within a PPF Framework

An increase in resources or an advance in technology can increase the production capabilities of an economy, leading to economic growth and a shift outward in the production possibilities frontier.

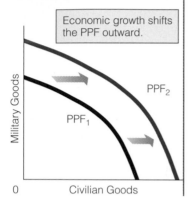

Economic growth shifts the PPF outward.

Technology

The body of skills and knowledge concerning the use of resources in production. An advance in technology commonly refers to the ability to produce more output with a fixed amount of resources or the ability to produce the same output with fewer resources.

To illustrate, suppose we move from inefficient point F to efficient point C. We produce more television sets and no fewer cars. What if we move from F to D? We produce more television sets and more cars. Finally, if we move from F to E, we produce more cars and no fewer television sets. Thus, moving from F can give us more of at least one good and no less of another good. In short, *productive inefficiency implies that gains are possible in one area without losses in another.*

UNEMPLOYED RESOURCES When the economy exhibits productive inefficiency, it is not producing the maximum output with the available resources and technology. One reason may be that the economy is not using all its resources; that is, some of its resources are unemployed, as at point F in Exhibit 5.

When the economy exhibits productive efficiency, it is producing the maximum output with the available resources and technology. This means it is using all its resources to produce goods; its resources are fully employed, and none are unemployed. At the productive efficient points A–E in Exhibit 5, there are no unemployed resources.

ECONOMIC GROWTH Economic growth refers to the increased productive capabilities of an economy. It is illustrated by a shift outward in the production possibilities frontier. Two major factors that affect economic growth are (1) an increase in the quantity of resources and (2) an advance in technology.

With an increase in the quantity of resources (e.g., through a new discovery of resources), it is possible to produce a greater quantity of output. In Exhibit 6, an increase in the quantity of resources makes it possible to produce both more military goods and more civilian goods. Thus, the PPF shifts outward from PPF_1 to PPF_2.

Technology refers to the body of skills and knowledge concerning the use of resources in production. An advance in technology commonly refers to the ability to produce more output with a fixed quantity of resources or the ability to produce the same output with a smaller quantity of resources.

Suppose an advance in technology allows more military goods and more civilian goods to be produced with the same quantity of resources. As a result, the PPF in Exhibit 6 shifts outward from PPF_1 to PPF_2. The outcome is the same as when the quantity of resources is increased.

SELF-TEST

(Answers to Self-Test questions are in the Self-Test Appendix.)

1. What does a straight-line production possibilities frontier (PPF) represent? What does a bowed-outward PPF represent?

2. What does the law of increasing costs have to do with a bowed-outward PPF?

3. A politician says, "If you elect me, we can get more of everything we want." Under what condition(s) is the politician telling the truth?

4. In an economy, only one combination of goods is productive efficient. True or false? Explain your answer.

Exchange or Trade

Exchange (Trade)

The process of giving up one thing for something else.

Exchange or **trade** is the process of giving up one thing for something else. Usually, money is traded for goods and services. Trade is all around us; we are involved with it every day. Few of us, however, have considered the full extent of trade.

economics 24/7

LIBERALS, CONSERVATIVES, AND THE PPF

Liberals and conservatives often pull in different economic directions. To illustrate, suppose our economy is currently at point A in Exhibit 7, producing X_2 of good X and Y_2 of good Y. Conservatives prefer point C to point A and try to convince the liberals and the rest of the nation to move to point C. Liberals, however, prefer point B to point A and try to persuade the conservatives and the rest of the nation to move to point B. Thus, we have a political tug of war.

Is there a way that both groups can get what they want? Yes, if there is economic growth so that the production possibilities frontier shifts outward from PPF_1 to PPF_2. On the new production possibilities frontier, PPF_2, point D represents the quantity of X that conservatives want and the quantity of Y that liberals want. At point D, conservatives have X_3 units of good X, which is what they would have had at point C, and liberals have Y_3 units of good Y, which is what they would have had at point B. Through economic growth, both conservatives and liberals can get what they want. The political tug of war will cease—at least for a while.

We say "for a while" because even at point D, there is scarcity. The wants of liberals and conservatives are both greater than the resources available to satisfy those wants. Starting at point D, liberals might push for a movement up the production possibilities frontier and conservatives for a movement down it.

Question to ponder: Does an increase in a family's income have the same effect as economic growth in a society? Does it eliminate or reduce the family tug of war—at least for a while?

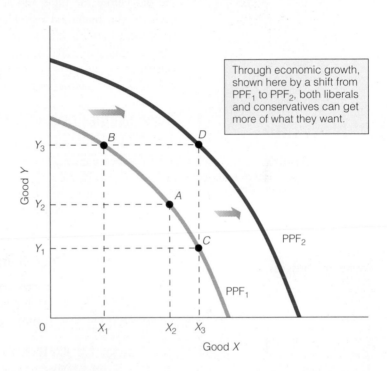

Through economic growth, shown here by a shift from PPF_1 to PPF_2, both liberals and conservatives can get more of what they want.

exhibit **7**

Economic Growth May End Political Battles, for a While

The economy is at point A, but conservatives want to be at point C and liberals want to be at point B. As a result, there is a political tug-of-war. Both conservatives and liberals can get the quantity of the good they want through economic growth. This is represented by point D on PPF_2.

Periods Relevant to Trade

There are three time periods relevant to the trading process. We discuss these relevant time periods next.

BEFORE THE TRADE Before a trade is made, a person is said to be in the **ex ante** position. For example, suppose Ramona has the opportunity to trade what she has, $2,000, for something she does not have, a big-screen television set. In the ex ante position, she wonders if she will be better off with (1) the television set or with (2) $2,000 worth of other goods. If she concludes that she will be better off with the television set than with

Ex Ante

Phrase that means "before," as in before a trade.

$2,000 worth of other goods, she will make the trade. Individuals will make a trade only if they believe ex ante (before) the trade that the trade will make them better off.

AT THE POINT OF TRADE Suppose Ramona now gives $2,000 to the person in possession of the television set. Does Ramona still believe she will be better off with the television set than with the $2,000? Of course she does. Her action testifies to this fact.

Ex Post

Phrase that means "after," as in after a trade.

AFTER THE TRADE After a trade is made, a person is said to be in the **ex post** position. Suppose two days have passed. Does Ramona still feel the same way about the trade as she did before the trade and at the point of trade? Maybe. Maybe not. She may look back on the trade and regret it. She may say that if she had it to do over again, she would not trade the $2,000 for the big-screen television set. In general, though, people expect a trade to make them better off, and usually, the trade meets their expectations. But there are no guarantees that a trade will meet expectations because no one in the real world can see the future.

Trade and the Terms of Trade

Trade refers to the process whereby "things" (money, goods, services, etc.) are given up to obtain something else. The **terms of trade** refer to *how much* of one thing is given up for *how much* of something else. For example, if $30 is traded for a best-selling book, the terms of trade are 1 bestseller for $30. If the price of a loaf of bread is $2.50, the terms of trade are 1 loaf of bread for $2.50. Buyers and sellers can always think of more advantageous terms of exchange. Buyers prefer lower prices, whereas sellers prefer higher prices.

Terms of Trade

How much of one thing is given up for how much of something else.

Thinking like AN ECONOMIST

A person buys a pair of shoes for $100. Later that day, the person says that he was "ripped off" by the shoe store owner; specifically, he says he paid too much for the shoes. Is this person arguing against trade or against the terms of trade? The economist knows that sometimes what sounds like a person arguing "against trade" is really his argument against the "terms of trade." Everyone can think of better terms of trade for himself. You buy a book for $40. Are there better terms of trade for you? Sure, you would have rather paid $30 for the book instead of $40. Sometimes, when it sounds as if we are arguing against trade, what we are really saying is this: "I wish I could have bought the good or service at better terms of trade than I did."

Costs of Trades

As always, economists consider both benefits and costs. They want to determine what costs are involved in a trade and whether the costs may prevent a trade from taking place.

UNEXPLOITED TRADES Suppose Smith wants to buy a red 1965 Ford Mustang in excellent condition. The maximum price she is willing and able to pay for the Mustang is $30,000. Also suppose that Jones owns a red 1965 Ford Mustang in excellent condition. The minimum price he is willing and able to sell the Mustang for is $23,000. Obviously, Smith's maximum buying price ($30,000) is greater than Jones's minimum selling price ($23,000), so a potential trade or exchange exists.

Will the potential trade between Smith and Jones become an actual exchange? The answer to this question may depend on the transaction costs. **Transaction costs** are the costs associated with the time and effort needed to search out, negotiate, and consummate a trade. To illustrate, neither Smith nor Jones may know that the other exists. Suppose Smith lives in Roanoke, Virginia, and Jones lives 40 miles away in Blacksburg, Virginia. Each needs to find the other, which may take time and money. Perhaps Smith can put an ad in the local Blacksburg newspaper stating that she is searching for a 1965 Ford Mustang in mint condition. Alternatively, Jones can put an ad in the local Roanoke newspaper stating that he has a 1965 Ford Mustang to sell. The ad may or may not be seen by the relevant party and then acted upon. Our point is a simple one: Transaction costs sometimes keep potential trades from turning into actual trades.

Transaction Costs

The costs associated with the time and effort needed to search out, negotiate, and consummate an exchange.

Consider another example. Suppose Kurt hates to shop for clothes because shopping takes too much time. He has to get in his car, drive to the mall, park the car, walk into the mall, look in different stores, try on different clothes, pay for the items, walk to and get back in his car, and drive home. Suppose Kurt spends an average of 2 hours when he shops, and he estimates that an hour of his time is worth $30. It follows, then, that Kurt incurs $60 worth of transaction costs when he buys clothes. Usually, he is not willing to incur the transaction costs necessary to buy a pair of trousers or a shirt.

Now, suppose we ask Kurt if he would be more willing to buy clothes if shopping was easier. Suppose, we say, the transaction costs associated with buying clothes could be lowered from $60 to less than $10. At lower transaction costs, Kurt says that he would be willing to shop more often.

How can transaction costs be lowered? Both people and computers can help lower the transaction costs of trades. For example, real estate brokers lower the transaction costs of selling and buying a house. Jim has a house to sell but doesn't know how to find a buyer. Karen wants to buy a house but doesn't know how to find a seller. Enter the real estate broker, who brings buyers and sellers together. In so doing, she lowers the transaction costs of buying and selling a house.

As another example, consider e-commerce on the Internet. Ursula can buy a book by getting in her car, driving to a bookstore, getting out of her car, walking into the bookstore, looking at the books on the shelves, taking a book to the cashier, paying for it, leaving the store, getting back in her car, and returning home. Or Ursula can buy a book over the Internet. She can click on one of the online booksellers, search for the book by title, read a short description of the book, and then click on 1-Click Buying. Buying on the Internet has lower transaction costs than shopping at a store because online buying requires less time and effort. Before online book buying and selling, were there potential book purchases and sales that weren't being turned into actual book purchases and sales? There is some evidence that there were.

TURNING POTENTIAL TRADES INTO ACTUAL TRADES Some people are always looking for ways to earn a profit. It would seem that one way to earn a profit is to turn potential trades into actual trades by lowering transaction costs. Consider the following example. Buyer Smith is willing to pay a maximum price of $400 for good X; Seller Jones is willing to accept a minimum price of $200 for good X. Currently, the transaction costs of the exchange are $500, evenly split between Buyer Smith and Seller Jones.

Buyer Smith thinks, "Even if I pay the lowest possible price for good X, $200, I will still have to pay $250 in transaction costs, bringing my total to $450. The maximum price I am willing to pay for good X is $400, so I will not make this purchase."

Seller Jones thinks, "Even if I receive the highest possible price for good X, $400, I will still have to pay $250 in transaction costs, leaving me with only $150. The minimum price I am willing to accept for good X is $200, so I will not make this sale."

This potential trade will not become an actual trade unless someone can lower the transaction costs. One role of an entrepreneur is to try *to turn potential trades into actual trades by lowering transaction costs.* Suppose Entrepreneur Brown can lower the transaction costs for Buyer Smith and Seller Jones to $10 each, asking $60 from each person for services rendered. Also, Entrepreneur Brown negotiates the price of good X at $300. Will the potential exchange become an actual exchange?

Buyer Smith thinks, "I am willing to pay a maximum of $400 for good X. If I purchase good X through Entrepreneur Brown, I will pay $300 to Seller Jones, $10 in transaction costs, and $60 to Brown. This is a total of $370, leaving me better off by $30. It is worthwhile for me to purchase good X."

Seller Jones thinks, "I am willing to sell good X for a minimum of $200. If I sell good X through Entrepreneur Brown, I will receive $300 from Buyer Smith and will have to pay $10 in transaction costs and $60 to Brown. That will leave me with $230, or $30 better off. It is worthwhile for me to sell good X."

Thus, an entrepreneur can earn a profit by finding a way to lower transaction costs. As a result, a potential exchange turns into an actual exchange.

Trades and Third-Party Effects

Consider two trades. In the first, Harriet pays 80 cents to Taylor for a pack of chewing gum. In this trade, both Harriet and Taylor are made better off (they wouldn't have traded otherwise), and no one is made worse off.

In the second trade, Bob pays $4 to George for a pack of cigarettes. Bob takes a cigarette, lights it, and smokes it. It happens that he is near Caroline when he smokes the cigarette, and she begins to cough because she is sensitive to cigarette smoke. In this trade, both Bob, who buys the cigarettes, and George, who sells the cigarettes, are made better off. But Caroline, who had nothing to do with the trade, is made worse off. In this exchange, a third party, Caroline, is adversely affected by the exchange between George and Bob.

These examples show that some trades affect only the parties involved in the exchange, and some trades have *third-party effects* (someone other than the parties involved in the exchange is affected). In the cigarette example, the third-party effect was negative; there was an adverse effect on Caroline, the third party. Sometimes economists call adverse third-party effects *negative externalities*. A later chapter discusses this topic in detail.

SELF-TEST

1. What are transaction costs? Are the transaction costs of buying a house likely to be greater or less than those of buying a car? Explain your answer.

2. Smith is willing to pay a maximum of $300 for good X, and Jones is willing to sell good X for a minimum of $220. Will Smith buy good X from Jones?

3. Give an example of a trade without third-party effects. Next, give an example of a trade with third-party effects.

Production, Trade, and Specialization

The first section of this chapter discusses production; the second section discusses trade. From these two sections, you might conclude that production and trade are unrelated activities. However, they are not: Before you can trade, you need to produce something. This section ties production and trade together and also shows how the benefits one receives from trade can be affected by how one produces.

Producing and Trading

To show how a change in production can benefit traders, we eliminate anything and everything extraneous to the process. Thus, we eliminate money and consider a barter, or moneyless, economy.

Economic Activities: Producing and Trading   Chapter 2   **43**

In this economy, there are two individuals, Elizabeth and Brian. They live near each other, and each engages in two activities: baking bread and growing apples. Let's suppose that within a certain period of time, Elizabeth can produce 20 loaves of bread and no apples, or 10 loaves of bread and 10 apples, or no bread and 20 apples. In other words, three points on Elizabeth's production possibilities frontier correspond to 20 loaves of bread and no apples, 10 loaves of bread and 10 apples, and no bread and 20 apples. As a consumer, Elizabeth likes to eat both bread and apples, so she decides to produce (and consume) 10 loaves of bread and 10 apples.

Within the same time period, Brian can produce 10 loaves of bread and no apples, or 5 loaves of bread and 15 apples, or no bread and 30 apples. In other words, these three combinations correspond to three points on Brian's production possibilities frontier. Brian, like Elizabeth, likes to eat both bread and apples, so he decides to produce and consume 5 loaves of bread and 15 apples. Exhibit 8 shows the combinations of bread and apples that Elizabeth and Brian can produce.

Elizabeth thinks that both she and Brian may be better off if each specializes in producing only one of the two goods and trading it for the other. In other words, Elizabeth should produce either bread or apples but not both. Brian thinks this may be a good idea but is not sure which good each person should specialize in producing.

An economist would advise each to produce the good that he or she can produce at a lower cost. In economics, a person who can produce a good at a lower cost than another person is said to have a **comparative advantage** in the production of that good.

Exhibit 8 shows that for every 10 units of bread Elizabeth does not produce, she can produce 10 apples. In other words, the opportunity cost of producing 1 loaf of bread *(B)* is 1 apple *(A)*:

> Opportunity costs for Elizabeth: $1B = 1A$
> $1A = 1B$

As for Brian, for every 5 loaves of bread he does not produce, he can produce 15 apples. So, for every 1 loaf of bread he does not produce, he can produce 3 apples. It follows, then, that for every 1 apple he chooses to produce, he forfeits 1/3 loaf of bread.

> Opportunity costs for Brian: $1B = 3A$
> $1A = \frac{1}{3}B$

Comparing opportunity costs, we see that Elizabeth can produce bread at a lower opportunity cost than Brian can. (Elizabeth forfeits 1 apple when she produces 1 loaf of bread, whereas Brian forfeits 3 apples when he produces 1 loaf of bread.) On the other hand, Brian can produce apples at a lower opportunity cost than Elizabeth can. We conclude that Elizabeth has a comparative advantage in the production of bread, and Brian has a comparative advantage in the production of apples.

Suppose each person specializes in the production of the good in which he or she has a comparative advantage. This means Elizabeth produces only bread and produces 20 loaves. Brian produces only apples and produces 30 apples.

Comparative Advantage

The situation where someone can produce a good at lower opportunity cost than someone else can.

Elizabeth		Brian	
Bread	**Apples**	**Bread**	**Apples**
20	0	10	0
10	10	5	15
0	20	0	30

exhibit **8**

Production by Elizabeth and Brian

This exhibit shows the combinations of goods each can produce individually in a given time period.

economics 24/7

JERRY SEINFELD, THE DOORMAN, AND ADAM SMITH

Oh, I get it. Why waste time making small talk with the doorman? I should just shut up and do my job, opening the door for you.

—The doorman, speaking to Jerry,
in an episode of *Seinfeld*

In a *Seinfeld* episode, Jerry comes across a doorman (played by actor Larry Miller) who seems to have a chip on his shoulder. While waiting for the elevator, Jerry sees the doorman reading a newspaper. Jerry looks over and says, "What about those Knicks?" (a reference to the New York Knicks professional basketball team). The doorman's response is, "What makes you think I wasn't reading the Wall Street page? Oh, I know, because I'm the uneducated doorman."

This exchange between the doorman and Jerry would be unlikely if Jerry had not lived in New York City or in some other large city. That's because doormen are usually found only in large cities. If you live in a city with a population less than 100,000, you may not find a single doorman in the entire city. There are few doormen even in cities with a population of 1 million.

This observation is not unique to us. It goes back to Adam Smith, who said that there is a direct relationship between the degree of specialization and the size of the market. Smith said:

> There are some sorts of industry, even of the lowest kind, which can be carried on nowhere but in a great town. A porter, for example, can find employment and subsistence in no other place. A village is by much too narrow a sphere for him; even an ordinary market town is scarce large enough to afford him constant occupation.[1]

Smith's observation that "some sorts of industry . . . can be carried on nowhere but in a great town" seems true. Some occupations and some goods can only be found in big cities. Try to find a doorman in North Adams, Michigan (population 514) or restaurant chefs who only prepare Persian, Yugoslavian, or Caribbean entrées in Ipswich, South Dakota (population 943).

[1] *An Inquiry into the Nature and Causes of the Wealth of Nations*, Adam Smith. Ed. Edwin Cannan, New York: Modern Library, 1965.

Thinking like AN ECONOMIST

We see many people specializing in the world in which we live. One person only works at accounting services, another only styles hair, a third only writes songs. Why do people specialize? Largely, it is because individuals have found that they are better off specializing in producing one good or service, selling that good or service for money, and then using the money to buy what they want. It is simply our story of Elizabeth and Brian occurring repeatedly with different pairs of individuals.

Now suppose that Elizabeth and Brian decide to trade 8 loaves of bread for 12 apples. In other words, Elizabeth produces 20 loaves of bread and then trades 8 of the loaves for 12 apples. After the trade, Elizabeth consumes 12 loaves of bread and 12 apples. Compare this situation with what she consumed when she didn't specialize and didn't trade. In that situation, she consumed 10 loaves of bread and 10 apples. Clearly, Elizabeth is better off when she specializes and trades than when she does not. But what about Brian?

Brian produces 30 apples and trades 12 of them to Elizabeth for 8 loaves of bread. In other words, he consumes 8 loaves of bread and 18 apples. Compare this situation with what he consumed when he didn't specialize and didn't trade. In that situation, he consumed 5 loaves of bread and 15 apples. Thus, Brian is also better off when he specializes and trades than when he does not.

Exhibit 9 summarizes consumption for Elizabeth and Brian. It shows that both Elizabeth and Brian make themselves better off by specializing in the production of one good and trading for the other.

Economic Activities: Producing and Trading   Chapter 2   **45**

		No Specialization and No Trade	Specialization and Trade	Gains from Specialization and Trade
Elizabeth	Consumption of Loaves of Bread	10	12	+2
	Consumption of Apples	10	12	+2
Brian	Consumption of Loaves of Bread	5	8	+3
	Consumption of Apples	15	18	+3

exhibit **9**

Consumption for Elizabeth and Brian With and Without Specialization and Trade

A comparison of the consumption of bread and apples before and after specialization and trade shows that both Elizabeth and Brian benefit from producing the good in which each has a comparative advantage and trading for the other good.

Profit and a Lower Cost of Living

The last column of Exhibit 9 shows the gains from specialization and trade. One way to view these gains is in terms of Elizabeth and Brian being better off when they specialize and trade than when they do not specialize and do not trade. In short, specialization and trade make people better off.

Another way to view these gains is in terms of *profit* and a *lower cost of living*. To illustrate, let's look again at Elizabeth. Essentially, Elizabeth undertakes two actions by specializing and trading. The first action is to produce more of one good (loaves of bread) than she produces when she does not specialize. The second action is to trade, or "sell," some of the bread for a "price" higher than the cost of producing the bread. Specifically, she "sells" 8 of the loaves of bread (to Brian) for a "price" of 12 apples. In other words, she "sells" each loaf of bread for a "price" of 1 1/2 apples. But Elizabeth can produce a loaf of bread for a cost of 1 apple. So she "sells" the bread for a "price" (1 1/2 apples) that's higher than her cost of producing the bread (1 apple). The difference is her profit.

Many people think that one person's profit is another person's loss. In other words, because Elizabeth earns a profit by specializing and trading, Brian must lose. But we know this is not the case. The cost to Brian of producing a loaf of bread is 3 apples. But he "buys" bread from Elizabeth for a "price" of only 1 1/2 apples. In other words, while Elizabeth is earning a profit, Brian's cost of living (what he has to forfeit to get a loaf of bread) is declining.

A Benevolent and All-Knowing Dictator Versus the Invisible Hand

Suppose a benevolent dictator governs the country where Brian and Elizabeth live. We assume that this benevolent dictator knows everything about almost every economic activity in his country. In other words, he knows Elizabeth's and Brian's opportunity costs of producing bread and apples.

Because the dictator is benevolent and because he wants the best for the people who live in his country, he orders Elizabeth to produce only loaves of bread and Brian to produce only apples. Next, he tells Elizabeth and Brian to trade 8 loaves of bread for 12 apples.

Afterward, he shows Exhibit 9 to Elizabeth and Brian. They are both surprised that they are better off having done what the benevolent dictator told them to do.

Now in the original story about Elizabeth and Brian, there was no benevolent, all-knowing dictator. There were only two people who were guided by their self-interest to specialize and trade. In other words, self-interest did for Elizabeth and Brian what the benevolent dictator did for them.

Adam Smith, the 18th-century Scottish economist and founder of modern economics, spoke about the *invisible hand* that "guided" individuals' actions toward a positive outcome that they did not intend. That is what happened in the original story about Elizabeth and Brian. Neither intended to increase the overall output of society; each intended only to make himself or herself better off.

SELF-TEST

1.   If George can produce either (a) 10X and 20Y or (b) 5X and 25Y, what is the opportunity cost to George of producing one more X?

2.   Harriet can produce either (a) 30X and 70Y or (b) 40X and 55Y; Bill can produce either (c) 10X and 40Y or (d) 20X and 20Y. Who has a comparative advantage in the production of X? of Y? Explain your answers.

A Reader Asks...

How Will Economics Help Me If I'm a History Major?

I'm a history major taking my first course in economics. But quite frankly, I don't see how economics will be of much use in my study of history. Any thoughts on the subject?

Economics often plays a major role in historical events. For example, many social scientists argue that economics played a large role in the collapse of communism. If communism had been able to produce the quantity and variety of goods and services that capitalism produces, perhaps the Soviet Union would still exist.

Fact is, understanding economics may help you understand many historical events or periods. If, as a historian, you study the Great Depression, you will need to know something about the stock market, tariffs, and more. If you study the California Gold Rush, you will need to know about supply, demand, and prices. If you study the history of prisoner-of-war camps, you will need to know about how and why

people trade and about money. If you study the Boston Tea Party, you will need to know about government grants of monopoly and about taxes.

Economics can also be useful in another way. Suppose you learn in your economics course what can and cannot cause inflation. We'll say you learn that X can cause inflation and that Y cannot. Then, one day, you read an article in which a historian says that Y caused the high inflation in a certain country and that the high inflation led to a public outcry, which was then met with stiff government reprisals. Without an understanding of economics, you might be willing to accept what the historian has written. But with your understanding of economics, you know that events could not have happened as the historian reports because Y, which the historian claims caused the high inflation, could not have caused the high inflation.

In conclusion, a good understanding of economics will not only help you understand key historical events but will also help you discern inaccuracies in recorded history.

! analyzing the scene

What does a point on a production possibilities frontier have to do with the collapse of the Soviet Union?

The former Soviet foreign minister said the Soviet Union had collapsed because of a conflict between the Kremlin and the Soviet people. What was the conflict? The conflict concerned where the economy of the Soviet Union chose to be located on its PPF. The Kremlin wanted a point that represented "more guns" (more military goods) and "less butter" (fewer civilian or consumer goods), whereas the people wanted a point that represented "fewer guns" and "more butter." In other words, the Kremlin wanted to be at one point on the PPF while the people wanted to be at another. It's unlikely the Soviet Union would have collapsed had the people and the Kremlin agreed on the point on the PPF to be at.

Why can't Bob get As in both biology and calculus, and what does Jim's desire to produce "more time" tell us about life?

Bob says he has to choose between an A in biology and an A in calculus. To make that statement, Bob must be thinking in terms of his PPF for "producing grades." His "grades PPF" would look like the straight line in Exhibit 1. Bob's likely biology grade is on the vertical axis (starting with an F at the origin and moving up to an A), and his calculus grade is on the horizontal axis (again starting with an F at the origin and moving across to an A). When Bob says that he must choose where he wants to get an A, he is saying that there is no point on his "grades PPF" that represents an A in both courses (given his resources, such as time, and his state of technology, such as his ability to learn the material). In other words, the point that represents two As is in his *unattainable region,* and the point that represents one A and, say, one B, is in his *attainable region.*

Jim's desire to produce "more time" tells us that he feels there is not enough of a particular resource (time) in which

to accomplish all his goals. More resources mean more goals can be met and fewer tradeoffs will be incurred.

What led Karen and Larry to specialize in doing certain tasks?

In the chapter we showed (numerically) how two people (Elizabeth and Brian) could make themselves better off by specializing and trading. What holds for Elizabeth and Brian also holds for Karen and Larry.

What did eBay do that really wasn't that hard?

On any given day, 16 million items in 27,000 different categories are listed for sale on eBay.com. What does eBay do? It brings buyers and sellers together.

Consider the situation years ago when the World Wide Web did not exist. Suppose a person in London found an old Beatles' record in his attic and decided he wanted to sell it. Unbeknownst to him, a person in Los Angeles wanted to buy exactly that old Beatles' record. But alas, the record never changed hands because neither the seller nor the buyer knew how to find the other or even if the other existed. In short, the transaction costs of completing the trade were just too high.

Years later, the Web came along, and with it, eBay. What eBay actually did was use the Web to lower the transaction costs of trading. eBay basically told the world: If you're a seller and want a buyer or if you're a buyer and want a seller, come to us.

Today, the London seller of the old Beatles' record can inexpensively be matched with the Los Angeles buyer. eBay and the Web are the "matchmakers." The potential traders go online to eBay where they become actual traders. eBay charges a small fee for creating the place where buyer and seller can find each other.

chapter summary

An Economy's Production Possibilities Frontier

- An economy's production possibilities frontier (PPF) represents the possible combinations of two goods that the economy can produce in a certain period of time under the conditions of a given state of technology and fully employed resources.

Increasing and Constant Opportunity Costs

- A straight-line PPF represents constant opportunity costs: Increased production of one good comes at constant opportunity costs.

- A bowed-outward (concave-downward) PPF represents the law of increasing opportunity costs: Increased production of one good comes at increased opportunity costs.

The Production Possibilities Frontier and Various Economic Concepts

- The PPF can be used to illustrate various economic concepts. Scarcity is illustrated by the frontier itself. Choice is illustrated by our knowing that we have to locate at some particular point either on the frontier or below it. In short, of the many attainable positions, one must be chosen. Opportunity cost is illustrated by a movement from one point on the PPF to another point on the PPF. Unemployed resources and productive inefficiency are illustrated by a point below the PPF. Productive efficiency and fully employed resources are illustrated by a point on the PPF. Economic growth is illustrated by a shift outward in the PPF.

Exchange or Trade

- The three time periods relevant to the trading process are (1) the ex ante period, which is the time before the trade is made; (2) the point of trade; and (3) the ex post period, which is the time after the trade has been made.
- There is a difference between trade and the terms of trade. Trade refers to the act of giving up one thing for something else. For example, a person may trade money for a car. The terms of trade refer to *how much* of one thing is traded for *how much* of something else. For example, how much money ($25,000? $30,000?) is traded for one car.

Transaction Costs

- Transaction costs are the costs associated with the time and effort needed to search out, negotiate, and consummate a trade. Some potential exchanges are not realized because of high transaction costs. Lowering transaction costs can turn a potential exchange into an actual exchange.
- One role of an entrepreneur is to try to lower transaction costs.

Comparative Advantage and Specialization

- Individuals can make themselves better off by specializing in the production of the good in which they have a comparative advantage and then trading some of that good for other goods. A person has a comparative advantage in the production of a good if he or she can produce the good at a lower opportunity cost than another person can.
- Individuals gain by specializing and trading. Specifically, they earn a profit by specializing in the production of the goods in which they have a comparative advantage.

key terms and concepts

Production Possibilities Frontier (PPF)	Productive Efficiency	(Exchange) Trade	Terms of Trade
	Productive Inefficiency	Ex Ante	Transaction Costs
Law of Increasing Opportunity Costs	Technology	Ex Post	Comparative Advantage

questions and problems

1 Describe how each of the following would affect the U.S. production possibilities frontier: (a) an increase in the number of illegal immigrants entering the country; (b) a war; (c) the discovery of a new oil field; (d) a decrease in the unemployment rate; (e) a law that requires individuals to enter lines of work for which they are not suited.

2 Explain how the following can be represented in a PPF framework: (a) the finiteness of resources implicit in the scarcity condition; (b) choice; (c) opportunity cost; (d) productive efficiency; (e) unemployed resources.

3 What condition must hold for the production possibilities frontier to be bowed outward (concave downward)? to be a straight line?

4 Give an example to illustrate each of the following: (a) constant opportunity costs and (b) increasing opportunity costs.

5 Why are most production possibilities frontiers for goods bowed outward (concave downward)?

6   Within a PPF framework, explain each of the following: (a) a disagreement between a person who favors more domestic welfare spending and one who favors more national defense spending; (b) an increase in the population; (c) a technological change that makes resources less specialized.

7   Some people have said that during the Cold War, the Central Intelligence Agency (CIA) regularly estimated (a) the total quantity of output produced in the Soviet Union and (b) the total quantity of civilian goods produced in the Soviet Union. Of what interest would these data, or the information that might be deduced from them, be to the CIA? (Hint: Think in terms of the PPF.)

8   Suppose a nation's PPF shifts inward as its population grows. What happens, on average, to the material standard of living of the people? Explain your answer.

9   "A nation may be able to live beyond its means, but the world cannot." Do you agree or disagree? Explain your answer.

10 Use the PPF framework to explain something in your everyday life that was not mentioned in the chapter.

11 Describe the three time periods relevant to the trading process.

12 Are all exchanges or trades beneficial to both parties in the ex post position? Explain your answer.

13 A person who benefits from a trade can be disgruntled over the terms of trade. Do you agree or disagree? Explain your answer.

14 Give an example of a negative third-party effect (negative externality).

working with numbers and graphs

1   Tina can produce any of the following combinations of goods X and Y: (a) $100X$ and $0Y$, (b) $50X$ and $25Y$, and (c) $0X$ and $50Y$. David can produce any of the following combinations of goods X and Y: (a) $50X$ and $0Y$, (b) $25X$ and $40Y$, and (c) $0X$ and $80Y$. Who has a comparative advantage in the production of good X? of good Y? Explain your answer.

2   Using the data in Problem 1, prove that both Tina and David can be made better off through specialization and trade.

3   Exhibit 6 represents an advance in technology that made it possible to produce more of both military and civilian goods. Represent an advance in technology that makes it possible to produce more of only civilian goods. Does this indirectly make it possible to produce more military goods? Explain your answer.

4   In the following figure, which graph depicts a technological breakthrough in the production of good X only?

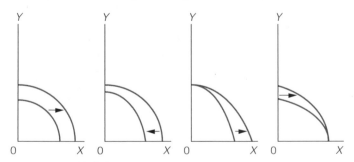

5   In the preceding figure, which graph depicts a change in the PPF that is a likely consequence of war?

6   If PPF_2 in the following graph is the relevant production possibilities frontier, then which points are unattainable? Explain your answer.

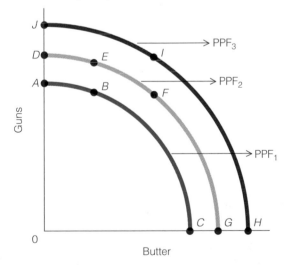

7   If PPF_1 in the preceding figure is the relevant production possibilities frontier, then which point(s) represent productive efficiency? Explain your answer.

Supply and Demand: Theory

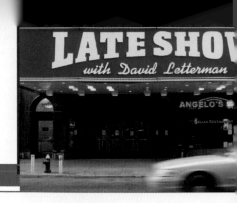

Setting the Scene

James Beider is a law student at Columbia University Law School. He lives on the Upper West Side of Manhattan, about thirty blocks from the school. The following events occurred on a day not too long ago.

9:03 A.M.

James is sitting in front of a computer in the law library at Columbia University. He's not checking on books but on the current prices of three stocks he owns (Wal-Mart, Microsoft, and Dell). He also checks on the exchange rate between the dollar and the euro. He plans to take a trip to Europe in the summer and is hoping the dollar will be stronger (against the euro) than it has been in the last few weeks. Last week, a person paid $1.10 for 1 euro; today, a person has to pay $1.28 for a euro. James mutters under his breath that if the dollar gets any weaker, he might have to cancel his trip.

1:30 P.M.

James is sitting in Tommy's Restaurant (three blocks from Columbia University), eating lunch with a few friends. His last class of the day is at 2 P.M. He picks up his cell phone and calls his apartment supervisor. No answer. James frowns as he puts his phone away. "What's wrong?" one friend asks. "I've been trying to get this

guy to fix my shower for two weeks now," James answers. "I'm just frustrated." "Ah, the joys of living in a rent-controlled apartment," his friend says.

4:55 P.M.

James and his girlfriend Kelly are in a taxi on their way to the Ed Sullivan Theater at 1697 Broadway to see the *Late Show with David Letterman*. James has wanted to see the show for two years and finally managed to get tickets. The tickets are free—but the wait time to obtain two tickets is approximately nine months.

11:02 P.M.

James is watching the 11 o'clock news as he eats a slice of cold pizza.

The TV reporter says, "The mayor said today that he is concerned that the city's burglary rate has been rising."

Cut to mayor at today's news conference.

"This city and this mayor are not going to be soft on crime. We're going to

do everything in our power to make sure that everyone knows that crime doesn't pay."

James says, "You tell 'em, mayor." Then he reaches for another slice of pizza.

? Here are some questions to keep in mind as you read this chapter:

- *At the time James checks stock prices, Wal-Mart is selling for $44.09, Microsoft for $23.75, and Dell for $21.75. Why doesn't Dell sell for more than Wal-Mart? Why does Microsoft sell for more than Dell? Why is the euro selling for $1.28 and not higher or lower?*

- *What does getting his shower fixed have to do with James living in a rent-controlled apartment?*

- *Why does it take so long (nine months) to get tickets to see the* Late Show with David Letterman?

- *Does the burglary rate have anything to do with how "hard" or "soft" a city is on crime?*

See analyzing the scene at the end of this chapter for answers to these questions.

A Note about Theories

Economists often build theories. They build **theories** to answer questions that do not have obvious answers. For example, they might build a theory to understand why interest rates rise at some times and fall at others, why the price of a car is $25,000 and not $27,000, or why some countries have higher economic growth rates than other countries. When building theories, economists omit certain variables or factors when trying to explain or understand something. To understand why, consider an analogy. Suppose you were to draw a map for a friend, showing him how to get from his house to your house. Would you draw a map that showed *every single thing* your friend would see on the trip from his house to yours, or would you simply draw the main roads and one or two landmarks? If you'd do the latter, you would be abstracting from reality; you would be omitting certain things.

You would "omit certain variables or factors" for two reasons. First, to get your friend from his house to yours, you don't need to include everything on your map. Simply noting main roads may be enough. Second, if you did note everything on your map, your friend might get confused. Giving too much detail could be as bad as giving too little. (Back in Chapter 1, you learned there is an efficient amount of almost everything. There is also an efficient amount of detail. There can be too much, too little, or just the right amount. Just the right amount is the efficient amount.)

When economists build a theory, they do the same thing you do when you draw a map. They abstract from reality; they leave out certain things. They focus on the major factors or variables that they believe will explain the phenomenon they are trying to understand.

This chapter deals with the theory of supply and demand. The objective of the theory is to try to understand why prices are what they are—for instance, why bread's price is $2 a loaf and not $20 a loaf or why a computer's price is $1,000 and not $10,000.

Theory
An abstract representation of the real world designed with the intent to better understand the world.

What Is Demand?

A **market** is any place people come together to trade. Economists often say that there are *two* sides to every market: a buying side and a selling side. The buying side of the market is usually referred to as the *demand* side; the selling side of the market is usually referred to as the *supply* side. Let's begin with a discussion of *demand*.

The word **demand** has a precise meaning in economics. It refers to:

1. the willingness and ability of buyers to purchase different quantities of a good
2. at different prices
3. during a specific time period (per day, week, etc.).[1]

For example, we can express part of John's demand for magazines by saying that he is willing and able to buy 10 magazines a month at $4 per magazine and that he is willing and able to buy 15 magazines a month at $3 per magazine.

Remember this important point about demand: Unless *both* willingness and ability to buy are present, there is no demand, and a person is not a buyer. For example, Josie may be willing to buy a computer but be unable to pay the price; Tanya may be able to buy a computer but be unwilling to do so. Neither Josie nor Tanya demands a computer, and neither is a buyer of a computer.

Market
Any place people come together to trade.

Demand
The willingness and ability of buyers to purchase different quantities of a good at different prices during a specific time period.

 If a person says that he wants a car, is this the same thing as saying that he demands a car?

No. Saying he "wants" a car does not imply that he has both the willingness and ability to buy a car. One must have both willingness and ability before one has demand.

---

[1]Demand takes into account *services* as well as goods. Goods are tangible and include such things as shirts, books, and television sets. Services are intangible and include such things as dental care, medical care, and an economics lecture. To simply the discussion, we refer only to goods.

The Law of Demand

Law of Demand

As the price of a good rises, the quantity demanded of the good falls, and as the price of a good falls, the quantity demanded of the good rises, *ceteris paribus.*

Will people buy more units of a good at lower prices than at higher prices? For example, will people buy more computers at $1,000 per computer than at $4,000 per computer? If your answer is yes, you instinctively understand the law of demand. The **law of demand** states that as the price of a good rises, the quantity demanded of the good falls, and as the price of a good falls, the quantity demanded of the good rises, *ceteris paribus.* Simply put, the law of demand states that the price of a good and the quantity demanded of the good are inversely related, *ceteris paribus:*

$$P\uparrow Q_d\downarrow$$
$$P\downarrow Q_d\uparrow \textit{ ceteris paribus}$$

where P = price and Q_d = quantity demanded.

Quantity demanded is the number of units of a good that individuals are willing and able to buy at a particular price during some time period. For example, suppose individuals are willing and able to buy 100 TV dinners per week at a price of $4 per dinner. Therefore, 100 units is the quantity demanded of TV dinners at $4.

What Does *Ceteris Paribus* Mean?

Ceteris Paribus

A Latin term meaning "all other things constant" or "nothing else changes."

When we defined the law of demand, we used the term **ceteris paribus**. This is a Latin term that means *all other things held constant* or *nothing else changes.* For example, an economist might say: "As the price of Pepsi-Cola rises, the quantity demanded of Pepsi-Cola falls, *ceteris paribus.*" Translated: If we raise the price of Pepsi-Cola, and nothing else changes—in other words, people's preferences stay the same, the recipe for Pepsi-Cola stays the same, and so on—then in response to the higher price of Pepsi-Cola, people will buy less Pepsi-Cola.

But some people ask, "Why would economists want to assume that when the price of Pepsi-Cola rises, nothing else changes? Don't other things change in the real world? Why assume things that we know are not true?"

Economists do not specify *ceteris paribus* because they want to say something false about the world. They specify it because they want to clearly define what they believe to be the real-world relationship between two variables. Look at it this way. If you drop a ball off the roof of a house, it will strike the ground *unless someone catches it.* This statement is true, and probably everyone would willingly accept it as true. But saying "unless someone catches it" is really no different than saying "assuming nothing else changes" or "*ceteris paribus.*"

Q&A

Please give another example to convey the meaning of why economists use the term **ceteris paribus**.

Wilson has eaten regular ice cream for years. Recently, he has been gaining weight. He decides to change from regular ice cream to low-fat ice cream. Now what do you expect will happen to his weight? If you think his weight will probably fall, then you are implicitly assuming "if nothing else changes." In other words, if Wilson doesn't change anything else in his life—how much ice cream he eats in total, how much he exercises each day, and so on—then his weight will decline by changing from eating regular to low-fat ice cream. Now an economist would simply put it this way: If Wilson changes from eating regular to low-fat ice cream, we can expect that he will lose weight, ceteris paribus.

Four Ways to Represent the Law of Demand

Here are four ways to represent the law of demand.

- **In Words.** We can represent the law of demand in words; we have done so already. Earlier we said that as the price of a good rises, quantity demanded falls, and as price falls, quantity demanded rises, *ceteris paribus.* That was the statement (in words) of the law of demand.

- **In Symbols.** We can also represent the law of demand in symbols, which we have also done earlier. In symbols, the law of demand is:

$$P\uparrow Q_d\downarrow$$
$$P\downarrow Q_d\uparrow \textit{ ceteris paribus}$$

Demand Schedule

The numerical tabulation of the quantity demanded of a good at different prices. A demand schedule is the numerical representation of the law of demand.

- **In a Demand Schedule.** A **demand schedule** is the numerical representation of the law of demand. A demand schedule for good X is illustrated in Exhibit 1(a).

- **As a Demand Curve.** In Exhibit 1(b), the four price-quantity combinations in part (a) are plotted and the points connected, giving us a (downward-sloping) demand curve. A **(downward-sloping) demand curve** is the graphical representation of the inverse relationship between price and quantity demanded specified by the law of demand. In short, a demand curve is a picture of the law of demand.

Two Prices: Absolute and Relative

In economics, there are absolute (or money) prices and relative prices. The **absolute price** is the price of the good in money terms. For example, the absolute price of a car might be $30,000. The **relative price** is the price of the good *in terms of another good*. For example, suppose the absolute price of a car is $30,000 and the absolute price of a computer is $2,000. The relative price of the car—that is, the price of the car *in terms of computers*—is 15 computers. A person gives up the opportunity to buy 15 computers when he or she buys a car.

$$\text{Relative price of a car (in terms of computers)} = \frac{\text{Absolute price of a car}}{\text{Absolute price of a computer}}$$
$$= \frac{\$30,000}{\$2,000}$$
$$= 15$$

Thus, the relative price of a car in this example is 15 computers.

Now let's compute the relative price of a computer—that is, the price of a computer in terms of a car:

$$\text{Relative price of a computer (in terms of cars)} = \frac{\text{Absolute price of a computer}}{\text{Absolute price of a car}}$$
$$= \frac{\$2,000}{\$30,000}$$
$$= \frac{1}{15}$$

Thus, the relative price of a computer in this example is 1/15 of a car. A person gives up the opportunity to buy 1/15 of a car when he or she buys a computer.

Now consider this question: What happens to the relative price of a good if its absolute price rises and nothing else changes? For example, if the absolute price of a car rises from $30,000 to $40,000, what happens to the relative price of a car? Obviously, it rises from 15 computers to 20 computers. In short, if the absolute price of a good rises and nothing else changes, then the relative price of the good rises too.

Why Does Quantity Demanded Go Down as Price Goes Up?

The law of demand states that price and quantity demanded are inversely related. This much you know. But you do know *why* quantity demanded moves in the opposite direction of price? We identify two reasons. The first reason is that *people substitute lower priced goods for higher priced goods*.

Often, many goods serve the same purpose. Many different goods will satisfy hunger, and many different drinks will satisfy thirst. For example, both orange juice and grapefruit juice will satisfy thirst. On Monday, the price of orange juice equals the price of grapefruit juice,

---

(Downward-Sloping) Demand Curve

The graphical representation of the law of demand.

Absolute (Money) Price

The price of a good in money terms.

Relative Price

The price of a good in terms of another good.

exhibit 1

Demand Schedule and Demand Curve

Part (a) shows a demand schedule for good X. Part (b) shows a demand curve, obtained by plotting the different price-quantity combinations in part (a) and connecting the points. On a demand curve, the price (in dollars) represents price per unit of the good. The quantity demanded, on the horizontal axis, is always relevant for a specific time period (a week, a month, and so on).

Demand Schedule for Good X

Price (dollars)	Quantity Demanded	Point in Part (b)
4	10	A
3	20	B
2	30	C
1	40	D

(a)

(b)

Thinking like **AN ECONOMIST**

The economist knows that it is possible for a good to go up in price at the same time as it becomes cheaper. (How can this happen?) To illustrate, suppose the absolute price of a pen is $1 and the absolute price of a pencil is 10 cents. The relative price of 1 pen, then, is 10 pencils. Now let the absolute price of a pen rise to $1.20 at the same time that the absolute price of a pencil rises to 20 cents. As a result, the relative price of 1 pen falls to 6 pencils. In other words, the absolute price of pens rises (from $1 to $1.20) at the same time as pens become relatively cheaper (in terms of how many pencils you have to give up to get a pen). Who would have thought it?

economics 24/7

TICKET PRICES AT DISNEY WORLD

The Walt Disney Company operates two major theme parks in the United States: Disneyland in California and Disney World in Florida. Every year, millions of people visit each site. The ticket price for visiting Disneyland or Disney World differs depending on how many days a person visits the theme park. For example, Disney World sells one- to ten-day tickets. On the day we checked, the price of a one-day ticket was $63 and the price of a ten-day ticket was $210.

Now if we take the price of a one-day ticket and multiply it by 10, we get $630, but oddly enough, the price of a ten-day ticket is not $630 but $210. Why does Disney World charge $420 less for a ten-day ticket rather than 10 times the one-day ticket price?

Disney World is effectively telling visitors that if they want to visit the theme park for one day, they have to pay $63. But if they want to visit the theme park for ten days, they don't

have to pay $63 for each additional day. They pay much less for additional days. But why?

An economic concept, the *law of diminishing marginal utility*, is the reason. The law of diminishing marginal utility states that as a person consumes additional units of a good, eventually, the utility from each additional unit of the good decreases. Assuming the law of diminishing marginal utility holds for Disney World, individuals will get more utility from the first day at Disney World than from, say, the second, third, or tenth day. The less utility or satisfaction a person gets from something, the lower the dollar amount he is willing to pay for it. Thus, a person would not be willing to pay as much for the second day at Disney World as the first, and he would not be willing to pay as much for the tenth day as the ninth and so on. Disney World knows this and therefore prices its ticket prices differently depending on how many days one wants to visit Disney World.

Law of Diminishing Marginal Utility

For a given time period, the marginal (additional) utility or satisfaction gained by consuming equal successive units of a good will decline as the amount consumed increases.

---

but on Tuesday, the price of orange juice rises. As a result, people will choose to buy less of the relatively higher priced orange juice and more of the relatively lower priced grapefruit juice. In other words, a rise in the price of orange juice will lead to a decrease in the quantity demanded of orange juice.

The second reason for the inverse relationship between price and quantity demanded has to do with the **law of diminishing marginal utility**, which states that for a given time period, the marginal (additional) utility or satisfaction gained by consuming equal successive units of a good will decline as the amount consumed increases. For example, you may receive more utility or satisfaction from eating your first hamburger at lunch than from eating your second and, if you continue, more utility from your second hamburger than from your third.

What does this have to do with the law of demand? Economists state that the more utility you receive from a unit of a good, the higher the price you are willing to pay for it; the less utility you receive from a unit of a good, the lower the price you are willing to pay for it. According to the law of diminishing marginal utility, individuals obtain less utility from additional units of a good. It follows that they will only buy larger quantities of a good at lower prices. And this is the law of demand.

Individual Demand Curve and Market Demand Curve

There is a difference between an individual demand curve and a market demand curve. An individual demand curve represents the price-quantity combinations of a particular

Quantity Demanded

Price	Jones		Smith		Other Buyers		All Buyers
$15	1		2		20		23
14	2		3		45		50
13	3		4		70		77
12	4	+	5	+	100	=	109
11	5	+	6	+	130	=	141
10	6		7		160		173

(a)

(b)

exhibit **2**

Deriving a Market Demand Schedule and a Market Demand Curve

Part (a) shows four demand schedules combined into one table. The market demand schedule is derived by adding the quantities demanded at each price. In (b), the data points from the demand schedule are plotted to show how a market demand curve is derived. Only two points on the market demand curve are noted.

good for a *single buyer.* For example, a demand curve could show Jones's demand for CDs. A market demand curve represents the price–quantity combinations of a particular good for *all buyers.* In this case, the demand curve would show all buyers' demand for CDs.

A market demand curve is derived by "adding up" individual demand curves, as we show in Exhibit 2. The demand schedules for Jones, Smith, and other buyers are shown in part (a). The market demand schedule is obtained by adding the quantities demanded at each price. For example, at $12, the quantities demanded are 4 units for Jones, 5 units for Smith, and 100 units for other buyers. Thus, a total of 109 units are demanded at $12. In part (b), the data points for the demand schedules are plotted and added to produce a market demand curve. The market demand curve could also be drawn directly from the market demand schedule.

A Change in Quantity Demanded Versus a Change in Demand

Economists often talk about (1) a change in quantity demanded and (2) a change in demand. Although "quantity demanded" may sound like "demand," they are not the same. In short, a "change in quantity demanded" *is not* the same as a "change in demand." (Read the last sentence at least two more times.) We use Exhibit 1 to illustrate the difference between "a change in quantity demanded" and "a change in demand."

A CHANGE IN QUANTITY DEMANDED Look at the horizontal axis in Exhibit 1, which is labeled "quantity demanded." Notice that quantity demanded is a *number*—such as 10, 20, 30, 40, and so on. More specifically, it is the number of units of a good that individuals are willing and able to buy at a particular price during some time period. In Exhibit 1, if the price is $4, then quantity demanded is 10 units of good X; if the price is $3, then quantity demanded is 20 units of good X.

> Quantity demanded = The *number* of units of a good that individuals are willing and able to buy at a particular price

Now, again looking at Exhibit 1, what can change quantity demanded from 10 (which it is at point A) to 20 (which it is at point B)? Or what has to change before quantity demanded will change? The answer is on the vertical axis of Exhibit 1. The only thing that can change the quantity demanded of a good is the price of the good, which is called **own price**.

Own Price

The price of a good. For example, if the price of oranges is $1, this is (its) own price.

> Change in quantity demanded = A *movement* from one point to another point on the same demand curve *caused* by a change in the price of the good

A CHANGE IN DEMAND Let's look again at Exhibit 1, this time focusing on the demand curve. Demand is represented by the *entire* curve. When an economist talks about a "change in demand," he or she is actually talking about a change—or shift—in the entire demand curve.

> Change in demand = Shift in demand curve

Demand can change in two ways: Demand can increase, and demand can decrease. Let's look first at an *increase* in demand. Suppose we have the following demand schedule.

Demand Schedule A	
Price	Quantity Demanded
$20	500
$15	600
$10	700
$ 5	800

The demand curve for this demand schedule will look like the demand curve labeled D_A in Exhibit 3(a).

exhibit 3

Shifts in the Demand Curve

In part (a), the demand curve shifts rightward from D_A to D_B. This shift represents an increase in demand. At each price, the quantity demanded is greater than it was before. For example, the quantity demanded at $20 increases from 500 units to 600 units. In part (b), the demand curve shifts leftward from D_A to D_C. This shift represents a decrease in demand. At each price, the quantity demanded is less. For example, the quantity demand at $20 decreases from 500 units to 400 units.

What does an increase in demand mean? It means that individuals are willing and able to buy more units of the good at each and every price. In other words, demand schedule *A* will change as follows:

Demand Schedule *B* (increase in demand)	
Price	Quantity Demanded
$20	~~500~~ 600
$15	~~600~~ 700
$10	~~700~~ 800
$ 5	~~800~~ 900

Whereas individuals were willing and able to buy 500 units of the good at $20, now they are willing and able to buy 600 units of the good at $20; whereas individuals were willing and able to buy 600 units of the good at $15, now they are willing and able to buy 700 units of the good at $15; and so on.

As shown in Exhibit 3(a), the demand curve that represents demand schedule *B* lies to the right of the demand curve that represents demand schedule *A*. We conclude that *an increase in demand is represented by a rightward shift in the demand curve and means that individuals are willing and able to buy more of a good at each and every price.*

Increase in demand = Rightward shift in the demand curve

Now let's look at a *decrease* in demand. What does a decrease in demand mean? It means that individuals are willing and able to buy less of a good at each and every price. In this case, demand schedule *A* will change as follows:

Demand Schedule *C* (decrease in demand)	
Price	Quantity Demanded
$20	~~500~~ 400
$15	~~600~~ 500
$10	~~700~~ 600
$ 5	~~800~~ 700

As shown in Exhibit 3(b), the demand curve that represents demand schedule *C* obviously lies to the left of the demand curve that represents demand schedule *A*. We conclude that *a decrease in demand is represented by a leftward shift in the demand curve and means that individuals are willing and able to buy less of a good at each and every price.*

Decrease in demand = Leftward shift in the demand curve

What Factors Cause the Demand Curve to Shift?

We know what an increase and decrease in demand mean: An increase in demand means consumers are willing and able to buy more of a good at every price. A decrease in demand means consumers are willing and able to buy less of a good at every price. We also know that an increase in demand is graphically portrayed as a rightward shift in a demand curve and a decrease in demand is graphically portrayed as a leftward shift in a demand curve.

But what factors or variables can increase or decrease demand? What factors or variables can shift demand curves? We identify and discuss these factors or variables in this section.

INCOME As a person's income changes (increases or decreases), his or her demand for a particular good may rise, fall, or remain constant.

Normal Good

A good the demand for which rises (falls) as income rises (falls).

Inferior Good

A good the demand for which falls (rises) as income rises (falls).

Neutral Good

A good the demand for which does not change as income rises or falls.

Substitutes

Two goods that satisfy similar needs or desires. If two goods are substitutes, the demand for one rises as the price of the other rises (or the demand for one falls as the price of the other falls).

Complements

Two goods that are used jointly in consumption. If two goods are complements, the demand for one rises as the price of the other falls (or the demand for one falls as the price of the other rises).

For example, suppose Jack's income rises. As a consequence, his demand for CDs rises. For Jack, CDs are a normal good. For a **normal good**, as income rises, demand for the good rises, and as income falls, demand for the good falls.

$$X \text{ is a normal good: If income} \uparrow \text{ then } D_X \uparrow$$
$$\text{If income} \downarrow \text{ then } D_X \downarrow$$

Now suppose Marie's income rises. As a consequence, her demand for canned baked beans falls. For Marie, canned baked beans are an inferior good. For an **inferior good**, as income rises, demand for the good falls, and as income falls, demand for the good rises.

$$Y \text{ is an inferior good: If income} \uparrow \text{ then } D_Y \downarrow$$
$$\text{If income} \downarrow \text{ then } D_Y \uparrow$$

Finally, suppose when George's income rises, his demand for toothpaste neither rises nor falls. For George, toothpaste is neither a normal good nor an inferior good. Instead, it is a neutral good. For a **neutral good**, as income rises or falls, the demand for the good does not change.

PREFERENCES People's preferences affect the amount of a good they are willing to buy at a particular price. A change in preferences in favor of a good shifts the demand curve rightward. A change in preferences away from the good shifts the demand curve leftward. For example, if people begin to favor Dan Brown novels to a greater degree than previously, the demand for Brown novels increases, and the demand curve shifts rightward.

PRICES OF RELATED GOODS There are two types of related goods: substitutes and complements. Two goods are **substitutes** if they satisfy similar needs or desires. For many people, Coca-Cola and Pepsi-Cola are substitutes. If two goods are substitutes, as the price of one rises (falls), the demand for the other rises (falls). For instance, higher Coca-Cola prices will increase the demand for Pepsi-Cola as people substitute Pepsi for the higher priced Coke (Exhibit 4(a)). Other examples of substitutes are coffee and tea, corn chips and potato chips, two brands of margarine, and foreign and domestic cars.

$$X \text{ and } Y \text{ are substitutes: If } P_X \uparrow \text{ then } D_Y \uparrow$$
$$\text{If } P_X \downarrow \text{ then } D_Y \downarrow$$

Two goods are **complements** if they are consumed jointly. For example, tennis rackets and tennis balls are used together to play tennis. If two goods are complements, as the price of one rises (falls), the demand for the other falls (rises). For example, higher tennis racket prices will decrease the demand for tennis balls, as Exhibit 4(b) shows. Other examples of complements are cars and tires, light bulbs and lamps, and golf clubs and golf balls.

$$A \text{ and } B \text{ are complements: If } P_A \uparrow \text{ then } D_B \downarrow$$
$$\text{If } P_A \downarrow \text{ then } D_B \uparrow$$

NUMBER OF BUYERS The demand for a good in a particular market area is related to the number of buyers in the area: more buyers, higher demand; fewer buyers, lower demand. The number of buyers may increase owing to a higher birthrate, increased immigration, the migration of people from one region of the country to another, and so on. The number of buyers may decrease owing to a higher death rate, war, the migration of people from one region of the country to another, and so on.

EXPECTATIONS OF FUTURE PRICE Buyers who expect the price of a good to be higher next month may buy the good now—thus increasing the current (or present) demand

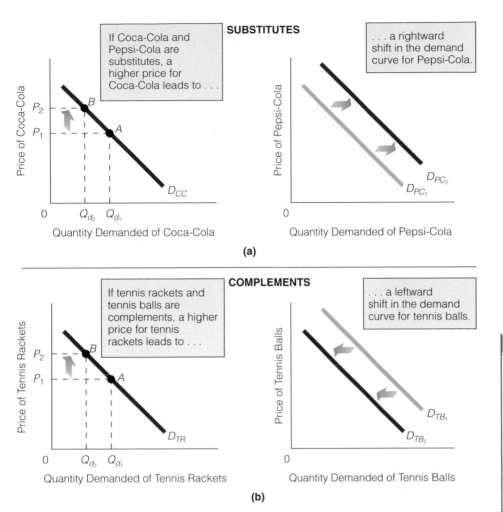

SUBSTITUTES

If Coca-Cola and Pepsi-Cola are substitutes, a higher price for Coca-Cola leads to . . .

. . . a rightward shift in the demand curve for Pepsi-Cola.

(a)

COMPLEMENTS

If tennis rackets and tennis balls are complements, a higher price for tennis rackets leads to . . .

. . . a leftward shift in the demand curve for tennis balls.

(b)

exhibit **4**

Substitutes and Complements

(a) Coca-Cola and Pepsi-Cola are substitutes: The price of one and the demand for the other are directly related. As the price of Coca-Cola rises, the demand for Pepsi-Cola increases. (b) Tennis rackets and tennis balls are complements: The price of one and the demand for the other are inversely related. As the price of tennis rackets rises, the demand for tennis balls decreases.

for the good. Buyers who expect the price of a good to be lower next month may wait until next month to buy the good—thus decreasing the current (or present) demand for the good.

For example, suppose you are planning to buy a house. One day, you hear that house prices are expected to go down in a few months. Consequently, you decide to delay your purchase of a house for a few months. Alternatively, if you hear that prices are expected to rise in a few months, you might go ahead and purchase a house now.

Movement Factors and Shift Factors

Economists often distinguish between (1) factors that can move us along curves and (2) factors that can shift curves.

The factors that move us along curves are sometimes called *movement* factors. In many economic diagrams—such as the diagram of the demand curve in Exhibit 1—the movement factor (price) is on the vertical axis.

The factors that actually shift the curves are sometimes called *shift* factors. The shift factors for the demand curve are income, preferences, the price of related goods, and so on. Often, the shift factors do not appear in the economic diagrams. For example, in Exhibit 1, the movement factor—price—is on the vertical axis, but the shift factors do not appear anywhere in the diagram. We just know what they are and that they can shift the demand curve.

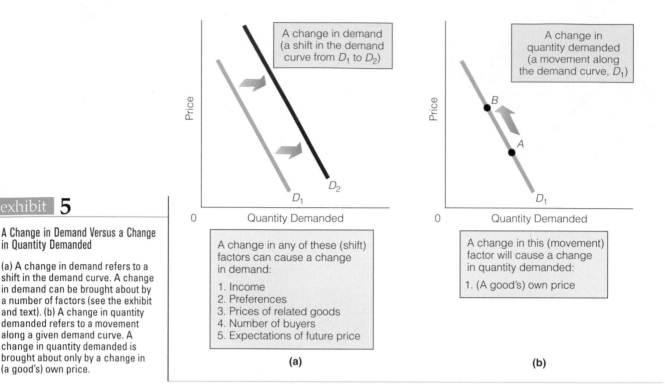

A Change in Demand Versus a Change in Quantity Demanded

(a) A change in demand refers to a shift in the demand curve. A change in demand can be brought about by a number of factors (see the exhibit and text). (b) A change in quantity demanded refers to a movement along a given demand curve. A change in quantity demanded is brought about only by a change in (a good's) own price.

When you see a curve in this book, first ask what factor will move us along the curve. In other words, what is the movement factor? Second, ask what factors will shift the curve. In other words, what are the shift factors? Exhibit 5 summarizes the shift factors that can change demand and the movement factors that can change quantity demanded.

SELF-TEST

(Answers to Self-Test questions are in the Self-Test Appendix.)

1. As Sandi's income rises, her demand for popcorn rises. As Mark's income falls, his demand for prepaid telephone cards rises. What kinds of goods are popcorn and telephone cards for the people who demand each?

2. Why are demand curves downward sloping?

3. Give an example that illustrates how to derive a market demand curve.

4. What factors can change demand? What factors can change quantity demanded?

Supply

Just as the word *demand* has a specific meaning in economics, so does the word *supply.* **Supply** refers to

Supply
The willingness and ability of sellers to produce and offer to sell different quantities of a good at different prices during a specific time period.

1. the willingness and ability of sellers to produce and offer to sell different quantities of a good

2. at different prices

3. during a specific time period (per day, week, etc.).

The Law of Supply

The **law of supply** states that as the price of a good rises, the quantity supplied of the good rises, and as the price of a good falls, the quantity supplied of the good falls, *ceteris paribus*. Simply put, the price of a good and the quantity supplied of the good are directly related, *ceteris paribus*. (Quantity supplied is the number of units sellers are willing and able to produce and offer to sell at a particular price.) The **(upward-sloping) supply curve** is the graphical representation of the law of supply (see Exhibit 6). The law of supply can be summarized as follows:

$$P\uparrow Q_S\uparrow$$
$$P\downarrow Q_S\downarrow \text{ ceteris paribus}$$

where P = price and Q_S = quantity supplied.

The law of supply holds for the production of most goods. It does not hold when there is no time to produce more units of a good. For example, suppose a theater in Atlanta is sold out for tonight's play. Even if ticket prices increased from $30 to $40, there would be no additional seats in the theater. There is no time to produce more seats. The supply curve for theater seats is illustrated in Exhibit 7(a). It is fixed at the number of seats in the theater, 500.[2]

The law of supply also does not hold for goods that cannot be produced over any period of time. For example, the violinmaker Antonio Stradivari died in 1737. A rise in the price of Stradivarius violins does not affect the number of Stradivarius violins supplied, as Exhibit 7(b) illustrates.

Why Most Supply Curves Are Upward Sloping

Think back to the discussion of the *law of increasing opportunity costs* in Chapter 2. That discussion shows that if the production possibilities frontier (PPF) is bowed outward, increasing costs exist. In other words, increased production of a good comes at increased opportunity costs. An upward-sloping supply curve simply reflects the fact that costs rise when more units of a good are produced.

Law of Supply
As the price of a good rises, the quantity supplied of the good rises, and as the price of a good falls, the quantity supplied of the good falls, *ceteris paribus*.

(Upward-Sloping) Supply Curve
The graphical representation of the law of supply.

exhibit **6**

A Supply Curve

The upward-sloping supply curve is the graphical representation of the law of supply, which states that price and quantity supplied are directly related, *ceteris paribus*. On a supply curve, the price (in dollars) represents price per unit of the good. The quantity supplied, on the horizontal axis, is always relevant for a specific time period (a week, a month, and so on).

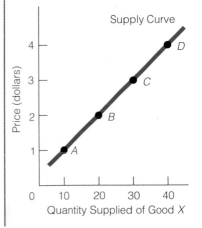

exhibit **7**

Supply Curves When There Is No Time to Produce More or No More Can Be Produced

The supply curve is not upward-sloping when there is no time to produce additional units or when additional units cannot be produced. In those cases, the supply curve is vertical.

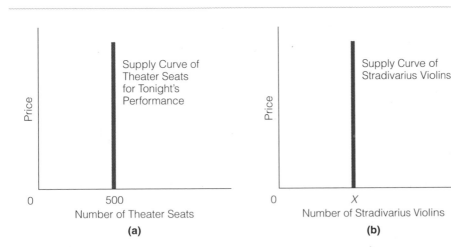

---

[2]The vertical supply curve is said to be *perfectly inelastic*.

THE MARKET SUPPLY CURVE An individual supply curve represents the price-quantity combinations for a single seller. The market supply curve represents the price-quantity combinations for all sellers of a particular good. Exhibit 8 shows how a market supply curve can be derived by "adding" individual supply curves. In part (a), a **supply schedule**, the numerical tabulation of the quantity supplied of a good at different prices, is given for Brown, Alberts, and other suppliers. The market supply schedule is obtained by adding the quantities supplied at each price, *ceteris paribus*. For example, at $11, the quantities supplied are 2 units for Brown, 3 units for Alberts, and 98 units for other suppliers. Thus, a total of 103 units are supplied at $11. In part (b), the data points for the supply schedules are plotted and added to produce a market supply curve. The market supply curve could also be drawn directly from the market supply schedule.

Supply Schedule
The numerical tabulation of the quantity supplied of a good at different prices. A supply schedule is the numerical representation of the law of supply.

Changes in Supply Mean Shifts in Supply Curves

Just as demand can change, so can supply. The supply of a good can rise or fall. What does it mean if the supply of a good increases? It means that suppliers are willing and able to produce and offer to sell more of the good at all prices. For example, suppose that in January sellers are willing and able to produce and offer for sale 600 shirts at $25 each and that in February they are willing and able to produce and sell 900 shirts at $25 each. An increase in supply shifts the entire supply curve to the right, as shown in Exhibit 9(a).

exhibit 8

Deriving a Market Supply Schedule and a Market Supply Curve

Part (a) shows four supply schedules combined into one table. The market supply schedule is derived by adding the quantities supplied at each price. In (b), the data points from the supply schedules are plotted to show how a market supply curve is derived. Only two points on the market supply curve are noted.

Price	Brown		Alberts		Other Suppliers		All Suppliers
$10	1		2		96		99
11	2	+	3	+	98	=	103
12	3	+	4	+	102	=	109
13	4		5		106		115
14	5		6		108		119
15	6		7		110		123

Quantity Supplied

(a)

(b)

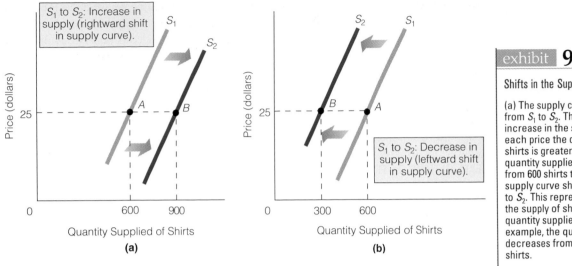

(a)

(b)

.

exhibit **9**

Shifts in the Supply Curve

(a) The supply curve shifts rightward from S_1 to S_2. This represents an increase in the supply of shirts: At each price the quantity supplied of shirts is greater. For example, the quantity supplied at $25 increases from 600 shirts to 900 shirts. (b) The supply curve shifts leftward from S_1 to S_2. This represents a decrease in the supply of shirts: At each price the quantity supplied of shirts is less. For example, the quantity supplied at $25 decreases from 600 shirts to 300 shirts.

The supply of a good decreases if sellers are willing and able to produce and offer to sell less of the good at all prices. For example, suppose that in January sellers are willing and able to produce and offer for sale 600 shirts at $25 each and that in February they are willing and able to produce and sell only 300 shirts at $25 each. A decrease in supply shifts the entire supply curve to the left, as shown in Exhibit 9(b).

What Factors Cause the Supply Curve to Shift?

We know the supply of any good can change. But what causes supply to change? What causes supply curves to shift? The factors that can change supply include (1) prices of relevant resources, (2) technology, (3) number of sellers, (4) expectations of future price, (5) taxes and subsidies, and (6) government restrictions.

PRICES OF RELEVANT RESOURCES Resources are needed to produce goods. For example, wood is needed to produce doors. If the price of wood falls, it becomes less costly to produce doors. How will door producers respond? Will they produce more doors, the same number of doors, or fewer doors? With lower costs and prices unchanged, the profit from producing and selling doors has increased; as a result, there is an increased (monetary) incentive to produce doors. Door producers will produce and offer to sell more doors at each and every price. Thus, the supply of doors will increase, and the supply curve of doors will shift rightward. If the price of wood rises, it becomes more costly to produce doors. Consequently, the supply of doors will decrease, and the supply curve of doors will shift leftward.

TECHNOLOGY In Chapter 2, technology is defined as the body of skills and knowledge concerning the use of resources in production. Also, an advance in technology refers to the ability to produce more output with a fixed amount of resources, thus reducing per-unit production costs. To illustrate, suppose it currently takes $100 to produce 40 units of a good. The per-unit cost is therefore $2.50. If an advance in technology makes it possible to produce 50 units at a cost of $100, then the per-unit cost falls to $2.00.

If per-unit production costs of a good decline, we expect the quantity supplied of the good at each price to increase. Why? The reason is that lower per-unit costs increase profitability and therefore provide producers with an incentive to produce more. For example, if corn growers develop a way to grow more corn using the same amount of water and other resources, it follows that per-unit production costs will fall, profitability will increase, and growers will want to grow and sell more corn at each price. The supply curve of corn will shift rightward.

NUMBER OF SELLERS If more sellers begin producing a particular good, perhaps because of high profits, the supply curve will shift rightward. If some sellers stop producing a particular good, perhaps because of losses, the supply curve will shift leftward.

EXPECTATIONS OF FUTURE PRICES If the price of a good is expected to be higher in the future, producers may hold back some of the product today (if possible, but perishables cannot be held back). Then, they will have more to sell at the higher future price. Therefore, the current supply curve will shift leftward. For example, if oil producers expect the price of oil to be higher next year, some may hold oil off the market this year to be able to sell it next year. Similarly, if they expect the price of oil to be lower next year, they might pump more oil this year than previously planned.

TAXES AND SUBSIDIES Some taxes increase per-unit costs. Suppose a shoe manufacturer must pay a $2 tax per pair of shoes produced. This tax leads to a leftward shift in the supply curve, indicating that the manufacturer wants to produce and offer to sell fewer pairs of shoes at each price. If the tax is eliminated, the supply curve shifts rightward.

Subsidy

A monetary payment by government to a producer of a good or service.

Subsidies have the opposite effect. Suppose the government subsidizes the production of corn by paying corn farmers $2 for every bushel of corn they produce. Because of the subsidy, the quantity supplied of corn is greater at each price, and the supply curve of corn shifts rightward. Removal of the subsidy shifts the supply curve of corn leftward. A rough rule of thumb is that we get more of what we subsidize and less of what we tax.

GOVERNMENT RESTRICTIONS Sometimes, government acts to reduce supply. Consider a U.S. import quota on Japanese television sets. An import quota, or quantitative restriction on foreign goods, reduces the supply of Japanese television sets in the United States. It shifts the supply curve leftward. The elimination of the import quota allows the supply of Japanese television sets in the United States to shift rightward.

Licensure has a similar effect. With licensure, individuals must meet certain requirements before they can legally carry out a task. For example, owner-operators of day-care centers must meet certain requirements before they are allowed to sell their services. No doubt, this reduces the number of day-care centers and shifts the supply curve of day-care centers leftward.

A Change in Supply Versus a Change in Quantity Supplied

A change in supply is not the same as a change in quantity supplied. A change in supply refers to a shift in the supply curve, as illustrated in Exhibit 10(a). For example, saying that the supply of oranges has increased is the same as saying that the supply curve for oranges has shifted rightward. The factors that can change supply (shift the supply curve) include prices of relevant resources, technology, number of sellers, expectations of future price, taxes and subsidies, and government restrictions.

A change in quantity supplied refers to a movement along a supply curve, as in Exhibit 10(b). The only factor that can directly cause a change in the quantity supplied of a good is a change in the price of the good, or own price.

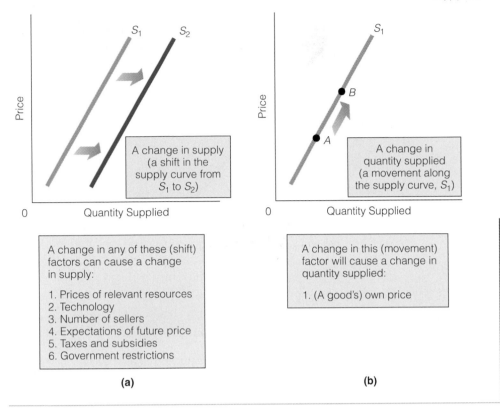

exhibit **10**

A Change in Supply Versus a Change in Quantity Supplied

(a) A change in supply refers to a shift in the supply curve. A change in supply can be brought about by a number of factors (see the exhibit and text). (b) A change in quantity supplied refers to a movement along a given supply curve. A change in quantity supplied is brought about only by a change in (a good's) own price.

SELF-TEST

1. What would the supply curve for houses (in a given city) look like for a time period of (a) the next ten hours and (b) the next three months?

2. What happens to the supply curve if each of the following occurs?
   a. There is a decrease in the number of sellers.
   b. A per-unit tax is placed on the production of a good.
   c. The price of a relevant resource falls.

3. "If the price of apples rises, the supply of apples will rise." True or false? Explain your answer.

The Market: Putting Supply and Demand Together

In this section, we put supply and demand together and discuss the market. The purpose of the discussion is to gain some understanding about how prices are determined.

Supply and Demand at Work at an Auction

Imagine you are at an auction where bushels of corn are bought and sold. At this auction, the auctioneer will adjust the corn price to sell all the corn offered for sale. The supply curve of corn is vertical, as in Exhibit 11. It intersects the horizontal axis at 40,000 bushels; that is, quantity supplied is 40,000 bushels. The demand curve for corn is downward sloping. Furthermore, suppose each potential buyer of corn is sitting in front of a computer that immediately registers the number of bushels he or she wants to buy. For example, if Nancy Bernstein wants to buy 5,000 bushels of corn, she simply keys

exhibit 11

Supply and Demand at Work at an Auction

Q_d = quantity demanded; Q_s = quantity supplied. The auctioneer calls out different prices, and buyers record how much they are willing and able to buy. At prices of $6.00, $5.00, and $4.00, quantity supplied is greater than quantity demanded. At prices of $1.25 and $2.25, quantity demanded is greater than quantity supplied. At a price of $3.10, quantity demanded equals quantity supplied.

Surplus (Excess Supply)

A condition in which quantity supplied is greater than quantity demanded. Surpluses occur only at prices above equilibrium price.

Shortage (Excess Demand)

A condition in which quantity demanded is greater than quantity supplied. Shortages occur only at prices below equilibrium price.

Equilibrium Price (Market-Clearing Price)

The price at which quantity demanded of the good equals quantity supplied.

Equilibrium Quantity

The quantity that corresponds to equilibrium price. The quantity at which the amount of the good that buyers are willing and able to buy equals the amount that sellers are willing and able to sell, and both equal the amount actually bought and sold.

Disequilibrium Price

A price other than equilibrium price. A price at which quantity demanded does not equal quantity supplied.

Disequilibrium

A state of either surplus or shortage in a market.

Equilibrium

Equilibrium means "at rest." Equilibrium in a market is the price-quantity combination from which there is no tendency for buyers or sellers to move away. Graphically, equilibrium is the intersection point of the supply and demand curves.

"5,000" into her computer. The auction begins. (Follow along in Exhibit 11 as we relay what is happening at the auction.) The auctioneer calls out the price:

• **$6.00.** The potential buyers think for a second, and then each registers the number of bushels he or she is willing and able to buy at that price. The total is 10,000 bushels, which is the quantity demanded of corn at $6.00. The auctioneer, realizing that 30,000 bushels of corn (40,000 − 10,000 = 30,000) will go unsold at this price, decides to lower the price per bushel to:

• **$5.00.** The quantity demanded increases to 20,000 bushels, but still the quantity supplied of corn at this price is greater than the quantity demanded. The auctioneer calls out:

• **$4.00.** The quantity demanded increases to 30,000 bushels, but the quantity supplied at $4.00 is still greater than the quantity demanded. The auctioneer drops the price down to:

• **$1.25.** At this price, the quantity demanded jumps to 60,000 bushels, but that is 20,000 bushels more than the quantity supplied. The auctioneer calls out a higher price:

• **$2.25.** The quantity demanded drops to 50,000 bushels, but buyers still want to buy more corn at this price than there is corn to be sold. The auctioneer calls out:

• **$3.10.** At this price, the quantity demanded of corn is 40,000 bushels and the quantity supplied of corn is 40,000 bushels. The auction stops. The 40,000 bushels of corn are bought and sold at $3.10 per bushel.

The Language of Supply and Demand: A Few Important Terms

If quantity supplied is greater than quantity demanded, a **surplus** or **excess supply** exists. If quantity demanded is greater than quantity supplied, a **shortage** or **excess demand** exists. In Exhibit 11, a surplus exists at $6.00, $5.00, and $4.00. A shortage exists at $1.25 and $2.25. The price at which quantity demanded equals quantity supplied is the **equilibrium price** or **market-clearing price**. In our example, $3.10 is the equilibrium price. The quantity that corresponds to the equilibrium price is the **equilibrium quantity**. In our example, it is 40,000 bushels of corn. Any price at which quantity demanded is not equal to quantity supplied is a **disequilibrium price**.

A market that exhibits either a surplus ($Q_s > Q_d$) or a shortage ($Q_d > Q_s$) is said to be in **disequilibrium**. A market in which quantity demanded equals quantity supplied ($Q_d = Q_s$) is said to be in **equilibrium** (identified by the letter E in Exhibit 11).

Moving to Equilibrium: What Happens to Price When There Is a Surplus or a Shortage?

What did the auctioneer do when the price was $6.00 and there was a surplus of corn? He lowered the price. What did the auctioneer do when the price was $2.25 and there was a shortage of corn? He raised the price. The behavior of the auctioneer can be summarized this way: If a surplus exists, lower the price; if a shortage exists, raise the price. This is how the auctioneer moved the corn market into equilibrium.

Not all markets have auctioneers. (When was the last time you saw an auctioneer in the grocery store?) But many markets act *as if* an auctioneer were calling out higher and lower prices until equilibrium price is reached. In many real-world auctioneerless markets, prices fall when there is a surplus and rise when there is a shortage. Why?

WHY DOES PRICE FALL WHEN THERE IS A SURPLUS? In Exhibit 12, there is a surplus at a price of $15: Quantity supplied (150 units) is greater than quantity demanded (50 units). Suppliers will not be able to sell all they had hoped to sell at $15. As a result, their inventories will grow beyond the level they hold in preparation for demand changes. Sellers will want to reduce their inventories. Some will lower prices to do so, some will cut back on production, others will do a little of both. As shown in the exhibit, there is a tendency for price and output to fall until equilibrium is achieved.

WHY DOES PRICE RISE WHEN THERE IS A SHORTAGE? In Exhibit 12, there is a shortage at a price of $5: Quantity demanded (150 units) is greater than quantity supplied (50 units). Buyers will not be able to buy all they had hoped to buy at $5. Some buyers will bid up the price to get sellers to sell to them instead of to other buyers. Some sellers, seeing buyers clamor for the goods, will realize that they can raise the price of the goods they have for sale. Higher prices will also call forth added output. Thus, there is a tendency for price and output to rise until equilibrium is achieved.

Take a look at Exhibit 13. It brings together much of what we have discussed about supply and demand.

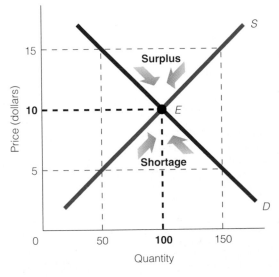

exhibit **12**

Moving to Equilibrium

If there is a surplus, sellers' inventories rise above the level they hold in preparation for demand changes. Sellers will want to reduce their inventories. As a result, price and output fall until equilibrium is achieved. If there is a shortage, some buyers will bid up price to get sellers to sell to them instead of to other buyers. Some sellers will realize they can raise the price of the goods they have for sale. Higher prices will call forth added output. Price and output rise until equilibrium is achieved. (Note: Recall that price, on the vertical axis, is price per unit of the good, and quantity, on the horizontal axis, is for a specific time period. In this text, we do not specify this on the axes themselves, but consider it to be understood.)

Price	Q_s	Q_d	Condition
$15	150	50	Surplus
10	100	100	Equilibrium
5	50	150	Shortage

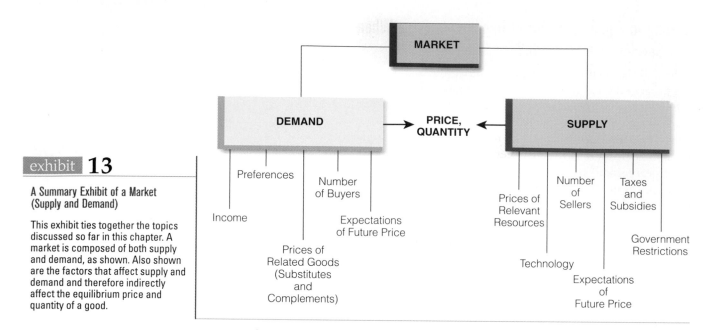

exhibit **13**

A Summary Exhibit of a Market (Supply and Demand)

This exhibit ties together the topics discussed so far in this chapter. A market is composed of both supply and demand, as shown. Also shown are the factors that affect supply and demand and therefore indirectly affect the equilibrium price and quantity of a good.

Speed of Moving to Equilibrium

On August 2, 2006, at 9:11 A.M. (Eastern time), the price of a share of IBM stock was $76.54. A few seconds later, the price had risen to $76.57. Obviously, the stock market is a market that equilibrates quickly. If demand rises, then initially there is a shortage of the stock at the current equilibrium price. The price is bid up, and there is no longer a shortage. All this happens in seconds.

Now consider a house offered for sale in any city in the United States. It is not uncommon for the sale price of a house to remain the same even though the house does not sell for months. For example, a person offers to sell her house for $400,000. One month passes, no sale; two months pass, no sale; three months pass, no sale; and so on. Ten months later, the house has still not sold, and the price is still $400,000.

Is $400,000 the equilibrium price of the house? Obviously not. At the equilibrium price, there would be a buyer for the house and a seller of the house (quantity demanded would equal quantity supplied). At a price of $400,000, there is a seller of the house but no buyer. The price of $400,000 is above equilibrium price. At $400,000, there is a surplus in the housing market; equilibrium has not been achieved.

Some people may be tempted to argue that supply and demand are at work in the stock market but not in the housing market. A better explanation, though, is that *not all markets equilibrate at the same speed*. While it may take only seconds for the stock market to go from surplus or shortage to equilibrium, it may take months for the housing market to do so.

Moving to Equilibrium: Maximum and Minimum Prices

The discussion of surpluses illustrates how a market moves to equilibrium, but there is another way to demonstrate this. Exhibit 14 shows the market for good X. Look at the first unit of good X. What is the *maximum price buyers would be willing to pay* for it? The answer is $70. This can be seen by following the dotted line up from the first unit of the good to the demand curve. What is the *minimum price sellers need to receive before they would be willing to sell* this unit of good X? It is $10. This can be seen by following the dotted

© ASSOCIATED PRESS, AP

economics 24/7

OVERBOOKING AND THE AIRLINES

Airlines often overbook flights; that is, they accept more reservations than there are seats available on a flight. They do this because they know that a certain (usually small) percentage of individuals with reservations will not show up. An empty seat means that the airline's cost per actual passenger on board is higher than it would be if the seat were occupied by a paying passenger. So airlines try to make sure there are few empty seats. One way to reduce the number of empty seats is to overbook.

A while back, when an airline was confronted with more people with reservations showing up for a flight than there were seats available, it would simply "bump" passengers. In other words, the airline would tell some passengers that they could not fly on a particular flight. Obviously, the bumped passengers were disappointed and angry.

One day while shaving, economist Julian Simon (1932–1998) came up with a better way to deal with overbooking. He argued that the airline should enter into a market transaction with those persons who had reserved seats for an overbooked flight. Instead of bumping people randomly, an airline should ask passengers to sell their seats back to the airline. Passengers who absolutely had to get from X to Y would not sell their seats, but passengers who did not have to get from X to Y right away might be willing to sell their ticket for a given flight.

Simon wrote the executives of various airlines and outlined the details of his plan. He even told them that the first airline that enacted the plan would likely reap larger sales. It could, after all, guarantee its passengers that they would not get bumped. Most airline executives wrote back and told him it was a reasonably good idea but unworkable.

Simon contacted various economists asking them to support his idea publicly. Some did; some didn't. For years, Simon pushed his idea with airline executives and government officials.

Then Alfred Kahn, an economist, was appointed chairman of the Civil Aeronautics Board. Simon contacted Kahn with his plan, and Kahn liked it. According to Simon, "Kahn announced something like the scheme in his first press conference. He also had the great persuasive skill to repackage it as a 'voluntary' bumping plan, and at the same time to increase the penalties that airlines must pay to involuntary bumpees, a nice carrot-and-stick combination."[3]

The rest, as people say, is history. Simon's plan has been in operation since 1978. Simon wrote, "The volunteer system for handling airline oversales exemplifies how markets can improve life for all concerned parties. In case of an oversale, the airline agent proceeds from lowest bidder upwards until the required number of bumpees is achieved. Low bidders take the next flight, happy about it. All other passengers fly as scheduled, also happy. The airlines can overbook more, making them happy too."[4]

[3]See Julian Simon's, "Origins of the Airline Oversales Auction System," at http://www.cato.org/pubs/regulation/regv17n2/reg17n2-simon.html.
[4]Ibid.

line up from the first unit to the supply curve. Because the maximum buying price is greater than the minimum selling price, the first unit of good X will be exchanged.

What about the second unit? For the second unit, buyers are willing to pay a maximum price of $60, and sellers need to receive a minimum price of $20. The second unit of good X will be exchanged. In fact, exchange will occur as long as the maximum buying price is greater than the minimum selling price. The exhibit shows that a total of four units of good X will be exchanged. The fifth unit will not be exchanged because the maximum buying price ($30) is less than the minimum selling price ($50).

In the process just described, buyers and sellers trade money for goods as long as both benefit from the trade. The market converges on a quantity of 4 units of good X and a price of $40 per unit. This is equilibrium. In other words, mutually beneficial trade drives the market to equilibrium.

Units of Good X	Maximum Buying Price	Minimum Selling Price	Result
1st	$70	$10	Exchange
2d	60	20	Exchange
3d	50	30	Exchange
4th	40	40	Exchange
5th	30	50	No Exchange

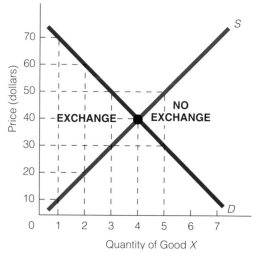

exhibit 14

Moving to Equilibrium in Terms of Maximum and Minimum Prices

As long as the maximum buying price is greater than the minimum selling price, an exchange will occur. This condition is met for units 1–4. The market converges on equilibrium through a process of mutually beneficial exchanges.

Equilibrium in Terms of Consumers' and Producers' Surplus

Equilibrium can be viewed in terms of two important economic concepts: consumers' surplus and producers' (or sellers') surplus. **Consumers' surplus** is the difference between the maximum buying price and the price paid by the buyer.

Consumers' Surplus (CS)

The difference between the maximum price a buyer is willing and able to pay for a good or service and the price actually paid. CS = Maximum buying price − Price paid

Consumers' surplus = Maximum buying price − Price paid

For example, if the highest price you would pay to see a movie is $10 and you pay $7 to see the movie, then you have received $3 consumers' surplus. Obviously, the more consumers' surplus consumers receive, the better off they are. Wouldn't you have preferred to pay, say, $4 to see the movie instead of $7? If you had paid only $4, your consumers' surplus would have been $6 instead of $3.

Producers' (or sellers') surplus is the difference between the price received by the producer or seller and the minimum selling price.

Producers' (Sellers') Surplus (PS)

The difference between the price sellers receive for a good and the minimum or lowest price for which they would have sold the good. PS = Price received − Minimum selling price

Producers' (sellers') surplus = Price received − Minimum selling price

Suppose the minimum price the owner of the movie theater would have accepted for admission is $5. But she doesn't sell admission for $5; she sells it for $7. Her producers' or sellers' surplus is $2. A seller prefers a large producers' surplus to a small one. The theater owner would have preferred to sell admission to the movie for $8 instead of $7 because then she would have received $3 producers' surplus.

Total surplus is the sum of the consumers' surplus and producers' surplus.

Total Surplus (TS)

The sum of consumers' surplus and producers' surplus. TS = CS + PS

Total surplus = Consumers' surplus + Producers' surplus

In Exhibit 15(a), consumers' surplus is represented by the shaded triangle. This triangle includes the area under the demand curve and above the equilibrium price. According to the definition, consumers' surplus is the highest price buyers are willing to pay

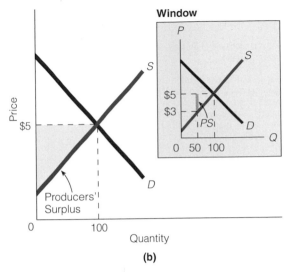

(a)

Consumers' Surplus (CS)

(b)

Producers' Surplus (PS)

exhibit **15**

Consumers' and Producers' Surplus

(a) Consumers' surplus. As the shaded area indicates, the difference between the maximum or highest amount buyers would be willing to pay and the price they actually pay is consumers' surplus. (b) Producers' surplus. As the shaded area indicates, the difference between the price sellers receive for the good and the minimum or lowest price they would be willing to sell the good for is producers' surplus.

(maximum buying price) minus the price they pay. For example, the window in (a) shows that buyers are willing to pay as high as $7 for the 50th unit but only pay $5. Thus, the consumers' surplus on the 50th unit of the good is $2. If we add the consumers' surplus on each unit of the good between and including the first and the 100th units (the equilibrium quantity), we obtain the shaded consumers' surplus triangle.

In Exhibit 15(b), producers' surplus is represented by the shaded triangle. This triangle includes the area above the supply curve and under the equilibrium price. Keep in mind the definition of producers' surplus—the price received by the seller minus the lowest price the seller would accept for the good. For example, the window in (b) shows that sellers would have sold the 50th unit for as low as $3 but actually sold it for $5. Thus, the producers' surplus on the 50th unit of the good is $2. If we add the producers' surplus on each unit of the good between and including the first and the 100th, we obtain the shaded producers' surplus triangle.

Now consider consumers' surplus and producers' surplus at the equilibrium quantity. Exhibit 16 shows that consumers' surplus at equilibrium is equal to areas $A + B + C + D$, and producers' surplus at equilibrium is equal to areas $E + F + G + H$. At any other exchangeable quantity, such as at 25, 50, or 75 units, both consumers' surplus and producers' surplus are less. For example, at 25 units, consumers' surplus is equal to area A, and producers' surplus is equal to area E. At 50 units, consumers' surplus is equal to areas $A + B$, and producers' surplus is equal to areas $E + F$.

Is there a special property to equilibrium? At equilibrium, both consumers' surplus and producers' surplus are maximized. In short, total surplus is maximized.

What Can Change Equilibrium Price and Quantity?

Equilibrium price and quantity are determined by supply and demand. Whenever demand changes, supply changes, or both change, equilibrium price and quantity change. Exhibit 17 illustrates eight different cases where this occurs. Cases (a)−(d) illustrate the four basic changes in supply and demand, where either supply or demand changes. Cases (e)−(h) illustrate changes in both supply and demand.

- (a) Demand rises (the demand curve shifts rightward), and supply is constant (the supply curve does not move). Equilibrium price rises, equilibrium quantity rises.

exhibit 16

Equilibrium, Consumers' Surplus, and Producers' Surplus

Consumers' surplus is greater at equilibrium quantity (100 units) than at any other exchangeable quantity. Producers' surplus is greater at equilibrium quantity than at any other exchangeable quantity. For example, consumers' surplus is areas $A + B + C$ at 75 units, but areas $A + B + C + D$ at 100 units. Producers' surplus is areas $E + F + G$ at 75 units, but areas $E + F + G + H$ at 100 units.

Quantity (units)	Consumers' Surplus	Producers' Surplus
25	A	E
50	$A + B$	$E + F$
75	$A + B + C$	$E + F + G$
100 (Equilibrium)	$A + B + C + D$	$E + F + G + H$

(a)

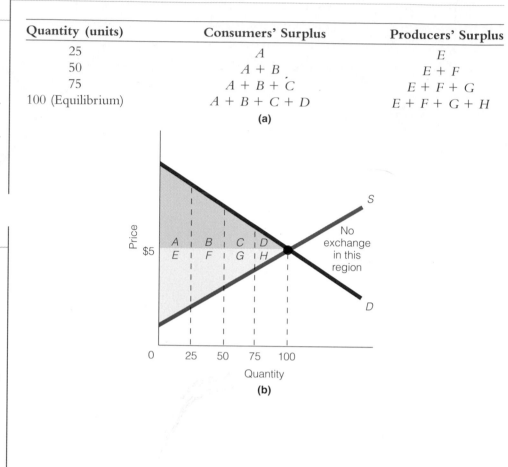

(b)

table 17

Equilibrium Price and Quantity Effects of Supply Curve Shifts and Demand Curve Shifts

The exhibit illustrates the effects on equilibrium price and quantity of a change in demand, a change in supply, or a change in both. Below each diagram the condition leading to the effects is noted, using the following symbols: (1) a bar over a letter means *constant* (thus, $\bar{S}$ means that supply is constant); (2) a downward-pointing arrow (↓) indicates a fall; (3) an upward-pointing arrow (↑) indicates a rise. A rise (fall) in demand is the same as a rightward (leftward) shift in the demand curve. A rise (fall) in supply is the same as a rightward (leftward) shift in the supply curve.

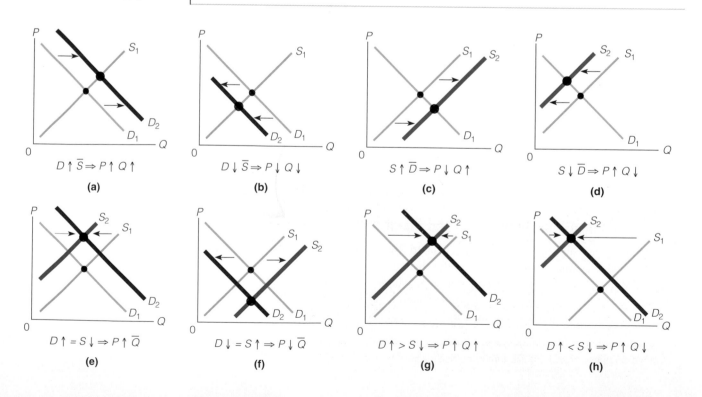

(a) $D \uparrow \bar{S} \Rightarrow P \uparrow Q \uparrow$

(b) $D \downarrow \bar{S} \Rightarrow P \downarrow Q \downarrow$

(c) $S \uparrow \bar{D} \Rightarrow P \downarrow Q \uparrow$

(d) $S \downarrow \bar{D} \Rightarrow P \uparrow Q \downarrow$

(e) $D \uparrow = S \downarrow \Rightarrow P \uparrow \bar{Q}$

(f) $D \downarrow = S \uparrow \Rightarrow P \downarrow \bar{Q}$

(g) $D \uparrow > S \downarrow \Rightarrow P \uparrow Q \uparrow$

(h) $D \uparrow < S \downarrow \Rightarrow P \uparrow Q \downarrow$

- (b) Demand falls, supply is constant. Equilibrium price falls, equilibrium quantity falls.
- (c) Supply rises, demand is constant. Equilibrium price falls, equilibrium quantity rises.
- (d) Supply falls, demand is constant. Equilibrium price rises, equilibrium quantity falls.
- (e) Demand rises and supply falls by an equal amount. Equilibrium price rises, equilibrium quantity is constant.
- (f) Demand falls and supply rises by an equal amount. Equilibrium price falls, equilibrium quantity is constant.
- (g) Demand rises by a greater amount than supply falls. Equilibrium price rises, equilibrium quantity rises.
- (h) Demand rises by a smaller amount than supply falls. Equilibrium price rises, equilibrium quantity falls.

SELF-TEST

1. When a person goes to the grocery store to buy food, there is no auctioneer calling out prices for bread, milk, and other items. Therefore, supply and demand cannot be operative. Do you agree or disagree? Explain your answer.

2. The price of a given-quality personal computer is lower today than it was five years ago. Is this necessarily the result of a lower demand for computers? Explain your answer.

3. What is the effect on equilibrium price and quantity of the following?
   a. A decrease in demand that is greater than the increase in supply
   b. An increase in supply
   c. A decrease in supply that is greater than the increase in demand
   d. A decrease in demand

4. At equilibrium quantity, what is the relationship between the maximum buying price and the minimum selling price?

5. If the price paid is $40 and the consumers' surplus is $4, then what is the maximum buying price? If the minimum selling price is $30 and producers' surplus is $4, then what is the price received by the seller?

Price Controls

Because scarcity exists, there is a need for a rationing device—such as dollar price. But price is not always permitted to be a rationing device. Sometimes, price is controlled. There are two types of price controls: price ceilings and price floors. In the discussion of price controls, the word *price* is used in the generic sense. It refers to the price of an apple, for example, the price of labor (wage), the price of credit (interest rate), and so on.

Price Ceiling: Definition and Effects

A **price ceiling** is a government-mandated maximum price above which legal trades cannot be made. For example, suppose the government mandates that the maximum price at which good X can be bought and sold is $8. It follows that $8 is a price ceiling. If $8 is below the equilibrium price of good X, as in Exhibit 18, any or all of the following effects may arise.[5]

Price Ceiling

A government-mandated maximum price above which legal trades cannot be made.

SHORTAGES At the $12 equilibrium price in Exhibit 18, the quantity demanded of good X (150) is equal to the quantity supplied (150). At the $8 price ceiling, a shortage exists. The quantity demanded (190) is greater than the quantity supplied (100). When a

---

[5]If the price ceiling is above the equilibrium price (say, $8 is the price ceiling and $4 is the equilibrium price), it has no effects. Usually, however, a price ceiling is below the equilibrium price.

exhibit **18**

A Price Ceiling

The price ceiling is $8 and the equilibrium price is $12. At $12, quantity demanded = quantity supplied. At $8, quantity demanded > quantity supplied. (Recall that price, on the vertical axis, always represents price per unit. Quantity, on the horizontal axis, always holds for a specific time period.)

shortage exists, there is a tendency for price and output to rise to equilibrium. But when a price ceiling exists, this tendency cannot be realized because it is unlawful to trade at the equilibrium price.

FEWER EXCHANGES At the equilibrium price of $12 in Exhibit 18, 150 units of good X are bought and sold. At the price ceiling of $8, 100 units of good X are bought and sold. (Buyers would prefer to buy 190 units, but only 100 are supplied.) We conclude that price ceilings cause fewer exchanges to be made.

Notice in Exhibit 18 that the demand curve is above the supply curve for all quantities less than 150 units. (At 150 units, the demand curve and the supply curve intersect and thus share the same point in the two-dimensional space.) This means the maximum buying price is greater than the minimum selling price for all units less than 150. In particular, the maximum buying price is greater than the minimum selling price for units 101 to 149. For example, buyers might be willing to pay $17 for the 110th unit, and sellers might be willing to sell the 110th unit for $10. But no unit after the 100th unit (not the 110th unit, not the 114th unit, not the 130th unit) will be produced and sold because of the price ceiling. In short, the price ceiling prevents mutually advantageous trades from being realized.

NONPRICE RATIONING DEVICES If the equilibrium price of $12 fully rationed good X before the price ceiling was imposed, it follows that a (lower) price of $8 can only partly ration this good. In short, price ceilings prevent price from rising to the level sufficient to ration goods fully. But if price is responsible for only part of the rationing, what accounts for the rest? The answer is some other (nonprice) rationing device, such as first come, first served (FCFS).

In Exhibit 18, 100 units of good X will be sold at $8, although buyers are willing to buy 190 units at this price. What happens? Possibly, good X will be sold on an FCFS basis for $8 per unit. In other words, to buy good X, a person must not only pay $8 per unit but also be one of the first people in line.

BUYING AND SELLING AT A PROHIBITED PRICE Buyers and sellers may regularly circumvent a price ceiling by making their exchanges "under the table." For example, some buyers may offer some sellers more than $8 per unit for good X. No doubt, some sellers will accept the offers. But why would some buyers offer more than $8 per unit when they

economics 24/7

TICKET SCALPING

I got two for Pavarotti.

—Ticket scalper

At a big rock concert, a major sports event, or a popular Broadway play, ticket scalpers are likely to be nearby trying to sell tickets. Many people do not like scalpers; they believe scalpers are taking advantage of them by charging many times more than the original supplier of the ticket charged. Some states have outlawed ticket scalping or permit it only if the scalper charges a limited amount, say, 5 to 10 percent more than the original ticket price. Scalpers who continue to practice their trade in defiance of the law are fined.

The question the economist asks is: Why does ticket scalping exist in the first place? The noneconomist may answer, "Because there is greed and selfishness in the world." But surely, greed and selfishness do not surface just for major sports events or Broadway plays. Ticket scalpers are not at all events, only some. Put the question this way: What condition is necessary before ticket scalping will exist?

If you think in terms of supply and demand, you will have the answer. Certainly, there will be no ticket scalping if the equilibrium price is initially charged for a ticket. At the equilibrium price, the quantity demanded of tickets will equal the quantity supplied.

Suppose the ticket price is above equilibrium. Will ticket scalping exist then? No, because at a price higher than equilibrium price, people will buy fewer tickets than there are tickets available. No one has ever seen a ticket scalper trying to sell a ticket that can be purchased from the ticket office.

Ticket scalping will exist only when the ticket price initially charged is lower than the equilibrium price. For example, suppose the equilibrium price to see a particular rock band is $80 a ticket, but only $50 a ticket is charged. Someone will likely buy the ticket for $50 and then turn around and sell it for $80. In other words, before ticket scalping exists, a profitable opportunity must present itself.

But why would a seller choose to sell tickets for less than equilibrium price? One answer is that the seller may not know what equilibrium price is in a particular setting. In other words, a seller may simply make a mistake and charge more or less than equilibrium price. Another answer is that the seller may be concerned about sacrificing the goodwill of her customers (many of whom she hopes will be repeat customers) if she charges the equilibrium price. For example, some Broadway theaters charge below equilibrium prices for tickets to plays. They even know they are charging below equilibrium prices because they know the prices the scalpers are getting paid. But as the president of one Broadway theater said, "Even though we could sell tickets for $100, we'd be cutting our throats because it would be a PR disaster for Broadway."

can buy good X for $8? The answer is because not all buyers can buy the amount of good X they want at $8. As Exhibit 18 shows, there is a shortage. Buyers are willing to buy 190 units at $8, but sellers are willing to sell only 100 units. In short, 90 fewer units will be sold than buyers would like to buy. Some buyers will go unsatisfied. How, then, does any one buyer make it more likely that sellers will sell to him or her instead of to someone else? The answer is by offering to pay a higher price. Because it is illegal to pay a higher price, the transaction must be made "under the table."

TIE-IN SALES In Exhibit 18, the maximum price buyers would be willing and able to pay per unit for 100 units of good X is $18. (This is the price on the demand curve at a quantity of 100 units.) The maximum legal price, however, is $8. This difference between two prices often prompts a **tie-in sale**, a sale whereby one good can be purchased only if another good is also purchased. For example, if Ralph's Gas Station sells gasoline to customers only if they buy a car wash, the two goods are linked together in a tie-in sale.

Tie-in Sale
A sale whereby one good can be purchased only if another good is also purchased.

Suppose that the sellers of good X in Exhibit 18 also sell good Y. They might offer to sell buyers good X at $8 only if the buyers agree to buy good Y at, say, $10. We choose $10 as the price for good Y because $10 is the difference between the maximum per-unit price buyers are willing and able to pay for 100 units of good X ($18) and the maximum legal price ($8).

In New York City and other communities with rent-control laws, tie-in sales sometimes result from rent ceilings on apartments. Occasionally, to rent an apartment, an individual must agree to buy the furniture in the apartment.

Thinking like
AN ECONOMIST
Economists think in terms of unintended effects. For example, a price ceiling policy intended to lower prices for the poor may cause shortages, the use of nonprice rationing devices, illegal market transactions, and tie-in sales. When we consider both the price ceiling and its effects, it is not clear that the poor have been helped. The economist knows that wanting to do good (for others) is not sufficient. It is important to know how to do good too.

Do Buyers Prefer Lower Prices to Higher Prices?

"Of course," someone might say, "buyers prefer lower prices to higher prices. What buyer would want to pay a higher price for anything?" But wait a minute. Price ceilings are often lower than equilibrium prices. Does it follow that buyers prefer price ceilings to equilibrium prices? Not necessarily. Price ceilings have effects that equilibrium prices do not: shortages, use of first come, first served as a rationing device, tie-in sales, and so on. A buyer could prefer to pay a higher price (an equilibrium price) than to pay a lower price and have to deal with the effects of a price ceiling. All we can say for certain is that buyers prefer lower prices to higher prices, *ceteris paribus*. As in many cases, the *ceteris paribus* condition makes all the difference.

Price Floor: Definition and Effects

Price Floor

A government-mandated minimum price below which legal trades cannot be made.

A **price floor** is a government-mandated minimum price below which legal trades cannot be made. For example, suppose the government mandates that the minimum price at which good X can be sold is $20. It follows that $20 is a price floor (see Exhibit 19). If the price floor is above the equilibrium price, the following two effects arise.[6]

SURPLUSES At the $15 equilibrium price in Exhibit 19, the quantity demanded of good X (130) is equal to the quantity supplied (130). At the $20 price floor, a surplus exists.

exhibit 19

A Price Floor

The price floor is $20 and the equilibrium price is $15. At $15, quantity demanded = quantity supplied. At $20, quantity supplied > quantity demanded.

[6]If the price floor is below the equilibrium price (say, $20 is the price floor and $25 is the equilibrium price), it has no effects. Usually, however, a price floor is above the equilibrium price.

The quantity supplied (180) is greater than the quantity demanded (90). A surplus is usually a temporary state of affairs. When a surplus exists, there is a tendency for price and output to fall to equilibrium. But when a price floor exists, this tendency cannot be realized because it is unlawful to trade at the equilibrium price.

FEWER EXCHANGES At the equilibrium price in Exhibit 19, 130 units of good X are bought and sold. At the price floor, 90 units are bought and sold. (Sellers want to sell 180 units, but buyers buy only 90.) We conclude that price floors cause fewer exchanges to be made.

SELF-TEST

1. Do buyers prefer lower prices to higher prices?

2. "When there are long-lasting shortages, there are long lines of people waiting to buy goods. It follows that the shortages cause the long lines." Do you agree or disagree? Explain your answer.

3. Who might argue for a price ceiling? a price floor?

A Reader Asks...

How Does Knowing About Supply and Demand Help Me?

Some things are interesting but not useful. Other things are useful but not interesting. For example, supply and demand are interesting but not useful. Learning how to fix a car is useful but not particularly interesting. Am I wrong? Have I missed something? Is knowledge of supply and demand useful? If it is, what can you do with it?

A knowledge of supply and demand can be used both to explain and to predict. Let's look at prediction first. Suppose you learn that the federal government is going to impose a quota on imported television sets. What will happen when the quota is imposed? With your knowledge of supply and demand, you can predict that the price of television sets will rise. In other words, you can use your knowledge of supply and demand to predict what will happen. Stated differently, you can use your knowledge of supply and demand to see into the future. Isn't the ability to see into the future useful?

Supply and demand also allows you to develop richer and fuller explanations of events. To illustrate, suppose there is a shortage of apples in country X. The cause of the shortage, someone says, is that apple growers in the country are simply growing too few apples. Well, of course, it's true that apple growers are growing "too few" apples compared to the number of apples consumers want to buy. But does this explanation completely account for the shortage of apples? Your knowledge of supply and demand will prompt you to ask why apple growers are growing too few apples. When you understand that quantity supplied is related to price, you understand that apple growers will grow more apples if the price of apples is higher. What is keeping the price of apples down? Could it be a price ceiling? Without a price ceiling, the price of apples would rise, and apple growers would grow (and offer to sell) more apples. The shortage of apples will vanish.

In other words, without a knowledge of supply and demand, you may have been content to explain the shortage of apples by saying that apple growers are growing too few apples. With your knowledge of supply and demand, you delve deeper into *why* apple growers are growing too few apples.

analyzing the scene

At the time James checks stock prices, Wal-Mart is selling for $44.09, Microsoft for $23.75, and Dell for $21.75. Why doesn't Dell sell for more than Wal-Mart? Why does Microsoft sell for more than Dell? Why is the euro selling for $1.28 and not higher or lower?

The price of each stock is determined by supply and demand. The price of Wal-Mart stock is higher than the price of Dell stock because the demand for Wal-Mart stock is higher than the demand for Dell stock and/or the supply of Wal-Mart stock is lower than the supply of Dell stock. Similar reasoning explains why Microsoft stock sells for more than Dell stock does.

The exchange rate between the euro and the dollar is also determined by supply and demand. Just as there is a demand for and supply of apples, oranges, houses, and computers, there is a demand for and supply of various currencies (e.g., the dollar and the euro). The dollar price James has to pay for a euro has to do with the demand for and supply of euros. Thus, supply and demand may determine whether or not James takes a trip to Europe this summer.

What does getting his shower fixed have to do with James living in a rent-controlled apartment?

James has been trying for two weeks to get his apartment supervisor to fix his shower. James's friend thinks it has taken so long because James lives in a rent-controlled apartment. (A rent-controlled apartment has a rent ceiling; James's rent is lower than the equilibrium, or market-clearing, rent.) Is James's friend right? With a rent ceiling, the quantity demanded of apartments is greater than the quantity supplied; that is, a shortage of apartments exists. The apartment supervisor knows there is a shortage of apartments and realizes he could rent the apartment easily if James moved. The supervisor is likely to be less responsive to James's request to fix the shower than he would be if the rental market were in equilibrium or surplus.

Why does it take so long (nine months) to get tickets to see the **Late Show with David Letterman?**

We know that the price of a ticket is zero (which is not the equilibrium or market-clearing price). At a price of zero, the quantity demanded of tickets is much greater than the quantity supplied. How are the tickets rationed? They're rationed on a first come, first served basis. James had to "stand in line," or "wait," for nine months to get tickets to see the show. That's one long line.

Does the burglary rate have anything to do with how "hard" or "soft" a city is on crime?

The law of demand holds for apples—raise the price of apples and fewer apples will be sold. But does the law of demand hold for burglary too? The mayor of New York City hinted that it does in a report on the 11 o'clock news. The mayor said, "This city and this mayor are not going to be soft on crime. We're going to do everything in our power to make sure that everyone knows that crime doesn't pay." He said these words in response to the rise in the city's burglary rate. Obviously, the mayor thinks that if the city raises the "price" a person has to pay for committing burglary (in terms of fines or jail time), there will be fewer burglaries.

chapter summary

Demand

- The law of demand states that as the price of a good rises, the quantity demanded of the good falls, and as the price of a good falls, the quantity demanded of the good rises, *ceteris paribus*. The law of demand holds that price and quantity demanded are inversely related.

- Quantity demanded is the total number of units of a good that buyers are willing and able to buy at a particular price.

- A (downward-sloping) demand curve is the graphical representation of the law of demand.

- Factors that can change demand and cause the demand curve to shift include income, preferences, prices of related goods (substitutes and complements), number of buyers, and expectations of future price.

- The only factor that can directly cause a change in the quantity demanded of a good is a change in the good's own price.

Absolute Price and Relative Price

- The absolute price of a good is the price of the good in money terms.
- The relative price of a good is the price of the good in terms of another good.

Supply

- The law of supply states that as the price of a good rises, the quantity supplied of the good rises, and as the price of a good falls, the quantity supplied of the good falls, *ceteris paribus*. The law of supply asserts that price and quantity supplied are directly related.
- The law of supply does not hold when there is no time to produce more units of a good or when goods cannot be produced at all (over any period of time).
- The upward-sloping supply curve is the graphical representation of the law of supply. More generally, a supply curve (no matter how it slopes) represents the relationship between price and quantity supplied.
- Factors that can change supply and cause the supply curve to shift include prices of relevant resources, technology, number of sellers, expectations of future price, taxes and subsidies, and government restrictions.
- The only factor that can directly cause a change in the quantity supplied of a good is a change in the good's own price.

The Market

- Demand and supply together establish equilibrium price and equilibrium quantity.
- A surplus exists in a market if, at some price, quantity supplied is greater than quantity demanded. A shortage exists if, at some price, quantity demanded is greater than quantity supplied.
- Mutually beneficial trade between buyers and sellers drives the market to equilibrium.

Consumers' Surplus, Producers' Surplus, and Total Surplus

- Consumers' surplus is the difference between the maximum buying price and price paid by the buyer.

    Consumers' surplus = Maximum buying price − Price paid

- Producers' (or sellers') surplus is the difference between the price the seller receives and minimum selling price.

    Producers' surplus = Price received − Minimum selling price

- The more consumers' surplus that buyers receive, the better off they are. The more producers' surplus that sellers receive, the better off they are.
- Total surplus is the sum of consumers' surplus and producers' surplus.
- Total surplus (the sum of consumers' surplus and producers' surplus) is maximized at equilibrium.

Price Ceilings

- A price ceiling is a government-mandated maximum price. If a price ceiling is below the equilibrium price, some or all of the following effects arise: shortages, fewer exchanges, nonprice rationing devices, buying and selling at prohibited prices, and tie-in sales.
- Consumers do not necessarily prefer (lower) price ceilings to (higher) equilibrium prices. They may prefer higher prices and none of the effects of price ceilings to lower prices and some of the effects of price ceilings. All we can say for sure is that consumers prefer lower prices to higher prices, *ceteris paribus*.

Price Floors

- A price floor is a government-mandated minimum price. If a price floor is above the equilibrium price, the following effects arise: surpluses and fewer exchanges.

key terms and concepts

Theory	Demand Curve	Normal Good	Law of Supply
Market	Absolute (Money) Price	Inferior Good	Supply Curve
Demand	Relative Price	Neutral Good	Supply Schedule
Law of Demand	Law of Diminishing	Substitutes	Subsidy
Ceteris Paribus	Marginal Utility	Complements	Surplus (Excess Supply)
Demand Schedule	Own Price	Supply	

Shortage (Excess Demand)	Equilibrium Quantity	Consumers' Surplus	Price Ceiling
Equilibrium Price (Market-Clearing Price)	Disequilibrium Price	Producers' (Sellers') Surplus	Tie-in Sale
	Disequilibrium	Total Surplus	Price Floor
	Equilibrium		

questions and problems

1 True or false? As the price of oranges rises, the demand for oranges falls, *ceteris paribus.* Explain your answer.

2 "The price of a bushel of wheat, which was $3.00 last month, is $3.70 today. The demand curve for wheat must have shifted rightward between last month and today." Discuss.

3 "Some goods are bought largely because they have 'snob appeal.' For example, the residents of Beverly Hills gain prestige by buying expensive items. In fact, they won't buy some items unless they are expensive. The law of demand, which holds that people buy more at lower prices than higher prices, obviously doesn't hold for the residents of Beverly Hills. The following rules apply in Beverly Hills: "high prices, buy; low prices, don't buy." Discuss.

4 "The price of T-shirts keeps rising and rising, and people keep buying more and more. T-shirts must have an upward-sloping demand curve." Identify the error.

5 Predict what would happen to the equilibrium price of marijuana if it were legalized.

6 Compare the ratings for television shows with prices for goods. How are ratings like prices? How are ratings different from prices? (Hint: How does rising demand for a particular television show manifest itself?)

7 Must consumers' surplus equal producers' surplus at equilibrium price? Explain your answer.

8 Many movie theaters charge a lower admission price for the first show on weekday afternoons than they do for a weeknight or weekend show. Explain why.

9 A Dell computer is a substitute for a Hewlett-Packard computer. What happens to the demand for Hewlett-Packard computers and the quantity demanded of Dell computers as the price of a Dell falls?

10 Describe how each of the following will affect the demand for personal computers: (a) a rise in incomes (assuming computers are a normal good); (b) a lower expected price for computers; (c) cheaper software; (d) computers become simpler to operate.

11 Describe how each of the following will affect the supply of personal computers: (a) a rise in wage rates; (b) an increase in the number of sellers of computers; (c) a tax placed on the production of computers; (d) a subsidy placed on the production of computers.

12 The law of demand specifies an inverse relationship between price and quantity demanded, *ceteris paribus.* Is the "price" in the law of demand absolute price or relative price? Explain your answer.

13 Use the law of diminishing marginal utility to explain why demand curves slope downward.

14 Explain how the market moves to equilibrium in terms of shortages and surpluses and in terms of maximum buying prices and minimum selling prices.

15 Identify what happens to equilibrium price and quantity in each of the following cases:
  a Demand rises and supply is constant
  b Demand falls and supply is constant
  c Supply rises and demand is constant
  d Supply falls and demand is constant
  e Demand rises by the same amount that supply falls
  f Demand falls by the same amount that supply rises
  g Demand falls by less than supply rises
  h Demand rises by more than supply rises
  i Demand rises by less than supply rises
  j Demand falls by more than supply falls
  k Demand falls by less than supply falls

16 Many of the proponents of price ceilings argue that government-mandated maximum prices simply reduce producers' profits and do not affect the quantity supplied of a good on the market. What must the supply curve look like before a price ceiling does not affect quantity supplied?

working with numbers and graphs

1 If the absolute price of good X is $10 and the absolute price of good Y is $14, then what is (a) the relative price of good X in terms of good Y and (b) the relative price of good Y in terms of good X?

2 Price is $10, quantity supplied is 50 units, and quantity demanded is 100 units. For every $1 rise in price, quantity supplied rises by 5 units and quantity demanded falls by 5 units. What is the equilibrium price and quantity?

3 Draw a diagram that shows a larger increase in demand than the decrease in supply.

4 Draw a diagram that shows a smaller increase in supply than the increase in demand.

5 At equilibrium in the following figure, what area(s) does consumers' surplus equal? producers' surplus?

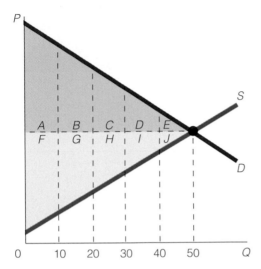

6 At what quantity in the preceding figure is the maximum buying price equal to the minimum selling price?

7 In the following figure, can the movement from point 1 to point 2 be explained by a combination of an increase in the price of a substitute and a decrease in the price of nonlabor resources? Explain your answer.

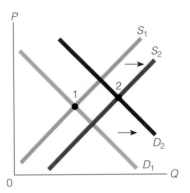

8 The demand curve is downward sloping, the supply curve is upward sloping, and the equilibrium quantity is 50 units. Show on a graph that the difference between the maximum buying price and minimum selling price is greater at 25 units than at 33 units.

9 Diagrammatically show and explain why a price ceiling that is above the equilibrium price will not prompt a tie-in sale.

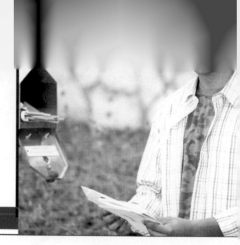

Supply and Demand: Practice

4

Setting the Scene

The following events occurred on a day in April.

3:15 P.M.

Bob Mason, 18 years old, walks to the mailbox in front of his house. He reaches inside the mailbox, pulls out the mail, and nervously looks through the letters. It's there. He's been anxiously waiting for the mail every day just for this letter. In the next few seconds, he'll learn whether or not he's been accepted by the college he so desperately wants to attend.

3:43 P.M.

Carl and Karen Jenkins, married one year, are in their real estate agent's car driving to the next house they'll look at today. Carl wonders out loud why houses are so expensive in their area. "A person can get twice the house for almost half the money in other parts of the country," he says.

5:15 P.M.

Carlos is on the freeway driving home from work. Traffic is heavy, as usual, and Carlos is driving about 30 mph at the moment. As he half listens to a talk show on the radio, Carlos picks up his cell phone and makes a call. Just as he ends his call, traffic slows down to 5 mph. "I'm not sure how much longer I can take these commutes," Carlos thinks. "This traffic is really getting ridiculous."

5:35 P.M.

Samantha Wilson is standing at the counter of American Airlines in the Dallas–Fort Worth Airport. She asks for an aisle seat for her flight. The response: "I'm afraid the only seats I have left are center seats."

 Here are some questions to keep in mind as you read this chapter:

- *What is the relationship between the probability of Bob Mason being admitted to the college of his choice and the tuition the college charges?*

- *Why are house prices higher in some parts of the country than in other parts of the country?*

- *What do supply, demand, and price have to do with Carlos driving 5 mph on a freeway on his way home from work?*

- *Why aren't any aisle seats left?*

See analyzing the scene at the end of this chapter for answers to these questions.

In this chapter we apply what we learned in the last chapter. In short, we take what we know about the law of demand, the law of supply, equilibrium price, price ceilings, consumers' surplus, etc., and then apply that knowledge to the real world.

Application 1: Why Do Colleges Use GPAs, ACTs, and SATs for Purposes of Admission?

At many colleges and universities, a student pays part of the price of his or her education (by way of tuition payments), and taxpayers and private donors pay part (by way of tax payments and charitable donations, respectively). Thus, the tuition that students pay to attend colleges and universities is usually less than the equilibrium tuition. To illustrate, suppose a student pays tuition T_1 at a given college or university. As shown in Exhibit 1, T_1 is below the equilibrium tuition, T_E. At T_1, the number of students who want to attend the university (N_1) is greater than the number of openings at the university (N_2); that is, quantity demanded is greater than quantity supplied. The university receives more applications for admission than there are places available. Something has to be done. But what?

The college or university is likely to ration its available space by a combination of money price and some other nonprice rationing devices. The student must pay the tuition, T_1, *and* meet the standards of the nonprice rationing devices. Colleges and universities usually use such things as GPAs (grade point averages), ACT scores, and SAT scores as rationing devices.

Thinking like **AN ECONOMIST** *The layperson sees a university that requires a GPA of 3.8 and an SAT score of 1900 or better for admission. An economist sees a rationing device. The economist then goes on to ask why this particular nonprice rationing device is used. He reasons that there would be no need for a nonprice rationing device if (dollar) price were fully rationing the good or service.*

SELF-TEST

(Answers to Self-Test questions are in the Self-Test Appendix).

1. Suppose the demand rises for admission to a university but both the tuition and the number of openings in the entering class remain the same. Will this affect the admission standards of the university? Explain your answer.

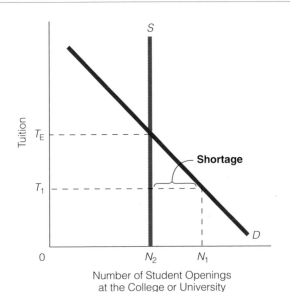

exhibit **1**

College and University Admissions

If the college or university charges T_1 in tuition (when T_E is the equilibrium tuition), a shortage will be generated. The college or university will then use some nonprice rationing device, such as GPAs, ACTs, and SATs, as admission criteria.

2.   Administrators and faculty at state colleges and universities often say that their standards of admission are independent of whether there is a shortage or surplus of openings at the university. Do you think this is true? Do you think that faculty and administrators ignore surpluses and shortages of openings when setting admission standards? Explain your answer.

Application 2: What Will Happen to the Price of Marijuana If the Purchase and Sale of Marijuana Are Legalized?

In the United States, the purchase or sale of marijuana is unlawful. However, there is still a demand for and supply of marijuana. There is also an equilibrium price of marijuana. Let's say that price is P_1.

Suppose that beginning tomorrow, the purchase and sale of marijuana become legal. Will P_1 rise, fall, or remain the same?

The answer, of course, depends on what we think will happen to the demand for and supply of marijuana. If the purchase and sale of marijuana are legal, then some people currently producing corn and wheat will likely choose instead to produce and sell marijuana. So, the supply of marijuana will rise. If nothing else changes, the price of marijuana will fall.

But something else is likely to change. If marijuana consumption is no longer illegal, then the number of people who want to buy and consume marijuana will likely rise. In other words, there will be more buyers of marijuana. This will increase the demand for marijuana.

Thus, decriminalizing the purchase and sale of marijuana is likely to shift both the marijuana demand and supply curves to the right. What happens to the price of marijuana depends on how much the curves shift. Three possibilities exist:

1.   The demand curve shifts to the right by the same amount as the supply curve shifts to the right. In this case, the price of marijuana will not change. (Try to visualize the demand and supply curves shifting.)

2.   The demand curve shifts to the right by more than the supply curve shifts to the right. In this case, the price of marijuana will rise. (Try to visualize the demand curve shifting to the right by more than the supply curve shifts to the right. Can you see the higher price on the vertical axis?)

3.   The supply curve shifts to the right by more than the demand curve shifts to the right. In this case, the price of marijuana will fall.

If you can't visualize the shifts of the demand and supply curves for the three possibilities, draw the original demand and supply curves, then draw the shift in each curve, and finally, identify the new equilibrium price.

SELF-TEST

1.   What will happen to the price of marijuana if the supply of marijuana increases by more than the demand for it?

2.   What will happen to the quantity of marijuana (purchased and sold) if the demand for marijuana rises by more than the supply of marijuana falls?

Application 3: Where Did You Get That Music?

In recent years, the recording industry feels it has suffered some reduced sales because of music piracy. People download music (or transfer files) from the Internet instead of buying the music on CDs sold by recording companies.

The recording industry, we expect, would like to reduce the amount of downloading and file transferring to zero. If zero piracy is not possible, the industry at least wants less than currently exists. In other words, if 100,000 songs are downloaded on an average day, the recording industry wants that number reduced to 50,000 or, even better, to 25,000. The fewer, the better. How can the recording industry get what it wants?

We can use a supply-and-demand framework to find out how to get less of something. Let's consider how to reduce the amount of apples purchased each day. Suppose buyers are currently buying 30,000 apples a day. What has to happen for fewer apples to be purchased each day? One of three things:

1. A higher price will cause apple buyers to move up their demand curves (change in quantity demanded) and purchase fewer apples.

2. A lower demand (shift leftward in the demand curve) will result in buyers purchasing fewer apples.

3. A lower supply (shift leftward in the supply curve) will result in buyers purchasing fewer apples.

The recording industry has tried all three—higher price, lower demand, and lower supply—in its attempt to reduce the amount of pirated music.

To try to lower supply, the recording industry brought a legal suit against certain companies, such as Napster, that made downloading possible. The recording industry charged Napster with "willful contributory and vicarious copyright infringement." By getting rid of the "middlemen" that made music trading (some would say music pirating) possible, the recording industry would lower the supply of music available on the Internet.

The recording industry also stated that it would sue scores of people who download music. This statement by the recording industry was intended to raise the price of downloading music. The message to downloaders was: You thought the cost of downloading music was zero, but it is not. We may sue you and force you to pay damages. This attempt to reduce the amount of downloaded music worked. Soon after the announcement, the number of Internet users who said they downloaded music fell from about 35 million to 18 million.

Not long ago, the recording industry ran TV commercials to try to lower the demand for downloading music. One commercial showed many of the people who work in the recording industry. The ad showed the artists, of course, but it also showed the technicians behind the scenes and the scores of other people who depend on the recording industry for their livelihood. The message was that there are hundreds of everyday people working behind the scenes, and when you download music instead of buying it, you hurt these people—you jeopardize their jobs and their families. The recording industry hoped to affect a person's preferences in a way that would lead to a decline in the demand for downloading music. The industry wanted a person to think, "I didn't know that I might put someone out of a job by downloading music. Maybe I shouldn't download anymore, or at least do less of it."

SELF-TEST

1.   On January 21, 2004, the recording industry filed lawsuits against 532 people it accused of illegally swapping copyrighted music on the Internet. What does this have to do with supply, demand, or price?

2.   Suppose the recording industry runs only a few TV commercials trying to lower demand for downloading music. Instead, it continually takes legal action against either the people who download the music or the companies that make downloading (and file transferring) possible. What might explain these actions?

Application 4: Television Shows During the Olympics

For two weeks in February 2006, NBC broadcast the Winter Olympics from Turin, Italy. During the two Olympic weeks, many of the other television networks chose to not broadcast new episodes of some of their regular prime-time shows. For example, for the person who usually watches *CSI* on Thursday night on CBS, the network ran a rerun of *CSI* instead of a new episode. Other networks chose to run old movies instead of their regular prime-time shows.

In Chapter 3, we learned that "expectations of future price" can affect the supply of a good. Can expectations of future price also affect the supply of a television show? What was CBS thinking when it decided to show a rerun of *CSI* during the Olympics instead of a new episode? It probably was thinking that the demand to watch *CSI* would be less during the Olympics than during other weeks. And if the demand for *CSI* is lower during the Olympics, how much an advertiser would pay for a half-minute commercial during that week is lower as well. In other words, CBS believed that the future price of a half-minute commercial in a non-Olympic week would be higher than in an Olympic week, so it reduced its supply of new *CSI* episodes in an Olympic week to zero and transferred what supply of new *CSI* episodes it had to non-Olympic weeks—when it could fetch a higher price for a half-minute commercial.

© JERRY LAMPEN/REUTERS/LANDOV

SELF-TEST

1.   How might the expectation of a higher price for houses affect the (current) demand for houses?

2.   How might the expectation of a lower price for cars affect the (current) demand for cars?

Application 5: Who Feeds Cleveland?

Rarely does anyone ask who feeds Cleveland or who feeds (the people in) any other city in the world for that matter. Most of us take it for granted that we somehow get fed. We go to the grocery store, we select certain items off the shelves, we pay for those items, and then we go home and eat the food. What more do we need to think about?

To understand just how much is involved, suppose you had the job of feeding Cleveland: You need to tell farmers how much corn, wheat, and soybeans to grow. You need to decide what the right price is for Cheerios and ketchup and milk. (How do you figure out these prices?) You need to send so many cartons of orange juice to various grocery stores. (We wonder whether you might send too much orange juice to one grocery store and not enough to another.)

To get the right amount of food to your local grocery store, literally hundreds of decisions have to be made along the way. Yet, no giant computer decides how much corn and wheat will be grown and how much orange juice will be sent to the grocery store at the corner of 13th Street and Main. No government bureaucracy in Washington, D.C., decides such things. As far as we know, we cannot point to a single person in the world and say: "She feeds Cleveland."

Well, if no one feeds Cleveland, then how does Cleveland get fed? The answer is "supply and demand feeds Cleveland." That's right, supply and demand, or what we have come to know as "the market." If the demand for Cheerios rises, the price rises, which prompts the manufacturer to produce more Cheerios. If the demand for corn rises, the price rises, which prompts corn farmers to plant and harvest more corn. If the demand for fat-free ice cream falls, then fat-free ice cream stays in the grocery freezer longer, and soon the price drops, which signals to ice cream manufacturers that they shouldn't produce as much fat-free ice cream.

A famous economist once said that if "supply and demand" or "the market" didn't naturally exist, it would have to be invented—and then it would be hailed as the greatest invention the world had ever seen. Of course, the market was not invented; it just is.

Who feeds Cleveland, New York, Chicago, New Orleans, London, Buenos Aires, and Paris?

And who feeds you?

Application 6: The Minimum Wage Law

Recall that a price floor is a legislated minimum price below which trades cannot legally be made. The *minimum wage* is a price floor—a government-mandated minimum price for labor. It affects the market for unskilled labor. In Exhibit 2, we assume the minimum

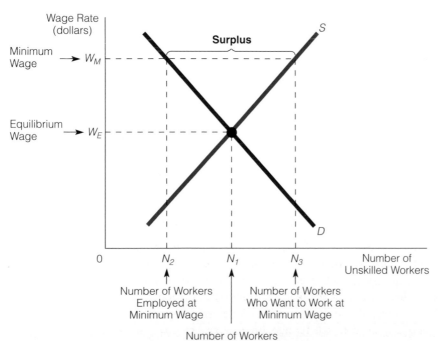

exhibit 2

Effects of the Minimum Wage

At a minimum wage of W_M an hour, there is a surplus of workers and fewer workers are employed than would be at the equilibrium wage W_E.

wage is W_M and the equilibrium wage is W_E. At the equilibrium wage, N_1 workers are employed. At the higher minimum wage, N_3 workers want to work but only N_2 actually do work. There is a surplus of workers equal to $N_3 - N_2$ in this unskilled labor market. In addition, fewer workers are working at the minimum wage (N_2) than at the equilibrium wage (N_1). Overall, the effects of the minimum wage are (1) a surplus of unskilled workers and (2) fewer workers employed.

Suppose two economists decide to test the theory that as the minimum wage rises, some unskilled workers will lose their jobs. They look at the number of unskilled workers before and after the minimum wage is raised, and surprisingly, they find that the number of unskilled workers is the same. Is this sufficient evidence to conclude that an increase in the minimum wage does not cause some workers to lose their jobs?

We'll leave that question hanging while we consider whether or not the economists have adequately tested their theory. Instead of focusing on the number of people who lose their jobs, suppose they look at the people who keep their jobs but have their hours reduced as a result of the higher minimum wage.

Let's look at an example. Suppose a local hardware store currently employs David and Francesca to work after school cleaning up and stocking shelves. The owner of the store pays each of them the minimum wage of, say, $5.15 an hour. Then, the minimum wage is raised to $6.75 an hour. Will either David or Francesca lose their jobs as a result? Not necessarily. Instead, the owner of the store could reduce the number of hours he employs the two workers. For example, instead of having each of them work 20 hours a week, he might ask each to work only 14 hours a week.[1]

Now, let's reconsider our original question: Has the higher minimum wage eliminated jobs? In a way, no. It has, however, reduced the number of hours a person works in a job. (Of course, if we define a job as including both a particular task and a certain number of hours completing that task, then the minimum wage increase has eliminated "part" of the job.) This discussion argues for changing the label on the horizontal axis in Exhibit 2 from "Number of Unskilled Workers" to "Number of Unskilled Labor Hours."

Thinking like
AN ECONOMIST
In economics, some questions relate to "direction" and some to "magnitude." For example, suppose someone asks, "If the demand for labor is downward sloping and the labor market is competitive, how will a minimum wage (above the equilibrium wage) affect employment?" This person is asking a question that relates to the direction of the change in employment. Usually, these types of questions can be answered by applying a theory. Applying the theory of demand, an economist might say, "At higher wages, the quantity demanded of labor, or the employment level, will be lower than at lower wages." The word **lower** *speaks to the directional change in employment.*

Now suppose someone asks, "How much will employment decline?" This person is asking a question that relates to magnitude. Usually, questions that deal with magnitude can be answered only through some kind of empirical (data-collecting and analyzing) work. In other words, we would have to collect employment figures at the equilibrium wage and at the minimum wage and then find the difference.

SELF-TEST

1. When the labor supply curve is upward sloping, a minimum wage law that sets the wage rate above its equilibrium level creates a surplus of labor. If the labor supply curve is vertical, does a surplus of labor still occur? Explain your answer.

2. Someone says that an increase in the minimum wage will not cause firms to hire fewer workers. What is this person assuming?

Application 7: Loud Talking at a Restaurant

We discussed the concept of equilibrium at length in the last chapter. Equilibrium in a competitive market comes at the point at which the quantity demanded of a good equals the quantity supplied of a good. Another way to describe equilibrium is as a state of affairs that exists after all adjustments have been made. To illustrate, consider a shortage

---

[1]Our two economists need to find data that relate not only to how many, if any, people lose their jobs as a result of the higher minimum wage but also to how many people who keep their jobs end up working fewer hours.

in a market. Here quantity demanded of a good is greater than quantity supplied. Is this consistent with all adjustments having been made? Absolutely not. Buyers will still find it in their interest to bid up prices.

Or consider a surplus in a market. Is this consistent with all adjustments having been made? No. Sellers will still find it in their interest to lower prices.

It is only at equilibrium where neither buyers nor sellers will have any incentive to do anything different. Buyers won't bid up prices and sellers won't lower prices. Both sides of the market—the buying side and the selling side—are content with things just the way they are.

Now economists often ask themselves if what they see in front of them at the current moment is or is not consistent with equilibrium. If there are no more adjustments to come, then equilibrium exists; if there are more adjustments to come, then equilibrium does not exist.

With this in mind, suppose you are at a restaurant with some friends. Over time, you notice that the volume of the people talking in the restaurant is getting louder. If volume can be measured on a scale from 1 to 10, the volume was at 4 when you entered the restaurant, but it has now risen to 7.

You ask yourself two questions. First, what caused the increase in volume; second, is the current volume at equilibrium?

The answer to the first question is that as more people were seated in the restaurant, the volume naturally went up. But then, as the volume naturally went up (because of more people talking), each person had an incentive to raise his own volume of speaking. In other words, you are at a table talking to your friends. Then you notice that it is getting louder in the restaurant. To be heard by your friends, you raise your volume of speech. But because you raise your volume of speech, the overall volume of speech in the restaurant goes up, and then somebody else, noticing that the volume has just increased, raises her volume of speech to be heard by her friends at her table.

Where does it all end? It ends at equilibrium, at the point at which no one has any incentive either to raise or lower his or her voice. It ends when all adjustments to one's own volume of speech are complete. This comes when everyone sees the additional benefits of raising his voice as equal to the additional costs of raising his voice. When this state of affairs exists, equilibrium has been achieved. Or in supply-and-demand terms, it comes when, for each person in the restaurant, the quantity demanded of a higher volume of speech is equal to the quantity supplied of a higher volume of speech that each person is willing to provide.

Thinking like **AN ECONOMIST** *Economists will often identify equilibrium in a competitive market as a desirable state of affairs. After all, it is at equilibrium that the sum of consumers' and producers' surplus is maximized and all "gains from trade" have been realized. But the economist knows that equilibrium is not necessarily descriptive of a desirable state of affairs. Think of the loud talking in a restaurant. Things may get so loud that everyone in the restaurant realizes that he or she would be better off if everyone spoke less loudly, but still, no one has an incentive to be the first person to speak less loudly. In other words, equilibrium is consistent with loud talking, a condition that no one is particularly fond of.*

Application 8: Price Ceiling in the Kidney Market

Just as there are people who want to buy houses, computers, and books, there are people who want to buy kidneys. These people have kidney failure and either will die without a new kidney or will have to endure years of costly and painful dialysis. This demand for kidneys is shown as D_K in Exhibit 3.

The supply of kidneys is shown as S_K in Exhibit 3. Notice that at $0 price, the quantity supplied of kidneys is 350. These kidneys are from people who donate their kidneys to others, asking nothing in return. They may donate their kidneys upon their death or may donate one of their two kidneys while living. We have drawn the supply curve as upward sloping because we assume that some people who today are unwilling to donate a kidney for $0 might be willing to do so for some positive dollar amount.

exhibit **3**

The Market for Kidneys

We have identified the demand for kidneys as D_K and the supply of kidneys as S_K. Given the demand for and supply of kidneys, the equilibrium price of a kidney is P_1. It does not follow, though, that simply because there is an equilibrium price, people will be allowed to trade at this price. Today, it is unlawful to buy and sell kidneys at any positive price. In short, there is a price ceiling in the kidney market and the ceiling is $0. At the price ceiling, there is a shortage of kidneys, a nonprice rationing device for kidneys (first-come-first-served), fewer kidney transplants (than there would be at P_1), and illegal purchases and sales of kidneys.

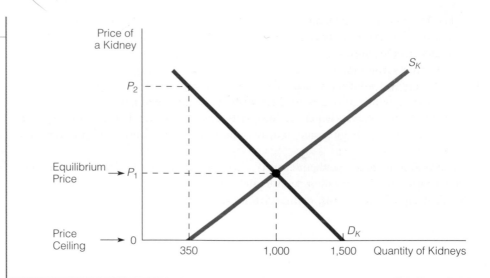

Specifically, we assume that as the price of a kidney rises, the quantity supplied of kidneys will rise.

If there were a free market in kidneys, the price of a kidney would be P_1 in Exhibit 3. At this price, 1,000 kidneys would be purchased and sold—1,000 kidney transplants would occur.

Today, there is no free market in kidneys. Buying or selling kidneys is illegal at any dollar amount. In essence, then, there is a price ceiling in the kidney market, and the ceiling is set at $0. What is the effect of this price ceiling?

If the demand curve for kidneys and the supply curve of kidneys intersected at $0, there would be neither a surplus nor a shortage of kidneys. But there is evidence that the demand and supply curves do not intersect at $0; they look more like those shown in Exhibit 3. In other words, there is a shortage of kidneys at $0: The quantity supplied of kidneys is 350 and the quantity demanded is 1,500. (Although these are not the actual numbers of kidneys demanded and supplied at $0, they are representative of the current situation in the kidney market.)

The last chapter described the possible effects of a price ceiling set below equilibrium price: shortages, nonprice rationing devices, fewer exchanges, tie-in sales, and buying and selling at prohibited prices (in other words, illegal trades). Are any of these effects occurring in the kidney market?

First, there is evidence of a shortage. In almost every country in the world, there are more people on national lists who want a kidney than there are kidneys available. Some of these people die waiting for a kidney.

Second, as just indicated, the nonprice rationing device used in the kidney market is (largely) first come, first served. A person who wants a kidney registers on a national waiting list. How long one waits is a function of how far down the list one's name appears.

Third, there are fewer exchanges; not everyone who needs a kidney gets a kidney. With a price ceiling of $0, only 350 kidneys are supplied. All these kidneys are from people who freely donate their kidneys. If P_1 were permitted, some people who are unwilling to supply a kidney (at $0) would be willing to do so. In short, monetary payment would provide the incentive for some people to supply a kidney. At P_1, 1,000 kidneys are demanded and supplied, so more people would get kidney transplants when the price of a kidney is P_1 (1,000 in total) than when the price of a kidney is $0 (350 in total). More transplants, of course, means fewer people die waiting for a kidney.

Fourth, kidneys are bought and sold at prohibited prices. People buy and sell kidneys today; they just do so illegally. There are stories of people paying between $25,000 and $200,000 for a kidney.

Some people argue that a free market in kidneys would be wrong. Such a system would place the poor at a disadvantage. Think of it: A rich person who needed a kidney could buy the kidney, but a poor person could not. The rich person would get a second chance at life, whereas the poor person would not. No one particularly enjoys contemplating this stark reality.

But consider another stark reality. If it is unlawful to pay someone for a kidney, fewer kidneys will be forthcoming. In other words, the quantity supplied of kidneys is less at $0 than at, say, $20,000. Fewer kidneys supplied mean fewer kidney transplants. And fewer kidney transplants mean more people will die from kidney failure.

SELF-TEST

1. A shortage of kidneys for transplants is a consequence of the price of a kidney being below equilibrium price. Do you agree or disagree? Explain your answer.

2. Assume the price ceiling in the kidney market is $0. Will there be a shortage of kidneys? Explain your answer.

Application 9: Healthcare and the Right to Sue Your HMO

A discussion of renters, landlords, and eviction notices is relevant to the right to sue an HMO. So we begin with an analysis of two laws related to eviction of a renter. Under law 1, a renter has 30 days to vacate an apartment after being served with an eviction notice. Under law 2, the renter has 90 days to vacate.

Landlords will find it less expensive to rent apartments under law 1 than under law 2. Under law 1, the most money a landlord can lose after serving an eviction notice is 30 days' rent. Under law 2, a landlord can lose 90 days' rent. Obviously, losing 90 days' rent is more costly than losing 30 days' rent.

A different supply curve of apartments exists under each law. The supply curve under law 1 (S_1 in Exhibit 4) lies to the right of the supply curve under law 2 (S_2 in the

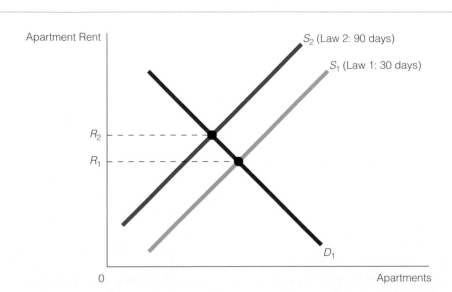

Apartment Rent and the Law

Under law 1, a renter has 30 days to leave an apartment after receiving an eviction notice from his or her landlord. Under law 2, a renter has 90 days to leave an apartment after receiving an eviction notice from his or her landlord. The cost to the landlord of renting an apartment is higher under law 2 than law 1, and so the supply curve of apartments under law 1 lies to the right of the supply curve of apartments under law 2. Different supply curves mean different rents. Apartment rent is higher under law 2 (R_2) than under law 1 (R_1).

exhibit). Again, that's because it is less expensive to supply apartments under law 1 than under law 2.

If the supply curve is different under the two laws, the equilibrium rent will be different too. As shown in Exhibit 4, the equilibrium rent will be lower under law 1 (R_1) than under law 2 (R_2).

In conclusion, under law 1, a renter pays lower rent (good) and has fewer days to vacate the apartment (bad). Under law 2, a renter pays a higher rent (bad) and has more days to vacate the apartment (good). Who pays for the additional days to vacate the apartment under law 2? The renter pays for these additional days by paying higher rent.

Now let's turn from apartments to healthcare. You may frequently hear people complain about their health maintenance organizations (HMOs). The complaints are diverse and wide-ranging. One common complaint is that patients cannot sue their HMOs in state courts for denial of benefits and poor-quality care. Some people argue that patients should have the right to sue their HMOs.

Let's consider two settings: one in which patients cannot sue their HMOs and one in which patients can sue. If patients cannot sue, an HMO's liability cost is lower than if patients can sue. A difference in liability costs will be reflected in different supply curves.

To illustrate, recall that any single point on a supply curve is the minimum price sellers need to receive for them to be willing and able to sell that particular unit of a good. Suppose when patients cannot sue, an HMO is willing and able to provide healthcare to John for $300 a month. If patients can sue, is the HMO still willing and able to provide healthcare to John for $300 a month? Not likely. Because of the higher liability cost due to the patient's ability to sue, the HMO is no longer willing and able to provide healthcare to John for $300 month. It will, however, be willing and able to provide healthcare to John for, say, $350 a month.

Saying a seller's minimum price for providing a good or service rises is the same as saying the seller's supply curve has shifted upward and to the left. In other words, the supply curve of HMO-provided healthcare will shift upward and to the left if patients have the right to sue. This is the same way the supply curve of apartments moved in Exhibit 4.

Will a difference in supply curves affect the price patients pay for their HMO-provided healthcare coverage? Yes. One effect of moving from a setting where patients do not have the right to sue to one where patients do have the right to sue is that patients will have to pay more for their HMO-provided healthcare coverage.

Economists don't determine whether patients having the right to sue is good or bad or right or wrong. Economists use their tools (in this instance, supply and demand) to point out that things people want, such as the right to sue their HMOs, often come with price tags. Individuals must decide whether the price they pay is worth what they receive in return.

SELF-TEST

1. Economists often say, "There is no such thing as a free lunch." How is this saying related to patients moving from a system where they cannot sue their HMOs to one where they can?

2. A professor tells her students that they can have an extra week to complete their research papers. Under what condition are the students better off with the extra week? Can you think of a case where the students would actually be worse off with the extra week?

Application 10: Being Late to Class

We usually think of the demand for goods and services that are traded in a market—goods such as oranges, computers, television sets, and cars and services such as hair-cutting services, attorney services, and so on. For goods and services that are traded in markets, the demand curve is downward sloping: The lower the price of the good or service, the more units of these goods and services buyers will want to buy; the higher the price of the good or service, the fewer units of these goods and services buyers will want to buy.

But we wonder if there is a demand for goods that are not traded in markets. For example, consider something like "being late to class." Does it makes sense to talk about the demand for being late to class? It makes sense if, in fact, being late to class is subject to the law of demand.

Are students more likely to be late to some classes than others? If so, might they be more likely to be late to classes where the instructor does not charge them a "price" for being late than to classes where the instructor does?

Consider a thought experiment. Two professors, Smith and Jones, each teach economics. Professor Smith tells students that for each time they are late to class, he will deduct one point from their final course grade. Professor Jones tells students that they should be on time to class but does not penalize them in any way if they are late. In which class would we expect students to more likely be late to class? If you answered "Professor Jones's class," then you are telling us that you believe there is a downward-sloping demand curve for being late to class.

To support the idea of a downward-sloping demand curve for being late to class, some professors point out that students are much less likely to be late to class on an exam day. Why? Because the price of being late to class on an exam day is higher than it is on most other days. Lateness on an exam day means the student has less time to complete the exam, which can adversely affect his or her grade.

> *Thinking like* **AN ECONOMIST** *The economist knows that the law of demand does not only hold for goods and services that are traded in a market. The law of demand sometimes holds for things that are not traded at all.*

SELF-TEST

1. What has to hold for there to be a downward-sloping demand curve for using foul language?

2. Do you think there is a downward-sloping demand curve for sneezing? Explain your answer.

Application 11: If Gold Prices Are the Same Everywhere, Then Why Aren't House Prices?

The price of an ounce of gold is the same everywhere in the world. For example, the price of an ounce of gold is the same in London as it is in New York City. House prices are not the same everywhere, though. For example, the median price of a house in Los Angeles, California, is higher than the median price of a house in Dubuque, Iowa. Why are gold prices the same everywhere while house prices are different?

To answer the question, let's look at what would happen if gold prices were not the same everywhere in the world. Let's assume the price of an ounce of gold is $250 in London and $300 in New York City. What happens? Obviously, this difference in prices for the same good presents a profit opportunity. People will buy gold in London for $250 an ounce, ship it to New York City, and sell it for $300 an ounce. If we ignore the costs of transporting the gold, a $50 profit per ounce is earned. When an opportunity exists for profit—by buying low and selling high—individuals are quick to try to capture the profit.

As gold is moved from London to New York City in search of profit, the supply of gold in London will fall, and the supply of gold in New York City will rise. A falling gold supply in London will push up the price of gold (from $250), and a rising gold supply in New York City will push down the price of gold (from $300). As the London gold price rises and the New York City gold price falls, a point will eventually be reached where the two prices are the same. When the London price and New York City price for gold are the same, profit cannot be earned by moving gold from London to New York City. In short, any difference in the price of gold in various locations will quickly be eliminated by changes in the supply of gold in the various locations.

Can the same hold for houses? If the price of a house in Los Angeles is higher than the price of a house in Dubuque, is it possible to move houses and land from Dubuque to Los Angeles? Of course not. We can't pick up a house and its lot in Dubuque and move them to Los Angeles, in the process reducing the supply of houses and land in Dubuque and increasing the supply of houses and land in Los Angeles. Because the supply of houses and land cannot be reshuffled the way the supply of gold can be, we expect differences in house prices in various locations but not differences in gold prices.

SELF-TEST

1.   What causes the price of gold to be the same in New York City and London?

2.   The price of a Honda Pilot is nearly the same in Miami as it is in Dallas. Why?

Application 12: Do You Pay for Good Weather?

Some places in the country are considered to have better weather than other places. For example, most people would say the weather in San Diego, California, is better than the weather in Fargo, North Dakota. Often, a person in San Diego will say, "You can't beat the weather today. And the good thing about it is that you don't have to pay a thing for it. It's free."

In one sense, the San Diegan is correct: There is no weather market. Specifically, no one comes around and asks San Diegans to pay a certain dollar amount for the weather on a given day.

But in another sense, the San Diegan is incorrect. The fact is that San Diegans indirectly pay for their good weather. How do they pay? To enjoy the weather in San Diego on a regular basis, you have to live in San Diego—you need to have housing. There is a demand for housing in San Diego just as there is a demand for housing in other places. Is the demand for housing in San Diego higher than it would be if the weather were not so good? Without the good weather, living in San Diego would not be as pleasurable, and therefore, the demand to live there would be lower. In short, the demand for housing in San Diego is higher because San Diego enjoys good weather. It follows that the price of housing is higher too. Thus, San Diegans indirectly pay for their good weather because they pay higher housing prices than they would if San Diego had bad weather.

Was our representative San Diegan right when he said the good weather was free?

SELF-TEST

1.   Give an example to illustrate that someone may "pay" for clean air in much the same way that she "pays" for good weather.

2.   If people pay for good weather, who ultimately receives the "good-weather payment"?

Application 13: Paying All Professors the Same Salary

In college, you take various courses. You may take courses in accounting, economics, English, and history. From your perspective, the professors in the courses may do much the same work. Each professor regularly comes to class, lectures and leads discussions, holds office hours, gives tests and exams, grades those tests and exams, and so on. Does it follow, then, that all professors of equal experience should be paid the same salary? In other words, if a professor in computer science with 10 years of experience earns $100,000 a year, should a professor in history with 10 years of experience earn $100,000 a year too? If your answer is yes, then what might the effects of such a policy be?

Let's again turn to supply and demand for an answer. Exhibit 5(a) shows the market for accounting professors; Exhibit 5(b) shows the market for history professors. In each market, there is a demand for and supply of professors. However, the equilibrium wage in the accounting market (W_A) is higher than the equilibrium wage in the history market (W_H).

If accounting and history professors are each paid their respective equilibrium wage, neither market will be in shortage or surplus. But pay both professors the same wage when their equilibrium wages are different, and shortages or surpluses will appear.

For example, suppose both accounting and history professors are paid the higher wage, W_A. The accounting market remains in equilibrium, but a surplus appears in the history market. There will be more historians who want to work at colleges (N_2) than colleges will hire (N_3).

Or suppose both accounting and history professors are paid the lower wage, W_H. The history market remains in equilibrium, but a shortage appears in the accounting market. Colleges will want to hire more accountants (N_2) than will be willing to work at the colleges (N_3).

Sitting in class, you may think that while the supply-and-demand analysis of the accounting and history markets is interesting, it does not affect you. What does it matter if your professors are paid the same or not?

But look at the number of professors hired in each market at the equilibrium wage and at the disequilibrium wage. In the accounting market, when the wage is W_A, N_1 accounting professors are hired. At W_H, only N_3 are hired because N_3 is the number of accounting professors who are willing and able to work at W_H. N_3 is less than N_1.

In the history market, when the wage is W_H, N_1 history professors are hired. At W_A, N_3 are hired because N_3 is the number of history professors colleges are willing and able to hire at W_A. N_3 is less than N_1.

exhibit **5**

Paying Professors the Same Salary

Suppose the market supply and demand conditions are as shown in (a) for accounting professors and as shown in (b) for history professors. Consequently, the equilibrium wage in the two markets would be different. As shown, the equilibrium wage for accounting professors (W_A) is higher than the equilibrium wage for history professors (W_H). What happens if both accounting and history professors are paid W_A? A surplus of history professors appears. What happens if both accounting and history professors are paid W_H? A shortage of accounting professors appears. Paying all college professors the same salary when there are differences in demand and supply creates shortages and surpluses.

(a) Market for Accounting Professors

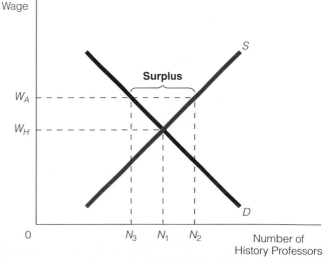

(b) Market for History Professors

In short, more professors are working at colleges teaching students when professors are paid equilibrium wages than when they are paid disequilibrium wages. So, how professors are paid affects the student-to-faculty ratio. Instead of 40 students per faculty member at disequilibrium wages, we might have 30 students per faculty member at equilibrium wages.

SELF-TEST

1. Suppose the supply of biology and computer science professors is the same but the demand for computer scientists is greater than the demand for biologists. Furthermore, suppose both biologists and computer scientists are paid the same wage. If a shortage exists in both fields, in which field is the shortage greater? Explain your answer.

2. Under what condition might an economist propose that all college professors (irrespective of their field) be paid the same?

Application 14: Price Floors and Winners and Losers

Exhibit 6 shows the demand for and supply of an agricultural foodstuff (corn, wheat, soybeans, etc.). If the market is allowed to move to equilibrium, the equilibrium price will be P_1, and the equilibrium quantity will be Q_1. Consumers' surplus will equal the area under the demand curve and above the equilibrium price: areas 1 + 2 + 3. Producers' surplus will equal the area under the equilibrium price and above the supply curve: areas 4 + 5. Total surplus, of course, is the sum of consumers' surplus and producers' surplus: areas 1 + 2 + 3 + 4 + 5.

Now suppose that the suppliers of the foodstuff argue for (and receive) a price floor, P_F. At this higher price, consumers do not buy as much as they once did. They now buy Q_2, whereas they used to buy Q_1. In addition, consumers' surplus is now only area 1, and producers' surplus is areas 2 + 4.

Obviously, consumers have been hurt by the new higher (government-mandated) price of P_F; specifically, they have lost consumers' surplus equal to areas 2 + 3.

exhibit 6

Agricultural Price Floors

The demand for and supply of an agricultural foodstuff are shown in this exhibit. The equilibrium price is P_1; consumers' surplus (CS) is areas 1 + 2 + 3; producers' surplus is areas 4 + 5. A price floor of P_F effectively transfers some of the consumers' surplus to producers in the form of a gain in producers' surplus. Specifically, at P_F, consumers' surplus is area 1 and producers' surplus is areas 2 + 4. Consumers are net losers because consumers' surplus has decreased by areas 2 + 3. Producers are net gainers because producers' surplus has increased from areas 4 + 5 to areas 2 + 4 and area 2 is larger than area 5. Overall, the economic pie of CS + PS has decreased from areas 1 + 2 + 3 + 4 + 5 to areas 1 + 2 + 4.

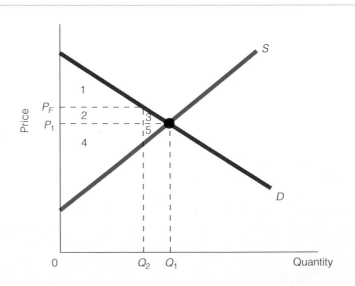

How have suppliers fared? Whereas their producers' surplus was equal to areas 4 + 5 at P_1, it is now equal to areas 2 + 4. (Area 2, which used to be part of consumers' surplus, has been transferred to producers and is now part of producers' surplus.) Whether or not producers are better off depends on whether or not area 2 (what they gain from P_F) is larger than area 5 (what they lose from P_F). Visually, we can tell that area 2 is larger than area 5, so producers are better off.

What is the overall effect of the price floor? Have producers gained more than consumers have lost, or have consumers lost more than producers have gained? To answer this question, we note that consumers lose areas 2 + 3 in consumers' surplus; producers gain area 2 in producers' surplus and lose area 5 in producers' surplus. So, the gains and losses are:

Losses to consumers: areas 2 + 3
Gains to producers: area 2
Losses to producers: area 5

Part of the loss to consumers is offset by the gain to producers (area 2), so net losses amount to areas 3 + 5. In other words, total surplus—the sum of consumers' surplus and producers' surplus—is lower than it was. Whereas it used to be areas 1 + 2 + 3 + 4 + 5, it now is areas 1 + 2 + 4. The total surplus lost is areas 3 + 5.

In short, (1) consumers lose, (2) producers gain, and (3) society (which is the sum of consumers and producers) loses.

You can think of this example in terms of a pie. Initially, the pie was made up of areas 1 + 2 + 3 + 4 + 5. This rather large pie registered all the gains of consumers and producers. After the price floor of P_F was imposed, the pie shrank to areas 1 + 2 + 4; in other words, the pie was smaller by areas 3 + 5.

A loss in total surplus—in our example, areas 3 + 5—is sometimes called a **deadweight loss**. It is the loss to society of not producing the competitive, or supply-and-demand-determined, level of output. In terms of Exhibit 6, it is the loss to society of producing Q_2 instead of producing Q_1.

Deadweight loss

The loss to society of not producing the competitive, or supply-and-demand-determined, level of output.

SELF-TEST

1.   Look at the area equal to areas 3 + 5 in Exhibit 6. If there is a price floor, this area ends up being a deadweight loss. It is the loss to society of not producing Q_1. Are there mutually beneficial trades that exist between Q_2 and Q_1, and if so, how do you know this?

2.   Why might producers argue for a price floor if it ends up making society worse off?

Application 15: College Superathletes

Let's consider a young man, 17 years old, who is one of the best high school football players in the country. As a superathlete, the young man will be recruited by many college and university football coaches. Every one of those colleges and universities will likely want its coach to be successful at getting the young athlete; after all, at many universities, athletics is a moneymaker.

Our superathlete decides to attend college *A,* where he receives a "full ride"—a full scholarship. How should this full scholarship be viewed? One way is to say the superathlete is charged zero tuition to attend the college. (In other words, whereas some students pay a price of $10,000 a year to attend the college, the superathlete pays nothing.)

Another way to view the full scholarship involves a two-step process. First, the college pays the superathlete a dollar amount equal to the full tuition. Second, it then charges the superathlete the full tuition. (In other words, the college gives the athlete $10,000 with one hand and then collects the $10,000 with the other hand.)

Although it ends up being the same for the athlete regardless of which way we view the full scholarship, for purposes of our analysis, let's view the full scholarship the second way: as a payment to the athlete combined with full price being charged. This way of viewing the scholarship leads to two important questions:

1. Can the college pay the athlete more than the full tuition of the college? In other words, if the full tuition is $10,000 a year, can the college pay the athlete, say, $15,000 a year?

2. Is the superathlete being paid what he is worth?

Because of NCAA rules, the answer to the first question is essentially no. The NCAA states that a college or university cannot pay a student to attend, and for all practical purposes, the NCAA views payment as anything more than a full scholarship. The NCAA takes the position that college athletes are amateurs, and amateurs cannot be paid to play their sport.

How does the NCAA rule affect our second question? What if the athlete's worth to the college or university is greater than the dollar amount of the full tuition? For example, suppose the athlete will increase the revenues of the college by $50,000 a year, and the full tuition is only $10,000 a year. In this case, the NCAA rule sets a price ceiling for the college. It sets a ceiling on what the college can pay an athlete. What is the effect of this price ceiling?

Let's consider the demand (on the part of various colleges) for a single superathlete and the supply of this single superathlete (see Exhibit 7). We assume that the supply curve is vertical at 1 "athletic services."

Now suppose the representative college charges tuition of $10,000. Because of the NCAA rule, this dollar amount is the effective price ceiling (or wage ceiling). Furthermore, let's suppose that the single college athlete's market equilibrium wage is $15,000. So, if the NCAA rule did not exist, the athlete's wage would rise to $15,000. This dollar amount is equal to areas $B + C$ in Exhibit 7. What is the consumers' surplus for the college that buys the athlete's services for $15,000? Obviously, it is equal to area A.

However, the NCAA rule stipulates that the college cannot pay the athlete more than $10,000 (full tuition). So, the athlete's payment falls from $15,000 to $10,000, or from areas $B + C$ to simply area C. The college's consumers' surplus increases to areas A

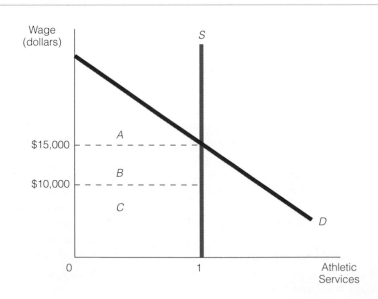

exhibit 7

The College Athlete

The exhibit shows the demand for and supply of a college athlete. If the market wage for the college athlete is $15,000, then the buyer of the athlete—in this case, the college—receives consumers' surplus equal to area A. If the wage can be held down to the tuition cost of attending the college—$10,000 in this example—then the college receives consumers' surplus of areas $A + B$.

+ *B*. Essentially, the NCAA rule transfers part of the athlete's income—area *B*—to the college in the form of greater consumers' surplus.

Just as the price floor in Application 14 leads to a transfer (from consumers to producers), a price ceiling leads to a transfer. The price ceiling set by the NCAA rule results in a transfer from the athlete to the college. In short, the athlete loses and the college gains. Moreover, in this case, the college gain in consumers' surplus equals the income loss for the athlete.

SELF-TEST

1. University *X* is a large university with a major football team. A new field house and track were just added to the university. How is this related to the discussion in this application?

2. Sometimes it is argued that if colleges paid student athletes, the demand for college sports would decline. In other words, the demand for college sports is as high as it is because student athletes are not paid (the way athletes in professional sports are paid). How would the analysis in this application change if we assume this argument is true?

Application 16: Supply and Demand on a Freeway

What does a traffic jam on a busy freeway in any large city have to do with supply and demand? Actually, it has quite a bit to do with supply and demand. Look at it this way: There is a demand for driving on the freeway and a supply of freeway space. The supply of freeway space is fixed (freeways do not expand and contract over a day, week, or month). The demand, however, fluctuates. It is higher at some times than at other times. For example, we would expect the demand for driving on the freeway to be higher at 8 A.M. (rush hour) than at 11 P.M. But even though the demand may vary, the money price for driving on the freeway is always the same—zero. A zero money price means that motorists do not pay tolls to drive on the freeway.

Exhibit 8 shows two demand curves for driving on the freeway: $D_{8 \text{ A.M.}}$ and $D_{11 \text{ P.M.}}$. We have assumed the demand at 8 A.M. is greater than at 11 P.M. We have also assumed that at $D_{11 \text{ P.M.}}$ and zero money price the freeway market clears: Quantity demanded of freeway space equals quantity supplied of freeway space. At the higher demand, $D_{8 \text{ A.M.}}$, however, this is not the case. At zero money price, a shortage of freeway space exists: Quantity demanded of freeway space is greater than quantity supplied of freeway space. The shortage appears in the form of freeway congestion and bumper-to-bumper traffic.

One way to eliminate the shortage is through an increase in the money price of driving on the freeway at 8 A.M. For example, as Exhibit 8 shows, a toll of 70 cents would clear the freeway market at 8 A.M.

If charging different prices (tolls) at different times of the day on freeways sounds like an unusual idea, consider how Miami Beach hotels price their rooms. They charge different prices for their rooms at different times of the year. During the winter months when the demand for vacationing in Miami Beach is high, the hotels charge higher prices than when the demand is (relatively) low. If different prices were charged for freeway space at different times of the day, freeway space would be rationed the same way Miami Beach hotel rooms are rationed.

©DAVID PAUL MORRIS/GETTY IMAGES

At 8 A.M. and $0 price, there is freeway congestion.

exhibit 8

Freeway Congestion and Supply and Demand

The demand for driving on the free-way is higher at 8 A.M. than at 11 P.M. At zero money price and $D_{11\ P.M.}$, the freeway market clears. At zero money price and $D_{8\ A.M.}$, there is a shortage of freeway space, which shows up as freeway congestion. At a price (toll) of 70 cents, the shortage is eliminated and freeway congestion disappears.

Before we leave this topic, let's consider the three alternatives usually proposed for freeway congestion. Some people propose tolls, some propose building more freeways, and others propose encouraging carpooling. Tolls deal with the congestion problem by adjusting price to its equilibrium level, as shown in Exhibit 8. Building more freeways deals with the problem by increasing supply. In Exhibit 8, it would be necessary to shift the supply curve of freeway space to the right so there is no longer any shortage of space at 8 A.M. More carpooling deals with the problem by decreasing demand. Two people in one car take up less space on a freeway than two people in two cars. In Exhibit 8, if through carpooling the demand at 8 A.M. begins to look like the demand at 11 P.M., then there is no longer a shortage of freeway space at 8 A.M.

> ### Thinking like AN ECONOMIST
> *The economist knows that when there are buyers and sellers of anything (bread, cars, or freeway space), only three conditions are possible—equilibrium, shortage, or surplus. When the economist sees traffic congestion, the first thing that comes to mind is that there is a shortage of road space. Buy why is there a shortage? The economist knows that shortages occur at prices below equilibrium price. In other words, price is too low.*

A final note: A fee to drive in the Central London area was introduced in 2003. Anyone going into or out of the Central London area between 7:00 A.M. and 6:30 P.M., Monday through Friday, must pay a fee of approximately $14. (Not everyone has to pay the fee. For example, taxi drivers, ambulance drivers, police vehicles, motorcycle drivers, and bicyclists do not have to pay the fee. The residents who live in the area receive a 90 percent discount.) Many people have claimed the fee a success because it has cut down on traffic and travel times and reduced pollution in the area.

Some people have urged New York City to institute a similar fee program to drive on certain streets in the city. On any given day in New York City, there are approximately 800,000 cars on the streets south of 60th Street in Manhattan. According to many, the city is "choking in traffic." We will have to wait to see if New York City goes the way of London.

SELF-TEST

1.   In Exhibit 8, at what price is there a surplus of freeway space at 8 A.M.?

2.   If the driving population increases in an area and the supply of freeway space remains constant, what will happen to freeway congestion? Explain your answer.

Application 17: What Does Price Have to Do with Getting to Class on Time?

Class starts at 10 o'clock in the morning. At 10:09, Pam Ferrario walks in late. She apologizes to the instructor, saying, "I've been on campus for 20 minutes, but I couldn't find a parking space." Her classmates nod, knowing full well what she is talking about. At Pam's university, especially between the hours of 8 A.M. and 2 P.M., parking spaces are hard to find.

This scene is replayed every day at many universities and colleges across the country. Students are late for class because on many days there isn't a parking space to be found. Why can't students find parking spaces? The immediate answer is because there is a shortage of parking spaces. But why is there a shortage of parking spaces? There is a shortage of parking spaces for the same reason there is any shortage: The equilibrium price is not being charged.

Who pays for the shortage of parking spaces? The students pay—not in money, but in time. Because students know parking spaces on campus are hard to find, they often leave home or work sooner than they would if there were no shortages. Or like Pam Ferrario, they pay by being late to class.

Are there alternatives to the *pay-in-time* and *pay-in-being-late-to-class* schemes for rationing campus parking spots? Some economists have suggested a *pay-in-price* scheme. For example, the university could install meters in the parking lot and raise the fee high enough so that between the hours of 8 A.M. and 2 P.M., the quantity demanded for parking spaces equals the quantity supplied.

Such suggestions are sometimes criticized on the basis that students must pay the parking fee, no matter how high, to attend classes. But that's not exactly true. Parking off campus and using public transportation are sometimes alternatives. But this is not really the main point. The issue isn't paying or not paying but choosing *how* to pay—in dollar price, time, or being late for class.

Some economists have taken the pay-in-price scheme further and have argued that parking spots should be auctioned on a yearly basis. In other words, a student would rent a parking spot for a year. This way, the student would always know that a parking spot would be open when he or she arrived at the campus. People who parked in someone else's spot would be ticketed by campus police.

Additionally, under this scheme, a student who rented a parking spot and chose not to use it between certain hours of the day could rent it to someone else during this period. So we would expect to see notices like this on campus billboards:

> *Thinking like*
> **AN ECONOMIST**   *The economist knows that just because someone doesn't pay a price in money terms, it doesn't mean there is no price to pay. People can pay for something in time. In fact, when money prices are below equilibrium levels, individuals usually pay in terms of something else (e.g., time).*

PARKING SPOT FOR RENT
Near Arts Building and Student Union. Ideal for liberal arts students. Available on a 2–12 hour basis between 12 noon and 12 midnight. Rate: $1 per hour. Call Jenny at 867-5309.

SELF-TEST

1. If a person pays for something in terms of time, he or she is really paying in terms of money. Do you agree or disagree? Explain your answer.

2. Suppose at the price of $1 a day for parking, quantity supplied is equal to quantity demanded. What happens if the demand for parking rises more than the supply of parking and the price of parking is kept constant at $1 a day?

Application 18: The Space Within Space

According to the law of supply, a rise in the price of housing will lead to an increase in the quantity supplied of housing. But can this happen if the number of houses, apartments, condos, and duplexes cannot increase?

Consider the following thought experiment. Suppose there are 100 houses in an area and that a law has been passed stating that no one can build another house in the area.

Now suppose the demand for housing in this particular area rises. We would expect the price of housing to rise. But will the quantity supplied rise as well? Perhaps your first answer is no; after all, a law has been passed stating that no one can build another house in the area.

But this doesn't necessarily mean that more housing can't become available. The higher the price of housing, the greater the incentive will be for people who already own houses to make some part of their houses available to others. For example, a couple living in a three-bedroom house might decide to rent one of the three rooms. A person living in a one-room house might be willing to share the house with a roommate.

This phenomenon is not unheard of, especially in large cities that have witnessed recent large increases in housing prices. For example, if you go online to Craigslist New York (http://newyork.craigslist.org/), you will find people who own houses, apartments, and condominiums advertising rooms, or even parts of rooms, for rent. (Craigslist is a centralized network of online urban communities featuring free classified advertisements.)

Application 19: 10 A.M. Classes in College

Suppose an economics class is offered in the same classroom at 10 A.M. in the morning and at 8 P.M. at night. Most students would prefer the 10 A.M. class to the 8 P.M. class. Notice in Exhibit 9 that the supply of seats in the class is the same at each time, but the demand to occupy those seats is not. Because the demand is greater for the 10 A.M. class than for the 8 P.M. class, the equilibrium price for the 10 A.M. class is higher than the equilibrium price for the 8 P.M. class.

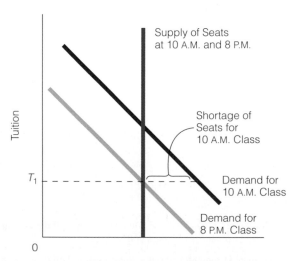

exhibit 9

The Supply and Demand for College Classes at Different Times

A given class is offered at two times, 10 A.M. and 8 P.M. The supply of seats in the classroom is the same at both times; however, the student demand for the 10 A.M. class is higher than the demand for the 8 P.M. class. The university charges the same tuition, T_1, regardless of which class a student takes. At this tuition, there is a shortage of seats for the 10 A.M. class. Seats are likely to be rationed on a first-come-first-served (first to register) basis or on seniority (seniors take precedence over juniors, etc.).

But the university or college charges the same tuition no matter what time students choose to take the class. The university doesn't charge students a higher tuition if they enroll in 10 A.M. classes than if they enroll in 8 P.M. classes.

Suppose tuition of T_1 is charged for all classes, and T_1 is the equilibrium tuition for 8 P.M. classes (see Exhibit 9). It follows that T_1 is below the equilibrium tuition for 10 A.M. classes. At T_1, the quantity demanded of seats for 10 o'clock classes will be greater than the quantity supplied; more students will want the 10 o'clock class than there is space available.

How will the university allocate the available seats? It may do it the same way that airlines ration aisle seats—that is, on a first come, first served basis. Students who are first to register get the 10 A.M. class; the latecomers have to take the 8 P.M. class. Or the university could ration these "high-demand classes" by giving their upper-class students (seniors) first priority.

> *Thinking like*
> **AN ECONOMIST**
> *The layperson sees students clamoring to get 10 A.M. classes and concludes that the demand is high for classes at this time. He then wonders why the university doesn't schedule more 10 A.M. classes. The economist knows that what the layperson sees is as much an effect of price as of demand. The demand for 10 A.M. classes may be high, but the quantity demanded may not be if the price is high enough. In fact, even though the demand for various classes at various times may be different, there is some set of prices that will make the quantity demanded of each class the same.*

SELF-TEST

1. Suppose college students are given two options. With option *A*, the price a student pays for a class is always the equilibrium price. For example, if the equilibrium price to take Economics 101 is $600 at 10 A.M. and is $400 at 4 P.M., then students pay more for the 10 A.M. class than they do for the 4 P.M. class. With option *B*, the price a student pays for a class is the same regardless of the time the class is taken. When given the choice between options *A* and *B*, many students would say they prefer option *B* to option *A*. Is this the case for you? If so, why would this be your choice?

2. How is the analysis of the 10 A.M. class similar to the analysis of a price ceiling in the kidney market?

Application 20: Who Pays the Tax?

Supply-and-demand analysis can be used to clear up one of the main myths of economics. Many people mistakenly believe that the placement of a tax determines the payment of a tax. In other words, if a tax is placed on the seller of a good, then it is the seller of the good that pays the full tax. But this need not be the case, as supply and demand help us to understand.

To illustrate, suppose the government imposes a tax on sellers of DVDs. They are taxed $1 for every DVD they sell. DVD sellers are told: "Sell a DVD and send $1 to the government." This government action changes equilibrium in the DVD market. To illustrate, in Exhibit 10, before the tax is imposed, the equilibrium price and quantity of DVDs is $15 and Q_1, respectively. The tax per DVD shifts the supply curve leftward from S_1 to S_2. The vertical distance between the two supply curves represents the $1 per DVD tax.

Why does the vertical distance between the two curves represent the $1 per DVD tax? That's because it matters to sellers how much they keep for each DVD sold, not how much buyers pay. If sellers are keeping $15 per DVD for Q_1 DVDs before the tax is imposed, then they want to keep $15 per DVD for Q_1 DVDs after the tax is imposed. But if the tax is $1, the only way they can keep $15 per DVD for Q_1 DVDs is to receive $16 per DVD. They receive $16 per DVD from buyers, turn over $1 to the government, and keep $15. In other words, each quantity on the new supply curve, S_2,

exhibit 10

Who Pays the Tax?

A tax placed on the sellers of DVDs shifts the supply curve from S_1 to S_2 and raises the equilibrium price from $15.00 to $15.50. Part of the tax is paid by buyers through a higher price paid ($15.50 instead of $15.00), and part of the tax is paid by sellers through a lower price kept ($14.50 instead of $15.00).

corresponds to a $1 higher price than it did on the old supply curve, S_1. *It does not follow, though—and this is critically important—that the new equilibrium price will be $1 higher than the old equilibrium price.*

The new equilibrium is at a price of $15.50 and a quantity of Q_2. Buyers pay $15.50 per DVD (after the tax is imposed) as opposed to $15.00 (before the tax was imposed). The difference between the new price and the old price is the amount of the $1.00 tax that buyers pay per DVD. In this example, buyers pay 50 cents, or one-half of the $1.00 tax per DVD.

Before the tax: Buyers pay $15.00.
After the tax: Buyers pay $15.50.

The sellers receive $15.50 per DVD from buyers (after the tax is imposed) as opposed to $15.00 per DVD (before the tax was imposed), but they do not get to keep $15.50 per DVD. One dollar has to be turned over to the government, leaving the sellers with $14.50. Before the tax was imposed, however, sellers received and kept $15.00 per DVD. As we noted, the relevant price to sellers is the price they get to keep. The difference between $15.00 and $14.50 is the amount of the tax per DVD that sellers pay. In this example, the sellers pay 50 cents, or one-half of the $1.00 tax per DVD.

Before the tax: Sellers receive $15.00 and keep $15.00.
After the tax: Sellers receive $15.50 and keep $14.50.

We conclude that the full tax was *placed* on the sellers, but they *paid* only one-half of the tax, whereas none of the tax was placed on buyers, but they paid one-half of the tax too. What is the lesson we learn through our supply-and-demand analysis? Government can place a tax on whomever it wants, but the laws of supply and demand determine who actually ends up paying the tax.

SELF-TEST

1. Is it necessarily the case that if government places a tax on the seller of a good, the seller of the good will end up paying the full tax?

2. In Application 20, explain why the vertical distance between the two supply curves is the (per-unit) tax.

A Reader Asks . . .

How Do I Find My Own Supply-and-Demand Applications?

I can understand an economist's applications of supply and demand, but I don't know how to apply supply and demand myself. How do I find my own supply-and-demand applications?

You can proceed in several ways, two of which we discuss here. First, you can heed the words of Robert Solow: "I am a supply-and-demand economist. When I come across something, I ask myself what is being transferred here and where does the supply come from and where does the demand come from."[2]

We can reformulate what Solow has said into a single question: *Is trade involved?* This is the relevant supply-and-demand question because supply and demand are about trade. In other words, when you observe something, simply ask: Is this about trade? If you are driving on a freeway, ask: Is driving on a freeway about trade? Specifically, is something being "bought" and "sold"? If so, what? If you are applying to college, ask: Is this about trade? What is being bought and sold?

A second way to proceed is to look for surpluses and shortages around you. Surpluses and shortages are manifestations of market disequilibrium. If you find them, you can be fairly sure that supply and demand are relevant. If you are sitting in a classroom with empty seats, ask: Is there a surplus or shortage here? In this case, of course, there is a surplus, which should lead you to think about price. Surpluses exist when prices are too high. Why is the price too high? If you observe more people applying to a particular college than the college will admit, ask: Is there a surplus or shortage here? In this case, there is a shortage, which again should lead you to think about price. Shortages exist when prices are too low. Why is price too low?

The key to finding your own supply-and-demand applications is to (1) observe things around you and then (2) ask questions about the things you observe. If you are sitting in a restaurant eating a meal, ask questions about what you observe. Is trade involved here? Yes. Is the restaurant filled to capacity, and is there a line of people waiting to get in? Yes. Are there more people who want to eat at this restaurant than there are spaces to accommodate them? Yes. Is there a shortage here? Yes. Why do shortages exist? Prices are too low. Why doesn't the restaurant raise its prices and eliminate the shortage?

The process isn't that hard, is it?

[2]Interview with Robert Solow. The entire interview is in *Economics* by Roger A. Arnold (St. Paul, Minn.: West Publishing Company, 1992).

! analyzing the scene

What is the relationship between the probability of Bob Mason being admitted to the college of his choice and the tuition the college charges?

Bob Mason is about to open the letter from the college he wants to attend. We don't know what the letter says, but we do know that the higher Bob's GPA and the smaller the gap between the equilibrium tuition and the tuition charged, the better Bob's chances of being accepted.

Why are house prices higher in some parts of the country than in other parts of the country?

Supply and demand explain the difference in house prices. In some parts of the country, the demand for houses (relative to the supply of houses) is high, perhaps because of good weather, excellent job opportunities, or a wide variety of fine entertainment. In other parts of the country, the demand for houses is low. Land (unlike gold) can't be moved to increase supply where demand is high, so house prices are higher in desirable locations than they are in less desirable locations, *ceteris paribus*.

What do supply, demand, and price have to do with Carlos driving 5 mph on a freeway on his way home from work?

Carlos is frustrated because congestion has caused traffic to slow to 5 mph on the freeway. Application 16 discusses how supply, demand, and price affect freeway traffic. If the price of driving on a freeway is below the equilibrium price, quantity demanded of freeway space is greater than quantity supplied. The result is a shortage of freeway space, and Carlos and other drivers having to drive more slowly than perhaps they would like.

Why aren't any aisle seats left?

When Samantha Wilson asks for an aisle seat, she's told that only center seats are left. Why are aisle seats taken before center seats? The short answer is because most people prefer aisle seats to center seats. Let's look a little further. A greater preference for aisle seats indicates a higher demand for aisle seats than for center seats. If the airlines charge the same price for both aisle and center seats and that price equals the equilibrium price for center seats, then there will likely be a shortage of aisle seats. The seats will be rationed partly by price and partly by first come, first served. Samantha doesn't get an aisle seat partly because of the airlines' pricing policy.

chapter summary

Why Do Colleges Use GPAs, ACTs, and SATs for Purposes of Admission?

- Colleges and universities charging students less than the equilibrium tuition for admission create a shortage of spaces at the colleges or universities. Consequently, colleges and universities have to impose some nonprice rationing device, such as GPAs or ACT or SAT scores.

Legalization of Marijuana

- If the purchase and sale of marijuana are legalized, the price of marijuana may rise, fall, or remain the same. The price will depend on whether the rise in the demand for marijuana is more than, less than, or equal to the rise in the supply of marijuana.

Where Did You Get That Music?

- The recording industry can do, and has done, three things to reduce the amount of music piracy. (1) Raise the price of downloading music. The industry has done this by pursuing legal suits against some individuals. (2) Reduce the supply of music that can be downloaded. The industry has done this by bringing suit against companies such as Napster. (3) Reduce the demand for downloadable music. The industry has done this by running TV commercials that send the message that if you download music you are affecting everyday workers in the recording industry in a negative way.

Television Shows During the Olympics

- If a television network expects that demand for a time-specific slot (e.g., its 8 P.M. time slot) is likely to be low, it is more likely to run a rerun than a new episode of a program.

The Minimum Wage

- A minimum wage (above equilibrium wage) reduces the number of unskilled workers working or reduces the number of unskilled labor hours purchased by employers.

Equilibrium (Loud Talking in a Restaurant)

- Equilibrium is a state of affairs that exists when no further adjustments will be made. Although equilibrium is a desirable state in a competitive market (at which quantity demanded equals quantity supplied), it does not necessarily follow that all equilibrium states are desirable. The example of loud talking in a restaurant makes our point.

Price Ceiling in the Kidney Market

- Currently, there is a price ceiling in the kidney market, and the price is set at $0. Many of the effects of a price ceiling (shortages, fewer exchanges, etc.) are seen in the kidney market.

Healthcare and the Right to Sue Your HMO

- The supply curve of HMO-provided healthcare will shift upward and to the left if patients have the right to sue. As a result, patients will pay more for their HMO-provided healthcare coverage when they have the right to sue than when they do not have the right to sue.

Being Late to Class

- There is a downward-sloping demand curve for some things that are not traded in markets. For example, there probably exists a downward-sloping demand curve for being late to class: The higher the price of being late to class, the less lateness students will consume; the lower the price of being late to class, the more lateness students will consume.

Gold Prices and House Prices

- Gold prices are the same everywhere in the world, but house prices are not. When the price of a good is higher in one location than in another location and that good can be moved from the lower priced location to the higher priced location, then the price of the good will end up being the same in both locations. Obviously, if the good cannot be moved from the lower priced location to the higher priced location, then the price of the good will not end up being the same in both locations.

Do You Pay for Good Weather?

- If good weather gives people utility, then the demand for and the price of housing will be higher in a city with good weather than in a city with bad weather. Conclusion: People who buy houses in good-weather locations indirectly pay for the good weather.

Paying All Professors the Same Salary

- Suppose the equilibrium wage rate as determined by supply and demand conditions is higher, say, for a biology professor than for a history professor. If both professors are paid the equilibrium wage in biology, then there will be a surplus of history professors. If both professors are paid the equilibrium wage in history, then there will be a shortage of biology professors.

Price Floors and Winners and Losers

- A price floor placed on an agricultural foodstuff ends up lowering consumers' surplus, raising producers' surplus, and creating a deadweight loss. In short, a price floor can transfer "surplus" from consumers to producers and leave society (as a whole) worse off too.

College Superathletes

- If a college superathlete receives a full scholarship to play a sport at a university and if the full scholarship is less than the equilibrium wage for the superathlete (because of a prohibition mandating that the athlete cannot be paid the difference between his higher equilibrium wage and the dollar amount of his full scholarship), then the university gains at the expense of the athlete.

Supply and Demand on a Freeway

- The effect of a disequilibrium price for driving on a freeway is a traffic jam. If the price to drive on a freeway is $0 and at this price the quantity demanded of freeway space is greater than the quantity supplied, then there will be a shortage of freeway space that will manifest itself as freeway congestion.

What Does Price Have to Do with Getting to Class on Time?

- If price doesn't fully ration campus parking spots, something will. The rationing device may be first-come-first-served, which often prompts students to leave for campus at earlier times than they would if price rationed parking spots.

10 A.M. Classes in College

- Colleges usually charge the same tuition for a class no matter when the class is taken. The supply of seats in the class may be the same at each time, but the demand for the class may be different at different times. At least for some classes, the quantity demanded of seats (in the class) will be greater than the quantity supplied. Thus, some nonprice rationing device will have to be used to achieve equilibrium.

Who Pays the Tax?

- The placement of a tax and the payment of a tax are two different things. For example, a tax placed on the seller of a good may be paid by both the seller and the buyer.

- In this chapter, we discuss a per-unit tax that was placed on the seller of a specific good (DVDs). This tax shifted the supply curve of DVDs leftward. The vertical distance between the old supply curve (before the tax) and the new supply curve (after the tax) was equal to the per-unit tax.

key terms and concepts

Deadweight Loss

questions and problems

1 Harvard, Yale, and Princeton all charge relatively high tuition. Still, each uses ACT and SAT scores as admission criteria. Are charging a relatively high tuition and using standardized test scores (as admission criteria) inconsistent? Explain your answer.

2 Suppose the purchase and sale of marijuana are legalized and the price of marijuana falls. What explains the lower price of marijuana?

3 The minimum wage in year 1 is $1 higher than the equilibrium wage. In year 2, the minimum wage is increased so that it is $2 above the equilibrium wage. We observe that the same number of people are working at the minimum wage in year 2 as in year 1. Does it follow that an increase in the minimum wage does not cause some workers to lose their jobs? Explain your answer.

4 Using supply-and-demand analysis, explain the recording industry's efforts to reduce the amount of pirated music.

5 In our discussion of the kidney market, we represent the demand curve for kidneys as downward sloping and the supply curve of kidneys as upward sloping. At the end of the discussion, we state, "If it is unlawful to pay someone for a kidney, fewer kidneys will be forthcoming. In other words, the quantity supplied of kidneys is less at $0 than at, say, $20,000. Fewer kidneys supplied mean fewer kidney transplants." Would there be fewer kidney transplants if the supply curve of kidneys is vertical? Explain your answer.

6 What do the applications about freeway congestion, campus parking, and 10 A.M. classes have in common?

7 Economics has been called the "dismal science" because it sometimes "tells us" that things are true when we would prefer they were false. For example, although there are no free lunches, might we prefer that there were? Was there anything in this chapter that you learned was true that you would have preferred to be false? If so, identify it. Then explain why you would have preferred it to be false.

8 In the discussion of healthcare and the right to sue your HMO, we state, "Saying a seller's minimum price for providing a good or service rises is the same as saying the seller's supply curve has shifted upward and to the left." Does it follow that if a seller's minimum price falls, the supply curve shifts downward and to the right? Explain your answer.

9 Application 12 explains that even though no one directly and explicitly pays for good weather ("Here is $100 for the good weather"), it is still possible to pay for good weather indirectly, such as through housing prices. Identify three other things (besides good weather) that you believe people pay for indirectly.

10 If the equilibrium wage for economics professors is higher than the equilibrium wage for history professors, which professors (do you think) are more likely to argue that all professors should be paid the same? Explain your answer.

11 Suppose there exists a costless way to charge drivers on the freeway. Under this costless system, tolls on the freeway would be adjusted according to traffic conditions. For example, when traffic is usually heavy, such as from 6:30 A.M. to 9:00 A.M. on a weekday, the toll to drive on the freeway would be higher than the toll would be when traffic is light. In other words, freeway tolls would be used to equate the demand for freeway space and the supply of freeway space. Would you be in favor of such a system to replace our current (largely, zero-price) system? Explain your answer.

12 Wilson walks into his Economics class ten minutes late because he couldn't find a place to park. Because of his tardiness, he doesn't hear the professor tell the class there will be a quiz at the next class session. At the next class session, Wilson is unprepared for the quiz and ends up failing it.

   a Might Wilson's failing the quiz have anything to do with the price of parking? Explain your answer.

   b Suppose Wilson says to his professor: "If this university had set equilibrium prices for parking, I wouldn't have been late to class, and therefore, I would have heard about the upcoming quiz, studied for it, and probably passed it. It's not my fault I failed the quiz. It's the university's fault for not setting the equilibrium price for parking." What would you say if you were the professor?

13 University A charges more for a class for which there is high demand than for a class for which there is low demand. University B charges the same for all classes. All other things being equal between the two universities, which university would you prefer to attend? Explain your answer.

14 Explain and diagrammatically represent how a price floor can bring about a transfer from consumers to producers.

15 Suppose the equilibrium wage for a college athlete is $40,000, but because of NCAA rules, the university can offer him only $22,000 (full tuition). How might the university administrators, coaches, or university alumni lure the college athlete to choose their school over others?

16 Consider the theater in which a Broadway play is performed. If tickets for all seats are the same price (say, $70), what economic effect might arise?

17 How does a grocery store know how much cereal, butter, and candy it should stock on its shelves?

working with numbers and graphs

1 The price to drive on a freeway is $0 at all times of the day. This price establishes equilibrium at 3 A.M. but is too low to establish equilibrium at 5 P.M. There is a shortage of freeway space at 5 P.M.

   a Graphically show and explain how carpooling may eliminate the shortage.

   b Graphically show and explain how building more freeways may eliminate the shortage.

2 Diagrammatically show and explain why there is a shortage of classroom space for some college classes and a surplus for others.

3 Smith has been trying to sell his house for six months, but so far, there are no buyers. Draw the market for Smith's house.

4 Explain and diagrammatically represent why the placement of a tax may be different than the payment of a tax.

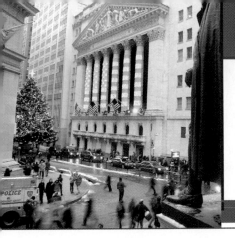

Setting the Scene

The following events occurred on a day in February.

7:42 A.M.

It's Thursday, and Franklin Smithies has just gotten off the subway at Park Place in the heart of the Financial District in lower Manhattan. He sips his morning cup of coffee as he walks toward his office. As he walks, he thinks about what awaits him. Franklin manages the stock portfolio of one of the largest pension funds in the country, and in a little less than hour, the BLS will issue a summary report on prices. What that report says will have much to do with how he spends the rest of his day.

8:30 A.M.

The U.S. Department of Labor, Bureau of Labor Statistics (BLS) releases this statement: Employment was virtually unchanged in December, while the unemployment rate, at 5.7 percent, continued to trend down.

8:30 A.M.

The BLS releases this statement: The Consumer Price Index for All Urban Consumers (CPI-U) decreased 0.1 percent in December, before seasonal adjustment.

10.07 A.M.

George Krenshaw, who has worked at T. R. Electronics for ten years, is called into his boss's office. George learns that the company has terminated his employment. "We have to cut back," his boss says. "We just don't have the business we once had."

3:18 P.M.

Catherine Lincoln picks up the phone to call her parents, both of whom are retired. When her father answers the phone, Catherine blurts out, "I got the job. And I got the salary I asked for—$50,000 a year." Her father replies, "That's a great salary—you're rich. You can easily live on that salary. After all, your mother and I lived comfortably on my first salary of $8,000 a year."

8:00 P.M.

Todd and Ellen are in their seats in the dark movie theater as the trailers play. They're waiting for the start of the movie.

Todd turns to Ellen and whispers, "I heard that this movie could end up being the biggest box-office hit of all time—even bigger than *Titanic*."

? Here are some questions to keep in mind as you read this chapter:

- *What does a report on prices have to do with what Franklin Smithies will do at work?*

- *How does the BLS compute the unemployment rate, and does it matter whether the unemployment rate is trending down or up?*

- *How does the BLS compute the consumer price index, and what does it matter whether prices are rising or falling?*

- *How long will George Krenshaw stay unemployed?*

- *Will Catherine be rich? How does her salary of $50,000 compare to her father's first salary of $8,000?*

- *What's the best way to compare the gross receipts of two movies?*

See **analyzing the scene** at the end of this chapter for answers to these questions.

How to Approach the Study of Macroeconomics

Before we begin our discussion of macroeconomic measurements, we need to take some time to discuss what macroeconomics is about and how best to approach the study of macroeconomics.

Macroeconomics is the branch of economics that deals with the entire economy. Most discussions in macroeconomics focus on one or more of the following:

1. Macroeconomic Problems
2. Macroeconomic Theories
3. Macroeconomic Policies
4. Different Views of How the Economy Works

We briefly discuss each next (see Exhibit 1).

Macroeconomic Problems

Here are a few macroeconomic problems:

1. High inflation rate
2. High unemployment rate
3. High interest rates
4. Low economic growth

When it comes to these macroeconomics problems and others, macroeconomists want to know two things: (1) What is the cause of the problem? and (2) What needs to be done to end the problem?

It is really no different from if you're going to see a physician about some health problem—say a regular stomachache. You might want to know the cause of the stomachache and then how to end the stomachache.

In this text, we will discuss a number of macroeconomic problems, including inflation, high unemployment, stagflation, low economic growth, and more.

Macroeconomic Theories

When macroeconomists encounter macroeconomic problems, certain questions naturally come to mind. For example, if interest rates are unusually high, a macroeconomist might wonder why interest rates are high sometimes but low at other times. If the inflation rate has recently gone up, a macroeconomist might wonder why the inflation rate went up now.

To answer their questions (questions that do not have obvious answers), macroeconomists often build theories. For example, a macroeconomist might build a theory to try to understand why interest rates are high in one year but not high in some other year; he or she might build a theory to try to understand why the inflation rate is low in one year but high in another year.

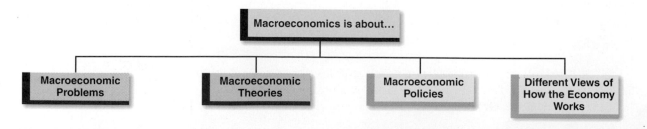

We will encounter a number of macroeconomic theories in our discussion of macroeconomics. We will encounter theories that attempt to explain such things as changes in the price level, changes in unemployment, changes in interest rates, and so on. Some of these theories will have names, such as the Keynesian theory of output or the monetarist theory of the price level. Often, the term that comes before the word theory, such as *Keynesian* or *monetarist theory of . . .* , refers to the macroeconomic school of thought that put forth the theory.

As you read through the macroeconomic chapters of this book, keep in mind that not all macroeconomists agree on the causes of certain macroeconomic problems. In other words, one macroeconomist might think that X is the cause of high unemployment, whereas another macroeconomist might think that the Y is the cause of high unemployment.

Macroeconomic Policies

To solve certain macroeconomic problems, macroeconomists often propose certain types of policies. Specifically, a macroeconomist might propose cutting tax rates to revive economic growth or cutting back the growth rate in the money supply to lower prices. The two types of macroeconomic policy that we will discuss include *fiscal policy* and *monetary policy*. Fiscal policy deals with changes in government expenditures and/or taxes. For example, a proposal to cut taxes is a fiscal policy measure. Monetary policy deals with changes in the money supply. For example, a proposal to decrease the rate of growth of the money supply is a monetary policy measure.

Different Views of How the Economy Works

We are not at the stage in the history of macroeconomics where we can say that all macroeconomists agree as to how the economy works. (This time in the history of macroeconomics may never come.) For example, some economists believe that the economy is inherently stable and self-regulating. A rough analogy comes from the field of medicine. For some illnesses, physicians believe that the human body has a way of curing itself. For example, in time, the human body usually heals itself of certain viruses (e.g., a cold or flu virus). In other words, the body is self-regulating; it can cure itself of certain ailments.

Some economists do not believe the economy is self-regulating. They see it as inherently unstable. In other words, the economy has certain forces within it that can (and sometimes do) cause it to get "ill" on its own.

Three Macroeconomic Organizational Categories

As we stated earlier, macroeconomics is the branch of economics that deals with the entire economy. The subject matter in macroeconomics includes (1) macroeconomic problems, (2) macroeconomic theories, (3) macroeconomic policies, (4) different views of how the economy works. To help you categorize what you learn in macroeconomics and to give you a better idea of what macroeconomics is about, we outline three macroeconomic organizational categories. We call these categories the

- P-Q category
- Self-Regulating–Economic Instability category
- Effective-Ineffective category

THE P-Q CATEGORY Macroeconomics deals with many variables, but two major variables are the *price level* and *Real GDP*. The price level is the weighted average of the prices of all goods and services. **Real GDP** is the value of the entire output produced annually

Real GDP
The value of the entire output produced annually within a country's borders, adjusted for price changes.

within a country's borders, adjusted for price changes. We discuss both the price level and Real GDP in depth later, but for now, you may simply want to view the price level as an average price and Real GDP as the quantity of output produced.

The symbol we use for the price level is P; the symbol we use for Real GDP is Q. Thus, we can talk about the P-Q category.

In macroeconomics, we have occasion to discuss numerous topics, such as inflation, deflation, unemployment, and so on. Many of these topics relate directly or indirectly to either P or Q. Here is a list of macroeconomic topics and how each relates to either P or Q.

Gross Domestic Product (GDP). P times Q.

Unemployment. Changes in unemployment are related to changes in Q.

Inflation. A rising P.

Deflation. A falling P.

Economic growth. Related to increasing Q.

Stagflation. A rising P combined with rising unemployment.

Business cycle. Recurrent swings up and down in Q.

Inflationary gap. The condition of the economy when Q is above its natural level.

Recessionary gap. The condition of the economy when Q is below its natural level.

Fiscal policy. Concerned with stabilizing P and increasing Q.

Monetary policy. Concerned with stabilizing P and increasing Q.

THE SELF-REGULATING-ECONOMIC INSTABILITY CATEGORY Consider the Great Depression of 1929–1933. During this period in U.S. history, unemployment skyrocketed, the production of goods and services plummeted (Q fell), prices fell (P fell), banks closed, savings were lost, and companies went bankrupt. What does this period indicate about the inherent properties of a market economy? Some observers argue that the Great Depression is proof of the inherent instability of a market (or capitalist) economy and demonstrates that natural economic forces, if left to themselves, may bring on human suffering.

Other observers see things differently. They argue that left to itself, the economy would never have nosedived into the Great Depression. They argue that the economy is inherently stable or self-regulating. The Great Depression, they believe, was largely caused and made worse by government tampering with the self-regulating and wealth-producing properties of a market economy.

Which came first? Did the market economy turn down under the weight of its own forces, producing massive unemployment, with government later stepping in to restrain the destructive market forces? Or was the market economy pushed into depression, and held there, by government economic tampering? The answer largely depends on how the inherent properties of a market economy are viewed. As economist Axel Leijonhufvud notes:

> The central issue in macroeconomic theory is—once again—the extent to which the economy, or at least its market sectors, may properly be regarded as a self-regulating system. . . . How well or badly, do its "automatic" mechanisms perform?[1]

THE EFFECTIVE-INEFFECTIVE CATEGORY Here the words *effective* and *ineffective* describe *fiscal policy* and *monetary policy*. **Fiscal policy** refers to changes in government expenditures and/or changes in taxes to achieve particular macroeconomic goals (e.g., low unemploy-

Fiscal Policy
Changes in government expenditures and/or changes in taxes to achieve particular macroeconomic goals.

---

[1]Axel Leijonhufvud, "Effective Demand Failures," *Swedish Journal of Economics* 75 (1973): 28.

ment, stable prices, etc.). **Monetary policy** refers to changes in the money supply, or the rate of growth of the money supply, to achieve particular macroeconomic goals.

Macroeconomists can take one of several positions with the effective-ineffective category. They can believe that fiscal and monetary policy are always effective (at meeting their goals), that both fiscal and monetary policy are ineffective, or that fiscal policy is effective and monetary policy is ineffective, and so on.

Often, a macroeconomist's position on the effectiveness-ineffectiveness of a policy is implicit in his or her view of how the economy works.

Monetary Policy
Changes in the money supply, or the rate of growth of the money supply, to achieve particular macroeconomic goals.

Macroeconomic Measures

Earlier, we presented three distinct macroeconomic categories—boxes, if you will, in which much of our macroeconomic discussion can be placed. In this section, we discuss the P of the P-Q category; in other words, we discuss the price level. In this section, we discuss how economists measure the price level.

Measuring Prices Using the CPI

As stated earlier, the **price level** is a weighted average of the prices of all goods and services. Economists measure the price level by constructing a **price index**. One major price index is the **consumer price index (CPI)**.

COMPUTING THE CPI The CPI is calculated by the Bureau of Labor Statistics (BLS) through its sampling of thousands of households and businesses. When a news report says that the "cost of living" increased by, say, 7 percent, it is usually referring to the CPI.[2]

The CPI is based on a representative group of goods and services purchased by a typical household. This representative group of goods is called the *market basket*. The market basket includes eight major categories of goods and services: food and beverages, housing, apparel, transportation, medical care, recreation, education and communication, and other goods and services. Some examples of these goods and services are breakfast cereal, milk, coffee, bedroom furniture, men's shirts, women's dresses, jewelry, new vehicles, airline fares, gasoline, prescription drugs, cable television, sports equipment, college tuition, postage, and haircuts.

To simplify our discussion, we assume the market basket includes only three goods instead of the many goods it actually contains. Our market basket consists of 10 pens, 5 shirts, and 3 pairs of shoes.

To calculate the CPI, we must first calculate the total dollar expenditure on the market basket in two years: the current year and the base year. The **base year** is a benchmark year that serves as a basis of comparison for prices in other years.

In Exhibit 2, we multiply the quantity of each good in the market basket (column 1) by its current-year price (column 2) to compute the current-year expenditure on each good (column 3). By adding the dollar amounts in column 3, we obtain the total dollar expenditure on the market basket in the current year. This amount is $167.

To find the total expenditure on the market basket in the base year, we multiply the quantity of each good in the market basket (column 1A) by its base-year price (column 2A) and then add these products (column 3A). This gives us $67.

Price Level
A weighted average of the prices of all good and services.

Price Index
A measure of the price level.

Consumer Price Index (CPI)
A widely cited index number for the price level; the weighted average of prices of a specific set of goods and services purchased by a typical household.

Base Year
The year chosen as a point of reference or basis of comparison for prices in other years; a benchmark year.

---

[2]Although changes in the CPI are often used to compute the change in the "cost of living," one's cost of living usually involves more than is measured by the CPI. For example, the CPI does not include income taxes, yet income taxes are a part of the cost of living for most people.

(1) Market Basket		(2) Current-Year Prices (per item)		(3) Current-Year Expenditures	(1A) Market Basket		(2A) Base-Year Prices (per item)		(3A) Base-Year Expenditures
10 pens	×	$ .70	=	$ 7.00	10 pens	×	$ .20	=	$ 2.00
5 shirts	×	14.00	=	70.00	5 shirts	×	7.00	=	35.00
3 pairs of shoes	×	30.00	=	90.00	3 pairs of shoes	×	10.00	=	30.00
				$167.00					**$67.00**

Total dollar expenditure on market basket in current year

Total dollar expenditure on market basket in base year

$$CPI = \left(\frac{\text{Total dollar expenditure on market basket in current year}}{\text{Total dollar expenditure on market basket in base year}}\right) \times 100$$

$$= \left(\frac{\$167}{\$67}\right) \times 100$$

$$= 249$$

Computing the Consumer Price Index

The exhibit uses hypothetical data to show how the CPI is computed. To find the "total dollar expenditure on market basket in current year," we multiply the quantities of goods in the market basket times their current-year prices and add these products. This gives us $167. To find the "total dollar expenditure on market basket in base year," we multiply the quantities of goods in the market basket times their base-year prices and add these products. This gives us $67. We then divide $167 by $67 and multiply the quotient by 100.

To find the CPI, we use the formula:

$$CPI = \frac{\text{Total dollar expenditure on market basket in current year}}{\text{Total dollar expenditure on market basket in base year}} \times 100$$

As shown in Exhibit 2, the CPI for our tiny economy is 249.

The consumer price index for the United States for the years 1959 to 2006 is shown in Exhibit 3.

MORE ABOUT THE BASE YEAR Recall that the base year is a benchmark year that serves as a basis of comparison for prices in other years. The CPI in the base year is 100. How do we know this? Well, look again at the formula for calculating the CPI. The numerator is the "total dollar expenditure on market basket in current year" and the denominator is the "total dollar expenditure on market basket in base year." In the base year, the current year *is* the base year, so the numerator and denominator are the same. The ratio is 1, and $1 \times 100 = 100$.

But if you look at Exhibit 3, you will notice that there is no year where the CPI is 100. Does this mean that there is no base year? Not at all. The base year has been defined by the government to be the period 1982–1984. Look at the CPI in each of the years 1982, 1983, and 1984. If we add the CPIs for the three years and divide by 3, we get 100: $(96.5 + 99.6 + 103.9)/3 = 100$.

Q&A

Is there a difference in economics between **price** *and* **price level**?

Yes. When the word price *is used, we are speaking about the single price of a good—such as the price of oranges, books, or shoes. When the word* price level *is used, we are talking about a weighted average of prices.*

WHEN WE KNOW THE CPI FOR VARIOUS YEARS, WE CAN COMPUTE THE PERCENTAGE CHANGE IN PRICES To find the percentage change in prices between any two years, we use the following formula:

$$\text{Percentage change in prices} = \left(\frac{CPI_{\text{later year}} - CPI_{\text{earlier year}}}{CPI_{\text{earlier year}}}\right) \times 100$$

For example, Exhibit 3 shows that the CPI in 1990 was 130.7, and the CPI in 2005 was 195.3. What was the percentage change in prices over this period of time? It was 49.43 percent: $[(195.3 - 130.7) \div 130.7] \times 100 = 49.43$. This means that from 1990 to

2005, prices increased 49.43 percent. You can think of the percentage change in prices this way: What cost $1 in 1990 cost approximately $1.49 in 2005.

Inflation and the CPI

Inflation is an increase in the price level and is usually measured on an annual basis. The *inflation rate* is the positive percentage change in the price level on an annual basis. For example, the inflation rate for 2000 is the percentage change in prices from the end of December 1999 through the end of December 2000. Although we do not show these data in a table, the CPI in December 1999 was 168.9, and the CPI in December 2000 was 174.6. This means the inflation rate in 2000 was approximately 3.4 percent.

When you know the inflation rate, you can find out whether your income is (1) keeping up with, (2) not keeping up with, or (3) more than keeping up with inflation. How you are doing depends on whether your income is rising by (1) the same percentage as, (2) a smaller percentage than, or (3) a greater percentage than the inflation rate, respectively. Another way to look at this is to compute and compare your real income for different years. **Real income** is a person's **nominal income** (or money income) adjusted for any change in prices. Real income is computed as follows:

$$\text{Real income} = \left(\frac{\text{Nominal income}}{\text{CPI}}\right) \times 100$$

CASE 1. KEEPING UP WITH INFLATION: REAL INCOME STAYS CONSTANT Jim earns $50,000 in year 1 and $55,000 in year 2. The CPI is 100 in year 1 and 110 in year 2. Jim's income has risen by 10 percent [(($55,000 − $50,000) / $50,000) × 100 = 10], and the inflation rate is 10 percent [((110 − 100) / 100) × 100 = 10]. Jim's income has risen by the same percentage as the inflation rate, so he has kept up with inflation. This is evident when we see that Jim's real income is the same in the two years. In year 1, it is $50,000, and in year 2, it is $50,000 too.

Real income year 1 = ($50,000/100) × 100 = $50,000
Real income year 2 = ($55,000/110) × 100 = $50,000

CASE 2. NOT KEEPING UP WITH INFLATION: REAL INCOME FALLS Karen earns $50,000 in year 1 and $52,000 in year 2. The CPI is 100 in year 1 and 110 in year 2. Karen's income has risen by 4 percent, and the inflation rate is 10 percent. Her income has risen by a smaller percentage than the inflation rate, so she has not kept up with inflation. Karen's real income has fallen from $50,000 in year 1 to $47,273 in year 2.

Real income year 1 = ($50,000/100) × 100 = $50,000
Real income year 2 = ($52,000/110) × 100 = $47,273

CASE 3. MORE THAN KEEPING UP WITH INFLATION: REAL INCOME RISES Carl earns $50,000 in year 1 and $60,000 in year 2. The CPI is 100 in year 1 and 110 in year 2. Carl's income has risen by 20 percent, and the inflation rate is 10 percent. His income has risen by a greater percentage than the inflation rate, so he has more than kept up with inflation. Carl's real income has risen from $50,000 in year 1 to $54,545 in year 2.

Real income year 1 = ($50,000/100) × 100 = $50,000
Real income year 2 = ($60,000/110) × 100 = $54,545

exhibit **3**

CPI, 1959–2006

Source: The data were reported at the Web site for the U.S. Department of Labor, Bureau of Labor Statistics. Site address http://www.bls.gov/home.htm

Year	CPI	Year	CPI
1959	29.1	1983	99.6
1960	29.6	1984	103.9
1961	29.9	1985	107.6
1962	30.2	1986	109.6
1963	30.6	1987	113.6
1964	31.0	1988	118.3
1965	31.5	1989	124.0
1966	32.4	1990	130.7
1967	33.4	1991	136.2
1968	34.8	1992	140.3
1969	36.7	1993	144.5
1970	38.8	1994	148.2
1971	40.5	1995	152.4
1972	41.8	1996	156.9
1973	44.4	1997	160.5
1974	49.3	1998	163.0
1975	53.8	1999	166.6
1976	56.9	2000	172.2
1977	60.6	2001	177.1
1978	65.2	2002	179.9
1979	72.6	2003	184.0
1980	82.4	2004	188.9
1981	90.9	2005	195.3
1982	96.5	2006	198.6

Inflation
An increase in the price level.

Real Income
Nominal income adjusted for price changes.

Nominal Income
The current-dollar amount of a person's income.

Thinking like
AN ECONOMIST

Comparing one thing with something else can be extremely useful. For example, in each of these three cases, we compared the percentage change in a person's nominal income with the inflation rate. Through this comparison, we learned something that we could not have learned by looking at either factor alone: how a person fared under inflation. Making comparisons is part of the economic way of thinking.

economics 24/7

DID PRESIDENT KENNEDY EARN MORE THAN TODAY'S PRESIDENT?

Today, the president of the United States earns an annual salary of $400,000. In 1962, when John F. Kennedy was president, he earned $100,000. Would you say that the president today is paid four times more than President Kennedy was paid?

At first glance, it may seem that today's president is paid more than Kennedy. We need to keep in mind, however, that when Kennedy was president, the prices of goods and services were much lower than today. In 1962, $100,000 would buy much more than $100,000 buys today. The question is, would it buy four times as much in 1962 as it buys today?

To get some idea of what a $100,000 salary in 1962 would equal in today's dollars, economists use the formula:

$$\text{Salary in today's dollars} = \text{Salary}_{\text{earlier year}} \times \left(\frac{\text{CPI}_{\text{current year}}}{\text{CPI}_{\text{earlier year}}} \right)$$

Suppose that by "today" we mean 2006. We want to find out what Kennedy's 1962 salary is equal to in 2006 dollars. The CPI in 2006 was 198.6, and the CPI in 1962 was 30.2. Filling in the formula, we see that Kennedy's salary in 1962 is equivalent to earning $657,616 in 2006.

$$\text{Kennedy's salary in 2006 dollars} = \$100,000 \times \left(\frac{198.6}{30.2} \right)$$
$$= \$657,616$$

President Kennedy, in 1962, earned more than the president today earns in terms of purchasing power. Kennedy earned the equivalent of $657,616 in today's dollars (2006), and the president today earns $400,000. In other words, Kennedy was paid the equivalent of $257,616 more than the president today is paid.

The Substitution Bias in Fixed-Weighted Measures

Look at Exhibit 2, where the CPI was first calculated. Notice that the market basket in both the current year and the base year is the same: 10 pens, 5 shirts, and 3 pairs of shoes. In the base year, the person bought 10 pens, 5 shirts, and 3 pairs of shoes, and even though the prices of all three of these items increased, she continued to buy the *same quantity* of each. This is like saying that Michael purchased two pounds of beef a week in 2005, and even though the price of beef increased between, say, 2005 and 2006, he continued to buy two pounds of beef a week. In reality, what Michael is likely to have done is *substitute,* say, chicken for beef *if the price of beef increased relatively more than the price of chicken during the time period in question.* In other words, Michael's buying behavior is likely to have responded to changes in *relative prices.*

Any price index that uses fixed quantities of goods, and therefore does not reflect the fact that people might substitute one good for another as the price of one good rises relative to another, is called a *fixed-weighted price index.* All fixed-weighted price measures have a *substitution bias*—they do not regularly account for the substitutions that individuals are likely to make. As a result of the substitution bias, a fixed-weighted price index can "overstate the cost of living." We explain how a fixed-weighted price index overstates the cost of living, in the following paragraphs.

Suppose a fixed-weighted price index—such as the CPI—is 100 in year 1 and 110 in year 2. Some people would loosely say that there has been a rise in the cost of living. In this context, a rise in the cost of living means that it takes more money in year 2 to purchase the same bundle of goods that was purchased in year 1. But this implicitly assumes that one's standard of living is obtained in only one way: *by purchasing a constant, or fixed, bundle of goods.* In reality, this probably isn't true. Different bundles of goods may represent *equivalent* standards of living.

For example, assume bundle *A* consists of two pounds of beef, one loaf of bread, and three boxes of Frosted Flakes cereal, and bundle *B* consists of two pounds of chicken, one loaf of bread, and three boxes of Honey Nut Cheerios. Furthermore, assume (1) bundles *A* and *B* represent equivalent standards of living; (2) a buyer is currently purchasing bundle *A,* which costs $100 over some time period; (3) the cost of purchasing bundle *A* rises to $110, prompting the buyer to substitute bundle *B* for bundle *A*; and (4) bundle *B* costs $100.

Has the cost of living increased for this person? If we base our answer on purchasing a fixed bundle of goods—bundle *A*—the answer is yes because the price of purchasing bundle *A* has risen from $100 to $110. But if we allow for substitutions (of bundles) and bundles *A* and *B* represent equivalent standards of living, then the answer is no because the cost of buying an equivalent bundle remains constant at $100. Many economists believe that allowing for substitutions is the only justifiable way of measuring the cost of living. Any method that does not allow for substitutions can result in overstating the change in the cost of living.

For many years, economists criticized the use of the CPI (a fixed-weighted price index), largely because the expenditure weights of the various goods and services in the market basket were changed only once a decade.[3] This meant that the market basket used to measure the CPI was the same for a decade or longer even though substitutions were taking place during this time. Today the BLS updates the expenditure weights of the market basket (used to compute the CPI) every two years.

GDP Implicit Price Deflator

Besides the CPI, there is another price index that is often cited: the *GDP deflator* or the *GDP implicit price deflator.* As you know, the CPI is based on a representative group of goods and services (the market basket) purchased by a typical household. Obviously, there are more goods and services produced in an economy than find their way into the market basket. The GDP implicit price deflator, unlike the CPI, is based on all goods and services produced in an economy.

Converting Dollars from One Year to Another

Suppose someone says, "Back in 1960, I had an annual salary of $10,000 a year. That sure isn't much these days." Of course, the person is right in one sense: An annual salary of $10,000 doesn't buy much these days. But was $10,000 a good salary back in 1960? It certainly could have been because prices in 1960 weren't as high as they are today. For example, the CPI was 29.6 in 1960, and it was 198.6 in 2006. In other words, one of the things that make a salary "good" or "not so good" is what the salary can buy.

Now suppose someone tells you that a $10,000 salary in 1960 is the same as a $67,094 salary today. Would you then better understand the 1960 $10,000 salary? Of course you would because you understand what it means to earn $67,094 today. Economists convert a past salary into a salary today by using this formula:

$$\text{Salary in today's (current) dollars} = \text{Salary}_{\text{earlier year}} \times \left(\frac{\text{CPI}_{\text{current year}}}{\text{CPI}_{\text{earlier year}}}\right)$$

---

[3]The "expenditure weights" refer to the quantities of each good in the market basket. For example, the expenditure weight for pens in our market basket in Exhibit 2 is 10.

economics 24/7

WHAT WAS A PENNY WORTH?

You are walking and you look down and see a penny. Do you stop and pick it up? Many people will say no, stating that it isn't worth their stopping and picking up a penny. After all, a penny is not worth very much, they say.

You buy a magazine at your campus store. The total price (including tax) comes to $6.02. You hand the cashier a $10 bill. Instead of giving you $3.98 in change, she reaches into the cup next to the cash register and pulls out two pennies; she gives you back $4 in change. It is easier for her to get the two pennies from the cup than to count out $3.98 in change. You say "thank you" and go on your way.

Another day comes, and this time you buy something for $5.99. You hand the cashier $6. When the cashier gives you back one penny in change, you drop the penny in the cup next to the cash register. One day you take from the cup, another day you give to the cup.

Twenty years ago, there was no penny cup next to cash registers. Why no penny cups then, but penny cups now? It's because 20 years ago a penny had more purchasing power than it does today. If a penny today had greater purchasing power than it does have, then you'd be less likely to drop a penny change into the penny cup; instead, you'd drop it in your pocket.

The discussion of cups and pennies gets us thinking. What was a penny worth, say, in 1900? A different way of asking the question: What coin today is equal to the purchasing power a penny had in 1900? The answer is a quarter. In other words, having a penny in 1900 was equivalent of having a quarter (25 cents today). It follows then that having four pennies in 1900 was the equivalent of having $1 today.

We leave you with the question we started out with, but this time we change the date. It is 1900 and you are walking along and you look down and see a penny. Do you stop and pick it up?

Assume the CPI today is the same as the most recent CPI in Exhibit 3 (which is the CPI for 2006). Using the formula, we get:

$$\text{Salary in 2006 dollars} = \$10,000 \times \left(\frac{198.6}{29.6}\right)$$
$$= \$67,094$$

SELF-TEST

(Answers to Self-Test questions are in the Self-Test Appendix.)

1. Explain how the CPI is calculated.

2. What is a base year?

3. In year 1, your annual income is $45,000 and the CPI is 143.6; in year 2, your annual income is $51,232 and the CPI is 150.7. Has your real income risen, fallen, or remained constant? Explain your answer.

Measuring Unemployment

Every month, the government surveys thousands of households to gather information about labor market activities. It uses the information from the survey to derive the number of Americans unemployed.

economics 24/7

ECONOMICS AT THE MOVIES

Some movies do better at the box office than other movies. For example, *Harry Potter and the Goblet of Fire*, released in 2005, earned higher gross receipts than *King Kong*, another movie released in 2005.

As of June 2006, the following list ranks the all-time top 10 movies in the United States in terms of gross receipts:

1. *Titanic* (1997)
2. *Star Wars* (1977)
3. *Shrek 2* (2004)
4. *E.T.: The Extra-Terrestrial* (1982)
5. *Star Wars: Episode I—The Phantom Menace* (1999)
6. *Spider-Man* (2002)
7. *Star Wars: Episode III—Revenge of the Sith* (2005)
8. *The Lord of the Rings: The Return of the King* (2003)
9. *Spider-Man 2* (2004)
10. *The Passion of the Christ* (2004)

Titanic, first on the list, earned gross receipts in the United States of $600 million, and *Star Wars*, in second place, earned $461 million. Comparing these two dollar amounts, it is easy to conclude that *Titanic* did better at the box office than *Star Wars* did.

But notice that *Titanic* was released in 1997 and *Star Wars* was released 20 years earlier in 1977. In other words, the receipts for *Titanic* are in 1997 dollars, and those for *Star Wars* are in 1977 dollars. To accurately compare the receipts of the two movies, we need to put them on an even footing. To do this, we need to change each movie's receipts into today's dollars. When we do this, *Star Wars* earned more than double what *Titanic* earned. Specifically, *Star Wars* earned $1.5 billion and *Titanic* earned $732 million.

What is the top grossing film of all time in today's dollars? It is *Gone with the Wind*, released in 1939. In today's dollars, it earned $2.7 billion.

Who Are the Unemployed?

The total population of the United States can be divided into two broad groups (Exhibit 4). One group consists of persons who are (1) under 16 years of age, (2) in the armed forces, or (3) institutionalized—that is, they are in a prison, mental institution, or home for the aged. The second group, which consists of all others in the total population, is called the *civilian noninstitutional population*.

The civilian noninstitutional population, in turn, can be divided into two groups: persons *not in the labor force* and persons in the *civilian labor force*. (Economists often refer to the "labor force" instead of the "civilian labor force.")

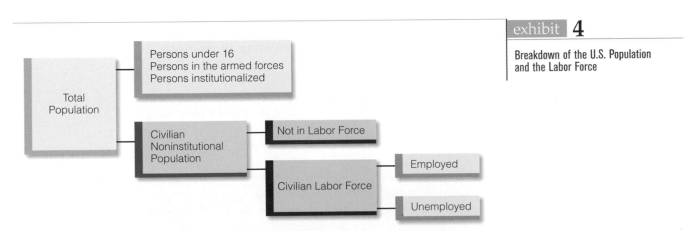

exhibit **4**

Breakdown of the U.S. Population and the Labor Force

$$\text{Civilian noninstitutional population} = \text{Persons not in the labor force} + \text{Persons in the labor force}$$

Persons not in the labor force are neither working nor looking for work. For example, people who are retired, who are engaged in own-home housework, or who choose not to work fall into this category.

Persons in the civilian labor force fall into one of two categories: *employed* or *unemployed*.

$$\text{Civilian labor force} = \text{Employed persons} + \text{Unemployed persons}$$

According to the BLS, employed persons consist of:

- All persons who did any work for pay or profit during the survey reference week.
- All persons who did at least 15 hours of unpaid work in a family-operated enterprise.
- All persons who were temporarily absent from their regular jobs because of illness, vacation, bad weather, industrial dispute, or various personal reasons.

According to the BLS, unemployed persons consist of:

- All persons who did not have jobs, made specific active efforts to find a job during the prior four weeks, and were available for work.
- All persons who were not working and were waiting to be called back to a job from which they had been temporarily laid off.

The Unemployment and Employment Rates

Unemployment Rate

The percentage of the civilian force that is unemployed: Unemployment rate = Number of unemployed persons/Civilian labor force.

The **unemployment rate** is the percentage of the civilian labor force that is unemployed. It is equal to the number of unemployed persons divided by the civilian labor force.

$$\text{Unemployment rate } (U) = \frac{\text{Number of unemployed persons}}{\text{Civilian labor force}}$$

Employment Rate

The percentage of the civilian noninstitutional population that is employed: Employment rate = Number of employed persons/Civilian noninstitutional population.

The **employment rate** (sometimes referred to as the *employment/population ratio*) is the percentage of the civilian noninstitutional population that is employed. It is equal to the number of employed persons divided by the civilian noninstitutional population:

$$\text{Employment rate } (E) = \frac{\text{Number of employed persons}}{\text{Civilian noninstitutional population}}$$

Notice that the sum of the unemployment rate and the employment rate will not equal 100 percent. In other words, if the unemployment rate is 6 percent, it does *not* follow that the employment rate is 94 percent. The denominator of the unemployment rate and the employment rate are not the same, so the two rates are percentages of different totals. The unemployment rate is a percentage of the civilian labor force. The employment rate is a percentage of the civilian noninstitutional population, which is a larger number than the civilian labor force.

Labor Force Participation Rate

The percentage of the civilian noninstitutional population that is in the civilian labor force. Labor force participation rate = Civilian labor force/Civilian noninstitutional population.

Finally, the **labor force participation rate** (LFPR) is the percentage of the civilian noninstitutional population that is in the civilian labor force.

$$\text{Labor force participation rate (LFPR)} = \frac{\text{Civilian labor force}}{\text{Civilian noninstitutional population}}$$

The LFPR may sound like the employment rate, but it is different. Although the denominator in both is the same, the numerator in the employment rate is the number of employed persons, and the numerator in the LFPR is the civilian labor force (which consists of both employed persons and unemployed persons). For this reason, some economists say that while the employment rate gives us the percentage of the population that is working, the LFPR gives us the percentage of the population that is *willing to work*.

Reasons for Unemployment

Usually, we think of an unemployed person as someone who has been fired or laid off from his or her job. Certainly, some unemployed persons fit this description, but not all of them do. According to the BLS, an unemployed person may fall into one of four categories.

1. **Job loser.** This is a person who was employed in the civilian labor force and was either fired or laid off. Most unemployed persons fall into this category.

2. **Job leaver.** This is a person employed in the civilian labor force who quits his or her job. For example, if Jim quit his job with company X and is looking for a better job, then he is a job leaver.

3. **Reentrant.** This is a person who was previously employed, hasn't worked for some time, and is currently reentering the labor force.

4. **New entrant.** This is a person who has never held a full-time job for two weeks or longer and is now in the civilian labor force looking for a job.

Unemployed persons = Job losers + Job leavers + Reentrants + New entrants

Discouraged Workers

Suppose Adam is fired from his job at company A in September. He looks for a job for about six months. During this time, he is considered an unemployed person and is counted in the unemployment rate. At the end of the sixth month, Adam is very discouraged; he doesn't think he will ever find a job, and so he stops looking. A month passes and he continues not to look for a job. Is Adam still considered an unemployed person? The answer is no. Remember, to be an unemployed person, you have to meet certain conditions, one of which is that you have to be actively looking for work. But Adam isn't actively looking for work, and he isn't waiting to be called back to a job or to report to a job. So Adam isn't unemployed. Because Adam is not unemployed, he does not get counted in the unemployment rate.

The BLS considers Adam a *discouraged worker*. You may think that for all practical purposes, a discouraged worker is the same as an unemployed person (because neither has a job). But they aren't the same for calculating the unemployment rate. The unemployed person gets counted, but the discouraged worker does not.

Some economists think that because discouraged workers are not considered unemployed, the unemployment rate is biased downward. Consequently, it doesn't really give us a good fix on the "real unemployment problem" in society.

Types of Unemployment

This section describes a few types of unemployment.

FRICTIONAL UNEMPLOYMENT Every day, demand conditions change in some markets, causing qualified individuals with transferable skills to leave some jobs and move to others. To illustrate, suppose there are two computer firms, A and B. For some reason, the demand falls for firm A's computers and the demand rises for firm B's computers. Consequently, firm A produces fewer computers. With fewer computers being produced,

economics 24/7

NATIONAL PUBLIC RADIO AND UNEMPLOYMENT FIGURES

We know that the unemployment rate is calculated by dividing the number of persons unemployed by the civilian labor force.

$$\text{Unemployment Rate} = \frac{\text{Number of unemployed persons}}{\text{Civilian labor force}}$$

Let's suppose that the number of unemployed persons is 100 and the civilian labor force is 1,000. It follows that the unemployment rate is 10 percent.

Suppose now that 10 of the unemployed persons become discouraged workers and stop looking for work. The number of unemployed persons falls to 90, and the civilian labor force (which consists of employed plus unemployed persons) becomes 990.

What is the unemployment rate now? It is 90 divided by 990, or 9.09 percent. In other words, the unemployment rate has dropped. But it hasn't dropped for the reason most people think the unemployment rate drops. It hasn't dropped because some of the unemployed persons found jobs. It dropped because some of the unemployed became so discouraged that they stopped looking for jobs.

This was the point an analyst on National Public Radio was making one day. According to the analyst, the recent unemployment figures "only look good" because so many of the unemployed have become discouraged and stopped looking for work.

It might be interesting to calculate an alternative unemployment rate, such as this one:

$$\text{Alternative Unemployment Rate} = \frac{\substack{\text{Number of unemployed persons} +\\ \text{Discouraged workers}}}{\substack{\text{Civilian labor force} +\\ \text{Discouraged workers}}}$$

In other words, let's compute an alternative unemployment rate that adds in discouraged workers both to the ranks of the unemployed and to the civilian labor force. In fact, the Bureau of Labor Statistics does just this. It computes what it calls "Total unemployed plus discouraged workers, as a percent of the civilian labor force plus discouraged workers."

On the day the analyst on NPR said that the unemployment rate "only looks good" (but implied that it wasn't so good), we checked the Bureau of Labor Statistics Web site to find the alternative unemployment rate we described earlier. It was down. In fact, it had been dropping for the past few months. The NPR analyst would have had a point if this alternative unemployment rate had been rising, but it hadn't. In short, the alternative unemployment rate we specified earlier tells us what the unemployment rate would look like if we include discouraged workers in our calculation.

© BLOOMBERG NEWS/LANDOV

firm *A* doesn't need as many employees, so it fires some employees. On the other hand, firm *B* produces more computers. With more computers being produced, firm *B* hires additional employees. The employees fired from firm *A* have skills that they can transfer to firm *B*—after all, both firms produce computers. However, it takes time for people to transfer from one firm to another. During this time, they are said to be frictionally unemployed.

The unemployment owing to the natural "frictions" of the economy, which is caused by changing market conditions and is represented by qualified individuals with transferable skills who change jobs, is called **frictional unemployment**. We use the symbol U_F to designate the frictional unemployment rate, which is the percentage of the labor force that is frictionally unemployed.

In a dynamic, changing economy like ours, there will always be frictional unemployment. Many economists believe that the basic cause of frictional unemployment is imperfect or incomplete information, which prevents individuals from leaving one job and finding another instantly.

Consider the situation where there are 1,000 job vacancies and 1,000 persons with the qualifications to fill the jobs. Will there be some unemployment? It is likely that there will be because not every one of the 1,000 job seekers will know where an available job is, nor will all employers give the job to the first applicant who knocks on the door (employers don't know if "better" applicants are around the corner). Matching qualified workers with jobs takes time.

STRUCTURAL UNEMPLOYMENT **Structural unemployment** is unemployment due to structural changes in the economy that eliminate some jobs and create other jobs for which the unemployed are unqualified. Most economists argue that structural unemployment is largely the consequence of automation (laborsaving devices) and long-lasting shifts in demand. The major difference between the frictionally unemployed and the structurally unemployed is that the latter do not have transferable skills. Their choice is between prolonged unemployment and retraining. For example, suppose there is a pool of unemployed automobile workers and a rising demand for computer analysts. If the automobile workers do not currently have the skills necessary to become computer analysts, they are structurally unemployed. We use the symbol U_S to designate the structural unemployment rate, which is the percentage of the labor force that is structurally unemployed.

NATURAL UNEMPLOYMENT Adding the frictional unemployment rate and the structural unemployment rate gives the **natural unemployment** rate (or natural rate of unemployment). We use the symbol U_N to designate the natural unemployment rate. Currently, most economists estimate the natural unemployment rate at between 4 and 6.5 percent.

$$\text{Natural unemployment rate } (U_N) =$$
$$\text{Frictional unemployment rate } (U_F) + \text{Structural unemployment rate } (U_S)$$

What Is Full Employment?

What do you think of when you hear the term *full employment*? Most people think full employment means that the actual or reported unemployment rate is zero. But a dynamic, changing economy can never have full employment of this type due to the frictional and structural changes that continually occur. In fact, it is natural for some unemployment to exist—some natural unemployment, that is. For this reason, economists *do not* equate full employment with a zero unemployment rate. Instead, for economists, *full employment exists when the economy is operating at its natural unemployment rate.* For example, if the natural unemployment rate is 5 percent, then full employment exists when the unemployment rate (in the economy) is 5 percent. In other words, the economy can be operating at full employment, and some people will be unemployed.

Cyclical Unemployment

The unemployment rate that exists in the economy is not always the natural rate. The difference between the existing unemployment rate and the natural unemployment rate is the **cyclical unemployment rate** (U_C).

$$\text{Cyclical unemployment rate } (U_C) =$$
$$\text{Unemployment rate } (U) - \text{Natural unemployment rate } (U_N)$$

When the unemployment rate (U) that exists in the economy is greater than the natural unemployment rate (U_N), the cyclical unemployment rate (U_C) is positive. For example, if $U = 8$ percent and $U_N = 5$ percent, then $U_C = 3$ percent. When the unemployment rate that exists in the economy is less than the natural unemployment rate, the cyclical unemployment rate is negative. For example, if $U = 4$ percent and $U_N = 5$ percent, then $U_C = -1$ percent.

Frictional Unemployment

Unemployment due to the natural "frictions" of the economy, which is caused by changing market conditions and is represented by qualified individuals with transferable skills who change jobs.

Structural Unemployment

Unemployment due to structural changes in the economy that eliminate some jobs and create other jobs for which the unemployed are unqualified.

Natural Unemployment

Unemployment caused by frictional and structural factors in the economy. Natural unemployment rate = Frictional unemployment rate + Structural unemployment rate.

Full Employment

The condition that exists when the unemployment rate is equal to the natural unemployment rate.

Cyclical Unemployment Rate

The difference between the unemployment rate and the natural unemployment rate.

economics 24/7

WHAT EXPLAINS THE INCREASING PERCENTAGE OF WOMEN IN THE LABOR FORCE?

In 1948 in the United States, 31 percent of all women 20 years old and older were working in the labor force. Today, that percentage is around 57 percent. What explains the percentage increase of women in the work force over the last half of the twentieth century? One explanation is that the "work culture" has changed over time. Often, in the United States in particular, the women's movement and feminism are given credit for this change in attitude.

There is, however, another explanation—one that has nothing to do with a changing culture but is purely economic in nature. Women have joined the work force in record numbers at the same time that it has become monetarily more advantageous to join the work force.

To illustrate, let's consider life at the end of the nineteenth century. In 1895, the average worker had to work 260 hours to earn enough money to buy a one-speed bicycle, 24 hours to earn enough to buy a cushioned chair, and 44 hours to earn enough to buy a 100-piece dinner set. More than 100 years later, in 2000, the average worker had to work only 7.2 hours to earn enough money to buy a one-speed bicycle, only 2.0 hours to earn enough to buy a cushioned chair, and only 3.6 hours to earn enough to buy a 100-piece dinner set. In other words, the average worker did not

have to work as many hours in 2000 as in 1895 to buy the same goods. This conclusion also holds for goods other than bicycles, cushioned chairs, and dinner sets. In fact, it holds for many if not most goods. The table below shows a few:[4]

When the average worker has to work only 7.2 hours to earn enough money to buy a bicycle compared to 260 hours, it follows that it is much more advantageous to work. Stated differently, using bicycles as our good, one hour of work in 1895 got the average worker 1/260 of a bicycle; but in 2000, it got the average worker about 1/7 of a bicycle. In other words, the hourly pay (in terms of bicycles) was much higher in 2000 than in 1895.

Economists would predict that more people would want to work the higher the wage rate for working (in terms of goods). In other words, the greater the benefits from working, the more people would choose to work. And this is exactly what we see. As the wage rate for working (in terms of bicycles, office chairs, dinner sets) has increased, women have joined the labor force in record numbers.

---

[4]The data are from Brad DeLong, an economist at the University of California, Berkeley, in his work *The Economic History of the Twentieth Century: Slouching Towards Utopia*. The work can be found at http://www.j-bradford-delong.net/TCEH/Slouch_title.html.

Time Needed for the Average Worker to Earn the Purchase Price of Various Goods

	Time to Earn in 1895 (hours)	Time to Earn in 2000 (hours)
One-speed bicycle	260	7.2
Cushioned office chair	24	2.0
100-piece dinner set	44	3.6
Hairbrush	16	2.0
Cane rocking chair	8	1.6
Solid gold locket	28	6.0
Encyclopedia Britannica	140	33.8
Steinway piano	2,400	1,107.6

SELF-TEST

1. What is the major difference between a person who is frictionally unemployed and one who is structurally unemployed?

2. If the cyclical unemployment rate is positive, what does this imply?

A Reader Asks...

Where Do I Go to Learn the Specifics of Jobs and Wages?

I'm a math major and I'll graduate from college in about a year. Is there a way for me to find out how much mathematicians earn and what types of jobs they perform?

No matter what your major is, you can learn about jobs and wages from the *Occupational Outlook Handbook.* The *Handbook* is on the Bureau of Labor Statistics Web site at http://stats.bls.gov/emp/.

According to the *Handbook,* mathematicians usually work as part of a team that includes economists, engineers, computer scientists, physicists, and others. In 2004, mathematicians held about 2,500 jobs. In addition, about 20,000 persons held faculty positions in mathematics at colleges and universities.

Many nonfaculty mathematicians work for the federal and state governments. The biggest employer of mathematicians in the federal government is the Department of Defense. In the private sector, major employers include research and testing services, educational services, security and commodity exchanges, and management and public relations services. In manufacturing, the pharmaceutical industry is the primary employer. Some mathematicians also work for banks, insurance companies, and public utilities.

Median annual earnings of mathematicians were $81,240 in 2004. The middle 50 percent earned between $60,050 and $101,360. The lowest 10 percent had earnings of less than $43,160, while the top 10 percent earned more than $120,900.

! analyzing the scene

What does a report on prices have to do with what Franklin Smithies will do at work?

Franklin manages the stock portfolio of one of the largest pension funds in the country. Often, stock portfolio managers use price reports to get a hint of what the Federal Reserve will do in the near future. (As we mentioned earlier in this chapter, the Federal Reserve is the monetary authority of the United States, capable of increasing and decreasing the money supply, influencing interest rates, etc.). For example, Franklin might reason: If prices have recently risen sharply, the Federal

Reserve may try to slow down price rises by raising interest rates. Higher interest rates may adversely affect the stocks I recently purchased, so the best thing for me to do is sell some stocks.

How does the BLS compute the unemployment rate, and does it matter whether the unemployment rate is trending down or up?

The BLS computes the unemployment rate by dividing the number of persons unemployed by the civilian labor force.

Most economists believe that it does matter whether or not the unemployment rate is trending down or up. All other things equal, an unemployment rate that is trending down indicates a stronger economy than one that is trending up.

How does the BLS compute the consumer price index, and what does it matter whether prices are rising or falling?

We show how to compute the CPI in Exhibit 2. It matters whether prices are rising or falling. For example, if prices are rising faster than, say, your nominal income, your real income will be falling.

How long will George Krenshaw stay unemployed?

This is a hard question to answer. We cannot say for sure if George Krenshaw will remain unemployed for two weeks, two months, or two years. How long he stays unemployed depends on the current and future state of the economy, how much time and effort he devotes to searching for another job, and other such things. We can make some general statements about the duration of his unemployment, though. For example, whether George Krenshaw is frictionally or structurally

unemployed matters to how long he stays unemployed. All other things being equal, George will stay unemployed longer if he is structurally unemployed than if he is frictionally unemployed. Recall that a person who is structurally unemployed does not have transferable skills, whereas a person who is frictionally unemployed does. The structurally unemployed person has to spend time retraining, whereas the frictionally unemployed person does not.

Will Catherine be rich? How does her salary of $50,000 compare to her father's first salary of $8,000?

Suppose Catherine's father earned the $8,000 in, say, 1960. By converting 1960 dollars into 2006 dollars, we find that earning $8,000 in 1960 is equivalent to earning $53,675 in 2006. So, Catherine's salary is $3,675 less than her father earned in 1960.

What's the best way to compare the gross receipts of two movies?

The best way to compare the gross receipts of the two movies is to convert both movies receipts into today's dollars. Then, receipts for both movies will be expressed in terms of the same year.

chapter summary

Measuring Prices

- One major price index is the consumer price index (CPI).

- $$CPI = \left(\frac{\text{Total dollar expenditure on market basket in current year}}{\text{Total dollar expenditure on market basket in base year}} \right) \times 100$$

- Percentage change in prices =
$$\left(\frac{CPI_{\text{later year}} - CPI_{\text{earlier year}}}{CPI_{\text{earlier year}}} \right) \times 100$$

- Inflation is an increase in the price level or price index.

- $$\text{Real income} = \left(\frac{\text{Nominal income}}{CPI} \right) \times 100$$

- Any price index that uses fixed quantities of goods, and therefore does not reflect the fact that people might substitute one good for another as the price of one good rises relative to another, is called a fixed-weighted price index. The substitution bias in a weighted price index can overstate the cost of living.

- A given dollar amount in an earlier year does not have the same purchasing power in a later year (or current

year) if prices are different in the two years. To convert a dollar amount in an earlier year into today's (or current) dollars, we use the formula:

Dollar amount in today's (current) dollars =

$$\text{Dollar amount}_{\text{earlier year}} \times \left(\frac{CPI_{\text{current year}}}{CPI_{\text{earlier year}}} \right)$$

Unemployment and Employment

- $$\text{Unemployment rate } (U) = \frac{\text{Number of unemployed persons}}{\text{Civilian labor force}}$$

- $$\text{Employment rate } (E) = \frac{\text{Number of employed persons}}{\text{Civilian noninstitutional population}}$$

- An unemployed person may be a job loser, a job leaver, a reentrant, or a new entrant.

- The unemployment rate may be biased downward because discouraged workers are not considered unemployed.

- Frictional unemployment, due to the natural "frictions" of the economy, is caused by changing market conditions and is represented by qualified individuals with transferable skills who change jobs.

- Structural unemployment is due to structural changes in the economy that eliminate some jobs and create others for which the unemployed are unqualified.

- Natural unemployment is caused by frictional and structural factors in the economy. The natural unemployment rate equals the sum of the frictional unemployment rate and the structural unemployment rate.

- Full employment is the condition that exists when the unemployment rate is equal to the natural unemployment rate.

- The cyclical unemployment rate is the difference between the existing unemployment rate and the natural unemployment rate.

key terms and concepts

Real GDP	Consumer Price Index (CPI)	Nominal Income	Frictional Unemployment
Fiscal Policy	Base Year	Unemployment Rate	Structural Unemployment
Monetary Policy	Inflation	Employment Rate	Natural Unemployment
Price Level	Real Income	Labor Force Participation Rate	Full Employment
Price Index			Cyclical Unemployment Rate

questions and problems

1   What does the CPI in the base year equal? Explain your answer.

2   Show that if the percentage rise in prices is equal to the percentage rise in nominal income, then one's real income does not change.

3   What does it mean if the expenditure weights of the market basket used to compute the CPI are changed?

4   How does structural unemployment differ from frictional unemployment?

5   What does it mean to say that the country is operating at full employment?

6   What is "natural" about natural unemployment?

7   What is the difference between the employment rate and the labor force participation rate?

8   If the unemployment rate is 4 percent, it does not follow that the employment rate is 96 percent. Explain why.

9   What criteria must be met for a person to be characterized as unemployed?

10   What is the difference between a job leaver and a reentrant?

11   How is a discouraged worker different from an unemployed worker?

working with numbers and graphs

1   Suppose there are 60 million people employed, 10 million unemployed, and 30 million not in the labor force. What does the civilian noninstitutional population equal?

2   Suppose there are 100 million people in the civilian labor force and 90 million people employed. How many people are unemployed? What is the unemployment rate?

3   Change the current-year prices in Exhibit 2 to $1 for pens, $28 for shirts, and $32 for a pair of shoes. What is the CPI for the current year based on these prices?

4   Jim earned an annual salary of $15,000 in 1965. What is this equivalent to in 2005 dollars? (Use Exhibit 3 to find the CPI in the years mentioned.)

5   A house cost $10,000 in 1976. What is this equivalent to in 2001 dollars? (Use Exhibit 3 to find the CPI in the years mentioned.)

6   Using the following data, compute (a) the unemployment rate, (b) the employment rate, and (c) the labor force participation rate.
Civilian noninstitutional population = 200 million
Number of employed persons = 126 million
Number of unemployed persons = 8 million

7   Based on the following data, compute (a) the unemployment rate, (b) the structural unemployment rate, and (c) the cyclical unemployment rate.
Frictional unemployment rate = 2 percent
Natural unemployment rate = 5 percent
Civilian labor force = 100 million
Number of employed persons = 82 million

8   Using Exhibit 3, compute the percentage change in prices between (a) 1966 and 1969, (b) 1976 and 1986, and (c) 1990 and 1999.

9   Assume the market basket contains $10X$, $20Y$, and $45Z$. The current-year prices for goods X, Y, and Z are $1, $4, and $6, respectively. The base-year prices are $1, $3, and $5, respectively. What is the CPI in the current year?

10 If the CPI is 150 and nominal income is $100,000, what does real income equal?

Macroeconomic Measurements, Part II: GDP and Real GDP

Setting the Scene

Listen to some conversations people were having not too long ago.

WALKING ACROSS THE UNIVERSITY OF KANSAS CAMPUS

Carmela:
How does the job situation look to you?

Oliver:
It's a little bleak. I thought employers would be knocking at my door after four years of college, but they're not. Just my luck—the economy has to be in a slump.

INSIDE A HOUSE IN CARBONDALE, ILLINOIS

Owner of the house:
How much do I owe you?

Plumber:
The bill comes to $185. I was wondering if you could pay me in cash. Would that be okay?

DRUG ENFORCEMENT AGENCY (DEA) HEADQUARTERS

First DEA official:
We just got a report that the banks in Miami are experiencing an unusually high demand for cash.

Second DEA official:
I'll call the Miami office.

A CLASSROOM, MICHIGAN STATE UNIVERSITY

Student:
I heard recently that China has a relatively large GDP. This seems odd to me because I thought China was still a relatively poor country. How can China have one of the highest gross domestic products in the world and be poor too? Am I missing something here?

WASHINGTON, D.C., METRO, 1 MILE FROM THE FOGGY BOTTOM STATION

First person:
The polls say that the economy is the number one issue for most people.

Second person:
In other words, "It's the economy, stupid!"

First person:
I guess so.

? Here are some questions to keep in mind as you read this chapter:

What does the state of the economy have to do with a college graduate's chances of getting a job?

Why does the plumber want to be paid in cash?

Why does the DEA care that people are demanding cash from banks in Miami?

How can a country have one of the highest GDPs in the world and be poor too?

What is the political relevance of the slogan, "It's the economy, stupid!"?

See analyzing the scene at the end of this chapter for answers to these questions.

Gross Domestic Product

In any given year, people in the United States produce goods and services. They produce television sets, books, pencil sharpeners, DVD players, attorney services, haircuts, and much more. Have you ever wondered what the total dollar value of all those goods and services is? In 2006, it was $13.2 trillion. In other words, in 2006, people living and working in the United States produced $13.2 trillion worth of goods and services. That dollar amount—$13.2 trillion—is what economists call the gross domestic product. Simply put, **gross domestic product (GDP)** is the *total market value of all final goods and services produced annually within a country's borders.*

Gross Domestic Product (GDP)
The total market value of all final goods and services produced annually within a country's borders.

Three Ways to Compute GDP

Consider a simple economy in which one good is produced and sold.

1.   Bob finds a seed and plants it. Sometime later, an orange tree appears.
2.   Bob pays Harry $5 in wages to pick and box the oranges.
3.   Next, Bob sells the oranges to Jim for $8.
4.   Jim turns the oranges into orange juice and sells the orange juice to Caroline for $10. Caroline drinks the juice.

What is the GDP in this simple economy? Is it $5, $13, $10, $18, or some other dollar amount?

Economists use three approaches to compute GDP: the expenditure approach, the income approach, and the value-added approach. The following paragraphs describe each approach in terms of our simple economy.

EXPENDITURE APPROACH To compute GDP using the expenditure approach, add the amount of money spent by buyers on *final goods and services*. The words "final goods and services" are important in computing GDP because not all goods are final goods. Some goods are *intermediate goods.*

Final Good
A good in the hands of its final user.

A **final good** (or service) is a good in the hands of the final user, or ultimate consumer. Think of buyers standing in line one after another. The first buyer in our simple economy was Jim. He bought oranges from Bob. The second buyer was Caroline, who bought orange juice from Jim.

Caroline is the final buyer in this economy; she is the final user, the ultimate consumer. No buyer comes after her. The good that she buys is the final good. In other words, the orange juice is the final good.

So, then, what are the oranges? Aren't they a final good too? No. The oranges are an *intermediate good*. An **intermediate good** is an input in the production of a final good. In other words, the oranges were used to produce orange juice (the final good).

Intermediate Good
A good that is an input in the production of a final good.

So, what does GDP equal if we use the expenditure approach to compute it? Again, it is the dollar amount spent by buyers for *final* goods and services. In our simple economy, there is only one buyer (Caroline), who spends $10 on one final good (orange juice). Thus, GDP in our tiny economy is $10.

You may be wondering why expenditures on only final goods are counted when computing GDP. The reason is because we would be *double counting* if we counted expenditures on both final goods *and* intermediate goods. **Double counting** refers to counting a good more than once when computing GDP. To illustrate, if we count both Caroline's purchase of the orange juice ($10) and Jim's purchase of the oranges ($8), we count the purchase of the oranges *twice*—once when the oranges are purchased by Jim and once when the oranges are in the orange juice.

Double Counting
Counting a good more than once when computing GDP.

INCOME APPROACH In our simple economy, income consists of wages and profits.[1] To compute GDP using the income approach, simply find the sum of all the wages and profits.

First, Harry earns $5 in wages.

Second, Bob's profit is $3: (1) Bob pays $5 to Harry, so the $5 is a cost to Bob; (2) Bob receives $8 for the oranges he sells to Jim; (3) $8 in revenue minus $5 in costs leaves Bob with $3 profit.

Third, Jim's profit is $2: (1) Jim pays $8 to Bob for the oranges, so the $8 is a cost to Jim; (2) Jim receives $10 for the orange juice he sells to Caroline; (3) $10 in revenue minus $8 in costs leaves Jim with $2 profit.

In our simple economy, the sum of Harry's wages, Bob's profit, and Jim's profit is $10. So GDP is equal to $10.

VALUE-ADDED APPROACH In our tiny economy, orange juice is sold for, or has a market value of, $10. How much of the $10 market value is attributable to Jim? Stated differently, how much of the $10 market value is *value added* by Jim? If your intuition tells you $2, then your intuition is correct. **Value added** is the dollar value contributed to a final good at each stage of production. That is, it is the difference between the dollar value of the output the producer sells and the dollar value of the intermediate goods the producer buys.

To compute GDP using the value-added approach, find the sum of the values added at all the stages of production. Bob buys no intermediate goods (he simply found a seed, planted it, and then hired Harry to pick and box oranges), but he sells the oranges to Jim for $8. In other words, valued added at this stage of production is $8.

Jim takes the oranges (an intermediate good he buys from Bob for $8) and turns them into orange juice that he sells to Caroline for $10. Value added at this stage of production is $2.

The sum of the values added at all (two) stages of production is $10, so GDP is equal to $10.

What GDP Omits

Some exchanges that take place in an economy are not included in GDP. As the following paragraphs indicate, these trades range from sales of used cars to illegal drug deals.

CERTAIN NONMARKET GOODS AND SERVICES If a family hires a person through the classified section of the newspaper to cook and clean, the service is counted in GDP. If family members perform the same tasks, however, their services are not counted in GDP. The difference is that, in the first case, a service is actually bought and sold for a price in a market setting, and in the other case, it is not.

Some nonmarket goods are included in GDP. For example, the market value of food produced on a farm and consumed by the farm family is estimated, and this imputed value is part of GDP.

---

[1]Later in the chapter, you will learn that in a large economy, such as the U.S. economy, income consists of more than wages and profits. To simplify the explanation, we have defined a tiny economy where only wages and profits exist.

Q&A *Could you give another example to illustrate the concept of double counting?*

Consider some of the intermediate goods used to make this book: glue, ink, and paper. In one sense, a book is simply another name for glue, ink, and paper together. In equation form, book = glue + ink + paper. Now, when computing GDP, if we count the purchase of the book and the purchases of glue, ink, and paper, we are counting what is on the left side of the equal sign in the equation (i.e., the book) and then adding it to what is on the right side of the equal sign in the equation (i.e., glue + ink + paper). That would be like saying 2 = 1 + 1, and counting both the 2 and the 1 + 1 to give a total of 4. Counting the 2 is enough; adding the 2 and the 1 + 1 is double counting.

Value Added
The dollar value contributed to a final good at each stage of production.

Q&A *You've defined GDP and said that there are three different approaches to computing it. No matter which approach we use—expenditure, income, or value-added—we get the same dollar amount. This much I understand. What I don't understand is how three fundamentally different approaches can give you the same dollar amount.*

Sometimes, different approaches are simply different ways of looking at the same thing. To illustrate, consider $10 that you spend for a book. Looking at things from your perspective, the $10 is an expenditure. *But consider it from the perspective of the bookseller. For her, the $10 is* income. *In short, what is an expenditure to one person is income to another person. Whether we measure income or expenditures, we get the same dollar amount.*

It is the same with computing GDP. The different approaches to computing GDP are simply different perspectives of looking at the same thing.

exhibit **1**

Size of the Underground Economy

Here we identify the size of the underground economy as a percentage of GDP for various countries in 2003.

Source: "Shadow Economies Around the World: What Do We Really Know?" Frederich Schneider, July 2004.

Country	Size of Underground Economy as Percentage of GDP
Australia	13.8%
Canada	15.4
France	14.8
Germany	16.8
Greece	28.3
Ireland	15.5
Italy	26.2
Japan	11.0
Norway	18.7
Spain	22.3
United States	8.6

Transfer Payment

A payment to a person that is not made in return for goods and services currently supplied.

exhibit **2**

GDP and Per Capita GDP, Selected Countries, 2005

Source: CIA World Factbook, 2006.

Country	GDP (billions)	Per capita GDP
Austria	$268	$32,700
China	8,859	6,800
Cuba	39	3,500
France	1,816	29,900
Germany	2,504	30,400
Mexico	1,066	10,000
Russia	1,589	11,100
United Kingdom	1,830	30,300
United States	12,360	41,800

UNDERGROUND ACTIVITIES, BOTH LEGAL AND ILLEGAL The underground economy consists of unreported exchanges that take place outside the normal recorded market channels. Some underground activities involve illegal goods (e.g., cocaine), and others involve legal goods and tax evasion.

Illegal goods and services are not counted in GDP because no record exists of such transactions. There are no written records of illegal drug sales, illegal gambling, and illegal prostitution. Nor are there written records of some legal activities that individuals want to keep from government notice. For example, a gardener might agree to do some gardening work only on the condition that he is paid in cash. Obviously, it is not illegal for a person to buy or sell gardening services, but still, the transaction might not be recorded if one or both parties do not want it to be. Why might the gardener want to be paid in cash? Perhaps he doesn't want to pay taxes on the income received—an objective more easily accomplished if there is no written record of the income being generated.

In Exhibit 1, we show the size of the underground economy as a percentage of GDP for various countries in 2003.

SALES OF USED GOODS GDP measures *current production* (i.e., occurring during the current year). A used car sale, for example, does not enter into the current-year statistics because the car was counted when it was originally produced.

FINANCIAL TRANSACTIONS The trading of stocks and bonds is not counted in GDP because it does not represent the production of new assets. It is simply the trading of existing assets (the exchange of stocks or bonds for money).

GOVERNMENT TRANSFER PAYMENTS A **transfer payment** is a payment to a person that is not made in return for goods and services currently supplied. Government transfer payments—such as Social Security benefits and veterans' benefits—are not counted in GDP because they do not represent payments to individuals for *current production*.

LEISURE Leisure is a good in much the same way that cars, houses, and shoes are goods. New cars, houses, and shoes are counted in GDP, but leisure is not because it is too difficult to quantify. The length of the workweek has fallen in the United States over the past years, indicating that the leisure time individuals have to consume has increased. But GDP computations do not take leisure into account.

GDP Is Not Adjusted for Bads Generated in the Production of Goods

Economic growth often comes with certain *bads*. For example, producing cars, furniture, and steel often generates air and water pollution—considered bads by most people. (Remember from Chapter 1 that a bad is anything from which individuals receive disutility.) GDP counts the goods and services, but it does not net out the air and water pollution. Thus, some economists argue that GDP overstates our overall economic welfare.

Per Capita GDP

If we divide a country's GDP by the population in the country, we get *per capita GDP*. For example, if a country has a GDP of $5 trillion and its population is 200 million, GDP per capita is $25,000. Exhibit 2 shows the GDP (in billions of dollars) and per capita GDP (in dollars) for various countries in 2005.

Is Either GDP or Per Capita GDP a Measure of Happiness or Well-Being?

Are the people in a country with a higher GDP or higher per capita GDP better off or happier than the people in a country with a lower GDP or lower per capita GDP? We

© IMAGE100/JUPITER IMAGES

economics 24/7

HAPPINESS AND THE ECONOMIST

In one survey, students at Harvard University were asked whether they would prefer (a) $50,000 a year while others got $25,000 a year or (b) $100,000 a year while others got $200,000 a year.

A majority of the students chose (a). In other words, they chose a lower absolute income but a higher relative income. They chose to be poorer in absolute terms, as long as they could be richer in relative terms.

Sometimes, researchers conclude from such a survey that an increase in one's absolute standard of living (say, as measured by per capita GDP) does not matter as much to happiness as a rise in one's relative standard of living (say, as measured by moving up from being "poor" to being "middle income" or from being "middle income" to being "rich"). In short, what matters is not so much how we are doing but how we are doing *relative to everyone else*.

Now the real question is whether or not survey results—such as the Harvard University student survey—are meaningful. For example, let's ask ourselves what we would observe if people care more about their relative standing than their absolute standing. Some economists have suggested that we would see more affluent people moving into poorer neighborhoods so that they could experience higher relative incomes. They go on to say that since we don't see this very often, it follows that individuals do not care about their relative income as much as the survey results suggest. As to something we would not see if people cared about their relative incomes, we would not see poor immigrants coming to a rich country; after all, when poor immigrants come to a rich country, they know they will be near the bottom of the income scale. Yet, they still come. Why? Perhaps it is because they enjoy a higher absolute income in the rich country than they would in the country they leave.

What can we learn about economists here? One key thing is economists don't always trust survey results—or what people say when answering certain questions. For economists, if we want to know something about people's preferences, we should observe how they act instead of noting what they say.

cannot answer that question because well-being and happiness are subjective. A person with more goods may be happier than a person with fewer goods, but possibly not. The person with fewer goods but a lot of leisure, little air pollution, and a relaxed way of life may be much happier than the person with many goods, little leisure, and a polluted, stressful environment.

We make this point to warn against reading too much into GDP figures. GDP figures are useful for obtaining an estimate of the productive capabilities of an economy, but they do not necessarily measure happiness or well-being.

> **Q&A** *Is it possible for a country to have a relatively large GDP but a relatively small per capita GDP?*
>
> *Yes. For example, look at Austria and China in Exhibit 2. Austria's GDP is much smaller than China's, but its per capita GDP is much larger.*

SELF-TEST

(Answers to Self-Test questions are in the Self-Test Appendix.)

1. Identify and explain the three approaches to computing GDP.

2. Suppose the GDP for a country is $0. Does this mean that there was no productive activity in the country? Explain your answer.

The Expenditure Approach to Computing GDP for a Real-World Economy

The last section explains the expenditure, income, and value-added approaches to computing GDP for a simple economy. This simple economy consisted of one person producing oranges, one person producing orange juice, and one person buying orange juice. Obviously, the U.S. economy is much more complex than this tiny economy is.

This section explains how the expenditure approach is used to compute GDP in a real-world economy like the U.S. economy. The next section explains how the income approach is used.

Expenditures in a Real-World Economy

Economists often talk about four sectors of the economy: (1) household sector, (2) business sector, (3) government sector, and (4) foreign sector. Economic actors in these sectors buy goods and services; in other words, they spend. The expenditures of the sectors are called, respectively, (1) *consumption;* (2) gross private domestic investment, or simply *investment;* (3) government consumption expenditures and gross investment, or simply *government purchases;* and (4) *net exports.*

CONSUMPTION **Consumption** *(C)* includes (1) spending on durable goods, (2) spending on nondurable goods, and (3) spending on services. Durable goods are goods that are expected to last for more than three years, such as refrigerators, ovens, or cars. Nondurable goods are goods that are not expected to last for more than three years, such as food. Services are intangible items such as lawn care, car repair, and entertainment. Consumption expenditures in the United States usually account for 70 percent of GDP. In short, consumption is the largest spending component of GDP.

INVESTMENT **Investment** *(I)* is the sum of (1) the purchases of newly produced capital goods, (2) changes in business inventories, sometimes referred to as **inventory investment**, and (3) the purchases of new residential housing.[2] The sum of the purchases of newly produced capital goods and the purchases of new residential housing is often referred to as **fixed investment**. In other words, investment = fixed investment + inventory investment. Fixed investment is the larger of the two components of investment.

GOVERNMENT PURCHASES **Government purchases** (G) include federal, state, and local government purchases of goods and services and gross investment in highways, bridges, and so on. **Government transfer payments**, which are payments to persons that are not made in return for goods and services currently supplied, are not included in government purchases. Social Security benefits and welfare payments are two examples of transfer payments; neither is a payment for current productive efforts.

NET EXPORTS People, firms, and governments in the United States sometimes purchase foreign-produced goods. These purchases are referred to as **imports** *(IM)*. Foreign residents, firms, and governments sometimes purchase U.S.-produced goods. These purchases are referred to as **exports** *(EX)*. If imports are subtracted from exports, we are left with **net exports** *(NX)*.

$$NX = EX - IM$$

---

[2]For purposes of computing GDP, the purchases of new residential housing (although undertaken by members of the household sector) are considered investment.

Consumption

The sum of spending on durable goods, nondurable goods, and services.

Investment

The sum of all purchases of newly produced capital goods, changes in business inventories, and purchases of new residential housing.

Inventory Investment

Changes in the stock of unsold goods.

Fixed Investment

Business purchases of capital goods, such as machinery and factories, and purchases of new residential housing.

Government Purchases

Federal, state, and local government purchases of goods and services and gross investment in highways, bridges, and so on.

Government Transfer Payments

Payments to persons that are not made in return for goods and services currently supplied.

Imports

Total domestic (U.S.) spending on foreign goods.

Exports

Total foreign spending on domestic (U.S.) goods.

Net Exports

Exports minus imports.

economics 24/7

GDP: PROCEED WITH CAUTION

Some people seem drawn to make incorrect comparisons between countries based on GDP figures. For example, a person might notice that Austria's GDP ($268 billion) is smaller than Germany's GDP ($2,504 billion) and conclude that Austrians are not as well off as Germans.

First, we would expect a country with a smaller population to have a smaller GDP than a country with a larger population. With fewer people, there is usually less output produced. Austria has a population of 8 million, whereas Germany has a population of 82 million. In other words, Germany has over 10 times the population of Austria, so we would expect it to have a higher GDP.

What we have said for GDP also holds for gross state product (GSP). For example, just as a country has a GDP, each state in the United States has a gross state product. The state with the largest GSP in 2004 was California with a GSP of $1.55 trillion. This is larger than the GDP of many countries, but then, California has a population greater than many countries.

Also, as we noted earlier in the chapter, it is not GDP (or GSP) that matters as much as it is per capita GDP (or per capita GSP). If you notice from Exhibit 2, Austria has a higher per capita GDP ($32,700) than does Germany ($30,400).

But even per capita GDP can be deceiving. When an economist states that the per capita GDP of, say, Austria, is $32,700, this is the dollar amount each person in Austria would have *if* the GDP of the country were divided up equally by the entire population—in other words, if everyone in the country had an equal slice of GDP.

But in actuality, not everyone in the country has an equal slice of GDP. Some people have a much smaller slice than other people. While one person may have a slice equal to $400,000, another person might have a slice equal to $7,000.

Finally, keep in mind the two ways we can witness an increase in GDP. GDP will rise if the inhabitants of a country actually produce more goods and services, and it will rise if output remains constant but only prices rise. A rise in GDP that is the result of only prices rising does not mean the same thing as a rise in GDP that is the result of prices remaining constant and output rising. Obviously, it means more to the overall standard of living of the people in the country if GDP rises because output is higher than because prices are higher.

The bottom line is that GDP is a useful economic variable, and it is readily measured and reported on. But we need to be careful that we don't use it incorrectly when making comparisons, discussing well-being, and so on.

Obviously, net exports (NX) can be positive or negative. If exports are greater than imports, then NX is positive; if imports are greater than exports, then NX is negative.

Computing GDP Using the Expenditure Approach

The expenditure approach to computing GDP sums the purchases of final goods and services made by the four sectors of the economy (see Exhibit 3). This may give you reason to pause because our earlier definition of GDP did not mention *purchases* of final goods and services. Rather, we defined GDP as the total market value of all final goods and services *produced* annually within a nation's borders.

The discrepancy is cleared up quickly when we note that national income accountants (persons who compute GDP for the government) assume that anything produced but not sold to consumers is "bought" by the firm that produced it. In other words, if a car is produced but not sold, it goes into business inventory and is consider "purchased"

Q&A   *What percentage of GDP was each of the components of GDP in 2005.*

In 2005, consumption was 70.4 percent of GDP, investment was 16.6 percent, government purchases were 18.9 percent, and net exports were –5.9 percent.

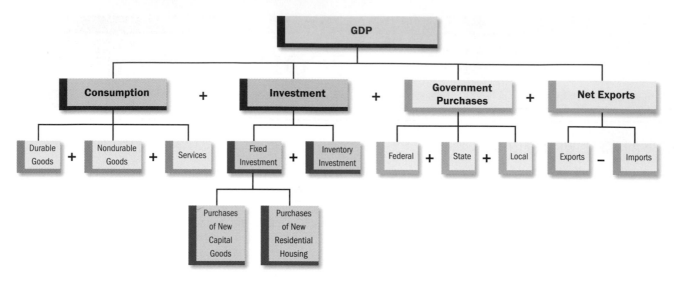

exhibit 3

The Expenditure Approach to Computing GDP

The expenditure components of GDP are consumption, investment, government purchases, and net exports. The exhibit shows what is included in each of these components.

by the firm that produced it. Thus, we can compute GDP by summing the purchases made by the four sectors of the economy. GDP equals consumption *(C)* plus investment *(I)* plus government purchases *(G)* plus net exports *(EX − IM)*.

$$GDP = C + I + G + (EX - IM)$$

Exhibit 4 shows the dollar amounts of the four components of GDP for the United States in 2006.

The Income Approach to Computing GDP for a Real-World Economy

Now let's look at how the income approach is used to compute GDP for a real-world economy. The two approaches should give us the same dollar figure for GDP. (Remember our simple orange juice economy?) Exhibit 5—a circular flow diagram of the economy—shows that in a simple economy, GDP computed by summing the purchases of the four sectors of the economy is equal to GDP computed by summing the income earned by the different resources. In other words, dollar purchases (or dollar expenditures) equal dollar income. Think of it in terms of a tiny

Q&A

Is there such a thing as a World GDP? If so, how much is it?

In 2005, the World GDP was $61 trillion.

exhibit 4

Components of GDP (Expenditure Approach)

The expenditure approach to computing GDP sums the purchase made by final users of goods and services. The expenditure components include consumption, investment, government purchases, and net exports. The data are for 2006.

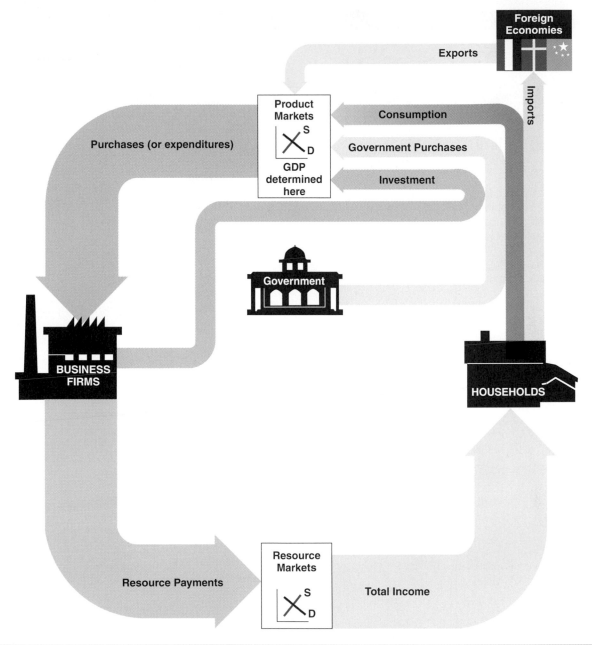

exhibit 5

The Circular Flow: Total Purchases (Expenditures) Equal Total Income in a Simple Economy

The exhibit shows an economy with four sectors: Households, Business Firms, Government, and Foreign Economies. Each sector purchases goods and services. The sum of these purchases is GDP [GDP = $C + I + G + (EX - IM)$].

The purchases (expenditures) made in product markets flow to business firms. Business firms then use these monies to buy resources in resource markets. In other words, these monies flow to the owners (suppliers) of land, labor, capital, and entrepreneurship. The sum of these resource payments is total income, which flows to households. In this simple economy, where some things have been ignored, total purchases (expenditures) equal total income. Because total purchases (expenditures) equal GDP and total purchases equal total income, it follows that GDP equals total income.

economy where one person buys 10 oranges for $1 each. His expenditures equal $10. But the $10 also represent income for the person who sold the buyer the oranges. An expenditure for one person is income for another.

economics 24/7

PER CAPITA GDP IN 1820

Most people are interested in knowing what the per capita GDP is today in different countries. Something else that is interesting, too, is the per capita GDP in different countries over the years. For example, wonder what country had the highest per capita GDP in, say, 1820? The answer is the Netherlands. What about 1900? That would be New Zealand. In the three tables in the exhibit, we identify the top 10 countries in various years in terms of per capita GDP.

1820

Rank	Country	Per capita GDP
1	Netherlands	$1,561
2	Australia	$1,528
3	Austria	$1,295
4	Belgium	$1,291
5	United States	$1,287
6	Denmark	$1,225
7	France	$1,218
8	Sweden	$1,198
9	Germany	$1,112
10	Italy	$1,092

1900

Rank	Country	Per capita GDP
1	New Zealand	$4,320
2	Australia	$4,299
3	United States	$4,096
4	Belgium	$3,652
5	Netherlands	$3,533
6	Switzerland	$3,531
7	Germany	$3,134
8	Denmark	$2,902
9	Austria	$2,901
10	France	$2,849

1950

Rank	Country	Per capita GDP
1	United States	$9,573
2	Switzerland	$8,939
3	New Zealand	$8,495
4	Venezuela	$7,424
5	Australia	$7,218
6	Canada	$7,047
7	Sweden	$6,738
8	Denmark	$6,683
9	Netherlands	$5,850
10	Belgium	$5,346

exhibit **6**

There are two steps involved in computing GDP using the income approach. First, we must compute national income. Second, we must adjust national income for certain things. The end result is GDP.

Computing National Income

National income is the sum of five components: (1) compensation of employees, (2) proprietors' income, (3) corporate profits, (4) rental income of persons, and (5) net interest. We discuss the details of each in the following paragraphs.

COMPENSATION OF EMPLOYEES Compensation of employees consists of wages and salaries paid to employees plus employers' contributions to Social Security and employee benefit plans plus the monetary value of fringe benefits, tips, and paid vacations. Compensation of employees is the largest component of national income. In 2006, compensation of employees in the United States was $7.4 trillion.

PROPRIETORS' INCOME Proprietors' income includes all forms of income earned by self-employed individuals and the owners of unincorporated businesses, including unincorporated farmers. Included in farm income is an estimate of the value of the food grown and consumed on farms.

CORPORATE PROFITS Corporate profits include all the income earned by the stockholders of corporations. Some of the profits are paid to stockholders in the form of dividends, some are kept within the firm to finance investments (these are called *undistributed profits* or *retained earnings*), and some are used to pay corporate profits taxes. (The portion of corporate profits used to pay corporate profits taxes is counted as income "earned" by households even though households do not receive the income.)

RENTAL INCOME (OF PERSONS) Rental income is the income received by individuals for the use of their nonmonetary assets (land, houses, offices). It also includes returns to individuals who hold copyrights and patents. Finally, it includes an imputed value to owner-occupied houses. For example, someone may own the house she lives in, and therefore not pay any rent, but for purposes of national income accounting, a rental value is imputed. In short, home ownership is viewed as a business that produces a service that is sold to the owner of the business.

NET INTEREST Net interest is the interest income received by U.S. households and government minus the interest they paid out.

NATIONAL INCOME We can summarize national income and its components as follows:

National income = Compensation of employees
+ Proprietors' income
+ Corporate profits
+ Rental income
+ Net interest

In 2006, national income in the United States was $11.5 trillion.

From National Income to GDP: Making Some Adjustments

After computing national income, you might think that there is nothing else to do—that national income should equal GDP. That's because we naturally think that every dollar spent is someone's income.

National Income

Total income earned by U.S. citizens and businesses, no matter where they reside or are located. National income is the sum of the payments to resources (land, labor, capital, and entrepreneurship). National income = compensation of employees + proprietors' income + corporate profits + rental income of persons + net interest.

But when we check the actual figures for national income and GDP, we find that they are not equal. In other words, not every dollar spent is someone else's income. For example, if Jones spends $10 to buy a book, $9.50 of the $10 might end up in the seller's pocket as income, but 50 cents of the $10 might go for taxes.

With this in mind, the income approach to computing GDP requires us to add certain things to national income and to subtract certain things from national income. The following equation and Exhibit 7 shows what must be added to and subtracted from national income to compute GDP. Keep the equation and exhibit in mind as you continue to read.

$$
\begin{aligned}
\text{GDP} = \ & \text{National income} \\
& - \text{Income earned from the rest of the world} \\
& + \text{Income earned by the rest of the world} \\
& + \text{Indirect business taxes} \\
& + \text{Capital consumption allowance} \\
& + \text{Statistical discrepancy}
\end{aligned}
$$

INCOME EARNED FROM THE REST OF THE WORLD, INCOME EARNED BY THE REST OF THE WORLD Consider that when we compute national income, we include the income earned by U.S. citizens who work and live in other countries, but we do not include the income earned by foreigners who work and live in the United States. If we want to compute GDP, we have to adjust for both these incomes. We do so by (1) subtracting from national income the income earned from the rest of the world (this is income U.S. citizens living abroad earned by producing and selling goods) and (2) adding to national income the income earned by the rest of the world (this is income non-U.S. citizens earned by producing and selling goods in the United States).

INDIRECT BUSINESS TAXES The main items that comprise indirect business taxes are excise taxes, sales taxes, and property taxes. These taxes are not part of national income because they are not considered a payment to any resource (land, labor, etc.). You should think of them as "monies collected by government" and not as payment to land, labor, capital, or entrepreneurship.

These indirect taxes are included in purchases of goods and services (you pay a sales tax when you buy most goods) and so are included when the expenditure approach is used to compute GDP. Therefore, we must add indirect business taxes to national income.

exhibit **7**

The Income Approach to Computing GDP

The exhibit identifies the components of national income and the adjustments necessary to compute GDP using the income approach.

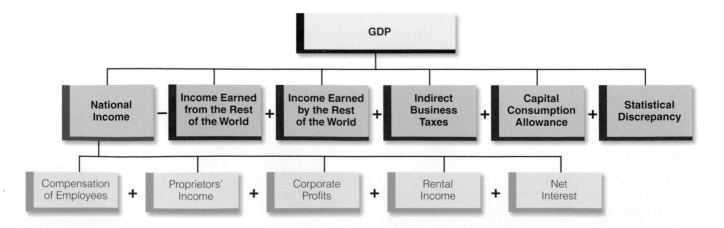

CAPITAL CONSUMPTION ALLOWANCE Some capital goods are used up in the production process through natural wear, obsolescence, or accidental destruction (e.g., the machinery that breaks down and cannot be repaired). The cost to replace these capital goods is called the **capital consumption allowance**, or **depreciation**. We add the capital consumption allowance, or depreciation, to national income because we want a measure of all the income earned in the economy. National income, by itself, doesn't include the income payments implicit in the capital consumption allowance.

Capital Consumption Allowance (Depreciation)
The estimated amount of capital goods used up in production through natural wear, obsolescence, and accidental destruction.

STATISTICAL DISCREPANCY GDP and national income are computed using different sets of data. Hence, statistical discrepancies or pure computational errors often occur and must be accounted for in the national income accounts.

Other National Income Accounting Measurements

Besides gross domestic product (GDP) and national income, three other national income accounting measurements are important. They are net domestic product, personal income, and disposable income. The five measurements—gross domestic product, national income, net domestic product, personal income, and disposable income—are often used interchangeably to measure the output produced and income earned in an economy.

Net Domestic Product

If we use the expenditure approach to compute GDP, we add consumption, investment, government purchases, and net exports. Investment (or more specifically, gross private domestic investment) includes fixed investment and inventory investment. Some of the fixed investment, however, is used to replace worn-out or obsolete capital goods. It is not used for the production of new goods. In short, gross private domestic investment contains within it the capital consumption allowance. If we subtract the capital consumption allowance from GDP, we are left with **net domestic product (NDP)**. NDP measures the total value of new goods available in the economy in a given year after worn-out capital goods have been replaced.

Net Domestic Product (NDP)
GDP minus the capital consumption allowance.

Net domestic product (NDP) = GDP – Capital consumption allowance

Personal Income

Not all income earned is received, and not all income received is earned. An example of "income earned but not received" is undistributed profits. Undistributed profits are earned by stockholders but not received by them. Instead, the undistributed profits are usually reinvested by the corporation. An example of "income received but not earned" is Social Security benefits.

Personal income is the amount of income that individuals actually receive. It is equal to national income minus such major earned-but-not-received items as undistributed corporate profits, social insurance taxes (Social Security contributions), and corporate profits taxes, plus transfer payments (which are received but not earned).

Personal Income
The amount of income that individuals actually receive. It is equal to national income minus undistributed corporate profits, social insurance taxes, and corporate profits taxes, plus transfer payments.

Personal income = National income
− Undistributed corporate profits
− Social insurance taxes
− Corporate profits taxes
+ Transfer payments

In 2006, personal income in the United States was approximately $10.8 trillion.

Disposable Income

The portion of personal income that can be used for consumption or saving is referred to as disposable personal income or simply **disposable income**. It is equal to personal income minus personal taxes (especially income taxes). Sometimes, disposable income is referred to as spendable income, take-home pay, or after-tax income.

Disposable income = Personal income – Personal taxes

In 2006, disposable income in the United States was approximately $9.4 trillion.

SELF-TEST

1. Describe the expenditure approach to computing GDP in a real-world economy.

2. Will GDP be smaller than the sum of consumption, investment, and government purchases if net exports are negative? Explain your answer.

3. If GDP is $400 billion and the country's population is 100 million, does it follow that each individual in the country has $40,000 worth of goods and services?

Real GDP

This section defines Real GDP, shows how to compute it, and then explains how it is used to measure economic growth.

Why We Need Real GDP

In 2002, U.S. GDP was about $10.5 trillion. One year later, in 2003, GDP was about $11.0 trillion. Although you know GDP was higher in 2003 than in 2002, do you know *the reason* GDP was higher in 2003 than in 2002?

As you think about your answer, let's look at GDP in a one-good economy. Suppose 10 units of this good are produced and each unit is sold for $10, so GDP in the economy is $100.

GDP = $10 × 10 units = $100

Now suppose GDP rises from $100 to $250. What caused it to rise? It could rise because price increased from $10 to $25:

GDP = $25 × 10 units = $250

Or it could rise because quantity of output produced increased from 10 units to 25 units:

GDP = $10 × 25 units = $250

Or it could rise because price increased to $12.50 and quantity increased to 20 units:

GDP = $12.50 × 20 units = $250

To gauge the health of the economy, economists want to know the *reason* for an increase in GDP. If GDP increased simply because price increased, then the economy is not growing. For an economy to grow, more output must be produced.

Because an increase in GDP can be due in part simply to an increase in price, a more meaningful measure is Real GDP. **Real GDP** is GDP adjusted for price changes.

Computing Real GDP

One way to compute Real GDP is to find the value of the output for the different years in terms of the same prices, the prices that existed in the base year. Let's look again at our one-good economy. Consider the following data.

Year	Price of Good X	Quantity Produced of Good X (units)	GDP
1	$10	100	$10 × 100 = **$1,000**
2	$12	120	$12 × 120 = **$1,440**
3	$14	140	$14 × 140 = **$1,960**

The data show *why* GDP is higher in subsequent years: GDP is higher because both price and quantity have increased. In other words, GDP rises because both price *and* quantity rise. Suppose we want to separate the part of GDP that is higher because quantity is higher from the part of GDP that is higher because price is higher. What we want then is Real GDP because Real GDP is the part of GDP that is higher because quantity (of output) is higher.

To compute Real GDP for any year, we simply multiply the quantity of the good produced in a given year by the price in the base year. Suppose we choose year 1 as the base year. So, to compute Real GDP in year 2, we simply multiply the quantity of the good produced in year 2 by the price of the good in year 1. To find Real GDP in year 3, we simply multiply the quantity of the good produced in year 3 by the price of the good in year 1.

Year	Price of Good X	Quantity Produced of Good X (units)	GDP	Real GDP
1 (Base Year)	$10	100	$10 × 100 = **$1,000**	$10 × 100 = **$1,000**
2	$12	120	$12 × 120 = **$1,440**	$10 × 120 = **$1,200**
3	$14	140	$14 × 140 = **$1,960**	$10 × 140 = **$1,400**

The General Equation for Real GDP

In the real world, there is more than one good and more than one price. The general equation used to compute Real GDP is:

$$\text{Real GDP} = \Sigma \,(\text{Base-year prices} \times \text{Current-year quantities})$$

Σ is the Greek capital letter *sigma*. Here it stands for *summation*. Thus, Real GDP is "the sum of all the current-year quantities times their base-year prices." In 2006, Real GDP in the United States was $11.4 trillion.

What Does It Mean If Real GDP Is Higher in One Year Than in Another Year?

If GDP is, say, $9 trillion in year 1 and $9.5 trillion in year 2, we cannot be sure why it has increased. Obviously, GDP can rise from one year to the next if (1) prices rise and output remains constant; (2) output rises and prices remain constant; or (3) prices and output rise.

However, if Real GDP is, say, $8 trillion in year 1 and $8.3 trillion in year 2, we *know* why it has increased. Real GDP rises only if output rises. In other words, Real GDP rises only if more goods and services are produced.

Real GDP, Economic Growth, and Business Cycles

Suppose there are two countries, *A* and *B*. In country *A*, Real GDP grows by 3 percent each year. In country *B*, Real GDP is the same each year: If Real GDP was $500 billion last year, it is $500 billion in the current year, and it will be $500 billion next year. In which of the two countries would you prefer to live, *ceteris paribus*?

Now consider another situation. Again suppose there are two countries, *C* and *D*. In country *C*, Real GDP takes a roller coaster ride: It alternates between rising and falling. It rises for some months, then falls, then rises again, then falls, and so on. In country *D*, Real GDP simply rises year after year. In which of the two countries would you prefer to live, *ceteris paribus*?

If you chose one country over the other in each of these two cases, then you are implicitly saying that Real GDP matters to you. One of the reasons economists study Real GDP is simply because Real GDP matters to you and others. In other words, because Real GDP is important to you, it is important to economists too.

Economists study two major macroeconomic topics that have to do with Real GDP. One topic is *economic growth;* the other is *business cycles.*

Economic Growth
Increases in Real GDP.

ECONOMIC GROWTH Annual **economic growth** has occurred if Real GDP in one year is higher than Real GDP in the previous year. For example, if Real GDP is $8.1 trillion in one year and $8.3 trillion in the next, the economy has witnessed economic growth. The growth rate is equal to the (positive) percentage change in Real GDP. The growth rate is computed using the following formula:

$$\text{Percentage change in Real GDP} = \left(\frac{\text{Real GDP}_{\text{later year}} - \text{Real GDP}_{\text{earlier year}}}{\text{Real GDP}_{\text{earlier year}}} \right) \times 100$$

Business Cycle
Recurrent swings (up and down) in Real GDP.

THE "UPS AND DOWNS" IN THE ECONOMY, OR THE BUSINESS CYCLE If Real GDP is on a roller coaster—rising and falling and rising and falling—the economy is said to be incurring a **business cycle**. Economists usually talk about four or five phases of the business cycle. We identify five phases in the following list and in Exhibit 8.

---

exhibit **8**

The Phases of the Business Cycle

The phases of a business cycle include the peak, contraction, trough, recovery, and expansion. A business cycle is measured from peak to peak.

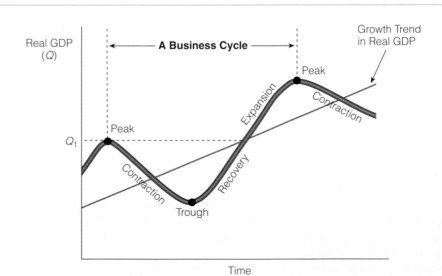

1. **Peak.** At the *peak* of the business cycle, Real GDP is at a temporary high. In Exhibit 8, Real GDP is at a temporary high at Q_1.

2. **Contraction.** The *contraction* phase represents a decline in Real GDP. According to the standard definition of *recession,* two consecutive quarter declines in Real GDP constitute a recession.

3. **Trough.** The low point in Real GDP, just before it begins to turn up, is called the *trough* of the business cycle.

4. **Recovery.** The *recovery* is the period when Real GDP is rising. It begins at the trough and ends at the initial peak. The recovery in Exhibit 7 extends from the trough until Real GDP is again at Q_1.

5. **Expansion.** The *expansion* phase refers to increases in Real GDP beyond the recovery. In Exhibit 8, it refers to increases in Real GDP above Q_1.

An entire business cycle is measured from peak to peak. The typical business cycle is approximately 4 to 5 years, although a few have been shorter and some have been longer.

NBER AND RECESSIONS In the contraction stage of the business cycle, we state that the "standard" definition of a recession is two consecutive quarter declines in Real GDP. This is not, however, the only definition of a recession.

On November 26, 2001, the National Bureau of Economic Research, which dates the business cycle, issued a press release. The first paragraph read:

 How many business cycles have there been in the United States?

According to the National Bureau of Economic Research, there have been 32 business cycles during the period 1854–2001.

> The NBER's Business Cycle Dating Committee has determined that a peak in business activity occurred in the U.S. economy in March 2001. A peak marks the end of an expansion and the beginning of a recession. The determination of a peak date in March is thus a determination that the expansion that began in March 1991 ended in March 2001 and a recession began. The expansion lasted exactly 10 years, the longest in the NBER's chronology.

According to this statement, the U.S. economy entered a recession in March 2001. That's because according to the NBER "a peak marks the end of an expansion and the beginning of a recession," and March 2001 was dated by the NBER as the peak of the business cycle. In other words, the U.S. economy was in a recession even though Real GDP had not declined for two consecutive quarters.

The NBER definition is different from the standard definition of a recession. According to the NBER, "a recession is a significant decline in activity spread across the economy, lasting more than a few months, visible in industrial production, employment, real income, and wholesale-retail trade."

macro Theme   In the last chapter, we identified three macroeconomic categories, one of which was the P-Q category. The P, you may remember, stands for the price level, and the Q stands for Real GDP. In the last chapter, we discussed how to measure the price level, P. In this chapter, we have discussed how to measure GDP and Real GDP, and we have discussed economic growth and the business cycle. Everything we have discussed in this chapter can be translated into P-Q language and placed in the P-Q category. For example, GDP is really P times Q. Real GDP is Q. Economic growth is increasing Q, and the business cycle is recurrent swings up and down in Q.

SELF-TEST

1. Suppose GDP is $6 trillion in year 1 and $6.2 trillion in year 2. What has caused the rise in GDP?

2. Suppose Real GDP is $5.2 trillion in year 1 and $5.3 trillion in year 2. What has caused the rise in Real GDP?

3. Can an economy be faced with endless business cycles and still have its Real GDP grow over time? Explain your answer.

A Reader Asks...

Where Can I Find the Most Recent Economic Data?

I've been learning about the CPI, GDP, the components of GDP, national income, and so on. Where can I find the recent data on these economic variables and others?

Your best bet for finding recent economic data is the Internet. The Economic Report of the President Web site at http://www.gpoaccess.gov/eop/index.html/ is a good place to start. Once at the site, click "Downloadable Reports/Tables" and then on the most recent year under "Statistical Tables."

Another good Web site you may want to visit is Economagic.com at http://www.economagic.com/. If you click the "Most Requested Series" link at this site, you will find data on prices, GDP, Real GDP, and so on.

If you are interested in business cycle data, go to the National Bureau of Economic Research Web site at http://www.nber.org/, click "Data," and then "Business Cycle Dates."

Finally, here is a short list of other Websites where you can find economic data:

- Economics Statistics Briefing Room at http://www.whitehouse.gov/fsbr/esbr.html
- Bureau of Economic Analysis at http://www.bea.gov/
- Bureau of Labor Statistics at http://stats.bls.gov/
- Congressional Budget Office at http://www.cbo.gov/
- U.S. Census Bureau at http://www.census.gov/

! analyzing the scene

What does the state of the economy have to do with a college graduate's chances of getting a job?

The state (or health) of the economy—as measured by the economic growth rate—is closely tied to whether business firms are hiring or firing. When the economy is growing, firms are usually hiring employees; when the economy is in a slump (a recession), firms are often firing employees. As far as one's job prospects go, it is better to be graduating when the economy is strong and growing than when it is weak and declining. In short, Real GDP may just be a "number"—but it's a number that affects people's lives.

Why does the plumber want to be paid in cash?

Why does the DEA care that people are demanding cash from banks in Miami?

Both questions relate to the underground economy where exchanges take place outside recorded market channels. Economists argue that the greater the demand for cash transactions relative to check and credit transactions, the more likely individuals want to transact business in the underground economy (outside the view of government). One reason to operate in the underground economy is because you do not want to pay taxes on income earned. This is likely the reason the plumber wants to be paid in cash.

Another reason to operate in the underground economy is because what you are buying or selling is illegal. The mission of the Drug Enforcement Administration (DEA) is to "bring to the criminal and civil justice system of the United States . . . those organizations and principal members of organizations, involved in the growing, manufacture, or distribution of controlled substances appearing in or destined for illicit traffic in the United States."[3] Illegal drugs are bought and sold for cash. (No checks or credit cards, please.) The fact that increasingly more cash was being withdrawn from Miami banks could be indicative of increased illegal drug purchases and sales in Miami. This is something that would obviously interest the DEA.

How can a country have one of the highest GDPs in the world and be poor too?

China's GDP of $8.859 trillion was one of the highest in the world in 2005. But even though China's GDP is large, so is its population (approximately 1.3 billion.) The Chinese per capita GDP (GDP divided by population) was approximately $6,800 in 2005, which was far lower than the per capita GDP in many countries in the world. In short, China has a relatively large GDP and a relatively small per capita GDP.

What is the political relevance of the slogan, "It's the economy, stupid!"?

In 1992, James Carville, who was Bill Clinton's political strategist in the 1992 presidential campaign, pinned a sign above his desk at Clinton headquarters in Little Rock, Arkansas. It read: "It's the economy, stupid!" The slogan was his way of keeping the Clinton campaign focused and "on message."

The state of the economy, it would seem, matters—and matters a lot—to voters. When voters are asked to identify the issue that is most important to them in, say, an upcoming presidential election, a large percentage say the economy. Can the state of the economy be used to predict election results? There is some evidence that it can be.

[3]From the DEA Mission Statement.

chapter summary

Gross Domestic Product

- Gross domestic product (GDP) is the total market value of all final goods and services produced annually within a country's borders.
- Any one of the following can be used to compute GDP: (1) expenditure approach, (2) income approach, or (3) value-added approach.
- To avoid the problem of double counting, only final goods and services are counted in GDP.
- GDP omits certain nonmarket goods and services, both legal and illegal underground activities, the sale of used goods, financial transactions, transfer payments, and leisure (even though leisure is a good). Finally, GDP is not adjusted for the bads (e.g., pollution) that sometimes accompany production.

Expenditures

- The expenditures on U.S. goods and services include consumption; gross private domestic investment, or investment; government consumption expenditures and gross investment, or government purchases; and net exports (exports − imports).
- Consumption includes spending on durable goods, nondurable goods, and services.
- Investment includes purchases of newly produced capital goods (fixed investment), changes in business inventories (inventory investment), and the purchases of new residential housing (also fixed investment).
- Government purchases include federal, state, and local government purchases of goods and services and gross investment in highways, bridges, and so on. Government purchases do not include transfer payments.
- Net exports equal the total foreign spending on domestic goods (exports) minus the total domestic spending on foreign goods (imports).

Computing GDP

- Using the expenditure approach, GDP $= C + I + G + (EX - IM)$. In other words, GDP equals consumption plus investment plus government purchases plus net exports.
- Using the income approach, GDP = National income − income earned from the rest of the world + income earned by the rest of the world + indirect business taxes + capital consumption allowance + statistical discrepancy.

Measurements Other Than GDP

- Net domestic product (NDP) equals gross domestic product (GDP) minus the capital consumption allowance.

  NDP = GDP − Capital consumption allowance

- National income equals the sum of resource, or factor, payments.

$$
\begin{aligned}
\text{National income} = \ &\text{Compensation of employees} \\
&+ \text{Proprietors' income} \\
&+ \text{Corporate profits} \\
&+ \text{Rental income} \\
&+ \text{Net interest}
\end{aligned}
$$

- Personal income equals national income minus undistributed corporate profits, social insurance taxes, and corporate profits taxes, plus transfer payments.

$$
\begin{aligned}
\text{Personal Income} = \ &\text{National income} \\
&- \text{Undistributed corporate profits} \\
&- \text{Social insurance taxes} \\
&- \text{Corporate profits taxes} \\
&+ \text{Transfer payments}
\end{aligned}
$$

- Disposable Income = Personal income − Personal taxes

Real GDP

- Real GDP is GDP adjusted for price changes. It is GDP in base-year dollars.

Economic Growth and Business Cycles

- Annual economic growth has occurred if Real GDP in one year is higher than Real GDP in the previous year.
- There are five phases to the business cycle: peak, contraction, trough, recovery, and expansion. A complete business cycle is measured from peak to peak.

key terms and concepts

Gross Domestic Product (GDP)	Consumption	Imports	Net Domestic Product (NDP)
Final Good	Investment	Exports	Personal Income
Intermediate Good	Inventory Investment	Net Exports	Disposable Income
Double Counting	Fixed Investment	National Income	Real GDP
Value Added	Government Purchases	Capital Consumption Allowance (Depreciation)	Economic Growth
Transfer Payment	Government Transfer Payments		Business Cycle

questions and problems

1 "I just heard on the news that GDP is higher this year than it was last year. This means that we're better off this year than last year." Comment.

2 Which of the following are included in the calculation of this year's GDP? (a) Twelve-year-old Johnny mowing his family's lawn; (b) Dave Malone buying a used car; (c) Barbara Wilson buying a bond issued by General Motors; (d) Ed Ferguson's receipt of a Social Security payment; (e) the illegal drug transaction at the corner of Elm and Fifth.

3 Discuss the problems you see in comparing the GDPs of two countries, say, the United States and the People's Republic of China.

4 The manuscript for this book was keyed by the author. Had he hired someone to do the keying, GDP would have been higher than it was. What other activities would increase GDP if they were done differently? What activities would decrease GDP if they were done differently?

5 Why does GDP omit the sales of used goods? of financial transactions? of government transfer payments?

6 A business firm produces a good this year that it doesn't sell. As a result, the good is added to the firm's inventory. How does this inventory good find its way into GDP?

7 Economists prefer to compare Real GDP figures for different years instead of comparing GDP figures. Why?

8 What is the difference between a recovery and an expansion?

9 Define each of the following terms:

   a   Contraction
   b   Business cycle
   c   Trough
   d   Disposable income
   e   Net domestic product

10 Explain why GDP can be computed either by measuring spending or by measuring income.

11 Does the expenditure approach to computing GDP measure U.S. spending on all goods, U.S. spending on only U.S. goods, or U.S. and foreign spending on only U.S. goods? Explain your answer.

12 In the first quarter of the year, Real GDP was $400 billion; in the second quarter, it was $398 billion; in the third quarter, it was $399 billion; and in the fourth quarter, it was $395 billion. Has there been a recession? Explain your answer.

working with numbers and graphs

1 Net exports are –$114 billion and exports are $857 billion. What are imports?

2 Consumption spending is $3.708 trillion, spending on nondurable goods is $1.215 trillion, and spending on services is $2.041 trillion. What does spending on durable goods equal?

3 Inventory investment is $62 billion and (total) investment is $1.122 trillion. What does fixed investment equal?

4 In year 1, the prices of goods X, Y, and Z are $2, $4, and $6 per unit, respectively. In year 2, the prices of goods X, Y, and Z are $3, $4, and $7, respectively. In year 2, twice as many units of each good are produced as in year 1. In year 1, 20 units of X, 40 units of Y, and 60 units of Z are produced. If year 1 is the base year, what does Real GDP equal in year 2?

5 Nondurable goods spending = $400 million, durable goods spending = $300 million, new residential housing spending = $200 million, and spending on services = $500 million. What does consumption equal?

6 According to the circular flow diagram in Exhibit 5, consumption spending flows into U.S. product markets but import spending does not. But U.S. households buy imported goods in U.S. markets, don't they? Explain.

7 How would you redraw the circular flow diagram in Exhibit 5 if you wanted to show (a) taxes that firms and households pay to government and (b) transfer payments that government makes to households?

8 National income = $500 billion, income earned from the rest of the world = $10 billion, income earned by the rest of the world = $12 billion, indirect business taxes = $2 billion, capital consumption allowance = $1 billion, and GDP = $525 billion. What does the statistical discrepancy equal?

9 GDP = $100 billion, NDP = $95 billion, and investment = $33 billion. What does the capital consumption allowance equal?

10 If Real GDP in year 1 is $487 billion and it is $498 billion in year 2, what is the economic growth rate equal to?

11 The following figure shows a business cycle. Identify each of the following as a phase of the business cycle:

a   Point A
b   Between point A and point B
c   Point B
d   Between point B and point C
e   Point D

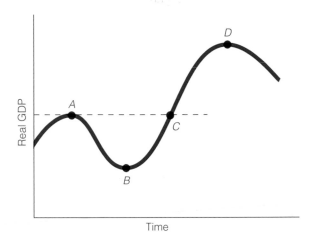

12 Using the following data, calculate (a) gross domestic product (GDP); (b) net domestic product (NDP); (c) national income (NI); (d) personal income (PI). All numbers are in billions of dollars.

Consumption	$1,149.5
Investment	400.3
Government purchases	425.3
Net exports	89.1
Capital consumption allowance	303.8
Indirect business taxes	213.3
Statistical discrepancy	4.4
Social Security insurance taxes	216.5
Transfer payments	405.6
Undistributed profits	91.0
Corporate profits taxes	77.7
Personal taxes	340.0
Dividends	0.0
Compensation of employees	800.0
Income earned from the rest of the world	50.0
Income earned by the rest of the world	56.0
Proprietors' income	400.0
Rental income	145.0
Net interest	23.0

Aggregate Demand and Aggregate Supply

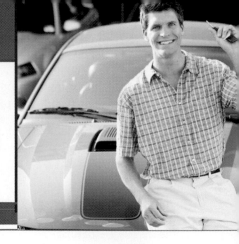

Setting the Scene

The following events occurred on a day in February.

10:13 A.M.

Toby Perkins, 22 years old, is looking at a car on a dealer's lot. He examines the right side of the car and then walks around to the left side. He opens the door and sits in the driver's seat. Just then, a car salesman walks up to the car. "That's a really nice car," are the salesman's first words. "I know," says Toby. "I wish interest rates were a little lower so I could buy it today." The car salesman says, "Oh, I'm sure we can work something out."

11:53 A.M.

Marcy, 23 years old, is sitting at the kitchen table looking at travel brochures for Ireland, England, France, Belgium, and Germany. Her mother enters the kitchen and asks, "Excited about your big trip?" "I guess," says Marcy. "Of course, the trip is getting more expensive by the minute." "What do you mean?" her mother asks. "The exchange rate," Marcy answers. "It's killing me. A couple of months ago, I could get euros for $1.10 each. Today, I'd have to pay $1.25 each. Two months ago, I could buy a British pound for $1.65. Today, I'd have to pay $1.85. If this trend continues, the trip will be too expensive, and I don't think I can go."

12:01 P.M.

Catherine Zavier walks by her economics professor's office. A notice is posted on the bulletin board next to the office door. She stops to read it: *Economics won't keep you out of the unemployment line, but at least if you're there, you'll know why.*

3:34 P.M.

An economist is sitting in the Oval Office of the White House, across the desk from the president of the United States. The president asks, "How does unemployment look for the next quarter?" The economist answers, "It's not good. I don't think Real GDP is going to be as high as we initially thought. The problem seems to be foreign income—it's just not growing at the rate we thought it was going to grow."

? Here are some questions to keep in mind as you read this chapter:

- *Why does Toby wish interest rates were lower? How can a change in interest rates affect a person's buying behavior?*

- *Why is Marcy's trip to Europe getting more expensive? How can a change in exchange rates affect a person's life?*

- *If you study economics and still end up in the unemployment line, will you really know why you're there?*

- *How can foreign income affect U.S. unemployment?*

See analyzing the scene at the end of this chapter for answers to these questions.

The Two Sides to an Economy

Just as there are two sides to a market, a buying side (demand) and a selling side (supply), there are two sides to an economy. There is a demand side and a supply side. The demand in an economy is referred to as *aggregate demand (AD);* the supply is referred to as *aggregate supply (AS).*

Macroeconomists often use the *AD-AS* framework of analysis to discuss the price level, GDP, Real GDP, unemployment, economic growth, and other major macroeconomic topics. In other words, all these topics can be and are discussed within the same framework. Discussing so many important economic topics within one framework, or with the same tools of analysis, often makes things easier for the student who is just beginning to study macroeconomics. The *AD-AS* framework has three parts: (1) aggregate demand (*AD*), (2) short-run aggregate supply (*SRAS*), and (3) long-run aggregate supply (*LRAS*).

Aggregate Demand

Recall from the last chapter that people, firms, and governments buy U.S. goods and services. **Aggregate demand** refers to the quantity demanded of these (U.S.) goods and services, or the quantity demanded of (U.S.) Real GDP, at various price levels, *ceteris paribus.* For example, the following whole set of data represents aggregate demand:

Aggregate Demand

Price Index	Quantity Demanded of Goods and Services (Quantity Demanded of Real GDP)
100	$1,200 billion worth of goods and services
110	$1,000 billion worth of goods and services
120	$800 billion worth of goods and services

An **aggregate demand (*AD*) curve** is the graphical representation of aggregate demand. An *AD* curve is shown in Exhibit 1. Notice that it is downward sloping, indicating an inverse relationship between the price level (*P*) and the quantity demanded of Real GDP (*Q*): As the price level rises, the quantity demanded of Real GDP falls, and as the price level falls, the quantity demanded of Real GDP rises, *ceteris paribus.*

Why Does the Aggregate Demand Curve Slope Downward?

Asking why the *AD* curve slopes downward is the same as asking why there is an inverse relationship between the price level and the quantity demanded of Real GDP. This inverse relationship, and the resulting downward slope of the *AD* curve, is explained by the real balance effect, the interest rate effect, and the international trade effect.

REAL BALANCE EFFECT (DUE TO A CHANGE IN THE PRICE LEVEL) The **real balance effect** states that the inverse relationship between the price level and the quantity demanded of Real GDP is established through changes in the value of **monetary wealth**, or money holdings.

To illustrate, consider a person who has $50,000 in cash. Suppose the price level falls. As this happens, the **purchasing power** of the person's $50,000 rises. That is, the $50,000, which once could buy 100 television sets at $500 each, can now buy 125 sets at $400 each. An increase in the purchasing power of the person's $50,000 is identical to saying that his monetary wealth has increased. (After all, isn't the $50,000 more valuable when it can buy more than when it can buy less?) And as he becomes wealthier, he buys more goods.

exhibit **1**

The Aggregate Demand Curve

The aggregate demand curve is downward-sloping, specifying an inverse relationship between the price level and the quantity demanded of Real GDP.

> **Aggregate Demand Curve**
> The price level and quantity demanded of Real GDP are inversely related.

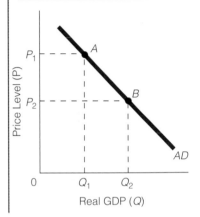

Aggregate Demand
The quantity demanded of all goods and services (Real GDP) at different price levels, *ceteris paribus.*

Aggregate Demand (*AD*) Curve
A curve that shows the quantity demanded of all goods and services (Real GDP) at different price levels, *ceteris paribus.*

Real Balance Effect
The change in the purchasing power of dollar-denominated assets that results from a change in the price level.

Monetary Wealth
The value of a person's monetary assets. Wealth, as distinguished from monetary wealth, refers to the value of all assets owned, both monetary and nonmonetary. In short, a person's wealth equals his or her monetary wealth (e.g., $1,000 cash) plus nonmonetary wealth (e.g., a car or a house).

Purchasing Power
The quantity of goods and services that can be purchased with a unit of money. Purchasing power and the price level are inversely related: As the price level goes up (down), purchasing power goes down (up).

In summary, a fall in the price level causes purchasing power to rise, which increases a person's monetary wealth. As people become wealthier, the quantity demanded of Real GDP rises.

Suppose the price level rises. As this happens, the purchasing power of the $50,000 falls. That is, the $50,000, which once could buy 100 television sets at $500 each, can now buy 80 sets at $625 each. A decrease in the purchasing power of the person's $50,000 is identical to saying that his monetary wealth has decreased. And as he becomes less wealthy, he buys fewer goods.

In summary, a rise in the price level causes purchasing power to fall, which decreases a person's monetary wealth. As people become less wealthy, the quantity demanded of Real GDP falls.

Interest Rate Effect

The changes in household and business buying as the interest rate changes (which, in turn, is a reflection of a change in the demand for or supply of credit brought on by price level changes).

INTEREST RATE EFFECT (DUE TO A CHANGE IN THE PRICE LEVEL)   The **interest rate effect** states that the inverse relationship between the price level and the quantity demanded of Real GDP is established through changes in household and business spending that is sensitive to changes in interest rates.

Let's consider a person who buys a fixed bundle of goods (food, clothing, and shelter) each week. Suppose the price level falls, increasing the purchasing power of the person's money. With more purchasing power (per dollar), she can purchase her fixed bundle of goods with less money. What does she do with (part of) this increase in her monetary wealth? She saves it. In terms of simple supply-and-demand analysis, the supply of credit increases. Subsequently, the price of credit, which is the interest rate, drops. As the interest rate drops, households and businesses borrow more, so they end up buying more goods. Thus, the quantity demanded of Real GDP rises.

Now suppose the price level rises, decreasing the purchasing power of the person's money. With less purchasing power (per dollar), she cannot purchase her fixed bundle of goods with the same amount of money. If she wants to continue to buy the fixed bundle of goods, she will need to acquire more money. In an effort to acquire more money, she goes to a bank and requests a loan. In terms of simple supply-and-demand analysis, the demand for credit increases. Subsequently, the interest rate rises. As the interest rate rises, households borrow less to finance, say, automobile purchases, and firms borrow less to finance new capital goods spending. Thus, the quantity demanded of Real GDP falls.

International Trade Effect

The change in foreign sector spending as the price level changes.

INTERNATIONAL TRADE EFFECT (DUE TO A CHANGE IN THE PRICE LEVEL)   The **international trade effect** states that the inverse relationship between the price level and the quantity demanded of Real GDP is established through foreign sector spending, which includes U.S. spending on foreign goods (imports) and foreign spending on U.S. goods (exports).

Suppose the price level in the United States falls. As this happens, U.S. goods become relatively cheaper than foreign goods. As a result, both Americans and foreigners buy more U.S. goods. The quantity demanded of (U.S.) Real GDP rises.

Suppose the price level in the United States rises. As this happens, U.S. goods become relatively more expensive than foreign goods. As a result, both Americans and foreigners buy fewer U.S. goods. The quantity demanded of (U.S.) Real GDP falls.

For a review of the three effects—real balance, interest rate, and international trade—see Exhibit 2.

ONE IMPORTANT WORD ON THE THREE EFFECTS   We explained that the aggregate demand curve is downward sloping because of the real balance, interest rate, and international trade effects. Keep in mind what caused these three effects: a change in the price level. In other words, when we were discussing, say, the interest rate effect, we were discussing the interest rate effect *of a change in the price level.*

exhibit **2**

Why the Aggregate Demand Curve
Is Downward-Sloping

This exhibit outlines the three effects
that explain why the *AD* curve is
downward-sloping. Each effect
relates to a change in the price level
(*P*) leading to a change in the quantity demanded of Real GDP (*Q*).

Type of Effect	How It Works	Graphical Representation of What Happens
Real Balance in Effect (due to a change in the price level)	*Price level falls* → purchasing power rises → monetary wealth rises → **buy more goods.**	
	Price level rises → purchasing power falls → monetary wealth falls → **buy fewer goods.**	
Interest Rate Effect (due to a change in the price level)	*Price level falls* → purchasing power rises → less money needed to buy fixed bundle of goods → save more → supply of credit rises → interest rate falls → businesses and households borrow more at lower interest rate → **buy more goods.**	
	Price level rises → purchasing power falls → borrow money in order to continue to buy fixed bundle of goods → demand for credit rises → interest rate rises → businesses and households borrow less at higher interest rate → **buy fewer goods.**	
International Trade Effect (due to a change in the price level)	*Price level in U.S. falls* relative to foreign price levels → U.S. goods relatively less expensive than foreign goods → both Americans and foreigners **buy more U.S. goods.**	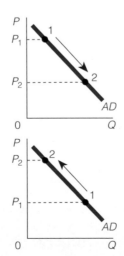
	Price level in U.S. rises relative to foreign price levels → U.S. goods relatively more expensive than foreign goods → both Americans and foreigners **buy fewer U.S. goods.**	

Why is this an important point? Because the interest rate can change due to things other than the price level changing, and not everything that changes the interest rate leads to a movement from one point to another point on the *AD* curve. Some things that change the interest rate can lead to a shift in the *AD* curve instead. We will have more to say about this later. For now, though, we ask that you simply keep in mind the *cause* of each of the three effects we discussed. That cause was a change in the price level—the variable on the vertical axis in Exhibit 1.

A Change in the Quantity Demanded of Real GDP Versus a Change in Aggregate Demand

A change in the quantity demanded of Real GDP is brought about by a change in the price level. As the price level falls, the quantity demanded of Real GDP rises, *ceteris paribus*. In Exhibit 3(a), a change in the quantity demanded of Real GDP is represented as a *movement* from one point (*A*) on AD_1 to another point (*B*) on AD_1.

A change in aggregate demand is represented in Exhibit 3(b) as a *shift* in the aggregate demand curve from AD_1 to AD_2. Notice that when the aggregate demand curve shifts, the quantity demanded of Real GDP changes even though the price level remains constant. For example, at a price level (index number) of 180, the quantity demanded of Real GDP on AD_1 in Exhibit 3(b) is $6.0 trillion. But at the same price level (180), the quantity demanded of Real GDP on AD_2 is $6.5 trillion.

Changes in Aggregate Demand: Shifts in the *AD* Curve

What can change aggregate demand? In other words, what can cause aggregate demand to rise and what can cause it to fall?

The simple answer is that aggregate demand changes when the spending on U.S. goods and services changes. If spending increases at a given price level, aggregate demand rises; if spending decreases at a given price level, aggregate demand falls. For example, suppose the price level in the economy is represented by the consumer price index and the index is currently 150 (CPI = 150). At this price level, U.S. residents,

exhibit **3**

A Change in the Quantity Demanded of Real GDP Versus a Change in Aggregate Demand

(a) A change in the quantity demanded of Real GDP is graphically represented as a *movement* from one point, *A*, on AD_1 to another point, *B*, on AD_1. A change in the quantity demanded of Real GDP is the result of a change in the price level. (b) A change in aggregate demand is graphically represented as a *shift* in the aggregate demand curve from AD_1 to AD_2.

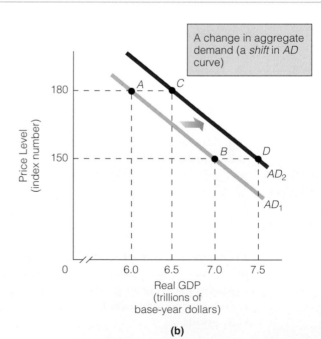

(a)   **(b)**

firms, and governments, along with foreigners, foreign firms, and foreign governments, want to buy, say, $7.0 trillion worth of U.S. goods and services. Then something changes, and all of a sudden, they want to buy $7.5 trillion worth of U.S. goods and services. Now, before you conclude that they want to buy more goods and services because the prices of goods and services have fallen, keep in mind that we haven't lowered the price level. The price level is still represented by the CPI, and it is still 150. In other words, all these people, firms, and governments want to buy more U.S. goods even though the prices of the goods and services have not changed.

When individuals, firms, and governments want to buy more U.S. goods and services even though the prices of these goods have not changed, then we say that aggregate demand has increased. As a result, the *AD* curve shifts to the right. Of course, when individuals, firms, and governments want to buy fewer U.S. goods and services at a given price level, then we say that aggregate demand has decreased. As a result, the *AD* curve shifts to the left.

Let's look again at Exhibit 3(b), which shows a change in aggregate demand (a shift in the *AD* curve). At point *B*, the price level is 150, and total expenditures on U.S. goods and services are $7.0 trillion. At point *D*, the price level is still 150, but total expenditures on U.S. goods and services have increased to $7.5 trillion. Why has aggregate demand moved from point *B* to point *D*; that is, what has caused the increase in total expenditures? To find out, we have to look at the components of total expenditures.

How Spending Components Affect Aggregate Demand

The last chapter identified four major spending components: consumption, investment, government purchases, and net exports. Let's keep the numbers simple and let $C = \$100$, $I = \$100$, $G = \$100$, $EX = \$50$, and $IM = \$15$. If $EX = \$50$ and $IM = \$15$, it follows that net exports (NX) equal the difference, or $35.

Using these dollar figures, we calculate that $335 is spent on U.S. goods and services. We get this dollar amount by finding the sum of consumption, investment, government purchases, and net exports.

Total expenditures on U.S. goods and services = $C + I + G + NX$

Obviously, this dollar amount will go up if (1) C rises, (2) I rises, (3) G rises, or (4) NX rises. In other words, a rise in consumption, investment, government purchases, or net exports will raise spending on U.S. goods and services:

$C\uparrow$, $I\uparrow$, $G\uparrow$, $NX\uparrow$ → Total expenditures on U.S. goods and services$\uparrow$

Now, what will cause spending on U.S. goods to go down? Obviously, it will decline if (1) C falls, (2) I falls, (3) G falls, or (4) NX falls.

$C\downarrow$, $I\downarrow$, $G\downarrow$, $NX\downarrow$ → Total expenditures on U.S. goods or services$\downarrow$

Because we now know what causes total expenditures on U.S. goods and services to change, we can relate the components of spending to (U.S.) aggregate demand. If, *at a given price level,* consumption, investment, government purchases, or net exports rise, aggregate demand will rise and the *AD* curve will shift to the right. If, *at a*

Q&A

Earlier it was stated, "If spending increases at a given price level, aggregate demand rises; if spending decreases at a given price level, aggregate demand falls." Why was it so important to say if spending increases "at a given price level." Won't spending increase if the price level drops? Isn't this why the AD curve is downward sloping?

If the price level drops, we move from one point on a given AD curve to another point on the same AD curve. For example, we move from point A to point B in Exhibit 3(a). Is this an increase in spending? Yes it is, but it is an increase in spending that is due to a decrease in the price level, holding all other things constant.

There can also be an increase in spending holding the price level constant. This is what we are talking about when the AD curve shifts.

To make sure we understand the difference, consider a simple example of your spending. The price of cookies goes down, and you end up buying more cookies each week. But is a lower price the only reason you might buy more cookies? The answer is probably no. You might buy more cookies (even though the price of cookies has not gone down) if, say, your income went up, your preferences changed in favor of cookies, or you were going to have a party and wanted to serve cookies, among other reasons.

This is all we are saying when we are discussing a shift in the AD curve. It is the result of more spending—at a given price level.

Thinking like AN ECONOMIST

The economist often thinks in terms of curves and movements along curves. Identify a given factor, and the economist will tell you whether it will lead to a movement along a curve or a shift in a curve. This may sound like so much nonsense to the layperson, but it is extremely important if you are studying economics. In some sense, the more able you are to think in terms of curves, movements along curves, and the factors that bring about both, the better.

given price level, consumption, investment, government purchases, or net exports fall, aggregate demand will fall and the *AD* curve will shift to the left. We can write these relationships as:

If, at a given price level, $C\uparrow$, $I\uparrow$, $G\uparrow$, $NX\uparrow$ then $AD\uparrow$

If, at a given price level, $C\downarrow$, $I\downarrow$, $G\downarrow$, $NX\downarrow$ then $AD\downarrow$

The flow charts in Exhibit 4 show how changes in spending components affect aggregate demand.

Factors That Can Change *C, I, G,* AND *NX (EX – IM)* and Therefore Can Change *AD*

What can change aggregate demand (*AD*) in the economy? You know that the answer is a change in consumption, investment, government purchases, or net exports (exports minus imports). So, for example, if someone asks you why *AD* increased, you may say because consumption (*C*) increased.

But suppose the person then asks, "But what caused consumption to increase?" In other words, your answer to one question simply leads to another question. If a change in consumption changes aggregate demand, what changes consumption? The same question can be asked about changes in investment, government purchases, and net exports (which means exports and imports). For example, if aggregate demand increased because investment increased, then what caused investment to increase?

This section looks at some of the (many) factors that can change consumption, investment, and net exports. A later chapter considers the factors that can change government purchases.

CONSUMPTION Four factors that can affect consumption are wealth, expectations about future prices and income, the interest rate, and income taxes.

Wealth

The value of all assets owned, both monetary and nonmonetary.

1. **Wealth.** Individuals consume not only on the basis of their present income but also on the basis of their **wealth**. Consider two individuals, each receiving an income of $50,000 a year. One has $75,000 in the bank, and the other has no assets at all. Which would you expect to spend more of her income on consumption goods this year? We would expect the person with the $75,000 in the bank to consume more. Greater wealth makes individuals feel financially more secure and thus more willing to spend.

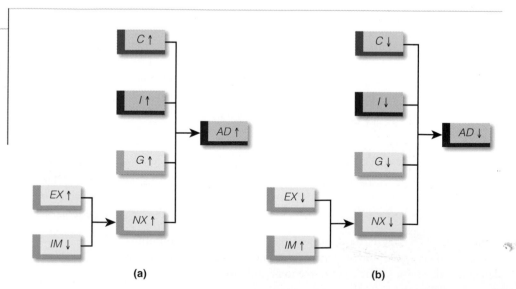

(a)   (b)

Increases in wealth lead to increases in consumption. If consumption increases, then aggregate demand rises and the AD curve shifts to the right. What will happen if wealth decreases? Decreases in wealth lead to a fall in consumption, which leads to a fall in aggregate demand. Consequently, the AD curve shifts to the left.

$$\text{Wealth}\uparrow \rightarrow C\uparrow \rightarrow AD\uparrow$$
$$\text{Wealth}\downarrow \rightarrow C\downarrow \rightarrow AD\downarrow$$

2. **Expectations about future prices and income.** If individuals expect higher prices in the future, they increase current consumption expenditures to buy goods at the lower current prices. This increase in consumption leads to an increase in aggregate demand. If individuals expect lower prices in the future, they decrease current consumption expenditures. This reduction in consumption leads to a decrease in aggregate demand.

   Similarly, expectation of a higher future income increases consumption, which leads to an increase in aggregate demand. Expectation of a lower future income decreases consumption, which leads to a decrease in aggregate demand.

$$\text{Expect higher future prices} \rightarrow C\uparrow \rightarrow AD\uparrow$$
$$\text{Expect lower future prices} \rightarrow C\downarrow \rightarrow AD\downarrow$$
$$\text{Expect higher future income} \rightarrow C\uparrow \rightarrow AD\uparrow$$
$$\text{Expect lower future income} \rightarrow C\downarrow \rightarrow AD\downarrow$$

3. **Interest rate.** Current empirical work shows that spending on consumer durables is sensitive to the interest rate. Many of these items are financed by borrowing, so an increase in the interest rate increases the monthly payment amounts linked to their purchase and thereby reduces their consumption. This reduction in consumption leads to a decline in aggregate demand. Alternatively, a decrease in the interest rate reduces monthly payment amounts linked to the purchase of durable goods and thereby increases their consumption. This increase in consumption leads to an increase in aggregate demand.

$$\text{Interest rate}\uparrow \rightarrow C\downarrow \rightarrow AD\downarrow$$
$$\text{Interest rate}\downarrow \rightarrow C\uparrow \rightarrow AD\uparrow$$

4. **Income taxes.** Let's consider personal income taxes, the tax a person pays on the income he or she earns. As income taxes rise, disposable income decreases. When people have less take-home pay to spend, consumption falls. Consequently, aggregate demand decreases. A decrease in income taxes has the opposite effect; it raises disposable income. When people have more take-home pay to spend, consumption rises and aggregate demand increases.

$$\text{Income taxes}\uparrow \rightarrow C\downarrow \rightarrow AD\downarrow$$
$$\text{Income taxes}\downarrow \rightarrow C\uparrow \rightarrow AD\uparrow$$

INVESTMENT Three factors that can change investment are the interest rate, expectations about future sales, and business taxes.

1. **Interest rate.** Changes in interest rates affect business decisions. As the interest rate rises, the cost of a given investment project rises and businesses invest less. As investment decreases, aggregate demand decreases. On the other hand, as the interest rate falls, the cost of a given investment project falls and businesses invest more. Consequently, aggregate demand increases.

$$\text{Interest rate}\uparrow \rightarrow I\downarrow \rightarrow AD\downarrow$$
$$\text{Interest rate}\downarrow \rightarrow I\uparrow \rightarrow AD\uparrow$$

Thinking like
AN ECONOMIST   *Let's back up for a minute and look at the recent past discussion. For example, we have said that if the dollar depreciates, U.S. exports will rise and U.S. imports will fall, which means in turn that U.S. net exports rise, which then causes aggregate demand to rise.*

If we were to summarize this type of argument, we'd say that a change in W leads to a change in X, which leads to a change in Y, which leads to change in Z. Let's call this kind of explanation the W-X-Y-Z explanation.

Economists often think in terms of one thing changing something else, which in turn changes still something else, and so on. Some people find this kind of thinking difficult. They ask: Why not simply say that W leads to Z instead of saying that W leads to X, which leads to Y, which leads to Z?

Well, that might make things easier (there would be less to remember), but what it gains in ease, it loses in completeness. It is best to explain just how one thing eventually leads to something else happening.

2. **Expectations about future sales.** Businesses invest because they expect to sell the goods they produce. If businesses become optimistic about future sales, investment spending grows and aggregate demand increases. If businesses become pessimistic about future sales, investment spending contracts and aggregate demand decreases.

Businesses become optimistic about future sales → $I\uparrow$ → $AD\uparrow$
Businesses become pessimistic about future sales → $I\downarrow$ → $AD\downarrow$

3. **Business taxes.** Businesses naturally consider expected after-tax profits when making their investment decisions. An increase in business taxes lowers expected profitability. With less profit expected, businesses invest less. As investment spending declines, aggregate demand declines. A decrease in business taxes, on the other hand, raises expected profitability and investment spending. This increases aggregate demand.

Business taxes $\uparrow$ → $I\downarrow$ → $AD\downarrow$
Business taxes $\downarrow$ → $I\uparrow$ → $AD\uparrow$

NET EXPORTS Two factors that can change net exports are foreign real national income and the exchange rate.

1. **Foreign real national income.** Just as Americans earn a national income, so do people in other countries. There is a foreign national income. By adjusting this foreign national income for price changes, we obtain foreign real national income. As foreign real national income rises, foreigners buy more U.S. goods and services. Thus, U.S. exports (*EX*) rise. As exports rise, net exports rise, *ceteris paribus*. As net exports rise, aggregate demand increases.

This process works in reverse too. As foreign real national income falls, foreigners buy fewer U.S. goods and exports fall. This lowers net exports, which reduces aggregate demand.

Foreign real national income $\uparrow$ → U.S. exports $\uparrow$ → U.S. net exports $\uparrow$ → $AD\uparrow$
Foreign real national income $\downarrow$ → U.S. exports $\downarrow$ → U.S. net exports $\downarrow$ → $AD\downarrow$

Exchange Rate

The price of one currency in terms of another currency.

Appreciation

An increase in the value of one currency relative to other currencies.

Depreciation

A decrease in the value of one currency relative to other currencies.

2. **Exchange rate.** The **exchange rate** is the price of one currency in terms of another currency; for example, $1.25 = 1 euro. A currency has **appreciated** in value if more of a foreign currency is needed to buy it. A currency has **depreciated** in value if more of it is needed to buy a foreign currency. For example, a change in the exchange rate from $1.25 = 1 euro to $1.50 = 1 euro means that more dollars are needed to buy 1 euro, and the euro has appreciated. And because more dollars are needed to buy 1 euro, the dollar has depreciated.

A depreciation in a nation's currency makes foreign goods more expensive. Consider an Irish coat that is priced at 200 euros when the exchange rate is $1.25 = 1 euro. To buy the Irish coat for 200 euros, an American has to pay $250 ($1.25 for each of 200 euros for a total of $250). Now suppose the dollar depreciates to $1.50 = 1 euro. The American now has to pay $300 for the coat.

This process is symmetrical, so an appreciation in a nation's currency makes foreign goods cheaper. For example, if the exchange rate goes from $1.25 = 1 euro to $1 = 1 euro, the Irish coat will cost the American $200.

The depreciation and appreciation of the U.S. dollar affect net exports. As the dollar depreciates, foreign goods become more expensive, Americans cut back on imported goods, and foreigners (whose currency has appreciated) increase their purchases of U.S. exported goods. If exports rise and imports fall, net exports increase and aggregate demand increases.

As the dollar appreciates, foreign goods become cheaper, Americans increase their purchases of imported goods, and foreigners (whose currency has depreciated) cut back on their purchases of U.S. exported goods. If exports fall and imports rise, net exports decrease, thus lowering aggregate demand.

Dollar depreciates → U.S. exports ↑ and U.S. imports ↓ → U.S. net exports ↑ → AD ↑
Dollar appreciates → U.S. exports ↓ and U.S. imports ↑ → U.S. net exports ↓ → AD ↓

See Exhibit 5 for a summary of the factors that change aggregate demand.

Can a Change in the Money Supply Change Aggregate Demand?

Changes in such factors as interest rates, business taxes, exchange rates, and so on can change aggregate demand (indirectly) by directly changing consumption, investment, and net exports. What about the money supply? Can a change in the money supply lead to a change in aggregate demand?

Suppose the money supply rises from, say, $1,350 billion to $1,400 billion. Will this result in an increase in aggregate demand? Most economists would say that it does, but they differ as to how the change in the money supply affects aggregate demand. One way to

If you had to summarize what this section is about, what would you say?

We'd say that it was about aggregate demand and those factors that can actually lead to shifts in the AD curve. This is best summarized by Exhibit 5.

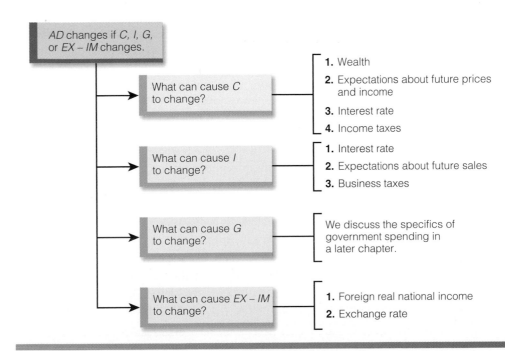

A CLOSER LOOK

Factors That Change Aggregate Demand

Aggregate demand (*AD*) changes whenever consumption (*C*), investment (*I*), government purchases (*G*), or net exports (*EX − IM*) change. The factors that can affect *C*, *I*, and *EX − IM*, thereby indirectly affecting aggregate demand, are listed.

AD changes if *C*, *I*, *G*, or *EX − IM* changes.

What can cause *C* to change?
1. Wealth
2. Expectations about future prices and income
3. Interest rate
4. Income taxes

What can cause *I* to change?
1. Interest rate
2. Expectations about future sales
3. Business taxes

What can cause *G* to change?
We discuss the specifics of government spending in a later chapter.

What can cause *EX − IM* to change?
1. Foreign real national income
2. Exchange rate

explain the effect (within the context of our discussion) is as follows: (1) A change in the money supply affects interest rates. (2) A change in interest rates changes consumption and investment. (3) A change in consumption and investment affects aggregate demand. Therefore, a change in the money supply is a catalyst in a process that ends with a change in aggregate demand. (We will have much more to say about the money supply and interest rates in later chapters.)

SELF-TEST

(Answers to Self-Test questions are in the Self-Test Appendix.)

1. Explain the real balance effect.

2. Explain what happens to the *AD* curve if the dollar appreciates relative to other currencies.

3. Explain what happens to the *AD* curve if personal income taxes decline.

Short-Run Aggregate Supply

Aggregate Supply

The quantity supplied of all goods and services (Real GDP) at different price levels, *ceteris paribus.*

Short-Run Aggregate Supply (SRAS) Curve

A curve that shows the quantity supplied of all goods and services (Real GDP) at different price levels, *ceteris paribus.*

Aggregate demand is one side of the economy; aggregate supply is the other side. **Aggregate supply** refers to the quantity supplied of all goods and services (Real GDP) at various price levels, *ceteris paribus.* Aggregate supply includes both short-run aggregate supply (*SRAS*) and long-run aggregate supply (*LRAS*). Short-run aggregate supply is discussed in this section.

Short-Run Aggregate Supply Curve: What It Is and Why It Is Upward Sloping

A **short-run aggregate supply (*SRAS*) curve** is illustrated in Exhibit 6. It shows the quantity supplied of all goods and services (Real GDP or output) at different price levels, *ceteris paribus.* Notice that the *SRAS* curve is upward sloping: As the price level rises, firms increase the quantity supplied of goods and services; as the price level drops, firms decrease the quantity supplied of goods and services. Why is the *SRAS* curve upward sloping? Economists have put forth a few explanations; we discuss two.

STICKY WAGES Some economists believe that wages are sticky, or inflexible. This may be because wages are "locked in" for a few years due to labor contracts entered into by workers and management. For example, management and labor may agree to lock in wages for the next one to three years. Both labor and management may see this as in their best interest. Management has some idea of what its labor costs will be during the time of the contract, and workers may have a sense of security knowing that their wages can't be lowered. Alternatively, wages may be sticky because of certain social conventions or perceived notions of fairness. Whatever the specific reason for sticky wages, let's see how they provide an explanation of an upward-sloping *SRAS* curve.

Firms pay *nominal wages* (e.g., $30 an hour), but they often decide how many workers to hire based on real wages. *Real wages* are nominal wages divided by the price level.

Real wage = Nominal wage/Price level

For example, suppose the nominal wage is $30 an hour, and the price level as measured by a price index is 1.50.[1] The real wage is therefore $20.

The quantity supplied of labor is *directly related* to the real wage: As the real wage rises, the quantity supplied of labor rises; as the real wage falls, the quantity supplied of labor falls. In short, more individuals are willing to work, and current workers are willing to work more, at higher real wages than at lower real wages.

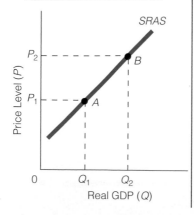

exhibit **6**

The Short-Run Aggregate Supply Curve

The short-run aggregate supply curve is upward-sloping, specifying a direct relationship between the price level and the quantity supplied of Real GDP.

Short-Run Aggregate Supply Curve
The price level and quantity supplied of Real GDP are directly related.

---

[1]Alternatively, you can view the price index as 1.50 times 100, or 150. In this case, the formula for the real wage would change to Real wage = (Nominal wage/Price level) × 100.

Real wage ↑ → *Quantity supplied* of labor ↑
Real wage ↓ → *Quantity supplied* of labor ↓

The quantity demanded of labor is *inversely related* to the real wage: As the real wage rises, the quantity demanded of labor falls; as the real wage falls, the quantity demanded of labor rises. Firms will employ more workers the cheaper it is to hire them.

Real wage ↑ → *Quantity demanded* of labor ↓
Real wage ↓ → *Quantity demanded* of labor ↑

With this as background, suppose a firm has agreed to pay its workers $30 an hour for the next three years and it has hired 1,000 workers. When it agreed to this nominal wage, it thought the price index would remain at 1.50 and the real wage would stay at $20.

Now suppose the price index *falls* to 1.25. When the price level falls to an index of 1.25, the real wage rises to $24 ($30/1.25). This is a higher real wage than the firm expected when it agreed to lock in nominal wages at $30 an hour. If the firm had known that the real wage would turn out to be $24 (and not remain at $20), it would never have hired 1,000 workers. It would have hired, say, 800 workers instead.

So what does the firm do? As we stated, there is an inverse relationship between the real wage and the quantity demanded of labor (the number of workers that firms want to hire). Now that the real wage has risen (from $20 to $24), the firm cuts back on its labor (say, from 1,000 to 800 workers). With fewer workers working, less output is produced.

In conclusion, if wages are sticky, a decrease in the price level (which pushes real wages up) will result in a decrease in output. This is what an upward-sloping *SRAS* curve represents: As the price level falls, the quantity supplied of goods and services declines.

WORKER MISPERCEPTIONS Another explanation for the upward-sloping *SRAS* curve holds that workers may misperceive real wage changes. To illustrate, suppose the nominal wage is $30 an hour and the price level as measured by a price index is 1.50. It follows that the real wage is $20. Now suppose the nominal wage falls to $25 and the price level falls to 1.25. The real wage is still $20 ($25/1.25 = $20), but workers may not know this. They will know their nominal wage has fallen (they know they are earning $25 an hour instead of $30 an hour). They also may know the price level is lower. But they may not know initially *how much* lower the price level is. For example, suppose they mistakenly believe the price level has fallen from 1.50 to 1.39. They will then think that their real wage has actually fallen from $20 ($30/1.50) to $17.98 ($25/1.39). In response to (the misperceived) falling real wage, workers may reduce the quantity of labor they are willing to supply. With fewer workers (resources), firms will end up producing less.

In conclusion, if workers misperceive real wage changes, then a fall in the price level will bring about a decline in output, which is illustrative of an upward-sloping *SRAS* curve.

What Puts the "Short Run" in *SRAS*?

According to most macroeconomists, the *SRAS* curve slopes upward because of sticky wages or worker misperceptions. No matter which explanation of the upward-sloping *SRAS* curve we accept, though, things are likely to change over time. Wages will not be sticky forever (labor contracts will expire), and workers will figure out that they misperceived real wage changes. It is only for a period of time—identified as the short run—that these issues are likely to be relevant.

Changes in Short-Run Aggregate Supply: Shifts in the *SRAS* Curve

A change in the quantity supplied of Real GDP is brought about by a change in the price level. A change in quantity supplied is shown as a *movement* along the *SRAS* curve. But what can change short-run aggregate supply? What can *shift* the *SRAS* curve? The factors that can shift the *SRAS* curve include wage rates, prices of nonlabor inputs, productivity, and supply shocks.

WAGE RATES Changes in wage rates have a major impact on the position of the *SRAS* curve because wage costs are usually a firm's major cost item. The impact of a rise or fall in equilibrium wage rates can be understood in terms of the following equation:

Profit per unit = Price per unit – Cost per unit

Higher wage rates mean higher costs and, at constant prices, translate into lower profits and a reduction in the number of units (of a given good) managers of firms will want to produce. Lower wage rates mean lower costs and, at constant prices, translate into higher profits and an increase in the number of units (of a given good) managers will decide to produce.

The impact of higher and lower equilibrium wages is shown in Exhibit 7. At the given price level, P_1 on $SRAS_1$, the quantity supplied of Real GDP is Q_1. When higher wage rates are introduced, a firm's profits at a given price level decrease. Consequently, the firm reduces production. In the diagram, this corresponds to moving from Q_1 to Q_2, which at the given price level is point B. Point B represents a point on a new aggregate supply curve ($SRAS_2$). Thus, a rise in equilibrium wage rates leads to a leftward shift in the aggregate supply curve. The steps are simply reversed for a fall in equilibrium wage rates.

PRICES OF NONLABOR INPUTS There are other inputs to the production process besides labor. Changes in their prices affect the *SRAS* curve in the same way as changes in wage rates do. An increase in the price of a nonlabor input (e.g., oil) shifts the *SRAS* curve leftward; a decrease in the price of a nonlabor input shifts the *SRAS* curve rightward.

PRODUCTIVITY *Productivity* describes the output produced per unit of input employed over some period of time. While various inputs can become more productive, let's consider the input labor. An increase in labor productivity means businesses will produce more output with the same amount of labor. This causes the *SRAS* curve to shift rightward. A decrease in labor productivity means businesses will produce less output with the same amount of labor. This causes the *SRAS* curve to shift leftward. A host of factors

Wage Rates and a Shift in the Short-Run Aggregate Supply Curve

A rise in wage rates shifts the short-run aggregate supply curve leftward. A fall in wage rates shifts the short-run aggregate supply curve rightward.

lead to increased labor productivity, including a more educated labor force, a larger stock of capital goods, and technological advancements.

SUPPLY SHOCKS Major natural or institutional changes on the supply side of the economy that affect aggregate supply are referred to as *supply shocks*. Bad weather that wipes out a large part of the midwestern wheat crop would be considered a supply shock. So would a major cutback in the supply of oil coming to the United States from the Middle East.

Supply shocks are of two varieties. *Adverse supply shocks* (such as the examples just given) shift the *SRAS* curve leftward, and *beneficial supply shocks* shift it rightward. Examples of the latter include a major oil discovery and unusually good weather leading to increased production of a food staple. These supply shocks are reflected in resource or input prices.

Exhibit 8 summarizes the factors that affect short-run aggregate supply.

SELF-TEST

1. If wage rates decline, explain what happens to the short-run aggregate supply (*SRAS*) curve.

2. Give an example of an increase in labor productivity.

3. Discuss the details of the worker misperceptions explanation for the upward-sloping *SRAS* curve.

Putting *AD* and *SRAS* Together: Short-Run Equilibrium

In this section, we put aggregate demand and short-run aggregate supply together to achieve short-run equilibrium in the economy. Aggregate demand and short-run aggregate supply determine the price level, Real GDP, and the unemployment rate in the short run.

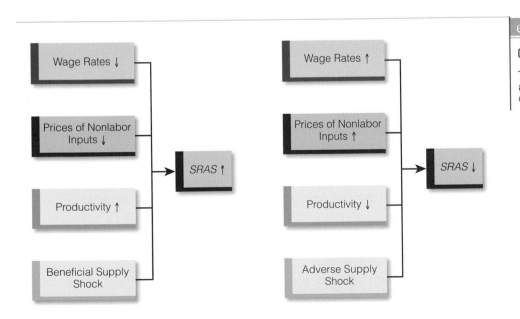

exhibit **8**

Changes in Short-Run Aggregate Supply

The flow charts show how short-run aggregate supply changes given changes in several factors.

economics 24/7

© TIM PAGE/CORBIS

THE VIETNAM WAR AND *AD-SRAS*

The tools of aggregate demand and aggregate supply are used in economics for explanatory and predictive purposes. Let's put ourselves in the position of an economist working with aggregate demand and aggregate supply. In the mid-1960s, the problem we are faced with is predicting the effect on Real GDP and the price level that will result from the economic actions associated with U.S. involvement in Vietnam. There are two main facts: (1) Beginning around 1965–1966, U.S. involvement in Vietnam escalated, with resulting increases in military spending. (2) During this period, the Federal Reserve increased the money supply. How would these actions affect Real GDP and the price level?

First, if we assume that taxes were not being raised to finance increased military spending, it follows that an increase in government military spending shifts the *AD*

curve rightward. The increase in the money supply also shifts the *AD* curve rightward. According to our *AD-SRAS* diagrammatics, a shift rightward in the *AD* curve will raise Real GDP and the price level. Did this actually happen? It did. During the period 1965–1969, Real GDP steadily increased, as did the inflation rate. It is interesting to look at the year-to-year changes in each factor. Here are the data:

Year	Real GDP (trillions of dollars)	Inflation rate
1965	$3.2	1.7%
1966	$3.4	2.7%
1967	$3.5	2.8%
1968	$3.6	4.2%
1969	$3.8	4.9%

How Short-Run Equilibrium in the Economy Is Achieved

Exhibit 9 shows an aggregate demand (*AD*) curve and a short-run aggregate supply (*SRAS*) curve. We consider the quantity demanded of Real GDP and the quantity supplied of Real GDP at three different price levels: P_1, P_2, and P_E.

At P_1, the quantity supplied of Real GDP (Q_2) is greater than the quantity demanded (Q_1). There is a surplus of goods. As a result, the price level drops, firms decrease output, and consumers increase consumption. Why do consumers increase consumption as the price level drops? (Hint: Think of the real balance, the interest rate, and the international trade effects.)

At P_2, the quantity supplied of Real GDP (Q_1) is less than the quantity demanded (Q_2). There is a shortage of goods. As a result, the price level rises, firms increase output, and consumers decrease consumption.

In instances of both surplus and shortage, economic forces are moving the economy toward *E*, where the quantity demanded of Real GDP equals the (short-run) quantity supplied of Real GDP. This is the point of **short-run equilibrium**. P_E is the short-run equilibrium price level; Q_E is the short-run equilibrium Real GDP.

A change in aggregate demand, short-run aggregate supply, or both will obviously affect the price level and/or Real GDP. For example, an increase in aggregate demand raises the equilibrium price level and, in the short run, Real GDP (Exhibit 10(a)). An

Short-Run Equilibrium

The condition that exists in the economy when the quantity demanded of Real GDP equals the (short-run) quantity supplied of Real GDP. This condition is met where the aggregate demand curve intersects the short-run aggregate supply curve.

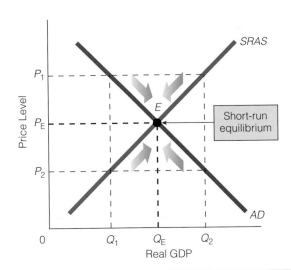

exhibit 9

Short-Run Equilibrium

At P_1, the quantity supplied of Real GDP is greater than the quantity demanded. As a result, the price level falls and firms decrease output. At P_2, the quantity demanded of Real GDP is greater than the quantity supplied. As a result, the price level rises and firms increase output. Short-run equilibrium occurs at point E, where the quantity demanded of Real GDP equals the (short-run) quantity supplied. This is at the intersection of the aggregate demand (AD) curve and the short-run aggregate supply ($SRAS$) curve. (Note: Although real-world AD and $SRAS$ curves can, and likely do, have some curvature to them, we have drawn both as straight lines, This does not affect the analysis. Whenever the analysis is not disturbed, we follow suit throughout this text.)

increase in short-run aggregate supply lowers the equilibrium price level and raises Real GDP (Exhibit 10(b)). A decrease in short-run aggregate supply raises the equilibrium price level and lowers Real GDP (Exhibit 10(c)).

Thinking in Terms of Short-Run Equilibrium Changes in the Economy

Earlier, you learned that certain factors can lead to a change in aggregate demand. You also learned that certain factors can lead to a change in short-run aggregate supply. Then you learned that if either aggregate demand or short-run aggregate supply changes, the price level and Real GDP will all change in the short run.

Exhibit 11 shows us how changes in AD or $SRAS$ can impact the economy and change P and Q. (Take a look at Exhibit 11 as we continue our discussion.) For example,

exhibit 10

Changes in Short-Run Equilibrium in the Economy

(a) An increase in aggregate demand increases the price level and Real GDP. (b) An increase in short-run aggregate supply decreases the price level and increases Real GDP. (c) A decrease in short-run aggregate supply increases the price level and decreases Real GDP.

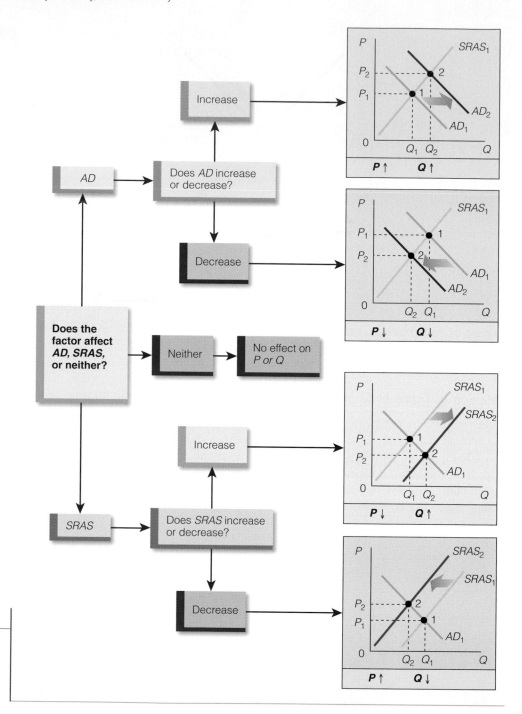

exhibit **11**

How a Factor Affects the Price Level and Real GDP in the Short Run

In the exhibit, P = price level and Q = Real GDP.

when a factor changes, the first thing we ask ourselves is whether the factor affects the AD curve or the $SRAS$ curve. If the answer is neither, then there will be no change in either curve.

If the answer is the AD curve, then we identify whether the AD curve shifts to the right or to the left. If the answer is the $SRAS$ curve, we identify whether the $SRAS$ curve shifts to the right or to the left.

After the shift in one or more curves, we identify the new equilibrium and identify what has happened to both the price level and Real GDP in the short run.

economics 24/7

AGGREGATE DEMAND, THE GREAT DEPRESSION, AND SCRABBLE

Economist Christina Romer writes, "At the broadest conceptual level, the Great Depression in the United States can be analyzed quite well with the simple aggregate supply–aggregate demand model familiar to introductory economics students. Between 1929 and 1933, a series of shocks caused aggregate demand to decline repeatedly in the United States. [In other words, the *AD* curve repeatedly shifted to the left.] These declines in aggregate demand moved the economy down along an upward-sloping aggregate supply curve. The net result was both progressively worsening unemployment and deflation."[2]

Certainly, a fall in aggregate demand can cause a rise in unemployment and a fall in prices. But can a repeated fall in aggregate demand lead to anything else? In an indirect way, it can. In fact, if it weren't for falling aggregate demand and the ensuing Great Depression, we might not have one of the more popular games people play—Scrabble.

Scrabble was invented by Alfred M. Butts of Poughkeepsie, New York. Before Butts invented Scrabble, he was an architect. Because of the Great Depression, he lost his job and couldn't find another. Wondering what to do with his time, he started analyzing different board games. He found that every game fell into one of three categories: number games, such as dice and bingo; move games, such as chess and checkers; and word games, such as anagrams.

Alfred Butts set out to create a board game that would combine chance and skill. He combined features of anagrams and crossword puzzles and called his game Criss Cross Word. The first boards of his Criss Cross Word game were hand drawn with his architectural drafting equipment. In time, Butts's game was purchased and renamed Scrabble.

[2]Christina Romer, "The Nation in Depression," *Journal of Economic Perspectives* (Spring 1993): 25.

To illustrate, suppose there is an adverse supply shock in the economy. We know this will shift the *SRAS* curve leftward.

Nothing has changed on the demand side of the economy, so the *AD* curve remains stable.

A leftward shift in the *SRAS* curve in the face of an unchanged *AD* curve ends up increasing the price level and decreasing Real GDP.

An Important Exhibit

Exhibit 12 brings together much of the material we have discussed in this chapter. To illustrate, much of our discussion up to this point has been about the economy in the short run; specifically, it has been about changes in the price level (*P*) and Real GDP (*Q*) in the short run.

Exhibit 12 tells us that changes in *AD* and *SRAS* will change the price level and Real GDP in the short run. Then we see what factors will actually change *AD* and what factors will change *SRAS*.

While following the process in Exhibit 12, consider what a fall in the interest rate will do to *P* and *Q* in the short run. We know that if the interest rate falls, both consumption (*C*) and investment (*I*) will rise. If both *C* and *I* rise, the *AD* will rise or the *AD* curve will shift rightward. If the *AD* curve shifts rightward, the price level (*P*) will rise and so will Real GDP (*Q*).

A Closer Look

exhibit 12

A Summary Exhibit of *AD* and *SRAS*

A CLOSER LOOK

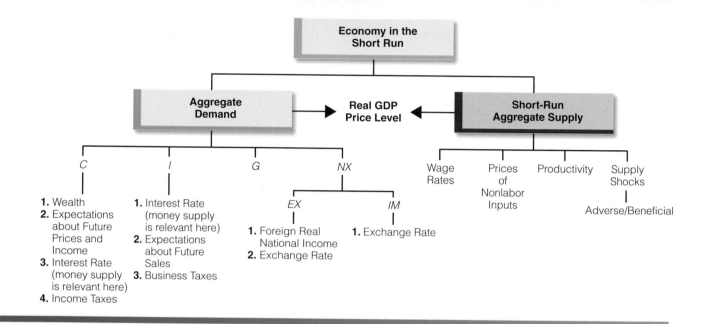

Long-Run Aggregate Supply

In this section, we discuss long-run aggregate supply and draw a long-run aggregate supply (*LRAS*) curve. We also discuss long-run equilibrium and explain how it differs from short-run equilibrium.

Going from the Short Run to the Long Run

Graphically, short-run equilibrium is at the intersection of the *AD* curve and the (upward-sloping) *SRAS* curve. As an earlier section explains, economists give different reasons for an upward-sloping *SRAS* curve. Recall that those reasons have to do with:

1. Sticky wages

2. Worker misperceptions

macro Theme

In an earlier chapter we discussed three macroeconomic categories, one of which was the *P-Q* category. We said that much of the work that is done in macroeconomics has to do with either *P*, the price level, or *Q*, Real GDP. In this chapter, we have shown how both *P* and *Q* are determined in the economy in the short run.

economics 24/7

REALITY CAN BE MESSY, AND CORRECT PREDICTIONS CAN BE DIFFICULT TO MAKE

In a textbook like this one, we can change one factor and then trace its effects through the economy, ultimately to the price level and Real GDP. To illustrate, suppose business taxes decline. We know this will lead to a rise in investment, which in turn will lead to a rise in *AD*. Now, assuming that *SRAS* has not changed, a rise in *AD* will lead to a rise in the price level and a rise in Real GDP. Here are the links again:

$$\text{Business taxes} \downarrow \rightarrow C \uparrow \rightarrow AD \uparrow \rightarrow P \uparrow Q \uparrow$$

where *C* = consumption, *AD* = aggregate demand, *P* = price level, and *Q* = Real GDP.

In reality, though, more than one thing could change at a time. Or at a minimum, two or more things could change within a few days or weeks of each other. To illustrate, let's suppose there is a factor on the demand side of the economy that changes at about the same time as a factor on the supply–side. Specifically, wealth rises at the same time as price of nonlabor inputs rises. What will ultimately happen to the price level and Real GDP? Well, let's break the problem down into small parts and proceed to find out.

1. We know that a rise in wealth will raise *AD*. The *AD* curve shifts rightward.

2. We know that a rise in nonlabor input prices will lower *SRAS*. The *SRAS* curve will shift leftward.

3. Because we have both the *AD* and *SRAS* curves changing at the same time, or about the same time, the overall change in the price level and Real GDP will depend on the relative shifts of the *AD* and *SRAS* curves.

4. Let's suppose the *AD* curve shifts rightward by more than the *SRAS* curve shifts leftward. (You may want to draw this.) As a result, the price level and Real GDP will rise.

5. If, however, the *AD* curve shifts rightward by less than the *SRAS* curve shifts leftward, then the price level will rise and Real GDP will fall.

6. Finally, if the *AD* curve shifts rightward to the same degree that the *SRAS* curve shifts leftward, Real GDP will not change and the price level will rise.

Sometimes, all this has something to say about economists' predictions. It is quite easy to put forth correct predictions in economics when only one thing changes and everything else remains constant. What is hard to do is put forth correct predictions when more than one thing changes at a time and when the things that change pull the economy in opposite directions. We have seen this through our example. Specifically, while the increase in *AD* tends to raise Real GDP, the decrease in *SRAS* tends to lower Real GDP. What will be the final effect on Real GDP? As we have seen, it depends on the relative shifts in *AD* and *SRAS*.

It follows, then, that short-run equilibrium identifies the Real GDP the economy produces when any of these two conditions hold.

In time, though, wages will become unstuck and misperceptions will turn into accurate perceptions. When this happens, the economy is said to be in the *long run*. In other words, in the long run, these two conditions do not hold.

An important macroeconomic question is: *Will the level of Real GDP the economy produces in the long run be the same as in the short run?* Most economists say that it will not be. They argue that in the long run, the economy produces the full–employment Real GDP or the **Natural Real GDP** (Q_N). The aggregate supply curve that identifies the output the economy produces in the long run is the **long-run aggregate supply (*LRAS*) curve**. It is portrayed as the vertical line in Exhibit 13.

Natural Real GDP

The Real GDP that is produced at the natural unemployment rate. The Real GDP that is produced when the economy is in long-run equilibrium.

Long-Run Aggregate Supply (*LRAS*) Curve

The *LRAS* curve is a vertical line at the level of Natural Real GDP. It represents the output the economy produces when wages and prices have adjusted to their (final) equilibrium levels and neither producers nor workers have any relevant misperceptions.

Long-Run Equilibrium

The condition that exists in the economy when wages and prices have adjusted to their (final) equilibrium levels and workers do not have any relevant misperceptions. Graphically, long-run equilibrium occurs at the intersection of the *AD* and *LRAS* curves.

exhibit **13**

Long-Run Aggregate Supply (*LRAS*) Curve

The *LRAS* curve is a vertical line at the level of Natural Real GDP. It represents the output the economy produces when all economywide adjustments have taken place and workers do not have any relevant misperceptions.

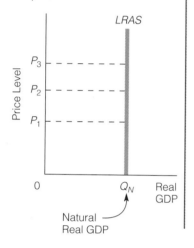

It follows that **long-run equilibrium** identifies the level of Real GDP the economy produces when wages and prices have adjusted to their (final) equilibrium levels and there are no misperceptions on the part of workers. Graphically, this occurs at the intersection of the *AD* and *LRAS* curves. Furthermore, the level of Real GDP that the economy produces in long-run equilibrium is Natural Real GDP (Q_N).

Short-Run Equilibrium, Long-Run Equilibrium, and Disequilibrium

There are two equilibrium states in an economy: short-run equilibrium and long-run equilibrium. These two equilibrium states are graphically shown in Exhibit 14.

In Exhibit 14(a), the economy is at point 1, producing Q_1 amount of Real GDP. Notice that at point 1, the quantity supplied of Real GDP (in the short run) is equal to the quantity demanded of Real GDP, and both are Q_1. The economy is in short-run equilibrium.

In Exhibit 14(b), the economy is at point 1, producing Q_N. In other words, it is producing Natural Real GDP. The economy is in long-run equilibrium when it produces Q_N.

Notice that in both short-run and long-run equilibrium, the quantity supplied of Real GDP equals the quantity demanded. So what is the difference between short-run equilibrium and long-run equilibrium? In long-run equilibrium, quantity supplied and demanded of Real GDP equal Natural Real GDP (see Exhibit 14(b)). But in short-run equilibrium, quantity supplied and demanded of Real GDP are either more than or less than Natural Real GDP.

Let's illustrate with numbers. Suppose Q_N = $9.0 trillion. In long-run equilibrium, quantity supplied of Real GDP = quantity demanded of Real GDP = $9.0 trillion. In short-run equilibrium, quantity supplied of Real GDP equals quantity demanded, but neither equals $9.0 trillion. For example, it could be that quantity supplied of Real GDP = quantity demanded of Real GDP = $8.5 trillion.

When the economy is in neither short-run equilibrium nor long-run equilibrium, it is said to be in *disequilibrium*. Essentially, disequilibrium is the state of the economy as it moves from one short-run equilibrium to another or from short-run equilibrium to long-run equilibrium. In disequilibrium, quantity supplied of Real GDP and quantity demanded of Real GDP are not equal.

exhibit **14**

Equilibrium States of the Economy

There are two equilibrium states in the economy: short-run equilibrium, shown in part (a), and long-run equilibrium, shown in part (b). During the time an economy moves from one equilibrium to another, it is said to be in disequilibrium.

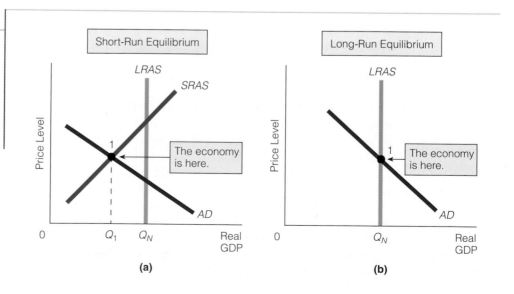

SELF-TEST

1. What is the difference between short-run equilibrium and long-run equilibrium?

2. Diagrammatically represent an economy that is in neither short-run equilibrium nor long-run equilibrium.

A Reader Asks...

Do My Job Prospects Depend on *AD* and *SRAS*?

Aggregate demand (*AD*) and short-run aggregate supply (*SRAS*) appear to determine Real GDP in the short run. Will *AD* and *SRAS* also influence my job prospects after I graduate from college?

Your job prospects will depend in part on your major, your grades, and your performance in job interviews. But your prospects will also depend on where the *AD* curve and the *SRAS* curve "intersect." That is, your job prospects will depend on whether *AD* and *SRAS* have been increasing, decreasing, or remaining constant.

To illustrate, suppose that some months before you graduate, interest rates rise and the dollar appreciates. An increase in interest rates tends to reduce durable goods spending and investment spending—so both consumption and investment decline. If the dollar appreciates, U.S. goods become more expensive for foreigners, so they buy less. Also, foreign goods become cheaper for Americans, so they buy more. The result is that exports fall and imports rise, or net exports decline.

If consumption, investment, and net exports fall, aggregate demand in the U.S. economy declines. In other words, the *AD* curve shifts to the left.

As a result of declining aggregate demand in the economy, there is a new short-run equilibrium. The new short-run equilibrium is at a lower Real GDP level. In other words, firms have cut back on the quantity of goods and services they produce. Many of the firms that cut back may be the ones at which you hope to find a job after college. Your job prospects look slightly less rosy than they did before the changes in the economy.

A statement in the magazine *The Economist* provides further evidence of the connection between the state of the economy and your job prospects. In its November 1, 2001, edition, the magazine stated, "the downturn [in the economy] is plainly bad news for the [MBA] students, especially since banking and consulting—two of the industries which, in less interesting times, reliably hire hundreds of MBAs—have curtailed their recruiting."

! analyzing the scene

Why does Toby wish interest rates were lower? How can a change in interest rates affect a person's buying behavior?

Some people will take out a loan to buy a car. A decrease in interest rates lowers the monthly payments on that loan. Given this, individuals are more likely to borrow funds, say, to buy a car the lower interest rates happen to be.

Why is Marcy's trip to Europe getting more expensive? How can a change in exchange rates affect a person's life?

Exchange rates are determined in much the same way interest rates are determined—by the forces of supply and demand. The price Marcy will pay for the goods and services she buys in Europe is affected by the dollar price she has to pay for the euro and the British pound. For example, suppose Marcy has reservations at a hotel in London that charges £70 a night. At an exchange rate £1 = $1.65, Marcy would pay $115.50 a night. But at an exchange rate of £1 = $1.85, she would have to pay $129.50 a night.

If you study economics and still end up in the unemployment line, will you really know why you're there?

You should have a better idea of why you might be in the unemployment line after reading this chapter than you did before reading it. According to the *AD-SRAS* framework in this chapter, changes in either *AD* or *SRAS* will change Real GDP in the short run. And changes in Real GDP will

affect the unemployment rate. You might be standing in the unemployment line because the economy's *AD* curve shifted to the left.

How can foreign income affect U.S. unemployment?

Foreign income is linked to the unemployment rate in the United States through changes in Real GDP. If foreign income falls, foreigners may buy fewer exports from the United States. And if U.S. export spending declines, so does aggregate demand for U.S.-produced goods and services. A decline in aggregate demand, in turn, leads to lower Real GDP in the short run. And a lower Real GDP is likely to come with a higher unemployment rate.

chapter summary

Aggregate Demand

- Aggregate demand refers to the quantity demanded of all goods and services (Real GDP) at different price levels, *ceteris paribus*.

- The aggregate demand (*AD*) curve slopes downward, indicating an inverse relationship between the price level and the quantity demanded of Real GDP.

- The aggregate demand curve slopes downward because of the real balance, interest rate, and international trade effects.

- The real balance effect states that the inverse relationship between the price level and the quantity demanded of Real GDP is established through changes in the value of a person's monetary wealth or money holdings. Specifically, a fall in the price level causes purchasing power to rise, which increases a person's monetary wealth. As people become wealthier, they buy more goods. A rise in the price level causes purchasing power to fall, which reduces a person's monetary wealth. As people become less wealthy, they buy fewer goods.

- The interest rate effect states that the inverse relationship between the price level and the quantity demanded of Real GDP is established through changes in household and business spending that is sensitive to changes in interest rates. If the price level rises, a person needs more money to buy a fixed bundle of goods. In an effort to acquire more money, the demand for credit rises, as does the interest rate. As the interest rate rises, businesses and households borrow less and buy fewer goods. Thus, the quantity demanded of Real GDP falls. If the price level falls, a person needs less money to buy a fixed bundle of goods. Part of the increase in a person's monetary wealth is saved, so the supply of credit rises, and the interest rate falls. As the interest rate falls, businesses and households borrow more and buy more goods. Thus, the quantity demanded of Real GDP rises.

- The international trade effect states that the inverse relationship between the price level and the quantity demanded of Real GDP is established through foreign sector spending. Specifically, as the price level in the United States rises, U.S. goods become relatively more expensive than foreign goods, and both Americans and foreigners buy fewer U.S. goods. The quantity demanded of (U.S.) Real GDP falls. As the price level in the United States falls, U.S. goods become relatively less expensive than foreign goods, and both Americans and foreigners buy more U.S. goods. The quantity demanded of (U.S.) Real GDP rises.

- At a given price level, a rise in consumption, investment, government purchases, or net exports will increase aggregate demand and shift the *AD* curve to the right. At a given price level, a fall in consumption, investment, government purchases, or net exports will decrease aggregate demand and shift the *AD* curve to the left.

Factors That Can Change C, I, and NX (EX – IM) and Therefore Can Change AD

- The following factors can change consumption: wealth, expectations about future prices and income, the interest rate, and income taxes. The following factors can change investment: the interest rate, expectations about future sales, and business taxes. The following factors can change net exports (exports – imports): foreign real national income and the exchange rate. A change in the money supply can affect one or more spending components (e.g., consumption) and therefore affect aggregate demand.

Short-Run Aggregate Supply

- Aggregate supply refers to the quantity supplied of all goods and services (Real GDP) at different price levels, *ceteris paribus*.

- The short-run aggregate supply (*SRAS*) curve is upward sloping, indicating a direct relationship between the price level and the quantity supplied of Real GDP.
- A decrease in wage rates, a decrease in the price of nonlabor inputs, an increase in productivity, and beneficial supply shocks all shift the *SRAS* curve to the right. An increase in wage rates, an increase in the price of nonlabor inputs, a decrease in productivity, and adverse supply shocks all shift the *SRAS* curve to the left.

Short-Run Equilibrium

- Graphically, short-run equilibrium exists at the intersection of the *AD* and *SRAS* curves. A shift in either or both of these curves can change the price level and Real GDP. For example, an increase in aggregate demand increases the price level and Real GDP, *ceteris paribus*.

Long-Run Aggregate Supply and Long-Run Equilibrium

- The long-run aggregate supply (*LRAS*) curve is vertical at the Natural Real GDP level.
- Graphically, long-run equilibrium exists at the intersection of the *AD* and *LRAS* curves. It is the condition that exists in the economy when all economywide adjustments have taken place and workers do not hold any (relevant) misperceptions. In long-run equilibrium, quantity demanded of Real GDP = quantity supplied of Real GDP = Natural Real GDP.

Three States of an Economy

- An economy can be in short-run equilibrium, long-run equilibrium, or disequilibrium.

key terms and concepts

Aggregate Demand	Purchasing Power	Appreciation	Short-Run Equilibrium
Aggregate Demand (*AD*) Curve	Interest Rate Effect	Depreciation	Natural Real GDP
Real Balance Effect	International Trade Effect	Aggregate Supply	Long-Run Aggregate Supply (*LRAS*) Curve
Monetary Wealth	Wealth	Short-Run Aggregate Supply (*SRAS*) Curve	Long-Run Equilibrium
	Exchange Rate		

questions and problems

1   Is aggregate demand a specific dollar amount? For example, would it be correct to say that aggregate demand is $9 trillion this year?

2   Explain each of the following: (a) real balance effect, (b) interest rate effect, and (c) international trade effect.

3   Graphically portray each of the following: (a) a change in the quantity demanded of Real GDP and (b) a change in aggregate demand.

4   The amount of Real GDP (real output) that households are willing and able to buy may change if there is a change in either (a) the price level or (b) some nonprice factor, such as wealth, interest rates, and so on. Do you agree or disagree? Explain your answer.

5   Explain what happens to aggregate demand in each of the following cases:
   a   The interest rate rises.
   b   Wealth falls.
   c   The dollar depreciates relative to foreign currencies.
   d   Households expect lower prices in the future.
   e   Business taxes rise.

6   Will a direct increase in the price of U.S. goods relative to foreign goods lead to a change in the quantity demanded of Real GDP or to a change in aggregate demand? Will a change in the exchange rate that subsequently increases the price of U.S. goods relative to foreign goods lead to a change in the quantity demanded of Real GDP or to a change in aggregate demand? Explain your answers.

7   Explain how each of the following will affect short-run aggregate supply:
   a   An increase in wage rates
   b   A beneficial supply shock
   c   An increase in the productivity of labor
   d   A decrease in the price of a nonlabor resource (e.g., oil)

8   What is the difference between a change in the quantity supplied of Real GDP and a change in short-run aggregate supply?

9   A change in the price level affects which of the following?
   a   The quantity demanded of Real GDP
   b   Aggregate demand
   c   Short-run aggregate supply
   d   The quantity supplied of Real GDP

10 In the short run, what is the impact on the price level, and Real GDP of each of the following:

   a   An increase in consumption brought about by a decrease in interest rates

   b   A decrease in exports brought about by an appreciation of the dollar

   c   A rise in wage rates

   d   A beneficial supply shock

   e   An adverse supply shock

   f   A decline in productivity

11 Identify the details of each of the following explanations for an upward-sloping *SRAS* curve:

   a   Sticky-wage explanation

   b   Worker-misperception explanation

12 What is the difference between short-run equilibrium and long-run equilibrium?

working with numbers and graphs

1 Suppose that at a price index of 154, the quantity demanded of (U.S.) Real GDP is $10.0 trillion worth of goods. Do these data represent aggregate demand or a point on an aggregate demand curve? Explain your answer.

2 Diagrammatically represent the effect on the price level and Real GDP in the short run of each of the following:

   a   An increase in wealth

   b   An increase in wage rates

   c   An increase in labor productivity

3 Diagrammatically represent the following and identify the effect on Real GDP and the price level in the short run:

   a   An increase in *SRAS* that is greater than the increase in *AD*

   b   A decrease in *AD* that is greater than the increase in *SRAS*

   c   An increase in *SRAS* that is less than the increase in *AD*

4 In the following figure, which part is representative of each of the following:

   a   A decrease in wage rates

   b   An increase in the price level

   c   A beneficial supply shock

   d   An increase in the price of nonlabor inputs

5 In the following figure, which of the points is representative of each of the following:

   a   The lowest Real GDP

   b   The highest Real GDP

   c   A decrease in *SRAS* that is greater than an increase in *AD*

(a)

(b)

(c)

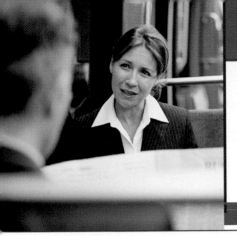
The Self-Regulating Economy

Setting the Scene Each weekday morning, approximately 100,000 New Yorkers ride the train from their homes on Long Island to their workplaces in Manhattan. Each weekday afternoon, those same 100,000 people take the return trip. Listen to a few conversations that occurred on a return trip one day in June. The time is 5:16 P.M.

FIRST CONVERSATION

Yvonne:
I don't know. Wages are rising, but then so is the unemployment rate. I may be the next to go. If I am, then I may have to move back in with my parents for a while.

Wendy:
That would be a shame after all you've been through these last few months.

Yvonne:
I know.

SECOND CONVERSATION

Robert:
I read today that people are starting to save more than they have in the past. I'm not sure that's good for the economy.

Charles:
Why wouldn't it be?

Robert:
Well, if everyone is saving more, who's going to be spending? Cut down on spending and we might just head straight into a recession.

THIRD CONVERSATION

Priscilla:
I read in the *Journal* that the president wants to lower taxes for businesses. That might stimulate production in the economy, but I'm not sure it will do anything for consumption. Don't people have to be able to buy the goods that businesses produce?

Jeff:
You remember Say's law from college, don't you? Supply creates its own demand.

Priscilla:
I'm not sure I ever believed that.

FOURTH CONVERSATION

José:
I think it's a little like when you have a cold or the flu. You don't need to see a doctor. In time, your body heals itself. That's sort of the way the economy works too. We don't really need government "coming to our rescue" every time the economy gets a cold.

Mark:
But what happens if the economy gets really sick? Can it heal itself then?

? Here are some questions to keep in mind as you read this chapter:

- *What does the economy have to do with Yvonne possibly having to move back in with her parents?*

- *Can people saving more be bad for the economy?*

- *What is Say's law and what does it say about production and consumption?*

- *According to José, how does the economy work?*

See **analyzing the scene** at the end of this chapter for answers to these questions.

The Classical View

The term *classical economics* is often used to refer to an era in the history of economic thought that stretched from about 1750 to the late 1800s or early 1900s. Although classical economists lived and wrote many years ago, their ideas are often employed by some modern-day economists.

✳ Classical Economists and Say's Law

You know from your study of supply and demand that there can be temporary shortages and surpluses in markets. For example, there may be a surplus in the apple market. But can there be a general surplus (a general glut of goods and services) in the economy? The classical economists thought not, largely because they believed in Say's law (named after J.B. Say). In its simplest version, **Say's law** states that supply creates its own demand.

Say's law is most easily understood in terms of a barter economy. Consider a person baking bread in a barter economy; he is a supplier of bread. According to Say, the baker works at his trade because he plans to demand other goods. As he is baking bread, the baker is thinking of the goods and services he will obtain in exchange for it. Thus, his act of supplying bread is linked to his demand for other goods. Supply creates its own demand.

If the supplying of some goods is simultaneously the demanding of other goods, then Say's law implies that there cannot be either (1) a general overproduction of goods (where supply in the economy is greater than demand in the economy) or (2) a general underproduction of goods (where demand in the economy is greater than supply in the economy).

Now suppose the baker is baking bread in a money economy. Does Say's law hold? Over a period of time, the baker earns an income as a result of his supplying bread. But what does he do with his income? One thing he does is buy goods and services. However, his demand for goods and services does not necessarily match the income that he generates through his actions as a supplier of bread. The baker may spend less than his full income because he engages in saving. Noting this, we might think that Say's law does not hold in a money economy because the act of supplying goods and services, and thus earning income, need not create an equal amount of demand.

But the classical economists disagreed. They argued that even in a money economy, where individuals sometimes spend less than their full incomes, Say's law still holds. Their argument was partly based on the assumption of interest rate flexibility.

Say's Law

Supply creates its own demand. Production creates demand sufficient to purchase all goods and services produced.

✳ Classical Economists and Interest Rate Flexibility

For Say's law to hold in a money economy, funds saved must give rise to an equal amount of funds invested; that is, what leaves the spending stream through one door must enter through another door. If not, then some of the income earned from supplying goods may not be used to demand goods (good-bye Say's law). As a result, there will be an overproduction of goods.

The classical economists argued that saving is matched by an equal amount of investment because of interest rate flexibility in the credit market. We explain their argument using Exhibit 1, where I represents investment and S represents saving.

Notice that I_1 is downward sloping, indicating an inverse relationship between the amount of funds firms invest and the interest rate (i). The reason for this is straightforward. The interest rate is the cost of borrowing funds. The higher the interest rate, the fewer funds firms borrow and invest; the lower the interest rate, the more funds firms borrow and invest.

Notice that S_1 is upward sloping, indicating a direct relationship between the amount of funds households save and the interest rate. The reason is that the higher the interest rate, the higher the reward for saving (or the higher the opportunity cost of consuming), and therefore, the fewer funds consumed and the more funds saved. Market-equilibrating forces

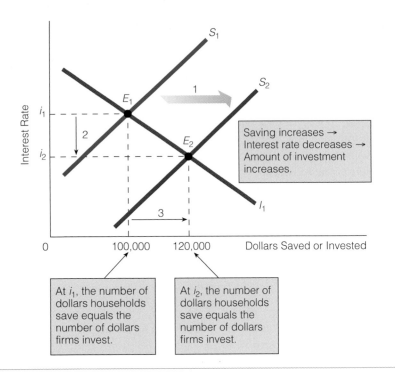

exhibit **1**

The Classical View of the Credit Market

In classical theory, the interest rate is flexible and adjusts so that saving equals investment. Thus, if saving increases and the saving curve shifts rightward from S_1 to S_2 (arrow 1), the increase in saving eventually puts pressure on the interest rate and moves it downward from i_1 to i_2 (arrow 2). A new equilibrium is established at E_2 (arrow 3), where once again the amount households save equals the amount firms invest.

move the credit market to interest rate i_1 and equilibrium point E_1. At E_1, the number of dollars households save ($100,000) equals the number of dollars firms invest ($100,000).

Suppose now that saving increases at each interest rate. In Exhibit 1, we represent this by a rightward shift in the saving curve from S_1 to S_2. The classical economists believed that an increase in saving will put downward pressure on the interest rate, moving it to i_2, thereby increasing the number of dollars firms invest. Ultimately, the number of dollars households save ($120,000) will once again equal the number of dollars firms invest ($120,000). Interest rate flexibility ensures that saving equals investment. (What goes out one door comes in the other door.) In short, changes in the interest rate uphold Say's law in a money economy where there is saving.

Let's use a few numbers to show exactly what classical economists were saying. Suppose that at a given price level, total expenditures (TE) in a very tiny economy are $5,000. We know that total expenditures (total spending on domestic goods and services) equal the sum of consumption (C), investment (I), government purchases (G), and net exports ($EX - IM$). If $C = \$3,000$, $I = \$600$, $G = \$1,200$, and $EX - IM = \$200$, then

$$TE = C + I + G + (EX - IM)$$
$$\$5,000 = \$3,000 + \$600 + \$1,200 + \$200$$

Furthermore, let's assume the $5,000 worth of goods and services that the four sectors of the economy want to purchase also happens to be the exact dollar amount of goods and services that suppliers want to sell.

Next, let's increase saving in the economy. Saving (S) is equal to the amount of a person's disposable income (Y_d) minus consumption (C). For example, if Harriet earns a disposable income of $40,000 a year and spends $38,000, she saves $2,000.

$$\text{Saving } (S) = \text{Disposable income } (Y_d) - \text{Consumption } (C)$$

For saving to increase, consumption must decrease. Let's say saving increases by $100; then, consumption must fall from $3,000 to $2,900. At first glance, this seems to imply that total expenditures will fall to $4,900. But classical economists disagreed. They said that investment will increase by $100, going from $600 to $700. Total expenditures will remain constant at $5,000 and will be equal to the dollar amount of goods and services suppliers want to sell.

$$TE = C + I + G + (EX - IM)$$
$$\$5,000 = \$2,900 + \$700 + \$1,200 + \$200$$

Exhibit 2 summarizes this discussion.

According to the classical view of the economy, then, Say's law holds both in a barter economy and in a money economy. In a money economy, according to classical economists, interest rates will adjust to equate saving and investment. Therefore, any fall in consumption (and consequent rise in saving) will be matched by an equal rise in investment. In essence, at a given price level, total expenditures will not decrease as a result of an increase in saving.

What does an increase in saving imply for aggregate demand (*AD*)? An earlier chapter explains that aggregate demand changes only if total spending in the economy changes at a given price level. Therefore, because there is no change in total spending as a result of an increase in saving, there is no change in aggregate demand.

macro *Theme*

Economists do not always agree as to how the economy works. What you have just read is the classical position on interest rate flexibility and an increase in saving matched by an equal increase in investment. What leaves the spending stream by one door enters through another door. In the next chapter, you will learn about a group of economists that take issue with this classical position. There are numerous debates in macroeconomics, as you soon will find out.

Classical Economists on Prices and Wages

exhibit 2

The Classical View of Say's Law in a Money Economy

According to classical economists, a decrease in consumption and subsequent increase in saving will be matched by an equal increase in investment. Thus, there is no change in total expenditures.

Classical economists believed that most, if not all, markets are competitive. That is, supply and demand operate in all markets. If, for example, there is a surplus of labor in the labor market, it will be temporary. Soon, the wage rate will decline, and the quantity supplied of labor will equal the quantity demanded of labor. Similarly, if there is a shortage of labor in the labor market, the wage rate will rise, and the quantity supplied will equal the quantity demanded.

What holds for wages in the labor market holds for prices in the goods and services market. Prices will adjust quickly to any surpluses or shortages, and equilibrium will be quickly reestablished.

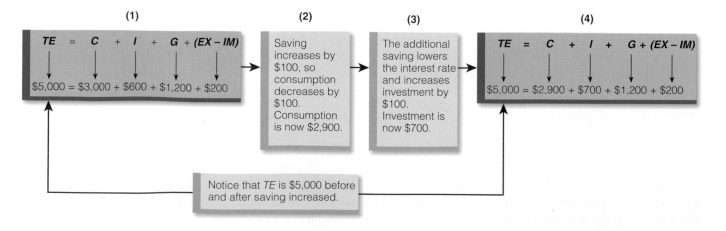

(1)

$$TE = C + I + G + (EX - IM)$$
$$\$5,000 = \$3,000 + \$600 + \$1,200 + \$200$$

(2) Saving increases by $100, so consumption decreases by $100. Consumption is now $2,900.

(3) The additional saving lowers the interest rate and increases investment by $100. Investment is now $700.

(4)

$$TE = C + I + G + (EX - IM)$$
$$\$5,000 = \$2,900 + \$700 + \$1,200 + \$200$$

Notice that *TE* is $5,000 before and after saving increased.

SELF-TEST

(Answers to Self-Test questions are in the Self-Test Appendix.)

1. Explain Say's law in terms of a barter economy.

2. According to classical economists, if saving rises and consumption spending falls, will total spending in the economy decrease? Explain your answer.

3. What is the classical position on prices and wages?

Three States of the Economy

You will need the basic background information provided in this section before we discuss the views of economists who believe the economy is self-regulating. Specifically, we discuss three states of the economy, the correspondence between the labor market and the three states of the economy, and more in this section.

Real GDP and Natural Real GDP: Three Possibilities

In the last chapter, Natural Real GDP is defined as the Real GDP that is produced at the natural unemployment rate. It is the Real GDP that is produced when the economy is in long-run equilibrium.

Economists often refer to the three states of an economy that are possible when we consider the relationship between Real GDP and Natural Real GDP. The possibilities are an economy operating at a level of Real GDP (1) less than Natural Real GDP, (2) greater than Natural Real GDP, or (3) equal to Natural Real GDP.

Three possible states of an economy are:

- Real GDP is less than Natural Real GDP.
- Real GDP is greater than Natural Real GDP.
- Real GDP is equal to Natural Real GDP.

Let's now give a name to each of these three possible states of the economy and graphically portray each.

REAL GDP IS LESS THAN NATURAL REAL GDP (RECESSIONARY GAP) Exhibit 3(a) shows an *AD* curve, an *SRAS* curve, and the *LRAS* curve. It also shows that Natural Real GDP (Q_N) is produced in the long run.

Short-run equilibrium is at the intersection of the *AD* and *SRAS* curves, so in part (a), short-run equilibrium is at point 1. The Real GDP level that the economy is producing at point 1 is designated by Q_1.

Now compare Q_1 with Q_N. Obviously, Q_1 is less than Q_N. In other words, the economy is currently producing a level of Real GDP in the short run that is less than its Natural Real GDP level.

When the Real GDP the economy is producing is less than its Natural Real GDP, the economy is said to be in a **recessionary gap**.

REAL GDP IS GREATER THAN NATURAL REAL GDP (INFLATIONARY GAP) In Exhibit 3(b), the *AD* and *SRAS* curves intersect at point 1, so short-run equilibrium is at point 1. The Real GDP level the economy is producing at point 1 is designated by Q_1.

Q&A

Are we saying here that an economy has to be in one of three states? Isn't this the case for markets too?

Yes. Think back to our discussion of a market in Chapter 3. You learned then that there were three possible relationships between the quantity demanded of a good and the quantity supplied: (1) quantity demand greater than quantity supplied; (2) quantity demanded less than quantity supplied; or (3) quantity demanded equal to quantity supplied. It is much the same with an economy. Real GDP can be either greater than, less than, or equal to Natural Real GDP.

Recessionary Gap

The condition where the Real GDP the economy is producing is less than the Natural Real GDP and the unemployment rate is greater than the natural unemployment rate.

(a)

(b)

(c)

exhibit 3

Real GDP and Natural Real GDP: Three Possibilities

In (a), the economy is currently in short-run equilibrium at a Real GDP level of Q_1. Q_N is Natural Real GDP or the potential output of the economy. Notice that $Q_1 < Q_N$. When this condition ($Q_1 < Q_N$) exists, the economy is said to be in a recessionary gap.

In (b), the economy is currently in short-run equilibrium at a Real GDP level of Q_1. Q_N is Natural Real GDP or the potential output of the economy. Notice that $Q_1 > Q_N$. When this condition ($Q_1 > Q_N$) exists, the economy is said to be in an inflationary gap.

In (c), the economy is currently operating at a Real GDP level of Q_1, which is equal to Q_N. In other words, the economy is producing its Natural Real GDP or potential output. When this condition ($Q_1 = Q_N$) exists, the economy is said to be in long-run equilibrium.

Inflationary Gap

The condition where the Real GDP the economy is producing is greater than the Natural Real GDP and the unemployment rate is less than the natural unemployment rate.

Compare Q_1 with Q_N. Obviously, Q_1 is greater than Q_N. In other words, the economy is currently producing a level of Real GDP in the short run that is greater than its Natural Real GDP level or potential output.

When the Real GDP the economy is producing is greater than its Natural Real GDP, the economy is said to be in an **inflationary gap**.

REAL GDP IS EQUAL TO NATURAL REAL GDP (LONG-RUN EQUILIBRIUM) In Exhibit 3(c), the *AD* and *SRAS* curves indicate that short-run equilibrium is at point 1. The Real GDP level the economy is producing at point 1 is designated by Q_1.

Again compare Q_1 and Q_N. This time, Q_1 is equal to Q_N. In other words, the economy is currently producing a level of Real GDP that is equal to its Natural Real GDP or potential output.

When the Real GDP the economy is producing is equal to its Natural Real GDP, the economy is in *long-run equilibrium*.

The Labor Market and the Three States of the Economy

If the economy can be in three possible states, so can the labor market. We identify the three possible states of the labor market and then tie each state to a possible state of the economy.

We know that the labor market consists of the demand for labor and the supply of labor. Like a goods market, the labor market can manifest (1) equilibrium, (2) a shortage, or (3) a surplus.

Three possible states of the labor market are:

* Equilibrium
* Shortage
* Surplus

Thinking like **AN ECONOMIST**   *The economist often thinks in threes. For the economist, there is either (1) a shortage, (2) a surplus, or (3) equilibrium in a market. Similarly, for the economist, an economy is either (1) in a recessionary gap, (2) in an inflationary gap, or (3) in long-run equilibrium.*

When equilibrium exists in the labor market, there are the same number of jobs available as the number of people who want to work. That is, the quantity demanded of labor is equal to the quantity supplied of labor.

When there is a shortage in the labor market, there are more jobs available than there are people who want to work. That is, the quantity demanded of labor is greater than the quantity supplied of labor.

When there is a surplus in the labor market, there are more people who want to work than there are jobs available; the quantity supplied of labor is greater than the quantity demanded of labor.

RECESSIONARY GAP AND THE LABOR MARKET If the economy is in a recessionary gap, is the labor market in equilibrium, shortage, or surplus? To simplify, suppose the economy is in a recessionary gap producing a Real GDP level of $9 trillion (worth of goods and services) when Natural Real GDP, or potential output, is $10 trillion.

The unemployment rate that exists when the economy produces Natural Real GDP is, of course, the natural unemployment rate. Is the unemployment rate that exists when the economy is in a recessionary gap producing $9 trillion worth of goods and services greater or less than the natural unemployment rate that exists when the economy is producing $10 trillion worth of goods and services? The answer is that the unemployment rate is greater than the natural unemployment rate because fewer workers are needed to produce a Real GDP of $9 trillion than are needed to produce a Real GDP of $10 trillion. *Ceteris paribus,* the unemployment rate will be higher at a Real GDP level of $9 trillion than it is at a level of $10 trillion.

We conclude that when the economy is in a recessionary gap, the unemployment rate is *higher* than the natural unemployment rate. This implies there is a surplus in the labor market: Quantity supplied of labor is greater than quantity demanded, or there are more people who want to work than there are jobs available.

> *If the economy is in a recessionary gap, the unemployment rate is higher than the natural unemployment rate, and a surplus exists in the labor market.*

INFLATIONARY GAP AND THE LABOR MARKET Now suppose the economy is in an inflationary gap producing a Real GDP level of $11 trillion (worth of goods and services) when Natural Real GDP, or potential output, is $10 trillion.

Again, the unemployment rate that exists when the economy produces Natural Real GDP is the natural unemployment rate. Is the unemployment rate that exists when the economy is producing $11 trillion worth of goods and services greater or less than the natural unemployment rate that exists when the economy is producing $10 trillion worth of goods and services? The answer is that the unemployment rate is less than the natural unemployment rate because more workers are needed to produce a Real GDP of $11 trillion than are needed to produce a Real GDP of $10 trillion. *Ceteris paribus,* the unemployment rate will be lower at a Real GDP level of $11 trillion than it is at a level of $10 trillion.

We conclude that when the economy is in an inflationary gap, the unemployment rate is *lower* than the natural unemployment rate. This implies that there is a shortage in the labor market: Quantity demanded of labor is greater than quantity supplied, or there are more jobs available than there are people who want to work.

> *If the economy is in an inflationary gap, the unemployment rate is less than the natural unemployment rate, and a shortage exists in the labor market.*

LONG-RUN EQUILIBRIUM AND THE LABOR MARKET Finally, suppose the economy is in long-run equilibrium. In other words, it is producing a Real GDP level equal to Natural Real GDP. It follows that in this state, the unemployment rate (that exists in the economy) is the same as the natural unemployment rate. This implies that there is neither a shortage nor a surplus in the labor market; instead, equilibrium exists in the labor market.

> *If the economy is in long-run equilibrium, the unemployment rate equals the natural unemployment rate, and equilibrium exists in the labor market.*

The following table summarizes three possible states of the economy and the related states of the labor market.

State of the Economy	What Do We Call It?	Relationship Between Unemployment Rate and Natural Unemployment Rate	State of the Labor Market
Real GDP < Natural Real GDP	Recessionary gap	Unemployment rate > Natural unemployment rate	Surplus exists
Real GDP > Natural Real GDP	Inflationary gap	Unemployment rate < Natural unemployment rate	Shortage exists
Real GDP = Natural Real GDP	Long-run equilibrium	Unemployment rate = Natural unemployment rate	Equilibrium exists

One Nagging Question: How Can the Unemployment Rate Be Less Than the Natural Unemployment Rate?

Recall that when the economy is in an inflationary gap, the unemployment rate is less than the natural unemployment rate. For example, if the natural unemployment rate is 5 percent, the unemployment rate may be 4 percent.

But how can the economy do better than the natural unemployment rate, which, after all, is equated with full employment or potential output? To explain, we need to use two production possibilities frontiers.

In Exhibit 4, the two production possibilities frontiers are the physical PPF (purple curve) and the institutional PPF (blue curve). The physical PPF illustrates different combinations of goods the economy can produce given the physical constraints of (1) finite resources and (2) the current state of technology.

The institutional PPF illustrates different combinations of goods the economy can produce given the physical constraints of (1) finite resources, (2) the current state of technology, and (3) any institutional constraints. Broadly defined, an institutional constraint is anything that prevents economic agents from producing the maximum Real GDP physically possible.

For example, the minimum wage law, which is an institutional constraint, specifies that workers must be paid a wage rate at least equal to the legislated minimum wage. One effect of this law is that unskilled persons whose value to employers falls below the legislated minimum wage will not be hired. Fewer workers mean less output produced, *ceteris*

exhibit **4**

The Physical and Institutional PPFs

A society has both a physical PPF and an institutional PPF. The physical PPF illustrates different combinations of goods the economy can produce given the physical constraints of (1) finite resources and (2) the current state of technology. The institutional PPF illustrates different combinations of goods the economy can produce given the physical constraints of (1) finite resources, (2) the current state of technology, and (3) any institutional constraints. The economy is at the natural unemployment rate if it is located on its institutional PPF, such as at points *A, B,* or *C.* An economy can never operate beyond its physical PPF, but it is possible for it to operate beyond its institutional PPF because institutional constraints are not always equally effective. If the economy does operate beyond its institutional PPF, such as at point *D,* then the unemployment rate in the economy is lower than the natural unemployment rate.

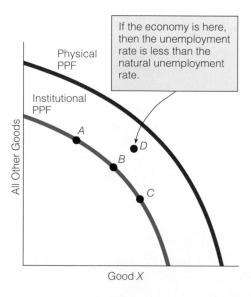

Good X

paribus. (This is why the institutional PPF lies closer to the origin than the physical PPF.)

Within the confines of society's physical and institutional constraints, there is a natural unemployment rate. This situation is represented by any point on the institutional PPF. In the exhibit, points *A*, *B*, and *C* are all such points.

An economy can never operate beyond its physical PPF, but it is possible for it to operate beyond its institutional PPF. For example, suppose inflation reduces the purchasing power of the minimum wage, thus reducing or eliminating the constraining properties of the minimum wage law on the unskilled labor market.[1] This would make one of society's institutional constraints ineffective, allowing the economy to temporarily move beyond the institutional constraint.

Logic dictates that if the economy is operating at the natural unemployment rate when it is located on its institutional PPF, then it must be operating at an unemployment rate lower than the natural rate when it is located beyond its institutional PPF (but below its physical PPF). Because society's institutional constraints are not always equally effective, it is possible for an economy to be operating at an unemployment rate below the natural rate.

> *Thinking like* **AN ECONOMIST**
>
> *Think of two economies, A and B, that have the identical physical PPF. Does it follow that they will also have the identical institutional PPF too? No, because one economy might have greater institutional constraints (on production) than the other economy. The size of the gap between the two frontiers is indicative of how far away a given economy is from achieving its potential. For example, if the gap between economy A's institutional PPF and physical PPF is greater than the gap between economy B's two frontiers, then economy A is farther away from realizing its potential (when it comes to output production) than is economy B.*

SELF-TEST

1. What is a recessionary gap? an inflationary gap?

2. What is the state of the labor market when the economy is in a recessionary gap? in an inflationary gap?

3. If the economy is in an inflationary gap, locate its position in terms of the two PPFs discussed in this section.

The Self-Regulating Economy

Some economists believe that the economy is self-regulating. This means that if the economy is not at the natural unemployment rate (or full employment)—that is, it is not producing Natural Real GDP—then it can move itself to this position. The notion of a self-regulating economy is a very classical notion, but it is also a view held by some modern-day economists. This section describes how a self-regulating economy works.

What Happens If the Economy Is in a Recessionary Gap?

If the economy is in a recessionary gap,

1. it is producing a Real GDP level that is less than Natural Real GDP,

2. the unemployment rate is greater than the natural unemployment rate, and

3. a surplus exists in the labor market.

Exhibit 5(a) illustrates this case for a Real GDP of $9 trillion and a Natural Real GDP of $10 trillion. What, if anything, happens in the economy?

---

[1] Inflation reduces the real (inflation-adjusted) minimum wage. If the minimum wage rate is $6 and the price level is 1.00, the real minimum wage is $6 ($6 divided by the price level, 1.00). If the price level rises to 2.00, then the real minimum wage rate falls to $3. The lower the real minimum wage, the greater the number of unskilled workers employers will hire because the demand curve for unskilled workers is downward sloping.

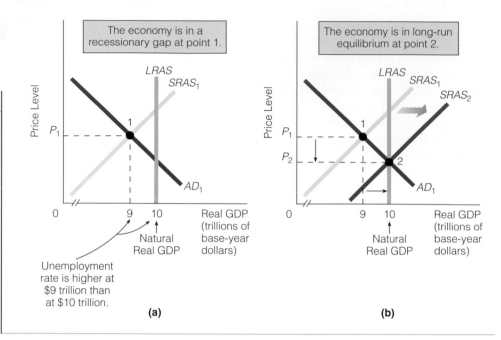

exhibit 5

The Self-Regulating Economy: Removing a Recessionary Gap

(a) The economy is at P_1 and Real GDP of $9 trillion. Because Real GDP is less than Natural Real GDP ($10 trillion), the economy is in a recessionary gap and the unemployment rate is higher than the natural unemployment rate. (b) Wage rates fall, and the short-run aggregate supply curve shifts from $SRAS_1$ to $SRAS_2$. As the price level falls, the real balance, interest rate, and international trade effects increase the quantity demanded of Real GDP. Ultimately, the economy moves into long-run equilibrium at point 2.

Q&A

Would it be correct to say that a self-regulating economy can "heal itself" of a recessionary gap?

Yes, that is correct. In other words, if the economy is "ill"—and the "illness" is called a recessionary gap—then its internal mechanism will kick in and eventually eliminate the recessionary gap.

According to economists who believe the economy is self-regulating, the surplus in the labor market begins to exert downward pressure on wages.[2] In other words, as old wage contracts expire, business firms will negotiate contracts that pay workers lower wage rates.

Recall from the last chapter that as wage rates fall, the $SRAS$ curve begins to shift to the right, ultimately moving from $SRAS_1$ to $SRAS_2$ in Exhibit 5(b). As a result of the increase in short-run aggregate supply, the price level falls. But as the price level falls, the quantity demanded of Real GDP rises due to the real balance, interest rate, and international trade effects (all of which were discussed in the last chapter). As the price level falls, the economy moves from one point on the AD curve to a point farther down the same curve. In Exhibit 5(b), this is a move from point 1 to point 2.

As long as the economy's Real GDP is less than its Natural Real GDP, the price level will continue to fall. Ultimately, the economy moves to long-run equilibrium at point 2, corresponding to P_2 and a Natural Real GDP of $10 trillion.

Recessionary gap →
Unemployment rate > Natural unemployment rate →
Surplus in labor market → Wages fall → $SRAS$ curve shifts to the right →
Economy moves into long-run equilibrium

What Happens If the Economy Is in an Inflationary Gap?

If the economy is in an inflationary gap,

1.   it is producing a Real GDP level that is greater than Natural Real GDP,

---

[2]In this discussion of how the self-regulating economy eliminates a recessionary gap, we have emphasized wages (in the labor market) adjusting downward. Other resource prices besides wages may fall as well.

© ASSOCIATED PRESS, AP

economics 24/7

HURRICANE KATRINA AND THE ECONOMY

Hurricane Katrina was a major hurricane that hit the central Gulf Coast on the morning of August 29, 2005. Katrina caused catastrophic damage along the coastlines of Louisiana, Mississippi, and Alabama. The levees that separated Lake Pontchartrain from the city of New Orleans were damaged by Katrina, ultimately leading to the flooding of about 80 percent of New Orleans.

How does something like Hurricane Katrina affect the economy? Is it possible to translate Katrina into our aggregate demand-aggregate supply framework of analysis?

Katrina is an adverse supply shock to the economy, thus shifting the SRAS curve to the left. Katrina essentially destroyed lives (labor) and capital (production facilities, oil platforms) and thus adversely affected the economy's ability to produce goods and services.

Think of what a shift leftward in the SRAS curve means in terms of Real GDP. It means either that there will be an absolute decline in Real GDP or that Real GDP will not grow by as much as it would have had Katrina not occurred. (With respect to the latter, Real GDP will not grow by as much as it would have had Katrina not occurred; think of Katrina as shifting the SRAS curve leftward at the same time that some forces in the economy are shifting the SRAS curve rightward. Even if the forces shifting the SRAS curve rightward are stronger than the forces, like Katrina, shifting the SRAS curve leftward, still the left-shifting forces have an effect on the final position of the SRAS curve.)

Soon after Katrina, both private and government economic groups changed their predictions of growth in Real GDP. For example, both Merrill Lynch and Bank of America revised their growth figures for Real GDP downward. The Congressional Budget Office (CBO) reported that the growth rate in Real GDP would decline by 0.5 to 1 percent due to Hurricane Katrina. The CBO also predicted that employment would fall by 400,000 persons due to Katrina.

What about the self-regulating properties of the economy? Could a hurricane like Katrina destabilize the economy permanently, thus producing an economy that became so destabilized that it couldn't find its way back to Natural Real GDP without, say, government intervention? According to economists who believe the economy is self-regulating, the answer is no. Even if Katrina moved the economy into a recessionary gap, the self-regulating properties of the economy would soon exert themselves and remove the economy from the recessionary gap. In other words, if Katrina happened to move Real GDP below its natural level, in time, wages would fall, the SRAS curve would shift rightward, and the economy would have self-regulated itself at its Natural Real GDP level.

2. the unemployment rate is less than the natural unemployment rate, and

3. a shortage exists in the labor market.

Exhibit 6(a) illustrates this case for a Real GDP of $11 trillion and a Natural Real GDP of $10 trillion. What happens in the economy in this situation?

Again, according to economists who believe the economy is self-regulating, the shortage in the labor market begins to exert upward pressure on wages. In other words, as old wage contracts expire, business firms will negotiate contracts that pay workers higher wage rates.

As wage rates rise, the SRAS curve begins to shift to the left, ultimately moving from $SRAS_1$ to $SRAS_2$ in Exhibit 6(b). As a result of the decrease in short-run aggregate supply, the price level rises. But as the price level rises,

Thinking like AN ECONOMIST

This short feature points out what economists often do. They take something from the real world—like Hurricane Katrina—and analyze it in terms of a particular model, theory, or view of the economy. For example, we have taken Hurricane Katrina and placed in within the context of AD-SRAS and a self-regulating economy. Out come certain results: Katrina will shift the SRAS curve leftward, it will either reduce Real GDP or reduce the overall growth in Real GDP, and it will not lead to permanently destabilizing effects in the economy. Visually, you might want to think of AD-SRAS as a box with a crank attached. Katrina is tossed into the box, the crank is turned, and out comes a certain analysis. What the economist has that the noneconomist often does not have is a framework of analysis.

exhibit 6

The Self-Regulating Economy: Removing an Inflationary Gap

(a) The economy is at P_1 and Real GDP of $11 trillion. Because Real GDP is greater than Natural Real GDP ($10 trillion), the economy is in an inflationary gap and the unemployment rate is lower than the natural unemployment rate. (b) Wage rates rise, and the short-run aggregate supply curve shifts from $SRAS_1$ to $SRAS_2$. As the price level rises, the real balance, interest rate, and international trade effects decrease the quantity demanded of Real GDP. Ultimately, the economy moves into long-run equilibrium at point 2.

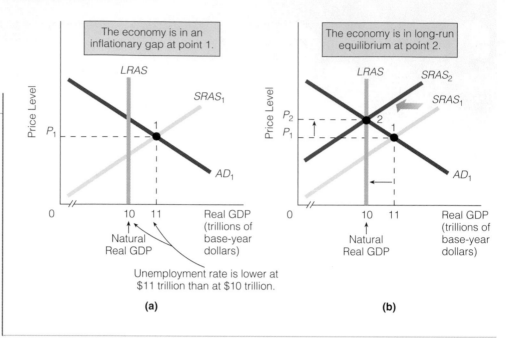

the quantity demanded of Real GDP falls due to the real balance, interest rate, and international trade effects. As the price level rises, the economy moves from one point on the AD curve to a point farther up the same curve. In Exhibit 6(b), this is a move from point 1 to point 2.

As long as the economy's Real GDP is greater than its Natural Real GDP, the price level will continue to rise. Ultimately, the economy moves to long-run equilibrium at point 2, corresponding to P_2, and a Natural Real GDP of $10 trillion.

Inflationary gap →
Unemployment rate < Natural unemployment rate →
Shortage in labor market → Wages rise → $SRAS$ curve shifts to the left →
Economy moves into long-run equilibrium

The Self-Regulating Economy: A Recap

We have shown that if the economy is in a recessionary gap, wage rates fall (along with other resource prices), and the $SRAS$ curve shifts to the right. As this happens, the price level falls and the economy moves down the AD curve. The economy moves in the direction of long-run equilibrium, ultimately achieving the Natural Real GDP level.

If the economy is in an inflationary gap, wage rates rise (along with other resource prices), and the $SRAS$ curve shifts to the left. As this happens, the price level rises and the economy moves up the AD curve. The economy moves in the direction of long-run equilibrium, ultimately achieving the Natural Real GDP level.

Flexible wage rates (and other resource prices) play a critical role in the self-regulating economy. For example, suppose wage rates are not flexible and do not fall in a recessionary gap. Then, the $SRAS$ curve will not shift to the right. But if the $SRAS$ curve does not shift to the right, the price level will not fall. And if the price level does not fall, the economy won't move down the AD curve toward long-run equilibrium. Similarly, if wage rates are not flexible and do not rise in an inflationary gap, then the economy won't move up the AD curve toward long-run equilibrium.

The economists who believe in a self-regulating economy—classical economists, monetarists, and new classical economists—believe that wage rates and other resource prices are *flexible* and move up and down in response to market conditions. Thus, these economists believe that *wage rates will fall* when there is a *surplus of labor.* They believe that *wage rates will rise* when there is a *shortage of labor.* You will see in the next chapter that the flexible wages and prices position taken by these economists has not gone unchallenged.

The following table summarizes how a self-regulating economy works for three possible states of the economy.

State of the Economy	What Happens If the Economy Is Self-Regulating?
Recessionary gap (Real GDP < Natural Real GDP)	Wages fall and *SRAS* curve shifts to the right until Real GDP = Natural Real GDP.
Inflationary gap (Real GDP >Natural Real GDP)	Wages rise and *SRAS* curve shifts to the left until Real GDP = Natural Real GDP.
Long-run equilibrium (Real GDP = Natural Real GDP)	No change in wages and no change in *SRAS.*

macro Theme   One of the macroeconomic categories we introduced in an earlier chapter was the *self-regulating–economic instability* category. We said then that some economists believe the economy is self-regulating, and other economists believe the economy is inherently unstable (or *not* self-regulating). This macro theme has started to be developed with this chapter. You just heard from economists who believe the economy is self-regulating. In later chapters, you will hear from economists who believe the economy is inherently unstable.

Policy Implication of Believing the Economy Is Self-Regulating

Classical, new classical, and monetarist economists believe that the economy is self-regulating. For these economists, full employment is the norm: The economy always moves back to Natural Real GDP. Stated differently, if the economy becomes "ill"—in the form of a recessionary or an inflationary gap—it certainly is capable of healing itself through changes in wages and prices. This belief in how the economy works has led these economists to advocate a macroeconomic policy of **laissez-faire**, or noninterference. In these economists' view, government does not have an economic management role to play.

Laissez-faire
A public policy of not interfering with market activities in the economy.

Changes in a Self-Regulating Economy: Short Run and Long Run

Let's consider how a change in aggregate demand affects the economy in the short run and the long run if the economy is self-regulating. In Exhibit 7(a), the economy is initially in long-run equilibrium at point 1. Suppose there is an increase in aggregate demand brought about by, say, an increase in government purchases (this possibility is discussed in the last chapter). The *AD* curve shifts right from AD_1 to AD_2, and in the short run, the economy moves to point 2 with both Real GDP and the price level higher than each was at point 1.

Now at point 2, the economy is in an inflationary gap. If the economy is self-regulating, wages will soon rise and the *SRAS* curve will shift to the left—ultimately from $SRAS_1$ to $SRAS_2$. The economy will end up at point 3 in long-run equilibrium.

Now let's examine the changes in the short run and in the long run. As a result of an increase in aggregate demand, Real GDP rises and the price level rises in the short run. In addition, because Real GDP rises, the unemployment rate falls. In the long run, when the economy is at point 3, it is producing exactly the same level of Real GDP that it was producing originally (Q_N) but at a higher price level.

Changes in a Self-Regulating Economy: Short Run and Long Run

In (a) the economy is initially at point 1 in long-run equilibrium. Aggregate demand rises and the AD curve shifts right from AD_1 to AD_2. The economy is at point 2 in the short run, with a higher Real GDP and a higher price level than at point 1. The economy is also in an inflationary gap at point 2. If the economy is self-regulating, wages will soon rise, the $SRAS$ curve will shift left from $SRAS_1$ to $SRAS_2$, and the economy will be in long-run equilibrium at point 3. At point 3, the economy is producing the same Real GDP as it did at point 1. In other words, in the long run, an increase in aggregate demand only raises the price level. In (b) the economy is initially at point 1 in long-run equilibrium. Aggregate demand falls and the AD curve shifts left from AD_1 to AD_2. The economy is at point 2 in the short run, with a lower Real GDP and a lower price level than at point 1. The economy is also in a recessionary gap. If the economy is self-regulating, wages will soon fall, the $SRAS$ curve will shift right from $SRAS_1$ to $SRAS_2$, and the economy will be in long-run equilibrium at point 3. At point 3, the economy is producing the same Real GDP as it did at point 1. In other words, in the long run, a decrease in aggregate demand only lowers the price level.

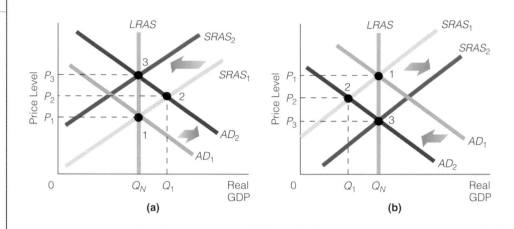

Conclusion: If the economy is self-regulating, an increase in aggregate demand can raise the price level and Real GDP in the short run, but in the long run, the only effect of an increase in aggregate demand is a rise in the price level. In other words, in the long run, all that we have to show for an increase in aggregate demand is higher prices.

Now let's consider what happens if aggregate demand falls. In Exhibit 7(b), the economy is initially in long-run equilibrium at point 1. Suppose there is a decrease in aggregate demand. The AD curve shifts left from AD_1 to AD_2, and in the short run, the economy moves to point 2 with both Real GDP and the price level lower than each was at point 1.

Now at point 2, the economy is in a recessionary gap. If the economy is self-regulating, wages will soon fall and the $SRAS$ curve will shift to the right—ultimately from $SRAS_1$ to $SRAS_2$. The economy will end up at point 3 in long-run equilibrium.

Again, let's examine the changes in the short run and in the long run. As a result of a decrease in aggregate demand, Real GDP falls and the price level falls in the short run. In addition, because Real GDP falls, the unemployment rate rises. In the long run, when the economy is at point 3, it is producing exactly the same level of Real GDP that it was producing originally (Q_N) but at a lower price level.

Conclusion: If the economy is self-regulating, a decrease in aggregate demand can lower the price level and Real GDP in the short run, but in the long run, the only effect of a decrease in aggregate demand is a lower price level.

Change in AD	In the Short Run	In the Long Run
$AD \uparrow$	$P \uparrow, Q \uparrow$	$P \uparrow$, Q does not change
$AD \downarrow$	$P \downarrow, Q \downarrow$	$P \downarrow$, Q does not change

Let's return to Exhibit 7(a) to clarify a point about long-run equilibrium. In the exhibit, the economy starts at point 1 in long-run equilibrium and then moves to point 2. At point 2, both the price level and Real GDP are higher than they were at point 1. In other words, if AD rises, both the price level and Real GDP rise in the short run. If the economy is self-regulating, it will not remain at point 2. Instead, it will move to point 3, where it is again in long-run equilibrium. At point 3, the price level is higher than it was at point 2, but Real GDP is lower. Why, then, don't we say that Real GDP is lower in the long run than it is in the short run instead of saying that Real GDP does not change in the long run? The answer is that the long run is measured from one long-run equilibrium point to another long-run equilibrium point. In terms of Exhibit 7(a), we look at the long run by comparing point 1 and point 3. When we make this comparison, we notice two things: The price level is higher at point 3 than at point 1, and Real GDP is the same at both points.

SELF-TEST

1. If the economy is self-regulating, what happens if it is in a recessionary gap?

2. If the economy is self-regulating, what happens if it is in an inflationary gap?

3. If the economy is self-regulating, how do changes in aggregate demand affect the economy in the long run?

A Reader Asks...

Why Don't All Economists Agree?

According to the text, not all economists believe the economy is self-regulating. Why don't all economists agree on how the economy works?

One reason (but not the only reason) is because economists can't undertake controlled experiments. In a controlled experiment, it is possible to change one variable, leave all other variables unchanged, and then see what happens. Whatever happens must be the result of the one variable you changed.

To illustrate, suppose you want to know whether or not increasing your intake of vitamin C will reduce the number of colds you get in a year. In a controlled experiment, you would increase your intake of vitamin C and everything else in your life would stay the same—the amount of sleep you get each night, the amount of exercise you get, the people you are around, and so on. Then you would observe whether or not you got fewer colds. If you did get fewer colds, you could be reasonably sure that it was because of your higher intake of vitamin C.

Now let's see what happens in economics because economists cannot run controlled experiments. Suppose Real GDP falls in February 2007. Economist *A* argues that the decline in Real GDP was due to higher interest rates in July 2006 and not to higher taxes in August 2006. Economist *B* argues just the opposite: The decline in Real GDP was due to higher taxes in August 2006 and not to higher interest rates in July 2006.

Obviously, economist *A* has a theory that states that a change in interest rates affects Real GDP but a change in taxes does not. Economist *B* has a theory that states that a change in taxes affects Real GDP but a change in interest rates does not. It would be nice to test each theory in a controlled environment: Change taxes and nothing else and see what happens; change interest rates and nothing else and see what happens. You can see that if we could do this, some of the disagreements between economists *A* and *B* are likely to disappear.

! analyzing the scene

What does the economy have to do with Yvonne possibly having to move back in with her parents?

Yvonne says that wages are rising but so is the unemployment rate. This is what happens if the economy is self-regulating and is removing itself from an inflationary gap. In an inflationary gap, the unemployment rate is below the natural unemployment rate. In time, wages rise and the *SRAS* curve shifts leftward. As the *SRAS* curve shifts leftward, Real GDP declines and the unemployment rate rises. Bottom line: Some people will become unemployed as the economy stabilizes itself at the natural unemployment rate. If Yvonne is one of these people, then she may have to move back in with her parents for a while.

Can people saving more be bad for the economy?

According to classical economists, if, say, households save more (and spend less), the interest rate will fall, prompting businesses to spend more. More important, the decline in household spending will be matched by an equal rise in business spending. In short, for classical economists, saving more does not lead to less spending in the economy. Saving more simply leads to a different configuration of spending (less consumption, more investment).

What is Say's law and what does it say about production and consumption?

According to Say's law, supply creates its own demand. Specifically, Say's law holds that the act of supplying goods (production) is linked to the act of demanding goods (consumption).

People don't produce without thinking about how they'll consume. Believers in Say's law often argue that a key way to stimulate consumption in the economy is to make it easier for businesses to produce more. They argue that more production leads to more consumption.

According to José, how does the economy work?

José says, "I think it's a little like when you have a cold or the flu. You don't need to see a doctor. In time, your body heals itself. That's sort of the way the economy works too." Obviously, José believes the economy is self-regulating and will heal itself. The economy will move itself out of either an inflationary gap or a recessionary gap and will settle down (eventually) in long-run equilibrium at the natural unemployment rate and Natural Real GDP.

chapter summary

Say's Law

- Say's law states that supply creates its own demand. All economists believe that Say's law holds in a barter economy. Here, there can be no general overproduction or underproduction of goods. Classical economists believed that Say's law also holds in a money economy. In their view, even if consumption drops and saving rises, economic forces are at work producing an equal increase in investment. According to classical economists, interest rates are flexible and equate the amount of saving and investment in an economy.

Classical Economists on Markets, Wages, and Prices

- Classical economists believed that most, if not all, markets are competitive and that wages and prices are flexible.

Three States of the Economy

- Natural Real GDP is the level of Real GDP that is produced when the economy is operating at the natural unemployment rate.
- The economy can be producing a Real GDP level that (1) is equal to Natural Real GDP, (2) is greater than Natural Real GDP, or (3) is less than Natural Real GDP. In other words, the economy can be in (1) long-

run equilibrium, (2) an inflationary gap, or (3) a recessionary gap, respectively.

- In long-run equilibrium, the Real GDP that the economy is producing is equal to the Natural Real GDP. The unemployment rate that exists in the economy is equal to the natural unemployment rate, and the labor market is in equilibrium.
- In a recessionary gap, the Real GDP that the economy is producing is less than the Natural Real GDP. The unemployment rate that exists in the economy is greater than the natural unemployment rate, and a surplus exists in the labor market.
- In an inflationary gap, the Real GDP that the economy is producing is greater than the Natural Real GDP. The unemployment rate that exists in the economy is less than the natural unemployment rate, and a shortage exists in the labor market.

The Institutional and Physical Production Possibilities Frontiers

- The physical PPF illustrates different combinations of goods the economy can produce given the physical constraints of (1) finite resources and (2) the current state of technology. The institutional PPF illustrates different combinations of goods the economy can produce given the physical constraints of (1) finite resources, (2) the current state of technology, and (3) any institutional constraints.

- If an economy is operating on its institutional PPF, it is operating at the natural unemployment rate. If it is operating at a point beyond the institutional PPF but below the physical PPF, it is operating at an unemployment rate less than the natural unemployment rate.

The Self-Regulating Economy

- Some economists (classical, new classical, monetarists) contend that the economy can eliminate both recessionary and inflationary gaps smoothly and quickly by itself.
- If the economy is self-regulating and in a recessionary gap, then the unemployment rate in the economy is greater than the natural unemployment rate, and a surplus exists in the labor market. As old wage contracts expire, wage rates fall. As a result, the SRAS curve shifts to the right, and the price level falls. As the price level falls, the quantity demanded of Real GDP rises. Ultimately, the economy will move into long-run equilibrium where it is producing Natural Real GDP.
- If the economy is self-regulating and in an inflationary gap, then the unemployment rate in the economy is less than the natural unemployment rate, and a shortage exists in the labor market. As old wage contracts expire, wage rates rise. As a result, the SRAS curve shifts to the left and the price level rises. As the price level rises, the quantity demanded of Real GDP falls. Ultimately, the economy will move into long-run equilibrium where it is producing Natural Real GDP.

key terms and concepts

Say's Law
Recessionary Gap
Inflationary Gap
Laissez-faire

questions and problems

1 What is the classical economics position with respect to (a) wages, (b) prices, and (c) interest rates?

2 According to classical economists, does Say's law hold in a money economy? Explain your answer.

3 According to classical economists, does an increase in saving shift the AD curve to the left? Explain your answer.

4 What does it mean to say the economy is in a recessionary gap? in an inflationary gap? in long-run equilibrium?

5 Describe the relationship of the (actual) unemployment rate to the natural unemployment rate in each of the following economic states: (a) a recessionary gap, (b) an inflationary gap, and (c) long-run equilibrium.

6 Diagrammatically represent an economy in (a) an inflationary gap, (b) a recessionary gap, and (c) long-run equilibrium.

7 Explain how an economy can operate beyond its institutional PPF but not beyond its physical PPF.

8 According to economists who believe in a self-regulating economy, what happens—step by step—when the economy is in a recessionary gap? What happens when the economy is in an inflationary gap?

9 If wage rates are not flexible, can the economy be self-regulating? Explain your answer.

10 Explain the importance of the real balance, interest rate, and international trade effects to long-run (equilibrium) adjustment in the economy.

11 Suppose the economy is self-regulating, the price level is 132, the quantity demanded of Real GDP is $4 trillion, the quantity supplied of Real GDP in the short run is $3.9 trillion, and the quantity supplied of Real GDP in the long run is $4.3 trillion. Is the economy in short-run equilibrium? Will the price level in long-run equilibrium be greater than, less than, or equal to 132? Explain your answers.

12 Suppose the economy is self-regulating, the price level is 110, the quantity demanded of Real GDP is $4 trillion, the quantity supplied of Real GDP in the short run is $4.9 trillion, and the quantity supplied of Real GDP in the long run is $4.1 trillion. Is the economy in short-run equilibrium? Will the price level in long-run equilibrium be greater than, less than, or equal to 110? Explain your answers.

working with numbers and graphs

1   In the following figure, which point is representative of:

   a   The economy on its *LRAS* curve
   b   The economy in a recessionary gap
   c   The economy in an inflationary gap

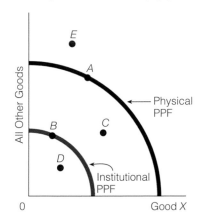

2   In the following figure, which of parts (a)–(c) is consistent with or representative of:

   a   The economy operating at the natural unemployment rate
   b   A surplus in the labor market
   c   A recessionary gap
   d   A cyclical unemployment rate of zero

3   Diagrammatically represent the following:

   a   An economy in which *AD* increases as it is self-regulating out of a recessionary gap
   b   An economy in which *AD* decreases as it is self-regulating out of an inflationary gap

4   Economist Jones believes there is always sufficient (aggregate) demand in the economy to buy all the goods and services supplied at full employment. Diagrammatically represent what the economy looks like for Jones.

5   Diagrammatically show what happens when the institutional constraints in the economy become less effective.

Economic Instability: A Critique of the Self-Regulating Economy

9

Setting the Scene

On a Sunday talk show, two economists are interviewed about their opinions on the economy.

MODERATOR:

The nation's unemployment rate has just risen. Will it continue to rise?

ECONOMIST 1:

I think it will remain where it is for some time. We'll need to stimulate the economy to bring down the unemployment rate.

ECONOMIST 2:

I disagree. The economy is self-regulating and the unemployment rate will soon begin to fall. There are already a few signs that wages are beginning to decline.

MODERATOR:

This week in Congress, various spending proposals were discussed. Some say that enacting these spending proposals will go a long way to raising spending in this country. Do you agree?

ECONOMIST 1:

I agree. I think a huge multiplier effect will kick in.

ECONOMIST 2:

Again, I would have to disagree. I think the multiplier effect will be rather small.

MODERATOR:

Well, then, what about the effect of the spending on output and prices? Will the additional spending lead to higher output and higher prices?

ECONOMIST 1:

I think it will lead to largely higher output with only a very tiny increase in the price level.

ECONOMIST 2:

I think it will lead to almost no change in output and to a significant uptick in the price level.

MODERATOR:

The data show that the savings rate is beginning to rise in the country. People are beginning to save a large slice of their paychecks. Will this help the economy?

ECONOMIST 1:

I'm not so sure it will. When people save more, they spend less, and a decline in overall spending could be hurtful at this time.

ECONOMIST 2:

I don't agree. An increase in saving will put downward pressure on interest rates, and businesses will invest more at lower interest rates. I don't see saving in as negative a way as my colleague.

? Here are some questions to keep in mind as you read this chapter:

- *Why do the two economists disagree over the predicted change in the unemployment rate?*

- *Why do the two economists disagree over the predicted change in spending?*

- *Why do the two economists disagree over the predicted change in output (Real GDP) and the price level?*

- *Why do the two economists disagree over the effect on spending of a rise in savings?*

See analyzing the scene at the end of this chapter for answers to these questions.

Questioning the Classical Position

John Maynard Keynes, an English economist, changed the way many economists viewed the economy. Keynes's major work, *The General Theory of Employment, Income and Money,* was published in 1936. Just prior to its publication, the Great Depression had plagued many countries of the world. Looking around at the world during that time, one had to wonder if the classical view of the economy wasn't wrong. After all, unemployment was sky high in many countries, and numerous economies had been contracting. Where was Say's law with its promise that there would not be general gluts? Where was the self-regulating economy healing itself of its depression illness? Where was full employment? And given the depressed state of the economy, could anyone any longer believe that laissez-faire was the right policy stance?

With the Great Depression as recent history, Keynes and the Keynesians thought that while their theory may not be right with respect to every detail, there certainly was enough evidence to say that the classical view of the economy was wrong.

Keynes challenged all four of the following beliefs on which the classical position of the economy was based: (1) Say's law holds, so insufficient demand in the economy is unlikely. (2) Wages, prices, and interest rates are flexible. (3) The economy is self-regulating. (4) Laissez-faire is the right and sensible economic policy to implement.

> ## *Theme* macro
>
> As we discussed in an earlier chapter, not all economists believe the economy is self-regulating; that is, the economy can move itself out of either a recessionary or inflationary gap and into long-run equilibrium at Natural Real GDP. For example, Keynesians believe that at times the economy can be inherently unstable. What does this mean? Simply put, it means an economy that is in, say, a recessionary gap might not be able to remove itself from the recessionary gap. Keep this in mind as you read this chapter.

Keynes's Criticism of Say's Law in a Money Economy

Let's review the position expressed by classical economists on Say's law in a money economy. According to classical economists, if consumption spending fell because saving increased, then total spending would not fall because the added saving would simply bring about more investment spending. This would happen through changes in the interest rate. The added saving would put downward pressure on the interest rate, and at a lower interest rate, businesses would borrow and invest more. Through changes in the interest rate, the amount of saving would always equal the amount invested.

Keynes disagreed. He didn't think that added saving would necessarily stimulate an equal amount of added investment spending. Exhibit 1 illustrates Keynes's point of view. As in the last chapter, we let consumption = $3,000, investment = $600, government purchases = $1,200, and net exports = $200. Then saving increases by $100, which lowers consumption to $2,900. According to the classical economists, investment rose by $100 at the same time, going from $600 to $700. Keynes asked: What guarantee is there that an increase in saving will be equally matched by an increase in investment? What if saving rises by $100 (which means consumption goes down by $100), but investment rises by, say, only $40 (instead of $100)? In this situation, the equation $TE = C + I + G + (EX - IM)$ changes from

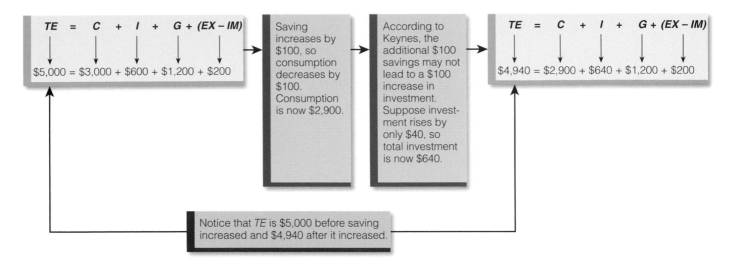

$TE = C + I + G + (EX - IM)$

$5,000 = 3,000 + 600 + 1,200 + 200$

Saving increases by $100, so consumption decreases by $100. Consumption is now $2,900.

According to Keynes, the additional $100 savings may not lead to a $100 increase in investment. Suppose investment rises by only $40, so total investment is now $640.

$TE = C + I + G + (EX - IM)$

$4,940 = 2,900 + 640 + 1,200 + 200$

Notice that *TE* is $5,000 before saving increased and $4,940 after it increased.

exhibit 1

Keynes's View of Say's Law in a Money Economy

According to Keynes, a decrease in consumption and subsequent increase in saving may not be matched by an equal increase in investment. Thus, a decrease in total expenditures may occur.

$$TE = \$3,000 + \$600 + \$1,200 + \$200$$
$$= \$5,000$$

to

$$TE = \$2,900 + \$640 + \$1,200 + \$200$$
$$= \$4,940$$

Thus, total expenditures decrease from $5,000 to $4,940. And if, at a given price level, total spending falls, so will aggregate demand. In other words, according to Keynes, it was possible for saving to increase and aggregate demand to fall.

Of course, a classical economist would retort that, as a result of a $100 increase in saving, interest rates would fall enough to guarantee that investment would increase by $100. But Keynes countered by saying that individuals save and invest for a host of reasons and that no single factor, such as the interest rate, links these activities.

Furthermore, Keynes believed that saving is more responsive to changes in income than to changes in the interest rate and that investment is more responsive to technological changes, business expectations, and innovations than to changes in the interest rate. In summary, whereas the classical economists believed that saving and investment depend on the interest rate, Keynes believed that both saving and investment depend on a number of factors that may be far more influential than the interest rate.

Consider the difference between Keynes and the classical economists on saving. As noted earlier, the classical economists held that saving is directly related to the interest rate: As the interest rate goes up, saving rises; as the interest rate goes down, saving falls, *ceteris paribus.*

Keynes thought this might not always be true. Suppose individuals are saving for a certain goal—say, a retirement fund of $100,000. They might save less per period at an interest rate of 10 percent than at an interest rate of 5 percent because a higher interest rate means that less saving is required per period to meet the goal within a set time. For example, if the interest rate is 5 percent, $50,000 in savings is needed to earn $2,500 in interest income per year. If the interest rate is 10 percent, only $25,000 in savings is needed to earn $2,500 in interest.

As to investment, Keynes believed that the interest rate is important in determining the level of investment, but he did not think it is as important as other variables, such as the expected rate of profit on investment. Keynes argued that if business expectations are pessimistic, then there is unlikely to be much investment, regardless of how low the interest rate is.

Keynes on Wage Rates

In the last chapter, we stated that if the unemployment rate in the economy is greater than the natural unemployment rate, a surplus exists in the labor market: The number of job seekers is high relative to the number of jobs available. Consequently, according to classical economists, wage rates will fall.

Keynes didn't believe the adjustment was so simple. Instead, he said, employees will naturally resist an employer's efforts to cut wages. Similarly, labor unions may resist wage cuts. In short, wage rates may be inflexible in a downward direction.

Suppose Keynes is correct and wage rates won't fall. Does this mean that if the economy is in a recessionary gap, it can't get itself out? The unequivocal answer is yes. If employee and labor union resistance prevent wage rates from falling, then the *SRAS* curve will not shift to the right. If the *SRAS* curve doesn't shift to the right, the price level won't come down. If the price level doesn't come down, buyers will not purchase more goods and services and remove the economy from a recessionary gap. In terms of Exhibit 2, the economy is stuck at point 1. It cannot get to point 2.

In summary, Keynes believed that the economy was inherently unstable—it may not automatically cure itself of a recessionary gap. It may not be self-regulating.

New Keynesians and Wage Rates

Many economists criticized early versions of the Keynesian theory on the ground that it didn't offer a rigorous and complete explanation for inflexible wages. Some of the later versions—put forth by New Keynesian economists—made up for this deficiency by focusing on, among other things, long-term contracts and efficiency reasons for firms paying higher-than-market wages.

For example, New Keynesians argue that long-term labor contracts are often advantageous for both employers and workers. Firms may perceive such benefits as (1) fewer labor negotiations (labor negotiations can be costly) and (2) a decreased likelihood of worker strikes (the firms avoid strikes during the time of the contract). Workers may perceive such benefits as (1) fewer strikes (which can be costly for them too) and (2) the sense of security long-term contracts provide.

Long-term contracts have costs as well as benefits for both firms and workers, but some economists believe that in many instances the benefits outweigh the costs and that firms and workers enter into the long-term contracts for mutually advantageous reasons. When they do, wage rates are "locked in" for the period of the contract and therefore cannot adjust downward. As a result, the economy may get stuck at point 1 in Exhibit 2 for a long time and experience high levels of unemployment for many years.

Efficiency Wage Models
These models hold that it is sometimes in the best interest of business firms to pay their employees higher-than-equilibrium wage rates.

As another example, New Keynesian economists who work with **efficiency wage models** believe there are solid microeconomic reasons for inflexible wages. They argue that firms sometimes find it in their best interest to pay wage rates above market-clearing levels. According to efficiency wage models, labor productivity depends on the wage rate the firm pays its employees. Specifically, a cut in wages can cause labor productivity to decline, which, in turn, raises the firm's costs. (Basically, these models say that you are more productive when you are paid a higher wage than when you are paid a lower wage.) By paying a higher-than-market wage, firms provide an incentive to workers to be productive and do less shirking, among other things. If shirking declines, so do the monitoring (management) costs of the firm.

Economist Robert Solow has argued that "the most interesting and important line of work in current macroeconomic theory is the attempt to reconstruct plausible

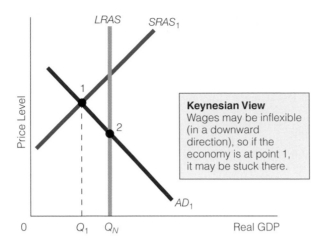

Keynesian View
Wages may be inflexible (in a downward direction), so if the economy is at point 1, it may be stuck there.

exhibit 2

The Economy Gets "Stuck" in a Recessionary Gap

If the economy is in a recessionary gap at point 1, Keynes held that wage rates may not fall. The economy may be stuck in the recessionary gap.

microeconomic underpinnings for a recognizably Keynesian macroeconomics."[1] Many Keynesian economists believe efficiency wage models can perform this task. They believe these models provide a solid microeconomic explanation for inflexible wages and thus are capable of explaining why continuing unemployment problems exist in some economies.

Keynes on Prices

Again, think back to the process classical economists (among others) believe occurs when a recessionary gap exists. Wage rates fall, the *SRAS* curve shifts to the right, and the price level begins to decrease . . . Now stop right there! Notice that we said "and the price level begins to decrease." This phrase tells us that classical economists believe that prices in the economy are flexible: They move up and down in response to market forces.

Keynes said that the internal structure of an economy is not always competitive enough to allow prices to fall. Recall from Chapter 3 how the forces of supply and demand operate when price is above equilibrium. In this case, a surplus is generated, and price falls until the quantity supplied of the good equals the quantity demanded. Keynes suggested that anticompetitive or monopolistic elements in the economy would sometimes prevent price from falling.

Before continuing, use the following chart to quickly review some of the differences in the views of the classical economists and Keynes.

	Classical Economists	**Keynes**
Say's Law	Holds in a money economy. In other words, all output produced will be demanded.	May not hold in a money economy. In other words, more output may be produced than will be demanded.
Savings	Amount saved and interest rate are directly related. Savers save more at higher interest rates and save less at lower interest rates.	Savers may not save more at higher interest rates or save less at lower interest rates. If savers have a savings goal in mind, then a higher interest rate means savers can save less and still reach their goal.

(Continued)

[1]Robert Solow, "Another Possible Source of Wage Stickiness," in *Efficiency Wage Models of the Labor Market*, ed. George Akerlof and Janet Yellen (Cambridge: Cambridge University Press, 1986), 41.

	Classical Economists	Keynes
Investment	Amount invested is inversely related to interest rate. Businesses invest more at lower interest rates and invest less at higher interest rates.	If expectations are pessimistic, a lower interest rate may not stimulate additional investment.
Prices	Flexible	May be inflexible downward
Wages	Flexible	May be inflexible downward

Is It a Question of the Time It Takes for Wages and Prices to Adjust?

Classical economists believed that both wages and prices are flexible and adjust downward in a recessionary gap. Keynes, however, suggested that wages and prices are not flexible (in a downward direction) and may not adjust downward in a recessionary gap.

Many economists today take a position somewhere between Keynes and the classical economists. For them, the question is not whether wages and prices are flexible downward, but *how long it takes for wages and prices to adjust downward.*

Consider Exhibit 3. Suppose the economy is currently in a recessionary gap at point 1. The relevant short-run aggregate supply curve is $SRAS_1$, where the wage rate is $10 per hour and the price level is P_1. Now, classical economists said the wage rate and price level would fall, whereas Keynes said this may not happen.

Did Keynes mean that if the economy is in a recessionary gap, *the wage rate will never fall and the price level will never adjust downward?* Most economists think not. The question is *how long* the wage rate and price level will take to fall. Will they fall in just a few weeks? Will they fall in a few months? Or will they take five years to fall? The question is relevant because the answer determines how long an economy will be in a recessionary gap, and thus, how long the economy takes to self-regulate.

Let's look at things this way: If it takes only a few weeks or months for wage rates to fall (say, to $8 an hour) and shift the short-run aggregate supply curve from $SRAS_1$ to $SRAS_2$ and for the price level to fall from P_1 to P_2, then for all practical purposes, the economy is almost instantaneously self-regulating. But if it takes years for

> ### Thinking like AN ECONOMIST
>
> *The economist knows that assumptions matter to conclusions. For example, we know (from the last chapter) that classical economists assumed that wages are flexible, and in this chapter, we learn that Keynes assumed that wages (at times) might be inflexible. This difference in assumptions will matter to our conclusions. For example, classical economists, assuming wages are flexible, will reach different conclusions than will Keynes, who is assuming wages are inflexible.*

A Question of How Long It Takes for Wage Rates and Prices to Fall

Suppose the economy is in a recessionary gap at point 1. Wage rates are $10 per hour, and the price level is P_1. The issue may not be whether wage rates and the price level fall, but how long they take to reach long-run levels. If they take a short time, then classical economists are right: the economy is self-regulating. If they take a long time—perhaps years—then Keynes is right: the economy is not self-regulating over any reasonable period of time.

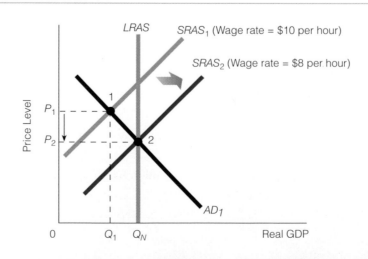

this to happen, the economy can hardly be considered self-regulating over any reasonable amount of time.

The classical position is that the time required before wages and prices adjust downward is short enough to call the economy self-regulating. The Keynesian position is that the time is long enough to say that the economy is not self-regulating. Instead, the Keynesians believe that the economy is inherently unstable: It can exist in a recessionary gap for a long time.

SELF-TEST

(Answers to Self-Test questions are in the Self-Test Appendix.)

1. What do Keynesians mean when they say the economy is inherently unstable?

2. "What matters is not whether the economy is self-regulating or not, but whether prices and wages are flexible and adjust quickly." Comment.

3. According to Keynes, why might aggregate demand be too low?

The Simple Keynesian Model

Economists build models and theories to better understand the economic world. A student will find many models and theories in economics. We have already discussed a few in this book: the theory of supply and demand, the theory of comparative advantage, and the classical theory of interest rates.

We turn now to a prominent macroeconomics model: the simple Keynesian model. In this section, we identify and discuss a few of the key components and themes of the model.

Assumptions

In the simple Keynesian model, certain simplifying assumptions hold. First, the price level is assumed to be constant until the economy reaches its full-employment or Natural Real GDP level.

Second, there is no foreign sector. In other words, the model represents a *closed economy*, not an *open economy*. It follows that total spending in the economy is the sum of consumption, investment, and government purchases.

Third, the monetary side of the economy is excluded.

The Consumption Function

Although Keynes was interested in the level of total spending in general, he was particularly concerned about consumption. Consumption (C) was a major concern because it is by far the largest slice of the total spending pie.

Keynes made three basic points about consumption:

1. Consumption depends on disposable income. (Disposable income, remember, is income minus taxes.)

2. Consumption and disposable income move in the same direction.

3. When disposable income changes, consumption changes by less.

These three points make a specific statement about the relationship between consumption and disposable income. The statement specifying this relationship is called the **consumption function**. We can write the consumption function as:

$$C = C_0 + (MPC)(Y_d)$$

Consumption Function

The relationship between consumption and disposable income. In the consumption function used here, consumption is directly related to disposable income and is positive even at zero disposable income: $C = C_0 + (MPC)(Y_d)$.

To understand the consumption function, you need to know what the variables represent. You know that C is consumption, and we use Y_d to specify disposable income. Let's look at MPC and C_0.

MPC stands for **marginal propensity to consume**, which is the ratio of the change in consumption to the change in disposable income:

Marginal Propensity to Consume (MPC)

The ratio of the change in consumption to the change in disposable income: $MPC = \Delta C/\Delta Y_d$.

Marginal propensity to consume = Change in consumption/Change in disposable income
$$MPC = \Delta C/\Delta Y_d$$

The symbol Δ stands for "change in." Thus, the MPC is equal to the change in consumption divided by the change in disposable income. To illustrate, suppose consumption rises from $800 to $900 as disposable income rises from $1,000 to $1,200. If we divide the change in consumption, which is $100, by the change in disposable income, which is $200, we see that the MPC equals 0.50. (Notice that the MPC is always a positive number between 0 and 1 because of Keynes's points 2 and 3 listed earlier.)

Autonomous Consumption

The part of consumption that is independent of disposable income.

C_0 is **autonomous consumption**. Autonomous consumption does not change as disposable income changes; it changes due to factors other than disposable income. Think of consumption (as specified by the consumption function) as made up of two parts. One part—the C_0 part—which is independent of disposable income, is called *autonomous consumption*. The second part—the $MPC(Y_d)$ part—which depends on disposable income, is called *induced consumption*.

The difference between autonomous consumption and induced consumption can be illustrated by example. Suppose your taxes are lowered; consequently, your disposable income rises. With more disposable income, you buy more goods and services (entertainment, books, DVDs). The increase in disposable income has *induced* you to consume more, hence the name *induced consumption*. Next, suppose your disposable income has not changed, but for some reason, you are consuming more. You might be consuming more medicine because you have recently become ill, or you might be consuming more car maintenance services because your car recently broke down. In short, you are consuming more of various goods and services even though your disposable income has not changed at all. This type of consumption is autonomous (independent) of disposable income, hence the name *autonomous consumption*.

Now, let's look again at the consumption function:

Consumption = Autonomous consumption
+ (Marginal propensity to consume)(Disposable income)
$$C = C_0 + (MPC)(Y_d)$$

Suppose $C_0 = \$800$, $MPC = 0.80$, and $Y_d = \$1,500$. By substituting these numbers into the consumption function, we find that $C = \$800 + (0.80)(\$1,500) = \$800 + \$1,200 = \$2,000$.

What will cause an increase in consumption? Consumption, C, will increase if any of the variables, C_0, MPC, or Y_d, increases. Thus, C can be increased in three ways:

1. **Raise autonomous consumption.** Suppose in our example that autonomous consumption, C_0, goes from $800 to $1,000. This would raise consumption to $2,200: $C = \$1,000 + (0.80)(\$1,500) = \$2,200$.

2. **Raise disposable income.** Suppose disposable income, Y_d, goes from $1,500 to $1,800. This would raise consumption to $2,240: $C = \$800 + (0.80)(\$1,800) = \$2,240$. This increase in consumption from $2,000 to $2,240 is due to an increase of $240 in induced consumption. Specifically, the increased consumption was induced by an increase in disposable income.

3. **Raise the MPC.** Suppose the MPC rises to 0.90. This would raise consumption to $2,150: $C = \$800 + (0.90)(\$1,500) = \$2,150$.

In Exhibit 4, we set C_0 equal to $200 billion and the MPC equal to 0.80; thus, $C = \$200$ billion $+ (0.8)(Y_d)$. We then calculated different levels of consumption (column 3) for different levels of disposable income (column 1).

Consumption and Saving

In Exhibit 4, we also calculated the saving levels (column 5) at the different disposable income levels. How did we calculate this? We know that $C = C_0 + (MPC)(Y_d)$, and we also know that households can only consume or save. So it follows that saving, S, is the difference between disposable income and consumption:

Saving = Disposable Income − Consumption
= Disposable Income − [Autonomous consumption
+ (Marginal propensity to consume)(Disposable income)]
$$S = Y_d − [C_0 + (MPC)(Y_d)]$$

The **marginal propensity to save (MPS)** is the ratio of the change in saving to the change in disposable income:

Marginal propensity to save = Change in saving/Change in disposable income
$$MPS = \Delta S/\Delta Y_d$$

Disposable income can be used only for consumption or saving; that is, $C + S = Y_d$. So any change to disposable income can only change consumption or saving. It follows that the marginal propensity to consume (MPC) plus the marginal propensity to save (MPS) must equal 1.

Marginal propensity to consume + Marginal propensity to save = 1
$$MPC + MPS = 1$$

In Exhibit 4, the MPC is 0.80, so the MPS is 0.20.

The Multiplier

We know from the consumption function that a rise in autonomous consumption (C_0) will raise consumption (C) and, in turn, raise total spending. But *how much* will total spending rise? If C_0 rises by $40 billion, will total spending rise by $40 billion? According to Keynes, total spending would not rise by $40 billion in this case. The rise in C_0 will act as a catalyst to additional spending, and total spending will rise by *more than* $40 billion.

Let's illustrate with a simple example. Suppose there are 10 people in the economy, represented by the letters *A–J*. Person *A* increases his autonomous consumption—specifically, he buys $40 more additional goods from person *B*. Now person *B* has witnessed

Q&A

One person's **MPC** *is higher than another person's* **MPC**. *What does this mean?*

Suppose Smith's MPC = 0.76 *and Brown's* MPC = 0.99. *It follows that out of every additional dollar of income, Smith will spend 76 cents and Brown will spend 99 cents.*

Marginal Propensity to Save (MPS)
The ratio of the change in saving to the change in disposable income: $MPS = \Delta S/\Delta Y_d$.

exhibit 4

Consumption and Saving at Different Levels of Disposable Income (in billions)

Our consumption function is $C = C_0 + (MPC)(Y_d)$, where C_0 has been set at $200 billion and $MPC = 0.80$. Saving is the difference between Y_d and C: $S = Y_d − [C_0 + (MPC)(Y_d)]$. All dollar amounts are in billions.

(1) Disposable Income Y_d	(2) Change in Disposable Income ΔY_d	(3) Consumption $C = C_0 + (MPC)(Y_d)$	(4) Change in Consumption	(5) Saving $S = Y_d − [C_0 + (MPC)(Y_d)]$	(6) Change in Saving
$ 800	$___	$ 840	$___	−$40	$___
1,000	200	1,000	160	0	40
1,200	200	1,160	160	40	40
1,400	200	1,320	160	80	40
1,600	200	1,480	160	120	40
1,800	200	1,640	160	160	40

an increase in his income; his income has risen by $40. According to Keynes, person B will spend some fraction of this additional income. How much he spends depends on his marginal propensity to consume (MPC). If his MPC is 0.80, then he will spend 80 percent of $40, or $32. Let's say he spends this additional $32 on goods he purchases from person C. Thus, person C's income rises by $32, and now she will spend some percentage of this additional income. Again, how much she will spend of the additional income depends on her MPC. If we again assume that the MPC is 0.80, then person C spends $25.60.

> Person A increases his *autonomous consumption* by $40 →
> This generates $40 *additional income* for person B →
> Person B increases his *consumption* by $32 →
> This generates $32 *additional income* for person C →
> Person C increases her *consumption* by $25.60 →
> And so on and so on.

The process whereby an initial rise in autonomous consumption leads to a rise in consumption for one person, generating additional income for another person, and leading to additional consumption spending by that person, and so on and so on is called the *multiplier process.*

Suppose we sum the initial rise in autonomous spending ($40) and all the additional spending it generated through the multiplier process. When the multiplier process ends, how much additional spending will have been generated? In other words, how much will total expenditures rise by?

Multiplier

The number that is multiplied by the change in autonomous spending to obtain the overall change in total spending. The multiplier (m) is equal to $1 / (1 - MPC)$. If the economy is operating below Natural Real GDP, then the multiplier turns out to be the number that is multiplied by the change in autonomous spending to obtain the change in Real GDP.

The answer depends on the value of the multiplier. The **multiplier** (m) is equal to 1 divided by $1 - MPC$.

$$\text{Multiplier } (m) = \frac{1}{1 - MPC}$$

For example, if the $MPC = 0.80$ (in each round of spending), then the multiplier equals 5:

$$\text{Multiplier } (m) = \frac{1}{1 - MPC}$$
$$= \frac{1}{1 - 0.80}$$
$$= \frac{1}{0.20}$$
$$= 5$$

Our original increase in autonomous consumption ($40) multiplied by the multiplier (5) equals $200. So in our example, a $40 increase in autonomous consumption would increase total spending $200.

Just as consumption has an autonomous spending component, so do investment and government purchases. The multiplier process holds for these sectors too. The process also holds for a decrease in autonomous spending by one of the sectors of total spending. So, in general,

Change in total spending = Multiplier × Change in autonomous spending

To illustrate, suppose many business owners become optimistic about the future of the economy. They believe that members of the household and government sectors will soon start buying more goods and services. In expectation of "better times," businesses buy more factories and capital goods, and so investment spending rises. Investment spending has risen even though there has been no change in income or Real GDP; hence, the rise is in autonomous investment spending. According to the multiplier analysis, this additional autonomous investment spending will change total spending by some

economics 24/7

THE MULTIPLIER GOES ON SPRING BREAK

During the week-long spring break, many college students put away their books, pack their shorts, swimsuits, and tanning oil, jump into their cars, and head for the beaches. As they are driving to Fort Lauderdale, Galveston, Myrtle Beach, Daytona Beach, San Diego, and other coastal cities, the multiplier is getting ready to go to work.

Look at it this way. When college students from around the country head for, say, Daytona Beach, they have dollars in their pockets. They will spend many of these dollars in Daytona Beach—on food and drink, motel rooms, dance clubs, and so on. As far as Daytona Beach is concerned, those dollars represent autonomous spending. More important, those dollars can raise the total income of Daytona Beach by some multiple of itself. College students buy pizzas, beer, and sodas. The people who sell these items find their incomes rising. They, in turn, spend some fraction of their increase in income, which generates additional income for still others, who spend some fraction of their increase in income, and so on and so on.

Let's take a hypothetical example. Suppose college students spend $7 million in Daytona Beach during spring break. If the *MPC* is, say, 0.60 in Daytona Beach and all the added income generated is spent in Daytona Beach, then college students will increase (nominal) income in Daytona Beach by $17.5 million.

Do the people who live in Daytona Beach want college students to visit their city during spring break? Many of them do because it means extra dollars in their pockets. College students from out of town, together with the multiplier, often make for robust economic times!

multiple. For example, if the multiplier is 5, then a $1 increase in autonomous investment will raise total spending by $5.

The Multiplier and Reality

We have discussed the multiplier in simple terms: A change in autonomous spending leads to a *greater change* in total spending. Also, in the simple Keynesian model, the change in total spending is *equal to* the change in Real GDP (assuming the economy is operating below Natural Real GDP). That's because in the model, prices are assumed to be constant until Natural GDP is reached; so any change in (nominal) total spending is equal to the change in *real* total spending.

We must note two points, however. First, the multiplier takes time to have an effect. In a textbook, it takes only seconds to go from an initial increase in autonomous spending to a multiple increase in either total spending or Real GDP. In the real world, this process takes many months.

Second, for the multiplier to increase Real GDP, *idle resources must exist at each spending round*. After all, if Real GDP is increasing (output is increasing) at each spending round, *idle resources must be available to be brought into production*. If this were not the case, then increased spending would simply result in higher prices without an increase in Real GDP. Simply put, there would be an increase in GDP but not in Real GDP.

Q&A   *Let me see if I have this correct. First, someone increases his or her autonomous spending—say, by $10. Second, this $10 spending generates more spending via the multiplier. For example, if the multiplier is 5, then total spending will increase by $50. Third, according to the Keynesian model, the increase in total spending (which is $50 in my example) will generate an increase in Real GDP of $50. Do I have this correct?*

Yes, you have it correct. We simply remind you that the reason the increase in total spending of $50 generates an increase in Real GDP of $50 is because prices are held constant in the model. We specified this earlier in the chapter.

SELF-TEST

1.   How is autonomous consumption different from consumption?

2.   If the *MPC* is 0.70, what does the multiplier equal?

3.   What happens to the multiplier as the *MPC* falls?

The Simple Keynesian Model in the *AD-AS* Framework

The first section of this chapter presented a few of Keynes's criticisms of the self-regulating economy or classical position. The second section identified and discussed some of the key components of the simple Keynesian model—in particular the consumption function and the multiplier. In this section, we analyze the simple Keynesian model in terms of the aggregate demand and aggregate supply (*AD-AS*) framework. In the next section, we discuss the simple Keynesian model in terms of the total expenditures and total production (*TE-TP*) framework.[2]

Shifts in the Aggregate Demand Curve

Because there is no foreign sector in the simple Keynesian model, total spending consists of consumption (*C*), investment (*I*), and government purchases (*G*). Because there is no monetary side of the economy, it follows that changes in any of these variables (*C, I, G*) can shift the *AD* curve. For example, a rise in consumption will shift the *AD* curve to the right; a decrease in investment will shift the *AD* curve to the left.

Now let's consider aggregate demand in terms of what we know about the consumption function and the multiplier. We know that a rise in autonomous consumption (C_0) will raise consumption (*C*) and therefore shift the *AD* curve to the right.

$$C_0 \uparrow \rightarrow C \uparrow \rightarrow AD \uparrow$$

How much the *AD* curve will shift due to the rise in autonomous consumption depends on the multiplier. Recall our earlier example in which autonomous consumption C_0 increases \$40 and the multiplier (*m*) is 5.

$$\text{Change in total spending} = \text{Multiplier} \times \text{Change in autonomous spending}$$
$$= m \times \Delta C_0$$
$$= 5 \times \$40$$
$$= \$200$$

Exhibit 5 illustrates how the *AD* curve shifts in this situation. We start with the original aggregate demand curve AD_1. Now, autonomous consumption (C_0) rises by \$40. This shifts the aggregate demand curve to AD_2. Does the *AD* curve stay here? No. Because of the multiplier, the initial autonomous consumption spending generates more spending, eventually pushing the *AD* curve to AD_3. In other words, at the end of the process, the *AD* curve has shifted from AD_1 to AD_3. Part of this shift (\$40) is due to the initial rise in autonomous consumption, and part of this shift (\$160) is due to the multiplier.

The Keynesian Aggregate Supply Curve

Earlier, we noted that in the simple Keynesian model, "the price level is assumed to be constant until it reaches its full-employment or Natural Real GDP level." What does this tell us about the Keynesian aggregate supply curve?

---

[2]Some instructors may choose to assign only one of these two sections. It is clear at the end of the chapter which questions and problems go with which sections of this chapter.

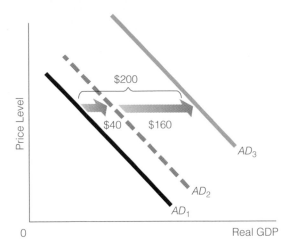

exhibit 5

The Multiplier and Aggregate Demand

An initial increase in autonomous consumption raises total spending and shifts the aggregate demand curve from AD_1 to AD_2. The AD curve does not end here, however. Because of the multiplier, the increase in autonomous spending generates additional incomes and additional spending, shifting the aggregate demand curve to AD_3.

Think back to the discussions of aggregate demand and aggregate supply in the last two chapters and in the first section of this chapter. In these discussions, the AD curve is downward–sloping, and the $SRAS$ curve is upward sloping. Given that the $SRAS$ curve is upward sloping, any shift in the AD curve (rightward or leftward) will automatically change (raise or lower) the price level. If the price level is assumed to be constant, then the Keynesian aggregate supple curve must have a horizontal section to it.

As shown in Exhibit 6, the Keynesian aggregate supply curve (outlined in this chapter and implicit in the simple Keynesian model) has both a horizontal section and a vertical section. The aggregate supply curve is horizontal until Q_N or Natural Real GDP because the simple Keynesian model assumes the price level is constant until Q_N is reached. With this AS curve, what happens in the economy when the AD curve shifts?

An increase in aggregate demand from AD_1 to AD_2 raises Real GDP from Q_1 to Q_2 but does not change the price level. (The price level remains at P_1.) On the other hand, once the economy has reached Q_N, any increases in aggregate demand do change the price level. For example, an increase in aggregate demand from AD_3 to AD_4 raises the price level from P_2 to P_3.

According to Keynes, a change in autonomous spending (e.g., a change in autonomous consumption) will stimulate additional spending in the economy. In our example, a rise in autonomous consumption of $40 generated an additional $160 worth of spending

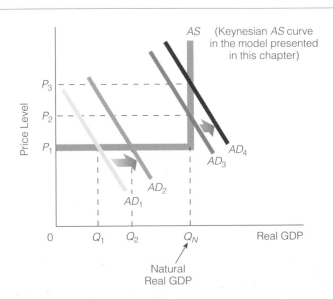

exhibit 6

The AS Curve in the Simple Keynesian Model

The AS curve in the simple Keynesian model is horizontal until Q_N (Natural Real GDP) and vertical at Q_N. It follows that any changes in aggregate demand in the horizontal section do not change the price level, but any changes in aggregate demand in the vertical section do change the price level.

economics 24/7

NEGATIVE SAVINGS AND HOUSE WEALTH

In 1932 and 1933, the savings rate in the United States was negative. These were years of the Great Depression, when the unemployment rate was high and businesses were collapsing.

The savings rate in the United States was also negative in 2005. But unemployment was not high in 2005, and businesses weren't collapsing. So what explains the negative savings rate? What explains the fact that many Americans were spending their entire income and then borrowing more to spend?

Some have suggested that it was rising house prices. In many places in the United States during the late 1990s and early 2000s, real estate prices rose dramatically. It was not uncommon in some parts of the country to have the price of a home double in a matter of a few years. This meant that a couple who bought a house earlier for, say, $150,000, now owned a house worth $300,000. Was there as much need to save when the booming real estate market had added $150,000 to the couple's net worth?

You can think of it this way: A couple in their mid-forties is busy working, earning an income, and saving part of that income for retirement and old age. All of a sudden, the house they own increases in value at a rate many times greater than the inflation rate. As a result of the rise in real estate prices, they, the owners of a house, become wealthier than they were before. Now there is not as great a need to save because they have just been handed a monetary bonus—special delivery, compliments of the real estate market. (Of course, whether they maintain their current house wealth depends on what happens to house prices in the future.)

In 2006, some people were wondering if real estate prices weren't ripe for a fall. What happens if the people who have spent their entire incomes, and gone into debt too, found themselves living in houses that were declining in value? What would happen if the "house wealth" they thought was there began to dissipate? Would they dramatically reduce their consumption spending and shift the *AD* curve in the economy leftward? And would this end up reducing Real GDP? Some economists thought so.

Q&A   *If the AD curve shifts rightward and stays within the horizontal section of the AS curve (in Exhibit 6), Real GDP will rise, but the price level will remain constant. Is this correct?*

Yes, it is correct.

so that total spending increased by $200. (The multiplier was 5 because we assumed the *MPC* was 0.80.)

Consider this question: Under what condition will a $200 *increase in total spending* lead to a $200 *increase in Real GDP?* The answer is when the aggregate supply curve is horizontal, which means (in the simple Keynesian model) when the economy is currently producing less than Natural Real GDP. In other words, the *AD* curve in the economy must be shifting rightward (due to the increased spending) but must be within the *horizontal section* of the Keynesian *AS* curve.

The Economy in a Recessionary Gap

According to classical and other economists (discussed in the last chapter), the economy is self-regulating. A recessionary gap or an inflationary gap is only a temporary state of affairs. In time, the economy moves into long-run equilibrium and produces Natural Real GDP (Q_N).

Keynes did not believe that the economy always works this way. He believed the economy could get stuck in a recessionary gap. As shown in Exhibit 7, this means the economy could be stuck at Q_1 (its equilibrium position) and be unable to get to Q_N on its own. In other words, the economy is at point *A,* and it is not able to get to point *B.* Keynes believed that the private sector—consisting of the household sector and business

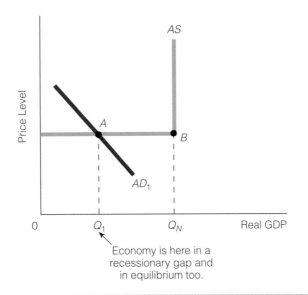

exhibit **7**

Can the Private Sector Remove the Economy from a Recessionary Gap?

The economy is at point A producing Q_1. Q_1 is less than Q_N, so the economy is in a recessionary gap. The questions is whether the private sector (consisting of consumption and investment spending) can remove the economy from the recessionary gap by increasing spending enough to shift the aggregate demand curve rightward to go through point B. Keynes believed that sometimes it could not. No matter how low interest rates fell, investment spending would not rise because of pessimistic business expectations with respect to future sales.

sector—may not be able to move the economy from point A to point B. Stated differently, neither consumption nor investment would rise enough to shift the aggregate demand curve from its current position (AD_1).

But suppose the interest rate in the economy falls. Won't this be enough to get businesses to invest more, and thus, won't the AD curve begin to shift rightward, headed for point B? Not necessarily, said Keynes. Remember, Keynes didn't believe that investment spending was always responsive to changes in interest rates. For example, suppose businesses are pessimistic about future sales, and the interest rate drops. Are businesses going to invest more just because interest rates have dropped, or might their pessimistic expectations of future sales be so strong that they don't invest more at the lower interest rate? Keynes believed that the latter scenario could be the case.

Government's Role in the Economy

In the self-regulating economy of the classical economists, government did not have a management role to play. The private sector (households and businesses) was capable of self-regulating the economy at its Natural Real GDP level.

Keynes believed the economy was not self-regulating; economic instability was a possibility. In other words, it was possible for the economy to get stuck in a recessionary gap.

Economic instability opens the door to government playing a role in the economy. According to Keynes, and to many Keynesians, if the private sector cannot self-regulate the economy at its Natural Real GDP level, then maybe it is incumbent for the government to help. In terms of Exhibit 7, maybe the government has a role to play in shifting the AD curve rightward so that it goes through point B. We discuss the role government might play in the economy in the next chapter.

The Theme of the Simple Keynesian Model

As portrayed in terms of AD and AS, the essence of the simple Keynesian model is:

1. The price level is constant until Natural Real GDP is reached.
2. The AD curve shifts if there are changes in C, I, or G.

Thinking like **AN ECONOMIST** *An economist's view of the economy and his policy suggestions are often linked. For example, classical economists and their modern-day counterparts, who view the economy as inherently stable, believe in a policy of laissez-faire: Government should keep its hands off the economy. Keynesians, however, who view the economy as inherently unstable, suggest that government has an economic role to play. In short, policy suggestions are sometimes a consequence of how one views the internal or inherent workings of an economy.*

3. According to Keynes, it is possible for the economy to be in equilibrium and in a recessionary gap too. In other words, the economy can be at point *A* in Exhibit 7.

4. The private sector may not be able to get the economy out of a recessionary gap. In other words, the private sector (households and businesses) may not be able to increase *C* or *I* enough to get the *AD* curve in Exhibit 7 to intersect the *AS* curve at point *B*.

5. The government may have a management role to play in the economy. According to Keynes, government may have to raise aggregate demand enough to stimulate the economy out of the recessionary gap and move it to its Natural Real GDP level.

SELF-TEST

1. What was Keynes's position with respect to the self-regulating properties of an economy?

2. What will happen to Real GDP if autonomous spending rises and the economy is operating in the horizontal section of the Keynesian *AS* curve? Explain your answer.

3. An economist who believes the economy is self-regulating is more likely to advocate laissez-faire than an economist who believes the economy is inherently unstable. Do you agree or disagree? Explain your answer.

The Simple Keynesian Model in the *TE-TP* Framework

A story can be translated into different languages, and an economic model can be presented in various frameworks. The last section presented the simple Keynesian model in terms of the familiar (diagrammatic) *AD-AS* framework of analysis.

But the simple Keynesian model was not first presented in terms of *AD-AS*. It was first presented in terms of the framework that we discuss in this section. This framework has been known by different names, three of which are the Keynesian cross, income-expenditure, and total expenditure-total production. Throughout our discussion, we shall refer to it as total expenditure-total production, or simply the *TE-TP* framework.

Deriving a Total Expenditures (*TE*) Curve

Just as we derived *AD* and *AS* curves in the *AD-AS* framework, we want to derive a total expenditures (*TE*) curve in the *TE-TP* framework. Total expenditures are the sum of its parts: consumption, investment, and government purchases. To derive a *TE* curve, we must first derive a diagrammatic representation of consumption, investment, and government purchases, as shown in Exhibit 8 and explained next.

1. **Consumption.** As disposable income rises, so does consumption. This is shown arithmetically in columns (1) and (3) of Exhibit 4. Exhibit 4 also shows that because the *MPC* is less than 1, consumption rises by less than disposable income rises. Consumption also rises as Real GDP rises but, again, by a smaller percentage. For example, if Real GDP rises by $100, consumption may rise by $80. In Exhibit 8(a), we have drawn consumption as an upward-sloping curve. Notice that as Real GDP rises from Q_1 to Q_2, consumption rises from $7 trillion to $7.5 trillion.

2. **Investment.** We are going to simplify things in deriving *TE*. Look at the investment curve in Exhibit 8(b). We assume investment is constant at $1 trillion whether Real GDP is Q_1 or Q_2.

3. **Government purchases.** We simplify the government spending curve too. In Exhibit 8(c), government purchases are constant at $1.5 trillion, regardless of the amount of Real GDP.

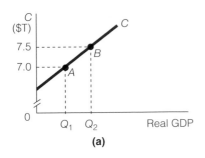

(a)

(b)

(c)

(d)

Consumption
($ Trillions)

At Q_1	7.0
At Q_2	7.5

Investment
($ Trillions)

At Q_1	1.0
At Q_2	1.0

Government Purchases
($ Trillions)

At Q_1	1.5
At Q_2	1.5

Total Expenditures
($ Trillions)

At Q_1	9.5
At Q_2	10.0

exhibit **8**

The Derivation of the Total Expenditures (*TE*) Curve

At different levels of Real GDP, we sum consumption (a), investment (b), and government purchases (c) to derive *TE* curve (d).

In Exhibit 8(d), we have derived a *TE* curve. We simply added the components of total expenditures at the two Real GDP levels, Q_1 and Q_2, plotted the relevant points, and then drew a line through the points. We see that at Q_1, total expenditures are $9.5 trillion, and at Q_2, they are $10.0 trillion. The *TE* curve is upward sloping.

What Will Shift the *TE* Curve?

The *TE* curve in the *TE-TP* framework plays the same role as the *AD* curve in the *AD-AS* framework. Just as the *AD* curve shifts if there is a change in *C*, *I*, or *G*, the *TE* curve shifts if there is a change in *C, I,* or *G.* For example, a rise in *C* will shift the *TE* curve upward; a decline in *I* will shift the *TE* curve downward.

Comparing Total Expenditures (*TE*) and Total Production (*TP*)

Businesses produce the goods and services that are bought by the three sectors of the economy (household, business, and government). Sometimes, though, businesses produce too much or too little in comparison to what the three sectors buy. For example, suppose businesses produce $10 trillion worth of goods and services, but the three sectors of the economy buy only $9.5 trillion worth of goods and services. In this case, businesses have produced too much relative to what the three sectors of the economy buy.

Or possibly, businesses produce $10 trillion worth of goods and services, but the three sectors of the economy buy $10.5 trillion worth of goods and services. In this case, businesses have produced too little relative to what the three sectors of the economy buy. (If you are wondering how the three sectors of the economy can possibly buy more than businesses produce, the answer has to do with goods that businesses hold in inventory. We will soon explain the process.)

Finally, it is possible for businesses to produce $10 trillion worth of goods and services and for the three sectors of the economy to buy exactly $10 trillion worth of goods and services. In this case, businesses have produced exactly the right amount of goods and services.

Thus, there are three possible states of the economy in the *TE-TP* framework. The total expenditures (*TE*) of the three sectors of the economy can be less than, greater than, or equal to the dollar value of total production (*TP*). In other words, each of the following states of the economy is possible:

$$TE < TP$$
$$TE > TP$$
$$TE = TP$$

Thinking like **AN ECONOMIST** *Where has the concept of "threes" come up before? When we discussed a single market (in Chapter 3), we said a market could be in equilibrium, shortage, or surplus. In other words, there were three possible states of a market. In Chapter 8, we said the economy could be producing a Real GDP level either greater than, less than, or equal to Natural Real GDP. In other words, in an economy, there are three possible states. Now we are saying that total expenditures (TE) can be either less than, greater than, or equal to total production. Once again, we are dealing with three possible states of an economy.*

According to many economists, if the economy is currently operating where *TE* < *TP* or *TE* > *TP* (both states are described as disequilibrium), it will eventually move to where *TE* = *TP* (where the economy is in equilibrium). The next section explains how this happens.

Moving from Disequilibrium to Equilibrium

Business firms hold an inventory of their goods to guard against unexpected changes in the demand for their product. For example, General Motors may hold an inventory of a certain type of car in case the demand for that car suddenly increases unexpectedly.

Although we know why business firms hold an inventory of their goods, we don't know *how much* inventory they will hold. For example, we don't know if General Motors will hold an inventory of 1,000 cars, 2,000 cars, or 10,000 cars. (Inventories are usually held in terms of, say, a 45- or 60-day supply, but we have simplified things here.) However, we do know that for General Motors, and all other business firms, there is some *optimum inventory.* This is "just the right amount" of inventory—not too much and not too little. With this in mind, consider two cases that illustrate how business inventory levels play an important role in the economy's adjustment from disequilibrium to equilibrium in the *TE-TP* framework.

CASE 1: *TE* < *TP* Assume business firms hold an optimum inventory level of $300 billion worth of goods. Then firms produce $11 trillion worth of goods and services, and the three sectors of the economy buy $10.8 trillion worth of goods and services. Thus, producers produce more than individuals buy ($TE < TP$). The difference adds to inventories, and inventory levels rise unexpectedly to $500 billion, which is $200 billion more than the $300 billion firms see as optimal.

This unexpected rise in inventories signals to firms that they have *overproduced*. Consequently, they cut back on the quantity of goods they produce. The cutback in production causes Real GDP to fall, bringing Real GDP closer to the (lower) output level that the three sectors of the economy are willing and able to buy. Ultimately, TP will equal TE.

CASE 2: *TE > TP* Assume business firms hold their optimum inventory level, $300 billion worth of goods. Then firms produce $10.4 trillion worth of goods, and members of the three sectors buy $10.6 trillion worth of goods. But how can individuals buy more than firms produce? The answer is that firms make up the difference out of inventory. In our example, inventory levels fall from $300 billion to $100 billion because individuals purchase $200 billion more of goods than firms produced (to be sold). This example illustrates why firms maintain inventories in the first place: to be able to meet an unexpected increase in sales.

The unexpected fall in inventories signals to firms that they have *underproduced*. Consequently, they increase the quantity of goods they produce. The rise in production causes Real GDP to rise, in the process bringing Real GDP closer to the (higher) real output that the three sectors are willing and able to buy. Ultimately, TP will equal TE.

The Graphical Representation of the Three States of the Economy in the *TE-TP* Framework

The three states of the economy are represented in Exhibit 9. Notice that there is a *TE* curve, which we derived earlier, and a *TP* curve, which is simply a 45-degree line. (It is called a 45-degree line because it bisects the 90-degree angle at the origin.) It is important to notice that at any point on the *TP* curve, total production is equal to Real GDP

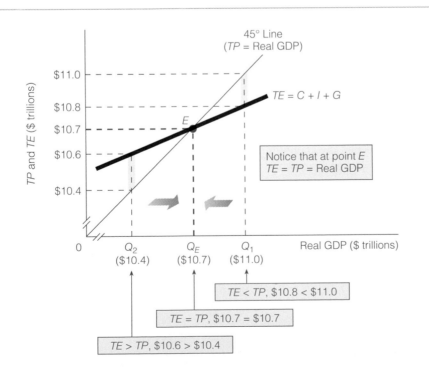

exhibit **9**

The Three States of the Economy in the *TE-TP* Framework

At Q_E, $TE = TP$ and the economy is in equilibrium. At Q_1, $TE < TP$. This results in an unexpected increase in inventories, which signals firms that they have overproduced, which leads firms to cut back production. The cutback in production reduces Real GDP. The economy tends to move from Q_1 to Q_E. At Q_2, $TE > TP$. This results in an unexpected decrease in inventories, which signals firms that they have underproduced, which leads firms to raise production. The increased production raises Real GDP. The economy tends to move from Q_2 to Q_E.

(TP = Real GDP).[3] This is because TP and Real GDP are different names for the same thing. Real GDP, remember, is simply the total market value of all final goods and services produced annually within a country's borders, adjusted for price changes.

Now let's look at three different Real GDP levels in the exhibit. We start with Q_1, where Real GDP = $11 trillion. At this Real GDP level, what does TE equal? What does TP equal? We see that TE is $10.8 trillion and TP is $11 trillion. This illustrates Case 1, in which producers produce more than individuals buy ($TE < TP$). The difference adds to inventories. This unexpected rise in inventories signals to firms that they have overproduced. Consequently, they cut back on the quantity of goods they produce. The cutback in production causes Real GDP to fall, ultimately bringing Real GDP down to Q_E ($10.7 trillion in the exhibit).

Now we look at Q_2, where Real GDP = $10.4 trillion. At this Real GDP level, TE equals $10.6 trillion and TP equals $10.4 trillion. This illustrates Case 2, in which the three sectors of the economy buy more goods and services than business firms have produced ($TE > TP$). Business firms make up the difference between what they have produced and what the three sectors of the economy buy through inventories. Inventories fall below optimum levels. Consequently, businesses increase the quantity of goods they produce. The rise in production causes Real GDP to rise, ultimately moving Real GDP up to Q_E ($10.7 trillion in the exhibit).

When the economy is producing Q_E, or $10.7 trillion worth of goods and services, it is in equilibrium. At this Real GDP level, TP and TE are the same, $10.7 trillion. The following table summarizes some key points about the state of the economy in the TE-TP framework.

State of the Economy	What Happens to Inventories?	What Do Firms Do?
$TE < TP$ Individuals are buying less output than firms produce.	Inventories rise above optimum levels.	Firms cut back production to reduce inventories to their optimum levels.
$TE > TP$ Individuals are buying more output than firms produce.	Inventories fall below optimum levels.	Firms increase production to raise inventories to their optimum levels.
$TE = TP$	Inventories are at their optimum levels.	Firms neither increase nor decrease production.

The Economy in a Recessionary Gap and the Role of Government

According to Keynes, the economy can be in equilibrium and in a recessionary gap too. We saw this in the last section for the simple Keynesian model in the AD-AS framework. (To review, look back at Exhibit 7.) Can the same situation exist in the TE-TP framework? Yes it can. For example, in Exhibit 9, the economy equilibrates at point E

---

[3]Earlier, we said that the TE curve plays the role in the TE-TP framework that the AD curve plays in the AD-AS framework. In other words, roughly speaking, the AD curve is the TE curve. Similarly, the TP curve plays the role in the TE-TP framework that the AS curve plays in the AD-AS framework. In other words, roughly speaking, the TP curve is the AS curve. In the AD-AS framework, equilibrium is at the intersection of the AD and AS curves. As you will soon learn, in the TE-TP framework, equilibrium is at the intersection of the TE and TP curves.

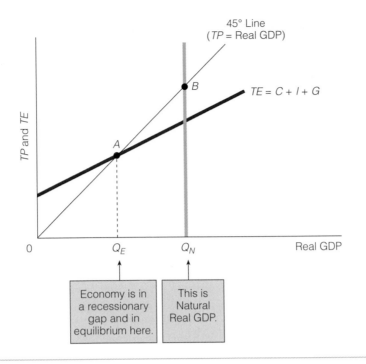

exhibit **10**

The Economy: In Equilibrium, and in a Recessionary Gap, Too

Using the *TE-TP* framework, the economy is currently in equilibrium at point *A*, producing Q_E. Natural Real GDP, however, is greater than Q_E, so the economy is in a recessionary gap as well as being in equilibrium.

and thus produces a Real GDP level of $10.7 trillion worth of goods and services. Is there any guarantee that the Real GDP level of $10.7 trillion is the Natural Real GDP level? Not at all. The economy could be in a situation like that shown in Exhibit 10. The economy is in equilibrium at point *A*, producing Q_E, but the Natural Real GDP level is Q_N. Because the economy is producing at a Real GDP level that is less than Natural Real GDP, it is in a recessionary gap.

How does the economy get out of the recessionary gap? Will the private sector (households and businesses) be capable of pushing the *TE* curve in Exhibit 10 upward so that it goes through point *B*, and thus Q_N is produced? According to Keynes, not necessarily. Keynes believed government may be necessary to get the economy out of a recessionary gap. For example, government may have to raise its purchases (raise *G*) so that the *TE* curve shifts upward and goes through point *B*.

macro
Theme   There are debates in macroeconomics. One debate concerns the issue of equilibrium in the economy: in other words, where the economy naturally ends up after all adjustments have been made. In the last chapter, we read about economists who believe that the economy is self-regulating and that an economy naturally ends up (in the long run) producing Natural Real GDP. In this chapter, we have read about economists who believe that the economy can be inherently unstable and that an economy can naturally end up producing a level of Real GDP less than Natural Real GDP. To the first group of economists, equilibrium is a desirable state of affairs; to the second group, equilibrium (where Real GDP is less than Natural Real GDP) is not a desirable state of affairs.

A Reader Asks...

Was Keynes a Revolutionary in Economics?

Even before I enrolled in an economics course, I had heard of the economist John Maynard Keynes. Could you tell me a little about his life? Also, I'd like to know if economists consider him a revolutionary in economics. If so, what did he revolutionize?

John Maynard Keynes was born in Cambridge, England, on June 5, 1883, and died at Tilton (in Sussex) on April 21, 1946. His father was John Neville Keynes, an eminent economist and author of *The Scope and Method of Political Economy*. Keynes's mother was one of the first female students to attend Cambridge University and for a time presided as mayor of the city of Cambridge.

Keynes was educated at Eton and at King's College, Cambridge, where he received a degree in mathematics in 1905. At Cambridge, he studied under the well-known and widely respected economist Alfred Marshall. In 1925, Keynes married Russian ballerina Lydia Lopokova. He was prominent in British social and intellectual circles and enjoyed art, theater, opera, debate, and collecting rare books.

Many economists rank Keynes's *The General Theory of Employment, Interest and Money* alongside Adam Smith's *Wealth of Nations* and Karl Marx's *Das Kapital* as the most influential economic treatises ever written. The book was published on February 4, 1936.

Before the publication of the *General Theory*, Keynes presented the ideas contained in the work in a series of university lectures that he gave between October 10, 1932, and December 2, 1935. Ten days after his last lecture, he sent off the manuscript of what was to become the *General Theory*.

Keynes's lectures were said to be both shocking (he was pointing out the errors of the Classical School) and exciting (he was proposing something new). One of the students at these lectures was Lorie Tarshis, who later wrote the first Keynesian introductory textbook, *The Elements of Economics*. In another venue, Tarshis wrote about the Keynes lectures and specifically about why Keynes's ideas were revolutionary.

I attended that first lecture, naturally awed but bothered. As the weeks passed, only a stone would not have responded to the growing excitement these lectures generated. So I missed only two over the four years—two out of the thirty lectures. And like others, I would feel the urgency of the task. No wonder! These were the years when everything came loose; when sober dons and excitable students seriously discussed such issues as: Was capitalism not doomed? Should Britain not take the path of Russia or Germany to create jobs? Keynes obviously believed his analysis led to a third means to prosperity far less threatening to the values he prized, but until he had developed the theory and offered it in print, he knew that he could not sway government. So he saw his task as supremely urgent. I was also a bit surprised by his concern over too low a level of output. I had been assured by all I had read that the economy would bob to the surface, like a cork held under water—and output would rise, of its own accord, to an acceptable level. But Keynes proposed something far more shocking: that the economy could reach an equilibrium position with output far below capacity. That was an exciting challenge, sharply at variance with the views of Pigou and Marshall who represented "The Classical (Orthodox) School" in Cambridge, and elsewhere.[4]

---

[4] L. Tarshis, "Keynesian Revolution," in *The New Palgrave: A Dictionary of Economics*, vol. 3 (London: Macmillan Press, 1987), p. 48.

The Theme of the Simple Keynesian Model

As portrayed in terms of *TE* and *TP,* the essence of the simple Keynesian model is:

1. The price level is constant until Natural Real GDP is reached.

2. The *TE* curve shifts if there are changes in *C, I,* or *G*.

3. According to Keynes, it is possible for the economy to be in equilibrium and in a recessionary gap too. In other words, the economy can be at point *A* in Exhibit 10.

4. The private sector may not be able to get the economy out of a recessionary gap. In other words, the private sector (households and businesses) may not be able to increase *C* or *I* enough to get the *TE* curve in Exhibit 10 to rise and pass through point *B*.

5. The government may have a management role to play in the economy. According to Keynes, government may have to raise *TE* enough to stimulate the economy out of the recessionary gap and move it to its Natural Real GDP level.

SELF-TEST

1. What happens in the economy if total production (*TP*) is greater than total expenditures (*TE*)?

2. What happens in the economy if total expenditures (*TE*) are greater than total production (*TP*)?

Thinking like
AN ECONOMIST

We have discussed the concept of equilibrium in terms of a market (Chapter 3) and in terms of an economy (this chapter). In Chapter 3, we described market equilibrium as the setting at which the quantity demanded of a good equals the quantity supplied of a good. We also hinted that equilibrium in a market is a desirable state of affairs because, at equilibrium, the sum of consumers' and producers' surplus is maximized and because all gains from trade have been realized.

In this chapter, however, we have hinted that equilibrium in an economy might not be a desirable state of affairs, especially if equilibrium comes at a level of Real GDP that is less than Natural Real GDP.

Keep in mind what equilibrium *means* to an economist. It means that the adjustment process has ended. In terms of our simple Keynesian model, it means that inventories are at their optimum levels so that firms do not have an incentive to either increase or decrease production.

There is nothing that necessitates an equilibrium position having to be a desirable state of affairs. In other words, just because an economist says that something is in equilibrium, it does not necessarily follow that equilibrium is desirable. In this chapter, we have seen where equilibrium in the economy (at a position at which Real GDP is less than Natural Real GDP) might not be a desirable state of affairs.

! analyzing the scene

Why do the two economists disagree over the predicted change in the unemployment rate?

Economist 1 believes the unemployment rate will remain at its current level unless something is done. Economist 2 believes the unemployment rate will soon decline. He says that wages are already beginning to fall. Economist 1 probably believes that the economy is not self-regulating and that the economy is stuck in a recessionary gap. Either that or he believes that wages and prices are not likely to come down any time soon, so the "self-regulating" property of the economy isn't likely to be operable any time soon. Economist 2 seems to believe that lower wages will shift the *SRAS* curve rightward, lowering the price level, and thus move the economy out of a recessionary gap. As the economy comes out of a recessionary gap, the unemployment rate will decline. In short, Economist 2 believes the economy is self-regulating (at Natural Real GDP) and Economist 1 does not.

Why do the two economists disagree over the predicted change in spending?

Economist 1 believes that an initial rise in (autonomous) spending will lead to a large change in total spending, and Economist 2 believes it will not. What is at the heart of their disagreement? Perhaps the two economists disagree on the current value of the marginal propensity to consume (*MPC*). The higher the *MPC*, the larger the multiplier and the larger the increase in total spending, given an initial rise in autonomous spending. To illustrate, suppose Economist 1 believes the *MPC* is 0.80 and Economist 2 believes the *MPC* is 0.40. For Economist 1, the multiplier is 5, but for Economist 2, it is 1.67. This means Economist 1 believes that an increase in autonomous spending of $1 will end up increasing total spending by $5, and Economist 2 believes that an increase in autonomous spending of $1 will end up increasing total spending by $1.67.

Why do the two economists disagree over the predicted change in output (Real GDP) and the price level?

Economist 1 believes the additional spending in the economy will lead to a large change in output and almost no change in the price level. Economist 2 believes the additional spending in the economy will lead to almost no change in output and to a substantial change in the price level. What is at the heart of their difference? Economist 1 views the increased spending as occurring within the horizontal section of the Keynesian aggregate supply (*AS*) curve. After all, if aggregate demand rises within the horizontal section of the *AS* curve, Real GDP will rise but the price level will not. Economist 2 views the increased spending as occurring within the vertical section of the Keynesian *AS* curve. In this case, a rise in aggregate demand leaves Real GDP unchanged but raises the price level.

Why do the two economists disagree over the effect on spending of a rise in savings?

Economist 1 believes an increase in saving may lead to a decline in total spending, and Economist 2 believes an increase in saving will not lead to a decline in total spending. What is at the heart of their difference? Economist 1 may believe that although an increase in saving will lead to a decline in the interest rate, investment spending is not responsive to the lower interest rate at this time. Economist 2 may believe the opposite: As saving rises, downward pressure on the interest rate will cause businesses to invest more at the lower interest rate, thus offsetting the decline in household spending.

chapter summary

Keynes on Wage Rates and Prices

- Keynes believed that wage rates and prices may be inflexible downward. He said that employees and labor unions would resist employer's wage cuts and that because of anticompetitive or monopolistic elements in the economy, prices would not fall.

Keynes on Say's Law

- Keynes did not agree that Say's law would necessarily hold in a money economy. He thought it was possible for consumption to fall (saving to increase) by more than investment increased. Consequently, a decrease in consumption (or increase in saving) could lower total expenditures and aggregate demand in the economy.

Consumption Function

- Keynes made three points about consumption and disposable income: (1) Consumption depends on disposable income. (2) Consumption and disposable income move in the same direction. (3) As disposable income changes, consumption changes by less. These three ideas are incorporated into the consumption function, $C = C_0 + (MPC)(Y_d)$, where C_0 is autonomous consumption, MPC is the marginal propensity to consume, and Y_d is disposable income.

The Multiplier

- A change in autonomous spending will bring about a multiple change in total spending. The overall change in spending is equal to $1/(1 - MPC)$ (the multiplier) times the change in autonomous spending.

The Simple Keynesian Model in the *AD-AS* Framework

- Changes in consumption, investment, and government purchases will change aggregate demand.
- A rise in *C, I,* or *G* will shift the *AD* curve to the right.
- A decrease in *C, I,* or *G* will shift the *AD* curve to the left.
- The aggregate supply curve in the simple Keynesian model has both a horizontal section and a vertical section. The "kink" between the two sections is at the Natural Real GDP level. If aggregate demand changes in the horizontal section of the curve (when the economy is operating below Natural Real GDP), there is a change in Real GDP but no change in the price level. If aggregate demand changes in the vertical section of the curve (when the economy is operating at Natural Real GDP), there is a change in the price level but no change in Real GDP.

The Simple Keynesian Model in the *TE-TP* Framework

- Changes in consumption, investment, and government purchases will change total expenditures.
- A rise in *C, I,* or *G* will shift the *TE* curve upward.
- A decrease in *C, I,* or *G* will shift the *TE* curve downward.

- If total expenditures (*TE*) equal total production (*TP*), the economy is in equilibrium. If *TE* < *TP*, the economy is in disequilibrium and inventories unexpectedly rise, signaling firms to cut back production. If *TE* > *TP*, the economy is in disequilibrium and inventories unexpectedly fall, signaling firms to increase production.

- Equilibrium occurs where *TE* = *TP*. The equilibrium level of Real GDP may be less than the Natural Real GDP level, and the economy may be stuck at this lower level of Real GDP.

A Keynesian Theme

- Keynes proposed that the economy could reach its equilibrium position with Real GDP below Natural Real GDP; that is, the economy can be in equilibrium and in a recessionary gap too. Furthermore, he argued that the economy may not be able to get out of a recessionary gap by itself. Government may need to play a management role in the economy.

key terms and concepts

Efficiency Wage Models	Marginal Propensity to Consume (*MPC*)	Autonomous Consumption	Marginal Propensity to Save (*MPS*)
Consumption Function			
Multiplier			

questions and problems

Questions 1–4 are based on the first section of the chapter, questions 5–7 are based on the second section, questions 8–14 are based on the third section, and questions 15–19 are based on the fourth section.

1 How is Keynes's position different from the classical position with respect to wages, prices, and Say's law?

2 Classical economists assumed that wage rates, prices, and interest rates were flexible and would adjust quickly. Consider an extreme case: Suppose classical economists believed wage rates, prices, and interest rates would adjust instantaneously. What would this imply the classical aggregate supply (*AS*) curve would look like? Explain your answer.

3 Give two reasons wage rates may not fall.

4 According to New Keynesian economists, why might business firms pay wage rates above market-clearing levels?

5 Given the Keynesian consumption function, how would a cut in income tax rates affect consumption? Explain your answer.

6 Explain how a rise in autonomous spending can increase total spending by some multiple.

7 A change in what factors will lead to a change in consumption?

8 According to Keynes, can an increase in saving shift the *AD* curve to the left? Explain your answer.

9 What factors will shift the *AD* curve in the simple Keynesian model?

10 According to Keynes, an increase in saving and decrease in consumption may lower total spending in the economy. But how could this happen if the increased saving lowers interest rates (as shown in the last chapter)? Wouldn't a decrease in interest rates increase investment spending, thus counteracting the decrease in consumption spending?

11 Can a person believe that wages are inflexible downward for, say, one year and also believe in a self-regulating economy? Explain your answer.

12 According to Keynes, can the private sector always remove the economy from a recessionary gap? Explain your answer.

13 What does the aggregate supply curve look like in the simple Keynesian model?

14 Suppose consumption rises and investment and government purchases remain constant. How will the *AD* curve shift in the simple Keynesian model? Under what condition will the rise in Real GDP be equal to the rise in total spending?

15 Explain how to derive a total expenditures (*TE*) curve.

16 What role do inventories play in the equilibrating process in the simple Keynesian model (as described in the *TE-TP* framework)?

17 Identify the three states of the economy in terms of *TE* and *TP*.

18 If Real GDP is $10.4 trillion in Exhibit 9, what is the state of business inventories?

19 How will a rise in government purchases change the *TE* curve in Exhibit 9?

working with numbers and graphs

Questions 1–2 are based on the second section of the chapter, questions 3–4 are based on the third section, and questions 5–8 are based on the fourth section.

1 Compute the multiplier in each of the following cases:

   a $MPC = 0.60$
   b $MPC = 0.80$
   c $MPC = 0.50$

2 Write an investment function (equation) that specifies two components: (a) autonomous investment spending and (b) induced investment spending.

3 Economist Smith believes that changes in aggregate demand affect only the price level, and economist Jones believes that changes in aggregate demand affect only Real GDP. What do the AD and AS curves look like for each economist?

4 Explain the following using the figure below.

   a   According to Keynes, aggregate demand may be insufficient to bring about the full-employment output level (or Natural Real GDP).
   b   A decrease in consumption (due to increased saving) is not matched by an increase in investment spending.

5 The TE curve in Exhibit 8(d) is upward sloping because the consumption function is upward sloping. Explain.

6 Look at Exhibit 8(d). What does the vertical distance between the origin and the point at which the TE curve cuts the vertical axis represent?

7 In the following figure, explain what happens if:

   a   The economy is at Q_1.
   b   The economy is at Q_2.

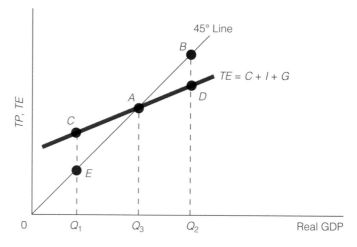

8 In the previous figure, if Natural Real GDP is Q_2, what state is the economy in at point A?

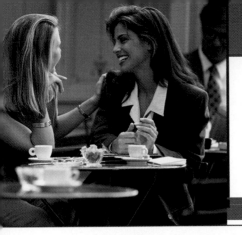

The Federal Budget and Fiscal Policy

Setting the Scene On any given day, individuals say a million and one things that relate to economics. Some of the things they say are true, and some are false. When false things are said, often the individuals don't realize what they are saying is false. Listen to some of the things people said recently.

9:42 A.M.

Georgia Dickens is sitting with a friend at a coffee shop. Georgia and her friend are talking about the new tax bill. Georgia thinks it would be wrong to cut tax rates at this time "because lower tax rates," she says, "will lead to a larger budget deficit—and the budget deficit is already plenty big."

10:37 A.M.

Alberto Cruz is in a colleague's office. Alberto's colleague has just told Alberto that she thinks "the rich in this country don't pay enough in taxes." Alberto asks her what percentage of income taxes the rich pay. His colleague says she isn't sure what the "exact percentage is," but she's pretty sure it isn't much.

12:14 P.M.

Marion Rosenthal and a friend, Alice Cummings, are having lunch at a small Italian restaurant. Marion says, "I think all this new federal government spending is really going to stimulate the economy." "What do you mean?" Alice asks. "Well," says Marion, "with more federal spending, there will be greater demand for goods in the economy, and this will get business to hire more people to produce the greater number of goods people are demanding." "I'm not sure it works that way," Alice says.

6:14 P.M.

The Mason family is eating dinner. Vivien Mason says, "I don't agree. I think we spend too much on food stamps. I bet we spend about $200 billion a year on food stamps." Frank Mason responds, "You may be right, but that doesn't mean we aren't spending too much on national defense too. I bet we spend 15 times more on national defense than we spend on food stamps." Karen Mason says, "But national security is the government's main job, don't you think? If we're not safe, it won't matter how much we spend on food stamps."

? Here are some questions to keep in mind as you read this chapter:

- *Do lower tax rates mean a larger deficit?*

- *Who are the rich and how much do they pay in taxes?*

- *Will increases in federal government spending increase aggregate demand in the economy?*

- *How much is spent on food stamps? On national defense?*

See **analyzing the scene** at the end of this chapter for answers to these questions.

The Federal Budget

The federal budget is composed of two, not necessarily equal, parts: government expenditures and tax revenues. You are familiar with the term *government purchases* from earlier chapters. *Government expenditures*—sometimes simply called *government spending*—are not the same as government purchases. *Government expenditures* are the sum of government purchases and (government) transfer payments.[1]

Government Expenditures

In 2005, the federal government spent $2.472 trillion. This was about 20.1 percent of GDP for that year. The following table shows government spending as a percentage of GDP in a few other years.

Year	Government Spending as a Percentage of GDP
1999	18.6
2000	18.4
2001	18.5
2002	19.4
2003	19.9
2004	19.9
2005	20.1

The bulk of the $2.472 trillion in government spending in 2005 was spent on four programs: Social Security, Medicare, Medicaid, and national defense. These four programs together accounted for 62 percent of all government spending in 2005. The following table shows the actual dollar amounts spent in various spending program categories.

Spending Program Category	Billions of Dollars
National Defense	$500
Social Security	519
Medicare	333
Medicaid	182
Unemployment Compensation	32
Food Stamps	33
Family Support	24
Child Nutrition	13
Veterans' Benefits	36
Federal Civilian Retirement Benefits	64
Administration of Justice	40
General Science, Space, and Technology	24
Agriculture	30
Net Interest on the Public Debt	177

---

[1]Remember from an earlier chapter that government purchases refer to the purchases of goods and services by government at all levels. Transfer payments are payments to persons that are not made in return for goods and services currently supplied, such as Social Security payments. In our discussions in this chapter, the terms *government expenditures, government spending, government purchases,* and *transfer payments* all refer to the *federal* government.

Government Tax Revenues

The federal government imposes taxes and fees that generate revenue. In 2005, government revenues totaled $2.154 trillion. This was 17.5 percent of GDP for the year. The following table shows government tax revenues as a percentage of GDP in a few other years.

Year	Government Tax Revenues as a Percentage of GDP
1999	20.0
2000	20.9
2001	19.8
2002	17.9
2003	16.5
2004	16.3
2005	17.5

The bulk of government tax revenues comes from three taxes: the individual income tax, the corporate income tax, and Social Security taxes. These three taxes together accounted for 93 percent of total government tax revenues in 2005. The following table shows the actual dollar amount raised in tax revenue by each tax and the tax revenue for each tax as a percentage of GDP.

Tax	Billions of Dollars	Percentage of 2005 GDP
Individual Income Tax	$927	7.5
Corporate Income Tax	278	2.3
Social Security Taxes	798	6.5
Other	154	1.3

The actual dollar amounts for these major taxes in various years (in billions of dollars) are shown in this table:

Year	Individual Income	Corporate Income	Social Security
2001	$994	151	694
2002	858	148	700
2003	794	132	713
2004	809	278	794

You can see from these tables that the individual income tax is a large portion of the government tax revenue pie. Let's look at this tax in more detail.

INCOME TAX STRUCTURES An income tax structure can be progressive, proportional, or regressive. Under a **progressive income tax**, the tax rate increases as a person's taxable income level rises. To illustrate, suppose Davidson pays taxes at the rate of 15 percent on a taxable income of $20,000. When his (taxable) income rises to, say, $30,000, he pays at a rate of 28 percent. And when his income rises to, say, $55,000, he pays at a rate of 31 percent. A progressive income tax is usually capped at some tax rate. Currently, the U.S. income tax structure is progressive. There are six (marginal) tax rates, ranging from a low of 10 percent to a high of 35 percent.

Under a **proportional income tax**, the same tax rate is used for all income levels. A proportional income tax is sometimes referred to as a *flat tax*. For example, if Kuan's taxable income is $10,000, she pays taxes at a rate of 10 percent; if her taxable income rises to $100,000, she still pays at a rate of 10 percent.

Progressive Income Tax

An income tax system in which one's tax rate rises as one's taxable income rises (up to some point).

Proportional Income Tax

An income tax system in which one's tax rate is the same no matter what one's taxable income is.

economics 24/7

TWO PLUMBERS, NEW YEAR'S EVE, AND PROGRESSIVE TAXATION

Many people believe that if two people do the same job, they should be paid the same dollar amount. This notion of *equal pay for equal work* often arises in discussions about the jobs performed by men and women. In other words, if a man and a woman do the same job, many people say that they should be paid the same dollar amount.

Sometimes the notion of equal pay for equal work is extended to *equal after-tax pay for equal work*. That is, if two people do the same job, then they should earn the same after-tax income. However, a progressive income tax structure sometimes makes this impossible.

To illustrate, suppose under a progressive income tax structure, a person who earns between $50,000 and $60,000 pays income tax at a tax rate of 20 percent. For every dollar earned over $60,000 but under $70,000, a person pays at a tax rate of 30 percent.

Now, let's consider two plumbers, Smith and Jones. By December 30, Jones has earned $58,000 for the year and Smith has earned $60,000. Each is asked to do the same

kind of plumbing job on December 31, New Year's Eve. Each plumber charges $1,000 for the job. Thus, Jones and Smith receive equal pay for equal work.

Let's look at the after-tax income that each receives for the job. On the additional $1,000 that Jones earns, she pays at a tax rate of 20 percent. So she pays $200 in taxes and gets to keep $800 in after-tax income. Smith, on the other hand, now has an income of $61,000 and thus falls into a higher marginal tax bracket. He pays at a tax rate of 30 percent on the additional $1,000. So Smith pays $300 in taxes and has $700 in after-tax income. Smith does the same job as Jones, but Smith earns only $700 in after-tax pay while Jones earns $800 in after-tax pay.

Our conclusion: The progressive income tax structure can turn *equal pay for equal work* into *unequal after-tax pay for equal work*. Stated differently, a person can be in favor of progressive income taxes or equal after-tax pay for equal work but not both. Sometimes, it is a matter of one or the other.

Regressive Income Tax

An income tax system in which one's tax rate declines as one's taxable income rises.

Under a **regressive income tax**, the tax rate decreases as a person's taxable income level rises. For example, Lowenstein's tax rate is 10 percent when her taxable income is $10,000 and 8 percent when her taxable income rises to $20,000.

See Exhibit 1 for a review of the three income tax structures.

WHO PAYS THE INCOME TAX? Economists often look at the tax situation for different income groups. For example, in 2005, the top 1 percent of income earners in the United States earned 16.5 percent of the total income earned that year and paid 33.7 percent of the total federal income taxes. The following data show the income and taxes for various income groups in 2005.

Income Group	Group's Share of Total Income	Group's Share of Federal Income Taxes
Top 1%	16.5%	33.7%
Top 5%	31.0	54.1
Top 10%	42.1	65.8
Top 25%	64.7	83.6
Top 50%	86.1	96.4
Bottom 50%	13.9	3.6

exhibit **1**

A CLOSER LOOK

Three Income Tax Structures

The three income tax structures outlined are the progressive, proportional, and regressive.

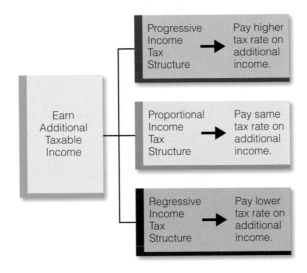

Budget Deficit, Surplus, or Balance

If government expenditures are greater than tax revenues, the federal government runs a **budget deficit**. If tax revenues are greater than government expenditures, the federal government runs a **budget surplus**. If government expenditures equal tax revenues, the federal government runs a **balanced budget**.

In 2005, government expenditures were $2.472 trillion and tax revenues were $2.154 trillion, so the federal government ran a budget deficit that year of $318 billion. Budget surpluses or deficits are projected for upcoming years. For the period 2006 to 2010, the government is projected to run the following deficits:

Year	Projected Budget Deficit (billions of dollars)
2006	$337
2007	270
2008	259
2009	241
2010	222

If the government spends more than its tax revenue and thus runs a budget deficit, where does it get the money to finance the deficit? In other words, if the government spends $100 and only has $70 in taxes, where does it get the $30 difference? The answer is that the federal government—actually it is the U.S. Treasury—borrows the $30. That is, it finances the budget deficit with borrowed funds.

Budget Deficit
Government expenditures greater than tax revenues.

Budget Surplus
Tax revenues greater than government expenditures.

Balanced Budget
Government expenditures equal to tax revenues.

Structural and Cyclical Deficits

Suppose the budget is currently balanced, and then Real GDP in the economy drops. As Real GDP drops, the tax base of the economy falls, and if tax rates are held constant, tax revenues will fall. Also, as a result of the decline in Real GDP, transfer payments (e.g., unemployment compensation) will rise. Thus, government expenditures will rise and tax revenues will fall. As a result, a balanced budget turns into a budget deficit. This budget deficit resulted from the downturn in economic activity, not from any current spending and taxing decisions by the government.

Cyclical Deficit

The part of the budget deficit that is a result of a downturn in economic activity.

Structural Deficit

The part of the budget deficit that would exist even if the economy were operating at full employment.

Economists use the term **cyclical deficit** to refer to that part of the budget deficit that is a result of a downturn in economic activity. The remainder of the deficit—or that part of the deficit that would exist if the economy were operating at full employment—is called the **structural deficit**. In other words,

Total budget deficit = Structural deficit + Cyclical deficit

To illustrate, suppose the economy is in a recessionary gap, government expenditures are currently $2.3 trillion, and tax revenues are $2.0 trillion. Thus, the (total) budget deficit is $300 billion. Economists estimate what government expenditures and tax revenues would be if the economy were operating at full employment. Assume they estimate government expenditures would be only $2.2 trillion and tax revenues would be $2.1 trillion. This means that the structural deficit—the deficit that would exist at full employment—is $100 billion. The cyclical deficit—the part of the budget deficit that is a result of economic downturn—is $200 billion.

The Public Debt

Public Debt

The total amount the federal government owes its creditors.

A budget deficit occurs when government expenditures are greater than tax revenues for a *single year*. The **public debt**, which is sometimes called the federal or national debt, is the *total* amount the federal government owes its creditors. The public debt was $8.5 trillion on October 5, 2006. You can find the public debt as of today on the Bureau of the Public Debt Web site at http://www.publicdebt.treas.gov/opd/opd.htm. The public debt was at its lowest on January 1, 1835, totaling $33,733.05 on that day.

SELF-TEST

(Answers to Self-Test questions are in the Self-Test Appendix.)

1. Explain the differences among progressive, proportional, and regressive income tax structures.

2. What percentage of all income taxes was paid by the top 5 percent of income earners in 2005? What percentage of total income did this income group receive in 2005?

3. What three taxes account for the bulk of federal tax revenues?

4. What is the cyclical budget deficit?

Fiscal Policy

As the last chapter explained, some economists believe the economy is inherently unstable. These economists argue that government should play a role in managing the economy because the economy can get stuck in a recessionary gap. They believe government should try to move the economy out of the recessionary gap and toward Natural Real GDP.

Fiscal Policy

Changes in government expenditures and/or taxes to achieve particular economic goals, such as low unemployment, stable prices, and economic growth.

One of the major ways government can influence the economy is through its *fiscal policy*. **Fiscal policy** refers to changes in government expenditures and/or taxes to achieve particular economic goals, such as low unemployment, price stability, and economic growth. We discuss fiscal policy in the following sections.

Some Relevant Fiscal Policy Terms

Expansionary fiscal policy refers to increases in government expenditures and/or decreases in taxes to achieve macroeconomic goals. **Contractionary fiscal policy** refers to decreases in government expenditures and/or increases in taxes to achieve these goals.

> Expansionary fiscal policy: Government expenditures up and/or taxes down
> Contractionary fiscal policy: Government expenditures down and/or taxes up

When changes in government expenditures and taxes are brought about deliberately through government actions, fiscal policy is said to be *discretionary*. For example, if Congress decides to increase government spending by, say, $10 billion in an attempt to lower the unemployment rate, this is an act of **discretionary fiscal policy**. In contrast, a change in either government expenditures or taxes that occurs automatically in response to economic events is referred to as **automatic fiscal policy**. To illustrate, suppose Real GDP in the economy turns down, causing more people to become unemployed. As a result, more people automatically receive unemployment benefits. These added unemployment benefits automatically boost government spending.

Two Important Notes

In your study of this chapter, keep in mind the following two important points:

1. In our discussion of fiscal policy in this chapter, we deal only with *discretionary fiscal policy*. In other words, we consider deliberate actions on the part of policymakers to affect the economy through changes in government spending and/or taxes.

2. We assume that any change in government spending is due to a change in government purchases and not to a change in transfer payments. Stated differently, we assume that transfer payments are constant so that changes in government spending are a reflection of changes in government purchases only.

Demand-Side Fiscal Policy

Fiscal policy can affect the demand side of the economy; that is, it can affect aggregate demand. This section focuses on how government spending and taxes can affect aggregate demand.

Shifting the Aggregate Demand Curve

How do changes in government purchases (*G*) and taxes (*T*) affect aggregate demand? Recall from an earlier chapter that a change in consumption, investment, government purchases, or net exports can change aggregate demand and therefore shift the *AD* curve. For example, an increase in government purchases (*G*) increases aggregate demand and shifts the *AD* curve to the right. A decrease in *G* decreases aggregate demand and shifts the *AD* curve to the left.[2]

A change in taxes (*T*) can affect consumption or investment or both and therefore can affect aggregate demand. For example, a decrease in income taxes increases disposable (after-tax) income, which permits individuals to increase their consumption. As consumption rises, the *AD* curve shifts to the right. An increase in taxes decreases disposable income, lowers consumption, and shifts the *AD* curve to the left.

---

[2]Later in this chapter, when we discuss crowding out, we question the effect of an increase in government purchases on aggregate demand.

Expansionary Fiscal Policy

Increases in government expenditures and/or decreases in taxes to achieve particular economic goals.

Contractionary Fiscal Policy

Decreases in government expenditures and/or increases in taxes to achieve particular economic goals.

Discretionary Fiscal Policy

Deliberate changes of government expenditures and/or taxes to achieve particular economic goals.

Automatic Fiscal Policy

Changes in government expenditures and/or taxes that occur automatically without (additional) congressional action.

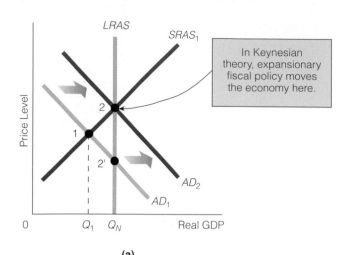

(a)
Expansionary Fiscal Policy
for a Recessionary Gap

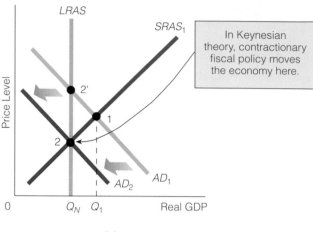

(b)
Contractionary Fiscal Policy
for an Inflationary Gap

exhibit **2**

Fiscal Policy in Keynesian Theory: Ridding the Economy of Recessionary and Inflationary Gaps

(a) In Keynesian theory, expansionary fiscal policy eliminates a recessionary gap. Increased government purchases, decreased taxes, or both lead to a rightward shift in the aggregate demand curve from AD_1 to AD_2, restoring the economy to the natural level of Real GDP, Q_N. (b) Contractionary fiscal policy is used to eliminate an inflationary gap. Decreased government purchases, increased taxes, or both lead to a leftward shift in the aggregate demand curve from AD_1 to AD_2, restoring the economy to the natural level of Real GDP, Q_N.

Fiscal Policy: A Keynesian Perspective

The model of the economy in Exhibit 2(a) shows a downward-sloping AD curve and an upward-sloping $SRAS$ curve. As you can see, the economy is initially in a recessionary gap at point 1. Aggregate demand is too low to move the economy to equilibrium at the Natural Real GDP level. The Keynesian prescription is to enact expansionary fiscal policy measures (an increase in government purchases or a decrease in taxes) to shift the aggregate demand curve rightward from AD_1 to AD_2 and move the economy to the Natural Real GDP level at point 2.

At this point, someone might ask: Why not simply wait for the short-run aggregate supply curve to shift rightward and intersect the aggregate demand curve at point 2'? The Keynesians usually respond that (1) the economy is stuck at point 1 and won't move naturally to point 2'—perhaps the economy is stuck because wage rates won't fall; or (2) the short-run aggregate supply curve takes too long to shift rightward, and in the interim, we must deal with the high cost of unemployment and a lower level of Real GDP.

In Exhibit 2(b), the economy is initially in an inflationary gap at point 1. In this situation, Keynesians are likely to propose a contractionary fiscal measure (a decrease in government purchases or an increase in taxes) to shift the aggregate demand curve leftward from AD_1 to AD_2 and move the economy to point 2.

In Exhibit 2, fiscal policy has worked as intended. In (a), the economy was in a recessionary gap, and expansionary fiscal policy eliminated the recessionary gap. In (b), the economy was in an inflationary gap, and contractionary fiscal policy eliminated the inflationary gap. In (a) and (b), fiscal policy is at its best and working as intended.

macro
Theme

In an earlier chapter, we said that economists don't always agree that economic policy is effective at, say, removing an economy from a recessionary or inflationary gap. Some economists believe that economic policy may be ineffective at removing an economy from a recessionary or inflationary gap. Specifically, some economists say that fiscal policy is effective, whereas others say that it is ineffective. You have just heard from the economists who say fiscal policy is effective. Now we turn to those who say fiscal policy could be ineffective.

economics 24/7

JFK AND THE 1964 TAX CUT

In 1962, John F. Kennedy was president of the United States and Walter Heller was one of Kennedy's economic advisors. Heller told the president that the economy needed a tax cut (a form of expansionary fiscal policy) to keep it from sputtering. In December, in a speech before the Economic Club of New York, President Kennedy said, "An economy hampered by restrictive tax rates will never produce enough revenue to balance our budget just as it will never produce enough jobs or enough profits."

Then in January 1963, he said, "It has become increasingly clear that the largest single barrier to full employment . . . and to a higher rate of economic growth is the unrealistically heavy drag of federal income taxes on private purchasing power, initiative and incentive."

Kennedy proposed expansionary fiscal policy—in the form of a tax cut—to raise economic growth and lower the unemployment rate. He proposed lowering the top individual income tax rate, the bottom individual income tax rate, the corporate income tax, and the capital gains tax. He was assassinated in Dallas before Congress passed his tax program, but Congress did pass it. What was the result?

When the tax bill passed in 1964, the unemployment rate was 5.2 percent; in 1965, it was down to 4.5 percent; in 1966, it was down further, to 3.8 percent. The tax cut is widely credited with bringing the unemployment rate down.

As for economic growth, when the tax cut was passed in 1964, it was 5.8 percent; one year later, in 1965, the growth rate was up to 6.4 percent; and in 1966, the growth rate was even higher, at 6.6 percent. Again, the tax cut received much of the credit for stimulating economic growth.

Crowding Out: Questioning Expansionary Fiscal Policy

Not all economists believe that fiscal policy works the way we have just described. Some economists bring up the subject of *crowding out*. **Crowding out** refers to a decrease in private expenditures (consumption, investment, etc.) that occurs as a consequence of increased government spending or the financing needs of a budget deficit.

Crowding out can be direct or indirect, as described in these two examples:

1. **Direct effect.** The government spends more on public libraries, and individuals buy fewer books at bookstores.[3]

2. **Indirect effect.** The government spends more on social programs and defense without increasing taxes; as a result, the size of the budget deficit increases. Consequently, the government must borrow more funds to finance the larger deficit. This increase in borrowing causes the demand for credit (or demand for loanable funds) to rise, which in turn causes the interest rate to rise. As a result, investment drops. More government spending indirectly leads to less investment spending.

TYPES OF CROWDING OUT Let's consider our first example, in which the government spends more on public libraries. To be specific, let's say that the government spends $2 billion more on public libraries. Suppose that after the government has spent $2 billion more on public libraries, consumers choose to spend not $1 less on books at bookstores. Obviously, then, there is no crowding out, or *zero crowding out*.

Crowding Out
The decrease in private expenditures that occurs as a consequence of increased government spending or the financing needs of a budget deficit.

---

[3] We are not saying that if the government spends more on public libraries, individuals will necessarily buy fewer books at bookstores; rather, if they do, this would be an example of crowding out. The same holds for example 2.

Complete Crowding Out

A decrease in one or more components of private spending completely offsets the increase in government spending.

Incomplete Crowding Out

The decrease in one or more components of private spending only partially offsets the increase in government spending.

Now, suppose that after the government has spent $2 billion more on public libraries, consumers choose to spend $2 billion less on books at bookstores. Obviously, crowding out exists, and the degree of crowding out is dollar for dollar. When $1 of government spending offsets $1 of private spending, **complete crowding out** is said to exist.

Finally, suppose that after the government has spent $2 billion more on public libraries, consumers end up spending $1.2 billion less on books at bookstores. Again, there is crowding out, but it is not dollar-for-dollar crowding out; it is not complete crowding out. In this case, incomplete crowding out exists. **Incomplete crowding out** occurs when the decrease in one or more components of private spending only partially offsets the increase in government spending.

The following table summarizes the different types of crowding out.

Type of Crowding Out	Example
Zero crowding out (sometimes called "no crowding out")	Government spends $2 billion more, and private sector spending stays constant.
Complete crowding out	Government spends $2 billion more, and private sector spends $2 billion less.
Incomplete crowding out	Government spends $2 billion more, and private sector spends $1.2 billion less.

GRAPHICAL REPRESENTATION OF CROWDING OUT If *complete* or *incomplete crowding out* occurs, it follows that expansionary fiscal policy will have less impact on aggregate demand and Real GDP than Keynesian theory predicts. Let's look at the graphical representation of crowding out.

Exhibit 3 illustrates the consequences of complete and incomplete crowding out. For comparison, the exhibit also includes the case in Keynesian theory where there is zero crowding out.

As we discuss Exhibit 3, keep in mind the three possibilities concerning crowding out:

- Zero crowding out (no crowding out)
- Incomplete crowding out
- Complete crowding out

In Exhibit 3, the economy is initially at point 1, with Real GDP at Q_1. In Keynesian theory, expansionary fiscal policy shifts the aggregate demand curve to AD_2 and moves

Zero (No), Incomplete, and Complete Crowding Out

The exhibit shows the effects of zero, incomplete, and complete crowding out in the *AD-AS* framework. Starting at point 1, expansionary fiscal policy shifts the aggregate demand curve to AD_2 and moves the economy to point 2 and Q_N. The Keynesian theory that predicts this outcome assumes zero, or no, crowding out; an increase in, say, government spending does not reduce private expenditures. With incomplete crowding out, an increase in government spending causes private expenditures to decrease by less than the increase in government spending. The net result is a shift in the aggregate demand curve to AD'_2. The economy moves to point 2' and Q'_2. With complete crowding out, an increase in government spending is completely offset by a decrease in private expenditures, and the net result is that aggregate demand does not increase at all. The economy remains at point 1 and Q_1.

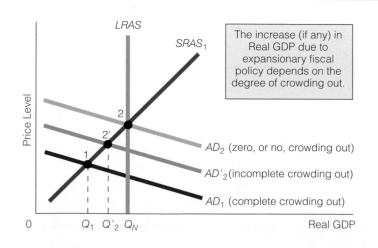

The increase (if any) in Real GDP due to expansionary fiscal policy depends on the degree of crowding out.

the economy to point 2. Among other things, this implicitly assumes there is zero crowding out (or no crowding out). Notice that Real GDP has increased from Q_1 to Q_N. It follows that the unemployment rate will fall from its level at Q_1 to a lower level at Q_N. Summary: If there is no crowding out, expansionary fiscal policy increases Real GDP and lowers the unemployment rate.

With incomplete crowding out, the aggregate demand curve only shifts (on net) to AD'_2 because the initial stimulus in aggregate demand due to increased government spending is *partially offset* by a fall in private expenditures. The economy moves to point $2'$. Notice that Real GDP has increased from Q_1 to Q'_2. It follows that the unemployment rate will fall from what it was at Q_1 to what it is at Q'_2. But also notice that the changes in both Real GDP and the unemployment rate are smaller with incomplete crowding out than they are with zero crowding out. Summary: If there is incomplete crowding out, expansionary fiscal policy increases Real GDP and lowers the unemployment rate but not as much as if there is zero crowding out.

In the case of complete crowding out, the initial stimulus in aggregate demand due to increased government spending is *completely offset* by a fall in private expenditures, and the aggregate demand curve does not move (on net) at all. Notice that Real GDP does not change, and neither does the unemployment rate. Summary: If there is complete crowding out, expansionary fiscal policy has no effect on the economy. The economy remains at point 1.

See Exhibit 4 for a summary flow chart of the different types of crowding out.

> **Thinking like AN ECONOMIST**
>
> *An ill person goes to the doctor and asks for some medicine. The doctor prescribes the medicine and the person goes home. After a few days, we learn that the medicine has not made the person well. It can be the same with some types of economic policy at certain times. Keep in mind what we are and are not saying here. We are not saying that economic policy is never effective; we are simply saying it is not necessarily effective. In our discussion of fiscal policy so far, crowding out is simply one reason fiscal policy may not be effective at times. Lags, which we discuss next, are another.*

A CLOSER LOOK

exhibit **4**

Expansionary Fiscal Policy (Government Spending Increases), Crowding Out, and Changes in Real GDP and the Unemployment Rate

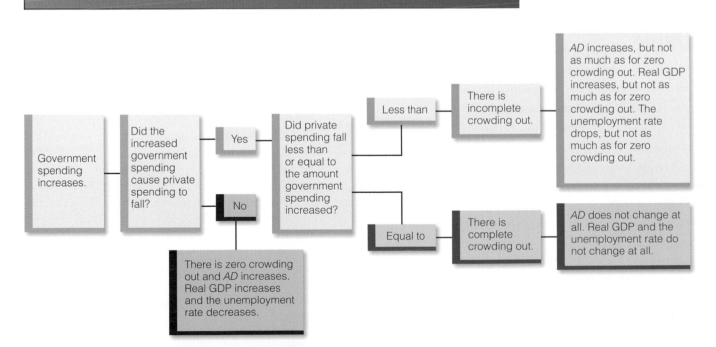

Lags and Fiscal Policy

Suppose we proved, beyond a shadow of a doubt, that there is no, or zero, crowding out. Would it then hold that fiscal policy should be used to solve the problems of inflationary and recessionary gaps? Many economists would answer not necessarily. The reason is that *lags* exist. There are five types of lags:

1. **The data lag.** Policymakers are not aware of changes in the economy as soon as they happen. For example, if the economy turns down in January, the decline may not be apparent for 2 to 3 months.

2. **The wait-and-see lag.** After policymakers are aware of a downturn in economic activity, they rarely enact counteractive measures immediately. Instead, they usually adopt a more cautious wait-and-see attitude. They want to be sure that the observed events are not just short-run phenomena.

3. **The legislative lag.** After policymakers decide that some type of fiscal policy measure is required, Congress or the president will have to propose the measure, build political support for it, and get it passed. This can take many months.

4. **The transmission lag.** After enacted, a fiscal policy measure takes time to be put into effect. For example, a discretionary expansionary fiscal policy measure mandating increased spending for public works projects will require construction companies to submit bids for the work, prepare designs, negotiate contracts, and so on.

5. **The effectiveness lag.** After a policy measure is actually implemented, it takes time to affect the economy. If government spending is increased on Monday, the aggregate demand curve does not shift rightward on Tuesday.

Taking these five lags together, some economists argue that discretionary fiscal policy is not likely to have the impact on the economy that policymakers hope. By the time the full impact of the policy is felt, the economic problem it was designed to solve (1) may no longer exist, (2) may not exist to the degree it once did, or (3) may have changed altogether.

Q&A

It seems to me that economists should get together and decide, once and for all, whether or not crowding out exists and whether or not the fiscal policy lags are substantive enough to destroy the effectiveness of fiscal policy. Why hasn't this been done?

Economists continue to work at getting definitive answers to some of the big macroeconomic questions, but unfortunately, things are not quite as easy as we might hope. There are unsettled questions in almost every field—medicine, chemistry, physics, biology, and so on. In this regard, economics is no different. By showing you that economists sometimes disagree and that they take different positions, you get an idea of some of the issues that inform their research.

Exhibit 5 illustrates the effect of lags. Suppose the economy is currently in a recessionary gap at point 1. The recession is under way before government officials recognize it. After it is recognized, however, Congress and the president consider enacting expansionary fiscal policy in the hope of shifting the AD curve from AD_1 to AD_2 so it will intersect the $SRAS$ curve at point 1′, at Natural Real GDP.

But in the interim, unknown to everybody, the economy is "healing," or regulating, itself. The $SRAS$ curve is shifting to the right. Government officials don't see this change because it takes time to collect and analyze data about the economy.

Thinking that the economy is not healing itself or not healing itself quickly enough, the government enacts expansionary fiscal policy. In time, the AD curve shifts rightward. But by the time the increased demand is felt in the goods and services market, the AD curve intersects the $SRAS$ curve at point 2. In short, the government has moved the economy from point 1 to point 2, and not, as it had desired, from point 1 to point 1′. The government has moved the economy into an inflationary gap. Instead of stabilizing and moderating the ups and downs in economic activity (the business cycle), the government has intensified the fluctuations.

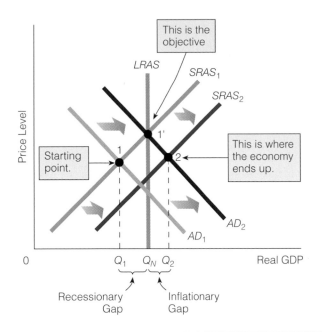

exhibit **5**

Fiscal Policy May Destabilize the Economy

In this scenario, the *SRAS* curve is shifting rightward (healing the economy of its recessionary gap), but this information is unknown to policymakers. Policymakers implement expansionary fiscal policy, and the *AD* curve ends up intersecting *SRAS₂* at point 2 instead of intersecting *SRAS₁* at point 1′. Policymakers thereby move the economy into an inflationary gap, thus destabilizing the economy.

Crowding Out, Lags, and the Effectiveness of Fiscal Policy

Economists who believe there is zero crowding out and lags are insignificant conclude that fiscal policy is effective at moving the economy out of a recessionary gap. Economists who believe crowding out is complete and/or lags are significant conclude that fiscal policy is ineffective at moving the economy out of a recessionary gap.

SELF-TEST

1. How does crowding out question the effectiveness of expansionary demand-side fiscal policy?

2. How might lags reduce the effectiveness of fiscal policy?

3. Give an example of the indirect effect of crowding out.

Supply-Side Fiscal Policy

Fiscal policy effects may be felt on the supply side as well as on the demand side of the economy. For example, a reduction in tax rates may alter an individual's incentive to work and produce, thus altering aggregate supply.

Marginal Tax Rates and Aggregate Supply

When fiscal policy measures affect tax rates, they may affect both aggregate supply and aggregate demand. Consider a reduction in an individual's marginal tax rate. The **marginal (income) tax rate** is equal to the change in a person's tax payment divided by the change in the person's taxable income.

Marginal tax rate = ΔTax payment /ΔTaxable income

Marginal (Income) Tax Rate

The change in a person's tax payment divided by the change in the person's taxable income: ΔTax payment/ΔTaxable income.

For example, if Serena's taxable income increases by $1 and her tax payment increases by $0.28, her marginal tax rate is 28 percent; if her taxable income increases by $1 and her tax payment increases by $0.35, then her marginal tax rate is 35 percent.

All other things held constant, lower marginal tax rates increase the incentive to engage in productive activities (work) relative to leisure and tax-avoidance activities.[4] As resources shift from leisure to work, short-run aggregate supply increases. If the lower marginal tax rates are permanent and not simply a one-shot affair, most economists predict that not only will the short-run aggregate supply curve shift rightward but the long-run aggregate supply curve will shift rightward too. Exhibit 6 illustrates the predicted effect of a permanent marginal tax rate cut on aggregate supply.

The Laffer Curve: Tax Rates and Tax Revenues

High tax rates are followed by attempts of ingenious men to beat them as surely as snow is followed by little boys on sleds.

—Arthur Okun, economist, 1928–1980

If (marginal) income tax rates are reduced, will income tax revenues increase or decrease? Most people think the answer is obvious—lower tax rates mean lower tax revenues. Economist Arthur Laffer explained why this may not be the case.

As the story is told, Laffer, while dining with a journalist at a restaurant in Washington, D.C., drew the curve in Exhibit 7 on a napkin. The curve came to be known as the **Laffer curve**. Laffer's objective was to explain the different possible relationships between tax rates and tax revenues.

In the exhibit, tax revenues are on the vertical axis and tax rates are on the horizontal axis. Laffer made three major points using the curve:

Laffer Curve

The curve, named after Arthur Laffer, that shows the relationship between tax rates and tax revenues. According to the Laffer curve, as tax rates rise from zero, tax revenues rise, reach a maximum at some point, and then fall with further increases in tax rates.

The Predicted Effect of a Permanent Marginal Tax Rate Cut on Aggregate Supply

A cut in marginal tax rates increases the attractiveness of productive activity relative to leisure and tax-avoidance activities and shifts resources from the latter to the former, thus shifting rightward both the short-run and the long-run aggregate supply curves.

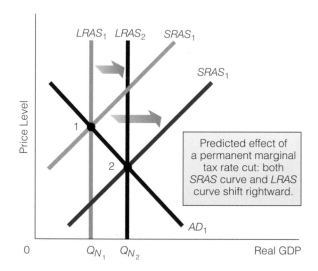

Predicted effect of a permanent marginal tax rate cut: both SRAS curve and LRAS curve shift rightward.

---

[4] When marginal tax rates are lowered, two things will happen: (1) individuals will have more disposable income and (2) the amount of money that individuals can earn (and keep) by working increases. As a result of effect 1, individuals will choose to work less. As a result of effect 2, individuals will choose to work more. Whether an individual works less or more on net depends on whether effect 1 is stronger than or weaker than effect 2. We have assumed that effect 2 is stronger than effect 1, so as marginal tax rates decline, the net effect is that individuals work more.

economics 24/7

© PRNEWSFOTO/SONY BMG MASTERWORKS

STAR WARS: EPISODE III–REVENGE OF THE SITH

The blockbuster movie *Star Wars: Episode III–Revenge of the Sith* was released on May 19, 2005. In its first four days, it earned a whopping $185 million.

As movie releases go, $185 million is an extraordinarily large dollar amount. Some people said this dollar amount indicated that the public was spending more money on going to the movies.

But is this necessarily true? Certainly, it doesn't have to be. There may be such a thing as "movie crowding out."

To illustrate, we assume the movie-going public spends $70 million each weekend on 10 movies. Let's say this dollar amount is evenly distributed across all 10 movies so that each movie earns $7 million. A blockbuster movie may simply have a larger share of the $70 million pie. The blockbuster may earn, say, $20 million, and the 9 remaining movies evenly divide the remaining $50 million. In other words, spending on the blockbuster comes at the expense of other movies on a dollar-for-dollar basis. Blockbuster spending crowds out nonblockbuster spending in much the same way that government spending can crowd out household spending.

Movie crowding out could also work another way. Perhaps because of the blockbuster, total spending on movies rises when the blockbuster is released. That is, the movie-going public increases the amount it spends on movies in the first few weekends after a blockbuster is released. Thus, spending may rise to, say, $100 million each weekend for 3 consecutive weekends after the release of a blockbuster. But then, the "blockbuster effect" fades away, and spending on movies falls below the usual $70 million per weekend. It may fall to, say, $50 million per weekend for a few weekends. Blockbuster spending has still "crowded out" nonblockbuster spending, although not as quickly as in the first case.

There is also a related issue. Perhaps a blockbuster doesn't crowd out other movie spending but does crowd out nonmovie spending. To illustrate, suppose because of a blockbuster, spending on movies actually does rise (over a year). The new average goes from $70 million each weekend to, say, $80 million. But because people are spending more on movies, they spend less on other things. In other words, "movie spending" crowds out "nonmovie spending." People end up spending less on books, restaurant meals, clothes, and so on. One sector of the economy (the movie sector) expands as another contracts.

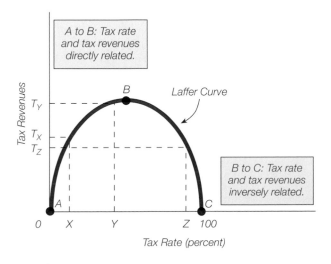

exhibit   **7**

The Laffer Curve

When the tax rate is either 0 or 100 percent, tax revenues are zero. Starting from a zero tax rate, increases in tax rates first increase (region *A* to *B*) and then decrease (region *B* to *C*) tax revenues. Starting from a 100 percent tax rate, decreases in tax rates first increase tax revenues (region *C* to *B*) and then decrease tax revenues (region *B* to *A*). This suggests there is some tax rate that maximizes tax revenues.

1. There are two (marginal) tax rates at which zero tax revenues will be collected—0 percent and 100 percent. Obviously, no tax revenues will be raised if the tax rate is zero, and if the tax rate is 100 percent, no one will work and earn income because the entire amount would be taxed away.

2. An increase in tax rates could cause tax revenues to increase. For example, an increase in tax rates from X percent to Y percent (see the exhibit) will increase tax revenues from T_X to T_Y.

3. A decrease in tax rates could cause tax revenues to increase. For example, a decrease in tax rates from Z percent to Y percent will increase tax revenues from T_Z to T_Y (see the exhibit). This was the point that brought public attention to the Laffer curve.

How can an *increase* in tax rates and a *decrease* in tax rates at different times both increase tax revenues? This can happen because of the interrelationship of tax rates, the **tax base**, and tax revenues.

Tax revenues equal the tax base times the (average) tax rate:[5]

$$\text{Tax revenues} = \text{Tax base} \times \text{(average) Tax rate}$$

For example, a tax rate of 20 percent multiplied by a tax base of $100 billion generates $20 billion of tax revenues.

Now, obviously, tax revenues are a function of two variables: (1) the tax rate and (2) the tax base. Whether tax revenues increase or decrease as the average tax rate is lowered depends on whether the tax base expands by a greater or lesser percentage than the percentage reduction in the tax rate. Exhibit 8 illustrates the point.

We start with a tax rate of 20 percent, a tax base of $100 billion, and tax revenues of $20 billion. We assume that as the tax rate is reduced, the tax base expands: The rationale is that individuals work more, invest more, enter into more trades, and shelter less income from taxes at lower tax rates.

However, the real question is: *How much* does the tax base expand following the tax rate reduction? Suppose the tax rate in Exhibit 8 is reduced to 15 percent. In Case 1, this increases the tax base to $120 billion: A 25 percent decrease in the tax rate (from 20 to 15 percent)

Tax Base

When referring to income taxes, the total amount of taxable income. Tax revenue = Tax base × (average) Tax rate.

Thinking like AN ECONOMIST   *Contrast the way economist Laffer thinks about a tax cut with the way the layperson thinks about it. The layperson probably believes that a reduction in tax rates will reduce tax revenues. The layperson focuses on the "arithmetic" of the situation. Laffer, however, focuses on the economic incentives. He asks: What does a lower tax rate imply in terms of a person's incentive to engage in productive activity? How does a lower tax rate affect one's trade-off between work and leisure? The layperson likely sees only the "arithmetic" effect of a tax cut; the economist sees the incentive effect.*

exhibit 8

Tax Rates, the Tax Base, and Tax Revenues

Tax revenues equal the tax base times the (average) tax rate. If the percentage reduction in the tax rate is greater than the percentage increase in the tax base, tax revenues decrease (Case 1). If the percentage reduction in the tax rate is less than the percentage increase in the tax base, tax revenues increase (Case 2). All numbers are in billions of dollars.

	(1) Tax Rate	(2) Tax Base	(3) Tax Revenues (1) × (2)	Summary
Start with:	20%	$100	$20	—
Case 1:	15	120	18	↓Tax rate ↓Tax revenues
Case 2:	15	150	22.5	↓Tax rate ↑Tax revenues

[5]First, the average tax rate is equal to an individual's tax payment divided by his or her taxable income (tax payment/taxable income). Second, a lower average tax rate requires a lower marginal tax rate. This follows from the average-marginal rule, which states that if the marginal magnitude is below the average magnitude, then the average is pulled down; if the marginal is above the average, the average is pulled up. Simply put, if an individual pays less tax on an additional taxable dollar (which is evidence of a marginal tax rate reduction), then his or her average tax naturally falls.

causes a 20 percent increase in the tax base (from $100 billion to $120 billion). Tax revenues drop to $18 billion. In Case 2, the tax base expands by 50 percent to $150 billion. Because the tax base increases by a greater percentage than the percentage decrease in the tax rate, tax revenues increase (to $22.5 billion).

Of course, either case is possible. In the Laffer curve, tax revenues increase if a tax rate reduction is made in the downward-sloping portion of the curve (between points *B* and *C* in Exhibit 8); tax revenues decrease following a tax rate reduction in the upward-sloping portion of the curve (between points *A* and *B*).

SELF-TEST

1. Give an arithmetic example to illustrate the difference between the marginal and average tax rates.

2. If income tax rates rise, will income tax revenues rise too?

A Reader Asks...

Are Americans Overtaxed?

On a television news program I was watching the other day, a person said that Americans are overtaxed. He went on to back this up by saying that Americans work from January 1 to around the end of April just to pay their taxes. If this is true, then perhaps Americans are overtaxed. What do the economists say, though? Do they say Americans are overtaxed?

Most economists do not usually comment on whether Americans are overtaxed, undertaxed, or taxed just the right amount. Instead, they mainly report on what taxes people pay, how much taxes people pay, and so on.

For example, what you heard on your television news program about how many days Americans work each year to pay their taxes is essentially correct. In 2005, the "average American taxpayer" worked from January 1 to April 17 to pay all her taxes (federal, state, and local). That is a total of 106 days out of a 365-day year. Is that too much? Some people, speaking for themselves, would say yes. After all, they might say, working almost one-third of the year just to pay your taxes is too much.

But consider a different measure of the tax burden: the ratio of tax revenues to GDP. This tax ratio for the United States is 29.7 percent, while the same ratio for Sweden is 54.2 percent, 45.3 percent for France, 37.9 percent for Germany, and 35.8 percent for Canada. The same people who said Americans were overtaxed might change their minds when they learn that the United States has a relatively lower tax burden than many other countries have.

Another issue to consider is how the tax burden is distributed among American workers. For example, in 2005, the top 1 percent of income earners in the United States paid 33.7 percent of all federal income taxes while the bottom 50 percent of all income earners paid 3.6 percent of all federal income taxes. Were the top 1 percent of income earners overtaxed and the bottom 50 percent undertaxed?

Finally, there is the issue of who benefits from the taxes. For example, suppose Smith pays $400 in taxes and Jones pays $200 in taxes. Is Smith overtaxed relative to Jones? Maybe not. Smith could receive $500 worth of benefits for the $400 he pays in taxes, whereas Jones could receive $100 worth of benefits for the $200 he pays in taxes. Even though Smith pays twice the taxes that Jones pays, Smith may consider himself much better off than Jones. And Jones may agree.

! analyzing the scene

Do lower tax rates mean a larger deficit?

Could Georgia be right when she says that lower taxes will increase the size of the budget deficit? She could be. It is certainly possible for a decrease in tax rates to lead to a decrease in tax revenues and a larger budget deficit. But this is not necessarily what will happen. Lower tax rates could lead to higher tax revenues and actually lead to a smaller budget deficit. What matters is whether the percentage cut in tax rates is larger or smaller than the percentage rise in the tax base.

Who are the rich and how much do they pay in taxes?

Alberto's colleague believes the rich don't pay enough taxes, but she isn't sure how much they do pay. Who are the rich? Are the rich the top 1 percent of income earners or are they the top 5 percent? Whoever you consider rich (the top 1 percent, the top 5 percent, or perhaps the top 10 percent), the percentage of income taxes they pay is shown in the text. Is there a lesson to learn here? One time on a television news show, a reporter asked a presidential candidate about his tax policy. The candidate said that he thought the rich should pay "their fair share." The reporter then asked the presidential candidate if he knew what share of federal income taxes were paid by the top 1 percent of income earners. The presidential candidate said he didn't know for sure, but he thought it was around 5 percent. He then went on to say that he thought it should be double or triple that—at least 10 or 15 percent. The reporter told the presidential candidate that the top 1 percent of income earners pay more than 33 percent of all federal income taxes. The presidential candidate didn't acknowledge the fact, nor did he miss a beat. He just went on talking.

Will increases in federal government spending increase aggregate demand in the economy?

This question brings up the issue of crowding out. If the increases in federal government spending do not crowd out private spending, then aggregate demand will rise in the economy. If there is, say, complete crowding out, aggregate demand will not change.

How much is spent on food stamps? On national defense?

Vivien suggests the U.S. government spends $200 billion on food stamps, and Frank believes 15 times more is spent on national defense than is spent on food stamps. However, in 2005, the federal government spent $33 billion on food stamps and $500 on national defense. Is there a lesson to learn here? People will always debate government expenditures. One person will think that more of the total spending pie should go for national defense, and someone else will think that less of the total spending pie should go for national defense. If you think that more should be spent on X and less on Y, then you should know how much is currently spent on X and Y. Economic data can readily be found at the following Web sites:

- Economic Statistics Briefing Room at http://www.whitehouse.gov/fsbr/esbr.html

- Bureau of Economic Analysis at http://www.bea.gov/

- Bureau of Labor Statistics at http://www.bls.gov/cpi/home.htm

- The Economic Report of the President at http://www.gpoaccess.gov/eop/index.html

- Budget of the United States Government at http://www.gpoaccess.gov/usbudget/index.html

- Congressional Budget Office at http://www.cbo.gov/

- U.S. Census Bureau at http://www.census.gov/

chapter summary

Government Spending

- In 2005, the federal government spent $2.472 trillion. This was 20.1 percent of the country's GDP. About 62 percent of the money went for Social Security, Medicare, Medicaid, and national defense.

Taxes

- In 2005, the federal government took in $2.154 trillion in tax revenues. Most of this came from three taxes: the individual income tax, the corporate income tax, and Social Security taxes.

- With a proportional income tax, everyone pays taxes at the same rate, whatever his or her income level. With a progressive income tax, a person pays taxes at a higher rate (up to some top rate) as his or her income level rises. With a regressive income tax, a person pays taxes at a lower rate as his or her income level rises.

- The federal income tax is a progressive income tax.

Deficits, Surpluses, and the Public Debt

- If government expenditures are greater than tax revenues, there is a budget deficit; if government expenditures are less than tax revenues, there is a budget surplus. If government expenditures equal tax revenues, there is a balanced budget. Budget deficits are predicted for the near future.

- A cyclical deficit refers to the part of the budget deficit that is a result of a downturn in economic activity.

- A structural deficit refers to the part of the deficit that would exist if the economy were operating at full employment.

- Total budget deficit = Structural deficit + Cyclical deficit.

- The public debt is the total amount the federal government owes its creditors.

Fiscal Policy: General Remarks

- Fiscal policy refers to changes in government expenditures and/or taxes to achieve particular economic goals. Expansionary fiscal policy refers to increases in government expenditures and/or decreases in taxes. Contractionary fiscal policy refers to decreases in government expenditures and/or increases in taxes.

Demand-Side Fiscal Policy: A Keynesian Perspective

- In Keynesian theory, demand-side fiscal policy can be used to rid the economy of a recessionary gap or an inflationary gap. A recessionary gap calls for expansionary fiscal policy, and an inflationary gap calls for contractionary fiscal policy. Ideally, fiscal policy changes aggregate demand by enough to rid the economy of either a recessionary gap or an inflationary gap.

Crowding Out

- Crowding out refers to the decrease in private expenditures that occurs as a consequence of increased government spending and/or the greater financing needs of a budget deficit. The crowding-out effect suggests that expansionary fiscal policy does not work to the degree that Keynesian theory predicts.

- Complete (incomplete) crowding out occurs when the decrease in one or more components of private spending completely (partially) offsets the increase in government spending.

Reasons Demand-Side Fiscal Policy May Be Ineffective

- Demand-side fiscal policy may be ineffective at achieving certain macroeconomic goals because of (1) crowding out and (2) lags.

Supply-Side Fiscal Policy

- When fiscal policy measures affect tax rates, they may affect both aggregate supply and aggregate demand. It is generally accepted that a marginal tax rate reduction increases the attractiveness of work relative to leisure and tax-avoidance activities and thus leads to an increase in aggregate supply.

- Tax revenues equal the tax base multiplied by the (average) tax rate. Whether tax revenues decrease or increase as a result of a tax rate reduction depends on whether the percentage increase in the tax base is greater or less than the percentage reduction in the tax rate. If the percentage increase in the tax base is greater than the percentage reduction in the tax rate, then tax revenues will increase. If the percentage increase in the tax base is less than the percentage reduction in the tax rate, then tax revenues will decrease.

key terms and concepts

Progressive Income Tax
Proportional Income Tax
Regressive Income Tax
Budget Deficit
Budget Surplus
Balanced Budget

Cyclical Deficit
Structural Deficit
Public Debt
Fiscal Policy
Expansionary Fiscal Policy

Contractionary Fiscal Policy
Discretionary Fiscal Policy
Automatic Fiscal Policy
Crowding Out
Complete Crowding Out

Incomplete Crowding Out
Marginal (Income) Tax Rate
Laffer Curve
Tax Base

questions and problems

1   Is it true that under a proportional income tax structure, a person who earns a higher income will pay more in taxes than a person who earns a lower income? Explain your answer.

2   A progressive income tax always raises more revenue than a proportional income tax. Do you agree or disagree? Explain your answer.

3   Explain two ways crowding out may occur.

4   Why is crowding out an important issue in the debate over the use of fiscal policy?

5   Some economists argue for the use of fiscal policy to solve economic problems; others argue against its use. What are some of the arguments on both sides?

6   The debate over using government spending and taxing powers to stabilize the economy involves more than technical economic issues. Do you agree or disagree? Explain your answer.

7   The Laffer curve, which shows (among other things) that a tax rate reduction can increase tax revenues, became very popular and was widely cited a couple of years before, during, and for a few years after the presidential election of 1980. Why do you think this happened?

8   Is crowding out equally likely under all economic conditions? Explain your answer.

9   Tax cuts will likely affect aggregate demand and aggregate supply. Does it matter which is affected more? Explain in terms of the *AD-AS* framework.

10   Explain how expansionary fiscal policy can, under certain conditions, destabilize the economy.

11   The economy is in a recessionary gap and both Smith and Jones advocate expansionary fiscal policy. Does it follow that both Smith and Jones favor "big government"?

12   Will tax cuts that are perceived to be temporary affect the *SRAS* and *LRAS* curves differently than tax cuts that are perceived to be permanent? Explain your answer.

working with numbers and graphs

Use the following table to answer questions 1–4.

Taxable Income	Taxes
$1,000–$5,000	10% of taxable income
$5,001–$10,000	$500 + 12% of everything over $5,000
$10,001–$15,000	$1,100 + 15% of everything over $10,000

1   If a person's income is $6,000, how much does he pay in taxes?

2   If a person's income is $14,000, how much does she pay in taxes?

3   What is the marginal tax rate on the 10,001st dollar? What is the marginal tax rate on the 10,000th dollar?

4   What is the average tax rate of someone with a taxable income of $13,766?

5   There are three income earners in society, and all three must pay income taxes. The taxable income of Smith is $40,000, the taxable income of Jones is $100,000, and the taxable income of Brown is $200,000.

a   How much tax revenue is raised under a proportional income tax where the tax rate is 10 percent? 15 percent?

b   Would a progressive tax with a rate of 5 percent on an income of $0–$40,000, a rate of 8 percent on everything over $40,000 and under $100,000, and a rate of 15 percent of everything over $100,000 raise more or less tax revenue than a proportional tax rate of 10 percent? Explain your answer.

6   Graphically show how fiscal policy works in the ideal case.

7   Graphically illustrate how government can use supply-side fiscal policy to get an economy out of a recessionary gap.

8   Graphically illustrate the following:

a   Fiscal policy destabilizes the economy.

b   Fiscal policy eliminates an inflationary gap.

c   Fiscal policy only partly eliminates a recessionary gap.

Money and Banking 11

Setting the Scene

The following events occurred at various times.

1595, LONDON, ENGLAND

William Shakespeare, sitting at a small wooden desk, writes:

Two households, both alike in dignity,
In fair Verona, where we lay our scene,
From ancient grudge break to new
    mutiny,
Where civil blood makes civil hands
    unclean.
From forth the fatal loins of these two
    foes
A pair of star-cross'd lovers take their life;
Whole misadventured piteous overthrows
Do with their death bury their parents'
    strife.
        —From Act 1, Prologue,
            Romeo and Juliet

APRIL 7, 1787, VIENNA, AUSTRIA

Ludwig van Beethoven, 16, arrives to take music lessons from Wolfgang Amadeus Mozart, 31. Mozart composes his "Quintet in C for Strings" this month.

SOMETIME IN 1885, EDINBURGH, SCOTLAND

Robert Louis Stevenson is having a nightmare. His wife wakes him up. He asks her why she woke him. For Stevenson, this nightmare is the beginning of what will turn out to be *The Strange Case of Dr. Jekyll and Mr. Hyde.* Here is a passage from the book: "It was on the moral side, and in my own person, that I learned to recognise the thorough and primitive duality of man; I saw that, of the two natures that contended in the field of my consciousness, even if I could rightly be said to be either, it was only because I was radically both; and from an early date . . . I had learned to dwell with pleasure, as a beloved daydream, on the thought of the separation of these elements."

JUNE 27, 1905, BERN, SWITZERLAND

Albert Einstein is sitting in a chair in his home. In three days, on June 30, 1905, he will submit his paper "On the Electrodynamics of Moving Bodies" to the leading German physics journal. The first few lines of that paper read: "It is known that Maxwell's electrodynamics—as usually understood at the present time—when applied to moving bodies, leads to asymmetries which do not appear to be inherent in the phenomena. Take, for example, the reciprocal electrodynamic action of a magnet and a conductor. The observable phenomenon here depends only on the relative motion of the conductor and the magnet, whereas the customary view draws a sharp distinction between the two cases in which either the one or the other of these bodies is in motion."

? Here is a question to keep in mind as you read this chapter:

- *What do William Shakespeare, Ludwig van Beethoven, Wolfgang Amadeus Mozart, Robert Louis Stevenson, and Albert Einstein have to do with money evolving out of a barter economy?*

See analyzing the scene at the end of this chapter for an answer to this question.

Money: What Is It and How Did It Come to Be?

The story of money starts with a definition and a history lesson. This section discusses what money is and isn't (the definition) and how money came to be (the history lesson).

Money: A Definition

To the layperson, the words *income, credit,* and *wealth* are synonyms for *money.* In each of the next three sentences, the word *money* is used incorrectly; the word in parentheses is the word an economist would use.

1. "How much money (income) did you earn last year?"
2. "Most of her money (wealth) is tied up in real estate."
3. "It sure is difficult to get much money (credit) in today's tight mortgage market."

In economics, the words *money, income, credit,* and *wealth* are not synonyms. The most general definition of **money** is any good that is widely accepted for purposes of exchange (payment for goods and services) and in the repayment of debts.

Money

Any good that is widely accepted for purposes of exchange and in the repayment of debt.

Three Functions of Money

Money has three major functions. It functions as a

1. medium of exchange,
2. unit of account, and
3. store of value.

MONEY AS A MEDIUM OF EXCHANGE If money did not exist, goods would have to be exchanged by **barter**. Suppose you wanted a shirt. You would have to trade some good in your possession, say, a jackknife, for the shirt. But first, you would have to locate a person who has a shirt and wants to trade it for a knife. In a money economy, this step is not necessary. You can simply (1) exchange money for a shirt or (2) exchange the knife for money and then the money for the shirt. The buyer of the knife and the seller of the shirt do not have to be the same person. Money is the medium through which exchange occurs; hence, it is a **medium of exchange**. As such, money reduces the *transaction costs* of making exchanges. Exchange is easier and less time-consuming in a money economy than in a barter economy.

Barter

Exchanging goods and services for other goods and services without the use of money.

Medium of Exchange

Anything that is generally acceptable in exchange for goods and services. A function of money.

MONEY AS A UNIT OF ACCOUNT A **unit of account** is a common measure in which values are expressed. Consider a barter economy. The value of every good is expressed in terms of all other goods, and there is no common unit of measure. For example, 1 horse might equal 100 bushels of wheat, or 200 bushels of apples, or 20 pairs of shoes, or 10 suits, or 55 loaves of bread, and so on. In a money economy, a person doesn't have to know the price of an apple in terms of oranges, pizzas, chickens, or potato chips, as would be the case in a barter economy. He or she only needs to know the price in terms of money. And because all goods are denominated in money, determining relative prices is easy and quick. For example, if 1 apple is $1 and 1 orange is 50 cents, then 1 apple = 2 oranges.

Unit of Account

A common measure in which relative values are expressed. A function of money.

Store of Value

The ability of an item to hold value over time. A function of money.

MONEY AS A STORE OF VALUE The **store of value** function refers to a good's ability to maintain its value over time. This is the least exclusive function of money because other goods—for example, paintings, houses, and stamps—can do this too. At times, money has not maintained its value well, such as during high inflationary periods. For the most

economics 24/7

IS MONEY THE BEST GIFT?

Consider what happens when one person gives another person a gift. First, the gift giver has to decide how much money to spend on the gift. Is it an amount between $10 and $20 or between $50 and $80? After the dollar range has been decided, the gift giver has to decide what to buy. Will it be a book, a shirt, a gift certificate to a restaurant, or what? Deciding what to buy requires the gift giver to guess the preferences of the gift recipient. This is no easy task, even if the gift giver knows the gift recipient fairly well. Often, guessing preferences is done poorly, which means that each year hundreds of thousands of people end up with gifts they would prefer not to have received. Every year, shirts go unworn, books go unread, and closets fill up with unwanted items.

At the end of a holiday season in 1993, Joel Waldfogel, then an economist at Yale University, asked a group of students two questions. First, he asked them what dollar value they would estimate was paid by the gift givers for all the holiday gifts they (the students) received. Second, he asked the students how much *they* would have paid to get the gifts they received. What Waldfogel learned was that, on average, gift recipients were willing to pay less for the gifts they received than gift givers paid for the gifts. For example, a gift recipient might be willing to pay $25 for a book that a gift giver bought for $30. The most conservative estimate put the average gift recipient's valuation at 90 percent of the buying price. This means that if the gift giver had given the cash value of the purchase instead of the gift itself, the recipient could then buy what was really wanted and been better off at no additional cost. In other words, some economists have concluded that when you don't know the preferences of the gift recipient very well, it just may be better to give money.

part, though, money has served as a satisfactory store of value. This allows us to accept payment in money for our productive efforts and to keep that money until we decide how we want to spend it.

From a Barter to a Money Economy: The Origins of Money

> The thing that differentiates man and animals is money.
> —Gertrude Stein

At one time, there was trade but no money. Instead, people bartered. They would trade 1 apple for 2 eggs, a banana for a peach.

Today, we live in a money economy. How did we move from a barter to a money economy? Did some king or queen issue the edict, "Let there be money"? Not likely. Money evolved in a much more natural, market-oriented manner.

Making exchanges takes longer (on average) in a barter economy than in a money economy. That's because the *transaction costs* of making exchanges are higher in a barter economy than they are in a money economy. Stated differently, the time and effort one has to incur to consummate an exchange are greater in a barter economy than in a money economy. To illustrate, suppose Smith, living in a barter economy, wants to trade apples for oranges. He locates Jones, who has oranges. Smith offers to trade apples for oranges, but Jones tells Smith that she does not like apples and would rather have peaches.

In this situation, Smith must either (1) find someone who has oranges and wants to trade oranges for apples or (2) find someone who has peaches and wants to trade peaches for apples, after which he must return to Jones and trade peaches for oranges.

Double Coincidence of Wants

In a barter economy, a requirement that must be met before a trade can be made. It specifies that a trader must find another trader who is willing to trade what the first trader wants and at the same time wants what the first trader has.

Thinking like AN ECONOMIST   *In our story of the emergence of money, we said that the people in a barter economy "accept good G because they know it can easily be traded for most other goods at a later time (unlike the item originally in their possession)." This brings up the role of self-interest. People in a barter economy simply wanted to make life easier on themselves; they wanted to cut down on the time and energy they were expending to obtain their preferred bundle of goods. In other words, it was out of self-interest that they began to accept the most marketable or acceptable of all goods—a process that eventually ended with money.*

Q&A   *Are we saying here that it was self-interest that got people out of a barter economy and into a money economy?*

Yes. Self-interest can lead to some things that are extremely useful and beneficial in life—such as money.

Suppose Smith continues to search and finds Brown, who has oranges and wants to trade oranges for (Smith's) apples. In economics terminology, Smith and Brown are said to have a **double coincidence of wants**. Two people have a double coincidence of wants if what the first person wants is what the second person has and what the second person wants is what the first person has. A double coincidence of wants is a necessary condition for trade to take place.

In a barter economy, some goods are more readily accepted in exchange than other goods are. This may originally be the result of chance, but when traders notice the difference in marketability, their behavior tends to reinforce the effect. Suppose there are 10 goods, *A–J*, and that good *G* is the most marketable (most acceptable) of the 10. On average, good *G* is accepted 5 of every 10 times it is offered in an exchange, while the remaining goods are accepted, on average, only 2 of every 10 times. Given this difference, some individuals accept good *G* simply because of its relatively greater acceptability, even though they have no plans to consume it. They accept good *G* because they know it can easily be traded for most other goods at a later time (unlike the item originally in their possession).

The effect snowballs. The more people accept good *G* for its relatively greater acceptability, the greater its relative acceptability becomes, which in turn causes more people to agree to accept it. This is how money evolved. When good *G*'s acceptance evolves to the point where good *G* is widely accepted for purposes of exchange, good *G* is money. Historically, goods that have evolved into money include gold, silver, copper, cattle, salt, cocoa beans, and shells.

Money in a Prisoner of War Camp

During World War II, an American, R. A. Radford, was captured and imprisoned in a POW camp. While in the camp, he made some observations about economic happenings, which he later described in the journal *Economica*. He noted that the Red Cross would periodically distribute packages to the prisoners that contained such goods as cigarettes, toiletries, chocolate, cheese, jam, margarine, and tinned beef. Not all the prisoners had the same preferences for the goods. For example, some liked chocolate more than others; some smoked cigarettes, and others did not. Because of their different preferences, the prisoners began to trade, say, a chocolate bar for some cheese, and a barter system emerged. After a short while, money appeared in the camp, but it was not U.S. dollars or any other government currency. The good that emerged as money—the good that was widely accepted for purposes of exchange—was cigarettes. As Radford noted, "The cigarette became the standard of value. In the permanent camp people started by wandering through the bungalows calling their offers—'cheese for seven [cigarettes]. . . . '"

Money, Leisure, and Output

Exchanges take less time in a money economy than in a barter economy because a double coincidence of wants is irrelevant. Everyone is willing to trade what he or she has for money. It follows that the movement from a barter to a money economy releases some time that people can use in different ways.

To illustrate, suppose it takes 10 hours a week in a barter economy to make trades, but it takes only 1 hour in a money economy. In a money economy, then, there are 9 hours a week that don't have to be spent making exchanges. How will people use these 9 hours? Some people will use them to work, other people will use them for leisure, and

economics 24/7

ENGLISH AND MONEY

In a world of barter, some goods are more widely accepted than other goods.

In a world of languages, some languages may be more widely used than other languages. Today, the most widely used language appears to be English.

English is spoken not only by native English speakers but by many other people around the world. English is the language of computers and the Internet. You can see English on posters everywhere in the world. You can hear English in pop songs sung in Tokyo. English is the working language of the Asian trade group ASEAN (Association of South East Asian Nations). It is the language of 98 percent of German research physicists and 83 percent of German research chemists. It is the official language of the European Central Bank, even though the bank is in Frankfurt, Germany. It is found in official documents in Phnom Penh, Cambodia. Singers all over the world sing in English. Alcatel, a French telecommunications company, uses English as its internal language. By 2050, half the world's population is expected to be proficient in English.

In a barter economy, if more people accept a particular good in exchange, then more people will want to accept that good. Might the same be true of a language? That is, if more people speak English, then will more non-English-speaking people want to learn English? Just as money lowers the transaction costs of making exchanges, English might lower the transaction costs of communicating.

Is the world evolving toward one universal language, and is that language English?

---

some people will divide the 9 hours between work and leisure. Thus, there is likely to be both more output (because of the increased production) and more leisure in a money economy than in a barter economy. In other words, a money economy is likely to be richer in both goods and leisure than is a barter economy.

A person's standard of living is, to a degree, dependent on the number and quality of goods he consumes and the amount of leisure he consumes. We would expect the average person's standard of living to be higher in a money economy than in a barter economy.

What Gives Money Its Value?

In the days when the dollar was backed by gold, people would say that gold gave paper money its value. Very few ever asked, "What gives gold its value?"

It is a myth that paper money has to be backed by some commodity (e.g., gold) before it can have value. Today, our money is not backed by gold. Our money has value because of its *general acceptability*. You accept a dollar bill in payment for your goods and services because you know others will accept the dollar bill in payment for their goods and services.

This system may sound odd, but suppose our money was not generally accepted. Suppose one day the grocery store clerk would not accept the paper dollars you offered as payment for the groceries you wanted to buy. Also, the plumber and the gas station attendant would not accept your paper dollars for fixing your kitchen drain and for servicing your car. If this were to happen, would you be as likely to accept paper dollars in exchange for what you sell? We think not. You accept paper dollars because you know that other people will accept paper dollars later when you try to spend them. Money has value to people because it is widely accepted in exchange for other goods that are valuable.

Defining the Money Supply

Money is any good that is widely accepted for purposes of exchange. Is a $10 bill money? Is a dime money? Is a checking account or a savings account money? What does money include? In other words, what is included in the money supply? Two of the more frequently used definitions of the money supply are M1 and M2.

M1

M1 is sometimes referred to as the *narrow definition of the money supply* or as *transactions money*. It is money that can be directly used for everyday transactions—to buy gas for the car, groceries to eat, and clothes to wear. **M1** consists of currency held outside banks (by members of the public for use in everyday transactions), checkable deposits, and traveler's checks.

M1

Includes currency held outside banks + checkable deposits + traveler's checks.

$$M1 = \text{Currency held outside banks} \\ + \text{Checkable deposits} \\ + \text{Traveler's checks}$$

Currency

Coins and paper money.

Federal Reserve Notes

Paper money issued by the Fed.

Checkable Deposits

Deposits on which checks can be written.

How are the components of M1 defined? **Currency** includes coins minted by the U.S. Treasury and paper money. About 99 percent of the paper money in circulation is **Federal Reserve notes** issued by the Federal Reserve District Banks. **Checkable deposits** are deposits on which checks can be written. There are different types of checkable deposits, including demand deposits, which are checking accounts that pay no interest, and NOW (negotiated order of withdrawal) and ATS (automatic transfer from savings) accounts, which do pay interest on their balances.

In June 2006, checkable deposits equaled $622 billion, currency held outside banks equaled $741 billion, and traveler's checks were $7 billion. M1, the sum of these figures, was $1,370 billion. The M1 money supply figures (for December) of the years 2000–2005 are shown in the following table.

Thinking like **AN ECONOMIST** *When a layperson hears the word* money, *she usually thinks of currency—paper money (dollar bills) and coins. For example, if you're walking along a dark street at night and a thief stops you and says, "Your money or your life," you can be sure he wants your currency. To an economist, though, money is more than simply currency. One definition of money (the M1 definition) is that it is currency, checkable deposits, and traveler's checks. (Still, if stopped by a thief, an economist would be unlikely to hand over his currency and then write a check too.)*

Year	M1 Money Supply (billions of dollars)
2000	$1,087
2001	1,182
2002	1,219
2003	1,304
2004	1,372
2005	1,368

M2

M2

Includes M1 + savings deposits (including money market deposit accounts) + small-denomination time deposits + money market mutual funds (retail).

M2 is sometimes referred to as the (most common) *broad definition of the money supply*. **M2** is made up of M1 plus savings deposits (including money market deposit accounts), small-denomination time deposits, and money market mutual funds (retail). In June 2006, M2 was $6,830 billion.

M2 = M1
+ Savings deposits (including money market deposit accounts)
+ Small-denomination time deposits
+ Money market mutual funds (retail)

Let's look at some of the components of M2. A **savings deposit**, sometimes called a *regular savings deposit,* is an interest-earning account at a commercial bank or thrift institution. (Thrift institutions include savings and loan associations, mutual savings banks, and credit unions.) Normally, checks cannot be written on savings deposits, and the funds in savings deposits can be withdrawn (at any time) without a penalty payment.

A **money market deposit account** (MMDA) is an interest-earning account at a bank or thrift institution. Usually, a minimum balance is required for an MMDA. Most MMDAs offer limited check-writing privileges. For example, the owner of an MMDA might be able to write only a certain number of checks each month, and/or each check may have to be above a certain dollar amount (e.g., $500).

A **time deposit** is an interest-earning deposit with a *specified maturity date.* Time deposits are subject to penalties for early withdrawal. Small-denomination time deposits are deposits of less than $100,000.

A **money market mutual fund** (MMMF) is an interest-earning account at a *mutual fund company.* MMMFs held by large institutions are referred to as institutional MMMFs. MMMFs held by all others (e.g., the MMMF held by an individual) are referred to as retail MMMFs. *Only retail MMMFs are part of M2.* Usually, a minimum balance is required for an MMMF account. Most MMMF accounts offer limited check-writing privileges.

The M2 money supply figures (for December) of the years 2000–2005 are as follows:

Year	M2 Money Supply (billions of dollars)
2000	$4,931
2001	5,451
2002	5,800
2003	6,079
2004	6,413
2005	6,672

Savings Deposit

An interest-earning account at a commercial bank or thrift institution. Normally, checks cannot be written on savings deposits, and the funds in a savings deposit can be withdrawn (at any time) without a penalty payment.

Money Market Deposit Account

An interest-earning account at a bank or thrift institution. Usually, a minimum balance is required for an MMDA. Most MMDAs offer limited check-writing privileges.

Time Deposit

An interest-earning deposit with a specified maturity date. Time deposits are subject to penalties for early withdrawal. Small-denomination time deposits are deposits of less than $100,000.

Money Market Mutual Fund

An interest-earning account at a mutual fund company. Usually, a minimum balance is required for an MMMF account. Most MMMF accounts offer limited check-writing privileges. Only retail MMMFs are part of M2.

Where Do Credit Cards Fit In?

Credit cards are commonly referred to as money—plastic money. But they are not money. A credit card is an instrument or document that makes it easier for the holder to obtain a loan. When Tina Ridges hands the department store clerk her MasterCard or Visa, she is, in effect, spending someone else's money (which already existed). The department store submits the claim to the bank, the bank pays the department store, and then the bank bills the holder of its credit card. By using her credit card, Tina has spent someone else's money, and she ultimately must repay her credit card debt with money. These transactions shift around the existing quantity of money between various individuals and firms but do not change the total.

economics 24/7

ECONOMICS ON THE YELLOW BRICK ROAD

I'll get you, my pretty.
> —Wicked Witch of the West in *The Wizard of Oz*

In 1893, the United States fell into economic depression: The stock market crashed, banks failed, workers were laid off, and many farmers lost their farms. Some people blamed the depression on the gold standard. They proposed that instead of only gold backing U.S. currency, there should be a bimetallic monetary standard in which both gold and silver backed the currency. This would lead to an increase in the money supply. Many people thought that with more money in circulation, the economic hard times would soon be a thing of the past.

One of the champions of silver was William Jennings Bryan, who was the Democratic candidate for the U.S. presidency in 1896. Bryan had established himself as a friend to the many Americans who had been hurt by the economic depression—especially farmers and industrial workers. Bryan's views were shared by L. Frank Baum, the author of *The Wonderful Wizard of Oz,* the book that was the basis for the 1939 movie *The Wizard of Oz.*

Baum blamed the gold standard for the hardships faced by farmers and workers during the Depression. Baum saw farmers and industrial workers as the "common man," and he saw William Jennings Bryan as the best possible hope for the common man in this country.

Numerous persons believe that Baum's most famous work, *The Wonderful Wizard of Oz,* is an allegory for the presidential election of 1896.[1] Some say that Dorothy, in the book and the movie, represents Bryan. Both Dorothy and Bryan were young (Bryan was a 36-year-old presidential candidate). Like the cyclone in the movie that transported Dorothy to the Land of Oz, the delegates at the 1896 Democratic convention lifted Bryan into a new political world, the world of presidential politics.

As Dorothy begins her travels to the Emerald City (Washington, D.C.) with Toto (who represents the Democratic party) to meet the Wizard of Oz, she travels down a yellow brick road (the gold standard). On her way, she meets the scarecrow (who represents the farmer), the tin man (who represents the industrial worker), and the cowardly lion, who some believe represents the Populist party of the time. (The Populist party was sometimes represented as a lion in cartoons of the time. It was a "cowardly" lion because, some say, it did not have the courage to fight an independent campaign for the presidency in 1896.) The message is clear: Bryan, with the help of the Democratic and Populist parties and the votes of the farmers and the industrial workers, will travel to Washington.

But then, when Dorothy and the others reach the Emerald City, they are denied their wishes, just as Bryan is denied the presidency. He loses the election to William McKinley.

But all is not over. There is still the battle with the Wicked Witch of the West, who wears a golden cap (gold standard). When the Wicked Witch sees Dorothy's silver shoes—they were changed to ruby shoes in the movie—she desperately wants them for their magical quality. But that is not to happen. Dorothy kills the Wicked Witch of the West; she then clicks her silver shoes together and they take her back home, where all is right with the world.

[1] The interpretation here is based on "William Jennings Bryan on the Yellow Brick Road" by John Geer and Thomas Rochon, *Journal of American Culture* (Winter 1993) and "The Wizard of Oz: Parable on Populism" by Henry Littlefield, *American Quarterly* (1964).

SELF-TEST

(Answers to Self-Test questions are in the Self-Test Appendix.)

1. Why (not how) did money evolve out of a barter economy?

2. If individuals remove funds from their checkable deposits and transfer them to their money market accounts, will M1 fall and M2 rise? Explain your answer.

3. How does money reduce the transaction costs of making trades?

How Banking Developed

Just as money evolved, so did banking. This section discusses the origins of banking. The discussion will shed some light on and aid in understanding modern banking.

The Early Bankers

Our money today is easy to carry and transport. But money was not always so portable. For example, when money was principally gold coins, carrying it about was neither easy nor safe. First, gold is heavy. Second, a person transporting thousands of gold coins can easily draw the attention of thieves. But storing gold at home can also be risky. Most individuals turned to their local goldsmith for help because he was already equipped with safe storage facilities. Goldsmiths were the first bankers. They took in other people's gold and stored it for them. To acknowledge that they held deposited gold, goldsmiths issued receipts called *warehouse receipts* to their customers.

After people's confidence in the receipts was established, they used the receipts to make payments instead of using the gold itself. (Gold was not only inconvenient for customers to carry, but it was also inconvenient for merchants to accept.) In short, the paper warehouse receipts circulated as money. For instance, if Franklin wanted to buy something from Mason that was priced at 10 gold pieces, he could simply give his warehouse receipt to Mason instead of going to the goldsmith, obtaining the gold, and then delivering it to Mason. For both Franklin and Mason, using the receipts was easier than dealing with the actual gold.

At this stage of banking, warehouse receipts were fully backed by gold; they simply represented gold in storage. Goldsmiths later began to recognize that on an average day, few people came to redeem their receipts for gold. Many individuals were simply trading the receipts for goods and seldom requested the gold that the receipts represented. In short, the receipts had become money, widely accepted for purposes of exchange.

Sensing opportunity, some goldsmiths began to lend some of the stored gold, realizing that they could earn interest on the loans without defaulting on their pledge to redeem the warehouse receipts when presented. In most cases, the borrowers of the gold also preferred warehouse receipts to the actual gold. Thus, the amount of gold represented by the warehouse receipts was greater than the actual amount of gold on deposit. The consequence of this lending activity was an increase in the money supply—measured in terms of gold and the paper warehouse receipts issued by the goldsmith-bankers.

This was the beginning of **fractional reserve banking**. Under a fractional reserve system, banks create money by holding on reserve only a fraction of the money deposited with them and lending the remainder. Our modern-day banking system operates under a fractional reserve banking arrangement.

Fractional Reserve Banking
A banking arrangement that allows banks to hold reserves equal to only a fraction of their deposit liabilities.

The Federal Reserve System

The next chapter discusses the structure of **the Fed** (the popular name for the **Federal Reserve System**) and the tools it uses to change the money supply. For now, we need only note that the Federal Reserve System is the central bank; essentially, it is a bank's bank. Its chief function is to control the nation's money supply.

Federal Reserve System (the Fed)
The central bank of the United States.

The Money Creation Process

This section describes the important money supply process, specifically, how the banking system, working under a fractional reserve requirement, creates money.

economics 24/7

© COLIN YOUNG-WOLFF/PHOTOEDIT

EBAY AND MATCH.COM

In our story of money emerging out of a barter economy, we learned that money lowered the transaction costs of making exchanges. In a barter economy, the transaction costs are relatively high to make exchanges because no one can be sure that the person who has what you want wants what you have. With the emergence of money, the transaction costs of making exchanges drop because everyone is willing to trade what he or she has for money.

Just as money has lowered the transaction costs of making exchanges, so has the Internet. Through the Internet, people can faster and more easily find other people they might want to exchange with.

Consider life before the Internet and before both eBay and Match.com. A person in London has an old Rolling Stones album he wants to sell. The problem is that he is not sure where the person is who might want to buy his album. Today, the person simply goes online to eBay and posts his Rolling Stones album for sale. In a matter of hours, perhaps,

people who want to buy the album are bidding on it. eBay and the Internet lower the transaction costs of bringing buyer and seller together.

Or consider Match.com, an online dating service. When people date each other, there is an exchange of sorts going on. Each person is effectively saying to the other, "I demand some of your time, which I hope you will supply to me."

One of the transaction costs of dating is actually finding a person to date. What Match.com and the Internet do is lower these transaction costs. It is a little like eBay, but what you are offering to "sell" is yourself. Instead of describing the Rolling Stones album you want to sell, you describe yourself. Then, in a sense, people "bid" on you by getting in touch.

What do money, eBay, and Match.com tell us about life? Simply this: People want to trade with each other, and part of being able to trade with each other is lowering the transaction costs of trading. Money, eBay, and Match.com fill the bill.

The Bank's Reserves and More

Reserves

The sum of bank deposits at the Fed and vault cash.

Many banks have an account with the Fed in much the same way that an individual has a checking account with a commercial bank. Economists refer to this account with the Fed as either a reserve account or bank deposits at the Fed. Banks also have currency or cash in their vaults—simply called vault cash—on the bank premises. The sum of (1) bank deposits at the Fed and (2) the bank's vault cash is (total bank) **reserves**.

$$\text{Reserves} = \text{Bank deposits at the Fed} + \text{Vault cash}$$

For example, if a bank currently has $4 million in deposits at the Fed and $1 million in vault cash, it has $5 million in reserves.

THE REQUIRED RESERVE RATIO AND REQUIRED RESERVES The Fed mandates that member commercial banks must hold a certain fraction of their checkable deposits in reserve form. What does "reserve form" mean here? It means in the form of "bank deposits at the Fed" and/or "vault cash" because the sum of these two equals reserves.

Required Reserve Ratio (r)

A percentage of each dollar deposited that must be held on reserve (at the Fed or in the bank's vault).

Required Reserves

The minimum amount of reserves a bank must hold against its checkable deposits as mandated by the Fed.

The fraction of checkable deposits that banks must hold in reserve form is called the **required reserve ratio (r)**. The dollar amount of deposits that must be held in reserve form is called **required reserves**. In other words, to find the required reserves for a given bank, multiply the required reserve ratio by checkable deposits (in the bank):

$$\text{Required reserves} = r \times \text{Checkable deposits}$$

For example, assume that customers have deposited $40 million in a neighborhood bank and that the Fed has set the required reserve ratio at 10 percent. It follows that required reserves for the bank equal $4 million (0.10 × $40 million = $4 million).

EXCESS RESERVES The difference between a bank's (total) reserves and its required reserves is its **excess reserves**:

Excess reserves = Reserves − Required reserves

For example, if the bank's (total) reserves are $5 million and its required reserves are $4 million, then it holds excess reserves of $1 million.

The important point about excess reserves is that banks use them to make loans. In fact, banks have a monetary incentive to use their excess reserves to make loans: If the bank uses the $1 million excess reserves to make loans, it earns interest income. If it does not make any loans, it does not earn interest income.

> **Q&A**
>
> *A bank has $100 million in checkable deposits and the required reserve ratio is 10 percent. How much of the $100 million does the bank need to have in reserves?*
>
> *The bank needs $10 million in reserves, or 10 percent of the $100 million. The remainder, or $90 million, consists of excess reserves, which can be used to make loans.*

Excess Reserves
Any reserves held beyond the required amount. The difference between (total) reserves and required reserves.

The Banking System and the Money Expansion Process

The banks in the banking system are prohibited from printing their own currency. Nevertheless, the banking system can create money by increasing checkable deposits. (Remember, checkable deposits are a component of the money supply. For example, M1 = currency held outside banks + checkable deposits + traveler's checks.)

The process starts with the Fed. For now, suppose the Fed prints $1,000 in new paper money and gives it to Bill. Bill takes the newly created $1,000 and deposits it in bank *A*. We can see this transaction in the following T-account. A **T-account** is a simplified balance sheet that records the *changes* in the bank's assets and liabilities.

T-Account
A simplified balance sheet that shows the changes in a bank's assets and liabilities.

Bank *A*		
Assets		**Liabilities**
Reserves +$1,000		Checkable deposits (Bill) +$1,000

Because the deposit initially is added to vault cash, *the bank's reserves have increased by $1,000*. The bank's liabilities also have increased by $1,000 because it owes Bill the $1,000 he deposited in the bank.

Next, the banker divides the $1,000 reserves into two categories: required reserves and excess reserves. The amount of required reserves depends on the required reserve ratio specified by the Fed. We'll set the required reserve ratio at 10 percent. This means the bank holds $100 in required reserves against the deposit and holds $900 in excess reserves. The previous T-account can be modified to show this:

Bank *A*		
Assets		**Liabilities**
Required reserves +$100		Checkable deposits (Bill) +$1,000
Excess reserves +$900		

On the left side of the T-account, the total is $1,000, and on the right side, the total is also $1,000. By dividing total reserves into required reserves and excess reserves, we can see how many dollars the bank is holding above the Fed requirements. These excess reserves can be used to make new loans.

Suppose bank *A* makes a loan of $900 to Jenny. The left (assets) side of the bank's T-account looks like this:

Bank *A*			
Assets		**Liabilities**	
Required reserves	+$100	See the next T-account.	
Excess reserves	+$900		
Loans	+$900		

Now, when bank *A* gives Jenny a $900 loan, it doesn't give her $900 cash. Instead, it opens a checking account for Jenny at the bank, and the balance in the account is $900. This is how things are shown in the T-account:

Bank *A*		
Assets	**Liabilities**	
See the previous T-account	Checkable deposits (Bill)	+$1,000
	Checkable deposits (Jenny)	+$ 900

Before we continue, *notice that the money supply has increased.* When Jenny borrowed $900 and the bank put that amount in her checking account, *no one else in the economy had any less money, and Jenny had more than before.* Consequently, the money supply has increased. (Think of M1 as equal to currency + checkable deposits + traveler's checks. Through the lending activity of the bank, checkable deposits have increased by $900, and there has been no change in the amount of currency or traveler's checks. It follows that M1 has increased.) In other words, the money supply is $900 more than it was previously.

Now suppose Jenny spends the $900 on a new computer. She writes a $900 check to the computer retailer, who deposits the full amount of the check in bank *B*. First, what happens to bank *A?* It uses its excess reserves to honor Jenny's check when it is presented by bank *B* and simultaneously reduces her checking account balance from $900 to zero. Bank *A*'s situation is shown here:

Bank *A*			
Assets		**Liabilities**	
Required reserves	+$100	Checkable deposits (Bill)	+$1,000
Excess reserves	$0		
Loans	+$900	Checkable deposits (Jenny)	$0

The situation for bank *B* is different. Because of the computer retailer's deposit, bank *B* now has $900 that it didn't have previously. This increases bank *B*'s reserves and liabilities by $900:

Bank *B*			
Assets		**Liabilities**	
Reserves	+$900	Checkable deposits	+$900
		(Computer Retailer)	

Note that the computer purchase has not changed the overall money supply. Dollars have simply moved from Jenny's checking account to the computer retailer's checking account.

The process continues in much the same way for bank *B* as it did earlier for bank *A*. Only a fraction (10 percent) of the computer retailer's $900 needs to be kept on reserve (required reserves on $900 = $90). The remainder ($810) constitutes excess reserves that can be lent to still another borrower. That loan will create $810 in new checkable deposits and thus expand the money supply by that amount. The process continues with banks *C, D, E,* and so on until the dollar figures become so small that the process comes to a halt. Exhibit 1 summarizes what happens as the $1,000 originally created by the Fed works its way through the banking system.

Looking back over the entire process, this is what has happened:

- The Fed created $1,000 worth of new money and gave it to Bill, who then deposited it in bank *A*.

- The reserves of bank *A* increased. The reserves of no other bank decreased.

- The banking system, with the newly created $1,000 in hand, made loans and, in the process, created checkable deposits for the people who received the loans.

- Remember, checkable deposits are part of the money supply. So in effect, by extending loans and, in the process, creating checkable deposits, the banking system has increased the money supply.

The $1,000 in new funds deposited in bank *A* was the basis of several thousand dollars' worth of new bank loans and new checkable deposits. In this instance, the $1,000 initially injected into the economy ultimately caused bankers to create $9,000 in new checkable deposits. When this amount is added to the newly created $1,000 the Fed

exhibit **1**

The Banking System Creates Checkable Deposits (Money)

In this exhibit, the required reserve ratio is 10 percent. We have assumed that there is no cash leakage and that excess reserves are fully lent out; that is, banks hold zero excess reserves.

(1) Bank	(2) New Deposits (new reserves)	(3) New Required Reserves	(4) Checkable Deposits Created by Extending New Loans (equal to new excess reserves)
A	$1,000.00	$100.00	$900.00
B	900.00	90.00	810.00
C	810.00	81.00	729.00
D	729.00	72.90	656.10
E	656.10	65.61	590.49
⋮	⋮	⋮	⋮
TOTALS (rounded)	$10,000	$1,000	$9,000

gave to Bill, the money supply has expanded by $10,000. A formula that shows this result is

$$\text{Maximum change in checkable deposits} = (1/r) \times \Delta R$$

where r = the required reserve ratio and ΔR = the change in reserves resulting from the original injection of funds.[2] In the equation, the reciprocal of the required reserve ratio $(1/r)$ is known as the **simple deposit multiplier**. The arithmetic for this example is

$$\begin{aligned}\text{Maximum change in checkable deposits} &= (1 / 0.10) \times \$1,000 \\ &= 10 \times \$1,000 \\ &= \$10,000\end{aligned}$$

Simple Deposit Multiplier
The reciprocal of the required reserve ratio, $1/r$.

Why Maximum? Answer: No Cash Leakages and Zero Excess Reserves

We made two important assumptions in our discussion of the money expansion process.

First, we assumed that all monies were deposited in bank checking accounts. For example, when Jenny wrote a check to the computer retailer, the retailer endorsed the check and deposited the full amount in bank B. In reality, the retailer might have deposited less than the full amount and kept a few dollars in cash. This is referred to as a **cash leakage**. If there had been a cash leakage of $300, then bank B would have received only $600, not $900. This would change the second number in column 2 in Exhibit 1 to $600 and the second number in column 4 to $540. Therefore, the total in column 2 of Exhibit 1 would be much smaller. A cash leakage that reduces the flow of dollars into banks means that banks have fewer dollars to lend. Fewer loans mean banks put less into borrowers' accounts, so less money is created than when cash leakages equal zero.

Second, we assumed that every bank lent all its excess reserves, leaving every bank with zero excess reserves. After Bill's $1,000 deposit, for example, bank A had excess reserves of $900 and made a new loan for the full amount. Banks generally want to lend all of their excess reserves to earn additional interest income, but there is no law, natural or legislated, that says every bank has to lend every penny of excess reserves. If banks do not lend all their excess reserves, then checkable deposits and the money supply will increase by less than in the original situation (where banks did lend all their excess reserves).

If we had not made our two assumptions, the change in checkable deposits would have been much smaller. Because we assumed no cash leakages and zero excess reserves, the change in checkable deposits is the *maximum* possible change.

Cash Leakage
Occurs when funds are held as currency instead of deposited into a checking account.

Who Created What?

The money expansion process described had two major players: (1) the Fed, which created the new $1,000, and (2) the banking system. Together they created or expanded the money supply by $10,000. The Fed directly created $1,000 and thus made it possible for banks to create $9,000 in new checkable deposits as a by-product of extending new loans.

An easy formula for finding the maximum change in checkable deposits brought about by the banking system (and *only* the banking system) is

$$\begin{aligned}&\text{Maximum change in checkable deposits} \\ &\text{(brought about by the banking system)} = (1/r) \times \Delta ER\end{aligned}$$

---

[2]Because only checkable deposits, and no other components of the money supply, change in this example, we could write "Maximum change in checkable deposits = $(1/r) \times \Delta R$" as "Maximum $\Delta M = (1/r) \times \Delta R$" where ΔM = the change in the money supply. In this chapter, the only component of the money supply that we allow to change is checkable deposits. For this reason, we can talk about changes in checkable deposits and the money supply as if they are the same—which they are, given our specification.

where r = the required reserve ratio and ΔER = the change in excess reserves of the first bank to receive the new injection of funds. The arithmetic for our example is

Maximum change in checkable deposits
(brought about by the banking system) = $(1 / 0.10) \times \$900$
$$= 10 \times \$900$$
$$= \$9,000$$

It Works in Reverse: The "Money Destruction" Process

In the preceding example, the Fed created $1,000 of new money and gave it to Bill, who then deposited it in bank *A*. This simple act created a multiple increase in checkable deposits and the money supply. The process also works in reverse. Suppose Bill withdraws the $1,000 and gives it back to the Fed. The Fed then destroys the $1,000. As a result, bank reserves decline. The multiple deposit contraction process is symmetrical to the multiple deposit expansion process.

Again, we set the required reserve ratio at 10 percent. The situation for bank *A* looks like this:

Bank *A*		
Assets		**Liabilities**
Reserves $-\$1000$		Checkable deposits (Bill) $-\$1,000$

Losing $1,000 in reserves places bank *A* in a *reserve deficiency position*. Specifically, it is $900 short. Remember, bank *A* held $100 reserves against the initial $1,000 deposit, so it loses $900 in reserves that backed other deposits ($1,000 − $100 = $900). If this is not immediately obvious, consider the following example.

Suppose the checkable deposits in a bank total $10,000, and the required reserve ratio is 10 percent. This means the bank must hold $1,000 in reserve form. Now let's suppose this is exactly what the bank holds in reserves, $1,000. (We'll assume the $1,000 is held as vault cash.) Is the bank reserve deficient at this point? No, it is holding exactly the right amount of reserves given its checkable deposits. Not one penny more, not one penny less.

Now, one day, a customer of the bank asks to withdraw $1,000. The bank teller goes to the vault, collects $1,000, and hands it to the customer. Two things have happened: (1) reserves of the bank have fallen by $1,000 and (2) checkable deposits in the bank have fallen by the same amount. In other words, checkable deposits go from $10,000 to $9,000.

Does the bank currently have reserves? The answer is no. The bank's reserves of $1,000 were given to the customer, so the bank has $0 in reserves. If the required reserve ratio is 10 percent, how much does the bank need in reserves, given that checkable deposits are now $9,000? The answer is $900. That is, the bank is $900 reserve deficient.

When a bank is reserve deficient, it must take immediate action to correct this situation. What can it do? One thing it can do is to reduce its outstanding loans. Funds from loan repayments can be applied to the reserve deficiency rather than used to extend new loans. As borrowers repay $900 worth of loans, they reduce their checking account balances by that amount, causing the money supply to decline by $900.

Let's assume that the $900 loan repayment to bank *A* is written on a check issued by bank *B*. After the check has cleared, reserves and customer deposits at bank *B* fall by $900. This situation is reflected in bank *B*'s T-account:

Bank B		
Assets		**Liabilities**
Reserves −$900		Checkable deposits −$900

Bank B now faces a situation similar to bank A's earlier situation. Losing $900 in reserves places bank B in reserve deficiency. It is $810 short. Remember, bank B held $90 in reserve form against the $900 deposit, so it loses $810 that backed other deposits ($900 − $90 = $810). Bank B seeks to recoup $810 by reducing its outstanding loans by an equal amount. If a customer is asked to pay off an $810 loan and does so by writing a check on his or her account at bank C, that bank's reserves and deposits both decline by $810. As a result, bank C is now in reserve deficiency; it is $729 short. Remember, bank C held $81 in reserve form against the $810 deposit, so it is short $729 that backed other deposits ($810 − $81 = $729).

As you can see, the figures are the same ones given in Exhibit 1, with the exception that each change is negative rather than positive. When Bill withdrew $1,000 from his account and returned it to the Fed (which then destroyed the $1,000), the money supply declined by $10,000.

Exhibit 2 shows the money supply expansion and contraction processes in brief.

We Change Our Example

Let's change our example somewhat. This time, the Fed does not create new money. Instead, let's consider Jack, who currently has $1,000 in cash in a shoebox in his bedroom. He decides that he doesn't want to keep this much cash around the house, so he takes it to bank A and opens a checking account. So far, this act does not change the money supply. Initially, the $1,000 in the shoebox was currency outside a bank and thus was part of the money supply. When Jack took the $1,000 from his shoebox and placed it in a bank, there was $1,000 less currency outside a bank and $1,000 more checkable deposits. So far, this act has changed the *composition* of the money supply but not its *size*.

The $1,000 could not create a multiple of itself when it was in a shoebox in Jack's bedroom. When the $1,000 is placed in a checking account, however, the banking system has $1,000 more reserves than before and thus has excess reserves that can be used to extend new loans and create new checkable deposits. This means the money supply can expand in much the same way as earlier. At maximum, the banking system can create $9,000 worth of new loans and checkable deposits. (We assume again that $r = 0.10$.) The primary difference between the two examples is their *starting point*. The first example started with the Fed creating new money. The second example began with Jack removing $1,000 from a shoebox and depositing it in a bank. Despite this difference, in both examples, the banking system created the identical maximum amount of new checkable deposits.

exhibit 2

The Money Supply Expansion and Contraction Processes

The money supply expands if reserves enter the banking system; the money supply contracts if reserves exit the banking system. In expansion, reserves rise; thus, excess reserves rise, more loans are made, and checkable deposits rise. Because checkable deposits are part of the money supply, the money supply rises. In contraction, reserves fall; thus, excess reserves fall, fewer loans are made, and checkable deposits fall. Because checkable deposits are part of the money supply, the money supply falls.

Money Supply Expansion

Money Supply Contraction

SELF-TEST

1. If a bank's deposits equal $579 million and the required reserve ratio is 9.5 percent, what dollar amount must the bank hold in reserve form?

2. If the Fed creates $600 million in new reserves, what is the maximum change in checkable deposits that can occur if the required reserve ratio is 10 percent?

3. Bank *A* has $1.2 million in reserves and $10 million in deposits. The required reserve ratio is 10 percent. If bank *A* loses $200,000 in reserves, by what dollar amount is it reserve deficient?

A Reader Asks . . .

Do People Desire to Economize on Time?

It takes less time to make exchanges in a money economy than in a barter economy. In other words, by moving from a barter economy to a money economy, individuals economize on time. Are there other examples in economics of individuals economizing on time?

Some economists have argued that one of the hallmarks of a money economy is the gradual reduction of "dead" time spent to consume a good or service. Examples abound. Today, the use of bar codes and scanners permits consumers to get through supermarket and department store lines faster. Touchtone telephones allow people to refill prescriptions without going to the pharmacy. With the Internet, we can make price comparisons without traveling from store to store and can order a wide variety of goods and services.[3]

Some economists go on to argue that brand names also help individuals economize on time. Instead of spending time making price and quality comparisons on everything we purchase, we sometimes rely on brand names to provide a certain level of service or quality. We can read a few pages of every book in a bookstore to see if a book looks "good enough to buy," or we can save time by just buying a book written by an author who has already satisfied our reading propensities. When traveling to a new city, we can spend time learning about the different local hotels, or we can save time by checking into a Marriott or Holiday Inn.

[3]Many of the examples in this feature come from "Time: Economics' Neglected Stepchild," by Gene Epstein, *Barron's*, December 31, 2001.

! analyzing the scene

What do William Shakespeare, Ludwig van Beethoven, Wolfgang Amadeus Mozart, Robert Louis Stevenson, and Albert Einstein have to do with money evolving out of a barter economy?

All of the individuals mentioned worked at one thing and one thing only. Shakespeare wrote plays, Beethoven and Mozart composed music, Robert Louis Stevenson wrote novels, and Einstein thought and wrote about the physical world. Would anyone have done what he did had he lived in a barter economy instead of in a money economy? It is doubtful. In a money economy, individuals usually specialize in the production of one good or service because they can do so. In a barter economy, specializing is extremely costly. For Shakespeare, it would mean writing plays all day and then going out and trying to trade what he had written that day for apples, oranges, chickens, and bread. Would the baker trade 2 loaves of bread for 2 pages of *Romeo and Juliet?* Would the brewer trade 2 quarts of brew for the chance to play a Mozart composition? Einstein, living in a barter economy, would soon learn that he did not have a double coincidence of wants with many people, and therefore, if he was going to eat and be housed, he would need to spend time baking bread, raising chickens, and building shelter instead of thinking about space and time. In a barter economy, trade is difficult, so people produce for themselves. In a money economy, trade is easy, and so individuals produce one thing, sell it for money, and then buy what they want with the money. The "William Shakespeare" who lived in a barter economy spent his days very differently from the William Shakespeare who lived in England in the 16th century.

chapter summary

What Money Is

- Money is any good that is widely accepted for purposes of exchange and in the repayment of debts.
- Money serves as a medium of exchange, a unit of account, and a store of value.
- Money evolved out of a barter economy as traders attempted to make exchange easier. A few goods that have been used as money include gold, silver, copper, cattle, rocks, and shells.
- Our money today has value because of its general acceptability.

The Money Supply

- M1 includes currency held outside banks, checkable deposits, and traveler's checks.
- M2 includes M1, savings deposits (including money market deposit accounts), small-denomination time deposits, and money market mutual funds (retail).
- Credit cards are not money. When a credit card is used to make a purchase, a liability is incurred. This is not the case when money is used to make a purchase.

The Money Creation Process

- Banks in the United States operate under a fractional reserve system in which they must maintain only a fraction of their deposits in the form of reserves (i.e., in the form of deposits at the Fed and vault cash). Excess reserves are typically used to extend loans to customers. When banks make these loans, they credit borrowers' checking accounts and thereby increase the money supply. When banks reduce the volume of loans outstanding, they reduce checkable deposits and reduce the money supply.
- A change in the composition of the money supply can change the size of the money supply. For example, suppose M1 = $1,000 billion, where the breakdown is $300 billion currency outside banks and $700 billion in checkable deposits. Now suppose the $300 billion in currency is put in a checking account in a bank. Initially, this changes the composition of the money supply but not its size. M1 is still $1,000 billion but now includes $0 in currency and $1,000 billion in checkable deposits. Later, when the banks have had time to create new loans (checkable deposits) with the new reserves provided by the $300 billion deposit, the money supply expands.

key terms and concepts

Money	Currency	Money Market Mutual Fund	Required Reserves
Barter	Federal Reserve Notes	Fractional Reserve Banking	Excess Reserves
Medium of Exchange	Checkable Deposits	Federal Reserve System (the Fed)	T-Account
Unit of Account	M2	Reserves	Simple Deposit Multiplier
Store of Value	Savings Deposit	Required Reserve Ratio (r)	Cash Leakage
Double Coincidence of Wants	Money Market Deposit Account		
M1	Time Deposit		

questions and problems

1 Does inflation, which is an increase in the price level, affect the three functions of money? If so, how?

2 Some economists have proposed that the Fed move to a 100 percent required reserve ratio. This would make the simple deposit multiplier 1 ($1/r = 1/1.00 = 1$). Do you think banks would argue for or against the move? Explain your answer.

3 Money makes trade easier. Would having a money supply twice as large as it is currently make trade twice as easy? Would having a money supply half its current size make trade half as easy?

4 Explain why gold backing is not necessary to give paper money value.

5 "Money is a means of lowering the transaction costs of making exchanges." Do you agree or disagree? Explain your answer.

6 If you were on an island with 10 other people and there was no money, do you think money would emerge on the scene? Why or why not?

7 Can M1 fall as M2 rises? Can M1 rise without M2 rising too? Explain your answers.

8 Why isn't a credit card money?

9 If Smith, who has a checking account at bank *A*, withdraws his money and deposits all of it into bank *B*, do reserves in the banking system change? Explain your answer.

10 If Jones, who has a checking account at bank *A*, withdraws her money, deposits half of it into bank *B*, and keeps the other half in currency, do reserves in the banking system change? Explain your answer.

11 Give an example that illustrates a change in the composition of the money supply.

12 Describe the money supply expansion process.

13 Describe the money supply contraction process.

14 Does a cash leakage affect the change in checkable deposits and the money supply expansion process? Explain your answer.

working with numbers and graphs

1 Suppose $10,000 in new dollar bills (never seen before) falls magically from the sky into the hands of Joanna Ferris. What are the minimum increase and the maximum increase in the money supply that may result? Assume the required reserve ratio is 10 percent.

2 Suppose Joanna Ferris receives $10,000 from her friend Ethel and deposits the money in a checking account. Ethel gave Joanna the money by writing a check on her checking account. Would the maximum increase in the money supply still be what you found it to be in question 1 where Joanna received the money from the sky? Explain your answer.

3 Suppose that instead of Joanna getting $10,000 from the sky or through a check from a friend, she gets the money from her mother, who had buried it in a can in her backyard. In this case, would the maximum increase in the money supply be what you found it to be in question 1? Explain your answer.

4 Suppose $r = 10$ percent and the Fed creates $20,000 in new money that is deposited in someone's checking account in a bank. What is the maximum change in the money supply as a result?

5 Suppose $r = 10$ percent and John walks into his bank, withdraws $2,000 in cash, and burns the money. What is the maximum change in the money supply as a result?

6 The Fed creates $100,000 in new money that is deposited in someone's checking account in a bank. What is the maximum change in the money supply if the required reserve ratio is 5 percent? 10 percent? 20 percent?

12 The Federal Reserve System

Setting the Scene

The major policymaking group in the Federal Reserve System is the Federal Open Market Committee (FOMC). The FOMC meets eight times a year, each time on a Tuesday. The meeting is held in the board room of the Federal Reserve Building. Decisions about monetary policy are, to a large degree, made by the FOMC. The following events occur at a typical FOMC meeting.

8:00 A.M.

The board room is swept for electronic bugs.

8:45–9:00 A.M.

People begin to arrive for the meeting. In addition to the 12 members of the FOMC, about 37 other people will be present at the meeting.

8:59 A.M.

The chairman of the Board of Governors of the Federal Reserve System walks through the door that connects his office to the board room and takes his place at the table.

9:00 A.M.

The FOMC meeting commences. The first agenda item is a presentation by the manager of the System Open Market Account at the Federal Reserve Bank of New York. He discusses the financial and foreign exchange markets and provides certain details about open market operations.

A LITTLE LATER

The director of research and statistics at the Federal Reserve Board presents the forecast of the U.S. economy. The forecast has previously been circulated to the FOMC members in the Greenbook (because the cover of the document is green). The latest economic data are reviewed and discussed.

A LITTLE LATER

The 12 members of the FOMC present their views of local and national economic conditions.

A LITTLE LATER

The director of monetary affairs presents policy options. These policy options have been previously circulated in the Bluebook (because the cover of the document is blue). The chairman of the Board of Governors gives his opinion of the economy and of the policy options.

A LITTLE LATER

A general discussion among all the members of the FOMC takes place. At issue: the state of the U.S. economy and current policy options. After the discussion, the chairman summarizes his sense of the policy options. Then, the members vote on the options. The chair votes first, the vice chair votes second, and the remaining FOMC members vote in alphabetical order.

A LITTLE LATER

The FOMC discusses the wording of the announcement it will make regarding what it has decided.

BETWEEN 11:30 A.M. AND 1:30 P.M.

The meeting usually adjourns.

2:15 P.M.

The decision of the FOMC is released to the public.

? Here is a question to keep in mind as you read this chapter:

How does the Fed expand or contract the money supply?

See analyzing the scene at the end of this chapter for the answer to this question.

The Structure and Functions of the Fed

The Federal Reserve System is the central bank of the United States. Other nations also have central banks, such as the Bank of Sweden, the Bank of England, the Banque de France, the Bank of Japan, the Deutsche Bundesbank, and so on.

The Structure of the Fed

The Federal Reserve System came into existence with the Federal Reserve Act of 1913 and began operations in November 1914. The act divided the country into Federal Reserve Districts. As Exhibit 1 shows, there are 12 districts; each has a Federal Reserve Bank with its own president.

Within the Fed, a 7-member **Board of Governors** coordinates and controls the activities of the Federal Reserve System. The board members serve 14-year terms and are appointed by the president with Senate approval. To limit political influence on Fed policy, the terms of the governors are staggered—with one new appointment every other year—so a president cannot "pack" the board. The president also designates one member as chairman of the board for a 4-year term.

The major policymaking group within the Fed is the **Federal Open Market Committee (FOMC)**. Authority to conduct **open market operations**—the buying and selling of government securities—rests with the FOMC (more on open market operations later). The FOMC has 12 members: the 7-member Board of Governors and 5 Federal Reserve District Bank presidents. The president of the Federal Reserve Bank of New York holds a permanent seat on the FOMC because a large amount of financial activity takes place in New York City and because the New York Fed is responsible for executing open market operations. The other four positions are rotated among the Federal Reserve District Bank presidents.

The most important responsibility of the Fed is to conduct monetary policy, or control the money supply. **Monetary policy** refers to changes in the money supply. More specifically, *expansionary monetary policy* refers to an increase in the money supply, and *contractionary monetary policy* refers to a decrease in the money supply. As you will learn in this chapter, the Fed has tools at its disposal to both increase and decrease the

Board of Governors

The governing body of the Federal Reserve System.

Federal Open Market Committee (FOMC)

The 12-member policymaking group within the Fed. The committee has the authority to conduct open market operations.

Open Market Operations

The buying and selling of government securities by the Fed.

Monetary Policy

Changes in the money supply, or in the rate of change of the money supply, to achieve particular macroeconomic goals.

exhibit **1**

Federal Reserve Districts and Federal Reserve Bank Locations

The boundaries of the Federal Reserve Districts, the cities in which a Federal Reserve Bank is located, and the location of the Board of Governors (Washington, D.C.) are all noted on the map.

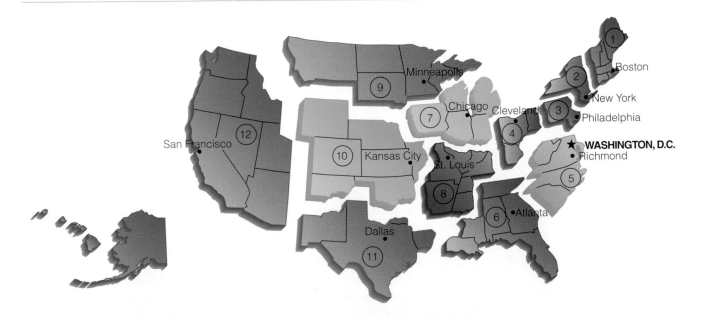

economics 24/7

© KYODO/LANDOV

SOME HISTORY OF THE FED

Slightly before the passage of the Federal Reserve Act in 1913, there was disagreement about how many districts and banks there should be. Many people thought there should be as few banks as possible—6 to 8—because concentrating activities in only a few cities would enhance efficiency and ease of operation. The Secretary of State at the time, William Jennings Bryan, wanted 50 district banks. He called for a "branch at every major crossroad." It was to be neither 6 nor 50; instead, there was a compromise. Section 2 of the Federal Reserve Act states that "not less than eight nor more than twelve cities" would be designated as Federal Reserve cities.

After the number of cities was determined to be 8 to 12, a commission was set up to identify both the boundaries of the Federal Reserve Districts and the locations of the district banks. The commission was composed of the Comptroller of the Currency, the Secretary of the Treasury, and the Secretary of Agriculture. They had to choose from among the 37 cities that had applied to be a location of a district bank. The commission settled on a 12-bank, 12-city plan. It decided the boundaries of the districts on the basis of trade. In other words, the commission decided the boundaries should include cities or towns that traded most with each other. If the residents of cities X and Y traded a lot with each other but the residents of city Z did not trade much with the residents of cities X and Y, then cities X and Y should be included in the same district but Z should not. Instead, city Z should be part of the district that included cities with which it traded.

Some commercial banks protested both the number of district banks and the boundaries decided on by the committee. These banks filed petitions for review of the plan with the Federal Reserve Board, thought to be the only group that could alter the plan.[1]

The petitions for review are said to have rekindled the debate about the actual number of district cities. Three members of the Federal Reserve Board wanted to reduce the number of district banks because they thought that half the banks were stronger than the other half were, and they wanted all banks to be of equal strength. Three other members of the Board wanted to stay with the original plan of 12 district banks. This left one member of the Board to break the tie. When it looked like that person's vote was going to be cast for a reduction in the number of district banks, one of the supporters of the original 12-bank plan went to the Attorney General of the United States. He asked the Attorney General for an opinion that stated the Board did not have the authority to alter the original plan. The Attorney General gave that opinion. The Board, afraid of attracting any negative publicity by disagreeing and challenging the opinion, accepted it.

---

[1]Before there was a Board of Governors of the Federal Reserve System, there was the Federal Reserve Board. The Banking Act of 1935, approved on August 23, 1935, changed the name of the Federal Reserve Board to the Board of Governors of the Federal Reserve System

---

money supply. In a later chapter, we will discuss monetary policy in detail and show how, under certain conditions, it can remove an economy from both recessionary and inflationary gaps.

The Functions of the Fed

The Fed has eight major responsibilities or functions. The first has already been mentioned.

1. **Control the money supply.** A full explanation of how the Fed does this comes later in this chapter.

2. **Supply the economy with paper money (Federal Reserve notes).** The Federal Reserve Banks have Federal Reserve notes on hand to meet the demands of the banks and the public. During the Christmas season, for example, more people withdraw larger-than-usual amounts of $1, $5, $20, $50, and $100 notes from banks. Banks need to replenish their vault cash, so they turn to their Federal Reserve

Banks. The Federal Reserve Banks meet this cash need by issuing more paper money (they act as passive suppliers of paper money). The money is actually printed at the Bureau of Engraving and Printing in Washington, D.C., but it is issued to commercial banks by the 12 Federal Reserve Banks.

3. **Provide check-clearing services.** When someone in San Diego writes a check to a person in Los Angeles, what happens to the check? The process by which funds change hands when checks are written is called the *check-clearing process*. The following process is summarized in Exhibit 2.

   a. Harry Saito writes a $1,000 check on his San Diego bank and sends it to Ursula Pevins in Los Angeles.

   b. Ursula takes the check to her local bank, endorses it, and deposits it in her checking account. The balance in her account rises by $1,000.

   c. Ursula's Los Angeles bank sends the check to its Federal Reserve District Bank, which is located in San Francisco. The Federal Reserve Bank of San Francisco increases the reserve account of the Los Angeles bank by $1,000 and decreases the reserve account of the San Diego bank by $1,000.

   d. The Federal Reserve Bank of San Francisco sends the check to Harry's bank in San Diego, which then reduces the balance in Harry's checking account by $1,000. Harry's bank in San Diego either keeps the check on record or sends it to Harry with his monthly bank statement.

4. **Hold depository institutions' reserves.** As noted in the last chapter, banks are required to keep reserves against customer deposits either in their vaults or in reserve accounts at the Fed. These accounts are maintained by the 12 Federal Reserve Banks for member banks in their respective districts.

5. **Supervise member banks.** Without warning, the Fed can examine the books of member commercial banks to see the nature of the loans the banks have made, monitor compliance with bank regulations, check the accuracy of bank records, and so on. If the Fed finds that a bank has not been maintaining established banking standards, it can pressure it to do so.

6. **Serve as the government's banker.** The federal government collects and spends large sums of money. As a result, it needs a checking account for many of the same

Q&A

What is the difference between the U.S. Treasury and the Fed?

The U.S. Treasury is a budgetary agency; the Fed is a monetary agency. When the federal government spends funds, the Treasury collects the taxes and borrows the funds needed to pay suppliers and others. In short, the Treasury has an obligation to manage the financial affairs of the federal government. Except for coins, the Treasury does not issue money. It cannot create money "out of thin air" as the Fed can. The Fed is principally concerned with the availability of money and credit for the entire economy. It does not issue Treasury securities. It does not have an obligation to meet the financial needs of the federal government. Its responsibility is to provide a stable monetary framework for the economy.

exhibit 2

The Check-Clearing Process

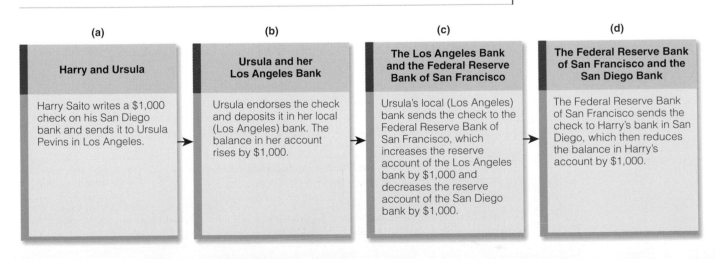

(a)	**(b)**	**(c)**	**(d)**
Harry and Ursula	**Ursula and her Los Angeles Bank**	**The Los Angeles Bank and the Federal Reserve Bank of San Francisco**	**The Federal Reserve Bank of San Francisco and the San Diego Bank**
Harry Saito writes a $1,000 check on his San Diego bank and sends it to Ursula Pevins in Los Angeles.	Ursula endorses the check and deposits it in her local (Los Angeles) bank. The balance in her account rises by $1,000.	Ursula's local (Los Angeles) bank sends the check to the Federal Reserve Bank of San Francisco, which increases the reserve account of the Los Angeles bank by $1,000 and decreases the reserve account of the San Diego bank by $1,000.	The Federal Reserve Bank of San Francisco sends the check to Harry's bank in San Diego, which then reduces the balance in Harry's account by $1,000.

reasons an individual does. Its primary checking account is with the Fed. The Fed is the government's banker.

7. **Serve as the lender of last resort.** A traditional function of a central bank is to serve as the lender of last resort for banks suffering cash management, or liquidity, problems.

8. **Serve as a fiscal agent for the Treasury.** The U.S. Treasury often issues (auctions) Treasury bills, notes, and bonds. These **U.S. Treasury securities** are sold to raise funds to pay the government's bills. The Federal Reserve District Banks receive the bids for these securities and process them in time for weekly auctions.

U.S. Treasury Securities
Bonds and bondlike securities issued by the U.S. Treasury when it borrows.

SELF-TEST

(Answers to Self-Test questions are in the Self-Test Appendix.)

1.   The president of which Federal Reserve District Bank holds a permanent seat on the Federal Open Market Committee (FOMC)?

2.   What is the most important responsibility of the Fed?

3.   What does it mean to say the Fed acts as "lender of last resort"?

Fed Tools for Controlling the Money Supply

The money supply is, say, $1.35 trillion one month and $1.40 trillion a few months later. How did this happen? The fact is that the Fed can change the money supply; it can cause the money supply to rise and to fall. The Fed has three tools at its disposal to change (or control) the money supply:

1.   open market operations

2.   the required reserve ratio

3.   the discount rate

This section explains how the Fed uses these tools to control the money supply.

Open Market Operations

When the Fed either buys or sells U.S. government securities in the financial markets, it is said to be engaged in *open market operations.*[2] Specifically, when it buys securities, it is engaged in an **open market purchase**; when it sells securities, it is engaged in an **open market sale**. The following paragraphs explain how an open market purchase or sale affects the money supply.

Open Market Purchase
The buying of government securities by the Fed.

Open Market Sale
The selling of government securities by the Fed.

OPEN MARKET PURCHASES When the Fed buys securities, someone has to sell securities. Suppose bank *ABC* in Denver is the seller. In other words, suppose the Fed buys $5 million worth of government securities from bank *ABC*.[3] When this happens, the securities leave the possession of bank *ABC* and go to the Fed.

Bank *ABC,* of course, wants something in return for the securities—it wants $5 million. The Fed pays for the government securities by increasing the balance in bank

---

[2]Actually, what the Fed buys and sells when it conducts open market operations are U.S. Treasury bills, notes, and bonds and government agency bonds. *Government securities* is a broad term that includes all of these financial instruments.

[3]If the Fed purchases a government security from a bank, where did the bank get the security in the first place? The answer is that banks often purchase government securities from the U.S. Treasury. It is possible that the bank purchased the government security from the U.S. Treasury months ago.

ABC's reserve account. In other words, if before bank *ABC* sold the securities to the Fed, it had $0 on deposit with the Fed, then after it sells the securities to the Fed, it has $5 million on deposit with the Fed.

At this point, someone will ask, "Where did the Fed get the $5 million to put into bank *ABC's* reserve account?" The answer, as odd as it seems, is: *out of thin air.* This simply means that the Fed has the legal authority to create money. What the Fed is effectively doing is deleting the "$0" balance in bank *ABC's* account and, with a few keystrokes, replacing it with the number 5 and 6 zeroes—$5,000,000.

As in the last chapter, we use T-accounts to show the changes to the accounts affected by the transaction. After the open market purchase, the Fed's T-account looks like this:

The Fed	
Assets	**Liabilities**
Government securities +$5 million	Reserves on deposit in bank *ABC's* account +$5 million

After the open market purchase, bank *ABC's* T-account looks like this:

Bank *ABC*	
Assets	**Liabilities**
Government securities −$5 million Reserves on deposit at the Fed +$5 million	No change

Recall that as the reserves of one bank increase with no offsetting decline in reserves for other banks, the money supply expands through a process of increased loans and checkable deposits. In summary, an open market purchase by the Fed ultimately increases the money supply.

OPEN MARKET SALES Sometimes, the Fed sells government securities to banks and others. Suppose the Fed sells $5 million worth of government securities to bank *XYZ* in Atlanta. The Fed surrenders the securities to bank *XYZ* and is paid with $5 million previously deposited in bank *XYZ's* reserve account at the Fed. In other words, the Fed simply reduces the balance in bank *XYZ's* reserve account by $5 million.

After the open market sale, the Fed's T-account looks like this:

 Q&A

Why would the Fed want to increase the money supply?

We will explain more about why the Fed may want to increase or decrease the money supply in the next two chapters, but for now, we can say that the Fed might want to increase the money supply at a certain time because it wants to move the economy out of a recessionary gap.

The Fed	
Assets	**Liabilities**
Government securities −$5 million	Reserves on deposit in bank *XYZ's* account −$5 million

Bank *XYZ's* T-account looks like this:

Bank *XYZ*	
Assets	**Liabilities**
Government securities +$5 million Reserves on deposit at the Fed −$5 million	No change

economics 24/7

FLYING IN WITH THE MONEY[4]

A banker at a commercial bank located about 200 miles from the Federal Reserve Bank of Minneapolis was frantic. There was a large crowd outside his bank, and the people wanted their money now. The banker got on the phone and called the Federal Reserve Bank in Minneapolis. He told the people at the Minneapolis Fed that there was a "mad run" on his bank. If the Fed did not come to his rescue soon, he would be out of currency and unable to give the customers of his bank their money.

Where was their money? Why didn't he have it to give to them? As the last chapter explained, banks need to have on hand only a fraction of their customers' deposits.

The Federal Reserve System responded to the call for currency. The Federal Reserve Bank of Minneapolis chartered a small plane, and two Fed officials took it, along with a half-million dollars in small-denomination bills, to the nearby town.

Upon approaching the town, the pilot flew the plane over Main Street to dramatize its arrival in the town: The Federal Reserve was flying in to the rescue. The plane landed at a nearby field. From the field, the Fed officials were escorted into town by the police, and the money was stacked in the bank's windows. The sight of all the money calmed the bank's customers, who were now assured they could get their money if they wanted. A banking panic was averted in a very dramatic way.

[4]This feature is based on "Born of a Panic: Forming the Federal Reserve System," *The Region* (August 1998).

Now that bank *XYZ*'s reserves have declined by $5 million, it is reserve deficient. As bank *XYZ* and other banks adjust to the lower level of reserves, they reduce their total loans outstanding, which reduces the total volume of checkable deposits and money in the economy.

A nagging question remains: What happened to the $5 million the Fed got from bank *XYZ*'s account? The answer is that it disappears from the face of the earth; it no longer exists. This is simply the other side of the "Fed can create money out of thin air" coin. The Fed can destroy money too; it can cause money to disappear into thin air.

Exhibit 3 summarizes how open market operations affect the money supply.

exhibit 3

Open Market Operations

An open market purchase increases reserves, which leads to an increase in the money supply. An open market sale decreases reserves, which leads to a decrease in money supply. (Note: We have assumed here that the Fed purchases government securities from and sells government securities to commercial banks.)

How Open Market Operations Affect the Money Supply

Fed Purchase of Government Securities → Increases Reserves → Increases Money Supply

Fed Sale of Government Securities → Decreases Reserves → Decreases Money Supply

The Required Reserve Ratio

The Fed can influence the money supply by changing the required reserve ratio. Recall from the last chapter that we can find the maximum change in checkable deposits (for a given change in reserves) by using the following formula:

$$\text{Maximum change in checkable deposits} = (1/r) \times \Delta R$$

For example, if reserves (R) increase by \$1,000 and the required reserve ratio (r) is 10 percent, then the maximum change in checkable deposits is \$10,000:

$$\text{Maximum change in checkable deposits} = (1/0.10) \times \$1,000$$
$$= 10 \times \$1,000$$
$$= \$10,000$$

Now suppose Fed officials increase the required reserve ratio from 10 percent to 20 percent. How will this change the amount of checkable deposits? The amount of checkable deposits will decline:

$$\text{Maximum change in checkable deposits} = (1/0.20) \times \$1,000$$
$$= 5 \times \$1,000$$
$$= \$5,000$$

If, instead, the Fed lowers the required reserve ratio to 5 percent, the maximum change in checkable deposits will increase:

$$\text{Maximum change in checkable deposits} = (1/0.05) \times \$1,000$$
$$= 20 \times \$1,000$$
$$= \$20,000$$

We conclude that an increase in the required reserve ratio leads to a decrease in the money supply, and a decrease in the required reserve ratio leads to an increase in the money supply. In other words, there is an inverse relationship between the required reserve ratio and the money supply. As r goes up, the money supply goes down; as r goes down, the money supply goes up.

The Discount Rate

In addition to providing loans to customers, banks themselves borrow funds when they need them. Consider bank ABC that currently has zero excess reserves. Then either of the following two events occurs:

- **Case 1:** Brian applies for a loan to buy new equipment for his horse ranch. The bank loan officer believes he is a good credit risk and that the bank could profit by granting him the loan. But the bank has no funds to lend.
- **Case 2:** Jennifer closes her checking account. As a result, the bank loses reserves and now is reserve deficient.

In Case 1, the bank wants funds so that it can make a loan to Brian and increase its profits. In Case 2, the bank needs funds to meet its **reserve requirement**. In either case, there are two major places the bank can go to acquire a loan: (1) the **federal funds market**, which means the bank goes to another bank for a loan, or (2) the Fed (the bank's Federal Reserve District Bank). At both places, the bank will pay an interest rate. The rate it pays for a loan in the federal funds market is called the **federal funds rate**. The rate it pays for a loan from the Fed is called the **discount rate** (also known as the primary credit rate). Bank ABC will try to minimize its costs by borrowing where the interest rate is lower, *ceteris paribus*. Usually, the discount rate is set one percentage point above the federal funds rate.

Reserve Requirement
The rule that specifies the amount of reserves a bank must hold to back up deposits.

Federal Funds Market
A market where banks lend reserves to one another, usually for short periods.

Federal Funds Rate
The interest rate in the federal funds market; the interest rate banks charge one another to borrow reserves.

Discount Rate
The interest rate the Fed charges depository institutions that borrow reserves from it.

Let us suppose, though, that the discount rate was lowered so that it is below the federal funds rate. What would happen? Banks would go to the Fed for loans instead of going to each other. Let's suppose bank *ABC* gets a loan from the Fed. If the Fed grants the bank a loan, the Fed's T-account looks like this:

The FED	
Assets	**Liabilities**
Loan to bank *ABC* +$1 million	Reserves on deposit in bank *ABC*'s account +$1 million

Bank *ABC*'s T-account reflects the same transaction from its perspective:

Bank *ABC*	
Assets	**Liabilities**
Reserves on deposit at the Fed +$1 million	Loan from the Fed +$1 million

Notice that when bank *ABC* borrows from the Fed, its reserves increase while the reserves of no other bank decrease. The result is increased reserves for the banking system as a whole, so the money supply increases. In summary: When a bank borrows at the Fed's discount window, the money supply increases.

On the other hand, when the discount rate is raised above the federal funds rate, banks will not borrow from the Fed. However, as the banks pay back their Fed loans previously taken out, reserves fall, and ultimately, the money supply declines.

A summary of the effects of the Fed's different monetary tools is shown in Exhibit 4.

THE FED, THE DISCOUNT RATE, AND THE FEDERAL FUNDS RATE Sometimes, news reports say that the Fed is thinking about changing the federal funds rate. But the Fed doesn't have direct control over the federal funds rate; it has direct control over the discount rate. The Fed can, however, indirectly affect the federal funds rate. Because the federal funds rate is a market interest rate determined by the supply of and demand for reserves, the Fed can change the supply of reserves through its open market operations. In other words, the Fed could, say, conduct an open market purchase and increase the supply of reserves in the banking system. In turn, this would impact the federal funds rate.

exhibit **4**

Fed Monetary Tools and Their Effects on the Money Supply

The following Fed actions increase the money supply: purchasing government securities on the open market, lowering the required reserve ratio, and lowering the discount rate relative to the federal funds rate. The following Fed actions decrease the money supply: selling government securities on the open market, raising the required reserve ratio, and raising the discount rate relative to the federal funds rate.

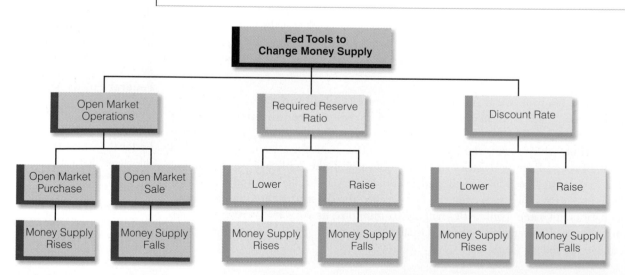

SELF-TEST

1. How does the money supply change as a result of (a) an increase in the discount rate, (b) an open market purchase, (c) an increase in the required reserve ratio?

2. What is the difference between the federal funds rate and the discount rate?

3. If bank *A* borrows $10 million from bank *B,* what happens to the reserves in bank *A?* in the banking system?

4. If bank *A* borrows $10 million from the Fed, what happens to the reserves in bank *A?* in the banking system?

A Reader Asks...

How Do I Get a Job at the Fed?

I'm a junior in college, majoring in economics. Are there any career opportunities at the Fed that I might apply for while I'm still a student?

The Fed operates both summer internships and a Cooperative Education Program for college students. The Fed's summer internship program is "designed to provide valuable work experience for undergraduate and graduate students considering careers in economics, finance, and computer science." The following three divisions at the Federal Reserve Board in Washington, D.C., regularly offer internships:

- Banking Supervision and Regulation
- Information Technology
- Research and Statistics

Summer internships are usually available to college sophomores, juniors, and seniors. The internships are usually unpaid and run from June 1 to September 1.

As an economics major, you may be interested in applying for an internship in the Division of Research and Statistics. This division collects economic and financial information and develops economic analyses that are used by the Board of Governors, the Federal Open Market Committee, and other Fed officials in formulating monetary and regulatory policies.

The Fed's Cooperative Education Program provides paid and unpaid professional work experience to undergraduate and graduate students in economics,

finance and accounting, information systems, and law. Here are the assignments in three of these areas:

- Economics: Students have the opportunity to apply their quantitative skills on projects in financial and nonfinancial areas, bank structure and competition, international trade, and foreign and exchange markets.

- Finance and Accounting: Students analyze the financial condition of domestic and foreign banking organizations and process applications filed by these financial institutions.

- Information Systems: Student assignments include creating public and intranet Web pages and assisting application developers in program maintenance, design, and coding.

Generally, employment in the Cooperative Education Program is for a summer or a year, although other assignment lengths are considered. Candidates are selected on the basis of scholastic achievement, recommendations, and completed coursework in relevant areas of study.

To obtain more information about the summer internships and the Cooperative Education Program, go to the Federal Reserve Web site at http://www.federalreserve.gov/, and click "Career Opportunities." You can also call the Fed's 24-hour job vacancy line at 1-800-448-4894.

analyzing the scene

How does the Fed expand or contract the money supply?

The 12 members of the FOMC decide the Fed's stance with respect to open market operations. This is one of the tools the Fed can use to increase or decrease the money supply. As discussed in this chapter, the Board of Governors of the Fed has two other tools—the discount rate and reserve requirements—that it can use to control the money supply. In all, the Fed has three principal tools to expand or contract the money supply.

chapter summary

The Federal Reserve System

- There are 12 Federal Reserve Districts. The Board of Governors controls and coordinates the activities of the Federal Reserve System. The Board is made up of 7 members, each appointed to a 14-year term. The major policymaking group within the Fed is the Federal Open Market Committee (FOMC). It is a 12-member group made up of the 7 members of the Board of Governors and 5 Federal Reserve District Bank presidents.

- The major responsibilities of the Fed are to (1) control the money supply, (2) supply the economy with paper money (Federal Reserve notes), (3) provide check-clearing services, (4) hold depository institutions' reserves, (5) supervise member banks, (6) serve as the government's banker, (7) serve as the lender of last resort, and (8) serve as a fiscal agent for the Treasury.

Controlling the Money Supply

- The following Fed actions increase the money supply: lowering the required reserve ratio, purchasing government securities on the open market, and lowering the discount rate relative to the federal funds rate. The following Fed actions decrease the money supply: raising the required reserve ratio, selling government securities on the open market, and raising the discount rate relative to the federal funds rate.

Open Market Operations

- An open market purchase by the Fed increases the money supply. An open market sale by the Fed decreases the money supply.

The Required Reserve Ratio

- An increase in the required reserve ratio leads to a decrease in the money supply. A decrease in the required reserve ratio leads to an increase in the money supply.

The Discount Rate

- An increase in the discount rate relative to the federal funds rate leads to a decrease in the money supply.

- A decrease in the discount rate relative to the federal funds rate leads to an increase in the money supply.

key terms and concepts

Board of Governors

Federal Open Market Committee (FOMC)

Open Market Operations

Monetary Policy

U.S. Treasury Securities

Open Market Purchase

Open Market Sale

Reserve Requirement

Federal Funds Market

Federal Funds Rate

Discount Rate

questions and problems

1 Identify the major responsibilities of the Federal Reserve System.

2 What is the difference between the Fed and the U.S. Treasury?

3 Explain how an open market purchase increases the money supply.

4 Explain how an open market sale decreases the money supply.

5 Suppose the Fed raises the required reserve ratio, a move that is normally thought to reduce the money supply. However, banks find themselves with a reserve deficiency after the required reserve ratio is increased and are likely to react by requesting a loan from the Fed. Does this action prevent the money supply from contracting as predicted?

6 Suppose bank *A* borrows reserves from bank *B*. Now that bank *A* has more reserves than previously, will the money supply increase?

7 Explain how a decrease in the required reserve ratio increases the money supply.

8 Suppose you read in the newspaper that all last week the Fed conducted open market purchases and that on Tuesday of last week it lowered the discount rate. What would you say the Fed was trying to do?

9 Explain how a check is cleared through the Federal Reserve System.

10 The Fed can change the discount rate directly and the federal funds rate indirectly. Explain.

11 What does it mean to say the Fed serves as the lender of last resort?

working with numbers and graphs

1 If reserves increase by $2 million and the required reserve ratio is 8 percent, then what is the maximum change in checkable deposits?

2 If reserves increase by $2 million and the required reserves ratio is 10 percent, then what is the maximum change in checkable deposits?

3 If the federal funds rate is 6 percent and the discount rate is 5.1 percent, to whom will a bank be more likely to go for a loan—another bank or the Fed? Explain your answer.

4 Complete the following table:

Federal Reserve Action	Effect on the Money Supply (up or down?)
Lower the discount rate	A
Conduct open market purchase	B
Lower required reserve ratio	C
Raise the discount rate	D
Conduct open market sale	E
Raise the required reserve ratio	F

Money and the Economy

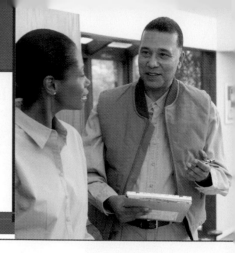

Setting the Scene

An increase or decrease in the money supply can have far-reaching effects in an economy. It can change Real GDP, the price level, the unemployment rate, and the interest rate. In an economics text, we see the effect of a change in the money supply in a diagram; in real life, we see it in the words and actions of everyday people. The following events occurred on different days not long ago.

JANUARY 5

Jan is getting her house remodeled. Today, her contractor told her that the price he pays for many of his supplies has increased quite dramatically and that the remodeling is going to end up costing "a little more." That night, Jan says to her husband, Mike, "I guess that's just the way life is sometimes. Costs go up, so prices go up." "I just wish it hadn't happened right now," Mike replies. "I know," Jan says. "We have so many expenses right now."

MARCH 13

Oliver and Roberta are thinking about buying a house. Mortgage rates are relatively low right now. "I heard someone say that the Fed is meeting next week and that they might lower interest rates more," Oliver says. Roberta asks, "Are you saying we should wait to buy a house?" "Well, maybe," Oliver answers.

JUNE 21

Jim has been out of a job for four months. He's in the kitchen talking to his brother, Sebastian. "I think someone has got to do something about the job situation," Jim says. "There are simply not that many jobs. I've been looking." Sebastian says, "I was watching the news and read a news blurb at the bottom of the TV screen. It said the Fed chairman was worried about the economy and that the Fed was likely to stimulate the economy soon. Maybe that will help." "What does the Fed have in mind?" asks Jim. "I'm not really sure," Sebastian answers.

? Here are some questions to keep in mind as you read this chapter:

• *Jan believes that she will end up paying more for her remodeling because her contractor's costs went up. Odd as it may sound, could Jan be the reason her contractor's costs went up?*

• *If the Fed wants to lower interest rates, are interest rates destined to go down? In short, can the Fed do what it wants to do?*

• *If the Fed does what Sebastian thinks it will do, will his brother, Jim, have a better chance of finding a job?*

See analyzing the scene at the end of this chapter for answers to these questions.

Money and the Price Level

Do changes in the money supply affect the price level in the economy? Classical economists believed so. Their position was based on the equation of exchange and the simple quantity theory of money.

The Equation of Exchange

The **equation of exchange** is an identity that states that the money supply (M) multiplied by velocity (V) must be equal to the price level (P) times Real GDP (Q).

$$MV \equiv PQ$$

The sign $\equiv$ means "must be equal to"; this is an identity. An identity is valid for all values of the variables.

You are familiar with the money supply, the price level, and Real GDP but not velocity. **Velocity** is the average number of times a dollar is spent to buy final goods and services in a year. For example, assume an economy has only five $1 bills. In January, the first of the $1 bills moves from Smith's hands to Jones's hands to buy good X. Then in June, it goes from Jones's hands to Brown's hands to buy good Y. And in December, it goes from Brown's hands to Peterson's hands to buy good Z. Over the course of the year, this dollar bill has changed hands 3 times.

The other dollar bills also change hands during the year. The second dollar bill changes hands 5 times; the third, 6 times; the fourth, 2 times; and the fifth, 7 times. Given this information, we can calculate the number of times a dollar changes hands on average in making a purchase. In this case, the number is 4.6. This number (4.6) is velocity.

In a large economy such as ours, it is impossible to simply count how many times each dollar changes hands; therefore, it is impossible to calculate velocity as in our example. Instead, a different method is used.

First, we calculate GDP; next, we calculate the average money supply; finally, we divide GDP by the average money supply to obtain velocity. For example, if $4,800 billion worth of transactions occur in a year and the average money supply during the year is $800 billion, a dollar must have been used an average of 6 times during the year to purchase goods and services. In symbols, we have

$$V \equiv GDP/M$$

GDP is equal to $P \times Q$, so this identity can be written

$$V \equiv (P \times Q)/M$$

Multiplying both sides by M, we get

$$MV \equiv PQ$$

which is the equation of exchange shown at the beginning of this section. Thus, the equation of exchange is derived from the definition of velocity.

The equation of exchange can be interpreted in different ways:

1. The money supply multiplied by velocity must equal the price level times Real GDP: $M \times V \equiv P \times Q$.

2. The money supply multiplied by velocity must equal GDP: $M \times V \equiv GDP$ (because $P \times Q = GDP$).

3. Total spending or expenditures (measured by MV) must equal the total sales revenues of business firms (measured by PQ): $MV \equiv PQ$.

Equation of Exchange

An identity stating that the money supply times velocity must be equal to the price level times Real GDP.

Velocity

The average number of times a dollar is spent to buy final goods and services in a year.

Can a given money supply, say, $1.2 trillion, end up supporting various GDP levels?

Yes. To illustrate, suppose the money supply is $100 and velocity is 2. It follows that GDP is $200. Now let velocity rise to 3. In turn, GDP rises to $300. In short, a given money supply of $100 is consistent with a GDP of $200 and with a GDP of $300.

The third way of interpreting the equation of exchange is perhaps the most intuitively easy to understand. It simply says that the total expenditures (of buyers) must equal the total sales (of sellers). Consider a simple economy where there is only one buyer and one seller. If the buyer buys a book for $20, then the seller receives $20. Stated differently, the money supply in the example, or $20, times velocity, 1, is equal to the price of the book, $20, times the quantity of the book.

From the Equation of Exchange to the Simple Quantity Theory of Money

The equation of exchange is an identity, not an economic theory. To turn it into a theory, we make some assumptions about the variables in the equation. Many 18th-century classical economists, as well as American economist Irving Fisher (1867–1947) and English economist Alfred Marshall (1842–1924), assumed (1) changes in velocity are so small that for all practical purposes velocity can be assumed to be constant (especially over short periods of time) and (2) Real GDP, or Q, is fixed in the short run. Hence, they turned the equation of exchange, which is simply true by definition, into a theory by assuming that both V and Q are fixed, or constant. With these two assumptions, we have the **simple quantity theory of money**: If V and Q are constant, we would predict that changes in M will bring about *strictly proportional* changes in P. In other words, the simple quantity theory of money predicts that changes in the money supply will bring about strictly proportional changes in the price level.

Simple Quantity Theory of Money

The theory that assumes that velocity (V) and Real GDP (Q) are constant and predicts that changes in the money supply (M) lead to strictly proportional changes in the price level (P).

Exhibit 1 shows the assumptions and predictions of the simple quantity theory. On the left side of the exhibit, the key assumptions of the simple quantity theory are noted: V and Q are constant. Also, $M \times V = P \times Q$ is noted. We use the equal sign ($=$) instead of the identity sign ($\equiv$) because we are speaking about the simple quantity theory and not the equation of exchange. (The $=$ sign here represents "is predicted to be equal"; i.e., given our assumptions, $M \times V$, or MV, is predicted to be equal to $P \times Q$, or PQ.)

Starting with the first row, the money supply is $500, velocity is 4, Real GDP (Q) is 1,000 units, and the price level, or price index, is $2.[1] Therefore, GDP equals $2,000. In the second row, the money supply increases by 100 percent, from $500 to $1,000, and both V and Q are constant, at 4 and 1,000, respectively. The price level moves from $2 to $4. On the right side of the exhibit, we see that a 100 percent increase in M predicts a 100 percent increase in P. Changes in P are predicted to be strictly proportional to changes in M.

exhibit **1**

Assumptions and Predictions of the Simple Quantity Theory of Money

The simple quantity theory of money assumes that both V and Q are constant. (A bar over each indicates this in the exhibit.) The prediction is that changes in M lead to strictly proportional changes in P. (Note: For purposes of this example, think of Q as "so many units of goods" and of P as the "average price paid per unit of these goods.")

M	$\times$	$\bar{V}$	$=$	P	$\times$	$\bar{Q}$	% Change in M	% Change in P
$ 500		4		$2		1,000		
1,000		4		4		1,000	+ 100%	+ 100%
1,500		4		6		1,000	+ 50	+ 50
1,200		4		4.80		1,000	− 20	− 20

[1] You are used to seeing Real GDP expressed as a dollar figure and a price index as a number without a dollar sign in front of it. We have switched things for purposes of this example because it is easier to think of Q as "so many units of goods" and P as "the average price paid per unit of these goods."

In the third row, M increases by 50 percent, and P is predicted to increase by 50 percent. In the fourth row, M decreases by 20 percent, and P is predicted to decrease by 20 percent.

In summary, the simple quantity theory assumes that both V and Q are constant in the short run and therefore predicts that changes in M lead to strictly proportional changes in P.

How well does the simple quantity theory of money predict? That is, do changes in the money supply actually lead to *strictly proportional* changes in the price level? For example, if the money supply goes up by 7 percent, does the price level go up by 7 percent? If the money supply goes down by 4 percent, does the price level go down by 4 percent? The answer is that the strict proportionality between changes in the money supply and the price level does not show up in the data (at least not very often). Generally, though, evidence supports the spirit (or essence) of the simple quantity theory of money—the higher the growth rate in the money supply, the greater the growth rate in the price level. To illustrate, we would expect that a growth rate in the money supply of, say, 40 percent, would generate a greater increase in the price level than, say, a growth rate in the money supply of 4 percent. And generally, this is what we see. For example, countries with more rapid increases in their money supplies often witness more rapid increases in their price levels than do countries that witness less rapid increases in their money supplies.

macro *Theme*

In Chapter 5, we noted that macroeconomists are very interested in what changes the variables P and Q. The simple quantity theory of money seeks to explain what leads to changes in P. The answer is fairly simple: Changes in the money supply lead to changes in the price level.

The Simple Quantity Theory of Money in an *AD-AS* Framework

You are familiar with the *AD-AS* framework from earlier chapters. In this section, we analyze the simple quantity theory of money in this framework.

THE *AD* CURVE IN THE SIMPLE QUANTITY THEORY OF MONEY The simple quantity theory of money builds on the equation of exchange. Recall that one way of interpreting the equation of exchange is that the total expenditures of buyers (measured by MV) must equal the total sales of sellers (measured by PQ). Thus, we are saying that MV is the total expenditures of buyers and PQ is the total sales of sellers. For now, we concentrate on MV as the total expenditures of buyers:

$$MV = \text{Total expenditures}$$

In an earlier chapter, total expenditures (TE) is defined as the sum of the expenditures made by the four sectors of the economy. In other words,

$$TE = C + I + G + (EX - IM)$$

Because $MV = TE$,

$$MV = C + I + G + (EX - IM)$$

Now recall that at a given price level, anything that changes $C, I, G, EX,$ or IM changes aggregate demand and thus shifts the aggregate demand (AD) curve. But MV equals $C + I + G + (EX - IM)$, so it follows that *a change in the money supply (M) or a change in velocity (V) will change aggregate demand and therefore lead to a shift in the AD curve.* Another way to say this is that aggregate demand depends on *both* the money supply and velocity.

Specifically, an increase in the money supply will increase aggregate demand and shift the AD curve to the right. A decrease in the money supply will decrease aggregate

© BETTMANN/CORBIS

economics 24/7

THE CALIFORNIA GOLD RUSH, OR AN APPLE FOR $72

Soon there was too much money in California and too little of everything else.

—J. S. Holiday, author of *The World Rushed In*

The only peacetime rise [in prices] comparable in total magnitude [to the 40 to 50 percent in prices from 1897 to 1914] followed the California gold discoveries in the early 1850s . . .

—Milton Friedman and Anna Schwartz, *A Monetary History of the United States, 1867–1960*

John Sutter was a Swiss immigrant who arrived in California in 1839. James Marshall, a carpenter, was building a sawmill for Sutter. On the chilly morning of January 24, 1848, Marshall was busy at work when something glistening caught his eye. He reached down and picked up the object. Marshall said to the workers he had hired, "Boys, by God I believe I have found a gold mine." Marshall later wrote, "I reached my hand down and picked it up; it made my heart thump, for I was certain it was gold. The piece was about half the size and shape of a pea. Then I saw another."

In time, Marshall and his workers came across more gold, and before long, people from all across the United States, and many other countries, headed to California. The California gold rush had begun.

The California gold rush, which resulted in an increase in the amount of money in circulation, provides an illustration of

how a fairly dramatic increase in the money supply can affect prices. As more gold was mined and the supply of money increased, prices began to rise. There was a general rise in prices across the country, but the earliest and most dramatic increases in prices occurred in and near the areas where gold was discovered. Near the gold mines, the prices of food and clothing sharply increased. For example, while a loaf of bread sold for 4 cents in New York (equivalent to 72 cents today), near the mines, the price was 75 cents (the equivalent of $13.50 today). Eggs sold for about $2 each (the equivalent of $36 today), apples for $4 (the equivalent of $72 today), a butcher's knife for $30 (the equivalent of $540 today), and boots went for $100 a pair (the equivalent of $1,800 today).

In San Francisco, land prices rose dramatically because of the city's relative closeness to the mines. Real estate that cost $16 (the equivalent of $288 today) before gold was discovered jumped to $45,000 (the equivalent of $810,000 today) in 18 months.

The sharp rise in prices that followed the California gold discoveries followed other gold discoveries too. For example, the gold stock of the world is estimated to have doubled from 1890 to 1914, due both to discoveries (in South Africa, Alaska, and Colorado) and to improved methods of mining and refining gold. During this period, world prices increased too.

demand and shift the *AD* curve to the left. An increase in velocity will increase aggregate demand and shift the *AD* curve to the right. A decrease in velocity will decrease aggregate demand and shift the *AD* curve to the left. But *in the simple quantity theory of money, velocity is assumed to be constant.* Thus, we are left with only changes in the money supply being able to shift the *AD* curve.

The *AD* curve for the simple quantity theory of money is shown in Exhibit 2(a). The *M, V* in parentheses next to the curve is a reminder of what factors can shift the *AD* curve. The bar over *V* (for velocity) indicates that velocity is assumed to be constant.

THE *AS* CURVE IN THE SIMPLE QUANTITY THEORY OF MONEY In the simple quantity theory of money, the level of Real GDP is assumed to be constant in the short run. Exhibit 2(b) shows Real GDP fixed at Q_1. The *AS* curve is vertical at this level of Real GDP.

> **Q&A**
>
> **In an earlier chapter, we learned that if AD rises, both P and Q will rise in the short run. Does that happen here too?**
>
> *In earlier chapters, an increase in AD led to a rise in both the price level (P) and Real GDP (Q) in the short run because the SRAS curve was upward sloping. This is not the case when dealing with the simple quantity theory of money, as we explain next.*

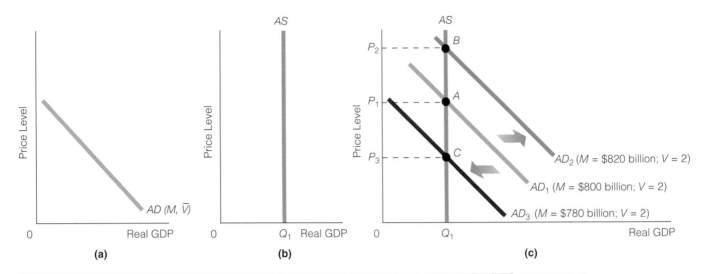

(a)   (b)   (c)

AD AND AS IN THE SIMPLE QUANTITY THEORY OF MONEY Exhibit 2(c) shows both the *AD* and *AS* curves in the simple quantity theory of money. Suppose AD_1 is initially operational. In the exhibit, AD_1 is based on a money supply of $800 billion and a velocity of 2. The price level is P_1.

Now suppose we increase the money supply to $820 billion. Velocity remains constant at 2. According to the simple quantity theory of money, the price level will increase. We see that it does. The increase in the money supply shifts the *AD* curve from AD_1 to AD_2 and pushes up the price level from P_1 to P_2.

Suppose that instead of increasing the money supply, we decrease it to $780 billion. Again, velocity remains constant at 2. According to the simple quantity theory of money, the price level will decrease. We see that it does. The decrease in the money supply shifts the *AD* curve from AD_1 to AD_3 and pushes down the price level from P_1 to P_3.

The Simple Quantity Theory of Money in the *AD-AS* Framework

(a) In the simple quantity theory of money, the *AD* curve is downward sloping. Velocity is assumed to be constant, so changes in the money supply will change aggregate demand. (b) In the simple quantity theory of money, Real GDP is fixed in the short run. Thus, the *AS* curve is vertical. (c) In the simple quantity theory of money, an increase in the money supply will shift the *AD* curve rightward and increase the price level. A decrease in the money supply will shift the *AD* curve leftward and decrease the price level.

Dropping the Assumptions That *V* and *Q* Are Constant

If we drop the assumptions that velocity (*V*) and Real GDP (*Q*) are constant, we have a more general theory of the factors that cause changes in the price level. Stated differently, changes in the price level depend on three variables:

1. money supply
2. velocity
3. Real GDP

To see this, let's again start with the equation of exchange.

$$M \times V \equiv P \times Q \qquad (1)$$

If the equation of exchange holds, it follows that:

$$P \equiv (M \times V)/Q \qquad (2)$$

Looking at equation 2, we can see that the money supply, velocity, and Real GDP determine the price level. In other words, the price level depends on the money supply, velocity, and Real GDP.

What kinds of changes in *M, V,* and *Q* will bring about inflation (an increase in the price level)? Obviously, *ceteris paribus,* an increase in *M* or *V* or a decrease in *Q* will cause

Q&A   *If the AS curve is vertical, then an increase in the money supply will shift the AD curve rightward, but this won't change Real GDP, although it will raise the price level, P. Is this correct?*

Yes, that is correct.

the price level to rise. For example, if velocity rises, *ceteris paribus,* the price level will rise. In other words, an increase in velocity is inflationary, *ceteris paribus.*

Inflationary Tendencies: $M\uparrow$, $V\uparrow$, $Q\downarrow$

What will bring about deflation (a decrease in the price level)? Obviously, *ceteris paribus,* a decrease in M or V or an increase in Q will cause the price level to fall. For example, if the money supply declines, *ceteris paribus,* the price level will drop. In other words, a decrease in the money supply is deflationary, *ceteris paribus.*

Deflationary Tendencies: $M\downarrow$, $V\downarrow$, $Q\uparrow$

SELF-TEST

(Answers to Self-Test questions are in the Self-Test Appendix.)

1. If M times V increases, why does P times Q have to rise?

2. What is the difference between the equation of exchange and the simple quantity theory of money?

3. Predict what will happen to the AD curve as a result of each of the following:
    a. The money supply rises.
    b. Velocity falls.
    c. The money supply rises by a greater percentage than velocity falls.
    d. The money supply falls.

Monetarism

Economists who call themselves *monetarists* have not been content to rely on the simple quantity theory of money. They *do not hold* that velocity is constant, nor do they hold that output is constant. Monetarist views on the money supply, velocity, aggregate demand, and aggregate supply are discussed in this section.

Monetarist Views

We begin with a brief explanation of the four positions held by monetarists. Then, we discuss how, based on these positions, monetarists view the economy.

VELOCITY CHANGES IN A PREDICTABLE WAY In the simple quantity theory of money, velocity is assumed to be constant. From this, it follows that any changes in aggregate demand are brought about by changes in the money supply only.

Monetarists do not assume velocity is constant. Instead, they assume that velocity can and does change. It is important to note, however, that monetarists believe velocity changes in a predictable way. Velocity does not change randomly, but rather, it changes in a way that can be understood and predicted. Monetarists hold that velocity is a function of certain variables—the interest rate, the expected inflation rate, the frequency with which employees receive paychecks, and more—and that changes in it can be predicted.

AGGREGATE DEMAND DEPENDS ON THE MONEY SUPPLY AND ON VELOCITY Earlier, we showed that total expenditures in the economy (TE) equal MV. To better understand the economy, some economists—such as Keynesians—focus on the spending components of TE, $C, I, G, EX,$ and IM. Other economists—such as monetarists—focus on the money supply (M) and velocity (V). For example, Keynesians often argue that changes in $C, I, G, EX,$ or IM can change aggregate demand, whereas monetarists often argue that M and V can change aggregate demand.

THE *SRAS* CURVE IS UPWARD SLOPING In the simple quantity theory of money, the level of Real GDP (Q) is assumed to be constant in the short run. So the aggregate supply curve is vertical, as shown in Exhibit 2. According to monetarists, Real GDP may change in the short run. It follows that monetarists believe that the *SRAS* curve is upward sloping.

THE ECONOMY IS SELF-REGULATING (PRICES AND WAGES ARE FLEXIBLE) Monetarists believe that prices and wages are flexible. It follows that monetarists believe the economy is self-regulating; it can move itself out of a recessionary or an inflationary gap and into long-run equilibrium producing Natural Real GDP.

> **macro**
> *Theme*   Recall that some economists believe the economy is self-regulating, and other economists believe the economy is inherently unstable. For example, both classical economists and monetarists believe the economy is inherently stable (or self-regulating), whereas Keynesians believe the economy can be inherently unstable (not self-regulating).

Monetarism and *AD-AS*

As we mentioned, monetarists tend to stress velocity and the money supply when discussing how the economy works. We describe the monetarist view using the *AD-AS* framework. Exhibit 3 helps to explain some of the highlights of monetarism. Each of the four parts (a)–(d) is considered separately.

PART (A) In (a), the economy is initially in long-run equilibrium producing Natural Real GDP (Q_N) at price level P_1. Monetarists believe that changes in the money supply will change aggregate demand. For example, suppose the money supply rises from $800 billion to $820 billion. If velocity is constant, the *AD* curve shifts to the right, from AD_1 to AD_2 in the exhibit. As a result, Real GDP rises to Q_1 and the price level rises to P_2. And of course, if Real GDP rises, the unemployment rate falls, *ceteris paribus*.

According to monetarists, the economy is in an inflationary gap at Q_1. Monetarists believe in a self-regulating economy. Thus, because the unemployment rate is less than the natural unemployment rate in an inflationary gap, soon wages will be bid up. This will cause the *SRAS* curve to shift leftward, from $SRAS_1$ to $SRAS_2$. The economy will return to long-run equilibrium, producing the same level of Real GDP as it did originally (Q_N) but at a higher price level.

We can separate what monetarists predict will happen to the economy in the short run due to an increase in the money supply from what they predict will happen in the long run. In the short run, Real GDP will rise and the unemployment rate will fall. In the long run, Real GDP will return to its natural level, as will the unemployment rate, and the price level will be higher.

PART (B) In (b), the economy is initially in long-run equilibrium, producing Natural Real GDP (Q_N) at price level P_1. A decrease in the money supply, holding velocity constant, will shift the *AD* curve to the left, from AD_1 to AD_2. This will reduce Real GDP to Q_1 and reduce the price level to P_2. Because Real GDP has fallen, the unemployment rate will rise.

According to monetarists, the economy in (b) is in a recessionary gap. Can the economy get itself out of a recessionary gap? Monetarists think so; they believe the economy is self-regulating. In time, wages will fall, the *SRAS* curve will shift to the right, and the economy will be back in long-run equilibrium producing Q_N—albeit at a lower price level.

(c)

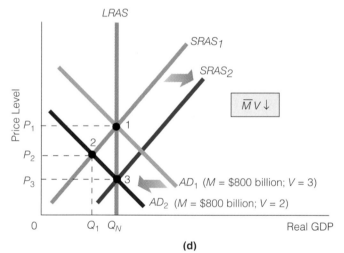

(d)

exhibit **3**

Monetarism in an *AD-AS* Framework

According to monetarists, changes in the money supply and velocity can change aggregate demand. In (a), an increase in the money supply shifts the *AD* curve to the right and raises Real GDP and the price level. Monetarists believe the economy is self-regulating; in time it moves back to its Natural Real GDP level at a higher price level. The same self-regulating properties are present in (b)–(d).

Again, we separate the short-run and long-run effects of a decrease in the money supply according to monetarists. In the short run, Real GDP will fall and the unemployment rate will rise. In the long run, Real GDP will return to its natural level, as will the unemployment rate, and the price level will be lower.

PART (C) Again, we start with the economy in long-run equilibrium. Now, instead of changing the money supply, we change velocity. An increase in velocity causes the *AD* curve to shift to the right, from AD_1 to AD_2. As a result, Real GDP rises, as does the price level. The unemployment rate falls as Real GDP rises.

According to monetarists, the economy is in an inflationary gap. In time, it will move back to long-run equilibrium. So in the short run, an increase in velocity raises Real GDP and lowers the unemployment rate. In the long run, Real GDP returns to its natural level, as does the unemployment rate, and the price level is higher.

PART (D) We start with the economy in long-run equilibrium. A decrease in velocity causes the *AD* curve to shift to the left, from AD_1 to AD_2. As a result, Real GDP falls, as does the price level. The unemployment rate rises as Real GDP falls.

According to monetarists, the economy is in a recessionary gap. In time, it will move back to long-run equilibrium. So in the short run, a decrease in velocity lowers

Real GDP and increases the unemployment rate. In the long run, Real GDP returns to its natural level, as does the unemployment rate, and the price level is lower.

The Monetarist View of the Economy

Based on our diagrammatic exposition of monetarism so far, we know the following about monetarists:

1. Monetarists believe the economy is self-regulating.

2. Monetarists believe changes in velocity and the money supply can change aggregate demand.

3. Monetarists believe changes in velocity and the money supply will change the price level and Real GDP in the short run but only the price level in the long run.

We need to make one other important point with respect to monetarists. But first, consider this question: Can a change in velocity offset a change in the money supply? To illustrate, suppose velocity falls and the money supply rises. By itself, a decrease in velocity will shift the *AD* curve to the left. And by itself, an increase in the money supply will shift the *AD* curve to the right. Can the decline in velocity shift the *AD* curve to the left by the same amount as the increase in the money supply shifts the *AD* curve to the right? This is, of course, possible. If it happens, then a change in the money supply would have no effect on Real GDP and the price level (in the short run) and on the price level (in the long run). In other words, we would have to conclude that changes in monetary policy may be ineffective at changing Real GDP and the price level.

Does this condition—a change in velocity completely offsetting a change in the money supply—occur often? Monetarists generally think not because they believe: (1) Velocity does not change very much from one period to the next; that is, it is relatively stable. (2) Changes in velocity are predictable, as mentioned earlier. In other words, monetarists believe velocity is relatively stable and predictable.

So in the monetarist view of the economy, changes in velocity are not likely to offset changes in the money supply. This means that *changes in the money supply will largely determine changes in aggregate demand and, therefore, changes in Real GDP and the price level.* For all practical purposes, an increase in the money supply will raise aggregate demand, increase both Real GDP and the price level in the short run, and increase the price level in the long run. A decrease in the money supply will lower aggregate demand, decrease both Real GDP and the price level in the short run, and decrease the price level in the long run.

SELF-TEST

1. What do monetarists predict will happen in the short run and in the long run as a result of each of the following (in each case, assume the economy is currently in long-run equilibrium)?
   a. Velocity rises.
   b. Velocity falls.
   c. The money supply rises.
   d. The money supply falls.

2. Can a change in velocity offset a change in the money supply (on aggregate demand)? Explain your answer.

Inflation

In everyday usage, the word *inflation* refers to any increase in the price level. Economists, though, like to differentiate between two types of increases in the price level: a one-shot increase and a continued increase. These two types of inflation are discussed in this section.

One-Shot Inflation

One-Shot Inflation
A one-time increase in the price level. An increase in the price level that does not continue.

One-shot inflation is exactly what it sounds like: It is a one-shot, or one-time, increase in the price level. Suppose the CPI for years 1 to 5 is as follows:

Year	CPI
1	100
2	110
3	110
4	110
5	110

Notice that the price level is higher in year 2 than in year 1, but after year 2, it does not change. In other words, it takes a "one-shot" jump in year 2 and then stabilizes. This is an example of one-shot inflation. One-shot inflation can originate on either the demand side or the supply side of the economy.

ONE-SHOT INFLATION: DEMAND-SIDE INDUCED In Exhibit 4(a), the economy is initially in long-run equilibrium at point 1. Suppose the aggregate demand curve shifts rightward from AD_1 to AD_2. As this happens, the economy moves to point 2, where the price level is P_2. At point 2 in Exhibit 4(b), the Real GDP the economy is producing (Q_2) is greater than Natural Real GDP. This means that the unemployment rate that exists in the economy is lower than the natural unemployment rate. Consequently, as old wage contracts expire, workers are paid higher wage rates because unemployment is relatively low. As wage rates rise, the $SRAS$ curve shifts leftward from $SRAS_1$ to $SRAS_2$. The long-run equilibrium position is at point 3. The price level and Real GDP at each of the three points are as follows:

Point	Price Level	Real GDP
1 (start)	P_1	$Q_1 = Q_N$
2	P_2	Q_2
3 (end)	P_3	$Q_1 = Q_N$

Notice that at point 3 the economy is at a higher price level than at point 1 but at the same Real GDP level.

Because the price level goes from P_1 to P_2 to P_3, you may think we have more than a one-shot increase in the price level. But because the price level stabilizes (at P_3), we cannot characterize it as continually rising. So the change in the price level is representative of one-shot inflation.

ONE-SHOT INFLATION: SUPPLY-SIDE INDUCED In Exhibit 5(a), the economy is initially in long-run equilibrium at point 1. Suppose the short-run aggregate supply curve shifts leftward from $SRAS_1$ to $SRAS_2$, say, because oil prices increase. As this happens, the economy moves to point 2, where the price level is P_2.

At point 2 in Exhibit 5(b), the Real GDP the economy is producing (Q_2) is less than Natural Real GDP. This means that the unemployment rate that exists in the economy is greater than the natural unemployment rate. Consequently, as old wage contracts expire, workers are paid lower wage rates because unemployment is relatively high. As wage rates fall, the short-run aggregate supply curve shifts rightward from $SRAS_2$ to $SRAS_1$. The long-run equilibrium position is at point 1 again. (If wage rates are somewhat inflex-

Q&A

Is it correct to say that one-shot inflation can originate on either the demand side or supply side of the economy?

Yes, that is a correct statement.

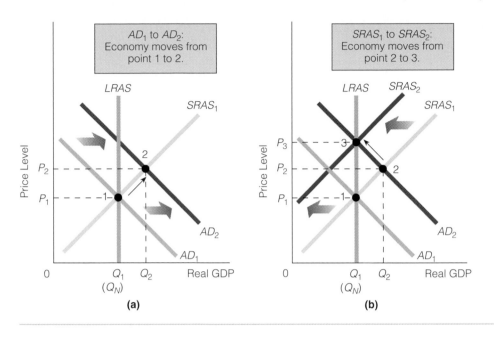

exhibit **4**

One-Shot Inflation: Demand-Side Induced

(a) The aggregate demand curve shifts rightward from AD_1 to AD_2. As a result, the price level increases from P_1 to P_2; the economy moves from point 1 to point 2. (b) Because the Real GDP the economy produces (Q_2) is greater than Natural Real GDP, the unemployment rate that exists is less than the natural unemployment rate. Wage rates rise, and the short-run aggregate supply curve shifts leftward from $SRAS_1$ to $SRAS_2$. Long-run equilibrium is at point 3.

ible, it may take a long time to move from point 2 back to point 1.) The price level and Real GDP at each of the three points are as follows:

Point	Price Level	Real GDP
1 (start)	P_1	$Q_1 = Q_N$
2	P_2	Q_2
1 (end)	P_1	$Q_1 = Q_N$

Because the price level initially increased from P_1 to P_2, this case is descriptive of one-shot inflation.

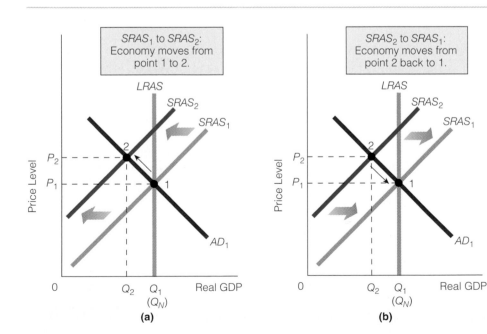

exhibit **5**

One-Shot Inflation: Supply-Side Induced

(a) The short-run aggregate supply curve shifts leftward from $SRAS_1$ to $SRAS_2$. As a result, the price level increases from P_1 to P_2; the economy moves from point 1 to point 2. (b) Because the Real GDP the economy produces (Q_2) is less than Natural Real GDP, the unemployment rate that exists is greater than the natural unemployment rate. Some economists argue that when this happens, wage rates will fall and the short-run aggregate supply curve will shift rightward from $SRAS_2$ (back to $SRAS_1$). Long-run equilibrium is at point 1.

CONFUSING DEMAND-INDUCED AND SUPPLY-INDUCED ONE-SHOT INFLATION Demand-induced and supply-induced one-shot inflation are easy to confuse.[2] To illustrate, suppose the Federal Reserve System increases the money supply. Because there is more money in the economy, there can be greater total spending at any given price level. Consequently, the *AD* curve shifts rightward.

Next, prices begin to rise. Soon after, wage rates begin to rise (because the economy is in an inflationary gap). Many employers, perhaps unaware that the money supply has increased, certainly are aware that they are paying their employees higher wages. Thus, it is possible that the employers will think the higher price level is due to higher wage rates and not to the increased money supply that preceded the higher wage rates. But they would be wrong. What may look like a supply-induced rise in the price level is really a demand-induced rise in the price level.

We can tell this same story in terms of the diagrams in Exhibit 4. In (a), the *AD* curve shifts rightward because, as we said, the money supply increases. Employers, however, are unaware of what has happened in part (a). What they see is part (b). They end up paying higher wage rates to their employees, and the *SRAS* curve shifts leftward. Unaware that the *AD* curve shifted rightward in (a) but aware that the *SRAS* curve shifted leftward in (b), the employers mistakenly conclude that the rise in the price level originated with a supply-side factor (higher wage rates) and not with a demand-side factor (an increase in the money supply).

> *Thinking like*
> **AN ECONOMIST**   *People tend to believe that what they see with their own eyes or experience in their daily lives causes the effects they notice. Witness, in our last example, employers' mistaken belief that the stimulus for the rise in the price level was a rise in wage rates (which they had experienced firsthand) and not an increase in the money supply (which they probably did not know had occurred). But the economist knows that the cause of a phenomenon may be far removed from our personal orbit. This awareness is part of the economic way of thinking.*

Continued Inflation

Suppose the CPI for years 1 to 5 is as follows:

Year	CPI
1	100
2	110
3	120
4	130
5	140

Notice that the CPI goes from 100 to 110, then from 110 to 120, and so on. Each year the CPI is higher than the year before. There is a continued increase in the price level. This is an example of **continued inflation**.

Continued Inflation
A continued increase in the price level.

FROM ONE-SHOT INFLATION TO CONTINUED INFLATION What can turn one-shot inflation into continued inflation? The answer is continued increases in aggregate demand. (Later, we will ask: But what leads to "continued increases in aggregate demand"?) The process is illustrated in Exhibit 6. (The diagram looks scary, but it isn't when you take it one step at a time.)

Beginning at point 1 in Exhibit 6(a), the aggregate demand curve shifts rightward from AD_1 to AD_2. The economy moves from point 1 to point 2. At point 2, the unemployment rate that exists in the economy is less than the natural unemployment rate. As a result, wage rates rise and cause the short-run aggregate supply curve to shift leftward from $SRAS_1$ to $SRAS_2$. The economy moves from point 2 to point 3. At point 3, the economy is in long-run equilibrium.

---

[2]Sometimes the terms *demand-side inflation* and *supply-side inflation* are used.

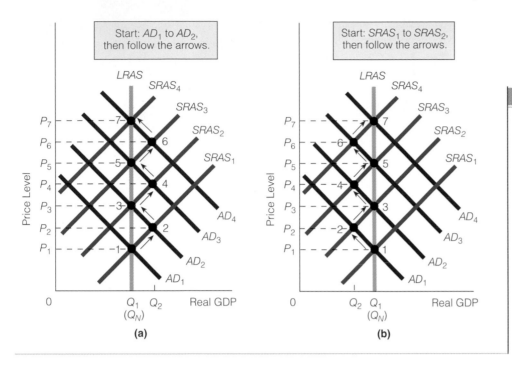

exhibit **6**

Changing One-Shot Inflation into Continued Inflation

(a) The aggregate demand curve shifts rightward from AD_1 to AD_2. The economy initially moves from point 1 to point 2 and finally to point 3. Continued increases in the price level are brought about through continued increases in aggregate demand.
(b) The short-run aggregate supply curve shifts leftward from $SRAS_1$ to $SRAS_2$. The economy initially moves from point 1 to point 2. The economy will return to point 1 unless there is an increase in aggregate demand. We see here, as in (a), that continued increases in the price level are brought about through continued increases in aggregate demand.

Suppose that at point 3 the economy experiences *another* rightward shift in the aggregate demand curve (to AD_3). The process repeats itself, and the economy moves from point 3 to point 4 to point 5. Still *another* rightward shift in the aggregate demand curve moves the economy from point 5 to point 6 to point 7. We have stopped at point 7, but we could have continued. Notice that the result of this process is a *continually rising price level*—from P_1 to P_7 and beyond. We conclude that continued increases in aggregate demand cause continued inflation.

Now let's look at continued inflation from the supply side of the economy. Beginning at point 1 in Exhibit 6(b), the short-run aggregate supply curve shifts leftward from $SRAS_1$ to $SRAS_2$. The economy moves from point 1 to point 2. At point 2, the unemployment rate that exists in the economy is greater than the natural unemployment rate. According to some economists, there is a natural tendency for wage rates to fall and the $SRAS$ curve to shift rightward, moving the economy back to point 1.

This natural tendency of the economy to return to point 1 will be offset, however, if the aggregate demand curve shifts rightward. Then, instead of moving from point 2 back to point 1, the economy moves from point 2 to point 3. At point 3, the economy is in long-run equilibrium, and a higher price level exists than existed at point 2.

Suppose the economy experiences another leftward shift in the aggregate supply curve (to $SRAS_3$). The economy moves from point 3 to point 4 and would naturally return to point 3 unless the aggregate demand curve shifts rightward. If the latter occurs, the economy moves to point 5. The same process moves the economy from point 5 to point 6 to point 7, where we have decided to stop. Notice that this process results in a continually rising price level—from P_1 to P_7 and beyond. Again, we conclude that *continued increases in aggregate demand cause continued inflation*.

CAN CONTINUED DECLINES IN *SRAS* CAUSE CONTINUED INFLATION? A natural question might be: Can continued declines in *SRAS* cause continued inflation? For example, suppose a labor union continually asks for and receives higher wages. As wages continually increase, the *SRAS* curve will continually shift leftward. Continued leftward shifts in *SRAS* will lead to a continually rising price level. Couldn't this happen? The answer is, it could

© NAJLAH FEANNY/CORBIS

economics 24/7

GRADE INFLATION: IT'S ALL RELATIVE

Inflation can sometimes be deceptive. To illustrate, suppose Jones produces and sells motorcycles. The average price for one of his motorcycles is $10,000. Unbeknownst to Jones, the Fed increases the money supply. Months pass, and then one day, Jones notices that the demand for his motorcycles has increased. Jones raises the prices of his motorcycles and earns a higher dollar income.

Jones is excited about earning more income. But soon he realizes that the prices of many of the things he buys have increased too. Food, clothing, and housing prices have all gone up. Jones is earning a higher dollar income, but he is also paying higher prices. In relative terms, Jones's financial position may be the same as it was before the price of motorcycles increased.

Now let's consider grade inflation. Beginning in the 1960s, the average GPA at most colleges and universities across the country began to rise. Whereas professors once gave out the full range of grades—A, B, C, D, and F—today, many professors give only As and Bs and a few Cs. It's been said that the "Gentleman's C," once a mainstay on many college campuses, has been replaced by the "Gentleperson's B."

Grade inflation can deceive you, just as general price inflation deceived Jones. To illustrate, suppose you get higher grades (without studying more or working harder). Your average grade goes from, say, C+ to B, and you believe you have an advantage over other college and university students. You reason that with higher grades, you will have a better chance of getting a good job or of getting into graduate school.

But this is true only if your grades go up *and no one else's do*. In other words, your relative position must improve. But grade inflation at thousands of colleges and universities across the country prevents this from happening. You get higher grades, but so does everyone else. Your GPA increases from, say, 2.90 to 3.60, but other students' GPAs also increase.

So do higher grades for you necessarily mean it will be easier for you to compete with others for a job or for admission to graduate school? No, not as long as other students are getting higher grades too. In essence, grade inflation, like general price inflation, is deceptive. When there is price inflation, you may initially think your financial position has improved because you are earning more for what you sell. But then you realize that you have to pay more for the things you buy. When there is grade inflation, you may initially think you have an advantage over other students because you are receiving higher grades. But then you learn that everyone else is receiving higher grades too. Your relative position may be the same as it was before grade inflation boosted your grades.

happen, but it isn't likely to happen. Remember, every time workers ask for and receive higher wages—shifting the *SRAS* curve leftward—Real GDP declines. And not as many workers are needed to produce a lower Real GDP as are needed to produce a higher Real GDP, so some of the workers will lose their jobs. It is doubtful labor unions would adopt a policy that put increasingly more of their members out of work.

Let's consider another argument against declines in *SRAS* causing continued inflation. If you go back to, say, 1960 and check both the CPI and the Real GDP level, you will find that the CPI today is higher than it was in 1960 and Real GDP is higher too. The higher price level means that since 1960, we have experienced continued inflation in the United States. But this continued inflation has accompanied (generally) a rising Real GDP. If the continued inflation of the past few decades had been caused by continued declines in *SRAS,* we wouldn't have had a rising Real GDP. We would have had a falling Real GDP (as *SRAS* declines, the price level rises and Real GDP falls). In short, the continued inflation in the United States had to be caused by continued increases in *AD* and not by continued decreases in *SRAS*.

THE BIG QUESTION: WHAT CAUSES CONTINUED INCREASES IN AGGREGATE DEMAND? So far, we know that continued increases in aggregate demand cause continued inflation. *But what causes continued increases in aggregate demand?*

To answer this question, recall that at a given price level, anything that increases total expenditures increases aggregate demand and shifts the *AD* curve to the right. With this in mind, consider an increase in the money supply. If there is more money in the economy, there can be greater total expenditures at a given price level. Consequently, aggregate demand increases and the *AD* curve shifts rightward.

Economists are widely agreed that the only factor that can change continually in such a way as to bring about continued increases in aggregate demand is the money supply. Specifically, continued increases in the money supply lead to continued increases in aggregate demand, which generate continued inflation.

Continued increases in the money supply → Continued increases in aggregate demand → Continued inflation

It is important to realize that the money supply is the *only* factor that can continually increase without causing a reduction in one of the four components of total expenditures—that is, consumption, investment, government purchases, or net exports.

We mention this because someone might ask: Can't government purchases continually increase and so cause continued inflation? There are two reasons this is unlikely to occur. First, there are both real and political limits beyond which government purchases cannot go. The real upper limit is 100 percent of GDP. We do not know what the political upper limit is, but it is likely to be less than 100 percent of GDP. In either case, once the limit is reached, government purchases can no longer increase.

Second, some economists argue that government purchases that are not financed with new money may crowd out one of the other expenditure components. (See the discussion of crowding out in an earlier chapter.) Thus, increases in government purchases are not guaranteed to raise total expenditures because if government purchases rise, consumption, say, may fall to the degree that government purchases have increased. For example, for every additional dollar government spends on public education, households may spend $1 less on private education.

The emphasis on the money supply as the only factor that can continue to increase and thus cause continued inflation has led most economists to agree with Nobel Laureate Milton Friedman that "inflation is always and everywhere a monetary phenomenon."

SELF-TEST

1. The prices of houses, cars, and television sets have increased. Has there been inflation?

2. Is continued inflation likely to be supply-side induced? Explain your answer.

3. What type of inflation is Milton Friedman referring to when he says that "inflation is always and everywhere a monetary phenomenon"?

Money and Interest Rates

Before we discuss how a change in the money supply affects interest rates, we review some of the ways changes in the money supply affect different economic variables.

What Economic Variables Are Affected by a Change in the Money Supply?

Throughout this text, we have talked about money and have shown how changes in the money supply affect different economic variables. Let's review some of these effects.

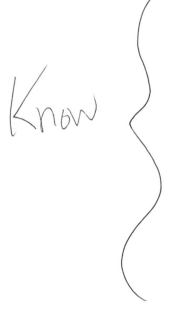

1. **Money and the supply of loans.** The last chapter discussed the actions of the Fed that change the money supply. For example, when the Fed undertakes an open market purchase, the money supply increases and reserves in the banking system increase. With greater reserves, banks can extend more loans. In other words, as a result of the Fed's conducting an open market purchase, the supply of loans rises. Similarly, when the Fed conducts an open market sale, the supply of loans decreases.

2. **Money and Real GDP.** This chapter shows how a change in the money supply can change aggregate demand and, therefore, change the price level and Real GDP in the short run. For example, look back at Exhibit 3(a). The economy starts at point 1, producing Q_N. An increase in the money supply shifts the AD curve rightward, from AD_1 to AD_2. In the short run, the economy moves to point 2 and produces a higher level of Real GDP (Q_1). Similarly, in the short run, a decrease in the money supply produces a lower level of Real GDP (see Exhibit 3(b)).

3. **Money and the price level.** This chapter also shows how a change in the money supply can change the price level. Again, look back at Exhibit 3(a). Initially, at point 1, the price level is P_1. An increase in the money supply shifts the AD curve rightward, from AD_1 to AD_2. In the short run, the price level in the economy moves from P_1 to P_2. In the long run, the economy is at point 3 and the price level is P_3. Exhibit 3(b) shows how a decrease in the money supply affects the price level.

Thus, we know that changes in the money supply affect (1) the supply of loans, (2) Real GDP, and (3) the price level. Is there anything else the money supply can affect? Many economists say that because the money supply affects the price level, it also affects the *expected inflation rate.*

The expected inflation rate is the inflation rate that you expect. For example, your expected inflation rate—the inflation rate you expect will be realized over the next year—may be 5 percent, 6 percent, or a different rate. Changes in the money supply affect the expected inflation rate—either directly or indirectly. We know from working with the equation of exchange that the greater the increase in the money supply, the greater the rise in the price level. And we would expect that the greater the rise in the price level, the higher the expected inflation rate, *ceteris paribus.* For example, we would predict that a money supply growth rate of, say, 10 percent a year generates a greater actual inflation rate, and a larger expected inflation rate, than a money supply growth rate of 2 percent a year.

To summarize: Changes in the money supply (or changes in the rate of growth of the money supply) can affect

1. the supply of loans,

2. Real GDP,

3. the price level, and

4. the expected inflation rate.

The Money Supply, the Loanable Funds Market, and Interest Rates

The loanable funds market is shown in Exhibit 7(a). The demand for loanable funds is downward sloping, indicating that borrowers will borrow more funds as the interest rate declines. The supply of loanable funds is upward sloping, indicating that lenders will lend more funds as the interest rate rises. The equilibrium interest rate, i_1 percent in the exhibit, is determined through the forces of supply and demand. If there is a surplus of loanable funds, the interest rate falls; if there is a shortage of loanable funds, the interest rate rises.

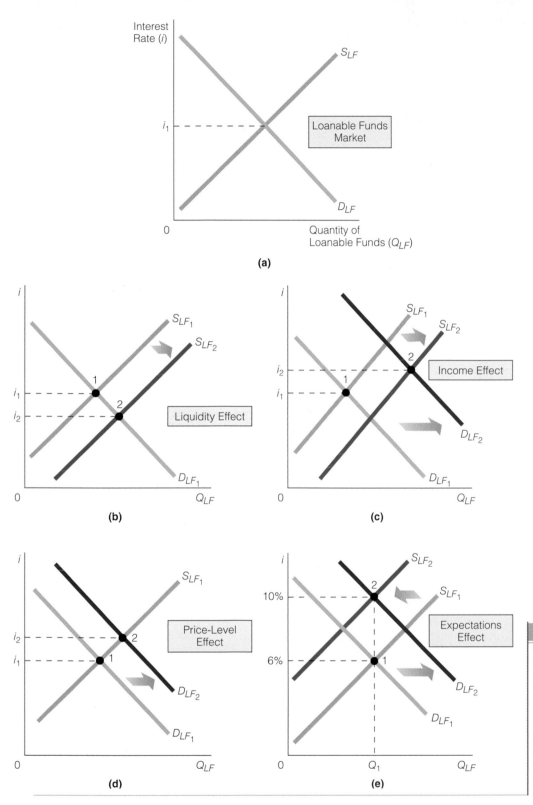

(a)

(b)

(c)

(d)

(e)

exhibit **7**

The Interest Rate and the Loanable Funds Market

The loanable funds market is shown in part (a). The demand for loanable funds is downward-sloping; the supply of loanable funds is upward-sloping. Part (b) shows the liquidity effect, part (c) shows the income effect, part (d) shows the price-level effect, and part (e) shows the expectations effect.

Anything that affects either the supply of loanable funds or the demand for loanable funds will obviously affect the interest rate. All four of the factors that are affected by changes in the money supply—the supply of loans, Real GDP, the price level, and the expected inflation rate—affect either the supply of or demand for loanable funds.

Liquidity Effect

The change in the interest rate due to a change in the supply of loanable funds.

THE SUPPLY OF LOANS A Fed open market purchase increases reserves in the banking system and therefore increases the supply of loanable funds. As a result, the interest rate declines (see Exhibit 7(b)). This change in the interest rate due to a change in the supply of loanable funds is called the **liquidity effect**.

REAL GDP A change in Real GDP affects both the supply of and demand for loanable funds. To understand this, you need to realize that there is (1) a link between supplying bonds and demanding loanable funds and (2) a link between demanding bonds and supplying loanable funds. In other words,

To *supply bonds* is to *demand loanable funds*.
To *demand bonds* is to *supply loanable funds*.

To explain, let's suppose corporations are the only economic actors that supply (sell) bonds and people (like you) are the only economic actors that demand (buy) bonds. Now, when a corporation supplies a bond, it is effectively seeking to borrow funds from you. It is saying, "If you will buy this bond from the corporation for, say, $10,000, the corporation promises to repay you $11,000 at some specified date in the future."

Thus, when the corporation supplies bonds for sale, it (the corporation) demands loanable funds (from you), and you, if you buy or demand the bonds, supply loanable funds to the corporation.

Think of a simpler transaction to understand how it is possible that when you supply one thing, you demand something else. When you *supply* the desk for sale that you produced, aren't you effectively *demanding* money? And isn't the person who buys, or *demands,* the desk from you effectively *supplying* money to you?

With this as background, let's now ask two questions. First, how does Real GDP affect the supply of loanable funds? When Real GDP rises, people's wealth is greater. (Real GDP consists of goods, and goods are one component of wealth.) When people became wealthier, they often demand more bonds (in much the same way that they may demand more houses, cars, and jewelry). But as we have just learned, to demand more bonds is to supply more loanable funds. So, when Real GDP rises, people (demand more bonds and thereby) supply more loanable funds.

Second, how does Real GDP affect the demand for loanable funds? When Real GDP rises, profitable business opportunities usually abound. Businesses decide to issue or supply more bonds to take advantage of these profitable opportunities. But again, we know that to supply more bonds is to demand more loanable funds. So, when Real GDP rises, corporations (issue or supply more bonds and thereby) demand more loanable funds.

Income Effect

The change in the interest rate due to a change in Real GDP.

In summary, then, when Real GDP increases, both the supply of and demand for loanable funds increase. What is the overall effect on the interest rate? Usually, the demand for loanable funds increases by more than the supply of loanable funds so that the interest rate rises. The change in the interest rate due to a change in Real GDP is called the **income effect**. See Exhibit 7(c).

THE PRICE LEVEL An earlier chapter discusses reasons the *AD* curve slopes downward. A downward-sloping *AD* curve is explained by (1) the real balance effect, (2) the interest rate effect, and (3) the international trade effect. With respect to the interest rate effect, we said: When the price level rises, the purchasing power of money falls, and people may increase their demand for credit or loanable funds to borrow the funds necessary to buy a fixed bundle of goods. This change in the interest rate due to a change in the price level is called the **price-level effect**. See Exhibit 7(d).

Price-Level Effect

The change in the interest rate due to a change in the price level.

THE EXPECTED INFLATION RATE A change in the expected inflation rate affects both the supply of and demand for loanable funds. To see how, let's suppose the expected inflation rate is currently zero. Let's also assume that when the expected inflation rate is zero, the

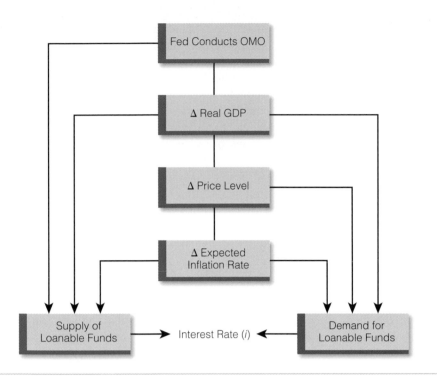

exhibit 8

How the Fed Affects the Interest Rate

This exhibit summarizes the way the Fed (through its monetary policy) affects the interest rate. For example, an open market operation (OMO) directly affects the supply of loanable funds and affects the interest rate. An OMO also affects Real GDP, the price level, and the expected inflation rate, and therefore indirectly affects either the supply of or demand for loanable funds, which in turn affects the interest rate.

equilibrium interest rate is 6 percent, as in Exhibit 7(e). Now suppose the expected inflation rate rises from 0 percent to 4 percent. What will this rise in the expected inflation rate do to the demand for and supply of loanable funds? Borrowers (demanders of loanable funds) will be willing to pay 4 percent more interest for their loans because they expect to be paying back the loans with dollars that have 4 percent less buying power than the dollars they are being lent. (Another way to look at this: If they wait to buy goods, the prices of the goods they want will have risen by 4 percent. To beat the price rise, they are willing to pay up to 4 percent more to borrow and purchase the goods now.) In effect, the demand for loanable funds curve shifts rightward so that at Q_1 borrowers are willing to pay a 4 percent higher interest rate. See Exhibit 7(e).

On the other side of the loanable funds market, the lenders (the suppliers of loanable funds) require a 4 percent higher interest rate to compensate them for the 4 percent less valuable dollars in which the loan will be repaid. In effect, the supply of loanable funds curve shifts leftward, so that at Q_1 lenders will receive an interest rate of 10 percent. See Exhibit 7(e).

Thus, an expected inflation rate of 4 percent increases the demand for loanable funds and decreases the supply of loanable funds so that the interest rate is 4 percent higher than it was when there was a zero expected inflation rate. A change in the interest rate due to a change in the expected inflation rate is referred to as the **expectations effect** (or *Fisher effect,* after economist Irving Fisher).

Exhibit 8 summarizes how a change in the money supply directly and indirectly affects the interest rate.

Expectations Effect
The change in the interest rate due to a change in the expected inflation rate.

THE DIFFERENCE BETWEEN THE PRICE-LEVEL EFFECT AND THE EXPECTATIONS EFFECT To many people, the price-level effect sounds the same as the expectations effect. After all, both have something to do with the price level. So what is the difference?

To illustrate the difference, consider a one-shot change in the money supply that ultimately moves the price level from a price index of 120 to a price index of 135. The price-level effect refers to the change in the interest rate that is related to the fact that the actual price level is rising. Think of the demand for loanable funds creeping up steadily as the price index rises from 120 to 121 to 122 to 123 and so on to 135. Once the price index has hit 135, there is no further reason for the demand for loanable funds to rise. After all, the price level isn't rising anymore. Now, as the price level is rising, people's expected inflation rate is rising. They may see (in their mind's eye) where the price level is headed (from 120 to 135) and adjust accordingly. Once the price level hits 135 (and given that we are talking about a one-shot change in the money supply), the expected inflation rate falls to zero. In other words, any change in the interest rate due to a rise in the expected inflation rate is now over, and therefore, the expected inflation rate no longer has an effect on the interest rate. But certainly, the price level still has an effect on the interest rate because the price level is higher than it was originally. In the end, the effect on the interest rate due to a rise in the price level remains, and the effect on the interest rate due to a rise in the expected inflation rate disappears.

So What Happens to the Interest Rate as the Money Supply Changes?

Suppose the Fed decides to raise the rate of growth of the money supply, say, from 3 percent to 5 percent a year. What effect will this have on the interest rate? Some people will quickly say, "It will lower the interest rate." They may be thinking that the only effect on the interest rate is the liquidity effect. In other words, as the Fed increases the rate of growth of the money supply, more reserves enter the banking system, more loans are extended, and the interest rate falls.

That would be the right answer if the only thing that an increase in the money supply growth rate did was to affect the supply of loanable funds. But as we have discussed, this isn't the only thing that happens. Real GDP changes, the price level changes, and the expected inflation rate changes, and changes in these factors affect the loanable funds market just as the Fed action did. Figuring out what happens to the interest rate is a matter of trying to figure out when each effect (liquidity, income, price-level, and expectations) occurs and how strong each effect is.

To illustrate, suppose everyone expects the Fed to continue to increase the money supply at a growth rate of 2 percent a year. Then, on January 1, the Fed announces that it will increase the rate of growth in the money supply to 4 percent and will begin open market purchases to effect this outcome immediately. It's possible that one second after the announcement, people's expected inflation rate rises. In other words, the expectations effect begins immediately and affects interest rates accordingly. On January 2, the interest rate is higher than it was one day earlier. At this point, someone could say, "See, an increase in the rate of growth in the money supply raises the interest rate." The problem with saying this, though, is that not all the effects (liquidity, income, etc.) have occurred yet. In time, the liquidity effect puts downward pressure on the interest rate. Suppose this begins to happen on January 15, and the interest rate begins to fall from what it was on January 2. Then, someone on January 15 could say, "It is obvious that an increase in the rate of growth of the money supply lowers interest rates."

Our point is: A change in the money supply affects the economy in many ways—changing the supply of loanable funds directly, changing Real GDP and therefore changing the demand for and supply of loanable funds, changing the expected inflation rate, and so on. The timing and magnitude of these effects determine changes in the interest rate.

The Nominal and Real Interest Rates

Nominal Interest Rate
The interest rate actually charged (or paid) in the market; the market interest rate. The nominal interest rate = Real interest rate + Expected inflation rate.

If you were to call a bank and ask what it charges for a given type of loan, the bank would quote some interest rate. The interest rate that it quotes is the interest rate we have been discussing. It is the interest rate that comes about through the interaction of the demand for and supply of loanable funds. Sometimes, this interest rate is called the **nominal interest rate** or market interest rate.

The nominal interest rate may not be the true cost of borrowing because part of the nominal interest rate is a reflection of the expected inflation rate. To illustrate, let's suppose the nominal interest rate is 9 percent, and the expected inflation rate is 2 percent. If you take out a loan for $10,000 at 9 percent, you will have to pay back the loan amount ($10,000) plus $900 in interest at the end of the year. In other words, for a $10,000 loan, you will have to repay $10,900.

Now let's suppose the expected inflation rate turns out to be the actual inflation rate. That is, people expected the inflation rate to be 2 percent, and it turns out to be 2 percent. In this case, the dollars you pay back will be worth less than the dollars you borrowed—by 2 percent. In other words, you borrowed dollars that were worth 2 percent more in purchasing power than the dollars you repaid.

This fact should be taken into account in determining your real cost of borrowing. Was the real cost of borrowing 9 percent or 7 percent? Economists would say it was 7 percent. The real cost of borrowing is sometimes called the **real interest rate**. It is equal to the nominal interest rate minus the expected inflation rate.[3]

> Real interest rate = Nominal interest rate – Expected inflation rate

Based on this equation, it follows that the nominal interest rate is equal to the real interest rate plus the expected inflation rate.

> Nominal interest rate = Real interest rate + Expected inflation rate

Real Interest Rate
The nominal interest rate minus the expected inflation rate. When the expected inflation rate is zero, the real interest rate equals the nominal interest rate.

SELF-TEST

1. If the expected inflation rate is 4 percent and the nominal interest rate is 7 percent, what is the real interest rate?

2. Is it possible for the nominal interest rate to immediately rise following an increase in the money supply? Explain your answer.

3. The Fed only affects the interest rate via the liquidity effect. Do you agree or disagree? Explain your answer.

[3] A broader definition is "Real interest rate = Nominal interest rate – Expected rate of change in the price level." This definition is useful because we will not always be dealing with an expected inflation rate; we could be dealing with an expected deflation rate.

A Reader Asks . . .

How Do We Know What the Expected Inflation Rate Equals?

Is there some way to figure out what the expected inflation rate equals at any given time?

One way to find out what the expected inflation rate equals is to look at the spread—the difference—between the yield on conventional bonds and the yield on indexed bonds with the same maturity. For example, we can look at the spread between the yield on a 10-year Treasury bond and the yield on an inflation-indexed 10-year Treasury bond.

Before we do this, let's look at the difference between a conventional bond and an inflation-indexed bond. An inflation-indexed bond guarantees the purchaser a certain real rate of return, but a conventional, or nonindexed, bond does not. For example, suppose you purchase an inflation-indexed, 10-year, $1,000 security that pays 4 percent interest. If there is no inflation, the annual interest payment is $40. But if the inflation rate is 3 percent, the bond issuer "marks up" the value of your security by 3 percent—from $1,000 to $1,030. Furthermore, your annual interest payment is 4 percent of this new higher amount; that is, it is 4 percent of $1,030, or $41.20.

Investors are willing to accept a lower yield on inflation-indexed bonds because they are receiving something with them that they are not receiving on conventional bonds—protection against inflation. So while a conventional bond may yield, say, 6 percent, an inflation-indexed bond may yield 4 percent.

What does the difference, or spread, signify? It is a measure of the inflation rate that investors expect will exist over the life of the bond.

To illustrate with some real numbers, we went to bloomberg.com and checked the yield on securities. An inflation-indexed 10-year Treasury bond had a yield of 1.72 percent. A conventional 10-year Treasury bond had a yield of 4.02. The difference, or spread, was 2.3 percent. This means that on this day, investors (or "the market") expected that the inflation rate was going to be 2.3 percent.

So, by checking the spread between yields on conventional and inflation-indexed bonds of the same maturity, you can see what the market expects the inflation rate will be. As the spread widens, the market expects a higher inflation rate; as the spread narrows, the market expects a lower inflation rate.

Once again, here is the process to follow:

1. Go to http://www.bloomberg.com.

2. Under "Market Data," click "Rates & Bonds."

3. Write down the yield on conventional 10-year Treasury bonds.

4. Write down the yield on inflation-indexed 10-year Treasury bonds.

5. Find the spread between the yields. The spread is the market's expected inflation rate.

6. By doing this daily, you can see if the market's perception of inflation is changing. For example, if the spread is widening, the market believes inflation will be increasing. If the spread is narrowing, the market believes inflation will be decreasing.

! analyzing the scene

Jan believes that she will end up paying more for her remodeling because her contractor's costs went up. Odd as it may sound, could Jan be the reason her contractor's costs went up?

Jan may not see the part she has played in her contractor's rising costs. She believes that the higher price she is going to end up paying is due to her contractor's higher costs. In other words, higher prices are caused by higher costs. But what she might not see is that higher demand (for remodeling) preceded the higher costs. In short, what looks like supply-side inflation to Jan could really be demand-side inflation. And she is on the demand side of the market in question.

If the Fed wants to lower interest rates, are interest rates destined to go down? In short, can the Fed do what it wants to do?

Oliver and Roberta are thinking about buying a house, and Oliver has recently heard that the Fed might lower interest rates. If the Fed wants to lower interest rates, will it be able to do so? The answer is not always. There is little doubt that the Fed can conduct an open market purchase and increase reserves in the banking system. In turn, this is likely to lead to an increased supply of loanable funds. If nothing else happens, interest rate will go down. This is the liquidity effect.

But the liquidity effect isn't the only effect of a change in the money supply. For example, suppose the market views the recent Fed action of increasing reserves in the banking system as inflationary. In short, the market's expected inflation rate rises. This will push the interest rate up.

The best we can say is: It's possible that the Fed, by increasing the supply of loanable funds, will lower (short-term) interest rates—but this depends on both the *timing* and *magnitude* of the liquidity and expectations effects.

If the Fed does what Sebastian thinks it will do, will his brother, Jim, have a better chance of finding a job?

Sebastian thinks that if the Fed "stimulates the economy," Jim might have a better chance of finding a job. Is he right?

The answer depends on a number of things. Stimulating the economy often refers to increasing the money supply (or the rate of growth of the money supply) so that the economy's *AD* curve shifts rightward. If the economy's *AS* curve is upward sloping (at least in the short run, as monetarists believe) and there is no change in velocity to offset the money supply-induced shift in the *AD* curve, then Real

GDP in the economy is likely to rise. With more goods and services being produced, Jim's chances of finding work will be better.

But suppose the *AS* curve is vertical (as classical economists assumed). Then a rise in the money supply will lead to higher prices and no change in Real GDP. In this case, Jim's

chances of getting a job might not be any better than before the Fed acted.

Our point is that the conditions in the economy determine the outcomes in the economy. If the *AS* curve is upward sloping, then a shift rightward in the *AD* curve leads to higher Real GDP. But if the *AS* curve is vertical, then a shift rightward in the *AD* curve leaves Real GDP unchanged.

chapter summary

The Equation of Exchange

- The equation of exchange is an identity: $MV \equiv PQ$. The equation of exchange can be interpreted in different ways: (1) The money supply multiplied by velocity must equal the price level times Real GDP: $M \times V \equiv P \times Q$. (2) The money supply multiplied by velocity must equal GDP: $M \times V \equiv$ GDP. (3) Total expenditures (measured by MV) must equal the total sales revenues of business firms (measured by PQ): $MV \equiv PQ$.

- The equation of exchange is not a theory of the economy. However, the equation of exchange can be turned into a theory by making assumptions about some of the variables in the equation. For example, if we assume that both V and Q are constant, then we have the simple quantity theory of money, which predicts that changes in the money supply cause *strictly proportional* changes in the price level.

- A change in the money supply or a change in velocity will change aggregate demand and therefore lead to a shift in the *AD* curve. Specifically, either an increase in the money supply or an increase in velocity will increase aggregate demand and therefore shift the *AD* curve to the right. A decrease in the money supply or a decrease in velocity will decrease aggregate demand and therefore shift the *AD* curve to the left.

- In the simple quantity theory of money, Real GDP is assumed to be constant in the short run. This means the *AS* curve is vertical. Also, velocity is assumed to be constant. This means the only thing that can change aggregate demand is a change in the money supply. In the face of a vertical *AS* curve, any change in the money supply shifts the *AD* curve and changes only the price level, not Real GDP.

Monetarism

- According to monetarists, if the economy is initially in long-run equilibrium, (1) an increase in the money supply will raise the price level and Real GDP in the short run and will raise only the price level in the long

run; (2) a decrease in the money supply will lower the price level and Real GDP in the short run and will lower only the price level in the long run; (3) an increase in velocity will raise the price level and Real GDP in the short run and will raise only the price level in the long run; (4) a decrease in velocity will lower the price level and Real GDP in the short run and will lower only the price level in the long run.

One-Shot Inflation and Continued Inflation

- One-shot inflation can result from an increase in aggregate demand or a decrease in short-run aggregate supply.

- For one-shot inflation to change to continued inflation, it is necessary and sufficient to have a continued increase in aggregate demand. Continued increases in the money supply cause continued increases in aggregate demand and continued inflation.

The Money Supply and Interest Rates

- Changes in the money supply can affect the interest rate via the liquidity, income, price-level, and expectations effects.

- The change in the interest rate due to a change in the supply of loanable funds is called the liquidity effect. The change in the interest rate due to a change in Real GDP is called the income effect. The change in the interest rate due to a change in the price level is called the price-level effect. The change in the interest rate due to a change in the expected inflation rate is called the expectations effect (or Fisher effect).

Nominal and Real Interest Rates

- Real interest rate = Nominal interest rate − Expected inflation rate
- Nominal interest rate = Real interest rate + Expected inflation rate

key terms and concepts

Equation of Exchange	One-Shot Inflation	Income Effect	Nominal Interest Rate
Velocity	Continued Inflation	Price-Level Effect	Real Interest Rate
Simple Quantity Theory of Money	Liquidity Effect	Expectations Effect	

questions and problems

1 What are the assumptions and predictions of the simple quantity theory of money? Does the simple quantity theory of money predict well?

2 In the simple quantity theory of money, the *AS* curve is vertical. Explain why.

3 In the simple quantity theory of money, what will lead to an increase in aggregate demand? In monetarism, what will lead to an increase in aggregate demand?

4 In monetarism, how will each of the following affect the price level in the short run?

　a　An increase in velocity
　b　A decrease in velocity
　c　An increase in the money supply
　d　A decrease in the money supply

5 Suppose the objective of the Fed is to increase Real GDP. To this end, it increases the money supply. Is there anything that can offset the increase in the money supply so that Real GDP does not rise? Explain your answer.

6 "A loaf of bread, a computer, and automobile tires have gone up in price; therefore, we are experiencing inflation." Do you agree or disagree with this statement? Explain your answer.

7 What is the difference in the long run between a one-shot increase in aggregate demand and a one-shot decrease in short-run aggregate supply?

8 "One-shot inflation may be a demand-side (of the economy) or a supply-side phenomenon, but continued inflation is likely to be a demand-side phenomenon." Do you agree or disagree with this statement? Explain your answer.

9 Explain how demand-induced one-shot inflation may appear as supply-induced one-shot inflation.

10 In recent years, economists have argued about what the true value of the real interest rate is at any one time and over time. Given that the Nominal interest rate = Real interest rate + Expected inflation rate, it follows that the Real interest rate = Nominal interest rate − Expected inflation rate. Why do you think there is so much disagreement over the true value of the real interest rate?

11 To a potential borrower, which would be more important—the nominal interest rate or the real interest rate? Explain your answer.

12 The money supply rises on Tuesday and by Thursday the interest rate has risen. Is this more likely the result of the income effect or the expectations effect? Explain your answer.

13 Suppose the money supply increased 30 days ago. Whether the nominal interest rate is higher, lower, or the same today as it was 30 days ago depends on what? Explain your answer.

working with numbers and graphs

1 How will things change in the *AD-AS* framework if a change in the money supply is completely offset by a change in velocity?

2 Graphically show each of the following:

    a   Continued inflation due to supply-side factors
    b   One-shot demand-induced inflation
    c   One-shot supply-induced inflation

3 Use the figure below to answer the following questions.

    a   The economy is at point *A* when there is a one-shot demand-induced inflation. Assuming no other changes in the economy, at what point will the economy settle (assuming the economy is self-regulating)?

    b   The economy is at point *A* when it is faced with two adverse supply-side shocks. The Fed tries to counter these shocks by increasing aggregate demand. What path will the economy follow?

Monetary Policy

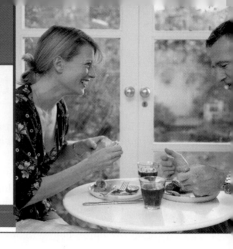

Setting the Scene The following conversations occurred recently.

1:34 P.M. MELANIE AND ANGELA ARE IN A LINE AT THE GROCERY STORE, WAITING TO PURCHASE SOME FOOD ITEMS FOR THE PARTY THEY'RE GIVING TONIGHT.

Melanie:
I really need to get another job. I'm just not making enough money.

Angela:
I know what you mean. You can never have enough money.

Melanie:
How true.

Grocery clerk:
That will be $124.76.

Melanie:
Here you go.

2:45 P.M. KAREN AND PETER ARE AT A LATE LUNCH.

Karen:
After lunch, I need to pick up a birthday gift for Zak.

Peter:
I'll go with you. I don't have to get back right away.

Karen:
The bill is $33.76. I'll put it on my MasterCard.

Peter:
Why don't you just use cash? It's not that much.

Karen:
I don't carry much cash anymore. I've only got $20 with me.

Peter:
Why don't you carry more cash than that?

Karen:
I'm not really sure.

3:34 P.M. QUENTIN IS SITTING IN THE MAIN LIBRARY OF THE UNIVERSITY.

He is thinking: It seems to me that the way to make a lot of money is to buy bonds when interest rates are headed down and sell bonds when interest rates are headed up. But how do I know when interest rates are headed up or down? That's the hard part, it seems to me.

5:00 P.M. THE ECONOMICS CLASS WILL END IN 15 MINUTES. A STUDENT ASKS A QUESTION.

Student:
So expansionary monetary policy increases Real GDP in the short run?

Economics professor:
Not always.

Student:
I don't understand.

? Here are some questions to keep in mind as you read this chapter:

- *Melanie agrees that "you can never have enough money," but she acts differently. How so?*

- *Why doesn't Karen carry more cash?*

- *Is Quentin right? Should he buy bonds when interest rates are headed down and sell bonds when they are headed up?*

- *How can expansionary monetary policy not increase Real GDP in the short run?*

See analyzing the scene at the end of this chapter for answers to these questions.

The Money Market

Like all markets, the money market has two sides: a demand side and a supply side.[1] Both are discussed in this section.

We discuss the money market for two reasons. First, we want to show how changes in the money market can affect the interest rate. The last chapter showed how changes in the demand for and supply of loanable funds can affect the interest rate. In this chapter, we show how changes in the demand for and supply of money can affect the interest rate. (Often, there is more than one way to discuss the determination of interest rates.)

Second, we want to show how changes in the money market can ripple outward and bring about changes in the goods and services market.

The Demand for Money

An illustration of the demand for a good puts the price of the good on the vertical axis and the quantity of the good on the horizontal axis. An illustration of the **demand for money (balances)** puts the price of holding money balances on the vertical axis and the quantity of money on the horizontal axis. But what is the price of holding money balances?

The price of holding money balances—specifically, the opportunity cost of holding money—is the interest rate. Money is one of many forms in which individuals may hold their wealth. By holding money, individuals forfeit the opportunity to hold that amount of their wealth in other forms. For example, the person who holds $1,000 in cash gives up the opportunity to purchase a $1,000 asset that yields interest (e.g., a bond). Thus, the interest rate is the opportunity cost of holding money. One pays the price of forfeited interest by holding money.

Exhibit 1(a) illustrates the demand for money (balances). As the interest rate increases, the opportunity cost of holding money increases, and individuals choose to hold less money. As the interest rate decreases, the opportunity cost of holding money decreases, and individuals choose to hold more money.

Demand for Money (Balances)
Represents the inverse relationship between the quantity demanded of money balances and the price of holding money balances.

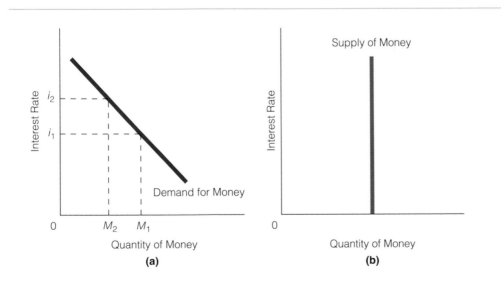

exhibit **1**

The Demand for and Supply of Money

(a) The demand curve for money is downward-sloping. (b) The supply curve of money is a vertical line at the quantity of money, which is largely, but not exclusively, determined by the Fed.

---

[1]In everyday language, the term *money market* is often used to refer to the market for short-term securities, where there is a demand for and supply of short-term securities. This is not the money market discussed here. In this money market, there is a demand for and supply of money.

The Supply of Money

Exhibit 1(b) shows the supply of money as a vertical line at the quantity of money, which is largely determined by the Fed. The money supply is not exclusively determined by the Fed because both banks and the public are important players in the money supply process, as discussed in earlier chapters. For example, when banks do not lend their entire excess reserves, the money supply is not as large as it is when they do.

Equilibrium in the Money Market

Equilibrium in the money market exists when the quantity demanded of money equals the quantity supplied. In Exhibit 2, equilibrium exists at the interest rate i_1. At a higher interest rate, i_2, the quantity supplied of money is greater than the quantity demanded, and there is an excess supply of money ("too much" money). At a lower interest rate, i_3, the quantity demanded of money is greater than the quantity supplied, and there is an excess demand for money ("too little" money). Only at i_1 are the quantity demanded and the quantity supplied of money equal. At i_1, there are no shortages or surpluses of money, no excess demands or excess supplies. Individuals are holding the amount of money they want to hold.

Transmission Mechanisms

Consider two markets: the money market and the goods and services market. Changes in the money market can ripple outward and affect the goods and services market. The routes, or channels, these ripple effects travel are known as the **transmission mechanism**. Economists have different ideas about (1) how changes in the money market affect the goods and services market and (2) whether the transmission mechanism is direct or indirect. We discuss two major transmission mechanisms: the Keynesian and the monetarist.

Transmission Mechanism
The routes, or channels, that ripple effects created in the money market travel to affect the goods and services market (represented by the aggregate demand and aggregate supply curves in the *AD-AS* framework).

macro Theme   In an earlier chapter, we said that not all economists agree as to how the economy works. What is coming up is two different views on how changes in the money market eventually affect the goods and services market.

Equilibrium in the Money Market

At an interest rate if i_1, the money market is in equilibrium: There is neither an excess supply of money nor an excess demand for money.

The Keynesian Transmission Mechanism: Indirect

The Keynesian route between the money market and the goods and services market is an indirect one. Refer to Exhibit 3, as the Keynesian transmission mechanism is described market by market in the following paragraphs.

1. **The money market.** Suppose the money market is in equilibrium at interest rate i_1 in part (a). Then, the Fed increases the reserves of the banking system through an open market purchase. This results in an increase in the money supply. The money supply curve shifts rightward from S_1 to S_2. The process increases the reserves of the banking system and therefore results in more loans being made. A greater supply of loans puts downward pressure on the interest rate, as reflected in the movement from i_1 to i_2.

2. **The investment goods market.** A fall in the interest rate stimulates investment. In the investment goods market in part (b), investment rises from I_1 to I_2.

3. **The goods and services market (*AD-AS* framework).** Recall from an earlier chapter that our Keynesian model has a horizontal aggregate supply curve in the goods and services market until full employment or Natural Real GDP is reached. The decline in the interest rate has brought about an increase in investment, as shown in part (b). Rising investment increases total spending in the economy and shifts the *AD* curve to the right in part (c). As a result, Real GDP rises from Q_1 to Q_2, and the price level does not change. Due to the increase in Real GDP, the unemployment rate (U) drops.

In summary, when the money supply increases, the Keynesian transmission mechanism works as follows: An increase in the money supply lowers the interest rate, which causes investment to rise and the *AD* curve to shift rightward. As a result, Real GDP increases. The process works in reverse for a decrease in the money supply.

$$\text{Money supply} \uparrow \rightarrow i \downarrow \rightarrow I \uparrow \rightarrow AD \uparrow \rightarrow Q \uparrow, \overline{P}, U \downarrow$$
$$\text{Money supply} \downarrow \rightarrow i \uparrow \rightarrow I \downarrow \rightarrow AD \downarrow \rightarrow Q \downarrow, \overline{P}, U \uparrow$$

The Keynesian Mechanism May Get Blocked

The Keynesian transmission mechanism is *indirect*. Changes in the money market *do not directly affect* the goods and services market (and thus Real GDP) because the investment goods market stands between the two markets. It is possible (although not likely) that the

exhibit **3**

The Keynesian Transmission Mechanism

The exhibit shows how the Keynesian transmission mechanism operates given an increase in the money supply. (a) An increase in the money supply brings on a lower interest rate. (b) As a result, investment increases. (c) As investment increases, total expenditures rise and the aggregate demand curve shifts rightward. Real GDP rises from Q_1 to Q_2.

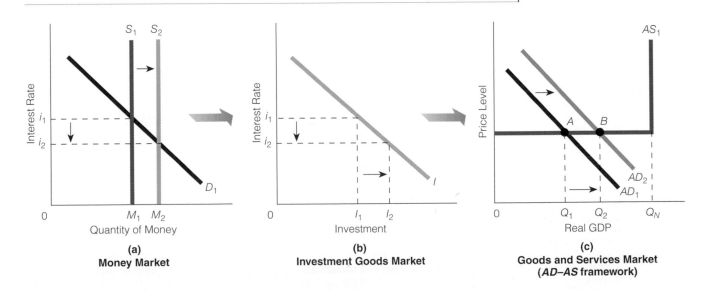

(a)	(b)	(c)
Money Market	**Investment Goods Market**	**Goods and Services Market** (*AD–AS* framework)

link between the money market and the goods and services market could be broken in the investment goods market. We explain.

INTEREST-INSENSITIVE INVESTMENT Some Keynesian economists believe that investment is not always responsive to interest rates. For example, when business firms are pessimistic about future economic activity, a decrease in interest rates will do little, if anything, to increase investment. When investment is completely insensitive to changes in interest rates, the investment demand curve is vertical, as in Exhibit 4(a).

Consider what happens to the Keynesian transmission mechanism described in Exhibit 3. If the investment demand curve is vertical (instead of downward sloping), a fall in interest rates will not increase investment; and if investment does not increase, neither will aggregate demand or Real GDP. In addition, unemployment won't fall. Thus, the Keynesian transmission mechanism would be short-circuited in the investment goods market, and the link between the money market in part (a) of Exhibit 3 and the goods and services market in part (c) would be broken.

$$\text{Money supply} \uparrow \rightarrow i \downarrow$$
$$\text{Investment insensitive to changes in } i \rightarrow \overline{I} \rightarrow \overline{AD} \rightarrow \overline{Q}, \overline{P}, \overline{U}$$

THE LIQUIDITY TRAP Keynesians have sometimes argued that the demand curve for money could become horizontal at some low interest rate. Before we discuss why this might occur, let's look at the consequences. Notice that in Exhibit 4(b), the demand curve for money becomes horizontal at i_1. This horizontal section of the demand curve for money is referred to as the **liquidity trap**.

What happens if the money supply is increased (e.g., from S_1 to S_2) when the money market is in the liquidity trap? The money market moves from point 1 to point 2, and individuals are willing to hold all the additional money supply at the given interest rate. What happens to the Keynesian transmission mechanism illustrated in Exhibit 3? Obviously, if an increase in the money supply does not lower the interest rate, then there will be no change in investment, aggregate demand, or Real GDP. The liquidity trap can break the link between the money market and the goods and services market.

$$\text{Money supply} \uparrow$$
$$\text{Liquidity trap} \rightarrow \overline{i} \rightarrow \overline{I} \rightarrow \overline{AD} \rightarrow \overline{Q}, \overline{P}, \overline{U}$$

Liquidity Trap
The horizontal portion of the demand curve for money.

---

exhibit **4**

Breaking the Link Between the Money Market and the Goods and Services Market: Interest-Insensitive Investment and the Liquidity Trap

The Keynesian transmission mechanism allows the link between the money market and the goods and services market to be broken in two places. (a) If investment is totally interest-intensive, a change in the interest rate will not change investment; therefore, aggregate demand and Real GDP will not change. (b) If the money market is in the liquidity trap, an increase in the money supply will not lower the interest rate. It follows that there will be no change in investment, aggregate demand or Real GDP.

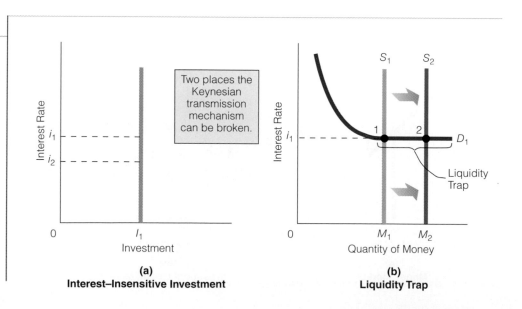

(a)
Interest–Insensitive Investment

(b)
Liquidity Trap

Because the Keynesian transmission mechanism is indirect, both *interest-insensitive investment demand* and the *liquidity trap* may occur. Therefore, Keynesians conclude, there may be times when monetary policy will be unable to increase Real GDP and decrease unemployment. Viewing the money supply as a string, some economists have argued that "you can't push on a string." In other words, you can't always force Real GDP up by increasing (pushing up) the money supply.

See Exhibit 5 for a review of the Keynesian transmission mechanism and how it may get blocked.

BOND PRICES, INTEREST RATES, AND THE LIQUIDITY TRAP The liquidity trap, or the horizontal section of the demand curve for money, seems to come out of the clear blue sky. Why might the demand curve for money become horizontal at some low interest rate? To understand an explanation of the liquidity trap, you must first understand the relationship between bond prices and interest rates.

Consider Jessica Howard, who buys good *X* for $100 today and sells it one year later for $110. What is her actual rate of return? It is 10 percent because the difference between the selling price and buying price ($10) divided by the buying price ($100) is 10 percent.

exhibit 5

The Keynesian View of Monetary Policy

According to the Keynesian transmission mechanism, if the Fed increases reserves in the banking system and therefore raises the money supply, the interest rate will drop, stimulating investment and aggregate demand. Consequently, Real GDP will rise, and the unemployment rate will drop. However, things may not work out this way if there is a liquidity trap or if investment is insensitive to changes in the interest rate.

A CLOSER LOOK

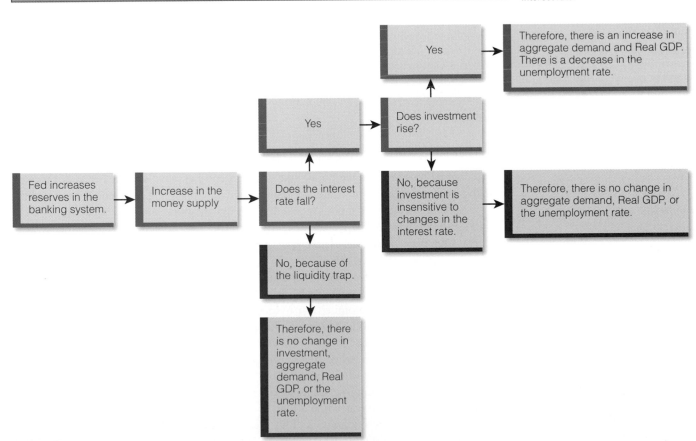

economics 24/7

IF YOU'RE SO SMART, THEN WHY AREN'T YOU RICH?

Upon meeting a professional economist, the general member of the public will often ask some economics-related question, such as: "What stocks should I buy?" "Is this a good time to buy bonds?" "Are interest rates going up?" "Where do you think the economy is headed?"

The professional economist will often answer the question. Usually, the professional economist explains things well enough so that the general member of the public thinks, "Yes, but if you're so smart [about the economy], then why aren't you rich?"

Fact is, some economists are rich, but many are not. Still, the question is a good one, and it helps us to understand the public's perception of economists and the science of economics.

So how can someone be smart about the economy and still not be rich? We use the inverse relationship between bond prices and interest rates to explain how this can be true. To become rich using the bond market, the rule to follow is simple: Buy bonds when you think interest rates are as high as they will go (because then bond prices will be low), and sell bonds when you think interest rates are as low as they will go (because then bond prices will be high). Buy low, sell high—that's the road to riches!

So to walk down the road to riches, all you have to do is be able to predict interest rates. Now you may think it should be easy for economists to predict interest rates. But it isn't. We illustrate just how difficult it is to predict interest rates by structuring our arguments in terms of the bond market.

We begin with the fundamentals. There is a demand for and supply of bonds in the bond market. The demand curve for bonds slopes downward: Buyers of bonds will buy more bonds at lower prices than at higher prices. The supply curve of bonds slopes upward: Suppliers of bonds will offer to sell more bonds at higher prices than at lower prices. In this regard, the demand for and supply of bonds is no different than the demand for and supply of any good (e.g., cars, computers, DVD players, etc.). Buyers will buy more bonds at lower prices, and suppliers will offer to sell more bonds at higher prices.

Thus, we know that the demand for and supply of bonds must work together to determine the price of bonds. A rise in the demand for bonds will raise the price of bonds, *ceteris paribus,* in the same way that a rise in the demand for television sets will raise the price of television sets. Similarly, an increase in the supply of bonds will lower the price

Now suppose good X is a bond. Jessica buys the bond for $100 and sells it one year later for $110. This time we phrase our question another way: What is her actual interest rate return, or what interest rate did Jessica earn? The answer is the same: 10 percent.

Staying with the example, suppose Jessica buys the bond for $90 instead of $100 but still sells it for $110. What is her interest rate return? It is 22 percent ($20/$90 is 22 percent). Our point is simple: *As the price of a bond decreases, the actual interest rate return, or simply the interest rate, increases.*

Let's look at a slightly more complicated example that illustrates the inverse relationship between bond prices and interest rates in another way. Suppose last year Rob Lewis bought a bond for $1,000 that promises to pay him $100 a year. The annual interest rate return is 10 percent ($100/$1,000 is 10 percent). Suppose, however, that market or nominal interest rates are higher now than they were last year when Rob bought his bond. Now bond suppliers have to promise to pay $120 a year to someone who buys a $1,000 bond.

What will this do to the price Rob can get in the market for his $1,000 bond bought last year, assuming he wants to sell it? Will anyone pay Rob $1,000 for an (old) bond that pays $100 a year when a new $1,000 bond that pays $120 a year can be purchased? The answer is a definite no. This means that Rob will have to lower the price of his bond below $1,000. How far below $1,000 will he have to lower it? The price will have to be far enough below $1,000 so that the interest rate return on his old bond will be competitive with (equal to) the interest rate return on new bonds.

of bonds in the same way that an increase in the supply of houses will lower the price of houses.

Recall from an earlier chapter the factors that will change demand and supply. For example, a change in income, preferences, prices of substitutes, and so on will change demand; a change in resource prices, (certain) taxes, and so on will change supply.

The same holds for the demand and supply of bonds. It isn't necessary in this discussion to describe the details of all the factors that can change the demand for and supply of bonds. Let's just say that factors *A–F* can change the demand for bonds and factors *G–L* can change the supply of bonds. Another way to say this is: The demand for bonds depends on factors *A, B, C, D, E,* and *F;* and the supply of bonds depends on factors *G, H, I, J, K,* and *L.*

We can now enumerate the reasons predicting interest rates is difficult:

1. We have to know how each of the factors *A–F* affects the demand for bonds. For example, does an increase in factor *B* increase or decrease the demand for bonds?
2. We have to know how each of the factors *G–L* affects the supply of bonds. Does a rise in factor *K* increase or decrease the supply of bonds?
3. If any of the factors *A–L* change, we have to know it. In other words, we need to know immediately which factors are changing. Suppose factor *C* changes, but we are unaware of it. A change in factor *C* changes the demand for bonds. A change in the demand for bonds changes the price of bonds. And as we have shown, if bond prices change, so do interest rates. Obviously, if we

didn't know that factor *C* changed, there would be no way we could predict the change in interest rates.
4. Even if we know which factors are changing, we still have to determine the impact that each (relevant) factor will have on the demand for and supply of bonds. Suppose a rise in factor *A* increases the demand for bonds, and a rise in factor *J* increases the supply of bonds. Now suppose *A* and *J* both rise. We can predict that the demand for bonds will rise and that the supply of bonds will rise, but we don't know how much each rises relative to the other.

If the demand for bonds rises by more than the supply of bonds, then the price of bonds will rise. (Can you show this graphically?) And if bond prices rise, interest rates fall.

But if the supply of bonds rises by more than the demand for bonds, the price of bonds will fall. (Can you show this graphically?) And if bond prices fall, interest rates rise.

Finally, if the supply of bonds rises by the same amount as the demand for bonds rises, the price of bonds will not change. And if bond prices don't change, neither do interest rates.

We conclude: To predict interest rates accurately, we need to know: (1) What factors affect the demand for and supply of bonds. Is it *A, B,* and *C,* or *A, B, D,* and *E?* (2) How those factors affect the demand for and supply of bonds. Does a rise in *A* increase or decrease the demand for bonds? (3) Which factors are changing? Did *B* just change? (4) How much bond demand and supply change given that some factors are changing. Did demand rise by more than supply, or did supply rise by more than demand?

Now do you see why not all economists are rich?

Rob's bond will sell for $833. At a price of $833, a buyer of his bond will receive $100 a year and an interest rate of 12 percent, which is the same interest rate he or she would receive by buying a new bond for $1,000 and receiving $120 a year. Thus, $100 is the same percentage of $833 as $120 is of $1,000—12 percent. We conclude that *the market interest rate is inversely related to the price of old or existing bonds.*

Keeping this in mind, consider the liquidity trap again. The reason an increase in the money supply does not result in an excess supply of money at a low interest rate is that individuals believe bond prices are so high (because low interest rates mean high bond prices) that an investment in bonds is likely to turn out to be a bad deal. Individuals would rather hold all the additional money supply than use it to buy bonds, which, they believe, are priced so high that they have no place to go but down.

The Monetarist Transmission Mechanism: Direct

In monetarist theory, there is a direct link between the money market and the goods and services market. The monetarist transmission mechanism is short. Changes in the money market have a direct impact on aggregate demand, as illustrated in Exhibit 6. An increase in the money supply from S_1 to S_2 in part (a) leaves individuals with an excess supply of money. As a result, they increase their spending on a wide variety of goods. Households buy more refrigerators, personal computers, television sets, clothes,

Q&A   *I want to make sure I have this correct. According to the Keynesian transmission mechanism, an increase in the money supply will lower the interest rate, which will then stimulate more investment spending, which will shift the AD curve to the right and end up raising Real GDP. But according to the monetarist transmission mechanism, an increase in the money supply will directly shift the AD curve to the right and end up raising Real GDP. In other words, there are "more steps" to get from the money market to the goods and services market in the Keynesian transmission mechanism than in the monetarist mechanism. Is this correct?*

Yes, that is correct.

and vacations. Businesses purchase additional machinery. The aggregate demand curve in part (b) is directly affected. In the short run, Real GDP rises from Q_1 to Q_2. The process works in reverse for a decrease in the money supply.

$$\text{Money supply} \uparrow \rightarrow AD \uparrow \rightarrow Q \uparrow, P \uparrow, U \downarrow$$
$$\text{Money supply} \downarrow \rightarrow AD \downarrow \rightarrow Q \downarrow, P \downarrow, U \uparrow$$

The Keynesian transmission mechanism from the money market to the goods and services market is indirect; the monetarist transmission mechanism is direct.

SELF-TEST

(Answers to Self-Test questions are in the Self-Test Appendix.)

1. Explain the inverse relationship between bond prices and interest rates.

2. "According to the Keynesian transmission mechanism, as the money supply rises, there is a direct impact on the goods and services market." Do you agree or disagree with this statement? Explain your answer.

3. Explain how the monetarist transmission mechanism works when the money supply rises.

Monetary Policy and the Problem of Inflationary and Recessionary Gaps

An earlier chapter explained how expansionary and contractionary fiscal policies might be used to rid the economy of recessionary and inflationary gaps, respectively. Later in that chapter, the effectiveness of fiscal policy was questioned. In this section, we discuss how monetary policy might be used to eliminate both recessionary and inflationary gaps.

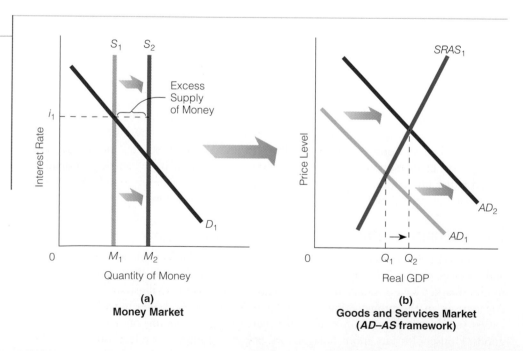

exhibit 6

The Monetarist Transmission Mechanism

The monetarist transmission mechanism is short and direct. Changes in the money market directly affect aggregate demand in the goods and services market. For example, an increase in the money supply leaves individuals with an excess supply of money that they spend on a wide variety of goods.

(a)
Money Market

(b)
Goods and Services Market
(AD–AS framework)

In Exhibit 7(a), the economy is in a recessionary gap at point 1; aggregate demand is too low to bring the economy into equilibrium at its natural level of Real GDP. Economist *A* argues that, in time, the short-run aggregate supply curve will shift rightward to point 2 (see Exhibit 7(b)), so it is best to leave things alone.

Economist *B* says that the economy will take too long to get to point 2 on its own, and in the interim, the economy is suffering the high cost of unemployment and a lower level of output.

Economist *C* maintains that the economy is stuck in the recessionary gap. Economists *B* and *C* propose **expansionary monetary policy** to move the economy to its Natural Real GDP level. An appropriate increase in the money supply will shift the aggregate demand curve rightward to AD_2, and the economy will be in long-run equilibrium at point 2′ (see Exhibit 7(c)). The recessionary gap is eliminated through the use of expansionary monetary policy.[2]

In Exhibit 8(a), the economy is in an inflationary gap at point 1. Economist *A* argues that, in time, the economy will move to point 2 (see Exhibit 8(b)), so it is best to leave things alone.

Economist *B* argues that it would be better to decrease the money supply (**contractionary monetary policy**) so that aggregate demand shifts leftward to AD_2, and the economy moves to point 2′ (see Exhibit 8(c)).

Economist *C* agrees with economist *B* and points out that the price level is lower at point 2′ than at point 2, although Real GDP is the same at both points.

Most Keynesians believe that the natural forces of the market economy work much faster and more assuredly in eliminating an inflationary gap than in eliminating a recessionary gap. In terms of Exhibits 7 and 8, they argue that it is much more likely the short-run aggregate supply curve in Exhibit 8(b) will shift leftward to point 2, eliminating

Expansionary Monetary Policy

The Fed increases the money supply.

Contractionary Monetary Policy

The Fed decreases the money supply.

---

[2]In a static framework, expansionary monetary policy refers to an increase in the money supply, and contractionary monetary policy refers to a decrease in the money supply. In a dynamic framework, expansionary monetary policy refers to an increase in the rate of growth of the money supply, and contractionary monetary policy refers to a decrease in the growth rate of the money supply. In the real world, where things are constantly changing, the growth rate of the money supply is more indicative of the direction of monetary policy.

exhibit **7**

Monetary Policy and a Recessionary Gap

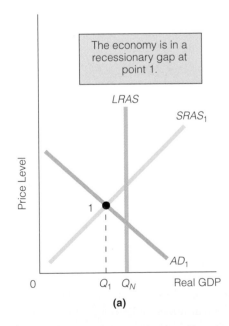

The economy is in a recessionary gap at point 1.

(a)

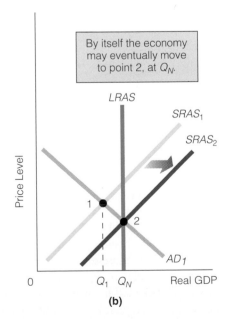

By itself the economy may eventually move to point 2, at Q_N.

(b)

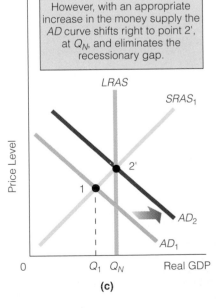

However, with an appropriate increase in the money supply the *AD* curve shifts right to point 2′, at Q_N, and eliminates the recessionary gap.

(c)

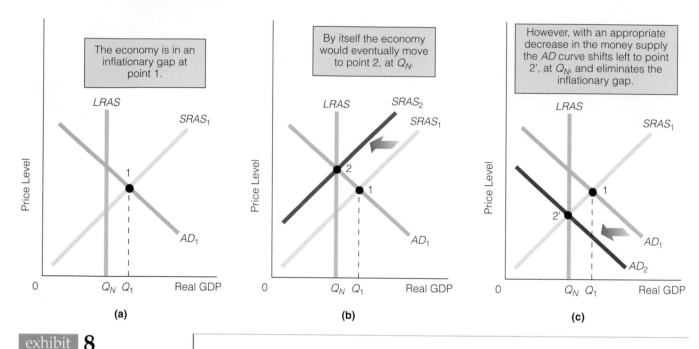

The economy is in an inflationary gap at point 1.

By itself the economy would eventually move to point 2, at Q_N.

However, with an appropriate decrease in the money supply the AD curve shifts left to point 2', at Q_N, and eliminates the inflationary gap.

(a)   (b)   (c)

exhibit **8**

Monetary Policy and an Inflationary Gap

the inflationary gap, than the short-run aggregate supply curve in Exhibit 7(b) will shift rightward to point 2, eliminating the recessionary gap. The reason is that wages and prices rise more quickly than they fall. (Recall that many Keynesians believe wages are inflexible in a downward direction.) Consequently, Keynesians are more likely to advocate expansionary monetary policy to eliminate a stubborn recessionary gap than contractionary monetary policy to eliminate a not-so-stubborn inflationary gap.

Theme **macro**   Notice the link between how an economist believes the economy works and the type of policy he or she proposes. For instance, suppose the economy is in a recessionary gap. We saw economist *A,* who believes the economy is self-regulating, propose that nothing should be done. In time, the economy would remove itself from the recessionary gap. But economist *C,* who believes the economy is stuck in a recessionary gap, proposed government action—specifically, expansionary monetary policy, which would shift the *AD* curve rightward and thus get the economy out of the recessionary gap.

Monetary Policy and the Activist-Nonactivist Debate

As an earlier chapter pointed out, some economists argue that fiscal policy is ineffective (owing to crowding out) or works in unintended and undesirable ways (owing to lags). Other economists, notably Keynesians, believe that neither is the case and that fiscal policy not only can, but also should be used to, smooth out the business cycle. This argument is part of the activist-nonactivist debate, which encompasses both fiscal and monetary policy. This section addresses *monetary policy* within the activist-nonactivist debate.

Activists argue that monetary policy should be deliberately used to smooth out the business cycle. They are in favor of economic **fine-tuning**, which is the (usually frequent) use of monetary policy to counteract even small undesirable movements in eco-

Activists

Persons who argue that monetary and fiscal policies should be deliberately used to smooth out the business cycle.

Fine-tuning

The (usually frequent) use of monetary and fiscal policies to counteract even small undesirable movements in economic activity.

nomic activity. Sometimes, the monetary policy they advocate is called either *activist* or *discretionary monetary policy.*

Nonactivists argue *against* the use of activist or discretionary monetary policy. Instead, they propose a rules-based monetary policy. Sometimes, the monetary policy they propose is called either *nonactivist* or *rules-based monetary policy.* An example of a rules-based monetary policy is one based on a predetermined steady growth rate in the money supply, such as allowing the money supply to grow 3 percent a year, no matter what is happening in the economy.

Nonactivists
Persons who argue against the deliberate use of discretionary fiscal and monetary policies. They believe in a permanent, stable, rule-oriented monetary and fiscal framework.

The Case for Activist (or Discretionary) Monetary Policy

The case for activist (or discretionary) monetary policy rests on three major claims:

1. **The economy does not always equilibrate quickly enough at Natural Real GDP.** Consider the economy at point 1 in Exhibit 7(a). Some economists maintain that, left to its own workings, the economy will eventually move to point 2 in part (b). Activists often argue that the economy takes too long to move from point 1 to point 2 and that too much lost output and too high an unemployment rate must be tolerated in the interim. They believe that an activist monetary policy speeds things along so that higher output and a lower unemployment rate can be achieved more quickly.

2. **Activist monetary policy works; it is effective at smoothing out the business cycle.** Activists are quick to point to the undesirable consequences of the constant monetary policy of the mid-1970s. In 1973, 1974, and 1975, the money supply growth rates were 5.5 percent, 4.3 percent, and 4.7 percent, respectively. These percentages represent a near constant growth rate in the money supply. The economy, however, went through a recession during this time (Real GDP fell between 1973 and 1974 and between 1974 and 1975). Activists argue that an activist and flexible monetary policy would have reduced the high cost the economy had to pay in terms of lost output and high unemployment.

3. **Activist monetary policy is flexible; nonactivist (rules-based) monetary policy is not.** Activists argue that flexibility is a desirable quality in monetary policy; inflexibility is not. The implicit judgment of activists is that the more closely monetary policy can be designed to meet the particulars of a given economic environment, the better. For example, at certain times, the economy requires a sharp increase in the money supply; at other times, a sharp decrease; at still other times, only a slight increase or decrease. Activists argue that activist (discretionary) monetary policy can change as the monetary needs of the economy change; nonactivist, rules-based, or "the-same-for-all-seasons" monetary policy cannot.

The Case for Nonactivist (or Rules-Based) Monetary Policy

The case for nonactivist (or rules-based) monetary policy also rests on three major claims:

1. **In modern economies, wages and prices are sufficiently flexible to allow the economy to equilibrate at reasonable speed at Natural Real GDP.** For example, nonactivists point to the sharp drop in union wages in 1982 in response to high unemployment. In addition, they argue that government policies largely determine the flexibility of wages and prices. For example, when government decides to cushion people's unemployment (e.g., through unemployment compensation), wages

Q&A *Economics would be much easier if all economists agreed on how the economy works and what should be done given a certain problem in the economy. Please comment.*

We agree with you. Economics would be easier if things were as you describe them. But they are not like that. And they are not like that in other fields too. For example, not all physicians agree as to how the body works and what to do if a problem (with the body) exists. Figuring out how the economy works is not as easy as we would like it to be, and so we naturally get different explanations for how someone thinks the economy works. Don't be disappointed because things aren't easy. Realize that we are dealing with complex things, which naturally give way to different explanations and to disagreements.

economics 24/7

HOW FAR DOES MONETARY POLICY REACH? OR MONETARY POLICY AND BLUE EYES

Two days before the beginning of the fall semester at a college in the Midwest, Suzanne, a student at the college, was waiting in line to register for classes. As she waited, she looked through the fall schedule. She had to take an economics principles course at 10 A.M.; two sections were listed at that time. The instructor for one section was Smith; Jones was the instructor for the other section. Suzanne, not knowing which section to take, asked the person behind her in line if he had ever taken a course from either instructor. The person said that he had taken a course with Smith and that Smith was very good. That was enough for Suzanne; she signed up for Smith's class.

While a student in Smith's class, Suzanne met the person whom she ended up marrying. His name is Bob. Suzanne often says to Bob, "You know, if that guy behind me in line that day had said that Smith wasn't a good teacher, or hadn't said anything at all, I might never have taken Professor Smith's class. I might have taken Jones's class instead, and I would never have met you. I'd probably be married to someone else right now."

While this story is untrue, still, it is representative of the many little things that happen every day. Little things can make big differences.

With this in mind, consider monetary policy (which is not really a little thing). Here is another story that is also not true but is still representative of something that, if it hasn't happened, certainly can.

A few years ago, Real GDP was far below its natural level. The Fed decided to increase the money supply. As a result, the AD curve in the economy shifted to the right. One of the first places to feel the new demand in the economy was Denver. Economic activity in Denver increased. Jake, who lived in Austin at the time, was out of work and looking for a job. He heard about the job prospects in Denver, and so one day, he got into his car and headed for Denver. Luckily for him, he got a job a few days after arriving in Denver. He rented an apartment near his job. He became a friend of Nick, who lived in the apartment across the hall.

Nick, knowing that Jake was new in town, asked Jake if he wanted a date with his girlfriend's friend Melanie. Jake said yes. Jake and Melanie ended up dating for 2 years; they've been married now for 10 years. They have 3 children, all of whom have blue eyes.

One day, the youngest child asked her mother why she had blue eyes. Her mother told her it's because both she and her daddy have blue eyes. And that's not an incorrect explanation, as far as it goes.

But we can't help wondering if the youngest child has blue eyes because of an event that took place years ago, an event that has to do with the Fed and the money supply. After all, if the Fed hadn't increased the money supply when it did, maybe Denver's job prospects wouldn't have been so healthy, and maybe Jake wouldn't have left Austin. But then, if Jake had not left Austin, he wouldn't have married Melanie and had 3 children, each with blue eyes. We're just speculating, of course.

will not fall as quickly as when government does nothing. Nonactivists believe that a laissez-faire, hands-off approach by government promotes speedy wage and price adjustments and therefore a quick return to Natural Real GDP.

2. **Activist monetary policies may not work.** Some economists argue that there are really two types of monetary policy: (1) monetary policy that is anticipated by the public and (2) monetary policy that is unanticipated. Anticipated monetary policy may not be effective at changing Real GDP or the unemployment rate. We discuss this subject in detail in the next chapter, but here is a brief explanation.

Suppose the public correctly anticipates that the Fed will soon increase the money supply by 10 percent. Consequently, the public reasons that aggregate demand will increase from AD_1 to AD_2, as shown in Exhibit 9, and prices will rise.

Workers are particularly concerned about the expected higher price level because they know higher prices decrease the buying power of their wages. In an attempt to maintain their real wages, workers bargain for and receive higher money wage rates—which shifts the short-run aggregate supply curve from $SRAS_1$ to $SRAS_2$ in Exhibit 9.

Now, if the $SRAS$ curve shifts leftward (owing to higher wage rates) to the same degree as the AD curve shifts rightward (owing to the increased money supply), Real GDP does not change. It stays constant at Q_1. Thus, *a correctly anticipated increase in the money supply will be ineffective at raising Real GDP.*

3. **Activist monetary policies are likely to be destabilizing rather than stabilizing; they are likely to make matters worse rather than better.** Nonactivists point to *lags* as the main reason that activist (or discretionary) monetary policies are likely to be destabilizing. (The total lag consists of the data, wait-and-see, legislative, transmission, and effectiveness lags discussed in an earlier chapter.) Nonactivists argue that a long lag (e.g., 12 to 20 months) makes it almost impossible to conduct effective activist monetary policy. They maintain that by the time the Fed's monetary stimulus arrives on the scene, the economy may not need any stimulus, and thus it will likely destabilize the economy. In this instance, the stimulus makes things worse rather than better.

Exhibit 10 illustrates the last point. Suppose the economy is currently in a recessionary gap at point 1. The recession is under way before Fed officials recognize it. After they are aware of the recession, however, the officials consider expanding the money supply in the hopes of shifting the AD curve from AD_1 to AD_2 so it will intersect the $SRAS$ curve at point 1′, at Natural Real GDP.

In the interim, however, unknown to everybody, the economy is regulating itself: The $SRAS$ curve is shifting to the right. Fed officials don't realize this shift is occurring because it takes time to collect and analyze data about the economy.

Thinking that the economy is not regulating itself, or not regulating itself quickly enough, Fed officials implement expansionary monetary policy. The AD curve shifts rightward. By the time the increased money supply is felt in the goods and services market,

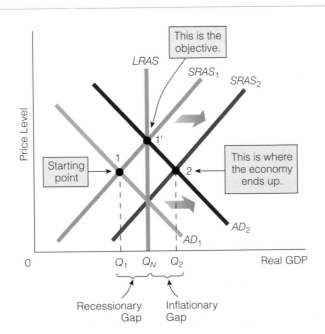

Ask an economist a question and you are likely to get a conditional answer. *For example, if you ask an economist whether monetary policy stabilizes or destabilizes the economy, she may answer that it can do either—depending on conditions. For instance, starting in a recessionary gap, if expansionary monetary policy shifts the AD curve rightward by just the right amount to intersect the SRAS curve and the LRAS curve at Natural Real GDP, then monetary policy stabilizes the economy. But if the monetary policy shifts the AD curve rightward by more than this amount, it may move the economy into an inflationary gap, thereby destabilizing the economy. If–then thinking is common in economics, as are if–then statements.*

the *AD* curve intersects the *SRAS* curve at point 2. In short, the Fed has moved the economy from point 1 to point 2 and not, as it had hoped, from point 1 to point 1′. The Fed has moved the economy into an inflationary gap. Instead of stabilizing and moderating the business cycle, the Fed has intensified it.

SELF-TEST

1. Why are Keynesians more likely to advocate expansionary monetary policy to eliminate a recessionary gap than contractionary monetary policy to eliminate an inflationary gap?

2. How might monetary policy destabilize the economy?

3. If the economy is stuck in a recessionary gap, does this make the case for activist (expansionary) monetary policy stronger or weaker? Explain your answer.

Nonactivist Monetary Proposals

In this section, we outline four nonactivist (or rules-based) monetary proposals.

A Constant-Money-Growth-Rate Rule

Many nonactivists argue that the sole objective of monetary policy is to stabilize the price level. To this end, they propose a *constant-money-growth-rate rule*. One version of the rule is:

> The annual money supply growth rate will be constant at the average annual growth rate of Real GDP.

For example, if the average annual Real GDP growth rate is approximately 3.3 percent, the money supply will be put on automatic pilot and will be permitted to grow at an annual rate of 3.3 percent. The money supply will grow at this rate regardless of the state of the economy.

Some economists predict that a constant-money-growth-rate rule will bring about a stable price level over time. This prediction is based on the equation of exchange ($MV = PQ$). If the average annual growth rate in Real GDP (Q) is 3.3 percent and the money supply (M) grows at 3.3 percent, the price level should remain stable over time. Advocates of this rule argue that in some years the growth rate in Real GDP will be below its average rate, causing an increase in the price level, and in other years the growth rate in Real GDP will be above its average rate, causing a fall in the price level, but over time the price level will be stable.

A Predetermined-Money-Growth-Rate Rule

Critics of the constant-money-growth-rate rule point out that it makes two assumptions: (1) Velocity is constant. (2) The money supply is defined correctly. These critics argue that there have been periods when velocity has not been constant. And it is not yet clear which definition of the money supply (M1, M2, or some broader monetary measure) is the proper one and therefore which money supply growth rate should be fixed.

Largely in response to the charge that velocity is not always constant, some nonactivists prefer the following rule:

> The annual growth rate in the money supply will be equal to the average annual growth rate in Real GDP minus the growth rate in velocity.

© BRAND X PICTURES/JUPITER IMAGES

economics 24/7

ASSET-PRICE INFLATION

During the years 1999–2004, the price level in the United States grew at a fairly modest annual average rate of 2.4 percent. But during those same years, asset prices (especially house prices) grew rapidly. In some cities, house prices increased by 25 to 40 percent. If the rapid rise in house prices had occurred in consumer prices instead, no doubt the Fed would have acted quickly to cool down the rise in consumer prices. In short, the Fed would have likely reduced the money supply.

So why doesn't the Fed act the same way when the rise in prices is in assets? Some economists have argued that it should. They argue that the Fed should target a broadly defined price level that includes both consumer prices and asset prices (e.g., house and stock prices). A few central banks—namely the European Central Bank, the Bank of England, and the Reserve Bank of Australia—have recently given some support to the view that monetary policy should sometimes consider the growth in asset prices (even when consumer price inflation is low). For example, in 2004, both the Bank of England and the Reserve Bank of Australia

began to adjust their respective monetary policy based on the rapid rise in asset prices in Great Britain and Australia.

In an article in *The Wall Street Journal* on February 18, 2004, Otmar Issing, the chief economist for the European Central Bank (ECB), discussed the role of a central bank in a world where consumer price inflation is low but asset price inflation is high. He states, "Just as consumer-price inflation is often described as a situation of 'too much money chasing too few goods,' asset-price inflation could similarly be characterized as 'too much money chasing too few assets.'" He goes on to say that central banks—all central banks—face a challenge in the future: how to deal with asset-price inflation in a way that is not harmful to the overall economy. He states, "As societies accumulate wealth, asset prices will have a growing influence on economic developments. The problem of how to design monetary policy under such circumstances is probably the biggest challenge for central banks in our times."[3]

---

[3]Otmar Issing, "Money and Credit," *The Wall Street Journal*, February 18, 2004.

In other words,

$$\%\Delta M = \%\Delta Q - \%\Delta V$$

With this rule, the growth rate of the money supply is not fixed. It can vary from year to year, yet it is predetermined in that it is dependent on the growth rates of Real GDP and velocity. For this reason, we call it the *predetermined-money-growth-rate rule.* To illustrate the workings of this rule, consider the following extended version of the equation of exchange:

$$\%\Delta M + \%\Delta V = \%\Delta P + \%\Delta Q$$

Suppose $\%\Delta Q$ is 3 percent and $\%\Delta V$ is 1 percent. The rule would specify that the growth rate in the money supply should be 2 percent. This would keep the price level stable; there would be a zero percent change in P:

$$\%\Delta M + \%\Delta V = \%\Delta P + \%\Delta Q$$
$$2\% + 1\% = 0\% + 3\%$$

The Fed and the Taylor Rule

Economist John Taylor has argued that there may be a middle ground, of sorts, between activist and nonactivist monetary policy. He has proposed that monetary authorities use a rule to guide them in making their discretionary decisions.

The rule that John Taylor has proposed has come to be known as the *Taylor rule.* The Taylor rule specifies how policymakers should set the target for the (nominal) federal funds rate. (Recall from an earlier chapter that the federal funds rate is the interest rate banks charge one another for reserves.) The "economic thinking" implicit in the Taylor rule is as follows: There is some federal funds rate target that is consistent with (1) stabilizing inflation around a rather low inflation rate and (2) stabilizing Real GDP around its full-employment level. Find this federal funds rate target and then use the tools of the Fed to hit the target.

The Taylor rule, which, according to Taylor, will find the right federal funds rate target, is:

Federal funds rate target = Inflation + Equilibrium real federal funds rate + ½ (Inflation gap) + ½ (Output gap)

Let's briefly discuss the four components of the rule:

- **Inflation.** This is the current inflation rate.
- **Equilibrium real federal funds rate.** The real federal funds rate is simply the nominal federal funds rate adjusted for inflation. Taylor assumes the equilibrium real federal funds rate is 2 percent.
- **½ inflation gap.** The inflation gap is the difference between the actual inflation rate and the target for inflation. Taylor assumes that an appropriate target for inflation is about 2 percent. If this target were accepted by policymakers, they would effectively be saying that they would not want an inflation rate higher than 2 percent.
- **½ output gap.** The output gap is the percentage difference between actual Real GDP and its full-employment or natural level.

For example, suppose the current inflation rate is 1 percent, the equilibrium real federal funds rate is 2 percent, the inflation gap is 1 percent, and the output gap is 2 percent. What is the federal funds rate target?

Federal funds rate target = Inflation + Equilibrium real federal funds rate
+ ½ (Inflation gap) + ½ (Output gap)
= 1% + 2% + ½ (1%) + ½ (2%)
= 4.5%

Inflation Targeting

Inflation Targeting
This requires the Fed to try to keep the inflation rate near a predetermined level.

Many economists today argue that the Fed should practice **inflation targeting**. Inflation targeting requires that the Fed try to keep the inflation rate near a predetermined level. There are three major issues that surround inflation targeting. The first deals with whether the inflation rate target should be a specific percentage rate (e.g., 2.5 percent) or should be a narrow range (e.g., 1.0–2.5 percent). Second, whether it is a specific percentage rate or range, what should that rate or range be? For example, if it is specific percentage rate, should it be, say, 2.0 percent or 3.5 percent? The last issue deals with whether the inflation rate target should be announced or not. In other words, if the Fed does adopt an inflation rate target of, say, 2.5 percent, should it tell the public that this is the inflation rate target?

Numerous central banks in the world do practice inflation targeting, and they do announce their targets. For example, the Bank of Canada has set a target of 2 percent (inflation), and it has been announcing its inflation target since 1991. Some other central banks that practice inflation targeting include the Bank of England, the Central Bank of Brazil, the Bank of Israel, and the Reserve Bank of New Zealand.

How would an inflation rate target work? Simply put, the Fed would undertake monetary policy actions so that the actual inflation rate stays near or at its inflation rate target. For example, if its target rate is 2 percent and the actual inflation rate is, say, 5 percent, it would cut back the growth rate in the money supply (or the absolute money supply) to bring the actual inflation rate nearer to the target rate.

The proponents of inflation targeting argue that such a policy is more in line with the Fed's objective of maintaining near price stability. The critics of inflation targeting often argue that such a policy will constrain the Fed at times—for example, when it might need to "overlook the target" to deal with a financial crisis.

SELF-TEST

1. Would a rules-based monetary policy produce price stability?

2. What is the inflationary gap? the output gap?

A Reader Asks...

Are There More Than Two Transmission Mechanisms?

A transmission mechanism describes "the routes, or channels, that ripples created in the money market travel to affect the goods and services market." We learned about the Keynesian and monetarist transmission mechanisms in this chapter. Are there other transmission mechanisms?

Yes, economists have put forth quite a few transmission mechanisms. We'll talk about a few.

One transmission mechanism focuses on monetary policy and stock prices. It says that when monetary policy is expansionary, the public finds itself with excess money. What does it do with the excess money? It buys stocks with the money. Greater demand for stocks drives up the price of stocks and increases the market value of firms. (The market value of a firm is the value investors believe a firm is worth; it is calculated by multiplying the number of shares outstanding by the current price per share.) As the market value of a firm rises, the firm decides to increase its investment spending. Higher investment, in turn, leads to greater aggregate demand and, in the short run, greater Real GDP.

Another transmission mechanism is similar to the one just described, but it focuses on consumption spending instead of investment spending. Again, we start with an increase in the money supply. Initially, the public finds itself with excess money. They use the money to buy stocks, and so the demand for and prices of stocks rise. Because stocks make up a part of a person's financial wealth, higher stock prices mean greater financial wealth for some people. What do people do with greater financial wealth? They spend some fraction of the increase in their financial wealth on consumer goods. As consumption rises, so does aggregate demand, and in the short run, Real GDP rises.

Another transmission mechanism looks at the effect of monetary policy on the exchange rate. According to this mechanism, an expansion in the money supply puts downward pressure on the interest rate (at least initially). As domestic interest rates fall, domestic dollar deposits become less attractive relative to deposits denominated in foreign currencies. As people move out of dollar-denominated deposits, the exchange-rate value of the dollar falls. In other words, the dollar depreciates relative to other currencies. Dollar depreciation and foreign currency appreciation make U.S. exports less expensive for foreigners and foreign imports more expensive for Americans. Exports rise and imports fall, so net exports rise. As a result of net exports rising, aggregate demand rises, and at least in the short run, so does Real GDP.

! analyzing the scene

Melanie agrees that "you can never have enough money," but she acts differently. How so?

Melanie agrees that you can never have enough money, and a few seconds later, she gives $124.76 to the grocery store clerk. If she really believed that you can never have enough money, she wouldn't have given up money for food. As explained earlier, a person can have "too much" money *relative to other things*.

Why doesn't Karen carry more cash?

How much cash Karen carries is related to the interest rate. We would expect her to carry less cash when the interest rate is high than when it is low.

Note that when Peter asks Karen why she carries so little cash, she says that she doesn't know. Do you think it's possible for a person to carry less cash as the interest rate (or opportunity cost of holding money) rises without knowing why she's doing so? In other words, is it possible for a person to respond to economic forces without knowing what those forces are?

Is Quentin right? Should he buy bonds when interest rates are headed down and sell bonds when they are headed up?

We know (1) bond prices and interest rates move in opposite directions, and (2) Quentin thinks he can make a lot of money by buying and selling bonds based on whether interest rates are decreasing or increasing. Quentin thinks that when interest rates are headed down, he should buy bonds. It follows that he believes bond prices are headed up, and so, he

should buy bonds now before they head up. Similarly, Quentin thinks that when interest rates are headed up, he should sell bonds. It follows that he believes bond prices are headed down, and so, he should sell bonds now before they go down in price. In short, Quentin is thinking correctly: Buy bonds when you think interest rates are going down, and sell bonds when you think interest rates are headed up.

However, Quentin was a little concerned about how he would know if interest rates were headed up or down. He is right to be concerned. Changes in interest rates are not easily predicted, as we explain in the feature, "If You're So Smart, Why Aren't You Rich?"

How can expansionary monetary policy not increase Real GDP in the short run?

You are accustomed to thinking that an increase in the money supply will shift the *AD* curve rightward. If the *SRAS* curve is upward sloping, it follows that Real GDP will rise (at least in the short run).

But now you learn that whether or not this outcome materializes depends on people's expectations. As shown in Exhibit 9, if people think expansionary monetary policy will lead to higher prices (because it shifts the *AD* curve rightward) and thus bargain for and receive higher wages, then the *SRAS* curve might shift leftward at the same time that the *AD* curve shifts to the right. If the *AD* curve shifts to the right to the same degree as the *SRAS* curve shifts to the left, then there will be no change in Real GDP. In other words, expansionary monetary policy might not "expand" Real GDP.

chapter summary

The Keynesian Transmission Mechanism

- The Keynesian route between the money market and the goods and services market is indirect. Changes in the money market must affect the investment goods market before the goods and services market is affected. Assuming that no liquidity trap exists and investment is not interest insensitive, the transmission mechanism works as follows for an increase in the money supply: An increase in the money supply lowers the interest rate and increases investment. This increases aggregate demand and thus shifts the *AD* curve rightward. Consequently, Real GDP rises, and the unemployment rate falls. Under the same assumptions, the transmission mechanism works as follows for a decrease in the money supply: A decrease in the money supply raises the interest rate and decreases investment. This decreases

aggregate demand and thus shifts the *AD* curve leftward. As a result, Real GDP falls, and the unemployment rate rises.

- The Keynesian transmission mechanism may be short-circuited either by the liquidity trap or by interest-insensitive investment. Both are Keynesian notions. If either is present, Keynesians predict that expansionary monetary policy will be unable to change Real GDP or unemployment.

The Monetarist Transmission Mechanism

- The monetarist route between the money market and the goods and services market is direct. Changes in the money supply affect aggregate demand. An increase in the money supply causes individuals to increase their spending on a wide variety of goods.

Bond Prices and Interest Rates

- Interest rates and the price of old or existing bonds are inversely related.

The Activist-Nonactivist Debate

- Activists argue that monetary policy should be deliberately used to smooth out the business cycle; they favor using activist, or discretionary, monetary policy to fine-tune the economy. Nonactivists argue against the use of discretionary monetary policy; they propose nonactivist, or rules-based, monetary policy.

- The case for discretionary monetary policy rests on three major claims: (1) The economy does not always equilibrate quickly enough at Natural Real GDP. (2) Activist monetary policy works. (3) Activist monetary policy is flexible, and flexibility is a desirable quality in monetary policy.

- The case for nonactivist monetary policy rests on three major claims: (1) There is sufficient flexibility in wages and prices in modern economies to allow the economy to equilibrate at reasonable speed at Natural Real GDP. (2) Activist monetary policies may not work. (3) Activist monetary policies are likely to make matters worse rather than better.

Nonactivist (or Rules-Based) Monetary Proposals

- The constant-money-growth-rate rule states that the annual money supply growth rate will be constant at the average annual growth rate of Real GDP.

- The predetermined-money-growth-rate rule states that the annual growth rate in the money supply will be equal to the average annual growth rate in Real GDP minus the growth rate in velocity.

- The Taylor rule holds that the federal funds rate should be targeted according to the following: Federal funds rate target = Inflation + Equilibrium real federal funds rate + ½ (Inflation gap) + ½ (Output gap).

- Inflation targeting requires the Fed to keep the inflation rate near a predetermined level.

key terms and concepts

Demand for Money (Balances)	Liquidity Trap	Contractionary Monetary Policy	Fine-tuning
Transmission Mechanism	Expansionary Monetary Policy	Activists	Nonactivists
			Inflation Targeting

questions and problems

1 Consider the following: Two researchers, *A* and *B,* are trying to determine whether eating fatty foods leads to heart attacks. The researchers proceed differently. Researcher *A* builds a model in which fatty foods may first affect *X* in one's body, and if *X* is affected, then *Y* may be affected, and if *Y* is affected, then *Z* may be affected. Finally, if *Z* is affected, the heart is affected, and the individual has an increased probability of suffering a heart attack. Researcher *B* doesn't proceed in this step-by-step fashion. She conducts an experiment to see if people who eat many fatty foods have more, fewer, or the same number of heart attacks as people who eat few fatty foods. Which researcher's methods have more in common with the research methodology implicit in the Keynesian transmission mechanism? Which researcher's methods have more in common with the research methodology implicit in the monetarist transmission mechanism? Explain your answer.

2 If bond prices fall, will individuals want to hold more or less money? Explain your answer.

3 It has been suggested that nonactivists are not concerned with the level of Real GDP and unemployment because most (if not all) nonactivist monetary proposals set as their immediate objective the stabilization of the price level. Discuss.

4 Suppose the combination of more accurate data and better forecasting techniques made it easy for the Fed to predict a recession 10 to 16 months in advance. Would this strengthen the case for activism or nonactivism? Explain your answer.

5 Suppose it were proved that there is no liquidity trap and investment is not interest insensitive. Would this be enough to disprove the Keynesian claim that expansionary monetary policy is not always effective at changing Real GDP? Why or why not?

6 Both activists and nonactivists make good points for their respective positions. Do you think there is anything an activist could say to a nonactivist to convince him or her to accept the activist position, and vice versa? If so, what is it? If not, why not?

7 The discussion of supply and demand in Chapter 3 noted that if two goods are substitutes, the price of one and the demand for the other are directly related. For example, if Pepsi-Cola and Coca-Cola are substitutes, an increase in the price of Pepsi-Cola will increase the demand for Coca-Cola. Suppose that bonds and stocks are substitutes. We know that interest rates and bond prices are inversely related. What do you predict is the relationship between stock prices and interest rates? Explain your answer.

8 Argue the case for and against a monetary rule.

9 How does inflation targeting work?

10 Conduct the following exercise. Pick any week of the year. Quickly read through all the issues of *The Wall Street Journal* for that week and write down the number of articles in which the word *Fed* is used, along with a brief summary of each article. Usually, the article will have to do with monetary policy. Many articles will also present opinions about what the Fed has done, is doing, and will do. The chief economist at a major firm may say that he thinks the Fed is positioning itself to ease up on money supply growth in the upcoming months. An economic forecaster at a major bank may say she thinks the newest member of the Board of Governors will be persuasive in arguing for inflation targeting. What is the point of this exercise? First, the large number of articles in which the Fed is mentioned will show you how important the Fed and monetary policy are to the economics, political, banking, and business communities. Second, the quotations from (supposedly) knowledgeable people will show you how much guessing and difference of opinion surround Fed monetary policy. Third, the factors cited as influencing Fed actions will give you a rough idea of how individuals think the Fed determines monetary policy.

After you conduct this exercise, sit down and reflect on the following questions:

a Is the Fed implementing an activist monetary policy?

b How does the Fed decide whether it should increase or decrease the rate of growth of the money supply?

c Would *The Wall Street Journal* publish so many articles about monetary policy if the United States had a rules-based monetary policy? If not, why not?

d Would I be better off or worse off if I could accurately predict monetary policy? What monetary institutions are needed for the accurate prediction of monetary policy?

If answers to these questions are not easily forthcoming, do not be concerned. As long as you can ask or recognize questions relevant to monetary policy and have some idea of what the answers may be, you are ready to join the interesting and continuing debate on monetary policy. That is an important accomplishment.

working with numbers and graphs

1 Bob bought a bond last year for $10,000 that promises to pay him $900 a year. This year, it is possible to buy a bond for $10,000 that promises to pay $1,000 a year. If Bob wants to sell his (old) bond, what is its price likely to be?

2 Sally bought a bond last year for $10,000 that promises to pay her $1,000 a year. This year, it is possible to buy a bond for $10,000 that promises to pay $800 a year. If Sally wants to sell her (old) bond, what is its price likely to be?

3 Suppose the annual average percentage change in Real GDP is 2.3 percent, and the annual average percentage change in velocity is 1.1 percent. Using the monetary rule discussed in the text, what percentage change in the money supply will keep prices stable (on average)?

4 Graphically show that the more interest insensitive the investment demand curve, the less likely monetary policy is effective at changing Real GDP.

5 Which panel in the figure to the right best describes the situation in each of (a)–(d)?

  a Expansionary monetary policy that effectively removes the economy from a recessionary gap

  b Expansionary monetary policy that is destabilizing

  c Contractionary monetary policy that effectively removes the economy from an inflationary gap

  d Monetary policy that is ineffective at changing Real GDP

6 Graphically portray the Keynesian transmission mechanism under the following conditions: (a) a decrease in the money supply; (b) no liquidity trap; (c) investment demand curve is downward sloping.

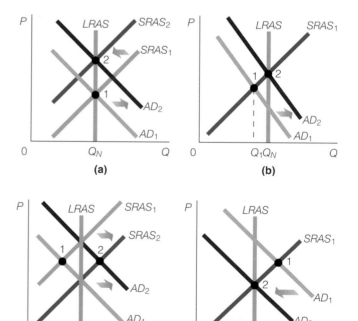

(a)   **(b)**   **(c)**   **(d)**

7 Graphically portray the monetarist transmission mechanism when the money supply declines.

8 According to the Taylor rule, if inflation is 5 percent, the inflation gap is 3 percent, and the output gap is 2 percent, what does the federal funds rate target equal?

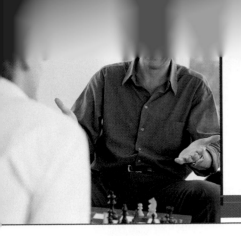

Setting the Scene

The following events occurred not long ago.

10:45 P.M. STEVEN WILSON'S HOUSE, EVANSTON, ILLINOIS

Steven has had a full day. It's almost time to go to bed, but before he does, Steven goes online to check the weather forecast for tomorrow. "Seventy percent chance of rain by midafternoon," the forecast reads. "I'd better put my umbrella out so I don't forget it tomorrow," Steven thinks to himself.

4:15 P.M. THE STATE FAIR, WICHITA, KANSAS

The fortuneteller's sign reads: "The Crystal Ball Never Lies. Your Fortune Told for $10." Three people wait in line to have their fortunes told. Robin, 16 years old, is the third person in line. "I'm just here for fun," Robin thinks to himself. "Still, I might as well ask the fortuneteller—just for fun—whether or not Stephanie will accept my invitation to the Friday night dance."

7:13 P.M. NICK AND MICHAEL, BROTHERS, ARE PLAYING CHESS IN THEIR HOME IN CANYON COUNTRY, CALIFORNIA.

Nick thinks, "If I move from e4 to e5, he'll probably move from f3 to c6, after which I'll move from b5 to c5. But it's the next step that worries me. What is the chance he'll then move from c3 to d6?" Nick then moves from e4 to e5. Michael thinks, "Nick probably thinks I'm going to move from f3 to c6, after which he'll probably move from b5 to c5. Maybe I should move from d3 to c7."

10:32 P.M. GEORGE IS WATCHING ONE OF HIS FAVORITE MOVIES, *THE GODFATHER*, ON TELEVISION. IT'S THE SCENE WHERE DON CORLEONE WARNS MICHAEL ABOUT BARZINI.

Don Corleone:
   Barzini will move against you first.

Michael:
   How?

Don Corleone:
   He will get in touch with you through someone you absolutely trust. That person will arrange a meeting, guarantee your safety . . .

   He rises and looks at Michael . . .

Don Corleone:
   . . . and at that meeting you will be assassinated.

? Here is a question to keep in mind as you read this chapter:

- *What does each of the events have to do with economics?*

See analyzing the scene at the end of this chapter for the answer to this question.

Phillips Curve Analysis

The *Phillips curve* is used to analyze the relationship between inflation and unemployment. We begin the discussion of the Phillips curve by focusing on the work of three economists: A. W. Phillips, Paul Samuelson, and Robert Solow.

The Phillips Curve

In 1958, A. W. Phillips of the London School of Economics published a paper in the economics journal *Economica*. The paper was titled "The Relation Between Unemployment and the Rate of Change of Money Wages in the United Kingdom, 1861–1957." As the title suggests, Phillips collected data about the rate of change in money wages, sometimes referred to as *wage inflation*, and *unemployment rates* in the United Kingdom over a period of time. He then plotted the rate of change in money wages against the unemployment rate for each year. Finally, he fit a curve to the data points (Exhibit 1).

AN INVERSE RELATIONSHIP The curve came to be known as the **Phillips curve**. Notice that the curve is downward sloping, suggesting that the rate of change of money wage rates (wage inflation) and unemployment rates are *inversely related*. This inverse relationship suggests a tradeoff between wage inflation and unemployment. Higher wage inflation means lower unemployment; lower wage inflation means higher unemployment.

Policymakers concluded from the Phillips curve that it was impossible to lower both wage inflation and unemployment; one could do one or the other. So the combination of low wage inflation and low unemployment was unlikely. This was the bad news.

The good news was that rising unemployment and rising wage inflation did not go together either. Thus, the combination of high unemployment and high wage inflation was unlikely.

Samuelson and Solow: The Phillips Curve Is Americanized

In 1960, two American economists, Paul Samuelson and Robert Solow, published an article in the *American Economic Review* in which they fit a Phillips curve to the U.S. economy from 1935 to 1959. Besides using American data instead of British data, they measured

Phillips Curve

A curve that originally showed the relationship between wage inflation and unemployment. Now it more often shows the relationship between price inflation and unemployment.

Why is there an inverse relationship between wage inflation and unemployment?

Early explanations focused on the state of the labor market, given changes in aggregate demand. When aggregate demand is increasing, businesses expand production and hire more employees. As the unemployment rate falls, the labor market becomes tighter and employers find it increasingly difficult to hire workers at old wages. Businesses must offer higher wages to obtain additional workers. Unemployment and money wage rates move in opposite directions.

The Original Phillips Curve

This curve was constructed by A. W. Phillips, using data for the United Kingdom from 1861 to 1913. (The relationship here is also representative of the experience of the United Kingdom through 1957.) The original Phillips curve suggests an inverse relationship between wage inflation and unemployment; it represents a wage inflation–unemployment tradeoff. (Note: Each dot represents a single year.)

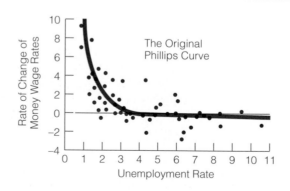

The Original Phillips Curve

price inflation rates (instead of wage inflation rates) against unemployment rates. They found an inverse relationship between (price) inflation and unemployment (see Exhibit 2).[1]

Economists concluded from the Phillips curve that **stagflation**, or high inflation together with high unemployment, was extremely unlikely. The economy could register (1) high unemployment and low inflation or (2) low unemployment and high inflation. Also, economists noticed that the Phillips curve presented policymakers with a *menu of choices*. For example, policymakers could choose to move the economy to any of the points on the Phillips curve in Exhibit 2. If they decided that a point like *A,* with high unemployment and low inflation, was preferable to a point like *D,* with low unemployment and high inflation, then so be it. It was simply a matter of reaching the right level of aggregate demand. To Keynesian economists, who were gaining a reputation for advocating fine-tuning the economy (i.e., using small-scale measures to counterbalance undesirable economic trends), this conclusion seemed consistent with their theories and policy proposals.

Stagflation

The simultaneous occurrence of high rates of inflation and unemployment.

The Controversy Begins: Are There Really Two Phillips Curves?

This section discusses the work of Milton Friedman and the hypothesis that there are two, not one, Phillips curves.

Things Aren't Always as We Thought

In the 1970s and early 1980s, economists began to question many of the conclusions about the Phillips curve. Their questions were largely prompted by events after 1969. Consider Exhibit 3, which shows U.S. inflation and unemployment rates for the years 1961–2003. The 1961–1969 period, which is shaded, depicts the original Phillips curve tradeoff between inflation and unemployment. The remaining period, 1970–2003, as a whole does not, although some subperiods, such as 1976–1979, do.

Focusing on the period 1970–2003, we note that stagflation—high unemployment and high inflation—is possible. For example, 1975, 1981, and 1982 are definitely years of stagflation. The existence of stagflation implies that a tradeoff between inflation and unemployment may not always exist.

Friedman and the Natural Rate Theory

Milton Friedman, in his presidential address to the American Economic Association in 1967 (published in the *American Economic Review*), attacked the idea of a *permanent* downward-sloping Phillips curve. Friedman's key point was that there are two, not one, Phillips curves: a short-run Phillips curve and a long-run Phillips curve. Friedman said, "There is always a temporary tradeoff between inflation and unemployment; there is no permanent tradeoff." In other words, *there is a tradeoff in the short run but not in the long run.* Friedman's discussion not only introduced two types of Phillips curves to the analysis but also opened the macroeconomics door wide, once and for all, to expectations theory—that is, to the idea that people's expectations about economic events affect economic outcomes.

exhibit **2**

The Phillips Curve and a Menu of Choices

Samuelson and Solow's early work using American data showed that the Phillips curve was downward-sloping. Economists reasoned that stagflation was extremely unlikely and that the Phillips curve presented policymakers with a menu of choices—point *A*, *B*, *C*, or *D*.

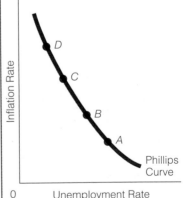

---

[1]Today, when economists speak of the Phillips curve, they are usually referring to the relationship between price inflation rates and unemployment rates instead of wage inflation rates and unemployment rates.

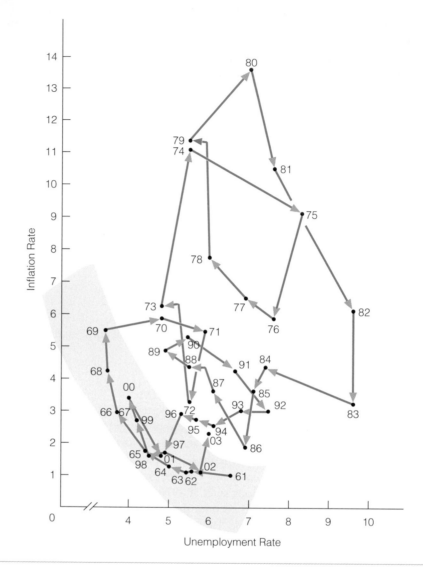

The Diagram That Raises Questions: Inflation and Unemployment, 1961–2003

The period 1961–1969 clearly depicts the original Phillips curve tradeoff between inflation and unemployment. The later period, 1970–2003, as a whole, does not. However, some sub-periods do, such as 1976–1979. The diagram presents empirical evidence that stagflation may exist; an inflation-unemployment tradeoff may not always hold.

Exhibit 4 illustrates both the short-run and long-run Phillips curves. We start with the economy in long-run equilibrium, operating at Q_1, which is equal to Q_N. This is shown in Window 1. In the main diagram, the economy is at point 1 at the natural rate of unemployment U_N. Further, and most important, *we assume that the expected inflation rate and the actual inflation rate are the same;* both are 2 percent.

Now suppose government *unexpectedly* increases aggregate demand from AD_1 to AD_2, as shown in Window 2. As a result, the *actual* inflation rate increases (say, to 4 percent), but in the short run (immediately after the increase in aggregate demand), individual decision makers do not know this. Consequently, the *expected* inflation rate remains at 2 percent. In short, aggregate demand increases at the same time that people's expected inflation rate remains constant. Because of this combination of events, certain things happen.

The higher aggregate demand causes temporary shortages and higher prices. Businesses then respond to higher prices and higher profits by increasing output. Higher output requires more employees, so businesses start hiring more workers. As job vacancies increase, many currently unemployed individuals find work. Furthermore, many of these newly employed persons accept the prevailing wage rate because they think the wages

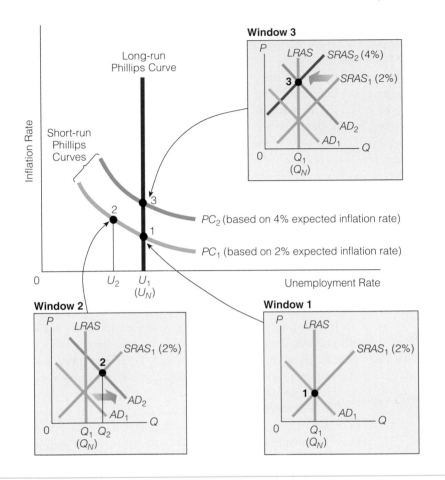

exhibit **4**

Short-Run and Long-Run Phillips Curves

Starting at point 1 in the main diagram, and assuming that the expected inflation rate stays constant as aggregate demand increases, the economy moves to point 2. As the expected inflation rate changes and comes to equal the actual inflation rate, the economy moves to point 3. Points 1 and 2 lie on a short-run Phillips curve. Points 1 and 3 lie on a long-run Phillips curve. (Note: The percentages in parentheses following the SRAS curves in the windows refer to the expected inflation rates.)

will have greater purchasing power (recall that they expect the inflation rate to be 2 percent) than, in fact, those wages will turn out to have.

So far, the results of an increase in aggregate demand with no change in the expected inflation rate are (1) an increase in Real GDP from Q_1 to Q_2 (see Window 2) and (2) a corresponding decrease in the unemployment rate from U_1 to U_2 (see the main diagram). Thus, the economy has moved from point 1 to point 2 in the main diagram.

This raises the question: Is point 2 a stable equilibrium? Friedman answered that it is not. He argued that *as long as the expected inflation rate is not equal to the actual inflation rate, the economy is not in long-run equilibrium.*

For Friedman, as for most economists today, the movement from point 1 to point 2 on PC_1 is a short-run movement. Economists refer to PC_1, along which short-run movements occur, as a *short-run Phillips curve.*

In time, inflation expectations begin to change. As prices continue to climb, wage earners realize that their real (inflation-adjusted) wages have fallen. In hindsight, they realize that they accepted nominal (money) wages based on an expected inflation rate (2 percent) that was too low. They revise their inflation expectations upward.

At the same time, some wage earners quit their jobs because they choose not to continue working at such low *real wages.* Eventually, the combination of some workers quitting their jobs and most (if not all) workers revising their inflation expectations upward causes wage rates to move upward.

Higher wage rates shift the short-run aggregate supply curve from $SRAS_1$ to $SRAS_2$ (see Window 3), ultimately moving the economy back to Natural Real GDP and to the natural rate of unemployment at point 3 (see the main diagram). The curve that connects point 1, where the economy started, and point 3, where it ended, is called the *long-run Phillips curve*.

Thus, the short-run Phillips curve exhibits a tradeoff between inflation and unemployment, whereas the long-run Phillips curve does not. This is the idea implicit in what has come to be called the **Friedman natural rate theory** (or the *Friedman "fooling" theory*). According to this theory, in the long run, the economy returns to its natural rate of unemployment, and the only reason it moved away from the natural unemployment rate in the first place was because workers were "fooled" (in the short run) into thinking the inflation rate was lower than it was.

How, specifically, do people's expectations relate to the discussion of the short- and long-run Phillips curves? To see how, again look at Exhibit 4. The economy starts out at point 1 in the main diagram. Then something happens in the economy: Aggregate demand increases. This raises the inflation rate, *but it takes some time before workers realize the change in the inflation rate.* In the interim, their expected inflation rate is "too low." And because their expected inflation rate is too low, workers are willing to work at jobs (and produce output) that they wouldn't work at if they perceived the inflation rate realistically.

But in time, workers do perceive the inflation rate realistically. In other words, the expected inflation rate is no longer too low—it has risen to equal the actual inflation rate. There is a predicted response in the unemployment rate and output as a result: The unemployment rate rises and output falls.

To summarize, because workers' expectations (of inflation) are, in the short run, inconsistent with reality, workers produce more output than they would have produced if those expectations were consistent with reality. Do you see how people's expectations can affect such real economic variables as Real GDP and the unemployment rate?

Exhibit 5 may also help explain the Friedman natural rate theory.

Friedman Natural Rate Theory
The idea that in the long run, unemployment is at its natural rate. Within the Phillips curve framework, the natural rate theory specifies that there is a long-run Phillips curve, which is vertical at the natural rate of unemployment.

Thinking like **AN ECONOMIST**   *A person says she bases her actions on reality. When it rains, she pulls out an umbrella; when she has a hard time seeing, she gets her eyes checked. People also base their actions on their perceptions of reality. That is what workers in the Friedman natural rate theory are doing. The inflation rate has actually increased, but workers don't perceive this change. Thus, in the short run (during the time period in which they misperceive reality), the workers do not base their actions on reality, but on their perception of reality.*

Theme **macro**   One of the biggest questions in macroeconomics is, How does the economy work? Or how do we explain what happens in the economy? With the introduction of expectations to our macroeconomic discussion, some economists are telling us that what happens in the economy has much to do with people's expectations. In other words, not only do real things in an economy—such as the amount of resources an economy makes use of, the current state of monetary policy, and so on—determine what happens in an economy, but also what "people think" determines what happens in an economy.

How Do People Form Their Expectations?

Implicit in the Friedman natural rate theory is a theory about how individuals form their expectations. Essentially, the theory holds that individuals form their expected inflation rate by looking at past inflation rates. To illustrate, let's suppose that the actual inflation rates in years 1–4 are 5 percent, 3 percent, 2 percent, and 2 percent, respectively. What do you think the inflation rate will be in year 5? Friedman assumes that people weight past inflation rates to come up with their expected inflation rate. For example, John may assign the following weights to the inflation rates in the past 4 years:

exhibit 5

Mechanics of the Friedman Natural Rate Theory

A CLOSER LOOK

The Friedman Natural Rate Theory

1. **Wages and prices are flexible.**
2. **Expectations are formed adaptively.**

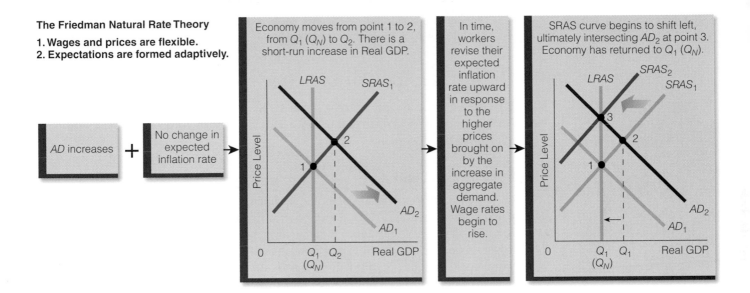

Year	Inflation Rate	Weight
1	5 percent	10%
2	3 percent	20%
3	2 percent	30%
4	2 percent	40%

In other words, as the upcoming year approaches, the weight assigned to the present year's inflation rate rises. Based on these weights, John forms his expected inflation rate (his "best guess" of the inflation rate in the upcoming year) by finding the weighted average of the inflation rates in the past 4 years.

$$\text{Expected inflation rate} = 0.10(5 \text{ percent}) + 0.20(3 \text{ percent})$$
$$+ 0.30(2 \text{ percent}) + 0.40(2 \text{ percent})$$
$$= 2.5 \text{ percent}$$

John's expected inflation rate is 2.5 percent.

Notice that in forming an expected inflation rate this way, the person is always looking to the past. He is, in a sense, looking over his shoulder to see what has happened and then, based on what has happened, "figuring out" what he thinks *will happen*. In economics, a person who forms an expected inflation rate this way is said to hold **adaptive expectations**. In short, the Friedman natural rate theory implicitly assumes that people hold adaptive expectations.

Some economists have argued this point. They believe that people do not form their expected inflation rate using adaptive expectations. Instead, they believe people hold *rational expectations*. We discuss this in the next section.

Adaptive Expectations

Expectations that individuals form from past experience and modify slowly as the present and the future become the past (as time passes).

SELF-TEST

(Answers to Self-Test questions are in the Self-Test Appendix.)

1. What condition must exist for the Phillips curve to present policymakers with a permanent menu of choices (between inflation and unemployment)?

2. Is there a tradeoff between inflation and unemployment? Explain your answer.

3. The Friedman natural rate theory is sometimes called the "fooling" theory. Who is being fooled and what are they being fooled about?

Rational Expectations and New Classical Theory

Rational expectations have played a major role in the Phillips curve controversy. The work of economists Robert Lucas, Robert Barro, Thomas Sargent, and Neil Wallace is relevant to this discussion.

Rational Expectations

In the early 1970s, a few economists, including Robert Lucas of the University of Chicago (winner of the 1995 Nobel Prize in Economics), began to question the short-run tradeoff between inflation and unemployment. Essentially, Lucas combined the natural rate theory with rational expectations.[2] (In this text, the natural rate theory built on adaptive expectations is called the *Friedman natural rate theory;* the natural rate theory built on rational expectations is called the *new classical theory.*)

Rational Expectations

Expectations that individuals form based on past experience and also on their predictions about the effects of present and future policy actions and events.

Before presenting the new classical theory, we define and discuss **rational expectations**. Rational expectations hold that individuals form the expected inflation rate not only on the basis of their past experience with inflation (looking over their shoulders) but also on their predictions about the effects of present and future policy actions and events. In short, the expected inflation rate is formed by looking at the past, present, and future. To illustrate, suppose the inflation rate has been 2 percent for the past 7 years. Then, the chairman of the Fed's Board of Governors speaks about "sharply stimulating the economy." Rational expectationists argue that the expected inflation rate might immediately jump upward based on the current words of the chairman.

A major difference between adaptive and rational expectations is the *speed* at which the expected inflation rate changes. If the expected inflation rate is formed adaptively, then it is slow to change. It is based only on the past, so individuals will wait until the present and the future become the past before they change their expectations. If the expected inflation rate is formed rationally, it changes quickly because it is based on the past, present, and future. One implication of rational expectations is that people anticipate policy.

Do People Anticipate Policy?

Suppose you chose people at random on the street and asked them this question: What do you think the Fed will do in the next few months? Do you think you would be more likely to receive (1) an intelligent answer or (2) the response, "What is the Fed?"

Most readers of this text will probably choose answer (2). There is a general feeling that the person on the street knows little about economics or economic institutions. The answer to our question "Do people anticipate policy?" seems to be no.

---

[2]Rational expectations appeared on the economic scene in 1961 when John Muth published "Rational Expectations and the Theory of Price Movements" in the journal *Econometrica*. For about 10 years, the article received little attention from the economics profession. Then, in the early 1970s, with the work of Robert Lucas, Thomas Sargent, Neil Wallace, Robert Barro, and others, the article began to be noticed.

But suppose you chose people at random on Wall Street and asked the same question. In this case, the answer to our larger question "Do people anticipate policy?" is likely to be yes.

We suggest that not all persons need to anticipate policy. *As long as some do*, the consequences may be the same *as if* all persons do. For example, Juanita Estevez is anticipating policy if she decides to buy 100 shares of SKA because her best friend, Tammy Higgins, heard from her friend, Kenny Urich, that his broker, Roberta Gunter, told him that SKA's stock is expected to go up. Juanita is anticipating policy because it is likely that Roberta Gunter obtained her information from a researcher in the brokerage firm who makes it his business to "watch the Fed" and to anticipate its next move.

Of course, anticipating policy is not done just for the purpose of buying and selling stocks. Labor unions hire professional forecasters to predict future inflation rates, which is important information to have during wage contract negotiations. Banks hire professional forecasters to predict inflation rates, which they incorporate into the interest rate they charge. Export businesses hire professional forecasters to predict the future exchange-rate value of the dollar. The average investor may subscribe to a business or investment newsletter to predict interest rates, the price of gold, or next year's inflation rate more accurately. The person thinking of refinancing his or her mortgage watches one of the many financial news shows on television to find out about the government's most recent move and how it will affect interest rates in the next 3 months.

New Classical Theory: The Effects of Unanticipated and Anticipated Policy

New classical theory makes two major assumptions: (1) expectations are formed rationally; (2) wages and prices are flexible. With these in mind, we discuss new classical theory in two settings: where policy is unanticipated and where policy is anticipated.

macro Theme In an earlier chapter, we said that not all economists agree on how economic policy (e.g., fiscal and monetary policy) works or even if it does work—say, at changing Real GDP. With our discussion of expectations, we are adding a new dimension to things. Now you will find that some economists believe economic policy might not work if it is anticipated but will work if it is unanticipated. In other words, if the policy is a "surprise," it has a much greater chance of working than if it isn't.

UNANTICIPATED POLICY Consider Exhibit 6(a). The economy starts at point 1, where $Q_1 = Q_N$. Unexpectedly, the Fed begins to buy government securities, and the money supply and aggregate demand increase. The aggregate demand curve shifts rightward from AD_1 to AD_2. Because the policy action was unanticipated, individuals are caught off guard, so the anticipated price level (P_1), on which the short-run aggregate supply curve is based, is not likely to change immediately. (This is similar to saying, as we did in the discussion of the Friedman natural rate theory, that individuals' expected inflation rate is less than the actual inflation rate.)

In the short run, the economy moves from point 1 to point 2, from Q_1 to Q_2. (In Phillips curve terms, the economy has moved up the short-run Phillips curve to a higher inflation rate and lower unemployment rate.) In the long run, workers correctly anticipate the higher price level and increase their wage demands accordingly. The short-run aggregate supply curve shifts leftward from $SRAS_1$ to $SRAS_2$, and the economy moves to point 3.

(a)

(b)

Rational Expectations in an *AD-AS* Framework

The economy is in long-run equilibrium at point 1 in both (a) and (b). In (a), there is an unanticipated increase in aggregate demand. In the short run, the economy moves to point 2. In the long run, it moves to point 3. In (b), the increase in aggregate demand is correctly anticipated. Because the increase is anticipated, the short-run aggregate supply curve shifts from *SRAS*$_1$ to *SRAS*$_2$ at the same time the aggregate demand curve shifts from *AD*$_1$ to *AD*$_2$. The economy moves directly to point 2, which is comparable to point 3 in (a).

ANTICIPATED POLICY Now consider what happens when policy is anticipated, in particular, when it is *correctly anticipated*. When individuals anticipate that the Fed will buy government securities and that the money supply, aggregate demand, and prices will increase, they will adjust their present actions accordingly. For example, workers will bargain for higher wages so that their real wages will not fall when the price level rises. As a result, the short-run aggregate supply curve will shift leftward from *SRAS*$_1$ to *SRAS*$_2$ *at the same time* that the aggregate demand curve shifts rightward from *AD*$_1$ to *AD*$_2$ (see Exhibit 6(b)). The economy moves directly from point 1 to point 2. Real GDP does not change; throughout the adjustment period, it remains at its natural level. It follows that the unemployment rate does not change either. There is no short-run tradeoff between inflation and unemployment. The short-run Phillips curve and the long-run Phillips curve are the same; the curve is vertical.

Policy Ineffectiveness Proposition (PIP)

Using rational expectations, we showed (see Exhibit 6) that *if the rise in aggregate demand is unanticipated, there is a short-run increase in Real GDP, but if the rise in aggregate demand is correctly anticipated, there is no change in Real GDP.* What are the implications of these results?

Let's consider the two types of macroeconomic policies—fiscal and monetary—that you have studied. Both of these policies can theoretically increase aggregate demand. For example, assuming there is no crowding out or incomplete crowding out, expansionary fiscal policy shifts the *AD* curve rightward. Expansionary monetary policy does the same. In both cases, expansionary policy is effective at increasing Real GDP and lowering the unemployment rate *in the short run*.

New classical economists question this scenario. They argue that if (1) the expansionary policy change is correctly anticipated, (2) individuals form their expectations rationally, and (3) wages and prices are flexible, then neither expansionary fiscal policy nor expansionary monetary policy will be able to increase Real GDP and lower the unemployment rate in the short run. This argument is called the **policy ineffectiveness proposition (PIP)**.

Policy Ineffectiveness Proposition (PIP)

If (1) a policy change is correctly anticipated, (2) individuals form their expectations rationally, and (3) wages and prices are flexible, then neither fiscal policy nor monetary policy is effective at meeting macroeconomic goals.

economics 24/7

RATIONAL EXPECTATIONS IN THE COLLEGE CLASSROOM

If people hold rational expectations, the outcome of a policy will be different if the policy is unanticipated than if it is anticipated. Specifically, unanticipated policy changes can move the economy away from the natural unemployment rate, but (correctly) anticipated policy changes cannot. Does something similar happen in a college classroom?

Suppose Ana's history class starts at 9:00 A.M., and it is "natural" for her to arrive 1 minute before class starts. In other words, her "natural waiting time" is 1 minute.

The first day of class, Ana arrives at 8:59, her instructor arrives at 8:59:30, and she starts class promptly at 9:00 A.M.

The second day of class, Ana arrives at 8:59, her instructor arrives at 9:01:30, and she starts class at 9:02 A.M. On this day, Ana has waited 3 minutes, which is above her natural waiting time of 1 minute.

The third, fourth, and fifth days of class are the same as the second. So for the second through fifth days, Ana is operating at above her natural waiting time.

Rational expectations hold that people will not continue to make the same mistake. In this case, Ana will take her professor's recent arrival time into account and adjust accordingly. On the sixth day of class, instead of arriving at 8:59,

Ana arrives at 9:01. This day, the instructor again arrives at 9:01:30 and begins class at 9:02 A.M. Ana has moved back to her natural waiting time of 1 minute.

Let's summarize our story so far: Ana has a natural waiting time that was met on the first day of class. On the second through fifth days of class, the professor obviously had a "change of policy" as to her arrival time. This change of policy was unanticipated by Ana, so she was fooled into waiting more than her natural waiting time. But Ana did not continue to make the same mistake. She adjusted to her professor's "policy change" and went back to her 1-minute natural waiting time.

Now let's change things a bit. Suppose at the end of the first day of class, the professor says, "I know I arrived to class at 8:59:30 today, but I won't do this again. From now on, I will arrive at 9:01:30."

In this situation, the professor has announced her policy change. Ana hears the announcement and therefore (correctly) anticipates what the professor will do from now on. With this information, she adjusts her behavior. Instead of arriving to class at 8:59, she arrives at 9:01. Thus, she has correctly anticipated her professor's policy change, and she will remain at her natural waiting time (she will not move from it, even temporarily).

Think what this means. If, under certain conditions, expansionary monetary and fiscal policy are not effective at increasing Real GDP and lowering the unemployment rate, the case for government fine-tuning the economy is questionable.

Keep in mind that new classical economists are not saying that monetary and fiscal policies are never effective. Instead, they are saying that monetary and fiscal policies are not effective *under certain conditions*—specifically, when (1) policy is correctly anticipated, (2) people form their expectations rationally, and (3) wages and prices are flexible.

Rational Expectations and Incorrectly Anticipated Policy

Let's make a small change this time. Suppose wages and prices are flexible, people form their expectations rationally, and they anticipate policy—but this time they anticipate policy *incorrectly*. What happens?

> ### Thinking like AN ECONOMIST
>
> There is a lot of if–then thinking in economics. ("If the price of a good falls and nothing else changes, then the quantity demanded of a good will rise.") That is what we have here. New classical economists are saying that if people anticipate policy correctly, and if people form their expectations rationally, and if wages and prices are flexible, then monetary and fiscal policies are not effective at changing Real GDP. Of course, this then begs the question of whether or not the conditional statements (the if statements) do actually hold in the real world.

To illustrate, consider Exhibit 7. The economy is in long-run equilibrium at point 1 where $Q_1 = Q_N$. People believe the Fed will increase aggregate demand by increasing the money supply, but they *incorrectly anticipate* the degree to which aggregate demand will be increased. Thinking aggregate demand will increase from AD_1 to AD_2, they immediately revise their anticipated price level to P_2 (the long-run equilibrium position of the AD_2 curve and the *LRAS* curve). As a result, the short-run aggregate supply curve shifts leftward from $SRAS_1$ to $SRAS_2$.

However, the actual increase in aggregate demand is less than anticipated, and the aggregate demand curve only shifts rightward from AD_1 to AD_2'. As a result, the economy moves to point 2′, to a lower Real GDP and a higher unemployment rate. We conclude that a policy designed to increase Real GDP and lower unemployment can do just the opposite if the policy is less expansionary than anticipated.

In the example just given, people incorrectly anticipated policy in a particular direction; that is, they mistakenly believed that the aggregate demand curve was going to shift to the right more than it actually did. In other words, they *overestimated the increase in aggregate demand*. If people can overestimate the increase in aggregate demand, then it is likely that they can *underestimate* the increase in aggregate demand too. In short, when discussing rational expectations, we get different outcomes in the short run depending on whether policy is (1) unanticipated, (2) anticipated correctly, (3) anticipated incorrectly in one direction, or (4) anticipated incorrectly in the other direction.

> **Q&A**
>
> *Are new classical economists saying that if people anticipate things correctly, we will get different economic outcomes than if they anticipate things, say, incorrectly in a particular direction?*
>
> *Yes, that is exactly what they are saying.*

How to Fall into a Recession Without Really Trying

Suppose the public witnesses the following series of events 3 times in 3 years.

1. The federal government runs a budget deficit. It finances the deficit by borrowing from the public (issuing Treasury bills, notes, and bonds).

2. The Fed conducts open market operations and buys many of the government securities.

3. Aggregate demand increases and the price level rises.

exhibit 7

The Short-Run Response to an Aggregate Demand-Increasing Policy That Is Less Expansionary Than Anticipated (in the New Classical Theory)

Starting at point 1, people anticipate an increase in aggregate demand from AD_1 to AD_2. Based on this, the short-run aggregate supply curve shifts leftward from $SRAS_1$ to $SRAS_2$. It turns out, however, that the aggregate demand curve only shifts rightward to AD_2' (less than anticipated). As a result, the economy moves to point 2′, to a lower Real GDP and a higher unemployment rate.

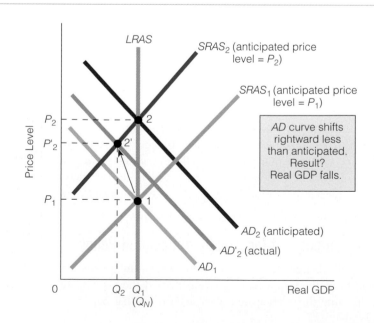

4. At the same time all this is going on, Congress says it will do whatever is necessary to bring inflation under control. The chairman of the Fed says the Fed will soon move against inflation.

5. Congress, the president, and the Fed do *not* move against inflation.

According to some economists, if the government says it will do *X* but continues to do *Y* instead, then people will see through the charade. They will equate "saying *X*" with "doing *Y*." In other words, the equation in their heads will read "Say *X* = Do *Y*." They will also always base their behavior on what they expect the government to do, not on what it says it will do.[3]

Now suppose the government changes; it says it will do *X* and actually does *X*. People will not know the government is telling the truth this time, and they will continue to think that saying *X* really means doing *Y*.

Some new classical economists say this is what happened in the early 1980s and that it goes a long way to explaining the 1981–1982 recession. They tell this story:

1. President Reagan proposed, and Congress approved, tax cuts in 1981.

2. Although some economists insisted the tax cuts would stimulate so much economic activity that tax revenues would increase, the public believed the tax cuts would decrease tax revenues and increase the size of the budget deficit (that existed at the time).

3. People translated larger budget deficits into more government borrowing.

4. They anticipated greater money supply growth connected with the larger deficits because they had seen this happen before.

5. Greater money supply growth would mean an increase in aggregate demand and in the price level.

6. The Fed said it would not increase the money supply, but it had said this before and it had acted contrarily, so few people believed the Fed this time.

7. The Fed actually did not increase the money supply as much as individuals thought it would.

8. This meant the monetary policy was not as expansionary as individuals had anticipated.

9. As a result, the economy moved to a point like 2′ in Exhibit 7. Real GDP fell and unemployment increased; a recession ensued.

The moral of the story, according to new classical economists, is that if the Fed says it is going to do *X*, then it had better do *X* because if it doesn't, the next time it says it is going to do *X*, no one will believe it and the economy may fall into a recession as a consequence. The recession will be an unintended effect of the Fed saying one thing and doing another in the past.

Q&A

We are not used to seeing expansionary monetary policy resulting in a decline in Real GDP, which is what Exhibit 7 shows. Isn't this a very unusual outcome? Usually, we think of expansionary monetary policy increasing Real GDP—at least in the short run.

You are correct that we usually think of expansionary monetary policy as increasing Real GDP in the short run. What we are saying with Exhibit 7, though, is that under certain conditions, expansionary monetary policy can result in declining Real GDP. How so? If people think that the Fed will increase the money supply by more than the Fed actually increases the money supply.

Thinking like AN ECONOMIST

Think of how economics might differ from chemistry. In chemistry, if you add 2 molecules of hydrogen to 1 molecule of oxygen, you always get water. But in economics, if you add expansionary monetary policy to an economy, you don't always get a rise in short-run Real GDP. Sometimes you can get a rise (when policy is unanticipated), at other times there will be no change in Real GDP (when policy is correctly anticipated), and at still other times there will be a decline in Real GDP (when policy is incorrectly anticipated in a particular direction). What is often frustrating to economists is that sometimes the layperson thinks that economics works the same way chemistry does: X plus Y should always give us Z. Sorry, but that is not the way things work in economics. The one thing that exists in economics (that is part of determining outcomes) that does not exist in chemistry is human beings. And what new classical economists teach us about those human beings is that their perceptions and anticipation of things (vis-à-vis reality) have a large part to play in determining outcomes.

---

[3]Rational expectations have sometimes been reduced to the adage, "Fool me once, shame on you; fool me twice, shame on me."

economics 24/7

THE BOY WHO CRIED WOLF (AND THE TOWNSPEOPLE WITH RATIONAL EXPECTATIONS)

You may know the fable about the boy and the wolf: There was a young boy who liked to play tricks on people. One day, the boy's father (a shepherd) had to go out of town. He asked his son to take care of the sheep while he was gone. While the boy was watching the sheep, he suddenly began yelling, "Wolf, wolf, wolf." The townspeople came running because they thought the boy needed help protecting the sheep from the wolf. When they arrived, they found the boy laughing at the trick he had played on them. The same thing happened two or three more times. Finally, one day, a real wolf appeared. The boy called, "Wolf, wolf, wolf," but no one came. The townspeople were not going to be fooled again. And so the wolf ate the sheep.

The fable about the boy and the wolf has something in common with a concept we discuss in this chapter: the unintended consequences of saying one thing and doing another.

In the new classical economic story of the 1981–1982 recession, the public incorrectly anticipated Fed policy, and as a result, the economy fell into a recession. But the reason the public incorrectly anticipated Fed policy was because, in the past, the Fed had said one thing and done another. It had said *X* but done *Y*.

It's the same with the boy and the wolf. The first few times the boy cried wolf, the townspeople found that there was no wolf and the boy was simply playing a trick on them. In their minds, crying "Wolf" came to equal "No Wolf." So, when the boy cried wolf the last time and actually meant it, no one from the town came to help him. And the wolf ate the sheep.

Just as the Fed might have learned that saying one thing and doing another can result in a recession, the boy learned that saying one thing and meaning another can result in sheep being killed. The moral of our story is that if you tell a lie again and again, people will no longer believe you when you tell the truth.

SELF-TEST

1. Does the policy ineffectiveness proposition (PIP) always hold?

2. When policy is unanticipated, what difference is there between the natural rate theory built on adaptive expectations and the natural rate theory built on rational expectations?

3. If expectations are formed rationally, does it matter whether policy is unanticipated, anticipated correctly, or anticipated incorrectly? Explain your answer.

New Keynesians and Rational Expectations

The new classical theory assumes complete flexibility of wages and prices. In this theory, an increase in the anticipated price level results in an immediate and equal rise in wages and prices, and the aggregate supply curve immediately shifts to the long-run equilibrium position.

In response to the assumption of flexible wages and prices, a few economists began to develop what has come to be known as the *New Keynesian rational expectations theory*. This theory assumes that rational expectations are a reasonable characterization of how expectations are formed but drops the new classical assumption of complete wage and price flexibility. Economists who work with this theory argue that long-term labor contracts often prevent wages and prices from fully adjusting to changes in the anticipated price level. (Prices and wages are somewhat sticky, rigid, or inflexible.)

Consider the possible situation at the end of the first year of a 3-year wage contract. Workers may realize that the anticipated price level is higher than they expected when they negotiated the contract but will be unable to do much about it because their wages are locked in for the next 2 years. Price rigidity might also arise because firms often engage in fixed-price contracts with their suppliers. As discussed in an earlier chapter, Keynesian economists today put forth microeconomic-based reasons long-term labor contracts and above-market wages are sometimes in the best interest of both employers and employees (efficiency wage theory).

To see what the theory predicts, look at Exhibit 8. The economy is initially in long-run equilibrium at point 1. The public anticipates an increase in aggregate demand from AD_1 to AD_2. As a result, the anticipated price level changes. Because of some wage and price rigidities, however, the short-run aggregate supply curve does not shift all the way from $SRAS_1$ to $SRAS_2$, and the economy does not move from point 1 to point 2 (as in new classical theory). The short-run aggregate supply curve shifts instead to $SRAS'_2$ because rigidities prevent complete wage and price adjustments. In the short run, the economy moves from point 1 to point 2', from Q_N to Q_A. Note that had the policy been unanticipated, Real GDP would have increased from Q_N to Q_{UA} in the short run.

The assumptions of the New Keynesian theory (rational expectations and some price and wage rigidities) seem more reasonable to me than the assumptions of other theories in this chapter (e.g., the Friedman natural rate theory or the new classical theory). Does it follow that the New Keynesian theory is right and the others are wrong?

Economists do not usually judge theories by how "reasonable" the assumptions of the theory seem. That's because we have all encountered theories with reasonable-sounding assumptions that ended up being wrong. (To give but one example of what we mean here, consider that at one time in the world's history, it seemed reasonable to assume that Earth was flat. But Earth is not flat.) Instead, economists judge a theory by how well it predicts and explains real-world events.

Looking at Things from the Supply Side: Real Business Cycle Theorists

Throughout this chapter, changes in Real GDP have originated on the demand side of the economy. When discussing the Friedman natural rate theory, the new classical theory, and the New Keynesian theory, we begin our analysis by shifting the AD curve to the right. Then we explain what happens in the economy as a result.

From the discussions in this chapter, it is possible to believe that all changes in Real GDP originate on the demand side of the economy. In fact, some economists believe this to be true. However, other economists do not. One group of such economists—called *real business cycle theorists*—believe that changes on the supply side of the economy can lead to changes in Real GDP and unemployment.

Real business cycle theorists argue that a decrease in Real GDP (which refers to the recessionary or contractionary part of a business cycle) can be brought about by a major supply-side change that reduces the capacity of the economy to produce. Moreover, they argue that what looks like a contraction in Real GDP originating on the demand side of the economy can be, in essence, the effect of what has happened on the supply side. Exhibit 9 helps explain the process.

We start with an adverse supply shock that reduces the capacity of the economy to produce. This is represented by a shift inward in the economy's production possibilities frontier or a leftward shift in the long-run aggregate supply curve from $LRAS_1$ to $LRAS_2$, which moves the economy from point A to point B. As shown in Exhibit 9, a leftward shift in the long-run aggregate supply curve means that Natural Real GDP has fallen.

As a result of the leftward shift in the $LRAS$ curve and the decline in Real GDP, firms reduce their demand for labor and scale back employment. Due to the lower demand for labor (which puts downward pressure on money wages) and the higher price level, real wages fall.

exhibit 8

The Short-Run Response to Aggregate Demand-Increasing Policy (in the New Keynesian Theory)

Starting at point 1, an increase in aggregate demand is anticipated. As a result, this short-run aggregate supply curve shifts leftward, but not all the way to $SRAS_2$ (as would be the case in the new classical model). Instead it shifts only to $SRAS'_2$ because of some wage and price rigidities; the economy moves to point 2' (in the short run), and Real GDP increases from Q_N to Q_A. If the policy had been unanticipated, Real GDP would have increased from Q_N to Q_{UA}.

Real Business Cycle Theory

We start with a supply-side change capable of reducing the capacity of the economy to produce. This is manifested by a leftward shift of the long-run aggregate supply curve from $LRAS_1$ to $LRAS_2$ and a fall in the Natural Real GDP level from Q_{N1} to Q_{N2}. A reduction in the productive capacity of the economy filters to the demand side of the economy and, in our example, reduces consumption, investment, and the money supply. The aggregate demand curve shifts leftward from AD_1 to AD_2.

As real wages fall, workers choose to work less, and unemployed persons choose to extend the length of their unemployment. Due to less work and lower real wages, workers have less income. Lower incomes soon lead workers to reduce consumption.

Because consumption has fallen, or businesses have become pessimistic (prompted by the decline in the productive potential of the economy), or both, businesses have less reason to invest. As a result, firms borrow less from banks, the volume of outstanding loans falls, and therefore, the money supply falls. A decrease in the money supply causes the aggregate demand curve to shift leftward, from AD_1 to AD_2 in Exhibit 9, and the economy moves to point C.

Real business cycle theorists sometimes point out how easy it is to confuse a demand-induced decline in Real GDP with a supply-induced decline in Real GDP. In our example, both the aggregate supply side and the aggregate demand side of the economy change, but the aggregate supply side changes first. If the change in aggregate supply is overlooked, and only the changes in aggregate demand are observed (or specifically, a change in one of the variables that can change aggregate demand, such as the money supply), then the contraction in Real GDP will appear to be demand induced. In terms of Exhibit 9, the leftward shift in the $LRAS$ curve would be overlooked, but the leftward shift in the AD curve would be observed, giving the impression that the contraction is demand induced.

If real business cycle theorists are correct, the cause–effect analysis of a contraction in Real GDP would be turned upside down. To take but one example, changes in the money supply may be an effect of a contraction in Real GDP (which originates on the supply side of the economy) and not its cause.

SELF-TEST

1.   *The Wall Street Journal* reports that the money supply has recently declined. Is this consistent with a demand-induced or supply-induced business cycle or both? Explain your answer.

2.   How are New Keynesians who believe people hold rational expectations different from new classical economists who believe people hold rational expectations?

A Reader Asks...

Do Expectations Matter?

What insights, if any, does the introduction of expectations into macroeconomics provide?

Think about your study of macroeconomics in earlier chapters. You learned that changes in such things as taxes, government purchases, interest rates, the money supply, and more could change Real GDP, the price level, and the unemployment rate. For example, starting at long-run equilibrium, a rise in the money supply will raise Real GDP and lower the unemployment rate in the short run and raise the price level in the long run. Or consider that an increase in productivity can shift the *SRAS* curve to the right and thus bring about a change in Real GDP and the price level. In short, most of this text discusses how changes in real variables can affect the economy.

With the introduction of expectations theory, we move to a different level of analysis. Now we learn that what people think can also affect the economy. In other words, not only can a change in the world's oil supply affect the economy—almost everyone would expect that—but so can whether or not someone believes that the Fed will increase the money supply.

Think back to our discussion of rational expectations and incorrectly anticipated policy. The economy is in long-run equilibrium when the Fed undertakes an expansionary monetary policy move. The Fed expects to increase the money supply by, say, $10 billion, but somehow, economic agents believe the increase in the money supply will be closer to $20 billion. In other words, economic agents think that the money supply will rise by more than it will rise. Does it matter that their thoughts are wrong? Expectations theory says that it does. As shown in Exhibit 7, wrong thoughts can lead to lower Real GDP and higher prices.

In conclusion, the insight that expectations theory provides is that what people think can affect Real GDP, unemployment, and prices. Who would have thought it?

! analyzing the scene

What does each of the events have to do with economics?

In each of the events, someone is thinking about the future. What will the weather be like tomorrow? What will the fortuneteller say about my chances of hearing a yes from Stephanie? What will my brother's next move be? How will someone move against Michael?

Also, in each case, the person's "best guess" of what the future holds likely will affect his current behavior. If Steven expects rain tomorrow, he will put out his umbrella today. If the fortuneteller tells Robin that Stephanie will not accept his invitation to the dance, he might be less likely to ask her. If one brother thinks the other brother will move to a certain square, then this will affect how he moves. If Michael believes that Barzini will come against him and that the person who arranges the meeting is working for Barzini, then he'll be more likely to move against both Barzini and the person (it's Tessio) who arranges the meeting.

An important part of rational expectations theory is looking to the future and anticipating what will happen. What one thinks "will happen" largely influences the actions one takes. This is what each of the four events has to do with economics.

The individual who goes from (1) expecting the Fed to raise the money supply, to (2) realizing that a greater money supply means higher prices, and who then (3) bargains for higher wages at work really isn't thinking much differently than Don Corleone when he tells Michael to prepare for Barzini. In both cases, something "bad" is headed one's way. In both cases, preparing for what's ahead can make all the difference. For the individual faced with higher prices on the horizon, preparing means bargaining for a higher money (or nominal) wage so that her real wage doesn't decline. For Michael, faced with Barzini in his future, preparing means saving his life.

chapter summary

The Phillips Curve

- A. W. Phillips plotted a curve to a set of data points that exhibited an inverse relationship between wage inflation and unemployment. This curve came to be known as the Phillips curve. From the Phillips curve relationship, economists concluded that neither the combination of low inflation and low unemployment nor the combination of high inflation and high unemployment was likely.

- Economists Samuelson and Solow fit a Phillips curve to the U.S. economy. Instead of measuring wage inflation against unemployment rates (as Phillips did), they measured price inflation against unemployment rates. They found an inverse relationship between inflation and unemployment rates.

- Based on the findings of Phillips and Samuelson and Solow, economists concluded the following: (1) Stagflation, or high inflation and high unemployment, is extremely unlikely. (2) The Phillips curve presents policymakers with a menu of choices between different combinations of inflation and unemployment rates.

Friedman Natural Rate Theory

- Milton Friedman pointed out that there are two types of Phillips curves: a short-run Phillips curve and a long-run Phillips curve. The short-run Phillips curve exhibits the inflation-unemployment tradeoff; the long-run Phillips curve does not. Consideration of both short-run and long-run Phillips curves opened macroeconomics to expectations theory.

- The Friedman natural rate theory holds that in the short run, a decrease (increase) in inflation is linked to an increase (decrease) in unemployment, but in the long run, the economy returns to its natural rate of unemployment. In other words, there is a tradeoff between inflation and unemployment in the short run but not in the long run.

- The Friedman natural rate theory was expressed in terms of adaptive expectations. Individuals formed their inflation expectations by considering past inflation rates. Later, some economists expressed the theory in terms of rational expectations. Rational expectations theory holds that individuals form their expected inflation rate by considering present and past inflation rates, as well as all other available and relevant information—in particular, the effects of present and future policy actions.

New Classical Theory

- Implicit in the new classical theory are two assumptions: (1) Individuals form their expectations rationally. (2) Wages and prices are completely flexible.

- In the new classical theory, policy has different effects (1) when it is unanticipated and (2) when it is anticipated. For example, if the public correctly anticipates an increase in aggregate demand, the short-run aggregate supply curve will likely shift leftward at the same time the aggregate demand curve shifts rightward. If the public does not anticipate an increase in aggregate demand (but one occurs), then the short-run aggregate supply curve will not shift leftward at the same time the aggregate demand curve shifts rightward; it will shift leftward sometime later. If policy is correctly anticipated, expectations are formed rationally, and wages and prices are completely flexible, then an increase or decrease in aggregate demand will change only the price level, not Real GDP or the unemployment rate. The new classical theory casts doubt on the belief that the short-run Phillips curve is always downward sloping. Under certain conditions, it may be vertical (as is the long-run Phillips curve).

- If policies are anticipated but not credible, and rational expectations are a reasonable characterization of how individuals form their expectations, then certain policies may have unintended effects. For example, if the public believes that aggregate demand will increase by more than it (actually) increases (because policymakers have not done in the past what they said they would do), then anticipated inflation will be higher than it would have been, the short-run aggregate supply curve will shift leftward by more than it would have, and the (short-run) outcomes of a policy that increases aggregate demand will be lower Real GDP and higher unemployment.

New Keynesian Theory

- Implicit in the New Keynesian theory are two assumptions: (1) Individuals form their expectations rationally. (2) Wages and prices are not completely flexible (in the short run).

- If policy is anticipated, the economic effects predicted by the new classical theory and the New Keynesian theory are not the same (in the short run). Because the New Keynesian theory assumes that wages and prices are not completely flexible in the short run, given an anticipated change in aggregate demand, the short-run aggregate supply curve cannot immediately shift to its long-run equilibrium position. The New Keynesian theory predicts that there is a short-run tradeoff between inflation and unemployment (in the Phillips curve framework).

Real Business Cycle Theory

- Real business cycle contractions (in Real GDP) originate on the supply side of the economy. A contraction in Real GDP might follow this pattern: (1) An adverse supply shock reduces the economy's ability to produce. (2) The *LRAS* curve shifts leftward. (3) As a result, Real GDP declines and the price level rises. (4) The number of persons employed falls, as do real wages, owing to a decrease in the demand for labor (which lowers money wages) and a higher price level. (5) Incomes decline. (6) Consumption and investment decline. (7) The volume of outstanding loans declines. (8) The money supply falls. (9) The *AD* curve shifts leftward.

key terms and concepts

Phillips Curve	Friedman Natural Rate	Adaptive Expectations	Policy Ineffectiveness
Stagflation	Theory	Rational Expectations	Proposition (PIP)

questions and problems

1 What is a major difference between adaptive and rational expectations? Give an example of each.

2 It has been said that the policy ineffectiveness proposition (connected with new classical theory) does not eliminate policymakers' ability to reduce unemployment through aggregate demand-increasing policies because they can always increase aggregate demand by more than the public expects. What might be the weak point in this argument?

3 Why does the new classical theory have the word *classical* associated with it? Also, why has it been said that the classical theory failed where the new classical theory succeeds, as the former could not explain the business cycle ("the ups and downs of the economy"), but the latter can?

4 Suppose a permanent downward-sloping Phillips curve existed and offered a menu of choices of different combinations of inflation and unemployment rates to policymakers. How do you think society would go about deciding which point on the Phillips curve it wanted to occupy?

5 Suppose a short-run tradeoff between inflation and unemployment currently exists. How would you expect this tradeoff to be affected by a change in technology that permits the wider dispersion of economic policy news? Explain your answer.

6 New Keynesian theory holds that wages are not completely flexible because of such things as long-term labor contracts. New classical economists often respond that experience teaches labor leaders to develop and bargain for contracts that allow for wage adjustments. Do you think the new classical economists have a good point? Why or why not?

7 What evidence can you point to that suggests individuals form their expectations adaptively? What evidence can you point to that suggests individuals form their expectations rationally?

8 Explain both the short-run and long-run movements of the Friedman natural rate theory, assuming expectations are formed adaptively.

9 Explain both the short-run and long-run movements of the new classical theory, assuming expectations are formed rationally and policy is unanticipated.

10 "Even if some people do not form their expectations rationally, this does not necessarily mean that the new classical theory is of no value." Discuss.

11 In the real business cycle theory, why can't the change in the money supply prompted by a series of events catalyzed by an adverse supply shock be considered the "cause" of the business cycle?

12 The expected inflation rate is 5 percent and the actual inflation rate is 7 percent. According to Friedman, is the economy in long-run equilibrium? Explain your answer.

working with numbers and graphs

1   Illustrate graphically what would happen in the short run and in the long run if individuals hold rational expectations, prices and wages are flexible, and individuals underestimate the decrease in aggregate demand.

2   In each of the following figures, the starting point is point 1. Which part illustrates each of the following?

   a   Friedman natural rate theory (short run)

   b   New classical theory (unanticipated policy, short run)

   c   Real business cycle theory

   d   New classical theory (incorrectly anticipated policy, overestimating increase in aggregate demand, short run)

   e   Policy ineffectiveness proposition (PIP)

3   Illustrate graphically what would happen in the short run and in the long run if individuals hold adaptive expectations, prices and wages are flexible, and there is a decrease in aggregate demand.

Setting the Scene

The following facts are related to your life.

FACT 1

If you had lived during the 1200s in Western Europe, your standard of living would not have been much different from what it would have been had you lived in the year 1000. In those 200 years, people's lives had not changed much. Of course, if you had lived during the 1400s in Western Europe, your standard of living would not have been much different from what it would have been had you lived in the year 1000. Fact is, had you lived during the 1700s in Western Europe, your standard of living would not have been much different from what it would have been had you lived in the year 1000. Most people living at these times did not live long enough to notice any economic growth. The world they were born into, and died in, was much the same decade after decade. Their parents, grandparents, and great grandparents lived much the same lives.

FACT 2

In 2005, the per capita Real GDP in North Korea grew 1 percent. Per capita real income in North Korea that year was $1,700. In contrast, the per capita real income in the United States was $41,800. So the average American was 24 times richer (in terms of material goods) than the average North Korean was.

If North Korea maintains its 1 percent growth rate in the future, per capita Real GDP will rise to $3,400 in the year 2077, which is slightly lower than the living standard of the average Cuban in 2005. But if North Korea can increase its growth rate to, say, 3 percent, then per capita Real GDP will rise to $3,400 in 2029, 48 years earlier.

FACT 3

In 2005, the per capita Real GDP in the United States was $41,800, and the economic growth rate was 3.5 percent. If the United States maintains its 3.5 percent growth rate in the future, then in 21 years, the per capita Real GDP will be *twice as large* as it was in 2005. But if the economic growth rate in the United States rises to, say, 4.0 percent, it will take only 18 years for per capita Real GDP to double. In other words, a 0.5 percent rise in the economic growth rate can double the material standard of living in the United States 3 years earlier.

FACT 4

About 24,000 people die every day from hunger or hunger-related causes. This is down from 35,000 ten years ago and 41,000 twenty years ago. Three-fourths of the deaths are children under the age of 5. The vast majority of people who die of hunger live in countries of the world that have experienced relatively little economic growth.

? Here are some questions to keep in mind as you read this chapter:

- *How is your life today different from the lives of your great grandparents?*

- *Does it matter to the average North Korean what the economic growth rate is in North Korea?*

- *Does it matter to the average American what the economic growth rate is in the United States?*

- *Might economic growth matter to hungry people?*

See analyzing the scene at the end of this chapter for answers to these questions.

A Few Basics About Economic Growth

Absolute Real Economic Growth

An increase in Real GDP from one period to the next.

Per Capita Real Economic Growth

An increase from one period to the next in per capita Real GDP, which is Real GDP divided by population.

The term *economic growth* refers either to absolute real economic growth or to per capita real economic growth. **Absolute real economic growth** is an increase in Real GDP from one period to the next. Exhibit 1 shows absolute real economic growth (or the percentage change in Real GDP) for the United States for the period 1993–2005.

Per capita real economic growth is an increase from one period to the next in per capita Real GDP, which is Real GDP divided by population.

Per capita Real GDP = Real GDP/Population

> *macro Theme* In an earlier chapter, we said that one of the two variables that macroeconomists are concerned with learning about is Real GDP, Q. Economic growth, the topic of this chapter, deals with factors that cause an increase in Q.

Do Economic Growth Rates Matter?

Suppose the (absolute) real economic growth rate is 4 percent in one country and 3 percent in another country. The difference in these growth rates may not seem very significant. But if these growth rates are sustained over a long period of time, the people who live in each country will see a real difference in their standard of living.

If a country's economic growth rate is 4 percent each year, its Real GDP will double in 18 years. If a country has a 3 percent annual growth rate, its Real GDP will double in 24 years. In other words, a country with a 4 percent growth rate can double its Real GDP in 6 fewer years than a country with a 3 percent growth rate. (As an aside, to calculate the time required for any variable to double, simply divide its percentage growth rate into 72. This is called the *rule of 72*.)

Let's look at economic growth rates in another way. Suppose two countries have the same population. Real GDP is $300 billion in country *A* and $100 billion in country *B*. Relatively speaking, country *A* is 3 times richer than country *B*. Now suppose the annual economic growth rate is 3 percent in country *A* and 6 percent in country *B*. In just 15 years, country *B* will be the richer country.

Growth Rates in Selected Countries

Suppose in a given year, country *A* has an economic growth rate (rate of growth in Real GDP) of 7 percent and country *B* has an economic growth rate of 1 percent. Does it

exhibit **1**

Absolute Real Economic Growth Rates for the United States, 1993–2005

This exhibit shows the absolute real economic growth rates (or percentage change in Real GDP) in the United States for the period 1993–2005.

Source: *Economic Report of the President*, 2006.

economics 24/7

GROWTH AND MORALITY[1]

There is more to life, liberty, and the pursuit of happiness than a faster car and an iPod nano.

—*The Economist*
November 10, 2005

Almost everyone agrees that economic growth, especially sustained economic growth, can produce more, better, and newer goods and services. But what else can it do, if anything? According to economist Benjamin Friedman, it can make people happier, more tolerant, more willing to settle disputes in a peaceful manner, and more inclined to favor an open and democratic society. It can also make people more willing to work toward improving the environment and reducing poverty.

The thought that economic growth can do more than give us more goods and services goes back to Adam Smith. According to Smith, it is when a nation is acquiring more—when it is getting richer—that most of the people are happy and comfortable. When a nation is only maintaining its wealth or when a nation's wealth is declining, its people are not as happy or as comfortable.

What Friedman essentially argues is that economists have looked at the benefits of economic growth too narrowly. They have stressed the rising material standard of living that comes with economic growth. But this, says Friedman, ignores the political, social, and moral aspects of economic

growth. In his book, *The Moral Consequences of Economic Growth*, he says that "a rising standard of living lies not just in the concrete improvements it brings to how individuals live but in how it shapes the social, political, and ultimately the moral character of a people."

If Friedman is correct that economic growth affects not only the economic life of people but their political, social, and moral life too, then we need to ask why this happens. Friedman says it is because people's sense of how well off they are is made relative to their (own) past. People feel happiest (and most tolerant of others) when they believe their standard of living is rising—in other words, if they are better off this year than last year. When this occurs, people care less of where they stand relative to other people. But if they are not witnessing an increase in their standard of living relative to their past, they then begin to care more about how they are doing relative to others. It is this comparison with others that usually results in frustration and (possible) social friction.

Friedman does not argue that there are absolutely no costs to growth. Instead, he simply makes the point that the benefits that emanate from growth may be greater and more far-reaching than we initially thought.

---

[1]This feature is based on "Why the Rich Must Get Richer," *The Economist*, November 10, 2005.

---

follow that the material standard of living in country *A* is higher than the material standard of living in country *B*? Not at all. A snapshot (in time) of the growth rate in two countries doesn't tell us anything about growth rates in previous years, nor does it speak to per capita Real GDP. For example, did country *A* have the same 7 percent growth rate last year and the year before? Does country *A* have a higher per capita Real GDP?

Now suppose the per capita Real GDP in country *C* is $30,000 and the per capita Real GDP in country *D* is $2,000. Does it follow that the material standard of living in country *C* is higher than the material standard of living in country *D*? Probably so, but not necessarily. We say not necessarily because we do not know the *income distribution* in either country. All a per capita Real GDP figure tells us is that *if* we were to divide a country's entire Real GDP *equally* among all the people in the country, each person would have a certain dollar

Thinking like AN ECONOMIST

Economic growth has been a major topic of discussion for economists for over two centuries. Adam Smith, the founder of modern economics, wrote a book on the subject that was published in 1776—An Inquiry into the Nature and Causes of the Wealth of Nations. In the book, Smith set out to answer the question of why some countries are rich and others are poor. Today, we'd ask: Why do some countries have a high per capita Real GDP and others have a low per capita Real GDP? For economists, getting the right answer to this question is of major importance to the lives of millions—if not billions—of people.

amount of Real GDP at his or her disposal. In reality, 2 percent of the population may have, say, 70 percent of the country's Real GDP as income, while the remaining 98 percent of the population shares only 30 percent of Real GDP as income.

With these qualifications specified, here are the economic growth rates and per capita Real GDP for selected countries in 2005.[2]

Country	Percentage Growth Rate in Real GDP	Per Capita Real GDP
Argentina	8.2	$13,600
Australia	2.7	32,000
Bangladesh	5.2	2,100
Belgium	1.5	31,800
Canada	2.9	32,900
Cuba	5.2	3,300
Egypt	4.5	4,400
Germany	0.8	29,700
Iran	4.8	8,100
Israel	4.3	22,000
Turkey	5.1	7,900
United States	3.5	41,800

Two Types of Economic Growth

Economic growth can be shown in two of the frameworks of analysis used so far in this book: the production possibilities frontier (PPF) framework and the *AD-AS* framework. Within these two frameworks, we consider two types of economic growth: (1) economic growth that occurs from an inefficient level of production and (2) economic growth that occurs from an efficient level of production.

ECONOMIC GROWTH FROM AN INEFFICIENT LEVEL OF PRODUCTION A production possibilities frontier is shown in Exhibit 2(a). Suppose the economy is currently operating at point *A,* below the PPF. Obviously, the economy is not operating at its Natural Real GDP level. If it were, the economy would be located on the PPF instead of below it. Instead, the economy is at an inefficient point or at an inefficient level of production.

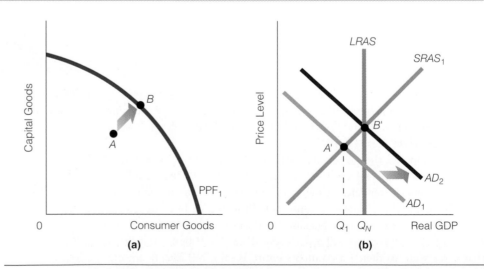

exhibit 2

Economic Growth from an Inefficient Level of Production

The economy is at Point *A* in (a) and at point *A'* in (b). Currently, the economy is at an inefficient point, or below Natural Real GDP. Economic growth is evidenced as a movement from point *A* to *B* in (a), and as a movement from *A'* to *B'* in (b).

[2] The source of these data is the *CIA World Factbook, 2006.*

Point A in Exhibit 2(a) corresponds to point A' in Exhibit 2(b). At point A', the economy is in a recessionary gap, operating below Natural Real GDP. Now suppose that through expansionary monetary or fiscal policy, the aggregate demand curve shifts rightward from AD_1 to AD_2. The economy is pulled out of its recessionary gap and is now producing Natural Real GDP at point B' in Exhibit 2(b).

What does the situation look like now in Exhibit 2(a)? Obviously, if the economy is producing at its Natural Real GDP level, it is operating at full employment or at the natural unemployment rate. This means the economy has moved from point A (below the PPF) to point B (on the PPF). The economy has moved from operating at an inefficient level of production to operating at an efficient level.

ECONOMIC GROWTH FROM AN EFFICIENT LEVEL OF PRODUCTION How can the economy grow if it is on the PPF in Exhibit 2(a)—exhibiting efficiency—or producing at the Natural Real GDP level in Exhibit 2(b)? The answer is that the PPF must shift to the right (or outward) in (a), or the *LRAS* curve must shift to the right in (b). In other words, if the economy is at point B in Exhibit 3(a), it can grow if the PPF shifts rightward from PPF_1 to PPF_2. Similarly, if the economy is at point B' in Exhibit 3(b), the only way Real GDP can be raised beyond Q_{N1} on a permanent basis is if the *LRAS* curve shifts to the right from $LRAS_1$ to $LRAS_2$.

Although we have described economic growth from both an inefficient and efficient level of production, usually when economists speak of economic growth, they are speaking about it from an efficient level of production. That is, they are talking about a shift rightward in the PPF or in the *LRAS* curve.

Economic Growth and the Price Level

Economic growth can occur with a falling price level, rising price level, or stable price level. To see this, look again at Exhibit 3(b). The *LRAS* curve shifts from $LRAS_1$ to $LRAS_2$. Three possible aggregate demand curves may be consistent with this new *LRAS* curve: AD_1, AD_2, or AD_3.

If AD_1 is the relevant *AD* curve, economic growth occurs with a declining price level. Before the *LRAS* curve shifted to the right, the price level was P_1; after the shift, it was lower, at P_2.

If AD_2 is the relevant *AD* curve, economic growth occurs with a stable price level. Before the *LRAS* curve shifted to the right, the price level was P_1; after the shift, it was the same, at P_1.

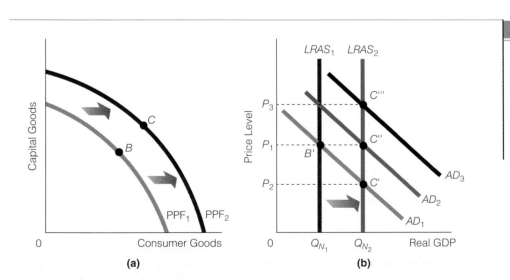

exhibit 3

Economic Growth from an Efficient Level of Production

The economy is at point B in (a) and at point B' in (b). Economic growth can only occur in (a) if the PPF shifts rightward from PPF_1 to PPF_2. It can only occur in (b) if the *LRAS* curve shifts from $LRAS_1$ to $LRAS_2$.

(a)   (b)

economics 24/7

HOW ECONOMIZING ON TIME CAN PROMOTE ECONOMIC GROWTH

If a society obtains more resources, its PPF will shift to the right, and economic growth is therefore possible. One way to obtain "more resources" is through a technological change or innovation that makes it possible to use fewer resources to produce a particular good. To illustrate, suppose there are 100 units of a given resource. Currently, 10 units of the resource are needed to produce 20 units of good X, and 90 units of the resource are used to produce 900 units of other goods.

Now suppose a technological change or innovation makes it possible to produce 20 units of good X with only 5 units of the resource. This means 95 units of the resource can be used to produce other goods. With more resources going to produce other goods, more other goods can be produced. Perhaps with 95 units of the resource going to produce other goods, 950 units of other goods can be produced. In short, a technological advance or innovation that saves resources in the production of one good makes growth possible.

With this in mind, consider the resource *time*. Usually, when people think of resources, they think of labor, capital, and natural resources. But time is a resource because it takes time (in much the same way that it takes labor or capital) to produce goods. Any technological advance that economizes on time frees up some time that can be used to produce other goods.

To illustrate, consider a simple everyday example. With today's computers, people can make calculations, write books, key reports, design buildings, and much more in less time than was necessary in the past. Thus, there is more time available to do other things. Having more time to produce other things promotes economic growth.

Let's consider something that is discussed in an earlier chapter—money. Does money economize on time? Before there was money, people made barter trades. In a barter economy, finding people to trade with takes time. Money economizes on this time. Because everyone accepts money, it is easier for people to acquire the goods and services they want. Money makes trading easier. It also makes trading quicker. In other words, it saves time. Money is a "technology" that saves time and promotes economic growth.

If AD_3 is the relevant AD curve, economic growth occurs with a rising price level. Before the $LRAS$ curve shifted to the right, the price level was P_1; after the shift, it was higher, at P_3.

In recent decades, the U.S. economy has witnessed economic growth with a rising price level. This means the AD curve has been shifting to the right at a faster rate than the $LRAS$ curve has been shifting to the right.

What Causes Economic Growth?

This section looks at some of the determinants of economic growth—that is, the factors that can shift the PPF or the $LRAS$ curve to the right. These factors include natural resources, labor, capital, technological advances, the property rights structure, and economic freedom. We then discuss some of the policies that promote economic growth.

Natural Resources

People often think that countries with a plentiful supply of natural resources experience economic growth, whereas countries short of natural resources do not. In fact, some countries with an abundant supply of natural resources have experienced rapid growth in the past (e.g., the United States), and others have experienced no growth or only slow growth.(e.g. Ghana, in certain years). Also, some countries that are short of natural resources, such as Singapore, have grown very fast. It appears that natural resources are neither a sufficient nor a necessary factor for growth: Countries rich in natural resources are not guaranteed economic growth, and countries poor in natural resources may grow economically. Having said all this, it is still more likely for a nation rich in natural resources to experience growth, *ceteris paribus*. For example, if a place such as Hong Kong, which has few natural resources, had been blessed with much fertile soil, instead of only a little, and many raw materials, instead of almost none, it might have experienced more economic growth than it has.

Labor

With more labor, it is possible to produce more output (more Real GDP), but whether the average productivity of labor rises, falls, or stays constant (as additional workers are added to the production process) depends on how productive the additional workers are relative to existing workers. If the additional workers are less productive than existing workers, labor productivity will decline. If they are more productive, labor productivity will rise. And if they are equally as productive, labor productivity will stay the same. (Note: Average labor productivity is total output divided by total labor hours. For example, if $6 trillion of output is produced in 200 billion labor hours, then average labor productivity is $30 per hour.)

Both an increase in the labor force and an increase in labor productivity lead to increases in Real GDP, but only an increase in labor productivity tends to lead to an increase in per capita Real GDP.

How then do we achieve an increase in labor productivity? One way is through increased education, training, and experience. These are increases in what economists call *human capital*. Another way is through (physical) capital investment. Combining workers with more capital goods tends to increase the productivity of the workers. For example, a farmer with a tractor is more productive than a farmer without one.

Capital

As just mentioned, capital investment can lead to increases in labor productivity and, therefore, not only to increases in Real GDP but also to increases in per capita Real GDP. But more capital goods do not fall from the sky. Recall that getting more of one thing often means forfeiting something else. To produce more capital goods, which are not directly consumable, present consumption must be reduced. Robinson Crusoe, alone on an island and fishing with a spear, must give up some of his present fish to weave a net (a physical capital good) with which he hopes to catch more fish.

If Crusoe gives up some of his present consumption—if he chooses not to consume now—he is, in fact, saving. There is a link between nonconsumption, or saving, and capital formation. As the saving rate increases, capital formation increases and so does economic growth.

Exhibit 4 shows that for the period 1970–1990, countries with higher investment rates largely tended to have higher per capita Real GDP growth rates. For example, investment was a higher percentage of GDP in Austria, Norway, and Japan than it was in the United States. And these countries experienced a higher per capita Real GDP growth rate than the United States did.

Technological Advances

Technological advances make it possible to obtain more output from the same amount of resources. Compare the amount of work that can be done by a business that uses computers with the amount accomplished by a business that does not use computers.

exhibit 4

Investment and Per Capita Real Economic Growth for Selected Countries, 1970–1990

Generally, but not always, those countries in which investment is a larger percentage of GDP have higher per capita Real GDP growth rates.

Source: Council of Economic Advisors, *Economic Report of the President*, 1997 (Washington, D.C.: U.S. Government Printing Office, 1997)

Technological advances may be the result of new capital goods or of new ways of producing goods. The use of computers is an example of a technological advance that is the result of a new capital good. New and improved management techniques are an example of a new way of producing goods.

Technological advances usually come as the result of companies, and a country, investing in research and development (R&D). Research and development is a general term that encompasses such things as scientists working in a lab to develop a new product and managers figuring out, through experience, how to motivate workers to work to their potential.

Free Trade as Technology

Suppose someone in the United States has invented a machine that can turn wheat into cars.[3] The only problem with the machine is that it works only in Japan. So people in the United States grow wheat and ship it to Japan. There, the machine turns the wheat into cars. The cars are then loaded on ships and brought to the United States.

Many economists say there is really no difference between a machine that can turn wheat into cars and free trade between countries. When there is free trade, people in the United States grow wheat and ship it to Japan. After a while the ships come back loaded with cars. This is exactly what happens with our mythical machine. There is really no discernible difference between a machine turning wheat into cars and trading wheat for cars. In both cases, wheat is given up to get cars.

If the machine is a technological advancement, then so is free trade, as many economists point out. In that technological advancements can promote economic growth, so can free trade.

Property Rights Structure

Some economists have argued that per capita real economic growth first appeared in areas that had developed a system of institutions and property rights that encouraged individuals to direct their energies to effective economic projects. Here, property rights

---

[3] The essence of this example comes from David Friedman, *Hidden Order* (New York: HarperCollins, 1996), 70.

economics 24/7

RELIGIOUS BELIEFS AND ECONOMIC GROWTH

For given religious beliefs, increases in church attendance tend to reduce economic growth. In contrast, for given church attendance, increases in some religious beliefs—notably heaven, hell, and an afterlife—tend to increase economic growth.[4]

—Robert Barro and Rachel McCleary

Economists have been studying economic growth for more than 200 years. Some of the questions they have asked and tried to answer include: Why are some nations rich and others poor? What causes economic growth? Why do some nations grow faster than other nations?

In our discussion of economic growth in this chapter, we identify and discuss a few of the causes of economic growth. We do not include any cultural determinants of economic growth. Some economic researchers argue that explanations for economic growth should be broadened to include cultural determinants. They argue that culture may influence personal traits, which may in turn affect economic growth. For example, personal traits such as honesty, thriftiness, willingness to work hard, and openness to strangers may be related to economic growth.

Two Harvard economists, Robert Barro and Rachel McCleary, have analyzed one such cultural determinant: the role that

religion plays in economic growth. Their work was based partly on the World Values Survey, which looked at a representative sample of people in 66 countries on all six inhabited continents between 1981 and 1997. The survey asked at least 1,000 people in each country about their basic values and beliefs: What is their religious affiliation? How often do they attend a religious service? Were they raised religiously or not?

Barro and McCleary found that economic growth responds negatively to church attendance (nations with a high rate of attendance at religious services grow more slowly than those with lower rates of attendance) but positively with religious beliefs in heaven, hell, and an afterlife. Specifically, in countries where the belief in heaven, hell, and an afterlife is strong, growth of gross domestic product runs about 0.5 percent higher than average. (This result takes into account other factors, such as education, that influence growth rates.) Perhaps more telling, the belief in hell matters more to economic growth than the belief in heaven. Barro and McCleary suggest that the religious beliefs stimulate growth because they help to sustain aspects of individual behavior that enhance productivity.

---

[4]Robert Barro and Rachel McCleary, "Religion and Economic Growth" (NBER Working Paper No. 9682).

refer to the range of laws, rules, and regulations that define rights for the use and transfer of resources.

Consider two property rights structures. In one structure, people are allowed to keep the full monetary rewards of their labor. In the other, people are allowed to keep only half. Many economists would predict that the first property rights structure would stimulate more economic activity than the second, *ceteris paribus*. Individuals will invest more, take more risks, and work harder when the property rights structure allows them to keep more of the monetary rewards of their investing, risk taking, and labor.

Economic Freedom

Some economists believe that economic freedom leads to economic growth. Countries in which people enjoy a large degree of economic freedom develop and grow more quickly than countries in which people have little economic freedom. The Heritage Foundation and *The Wall Street Journal* have joined together to produce an "index of economic freedom." This index is based on 50 independent variables divided into 10

> *Thinking like*
> **AN ECONOMIST**   *When looking at the causes of economic growth, economists think in terms of both tangibles and intangibles. The tangibles include natural resources, labor, capital, and technological advances. The intangibles include the property rights structure, which directly affects individuals' incentives to apply the tangibles to the production of goods and services. No amount of natural resources, labor, capital, and technological advances can do it alone. People must be motivated to put them all together. In addition, the degree of motivation affects the result. In a world where it is easy to think that only those things that occupy physical space matter, the economist is there to remind us that we often need to look further.*

broad categories of economic freedom, such as trade policy, monetary policy, property rights structure, regulation, fiscal burden of government, and so on. For example, a country with few tariffs and quotas (trade policy) is considered to have more economic freedom than a country with many tariffs and quotas.

The index is a number between 1 and 5. A country with a great deal of economic freedom has a low index, and a country with little economic freedom has a high index. Thus, free countries have an index between 1.00 and 1.95; mostly free countries, between 2.00 and 2.95; mostly unfree countries, between 3.00 and 3.95; and repressed countries, between 4.00 and 5.00.

The data show that economic freedom and Real GDP per capita are correlated. For the most part, the more economic freedom the people of a country experience, the higher the Real GDP per capita. Some economists believe there is a "cause and effect" relationship: Greater economic freedom causes greater economic wealth.

Policies to Promote Economic Growth

Recall from earlier in this chapter that economic growth can occur from either (1) an inefficient level of production or (2) an efficient level of production. When the economy is situated below its PPF, demand-inducing expansionary monetary or fiscal policy is often advocated. Its objective is to increase aggregate demand enough to raise Real GDP (and lower the unemployment rate). We refer to such policies as *demand-side policies.*

There are *supply-side policies* too. These policies are designed to shift the PPF and the *LRAS* curve to the right. The best way to understand the intent of these policies is to first recall the factors that cause economic growth. These factors include natural resources, labor, increases in human capital, increases in (physical) capital investment, technological advances, property rights structure, and economic freedom. Any policies that promote these factors tend to promote economic growth. Two supply-side policies that do this are lowering taxes and reducing regulation.

TAX POLICY Some economists propose cutting taxes on such activities as working and saving to increase the productive capacity of the economy. For example, some economists say that if the marginal income tax rate is cut, workers will work more. As they work more, output will increase.

Other economists argue that if the tax is lowered on income placed in saving accounts, the return from saving will increase and thus the amount of saving will rise. In turn, this will make more funds available for investment, which will lead to greater capital goods growth and higher labor productivity. Ultimately, per capita Real GDP will increase.

REGULATORY POLICY Some economists say that some government regulations increase the cost of production for business and, consequently, reduce output. These economists are mainly referring to the costs of regulation, which may take the form of spending hours on required paperwork, adding safety features to a factory, or buying expensive equipment to reduce pollution emissions. On net, the benefits of these policies may be greater than, less than, or equal to the costs, but certainly, sometimes the costs are evidenced in the form of less output.

Economists who believe the benefits do not warrant the costs often argue for some form of deregulation. In addition, some economists are trying to make the costs of regulation more visible to policymakers so that regulatory policy will take into account all the benefits and all the costs.

WHAT ABOUT INDUSTRIAL POLICY? **Industrial policy** is a deliberate government policy of "watering the green spots," or aiding industries that are most likely to be successful in the world marketplace.

The proponents of industrial policy argue that government needs to work with business firms in the private sector to help them compete in the world marketplace. In particular, they argue that government needs to identify the industries of the future—biotechnology, telecommunications, robotics, and computers and software—and help these industries grow and develop now. The United States will be disadvantaged in a relative sense, they argue, if governments of other countries aid some of their industries and the United States does not aid some of its own industries.

Critics maintain that however good the intentions, industrial policy does not always turn out the way its proponents would like for three reasons. First, in deciding which industries to help, government may favor the industries with the most political influence, not the industries that it makes economic sense to help. Critics argue that elected government officials are not beyond rewarding people who have helped them win elections. Thus, industrial policy may turn out to be a way to reward friends and injure enemies rather than good economic policy.

Second, critics argue that the government officials who design and implement industrial policy aren't really smart enough to know which industries will be the industries of the future. Thus, they shouldn't try to impose their uninformed guesses about the future on the economy.

Finally, critics argue that government officials who design and implement industrial policy are likely to hamper economic growth if they provide protection to some industries. For example, suppose the United States institutes an industrial policy. U.S. government officials decide that the U.S. computer industry needs to be protected from foreign competition. In their effort to aid the computer industry, they impose tariffs and quotas on foreign competitors. This action might prompt foreign nations to retaliate by placing tariffs and quotas on U.S. computers. In the end, we might simply have less free trade in the world. This would hurt consumers because they would have to pay higher prices. It would hurt the people who work for export companies because many of them would lose their jobs. And the reduction in trade would prevent the U.S. computer industry from selling in the world marketplace. The end result would be the opposite of what the policy wants to accomplish.

Industrial Policy
A deliberate policy by which government "waters the green spots," or aids industries that are most likely to be successful in the world marketplace.

Economic Growth and Special Interest Groups

Certain economic policies can promote economic growth, but will these policies necessarily be chosen? Or will nongrowth-promoting policies more likely be chosen?

To illustrate, consider two types of economic policies: growth-promoting policies and transferring-promoting policies. A growth-promoting policy increases Real GDP; it enlarges the size of the economic pie. A transfer-promoting policy leaves the size of the economic pie unchanged, but it increases the size of the slice of the pie that one group gets relative to another group.

For example, suppose group *A,* a special interest group, currently gets 1/1,000 of the economic pie, and the economic pie is $1,000. It follows that the group gets a $1 slice of the economic pie. Group *A* wants to get more than a $1 slice. It can do this in one of two ways. The first way is to lobby for a policy that increases the size of its slice of the given economic pie. In other words, group *A* gets a larger slice (say, a $2 slice) at the expense of someone else getting a smaller slice. Alternatively, group *A* can lobby for a policy that increases the size of the pie—say, from $1,000 to $1,500. (Will group *A* get the full increase of $500? Not at all. It only gets 1/1,000 of the increase, or 50 cents.) So group *A* has to decide whether it is better for it to lobby for a growth-promoting policy (where it gets 1/1,000 of any increase in Real GDP) or if it is better for it to lobby for a transfer-promoting policy (where it gets 100 percent of any transfer).

According to Mancur Olson, in his *The Rise and Decline of Nations,* special interest groups are more likely to argue for transfer-promoting policies than growth-promoting policies. The cost-benefit calculation of each policy makes it so.[5]

How does this behavior by special interest groups affect economic growth? Simply that the more special interest groups in a country, the more likely that transfer-promoting policies will be lobbied for instead of growth-promoting policies because individuals will try to get a larger slice of a constant-size economic pie rather than trying to increase the size of the pie. In short, numerous and politically strong special interest groups are detrimental to economic growth.

SELF-TEST

(Answers to Self-Test questions are in the Self-Test Appendix.)

1.   "Economic growth refers to an increase in GDP." Comment.

2.   Country *A* has witnessed both economic growth and a rising price level during the past two decades. What does this imply about the *LRAS* and *AD* curves?

3.   How can capital investment promote economic growth?

New Growth Theory

Beginning in the 1980s, economists began discussing economic growth in ways different from the way it was discussed in previous decades. More attention was placed on technology, ideas, and education. The discussion takes place under the rubric "new growth theory."

What Was Wrong with the Old Theory? Or What's New with New Growth Theory?

To talk about *new growth theory* assumes there was a theory of economic growth that came before it. Before new growth theory, there was *neoclassical growth theory.* Some economists believe that new growth theory came to exist to answer some of the questions that neoclassical growth theory could not, in much the same way that a new medical theory may arise to answer questions that an old medical theory can't answer.

Neoclassical growth theory emphasized two resources: labor and capital. Within neoclassical growth theory, technology was discussed but only in a very shallow way. Technology, it was said, was exogenous; that is, it came from outside the economic system. Stated differently, technology was something that "fell out of the sky," that was outside our control, that we simply accepted as a given.

New growth theory holds that technology is endogenous; it is a central part of the economic system. More important, the technology that is developed—both the amount and the quality—depends on the amount of resources we devote to it: The more resources that go to develop technology, the more and better technology is developed.

Paul Romer, whose name is synonymous with new growth theory, asks us to think about technology the way we think about prospecting for gold. For one individual, the chances of finding gold are so small that if one did find gold, it would simply be viewed as good luck. However, if there are 10,000 individuals mining for gold across a wide geographical area, the chances of finding gold would greatly improve. As with gold, so

---

[5]Mancur Olson, *The Rise and Decline of Nations* (New Haven, CT, and London: Yale University Press, 1982).

© ANNE KNUDSEN

economics 24/7

PROFESSORS, STUDENTS, AND IDEAS

Paul Romer, the founder of new growth theory, emphasizes ideas and knowledge as catalysts of economic growth. Ideas and knowledge don't fall from the sky, though; they need to be produced. According to Romer, one way to produce more ideas and knowledge is by investing in research and development (R&D).

But R&D can proceed in different ways. One way, the way Romer believes is currently in operation, is what he calls the linear model of science and discovery. In a business firm, this model is applied in the following way: The firm has an R&D department that is responsible for coming up with new ideas and new knowledge. After the R&D department has done its job, the rest of the firm is responsible for turning the knowledge or idea into a product that will sell. In short, the process begins with an idea, gets turned into a product (or service), and is then marketed and distributed.

According to Romer, the linear model is the wrong way to proceed. Scientists, engineers, and others can come up with new ideas and new knowledge, but it is not just new knowledge for knowledge's sake that is needed. We need new knowledge to solve the problems that we already have. Romer advocates the use of marketlike mechanisms to focus research efforts.

Romer believes that one of the problems with the present system is that universities are not producing the kinds of scientists and engineers that the private sector needs. Universities are training and producing scientists and engineers who are copies of their professors and are not necessarily the scientists and engineers needed in the marketplace. He believes there are many areas in the private sector where the demand for scientists is not being met.

Why are colleges and universities producing the "wrong" kinds of scientists and engineers? One reason, Romer argues, is that the federal government gives research monies to professors (including monies for research assistants), and then the professors hire the assistants to do what the professors want them to do. In other words, people are trained in areas that professors want them to be trained in, areas that interest the professors. But what interests professors? They are interested in research grants, many of which are given out by the federal government. Thus, professors have an incentive to respond to the research priorities of the federal government. So the federal government indirectly controls much of the research.

Romer proposes a change: Give students and businesses some control over research funds. He says, "The approach I prefer is one where you give students more control over their own funds. Instead of giving the money for student fellowship positions to the research professor in the department, why not give it to the student? That way a student could take the fellowship and say, 'I've seen the numbers. I know I can't get a job if I get a math Ph.D., but if I go into bio-informatics, there is a huge demand for people right now.' If the students could control the funds, the universities would start to cater to their demands, which would be in line with the market and the private sector's needs."[6]

The same outcome, Romer believes, would be forthcoming if businesses had some control over (federal) research monies that go to universities. Businesses would direct the monies into financing research that could help answer questions and solve problems in the private sector.

---

[6]See the interview with Paul Romer by Joel Jutzman in *Strategy and Business* (first quarter 1997): 11.

---

with technological advances. If one person is trying to advance technology, his or her chances of success are much smaller than if hundreds or thousands of persons are trying.

New growth theory also emphasizes the process of discovering and formulating ideas. According to Romer, discovering and implementing new ideas are what causes economic growth.

To explain, we consider the difference between *objects* and *ideas*. Objects are material, tangible things—such as natural resources and capital goods. One of the arguments often made as to why some countries are poor is that they lack objects (natural resources and capital goods). The retort to this argument is that some countries that have had very few objects have been able to grow economically. For example, in the 1950s, Japan had few natural resources and capital goods (it still doesn't have an abundance of natural resources), but still it grew economically. Some economists believe that Japan grew because it had access to ideas or knowledge.

Discovery, Ideas, and Institutions

If the process of discovering ideas is important to economic growth, then it behooves us to figure out ways to promote the discovery process. One way is for business firms not to get locked into doing things one way and one way only. They must let their employees—from the inventor in the lab to the worker on the assembly line—try new ways of doing things. Some might carry this further: Businesses need to create an environment that is receptive to new ideas. They need to encourage their employees to try new ways of doing things.

Employee flexibility, which is a part of the discovery process, is becoming a larger part of the U.S. economy. To some degree, this is seen in the amount of time and effort firms devote to discovery in contrast to the amount of time they devote to actually manufacturing goods. Consider the computer software business. Millions of dollars and hundreds of thousands of work hours are devoted to coming up with new and useful software, whereas only a tiny fraction of the work effort and hours go into making, copying, and shipping the disks or CDs that contain the software.

Expanding Our Horizons

Let's return to Paul Romer. Romer has said that "economic growth occurs whenever people take resources and rearrange them in ways that are more valuable."[7] Let's focus on the word "rearrange." We can think of rearranging as in "rearranging the pieces of a puzzle," as in "changing the ingredients in a recipe," or as in "rearranging the way a worker goes about his or her daily work." When we rearrange anything, we do that "thing" differently. Sometimes, differently is better, and sometimes, it is worse.

Think of the way you study for a test. Perhaps you read the book first, then go back and underline, then study the book, and then finally study your lecture notes. Would it be better to study differently? Often, you won't know until you try.

As with studying for a test, so it is with producing a car, computer software, or a shopping mall. We do not find the better ways of doing things unless we experiment. And with repeated experiments, we often discover new and better ideas, ideas that ultimately lead to economic growth.

Consider the research and development of new medicines. Sometimes, what makes a mildly effective medicine into a very effective medicine is a change in one or two molecules of a certain chemical. In other words, small changes—changes perhaps no one would ever think would matter—can make a large difference. There is a policy prescription that follows from this knowledge: We should think of ways to make the process of discovering ideas, experimenting with different ways of doing things, and developing new technology more likely. Without this, we are likely to diminish our growth potential.

Stated differently, if we believe ideas are important to economic growth, then we need to have ideas about how to generate more ideas. Paul Romer calls these meta-ideas: ideas about how to support the production and transmission of other ideas.

Some ways have been proposed. Perhaps we need to invest more funds in education or research and development. Or perhaps we need to find ways to better protect people's ideas (few people will invest the time, money, and effort to discover better ideas if those ideas can easily be stolen) and so on.

---

[7]See the interview with Paul Romer by Joel Kurtzman in *Strategy and Business* (first quarter 1997): 11

In the 21st century, countries with the most natural resources and capital goods aren't likely to be the ones that grow the fastest. If new growth theory is correct, it will be countries that have discovered how to encourage and develop the most and best ideas.

SELF-TEST

1. What are two worries about future economic growth?

2. If technology is endogenous, what are the implications for economic growth?

3. According to new growth theory, what countries will grow the fastest in this century?

A Reader Asks...

Can an Understanding of How Economies Grow Help Me?

This chapter explains that economic growth is largely a function of, or dependent on, such things as the amount of labor and capital an economy employs, technological advancements, the property rights structure, and so on. Can these factors translate into personal income growth? For example, if my objective is to "grow" my income over time, will knowing how economies grow provide me with any information on how to cultivate the growth of my income?

Let's recall the factors that are important to economic growth: (1) natural resources, (2) labor, (3) capital, (4) technological advances, (5) the property rights structure, and (6) economic freedom. In terms of personal income growth, counterparts exist for some of these factors. For example, an individual's natural talent might be the counterpart of a country's natural resources. Just as a country might be "lucky" to have plentiful natural resources, so might an individual be

lucky to be born with a natural talent, especially a talent that others value highly.

Two factors directly relevant to your income growth are labor and (human) capital. We know that more labor and greater labor productivity promote economic growth. Similarly, for an individual, more labor expended and greater labor productivity often lead to income growth. How can you "expend more labor"? The answer is by working more hours. How can you increase your labor productivity? As we said earlier in the chapter, "one way is through increased education, training, and experience." In other words, acquire more *human capital*. Simply put, one way to increase your income is to work more; another way is to work better.

Finally, consider the role the property rights structure and economic freedom play in income growth. We often observe people migrating to places where the property rights structure and level of economic freedom are conducive to their personal income growth. For example, very few people in the world migrate to North Korea, but many people migrate to the United States.

! analyzing the scene

How is your life today different from the lives of your great grandparents? Does it matter to the average North Korean what the economic growth rate is in North Korea? Does it matter to the average American what the economic growth rate is in the United States? Might economic growth matter to hungry people?

If you have always lived in a country that has experienced many years of economic growth, you might not realize how

economic growth affects your life. Some have said that economic growth is one of those things you don't notice until you are without it. In other words, you don't recognize the benefits of economic growth until the benefits are no longer there. In this regard, economic growth is like many of the things that make us better off but that we take for granted.

For example, how many of us think of the importance of antibiotics to our lives? Before Alexander Fleming discovered penicillin in 1928, there were no antibiotics. In a world without antibiotics, individuals regularly died from simple bacterial infections. David Ricardo, the famous 19th-century economist, died of an ear infection at the age of 51—an ear infection that could have been cured easily with a few doses of antibiotics.

Those of us alive today often take economic growth for granted, perhaps because we were born at a time and in a country that has experienced quite a bit of economic growth.

Think back to the year 1865, the last year of the American Civil War. Suppose there had been no economic growth in the United States in any year since 1865. What would your life be like today? How different would your life be?

In addition, economic growth often occurs slowly over time, and perhaps that's why we don't take much notice of it. But like antibiotics, it would be sorely missed if it weren't here. In short, economic growth makes a huge difference to the way we live.

chapter summary

Economic Growth

- Absolute real economic growth refers to an increase in Real GDP from one period to the next.

- Per capita real economic growth refers to an increase from one period to the next in per capita Real GDP, which is Real GDP divided by population.

- Economic growth can occur starting from an inefficient level of production or from an efficient level of production.

Economic Growth and the Price Level

- Usually, economists talk about economic growth as a result of a shift rightward in the PPF or in the *LRAS* curve.

- Economic growth can occur along with (1) an increase in the price level, (2) a decrease in the price level, or (3) no change in the price level.

Causes of Economic Growth

- Factors related to economic growth include natural resources, labor, capital, technological advances, the property rights structure, and economic freedom.

- Countries rich in natural resources are not guaranteed economic growth, and countries poor in natural resources may grow economically. Nevertheless, a country with more natural resources can evidence more economic growth, *ceteris paribus.*

- An increase in the amount of labor or in the quality of labor (as measured by increases in labor productivity) can lead to economic growth.

- More capital goods can lead to increases in economic growth. Capital formation, however, is related to saving: As the saving rate increases, capital formation increases.

- Technological advances may be the result of new capital goods or of new ways of producing goods. In either case, technological advances lead to economic growth.

- Economic growth is not unrelated to the property rights structure in the country. Individuals will invest more, take more risks, and work harder—thus, there is likely to be greater economic growth—when the property rights structure allows them to keep more of the fruits of their investing, risk taking, and labor, *ceteris paribus.*

- For the most part, the more economic freedom the people of a country experience, the higher the Real GDP per capita.

Policies to Promote Economic Growth

- Both demand-side and supply-side policies can be used to promote economic growth. Demand-side policies focus on shifting the *AD* curve to the right. Supply-side policies focus on shifting the *LRAS* curve to the right.

- Some economists propose cutting taxes on such activities as saving and working to increase the productive capacity of the economy. Other economists argue that regulations on business should be relaxed to increase the productive capacity of the economy.

- Industrial policy is a deliberate government policy of "watering the green spots," or aiding industries that are most likely to be successful in the world marketplace.

- Industrial policy has both proponents and opponents. The proponents argue that the government needs to identify the industries of the future and help these industries grow and develop now. The United States will fall behind, they argue, if it does not adopt an industrial policy while some other countries do. The opponents of industrial policy argue that the government doesn't know which industries it makes economic sense to help and that industrial policy is likely to become protectionist and politically motivated.

Economic Growth and Special Interest Groups

- According to Mancur Olson, the more special interest groups in a country, the more likely that transfer-promoting policies will be lobbied for instead of growth-promoting policies because individuals will try to get a larger slice of a constant-size economic pie rather than trying to increase the size of the pie.

New Growth Theory

- New growth theory holds that technology is endogenous as opposed to neoclassical growth theory, which holds that technology is exogenous. When something is endogenous, it is part of the economic system, under our control or influence. When something is exogenous, it is not part of the system; it is assumed to be given to us, often mysteriously through a process that we do not understand.

- According to Paul Romer, discovering and implementing new ideas are what causes economic growth.

- Certain institutions can promote the discovery of new ideas and therefore promote economic growth.

key terms and concepts

Absolute Real Economic Growth

Per Capita Real Economic Growth

Industrial Policy

questions and problems

1 Why might per capita real economic growth be a more useful measurement than absolute real economic growth?

2 What does it mean to say "natural resources are neither a sufficient nor a necessary factor for growth"?

3 How do we compute (average) labor productivity?

4 Is it possible to have more workers working, producing a higher Real GDP, at the same time that labor productivity is declining? Explain your answer.

5 How does an increased saving rate relate to increased labor productivity?

6 Economic growth doesn't simply depend on having more natural resources, more or higher quality labor, more capital, and so on; it depends on people's incentives to put these resources together to produce goods and services. Do you agree or disagree? Explain your answer.

7 It is possible to promote economic growth from either the demand side or the supply side. Do you agree or disagree? Explain your answer.

8 What is *new* about new growth theory?

9 How does discovering and implementing new ideas cause economic growth?

10 Explain how each of the following relates to economic growth: (a) technological advance, (b) labor productivity, (c) natural resources, (d) education, (e) special interest groups.

11 Explain how free trade is a form of technology.

12 What is Paul Romer's position on the best way to proceed with research and development?

working with numbers and graphs

1 The economy of country X is currently growing at 2 percent a year. How many years will it take to double the Real GDP of country X?

2 Diagrammatically represent each of the following: (a) economic growth from an inefficient level of production and (b) economic growth from an efficient level of production.

3 Diagrammatically represent each of the following: (a) economic growth with a stable price level, (b) economic growth with a rising price level, and (c) economic growth with a falling price level.

Setting the Scene

George McClintock, 45 years old, lives in Bridgeport, Connecticut. He works for a pharmaceutical company. The following events happened one day in May.

8:04 A.M.

As he's driving to work, George is listening to a news report on the radio. The reporter says that some group (George didn't catch the name of the group) is urging people to trade in their SUVs for smaller cars. The group argues that smaller, more gas-efficient cars will reduce the amount of air pollution and make for a more healthful environment. George wonders if he should trade in his SUV and "do his part."

3:33 P.M.

George is in a meeting that has been called to discuss the prices of the company's new products. Some of his coworkers think the company should raise the price of one of its products by 5 percent; others are arguing against a price rise. One person at the meeting says, "How can we lose by raising the price? Currently, we sell 2,000 units a day at $40 a unit. If we raise the price $2, we can bring in $4,000 more every day."

4:56 P.M.

Driving home after work, George is listening to a report on the radio about an earthquake in Los Angeles. In one area of LA, the earthquake destroyed many of the apartment buildings. A news reporter says, "If anything, the earthquake will drive up the price of water and apartment rents."

? Here are some questions to keep in mind as you read this chapter:

• *If everyone with an SUV trades it in for a smaller, more efficient car, will air pollution be reduced?*

• *If the pharmaceutical company raises the price of one of its products by 5 percent, will its total revenue rise?*

• *If the LA earthquake does result in higher apartment rents, does it follow that apartment landlords will have greater total revenue?*

See analyzing the scene at the end of this chapter for answers to these questions.

How to Approach the Study of Microeconomics

Before we begin our discussion of microeconomics, we need to take some time to discuss what microeconomics is about and how best to approach the study of microeconomics. Microeconomics is the branch of economics that deals with human behavior and choices as they relate to relatively small units: an individual, a firm, an industry, a single market.

There are some key players in microeconomics—players we will discuss time and again. The key microeconomic players are:

1. consumers
2. business firms
3. factor (or resource) owners

Each of these three microeconomic players will have an objective (or goal), face some constraints, and have to make choices. In a way, all of microeconomics is really about three things:

1. objectives
2. constraints
3. choices

Let's discuss each of the three players in terms of its objectives, constraints, and choices.

Consumers

Consumers buy goods and services produced by firms. This advances their *objective* of trying to maximize their utility or satisfaction. Yet very few people can buy all the goods they might like to consume. Consumers' purchases are *constrained* by their limited incomes and by the positive prices for each good. Each purchase subtracts from the consumer's available income and eventually nothing remains. Given limited purchasing ability, the consumer will attempt to gain as much utility as possible from each dollar spent. In practice, this is done by *choosing* to use *marginal analysis* in making consumption decisions—by comparing the additional (or marginal) benefits and additional (or marginal) costs of each purchase.

Firms

Firms *hire* productive factors or resources, combine them in a certain way to *produce* a final good, and then *sell* that good to consumers. In short, firms play two roles in the economy: They are the buyers of factors and the sellers of goods.

FIRMS AS BUYERS   When they hire workers and other productive factors, the *objective* of firms is to maximize profit. Among other things, this implies that they will hire a mix of factors that will minimize their costs of producing the desired amount of output. Their hiring decisions are *constrained* by the positive price of factors and by the need to cover opportunity costs. Firms achieve their objectives by *choosing* to hire only factors that contribute more at the margin to the firm's output and sales receipts than the additional cost of employing them.

FIRMS AS SELLERS   The *objective* here is to maximize profit. In their attempt to maximize profit, firms (as sellers) will have to *choose* what quantity of the good or service they will produce and *choose* what price to charge. The *constraints* placed on sellers comes from consumers, who search for lower prices and higher quality, and from competitors, who attempt to undercut prices charged by other sellers or produce a more desirable good or service.

Factor Owners

Factor owners (or resource owners) sell the factors or resources to firms that firms use to produce goods and services. The *objective* of factor owners is to maximize the income they earn from selling their factors. Since factors are not infinite, factor owners are *constrained* by the prices paid for their services in the marketplace and by the finite amount of factors they have to sell. For example, you, as the owner of your labor, can sell only as much labor as you have in a 24-hour day (where approximately 8 hours each day are needed for sleep). Factor owners achieve their objective by *choosing* to sell those units (of the factor) for which the additional (marginal) benefits, in terms of price offered for the resource, are greater than or equal to the additional (marginal) cost. For example, how much of your labor you choose to sell will depend on the value you place on what you could be doing if you didn't work (your opportunity costs) in relation to the price you are offered for one hour's worth of your labor.

Choices Are Made in Market Settings

The choices of consumers, firms, and factor owners are not made in a vacuum; instead, they are made in market settings. Not all market settings are alike. In other words, the setting (or environment) in which consumers, firms, and factor owners make choices may differ from one time to the next. To illustrate, consumers might make choices in one market setting that has many buyers and many sellers and later make choices in a market setting that has many buyers and only a few sellers. Much of our discussion of microeconomics will focus on the various market settings in which choices are made.

Recap

What should you look for as you begin your study of microeconomics?

1. You should look for the different players—consumers, firms, and factor owners.
2. You should identify the objective of each.
3. You should identify the constraint(s) that each faces.
4. You should focus on the way the economic player chooses within those constraints.
5. You should keep in mind the environment—or the market setting—in which all this takes place.

Elasticity: Part 1

The law of demand states that price and quantity demanded are inversely related, *ceteris paribus*. But it doesn't tell us by what percentage quantity demanded changes as price changes. Suppose price rises by 10 percent. As a result, quantity demanded falls. But by what percentage does it fall? The notion of price elasticity of demand can help answer this question. The general concept of elasticity provides a technique for estimating the response of one variable to changes in some other variable. It has numerous applications in economics.

Price Elasticity of Demand

Have you ever watched any of the TV shopping networks, such as QVC or the Home Shopping Network? Every now and then, the people on these networks will offer computers for sale. For example, QVC will often advertise Dell computers for sale. You may hear the following: "Today, we're offering this Dell computer, along with a printer, digital camera, flat-panel monitor, and scanner all for the unbelievable price of $1,700."

No matter how many computers QVC sells with its offer, one question almost always pops into the minds of the top managers of both QVC and Dell. It is, "How many more computers could we have sold if the price had been, say, $100 lower?" A similar question is, "How many fewer computers would we have sold if the price had been, say, $100 higher?"

Specifically, QVC and Dell managers want to know the *price elasticity of demand* for the computer being offered for sale. **Price elasticity of demand** is a measure of the responsiveness of quantity demanded to changes in price. More specifically, it addresses the "percentage change in quantity demanded for a given percentage change in price."

Price Elasticity of Demand

A measure of the responsiveness of quantity demanded to changes in price.

Let's say that QVC raises the price of the computer by 10 percent, and as a result, quantity demanded for the computer falls by 20 percent. The percentage change in quantity demanded—20 percent—divided by the percentage change in price—10 percent—is called the *coefficient of price elasticity of demand* (E_d).

$$E_d = \frac{\text{Percentage change in quantity demanded}}{\text{Percentage change in price}} = \frac{\%\Delta Q_d}{\%\Delta P}$$

In the formula, E_d = coefficient of price elasticity of demand, or simply elasticity coefficient; % = percentage; and Δ stands for "change in."

If we carry out the calculation in our simple example—where quantity demanded changes by 20 percent and price changes by 10 percent—we get the number 2. An economist would say either, "The coefficient of price elasticity of demand is 2" or, more simply, "Price elasticity of demand is 2."

Q&A

What does "price elasticity of demand is 2" mean?

A price elasticity of demand equal to 2 means that the percentage change in quantity demanded will be 2 times any percentage change in price.[1] If price changes 5 percent, quantity demanded will change 10 percent; if price changes 10 percent, quantity demanded will change 20 percent.

WHERE IS THE MISSING MINUS SIGN? You know that price and quantity demanded move in opposite directions: When price rises, quantity demanded falls; when price falls, quantity demanded rises. In our previous example, when price rises by 10 percent, quantity demanded falls by 20 percent. Now, when you divide a *minus 20 percent* by a *positive 10 percent,* you don't get 2; you get −2. Instead of saying that the price elasticity of demand is 2, you might think the price elasticity of demand is −2. However, by convention, economists usually simplify things by speaking of the absolute value of the price elasticity of demand; thus, they drop the minus sign.

FORMULA FOR CALCULATING PRICE ELASTICITY OF DEMAND Using percentage changes to calculate price elasticity of demand can lead to conflicting results depending on whether price rises or falls. Therefore, economists use the following formula to calculate price elasticity of demand.[2]

$$E_d = \frac{\dfrac{\Delta Q_d}{Q_{d\,\text{Average}}}}{\dfrac{\Delta P}{P_{\text{Average}}}}$$

In the formula, ΔQ_d stands for the absolute change in Q_d. For example, if Q_d changes from 50 units to 100 units, then ΔQ_d is 50 units. ΔP stands for the absolute change in price. For example, if price changes from $12 to $10, then ΔP is $2. $Q_{d\,\text{Average}}$ stands for the average of the two quantities demanded, and P_{Average} stands for the average of the two prices.

---

[1] This assumes we are changing price from its current level.
[2] This formula is sometimes called the midpoint formula for calculating price elasticity of demand.

For the price and quantity demanded data in Exhibit 1, the calculation is

$$E_d = \frac{\frac{50}{75}}{\frac{2}{11}} = 3.67$$

Because we use the "average price" and "average quantity demanded" in our price elasticity of demand equation, 3.67 may be considered the price elasticity of demand at a point *midway between the two points identified on the demand curve.* For example, in Exhibit 1, 3.67 is the price elasticity of demand between points A and B on the demand curve.

Elasticity Is Not Slope

There is a tendency to think that slope and price elasticity of demand are the same, but they are not. Suppose we identify a third point on the demand curve in Exhibit 1. The following table shows the price and quantity demanded for our three points.

Point	Price	Quantity Demanded
A	$12	50
B	10	100
C	8	150

To calculate the *price elasticity of demand* between points A and B, we divide the percentage change in quantity demanded (between the two points) by the percentage change in price (between the two points). Using the price elasticity of demand formula, we get 3.67.

The *slope of the demand curve* between points A and B is the ratio of the change in the variable on the vertical axis to the change in the variable on the horizontal axis.

$$\text{Slope} = \frac{\Delta \text{Variable on vertical axis}}{\Delta \text{Variable on horizontal axis}} = \frac{-2}{50} = -0.04$$

Now let's calculate the price elasticity of demand and the slope between points B and C. The price elasticity of demand is 1.80; the slope is still −0.04.

From Perfectly Elastic to Perfectly Inelastic Demand

Look back at the equation for the elasticity coefficient and think of it as

$$E_d = \frac{\text{Percentage change in quantity demanded}}{\text{Percentage change in price}} = \frac{\text{Numerator}}{\text{Denominator}}$$

Focusing on the numerator and denominator, we realize that (1) the numerator can be greater than the denominator, (2) the numerator can be less than the denominator, or (3) the numerator can be equal to the denominator. These three cases, along with two peripherally related cases, are discussed in the following paragraphs. Exhibits 2 and 3 provide summaries of the discussion.

Elasticity Coefficient	Responsiveness of Quantity Demanded to a Change in Price	Terminology
$E_d > 1$	Quantity demanded changes proportionately more than price changes: $\%\Delta Q_d > \%\Delta P$.	Elastic
$E_d < 1$	Quantity demanded changes proportionately less than price changes: $\%\Delta Q_d < \%\Delta P$.	Inelastic
$E_d = 1$	Quantity demanded changes proportionately to price change: $\%\Delta Q_d = \%\Delta P$.	Unit elastic
$E_d = \infty$	Quantity demanded is extremely responsive to even very small changes in price.	Perfectly elastic
$E_d = 0$	Quantity demanded does not change as price changes.	Perfectly inelastic

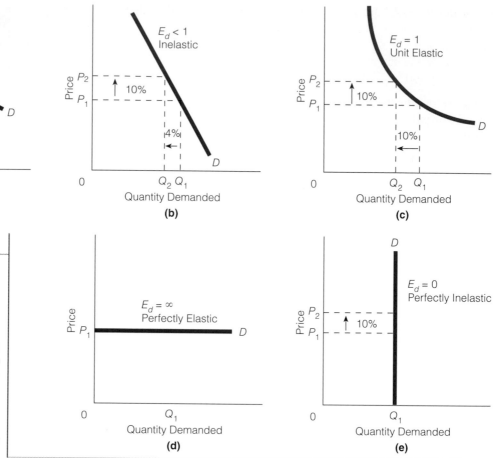

exhibit 3

Graphical Representation of Price Elasticity of Demand

(a) The percentage change in quantity demanded is greater than the percentage change in price: $E_d > 1$ and demand is elastic. (b) The percentage change in quantity demanded is less than the percentage change in price: $E_d < 1$ and demand is inelastic. (c) The percentage change in quantity demand is equal to percentage change in price: $E_d = 1$ and demand is unit elastic. (d) A small change in price reduces quantity demanded to zero: $E_d = \infty$ and demand is perfectly elastic. (e) A change in price does not change quantity demanded: $E_d = 0$ and demand is perfectly inelastic.

Elastic Demand

The percentage change in quantity demanded is greater than the percentage change in price. Quantity demanded changes proportionately more than price changes.

Inelastic Demand

The percentage change in quantity demanded is less than the percentage change in price. Quantity demanded changes proportionately less than price changes.

Unit Elastic Demand

The percentage change in quantity demanded is equal to the percentage change in price. Quantity demanded changes proportionately to price changes.

ELASTIC DEMAND ($E_d > 1$) If the numerator (percentage change in quantity demanded) is greater than the denominator (percentage change in price), the elasticity coefficient is greater than 1 and demand is **elastic**. This means, of course, that quantity demanded changes proportionately more than price changes. A 10 percent increase in price causes, say, a 20 percent reduction in quantity demanded ($E_d = 2$).

Percentage change in quantity demanded > Percentage change in price →
$E_d > 1$ → Demand is elastic

INELASTIC DEMAND ($E_d < 1$) If the numerator (percentage change in quantity demanded) is less than the denominator (percentage change in price), the elasticity coefficient is less than 1 and demand is **inelastic**. This means that quantity demanded changes proportionately less than price changes. A 10 percent increase in price causes, say, a 4 percent reduction in quantity demanded ($E_d = 0.4$).

Percentage change in quantity demanded < Percentage change in price →
$E_d < 1$ → Demand is inelastic

UNIT ELASTIC DEMAND ($E_d = 1$) If the numerator (percentage change in quantity demanded) equals the denominator (percentage change in price), the elasticity coefficient is 1. This means quantity demanded changes proportionately to price changes. For example, a 10 percent increase in price causes a 10 percent decrease in quantity demanded ($E_d = 1$). In this case, demand exhibits unitary elasticity or is **unit elastic**.

Percentage change in quantity demanded = Percentage change in price →
$E_d = 1$ → Demand is unit elastic

PERFECTLY ELASTIC DEMAND ($E_d = \infty$) If quantity demanded is extremely responsive to changes in price, demand is **perfectly elastic**. For example, buyers are willing to buy all units of a seller's good at $5 per unit but nothing at $5.10. A small percentage change in price causes an extremely large percentage change in quantity demanded (from buying all to buying nothing). The percentage is so large, in fact, that economists say it is "infinitely large."

PERFECTLY INELASTIC DEMAND ($E_d = 0$) If quantity demanded is completely unresponsive to changes in price, demand is **perfectly inelastic**. A change in price causes no change in quantity demanded. For example, suppose the price of Dogs Love It dog food rises 10 percent (from $10 to $11), and Jeremy doesn't buy any less of it per week for his dog. It follows that Jeremy's demand for Dogs Love It dog food is perfectly inelastic between a price of $10 and $11.

Perfectly Elastic Demand

A small percentage change in price causes an extremely large percentage change in quantity demanded (from buying all to buying nothing).

Perfectly Inelastic Demand

Quantity demanded does not change as price changes.

PERFECTLY ELASTIC AND PERFECTLY INELASTIC DEMAND CURVES You are used to seeing downward-sloping demand curves. Now, Exhibit 3 shows two demand curves that are not downward sloping. You may be thinking: Aren't all demand curves supposed to be downward sloping because according to the law of demand, an inverse relationship exists between price and quantity demanded? The answer is that in the real world, no demand curves are perfectly elastic (horizontal) or perfectly inelastic (vertical) at all prices. Thus, the perfectly elastic and perfectly inelastic demand curves in Exhibit 3 should be viewed as representations of the extreme limits between which all real-world demand curves fall.

However, a few real-world demand curves do *approximate* the perfectly elastic and inelastic demand curves in (d) and (e) of Exhibit 3. In other words, they come very close. For example, the demand for a particular farmer's wheat approximates the perfectly elastic demand curve in (d). A later chapter discusses the perfectly elastic demand curve for firms in perfectly competitive markets.

Price Elasticity of Demand and Total Revenue (Total Expenditure)

Total revenue (TR) of a seller equals the price of a good times the quantity of the good sold.[3] For example, if the hamburger stand down the street sells 100 hamburgers today at $1.50 each, its total revenue is $150.

Suppose the hamburger vendor raises the price of hamburgers to $2 each. What do you predict will happen to total revenue? Most people say it will increase; there is a widespread belief that higher prices bring higher total revenue. But total revenue may increase, decrease, or remain constant.

Suppose price rises to $2, but because of the higher price, the quantity of hamburgers sold falls to 50. Total revenue is now $100 (whereas it was $150). Whether total revenue rises, falls, or remains constant after a price change depends on whether the percentage change in quantity demanded is less than, greater than, or equal to the percentage change in price. Thus, price elasticity of demand influences total revenue.

Total Revenue (TR)
Price times quantity sold.

Q&A *Are we saying here that as the price of a good rises, the total revenue a firm receives for selling the good may go down? Isn't this counterintuitive?*

Whether or not it is counterintuitive is not the main issue. What matters is whether or not it is right. In what we plan to show next, as price goes up, total revenue can go up, down, or stay the same—depending on elasticity of demand.

ELASTIC DEMAND AND TOTAL REVENUE If demand is elastic, the percentage change in quantity demanded is greater than the percentage change in price. Given a price rise of, say, 5 percent, quantity demanded falls by more than 5 percent—say, 8 percent. What happens

[3]In this discussion, *total revenue* and *total expenditure* are equivalent terms. Total revenue equals price times the quantity sold. Total expenditure equals price times the quantity purchased. If something is sold, it must be purchased, making total revenue equal to total expenditure. The term *total revenue* is used when looking at things from the point of view of the sellers in a market. The term *total expenditure* is used when looking at things from the point of view of the buyers in a market. Buyers make expenditures; sellers receive revenues.

Q&A

How, again, do we know that if demand is elastic, it follows that total revenue falls as price rises?

First, keep in mind what elastic demand means. It means that the percentage change in quantity demanded changes more than the percentage change in price. Now let's say that price rises by 5 percent. We know that quantity demanded will change by more than 5 percent; let's say quantity demanded changes by 10 percent. So now we have price going up by 5 percent and quantity demanded going down by 10 percent. What happens to total revenue? The 5 percent higher price is pushing total revenue up, but the 10 percent lower quantity demanded is pushing total revenue down by more. On net, then, total revenue falls. We conclude that if demand is elastic, a rise in price will bring about a decrease in total revenue.

to total revenue? Because quantity demanded falls, or sales fall off, by a greater percentage than the percentage rise in price, total revenue decreases. In short, if demand is elastic, a price rise decreases total revenue.

$$\text{Demand is elastic: } P\uparrow \rightarrow TR\downarrow$$

What happens to total revenue if demand is elastic and price falls? In this case, quantity demanded rises (price and quantity demanded are inversely related) by a greater percentage than the percentage fall in price, causing total revenue to increase. In short, if demand is elastic, a price fall increases total revenue.

$$\text{Demand is elastic: } P\downarrow \rightarrow TR\uparrow$$

Exhibit 4(a) may help you see the relationship between a change in price and total revenue if demand is elastic. The exhibit shows elastic demand between points A and B on the demand curve. At point A, price is P_1 and quantity demanded is Q_1. Total revenue is equal to the rectangle $0P_1AQ_1$. Now suppose we lower price to P_2. Total revenue is now the rectangle $0P_2BQ_2$. You can see that the rectangle $0P_2BQ_2$ (after the price decline) is larger than rectangle $0P_1AQ_1$. In other words, if demand is elastic and price declines, total revenue will rise.

Of course, when price moves in the opposite direction, rising from P_2 to P_1, then the total revenue rectangle becomes smaller. In other words, if demand is elastic and price rises, total revenue will fall.

INELASTIC DEMAND AND TOTAL REVENUE If demand is inelastic, the percentage change in quantity demanded is less than the percentage change in price. If price rises, quantity demanded falls but by a smaller percentage than the percentage rise in price. As a result, total revenue increases. So if demand is inelastic, a price rise increases total revenue. However, if price falls, quantity demanded rises by a smaller percentage than the percentage fall in price and total revenue decreases. If demand is inelastic, a price fall decreases total revenue. If demand is inelastic, price and total revenue are directly related.

$$\text{Demand is inelastic: } P\uparrow \rightarrow TR\uparrow$$
$$\text{Demand is inelastic: } P\downarrow \rightarrow TR\downarrow$$

exhibit 4

Price Elasticity of Demand and Total Revenue

In (a) demand is elastic between points A and B. A fall in price, from P_1 to P_2, will increase the size of the total revenue rectangle from $0P_1AQ_1$ to $0P_2BQ_2$. A rise in price, from P_2 to P_1, will decrease the size of the total revenue rectangle from $0P_2BQ_2$ to $0P_1AQ_1$. In other words, when demand is elastic, price and total revenue are inversely related. In (b) demand is inelastic between points A and B. A fall in price, from P_1 to P_2, will decrease the size of the total revenue rectangle from $0P_1AQ_1$ to $0P_2BQ_2$. A rise in price, from P_2 to P_1, will increase the size of the total revenue rectangle from $0P_2BQ_2$ to $0P_1AQ_1$. In other words, when demand is inelastic, price and total revenue are directly related.

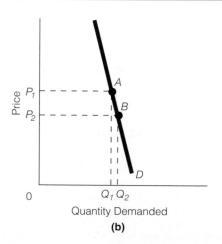

economics 24/7

DRUG BUSTS AND CRIME

Most people believe the sale or possession of drugs such as cocaine and heroin should be illegal. But sometimes, laws may have unintended effects? Do drug laws have unintended effects? Let's analyze the enforcement of drug laws in terms of supply, demand, and price elasticity of demand.

Suppose for every $100 of illegal drug sales, 60 percent of the $100 paid is obtained by illegal means. That is, buyers of $100 worth of illegal drugs obtain $60 of the purchase price from criminal activities such as burglaries, muggings, and so on.

We assume the demand for and supply of cocaine in a particular city are represented by D_1 and S_1 in Exhibit 5. The equilibrium price of $50 an ounce and the equilibrium quantity of 1,000 ounces give cocaine dealers a total revenue of $50,000. If 60 percent of this total revenue is obtained by the criminal activities of cocaine buyers, then $30,000 worth of crime has been committed to purchase the $50,000 worth of cocaine.

Now suppose there is a drug bust in the city. As a result, the drug enforcement authorities reduce the supply of cocaine. The supply curve shifts leftward from S_1 to S_2. The equilibrium price rises to $120 an ounce, and the equilibrium quantity falls to 600 ounces. The demand for cocaine is inelastic between the two prices, at 0.607. When demand is inelastic, an increase in price will raise total revenue. The total revenue received by cocaine dealers is now $72,000. If, again, we assume that 60 percent of the total revenue paid comes from criminal activity, then $43,200 worth of crime has been committed to purchase the $72,000 worth of cocaine.

Our conclusion: If the demand for cocaine is inelastic and people commit crimes to buy drugs, then a drug bust can actually increase the amount of drug-related crime. Obviously, this is an unintended effect of the enforcement of drug laws.

exhibit 5

Drug Busts and Drug-Related Crime

In the exhibit, P = price of cocaine, Q = quantity of cocaine, and TR = total revenue from selling cocaine. At a price of $50 for an ounce of cocaine, equilibrium quantity is 1,000 ounces and total revenue is $50,000. If $60 of every $100 cocaine purchase is obtained through crime, then $30,000 worth of crime is committed to purchase $50,000 worth of cocaine. As a result of a drug bust, the supply of cocaine shifts leftward; the price rises and the quantity falls. Because we have assumed the demand for cocaine is inelastic, total revenue rises to $72,000. Sixty percent of this comes from criminal activities, or $43,200.

	P	Q	TR	Dollar Amount of TR Obtained Through Crime
Before Drug Bust	$50	1,000	$50,000	$30,000
After Drug Bust	120	600	72,000	43,200

economics 24/7

© CREATAS IMAGES / JUPITER IMAGES

WILL HIGH TAXES ON CIGARETTES REDUCE SMOKING?

In recent years, there have been attempts to raise the taxes on cigarettes. The stated purpose of the increase in taxes is to make smoking more expensive in the hope that people will quit smoking, reduce the amount they smoke, or never start smoking.

But will higher taxes on cigarettes cause millions of smokers to stop or cut back on smoking? Will it prevent many teenagers from starting to smoke and reduce the number of teenagers who are smoking? If the demand curve for cigarettes is downward sloping, higher cigarette prices (brought about by higher taxes) will decrease the quantity demanded of cigarettes. But the question is: How much? Thus, price elasticity of demand is needed for the analysis.

To take an extreme case, suppose the demand curve for cigarettes is perfectly inelastic between the current price and the new higher price brought about through higher taxes. In this case, the quantity demanded of cigarettes will not change. If the demand curve is inelastic (but not perfectly inelastic), the percentage decline in the quantity demanded of cigarettes will be less than the percentage increase in the price of cigarettes.

The anti-tobacco lobby would prefer that the demand curve for cigarettes be highly elastic. In this case, the percentage change in the quantity demanded of cigarettes will be greater than the percentage change in price. Many more people will stop smoking if cigarette demand is elastic than if it is inelastic.

Another consideration is that the elasticity of demand for cigarettes may be different for adults than it is for teenagers. In fact, some studies show that teenagers are much more sensitive to cigarette price than adults are. In other words, the elasticity of demand for cigarettes is greater for teenagers than for adults.

One study found the elasticity of demand for cigarettes to be 0.35 (in the long run). This study did not separate adult smoking and teenage smoking. Another study looked at only teenage smoking and concluded that for every 10 percent rise in price, quantity demanded would decline by 12 percent. In other words, demand for cigarettes by teenagers is elastic. For those who want to use higher cigarette taxes as a means of curtailing teenage smoking, that is encouraging news.

You can see the relationship between inelastic demand and total revenue in Exhibit 4(b), where demand is inelastic between points *A* and *B* on the demand curve. If we start at P_1 and lower price to P_2, the total revenue rectangle goes from $0P_1AQ_1$ to the smaller total revenue rectangle $0P_2BQ_2$. In other words, if demand is inelastic and price falls, total revenue will fall.

Moving from the lower price, P_2, to the higher price, P_1, does just the opposite. If demand is inelastic and price rises, the total revenue rectangle becomes larger; that is, total revenue rises.

UNIT ELASTIC DEMAND AND TOTAL REVENUE If demand is unit elastic, the percentage change in quantity demanded equals the percentage change in price. If price rises, quantity demanded falls by the same percentage as the percentage rise in price. Total revenue does not change. If price falls, quantity demanded rises by the same percentage as the percentage fall in price. Again, total revenue does not change. If demand is unit elastic, a rise or fall in price leaves total revenue unchanged.

Thinking like
AN ECONOMIST

The layperson asks what happens to total revenue as price rises. The economist says, "It depends." But what does it depend on? The answer is price elasticity of demand. If demand is elastic, total revenue will fall; if demand is inelastic, total revenue will rise; and if demand is unit elastic, total revenue will not change. Often, the layperson seeks "one definitive answer" to his or her question. But often, what the economist gives is a "conditional answer": Given a particular condition, the answer is X, but given another condition, the answer is Y.

Demand is unit elastic: $P\uparrow \rightarrow \overline{TR}$

Demand is unit elastic: $P\downarrow \rightarrow \overline{TR}$

For a review of the relationship between price elasticity of demand and total revenue, see Exhibit 6.

SELF-TEST

(Answers to Self-Test questions are in the Self-Test Appendix.)

1. On Tuesday, price and quantity demanded are $7 and 120 units, respectively. Ten days later, price and quantity demanded are $6 and 150 units, respectively. What is the price elasticity of demand between the price of $7 and the price of $6?

2. What does a price elasticity of demand of 0.39 mean?

3. Identify what happens to total revenue as a result of each of the following: (a) price rises and demand is elastic; (b) price falls and demand is inelastic; (c) price rises and demand is unit elastic; (d) price rises and demand is inelastic; (e) price falls and demand is elastic.

4. Alexi says, "When a seller raises his price, his total revenue rises." What is Alexi implicitly assuming?

Elasticity: Part 2

This section discusses the elasticity ranges of a straight-line downward-sloping demand curve and the determinants of price elasticity of demand.

Price Elasticity of Demand Along a Straight-Line Demand Curve

The price elasticity of demand for a straight-line downward-sloping demand curve varies from highly elastic to highly inelastic. To illustrate, consider the price elasticity of demand at the upper range of the demand curve in Exhibit 7(a). No matter whether the price falls from $9 to $8 or rises from $8 to $9, using the price elasticity of demand formula (identified earlier in the chapter), we calculate price elasticity of demand as 5.66.[4]

Now consider the price elasticity of demand at the lower range of the demand curve in Exhibit 7(a). Whether the price falls from $3 to $2 or rises from $2 to $3, we calculate the price elasticity of demand as 0.33.

In other words, along the range of the demand curve we have identified, price elasticity goes from being greater than 1 (5.66) to being less than 1 (0.33). Obviously, on its way from being greater than 1 to being less than 1, price elasticity of demand must be equal to 1. In Exhibit 7(a), we have identified price elasticity of demand as equal to 1 at the *midpoint* of the demand curve.[5]

What do the elastic and inelastic ranges along the straight-line downward-sloping demand curve mean in terms of total revenue? If we start in the elastic range of the demand curve in Exhibit 7(a) and lower price, total revenue rises. This is shown in Exhibit 7(b). That is, as price is coming down within the elastic range of the demand curve in (a), total revenue is rising in (b).

When price has fallen enough such that we move into the inelastic range of the demand curve in (a), further price declines simply lower total revenue, as shown in (b). It

exhibit **6**

Elasticities, Price Changes, and Total Revenue

If demand is elastic, a price rise leads to a decrease in total revenue (*TR*), and a price fall leads to an increase in total revenue. If demand is inelastic, a price rise leads to an increase in total revenue and a price fall leads to a decrease in total revenue. If demand is unit elastic, a rise or fall in price does not change total revenue.

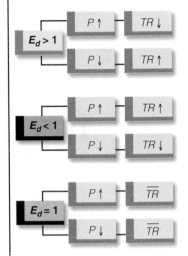

---

[4]Keep in mind that our formula uses the average of the two prices and the average of the two quantities demanded. You may want to look back at the formula to refresh your memory.

[5]For any straight-line downward-sloping demand curve, price elasticity of demand equals 1 at the midpoint of the curve.

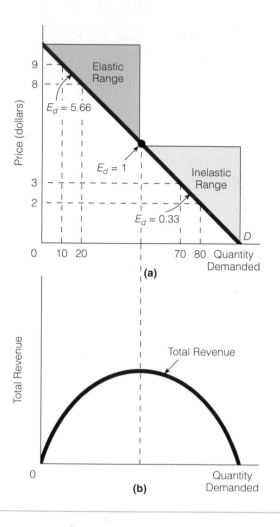

exhibit 7

Price Elasticity of Demand Along a Straight-Line Demand Curve

In (a), the price elasticity of demand varies along the straight-line downward-sloping demand curve. There is an elastic range to the curve (where $E_d > 1$) and an inelastic range (where $E_d < 1$). At the midpoint of any straight-line downward-sloping demand curve, price elasticity of demand is equal to 1 ($E_d = 1$).

Part (b) shows that in the elastic range of the demand curve, total revenue rises as price is lowered. In the inelastic range of the demand curve, further price declines result in declining total revenue. Total revenue reaches its peak when price elasticity of demand equals 1.

holds, then, that total revenue is at its highest—its peak—when price elasticity of demand equals 1.

Determinants of Price Elasticity of Demand

The following four factors are relevant to the determination of price elasticity of demand:

1. Number of substitutes
2. Necessities versus luxuries
3. Percentage of one's budget spent on the good
4. Time

Because all four factors interact, we hold all other things constant as we discuss each.

NUMBER OF SUBSTITUTES Suppose good *A* has 2 substitutes and good *B* has 15 substitutes. Assume that each of the 2 substitutes for good *A* is as good (or close) a substitute for that good as each of the 15 substitutes is for good *B*.

Let the price of each good rise by 10 percent. The quantity demanded of each good decreases. Will the percentage change in quantity demanded of good *A* be greater or less than the percentage change in quantity demanded of good *B*? That is, will quantity demanded be more responsive to the 10 percent price rise for the good that has 2 sub-

economics 24/7

WHY DO COMPANIES HIRE CELEBRITIES?

Many companies hire celebrities to advertise their products. In the past, Shaquille O'Neal was hired to advertise Burger King, Shakira was hired to advertise Pepsi, Jerry Seinfeld to advertise American Express, Celine Dion to advertise Chrysler, Tim McGraw to advertise Anheuser-Busch, and Michael Jordan to advertise products such as Gatorade and Nike.

Why do companies hire celebrities to pitch their wares? The obvious answer is to get the attention of consumers. When people see a sports star, television star, model, or movie star talking about a product, they are likely to take notice.

But there are other ways companies can get the attention of consumers, so maybe another factor is involved. Some economists have hypothesized that this other factor is related to price elasticity of demand and total revenue.

Consider the case of basketball star Shaquille O'Neal, who has advertised Burger King in the past. What message was Burger King trying to convey with its ads showing Shaq ordering a Whopper? The message may have been this: For Shaq, there is only one hamburger—no substitutes.

If the buying public accepts this message—if buyers believe there are no substitutes for a Whopper or if they want to do what Shaq does—then the price elasticity of a Whopper declines. The fewer substitutes, the lower the price elasticity of demand.

And if it is possible to get the demand for Whoppers to become inelastic (at least for a short range of the demand curve above current price), then Burger King can raise both price and total revenue. Remember, if demand is inelastic, an increase in price leads to higher total revenue.

Does Burger King want to increase its total revenue? Under the conditions stated here, it certainly does.

It's true that, at a higher price, fewer Whoppers will be sold. But profit is the objective, not number of Whoppers sold. Profit is the difference between total revenue and total cost. If the demand for a Whopper is inelastic, a price increase will raise total revenue. It will also mean fewer Whoppers sold, which will lower costs. If revenues rise and costs decline, profits rise.

Our concluding point is a simple one: The discussion of price elasticity of demand in this chapter isn't as far removed from the discussions in the offices of major companies and advertising firms as you may have thought.

stitutes (good *A*) or for the good that has 15 substitutes (good *B*)? The answer is the good with 15 substitutes, good *B*. This occurs because the greater the opportunities for substitution (there is more chance of substituting a good for *B* than of substituting a good for *A*), the greater the cutback in the quantity of the good purchased as its price rises. When the price of good *A* rises 10 percent, people can turn to 2 substitutes. Quantity demanded of good *A* falls, but not by as much as if 15 substitutes had been available, as there were for good *B*.

The relationship between the availability of substitutes and price elasticity is clear: *The more substitutes for a good, the higher the price elasticity of demand; the fewer substitutes for a good, the lower the price elasticity of demand.*

For example, the price elasticity of demand for Chevrolets is higher than the price elasticity of demand for all cars. This is because there are more substitutes for Chevrolets than there are for cars. Everything that is a substitute for a car (bus, train, walking, bicycle, etc.) is also a substitute for a specific type of car, such as a Chevrolet; but some things that are substitutes for a Chevrolet (Ford, Toyota, Chrysler, Mercedes-Benz, etc.) are not substitutes for a car. Instead, they are simply types of cars.

Thus, the relationship above can be stated as: *The more broadly defined the good, the fewer the substitutes; the more narrowly defined the good, the greater the substitutes.* There are

Q&A **Is price elasticity of demand greater for computers or for Sony computers?**

Ask yourself which good—computers or Sony computers—has more substitutes. The answer is Sony computers. Thus, it follows that the elasticity of demand is greater for Sony computers than it is for computers.

Q&A **Are we saying that the demand for, say, gasoline is elastic and the demand for, say, paper, is inelastic because one usually spends a larger percentage of his budget on gasoline (for the car) than on paper?**

First, we are not saying that the demand for gasoline is elastic and the demand for paper is inelastic. The words elastic *and* inelastic *come with precise definitions. Elastic means that the percentage change in quantity demanded is greater than the percentage change in price so that $E_d > 1$. We do not know if gasoline has $E_d > 1$. Similarly, we do not know if the demand for paper is inelastic so that $E_d < 1$.*

What we are saying is that if gasoline consumption is a larger percentage of the budget than paper consumption, it follows that the elasticity of demand for gasoline is greater than the elasticity of demand for paper. In other words, E_d is a larger number for gasoline than it is for paper. Whether it is greater than 1 or less than 1, we cannot say without actual data.

Q&A **Would the elasticity of demand for gasoline be greater in the short run or in the long run?**

In the long run. If the price of gasoline rises, the consumption of gasoline does not fall dramatically in the short run. For example, motorists don't immediately stop driving big gas-guzzling cars. As time passes, however, many car owners trade in their big cars for compact cars. Car buyers become more concerned with the miles a car can travel per gallon of gas. People begin to form carpools. As a result, gasoline consumption ends up falling more in the long run.

more substitutes for this economics textbook than there are for textbooks. There are more substitutes for Coca-Cola than there are for soft drinks.

NECESSITIES VERSUS LUXURIES Generally, *the more that a good is considered a luxury (a good that we can do without) rather than a necessity (a good that we can't do without), the higher the price elasticity of demand.* For example, consider two goods—jewelry and a medicine for controlling high blood pressure. If the price of jewelry rises, it is easy to cut back on jewelry purchases. No one really needs jewelry to live. However, if the price of the medicine for controlling one's high blood pressure rises, it is not so easy to cut back on it. We expect the price elasticity of demand for jewelry to be higher than the price elasticity of demand for medicine used to control high blood pressure.

PERCENTAGE OF ONE'S BUDGET SPENT ON THE GOOD Claire Rossi has a monthly budget of $3,000. Of this monthly budget, she spends $3 per month on pens and $400 per month on dinners at restaurants. In percentage terms, she spends 0.1 percent of her monthly budget on pens and 13 percent of her monthly budget on dinners at restaurants. Suppose both the price of pens and the price of dinners at restaurants double. Would Claire be more responsive to the change in the price of pens or the change in the price of dinners at restaurants? The answer is the change in the price of dinners at restaurants. The reason is that a doubling in price of a good on which Claire spends 0.1 percent of her budget is not felt as strongly as a doubling in price of a good on which she spends 13 percent. Claire is more likely to ignore the doubling in the price of pens than she is to ignore the doubling in the price of dinners at restaurants. Buyers are (and thus quantity demanded is) more responsive to price the larger the percentage of their budget that goes for the purchase of the good. *The greater the percentage of one's budget that goes to purchase a good, the higher the price elasticity of demand; the smaller the percentage of one's budget that goes to purchase a good, the lower the price elasticity of demand.*

TIME As time passes, buyers have greater opportunities to be responsive to a price change. If the price of electricity went up today, and you knew about it, you probably would not change your consumption of electricity today as much as you would 3 months from today. As time passes, you have more chances to change your consumption by finding substitutes (natural gas), changing your lifestyle (buying more blankets and turning down the thermostat at night), and so on. We conclude: *The more time that passes (since the price change), the higher the price elasticity of demand for the good; the less time that passes, the lower the price elasticity of demand for the good.*[6] In other words, price elasticity of demand for a good is higher in the long run than in the short run.

---

[6]If we say, "The more time that passes (since the price change), the higher the price elasticity of demand," wouldn't it follow that price elasticity of demand gets steadily larger? For example, might it be that on Tuesday the price of good X rises, and 5 days later, $E_d = 0.70$, 10 days later it is 0.76, and so on toward infinity? This is not exactly the case. Obviously, there comes a time when quantity demanded is no longer adjusting to a change in price (just as there comes a time when there are no longer any ripples in the lake from the passing motorboat). Our conditional statement ("the more time that passes . . .") implies this condition

SELF-TEST

1. If there are 7 substitutes for good *X* and demand is inelastic, does it follow that if there are 9 substitutes for good *X*, demand will be elastic? Explain your answer.

2. Price elasticity of demand is predicted to be higher for which good of the following combinations of goods: (a) Dell computers or computers; (b) Heinz ketchup or ketchup; (c) Perrier water or water? Explain your answers.

Other Elasticity Concepts

This section looks at three other elasticities: cross elasticity of demand, income elasticity of demand, and price elasticity of supply.

Cross Elasticity of Demand

Cross elasticity of demand measures the responsiveness in the quantity demanded of one good to changes in the price of another good. It is calculated by dividing the percentage change in the quantity demanded of one good by the percentage change in the price of another good.

Cross Elasticity of Demand
Measures the responsiveness in quantity demanded of one good to changes in the price of another good.

$$E_c = \frac{\text{Percentage change in quantity demanded of one good}}{\text{Percentage change in price of another good}}$$

where E_c stands for the coefficient of cross elasticity of demand, or elasticity coefficient.[7]

This concept is often used to determine whether two goods are substitutes or complements and the degree to which one good is a substitute for or complement to another. Consider two goods: Skippy peanut butter and Jif peanut butter. Suppose that when the price of Jif increases by 10 percent, the quantity demanded of Skippy increases by 45 percent. The cross elasticity of demand for Skippy with respect to the price of Jif is written

$$E_c = \frac{\text{Percentage change in quantity demanded of Skippy}}{\text{Percentage change in price of Jif}}$$

In this case, the cross elasticity of demand is a positive 4.5. When the cross elasticity of demand is positive, the percentage change in the quantity demanded of one good (numerator) moves in the same direction as the percentage change in the price of another good (denominator). This is representative of goods that are substitutes. As the price of Jif rises, the demand curve for Skippy shifts rightward, causing the quantity demanded of Skippy to increase at every price.[8] We conclude that if $E_c > 0$, the two goods are substitutes.

$$E_c > 0 \rightarrow \text{Goods are substitutes}$$

If the elasticity coefficient is negative, $E_c < 0$, then the two goods are complements.

$$E_c < 0 \rightarrow \text{Goods are complements}$$

A negative cross elasticity of demand occurs when the percentage change in the quantity demanded of one good (numerator) and the percentage change in the price of another good (denominator) move in opposite directions. Consider an example. Suppose

---

[7] A question normally arises: How can E_d and E_c both be the elasticity coefficient? It is a matter of convenience. When speaking about price elasticity of demand, the coefficient of price elasticity of demand is referred to as the "elasticity coefficient." When speaking about cross elasticity of demand, the coefficient of cross elasticity of demand is referred to as the "elasticity coefficient." The practice holds for other elasticities as well.

[8] Recall that if two goods are substitutes, a rise in the price of one good causes the demand for the other good to increase.

economics 24/7

©PHOTODISC BLUE/GETTY IMAGES

ARE CHILDREN SUBSTITUTES OR COMPLEMENTS?

Not all parents are alike. Some parents spend a lot of time with their children; others do not. Some parents (with similar incomes) spend a lot of money on their children; others do not. Some parents are strict disciplinarians; others are not. Which parental behavioral differences are significant? For example, if parents A and parents B spend different amounts of time reading to their children at bedtime, is this difference significant? Are children who are read to a lot different from children who are read to very little or not at all? If not, then perhaps this parental difference does not matter.

One difference in parental behavior that may be significant is whether parents treat their children as substitutes or as complements. To illustrate, suppose Bob is the father of two boys, Zack, 4 years old, and Dylan, 6 years old. Bob spends time with each of his boys, and the amount of time he spends with each boy often depends on the "price" the son "charges" his father to be with him. For example, Zack is a little harder to be around than Dylan (he asks for more things from his father, he doesn't seem to be as happy doing certain things, etc.), so the "price" Bob has to pay to be around Zack is higher than the price he has to pay to be around Dylan.

How will a change in the price each son charges his father influence the time the father spends with the other son? This question involves cross elasticity of demand, where

$$E_c = \frac{\text{Percentage change in quantity demanded of time spent with Dylan}}{\text{Percentage change in price Zack charges his father to be with him}}$$

Suppose Zack increases the price he charges his father to be with him. He demands more of his father, he seems less content when his father suggests certain activities, and so

on. How will Bob react? If an increase in the price he has to pay to be with Zack increases the amount of time he wants to spend with Dylan, then as far as Bob is concerned, Dylan and Zack are substitutes ($E_c > 0$). But if an increase in the price he has to pay to be with Zack causes Bob to decrease the time he spends with Dylan, then Dylan and Zack are complements ($E_c < 0$).

In the first case, where the two boys are substitutes, the father may be saying, "I like to be with both my boys, but if one makes it harder for me to be with him, I'll spend less time with him and I'll spend more time with the other." In the second case, where the two boys are complements, the father may be saying, "I like to be with both my boys, but if one makes it harder for me to be with him, I'll spend less time with him and less time with the other too."

Does it matter to the two boys whether they are viewed by their father as substitutes or complements? Consider things from Dylan's perspective. Suppose he wants his father to spend more time with him. If Zack raises the price to his father of being with him (Zack) and Dylan and Zack are substitutes, then Dylan will benefit from Zack's raising the price. His father will spend less time with Zack and more with him. But if Zack and Dylan are complements, an increase in the price Zack charges his father to be with him (Zack) will cause his father to spend less time with Dylan.

Will Dylan act differently to Zack depending on whether he perceives himself as a substitute or as a complement? If he perceives himself as a substitute, he may urge Zack to act up with Dad, knowing that this means Dad will spend more time with him, Dylan. But if he perceives himself as a complement, he may urge Zack to be good with Dad, knowing that if Zack charges his father a lower price to be around him (Zack), this will increase the amount of time the father will spend with Dylan.

the price of cars increases by 5 percent, and the quantity demanded of car tires decreases by 10 percent. Calculating the cross elasticity of demand, we have −10 percent/5 percent = −2. Cars and car tires are complements.

The concept of cross elasticity of demand can be very useful. Suppose a company sells cheese. A natural question might be: What goods are substitutes for cheese? The answer would help identify the company's competitors. The company could find out which goods are substitutes for cheese by calculating the cross elasticity of demand between cheese and other goods. A positive cross elasticity of demand would indicate the two goods were substitutes, and the higher the cross elasticity of demand, the greater the degree of substitution.

Income Elasticity of Demand

Income elasticity of demand measures the responsiveness of quantity demanded to changes in income. It is calculated by dividing the percentage change in quantity demanded of a good by the percentage change in income.

$$E_y = \frac{\text{Percentage change in quantity demanded}}{\text{Percentage change in income}}$$

where E_y = coefficient of income elasticity of demand, or elasticity coefficient.

Income elasticity of demand is positive, $E_y > 0$, for a *normal good*. Recall that a normal good is one whose demand, and thus quantity demanded, increases, given an increase in income. Thus, the variables in the numerator and denominator in the income elasticity of demand formula move in the same direction for a normal good.

$$E_y > 0 \rightarrow \text{Normal good}$$

In contrast to a normal good, the demand for an *inferior good* decreases as income increases. Income elasticity of demand for an inferior good is negative, $E_y < 0$.

$$E_y < \rightarrow \text{Inferior good}$$

To calculate the income elasticity of demand for a good, we use the same approach that we used to calculate price elasticity of demand.

$$E_y = \frac{\frac{\Delta Q_d}{Q_{d\,\text{Average}}}}{\frac{\Delta Y}{Y_{\text{Average}}}}$$

where $Q_{d\,\text{Average}}$ is the average quantity demanded and Y_{Average} is the average income.

Suppose income increases from \$500 to \$600 per month, and as a result, quantity demanded of good X increases from 20 units to 30 units per month. We have

$$E_y = \frac{\frac{10}{25}}{\frac{100}{550}} = 2.2$$

E_y is a positive number, so good X is a normal good. Also, because $E_y > 1$, demand for good X is said to be **income elastic**. This means the percentage change in quantity demanded of the good is greater than the percentage change in income. If $E_y < 1$, the demand for the good is said to be **income inelastic**. If $E_y = 1$, then the demand for the good is **income unit elastic**.

Price Elasticity of Supply

Price elasticity of supply measures the responsiveness of quantity supplied to changes in price. It is calculated by dividing the percentage change in quantity supplied of a good by the percentage change in the price of the good.

$$E_s = \frac{\text{Percentage change in quantity supplied}}{\text{Percentage change in price}}$$

where E_s stands for the coefficient of price elasticity of supply, or elasticity coefficient. We use the same approach to calculate price elasticity of supply that we used to calculate price elasticity of demand.

Income Elasticity of Demand
Measures the responsiveness of quantity demanded to changes in income.

Income Elastic
The percentage change in quantity demanded of a good is greater than the percentage change in income.

Income Inelastic
The percentage change in quantity demanded of a good is less than the percentage change in income.

Income Unit Elastic
The percentage change in quantity demanded of a good is equal to the percentage change in income.

Price Elasticity of Supply
Measures the responsiveness of quantity supplied to changes in price.

In addition, supply can be classified as elastic, inelastic, unit elastic, perfectly elastic, or perfectly inelastic (Exhibit 8). Elastic supply ($E_s > 1$) refers to a percentage change in quantity supplied that is greater than the percentage change in price.

Percentage change in quantity supplied > Percentage change in price →
$E_s > 1$ → Elastic supply

Inelastic supply ($E_s < 1$) refers to a percentage change in quantity supplied that is less than the percentage change in price.

Percentage change in quantity supplied < Percentage change in price →
$E_s < 1$ → Inelastic supply

Unit elastic supply ($E_s = 1$) refers to a percentage change in quantity supplied that is equal to the percentage change in price.

Percentage change in quantity supplied = Percentage change in price →
$E_s = 1$ → Unit elastic supply

Perfectly elastic supply ($E_s = \infty$) represents the case where a small change in price changes quantity supplied by an infinitely large amount (and thus, the supply curve, or a portion of the overall supply curve, is horizontal). Perfectly inelastic supply ($E_s = 0$) represents the case where a change in price brings no change in quantity supplied (and thus, the supply curve, or a portion of the overall supply curve, is vertical).

See Exhibit 9 for a summary of the elasticity concepts.

exhibit **8**

Price Elasticity of Supply

(a) The percentage change in quantity supplied is greater than the percentage change in price: $E_s > 1$ and supply is elastic. (b) The percentage change in quantity supplied is less than the percentage change in price: $E_s < 1$ and supply is inelastic. (c) The percentage change in quantity supplied is equal to the percentage change in price: $E_s = 1$ and supply is unit elastic. (d) A small change in price changes quantity supplied by an infinite amount: $E_s = \infty$ and supply is perfectly elastic. (e) A change in price does not change quantity supplied: $E_s = 0$ and supply is perfectly inelastic.

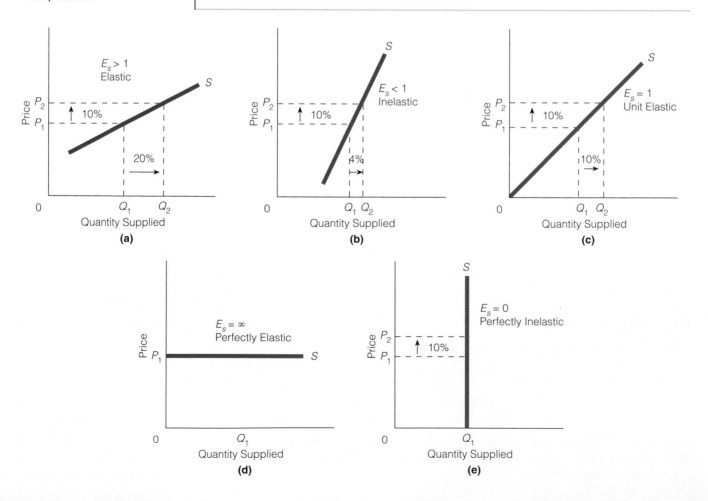

Type	Calculation	Possibilities	Terminology
Price elasticity of demand	$\dfrac{\text{Percentage change in quantity demanded}}{\text{Percentage change in price}}$	$E_d > 1$ $E_d < 1$ $E_d = 1$ $E_d = \infty$ $E_d = 0$	Elastic Inelastic Unit elastic Perfectly elastic Perfectly inelastic
Cross elasticity of demand	$\dfrac{\text{Percentage change in quantity demanded of one good}}{\text{Percentage change in price of another good}}$	$E_c < 0$ $E_c > 0$	Complements Substitutes
Income elasticity of demand	$\dfrac{\text{Percentage change in quantity demanded}}{\text{Percentage change in income}}$	$E_y > 0$ $E_y < 0$ $E_y > 1$ $E_y < 1$ $E_y = 1$	Normal good Inferior good Income elastic Income inelastic Income unit elastic
Price elasticity of supply	$\dfrac{\text{Percentage change in quantity supplied}}{\text{Percentage change in price}}$	$E_s > 1$ $E_s < 1$ $E_s = 1$ $E_s = \infty$ $E_s = 0$	Elastic Inelastic Unit elastic Perfectly elastic Perfectly inelastic

exhibit **9**

Summary of the Four Elasticity Concepts

Price Elasticity of Supply and Time

The longer the period of adjustment to a change in price, the higher the price elasticity of supply. (We are referring to goods whose quantity supplied can increase with time. This covers most goods. It does not, however, cover original Picasso paintings.) There is an obvious reason for this: Additional production takes time.

For example, suppose the demand for new housing increases in your city. Further, suppose this increase in demand occurs all at once on Tuesday. This places upward pressure on the price of housing. Will the number of houses supplied be much different on Saturday than it was on Tuesday? No, it won't. It will take time for suppliers to determine whether the increase in demand is permanent. If they decide it is a temporary state, not much will be done. If contractors decide it is permanent, they need time to move resources from the production of other things into the production of additional new housing. Simply put, the change in quantity supplied of housing is likely to be different in the long run than in the short run, given a change in price. This translates into a higher price elasticity of supply in the long run than in the short run.

SELF-TEST

1. What does an income elasticity of demand of 1.33 mean?

2. If supply is perfectly inelastic, what does this signify?

Thinking like
AN ECONOMIST
In a way, this chapter is about ratios. Ratios describe how one thing changes (the numerator) relative to a change in something else (the denominator). For example, when we discuss price elasticity of demand, we investigate how quantity demanded changes as price changes; when we discuss income elasticity of demand, we explore how quantity demanded changes as income changes. Economists often think in terms of ratios because they are often comparing the change in one variable to the change in another variable.

A Reader Asks...

Is the Type of Thinking Inherent in Elasticity Useful?

The elasticity concepts in this chapter are interesting, and I'm sure they're useful to business firms. But I don't really see how thinking about elasticities helps me in any fundamental way. Any comments?

Elasticity (price, income, supply, cross) relates to a change in one thing relative to a change in something else. Thinking in terms of these types of relationships can help you gain insight into certain phenomena. For example, consider this question: If a company is forced to pay its employees higher wage rates ($20 an hour instead of $18 an hour), will the higher wage rate result in the company paying a larger total amount in wages (say, $500,000 a month instead of $400,000)?

Now the answer most people will give is yes. They reason this way: Multiplying a given number of hours worked by $20 results in a greater total dollar amount than multiplying the number of hours by $18.

Thinking elastically, we know that changing one thing can lead to a change in something else. Specifically, we know that an increase in wage rates can affect the number of hours worked. Companies may not hire as many employees or may not have their employees work as many hours if the wage rate is $20 an hour than if it is $18 an hour. In short, hours worked are likely to fall as wage rates rise. Whether the total amount the firm pays in wages rises, falls, or remains constant depends on the percentage rise in wage rates relative to the percentage fall in hours worked. For example, if the percentage increase in wage rates is less than the percentage decline in hours worked, the total amount paid in wages will decline. We could not have easily come up with this conclusion had we not looked at the percentage change in one thing relative to the percentage change in something else. This type of thinking, of course, is inherent in the elasticity concepts discussed in this chapter.

! analyzing the scene

If everyone with an SUV trades it in for a smaller, more efficient car, will air pollution be reduced? If the pharmaceutical company raises the price of one of its products by 5 percent, will its total revenue rise? If the LA earthquake does result in higher apartment rents, does it follow that apartment landlords will have greater total revenue?

The theme in all of these questions is the same: One thing actually changes or a change is proposed, and you are asked to wonder what the effect of the change might be. Let's consider each question separately.

If people trade in their SUVs for small, gas-efficient cars, will air pollution be reduced? The answer is not necessarily. When people have small cars, they may increase the amount they drive because the cost per mile is less for a small car than for an SUV. For example, suppose it takes $2 worth of gas to drive 15 miles in an SUV and $2 worth of gas to drive 25 miles in a Honda Civic. On a per mile basis, the cost would

be 13 cents a mile in an SUV and 8 cents a mile in a Honda Civic. If the demand curve for driving is downward sloping, people will drive more at 8 cents a mile than at 13 cents a mile. The question is: How much more will they drive? Certainly, the possibility exists that drivers will drive so much more (in their small cars as opposed to their big SUVs) that the amount of air pollution (due to driving more) increases instead of decreases. In other words, the small cars might emit less pollution than SUVs per mile traveled, but if drivers travel significantly more miles in their smaller cars than in their SUVs, we might end up with more instead of less air pollution.

Now let's turn to the pharmaceutical company and prices. Will the company take in more total revenue if it raises the price of a particular product? Yes, if the demand for the product is inelastic between the old (lower) price and the new (higher) price. No, if the demand for the product is elastic between the old (lower) price and the new (higher) price.

Finally, will the LA earthquake cause a rise in apartment rents? Yes, because as the supply of apartments falls (due to the earthquake), the demand for apartments intersects the supply of apartments higher up the demand curve and brings about a higher dollar rent. But it doesn't necessarily follow that higher apartment rents will increase total revenue for apartment owners—in much the same way that it did not neces-sarily follow that a higher product price will increase total revenue for the pharmaceutical company. It all depends on price elasticity of demand. If the demand for apartments is inelastic between the old (lower, pre-earthquake) rents and the new (higher, post-earthquake) rents, total apartment revenue will rise. If the demand for apartments is elastic, total revenue will fall.

chapter summary

Price Elasticity of Demand

- Price elasticity of demand is a measure of the responsiveness of quantity demanded to changes in price:

$$E_d = \frac{\text{Percentage change in quantity demanded}}{\text{Percentage change in price}}$$

- If the percentage change in quantity demanded is greater than the percentage change in price, demand is elastic. If the percentage change in quantity demanded is less than the percentage change in price, demand is inelastic. If the percentage change in quantity demanded is equal to the percentage change in price, demand is unit elastic. If a small change in price causes an infinitely large change in quantity demanded, demand is perfectly elastic. If a change in price causes no change in quantity demanded, demand is perfectly inelastic.

- The coefficient of price elasticity of demand (E_d) is negative, signifying the inverse relationship between price and quantity demanded. For convenience, however, the absolute value of the elasticity coefficient is used.

Total Revenue and Price Elasticity of Demand

- Total revenue equals price times quantity sold. Total expenditure equals price times quantity purchased. Total revenue equals total expenditure.

- If demand is elastic, price and total revenue are inversely related: As price rises (falls), total revenue falls (rises).

- If demand is inelastic, price and total revenue are directly related: As price rises (falls), total revenue rises (falls).

- If demand is unit elastic, total revenue is independent of price: As price rises (falls), total revenue remains constant.

Determinants of Price Elasticity of Demand

- The more substitutes for a good, the higher the price elasticity of demand; the fewer substitutes for a good, the lower the price elasticity of demand.

- The more that a good is considered a luxury instead of a necessity, the higher the price elasticity of demand.

- The greater the percentage of one's budget that goes to purchase a good, the higher the price elasticity of demand; the smaller the percentage of one's budget that goes to purchase a good, the lower the price elasticity of demand.

- The more time that passes (since a price change), the higher the price elasticity of demand; the less time that passes, the lower the price elasticity of demand.

Cross Elasticity of Demand

- Cross elasticity of demand measures the responsiveness in the quantity demanded of one good to changes in the price of another good:

$$E_c = \frac{\text{Percentage change in quantity demanded of one good}}{\text{Percentage change in price of another good}}$$

- If $E_c > 0$, two goods are substitutes. If $E_c < 0$, two goods are complements.

Income Elasticity of Demand

- Income elasticity of demand measures the responsiveness of quantity demanded to changes in income:

$$E_y = \frac{\text{Percentage change in quantity demanded}}{\text{Percentage change in income}}$$

- If $E_y > 0$, the good is a normal good. If $E_y < 0$, the good is an inferior good.

- If $E_y > 1$, demand is income elastic. If $E_y < 1$, demand is income inelastic. If $E_y = 1$, demand is income unit elastic.

Price Elasticity of Supply

- Price elasticity of supply measures the responsiveness of quantity supplied to changes in price:

$$E_s = \frac{\text{Percentage change in quantity supplied}}{\text{Percentage change in price}}$$

- If the percentage change in quantity supplied is greater than the percentage change in price, supply is elastic. If the percentage change in quantity supplied is less than the percentage change in price, supply is inelastic. If the percentage change in quantity supplied is equal to the percentage change in price, supply is unit elastic.

- Price elasticity of supply is higher in the long run than in the short run.

key terms and concepts

Price Elasticity of
   Demand

Elastic Demand

Inelastic Demand

Unit Elastic Demand

Perfectly Elastic Demand

Perfectly Inelastic
   Demand

Total Revenue (*TR*)

Cross Elasticity of
   Demand

Income Elasticity of
   Demand

Income Elastic

Income Inelastic

Income Unit Elastic

Price Elasticity of Supply

questions and problems

1 Explain how a seller can determine whether the demand for his or her good is inelastic, elastic, or unit elastic between two prices.

2 Suppose the current price of gasoline at the pump is $1 per gallon and that 1 million gallons are sold per month. A politician proposes to add a 10-cent tax to the price of a gallon of gasoline. She says the tax will generate $100,000 tax revenues per month (1 million gallons × $0.10 = $100,000). What assumption is she making?

3 Suppose a straight-line downward-sloping demand curve shifts rightward. Is the price elasticity of demand higher, lower, or the same between any two prices on the new (higher) demand curve than on the old (lower) demand curve?

4 Suppose Austin, Texas, is hit by a tornado that destroys 25 percent of the housing in the area. Would you expect the total expenditure on housing after the tornado to be greater than, less than, or equal to what it was before the tornado?

5 Which good in each of the following pairs of goods has the higher price elasticity of demand? (a) airline travel in the short run or airline travel in the long run; (b) television sets or Sony television sets; (c) cars or Toyotas; (d) telephones or AT&T telephones; (e) popcorn or Orville Redenbacher's popcorn?

6 How might you determine whether toothpaste and mouthwash manufacturers are competitors?

7 Assume the demand for product *A* is perfectly inelastic. Further, assume that the buyers of *A* get the funds to pay for it by stealing. If the supply of *A* decreases, what happens to its price? What happens to the amount of crime committed by the buyers of *A*?

8 Suppose you learned that the price elasticity of demand for wheat is 0.7 between the current price for wheat and a price $2 higher per bushel. Do you think farmers collectively would try to reduce the supply of wheat and drive the price up $2 higher per bushel? Why? Assuming that they would try to reduce supply, what problems might they have in actually doing so?

9 In 1947, the U.S. Department of Justice brought a suit against the DuPont Company (which at the time sold 75 percent of all the cellophane in the United States) for monopolizing the production and sale of cellophane. In court, the DuPont Company tried to show that cellophane was only one of several goods in the market in which it was sold. It argued that its market was not the cellophane market but the "flexible packaging materials" market, which included (besides cellophane) waxed paper, aluminum foil, and so forth. DuPont pointed out that it had only 20 percent of all sales in this more broadly defined market. Using this information, discuss how the concept of cross elasticity of demand would help establish whether DuPont should have been viewed as a firm in the cellophane market or as a firm in the "flexible packaging materials" market.

working with numbers and graphs

1   A college raises its annual tuition from $2,000 to $2,500, and its student enrollment falls from 4,877 to 4,705. Compute the price elasticity of demand. Is demand elastic or inelastic?

2   As the price of good X rises from $10 to $12, the quantity demanded of good Y rises from 100 units to 114 units. Are X and Y substitutes or complements? What is the cross elasticity of demand?

3   The quantity demanded of good X rises from 130 to 145 units as income rises from $2,000 to $2,500 a month. What is the income elasticity of demand?

4   The quantity supplied of a good rises from 120 to 140 as price rises from $4 to $5.50. What is the price elasticity of supply?

5   In the following figure, what is the price elasticity of demand between the two prices on D_1? on D_2?

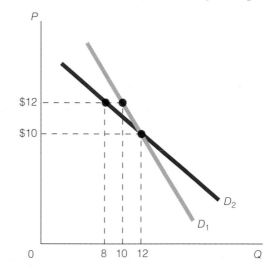

Consumer Choice: Maximizing Utility and Behavioral Economics

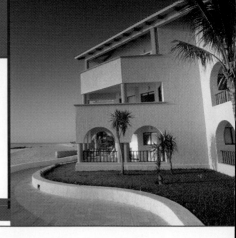

Setting the Scene

Zach and Viv Harris have been married for 6 years and have 2 children, 4-year-old Adrian and 2-year-old Michael. Zach and Viv are looking to the future, when their children begin school. Both parents think that the school district in which they reside leaves something to be desired. They would like to move to the east side of town where there are better schools.

Zach:
I think the kids would be better off if we just went ahead and moved.

Viv:
But house prices are so much higher on the east side. Do you think we can afford to move there?

Zach:
I don't think we can afford not to move there. You know the schools are better on the other side of town.

Viv:
That's what I've heard. The kids seem to get higher scores on standardized tests.

Zach:
I suppose the kids will miss their friends, but they're probably young enough that they'll adjust.

Viv:
What do you think about staying here and sending the kids to a private school?

Zach:
Private schools are getting pretty expensive. I really don't want to pay for a private school.

Viv:
I don't want to either. I just think we should look at all our options.

BARBARA AND STEVE OBERLIN ARE LOOKING FOR A HOUSE TO BUY. THEY'RE CONSIDERING TWO HOUSES FOR SALE ON THE SAME STREET. ONE OF THE HOUSES HAS AN OCEAN VIEW; THE OTHER DOES NOT.

Barbara:
I like that ocean view.

Steve:
Who wouldn't? But the house is pricey. The one down the street is essentially the same house.

Barbara:
But without the view.

Steve:
Yeah, I know. Maybe we should think about it some more.

Barbara:
I guess it comes down to how much we're willing to pay for the view.

Steve:
What's the most you think we should pay?

Barbara:
I'm not sure. What do you think?

Steve:
I'm not sure either.

? Here are some questions to keep in mind as you read this chapter:

- *How is buying a house in a good school district like sending children to a private school?*

- *What is the price of an ocean view?*

See analyzing the scene at the end of this chapter for answers to these questions.

Utility Theory

Water is cheap and diamonds are expensive. But water is necessary to life and diamonds are not. Isn't it odd—paradoxical?—that what is necessary to life is cheap and what is not necessary is expensive? Eighteenth-century economist Adam Smith wondered about this question. He observed that often things that have the greatest value in use, or are the most useful, have a relatively low price, and things that have little or no value in use have a high price. Smith's observation came to be known as the **diamond-water paradox**, or the paradox of value. The paradox challenged economists, and they sought a solution to it. This section begins to develop parts of the solution they found.

Utility: Total and Marginal

Saying that a good gives you **utility** is the same as saying that it has the power to satisfy your wants or that it gives you satisfaction. For example, suppose you buy your first unit of good X. You obtain a certain amount of utility, say, 10 **utils** from it. (Utils are an artificial construct used to "measure" utility; we realize you have never seen a util—no one has.)

You buy a second unit of good X. Once again, you get a certain amount of utility from this second unit, say, 8 utils. You purchase a third unit and receive 7 utils. The sum of the amount of utility you obtain from each of the 3 units is the *total utility* you receive from purchasing good X—which is 25 utils. **Total utility** is the total satisfaction one receives from consuming a particular quantity of a good (in this example, 3 units of good X).

Total utility is different from marginal utility. **Marginal utility** is the *additional* utility gained from consuming an additional unit of good X. Marginal utility is the change in total utility divided by the change in the quantity consumed of a good:

$$MU = \frac{\Delta TU}{\Delta Q}$$

where the change in the quantity consumed of a good is usually equal to 1 unit.

To illustrate, suppose you receive 10 utils of total utility from consuming 1 apple and 19 utils of total utility from consuming 2 apples. What is the marginal utility of the second apple, or what is the additional utility of consuming an additional apple? It is 9 utils.

Notice that as a person consumes more apples, total utility rises (column 2); however, at the same time total utility is rising, marginal utility (additional utility received from the additional apple) is falling (column 3). In other words, the numbers in column 2 rise as the numbers in column 3 fall.

Law of Diminishing Marginal Utility

Do you think the marginal utility of the second unit is greater than, less than, or equal to the marginal utility of the first unit? Before answering, consider the difference in marginal utility between the third unit and the second unit or between the fifth unit and the fourth unit (had we extended the number of units consumed). In general, we are asking whether the marginal utility of the unit that comes next is greater than, less than, or equal to the marginal utility of the unit that comes before.

Economists have generally answered "less than." The **law of diminishing marginal utility** states that for a given time period, the marginal utility gained by consuming equal successive units of a good will decline as the amount consumed increases. In terms of our artificial units, utils, this means that the number of utils gained by consuming the

Diamond-Water Paradox

The observation that things that have the greatest value in use sometimes have little value in exchange and things that have little value in use sometimes have the greatest value in exchange.

Utility

A measure of the satisfaction, happiness, or benefit that results from the consumption of a good.

Util

An artificial construct used to measure utility.

Total Utility

The total satisfaction a person receives from consuming a particular quantity of a good.

Marginal Utility

The additional utility a person receives from consuming an additional unit of a particular good.

Thinking like **AN ECONOMIST** *The economist knows that the total utility of something can be rising as the marginal utility of that something is falling. In fact, this is often the case. To illustrate, look at the table that follows:*

(1) Number of apples consumed	(2) Total Utility (utils)	(3) Marginal Utility (utils)
1	10	10
2	19	9
3	27	8

Law of Diminishing Marginal Utility

The marginal utility gained by consuming equal successive units of a good will decline as the amount consumed increases.

first unit of a good is greater than the number of utils gained by consuming the second unit (which is greater than the number gained by the third, which is greater than the number gained by the fourth, etc.).

The law of diminishing marginal utility is illustrated in Exhibit 1. The table in part (a) shows both the total utility of consuming a certain number of units of a good and the marginal utility of consuming additional units. The graph in part (b) shows the total utility curve for the data in part (a), and the graph in part (c) shows the marginal utility curve for the data in part (a). Notice how the graphs in (b) and (c) show that total utility can increase as marginal utility decreases. This relationship between total utility and marginal utility is important in unraveling the diamond-water paradox.

The law of diminishing marginal utility is based on the idea that if a good has a variety of uses but only 1 unit of the good is available, then the consumer will use the first unit to satisfy his or her most urgent want. If 2 units are available, the consumer will use the second unit to satisfy a less urgent want.

To illustrate, suppose that good *X* can be used to satisfy wants *A* through *E,* with *A* being the most urgent want and *E* being the least urgent want. Also, *B* is more urgent than *C, C* is more urgent than *D,* and *D* is more urgent than *E.* We can chart the wants as follows:

		WANTS		
A	*B*	*C*	*D*	*E*
Most Urgent				Least Urgent

exhibit 1

Total Utility, Marginal Utility, and the Law of Diminishing Marginal Utility

TU = total utility and MU = marginal utility. (a) Both total utility and marginal utility are expressed in utils. Marginal utility is the change in total utility divided by the change in the quantity consumed of the good, $MU = \Delta TU/\Delta Q$. (b) Total utility curve. (c) Marginal utility curve. Together, (b) and (c) demonstrate that total utility can increase (b) as marginal utility decreases (c).

(1) Units of Good X	(2) Total Utility (utils)	(3) Marginal Utility (utils)
0	0	—
1	10	10
2	19	9
3	27	8
4	34	7
5	40	6

(a)

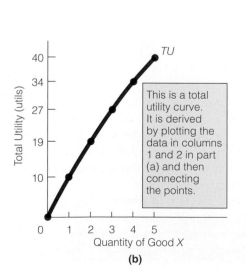

This is a total utility curve. It is derived by plotting the data in columns 1 and 2 in part (a) and then connecting the points.

(b)

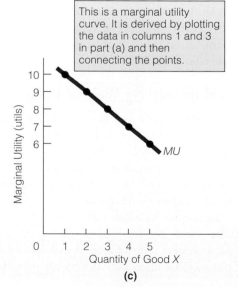

This is a marginal utility curve. It is derived by plotting the data in columns 1 and 3 in part (a) and then connecting the points.

(c)

economics 24/7

CUBAN CIGARS, CHILEAN GRAPES

The law of diminishing marginal utility explains why people trade. To illustrate, consider two people, Smith and Jones. Smith has 100 apples and Jones has 100 oranges. As Smith consumes her apples, marginal utility declines. Her tenth apple doesn't give her as much utility as her ninth and so on. The same is true for Jones with respect to oranges. In other words, as Smith and Jones consume successive units of what they have, marginal utility falls.

At some point, Smith's marginal utility of consuming another apple is likely less than her marginal utility of consuming something different—say, an orange. And at some point, Jones's marginal utility of consuming another orange is likely less than his marginal utility of consuming something different—say, an apple. When this point comes, Smith and Jones will trade. For Smith, the marginal utility of an apple will be less than the marginal utility of an orange, and she will gladly trade an apple for an orange. For Jones, the marginal utility of an orange will be less than the marginal utility of an apple, and he will gladly trade an orange for an apple.

Suppose the law of diminishing marginal utility did not exist. Smith would have the same marginal utility when she consumed her first and her one-hundredth apple, and this marginal utility would always be greater than her marginal utility of an orange. The same would be true for Jones with respect to oranges. In this case, Smith and Jones would not trade with each other. It is the law of diminishing marginal utility, at work on both apples and oranges, that gets Smith and Jones to eventually trade with each other.

What holds for individuals in the same country holds for individuals from different countries. Cubans may like cigars, but at some point, the marginal utility of a cigar is less than the marginal utility of some good produced in another country, and Cubans are happy to trade cigars for other goods. Chileans might like grapes, but at some point, the marginal utility of a grape is less than the marginal utility of some good produced in another country, and Chileans are then happy to trade grapes for other goods.

Suppose the first unit of good X can satisfy any one—but only one—of wants A through E. Which want will an individual choose to satisfy? The answer is the most urgent want—A. The individual chooses to satisfy A instead of B, C, D, or E because people will ordinarily satisfy their most urgent want before all others. If you were dying of thirst in a desert (having gone without water for 3 days)

© A. INDEN/ZEFA/CORBIS

Q&A

When I first started playing chess, I received less utility (per game) than I do now as an accomplished chess player. Doesn't this observation invalidate the law of diminishing marginal utility?

Some economists think not. They argue that a person's first game of chess may not be the same good as his one-hundredth game. Although to an onlooker the first and the one-hundredth games may appear much alike (they use the same board and so forth), from the viewpoint of the chess player, there may be a large difference between the first game of chess and the one-hundredth game (in terms of how well he knows the game). In fact, the difference may be so large that we are dealing with two different goods.

and came across a quart of water, would you drink it or use it to wash your hands? You would drink it, of course. You would satisfy your most urgent want first. Washing your hands in the water would give you less utility than drinking the water.

THE MILLIONAIRE AND THE PAUPER: WHAT THE LAW SAYS AND DOESN'T SAY Who gets more utility from one more dollar, a poor man or a millionaire? Most people would say that a poor man gets more utility from one more dollar because the poor man has so many fewer dollars than the millionaire. "What's an extra dollar to a millionaire?" they ask. Then they answer, "Nothing. A millionaire has so many dollars, one more doesn't mean a thing."

Thinking like **AN ECONOMIST**

The economist knows that what "looks true" or "seems true" may not "be true." It may seem only reasonable to believe that the millionaire receives less utility from an additional dollar than a pauper. But this does not make it so. At one time, it only seemed reasonable to believe that the world was flat, but we know that the world is not flat.

Some people think the law of diminishing marginal utility substantiates the claim that a millionaire gets less utility from one more dollar than a poor man does. Unfortunately, though, this is a misreading of the law. In terms of this example, the law says that for the millionaire, an additional dollar is worth less than the dollar that preceded it; and for the poor man, an additional dollar is worth less than the dollar that preceded it. Let's say the millionaire has $2 million, and the poor man has $1,000. We now give each of them one more dollar. The law of diminishing marginal utility says (1) the additional dollar is worth less to the millionaire than her two-millionth dollar, and (2) the additional dollar is worth less to the poor man than his one-thousandth dollar. That is all the law says. We do not and cannot know whether the additional dollar is worth more or less to the millionaire than it is to the poor man. In summary, the law says something about the millionaire and about the poor man (both persons value the last dollar less than the next-to-last dollar), but it does not say anything about the millionaire's utility compared to the poor man's utility.

Interpersonal Utility Comparison

Comparing the utility one person receives from a good, service, or activity with the utility another person receives from the same good, service, or activity.

To compare the utility the millionaire gets from the additional dollar with the utility the poor man gets from it is to fall into the trap of making an **interpersonal utility comparison**. The utility obtained by one person cannot be scientifically or objectively compared with the utility obtained from the same thing by another person because utility is subjective. Who knows for certain how much satisfaction (utility) the millionaire gets from the additional dollar compared with that of the poor man? The poor man may care little for money; he may shun it, consider the love of it the root of all evil, and prefer to consume the things in life that do not require money. On the other hand, the millionaire may be interested only in amassing more money. We should not be so careless as to "guess" at the utility one person obtains from consuming a certain item, compare it to our "guess" of the utility another person obtains from consuming the same item, and then call these "guesses" scientific facts.

The Solution to the Diamond-Water Paradox

Goods have both total utility and marginal utility. Take water, for example. Water is extremely useful; we cannot live without it. We would expect its total utility (its total usefulness) to be high. But we would expect its marginal utility to be low because water is relatively plentiful. As the law of diminishing marginal utility states, the utility of successive units of a good diminishes as consumption of the good increases. In short, water is immensely useful, but there is so much of it that individuals place relatively little value on another unit of it.

In contrast, diamonds are not as useful as water. We would expect the total utility of diamonds to be lower than the total utility of water. However, we would expect the marginal utility of diamonds to be high. Why? There are relatively few diamonds in the world, so the consumption of diamonds (in contrast to the consumption of water) takes place at relatively high marginal utility. Diamonds, which are rare, get used only for their few valuable uses. Water, which is plentiful, gets used for its many valuable uses and for its not-so-valuable uses (e.g., spraying the car with the hose for 2 more minutes even though you are 99 percent sure that the soap is fully rinsed off).

In conclusion, the total utility of water is high because water is extremely useful. The total utility of diamonds is low in comparison because diamonds are not as useful as water. The marginal utility of water is low because water is so plentiful that people end up consuming it at low marginal utility. The marginal utility of diamonds is high because diamonds are so scarce that people end up consuming them at high marginal utility.

Do prices reflect total or marginal utility? Marginal utility.

SELF-TEST

(Answers to Self-Test questions are in the Self-Test Appendix.)

1. State and solve the diamond-water paradox.

2. If total utility is falling, what does this imply for marginal utility? Give an arithmetical example to illustrate your answer.

3. When would the total utility of a good and the marginal utility of a good be the same?

Consumer Equilibrium and Demand

This section identifies the condition necessary for consumer equilibrium and then discusses the relationship between equilibrium and the law of demand. The analysis is based on the assumption that individuals seek to maximize utility.

Equating Marginal Utilities per Dollar

Suppose there are only two goods in the world: apples and oranges. At present, a consumer is spending his entire income consuming 10 apples and 10 oranges a week. We assume that for a particular week, the marginal utility and price of each are as follows:[1]

$$MU_{oranges} = 30 \text{ utils}$$
$$MU_{apples} = 20 \text{ utils}$$
$$P_{oranges} = \$1$$
$$P_{apples} = \$1$$

So the consumer's marginal (last) dollar spent on apples returns 20 utils per dollar, and his marginal (last) dollar spent on oranges returns 30 utils per dollar. The ratio MU_O/P_O (O = oranges) is greater than the ratio MU_A/P_A (A = apples): $MU_O/P_O > MU_A/P_A$.

If the consumer found himself in this situation one week, he would redirect his purchases of apples and oranges the next week. He would think: If I buy an orange, I receive more utility (30 utils) than if I buy an apple (20 utils). It's better to buy 1 more orange with \$1 and 1 less apple. I gain 30 utils from buying the orange, which is 10 utils more than if I buy the apple.

 Can you give a numerical example that illustrates the solution to the diamond-water paradox?

Look at the two tables below.

Units of water	MU (utils)	Units of diamonds	MU (utils)
1	100	1	60
2	99	2	59
–			
–			
100	1		

In the first two columns, we show the marginal utility of different units of water. In the second two columns, we show the marginal utility of different units of diamonds.

Notice that the first unit of water brings greater marginal utility (100 utils) than the first unit of diamonds (60 utils). If there were no more than 1 unit of each good in the world, water would likely be more expensive than diamonds. But there is more than 1 unit of each good in the world. We have assumed that there are 100 units of water and 2 units of diamonds.

Because there is so much more water than diamonds, we end up consuming water around the one-hundredth unit (where marginal utility is low) and consuming diamonds around the second unit (where marginal utility is high).

---

[1] You may wonder where we get these marginal utility figures. They are points on hypothetical marginal utility curves such as the one in Exhibit 1. The important point is that one number is greater than the other. We could easily have picked other numbers, such as 300 and 200.

What happens as the consumer buys 1 more orange and 1 less apple? The marginal utility of oranges falls (recall what the law of diminishing marginal utility says happens as a person consumes additional units of a good), and the marginal utility of apples rises (the consumer is consuming fewer apples). Because the consumer has bought 1 more orange and 1 less apple, he now has 11 oranges and 9 apples. At this new combination of goods,

$$MU_{oranges} = 25 \text{ utils}$$
$$MU_{apples} = 25 \text{ utils}$$
$$P_{oranges} = \$1$$
$$P_{apples} = \$1$$

Now, the ratio MU_O/P_O equals the ratio MU_A/P_A. The consumer is getting exactly the same amount of utility (25 utils) per dollar from each of the 2 goods. There is no way for the consumer to redirect his purchases (buy more of 1 good and less of another good) and have more utility. Thus, the consumer is in equilibrium. In short, a consumer is in equilibrium when he or she derives the same marginal utility per dollar for all goods. The condition for **consumer equilibrium** is

$$\frac{MU_A}{P_A} = \frac{MU_B}{P_B} = \frac{MU_C}{P_C} = \ldots = \frac{MU_Z}{P_Z}$$

where the letters $A–Z$ represent all the goods a person buys.[2]

A person in consumer equilibrium has *maximized his total utility*. By spending his dollars on goods that give him the greatest marginal utility and in the process bringing about the consumer equilibrium condition, he is adding as much to his total utility as he can possibly add.

Maximizing Utility and the Law of Demand

Suppose a consumer is currently in equilibrium; that is,

$$\frac{MU_O}{P_O} = \frac{MU_A}{P_A}$$

When the consumer is in equilibrium, he or she is maximizing utility.

Now suppose the price of oranges falls. The situation now becomes this:

$$\frac{MU_O}{P_O} > \frac{MU_A}{P_A}$$

The consumer will attempt to restore equilibrium by buying more oranges. This behavior—buying more oranges when the price of oranges falls—is consistent with the law of demand.

We conclude: The consumer's attempt to reach equilibrium—which is simply another way of saying that the consumer is seeking to maximize utility—is consistent with the law of demand. In short, utility maximization is consistent with the law of demand.

Should the Government Provide the Necessities of Life for Free?

Sometimes, you will hear people say, "Food and water are necessities of life. No one can live without them. It is wrong to charge for these goods. The government should provide them free to everyone."

Or you might hear, "Medical care is a necessity to those who are sick. Without it, people will either experience an extremely low quality

Consumer Equilibrium

Occurs when the consumer has spent all income and the marginal utilities per dollar spent on each good purchased are equal: $MU_A/P_A = MU_B/P_B = \ldots = MU_Z/P_Z$, where the letters $A–Z$ represent all the goods a person buys.

Thinking like **AN ECONOMIST** *The economist knows that if certain things are true, then certain other things follow. To illustrate, if people seek to maximize utility, then the law of demand follows. How so? Start in consumer equilibrium where the marginal utility-price ratio (MU/P) for good A equals the marginal utility-price ratio for good B: $MU_A/P_A = MU_B/P_B$. Now let the price of good A fall. We now get $MU_A/P_A > MU_B/P_B$. To increase his utility, the person in this position buys more A (and less B). In other words, to increase his utility (maximize utility), the person buys more of a good when the price of the good falls.*

[2] We are assuming here that the consumer exhausts his or her income and that saving is treated as a good.

economics 24/7

HOW YOU PAY FOR GOOD WEATHER

Suppose there are two cities that are alike in every way except one—the weather. We'll call one city Good-Weather City (*GWC*) and the other Bad-Weather City (*BWC*). In *GWC*, temperatures are moderate all year (75 degrees) and the sky is always blue. In *BWC*, the winter brings snow and freezing rain, and the summer brings high humidity and high temperatures. *BWC* has all the forms of weather that people dislike. We assume people get more utility from living in good weather than from living in bad weather. We also assume the median price of a home in the two cities is the same—$200,000.

In terms of marginal utility and housing prices,

$$\frac{MU_{GWC}}{P_{H,GWC}} > \frac{MU_{BWC}}{P_{H,BWC}}$$

That is, the marginal utility of living in *GWC* (MU_{GWC}) divided by the price of a house in *GWC* ($P_{H,GWC}$) is greater than the marginal utility of living in *BWC* (MU_{BWC}) divided by the price of a house in *BWC* ($P_{H,BWC}$). In other words, there is greater utility per dollar in *GWC* than in *BWC*.

What will people do? At least some people will move from *BWC* to *GWC*. The people in *BWC* who want to move will put their houses up for sale. This will increase the supply of houses for sale and lower the price. As these people move to *GWC*, they increase the demand for houses, and house prices in *GWC* begin to rise.

This process will continue until the price of a house in *GWC* has risen high enough, and the price of a house in *BWC* has fallen low enough, so that the *MU/P* ratios in the two cities are the same. In other words, the process continues until this condition is reached:

$$\frac{MU_{GWC}}{P_{H,GWC}} = \frac{MU_{BWC}}{P_{H,BWC}}$$

When this has occurred, one receives the same utility per dollar in the two cities. In other words, the two cities are the same.

Now let's consider a young couple that has to choose between living in the two cities. Is it clear that the young couple will choose *GWC* instead of *BWC* because *GWC* has a better climate? Not at all. *GWC* has a better climate than *BWC*, but *BWC* has lower housing prices. One partner says, "Let's live in *GWC*. Think of all that great weather we'll enjoy. We can go outside every day." The other partner says, "But if we live in *BWC*, we can have either a much bigger and better house for the money or more money to spend on things other than housing. Think of the better cars and clothes we'll be able to buy or the vacations we'll be able to take because we won't have to spend as much money to buy a house."

What has happened is that the initial greater satisfaction of living in *GWC* (the higher utility per dollar) has been eroded by people moving to *GWC* and raising housing prices. *GWC* doesn't look as good as it once did.

On the other hand, *BWC* doesn't look as (relatively) bad as it once did. It still doesn't have the good climate that *GWC* has, but it has lower housing prices now. The utility per dollar of living in *BWC* has risen as a consequence of housing prices falling.

As long as one city is better (in some way) than another, people will move to the relatively better city. In the process, they will change things just enough so that it is no longer relatively better. In the end, you have to pay for paradise.

of life (you can't experience a high quality of life when you're sick) or die. Making people pay for medical care is wrong. The government should provide it free to the people who need it."

Each of these statements labels something as a necessity of life (food and water, medical care) and then makes the policy proposal that government should provide the necessity for free.

Suppose government did give food, water, and medical care to everyone for free—at zero price (although not at zero taxes). At zero price, people would want to consume these goods up to the point of zero marginal utility for each good. They would do so because if the marginal utility of the good (expressed in dollars) is greater than its price, one could derive more utility from purchasing the good than one would lose in parting with the dollar price of the good. That is, if the price of a good is $5, an individual will continue consuming it as long as the marginal utility she derives from it is greater than $5. If the price is $0, she will continue to consume the good as long as the marginal utility she derives from it is greater than $0.

Resources must be used to produce every unit of a good consumed. If the government uses scarce resources to provide goods that have low marginal utility (which food, water, and medical care would have at zero price), then fewer resources are available to produce other goods. However, if some resources are withdrawn from producing these low-utility goods, total utility would fall very little. The resources could then be redirected to producing goods with a higher marginal utility, thereby raising total utility.

The people who argue that certain goods should be provided free implicitly assume that the not-so-valuable uses of food, water, and medical care are valuable enough to warrant a system of taxes to pay for the complete provision of these goods at zero price. It is questionable, however, if the least valuable uses of food, water, and medical care are worth the sacrifices of other goods that would necessarily be forfeited if more of these goods were produced.

Think about this: Currently, water is relatively cheap, and people use it to satisfy its more valuable uses and its not-so-valuable uses too. But suppose water was cheaper than it is. Suppose it had a zero price. Would it be used to satisfy its more valuable uses, its not-so-valuable uses, and its absolutely least valuable use? If food had a zero price, would it be used to satisfy its more valuable uses, its not-so-valuable uses, and its absolutely least valuable use (food fights perhaps)?

SELF-TEST

1.   Alesandro purchases two goods, X and Y, and the utility gained for the last unit purchased of each is 16 utils and 23 utils, respectively. The prices of X and Y are $1 and $1.75, respectively. Is Alesandro in consumer equilibrium? Explain your answer.

2.   In a two-good world, in which the goods are A and B, what does it mean to be in consumer disequilibrium?

Behavioral Economics

Economists are interested in how people behave. This chapter has shown how economists predict people will behave when the MU/P ratio for one good is greater than it is for another good. In this situation, economic theory predicts that individuals will buy more of the good with the higher MU/P ratio and less of the good with the lower MU/P ratio. In other words, individuals, seeking to maximize their utility, buy more of one good and less of another good until the MU/P ratio for all goods is the same.

In traditional economic theories and models, individuals are assumed to be rational, self-interested, and consistent. For about the last 30 years, behavioral economists have challenged the traditional economic models. Behavioral economists argue that some human behavior does not fit neatly—at a minimum, easily—into the traditional economic framework. In this section, we describe some of the findings of behavioral economists.

Are People Willing to Reduce Others' Incomes?

Two economists, Daniel Zizzo and Andrew Oswald, set up a series of experiments with 4 groups, each with 4 people. Each person was given the same amount of money and asked to gamble with the new money. At the end of each act of gambling, 2 of the 4 persons in each group had won money and 2 had lost money. Then each of the 4 people in each group was given the opportunity to pay some amount of money to reduce the take of the others in the group. To illustrate, suppose in the group consisting of Smith, Jones, Brown, and Adams, Smith and Adams had more money after gambling, and Jones and Brown had less money. All four were given the opportunity to reduce the amount of money held by the others in the group. For example, Brown could pay to reduce Smith's money, Jones could pay to reduce Adams's, and so on.

At this point, some people argue that no one will spend his money to hurt someone else if it means leaving himself poorer. However, Zizzo and Oswald found that 62 percent of the participants did just that: They made themselves worse off to make someone else worse off.

Why might people behave this way? One explanation is that individuals are concerned with relative rank and status more than with absolute well-being. Thus, the poorer of the two individuals doesn't mind paying, say, 25 cents if it means he can reduce the richer person's take by, say, $1. After the 25 cents is spent by the poorer person, the gap between him and the richer person is smaller.

Some economists argue that such behavior is irrational and inconsistent with utility maximization. Other economists say it is no such thing. They argue that if people get utility from relative rank, then, in effect, what is happening is that people are buying a move up the relative rank ladder by reducing the size of the gap between themselves and others.

Is $1 Always $1?

Do people treat money differently depending on where it comes from? Traditional economics argues that they should not—after all, a dollar is a dollar is a dollar. Specifically, $1 that someone gives to you as a gift is no different from $1 you earn or $1 you find on the street. When people treat some dollars differently from other dollars, they are *compartmentalizing*. They are saying that dollars in some compartments (of their minds) are valued differently from dollars in other compartments.

Let's consider the following situation. Suppose you plan to see a Broadway play, the ticket for which costs $100. You buy the $100 ticket on Monday to see the play on Friday night. When Friday night arrives, you realize you have lost the ticket. *Do you spend another $100 to buy another ticket (assuming another ticket can be purchased)?*[3]

Now let's change the circumstances slightly. Suppose instead of buying the ticket on Monday, you plan to buy the ticket at the ticket window on Friday night. At the ticket window on Friday night, you realize you have lost $100 somewhere between home and the theater. *Assuming you still have enough money to buy a $100 ticket to the play, do you buy it?*

Now, regardless of how you answer each question, some economists argue that your answers should be consistent. If you say no to the first question, you should say no to the second question. If you say yes to the first question, you should say yes to the second question. That's because the two questions, based on two slightly different settings, essentially present you with the same choice.

However, many people, when asked the two questions, say that they will not pay an additional $100 to buy a second ticket (having lost the first $100 ticket) but will spend an additional $100 to buy a first ticket (having lost $100 in cash between home and the theater). Why? Some people argue that spending an additional $100 on an additional

> **Q&A** *Could you give an example of a person who benefits in absolute terms but finds himself declining in relative terms?*
>
> *Look at the table that follows.*
>
> | Person | Dollar Income |
> | --- | --- |
> | A | $100,000 |
> | B | 80,000 |
> | C | 60,000 |
> | D | 40,000 |
> | E | 20,000 |
>
> *Person B has a dollar income of $80,000, and his income is the second highest of the five persons. Now suppose everyone's income rises by $100,000—except for B's income. His income rises by $20,000. In absolute dollar terms, B is better off. But in relative terms, his income is now the lowest of the five persons. His income rises in absolute terms (going from $80,000 to $100,000) but falls in relative terms (going from second highest to lowest).*

---

[3]The example comes from Gary Belsky and Thomas Gilovich, *Why Smart People Make Big Money Mistakes and How to Correct Them* (New York: Simon & Schuster, 1999).

ticket is the same as paying $200 to see the play—and that is just too much to pay. However, they don't see themselves as spending $200 to see the play when they lose $100 and pay $100 for a ticket. In either case, though, $200 is gone.

Behavioral economists argue that people who answer the two questions differently (yes to one and no to the other) are compartmentalizing. They are treating two $100 amounts in two different ways—as if they come from two different compartments. For example, the person who says she will not buy a second $100 ticket (having lost the first $100 ticket) but will buy a first ticket (having lost $100 cash) is effectively saying by her behavior that $100 lost on a ticket is different from $100 lost in cash.

Let's consider another situation. Suppose you earn $1,000 by working hard at a job and also win $1,000 at the roulette table in Las Vegas. Would you feel freer to spend the $1,000 won in Las Vegas than to spend the $1,000 you worked hard to earn? If the answer is yes, then you are treating money differently depending on where it came from and what you had to do to get it. Nothing is necessarily wrong or immoral about that, but still, it is interesting because $1,000 is $1,000 is $1,000—no matter where it came from and no matter what you had to do to get it.

Finally, let's look at an experiment conducted by two marketing professors. Drazen Prelec and Duncan Simester once organized a sealed-bid auction to a Boston Celtics basketball game. Half the participants in the auction were told that if they had the winning bid, they had to pay in cash. The other half of the participants were told that if they had the winning bid, they had to pay with a credit card.

One would think that the average bid from the people who had to pay cash would be the same as the average bid from the people who had to pay with a credit card—assuming that the two groups were divided randomly and that no group showed a stronger or weaker preference for seeing the Celtics game. But this didn't happen. The average bid of the people who had to pay with a credit card was higher than the average bid of the people who had to pay with cash. Using a credit card somehow caused people to bid higher dollar amounts than they would have bid had they known they were going to pay cash. Money from the credit card compartment seemed to be more quickly or easily spent than money from the cash compartment.

Coffee Mugs and the Endowment Effect

In one economic experiment, coffee mugs were allocated randomly to half the people in a group. Each person with a mug was asked to state a price at which he would be willing to sell his mug. Each person without a mug was asked to state a price at which he would be willing to buy a mug.

It turns out that, even though the mugs were allocated randomly (dispelling the idea that somehow the people who received a mug valued it more than the people who did not receive one), the lowest price at which the owner would sell the mug was, on average, higher than the highest price at which a buyer would pay to buy a mug. It is as if sellers said they wouldn't sell mugs for less than $15, and buyers said they wouldn't buy mugs for more than $10.

This outcome—which is called the *endowment effect*—is odd. It's odd because even though there is absolutely no reason to believe that the people who received the mugs valued them more than the people who didn't receive them, it turns out that people place a higher value on something (like a mug) simply because they own it. In other words, people seem to show an inclination to hold on to what they have.

If this applies to you, think of what it means. When you go into a store to buy a sweater, you say the sweater is worth no more to you than, say, $40, and you are not willing to pay more than $40 for it. But if someone gave you the sweater as a gift and you were asked to sell it, you wouldn't be willing to sell it for less than, say, $50. Simply owning the sweater makes it more valuable to you.

Economist David Friedman says that such behavior is not limited to humans.[4] He points out that some species of animals exhibit territorial behavior—that is, they are more likely to fight to keep what they have than fight to get what they don't have. As Friedman notes, "It is a familiar observation that a dog will fight harder to keep his own bone than to take another dog's bone."

Friedman argues that this type of behavior in humans makes perfect sense in a hunter-gatherer society. Here is what Friedman has to say:

> Now consider the same logic [found in the fact that a dog will fight harder to keep the bone he has than to take a bone from another dog] in a hunter-gatherer society—in which there are no external institutions to enforce property rights. Imagine that each individual considers every object in sight, decides how much each is worth to him, and then tries to appropriate it, with the outcome of the resulting Hobbesian struggle determined by some combination of how much each wants things and how strong each individual is. It does not look like a formula for a successful society, even on the scale of a hunter-gatherer band.
>
> There is an alternative solution, assuming that humans are at least as smart as dogs, robins, and fish. Some method, possibly as simple as physical possession, is used to define what "belongs to" whom. Each individual then commits himself to fight very hard to protect his "property"—much harder than he would be willing to fight in order to appropriate a similar object from someone else's possession—with the commitment made via some psychological mechanism presumably hardwired into humans. The result is both a considerably lower level of (risky) violence and a considerably more prosperous society.
>
> The fact that the result is attractive does not, of course, guarantee that it will occur—evolution selects for the reproductive interest of the individual, not the group. But in this case they are the same. To see that, imagine a population in which some individuals have adopted the commitment strategy [outlined above—that is, fighting for what you physically possess], and some have adopted different commitment strategies—for example, a strategy of fighting to the death for whatever they see as valuable. It should be fairly easy to see that individuals in the first group will, on average, do better for themselves—hence have (among other things) greater reproductive success—than those in the second group.
>
> How do I commit myself to fight very hard for something? One obvious way is some psychological quirk that makes that something appear very valuable to me. Hence the same behavior pattern that shows up as territorial behavior in fish and ferocious defense of bones in dogs shows up in Cornell students [who were given the coffee mugs] as an endowment effect. Just as in the earlier cases, behavior that was functional in the environment in which we evolved continues to be observed, even in an environment in which its function has largely disappeared.[5]

We value X more highly if we have it than if we do not have it because such behavior at one point in our evolution made possible a system of property rights in a world where the alternative was the Hobbesian jungle.

Does the Endowment Effect Hold Only for New Traders?

The endowment effect has not gone untested. John List, an economist at the University of Maryland, wanted to know if new traders were more likely to experience the endowment effect than experienced traders were. He went to a sports-card exchange where people trade regularly. In one experiment, he took aside a group of card fans and gave them such things as sports autographs and sports badges. He then gave them the opportunity to trade. It turned out that the more experience the trader had (at trading such items), the less prone he or she was to the endowment effect.

One criticism of this experiment was that novice traders were less likely to trade than were experienced traders because novices were not sure what the sports autographs

---

[4]See his "Economics and Evolutionary Psychology" at his Web site, http://www.daviddfriedman.com/JLE/jie.htm.
[5]Ibid., p. 10.

were worth. To meet this criticism, List conducted another experiment with chocolate and coffee mugs where he was sure everyone did know the values of the items. Once again, there was some endowment effect, but it was not as strong as in the sports memorabilia case, and—more important—it was only present with newer traders. In other words, experience as a trader seems to make one less prone to the endowment effect.

SELF-TEST

1. Brandon's grandmother is very cautious about spending money. Yesterday, she gave Brandon a gift of $100 for his birthday. Brandon also received a gift of $100 from his father, who isn't nearly as cautious about spending money as Brandon's grandmother is. Brandon believes that it would somehow be wrong to spend his grandmother's gift on frivolous things, but it wouldn't be wrong to spend his father's gift on such things. Is Brandon compartmentalizing? Explain your answer.

2. Summarize David Friedman's explanation of the endowment effect.

A Reader Asks . . .

Do People Really Equate Marginal Utility-Price Ratios?

Am I expected to believe that real people actually go around with marginal utility-price ratios in their heads and that they behave according to how these ratios change? After all, most people don't even know what marginal utility is.

We could answer that most people may not know the laws of physics, but this doesn't prevent their behavior from being consistent with the laws of physics. But we present a different argument. First, let's review how a person who equates MU/P ratios behaves in accordance with the law of demand. When the MU/P ratio for good A is equal to the MU/P ratio for good B, the person is in consumer equilibrium. Suppose the price of good A falls so that the MU/P ratio for good A is now greater than the MU/P ratio for B. What does the individual do? To maximize utility, we predict that the person will buy more of good A because he receives more utility per dollar buying A than he does buying B. Buying more A when the price of good A declines—to maximize utility—is consistent with the law of demand, which states that price and quantity demanded are inversely related, *ceteris paribus*. In other words, to act in accordance with the law of demand is consistent with equating MU/P ratios.

Now our real question is, "Is it possible that people act in a manner consistent with the law of demand, even though they don't know what the law of demand says?" If the answer is yes, then they are acting *as if* they are equating MU/P ratios in their heads.

But let's not talk about people for a minute. Let's talk about rats. Certainly, rats do not understand what marginal utility is. They will not be able to define it, compute it, or do anything else with it. But do they act *as if* they equate MU/P ratios? Do they observe the law of demand?

With these questions in mind, consider an experiment conducted by economists at Texas A&M University, who undertook to study the "buying" behavior of two white rats. Each rat was put in a laboratory cage with two levers. By pushing one lever, a rat obtained root beer; by pushing the other lever, it obtained nonalcoholic collins mix. Every day, each rat was given a "fixed income" of 300 pushes. (When the combined total of pushes on the two levers reached 300, the levers could not be pushed down until the next day.) The prices of root beer and collins mix were both 20 pushes per milliliter of beverage. Given this income and the price of root beer and collins mix, one rat settled in to consuming 11 milliliters of root beer and 4 milliliters of collins mix. The other rat settled in to consuming almost all root beer.

Then the prices of the two beverages were changed. The price of collins mix was halved while the price of root beer was doubled.[6] Using economic theory, we would predict that with these new prices, the consumption of collins mix would increase and the consumption of root beer would decrease. This is exactly what happened. Both rats began to consume more collins mix and less root beer. In short, both rats had

downward-sloping demand curves for collins mix and root beer.

The point? If the behavior of rats is consistent with the law of demand and the law of demand is consistent with equating MU/P ratios, then do you really have to know you are equating MU/P ratios before you can be doing it? Obviously not.

---

[6] The researchers raised the price of root beer by reducing the quantity of root beer dispensed per push. This is the same as increasing the number of pushes necessary to obtain the original quantity of root beer.

! analyzing the scene

How is buying a house in a good school district like sending children to a private school?

Zach and Viv are thinking of moving to the east side of town to be in a better school district. Better-than-average public schools come with a price tag, though. The price tag is generally attached to the houses located in the better-than-average school district. In short, houses in better-than-average school districts have a higher price than houses in average or below-average school districts, *ceteris paribus*. Zach doesn't want to stay in the current house and send their children to a private school because he doesn't want to pay for a private school. But he will have to pay for better schooling one way or another: Either buy the higher priced house in the better-than-average school district or stay in the old house and pay for a private school.

What is the price of an ocean view?

In the feature "How You Pay for Good Weather," we explain how a house located in a city with good weather will be priced higher than a house located in a city with bad weather. We pay a premium for things that are "above average" (like the house in the good-weather city), and we receive a discount for things that are "below average" (like the house in the bad-weather city). A house located in a good school district is similar to a house in a good-weather city.

Now, let's consider the price of an ocean view. Barbara and Steve are looking at two houses on the same street. The houses are similar except that one has an ocean view and the other doesn't. The price of the ocean view is the dollar difference between the prices of the two houses. If, for example, the house with the view is priced at $750,000 and the house without the view is priced at $500,000, then the price of the ocean view is $250,000.

chapter summary

The Law of Diminishing Marginal Utility

- The law of diminishing marginal utility holds that as the amount of a good consumed increases, the marginal utility of the good decreases.

- The law of diminishing marginal utility should not be used to make interpersonal utility comparisons. For example, the law does not say that a millionaire receives less (or more) utility from an additional dollar than a poor man receives. Instead, it says that for both the

millionaire and the poor man, the last dollar has less value for both the millionaire and the poor man than the next-to-last dollar has.

The Diamond-Water Paradox

- The diamond-water paradox states that what has great value in use sometimes has little value in exchange, and what has little value in use sometimes has great value in exchange. A knowledge of the difference between total utility and marginal utility is necessary to unravel the diamond-water paradox.

- A good can have high total utility and low marginal utility. For example, water's total utility is high, but because water is so plentiful, its marginal utility is low. In short, water is immensely useful, but it is so plentiful that individuals place relatively low value on another unit of it. In contrast, diamonds are not as useful as water, but because there are few diamonds in the world, the marginal utility of diamonds is high. In summary, a good can be extremely useful and have a low price if the good is in plentiful supply (high value in use, low value in exchange). On the other hand, a good can be of little use and have a high price if the good is in short supply (low value in use, high value in exchange).

Consumer Equilibrium

- Individuals seek to equate marginal utilities per dollar. For example, if a person receives more utility per dollar spent on good A than on good B, she will reorder her purchases and buy more A and less B. There is a tendency to move away from the condition $MU_A/P_A > MU_B/P_B$ to the condition $MU_A/P_A = MU_B/P_B$. The latter condition represents consumer equilibrium (in a two-good world).

Marginal Utility Analysis and the Law of Demand

- Marginal utility analysis can be used to illustrate the law of demand. The law of demand states that price and quantity demanded are inversely related, *ceteris paribus*. Starting from consumer equilibrium in a world in which there are only two goods, A and B, a fall in the price of A will cause MU_A/P_A to be greater than MU_B/P_B. As a result, the consumer will purchase more of good A to restore herself to equilibrium.

Behavioral Economics

- Behavioral economists argue that some human behavior does not fit neatly—at a minimum, easily—into the traditional economic framework.

- Behavioral economists believe they have identified human behaviors that are inconsistent with the model of men and women as rational, self-interested, and consistent. These behaviors include the following: (1) Individuals are willing to spend some money to lower the incomes of others even if it means their incomes will be lowered. (2) Individuals don't always treat $1 as $1; some dollars seem to be treated differently from other dollars. (3) Individuals sometimes value X more if it is theirs than if it isn't theirs and they are seeking to acquire it.

key terms and concepts

Diamond-Water Paradox	Util	Marginal Utility	Interpersonal Utility Comparison
Utility	Total Utility	Law of Diminishing Marginal Utility	Consumer Equilibrium

questions and problems

1 "If we take $1 away from a rich person and give it to a poor person, the rich person loses less utility than the poor person gains." Comment.

2 Is it possible to get so much of a good that it turns into a bad? If so, give an example.

3 If a person consumes fewer units of a good, will marginal utility of the good increase as total utility decreases? Why or why not?

4 Assume the marginal utility of good A is 4 utils and its price is $2, and the marginal utility of good B is 6 utils and its price is $1. Is the individual consumer maximizing (total) utility if she spends a total of $3 by buying one unit of each good? If not, how can more utility be obtained?

5 Individuals who buy second homes usually spend less for them than they do for their first homes. Why is this the case?

6 Describe five everyday examples of you or someone else making an interpersonal utility comparison.

7 Is there a logical link between the law of demand and the assumption that individuals seek to maximize utility? (Hint: Think of how the condition for consumer equilibrium can be used to express the inverse relationship between price and quantity demanded.)

8 List five sets of two goods (each set is composed of two goods; e.g., diamonds and water are one set) where the good with the greater value in use has a lower value in exchange than does the good with the lower value in use.

9 Do you think people with high IQs are in consumer equilibrium (equate marginal utilities per dollar) more often than people with low IQs? Why or why not?

10 What is the endowment effect?

11 After each toss of the coin, one person has more money and one person has less. If the person with less money cares about relative rank and status, will he be willing to pay, say, $1 to reduce the other person's winnings by, say, 50 cents? Will he be willing to pay 25 cents to reduce the other person's winnings by $1? Explain your answers.

working with numbers and graphs

1 The marginal utility for the third unit of X is 60 utils, and the marginal utility for the fourth unit of X is 45 utils. If the law of diminishing marginal utility holds, what is the minimum total utility?

2 Fill in blanks A–D in the following table.

Units of Good Consumed	Total Utility (utils)	Marginal Utility (utils)
1	10	10
2	19	A
3	B	8
4	33	C
5	35	D

3 The total utilities of the first 5 units of good X are 10, 19, 26, 33, and 40 utils, respectively. In other words, the total utility of 1 unit is 10 utils, the total utility of 2 units is 19 utils, and so on. What is the marginal utility of the third unit?

Use the following table to answer Questions 4 and 5.

Units of Good X	TU of Good X (utils)	Units of Good Y	TU of Good Y (utils)
1	20	1	19
2	35	2	32
3	48	3	40
4	58	4	45
5	66	5	49

4 If George spends $5 (total) a week on good X and good Y, and if the price of each good is $1 per unit, then how many units of each good does he purchase to maximize utility?

5 Given the number of units of each good George purchased in Question 4, what is his total utility?

6 Draw the marginal utility curve for a good that has constant marginal utility.

7 The marginal utility curve for units 3–5 of good X is below the horizontal axis. Draw the corresponding part of the total utility curve for good X.

Budget Constraint and Indifference Curve Analysis

This chapter uses marginal utility theory to discuss consumer choice. Sometimes budget constraint and indifference curve analysis is used instead, especially in upper-division economics courses. We examine this important topic in this appendix.

The Budget Constraint

Budget Constraint

All the combinations or bundles of two goods a person can purchase given a certain money income and prices for the two goods.

Societies have production possibilities frontiers, and individuals have **budget constraints**. The budget constraint is built on two prices and the individual's income. To illustrate, consider O'Brien, who has a monthly income of $1,200. In a world of two goods, X and Y, O'Brien can spend his total income on X, he can spend his total income on Y, or he can spend part of his income on X and part on Y. Suppose the price of X is $100 and the price of Y is $80. Given this, if O'Brien spends his total income on X, he can purchase a maximum of 12 units; if he spends his total income on Y, he can purchase a maximum of 15 units. Locating these two points on a two-dimensional diagram and then drawing a line between them, as shown in Exhibit 1, gives us O'Brien's budget constraint. Any point on the budget constraint, as well as any point below it, represents a possible combination (bundle) of the two goods available to O'Brien.

Slope of the Budget Constraint

The slope of the budget constraint has special significance. The absolute value of the slope represents the relative prices of the two goods, X and Y. In Exhibit 1, the slope, or

The Budget Constraint

An individual's budget constraint gives us a picture of the different combinations (bundles) of two goods available to the individual. (We assume a two-good world; for a many-good world, we could put one good on one axis and "all other goods" on the other axis.) The budget constraint is derived by finding the maximum amount of each good an individual can consume (given his or her income and the prices of the two goods) and connecting these two points.

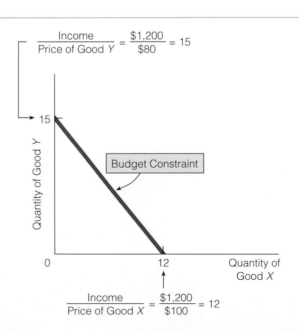

$$\frac{\text{Income}}{\text{Price of Good } Y} = \frac{\$1{,}200}{\$80} = 15$$

$$\frac{\text{Income}}{\text{Price of Good } X} = \frac{\$1{,}200}{\$100} = 12$$

P_X/P_Y, is equal to 1.25, indicating that the relative price of 1 unit of X is 1.25 units of Y.

What Will Change the Budget Constraint?

The budget constraint is built on two prices and the individual's income. This means that if any of the three variables changes (either of the prices or the individual's income), the budget constraint changes. Not all changes are alike, however. Consider a fall in the price of good X from $100 to $60. With this change, the maximum number of units of good X purchasable with an income of $1,200 rises from 12 to 20. The budget constraint revolves away from the origin, as shown in Exhibit 2(a). Notice that the number of O'Brien's possible combinations of the two goods increases; there are more bundles of the two goods available after the price decrease than before.

Consider what happens to the budget constraint if the price of good X rises. If it goes from $100 to $150, the maximum number of units of good X falls from 12 to 8. The budget constraint revolves toward the origin. As a consequence, the number of bundles available to O'Brien decreases. We conclude that a change in the price of either good changes the slope of the budget constraint, with the result that relative prices and the number of bundles available to the individual also change.

We turn now to a change in income. If O'Brien's income rises to $1,600, the maximum number of units of X rises to 16 and the maximum number of units of Y rises to 20. The budget constraint shifts rightward (away from the origin) and is parallel to the old budget constraint. As a consequence, the number of bundles available to O'Brien increases (Exhibit 2(b)). If O'Brien's income falls from $1,200 to $800, the extreme end points on the budget constraint become 8 and 10 for X and Y, respectively. The budget constraint shifts leftward (toward the origin) and is parallel to the old budget constraint. As a consequence, the number of bundles available to O'Brien falls (Exhibit 2(b)).

Indifference Curves

An individual can, of course, choose any bundle of the two goods on or below the budget constraint. We assume that she spends her total income and therefore chooses a point on the budget constraint. This raises two important questions: (1) Which bundle of the many bundles of the two goods does the individual choose? (2) How does the individual's chosen combination of goods change given a change in prices or income? Both

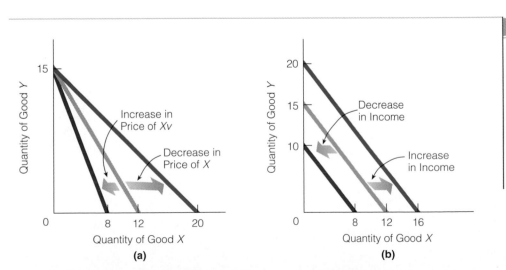

exhibit **2**

Changes in the Budget Constraint

(a) A change in the price of good X or good Y will change the slope of the budget constraint. (b) A change in income will change the position of the budget constraint while the slope remains constant. Whenever a budget constraint changes, the number of combinations (bundles) of the two goods available to the individual changes too.

questions can be answered by combining the budget constraint with the graphical expression of the individual's preferences—that is, indifference curves.

Constructing an Indifference Curve

Is it possible to be indifferent between two bundles of goods? Yes, it is. Suppose bundle *A* consists of 2 pairs of shoes and 6 shirts and bundle *B* consists of 3 pairs of shoes and 4 shirts. A person who is indifferent between these two bundles is implicitly saying that it doesn't matter which bundle he has; one is as good as the other. He is likely to say this, though, only if he receives equal total utility from the two bundles. If this were not the case, he would prefer one bundle to the other.

If we tabulate all the different bundles from which the individual receives equal utility, we have an **indifference set**. We can then plot the data in the indifference set and draw an **indifference curve**. Consider the indifference set illustrated in Exhibit 3(a). There are four bundles of goods, *A–D*; each bundle gives the same total utility as every other bundle. These equal-utility bundles are plotted in Exhibit 3(b). Connecting these bundles in a two-dimensional space gives us an indifference curve.

Characteristics of Indifference Curves

Indifference curves for goods have certain characteristics that are consistent with reasonable assumptions about consumer behavior.

1. **Indifference curves are downward-sloping (from left to right).** The assumption that consumers always prefer more of a good to less requires that indifference curves slope downward left to right. Consider the alternatives to downward-sloping: vertical, horizontal, and upward-sloping (left to right). A horizontal or vertical curve would combine bundles of goods some of which had more of one good and no less of another good than other bundles (Exhibit 4(a–b)). (If bundle *B* contains more of one good and no less of another good than bundle *A*, would an individual be *indifferent* between the two bundles? No, he or she wouldn't. Individuals prefer more to less.) An upward-sloping curve would combine bundles of goods some of which had more of *both* goods than other bundles (Exhibit 4(c)). A simpler way of putting

---

Indifference Set

Group of bundles of two goods that give an individual equal total utility.

Indifference Curve

Represents an indifference set. A curve that shows all the bundles of two goods that give an individual equal total utility.

---

exhibit 3

An Indifference Set and an Indifference Curve

An indifference set is a number of bundles of two goods in which each bundle yields the same total utility. An indifference curve represents an indifference set. In this exhibit, data from the indifference set (a) are used to derive an indifference curve (b).

	An Indifference Set	
Bundle	**Milk (units)**	**Orange Juice (units)**
A	8	3
B	5	4
C	3	5
D	2	6

(a)

(b)

(a)   (b)   (c)

exhibit **4**

Indifference Curves for Goods Do Not Look Like This

(a) Bundle *B* has more milk and no less orange juice than bundle *A*, so an individual would prefer *B* to *A* and not be indifferent between them.
(b) Bundle *B* has more orange juice and no less milk than bundle *A*, so an individual would prefer *B* to *A* and not be indifferent between them.
(c) Bundle *B* has more milk and more orange juice than bundle *A*, so an individual would prefer *B* to *A* and not be indifferent between them.

it is to say that indifference curves are downward-sloping because a person has to get more of one good in order to maintain his or her level of satisfaction (utility) when giving up some of another good.

2. **Indifference curves are convex to the origin.** This implies that the slope of the indifference curve becomes flatter as we move down and to the right along the indifference curve. For example, at 8 units of milk (point *A* in Exhibit 3(b)), the individual is willing to give up 3 units of milk to get an additional unit of orange juice (and thus move to point *B*). At point *B*, where she has 5 units of milk, she is willing to give up only 2 units of milk to get an additional unit of orange juice (and thus move to point *C*). Finally, at point *C*, with 3 units of milk, she is now willing to give up only 1 unit of milk to get an additional unit of orange juice. We conclude that the more of one good that an individual has, the more units he or she will give up to get an additional unit of another good; the less of one good that an individual has, the fewer units he or she will give up to get an additional unit of another good. Is this reasonable? The answer is yes. Our observation is a reflection of diminishing marginal utility at work. As the quantity of a good consumed increases, the marginal utility of that good decreases; therefore we reason that the more of one good an individual has, the more units he or she can (and will) sacrifice to get an additional unit of another good and still maintain total utility. Stated differently, if the law of diminishing marginal utility did not exist then it would not make sense to say that indifference curves of goods are convex to the origin.

An important peripheral point about marginal utilities is that *the absolute value of the slope of the indifference curve*—which is called the **marginal rate of substitution**—*represents the ratio of the marginal utility of the good on the horizontal axis to the marginal utility of the good on the vertical axis:*

$$\frac{MU_{\text{good on horizontal axis}}}{MU_{\text{good on vertical axis}}}$$

Let's look carefully at the words in italics. First, we said that the absolute value of the slope of the indifference curve is the marginal rate of substitution. The marginal rate of substitution (*MRS*) is the amount of one good an individual is willing to give up to obtain an additional unit of another good and maintain equal total utility. For example, in Exhibit 3(b), we see that moving from point *A* to point *B*, the individual is willing to give up 3 units of milk to get an additional unit of

Marginal Rate of Substitution

The amount of one good an individual is willing to give up to obtain an additional unit of another good and maintain equal total utility.

orange juice, with total utility remaining constant (between points *A* and *B*). The marginal rate of substitution is therefore 3 units of milk for 1 unit of orange juice in the area between points *A* and *B*. And as we said, the absolute value of the slope of the indifference curve, the marginal rate of substitution, is equal to the ratio of the *MU* of the good on the horizontal axis to the *MU* of the good on the vertical axis. How can this be? Well, if it is true that an individual giving up 3 units of milk and receiving 1 unit of orange juice maintains her total utility, it follows that (in the area under consideration) the marginal utility of orange juice is approximately three times the marginal utility of milk. In general terms

Absolute value of the slope of the indifference curve = Marginal rate of substitution

$$= \frac{MU_{\text{good on horizontal axis}}}{MU_{\text{good on vertical axis}}}$$

3. **Indifference curves that are farther from the origin are preferable because they represent larger bundles of goods.** Exhibit 3(b) shows only one indifference curve. However, different bundles of the two goods exist and have indifference curves passing through them. These bundles have less of both goods or more of both goods than those in Exhibit 3(b). Illustrating a number of indifference curves on the same diagram gives us an **indifference curve map**. Strictly speaking, an indifference curve map represents a number of indifference curves for a given individual with reference to two goods. A "mapping" is illustrated in Exhibit 5.

   Notice that although only five indifference curves have been drawn, many more could have been added. For example, there are many indifference curves between I_1 and I_2.

   Also notice that the farther away from the origin an indifference curve is, the higher total utility it represents. You can see this by comparing point *A* on I_1 and point *B* on I_2. At point *B*, there is the same amount of orange juice as at point *A* but more milk. Point *B* is therefore preferable to point *A*, and because *B* is on I_2 and *A* is on I_1, I_2 is preferable to I_1. The reason for this is simple: An individual receives more utility at any point on I_2 (because more goods are available) than at any point on I_1.

Indifference Curve Map

Represents a number of indifference curves for a given individual with reference to two goods.

An Indifference Map

A few of the many possible indifference curves are shown. Any point in the two-dimensional space is on an indifference curve. Indifference curves farther away from the origin represent greater total utility than those closer to the origin.

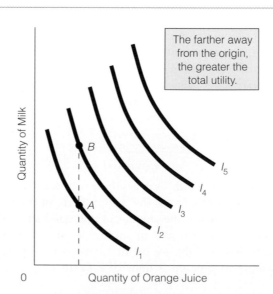

The farther away from the origin, the greater the total utility.

4. **Indifference curves do not cross (intersect).** Indifference curves do not cross because individuals' preferences are **transitive**. Consider the following example. If Kristin prefers Coca-Cola to Pepsi-Cola and she also prefers Pepsi-Cola to root beer, then it follows that she prefers Coca-Cola to root beer. If she preferred root beer to Coca-Cola, she would be contradicting her earlier preferences. To say that an individual has transitive preferences means that he or she maintains a logical order of preferences during a given time period. Consider what indifference curves that crossed would represent. In Exhibit 6, indifference curves I_1 and I_2 intersect at point A. Notice that point A lies on both I_1 and I_2. Comparing A and B, we hold that the individual must be indifferent between them because they lie on the same indifference curve. The same holds for A and C. But if the individual is indifferent between A and B and between A and C, it follows that she must be indifferent between B and C. But C has more of both goods than B, and thus the individual will not be indifferent between B and C; she will prefer C to B. We cannot have transitive preferences and make sense of crossing indifference curves. We can, however, have transitive preferences and make sense of non-crossing indifference curves. We go with the latter.

Transitivity

The principle whereby if A is preferred to B, and B is preferred to C, then A is preferred to C.

The Indifference Map and the Budget Constraint Come Together

At this point, we bring the indifference map and the budget constraint together to illustrate consumer equilibrium. We have the following facts: (1) The individual has a budget constraint. (2) The absolute value of the slope of the budget constraint is the relative prices of the two goods under consideration, say, P_X/P_Y. (3) The individual has an indifference map. (4) The absolute value of the slope of the indifference curve at any point is the marginal rate of substitution, which is equal to the marginal utility of one good divided by the marginal utility of another good; for example, MU_X/MU_Y.

With this information, what is the necessary condition for consumer equilibrium? Obviously, the individual will try to reach a point on the highest indifference curve she can reach. This point will be where the slope of the budget constraint is equal to the slope of an indifference curve (or where the budget constraint is tangent to an indifference curve). At this point, consumer equilibrium is established and the following condition holds:

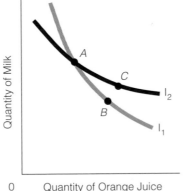

exhibit 6

Crossing Indifference Curves Are Inconsistent with Transitive Preferences

Point *A* lies on both indifference curves I_1 and I_2. This means that the individual is indifferent between *A* and *B* and between *A* and *C,* which results in her (supposedly) being indifferent between *B* and *C*. But individuals prefer "more to less" (when it comes to goods) and, thus, would prefer *C* to *B*. We cannot have transitive preferences and make sense of crossing indifference curves.

Slope of budget constraint = slope of indifference curve

$$\frac{P_X}{P_Y} = \frac{MU_X}{MU_Y}$$

This condition is met in Exhibit 7 at point E. Note that this condition looks similar to the condition for consumer equilibrium earlier in this chapter. By rearranging the terms in the condition, we get[1]

$$\frac{MU_X}{P_X} = \frac{MU_Y}{P_Y}$$

From Indifference Curves to a Demand Curve

We can now derive a demand curve within a budget constraint–indifference curve framework. Exhibit 8(a) shows two budget constraints, one reflecting a $10 price for good X and the other reflecting a $5 price for good X. Notice that as the price of X falls, the consumer moves from point A to point B. At B, 35 units of X are consumed; at A, 30 units of X were consumed. We conclude that a lower price for X results in greater consumption of X. By plotting the relevant price and quantity data, we derive a demand curve for good X in Exhibit 8(b).

exhibit 7

Consumer Equilibrium

Consumer equilibrium exists at the point where the slope of the budget constraint is equal to the slope of an indifference curve, or where the budget constraint is tangent to an indifference curve. In the exhibit, this point is E. Here $P_X/P_Y = MU_X/MU_Y$, or rearranging, $MU_X/P_X = MU_Y/P_Y$.

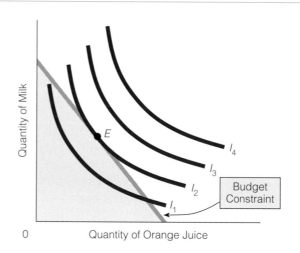

---

[1]Start with $P_X/P_Y = MU_X/MU_Y$ and cross multiply. This gives $P_X MU_Y = P_Y MU_X$. Next divide both sides by P_X. This gives $MU_Y = P_Y MU_X/P_X$. Finally, divide both sides by P_Y. This gives $MU_Y/P_Y = MU_X/P_X$.

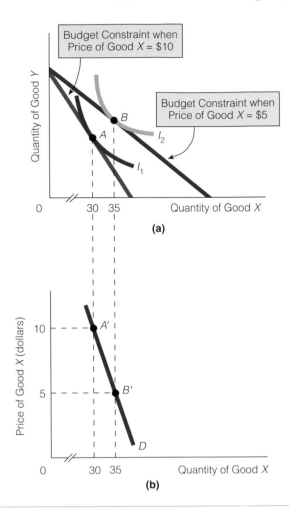

(a)

(b)

exhibit **8**

**From Indifference Curves
to a Demand Curve**

(a) At a price of $10 for good X, con-
sumer equilibrium is at point A with
the individual consuming 30 units of
X. As the price falls to $5, the budget
constraint moves outward (away
from the origin), and the consumer
moves to point B and consumes 35
units of X. Plotting the price-quantity
data for X gives a demand curve for
X in (b).

appendix summary

- A budget constraint represents all combinations of bundles of two goods a person can purchase given a certain
money income and prices for the two goods.

- An indifference curve shows all the combinations or
bundles of two goods that give an individual equal total
utility.

- Indifference curves are downward-sloping, convex to
the origin, and do not cross. The farther away from the

origin an indifference curve is, the greater total utility it
represents for the individual.

- Consumer equilibrium is at the point where the slope
of the budget constraint equals the slope of the indifference curve.

- A demand curve can be derived within a budget con-
straint-indifference curve framework.

questions and problems

1 Diagram the following budget constraints:

   a   Income = \$4,000; P_X = \$50; P_Y = \$100

   b   Income = \$3,000; P_X = \$25; P_Y = \$200

   c   Income = \$2,000; P_X = \$40; P_Y = \$150

2 Explain why indifference curves (a) are downward-sloping, (b) are convex to the origin, and (c) do not cross.

3 Explain why consumer equilibrium is equivalent whether using marginal utility analysis or using indifference curve analysis.

4 Derive a demand curve using indifference curve analysis.

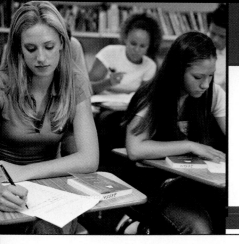

Production and Costs 19

Setting the Scene

The following events occurred one day recently.

8:45 A.M.

Olaf, who owns a small chair company, has incurred $76 in costs in producing a particular type of chair. Initially, he priced the chair at $150, but no one wanted to buy the chair at that price. Last week, he put the chair on sale for $109; still no one purchased it. Today, he's wondering if he should sell the chair for less than his cost to produce it.

10:19 A.M.

Lisa, a junior at a large public university in the South, is majoring in computer science. In a little over a year, she will graduate with a degree in computer science. She just has one problem: She doesn't like computer science. People keep telling her to stick with it. After all, they say, you can't quit now after investing nearly four years in computer science. Besides, they add, computer scientists usually earn more in their first jobs than individuals who have selected other majors. Lisa feels torn; she isn't sure what she should do.

2:56 P.M.

Ursula is in her chemistry class taking a multiple-choice test. She realizes that she doesn't know the answers to most of the questions on the test. Ian and Charles sit next to her. She could easily look over and check her answers against theirs. But she doesn't. It's not because Ursula feels particularly guilty about cheating . . . it's something else.

5:05 P.M.

Quentin Hammersmith is driving home after work, thinking about his job. He's worked for Smithies and Brown, an accounting firm, for 10 years. He finds the work rewarding—but lately he's thought about quitting his job and doing what he's always wanted to do. He's always wanted to own and operate a sports bar. But every time he's about ready to quit, he reminds himself of his $150,000 salary at the accounting firm.

? Here are some questions to keep in mind as you read this chapter:

- *Should Olaf sell the chair for a price below his cost?*

- *What would you do if you were Lisa?*

- *What keeps Ursula from cheating?*

- *Would Quentin be more likely to quit his accounting job to own a sports bar if he earned a salary of $60,000 a year instead of $150,000 a year?*

See analyzing the scene at the end of this chapter for answers to these questions.

Why Firms Exist

Business Firm

An entity that employs factors of production (resources) to produce goods and services to be sold to consumers, other firms, or the government.

A **business firm** is an entity that employs resources, or factors of production, to produce goods and services to be sold to consumers, other firms, or the government. This section explores a basic question: Why do firms exist? The answer to this question leads to discussions of worker behavior, markets, and questions a firm must answer.

The Market and the Firm: Invisible Hand Versus Visible Hand

In our discussion of supply and demand, the market guides and coordinates individuals' actions. Moreover, the market does this in an impersonal manner. No one orders buyers to reduce quantity demanded when price increases; they just do it. No one orders sellers to increase quantity supplied when price increases; they just do it. No one orders more resources to be moved into the production of personal computers when the demand and price for personal computers increase. The market guides individuals from the production of one good into the production of another good. It coordinates individuals' actions so that suppliers and demanders find mutual satisfaction at equilibrium. As economist Adam Smith observed, individuals in a market setting are "led by an invisible hand to promote an end which was no part of their intention."

Contrast the invisible hand of the market with the visible hand of a manager in a firm. Who tells the employee on the assembly line to make more computer chips? The manager does. Who tells the employee to design a new engine, to paint the lamps green, to put steak and lobster on the menu? The manager does. Thus, both the invisible hand of the market and the visible hand of the manager of a firm guide and coordinate individuals' actions. There is, in other words, both **market** and **managerial coordination**.

If the market is capable of guiding and coordinating individuals' actions, why did firms (and managers) arise in the first place? Thus, we return to our original question: Why do firms exist?

Market Coordination

The process in which individuals perform tasks, such as producing certain quantities of goods, based on changes in market forces, such as supply, demand, and price.

Managerial Coordination

The process in which managers direct employees to perform certain tasks.

The Alchian and Demsetz Answer

Economists Armen Alchian and Harold Demsetz suggest that firms are formed when benefits can be obtained from individuals working as a team.[1] Sometimes, the sum of what individuals can produce as a team is greater than the sum of what they can produce alone:

$$\text{Sum of team production} > \text{Sum of individual production}$$

Consider 11 individuals, all making shoe boxes. Each working alone produces 10 shoe boxes per day, for a total daily output of 110 shoe boxes. If they work as a team, however, the same 11 individuals can produce 140 shoe boxes. The added output (30 shoe boxes) may be reason enough for them to work together as a team and form a firm.

Shirking in a Team

Shirking

The behavior of a worker who is putting forth less than the agreed-to effort.

Although forming a firm can increase output, team production can have problems that do not occur in individual production. One problem of team production is **shirking**, which occurs when workers put forth less than the agreed-to effort. The amount of shirking increases in teams because the costs of shirking to individual team members are lower than when they work alone.

---

[1]Armen Alchian and Harold Demsetz, "Production, Information Costs, and Economic Organization," *American Economic Review* 62 (December 1972): 777–795.

Consider five individuals, Alice, Bob, Carl, Denise, and Elizabeth, who form a team to produce light bulbs because they realize that the sum of their team production will be more than the sum of their individual production. They agree to team-produce light bulbs, sell the light bulbs, and split the proceeds five equal ways. On an average day, they produce 140 light bulbs and sell each one for $2. Total revenue per day is $280, with each of the five team members receiving $56. Then Carl begins to shirk. Owing to his shirking, production falls to 135 light bulbs per day and total revenue falls to $270 per day. Each person now receives $54. Notice that while Carl did all the shirking, Carl's reduction in pay was only $2, one-fifth of the $10 drop in total revenue.

In situations (such as team production) where one person receives all the benefits from shirking and pays only a part of the costs, economists predict there will be more shirking than in the situation where the person who shirks bears the full cost of his or her shirking.

THE MONITOR (MANAGER): TAKING CARE OF SHIRKING   The **monitor** (or manager) plays an important role in the firm. The monitor reduces the amount of shirking by firing shirkers and rewarding the productive members of the firm. In doing this, the monitor can preserve the benefits that often come with team production (increased output) and reduce, if not eliminate, the costs associated with team production (increased shirking). But this raises a question: *Who or what monitors the monitor?* That is, *how can the monitor be kept from shirking?*

One possibility is to give the monitor an incentive not to shirk by making him or her a **residual claimant** of the firm. A residual claimant receives the excess of revenues over costs (profits) as income. If the monitor shirks, then profits are likely to be lower (or even zero or negative), and therefore, the monitor will receive less income.

> **Monitor**
>
> Person in a business firm who coordinates team production and reduces shirking.

> **Residual Claimants**
>
> Persons who share in the profits of a business firm.

Ronald Coase on Why Firms Exist

Ronald Coase, winner of the 1991 Nobel Prize in Economics, argued that "the main reason why it is profitable to establish a firm would seem to be that there is a cost of using the price mechanism."[2] Stated differently, firms exist to economize on buying and selling everything, or they exist to reduce transaction costs.

Consider an example. Suppose it takes 20 different operations to produce good X. One way to produce good X, then, is to enter into a separate contract with everyone necessary to complete the 20 different operations. If we assume that one person completes one and only one operation, then we have 20 different contracts. Obviously, there are costs associated with preparing and monitoring these various contracts. A firm is a recipe for reducing these costs. It effectively replaces many contracts with one.

Here is what Coase had to say:

> *The costs of negotiating and concluding a separate contract for each exchange transaction which takes place on a market must also be taken into account. . . . It is true that contracts are not eliminated when there is a firm, but they are greatly reduced. A factor of production (or the owner thereof) does not have to make a series of contracts as would be necessary, of course, if this co-operation were a direct result of the working of the price mechanism. For this series of contracts is substituted one. At this state, it is important to note the character of the contract into which a factor enters that is employed within a firm. The contract is one whereby the factor [the employee], for a certain remuneration (which may be fixed or fluctuating), agrees to obey the directions of an entrepreneur within certain limits.*[3]

---

[2]Ronald Coase, "The Nature of the Firm," *Economica* (November 1937).
[3]Ibid.

Markets: Outside and Inside the Firm

What do we see when we put the firm under the microeconomic microscope? Basically, we see a market of sorts at work. Economics is largely about trades or exchanges; it is about market transactions. In supply-and-demand analysis, the exchanges are between buyers of goods and services and sellers of goods and services. In the theory of the firm, the exchanges take place at two levels: (1) at the level of individuals coming together to form a team and (2) at the level of workers "choosing" a monitor.

Let's look at the theory of the firm in the context of exchange. Individuals initially come together because they realize that the sum of what they can produce as a team is greater than the sum of what they can produce as individuals. In essence, each individual "trades" working alone for working in a team. Later, after the team has been formed, the team members learn that shirking reduces the amount of the added output they came together to capture in the first place. Now the team members enter into another trade or market transaction. They trade some control over their daily behavior—specifically, they trade an environment in which the cost of shirking is low for an environment in which the cost of shirking is high—to receive a larger absolute amount of the potential benefits that drew them together. It is in this trade that the monitor appears: Some individuals "buy" the monitoring services that other individuals "sell."

As you continue your study of microeconomics, look for the "markets" that appear at different levels of analysis.

The Firm's Objective: Maximizing Profit

Profit

The difference between total revenue and total cost.

Firms produce goods to sell the goods. Economists assume that a firm's objective in producing and selling goods is to maximize profit. **Profit** is the difference between total revenue and total cost.

$$\text{Profit} = \text{Total revenue} - \text{Total cost}$$

Recall that *total revenue* is equal to the price of a good multiplied by the quantity of the good sold. For example, if a business firm sells 100 units of X at $10 per unit, its total revenue is $1,000.

Almost everyone defines total revenue the same way, but a disagreement sometimes arises as to what total cost should include. To illustrate, suppose Jill currently works as an attorney earning $80,000 a year. One day, dissatisfied with her career, Jill quits her job as an attorney and opens a pizzeria. After one year of operating the pizzeria, Jill sits down to compute her profit. She sold 20,000 pizzas at a price of $10 per pizza, so her total revenue (for the year) is $200,000. Jill computes her total costs by adding the dollar amounts she spent for everything she bought or rented to run the pizzeria. She spent $2,000 on plates, $3,000 on cheese, $4,000 on soda, $20,000 for rent in the mall where the pizzeria is located, $2,000 for electricity, and so on. The dollar payments Jill made for everything she bought or rented are called her *explicit costs*. An **explicit cost** is a cost

Explicit Cost

A cost incurred when an actual (monetary) payment is made.

that is incurred when an actual (monetary) payment is made. So Jill sums her explicit costs, which turn out to be $90,000. Then she computes her profit by subtracting $90,000 from $200,000. This gives her a profit of $110,000.

A few days pass before Jill tells her friend Marian that she earned a $110,000 profit her first year of running the pizzeria. Marian asks: "Are you sure your profit is $110,000?" Jill assures her that it is. "Did you count the salary you earned as an attorney as a cost?" Marian asks. Jill tells Marian that she did not count the $80,000 salary as a cost of running the pizzeria because the $80,000 is not something

Thinking like **AN ECONOMIST**   *The economist wants to know what a person "gives up" when she goes into business for herself. What she gives up isn't only the money she pays for resources (to run the business), but she also gives up the job she would have had (and the income she would have been earning) had she not gone into business for herself.*

© IMAGE SOURCE/JUPITER IMAGES

economics 24/7

DO SECRETARIES WHO WORK FOR INVESTMENT BANKS EARN MORE THAN SECRETARIES WHO WORK FOR HOTELS?[4]

A person who lives in Des Moines, Iowa, pays the same price for a Snickers candy bar as a person who lives in Tucson, Arizona; a person who lives in Billings, Montana, pays the same price for a soft drink as a person who lives in Orlando, Florida. Many goods fetch the same price no matter where they are bought and sold.

If many of the same goods fetch the same price, do many of the people who do the same work earn the same wage? For example, will secretaries at different types of businesses earn the same wage? Probably not. There is some evidence that not all firms pay workers doing identical jobs the same wage. Industries where profits are higher tend to pay workers higher wages. For example, secretaries in investment banks tend to earn more than secretaries in hotels. Cleaners in law firms earn more than cleaners in hotels. Mexican truck drivers who deliver oil earn more than drivers who deliver corn. British clerical workers earn more in the computer industry than in the textile industry.

One explanation of this difference in wage rates is that secretaries working in high-profit industries are paid more than secretaries working in low-profit industries because they do more or harder work. But there is not much evidence that this is true.

Another explanation of the difference is that the higher wage rate in some industries compensates for the relative unpleasantness of work in that industry. Although wages do adjust for the degree of risk on the job, the amount of unpleasantness, and so on, there seems to be no evidence

that this is the case in the examples mentioned. A secretary who works in an investment bank doesn't seem to have a more pleasant or less pleasant work environment than a secretary who works in a hotel.

Then, what does explain the difference in wage rates? Some efficiency wage theorists have hypothesized that above-equilibrium wages are paid by many high-profit industries because the managerial cost of monitoring employees in these industries is higher. They argue that in a high-profit industry, a manager's time is more valuable. In this setting, it is particularly costly for managers to monitor employees—that is, to make sure they do not shirk. Managers know that if they pay workers above-equilibrium wages, the workers will be less likely to shirk. Workers don't want to take the chance of losing jobs that pay them more than they can earn elsewhere. Therefore, to a large degree, the higher wage acts as an incentive for workers to monitor themselves. Managers in high-profit industries find it less costly to pay the higher wages that ensure employees will monitor themselves than to spend their valuable time monitoring employees. In short, if an investment banker doesn't want to waste her time monitoring her secretary's output, the easiest and least costly way to do this is to pay him more than he could earn in another job.

---

[4] This feature is based on "When Paying More Costs Less," *The Economist* (May 30–June 5, 1998), and Shailendra Raj Mehta, "The Law of One Price and a Theory of the Firm: A Ricardian Perspective on Interindustry Wages," *Rand Journal of Economics* (Spring 1998).

---

she "paid out" to run the pizzeria. "I wrote a check to my suppliers for the pizza ingredients, soda, dishes, and so on," Jill says, "but I didn't write a check to anyone for the $80,000."

Marian says that although Jill did not "pay out" $80,000 in salary to run the pizzeria, still she forfeited $80,000 to run the pizzeria. "What you could have earned but didn't is a cost to you of running the pizzeria," says Marian.

Jill's $80,000 salary is what economists call an *implicit cost*. An **implicit cost** is a cost that represents the value of resources used in production for which no actual (monetary) payment is made. It is a cost incurred as a result of a firm using resources that it owns or that the owners of the firm contribute to it.

Implicit Cost

A cost that represents the value of resources used in production for which no actual (monetary) payment is made.

If total cost is computed as explicit costs plus implicit costs, then Jill's total cost of running the pizzeria is $90,000 plus $80,000, or $170,000. Subtracting $170,000 from a total revenue of $200,000 leaves a profit of $30,000.

> ### *micro* Theme
>
> In an earlier chapter, we mentioned that economic actors (e.g., firms, consumers, resource owners, etc.) have objectives. The objective of the business firm is to maximize profit.

Accounting Profit Versus Economic Profit

Accounting Profit

The difference between total revenue and explicit costs.

Economists refer to the first profit that Jill calculated ($110,000) as *accounting profit*. **Accounting profit** is the difference between total revenue and total cost, where total cost equals explicit costs (see Exhibit 1(a)).

Accounting profit = Total revenue − Total cost (Explicit costs)

Economic Profit

The difference between total revenue and total cost, including both explicit and implicit costs.

Economists refer to the second profit calculated ($30,000) as *economic profit*. **Economic profit** is the difference between total revenue and total cost, where total cost equals the sum of explicit and implicit costs (see Exhibit 1(b)).

Economic profit = Total revenue − Total cost (Explicit costs + Implicit costs)

Let's consider another example that explains the difference between explicit and implicit costs. Suppose a person has $100,000 in the bank, earning an interest rate of 5 percent a year. This amounts to $5,000 in interest a year. Now suppose this person takes the $100,000 out of the bank to start a business. The $5,000 in *lost interest* is included in the implicit costs of owning and operating the firm. To see why, let's change the example somewhat. Assume the person does not use her $100,000 in the bank to start a business. Suppose she leaves her $100,000 in the bank and instead takes out a $100,000 loan at an interest rate of 5 percent. The interest she has to pay on the loan—$5,000 a year—certainly would be an explicit cost and would take away from overall profit. It just makes sense, then, to count the $5,000 interest the owner doesn't earn if she uses her own $100,000 to start the business (instead of taking out a loan) as a cost, albeit an implicit cost.

exhibit **1**

Accounting and Economic Profit

Accounting profit equals total revenue minus explicit costs. Economic profit equals total revenue minus both explicit and implicit costs.

Zero Economic Profit Is Not as Bad as It Sounds

Economic profit is usually lower (never higher) than accounting profit because economic profit is the difference between total revenue and total cost, where total cost is the sum of explicit and implicit costs, whereas accounting profit is the difference between total revenue and only explicit costs. Thus, it is possible for a firm to earn both a positive accounting profit and a zero economic profit. In economics, a firm that makes a zero economic profit is said to be earning a **normal profit**.

Normal profit = Zero economic profit

Should the owner of a firm be worried if he has made zero economic profit for the year just ending? The answer is no. A zero economic profit—as bad as it may sound—means the owner has generated total revenue sufficient to cover total cost—that is, *both explicit and implicit costs*. If, for example, the owner's implicit cost is a (forfeited) $100,000 salary working for someone else, then earning a zero economic profit means he has done as well as he could have done in his next best (alternative) line of employment.

When we realize that zero economic profit (or normal profit) means "doing as well as could have been done," we understand that it isn't bad to make zero economic profit. Zero accounting profit, however, is altogether different; it implies that some part of total cost has not been covered by total revenue.

Normal Profit

Zero economic profit. A firm that earns normal profit is earning revenue equal to its total costs (explicit plus implicit costs). This is the level of profit necessary to keep resources employed in that particular firm.

Q&A *When most people use the word* profit, *do they mean accounting profit or economic profit?*

They probably mean accounting profit. Still, in this text, when we use the term profit, *we are referring to economic profit.*

SELF-TEST

(Answers to Self-Test questions are in the Self-Test Appendix.)

1. Will individuals form teams or firms in all settings?

2. Suppose everything about two people is the same except that one person currently earns a high salary and the other person currently earns a low salary. Which is more likely to start his or her own business and why?

3. Is accounting or economic profit larger? Why?

4. When can a business owner be earning a profit but not covering his costs?

Production

Production is a transformation of resources or inputs into goods and services. You may think of production the way you might think of making a cake. It takes certain ingredients to make a cake—sugar, flour, and so on. Similarly, it takes certain resources, or inputs, to produce a computer, a haircut, a piece of furniture, or a house.

Economists often talk about two types of inputs in the production process: fixed and variable. A **fixed input** is an input whose quantity cannot be changed as output changes. To illustrate, suppose the McMahon and McGee Bookshelf Company has rented a factory under a six-month lease: McMahon and McGee, the owners of the company, have contracted to pay the $2,500 monthly rent for six months—no matter what. Whether McMahon and McGee produce 1 bookshelf or 7,000 bookshelves, the $2,500 rent for the factory must be paid. The factory is an input in the production process of bookshelves; specifically, it is a fixed input.

A **variable input** is an input whose quantity can be changed as output changes. Examples of variable inputs for the McMahon and McGee Bookshelf Company include wood, paint, nails, and so on. These inputs can (and most likely will) change as the production of bookshelves changes. As more bookshelves are produced, more of

Fixed Input

An input whose quantity cannot be changed as output changes.

Variable Input

An input whose quantity can be changed as output changes.

these inputs will be purchased by McMahon and McGee; as fewer bookshelves are produced, fewer of these inputs will be purchased. Labor might also be a variable input for McMahon and McGee. As they produce more bookshelves, they might hire more employees; as they produce fewer bookshelves, they might lay off some employees.

If any of the inputs of a firm are fixed inputs, then it is said to be producing in the *short run*. In other words, the **short run** is a period of time in which some inputs are fixed.

If none of the inputs of a firm are fixed inputs—if all inputs are variable—then the firm is said to be producing in the *long run*. In other words, the **long run** is a period of time in which all inputs can be varied (no inputs are fixed).

When firms produce goods and services and then sell them, they necessarily incur costs. In this section, we discuss the production activities of the firm in the short run, a discussion that leads to the law of diminishing marginal returns and marginal costs. In the next section, we tie the production of the firm to all the costs of production in the short run. We then turn to an analysis of production in the long run.

Short Run

A period of time in which some inputs in the production process are fixed.

Long Run

A period of time in which all inputs in the production process can be varied (no inputs are fixed).

Q&A

What is the best way to understand the difference between the short run and the long run? Is the long run longer than the short run? For example, if the short run is 6 months, is the long run something longer than 6 months?

This is not the right way to differentiate the short run from the long run. Think of each as a period of time during which some condition exists. The short run is that period of time during which at least one input is fixed. This could be a period of 6 months, 2 years, and so on. The long run is not necessarily longer in months and years than the short run. It is simply that period of time during which all inputs are variable (i.e., no input is fixed). In terms of days, weeks, and months, the short run could be a longer period of time than the long run.

Production in the Short Run

Suppose two inputs (or resources), labor and capital, are used to produce some good. Furthermore, suppose one of those inputs—capital—is fixed. Obviously, because an input is fixed, the firm is producing in the short run.

Column 1 of Exhibit 2 shows the units of the fixed input, capital. Notice that capital is fixed at 1 unit. Column 2 shows different units of the variable input, labor. Notice that we go from 0 units of labor through 10 units of labor (10 workers). Column 3 shows the quantities of output produced with 1 unit of capital and different amounts of labor. (The quantity of output is sometimes referred to as the *total physical product*, or *TPP.*) For example, 1 unit of capital and 0 units of labor produce 0 output; 1 unit of capital and 1 unit of labor produce 18 units of output; 1 unit of capital and 2 units of labor produce 37 units of output; 1 unit of capital and 3 units of labor produce 57 units of output; and so on.

---

exhibit 2

Production in the Short Run and the Law of Diminishing Marginal Returns

In the short run, as additional units of a variable input are added to a fixed input, the marginal physical product of the variable input may increase at first. Eventually, the marginal physical product of the variable input decreases. The point at which marginal physical product decreases is the point at which diminishing marginal returns have set in.

(1) Fixed Input, Capital (units)	(2) Variable Input, Labor (workers)	(3) Quantity of Output, Q (units)	(4) Marginal Physical Product of Variable Input (units) $\Delta(3)/\Delta(2)$
1	0	0	
			18
1	1	18	
			19
1	2	37	
			20
1	3	57	
			19
1	4	76	
			18
1	5	94	
			17
1	6	111	
			16
1	7	127	
			10
1	8	137	
			−4
1	9	133	
			−8
1	10	125	

Column 4 shows the marginal physical product of the variable input. The **marginal physical product (MPP)** of a variable input is equal to the change in output that results from changing the variable input by one unit, *holding all other inputs fixed.* In our example, the variable input is labor, so here we are talking about the *MPP* of labor. Specifically, the *MPP* of labor is equal to the change in output, *Q*, that results from changing labor, *L*, by one unit, *holding all other inputs fixed.*

$$MPP = \frac{\Delta Q}{\Delta L}$$

Notice that the marginal physical product of labor first rises (from 18 to 19 to 20), then falls (from 20 to 19 to 18 to 17 to 16 to 10), and then becomes negative (–4 and –8). When the *MPP* is rising, we say there is increasing *MPP*, when it is falling, there is diminishing *MPP*, and when it is negative, there is negative *MPP*.

Focus on the point at which the *MPP* first begins to decline—with the addition of the fourth worker. The point at which the marginal physical product of labor first declines is the point at which diminishing marginal returns are said to have "set in." Diminishing marginal returns are common in production—so common, in fact, that economists refer to the **law of diminishing marginal returns** (or the law of diminishing marginal product). The law of diminishing marginal returns states that *as ever-larger amounts of a variable input are combined with fixed inputs, eventually, the marginal physical product of the variable input will decline.*

Some persons ask, "But why does the *MPP* of the variable input eventually decline?" To answer this question, think of adding agricultural workers (variable input) to 10 acres of land (fixed input). The workers must clear the land, plant the crop, and then harvest the crop. In the early stages of adding labor to the land, perhaps the *MPP* rises or remains constant. But eventually, as we continue to add more workers to the land, there comes a point when the land is overcrowded with workers. Workers are stepping around each other, stepping on the crops, and so on. Because of these problems, output growth begins to slow.

You may be wondering why the firm in Exhibit 2 would ever hire beyond the third worker. After all, the *MPP* of labor is at its highest (20) with the third worker. Why hire the fourth worker if the *MPP* of labor falls to 19? The reason the firm may hire the fourth worker is because this worker adds output. It would be one thing if the quantity of output was 57 units with three workers and fell to 55 units with the addition of the fourth worker. But this isn't the case here. With the addition of the fourth worker, output rises from 57 units to 76 units. The firm has to ask and answer two questions: (1) What can the additional 19 units of output be sold for? (2) What does it cost to hire the fourth worker? Suppose the additional 19 units can be sold for $100, and it costs the firm $70 to hire the fourth worker. Will the firm hire the fourth worker? Yes.

Marginal Physical Product (MPP)

The change in output that results from changing the variable input by one unit, holding all other inputs fixed.

Law of Diminishing Marginal Returns

As ever-larger amounts of a variable input are combined with fixed inputs, eventually, the marginal physical product of the variable input will decline.

Thinking like **AN ECONOMIST**   *In economics, when making decisions, it is usually the case that you compare one thing to something else. To illustrate, suppose you need to decide how much time to devote to studying. Would you consider only the additional benefits of spending more time studying, or would you consider the additional benefits and costs of spending more time studying? You would want to consider both the additional benefits and costs of spending more time studying.*

The same idea comes into play when a firm has to decide how many workers to hire. It wouldn't want to consider only the additional benefits of hiring more workers (let's say as measured by the additional output they produce times the price the additional output could be sold for). Instead, it would want to consider the additional benefits of hiring more workers against the additional costs of hiring more workers.

Theme **micro**   In an earlier chapter, we mentioned that economic actors (firms, consumers, resource owners) have to make choices. Often, economic actors make their choices by comparing one thing with another. More formally, they usually are comparing the "additional benefits" of an action with the "additional costs" of an action.

Marginal Physical Product and Marginal Cost

A firm's costs are tied to its production. Specifically, the *marginal cost (MC)* of producing a good is a reflection of the marginal physical product *(MPP)* of the variable input. Our objective in this section is to prove that this last statement is true. But before we can do this, we need to define and discuss some economic cost concepts.

SOME ECONOMIC COST CONCEPTS Recall our earlier discussion of fixed inputs and variable inputs. Certainly, a cost is incurred whenever a fixed input or variable input is employed in the production process. The costs associated with fixed inputs are called **fixed costs**. The costs associated with variable inputs are called **variable costs**.

Because the quantity of a fixed input does not change as output changes, fixed costs do not change as output changes. Payments for such things as fire insurance (the same amount every month), liability insurance, and the rental of a factory and machinery are usually considered fixed costs. Whether the business produces 1, 10, 100, or 1,000 units of output, it is likely that the rent for its factory will not change. It will be whatever amount was agreed to with the owner of the factory for the duration of the rental agreement.

Because the quantity of a variable input changes with output, so do variable costs. For example, it takes labor, wood, and glue to produce wooden bookshelves. It is likely that the quantity of all these inputs (labor, wood, and glue) will change as the number of wooden bookshelves produced changes.

Fixed Costs

Costs that do not vary with output; the costs associated with fixed inputs.

Variable Costs

Costs that vary with output; the costs associated with variable inputs.

 exhibit 3

Marginal Physical Product and Marginal Cost

(a) The marginal physical product of labor curve. The curve is derived by plotting the data from columns 2 and 4 in the exhibit. (b) The marginal cost curve. The curve is derived by plotting the data from columns 3 and 8 in the exhibit. Notice that as the *MPP* curve rises, the *MC* curve falls; and as the *MPP* curve falls, the *MC* curve rises.

(1) Fixed Input, Capital (units)	(2) Variable Input, Labor (workers)	(3) Quantity of Output, Q (units)	(4) Marginal Physical Product of Variable Input (units) $\Delta(3)/\Delta(2)$	(5) Total Fixed Cost (dollars)	(6) Total Variable Cost (dollars)	(7) Total Cost (dollars) (5) + (6)	(8) Marginal cost (dollars) $\Delta(7)/\Delta(3)$
1	0	0		$40	$ 0	$ 40	
1	1	18	18	40	20	60	$1.11
1	2	37	19	40	40	80	$1.05
1	3	57	20	40	60	100	$1.00
1	4	76	19	40	80	120	$1.05
1	5	94	18	40	100	140	$1.11
1	6	111	17	40	120	160	$1.17
1	7	127	16	40	140	180	$1.25

(a)

(b)

The sum of fixed costs and variable costs is **total cost (TC)**. If total fixed costs (TFC) are $100 and total variable costs (TVC) are $300, then total cost (TC) is $400.

$$TC = TFC + TVC$$

Now that we know what total cost is, we can formally define marginal cost. **Marginal cost (MC)** is the change in total cost, TC, that results from a change in output, Q.

$$MC = \frac{\Delta TC}{\Delta Q}$$

Total Cost (TC)

The sum of fixed costs and variable costs.

Marginal Cost (MC)

The change in total cost that results from a change in output: $MC = \Delta TC/\Delta Q$.

THE LINK BETWEEN MPP AND MC In Exhibit 3, we establish the link between the marginal physical product of a variable input and marginal cost. The first four columns present much of the same data first presented in Exhibit 2. Essentially, column 3 shows the different quantities of output produced by 1 unit of capital (fixed input) and various amounts of labor (variable input), and column 4 shows the MPP of labor. Exhibit 3(a) shows the MPP curve, which is based on the data in column 4. Notice that the MPP curve first rises and then falls.

In column 5, we have identified the total fixed cost (TFC) of production as $40. (Recall that fixed costs do not change as output changes.) For column 6, we have assumed that each worker is hired for $20, so when there is only 1 worker, total variable cost (TVC) is $20; when there are 2 workers, total variable cost is $40; and so on. Column 7 shows total cost at various output levels; the total cost figures in this column are simply the sum of the fixed costs in column 5 and the variable costs in column 6. Finally, in column 8, we compute marginal cost. Exhibit 3(b) shows the MC curve, which is based on the data in column 8.

Let's focus on columns 4 and 8 in Exhibit 3, which show the MPP and MC, respectively. Notice that when the MPP is rising (from 18 to 19 to 20), marginal cost is decreasing (from $1.11 to $1.05 to $1.00), and when the MPP is falling (from 20 to 19 etc.), marginal cost is increasing (from $1.00 to $1.05 etc.). In other words, the MPP and MC move in opposite directions. You can also see this by comparing the MPP curve with the MC curve. When the MPP curve is going up, the MC curve is moving down, and when the MPP curve is going down, the MC curve is going up. Of course, all this is common sense: As marginal physical product rises, or to put it differently, as the productivity of the variable input rises, we would expect costs to decline. And as the productivity of the variable input declines, we would expect costs to rise.

In conclusion, then, what the MC curve looks like depends on what the MPP curve looks like. Recall that the MPP curve must have a declining portion because of the law of diminishing marginal returns. So if the MPP curve first rises and then (when diminishing marginal returns set in) falls, it follows that the MC curve must first fall and then rise.

ANOTHER WAY TO LOOK AT THE RELATIONSHIP BETWEEN MPP AND MC An easy way to see that marginal physical product and marginal cost move in *opposite directions* involves reexamining the definition of marginal cost. Recall that marginal cost is defined as the change in total cost divided by the change in output. The change in total cost is the additional cost of an additional unit of the variable input (see Exhibit 3). The change in output is the marginal physical product of the variable input. Thus, marginal cost is equal to the additional cost of an additional unit of the variable input divided by the input's marginal physical product. In Exhibit 3, the variable input is labor, so $MC = W/MPP$, where MC = marginal cost, W = wage, and MPP = marginal physical product of labor. The following table reproduces column 4 from Exhibit 3, notes the wage, and computes MC using the equation $MC = W/MPP$.

*Suppose an **MPP** curve is entirely horizontal. What would the corresponding **MC** curve look like?*

The MC curve would be horizontal too. Look at it this way: (1) If the MPP curve is entirely horizontal, it means that MPP is constant—it neither rises nor falls. (2) We know that the MC curve declines as the MPP curve rises and the MC curve rises as the MPP curve falls. Well, then, if the MPP curve neither rises nor falls, it follows that the MC curve neither falls nor rises.

MPP	Variable Cost (W)	$W/MPP = MC$
18 units	$20	$20/18 = $1.11
19	20	20/19 = 1.05
20	20	20/20 = 1.00
19	20	20/19 = 1.05
18	20	20/18 = 1.11
17	20	20/17 = 1.17
16	20	20/16 = 1.25

Now, compare the marginal cost figures in the last column in the table above with the marginal cost figures in column 8 of Exhibit 3. Whether marginal cost is defined as equal to $\Delta TC/\Delta Q$ or as equal to W/MPP, the result is the same. The latter way of defining marginal cost, however, explicitly shows that as MPP rises, MC falls, and as MPP falls, MC rises.

$$\frac{W}{MPP \uparrow} = MC \downarrow$$

$$\frac{W}{MPP \downarrow} = MC \uparrow$$

Average Productivity

When the word *productivity* is used in the press or by the layperson, what is usually referred to is *average physical product* instead of *marginal physical product*. To illustrate the difference, suppose 1 worker can produce 10 units of output a day and 2 workers can produce 18 units of output a day. Marginal physical product is 8 units (MPP of labor $= \Delta Q/\Delta L$). Average physical product, which is output divided by the quantity of labor, is equal to 9 units.

$$AP \text{ of labor} = Q/L$$

Usually, when the term *labor productivity* is used in the newspaper and in government documents, it refers to the average (physical) productivity of labor on an hourly basis. By computing the average productivity of labor for different countries and noting the annual percentage changes, we can compare labor productivity between and within countries. Government statisticians have chosen 1992 as a benchmark year (a year against which we measure other years). They have also set a productivity index, which is a measure of productivity, for 1992 equal to 100. By computing a productivity index for other years and noting whether each index is above, below, or equal to 100, they know whether productivity is rising, falling, or remaining constant, respectively. Finally, by computing the percentage change in productivity indexes from one year to the next, they know the rate at which productivity is changing.

Suppose the productivity index for the United States is 120 in year 1 and 125 in year 2. The productivity index is higher in year 2 than in year 1, so labor productivity increased over the year; that is, output produced increased per hour of labor expended.

SELF-TEST

1. If the short run is 6 months, does it follow that the long run is longer than 6 months? Explain your answer.

2. "As we add more capital to more labor, eventually the law of diminishing marginal returns will set in." What is wrong with this statement?

3. Suppose a marginal cost (MC) curve falls when output is in the range of 1 unit to 10 units, flattens out and remains constant over an output range of 10 units to 20 units, and then rises over a range of 20 units to 30 units. What does this have to say about the marginal physical product (MPP) of the variable input?

economics 24/7

HIGH SCHOOL STUDENTS, STAYING OUT LATE, AND MORE

Can marginal cost affect a person's behavior? Let's analyze two different situations in which it might.

High School Students and Staying Out Late
A 16-year-old high school student asks her parents if she can have the car tonight. She says she plans to go with some friends to a concert. Her parents ask what time she will get home. She says that she plans to be back by midnight.

The girl's parents tell her that she can have the car and that they expect her home by midnight. If she's late, she will lose her driving privileges for a week.

Now suppose it is later that night. In fact, it is midnight and the 16-year-old is 15 minutes away from home. When she realizes she can't get home until 12:15 A.M., will she continue on home? She may not. The marginal cost of staying out later is now zero. In short, whether she arrives home at 12:15, 1:15, or 2:25, the punishment is the same: She will lose her driving privileges for a week. There is no additional cost for staying out an additional minute or an additional hour. There may, however, be additional benefits. Her "punishment" places a zero marginal cost on staying out after midnight. Once midnight has come and gone, the additional cost of staying out later is zero.

No doubt her parents would prefer her to get home at, say, 12:01 rather than at 1:01 or even later. If this is the case, then they should not have made the marginal cost of staying out after midnight zero. What they should have done is increased the marginal cost of staying out late for every minute (or 15-minute period) the 16-year-old was late. In other words, one of the parents might have said, "For the first 15 minutes you're late, you'll lose 1 hour of driving

privileges, for the second 15 minutes you're late, you'll lose 2 hours of driving privileges, and so on." This would have presented our teen with a rising marginal cost of staying out late. With a rising marginal cost, it is more likely she will get home close to midnight.

Crime
Suppose the sentence for murder in the first degree is life imprisonment and the sentence for burglary is 10 years. In a given city, the burglary rate has skyrocketed in the past few months. Many of the residents have become alarmed. They have called on the police and other local and state officials to do something about the rising burglary rate.

Someone proposes that the way to lower the burglary rate is to increase the punishment for burglary. Instead of only 10 years in prison, make the punishment stiffer. In his zeal to reduce the burglary rate, a state legislator proposes that burglary carry the same punishment as first-degree murder: life in prison. That will certainly get the burglary rate down, he argues. After all, who will take the chance of committing a burglary if he knows that if he gets caught and convicted, he will spend the rest of his days in prison?

Unfortunately, by making the punishment for burglary and murder the same, the marginal cost of murdering someone that a person is burglarizing falls to zero. To illustrate, suppose Smith is burglarizing a home and the residents walk in on him. Smith realizes the residents can identify him as the burglar, so he shoots and kills them. What does it matter? If he gets apprehended for burglary, the penalty will be the same as it is for murder. Raising the cost of burglary from 10 years to life imprisonment may reduce the number of burglaries, but it may have the unintended effect of raising the murder rate.

Costs of Production: Total, Average, Marginal

In this section, we continue our discussion of the costs of production. The easiest way to see the relationships among the various costs is with the example in Exhibit 4.

Column 1 of Exhibit 4 shows the various quantities of output, ranging from 0 units to 10 units.

Column 2 shows the total fixed costs of production. We have set *TFC* at $100. Recall that fixed costs do not change as output changes. Therefore, *TFC* is $100 when output is 0 units, 1 unit, or 2 units, and so on. Because *TFC* does not change as *Q* changes, the *TFC* curve in the exhibit is a horizontal line at $100.

(1) Quantity of Output, Q (units)	(2) Total Fixed Cost (TFC)	(3) Average Fixed Cost (AFC) AFC = TFC/Q = (2)/(1)	(4) Total Variable Cost (TVC)	(5) Average Variable Cost (AVC) AVC = TVC/Q = (4)/(1)
0	$100	—	$ 0	—
1	100	$100.00	50	$50.00
2	100	50.00	80	40.00
3	100	33.33	100	33.33
4	100	25.00	110	27.50
5	100	20.00	130	26.00
6	100	16.67	160	26.67
7	100	14.28	200	28.57
8	100	12.50	250	31.25
9	100	11.11	310	34.44
10	100	10.00	380	38.00

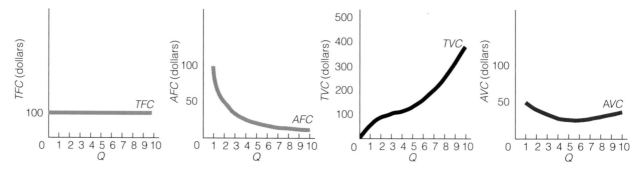

exhibit 4

Total, Average, and Marginal Costs

TFC equals $100 (column 2) and TVC is as noted in column 4. From the data, we calculate AFC, AVC, TC, ATC, and MC. The curves associated with TFC, AFC, TVC, AVC, TC, ATC, and MC are shown in diagrams at the bottom of the corresponding columns. (Note: Scale is not the same for all diagrams.)

Average Fixed Cost (AFC)

Total fixed cost divided by quantity of output: AFC = TFC / Q.

Average Variable Cost (AVC)

Total variable cost divided by quantity of output: AVC = TVC / Q.

Average Total Cost (ATC), or Unit Cost

Total cost divided by quantity of output: ATC = TC / Q.

In column 3, we have computed *average fixed cost*. **Average fixed cost (AFC)** is total fixed cost divided by quantity of output.

$$AFC = TFC/Q$$

For example, look at the fourth entry in column 3. How did we get a dollar amount of $33.33? We simply took *TFC* at 3 units of output, which is $100, and divided by 3. Notice that the *AFC* curve in the exhibit continually declines.

In column 4, we have simply entered some hypothetical data for total variable cost (*TVC*). The *TVC* curve in the exhibit rises because it is likely that variable costs will increase as output increases.

In column 5, we have computed average variable cost. **Average variable cost (AVC)** is total variable cost divided by quantity of output.

$$AVC = TVC/Q$$

For example, look at the third entry in column 5. How did we get a dollar amount of $40.00? We simply took *TVC* at 2 units of output, which is $80, and divided by 2. Notice that the *AVC* curve declines and then rises.

Column 6 shows total cost (*TC*). Total cost is the sum of total variable cost and total fixed cost. Notice that the *TC* curve does not start at zero. Why not? Because even when output is zero, there are some fixed costs. In this example, total fixed cost (*TFC*) at zero output is $100. It follows, then, that the total cost (*TC*) curve starts at $100 instead of at $0.

Column 7 shows *average total cost*. **Average total cost (ATC)** is total cost divided by quantity of output. Average total cost is sometimes called *unit cost*.

$$ATC = TC/Q$$

exhibit **4**

Continued

(6) **Total Cost** **(TC)** $TC = TFC + TVC$ $= (2) + (4)$	(7) **Average Total Cost** **(ATC)** $ATC = TC/Q$ $= (6)/(1)$	(8) **Marginal Cost (MC)** $MC = \Delta TC/\Delta Q$ $= \Delta(6)/\Delta(1)$
$100.00	—	—
150.00	$150.00	$50.00
180.00	90.00	30.00
200.00	66.67	20.00
210.00	52.50	10.00
230.00	46.00	20.00
260.00	43.33	30.00
300.00	42.86	40.00
350.00	43.75	50.00
410.00	45.56	60.00
480.00	48.00	70.00

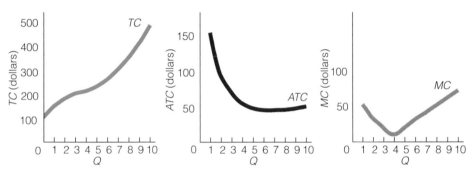

Alternatively, we can say that *ATC* equals the sum of *AFC* and *AVC*.

$$ATC = AFC + AVC$$

To understand why this makes sense, remember that $TC = TFC + TVC$. Thus, if we divide all total magnitudes by quantity of output (Q), we necessarily get $ATC = AFC + AVC$. Notice that the *ATC* curve falls and then rises.

Column 8 shows marginal cost (*MC*). Recall that marginal cost is the change in total cost divided by the change in output.

$$MC = \Delta TC / \Delta Q$$

The *MC* curve has a declining portion and a rising portion. What is happening to the *MPP* of the variable input when *MC* is declining? The *MPP* is rising. What is happening to the *MPP* of the variable input when *MC* is rising? *MPP* is falling. Obviously, the low point on the *MC* curve is when diminishing marginal returns set in.

The *AVC* and *ATC* Curves in Relation to the *MC* Curve

What do the average total and average variable cost curves look like in relation to the marginal cost curve? To explain, we need to discuss the **average-marginal rule**, which is best defined with an example.

Suppose there are 20 persons in a room and each person weighs 170 pounds. Your task is to calculate the average weight. This is accomplished by adding the individual

Thinking like
AN ECONOMIST   *Economists often deduce things from what they know. We just did this when discussing* MPP *and* MC. *Here is what we know: (1)* MPP *and* MC *are inversely related; as* MPP *rises,* MC *falls, and as* MPP *falls,* MC *rises. (2) When diminishing marginal returns "kick in,"* MPP *begins to decline. We deduce then that (3) when diminishing marginal returns kick in,* MC *begins to rise.*

Average-Marginal Rule

When the marginal magnitude is above the average magnitude, the average magnitude rises; when the marginal magnitude is below the average magnitude, the average magnitude falls.

weights and dividing by 20. Obviously, this average weight will be 170 pounds. Now let an additional person enter the room. We shall refer to this additional person as the marginal (additional) person and the additional weight he brings to the room as the marginal weight.

Let's suppose the weight of the marginal person is 275 pounds. The average weight based on the 21 persons now in the room is 175 pounds. The new average weight is greater than the old average weight. The average weight was pulled up by the weight of the additional person. In short, *when the marginal magnitude is above the average magnitude, the average magnitude rises.* This is one part of the average-marginal rule.

Suppose the weight of the marginal person is less than the average weight of 170 pounds, for example, 65 pounds. Then the new average is 165 pounds. In this case, the average weight was pulled down by the weight of the additional person. Thus, *when the marginal magnitude is below the average magnitude, the average magnitude falls.* This is the other part of the average-marginal rule.

$$\text{Marginal} < \text{Average} \rightarrow \text{Average} \downarrow$$
$$\text{Marginal} > \text{Average} \rightarrow \text{Average} \uparrow$$

We can apply the average-marginal rule to find out what the average total and average variable cost curves look like in relation to the marginal cost curve. The following analysis holds for both the average total cost curve and the average variable cost curve.

We reason that

1. if marginal cost is below (less than) average variable cost, average variable cost is falling;

2. if marginal cost is above (greater than) average variable cost, average variable cost is rising.

This reasoning implies that the relationship between the average variable cost curve and the marginal cost curve must look like that in Exhibit 5(a). In Region 1 of (a), marginal cost is below average variable cost, and consistent with the average-marginal rule, average variable cost is falling. In Region 2 of (a), marginal cost is above average variable cost, and average variable cost is rising. In summary, the relationship between the average

exhibit **5**

Average and Marginal Cost Curves

(a) The relationship between *AVC* and *MC*. (b) The relationship between *ATC* and *MC*. The *MC* curve intersects both the *AVC* and *ATC* curves at their respective low points (*L*). This is consistent with the average-marginal rule. (c) The *AFC* curve declines continuously.

MC curve cuts both *AVC* and *ATC* curves at their respective low points.

economics 24/7

WHAT MATTERS TO GLOBAL COMPETITIVENESS?

What does a country need to do to be competitive in the global marketplace? The usual answer is that it needs to produce goods that people in other countries want to buy at prices they want to pay. For example, for the United States to be competitive in the global car and computer markets, U.S. firms must produce cars and computers at prices that people all over the world are willing and able to pay.

Price is a major factor in the race to be competitive in the global market. If U.S. firms charge higher prices for their cars than German and Japanese firms charge for their similar-quality cars, then it is unlikely that U.S. firms will be competitive in the global car market. We conclude: If U.S. firms are to be competitive in the global market, they must keep their prices down, all other things equal.

But how do firms keep their prices down? One way is to keep their unit cost, or average total cost, down. Look at it this way:

Profit per unit = Price per unit − Unit cost (or ATC)

The lower unit cost is, the lower price can go and still earn the producer/seller an acceptable profit per unit. That is, to be competitive on price, firms must be competitive on unit cost; they need to find ways to lower unit cost. This chapter shows how unit cost will decline when marginal cost (*MC*) is below unit cost (*ATC*). In other words, to lower *ATC*, marginal cost must fall and go below (current) average total cost. But how do firms get *MC* to fall and eventually go below current *ATC*? This chapter also explains that before *MC* can decline, marginal physical product (*MPP*) must rise.

Let's summarize our analysis so far: To be competitive in the global marketplace, U.S. firms must be competitive on price. To be competitive on price, firms must be competitive on unit cost (*ATC*). This requires that firms get their *MC* to decline and, ultimately, go below their current *ATC*. And the way to get *MC* to decline and go below current *ATC* is to raise the marginal productivity (*MPP*) of the inputs the firms use. To a large degree, the key to becoming or staying globally competitive is to find and implement ways to increase factor productivity.

How do you fit into the picture? Your education may affect the marginal physical product (*MPP*) of labor. As you learn more things and become more skilled (more productive)—and as many others do too—the *MPP* of labor in the United States rises. This, in turn, lowers firms' marginal cost, which ideally will decline enough to pull both average variable and average total costs down. As this happens, U.S. firms can become more competitive on price and still earn a profit.

---

variable cost curve and the marginal cost curve in Exhibit 5(a) is consistent with the average-marginal rule.

In addition, because average variable cost is pulled down when marginal cost is below it and pulled up when marginal cost is above it, it follows that the marginal cost curve must intersect the average variable cost curve at the latter's lowest point. This lowest point is point *L* in Exhibit 5(a).

The same relationship that exists between the *MC* and *AVC* curves also exists between the *MC* and *ATC* curves, as shown in Exhibit 5(b). In Region 1 of (b), marginal cost is below average total cost, and consistent with the average-marginal rule, average total cost is falling. In Region 2 of (b), marginal cost is above average total cost, and average total cost is rising. It follows that the marginal cost curve must intersect the average total cost curve at the latter's lowest point.

What about the average fixed cost curve? Is there any relationship between it and the marginal cost curve? The answer is no. We can indirectly see why by recalling that average fixed cost is simply total fixed cost (which is constant over output) divided by output ($AFC = TFC/Q$). As output (Q) increases and total fixed cost (TFC) remains

Suppose MC is rising. Does it follow that ATC must be rising too?

No, because MC *can be rising and still be below (less than)* ATC. *For example, take another look at Exhibit 5(b). In Region 1, you will find* MC *both falling and rising (i.e., there is a falling and rising part to the* MC *curve in Region 1). Notice, though, that in the entire Region 1,* ATC *is falling. In other words,* MC *can be falling or rising, and still* ATC *can be continually declining. Whether or not* MC *is rising or falling is not what counts. What counts is whether* MC *is above (greater than) or below (less than)* ATC. *If it is below, then* ATC *will decline; if it is above, then* ATC *will rise.*

constant, it follows that average fixed cost (TFC/Q) must decrease continuously (see Exhibit 5(c)).

Tying Short-Run Production to Costs

As we have said before, costs are tied to production. To see this explicitly, let's summarize some of our earlier discussions (see Exhibit 6).

We assume production takes place in the short run, so there is at least one fixed input. Suppose we initially add units of a variable input to the fixed input, and the marginal physical product of the variable input (e.g., labor) rises. As a result of MPP rising, marginal cost (MC) falls. When MC has fallen enough to be below average variable cost (AVC), we know from the average-marginal rule that AVC will begin to decline. Also, when MC has fallen enough to be below average total cost (ATC), ATC will begin to decline.

Eventually, though, the law of diminishing marginal returns will set in. When this happens, the MPP of the variable input declines. As a result, MC rises. When MC has risen enough to be above AVC, AVC will rise. Also, when MC has risen enough to be above ATC, ATC will rise.

We conclude: What happens in terms of production (Is MPP rising or falling?) affects MC, which in turn eventually affects AVC and ATC. In short, the cost of a good is tied to the production of that good.

One More Cost Concept: Sunk Cost

Sunk Cost

A cost incurred in the past that cannot be changed by current decisions and therefore cannot be recovered.

Sunk cost is a cost incurred in the past that cannot be changed by current decisions and therefore cannot be recovered. For example, suppose a firm must purchase a $10,000 government license before it can legally produce and sell lamp poles. Furthermore, suppose the government will not buy back the license or allow it to be resold. The $10,000

exhibit 6

Tying Production to Costs

What happens in terms of production (*MPP* rising or falling) affects *MC*, which in turn eventually affects *AVC* and *ATC*.

A CLOSER LOOK

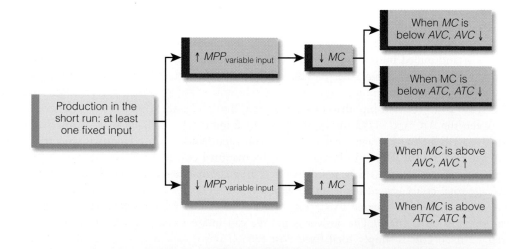

the firm spends to purchase the license is a sunk cost. It is a cost that, after it has been incurred (the $10,000 was spent), cannot be changed by a current decision (the firm cannot go back into the past and undo what was done) and cannot be recovered (the government will neither buy back the license nor allow it to be resold).

Let's consider another example of a sunk cost. Suppose Jeremy buys a movie ticket, walks into the theater, and settles down to watch the movie. Thirty minutes into the movie, he realizes that he hates it. The money he paid for the ticket is a sunk cost. The cost was incurred in the past, it cannot be changed, and it cannot be recovered. (We are assuming that movie theaters do not give your money back if you dislike the movie.)

ECONOMISTS' ADVICE: IGNORE SUNK COSTS Economists advise individuals to ignore sunk costs. To illustrate, consider the case of Jeremy who bought the movie ticket but dislikes the movie. Given the constraints in this case, the movie ticket is a sunk cost. Now suppose Jeremy says the following to himself as he is watching the movie:

> I paid to watch this movie, but I really hate it. Should I get up and walk out or should I stay and watch the movie? I think I'll stay and watch the movie because if I leave, I'll lose the money I paid for the ticket.

Can you see the error Jeremy is making? He believes that if he walks out of the theater, he will lose the money he paid for the ticket. But he has already lost the money he paid for the ticket. Whether he stays and watches the movie or leaves, the money he paid for the ticket is gone forever. It is a sunk cost.

An economist would advise Jeremy to ignore what has happened in the past and can't be undone. In other words, ignore sunk costs. Instead, Jeremy should simply ask and answer these questions: What do I gain (what are my benefits) if I stay and watch the movie? What do I lose (what are my costs) if I stay and watch the movie? (Not: What have I already lost? Nothing can be done about what has already been lost.)

If what Jeremy expects to gain by staying and watching the movie is greater than what he expects to lose, he should stay and watch the movie. However, if what he expects to lose by staying and watching the movie is greater than what he expects to gain, he should leave.

To see this more clearly, suppose again that Jeremy has decided to stay and watch the movie *because he doesn't want to lose the price of the movie ticket*. Two minutes after he has made this decision, you walk up to Jeremy and offer him $200 to leave the theater. What do you think Jeremy will do now? Do you think he will say, "I can't leave the movie theater because if I do, I will lose the price of the movie ticket"? Or do you think he is more likely to say, "Sure, I'll take the $200 and leave the movie theater"?

Most people will say that Jeremy will take the $200 and leave the movie theater. Why? The simple reason is because if he doesn't leave, he loses the opportunity to receive $200.

Well, wouldn't he have forfeited something—albeit not $200—if he stayed at the movie theater before the $200 was offered? (Might he have given up at least $1 in benefits doing something else?) In short, didn't he have some opportunity cost of staying at the movie theater before the $200 was offered? Surely he did. The problem is that somehow, by letting sunk cost influence his decision, Jeremy was willing to ignore this opportunity cost of staying at the theater. All the $200 did was to make this opportunity cost of staying at the movie theater obvious.

Thinking like AN ECONOMIST

In economics, it is important to learn what comes before a particular event. To illustrate, suppose ATC is rising at this moment. Can you see the process that brought this particular event (ATC rising) at this particular moment?

Let's take one step back at a time. ATC is rising because (one step back) MC rose to a level above ATC. But why did MC rise to a level above ATC or why is MC rising at all? MC is rising because MPP (one step back) is declining. But why is MPP declining? MPP is declining because (one step back) the law of diminishing marginal returns set in.

When you look at a tree, you see a tree with branches and leaves. If you "look back" though, you can see the seed that was planted that grew into the tree. It is the same in economics. When you look at rising ATC, most of us simply see "rising ATC." But if you look far enough back, you can see the law of diminishing marginal returns "growing" into "rising ATC."

economics 24/7

"I HAVE TO BECOME AN ACCOUNTANT"

Don: I don't like accounting, but I have to become an accountant.

Mike: Why?

Don: Because I've spent four years in college studying accounting. I spent all that money and time on accounting; I have to get some benefits from it.

Mike: The money and time you spent on accounting are sunk costs. You can't get those back.

Don: Sure I can. All I have to do is work as an accountant. I'll be earning a good income and getting my "college investment" to pay off.

Mike: It sounds to me as if you're letting your four years in college studying accounting determine what you will do for the rest of your work life. Why do that?

Don: Because accounting is all I know how to do.

Mike: If you could do it over, what would you study and do?

Don: I'd study English literature and then I'd become a high school teacher.

Mike: Can't you still do that? You're only 24 years old.

Don: Sure, but that would mean my last 4 years in college were completely wasted. I'm not going to waste them.

Mike: Again, you're letting your past determine what you do now and in the future.

Don: It sounds like you're telling me to get out of accounting.

Mike: I'm not advising you to stay in or to get out of accounting. I'm simply saying that the time and money you spent getting a degree in accounting are sunk costs and that you shouldn't let sunk costs determine what you will do with your life.

Don: It still seems as if you're advising me to get out of accounting.

Mike: But that's not true. I'm simply saying that you should look at the benefits and costs of being an accountant—starting at this moment in time. You shouldn't look over your shoulder and say that because you "invested" four years in accounting that you now have to become an accountant. Those four years are gone; you can never get them back. And you shouldn't try.

Don: In other words, starting from this moment in time, I should ask myself what the costs and benefits are of becoming an accountant. If the costs are greater than the benefits, I should not become one, but if the benefits are greater than the costs, I should become one.

Mike: That's right. Let me put it to you this way. Suppose tomorrow the bottom fell out of the accounting market. Accountants couldn't earn even $100 a month. Would you still want to be an accountant?

Now consider the following situation: Suppose Alicia purchases a pair of shoes, wears them for a few days, and then realizes they are uncomfortable. Furthermore, suppose she can't return the shoes for a refund. Are the shoes a sunk cost? Would an economist recommend that Alicia simply not wear the shoes? An economist would consider the shoes a sunk cost because the purchase of the shoes represents a cost (1) incurred in the past that (2) cannot be changed by a current decision and (3) cannot be recovered. An economist would recommend that Alicia not base her current decision to wear or not wear the shoes on what has happened and cannot be changed. If Alicia lets what she has done, and can't undo, influence her present decision, she runs the risk of compounding her mistake.

To illustrate, if Alicia decides to wear the uncomfortable shoes because she thinks it is a waste of money not to, then she may end up with an even bigger loss: certainly less comfort and possibly a trip to the podiatrist later. The relevant question she must ask herself is, "What will I give up by wearing the uncomfortable shoes?" and not, "What did I give up by buying the shoes?"

The message here is that only the future can be affected by a present decision, never the past. Bygones are bygones; sunk costs are sunk costs.

Don: No way. It wouldn't make any sense. I couldn't earn enough income.

Mike: Well, if you wouldn't become an accountant because the benefits ($100 a month) are too low relative to the costs, doesn't it make sense not to become an accountant if the costs are too high relative to the benefits?

Don: What do you mean?

Mike: Well, suppose the bottom does not fall out of the accounting market, and you can earn $4,000 a month working as an accountant. The question now is: How much do you have to give up, say, in terms of less utility, to get this $4,000 a month? If you would be happy as an English literature teacher, although earning less than you would earn as an accountant, and unhappy as an accountant, then the cost of becoming an accountant and not a teacher may be more than $4,000 a month.

Don: I agree that if I become an accountant, I will have to give up some happiness. But if I don't become an accountant and become a high school teacher instead, I will have to give up some income because I probably would earn less as a teacher than as an accountant. And by the way, income gives me some happiness.

Mike: I agree. But now you're at least looking at the choice you have to make without considering something in the past that you can't change—that is, studying accounting in college.

Don: How so?

Mike: You're asking yourself what the benefits will be of becoming an accountant, and your answer seems to be the happiness or utility you'll receive from $4,000 a month. You're then asking yourself what the costs will be of becoming an accountant, and you seem to be saying that you'll have to forfeit some happiness. The question then becomes: Will the $4,000 a month provide you with enough utility to overcome the disutility you will feel because you're unhappy working as an accountant?

Don: But by doing this, how am I ignoring sunk cost? All this seems to tell me is that economics is about utility, not money.

Mike: You're ignoring the sunk cost of obtaining an accounting degree because when you consider the costs of becoming an accountant, you are considering only what you will (in the future) give up if you become one. You're not considering what you already have (in the past) given up and that cannot be changed.

Don: And are you suggesting that this is what I should do—only consider future costs and not sunk costs?

Mike: Yes, because you're better off not trying to change something that cannot be changed. It would be a little like your trying to change the weather. You can't do it, and you shouldn't waste your time and energy trying. If you do try, you're simply forfeiting other things that you could be accomplishing.

Don: In other words, I shouldn't try to get back the sunk costs I incurred getting an accounting degree because trying to do this means that I'll be forfeiting the opportunity to do other things. I'd be compounding an error. I'd be trying to get back something I can't get back and, in the process, losing some important time, energy, and perhaps money that I could be using in a more "utility productive" way.

Mike: That's right.

BEHAVIORAL ECONOMICS AND SUNK COST In one real-life experiment, two researchers randomly distributed discounts to buyers of subscriptions to Ohio University's 1982–1983 theater season.[5] One group of ticket buyers paid the normal ticket price of $15 per ticket, a second group received $2 off per ticket, and a third group received $7 off per ticket. In short, some buyers paid lower ticket prices than other buyers did.

The researchers found that people who paid more for their tickets attended the theater performances more often than those who paid less for their tickets. Now some people argue that this is because the people who paid more for their tickets somehow wanted to attend the theater more than those who paid less. But this isn't likely because the discounts to buyers were distributed randomly.

Thinking like
AN ECONOMIST *The economist knows that an understanding of sunk cost helps us to see the truth of the old saying, "Don't cry over spilled milk." Milk that has been spilled cannot be unspilled, so crying over it doesn't change a thing. If it did—if, by crying, you could unspill the milk—then by all means go ahead and cry*

---

[5]Hal Arkes and Catherine Blumer, "The Psychology of Sunk Cost," *Organizational Behavior and Human Decision Processes* 124 (1985).

Microeconomics emphasizes that all economic actors deal with objectives, constraints, and choices. Let's focus briefly on constraints. All economic actors would prefer to have fewer rather than more constraints and to have constraints that offer more rather than less latitude. For example, a firm would probably prefer to be constrained in having to buy its resources from five suppliers rather than from only one supplier. A consumer would rather have a budget constraint of \$4,000 a month instead of \$2,000 a month.

Think of two persons, A and B. Person A considers sunk cost when she makes a decision, and person B ignores it when she makes a decision. Does one person face fewer constraints, ceteris paribus? The answer is that the person who ignores sunk cost when making a decision, person B, faces fewer constraints. What person A does, in fact, is act as if a constraint is there—the constraint of sunk cost, the constraint of having to rectify a past decision—when it really exists only because person A thinks it does.

In this sense, the "constraint" of sunk cost is very different from the constraint of, say, scarcity. Whether a person believes it or not, scarcity exists. People are constrained by scarcity, as they are by the force of gravity, whether they know it or not. But people are not constrained by sunk cost if they choose not to be constrained by it. If you choose to let bygones be bygones, if you realize that sunk cost is a cost that has been incurred and cannot be changed, then you will not be constrained by it when making a current decision.

Economists look at things this way: There are already enough constraints in the world. You are not made better off by behaving as if there is one more than there actually is.

Instead, what seems to be the case here is that the more someone paid for the ticket (and everyone paid for his or her ticket before the night of the theater performance), the greater the sunk cost. And the greater the sunk cost, the more likely individuals were to attend the theater performance. In other words, (at least some) people were not ignoring sunk cost.

SELF-TEST

1. Identify two ways to compute average total cost (ATC).

2. Would a business ever sell its product for less than cost? Explain your answer.

3. What happens to unit costs as marginal costs rise? Explain your answer.

4. Do changes in marginal physical product influence unit costs? Explain your answer.

Production and Costs in the Long Run

This section discusses production and long-run costs. As noted previously, in the long run, there are no fixed inputs and no fixed costs. Consequently, the firm has *greater flexibility* in the long run than in the short run.

Long-Run Average Total Cost Curve

In the short run, there are fixed costs and variable costs; therefore, total cost is the sum of the two. But in the long run, there are no fixed costs, so variable costs *are* total costs. This section focuses on (1) what the long-run average total cost ($LRATC$) curve is and (2) what it looks like.

Consider the manager of a firm that produces bedroom furniture. When all inputs are variable, the manager must decide what the situation of the firm should be in the (upcoming) short-run period. For example, suppose he needs to determine the size of the plant; that is, he must decide whether the plant will be small, medium, or large. After this decision is made, he is locked into a specific plant size; he is locked in for the short run.

Associated with each of the three different plant sizes is a short-run average total cost ($SRATC$) curve. (We discuss both short-run and long-run average total cost curves here, so we distinguish between the two with prefixes: SR for short run and LR for long run.) The three short-run average total cost curves, representing the different plant sizes, are illustrated in Exhibit 7(a).

Suppose the manager of the firm wants to produce output level Q_1. Which plant size will he choose? Obviously, he will choose the plant size represented by $SRATC_1$ because this gives a lower unit cost of producing Q_1 than the plant size represented by $SRATC_2$. The latter plant size has a higher unit cost of producing Q_1 (\$6 as opposed to \$5).

Suppose, though, the manager chooses to produce Q_2. Which plant size will he choose now? He will choose the plant size represented by $SRATC_3$ because the unit cost of producing Q_2 is lower with the plant size represented by $SRATC_3$ than it is with the plant size represented by $SRATC_2$.

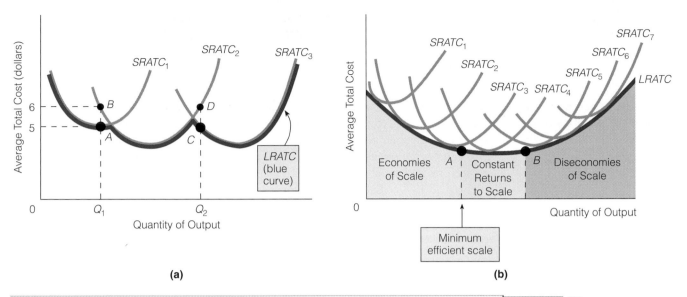

(a)   **(b)**

exhibit **7**

Long-Run Average Total Cost Curve (LRATC)

(a) There are three short-run average total cost curves for three different plant sizes. If these are the only plant sizes, the long-run average total cost curve is the heavily shaded, blue scalloped curve. (b) The long-run average total cost curve is the heavily shaded, blue smooth curve. The *LRATC* curve in (b) is not scalloped because it is assumed that there are so many plant sizes that the *LRATC* curve touches each *SRATC* curve at only one point.

If we were to ask the same question for every (possible) output level, we would derive the **long-run average total cost (LRATC)** curve. The *LRATC* curve shows the lowest unit cost at which the firm can produce any given level of output. In Exhibit 7(a), it is those portions of the three *SRATC* curves that are tangential to the blue curve. The *LRATC* curve is the scalloped blue curve.

Exhibit 7(b) shows a host of *SRATC* curves and one *LRATC* curve. In this case, the *LRATC* curve is not scalloped, as it is in part (a). The *LRATC* curve is smooth in part (b) because we assume there are many plant sizes in addition to the three represented in (a). In other words, although they have not been drawn, short-run average total cost curves representing different plant sizes exist in (b) between $SRATC_1$ and $SRATC_2$ and between $SRATC_2$ and $SRATC_3$ and so on. In this case, the *LRATC* curve is smooth and touches each *SRATC* curve at one point.

Economies of Scale, Diseconomies of Scale, and Constant Returns to Scale

Suppose two inputs, labor and capital, are used together to produce a particular good. If inputs are increased by some percentage (say, 100 percent) and output increases by a greater percentage (more than 100 percent), then unit costs fall and **economies of scale** are said to exist.

For example, suppose good X is made with two inputs, Y and Z, and it takes $20Y$ and $10Z$ to produce 5 units of X. The cost of each unit of input Y is $1, and the cost of each unit of input Z is $1. Thus, a total cost of $30 is required to produce 5 units of X. The unit cost (average total cost) of good X is $6 ($ATC = TC/Q$). Now consider a doubling of inputs Y and Z to $40Y$ and $20Z$ and a more than doubling in output, say, to 15 units of X. This means a total cost of $60 is required to produce 15 units of X, and the unit cost (average total cost) of good X is $4.

An increase in inputs can have two other results. If inputs are increased by some percentage and output increases by an equal percentage, then unit costs remain constant and **constant returns to scale** are said to exist. If inputs are increased by some percentage and output increases by a smaller percentage, then unit costs rise and **diseconomies of scale** are said to exist.

The three conditions can easily be seen in the *LRATC* curve in Exhibit 7(b). If economies of scale are present, the *LRATC* curve is falling, if constant returns to scale are present, the curve is flat, and if diseconomies of scale are present, the curve is rising.

Long-Run Average Total Cost (LRATC) Curve
A curve that shows the lowest (unit) cost at which the firm can produce any given level of output.

Economies of Scale
Exist when inputs are increased by some percentage and output increases by a greater percentage, causing unit costs to fall.

Constant Returns to Scale
Exist when inputs are increased by some percentage and output increases by an equal percentage, causing unit costs to remain constant.

Diseconomies of Scale
Exist when inputs are increased by some percentage and output increases by a smaller percentage, causing unit costs to rise.

Economies of scale → LRATC is falling
Constant returns to scale → LRATC is constant
Diseconomies of scale → LRATC is rising

If, in the production of a good, economies of scale give way to constant returns to scale or diseconomies of scale, as in Exhibit 7(b), the point at which this occurs is referred to as the minimum efficient scale. The **minimum efficient scale** is the lowest output level at which average total costs are minimized. Point *A* represents the minimum efficient scale in Exhibit 7(b).

What is the significance of the minimum efficient scale of output? Its significance can be seen by looking at the long-run average total cost curve between points *A* and *B* in Exhibit 7(b). Between points *A* and *B,* there are constant returns to scale; the average total cost is the same over the various output levels between the two points. This means that larger firms (firms producing greater output levels) within this range do not have a cost advantage over smaller firms that operate at the minimum efficient scale.

Keep in mind that economies of scale, diseconomies of scale, and constant returns to scale are only relevant in the long run. Implicit in the definition of the terms, and explicit in the example of economies of scale, all inputs necessary to the production of a good are changeable. Because no input is fixed, economies of scale, diseconomies of scale, and constant returns to scale must be relevant only in the long run.

Minimum Efficient Scale
The lowest output level at which average total costs are minimized.

Q&A *What is the difference between diminishing marginal returns and diseconomies of scale?*

Diminishing marginal returns are the result of using, say, a given plant size more intensively (adding more labor to a fixed amount of capital). Diseconomies of scale result from changes in the size of the plant.

Why Economies of Scale?

Up to a certain point, long-run unit costs of production fall as a firm grows. There are two main reasons for this: (1) Growing firms offer greater opportunities for employees to specialize. Individual workers can become highly proficient at more narrowly defined tasks, often producing more output at lower unit costs. (2) Growing firms (especially large, growing firms) can take advantage of highly efficient mass production techniques and equipment that ordinarily require large setup costs and thus are economical only if they can be spread over a large number of units. For example, assembly line techniques are usually "cheap" when millions of units of a good are produced but are "expensive" when only a few thousand units are produced.

Why Diseconomies of Scale?

Diseconomies of scale usually arise at the point where a firm's size causes coordination, communication, and monitoring problems. In very large firms, managers often find it difficult to coordinate work activities, communicate their directives to the right persons in satisfactory time, and monitor personnel effectively. The business operation simply gets "too big." There is, of course, a monetary incentive not to pass the point of operation where diseconomies of scale exist. Firms will usually find ways to avoid diseconomies of scale. They will reorganize, divide operations, hire new managers, and so on.

Minimum Efficient Scale and Number of Firms in an Industry

Some industries are composed of a smaller number of firms than other industries are. Or we can say there is a different degree of concentration in different industries.

The minimum efficient scale (*MES*) as a percentage of U.S. consumption or total sales is not the same for all industries. For example, in industry *X, MES* as a percentage of total sales might be 6.6, and in industry *Y,* it might be 2.3. This means the firms in industry *X* reach the minimum efficient scale of plant, and thus exhaust economies of scale, at an output level of 6.6 percent of total industry sales, whereas the firms in industry *Y* experience economies of scale only up to an output level of 2.3 percent of total industry sales. Ask yourself in which industry you would expect to find fewer firms? The answer is in industry X. By dividing the MES as a percentage of total sales into 100, we can estimate the number of efficient firms it takes to satisfy total consumption for a particular product. For the product produced by industry X, it takes 15 firms ($100/6.6 = 15$). For the product produced by industry Y, it takes 43 firms.

Shifts in Cost Curves

In discussing the shape of short-run and long-run cost curves, we assumed that certain factors remained constant. We discuss a few of these factors here and describe how changes in them can shift cost curves.

Taxes

Consider a tax on each unit of a good produced. Suppose company X has to pay a tax of $3 for each unit of X it produces. What effects will this have on the firm's cost curves? Will the tax affect the firm's fixed costs? No, it won't. The tax is paid only when output is produced, and fixed costs are present even if output is zero. (Note that if the tax is a lump-sum tax, requiring the company to pay a lump sum no matter how many units of X it produces, the tax will affect fixed costs.) We conclude that the tax does not affect fixed costs and therefore cannot affect average fixed cost.

Will the tax affect variable costs? Yes, it will. As a consequence of the tax, the firm has to pay more for each unit of X it produces. Because variable costs rise, so does total cost. This means that average variable cost and average total cost rise, and the representative cost curves shift upward. Finally, because marginal cost is the change in total cost divided by the change in output, marginal cost rises and the marginal cost curve shifts upward.

Input Prices

A rise or fall in variable input prices causes a corresponding change in the firm's average total, average variable, and marginal cost curves. For example, if the price of steel rises, the variable costs of building skyscrapers rise, and so must average variable cost, average total cost, and marginal cost. The cost curves shift upward. If the price of steel falls, the opposite effects occur.

Technology

Technological changes often bring either (1) the capability of using fewer inputs to produce a good (e.g., the introduction of the personal computer reduced the hours necessary to key and edit a manuscript) or (2) lower input prices (e.g., technological improvements in transistors have led to price reductions in the transistor components of calculators). In either case, technological changes of this variety lower variable costs and, consequently, lower average variable cost, average total cost, and marginal cost. The cost curves shift downward.

SELF-TEST

1. Give an arithmetical example to illustrate economies of scale.

2. What would the $LRATC$ curve look like if there were always constant returns to scale? Explain your answer.

3. Firm A charged $4 per unit when it produced 100 units of good X, and it charged $3 per unit when it produced 200 units. Furthermore, the firm earned the same profit per unit in both cases. How can this happen?

A Reader Asks...

Will a Knowledge of Sunk Cost Help Prevent Me from Making a Mistake in the Stock Market?

I have a friend who bought some stock at $40 a share. Soon after she bought the stock, it fell to $30 a share. I asked my friend if she planned to sell the stock. She said that she couldn't because if she did, she would take a $10 loss per share of stock. Is she looking at things correctly?

No. Your friend is letting a past decision (the purchase of stock at $40 a share) influence a present decision (whether or not to sell the stock).

Let's go back in time to when your friend was thinking about whether or not to buy the stock. Before she made the purchase, she must have asked herself this question: "Do I think the price of the stock will rise or fall?" She must have thought the price of the stock would rise or else she wouldn't have purchased it.

Why, then, doesn't she ask herself the same question now that the price of the stock has fallen? Why not ask, "Do I think the price of the stock will rise or fall?" Isn't this the best question she can ask herself? If she thinks the price of the stock will rise, then she should not sell the stock. But if she thinks the price will fall, then she should sell the stock before it falls further in price.

Instead, she lets her present be influenced by her past. She cannot change the past; she cannot change the fact that the price of her stock has fallen $10 per share. The $10 per share fall in price is a sunk cost. It is something that happened in the past and cannot be changed by a current decision. If she doesn't ignore sunk cost, she risks losing even more than she already has lost.

! analyzing the scene

Should Olaf sell the chair for a price below his cost? What would you do if you were Lisa?

Are both Olaf and Lisa looking at a sunk cost? Let's consider Olaf's situation. When someone says that he's going to sell something for below cost, usually we wonder what's wrong with him. How can Olaf make any profit if he sells the chair below his cost? Well, sometimes things don't turn out the way people would like. Profit is not guaranteed. The two options Olaf might have now are (1) don't sell the chair for less than cost and therefore don't sell the chair or (2) sell the chair below cost. If the choice is between not receiving any money for the chair and receiving some money for the chair, it is better to receive some money than no money. The $76 Olaf spent on producing the chair is a sunk cost. He cannot get back the $76. Now the choice is between selling the chair—at whatever price he can get—and ending up with some money or refusing to sell the chair and ending up with no money.

Now let's consider Lisa, a computer science major who doesn't like computer science. People tell her to stay with computer science because it pays well and because she has already invested so many years in the major. However, Lisa cannot change the past, and she should not let something she cannot change affect her future. She needs to ignore the past because the past is a sunk cost. Instead, she must ask herself what her future will be like if she continues in computer science and what her future will be like if she chooses to give up computer science and do something she likes better. For a feature that directly touches on this subject, read "I Have to Become an Accountant."

What keeps Ursula from cheating?

If Ursula doesn't feel any guilt from cheating, then why doesn't she cheat? The first and obvious answer is that she is afraid of being caught. But suppose there is no chance of her being caught. Will she cheat then? The answer is "not necessarily."

Whether she cheats or not actually has something to do with the average-marginal rule. People usually cheat by copying the work of someone they believe is smarter than they are. Suppose Ursula believes that her grade on the test will be 65 and that Ian and Charles will each receive a grade of 60 on the test. Her 65 can be viewed as the "average grade" and the grade of Ian and Charles as the "marginal grade." Because the marginal is less than the average, the marginal will pull the average down. There's no need to cheat if copying someone else's work will lower your grade. Ursula is likely to cheat only if she believes her grade will rise by cheating. But this will only occur if Ian and Charles are better students than she is. If a teacher wants to minimize cheating on a test, he or she should sit people with similar grades together.

Would Quentin be more likely to quit his accounting job to own a sports bar if he earned a salary of $60,000 a year instead of $150,000 a year?

The less Quentin gives up if he leaves his job as an accountant, the more likely he will leave his job as an accountant. Forfeiting $60,000 is easier than forfeiting $150,000, so the answer to the question is yes. There are benefits (to Quentin) of owning and operating a sports bar, but there are costs too. Some of those costs are explicit (rent for the bar, pretzels, TV sets, beer, etc.), and some of those costs are implicit (specifically, his salary as an accountant). Quentin is likely to consider both explicit and implicit costs in deciding whether or not to quit his job to own and operate a sports bar.

chapter summary

The Firm

- Alchian and Demsetz argue that firms are formed when there are benefits from individuals working as a team—specifically, when the sum of what individuals can produce as a team is greater than the sum of what individuals can produce alone: sum of team production > sum of individual production.

- There are both advantages and disadvantages to team production. The chief advantage (in many cases) is the positive difference between the output produced by the team and the sum of the output produced by individuals working alone. The chief disadvantage is the increased shirking in teams. The role of the monitor (manager) in the firm is to preserve the increased output and reduce or eliminate the increased shirking. The monitors have a monetary incentive not to shirk their monitoring duties when they are residual claimants.

- Ronald Coase argued that firms exist to reduce the "costs of negotiating and concluding a separate contract for each exchange transaction which takes place on a market." In short, firms exist to reduce transaction costs.

Explicit Cost and Implicit Cost

- An explicit cost is incurred when an actual (monetary) payment is made. An implicit cost represents the value of resources used in production for which no actual (monetary) payment is made.

Economic Profit and Accounting Profit

- Economic profit is the difference between total revenue and total cost, including both explicit and implicit costs. Accounting profit is the difference between total revenue

and explicit costs. Economic profit is usually lower (never higher) than accounting profit. Economic profit (not accounting profit) motivates economic behavior.

Production and Costs in the Short Run

- The short run is a period in which some inputs are fixed. The long run is a period in which all inputs can be varied. The costs associated with fixed and variable inputs are referred to as fixed costs and variable costs, respectively.

- Marginal cost is the change in total cost that results from a change in output.

- The law of diminishing marginal returns states that as ever-larger amounts of a variable input are combined with fixed inputs, eventually, the marginal physical product of the variable input will decline. As this happens, marginal cost rises.

- The average-marginal rule states that if the marginal magnitude is above (below) the average magnitude, the average magnitude rises (falls).

- The marginal cost curve intersects the average variable cost curve at its lowest point. The marginal cost curve intersects the average total cost curve at its lowest point. There is no relationship between marginal cost and average fixed cost.

Production and Costs in the Long Run

- In the long run, there are no fixed costs, so variable costs equal total costs.

- The long-run average total cost curve is the envelope of the short-run average total cost curves. It shows the lowest unit cost at which the firm can produce any given level of output.

- If inputs are increased by some percentage and output increases by a greater percentage, then unit costs fall and economies of scale exist. If inputs are increased by some percentage and output increases by an equal percentage, then unit costs remain constant and constant returns to scale exist. If inputs are increased by some percentage and output increases by a smaller percentage, then unit costs rise and diseconomies of scale exist.
- The minimum efficient scale is the lowest output level at which average total costs are minimized.

Sunk Cost

- Sunk cost is a cost incurred in the past that cannot be changed by current decisions and therefore cannot be recovered. A person or firm that wants to minimize losses will hold sunk costs to be irrelevant to present decisions.

Shifts in Cost Curves

- A firm's cost curves will shift if there is a change in taxes, input prices, or technology.

key terms and concepts

Business Firm	Accounting Profit	Law of Diminishing Marginal Returns	Average Total Cost (ATC), or Unit Cost
Market Coordination	Economic Profit	Fixed Costs	Average-Marginal Rule
Managerial Coordination	Normal Profit	Variable Costs	Sunk Cost
Shirking	Fixed Input	Total Cost (TC)	Long-Run Average Total Cost (LRATC) Curve
Monitor	Variable Input	Marginal Cost (MC)	
Residual Claimant	Short Run	Average Fixed Cost (AFC)	Economies of Scale
Profit	Long Run		Constant Returns to Scale
Explicit Cost	Marginal Physical Product (MPP)	Average Variable Cost (AVC)	Diseconomies of Scale
Implicit Cost			Minimum Efficient Scale

questions and problems

1   Explain the difference between managerial coordination and market coordination.

2   Is the managerial coordination that goes on inside a business firm independent of market forces? Explain your answer.

3   Explain why even conscientious workers will shirk more when the cost of shirking falls.

4   Illustrate the average-marginal rule in a noncost setting.

5   "A firm that earns only normal profit is not covering all its costs." Do you agree or disagree? Explain your answer.

6   The average variable cost curve and the average total cost curve get closer to each other as output increases. What explains this?

7   When would total costs equal fixed costs?

8   Is studying for an economics exam subject to the law of diminishing marginal returns? If so, what is the fixed input? What is the variable input?

9   Some individuals decry the decline of the small family farm and its replacement with the huge corporate megafarm. Discuss the possibility that this is a consequence of economies of scale.

10   We know there is a link between productivity and costs. For example, recall the link between the marginal physical product of the variable input and marginal cost. With this in mind, what link might there be between productivity and prices?

11   Some people's everyday behavior suggests that they do not hold sunk costs irrelevant to present decisions. Give some examples different from those discussed in this chapter.

12   Explain why a firm might want to produce its good even after diminishing marginal returns have set in and marginal cost is rising.

13   People often believe that large firms in an industry have cost advantages over small firms in the same industry.

For example, they might think a big oil company has a cost advantage over a small oil company. For this to be true, what condition must exist? Explain your answer.

14 The government says that firm *X* must pay $1,000 in taxes simply because it is in the business of producing a good. What cost curves, if any, does this tax affect?

15 Based on your answer to question 14, does *MC* change if *TC* changes?

16 Under what condition would Bill Gates be the richest person in the United States and earn zero economic profit?

working with numbers and graphs

1 Determine the appropriate dollar amount for each lettered space.

(1) Quantity of Output, Q (units)	(2) Total Fixed Cost (dollars)	(3) Average Fixed Cost (AFC)	(4) Total Variable Cost (TVC)	(5) Average Variable Cost (AVC)	(6) Total Cost (TC)	(7) Average Total Cost (ATC)	(8) Marginal cost (MC)
0	$200	A	$0		V		
1	200	B	30	L	W	GG	QQ
2	200	C	50	M	X	HH	RR
3	200	D	60	N	Y	I	SS
4	200	E	65	O	Z	JJ	TT
5	200	F	75	P	AA	KK	UU
6	200	G	95	Q	BB	LL	VV
7	200	H	125	R	CC	MM	WW
8	200	I	165	S	DD	NN	XX
9	200	J	215	T	EE	OO	YY
10	200	K	275	U	FF	PP	ZZ

2 Give a numerical example to show that as marginal physical product (*MPP*) rises, marginal cost (*MC*) falls.

3 Price = $20, quantity = 400 units, unit cost = $15, implicit costs = $4,000. What does economic profit equal?

4 If economic profit equals accounting profit, what do implicit costs equal?

5 If accounting profit is $400,000 greater than economic profit, what do implicit costs equal?

6 If marginal physical product is continually declining, what does marginal cost look like? Explain your answer.

7 If the *ATC* curve is continually declining, what does this imply about the *MC* curve? Explain your answer.

Perfect Competition 20

Setting the Scene

The following events occurred on a day in July.

11:12 A.M.

Pam Weatherspoon owns 2,000 shares of Wal-Mart stock. She has been thinking about selling 500 shares of the stock. Today, she goes online to find the current selling price of Wal-Mart stock; it's $58.68 a share. She decides to sell the 500 shares at this per-share price.

2:30 P.M.

Ricky Amador started his company, Amador Electronics, 10 years ago. Last year, he took a loss—his first loss in 10 years. He's thinking it might be a good idea to go out of business.

2:54 P.M.

A U.S. senator is speaking on a newly proposed tax bill. Some members of the Senate are walking about, some are at their desks reading, and a few are listening to the U.S. senator speak.

The senator says, "Certain companies in our country have been reaping huge windfall profits over the past year. I am not against profits—not when people work for them. But when huge profits are handed to certain firms not because the firms did anything to make their product a better product, not because they served the buying public better, and not because they built a better mousetrap, well then I have to say that something is wrong with those profits. In the America of today, certain companies are reaping huge windfall profits simply because the demand for their product increased. Unearned profits must be taxed at a higher rate than earned profits—or else we do not live in a fair and just society."

3:08 P.M.

Steven Pickering manufactures and sells small fans—the type a person might buy for an office. As he walks out of his factory to his car, Steven is wondering how many fans he should produce in the upcoming six-month period.

3:23 P.M.

A TV executive is in her office, looking out the window. She's thinking about one of the networks hottest TV shows. Last year, the show was the network's biggest profit maker. This year, the stars of the show are asking for huge salary increases. The TV executive wonders if the show would be as successful without two of the six major cast members. She also wonders if the stars are worth the salaries they want.

> **?** Here are some questions to keep in mind as you read this chapter:
>
> - *If Pam had decided to sell 400 shares of Wal-Mart stock instead of 500 shares, could she have sold each share for more than $58.68?*
>
> - *Should a company shut down if it is incurring a loss?*
>
> - *What will happen if taxes are imposed on companies because demand for their products has increased?*
>
> - *How does a business owner decide how much of his or her product to produce?*
>
> - *Why do profits sometimes get turned into salaries?*
>
> See analyzing the scene at the end of this chapter for answers to these questions.

Market Structures

Every firm shares two things with all other firms. First, every firm has to answer certain questions. These questions are:

1. What price should the firm charge for the good it produces and sells?

2. How many units of the good should the firm produce?

3. How much of the various resources that the firm needs to produce its good should it buy?

Market Structure

The particular environment of a firm, the characteristics of which influence the firm's pricing and output decisions.

Perfect Competition

A theory of market structure based on four assumptions: There are many sellers and buyers, sellers sell a homogeneous good, buyers and sellers have all relevant information, and there is easy entry into and exit from the market.

In short, regardless of whether a firm sells shirts or cars, whether it is large or small, whether it is located in Georgia or Maine, it must answer all three of these questions, period.

Second, every firm is like all other firms in that every firm finds itself operating within a certain *market structure*. A **market structure** is a firm's particular environment or setting, the characteristics of which influence the firm's pricing and output decisions.

Economists often discuss four different market structures: perfect competition, monopoly, monopolistic competition, and oligopoly. This chapter focuses on perfect competition; the next chapter, on monopoly; and the following chapter, on monopolistic competition and oligopoly. Essentially, in these three chapters, we outline the various theories that relate to each of the four market structures. Within these theories, you will see how firms go about answering the first two questions that all firms must answer. We begin to explain how the last question is answered when we discuss factor markets (later in the text).

Thinking like AN ECONOMIST

When we were discussing supply and demand (in Chapter 3), we briefly discussed what a theory is and why economists build theories. We are beginning to build a theory in this chapter—the theory of perfect competition. In every theory, assumptions are made. Do the assumptions of a theory have to be perfectly descriptive, or else are they useless? Most economists think not. Economists do not judge the worthiness of theories by how realistic the assumptions of the theory are. They judge the worthiness of the theory by how well it predicts real-world events. For example, the third assumption we made in the theory of perfect competition—buyers and sellers have all relevant information about prices, product quality, sources of supply, and so forth—may seem unrealistic. After all, can buyers and sellers really have all relevant information? The answer is they may not. But they may have enough of the relevant information (90 percent instead of 100 percent) so that things "turn out" the way they would if they had all relevant information.

What is our main point? Simply this: Even though a theory's assumptions may not be 100 percent accurate, they may be, as economist Milton Friedman has noted, "sufficiently good approximations for the purpose at hand."

The Theory of Perfect Competition

In this section, we begin our discussion of the theory of **perfect competition**, which is built on four assumptions:

1. **There are many sellers and many buyers, none of which is large in relation to total sales or purchases.** This assumption speaks to both demand (number of buyers) and supply (number of sellers). Because there are many buyers and sellers, it is reasonably assumed that each buyer and each seller acts independently of other buyers and sellers, respectively, and each is so small a part of the market that he or she has no influence on price.

2. **Each firm produces and sells a homogeneous product.** This means each firm sells a product that is indistinguishable from all other firms' products in a given industry. (For example, a buyer of wheat cannot distinguish between Farmer Stone's wheat and Farmer Gray's wheat.) As a consequence, buyers are indifferent to the sellers of the product.

3. **Buyers and sellers have all relevant information about prices, product quality, sources of supply, and so forth.** Buyers and sellers know who is selling what, at what prices, at what quality, and on what terms. In short, they know everything that relates to buying, producing, and selling the product.

4. **Firms have easy entry and exit.** New firms can enter the market easily, and existing firms can exit the market easily. There are no barriers to entry or exit.

economics 24/7

AMAZON: THERE MAY NOT BE ANY CAPPUCCINO, BUT THERE ARE MILLIONS OF BOOKS

Book superstores seem to be springing up everywhere in recent years. Usually, these superstores are about 25,000 square feet and have comfortable chairs and a coffee area. You can relax with a hot cup of cappuccino as you browse through a book you pulled off the seemingly endless rows of shelves. Companies such as Borders, Crown, Books-a-Million, and Barnes & Noble have been opening book superstores all over the country.

So far, superstores have been profitable ventures for Barnes & Noble. On average, a book superstore costs about $2 million to create and generates more than $6 million in total revenues in its first year.

When there are positive economic profits such as these, firms outside the market will enter to compete for a share of the positive profits earned by existing firms. In the book-selling market, the Internet has made this easier to do. Now, instead of building a $2 million physical superstore, it is possible to "build" a book superstore in cyberspace. In other words, it is possible to compete with Barnes & Noble, Crown, and Borders—firms that have physical superstores—by selling books via the Internet.

Amazon entered the book superstore market because the brick-and-mortar superstores had proved there were profits in the market. But Amazon entered the market in a way that had never been done before—through cyberspace. In April 1997, CEO Jeff Bezos said that a list of Amazon's 2.5 million titles would fill 14 New York City phone books. In other words, in the world of book superstores, Amazon is the super book superstore.

So what have we learned? First, when there are positive economic profits in a competitive market, new firms will enter the market. This is what Amazon did. Second, it is possible to enter a market today—as opposed to only a few years ago—through cyberspace. The Internet has given potential competitors another road they can travel to enter new markets.

Before discussing the perfectly competitive firm in the short run and in the long run, we discuss some of the characteristics of the perfectly competitive firm that result from these four assumptions.

A Perfectly Competitive Firm Is a Price Taker

A perfectly competitive firm is a **price taker**. A price taker is a seller that does not have the ability to control the price of the product it sells; it takes the price determined in the market. For example, if Farmer Stone is a price taker, it follows that he can increase or decrease his output without significantly affecting the price of the product he sells.

Why is a perfectly competitive firm a price taker? A firm is restrained from being anything but a price taker if it finds itself one among many firms where its supply is small relative to the total market supply (assumption 1 in the theory of perfect competition), and it sells a homogeneous product (assumption 2) in an environment where buyers and sellers have all relevant information (assumption 3).

Some people might suggest that the assumptions of the theory of perfect competition give economists what they want. Economists want the perfectly competitive firm to be a price taker, and so they choose the assumptions that will make this so. But this isn't the case. Economists start out with certain assumptions and then logically conclude that the firm for which these assumptions hold, or that behaves as if these assumptions hold, is a price taker; that is, it has no control over price. Afterward, economists test the theory by observing whether it accurately predicts and explains the real-world behavior of some firms.

Price Taker

A seller that does not have the ability to control the price of the product it sells; it takes the price determined in the market.

Q&A

An earlier chapter notes that demand curves are downward sloping. Now it appears that the demand curve for a perfectly competitive firm is not downward sloping but horizontal. How can this happen?

To answer this question, we emphasize the distinction between the market demand curve and a single firm's demand curve.

The market demand curve in Exhibit 1(a) is downward sloping, positing an inverse relationship between price and quantity demanded, ceteris paribus. The single perfectly competitive firm's demand curve does not contradict this relationship; it simply represents the pricing situation in which the single perfectly competitive firm finds itself. Recall from an earlier chapter that the more substitutes for a good, the higher the price elasticity of demand. In the perfectly competitive market setting, there are many substitutes for the firm's product—so many, in fact, that the firm's demand curve is perfectly elastic.

A single perfectly competitive firm's supply is such a small percentage of the total market supply that the firm cannot perceptibly influence price by changing its quantity of output. To put it differently, the firm's supply is so small compared with the total market supply that the inverse relationship between price and quantity demanded, although present, cannot be observed on the firm's level, although it is observable on the market level.

The Demand Curve for a Perfectly Competitive Firm Is Horizontal

In the perfectly competitive setting, there are many sellers and many buyers. Together, all buyers make up the market demand curve; together, all sellers make up the market supply curve. An equilibrium price is established at the intersection of the market demand and market supply curves (Exhibit 1(a)).

When the equilibrium price has been established, a single perfectly competitive firm faces a horizontal (flat, perfectly elastic) demand curve at the equilibrium price (Exhibit 1(b)). In short, the firm "takes" the equilibrium price as given—hence, the firm is a price taker—and sells all quantities of output at this price.[1]

WHY DOES A PERFECTLY COMPETITIVE FIRM SELL AT EQUILIBRIUM PRICE? If a perfectly competitive firm tries to charge a price higher than the market-established equilibrium price, it won't sell any of its product. This is because the firm sells a homogeneous product, its supply is small relative to the total market supply, and all buyers are informed about where they can obtain the product at the lower price.

exhibit 1

Market Demand Curve and Firm Demand Curve in Perfect Competition

(a) The market, composed of all buyers and sellers, establishes the equilibrium price. (b) A single perfectly competitive firm then faces a horizontal (flat, perfectly elastic) demand curve. We conclude that the firm is a price taker; it "takes" the equilibrium price established by the market and sells any and all quantities of output at this price. (The capital *D* represents the market demand curve; the lowercase *d* represents the single firm's demand curve.)

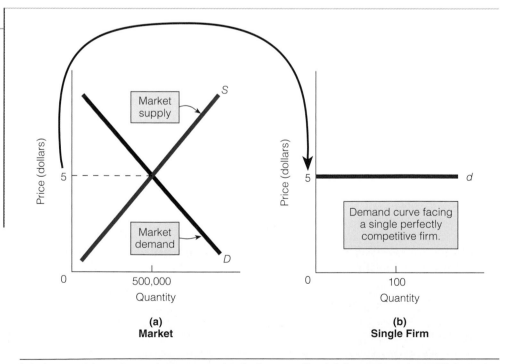

(a)
Market

(b)
Single Firm

[1]The horizontal demand curve does not mean that the firm can sell an infinite amount at the equilibrium price; rather, it means that price will be virtually unaffected by the variations in output that the firm may find it practicable to make.

economics 24/7

DO CHURCHES COMPETE?

This chapter discusses the competition between business firms for customers. Do religions compete in the same way business firms do? Some economists think so; they go on to say that problems often arise when one religion tries to use government to prevent other religions from competing with it.

To illustrate, the United States has a rather open and free religious environment. The First Amendment of the U.S. Constitution states, "Congress shall make no law respecting an establishment of religion, or prohibiting the free exercise thereof." It would be unconstitutional, for example, for the U.S. government to say that only Christianity could be practiced in the United States. That would be similar to saying that only Microsoft could sell software in the United States, that only NBC could broadcast television programs, or that only Harvard University could grant degrees of higher education.

When the Founding Fathers made it unconstitutional for government to favor one religion over another, they essentially made it impossible for any one religion to have a competition-free environment. Although Christianity is the major religion in the United States, one can "purchase" spirituality, codes of conduct, moral guides, and so on from other religions.

Because religions in the United States have to compete with other religions—for believers or, if we are to take the market analogy further, for "customers"—they serve people better. A religion that has to compete provides a higher quality product than a religion that doesn't have to compete. Even within Christianity, different denominations compete. The Southern Baptist Church has to compete with the Methodist Church, and the Methodist Church competes with the Southern Baptists. Today, the competition between denominations and between religions has provided the United States with a wide variety of religious experiences and institutions.

Contrast the United States with some Islamic countries. In some Islamic countries, especially those where the Islamic clergy occupy high positions of state, it is unlawful to openly practice other religions or even to conduct oneself in a way that is contrary to the cleric's interpretation of Islam. In such countries, government has effectively established one religion. Is that one religion and the people in that country better off because of it? To economists, a single producer in a market, whether it's a software producer or a producer of religious doctrine, doesn't serve its customers or believers well. Competition drives producers to try and do better.

If the firm wants to maximize profits, it will not offer to sell its good at a lower price than the equilibrium price. Why should it? It can sell all it wants at the market-established equilibrium price.

The equilibrium price is the only relevant price for the perfectly competitive firm.

The Marginal Revenue Curve of a Perfectly Competitive Firm Is the Same as Its Demand Curve

Recall that total revenue is the price of a good multiplied by the quantity sold. If the equilibrium price is $5, as in Exhibit 2(a), and the perfectly competitive firm sells 3 units of its good, its total revenue is $15. Now suppose the firm sells an additional unit, bringing the total number of units sold to 4. Its total revenue is now $20.

A firm's **marginal revenue (MR)** is the change in total revenue (TR) that results from selling one additional unit of output (Q); that is,

$$MR = \Delta TR / \Delta Q$$

Marginal Revenue (MR)

The change in total revenue that results from selling one additional unit of output.

(1) Price	(2) Quantity	(3) Total Revenue = (1) × (2)	(4) Marginal Revenue = ΔTR/ΔQ = Δ(3)/Δ(2)
$5	1	$ 5	$5
5	2	10	5
5	3	15	5
5	4	20	5

(a)

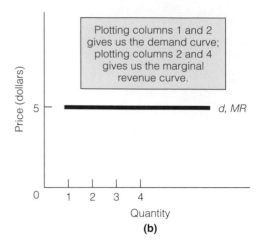

Plotting columns 1 and 2 gives us the demand curve; plotting columns 2 and 4 gives us the marginal revenue curve.

(b)

exhibit 2

The Demand Curve and the Marginal Revenue Curve for a Perfectly Competitive Firm

(a) By computing marginal revenue, we find that it is equal to price. (b) By plotting columns 1 and 2, we obtain the firm's demand curve; by plotting columns 2 and 4, we obtain the firm's marginal revenue curve. The two curves are the same.

Column 4 in Exhibit 2(a) shows that the firm's marginal revenue ($5) at any output level is always equal to the equilibrium price ($5). We conclude that for a perfectly competitive firm, price is equal to marginal revenue ($P = MR$).

For a Perfectly Competitive Firm, $P = MR$

If price is equal to marginal revenue, it follows that *the marginal revenue curve for the perfectly competitive firm is the same as its demand curve.*

A demand curve plots price against quantity, whereas a marginal revenue curve plots marginal revenue against quantity. If price equals marginal revenue, then the demand curve and marginal revenue curve are the same (Exhibit 2(b)).

For a Perfectly Competitive Firm, Demand Curve = Marginal Revenue Curve

Theory and Real-World Markets

The theory of perfect competition describes how firms act in a market structure where (1) there are many buyers and sellers, none of which is large in relation to total sales or purchases; (2) sellers sell a homogeneous product; (3) buyers and sellers have all relevant information; and (4) there is easy entry and exit. These assumptions are closely met in some real-world markets. Examples include some agricultural markets and a small subset of the retail trade. The stock market, where there are hundreds of thousands of buyers and sellers of stock, is also sometimes cited as an example of perfect competition.

The four assumptions of the theory of perfect competition are also *approximated* in some real-world markets. In such markets, the number of sellers may not be large enough for every firm to be a price taker, but the firm's control over price may be negligible. The amount of control may be so negligible, in fact, that the firm acts *as if* it were a perfectly competitive firm.

Similarly, buyers may not have all relevant information concerning price and quality, but they may still have a great deal of information, and the information they do not have may not matter. The products that the firms in the industry sell may not be homogeneous, but the differences may be inconsequential.

In short, a market that does not *exactly* meet the assumptions of perfect competition may nonetheless *approximate* those assumptions to such a degree that it behaves *as if* it were a perfectly competitive market. If so, the theory of perfect competition can be used to predict the market's behavior.

SELF-TEST

(Answers to Self-Test questions are in the Self-Test Appendix.)

1. If a firm is a price taker, it does not have the ability to control the price of the product it sells. What does this mean?

2. Why is a perfectly competitive firm a price taker?

3. The horizontal demand curve for the perfectly competitive firm signifies that it cannot sell any of its product for a price higher than the market equilibrium price. Why can't it?

4. Suppose the firms in a real-world market do not sell a homogeneous product. Does it necessarily follow that the market is not perfectly competitive?

Perfect Competition in the Short Run

The perfectly competitive firm is a price taker. So for a perfectly competitive firm, price is equal to marginal revenue, $P = MR$, and therefore, the firm's demand curve is the same as its marginal revenue curve. This section discusses the amount of output the firm will produce in the short run.

> **micro Theme**
>
> If you want to predict economic behavior, ask yourself what the objective is for the economic actor (whose behavior you want to predict). In the last chapter, we stated that the firm's objective is to maximize profit. Because we know what the firm's objective is, we have an insight into what its behavior will be. Simply stated, there are certain behaviors consistent with trying to maximize profit and certain behaviors that are inconsistent with trying to maximize profit. Much of the material we discuss in this section can be viewed as "actions that are consistent with a firm attempting to maximize profit."

What Level of Output Does the Profit-Maximizing Firm Produce?

Consider the situation in Exhibit 3. The perfectly competitive firm's demand curve and marginal revenue curve (which are the same) are drawn at the equilibrium price of $5. The firm's marginal cost curve is also shown. On the basis of these curves, what quantity of output will the firm produce?

exhibit 3

The Quantity of Output the Perfectly Competitive Firm Will Produce

The firm's demand curve is horizontal at the equilibrium price. Its demand curve is its marginal revenue curve. The firm produces that quantity of output at which $MR = MC$.

The firm will continue to increase its quantity of output as long as marginal revenue is greater than marginal cost. It will not produce units of output for which marginal revenue is less than marginal cost. We conclude that the firm will stop increasing its quantity of output when marginal revenue and marginal cost are equal. The **profit-maximization rule** for a firm says: *Produce the quantity of output at which $MR = MC$.*[2] In Exhibit 3, $MR = MC$ at 125 units of output.

Profit-Maximization Rule

Profit is maximized by producing the quantity of output at which $MR = MC$.

For the perfectly competitive firm, the profit-maximization rule can be written as $P = MC$ because for the perfectly competitive firm, $P = MR$. In perfect competition, profit is maximized when

$$P = MR = MC$$

micro *Theme*

Firms have objectives, face constraints, and have to make choices. The perfectly competitive firm's objective is to maximize profit. It faces the constraint of having to sell its output at the market-determined price—and only at that price. It chooses to produce the quantity of output at which $MR = MC$.

Q&A

Why doesn't the firm in Exhibit 3 stop producing at 50 units of output?

This is where the largest difference between marginal revenue and marginal cost occurs. Why does the firm continue to produce until marginal revenue equals marginal cost?

If the firm had stopped producing with unit 50, it wouldn't have produced unit 51, which comes with a marginal revenue that is greater than marginal cost. Nor would it have produced unit 52, for which marginal revenue is also greater than marginal cost. In short, the firm would not have produced some units of output for which a marginal (additional) profit could have been earned; thus, it would not have been maximizing profit. What matters is whether MR is greater than MC, not how much greater MR is than MC.

The Perfectly Competitive Firm and Resource Allocative Efficiency

Resources (or inputs) are used to produce goods and services; for example, wood may be used to produce a chair. The resources used in the production of goods have a certain exchange value to the buyers of the goods. This exchange value is approximated by the price that people pay for the good. When Smith buys a chair for $100, we know that Smith values the resources used to produce the chair by at least $100.

Wood that is used to produce chairs can't be used to produce desks. Hence, there is an opportunity cost of producing chairs that is best measured by its marginal cost.

Now suppose 100 chairs are produced, and at this quantity, price is greater than marginal cost; for example, price is $100 and marginal cost is $75. What does this mean? Obviously, it means that buyers place a higher value on wood when it is used to produce chairs than when it is used to produce some alternative good.

Producing a good—any good—until price equals marginal cost ensures that all units of the good are produced that are of greater value to buyers than the alternative goods that might have been produced. Stated differently, a firm that produces the quantity of output at which price equals marginal cost ($P = MC$) is said to exhibit **resource allocative efficiency**.

Resource Allocative Efficiency

The situation that exists when firms produce the quantity of output at which price equals marginal cost: $P = MC$.

Does the perfectly competitive firm exhibit resource allocative efficiency? We know two things about this firm so far. First, it produces the quantity of output at which $MR = MC$. Second, for the perfectly competitive firm, $P = MR$. Well, if the perfectly competitive firm produces the output at which $MR = MC$ and for this firm, $P = MR$, then it naturally follows that it produces the output at which $P = MC$. In short, the perfectly competitive firm is resource allocative efficient.

An important point to note is that for a perfectly competitive firm, profit maximization and resource allocative efficiency are not at odds. (Might they be for other market

---

[2]The profit-maximization rule is the same as the loss-minimization rule because it is impossible to maximize profits without minimizing losses. The profit-maximization rule holds for *all firms,* not just perfectly competitive firms.

structures? See the next two chapters.) The perfectly competitive firm seeks to maximize profit by producing the quantity of output at which $MR = MC$, and because for the firm, $P = MR$, it automatically accomplishes resource allocative efficiency ($P = MC$) when it maximizes profit ($MR = MC$).

To Produce or Not to Produce: That Is the Question

The following cases illustrate three applications of the profit-maximization (loss-minimization) rule by a perfectly competitive firm.

CASE 1: PRICE IS ABOVE AVERAGE TOTAL COST Exhibit 4(a) illustrates the perfectly competitive firm's demand and marginal revenue curves. If the firm follows the profit-maximization rule and produces the quantity of output at which marginal revenue equals marginal cost, it will produce 100 units of output. This will be the profit-maximizing quantity of output. Notice that at this quantity of output, price is above average total cost. Using the information in the exhibit, we can make the following calculations:

Case 1

Equilibrium price (P)	= $15
Quantity of output produced (Q)	= 100 units
Total revenue ($P \times Q = \$15 \times 100$)	= $1,500
Total cost ($ATC \times Q = \$11 \times 100$)	= $1,100
Total variable cost ($AVC \times Q = \$7 \times 100$)	= $700
Total fixed cost ($TC - TVC = \$1,100 - \$700$)	= $400
Profits ($TR - TC = \$1,500 - \$1,100$)	= $400

We conclude that if price is above average total cost for the perfectly competitive firm, the firm maximizes profits by producing the quantity of output at which $MR = MC$.

CASE 2: PRICE IS BELOW AVERAGE VARIABLE COST Exhibit 4(b) illustrates the case in which price is below average variable cost. The equilibrium price at which the perfectly competitive firm sells its good is $4. At this price, total revenue is less than both total cost and total variable cost, as the following calculations indicate. To minimize its loss, the firm should shut down.

Case 2

Equilibrium price (P)	= $4
Quantity of output produced (Q)	= 50 units
Total revenue ($P \times Q = \$4 \times 50$)	= $200
Total cost ($ATC \times Q = \$13 \times 50$)	= $650
Total variable cost ($AVC \times Q = \$5 \times 50$)	= $250
Total fixed cost ($TC - TVC = \$650 - \$250$)	= $400
Profits ($TR - TC = \$200 - \$650$)	= -$450

If the firm produces in the short run, it will take a loss of $450. If it shuts down, its loss will be less. It will lose its fixed costs, which amount to the difference between total cost and variable cost ($TFC + TVC = TC$, so $TC - TVC = TFC$). This is $400 ($650 - $250). So between the two options of producing in the short run or shutting down, the firm minimizes its losses by choosing to shut down ($Q = 0$). It will lose $400 by shutting down, whereas it will lose $450 by producing in the short run.

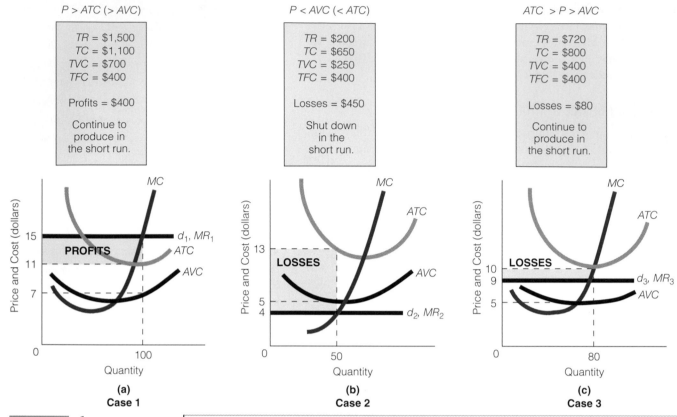

$P > ATC (> AVC)$

TR = $1,500
TC = $1,100
TVC = $700
TFC = $400

Profits = $400

Continue to
produce in
the short run.

$P < AVC (< ATC)$

TR = $200
TC = $650
TVC = $250
TFC = $400

Losses = $450

Shut down
in the
short run.

$ATC > P > AVC$

TR = $720
TC = $800
TVC = $400
TFC = $400

Losses = $80

Continue to
produce in
the short run.

(a)
Case 1

(b)
Case 2

(c)
Case 3

exhibit 4

**Profit Maximization and Loss
Minimization for the Perfectly
Competitive Firm: Three Cases**

(a) In Case 1, TR > TC and the firm
earns profits. It continues to produce
in the short run. (b) In Case 2, TR <
TC and the firm takes a loss. It shuts
down in the short run because it minimizes its losses by doing so; it is better to lose $400 in fixed costs than to
take a loss of $450. (c) In Case 3, TR
< TC and the firm takes a loss. It
continues to produce in the short run
because it minimizes its losses by
doing so; it is better to lose $80 by
producing than to lose $400 in fixed
costs.

We conclude that if price is below average variable cost, the perfectly competitive
firm minimizes losses by choosing to shut down—that is, by not producing.

CASE 3: PRICE IS BELOW AVERAGE TOTAL COST BUT ABOVE AVERAGE VARIABLE COST Exhibit
4(c) illustrates the case in which price is below average total cost but above average variable cost. Here the equilibrium price at which the perfectly competitive firm sells its
good is $9. If the firm follows the profit-maximization rule, it will produce 80 units of
output. At this price and quantity of output, total revenue is less than total cost (hence,
there will be a loss), but total revenue is greater than total variable cost. The calculations
are as follows:

Case 3		
Equilibrium price (P)	=	$9
Quantity of output produced (Q)	=	80 units
Total revenue ($P \times Q = \$9 \times 80$)	=	$720
Total cost ($ATC \times Q = \$10 \times 80$)	=	$800
Total variable cost ($AVC \times Q = \$5 \times 80$)	=	$400
Total fixed cost ($TC - TVC = \$800 - \$400$)	=	$400
Profits ($TR - TC = \$720 - \$800$)	=	−$80

If the firm decides to produce in the short run, it will take a loss of $80. Should it
shut down instead? If it does, it will lose its fixed costs, which, in this case, are $400 ($TC$
− TVC = $800 − $400). It is better to continue to produce in the short run than to
shut down. Losses are minimized by producing.

We conclude that if price is below average total cost but above average variable cost,
the perfectly competitive firm minimizes its losses by continuing to produce in the short
run instead of shutting down.

SUMMARY OF CASES 1–3 We conclude: *A perfectly competitive firm produces in the short run as long as price is above average variable cost (Cases 1 and 3). A perfectly competitive firm shuts down in the short run if price is less than average variable cost (Case 2).*

$$P > AVC \rightarrow \text{Firm produces}$$
$$P < AVC \rightarrow \text{Firm shuts down}$$

We can summarize the same information in terms of total revenue and total variable costs. *A perfectly competitive firm produces in the short run as long as total revenue is greater than total variable costs (Cases 1 and 3). A perfectly competitive firm shuts down in the short run if total revenue is less than total variable costs (Case 2).*

$$TR > TVC \rightarrow \text{Firm produces}$$
$$TR < TVC \rightarrow \text{Firm shuts down}$$

Exhibit 5 reviews some of the material discussed in this section.

The Perfectly Competitive Firm's Short-Run Supply Curve

The perfectly competitive firm produces (supplies output) in the short run if price is above average variable cost. It shuts down (does not supply output) if price is below average variable cost. It follows that the **short-run supply curve** of the firm is that portion of its marginal cost curve that lies above the average variable cost curve. Only a price above average variable cost will induce the firm to supply output. The short-run supply curve of the perfectly competitive firm is illustrated in Exhibit 6.

From Firm to Market (Industry) Supply Curve

After we know that the perfectly competitive firm's short-run supply curve is the part of its marginal cost curve above its average variable cost curve, it is a simple matter to derive the **short-run market (industry) supply curve**.[3] We horizontally "add" the short-run supply curves for all firms in the perfectly competitive market or industry.

> **Short-Run (Firm) Supply Curve**
>
> The portion of the firm's marginal cost curve that lies above the average variable cost curve.

Q&A *I thought the entire* **MC** *curve would have been the firm's supply curve.* **But it isn't, is it?**

No it isn't. Only that part of the firm's MC *curve that lies above the firm's* AVC *curve turns out to be the firm's supply curve.*

> **Short-Run Market (Industry) Supply Curve**
>
> The horizontal "addition" of all existing firms' short-run supply curves.

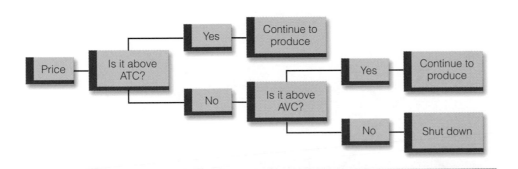

A CLOSER LOOK

---

[3]In discussing market structures, the words *industry* and *market* are often used interchangeably when a single-product industry is under consideration, which is the case here.

exhibit 6

exhibit 6

The Perfectly Competitive Firm's Short-Run Supply Curve

The short-run supply curve is that portion of the firm's marginal cost curve that lies above the average variable cost curve.

exhibit 7

Deriving the Market (Industry) Supply Curve for a Perfectly Competitive Market

In (a) we "add" (horizontally) the quantity supplied by each firm to derive the market supply curve. The market supply curve and the market demand curve are shown in (b). Together, they determine equilibrium price and quantity.

Consider, for simplicity, an industry made up of three firms, *A, B,* and *C* (see Exhibit 7(a)). At a price of P_1, firm *A* supplies 10 units, firm *B* supplies 8 units, and firm *C* supplies 18 units. One point on the market supply curve thus corresponds to P_1 on the price axis and 36 units (10 + 8 + 18 = 36) on the quantity axis.[4] If we follow this procedure for all prices, we have the short-run market supply curve. This market supply curve is shown in the market setting in part (b) of the exhibit.

This market supply curve is used along with the market demand curve (derived in Chapter 3) to determine equilibrium price and quantity.

Why Is the Market Supply Curve Upward Sloping?

Recall that in Chapter 3, when the demand and supply curves were introduced, the supply curve was drawn upward sloping. The supply curve is upward sloping because of the law of diminishing marginal returns. To see this, consider the following questions and answers.

Question 1: Why do we draw market supply curves upward sloping?
Answer: Because market supply curves are the horizontal "addition" of firms' supply curves, and firms' supply curves are upward sloping.

Question 2: But why are firms' supply curves upward sloping?
Answer: Because the supply curve for each firm is that portion of its marginal cost (*MC*) curve that is above its average variable cost (*AVC*) curve—and this portion of the *MC* curve is upward sloping.

---

[4]We add one qualification: Each firm's supply curve is drawn on the assumption that the prices of the variable inputs are constant.

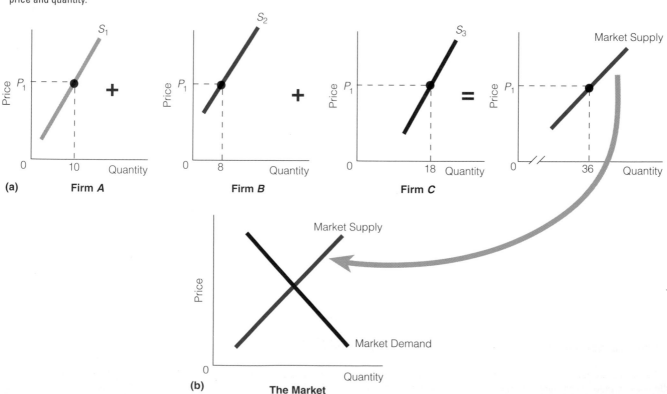

economics 24/7

WHAT DO AUDREY HEPBURN, LUCILLE BALL, AND BUGS BUNNY HAVE IN COMMON?

The U.S. Postal Service has issued certain special, collectors' stamps in the past. These stamps have had likenesses of Audrey Hepburn, Harry Houdini, James Dean, Lucille Ball, The Beatles, Niagara Falls, Alfred Hitchcock, Daffy Duck, and Bugs Bunny.

Why does the U.S. Postal Service issue these special, collectors' stamps? To find out, let's analyze stamps from the point of view of the Postal Service.

Most people buy stamps to send letters or other items through the mail. When a stamp is placed on a letter, the Postal Service is required to deliver the letter to the address on the envelope. Suppose the unit variable cost (AVC) of producing a stamp is 7 cents, regardless of the likeness on the front, and the unit variable cost of delivering a letter with a stamp on it is 19 cents. The sum of the unit variable costs of producing the stamp and delivering the letter is 26 cents.

$$AVC \text{ stamp} = $$
$$AVC \text{ producing the stamp} + AVC \text{ delivering the letter}$$

For purposes of simplicity, we assume $AFC = 0$; so $AVC = ATC$. In other words, the per-unit cost of the stamp is 26 cents. It follows, then, that if the price of a stamp is 39 cents, the U.S. Postal Service earns a per-unit profit of 13 cents per stamp issued and used.

Now suppose the U.S. Postal Service wants to increase its per-unit profit. How might it do this? One way is to issue stamps that people wouldn't put on items to be mailed. That is, issue stamps that people want to collect.

This brings us to the special, collectors' stamps the U.S. Postal Service issues and sells. Many people buy these stamps but do not use them to mail letters. They buy the stamps to collect them. But if people buy these stamps to collect them and not to use them, the U.S. Postal Service doesn't incur the unit variable cost of delivering mail for these special stamps. This means the average total cost of the collectors' stamp falls by the AVC of delivering the letter, which in turn means the ATC of the stamp falls to 7 cents (the AVC of producing the stamp). Consequently, the profit per unit for issuing collectors' stamps rises to 32 cents for a 39-cent stamp.

Question 3: But why do MC curves have an upward-sloping portion?

Answer: Because of the law of diminishing marginal returns. Remember that according to the law of diminishing marginal returns, the marginal physical product (MPP) of a variable input eventually declines. When this happens, the MC curve begins to rise. We conclude that because of the law of diminishing marginal returns, MC curves are upward-sloping, and because MC curves are upward sloping, so are market supply curves.

Q&A *We saw an upward-sloping supply curve back in Chapter 3 when we learned about supply and demand. Are you saying that the upward-sloping supply curve in Chapter 3 was derived by (1) summing the individual supply curves for the firms in the market and (2) those individual supply curves for the firms were simply that part of their MC curves above their AVC curves?*

That is exactly what we are saying.

SELF-TEST

1.   If a firm produces the quantity of output at which $MR = MC$, does it follow that it earns profits?

2.   In the short run, if a firm finds that its price (P) is less than its average total cost (ATC), should it shut down its operation?

3. The layperson says that a firm maximizes profits when total revenue (*TR*) minus total cost (*TC*) is as large as possible and positive. The economist says that a firm maximizes profits when it produces the level of output at which *MR* = *MC*. Explain how the two ways of looking at profit maximization are consistent.

4. Why are market supply curves upward sloping?

Perfect Competition in the Long Run

The number of firms in a perfectly competitive market may not be the same in the short run as in the long run. For example, if the typical firm is making economic profits in the short run, new firms will be attracted to the industry, and the number of firms will increase. If the typical firm is sustaining losses, some existing firms will exit the industry, and the number of firms will decrease. This process is explained in greater detail later in this section. We begin by outlining the conditions of long-run competitive equilibrium.

The Conditions of Long-Run Competitive Equilibrium

Long-Run Competitive Equilibrium

The condition where *P* = *MC* = *SRATC* = *LRATC*. There are zero economic profits, firms are producing the quantity of output at which price is equal to marginal cost, and no firm has an incentive to change its plant size.

The following conditions characterize **long-run competitive equilibrium**:

1. **Economic profit is zero: Price (*P*) is equal to short-run average total cost (*SRATC*).**

$$P = SRATC$$

The logic of this condition is clear when we analyze what will happen if price is above or below short-run average total cost. If it is above, positive economic profits will attract firms to the industry to obtain the profits. If price is below, losses will result and some firms will want to exit the industry. Long-run competitive equilibrium cannot exist if firms have an incentive to enter or exit the industry in response to positive economic profits or losses, respectively. For long-run equilibrium to exist, there can be no incentive for firms to enter or exit the industry. This condition is brought about by zero economic profit (normal profit), which is a consequence of the equilibrium price being equal to short-run average total cost.

2. **Firms are producing the quantity of output at which price (*P*) is equal to marginal cost (*MC*).**

$$P = MC$$

As previously noted, perfectly competitive firms naturally move toward the output level at which marginal revenue, or price because *MR* = *P* for a perfectly competitive firm, equals marginal cost.

3. **No firm has an incentive to change its plant size to produce its current output; that is, *SRATC* = *LRATC* at the quantity of output at which *P* = *MC*.**

To understand this condition, suppose *SRATC* > *LRATC* at the quantity of output established in condition 2. If this is the case,

Thinking like **AN ECONOMIST**

Perhaps as you have noticed by now, the concept of equilibrium is an important one in economics. But why? Because equilibrium is where things are headed; in a way, it is the destination point. To illustrate, suppose that firms in a perfectly competitive market are currently earning positive economic profit. At this point, there are, say, 100 firms in the market. Are things likely to stay this way? Is the number of firms likely to remain at 100? The answer is no. Because firms are earning positive profits, firms not currently in the market will join the market, pushing the number of firms upward from 100. Only when all firms are earning normal profit (zero economic profit) will things remain the way they are. Only then will the market be in equilibrium.[5]

When you get on a train in, say, Los Angeles that is headed for New York City, you are fairly sure the trip is not over until you reach New York City. It is not as easy to know when the "trip" is over in economics. Theoretically, we know the trip is over when equilibrium has been reached. But then it is incumbent upon the economist to define the conditions that specify equilibrium.

[5]We are assuming here that our other long-run equilibrium conditions hold, such as no firms want to change plant size and there is no incentive for any firm to produce any more or any less output.

the firm has an incentive to change plant size in the long run because it wants to produce its product with the plant size that will give it the lowest average total cost (unit cost). It will have no incentive to change plant size when it is producing the quantity of output at which price equals marginal cost and *SRATC* equals *LRATC*.

$$SRATC = LRATC$$

The three conditions necessary for long-run competitive equilibrium can be stated as: Long-run competitive equilibrium exists when $P = MC = SRATC = LRATC$ (Exhibit 8).

In conclusion, long-run competitive equilibrium exists when firms have no incentive to make any changes. Specifically, long-run competitive equilibrium exists when:

1. There is no incentive for firms to enter or exit the industry.
2. There is no incentive for firms to produce more or less output.
3. There is no incentive for firms to change plant size.

The Perfectly Competitive Firm and Productive Efficiency

A firm that produces its output at the lowest possible per-unit cost (lowest *ATC*) is said to exhibit **productive efficiency**. The perfectly competitive firm does this in long-run equilibrium, as shown in Exhibit 8. Productive efficiency is desirable from society's standpoint because it means that perfectly competitive firms are economizing on society's scarce resources and therefore not wasting them.

To illustrate, suppose the lowest unit cost at which good X can be produced is $3—this is the minimum *ATC*. If a firm produces 1,000 units of good X at this unit cost, its total cost is $3,000. Now suppose the firm produces good X not at its lowest unit cost of $3 but at a slightly higher unit cost of $3.50. Total cost now equals $3,500. This means resources worth $500 were employed producing good X that could have been used to produce other goods had the firm exhibited productive efficiency. Society could have been "richer" in goods and services, but now it is not.

Productive Efficiency

The situation that exists when a firm produces its output at the lowest possible per-unit cost (lowest *ATC*).

Industry Adjustment to an Increase in Demand

An increase in market demand for a product can throw an industry out of long-run competitive equilibrium. Suppose we start at long-run competitive equilibrium, where

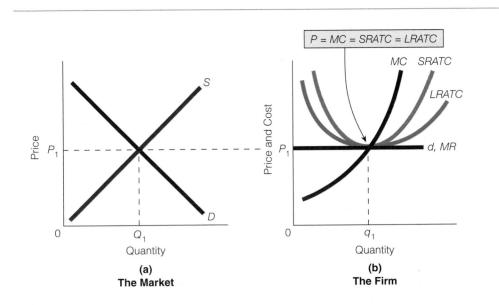

exhibit **8**

Long-Run Competitive Equilibrium

(a) Equilibrium in the market. (b) Equilibrium for the firm. In (b), $P = MC$ (the firm has no incentive to move away from the quantity of output at which this occurs, q_1); $P = SRATC$ (there is no incentive for firms to enter or exit the industry); and $SRATC = LRATC$ (there is no incentive for the firm to change its plant size).

(a)
The Market

(b)
The Firm

$P = MC = SRATC = LRATC$ (see Exhibit 9). Then market demand rises for the product produced by the firms in the industry. What happens? Equilibrium price rises. As a consequence, the demand curve faced by an individual firm (which is its marginal revenue curve) shifts upward.

exhibit **9**

The Process of Moving from One Long-Run Competitive Equilibrium Position to Another

This exhibit describes what happens on both the market level and the firm level when demand rises and throws an industry out of long-run competitive equilibrium.

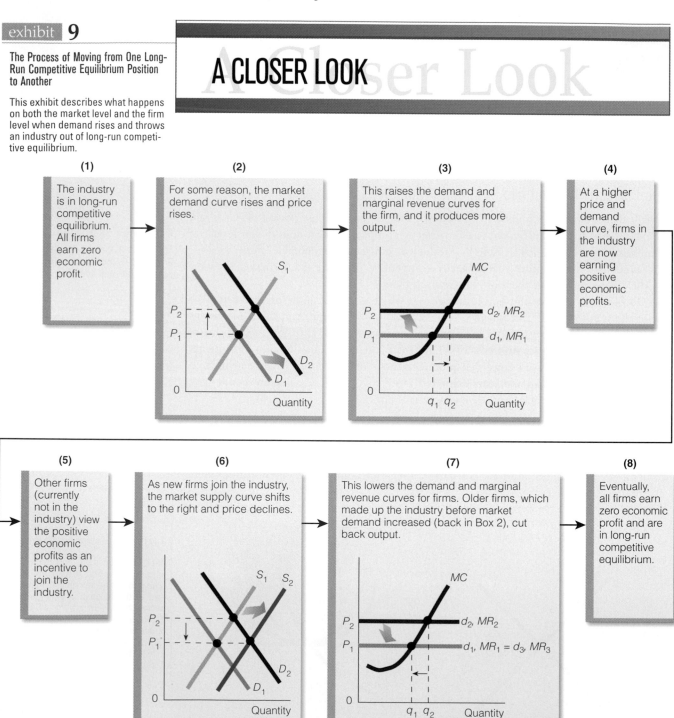

A CLOSER LOOK

(1) The industry is in long-run competitive equilibrium. All firms earn zero economic profit.

(2) For some reason, the market demand curve rises and price rises.

(3) This raises the demand and marginal revenue curves for the firm, and it produces more output.

(4) At a higher price and demand curve, firms in the industry are now earning positive economic profits.

(5) Other firms (currently not in the industry) view the positive economic profits as an incentive to join the industry.

(6) As new firms join the industry, the market supply curve shifts to the right and price declines.

(7) This lowers the demand and marginal revenue curves for firms. Older firms, which made up the industry before market demand increased (back in Box 2), cut back output.

(8) Eventually, all firms earn zero economic profit and are in long-run competitive equilibrium.

Next, *existing firms* in the industry increase quantity of output because marginal revenue now intersects marginal cost at a higher quantity of output. In the long run, new firms begin to enter the industry because price is currently above average total cost, and there are positive economic profits.

As new firms enter the industry, the market (industry) supply curve shifts rightward. As a consequence, equilibrium price falls. It falls until long-run competitive equilibrium is reestablished—that is, until there is, once again, zero economic profit.

If you look at the process again, from the initial increase in market demand to the reestablishment of long-run competitive equilibrium, you will notice that price increased in the short run (owing to the increase in demand) and then decreased in the long run (owing to the increase in supply). Also, profits increased (owing to the increase in demand and consequent increase in price) and then decreased (owing to the increase in supply and consequent decrease in price). They went from zero to some positive amount and then back to zero.

The *up-and-down* movements in both price and profits in response to an increase in demand are important to note. Why? Because too often people see only the primary upward movements in both price and profits and ignore or forget the secondary downward movements. The secondary effects in price and profits are as important as the primary effects.

The process of adjustment to an increase in demand brings up an important question. If price first rises owing to an increase in market demand and later falls owing to an increase in market supply, will the new equilibrium price be greater than, less than, or equal to the *original* equilibrium price? (In Exhibit 9, it is shown as equal to the original equilibrium price, but this need not be the case.)

For example, if the equilibrium price is $10 before the increase in market demand, will the new equilibrium price (after market and firm adjustments have taken place) be greater than, less than, or equal to $10? The answer depends on whether increasing cost, decreasing cost, or constant cost, respectively, describes the industry in which the increase in demand has taken place.

CONSTANT-COST INDUSTRY In a **constant-cost industry**, average total costs (unit costs) do not change as output increases or decreases when firms enter or exit the market or industry. If market demand increases for a good produced by firms in a constant-cost industry, price will initially rise and then will finally fall to its original level. This is illustrated in Exhibit 10(a).

We start from a position of long-run competitive equilibrium where there are zero economic profits. This is at point 1. Then, demand increases and price rises from P_1 to P_2. At P_2, there are positive economic profits, which cause the firms currently in the industry to increase output. We move up the supply curve, S_1, from point 1 to point 2. Next, new firms, drawn by the profits, enter the industry, causing the supply curve to shift rightward.

For a constant-cost industry, output is increased without a change in the price of inputs. Because of this, the firms' cost curves do not shift. But if costs do not rise to reduce the profits in the industry, then price must fall. (Profits can be reduced in two ways: through a rise in costs or a fall in price.) Price must fall to its original level (P_1) before profits can be zero. This implies that the supply curve shifts rightward by the same amount that the demand curve shifts rightward. In the exhibit, this is a shift from S_1 to S_2. The two long-run equilibrium points (1 and 3), where economic profits are zero, define the **long-run (industry) supply (LRS) curve**. A constant-cost industry is characterized by a horizontal long-run supply curve.

Constant-Cost Industry
An industry in which average total costs do not change as (industry) output increases or decreases when firms enter or exit the industry, respectively.

Long-Run (Industry) Supply (LRS) Curve
Graphic representation of the quantities of output that the industry is prepared to supply at different prices after the entry and exit of firms are completed.

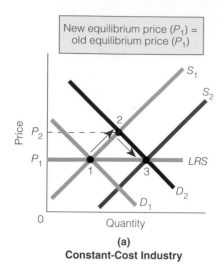

New equilibrium price (P_1) = old equilibrium price (P_1)

(a)
Constant-Cost Industry

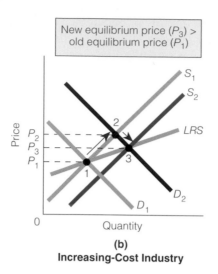

New equilibrium price (P_3) > old equilibrium price (P_1)

(b)
Increasing-Cost Industry

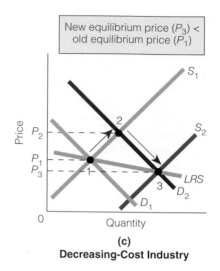

New equilibrium price (P_3) < old equilibrium price (P_1)

(c)
Decreasing-Cost Industry

exhibit 10

Long-Run Industry Supply Curves

LRS = long-run industry supply. Each part illustrates the same scenario, but with different results depending on whether the industry has (a) constant costs, (b) increasing costs, or (c) decreasing costs. In each part, we start at long-run competitive equilibrium (point 1). Demand increases, price rises from P_1 to P_2, and there are positive economic profits. Consequently, existing firms increase output and new firms are attracted to the industry. In (a), input costs remain constant as output increases, so the firms' cost curves do not shift. Profits fall to zero through a decline in price. This implies that in a constant-cost industry, the supply curve shifts rightward by the same amount as the demand curve shifts rightward. In (b), input costs increase as output increases. Profits are squeezed by a combination of rising costs and falling prices. The new equilibrium price (P_3) for an increasing-cost industry is higher than the old equilibrium price (P_1). In (c), input costs decrease as output increases. The new equilibrium price (P_3) for a decreasing-cost industry is lower than the old equilibrium price (P_1).

Increasing-Cost Industry

An industry in which average total costs increase as output increases and decrease as output decreases when firms enter and exit the industry, respectively.

Decreasing-Cost Industry

An industry in which average total costs decrease as output increases and increase as output decreases when firms enter and exit the industry, respectively.

INCREASING-COST INDUSTRY In an **increasing-cost industry**, average total costs (unit costs) increase as output increases and decrease as output decreases when firms enter and exit the industry, respectively. If market demand increases for a good produced by firms in an increasing-cost industry, price will initially rise and then will finally fall to a level above its original level.

Consider the situation in Exhibit 10(b). We start, as before, in long-run competitive equilibrium at point 1. Demand increases and price rises from P_1 to P_2. This brings about positive economic profits, which cause firms in the industry to increase output and new firms to enter the industry. So far, this is the same process as for a constant-cost industry. However, in an increasing-cost industry, as firms purchase more inputs to produce more output, some input prices rise and cost curves shift. In short, as industry output increases, profits are caught in a two-way squeeze: Price is coming down, and costs are rising. If costs are rising as price is falling, then it is not necessary for price to fall to its original level before zero economic profits rule once again. Price will not have to fall so far to restore long-run competitive equilibrium in an increasing-cost industry as in a constant-cost industry. We would expect, then, that when an increasing-cost industry experiences an increase in demand, the new equilibrium price will be higher than the old equilibrium price. This means the supply curve shifts rightward by less than the demand curve shifts rightward. An increasing-cost industry is characterized by an upward-sloping long-run supply curve.

DECREASING-COST INDUSTRY In a **decreasing-cost industry**, average total costs (unit costs) decrease as output increases and increase as output decreases when firms enter and exit the industry, respectively. If market demand increases for a good produced by firms in a decreasing-cost industry, price will initially rise and then will finally fall to a level below its original level. In Exhibit 10(c), price moves from P_1 to P_2 and then to P_3. In such an industry, average total costs decrease as new firms enter the industry, so price must fall below its original level to eliminate profits. A decreasing-cost industry is characterized by a downward-sloping long-run supply curve.

What Happens as Firms Enter an Industry in Search of Profits?

In 1969, the first handheld calculator was introduced in the United States; it sold for $395. In 1975, Sony sold the first videocassette recorder (VCR) for a price of $1,400. In 1977, Apple Computer Corporation sold the first personal computer—it had only 4K random access memory (RAM)—for just under $1,300. In 2007, the prices of all three goods were much lower in both nominal and real (inflation-adjusted) terms, and the quality was generally much higher than when the goods were introduced. Handheld calculators of higher quality than the one introduced in 1969 were selling for approximately $10. Videocassette recorders of higher quality than those in 1975 were selling for approximately $109. Personal home computers of much higher quality than those in 1977 were selling for approximately $499.

What brought about this sharp decrease in price and increase in quality? The entry of new firms into the calculator, VCR, and personal computer industries was partly responsible. Positive economic profits, realized by the first companies in the different industries, attracted new firms, the supply of the goods increased, and prices fell.[6] These examples illustrate how easy entry into a market can affect price and profits. They also suggest the potential benefits that incumbent firms can enjoy if they can successfully limit entry into the industry.

> ### *Thinking like* AN ECONOMIST
>
> Members of the public often see "profit" as something left over after all costs have been incurred. Economists see it as this, but they also see it as something more. Profit is a signal; specifically, it is a signal to firms not earning it. To illustrate, suppose there are 25 firms in a market, all of which are earning profit. That profit is essentially saying to firms that are not in the market: "Hey, come over here and get me." Firms (not in the market) then proceed to enter the market in which profit can be earned. As a result, the supply of the good (connected to the profit) rises and price begins to fall.

Industry Adjustment to a Decrease in Demand

Demand can decrease as well as increase. The analysis outlined for an increase in demand can be reversed to explain industry adjustment to a decrease in demand. Starting at long-run competitive equilibrium, market demand decreases. As a consequence, in the short run, the equilibrium price falls, effectively shifting the firm's demand curve (marginal revenue curve) downward. Following this, some firms in the industry will decrease production because marginal revenue intersects marginal cost at a lower level of output, and some firms will shut down.

In the long run, some firms will leave the industry because price is below average total cost, and they are suffering continual losses. As firms leave the industry, the market supply curve shifts leftward. As a consequence, the equilibrium price rises. It will rise until long-run competitive equilibrium is reestablished—that is, until there are, once again, zero economic profits (instead of negative economic profits). Whether the new equilibrium price is greater than, less than, or equal to the original equilibrium price depends on whether decreasing cost, increasing cost, or constant cost, respectively, describes the industry in which demand decreased.

Differences in Costs, Differences in Profits: Now You See It, Now You Don't

Suppose two farmers, Hancock and Cordero, produce wheat. Farmer Cordero grows his wheat on fertile land; Farmer Hancock grows her wheat on poor soil. Both farmers sell their wheat for the same price, but because of the difference in the quality of their land, Cordero has lower average total costs than Hancock, as shown in Exhibit 11.

If we compare the initial situations for the two farmers (each farmer's ATC_1), we notice that Cordero is earning profits and Hancock is not. Cordero is earning profits because he pays lower average total costs than Hancock as a consequence of farming higher quality land. But is this situation likely to continue? Is Cordero likely to continue earning profits? The answer is no.

Individuals will bid up the price of the fertile land that Cordero farms vis-à-vis the poor-quality land that Hancock farms. In other words, if Cordero is renting his farmland, the rent he pays will increase to reflect the superior quality of the land. The rent will increase by an amount equal to the profits per time period—that is, an amount

---

[6]Changes in technology also occurred at about this time.

exhibit 11

Differences in Costs, Differences in Profits: Now You See It, Now It's Gone

At ATC_1 for both farmers, Cordero earns profits and Hancock does not. Cordero earns profits because the land he farms is of higher quality (more productive) than Hancock's land. Eventually, this fact is taken into account, by Cordero either paying higher rent for the land or incurring implicit costs for it. This moves Cordero's ATC curve upward to the same level as Hancock's, and Cordero earns zero economic profits. The profits have gone as payment (implicit or explicit) for the higher quality, more productive land.

(a)
Farmer Hancock

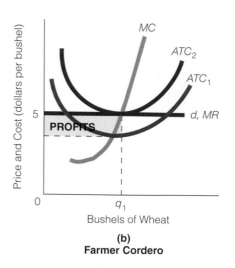

(b)
Farmer Cordero

equal to the shaded portion in Exhibit 11(b). If Cordero owns the land, the superior quality of the land will have a higher implicit cost attached to it (Cordero can rent it for more than Hancock can rent her land, assuming Hancock owns her land). This fact will be reflected in the average total cost curve.

In Exhibit 11(b), ATC_2 reflects either the higher rent Cordero must pay for the superior land or the full implicit cost he incurs by farming land he owns. In either case, when the average total cost curve reflects all costs, Cordero will be in the same situation as Hancock; he, too, will be earning zero economic profits.

Where has the profit gone? It has gone as payment for the higher quality, more productive resource responsible for the lower average total costs in the first place. Consequently, average total costs are no longer relatively lower for the person or firm that employs the higher quality, more productive resource or input.

Profit and Discrimination

A firm's discriminatory behavior can affect its profits in the context of the model of perfect competition. Let's start at the position of long-run competitive equilibrium where firms are earning zero economic profits. Consider the owner of a firm who chooses not to hire an excellent worker (a worker who is above average, let's say) simply because of that worker's race, religion, or gender.

If the owner of the firm discriminates in any way, what happens to his profits? If he chooses not to employ high-quality employees because of their race, religion, or gender, then his costs will rise above the costs of his competitors who hire the best employees—irrespective of race, religion, or gender. Because he is initially earning zero profit, where $TR = TC$, this act of discrimination will raise TC and push him into taking economic losses.

If the owner in the example is instead a manager, he may lose his job. Owners may decide to replace managers of firms earning subnormal profits. Thus, profit maximization by shareholders works to reduce discrimination.

Our conclusion is that if a firm is in a perfectly competitive market structure, it will pay penalties if it chooses to discriminate. This is not to say that discrimination will disappear. It only says that discrimination comes with a price tag. And according to economic theory, the more something costs, the less of it there will be, *ceteris paribus*.

SELF-TEST

1. If firms in a perfectly competitive market are earning positive economic profits, what will happen?

2. If firms in a perfectly competitive market want to produce more output, is the market in long-run equilibrium?

3. If a perfectly competitive market in long-run equilibrium witnesses an increase in demand, what will happen to price?

4. Suppose two firms produce computer software. Firm *A* employs a software genius at the same salary that firm *B* employs a mediocre software engineer. Will the firm that employs the software genius earn higher profits than the other firm, *ceteris paribus*?

Topics for Analysis Within the Theory of Perfect Competition

This section briefly analyzes three topics within the theory of perfect competition: higher costs and higher prices, advertising, and setting prices.

Do Higher Costs Mean Higher Prices?

Suppose there are 600 firms in an industry. Each firm sells the identical product at the same price. Suppose one of these firms experiences a rise in its marginal costs of production. Someone immediately comments, "Higher costs for the firm today, higher prices for the consumer tomorrow." Her assumption is that firms that experience a rise in costs simply pass on these higher costs to consumers in the form of higher prices.

Will this occur in a perfectly competitive market structure? Remember that each firm in the industry is a price taker; furthermore, only one firm has experienced a rise in marginal costs. Because this firm supplies only a tiny percentage of the total market supply, it is unlikely that the market supply curve will undergo more than a negligible change. And if the market supply curve does not change, neither will equilibrium price. In short, a rise in costs incurred by one of many firms does not mean consumers will pay higher prices. The situation would have been different, of course, if many of the firms in the industry had experienced a rise in costs. In this case, the market supply curve would have been affected, along with price.

Will the Perfectly Competitive Firm Advertise?

Do individual farmers advertise? Have you ever seen an advertisement for, say, Farmer Johnson's milk? We think not. First, Farmer Johnson sells a homogeneous product, so advertising his milk is the same as advertising every dairy farmer's milk. Second, Farmer Johnson is in a perfectly competitive market, so he can sell all the milk he wants at the going price. Why should he advertise? From his viewpoint, advertising has costs and no benefits.

Will a perfectly competitive industry advertise? For example, if Farmer Johnson won't advertise his milk, will the milk industry advertise milk? It may. The industry as a whole may advertise milk in the hope of shifting the market demand curve for milk to the right. This is actually what the milk industry hopes to do with its commercial message, "Got milk?"

Thinking like **AN ECONOMIST**

Sometimes, two or more explanations may seem equally reasonable. For example, observing that all firms within an industry sell their products for the same price, both the explanation that the firms collude on price and the explanation that the firms are price takers seem equally reasonable. But for the economist, a reasonable explanation is not sufficient; she wants the correct explanation. The economist is skeptical of any explanation that simply sounds reasonable. She needs evidence that supports the explanation.

Supplier-Set Price Versus Market-Determined Price: Collusion or Competition?

Suppose the only thing you know about a particular industry is that all firms within it sell their products at the same price. To explain this, some people argue that the firms are colluding—that is, the firms come together, pick a price, and stick to it.

This, of course, is one way all firms can arrive at the same price for their products. But it is not the only way. Another way has been described in this chapter. It could be that all firms are price takers; that is, the firms are in a perfectly competitive market structure. In this case, there is no collusion.

SELF-TEST

1. In a perfectly competitive market, do higher costs mean higher prices?

2. Suppose you see a product advertised on television. Does it follow that the product cannot be produced in a perfectly competitive market?

A Reader Asks . . .

Does Job Security Have Anything to Do with Fixed and Variable Costs?

What is the relationship among fixed, variable, and total costs, the firm's shutdown decision, and employee job security?

Consider the total fixed cost–total cost ratio (TFC/TC) for firms. The greater the ratio—that is, the larger TFC is relative to TC—the more likely the firm will operate in the short run; the smaller the ratio, the less likely the firm will operate in the short run. It follows that the more likely the firm will operate in the short run, the greater the job security for the employees of the firm; the less likely the firm will operate in the short run, the less job security for the employees of the firm.

To illustrate, suppose two firms, X and Y, have the following costs and ratios:

Notice that the two firms have the same total cost ($600) but that the fixed and variable costs are different percentages of total cost for the two firms. Firm X has a lower TVC/TC ratio and a higher TFC/TC ratio than firm Y has. If total revenue falls to, say, $499, firm Y will shut down because its total revenue will be less than its total variable cost (TVC). However, firm X will continue to operate. For firm X, total revenue will have to fall below $400 before it will shut down. In other words, the firm with the higher TFC/TC ratio (firm X) stays operational longer than the firm with the lower TFC/TC ratio (firm Y). It follows, then, that if everything else is equal between the two firms, an employee working for firm X is less likely to be laid off due to declining total revenue than is an employee working for firm Y.

Firm X	Firm Y
$TC = \$600$	$TC = \$600$
$TVC = \$400$	$TVC = \$500$
$TFC = \$200$	$TFC = \$100$
$TVC/TC = \$400/\$600 = 0.66$	$TVC/TC = \$500/\$600 = 0.83$
$TFC/TC = \$200/\$600 = 0.33$	$TFC/TC = \$100/\$600 = 0.17$

! analyzing the scene

If Pam had decided to sell 400 shares of Wal-Mart stock instead of 500 shares, could she have sold each share for more than $58.68?

Could Pam have received a higher per-share price if she had decided to sell fewer shares? In other words, is the market price "somewhat" under Pam's control? The answer is no. Her shares are such a small percentage of the total shares of Wal-Mart stock that if she holds back 100 shares (sells 400 shares instead of 500 shares), it is unlikely that she can affect the market price of Wal-Mart stock. In short, Pam is a price taker: She takes the market price as given.

Should a company shut down if it is incurring a loss?

Ricky Amador's company incurred a loss last year, and he wonders if he should shut down the company. However, a loss does not necessarily mean that shutting down is the best option. A loss occurs any time a firm sells its good for less than its unit costs (or *ATC*). But if price is above *AVC* (even though it is below *ATC*), it will still be better for the company to continue to operate in the short run than to shut down. Ricky Amador should look at the price he charges for his good in relation to his *AVC*. If price is above *AVC*, continue to operate; if price is below *AVC*, shut down.

What will happen if taxes are imposed on companies because demand for their products has increased?

A U.S. senator argues for a higher tax on "unearned profits" than on earned profits. According to the senator, unearned profits are profits that a company acquired because the demand for its product increased; they are not profits that the company earned because it produced a better good and so on. The senator is looking at profits as a dollar amount (which is the way many people look at profits). What he doesn't see (or if he sees, he doesn't indicate) is that profits direct resources.

To illustrate, suppose government taxes away all the profits of a company whose profits are the result of increasing demand. For example, the demand for good *X* rises, and in the short run, price and profits rise, and the government taxes away all these profits.

However, by increasing demand, the buying public was sending a signal to producers to produce more of good *X*. If current firms are permitted to keep the higher profits, then other firms will enter the industry and start to compete with them. In the process of the new firms competing with the old existing firms, more of good *X* will be produced, which the buying public was saying it wanted.

By taxing the profits away, government will prevent new firms from joining the industry and producing more of good *X*. And without the supply response from new firms, government will prevent price from falling. In terms of Exhibit 9, the process will stop at Step 4 and will not be able to go to Step 6 (more output and price back to its original level).

How does a business owner decide how much of his or her product to produce?

Steven Pickering, who manufactures and sells small fans, wonders how many fans he should produce in the upcoming 6-month period. What would we advise? The answer is consistent with good common sense: Keep producing as long as the additional revenue (or marginal revenue) of producing and selling an additional fan is greater than the additional cost (or marginal cost) of producing and selling an additional fan. He should produce the number of fans at which $MR = MC$.

Why do profits sometimes get turned into salaries?

This scene is similar to the situation for farmers Cordero and Hancock. Recall that Cordero earned profits, and Hancock did not. But Cordero earned profits because he was farming higher quality land than Hancock was farming. In time, Cordero's profits were turned into higher land payments—that is, payments for the higher quality, more productive resource responsible for the original profits.

Just as land is a resource for a farmer, the stars of the TV show are a resource for the network. If the network's profits are the result of the actors' superior acting, then the actors' superior acting is much like the higher quality land in the Cordero and Hancock example. In the end, it is likely that the higher profits for the network will go as payments for the higher quality, more productive resource responsible for the profits. Thus, the profits will be turned into higher salaries for the actors.

chapter summary

The Theory of Perfect Competition

- The theory of perfect competition is built on four assumptions: (1) There are many sellers and many buyers, none of which is large in relation to total sales or purchases. (2) Each firm produces and sells a homogeneous product. (3) Buyers and sellers have all relevant information with respect to prices, product quality, sources of supply, and so on. (4) There is easy entry into and exit from the industry.

- The theory of perfect competition predicts the following: (1) Economic profits will be squeezed out of the industry in the long run by the entry of new firms; that is, zero economic profit exists in the long run. (2) In equilibrium, firms produce the quantity of output at which price equals marginal cost. (3) In the short run, firms will stay in business as long as price covers average variable costs. (4) In the long run, firms will stay in business as long as price covers average total costs. (5) In the short run, an increase in demand will lead to a rise in price; whether the price in the long run will be higher than, lower than, or equal to its original level depends on whether the firm is in an increasing-, decreasing-, or constant-cost industry.

The Perfectly Competitive Firm

- A perfectly competitive firm is a price taker. It sells its product only at the market-established equilibrium price.

- The perfectly competitive firm faces a horizontal (flat, perfectly elastic) demand curve. Its demand curve and its marginal revenue curve are the same.

- The perfectly competitive firm (as well as all other firms) maximizes profits (or minimizes losses) by producing the quantity of output at which $MR = MC$.

- For the perfectly competitive firm, price equals marginal revenue.

- A perfectly competitive firm is resource allocative efficient because it produces the quantity of output at which $P = MC$.

Production in the Short Run

- If $P > ATC\ (> AVC)$, the firm earns economic profits and will continue to operate in the short run.

- If $P < AVC\ (< ATC)$, the firm takes losses. It will shut down because the alternative (continuing to produce) increases the losses.

- If $ATC > P > AVC$, the firm takes losses. Nevertheless, it will continue to operate in the short run because the alternative (shutting down) increases the losses.

- The firm produces in the short run only when price is greater than average variable cost. Therefore, the portion of its marginal cost curve that lies above the average variable cost curve is the firm's short-run supply curve.

Conditions of Long-Run Competitive Equilibrium

- Long-run competitive equilibrium exists when (1) there is no incentive for firms to enter or exit the industry, (2) there is no incentive for firms to produce more or less output, and (3) there is no incentive for firms to change plant size. We formalize these conditions as follows: (1) Economic profits are zero. (This is the same as saying there is no incentive for firms to enter or exit the industry.) (2) Firms are producing the quantity of output at which price is equal to marginal cost. (This is the same as saying there is no incentive for firms to produce more or less output. After all, when $P = MC$, it follows that $MR = MC$ for the perfectly competitive firm, and thus, the firm is maximizing profits.) (3) $SRATC = LRATC$ at the quantity of output at which $P = MC$. (This is the same as saying firms do not have an incentive to change plant size.)

- A perfectly competitive firm exhibits productive efficiency because it produces its output in the long run at the lowest possible per-unit cost (lowest ATC).

Industry Adjustment to a Change in Demand

- In a constant-cost industry, an increase in demand will result in a new equilibrium price equal to the original equilibrium price (before demand increased). In an increasing-cost industry, an increase in demand will result in a new equilibrium price higher than the original equilibrium price. In a decreasing-cost industry, an increase in demand will result in a new equilibrium price lower than the original equilibrium price.

- The long-run supply curve for a constant-cost industry is horizontal (flat, perfectly elastic). The long-run supply curve for an increasing-cost industry is upward sloping. The long-run supply curve for a decreasing-cost industry is downward sloping.

key terms and concepts

Market Structure

Perfect Competition

Price Taker

Marginal Revenue (*MR*)

Profit-Maximization Rule

Resource Allocative
Efficiency

Short-Run (Firm) Supply
Curve

Short-Run Market
(Industry) Supply Curve

Long-Run Competitive
Equilibrium

Productive Efficiency

Constant-Cost Industry

Long-Run (Industry)
Supply (*LRS*) Curve

Increasing-Cost Industry

Decreasing-Cost Industry

questions and problems

1 True or false: The firm's entire marginal cost curve is its short-run supply curve. Explain your answer.

2 True or false: In a perfectly competitive market, firms always operate at the lowest per-unit cost. Explain your answer.

3 "Firm *A,* one firm in a competitive industry, faces higher costs of production. As a result, consumers end up paying higher prices." Discuss.

4 Suppose all firms in a perfectly competitive market structure are in long-run equilibrium. Then demand for the firms' product increases. Initially, price and economic profits rise. Soon afterward, the government decides to tax most (but not all) of the economic profits, arguing that the firms in the industry did not earn the profits. They were simply the result of an increase in demand. What effect, if any, will the tax have on market adjustment?

5 Explain why one firm sometimes appears to be earning higher profits than another but in reality is not.

6 For a perfectly competitive firm, profit maximization does not conflict with resource allocative efficiency. Do you agree? Explain your answer.

7 The perfectly competitive firm does not increase its quantity of output without limit even though it can sell all it wants at the going price. Why not?

8 Suppose you read in a business magazine that computer firms are reaping high profits. With the theory of perfect competition in mind, what do you expect to happen over time to the following: computer prices, the profits of computer firms, the number of computers on the market, the number of computer firms?

9 In your own words, explain resource allocative efficiency.

10 The term *price taker* can apply to buyers as well as sellers. A price-taking buyer is one who cannot influence price by changing the amount she buys. What goods do you buy for which you are a price taker? What goods do you buy for which you are not a price taker?

11 Why study the theory of perfect competition if no real-world market completely satisfies all of the theory's assumptions?

12 Explain why a perfectly competitive firm will shut down in the short run if price is lower than average variable cost but will continue to produce if price is below average total cost but above average variable cost.

13 In long-run competitive equilibrium, $P = MC = SRATC = LRATC$. Because $P = MR$, we can write the condition as $P = MR = MC = SRATC = LRATC$. Now let's look at the condition as consisting of four parts: (a) $P = MR$, (b) $MR = MC$, (c) $P = SRATC$, and (d) $SRATC = LRATC$. To explain (b), why $MR = MC$, we say that this condition exists because the perfectly competitive firm attempts to maximize profits and this is how it does it. What are the explanations for (a), (c), and (d)?

14 Suppose the government imposes a production tax on one perfectly competitive firm in an industry. For each unit the firm produces, it must pay $1 to the government. Will consumers in this market end up paying higher prices because of the tax? Why or why not?

15 Why is the marginal revenue curve for a perfectly competitive firm the same as its demand curve?

16 Many plumbers charge the same price for coming to your house to fix a kitchen sink. Is this because plumbers are colluding together on price?

17 Do firms in a perfectly competitive market exhibit productive efficiency? Why or why not?

working with numbers and graphs

1   Given the following information, state whether the perfectly competitive firm should shut down or continue to operate in the short run.

   a $Q = 100; P = \$10; AFC = \$3; AVC = \$4$
   b $Q = 70; P = \$5; AFC = \$2; AVC = \$7$
   c $Q = 150; P = \$7; AFC = \$5; AVC = \$6$

2   If total revenue increases at a constant rate, what does this imply about marginal revenue?

3   Using the following table, what quantity of output should the firm produce? Explain your answer.

Q	TR	TC
0	$0	$0
1	100	50
2	200	110
3	300	180
4	400	260
5	500	360
6	600	480

4   Is the firm in Question 3 a perfectly competitive firm? Explain your answer.

5   Explain how a market supply curve is derived.

6   Draw the following:

   a   A perfectly competitive firm that earns profits
   b   A perfectly competitive firm that incurs losses but will continue operating in the short run
   c   A perfectly competitive firm that incurs losses and will shut down in the short run

7   Why is the perfectly competitive firm's supply curve that portion of its marginal cost curve that is above its average variable cost curve?

8   In the following figure, what area(s) represent(s) the following at Q_1?

   a   Total cost
   b   Total variable cost
   c   Total revenue
   d   Loss (negative profit)

9   Why does the *MC* curve cut the *ATC* curve at the latter's lowest point?

10 Suppose all firms in a perfectly competitive market are in long-run equilibrium. Illustrate what a perfectly competitive firm will do if market demand rises.

Monopoly 21

*Setting
the Scene* The following events occurred on a day in April.

10:01 A.M.

Jackson is looking at cars at a Toyota dealership. A car salesman walks over and asks him what car he likes. Jackson tells him. Then the salesman asks Jackson what he does for a living. Jackson wonders what that question has to do with anything, but still he answers. He tells the salesman that he is "an attorney, here in town." "What kind of law do you practice?" the salesman asks.

12:33 P.M.

A musical artist is in the office of one of BT Productions' executives. She is arguing about the price the company wants to charge for her latest CD. "I think the price should be at least $2 lower," she says. "We don't," says the executive. "Don't forget," he adds, "your royalties are tied to our revenues."

9:44 P.M.

Two years ago, Carl Wilson opened the only restaurant in a rather large town that provided its customers with "mud wrestling while you eat." Granted, it was a novel idea, and it was written up in the local newspaper. One columnist wrote, "Mr. Wilson is an entrepreneur. He has come up with a new kind of restaurant. I could even say that, as things stand right now, he is a monopolist; after all, he is the only restaurateur within a 100-mile radius that offers his patrons mud wrestling while they eat."

Tonight, Carl Wilson is sitting in his living room watching television. He has just decided to close his restaurant. It seems that very few people want to eat at a restaurant that provides mud wrestling as entertainment.

? Here are some questions to keep in mind as you read this chapter:

- *Is the car salesman simply making small talk by asking Jackson what he does for a living?*

- *Why does the musical artist want to price her CD lower than the BT Productions executive wants to price it?*

- *Did Carl Wilson think his one-of-a-kind restaurant bestowed monopoly status on him—and therefore, he just couldn't fail?*

See analyzing the scene at the end of this chapter for answers to these questions.

© BANANASTOCK/JUPITER IMAGES

The Theory of Monopoly

Monopoly

A theory of market structure based on three assumptions: There is one seller, it sells a product for which no close substitutes exist, and there are extremely high barriers to entry.

The last chapter discussed one market structure theory—the theory of perfect competition. At the opposite end of the market structure spectrum is the theory of **monopoly**. The theory of monopoly is built on three assumptions:

1. **There is one seller.** This means that the firm is the industry. Contrast this situation with perfect competition, where many firms make up the industry.

2. **The single seller sells a product for which there are no close substitutes.** Because there are no close substitutes for its product, the single seller—the monopolist or monopoly firm—faces little, if any, competition.

3. **There are extremely high barriers to entry.** In the theory of perfect competition, we assume it is easy for a firm to enter the industry. In the theory of monopoly, we assume it is very hard (if not impossible) for a firm to enter the industry. Extremely high barriers keep out new firms.

Examples of monopoly include many public utilities (local public utilities such as electricity, water, and gas companies) and the U.S. Postal Service (in the delivery of first-class mail).

Barriers to Entry: A Key to Understanding Monopoly

If a firm is a single seller of a product, why don't other firms enter the market and produce the same product? Legal barriers, economies of scale, or one firm's exclusive ownership of a scarce resource may make it difficult or impossible for new firms to enter the market.

Public Franchise

A right granted to a firm by government that permits the firm to provide a particular good or service and excludes all others from doing the same.

LEGAL BARRIERS Legal barriers include public franchises, patents, and government licenses. A **public franchise** is a right granted to a firm by government that permits the firm to provide a particular good or service and excludes all others from doing the same (thus eliminating potential competition by law). For example, the U.S. Postal Service has been granted the exclusive franchise to deliver first-class mail. Many public utilities operate under state and local franchises, as do food and gas suppliers along many state turnpikes.

In the United States, patents are granted to inventors of a product or process for a period of 20 years. During this time, the patent holder is shielded from competitors; no one else can legally produce and sell the patented product or process. The rationale behind patents is that they encourage innovation in an economy. It is argued that few people will waste their time and money trying to invent a new product if their competitors can immediately copy the product and sell it.

Entry into some industries and occupations requires a government-granted license. For example, radio and television stations cannot operate without a license from the Federal Communications Commission (FCC). In most states, a person needs to be licensed to join the ranks of physicians, dentists, architects, nurses, embalmers, barbers, veterinarians, and lawyers, among others.

Some cities also use licensing as a form of legal barrier. For example, the Taxi & Limousine Commission requires a person to have a taxi license, called a *taxi medallion,* to own and operate a taxi in New York City. A taxi medallion is similar to a business license; a person needs it to lawfully operate a taxicab business.

economics 24/7

MONOPOLY AND THE BOSTON TEA PARTY

The original meaning of the word *monopoly* was "an exclusive right to sell something." At one time, kings and queens granted monopolies to people in their favor. The monopoly entitled the person to be the sole producer or seller of a particular good. If anyone dared to compete with him, then the king or queen could have that person fined or imprisoned.

The issue of monopoly comes up in the early history of the United States. In 1767, the British Parliament passed the Townsend Acts. These acts imposed taxes (or duties) on various products that were imported into the American colonies. The taxes were so hated in the colonies that they prompted protest and noncompliance. The taxes were repealed in 1770, except for one—the tax on tea. Some historians state that the British Parliament left the tax on tea to

show the colonists that it had the right to raise tax revenue without seeking colonial approval. To get around the tax, the colonists started to buy tea from Dutch traders.

Then, in 1773, the British East India Company was in financial trouble. To help solve its financial problems, it sought a special privilege—a monopoly—from the British Parliament. In response, Parliament passed the Tea Act, which granted the British East India Company the sole right—the monopoly right—to export tea to the colonies. The combination of the tax and the monopoly right given to the British East India Company angered the colonists and is said to have led to the Boston Tea Party on December 16, 1773. The colonists who took part in the Boston Tea Party threw overboard 342 chests of tea owned by the monopoly-wielding British East India Company.

The number of taxi medallions (licenses) has been fixed at about 12,000 for many years. The price of a medallion changes according to changes in the demand for medallions. In 1976, a medallion was about $45,000; in 1988, it was $125,000; and in January 2004, it was $242,000. Obviously, many people find $242,000 a barrier to entering the taxi business. Thus, many economists believe that taxi medallions in New York City are a form of legal barrier.

ECONOMIES OF SCALE In some industries, low average total costs (low unit costs) are obtained only through large-scale production. Thus, if new entrants are to compete in the industry, they must enter it on a large scale. But having to produce on this scale is risky and costly and therefore acts as a barrier to entry. If economies of scale are so pronounced that only one firm can survive in the industry, this firm is called a **natural monopoly**. Often-cited examples of natural monopoly include public utilities that provide gas, water, and electricity. A later chapter discusses government regulation of a natural monopoly.

Natural Monopoly
The condition where economies of scale are so pronounced that only one firm can survive.

EXCLUSIVE OWNERSHIP OF A NECESSARY RESOURCE Existing firms may be protected from the entry of new firms by the exclusive or near-exclusive ownership of a resource needed to enter the industry. The classic example is the Aluminum Company of America (Alcoa), which for a time controlled almost all sources of bauxite in the United States. Alcoa was the sole producer of aluminum in the country from the late 19th century until the 1940s. Many people today view the De Beers Company of South Africa as a monopoly because it controls a large percentage of diamond production and sales. Strictly speaking, De Beers is more of a marketing cartel than a monopolist, although, as discussed in the next chapter, a successful cartel acts much like a monopolist.

What Is the Difference Between a Government Monopoly and a Market Monopoly?

Sometimes, high barriers to entry exist because competition is legally prohibited; sometimes, they exist independently. When high barriers take the form of public franchises, patents, or government licenses, competition is *legally* prohibited. When high barriers take the form of economies of scale or exclusive ownership of a resource, competition is not legally prohibited. In these latter cases, nothing legally prohibits rival firms from entering the market and competing, even though they may choose not to do so. The high barrier to entry does not have a sign attached to it that reads: "No competition allowed."

Some economists use the term *government monopoly* to refer to a monopoly that is legally protected from competition and the term *market monopoly* to refer to a monopoly that is not legally protected from competition. But these terms do not imply that one type is better or worse than the other.

SELF-TEST

(Answers to Self-Test questions are in the Self-Test Appendix.)

1. John states that there are always some close substitutes for the product any firm sells; therefore, the theory of monopoly (which assumes no close substitutes) cannot be useful. Comment.

2. How do economies of scale act as a barrier to entry?

3. How is a movie superstar like a monopolist?

Monopoly Pricing and Output Decisions

Price Searcher

A seller that has the ability to control to some degree the price of the product it sells.

A monopolist is a **price searcher**; that is, it is a seller that has the ability to control to some degree the price of the product it sells. In contrast to a price taker, a price searcher can raise its price and still sell its product—although not as many units as it could sell at the lower price. The pricing and output decisions of the price-searching monopolist are discussed in this section.

> **micro Theme**
> In an earlier chapter, we mentioned that microeconomics has a lot to do with (1) objectives, (2) constraints, and (3) choices. Think of both a perfectly competitive firm and a monopoly firm in terms of constraints. The perfectly competitive firm is constrained in that it cannot raise its price (above the market-equilibrium price) and still sell some of its good. The monopoly firm, though, is not constrained this way. It can raise its price and still sell some of its good.

The Monopolist's Demand and Marginal Revenue

In the theory of monopoly, the monopoly firm is the industry, and the industry is the monopoly firm—they are the same. It follows that the demand curve for the monopoly firm *is* the market demand curve, which is downward sloping. A downward-sloping demand curve posits an inverse relationship between price and quantity demanded: More is sold at lower prices than at higher prices, *ceteris paribus*. Unlike the perfectly competitive firm, the monopolist can raise its price and still sell its product (though not as much).

Suppose a monopolist wants to sell an additional unit of its product. What must it do? Because it faces a downward-sloping demand curve, it must necessarily lower price.

For example, let's assume the monopoly seller originally planned to sell 2 units of X a day at $10 each and now wishes to sell 3 units a day. To sell more units, it must lower price, say, to $9.75. It sells the 3 units at $9.75 each.[1]

So to sell an additional unit, a monopoly firm must lower price on all previous units. Note that *previous* and *additional* don't refer to an actual sequence of events. A firm doesn't sell 100 units of a good and then decide to sell one more unit. The firm is in an either–or situation. Either the firm sells 100 units over some period of time, or it sells 101 units over the same period of time. If the firm wants to sell 101 units, the price per unit must be lower than if it wants to sell 100 units.

A monopoly seller both gains and loses by lowering price. As Exhibit 1 shows, the monopolist in our example gains $9.75, the price of the additional unit sold, because price was lowered. It loses 50 cents—25 cents on the first unit it used to sell at $10 plus 25 cents on the second unit it used to sell at $10.

Gains are greater than losses; the monopolist's net gain from selling the additional unit of output is $9.25 ($9.75 − $0.50 = $9.25). This is the monopolist's *marginal revenue:* the change in total revenue that results from selling one additional unit of output. (Total revenue is $20 when 2 units are sold at $10 each. Total revenue is $29.25 when 3 units are sold at $9.75 each. The change in total revenue that results from selling one additional unit of output is $9.25.)

Notice that the price of the good ($9.75) is greater than the marginal revenue ($9.25), $P > MR$. This is the case for a monopoly seller or any price searcher. (Recall that for the firm in perfect competition, $P = MR$.)

For a monopolist, $P > MR$

The Monopolist's Demand and Marginal Revenue Curves Are Not the Same: Why Not?

In perfect competition, the firm's demand curve *is* the same as its marginal revenue curve. In monopoly, the firm's demand curve is not the same as its marginal revenue curve. The monopolist's demand curve lies above its marginal revenue curve.

(1) P	(2) Q	(3) TR	(4) MR
$10.00	2	$20.00	—— $9.25
9.75	3	29.25	

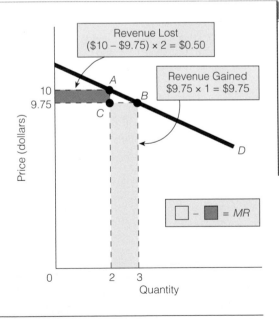

exhibit **1**

The Dual Effects of a Price Reduction on Total Revenue

To sell an additional unit of its good, a monopolist needs to lower price. This price reduction both gains revenue and loses revenue for the monopolist. In the exhibit, the revenue gained and revenue lost are shaded and labeled. Marginal revenue is equal to the larger shaded area minus the smaller shaded area.

[1]This discussion is about how a single-price monopolist behaves. This is a monopolist that sells all units of its product for the same price. Later, we discuss a price-discriminating monopolist.

exhibit 2

Demand and Marginal Revenue Curves

The demand curve plots price and quantity. The marginal revenue curve plots marginal revenue and quantity. For a monopolist, $P > MR$, so the marginal revenue curve must lie below the demand curve. (Note that when a demand curve is a straight line, the marginal revenue curve bisects the horizontal axis halfway between the origin and the point where the demand curve intersects the horizontal axis.)

The demand curve plots price and quantity (P and Q); the marginal revenue curve plots marginal revenue and quantity (MR and Q). Because price is greater than marginal revenue for a monopolist, its demand curve necessarily lies *above* its marginal revenue curve. (Note that price and marginal revenue are the same for the first unit of output, so the demand curve and the marginal revenue curve will share one point in common.) The relationship between a monopolist's demand and marginal revenue curves is illustrated in Exhibit 2.

Price and Output for a Profit-Maximizing Monopolist

The monopolist that seeks to maximize profit produces the quantity of output at which $MR = MC$ (as did the profit-maximizing perfectly competitive firm) and *charges the highest price per unit at which this quantity of output can be sold.*

In Exhibit 3, the highest price at which Q_1, the quantity at which $MR = MC$, can be sold is P_1. Notice that at Q_1, the monopolist charges a price that is greater than marginal cost, $P > MC$. Therefore, the monopolist is *not* resource allocative efficient.

Whether profits are earned depends on whether P_1 is greater or less than average total cost at Q_1. In short, the profit-maximizing price may be the loss-minimizing price. Monopoly profits and monopoly losses are illustrated in Exhibit 4.

Some people argue that it is unrealistic to suggest that a monopolist can take a loss. They say that if the monopolist is the only seller in the industry, then it is guaranteed a profit. But just because a firm is the only seller of a particular product does not guarantee it will earn profits. Remember, a monopolist cannot charge any price it wants for its good; it charges the highest price that the demand curve allows it to charge. In some instances, the highest price may be lower than the firm's average total costs (unit costs). If so, the monopolist incurs a loss, as shown in Exhibit 4(b).

If a Firm Maximizes Revenue, Does It Automatically Maximize Profit Too?

We assume that all firms, whether price searchers or price takers, seek to maximize profit. Many people easily fall into the trap of thinking that the price that maximizes total revenue is necessarily the price that maximizes profit. In other words, the higher

exhibit 3

The Monopolist's Profit-Maximizing Price and Quantity of Output

The monopolist produces the quantity of output (Q_1) at which $MR = MC$, and charges the highest price per unit at which this quantity of output can be sold (P_1). Notice that at the profit-maximizing quantity of output, price is greater than marginal cost, $P > MC$.

(a)
Monopoly Profits

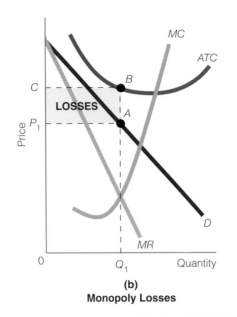

(b)
Monopoly Losses

exhibit 4

Monopoly Profits and Losses

A monopoly seller is not guaranteed any profits. In (a), price at above average total cost at Q_1, the quantity of output at which $MR = MC$. Therefore, TR (the area $0P_1BQ_1$) is greater than TC (the area $0CAQ_1$), and profits equal the area CP_1BA. In (b), price is below average total cost at Q_1. Therefore, TR (the area $0P_1AQ_1$) is less than TC (the area $0CBQ_1$) and losses equal the area P_1CBA.

the firm's total revenue (TR), the higher the firm's profit. But this is not necessarily the case. To illustrate, suppose $TR = \$100$, $TFC = \$40$, and $TVC = \$20$. Because $TC = TFC + TVC$, it follows that $TC = \$60$. The firm's profit, which is TR minus TC, is $40.

Now suppose the firm can sell one more unit of a good and raise its TR to $105. Should it sell one more unit of the good? The answer is that it depends; specifically, it depends on how much more it costs to produce one more unit. Suppose producing one more unit raises the firm's TVC to $30. Again, $TC = TFC + TVC$, and because TVC has risen to $30, TC rises to $70. The difference between TR and TC is now $35 ($105 − $70). Thus, selling one more unit of the good raises TR from $100 to $105, but it lowers profit from $40 to $35. A firm seeks to maximize profit, not total revenue.

Under one condition, maximizing revenue will be the same as maximizing profit. Can you guess the condition? It is when TC is constant. Of course, the only time TC is constant is when it is composed of only TFC; that is, variable costs are zero. To illustrate, suppose $TR = \$100$, $TFC = \$40$, and $TVC = \$0$. Because $TVC = \$0$, it follows that $TC = TFC = \$40$.

Now again suppose that if the firm sells one more unit of a good, its TR will rise to $105. Should it sell one more unit? The answer is obviously yes. That's because, in this case, $TC = TFC$ (and TFC is constant), so TC remains at $40. The firm increases its total revenue and its profit by $5 if it sells an additional unit of the good.

We conclude that maximizing profit is not consistent with maximizing revenue when variable costs exist. But when variable costs do not exist (i.e., variable costs are zero), then maximizing profit is consistent with maximizing revenue.

Q&A *In the last chapter, we learned that a perfectly competitive firm produces the quantity of output at which MR = MC. The monopoly firm does the same thing, correct? I would have thought that a perfectly competitive firm and monopoly firm would have acted differently in this regard.*

First, you are correct that both the monopoly firm and the perfectly competitive firm choose to produce the quantity of output for which MR = MC. Think about why this happens. Each firm would want to produce as long as its additional revenue (MR) is greater than its additional cost (MC), and it wouldn't want to produce where its additional cost (MC) was greater than its additional revenue (MR). That only leaves producing the quantity of output at which MR = MC.

Q&A *Can you give an example of when it might be bad for a firm to try to maximize its total revenue?*

Suppose the firm's total revenue is currently $100 and its total cost is $99. It follows that it is earning a $1 profit. Now suppose the firm can sell one more unit of its good and increase its total revenue to $102, but at the same time, it raises its total cost to $106. Although $102 of revenue is greater than $100, if the firm seeks to increase its total revenue by $2 (make its total revenue as large as possible), it will end up incurring a loss of $4.

Perfect Competition and Monopoly

We discussed perfect competition in the last chapter and monopoly in this chapter. Perfect competition and monopoly are at opposite ends of the (market structure) spectrum. This means there are major differences between them. In this section, we discuss those differences.

Price, Marginal Revenue, and Marginal Cost

Here are two key differences between perfect competition and monopoly:

1.　For the perfectly competitive firm, $P = MR$; for the monopolist, $P > MR$. The perfectly competitive firm's demand curve *is* its marginal revenue curve; the monopolist's demand curve *lies above* its marginal revenue curve.

2.　The perfectly competitive firm charges a price equal to marginal cost; the monopolist charges a price greater than marginal cost.

Perfect competition: $P = MR$ and $P = MC$
Monopoly: $P > MR$ and $P > MC$

Monopoly, Perfect Competition, and Consumers' Surplus

A monopoly firm differs from a perfectly competitive firm in terms of how much consumers' surplus buyers receive. To illustrate, consider Exhibit 5, which shows a downward-sloping market demand curve, a downward-sloping marginal revenue curve, and a horizontal marginal cost (MC) curve. Although you are used to seeing upward-sloping marginal cost curves, there is nothing to prevent marginal cost from being constant over some range of output. A horizontal MC curve simply means that marginal cost is constant. If the market in Exhibit 5 is perfectly competitive, the demand curve *is* the marginal revenue curve. Therefore, the profit-maximizing output is Q_{PC}.[2] The buyer will pay P_{PC} per

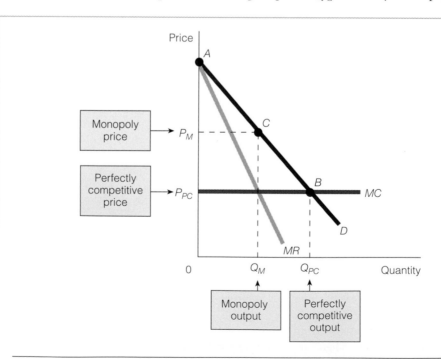

exhibit 5

Monopoly, Perfect Competition, and Consumers' Surplus

If the market in the exhibit is perfectly competitive, the demand curve is the marginal revenue curve. The profit-maximizing output is Q_{PC} and price is P_{PC}. Consumers' surplus is the area $P_{PC}AB$. If the market is a monopoly market, the profit-maximizing output is Q_M and price is P_M. In this case, consumers' surplus is the area P_MAC. Consumers' surplus is greater in perfect competition than in monopoly; it is greater by the area $P_{PC}P_MCB$.

[2]Keep in mind that we are looking at the market demand curve, not the firm's demand curve. This is why the demand curve is downward sloping. All market demand curves are downward sloping.

unit of the good. Recall that consumers' surplus is the area under the demand curve and above the price. For the perfectly competitive firm, consumers' surplus is the area $P_{PC}AB$.

Now suppose the market is a monopoly market. In this case, the demand curve and the marginal revenue curve are different. The profit-maximizing output is where the MR curve intersects the MC curve; thus, the profit-maximizing output is Q_M. The price the buyer pays is P_M. Consumers' surplus in the monopoly case is P_MAC.

Obviously, consumers' surplus is greater in the perfectly competitive case than in the monopoly case. How much greater? It is greater by the area $P_{PC}P_MCB$. Stated differently, this is the loss in consumers' surplus due to monopolization.

Monopoly or Nothing?

Suppose you could push one of two buttons to determine the conditions under which a particular good is produced. If you push the first button, the good is produced under the conditions of perfect competition. If you push the second button, the good is produced under the conditions of monopoly. Which button would you push?

From a consumer's perspective, pushing the first button and producing the good under the conditions of perfect competition would seem to be the better choice. After all, perfect competition provides more output than monopoly and a lower price. In short, there is more consumers' surplus. Perfect competition would seem to be superior to monopoly.

But life doesn't always present a choice between perfect competition and monopoly. Sometimes, it presents a choice between monopoly and nothing. To illustrate, consider Exhibit 6, which shows the demand curve for a good along with the relevant marginal revenue curve. The exhibit also shows two sets of MC and ATC curves. Let's assume that MC_1 and ATC_1 are the relevant cost curves. Notice that because the MC_1 curve is so far above the MR curve, there is no intersection point. In other words, there is no profit-maximizing quantity of output for a firm to produce. Simply put, although there is demand for the particular good, the costs of producing the good are so high that no firm would produce it. Given this situation, consumers receive no consumers' surplus from the purchase and consumption of the good.

Now suppose a firm—one single firm—is able to lower costs to MC_2 and ATC_2. Now marginal cost is low enough for the firm to produce the good. The firm produces Q_M and charges a price of P_M. The area $P_M AB$ is equal to consumers' surplus.

exhibit **6**

Monopoly or Nothing?

We start with the demand and marginal revenue curves and with MC_1 = ATC_1. Because cost is "so high," no firm produces the good. Later, a single firm figures out how to lower cost to MC_2 = ATC_2. This firm produces Q_M and charges the monopoly price of P_M per unit. Is monopoly preferable to no firm producing the good? From a consumer's perspective, the answer is yes. Consumers' surplus is zero when no firm produces the good, and consumers' surplus is area $P_M AB$ when the monopoly firm produces the good.

The economist tells us that it is better to compare real alternatives with other real alternatives instead of with unreal alternatives. In the preceding discussion, this means it is better to compare (1) monopoly with nothing than (2) monopoly with perfect competition when nothing is a real alternative and perfect competition is not. In short, we need to compare (1) "what is" with "what is" and not (2) "what is" with "what we wish it would be."

No doubt the firm producing this good and charging a price of P_M is a monopoly firm. But are consumers better off having a monopoly firm produce the good than having no firm produce it? If no firm produces the good (because costs are just too high), consumers' surplus is zero. But when the monopoly firm produces the good, consumers' surplus is positive.

So under certain conditions, a monopoly may be created in a market because a firm figures out a way to lower the cost of producing a good to a level that makes it worthwhile to produce. Of course, once the monopoly firm exists, consumers would prefer that the good be produced under perfect competition than under monopoly conditions. But that is not always the relevant choice. Sometimes, the choice is between monopoly and nothing, and when this is the choice, the consumers' surplus is greater with monopoly than it is with nothing.

SELF-TEST

1. Why does the monopolist's demand curve lie above its marginal revenue curve?

2. Is a monopolist guaranteed to earn profits?

3. Is a monopolist resource allocative efficient? Why or why not?

4. A monopolist is a price searcher. Why do you think it is called a price searcher? What is it searching for?

The Case Against Monopoly

Monopoly is often said to be inefficient in comparison with perfect competition. This section examines some of the shortcomings associated with monopoly.

The Deadweight Loss of Monopoly

Exhibit 7 shows demand, marginal revenue, marginal cost, and average total cost curves. We have made the simplifying assumption that the product is produced under constant-cost conditions; as a consequence, marginal cost equals long-run average total cost.

exhibit 7

Deadweight Loss and Rent Seeking as Costs of Monopoly

The monopolist produces Q_M, and the perfectly competitive firm produces the higher output level Q_{PC}. The deadweight loss of monopoly is the triangle (DCB) between these two levels of output. Rent-seeking activity is directed to obtaining the monopoly profits, represented by the area $P_{PC}P_MCD$. Rent seeking is a socially wasteful activity because resources are expended to transfer income rather than to produce goods and services.

If the product is produced under perfect competition, output Q_{PC} is produced and is sold at a price of P_{PC}. At the competitive equilibrium output level, $P = MC$.

If the product is produced under monopoly, output Q_M is produced and is sold at a price of P_M. At the monopoly equilibrium, $P > MC$.

Greater output is produced under perfect competition than under monopoly. The net value of the difference in these two output levels is said to be the **deadweight loss of monopoly**. In Exhibit 7, the value to buyers of increasing output from Q_M to Q_{PC} is equal to the maximum amount they would pay for this increase in output. This amount is designated by the area $Q_M CBQ_{PC}$. The costs that would have to be incurred to produce this additional output are designated by the area $Q_M DBQ_{PC}$. The difference between the two is the triangle DCB. *This is the amount buyers value the additional output over and above the costs of producing the additional output.* It is the loss attached to not producing the competitive quantity of output. The triangle DCB is referred to as the *deadweight loss triangle*.

We conclude that monopoly produces a quantity of output that is "too small" in comparison to the quantity of output produced in perfect competition. This difference in output results in a welfare loss to society.

Arnold Harberger was the first economist who tried to determine the actual size of the deadweight loss cost of monopoly in the manufacturing sector of the U.S. economy. He estimated the deadweight loss to be a small percentage of the economy's total output. Additional empirical work by other economists puts the figure at approximately 1 percent of total output.

Deadweight Loss of Monopoly

The net value (value to buyers over and above costs to suppliers) of the difference between the monopoly quantity of output (where $P > MC$) and the competitive quantity of output (where $P = MC$). The loss of not producing the competitive quantity of output.

Rent Seeking

Sometimes, individuals and groups try to influence public policy in the hope of redistributing (transferring) income from others to themselves. To illustrate, look again at the perfectly competitive outcome in Exhibit 7. The market produces Q_{PC} output and charges a price of P_{PC}.

Suppose one of the many firms that is currently producing some of Q_{PC} asks the government to grant it a monopoly. For example, of the 100 firms currently producing Q_{PC}, one firm, firm A, asks the government to prevent the 99 remaining firms from competing with it. Let's consider the benefits for firm A of becoming a monopolist (single seller). Currently, it is earning zero economic profit because it is selling at a price that equals ATC. If it becomes a monopolist, though, it will earn profits equal to the area $P_{PC} P_M CD$ in Exhibit 7. These profits are the result of a *transfer* from buyers to the monopolist.

To see this, let's go back to our discussion of consumers' surplus. If the market in Exhibit 7 is perfectly competitive, consumers' surplus is equal to the area $P_{PC} AB$; if the market is monopolized, consumers' surplus is equal to the area $P_M AC$. The difference is the area $P_{PC} P_M CB$, the area that represents the loss in consumers' surplus if the market is monopolized. Part of this area—$P_{PC} P_M CD$—is transferred to the monopolist in terms of profits. *In other words, if the market is monopolized, part of the consumers' surplus that is lost to buyers becomes profits for the monopolist.* (The other part is the deadweight loss of monopoly, identified by the deadweight loss triangle.)

If firm A tries to get the government to transfer "income" or consumers' surplus from buyers to itself, it is undertaking a *transfer-seeking activity*. In economics, these transfer-seeking activities are usually called **rent seeking**. In other words, firm A is rent seeking.[3]

Rent Seeking

Actions of individuals and groups who spend resources to influence public policy in the hope of redistributing (transferring) income to themselves from others.

[3]The word *rent* (used in this context) often confuses people. In everyday life, *rent* refers to the payment for an apartment. In economics, rent, or more formally, economic rent, is a payment in excess of opportunity cost. The term *rent* was introduced by economist Anne Krueger in her article "The Political Economy of the Rent-Seeking Society," *American Economic Review* 64 (June 1974): 291–303.

Here is an economics joke: Two economists are walking down the street. One sees a $10 bill lying on the sidewalk and asks, "Isn't that a $10 bill?" "Obviously not," says the other. "If it were, someone would have already picked it up."

This joke tells us something about how economists think. Specifically, economists believe that if the opportunity for gain exists, it won't last long because someone will grab it—quickly. By the time you come along, it's gone.

Think of this in terms of what Gordon Tullock has said about monopoly. As a seller, being a monopolist is better than being a competitive firm. Like a $10 bill lying on the sidewalk, a monopoly position is "worth something." Just as people will pick up a $10 bill on the sidewalk, they'll try to become monopolists.

This brings up the whole topic of rent seeking, to which Tullock first called our attention. Just as people will bend down to pick up the $10 bill, so will they invest resources in an attempt to capture the monopoly rents. In other words, no opportunity for gain is likely to be ignored.

Economist Gordon Tullock has made the point that rent-seeking behavior is individually rational but socially wasteful. To see why, let's say the profits in Exhibit 7 are equal to $10 million. That is, the area $P_{PC}P_MCD$ is equal to $10 million. Firm A wants the $10 million in profits, so it asks the government for a monopoly favor because it wants the government to prevent 99 firms from competing with it.

Firm A will not get its monopoly privilege simply by asking for it. The firm will have to spend money and time to convince government officials that it should be given this monopoly privilege. It will have to hire lobbyists, take politicians and other government officials to dinner, and perhaps give donations to certain politicians. Firm A will have to spend resources to get what it wants, and all the resources firm A uses to try to bring about a transfer from buyers to itself are wasted, says Tullock. How so? Well, resources used to bring about a transfer can't be used to produce shoes, computers, television sets, and many other things that people would like to buy. The resources are used to try to transfer income from one party to another. They aren't used to produce more goods and services.

Ask yourself what society would look like if no one produced anything but only invested time and money in rent seeking. Jones would try to get what is Smith's, Smith would try to get what is Brown's, and Brown would try to get what is Thompson's. No one would produce anything; everyone would simply spend time and money trying to get what currently belongs to someone else. In this world, who would produce the food, the computers, and the cars? The answer is no one.

Tullock makes the point that the resource cost of rent seeking should be added to the deadweight loss of monopoly. This addition, according to Tullock, makes the overall cost of monopoly to society higher than anyone initially thought.

X-Inefficiency

Economist Harvey Leibenstein maintains that the monopolist is not under pressure to produce its product at the lowest possible cost. The monopolist can produce its product above the lowest possible unit cost and still survive. Certainly, the monopolist benefits if it can and does lower its costs, but the point is that it doesn't have to in order to survive (with the proviso that average total costs cannot rise so high as to be higher than price). Leibenstein refers to a monopolist operating at higher than the lowest possible cost, and to the organizational slack that is directly tied to this, as **X-inefficiency**.

It is hard to obtain accurate estimates of X-inefficiency, but whatever its magnitude, there are forces working to mitigate it. For example, if a market monopoly is being run inefficiently, other people realizing this may attempt to buy the monopoly and, if successful, lower costs to make higher profits.

X-Inefficiency

The increase in costs and organizational slack in a monopoly resulting from the lack of competitive pressure to push costs down to their lowest possible level.

Price Discrimination

Price Discrimination

Occurs when the seller charges different prices for the product it sells and the price differences do not reflect cost differences.

In our discussions about monopoly, we have assumed that the monopoly seller sells all units of its product for the same price (it is a single-price monopolist). However, this is not always the case. Under certain conditions, a monopolist could practice **price discrimination**. This occurs when the seller charges different prices for the product it sells, and the price differences do not reflect cost differences.

Types of Price Discrimination

There are three types of price discrimination: perfect price discrimination, second-degree price discrimination, and third-degree price discrimination.

Suppose a monopolist produces and sells 1,000 units of good X. If it sells each unit separately and charges the highest price each consumer would be willing to pay for the product rather than go without it, the monopolist is said to practice **perfect price discrimination**. This is sometimes called *discrimination among units*.

If it charges a uniform price per unit for one specific quantity, a lower price for an additional quantity, and so on, the monopolist practices **second-degree price discrimination**. This is sometimes called *discrimination among quantities*. For example, the monopolist might sell the first 10 units for $10 each, the next 20 units for $9 each, and so on.

If it charges a different price in different markets or charges a different price to different segments of the buying population, the monopolist practices **third-degree price discrimination**. This is sometimes called *discrimination among buyers*. For example, if your local pharmacy charges senior citizens lower prices for medicine than it charges nonsenior citizens, it practices third-degree price discrimination.

Why a Monopolist Wants to Price Discriminate

Suppose these are the maximum prices at which the following units of a product can be sold: first unit, $10; second unit, $9; third unit, $8; fourth unit, $7. If the monopolist wants to sell 4 units, and it charges the same price for each unit (it is a single-price monopolist), its total revenue is $28 ($7 × 4).

Now suppose the monopolist can and does practice perfect price discrimination. It charges $10 for the first unit, $9 for the second unit, $8 for the third unit, and $7 for the fourth unit. Its total revenue is $34 ($10 + $9 + $8 + $7). A comparison of total revenue when the monopolist does and does not price discriminate explains why the monopolist would want to price discriminate. A perfectly price-discriminating monopolist receives the maximum price for each unit of the good it sells; a single-price monopolist does not.

For the monopolist who practices perfect price discrimination, price equals marginal revenue, $P = MR$. To illustrate, when the monopolist sells its second unit for $9 (having sold the first unit for $10), its total revenue is $19—or its marginal revenue is $9, which is equal to price.

Conditions of Price Discrimination

It is obvious why the monopolist would want to price discriminate. But what conditions must exist before it can? To price discriminate, the following conditions must hold:

1. The seller must exercise some control over price; that is, it must be a price searcher.
2. The seller must be able to distinguish among buyers who would be willing to pay different prices.
3. It must be impossible or too costly for one buyer to resell the good to other buyers. The possibility of **arbitrage**, or "buying low and selling high," must not exist.

If the seller is not a price searcher (if it is a price taker), it has no control over price and therefore cannot sell a good at different prices to different buyers. Also, unless the seller can distinguish among buyers who would pay different prices, it cannot price discriminate. After all, how would it know whom to charge the higher (lower) prices? Finally, if a buyer can resell the good, there can be no price discrimination because buyers who buy the good at a lower price will simply turn around and sell the good to other buyers for a price lower than the seller's higher price. In time, no one will pay the higher price.

Perfect Price Discrimination

Occurs when the seller charges the highest price each consumer would be willing to pay for the product rather than go without it.

Second-Degree Price Discrimination

Occurs when the seller charges a uniform price per unit for one specific quantity, a lower price for an additional quantity, and so on.

Third-Degree Price Discrimination

Occurs when the seller charges different prices in different markets or charges a different price to different segments of the buying population.

Arbitrage

Buying a good at a low price and selling the good for a higher price.

Q&A

When a firm price discriminates, doesn't one consumer end up paying a higher price because some other consumer pays a lower price?

Some people argue that if a firm charges one person $40 for its product and charges another person only $33, the first person is paying a higher price so the second person can pay a lower price. But this is not the case. Suppose there are two persons, O'Neill and Stevens. The maximum price O'Neill will pay for good X is $40; the maximum price Stevens will pay for good X is $33. If a monopolist can and does perfectly price discriminate, it charges O'Neill $40 and charges Stevens $33.

Is O'Neill somehow paying the higher price so that Stevens can pay the lower price? It is easy to see that O'Neill is not by considering whether the monopolist would have charged O'Neill a price under $40 if Stevens's maximum price had been $39 instead of $33. Probably it wouldn't. Why should it when it could have received O'Neill's maximum price of $40?

Our point is that the perfectly price-discriminating monopolist tries to get the highest price *from each customer*, irrespective of what other customers pay. In short, the price O'Neill is charged is independent of the price Stevens is charged.

---

exhibit 8

Comparison of a Perfectly Competitive Firm, Single-Price Monopolist, and Perfectly Price-Discriminating Monopolist

For both the perfectly competitive firm and the perfectly price-discriminating monopolist, $P = MR$ and the demand curve is the marginal revenue curve. Both produce where $P = MC$. The single-price monopolist, however, produces where $P > MC$ because for it, $P > MR$ and its demand curve lies above its marginal revenue curve. One different between the perfectly competitive firm and the perfectly price-discriminating monopolist is that the former charges the same price for each unit of the good it sells and the latter charges a different price for each unit of the good it sells.

Moving to $P = MC$ Through Price Discrimination

We learned in the last chapter that the perfectly competitive firm exhibits resource allocative efficiency; it produces the quantity of output at which $P = MC$. We learned earlier in this chapter that the single-price monopolist produces the quantity of output at which $P > MC$. The single-price monopolist produces an inefficient level of output. But what about the monopolist that can and does practice perfect price discrimination? Does it also produce an inefficient level of output?

The answer is no. A perfectly price-discriminating monopolist does not lower price on all previous units to sell an additional unit of its product. For it, $P = MR$ (as is the case for the perfectly competitive firm). Naturally, when the perfectly price-discriminating monopolist produces the quantity of output at which $MR = MC$, it automatically produces the quantity where $P = MC$. In short, the perfectly price-discriminating monopolist and the perfectly competitive firm both exhibit resource allocative efficiency.

Some important points are reviewed in Exhibit 8. In part (a), the perfectly competitive firm produces where $P = MC$. In part (b), the single-price monopolist produces where $P > MC$. In part (c), the perfectly price-discriminating monopolist produces where

(a)
Perfectly Competitive Firm

(b)
Single-Price Monopolist

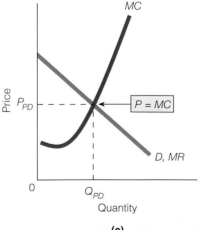

(c)
Perfectly Price-Discriminating Monopolist

economics 24/7

AMAZON AND PRICE DISCRIMINATION[4]

Not too long ago, Amazon, the online retailer charged different customers different prices for DVDs. For example, it charged some customers $74.99 for the movie *Planet of the Apes,* while it charged other customers $64.99 for the same movie. Who was charged the higher price? In this case, Amazon charged the higher price to persons who used Internet Explorer as a browser, and it charged the lower price to persons who used Netscape Navigator as a browser. At other times, Amazon charged different customers different prices depending on whether they were repeat buyers or first-time buyers and depending on what Internet service provider they used.

How does Amazon know which customers are willing to pay a higher price for a DVD and which customers are not? An Amazon spokesperson said that the price differences on certain DVDs were the result of tests that the company performs to reevaluate various aspects of its Web site, such as the navigation system, what the home page looks like, overall site design, and product pricing. Some economists speculated that it had much to do with maximizing profits.

As stated in this chapter, one condition of price discrimination is that sellers must be able to distinguish among buyers who would be willing to pay different prices. For example, book publishers do this through their sales of hardcover and paperback books. Most books are first offered in hardcover, and the people who are least price sensitive buy the hardcover book. Later, the book is released as a paperback. Then the persons who are most price sensitive buy the book in paperback form.

The Internet makes such market segmentation as that used by book publishers seem rather crude. Online sellers often ask for (and receive) market information from their customers. This information can be analyzed and categorized to give the seller some idea of the likelihood of a particular customer paying a higher price for a particular good. For example, customers who live in a certain zip code area or in a particular state (a high-income state as opposed to a low-income state) may be more likely to pay a higher price for a good than customers who live in a different zip code area or state.

[4]This feature is based on "Reckonings: What Price Fairness?" by Paul Krugman, *New York Times,* October 4, 2000.

$P = MC.$ Notice one important difference between the perfectly competitive firm and the perfectly price-discriminating monopolist. Although both produce where $P = MC,$ the perfectly competitive firm charges the same price for each unit of the good it sells, and the perfectly price-discriminating monopolist charges a different price for each unit of the good it sells.

You Can Have the Comics, Just Give Me the Coupons

Third-degree price discrimination, or discrimination among buyers, is sometimes employed through the use of cents-off coupons. (Remember that third-degree price discrimination exists if a seller sells the same product at different prices to different segments of the population.)

One of the conditions of price discrimination is that the seller has to be able to distinguish among customers who would be willing to pay different prices. Would people who value their time highly be

Thinking like AN ECONOMIST

Looks can be deceiving. It certainly looks like the perfectly price-discriminating monopolist charges one customer a higher price because some other customer is paying a lower price. But it is only when we note that the monopolist would want to charge the "highest price to each customer" that we see the error in our thinking. The seller may be selling his goods at a low price to one customer and at a high price to another, but we can be sure he wants to sell at the "highest low price" he can sell at.

economics 24/7

WHY DO DISTRICT ATTORNEYS PLEA-BARGAIN?

On the television series *Law & Order,* the assistant district attorney often offers the accused a chance to plead to a lesser charge in return for providing information about a crime or for agreeing to testify against someone. In short, the assistant district attorneys on *Law & Order* are willing to plea-bargain.

To some people, a district attorney who plea-bargains is similar to a seller who price discriminates. Let's analyze plea bargaining to see whether or not this is true. Suppose two people, Smith and Jones, have committed the same crime. The district attorney has the same type and amount of evidence against each person, and the chance of a successful prosecution is approximately the same for each case. A successful prosecution will end in each person going to prison for 25 years.

Now suppose the district attorney offers Smith a plea bargain. In exchange for Smith's testimony against Brown, who is someone the DA's office has been after for a long time, Smith will be charged with a lesser crime and will have to serve only 5 years in prison. Thus, Smith can pay a smaller price for his crime than Jones must pay. In other words, each person commits the same crime and each has an equal chance of being successfully prosecuted for that crime, but Smith (if he accepts the plea bargain) will serve 5 years in prison and Jones will serve 25 years.

Do district attorneys want to plea-bargain for a reason analogous to why sellers want to price discriminate?[5] A seller wants to price discriminate because it raises her total revenue without affecting her costs. Recall the example in the text: $10 is the highest price at which the first unit of a good can be sold, $9 is the highest price for the second unit, $8 is the highest price for the third unit, and $7 is the highest price for the fourth unit. A single-price monopolist that wants to sell 4 units of the good charges a price of $7 per unit and earns total revenue of $28. But a perfectly price-discriminating monopolist charges the highest price per unit and gains total revenue of $34. In other words, price discrimination leads to higher total revenue.

District attorneys do not want to maximize total revenue, but they may want to maximize the number of successfully prosecuted crimes given certain budget constraints. Just as price discrimination leads to higher total revenue, plea bargaining may lead to more successfully prosecuted crimes. Let's consider Smith and Jones again. Each has committed the same crime. Without a plea bargain, each person goes to prison for 25 years. But if the DA offers Smith 5 years, and in return, Smith helps the DA send Brown to prison, then because of the plea bargain, three crimes are successfully prosecuted—the crimes committed by Smith, Jones, and Brown.

Finally, just as certain conditions have to be met before a seller can price discriminate, certain conditions have to be satisfied before district attorneys can plea-bargain successfully.

To price discriminate, a seller must exercise some control over the price of the product she sells. To plea-bargain, a district attorney has to exercise some control over the sentence for the accused. In reality, district attorneys do exercise some control over sentences because they largely control the charges against the accused. If they reduce the charges (say, from murder to manslaughter), they automatically affect the sentence.

A seller who price discriminates has to be able to distinguish among customers who would be willing to pay different prices for the good she sells. Similarly, a district attorney has to be able to distinguish between accused persons who do and do not have something to "sell" to the authorities. District attorneys seem to be able to do this. In many cases, the accused person who has something to "sell" will say so.

Finally, for price discrimination to exist, arbitrage has to be impossible or too costly. Obviously, it is impossible to resell a plea bargain.

---

[5]Be careful here. We are not saying that a plea bargain is an act of price discrimination, broadly defined. We are saying that there are similarities between why sellers want to price discriminate and why district attorneys want to plea-bargain. Later in the feature, we explain that, just as certain conditions need to be met to price discriminate, certain conditions need to be met for district attorneys to offer plea bargains—and there seems to be a rough similarity between the two sets of conditions.

willing to pay a higher price for a product than people who do not? Some sellers think so. They argue that people who place a high value on their time want to economize on the shopping time connected with the purchase of the product. If sellers want to price discriminate between these two types of customers—charging more to customers who value time more and charging less to customers who value time less—they must determine the category into which each of their customers falls.

How would you go about this if you were a seller? What many real-world sellers do is place cents-off coupons in newspapers and magazines. They hypothesize that people who place a relatively low value on their time are willing to spend it clipping and sorting coupons. People who place a relatively high value on their time are not.

In effect, things work much like the following in, say, a grocery store:

1. The posted price for all products is the same for all customers.

2. Both Linda and Josh put product X in their shopping carts.

3. When Linda gets to the checkout counter, the clerk asks, "Do you have any coupons today?" Linda says no. She is therefore charged the posted price for all products, including X.

4. When Josh gets to the checkout counter, the clerk asks, "Do you have any coupons today?" Josh says yes and gives the clerk a coupon for product X. Josh pays a lower price for product X than Linda pays.

Thus, one of the uses of the cents-off coupon is to make it possible for the seller to charge a higher price to one group of customers than to another group. (We say one of the uses because cents-off coupons are also used to induce customers to try a product.)

micro Theme

In an earlier chapter, we mentioned that microeconomics is about objectives, constraints, and choices. We have talked about three types of firms so far. In the last chapter, we discussed a perfectly competitive firm. In this chapter, we discussed both the single-price and perfectly price-discriminating monopolist.

All three firms have the same objective: to maximize profit. All three firms face constraints, although not always the same constraints. For example, the single-price monopolist is constrained to selling its good for the same price to each customer, whereas the price-discriminating monopolist is not.

Finally, all three firms make choices such as choosing what quantity of output to produce, what price to charge, and so on.

SELF-TEST

1. What are some of the "costs," or shortcomings, of monopoly?

2. What is the deadweight loss of monopoly?

3. Why must a seller be a price searcher (among other things) before he can price discriminate?

A Reader Asks...

Do Colleges and Universities Price Discriminate?

At the university I attend, scholarships are given to students with low incomes, excellent grades, or athletic ability. Are these scholarships a form of price discrimination?

Let's ask this question: Do scholarships to these types of students (low income, high academic ability, high athletic ability) satisfy the definition of price discrimination? The low-income student might not come to the university unless he or she receives a lower tuition price (than other students pay). The university price discriminates because the scholarship, in effect, reduces the tuition the low-income student has to pay. The excellent student and the athlete have numerous universities competing for them. In other words, both have a high elasticity of demand for education at a given university because they have so many substitutes (other universities) from which to choose. Consequently, a university will have to offer them a lower tuition price to secure them as students. The university price discriminates through an academic scholarship

for the excellent student and an athletic scholarship for the athlete.

Now, let's consider whether or not the university meets the conditions of a price discriminator. First, it is a price searcher. Not all universities are alike, nor do they sell a homogeneous good as they would in the case of perfect competition (price taker).

Second, the university can distinguish among students (customers) who would be willing to pay different prices. For example, the student with few universities seeking him would probably be willing to pay more than the student with many options.

Third, the service being purchased cannot be resold to someone else. For example, it is difficult to resell an economics lecture. You could, of course, tell someone what was covered in the lecture, perhaps for a small payment or a promise to do the same for you at a later time, but this would be similar to telling someone about a movie instead of the person seeing the movie herself. It is often difficult or impossible to resell something that is consumed on the premises.

! analyzing the scene

Is the car salesman simply making small talk by asking Jackson what he does for a living?

One of the conditions for price discrimination is that the seller "must be able to distinguish among buyers who would be willing to pay different prices." "Willingness to pay" is, of course, not the same as "ability to pay," but that might not prevent the car salesmen from thinking that the two are strongly correlated. Why does the salesman ask Jackson a question that relates to his income? The salesman may simply be trying to get some idea of what Jackson can afford to pay. What he thinks Jackson can afford to pay may influence future price negotiations between Jackson and the salesman.

All this is reminiscent of an old episode of *The Cosby Show* on television. Dr. Huxtable (played by Bill Cosby) was

thinking of buying a new car. He went to the new car showroom with a friend. Dr. Huxtable made sure to "dress down" because he didn't want the car salesman to think he earned a high income. Dr. Huxtable is standing there negotiating the price with the salesman when all of a sudden his friend, who is on the other side of the showroom, yells out to him, "Dr. Huxtable . . ." Cosby grimaces as he now knows the cat is out of the bag.

Why does the musical artist want to price her CD lower than the BT Productions executive wants to price it?

The BT Productions executive wants to maximize the company's profit, which is the difference between the company's total revenue and its total cost. The musical artist receives a percentage of total revenue, not a percentage of profit, so she wants to maximize total revenue. She wants the total revenue to be as large as possible because a 10 percent royalty rate of, say, $10 million is larger than a 10 percent royalty rate of $7 million. The price that will maximize profit is not the same as the price that will maximize total revenue, and so the company executive and musical artist have different opinions on the best price to charge for the CD.

Let's look at Exhibit 9, which shows a demand curve and a marginal revenue curve for the CD. Note that there are two marginal cost curves. The one for the music company is positive and (we have assumed) constant. The other marginal cost curve is for the musical artist and is zero at all levels of output because we assume the artist does not have any costs of actually producing and selling the CD (this is the music company's job). In all, the exhibit shows one demand curve, one marginal revenue curve, and two marginal cost curves. (Most artists receive a fixed percentage of total receipts from the sale of their CDs, so the music company's demand and marginal revenue curves are relevant for the artist.) The artist wants to sell the quantity of CDs at which marginal revenue equals her marginal cost. This is at Q_A. The highest price per CD at which this quantity of CDs can be sold is P_A. This is the artist's best price. Because the artist is paid a fixed percentage of total sales revenues, she wants to maximize revenues. This occurs where $MR = 0$. (How so? If the artist has maximized total revenue, this means there is no *additional revenue* to be obtained. In other words, marginal revenue is zero.)

Assuming the music company wants to maximize profits, it will want to sell that quantity of CDs at which marginal revenue equals its marginal cost. This is at Q_{BT}. The highest price per CD at which this quantity of CDs can be sold is

P_{BT}. Notice that P_{BT} is higher than P_A—the best price for the music company is higher than the best price for the artist.

Did Carl Wilson think his one-of-a-kind restaurant bestowed monopoly status on him—and therefore, he just couldn't fail?

A firm can be the single seller of a good for which there are no close substitutes—that is, it can be a monopoly—and still fail. Monopoly is no guarantee of success. Success—that is, earning a profit—means that the firm sells its good for a price that is greater than its average total cost (*ATC*). The highest price a firm can charge is determined by the demand curve it faces. If demand is low, the price it can charge is likely to be low, *ceteris paribus*. In fact, the price may be so low that the firm's *ATC* is higher. Obviously, the demand for restaurants that offer mud wrestling while you eat is fairly low.

The Music Company and the Musical Artist Opt for Different Prices

The artist faces zero costs of producing and selling the CD; BT Productions, the music company, faces positive (and we assume) constant marginal costs. Both the artist and the music company may want to equate marginal revenue and marginal cost, but they do not have the same marginal cost. The artist wants Q_A CDs produced and sold at a price of P_A; the music company wants Q_{BT} CDs produced and sold at a price of P_{BT}.

chapter summary

The Theory of Monopoly

- The theory of monopoly is built on three assumptions: (1) There is one seller. (2) The single seller sells a product for which there are no close substitutes. (3) There are extremely high barriers to entry into the industry.

- High barriers to entry may take the form of legal barriers (public franchise, patent, government license), economies of scale, or exclusive ownership of a scarce resource.

Monopoly Pricing and Output

- The profit-maximizing monopolist produces the quantity of output at which $MR = MC$ and charges the highest price per unit at which this quantity of output can be sold.

- For the single-price monopolist, $P > MR$; therefore, its demand curve lies above its marginal revenue curve.

- The single-price monopolist sells its output at a price higher than its marginal cost, $P > MC$, and therefore is *not* resource allocative efficient.

- Consider a perfectly competitive market and a monopoly market, each with the same demand and marginal cost curves. Consumers' surplus is greater in the perfectly competitive market.

Rent Seeking

- Activity directed at competing for and obtaining transfers is referred to as rent seeking. From society's perspective, rent seeking is a socially wasteful activity. People use resources to bring about a transfer of income from others to themselves instead of producing goods and services.

Price Discrimination

- Price discrimination occurs when a seller charges different prices for its product and the price differences are not due to cost differences.

- Before a seller can price discriminate, certain conditions must hold: (1) The seller must be a price searcher. (2) The seller must be able to distinguish among customers who would be willing to pay different prices. (3) It must be impossible or too costly for a buyer to resell the good to others.

- A seller that practices perfect price discrimination (charges the maximum price for each unit of product sold) sells the quantity of output at which $P = MC$. It exhibits resource allocative efficiency.

- The single-price monopolist is said to produce too little output because it produces less than would be produced under perfect competition. This is not the case for a perfectly price-discriminating monopolist.

key terms and concepts

Monopoly

Public Franchise

Natural Monopoly

Price Searcher

Deadweight Loss of Monopoly

Rent Seeking

X-Inefficiency

Price Discrimination

Perfect Price Discrimination

Second-Degree Price Discrimination

Third-Degree Price Discrimination

Arbitrage

questions and problems

1   The perfectly competitive firm exhibits resource allocative efficiency ($P = MC$), but the single-price monopolist does not. What is the reason for this difference?

2   Because the monopolist is a single seller of a product with no close substitutes, is it able to obtain any price for its good that it wants? Why or why not?

3   When a single-price monopolist maximizes profits, price is greater than marginal cost. This means that buyers would be willing to pay more for additional units of output than the units cost to produce. Given this, why doesn't the monopolist produce more?

4   Is there a deadweight loss if a firm produces the quantity of output at which price equals marginal cost? Explain.

5   It has been noted that rent seeking is individually rational but socially wasteful. Explain.

6   Occasionally, students accuse their instructors, rightly or wrongly, of practicing grade discrimination. These students claim that the instructor "charges" some students a higher price for a given grade than he or she "charges" other students (by requiring some students to do more or better work). Unlike price discrimination, grade discrimination involves no money. Discuss the similarities and differences between the two types of discrimination. Which do you prefer less or perhaps dislike more? Why?

7   Make a list of real-world price discrimination practices. Do they meet the conditions posited for price discrimination?

8   For many years in California, car washes would advertise "Ladies' Day." On one day during the week, a woman could have her car washed for a price lower than a man could have his car washed. Some people argued that this was a form of sexual discrimination. A California court accepted the argument and ruled that car washes could no longer have a Ladies' Day. Do you think this was a case of sexual discrimination or price discrimination? Explain your answer.

9   Make a list of market monopolies and a list of government monopolies. Which list is longer? Why do you think this is so?

10 Fast-food stores often charge higher prices for their products in high-crime areas than they charge in low-crime areas. Is this an act of price discrimination? Why or why not?

11 In general, coupons are more common on small-ticket items than they are on big-ticket items. Explain why.

12 A firm maximizes its total revenue. Does it follow that it has automatically maximized its profit too? Why or why not?

working with numbers and graphs

1   Draw a graph that shows a monopoly firm incurring losses.

2   A monopoly firm is currently earning positive economic profit. The owner of the firm decides to sell it. He asks for a price that takes into account the economic profit. Explain and diagrammatically show what this does to the average total cost (ATC) curve of the firm.

3   Suppose a single-price monopolist sells its output (Q_1) at P_1. Then it raises its price to P_2 and its output falls to Q_2. In terms of Ps and Qs, what does marginal revenue equal?

Use the following figure to answer Questions 4–6.

4   If the market is perfectly competitive, what does profit equal?

5   If the market is a monopoly market, what does profit equal?

6   Redraw the figure and label consumers' surplus when the market is perfectly competitive and when it is monopolized.

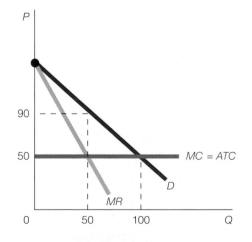

Monopolistic Competition, Oligopoly, and Game Theory

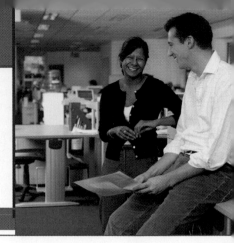

Setting the Scene

Carl and Amanda, two professors at a nearby college, were discussing grades one day recently.

AMANDA:

The grading distribution is becoming increasingly skewed toward the top end—toward the A end of the spectrum. At Harvard in 1966, 22 percent of all grades were As, but in 2002, the percentage of As was about 46 percent. It's the same at other colleges and universities, including right here where we teach.

CARL:

I know. I'm fairly sure that I give out more high grades today than I did years ago when I first started teaching. Students who receive a B from me today would have received a C or lower 15 years ago.

AMANDA:

What do you think explains the changes in the grading distribution? Could students be getting smarter or professors getting better at teaching?

CARL:

It's somewhat hard for me to believe that the average student at Harvard in 1966 wasn't as smart, or as hardworking, as the average student at Harvard in 2002. Or that somehow Harvard professors in 1966 were less talented instructors than Harvard professors in 2002. I think it must be grade inflation. It appears to me that professors are giving higher grades today for

work that in the past would have earned a lower grade. In other words, C work in 1966 now becomes B+ or A− work.

AMANDA:

I think I agree with you. But how can we get away from the current distribution? If I do away with grade inflation in my class and you and others do not, then I just place my students at a disadvantage relative to your students.

CARL:

I know. In a way, we seem to be trapped.

? Here is a question to keep in mind as you read this chapter:

• *If Carl and Amanda both want to end grade inflation, why don't they just do it?*

See analyzing the scene at the end of this chapter for an answer to this question.

The Theory of Monopolistic Competition

The theory of **monopolistic competition** is built on three assumptions:

1. **There are many sellers and buyers.** This assumption holds for perfect competition too. For this reason, you might think the monopolistic competitor should be a price taker, but this is not the case. It is a price searcher, basically because of the next assumption.

2. **Each firm (in the industry) produces and sells a slightly differentiated product.** Differences among the products may be due to brand names, packaging, location, credit terms connected with the sale of the product, friendliness of the salespeople, and so forth. Product differentiation may be real or imagined. For example, aspirin may be aspirin, but if some people view a name-brand aspirin (such as Bayer) as better than a generic brand, product differentiation exists.

3. **There is easy entry and exit.** Monopolistic competition resembles perfect competition in this respect. There are no barriers to entry and exit, legal or otherwise.

Examples of monopolistic competition include retail clothing, computer software, restaurants, and service stations.

Monopolistic Competition
A theory of market structure based on three assumptions: many sellers and buyers, firms producing and selling slightly differentiated products, and easy entry and exit.

The Monopolistic Competitor's Demand Curve

The perfectly competitive firm has many rivals, all producing the same good, and so there are an endless number of substitutes for the good it produces. The elasticity of demand for its product is extremely high—so high, in fact, that the demand curve it faces is horizontal (for all practical purposes).

The monopoly firm has practically no rivals, and it produces a good for which there are no substitutes. The elasticity of demand for its product is low, and its downward-sloping demand curve reflects this fact.

What is the situation for the monopolistic competitor? Like the perfectly competitive firm, it has many rivals. But unlike the perfectly competitive firm, its rivals don't sell exactly the same product the monopolistic competitor sells. There are substitutes for its product, but not perfect substitutes. Because of this, the elasticity of demand for its product is not as great as that of the perfectly competitive firm. Nor does its demand curve look like the demand curve faced by the perfectly competitive firm. The monopolistic competitor's demand curve is not horizontal; it is downward sloping.

Q&A *It seems that one way to differentiate between firms in different market structures is in terms of the number and quality of substitutes each faces. Is this correct?*

Yes. As we have just said, the perfectly competitive firm has a lot of perfect substitutes for the good it sells; the monopoly firm has no good substitutes for the good it sells; and the monopolistic competitive firm has substitutes for the good it sells, but not perfect substitutes.

The Relationship Between Price and Marginal Revenue for a Monopolistic Competitor

Because a monopolistic competitor faces a downward-sloping demand curve, it has to lower price to sell an additional unit of the good it produces. (It is a price searcher.) For example, let's say that it can sell 3 units at $10 each but that it has to lower its price to $9 to sell 4 units. It follows that its marginal revenue is $6 (total revenue at 3 units is $30 and total revenue at 4 units is $36), which is below its price of $9. Thus, for the monopolistic competitor $P > MR$.

Output, Price, and Marginal Cost for the Monopolistic Competitor

The monopolistic competitive firm is the same as both the perfectly competitive firm and the monopoly firm in one regard. It produces the quantity of output at which

$MR = MC$. We see this in Exhibit 1, where the firm produces q_1. What price does the monopolistic competitor charge for this quantity? Answer: The highest price it can charge. This is P_1 in the exhibit.

For the monopolistic competitor, $P > MR$. Because the monopolistic competitor produces the quantity of output at which $MR = MC$, it follows that it must produce a level of output at which price is greater than marginal cost, $P > MC$. This is obvious in Exhibit 1.

Will There Be Profits in the Long Run?

Suppose the firms in a monopolistic competitive market are currently earning profits, such as the firm in Exhibit 1. Will they continue to earn profits in the long run? Most likely, they won't. The assumption of easy entry and exit precludes this. If firms in the industry are earning profits, new firms will enter the industry and reduce the demand that each firm faces. In other words, the demand curve for each firm may shift to the left. Eventually, competition will reduce economic profits to zero in the long run, as shown for the monopolistic competitive firm in Exhibit 2.

Notice that the answer to the question of whether firms will continue to earn profits in the long run was, "Most likely, they won't" instead of, "no." In monopolistic competition, new firms usually produce a *close substitute* for the product produced by existing firms rather than the *identical* product produced in perfect competition. Is this enough of a difference to upset the zero economic profit condition in the long run? In some instances, it may be. An existing firm may differentiate its product sufficiently in the minds of buyers such that it continues to earn profits, even though new firms enter the industry and compete with it.

Firms that try to differentiate their products from those of other sellers in ways other than price are said to be engaged in *nonprice competition*. This may take the form of advertising or of trying to establish a well-respected brand name, among other things. For example, soft drink companies' advertising often tries to stress the uniqueness of their product. In the past, Dr. Pepper has been advertised as "the unusual one," 7-Up as "the uncola." Apple has a well-respected name in personal computers, Bayer in aspirin,

---

exhibit 1

The Monopolistic Competitive Firm's Output and Price

The monopolistic competitor produces that quantity of output for which $MR = MC$. This is q_1 in the exhibit. It charges the highest price consistent with this quantity, which is P_1.

At q_1, $P > MC$

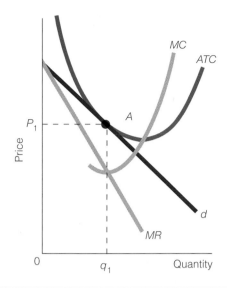

exhibit **2**

Monopolistic Competition in the Long Run

Because of easy entry into the industry, there are likely to be zero economic profits in the long run for a monopolistic competitor. In other words, $P = ATC$.

Marriott in hotels. Such well-respected names sometimes sufficiently differentiate products in the minds of buyers so that short-run profits are not easily, or completely, eliminated by the entry of new firms into the industry.

> **micro Theme**
>
> We have studied various firms over the past three chapters. We have learned, so far, that a firm either faces (1) a horizontal demand curve or (2) a downward-sloping demand curve. Another way of putting this is to say that a firm is either (1) a price taker or a (2) price searcher. If it faces a horizontal demand curve (which means it can only sell its good at the market-equilibrium price), then it is a price taker. If it faces a downward-sloping demand curve (which means it can sell some of its good at different prices, albeit less at higher prices), then it is a price searcher. In other words, the firms you encounter in the real world are either price takers or price searchers.

Excess Capacity: What Is It, and Is It "Good" or "Bad"?

The theory of monopolistic competition makes one major prediction, which is generally referred to as the **excess capacity theorem**. The theorem states that in equilibrium, a monopolistic competitor will produce an output smaller than the one that would minimize its unit costs of production.

To illustrate, look at point A in Exhibit 3(a). At this point, the monopolistic competitor is in long-run equilibrium because profits are zero ($P = ATC$). Notice that point A *is not* the lowest point on the average total cost curve. The lowest point on the ATC curve is point L. We conclude that in long-run equilibrium, when the monopolistic competitor earns zero economic profits, it is not producing the quantity of output at which average total costs (unit costs) are minimized for the given scale of plant. Exhibit 3 contrasts the perfectly competitive firm and the monopolistic competitor in long-run equilibrium. In part (b), the perfectly competitive firm is earning zero economic profits, and price (P_{C1}) equals average total cost (ATC). Furthermore, the point at which price equals average total cost (point L) is the lowest point on the ATC curve. In long-run equilibrium, the perfectly competitive firm produces the quantity of output at which unit costs are minimized.

Excess Capacity Theorem

States that a monopolistic competitor in equilibrium produces an output smaller than the one that would minimize its costs of production.

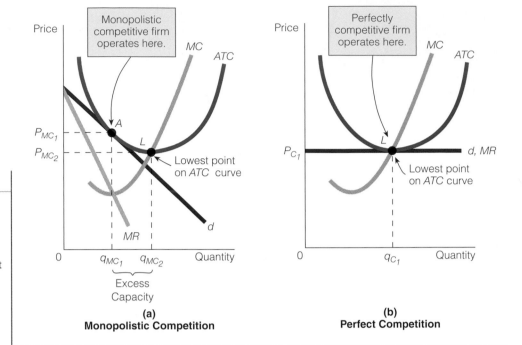

exhibit 3

A Comparison of Perfect Competition and Monopolistic Competition: The Issue of Excess Capacity

The perfectly competitive firm produces a quantity of output consistent with lowest unit costs. The monopolistic competitor does not. If it did, it would produce instead q_{MC2} of q_{MC1}. The monopolistic competitor is said to underutilize its plant size or to have excess capacity.

Now look back at part (a). The monopolistic competitor is earning zero economic profits, and price (P_{MC1}) equals average total cost. As previously noted, the monopolistic competitor does not produce the quantity of output at which unit costs are minimized. If it did, it would produce q_{MC2}. For this reason, it has been argued that the monopolistic competitor produces "too little" output (q_{MC1} instead of q_{MC2}) and charges "too high" a price (P_{MC1} instead of P_{MC2}). With respect to the former, "too little" output translates into the monopolistic competitor underutilizing its present plant size. It is said to have *excess capacity*. In part (a), the excess capacity is equal to the difference between q_{MC2} and q_{MC1}.

It is sometimes argued that the monopolistic competitor operates at excess capacity because it faces a downward-sloping demand curve. Look once again at Exhibit 3(a). The only way the firm would not operate at excess capacity is if its demand curve were tangent to the *ATC* curve at point *L*—the lowest point on the *ATC* curve. But for this to occur, the demand curve *would have to be horizontal*, which would require homogeneous products. It is impossible for a downward-sloping demand curve to be tangent to the *ATC* curve at point *L*.

In short, *the monopolistic competitor operates at excess capacity as a consequence of its downward-sloping demand curve,* and its downward-sloping demand curve is a consequence of differentiated products. We leave you with a question many economists ask but do not always answer the same way: *If excess capacity is the price we pay for differentiated products (more choice), is it too high a price?*

micro Theme

One way economists differentiate one firm from another is in terms of the outcomes that flow from its choices. For example, we saw (in an earlier chapter) that a perfectly competitive firm is both resource allocative efficient (which means it produces the quantity of output at which $P = MC$) and productive efficient (which means it produces the quantity of output at which *ATC* is minimized). In contrast, the monopolistic competitive firm is neither resource allocative efficient nor productive efficient, as we discuss next.

The Monopolistic Competitor and Two Types of Efficiency

An earlier chapter explains that a firm is resource allocative efficient if it charges a price that is equal to marginal cost, $P = MC$. Because the monopolistic competitive firm charges a price that is greater than marginal cost ($P > MC$), it is not resource allocative efficient.

An earlier chapter also explains that a firm is productive efficient if it charges a price that is equal to its lowest ATC. Because the monopolistic competitor operates at excess capacity, it is not productive efficient.

Advertising and Designer Labels

Suppose you own a business that is considered a monopolistic competitive firm. Your business is one of many sellers, you sell a product slightly differentiated from the products of your competitors, and there is easy entry into and exit from the industry. Would you rather your business were a monopoly firm instead? Wouldn't it be better for you to be the only seller of a product than to be one of many sellers? Most business owners would say that it is better to be a monopoly firm than a monopolistic competitive firm. This being the case, we consider how monopolistic competitors may try to become monopolists.

One possibility is through advertising. If a monopolistic competitor can, through advertising, persuade the buying public that her product is *more than just slightly differentiated* from those of her competitors, she stands a better chance of becoming a monopolist. (Remember, a monopolist produces a good for which there are no close substitutes.)

Consider an example. Many firms produce men's and women's jeans. To many people, the jeans produced by these firms look very much alike. How, then, does any one firm differentiate its product from the pack? It could add a "designer label" to the jeans to suggest that the jeans are unique—that they are the only Levi's jeans, for example. Or through advertising, it could try to persuade the buying public that its jeans are "the" jeans worn by the most famous, best-looking people living and vacationing in the most exciting places in the world.

We are not concerned here with whether or not the advertising is successful in meeting its objective. Our point is that firms sometimes use advertising to try to differentiate their products from their competitors' products.

Q&A

*One thing seems odd to me. Both the perfectly competitive firm and the monopolistic competitive firm produce the quantity of output at which **MR = MC**. And both charge the highest price (per unit) they can charge. In other words, they make the same choices with respect to "how much to produce" and "what price to charge." But even though they make the same choices, the outcomes of their choices are different. The perfectly competitive firm is resource allocative efficient and productive efficient, whereas the monopolistic competitive firm is neither. How can you make the same choices and get different outcomes?*

The different outcomes are a result of the perfectly competitive firm facing a horizontal demand curve and the monopolistic competitive firm facing a downward-sloping demand curve. The demand curve difference (between the two firms) is enough of a difference to make the same choices result in different outcomes.

SELF-TEST

(Answers to Self-Test questions are in the Self-Test Appendix.)

1. How is a monopolistic competitor like a monopolist? How is it like a perfect competitor?

2. Why do monopolistic competitors operate at excess capacity?

Oligopoly: Assumptions and Real-World Behavior

Unlike perfect competition, monopoly, and monopolistic competition, there is no one theory of **oligopoly**. However, the different theories of oligopoly do have the following common assumptions:

Oligopoly
A theory of market structure based on three assumptions: few sellers and many buyers, firms producing either homogeneous or differentiated products, and significant barriers to entry.

1. **There are few sellers and many buyers.** It is usually assumed that the few firms of an oligopoly are interdependent; each one is aware that its actions influence the other firms and that the actions of the other firms affect it. This interdependence among firms is a key characteristic of oligopoly.

2. **Firms produce and sell either homogeneous or differentiated products.** Aluminum is a homogeneous product produced in an oligopolistic market; cars are a differentiated product produced in an oligopolistic market.

3. **There are significant barriers to entry.** Economies of scale are perhaps the most significant barrier to entry in oligopoly theory, but patent rights, exclusive control of an essential resource, and legal barriers also act as barriers to entry.

The oligopolist is a price searcher. Like all other firms, it produces the quantity of output at which $MR = MC$.

Which industries today are dominated by a small number of firms; that is, which industries are oligopolistic? Economists have developed the *concentration ratio* to help

Concentration Ratio

The percentage of industry sales (or assets, output, labor force, or some other factor) accounted for by *x* number of firms in the industry.

answer this question. The **concentration ratio** is the percentage of industry sales (or assets, output, labor force, or some other factor) accounted for by *x* number of firms in the industry. The "*x* number" in the definition is usually four or eight, but it can be any number (although it is usually small).

Four-Firm Concentration Ratio: CR_4 = Percentage of industry sales accounted for by four largest firms

Eight-Firm Concentration Ratio: CR_8 = Percentage of industry sales accounted for by eight largest firms

A high concentration ratio implies that few sellers make up the industry; a low concentration ratio implies that more than a few sellers make up the industry.

Suppose we calculate a four-firm concentration ratio for industry Z. Total industry sales for a given year are $5 million, and the four largest firms in the industry account for $4.5 million in sales. The four-firm concentration ratio would be 0.90, or 90 percent ($4.5 million is 0.90 of $5 million). Industries with high four- and eight-firm concentration ratios in recent years include cigarettes, cars, tires, cereal breakfast foods, farm machinery, and soap and other detergents, to name a few.

Although concentration ratios are often used to determine the extent (or degree) of oligopoly, they are not perfect guides to industry concentration. Most important, they do not take into account foreign competition and competition from substitute domestic goods. For example, the U.S. automobile industry is concentrated, but it still faces stiff competition from abroad. A more relevant concentration ratio for this particular industry might be one computed on a worldwide basis.

Price and Output Under Three Oligopoly Theories

There is not just one theory of oligopoly; there are many. We present three in this section: the cartel theory, the kinked demand curve theory, and the price leadership theory.

The Cartel Theory

Cartel Theory

In this theory of oligopoly, oligopolistic firms act as if there were only one firm in the industry.

Cartel

An organization of firms that reduces output and increases price in an effort to increase joint profits.

The key behavioral assumption of the **cartel theory** is that oligopolists in an industry act as if there were only one firm in the industry. In short, they form a cartel to capture the benefits that would exist for a monopolist. A **cartel** is an organization of firms that reduces output and increases price in an effort to increase joint profits.

Let's consider the benefits that may arise from forming and maintaining a cartel. Exhibit 4 shows an industry in long-run competitive equilibrium. Price is P_1 and quantity of output is Q_1. The industry is producing the output at which price equals marginal cost, and there are zero economic profits. Now suppose the firms that make up the industry form a cartel and reduce output to Q_C. The new price is P_C (cartel price), and there are profits equal to the area $CP_C AB$, which can be shared among the members of the cartel. With no cartel, there are no profits; with a cartel, profits are earned. Thus, the firms have an incentive to form a cartel and to behave cooperatively rather than competitively.

However, firms may not be able to form a cartel, even though they have a profit incentive to do so. Also, even if they are able to form the cartel, the firms may not be able to maintain it successfully. Firms that wish to form and maintain a cartel will encounter several problems, in addition to the fact that legislation prohibits certain types of cartels in the United States. Organizing and forming a cartel involves costs as well as benefits.[1]

THE PROBLEM OF FORMING THE CARTEL Even if it were legal, getting the sellers of an industry together to form a cartel can be costly, even when the number of sellers is small. Each potential cartel member may resist incurring the costs of forming the cartel because it stands to benefit more if another firm does the work. In other words, each potential member has an incentive to be a free rider—that is, to stand by and take a free ride on the actions of others.

THE PROBLEM OF FORMULATING CARTEL POLICY Suppose the first problem is solved, and potential cartel members form a cartel. Now comes the problem of formulating policy. For example, firm A might propose that each cartel member reduce output by 10 percent, while firm B advocates that all bigger cartel members reduce output by 15 percent and all smaller members reduce output by 5 percent. There may be as many policy proposals as there are cartel members. Reaching agreement may be difficult. Such disagreements are harder to resolve the greater the differences among cartel members in costs, size, and so forth.

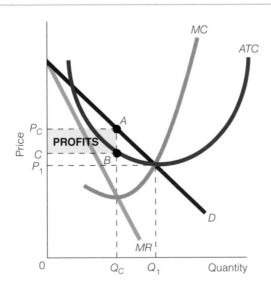

exhibit **4**

The Benefits of a Cartel (to Cartel Members)

We assume the industry is in long-run competitive equilibrium, producing Q_1 and charging P_1. There are no profits. A reduction in output to Q_C through the formation of a cartel raises prices to P_C and brings profits of $CP_C AB$. (Note: In an earlier chapter, a horizontal demand curve faces the *firm*. Here a downward-sloping demand curve faces the *industry*. Don't be misled by this difference. No matter what type of demand curve we use, long-run competitive equilibrium is where $P = MC = SRATC = LRATC$.)

---

[1]Sometimes, economists discuss the benefits and costs of organizing a cartel without specifying the market structure. We have followed suit here by broadening our discussion of cartel theory to include market structures other than oligopoly. This will be noticeable in places. For example, even though there are few sellers in oligopoly, we discuss cartel theory in the context of both few and many sellers.

economics 24/7

HOW IS A NEW YEAR'S RESOLUTION LIKE A CARTEL AGREEMENT?

In a cartel, one firm makes an agreement with another firm or firms. In a New Year's resolution, you essentially make an agreement with yourself. So both cases—the cartel and the resolution—involve an agreement.

Both cases also raise the possibility of cheating on the agreement. Suppose your New Year's resolution is to exercise more, take better notes in class, and read one "good" book a month. You might set such objectives for yourself because you know you will be better off in the long run if you do these things. But then, the short run interjects itself into the picture. You have to decide between exercising today or plopping down in your favorite chair and watching some television. You have to decide between starting to read *Moby Dick* or catching up on the latest entertainment news in *People* magazine. The part of you that wants to hold to the resolution is at odds with the part of you that wants to watch television or read *People*. Often, the television-watching, *People*-reading part wins out. It is just too easy to break a New Year's resolution—as you probably already know.

Similarly, it is easy to break a cartel agreement. For the firm that has entered into the agreement, the lure of higher

profits is often too strong to resist. In addition, the firm is concerned that if it doesn't break the agreement (and cheat), some other firm might, and then it will have lost out completely.

In short, both resolutions and cartel agreements take a lot of willpower to hold them together. And willpower, it seems, is in particularly short supply.

What, if anything, can take the place of willpower? What do both a resolution and a cartel agreement need to sustain long life? The answer is something or someone who will exact some penalty from the party that breaks the resolution or cartel agreement. Government sometimes plays this role for firms. Family members and friends occasionally play this role for individuals by reminding or reprimanding them if they fail to live up to their resolutions. (Usually, though, family members and friends are not successful.)

We conclude the following: First, an agreement is at the heart of both a New Year's resolution and a cartel. Second, both the resolution and the cartel are subject to cheating behavior. Third, if the resolution and the cartel are to sustain long life, they often need someone or something to prevent each party from breaking the agreement.

THE PROBLEM OF ENTRY INTO THE INDUSTRY Even if the cartel members manage to agree on a policy that generates high profits, those high profits will provide an incentive for firms outside the industry to join the industry. If current cartel members cannot keep new suppliers from entering, the cartel is likely to break up.

THE PROBLEM OF CHEATING As paradoxical as it first appears, after the cartel agreement is made, cartel members have an incentive to cheat on the agreement. Consider Exhibit 5, which shows a *representative firm* of the cartel. We compare three situations for this firm: (1) the situation before the cartel is formed; (2) the situation after the cartel is formed when all members adhere to the cartel price; and (3) the situation if the firm cheats on the cartel agreement, but the other cartel members do not.

Before the cartel is formed, the firm is in long-run competitive equilibrium; it produces output q_1 and charges price P_1. It earns zero economic profits. Next, it reduces its output to q_C as directed by the cartel (the cartel has set a quota for each member), and it charges the cartel price of P_C. Now the firm earns profits equal to the area $CP_C AB$.

What happens if the firm cheats on the cartel agreement and produces q_{CC} instead of the stipulated q_C? As long as other firms do not cheat, this firm views its demand curve as horizontal at the cartel price (P_C). The reason is simple: It is one of a number of

Quantity firm produces when it adheres to cartel agreement; profits = CP_CAB

Quantity firm produces when there is no cartel agreement; profits = 0

Quantity firm produces when it cheats on the cartel agreement, but other firms do not; profits = FP_CDE

exhibit 5

The Benefits of Cheating on the Cartel Agreement

The situation for a representative firm of a cartel: in long-run competitive equilibrium, it produces q_1 and charges P_1, earning zero economic profits. As a consequence of the cartel agreement, it reduces output to q_C and charges P_C. Its profits are the area CP_CAB. If it cheats on the cartel agreement and others do not, the firm will increase output to q_{CC} and reap profits of FP_CDE. Note, however, that if this firm can cheat on the cartel agreement, so can others. Given the monetary benefits gained by cheating, it is likely that the cartel will exist for only a short time.

firms, so it cannot affect price by changing output. Therefore, it can produce and sell additional units of output without lowering price. We conclude that if the firm cheats on the cartel agreement and other firms do not, then the cheating firm can increase its profits from the smaller amount CP_CAB to the larger amount FP_CDE. Of course, if all firms cheat, the cartel members are back where they started—with no cartel agreement and at price P_1.

This analysis illustrates a major theme of cartels: Firms have an incentive to form a cartel, but once it is formed, they have an incentive to cheat. As a result, some economists have concluded that even if cartels are formed successfully, it is unlikely that they will be effective for long.

The Kinked Demand Curve Theory

The behavioral assumption in the **kinked demand curve theory** is that if a single firm lowers price, other firms will do likewise, but if a single firm raises price, other firms will not follow suit. Suppose there are five firms in an industry, A, B, C, D, and E. If firm A raises its price, the other firms maintain their prices. If firm A cuts its price, the other firms match the price cut.

The kinked demand curve theory was developed in the 1930s by Paul Sweezy. We explain the theory using the example in Exhibit 6. The current price charged by the firm is $25. If the firm raises its price to $27, other firms will not match it, and therefore, the firm's sales will drop (from 20 to 10). In short, the demand curve for the firm above $25 is highly elastic. However, if the firm lowers its price to, say, $23, other firms will match the price cut, and therefore, the firm's sales will not increase by much (only from 20 to 22). Demand is much less elastic below $25 than above it. We conclude that

Thinking like **AN ECONOMIST**

In economics, there are moving targets. Consider the target of higher profits for the firms in an oligopolistic industry. After the firms form a cartel to capture the higher profits, the target of higher profits moves—to where a cartel member must cheat on the cartel to "hit" it. But if all cartel members take aim at the target's new position, the target moves back to its original position—to where cartel members must agree to stop cheating.

The layperson may think that an economic objective, or economic target, is stationary. All that an economic actor has to do to hit it is take careful aim. But the economist knows that sometimes the target moves, and careful aim is not always enough.

Kinked Demand Curve Theory

A theory of oligopoly that assumes that if a single firm in the industry cuts prices, other firms will do likewise, but if it raises price, other firms will not follow suit. The theory predicts price stickiness or rigidity.

there is a kink in the firm's demand curve at the current price (point *K* in Exhibit 6). The kink signifies that other firms respond radically differently to a single firm's price hikes than to its price cuts.

Actually, there are two demand curves and two marginal revenue curves in the kinked demand curve theory, as shown in the window in Exhibit 6. Only the thicker portions of the curves in the window are relevant, however, and thus appear in the main diagram. To illustrate, starting at a price of $25, the firm believes price cuts will be matched but price hikes will not. So when considering a price cut, the firm believes it faces the more inelastic of the two demand curves, d_2, and the corresponding marginal revenue curve, MR_2. But when considering a price hike, the firm believes it faces the more elastic of the two demand curves, d_1, and the corresponding marginal revenue curve, MR_1. It follows that the firm's demand curve includes part of d_1 and part of d_2; the firm's marginal revenue curve includes part of MR_1 and part of MR_2. This occurs because the theory assumes the market reacts one way to a price cut and a different way to a price hike.

PRICE RIGIDITY Look at the marginal revenue curve for the oligopolist in the main diagram of Exhibit 6. Directly below the kink, it drops sharply. In fact, the marginal revenue curve can be viewed as three segments: a line from point *A* to point *B*, which corresponds to the upper part of the demand curve; a gap between points *B* and *C* directly below the kink in the demand curve; and a line from point *C* onward, which corresponds to the lower part of the demand curve (from point *K* onward).

The gap between points *B* and *C* represents the sharp change in marginal revenue that occurs when price is lowered below the kink on the demand curve. The gap helps explain why prices might be less flexible (more rigid) in oligopoly than in other market structures.

Recall that the oligopolistic firm produces the output at which $MR = MC$. For the firm in Exhibit 6, though, marginal cost (*MC*) can change between points *B* and *C*, and the firm will continue to produce the same quantity of output and charge the same price. For example, an increase in marginal cost from MC_1 to MC_2 will not lead to a change in production levels or price.

To put it differently, prices are "sticky" if oligopolistic firms face kinked demand curves. Costs can change within certain limits, and such firms will not change their prices because they expect that none of their competitors will follow their price hikes, but all will match their price cuts.

exhibit 6

Kinked Demand Curve Theory

The key behavioral assumption of the theory is that rival firms will not match a price hike but will match a price cut. The theory predicts that changes in marginal costs between *B* and *C* will not cause changes in price or output. The window in the exhibit shows two demand curves and two marginal revenue curves. The firm believes it faces d_2, the more inelastic demand curve, if it cuts price; the firm believes it faces d_1, the more elastic demand curve, when it raises price. The relevant portions of each demand curve are indicated by heavy lines. Only the relevant parts of the demand and marginal revenue curves are shown in the main diagram.

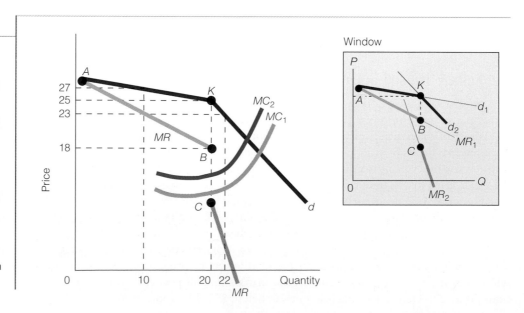

All firms have to make choices—how much to produce, how much to charge, and so on. When the perfectly competitive firm makes such choices, it does not strategize. It doesn't say: I will do *W* if my competitors do *X*, but I will do *Y* if my competitors do *Z*. However, when it comes to oligopoly, there is strategizing. For example, one oligopolistic firm in a given market might lower price if other oligopolistic firms in the market lower price, but it won't raise price if other firms raise price. In other words, in an oligopolistic market (compared with a perfectly competitive market), one firm's behavior depends to a greater degree on the behavior of other firms.

CRITICISMS OF THE KINKED DEMAND CURVE THEORY The kinked demand curve (and resulting *MR* curve) posits that prices in oligopoly will be less flexible (or more rigid) than in other market structures. The theory has been criticized on both theoretical and empirical grounds.

On a theoretical level, looking at Exhibit 6, the theory fails to explain how the original price of $25 came about. In other words, why does the kink come at $25? The theory is better at explaining things after the kink (the current price) has been identified than in explaining the placement of the kink. On empirical grounds, the theory has been challenged as a general theory of oligopoly. For example, economist George Stigler found no evidence that the oligopolists he examined were more reluctant to match price increases than price cuts, which calls into question the behavioral assumption behind the kinked demand curve theory.

The Price Leadership Theory

The key behavioral assumption in the **price leadership theory** is that one firm in the industry—called the dominant firm—determines price, and all other firms take this price as given. Suppose there are 10 firms in an industry, *A–J*, and that firm *A* is the dominant firm; also suppose firm *A* is much larger than its rival firms. (The dominant firm need not be the largest firm in the industry; it could be the low-cost firm.) The dominant firm sets the price that maximizes its profits, and all other firms take this price as given. All other firms, then, are seen as price takers; thus, they will equate price with their respective marginal costs.

This explanation suggests that the dominant firm acts without regard to the other firms in the industry and simply forces the other firms to adapt. This is not quite correct. The dominant firm sets the price based on information it has about the other firms in the industry, as shown in Exhibit 7.

Part (a) shows the market demand curve and the horizontal sum of the marginal cost curves of the fringe firms (all firms other than the dominant firm). Because these fringe firms are price takers, the marginal cost curve in (a) is their supply curve. The dominant firm observes that at a price of P_1, the fringe firms alone can supply the entire market. They will supply Q_1. In short, P_1 and Q_1 define the situation in the industry or market that excludes the dominant firm.

Now add the dominant firm. It derives its demand curve, D_{DN}, by noting how much is left for it to supply at each given price. For example, at a price of P_1, the fringe firms would supply the entire market, and nothing would be left for the dominant firm to supply. So a price of P_1 and an output of zero is one point on the dominant firm's demand curve, as shown in part (b). (Sometimes, the dominant firm's demand curve is

Price Leadership Theory

In this theory of oligopoly, the dominant firm in the industry determines price, and all other firms take their price as given.

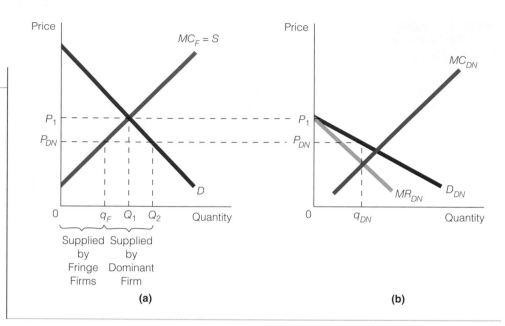

exhibit **7**

Price Leadership Theory

There is one dominant firm and a number of fringe firms. (a) The horizontal sum of the marginal cost curves of the fringe firms is their supply curve. At P_1, the fringe firms supply the entire market. (b) The dominant firm derives its demand curve by computing the difference between market demand, D, and MC_F at each price below P_1. It then produces q_{DN} (where $MR_{DN} = MC_{DN}$) and charges P_{DN}. P_{DN} becomes the price that the fringe firms take. They equate price and marginal cost and produce q_F in (a). The remainder of the output—the difference between Q_2 and q_F—is produced by the dominant firm.

referred to as the *residual demand curve* for obvious reasons.) The dominant firm continues to locate other points on its demand curve by noting the difference between the market demand curve (D) and MC_F at each price below P_1.

After the dominant firm calculates its residual demand curve, it produces the quantity of output at which its marginal revenue equals its marginal cost. This level is q_{DN} in Exhibit 7(b). It charges the highest price for this quantity of output, which is P_{DN}. This is the price that the dominant firm sets and the fringe firms take. Because they act as price takers, the fringe firms equate P_{DN} with marginal cost and produce q_F, as shown in part (a). The remainder of the total output produced by the industry—the difference between Q_2 and q_F—is produced by the dominant firm. This means that the distance from the origin to q_{DN} in (b) is equal to the difference between Q_2 and q_F in (a).

At one time or another, the following firms have been price leaders in their industries: R. J. Reynolds (cigarettes), General Motors (autos), Kellogg's (breakfast cereals), and Goodyear Tire and Rubber (tires).

SELF-TEST

1.   The text states, "Firms have an incentive to form a cartel, but once it is formed, they have an incentive to cheat." What, specifically, is the incentive to form the cartel, and what is the incentive to cheat on the cartel?

2.   What explains the kink in the kinked demand curve theory of oligopoly?

3.   According to the price leadership theory of oligopoly, how does the dominant firm determine what price to charge?

Game Theory, Oligopoly, and Contestable Markets

Of the four market structures (perfect competition, monopoly, monopolistic competition, and oligopoly), oligopoly is often described as the most difficult to analyze. Analysis is difficult because of the interdependence among firms in an oligopolistic market. Economists often use game theory to get a workable understanding of this interdependence of oligopoly firms. **Game theory** is a mathematical technique used to analyze the behavior of decision makers who (1) try to reach an optimal position through game playing or the use of strategic behavior, (2) are fully aware of the interactive nature of the process at hand, and (3) anticipate the moves of other decision makers.

In this section, we describe a famous game in game theory and then use it to discuss oligopoly behavior. We also discuss the issue of contestable markets.

Prisoner's Dilemma

A well-known game in game theory, called *prisoner's dilemma*, illustrates a case where individually rational behavior leads to a jointly inefficient outcome. It has been described this way: "You do what is best for you, I'll do what is best for me, and somehow we end up in a situation that is not best for either of us." The mechanics of the prisoner's dilemma game are explained in this section.

THE FACTS Two men, Bob and Nathan, are arrested and charged with jointly committing a crime. They are put in separate cells so that they cannot communicate with each other. The district attorney goes to each man separately and says the following:

- If you confess to the crime and agree to turn state's evidence and your accomplice does not confess, I will let you off with a $500 fine.
- If your accomplice confesses to the crime and agrees to turn state's evidence and you do not confess, I will fine you $5,000.
- If both you and your accomplice remain silent and refuse to confess to the crime, I will charge you with a lesser crime, which I can prove you committed, and both you and your accomplice will pay fines of $2,000.
- If both you and your accomplice confess, I will fine each of you $3,000.

THE OPTIONS AND CONSEQUENCES Each man has two choices: confess or not confess. These choices are shown in the grid in Exhibit 8. According to the possibilities laid out by the district attorney, if both men do not confess, each pays a fine of $2,000. This is shown in box 1 in the exhibit.

If Nathan confesses and Bob does not, then Nathan gets off with the light fine of $500 and Bob pays the stiff penalty of $5,000. This is shown in box 2.

If Nathan does not confess and Bob confesses, then Nathan pays the stiff penalty of $5,000 and Bob pays the light fine of $500. This is shown in box 3.

Finally, if both men confess, each pays $3,000. This is shown in box 4.

Game Theory

A mathematical technique used to analyze the behavior of decision makers who try to reach an optimal position for themselves through game playing or the use of strategic behavior, are fully aware of the interactive nature of the process at hand, and anticipate the moves of other decision makers.

Nathan's Choices

	Not Confess	Confess
Not Confess	**1** Nathan pays $2,000. Bob pays $2,000.	**2** Nathan pays $500. Bob pays $5,000.
Confess	**3** Nathan pays $5,000. Bob pays $500.	**4** Nathan pays $3,000. Bob pays $3,000.

Bob's Choices

exhibit **8**

Prisoner's Dilemma

Nathan and Bob each have two choices: confess or not confess. No matter what Bob does, it is always better for Nathan to confess. No matter what Nathan does, it is always better for Bob to confess. Both Nathan and Bob confess and end up in box 4 where each pays a $3,000 fine. Both men would have been better off had they not confessed. That way they would have ended up in box 1 paying a $2,000 fine.

WHAT NATHAN THINKS Nathan considers his choices and their possible outcomes. He reasons to himself, "I have two options, confess or not confess, and Bob has the same two options. Let me ask myself two questions:

- *"If Bob chooses not to confess, what is the best thing for me to do?* The answer is confess because if I do not confess, I will end up in box 1 paying $2,000, but if I confess I will end up in box 2 paying only $500. No doubt about it, if Bob chooses not to confess, I should confess.

- *"If Bob chooses to confess, what is the best thing for me to do?* The answer is confess because if I do not confess, I will end up in box 3 paying $5,000, but if I confess I will pay $3,000. No doubt about it, if Bob chooses to confess, I should confess."

NATHAN'S CONCLUSION Nathan concludes that no matter what Bob chooses to do, not confess or confess, he is always better off if he confesses. Nathan decides to confess to the crime.

THE SITUATION IS THE SAME FOR BOB Bob goes through the same mental process that Nathan does. Asking himself the same two questions Nathan asked himself, Bob gets the same answers and draws the same conclusion. Bob decides to confess to the crime.

THE OUTCOME The DA goes to each man and asks what he has decided. Nathan says, "I confess." Bob says, "I confess." The outcome is shown in box 4 with each man paying a fine of $3,000.

LOOK WHERE THEY COULD BE Is there an outcome, represented by one of the four boxes, that is better for both Nathan and Bob than the outcome where each pays $3,000? Yes, there is; it is box 1. In box 1, both Nathan and Bob pay $2,000. To get to box 1, all the two men had to do was keep silent and not confess.

CHANGING THE GAME What would happen if the DA gave Nathan and Bob another chance? Suppose she tells them that she will not accept their confessions. Instead, she wants them to talk it over together for 10 minutes, after which time she will come back, place each man in a separate room, and ask for his decision. The second time, she will accept each man's decision, no matter what.

Will this change the outcome? Most people will say yes, arguing that Nathan and Bob will now see that their better choice is to remain silent so that each ends up with a $2,000 fine instead of a $3,000 fine. Let's assume this happens, and Nathan and Bob enter into an agreement to remain silent.

NATHAN'S THOUGHTS ON THE WAY TO HIS ROOM The DA returns and takes Nathan to a separate room. On the way, Nathan thinks to himself, "I'm not sure I can trust Bob. Suppose he goes back on our agreement and confesses. If I hold to the agreement and he doesn't, he'll end up with a $500 fine and I'll end up paying $5,000. Of course, if I break the agreement and confess and he holds to the agreement, then I'll reduce my fine to $500. Maybe the best thing for me to do is break the agreement and confess, hoping that he doesn't and I'll pay only $500. If I'm not so lucky, at least I'll protect myself from paying $5,000."

Once in the room, the DA asks Nathan what his decision is. He says, "I confess."

THE SITUATION IS THE SAME FOR BOB Bob sees the situation the same way Nathan does and again chooses to confess.

THE OUTCOME AGAIN Both men end up confessing a second time. Each pays $3,000, realizing that if they had been silent and kept to their agreement, their fine would be only $2,000 each.

Oligopoly Firms' Cartels and the Prisoner's Dilemma

Think back to our discussion of the cartel theory of oligopoly. Were the oligopoly firms that entered into a cartel agreement in a prisoner's dilemma? Most economists answer yes. To illustrate, suppose there are two firms, *A* and *B*, that produce and sell the same product and are in stiff competition with each other. Currently, the competition between them is so stiff that each earns only $10,000 profits. Soon, the two firms decide to enter into a cartel agreement in which each agrees to raise prices and, after prices are raised, not to undercut the other. If they hold to the agreement, each firm will earn profits of $50,000. But if one firm holds to the cartel agreement and the other does not, the one that does not will earn profits of $100,000 and the one that does will earn $5,000 profits. Of course, if neither holds to the agreement, then both will be back where they started—earning $10,000 profits. The choices for the two firms and the possible outcomes are outlined in Exhibit 9.

Each firm is likely to behave the way the two prisoners did in our prisoner's dilemma. Each firm will see the chance to earn $100,000 by breaking the agreement (instead of $50,000 by holding to it); each will also realize that if it does not break the agreement and the other firm does, it will be in a worse situation than when it was in stiff competition with the other firm. Most economists predict that the two firms will end up in box 4 in Exhibit 9, earning the profits they did before they entered into the agreement. In summary, they will cheat on the cartel agreement and again be in competition—the very situation they wanted to escape.

Is there any way out of the prisoner's dilemma for the two firms? The only way out is to have some entity actually enforce the cartel agreement so that the two firms do not cheat. As odd as it may sound, sometimes government has played this role. We say this "sounds odd" because normally we think of government as trying to break up cartel agreements. After all, cartel agreements are illegal. Nevertheless, sometimes government acts as the enforcer, and not the eliminator, of the cartel agreement.

Consider the Civil Aeronautics Board (CAB) in the days of airline regulation. The CAB was created to protect the airlines from "cutthroat competition." It had the power to set airfares, allocate air routes, and prevent the entry of new carriers into the airline industry. In the days before deregulation, the federal government's General Accounting Office estimated that airline fares would have been, on average, as much as 52 percent

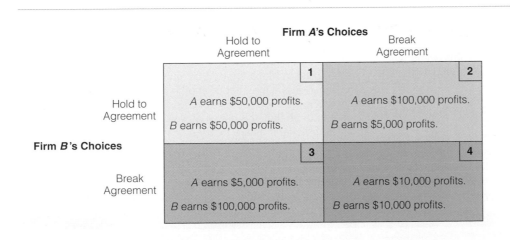

exhibit **9**

Cartels and Prisoner's Dilemma

Many economists suggest that firms trying to form a cartel are in a prisoner's dilemma situation. Both firms *A* and *B* earn higher profits holding to a (cartel) agreement than not, but each will earn even higher profits if it breaks the agreement while the other firm holds to it. If cartel formation is a prisoner's dilemma situation, we predict that cartels will be short-lived.

economics 24/7

AN ECONOMIC THEORY OF THE MAFIA

The U.S. government prohibits its residents from engaging in certain activities. With only a few exceptions, it forbids residents from being either buyers or sellers of illegal drugs, prostitution services, or gambling services. Because government is willing to punish anyone who goes against its prohibitions, there is a high barrier to entering the illegal drug, prostitution, and gambling markets.

Of course, not everyone has abided by the government's prohibitions; there are both buyers and sellers of illegal goods and services in spite of the high barrier. One of the historically biggest sellers in these markets is the Mafia. (The term Mafia has been adopted internationally to refer to an organized crime unit that sells illegal goods and services and is willing to use extreme force [violence] to protect what it perceives as its business interests.) In reality, numerous Mafia firms (sometimes referred to as families) benefit from the high barrier to entry established by the government. Each Mafia firm faces a higher demand curve than it would if there were no legal barriers to entry. Consequently, prices and profits are higher for the few Mafia firms that supply the market.[2]

The question each Mafia firm has to ask itself is: Could its profits be even higher without the other Mafia firms? In economic terms, the question becomes: Are there benefits from moving from being one of a few oligopoly firms to being the sole monopoly firm? Or stated differently, are there benefits from facing the entire market demand curve instead of only some fraction of it?

There are benefits, of course, but there are also costs in trying to obtain the benefits. How can a Mafia firm obtain the benefits of a monopoly? It can try to put other Mafia firms out of business by offering higher quality goods and services, lower prices, better credit terms, better delivery, and so on. Or it can try to eliminate (literally, kill) the members of the other Mafia firms. What will be the costs of using these methods?

If any one Mafia firm tries to kill its competitors, then the other Mafia firms will likely band together against it. To understand why, consider five Mafia firms, *A–E*. Firm *A* tries to eliminate firm *B* by killing the members of the firm. Firms *C–E* know that if firm *A* is successful, it will probably try to eliminate them next. They will then band together with firm

B to try to eliminate firm *A*. In short, each firm will soon realize that trying to kill its competition is not likely to be a successful strategy.

Now consider the option of trying to outcompete rivals by offering lower prices, higher quality, and so on. Will the Mafia firms proceed this way? Perhaps not. They may recognize that stiff competition among them may simply reduce their profits.

The Mafia firms may choose a third option: They may agree to form a cartel. Often in the past, Mafia cartel agreements have taken the form of dividing up the market. Each Mafia firm gets a certain geographic area in which it can exclusively supply all illegal goods and services.

But economists know that cartel agreements are notoriously unstable because there are often huge benefits from breaking the cartel agreement when others do not. Once the Mafia firms form a cartel agreement, each firm is in a prisoner's dilemma. In the end, the firms soon learn that cheating behavior puts everyone in a worse position. How then do Mafia firms make sure that each cooperates and holds to the cartel agreement? Who or what will enforce the Mafia cartel agreements?

Economist Robert Axelrod reports that the only strategy that seemingly solves the (repeated) prisoner's dilemma game and gets participants to cooperate with each other instead of cheating on each other is tit for tat. The tit-for-tat strategy is simple: You give to others what you get from them. When individuals know that they will get what they give, they will want to give (to others) what they want to receive from them. And what they want is cooperation—that is, holding to the cartel agreement. They want to make sure they are in box 1 of the prisoner's dilemma payoff matrix, not box 4 (see Exhibit 8).

Applied to Mafia firms, tit for tat works this way: If one Mafia family kills a member of another family, then the second family must kill someone in the first family. The message has to be that you get whatever you give. There is evidence that Mafia firms are rather efficient practitioners of tit for tat.

---

[2]We assume throughout our discussion that each Mafia firm faces constant marginal cost and therefore constant unit cost.

lower if the CAB had not been regulating them. Clearly, the CAB was doing for the airlines what an airline cartel would have done—prevent price competition, allocate routes, and prevent new entries into the industry.

In a similar vein, Judge Richard Posner has observed that "the railroads supported the enactment of the first Interstate Commerce Act, which was designed to prevent railroads from price discrimination, because discrimination was undermining the railroad's cartels."[3]

Are Markets Contestable?

The discussion of market structures, from perfect competition to oligopoly, has focused on the *number of sellers* in each market structure. In perfect competition, there are many sellers; in monopoly, there is one; in monopolistic competition, there are many; in oligopoly, there are few. The message is that the number of sellers in a market influences the behavior of the sellers within the market. For example, the monopoly seller is more likely to restrict output and charge higher prices than is the perfect competitor.

Some economists have shifted the emphasis from the number of sellers in a market to the issue of *entry into and exit from an industry.* This focus is a result of the work of William Baumol and other economists who have put forth the idea of contestable markets.

A **contestable market** is one in which the following conditions are met:

1. **There is easy entry into the market and costless exit from the market.**

2. **New firms entering the market can produce the product at the same cost as current firms.**

3. **Firms exiting the market can easily dispose of their fixed assets by selling them elsewhere** (less depreciation; thus, fixed costs are not sunk but recoverable).

To illustrate, suppose there are currently eight firms in an industry, all of which are earning profits. Firms outside the industry notice this and decide to enter the industry (nothing prevents entry). They acquire the necessary equipment and produce the product at the same cost as current producers do. Time passes, and the firms that entered the industry decide to exit it. They can either switch their machinery into another line of production or sell their equipment for what they paid for it, less depreciation.

Perhaps the most important element of a contestable market is "hit-and-run" entry and exit. New entrants can enter—hit—produce the product and take profits from current firms and then exit costlessly—run.

The theory of contestable markets has been criticized because of its assumptions— in particular, the assumption that there is extremely free entry into and costless exit from the industry. However, although this theory, like most theories, does not perfectly describe the real world, this does not of itself destroy the theory's usefulness.

At a minimum, contestable markets theory has rattled orthodox market structure theory. Here are a few of its conclusions:

1. Even if an industry is composed of a small number of firms, or simply one firm, this is not evidence that the firms perform in a noncompetitive way. They might be extremely competitive if the market they are in is contestable.

2. Profits can be zero in an industry even if the number of sellers in the industry is small.

3. If a market is contestable, inefficient producers cannot survive. Cost inefficiencies invite lower cost producers into the market, driving price down to minimum *ATC* and forcing inefficient firms to change their ways or exit the industry.

Contestable Market
A market in which entry is easy and exit is costless, new firms can produce the product at the same cost as current firms, and exiting firms can easily dispose of their fixed assets by selling them.

---

[3]Richard A. Posner, "Theories of Regulation," *Bell Journal of Economics and Management Science* 5 (Autumn): 337.

4. If, as conclusion 3 suggests, a contestable market encourages firms to produce at their lowest possible average total cost and charge $P = ATC$, it follows that they will also sell at a price equal to marginal cost. (Recall that the marginal cost curve intersects the average total cost curve at its minimum point.)

The theory of contestable markets has also led to a shift in policy perspectives. To some (but certainly not all) economists, the theory suggests a new way to encourage firms to act as perfect competitors. Rather than direct interference in the behavioral patterns of firms, efforts should perhaps be directed at lowering entry and exit costs.

A Review of Market Structures

With the discussion of oligopoly, examination of the four different market structures—perfect competition, monopoly, monopolistic competition, and oligopoly—comes to an end. Exhibit 10 reviews some of the characteristics and consequences of the different market structures.

The first four columns of the exhibit simply summarize the characteristics of the different market structures. The last column notes the long-run market tendency of price and average total cost in the different market structures. The relationship between price and ATC indicates whether long-run profits are possible. Note that three of the four market structures (monopoly, monopolistic competition, and oligopoly) have superscript letters beside the possible profits. These letters refer to notes that describe alternative market tendencies given different conditions. For example, the market tendency in oligopoly is $P > ATC$ and for profits to exist in the long run. The reason is that there are significant barriers to entry in oligopoly, so short-run profits cannot be reduced by competition from new firms entering the industry. However, the market tendency of price and average total cost may be different if the particular oligopolistic market is contestable.

Applications of Game Theory

Game theory, especially prisoner's dilemma, is applicable in a number of real-world situations. In this section, we discuss a few of these applications.

Grades and Partying

Your economics professor announces in class one day that on the next test, she will give the top 10 percent of the students in the class As, the next 15 percent Bs, and so on. You realize it takes less time studying to get, say, a 60 than a 90 on the test, so you hope everyone studies only a little. That way, you can study only a little and earn a high letter grade. But of course, everyone in the class is thinking the same thing.

exhibit **10**

Characteristics and Consequences
of Market Structures

Market Structure	Number of Sellers	Type of Product	Barriers to Entry	Long-Run Market Tendency of Price and *ATC*
Perfect competition	Many	Homogeneous	No	$P = ATC$ (zero economic profits)
Monopoly	One	Unique	Yes	$P > ATC$ (positive economic profits)[a, c]
Monopolistic competition	Many	Slightly differentiated	No	$P = ATC$ (zero economic profits)[b]
Oligopoly	Few	Homogeneous or differentiated	Yes	$P > ATC$ (positive economic profits)[a, c]

a. It is possible for positive profits to turn to zero profits through the capitalization of profits or rent-seeking activities.
b. It is possible for the firm to earn positive profits in the long run if it can differentiate its product sufficiently in the minds of the buying public.
c. It is possible for positive profits to turn to zero profits if the market is contestable.

Envision yourself entering into an agreement with your fellow students. You say the following to them one day:

There are 30 students in our class. Each of us can choose to study either 2 hours or 4 hours for the test. Our relative standing in the class will be the same whether we all study for 2 hours or all study for 4 hours. So why don't we all agree to study for only 2 hours. That way, we have 2 extra hours to do other things. I'd rather receive my B by studying only 2 hours instead of by having to study 4 hours.

Suppose everyone agrees with the logic of the argument and agrees to study only 2 hours. Of course, once everyone has agreed to this, there is an incentive to cheat on the agreement and study more. If everyone else in your class agrees to study 2 hours and you study 4 hours, you increase your relative standing in the class. You go from, say, a B to an A.

You and the other students in your class are in a prisoner's dilemma. Look at Exhibit 11, which shows the payoffs for you and for Jill, a representative other student. If both you and Jill study 4 hours, each receives an 85, which is a B (box 4). With your professor's new relative grading plan, if you study 2 hours and Jill studies 2 hours, the grade for each of you falls to 65, but now 65 is a B (box 1). In other words, comparing box 4 with box 1, box 1 is better because you receive the same letter grade (B) in both cases but spend less time studying.

Of course, once you and Jill agree to lower your study time from 4 hours to 2 hours, each of you has an incentive to cheat on the agreement. If you study 4 hours and Jill studies 2 hours, then you raise your grade to an 85, which is now an A, while Jill's grade is 65, which now becomes a C (box 2). Of course, if Jill studies 4 hours and you study 2 hours, then Jill raises her grade to an 85, which is now an A, while your grade is 65, which is now a C (box 3).

No matter what you think Jill is going to do, the best thing for you to do is study 4 hours.[4] The same holds for Jill with respect to whatever you choose to do. The outcome then is box 4, where both of you study 4 hours.

Ideally, what you need (and Jill needs too) is a way to enforce your agreement not to study more than 2 hours. How might students do this? One way is to party. That's right—party. If you can get all the students in your class together and party, you can be fairly sure that no one is studying too much.

Think about this: Students in the same class understand that (1) some professors set aside some percentage of As for the top students in the class (no matter how low the top

exhibit 11

Studying and Grades

Suppose your letter grade in class depends on how well you do relative to others. In this setting, you and the other students are in a prisoner's dilemma, which is shown here. If both you and Jill (a representative other student) each study 4 hours, each of you earns a point grade of 85, which is a B (box 4). If each of study 2 hours, each of you earn a point grade of 65, which is a B (box 1). Box 1 is preferred over box 4 because you get the same letter grade in each box, but you study less in box 1 than in box 4.

If you study 4 hours while Jill studies 2 hours, your point grade rises to 85 and Jill's point grade remains at 65. In this case, 85 is an A and 65 is a C (box 2). You are better off and Jill is worse off.

If you study 2 hours while Jill studies 4 hours, Jill's point grade rises to 85 and your point grade remains at 65. Jill earns a letter grade of A, and you earn a letter grade of C.

No matter what Jill decides to do—study 2 or 4 hours—it is always better for you to study 4 hours (assuming the costs of studying additional hours are less than the benefits of studying additional hours). The same holds for Jill. Our outcome, then, is box 4, where both you and Jill study 4 hours.

	Study 2 Hours	**You**	Study 4 Hours
Jill Study 2 Hours	You: 65, B Jill: 65, B	1	2 You: 85, A Jill: 65, C
Study 4 Hours	You: 65, C Jill: 85, A	3	4 You: 85, B Jill: 85, B

---

[4]We are assuming that the cost of studying 2 additional hours is lower than the benefits you receive by raising your grade one letter.

is) and (2) they are in a prisoner's dilemma. They realize it would be better for them to cooperate and study less than to compete and study more. Instead of actually entering into an agreement to study less (sign on the dotted line), they "think up" ways to keep the studying time down. One way to keep the studying time down—one way to enforce the implicit and unspoken agreement not to study too much—is to do things with others that do not entail studying. One "institution" that satisfies all requirements is partying—everyone is together not studying.

The Arms Race

During much of the Cold War, the United States and the Soviet Union engaged in an arms race. Both countries were producing armaments that were directed at the other. Occasionally, representatives of the two countries would meet and try to slow down the arms race. The United States would agree to cut armaments production if the Soviet Union did, and vice versa. Many arms analysts generally agreed that the arms agreements between the United States and the Soviet Union were unsuccessful. In other words, representatives of the two countries would meet and enter into an agreement not to compete so heavily in arms production. But then, the countries would end up competing on arms production.

Were the two countries in a prisoner's dilemma? Look at Exhibit 12. When both the United States and the Soviet Union were competing on arms production, they were in box 4, each receiving a utility level of 7. Their collective objective was to move from box 4 to box 1, where each cooperated with the other and reduced its armaments production. In box 1, each country received a utility level of 10. The arms agreements that the United States and the Soviet Union entered into were an attempt to get to box 1.

Of course, after the agreement was signed, each country had an incentive to cheat on the agreement. Certainly, the United States would be better off if it increased its armaments production while the Soviet Union cut back its production. Then, the United States could establish clear military superiority over the Soviet Union. The same held for the Soviet Union with respect to the United States.

Looking at the payoff matrix in Exhibit 12, it is easy to see that the best strategy for the United States was to compete; the same holds for the Soviet Union. And so the two countries ended up in box 4, racing to outproduce the other in arms.

Speed Limit Laws

Envision a world with no law against speeding. In this world, you and everyone else speeds. With everyone speeding, a good number of accidents occur each day, some of which may involve you. In time, everyone decides that something has to be done

exhibit **12**

An Arms Race

In the days of the Cold War, the United States and the Soviet Union were said to be in an arms race. Actually, the arms race was a result of the two countries being in a prisoner's dilemma. Start with each country racing to produce more military goods than the other country; that is, each country is in box 4. In their attempt to move to box 1, they enter into an arms agreement (to reduce the rate at which they produce arms). But no matter what the Soviet Union does (hold to the arms agreement or break it), it is always better for the United States o break the agreement. The same holds for the Soviet Union with respect to the United States. The two countries end up in box 4. (Note: In the exhibit, the higher the number, the better the position for the country.)

	United States	
	Hold to Arms Agreement	Break Arms Agreement
Soviet Union Hold to Arms Agreement	**1** United States, 10 Soviet Union, 10	**2** United States, 15 Soviet Union, 5
Break Arms Agreement	**3** United States, 5 Soviet Union, 15	**4** United States, 7 Soviet Union, 7

about the speeding. It is just too dangerous, everyone admits, to let the speeding continue.

Someone offers a proposal: "Let's agree that we will post signs on the road that state the maximum speed. Furthermore, let's agree here and now that we will all obey the speed limits." The proposal sounds like a good one, and so everyone agrees to follow it.

Of course, as we know by now, once the agreement not to speed is made, we have a prisoner's dilemma. Each person will be better off if he (and he alone) speeds while everyone else obeys the speed limit. In the beginning, everyone agrees to the speed limit; in the end, however, everyone breaks it.

What is missing, of course, is an effective enforcement mechanism. To move the speeders out of the classic prisoner's dilemma box (box 4 in our earlier examples) to box 1, someone or something has to punish people who do not cooperate with others. A law against speeding—backed up by the police and court system—solves the prisoner's dilemma. The law, the police, and the court system change the payoff for cheating on the agreement.

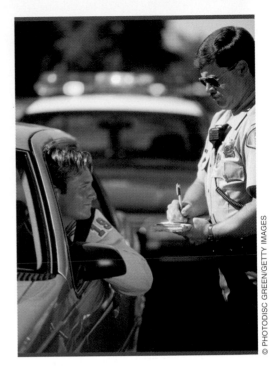

© PHOTODISC GREEN/GETTY IMAGES

The Fear of Guilt as an Enforcement Mechanism

Might there be a social purpose for guilt? Might there be a good reason for feeling guilty? With these two questions in mind, consider the following. John and Mary decide to get married. As part of their wedding vows, they promise to remain faithful to each other. In other words, each promises the other that he or she will not cheat.

Of course, once an agreement is made between two parties, often each party will be better off if one party cheats and the other does not. In the case of John and Mary, John may think, "I can gain utility by cheating on Mary." Of course, Mary can think the same thing with respect to John. Their utility payoffs are shown in Exhibit 13.

Notice in part (a) that both Mary and John receive a utility level of 15 when one cheats but the other does not. Possibly, if each person felt some guilt over cheating on his or her partner, the utility level would be something lower than 15. In some sense, both Mary and John might prefer to feel guilty when cheating. After all, both would prefer to be in box 1, where neither is cheating, than in box 4, where both are cheating. In short, given that box 1 is better than box 4 for both Mary and John, we would expect that both would opt for some enforcement mechanism that prevented them from moving away from box 1. Think back to the speeding example. Don't the speeders actually want a law against speeding that is enforced by the police and courts?

Of course, there is no outside enforcement mechanism for John and Mary. But an internal sense of guilt over cheating might be a good substitute for an external enforcement mechanism. Instead of the police and the court system putting John and Mary in prison for cheating, each one's sense of guilt will put him or her in a personal jail. (Isn't this what someone is implying by saying, "There is no way I can do that; I would feel too guilty." In other words, many people want to prevent themselves from suffering the pangs of guilt in much the same way they don't want to suffer the pain of prison. Both guilt pangs and prison are *bads*. Both come with disutility.)

Suppose, as shown in Exhibit 13(b), a sense of guilt would change Mary's utility level in box 2 from 15 to 4 and would change John's utility level in box 3 from 15 to 4. Then, neither Mary nor John would find it advantageous to cheat on the other if his or her spouse did not cheat.[5]

---

[5]Of course, the way we have structured the payoff matrix, each finds it advantageous to cheat on the other if the other cheats. If Mary does not cheat on John, then John is better off not cheating than cheating, but if Mary cheats on John, and John knows that Mary is cheating on him, then he is better off cheating than not cheating.

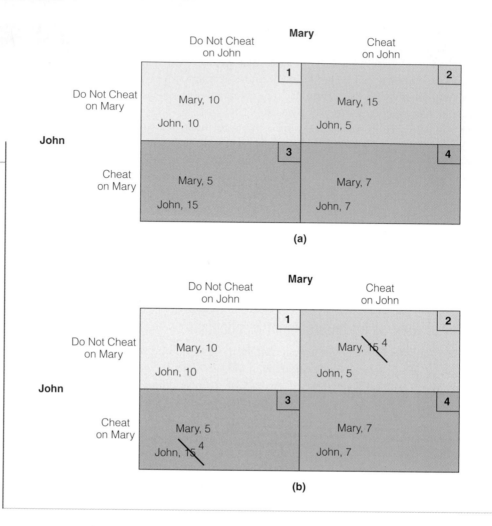

exhibit 13

Cheating and Guilt

Does guilt sometimes serve a useful social purpose? John and Mary are married and may be in a prisoner's dilemma. If Mary cheats on John, but John doesn't cheat on Mary, Mary may be better off and therefore moves from box 1 to box 2 in part (a). If John cheats on Mary, but Mary doesn't cheat on John, John may be better off and therefore moves from box 1 to box 3 in (a). Of course, if both cheat, they both end up in box 4, which is inferior for both to box 1. A sense of guilt for each person may change the payoffs in part (a). If each person feels guilty about cheating, then the payoff from cheating is lowered. Look at the new payoffs for each person in part (b). The payoff for cheating goes from 15 to 4 for both Mary and John. With the new, lower payoffs (resulting from a sense of guilt over cheating), both Mary and John remove themselves from a prisoner's dilemma and therefore are more likely to end up in box 1, a box that is better for both.

We end with a question: When is guilt good? One answer is that when the fear of guilt allows two people to remove themselves from a setting they would prefer not to be in to a better setting. If the fear of guilt moves Mary and John from box 4 to box 1 (which is what they want), then the fear of guilt is good.

A Reader Asks...

Are Some Prisoner's Dilemmas Good and Others Bad?

Are there times when we're glad that people are in a prisoner's dilemma and times when we're not glad? In other words, are there some settings in which we actually want people to end up in box 4 instead of box 1 and other settings in which we want people to end up in box 1 instead of box 4?

Let's look again at two of the prisoner's dilemma settings in the chapter. In one of our settings, two competing sellers enter into a cartel agreement to reduce or eliminate the competition between them. If the cartel agreement is successful, sellers are better off and consumers are worse off. If the cartel agreement is unsuccessful (if the cartel agreement is broken by one or both of the sellers), then sellers are worse off and consumers are better off.

The sellers, as you know, are in a prisoner's dilemma. Each seller agrees to cooperate with the other (to reduce or eliminate cooperation) but also has an incentive to cheat on the agreement. The incentive to cheat (and make oneself better off at the other's expense) is what gets each seller to break the cartel agreement. Outcome: Competition between sellers means benefits for consumers.

Consumers should be glad that sellers are in a prisoner's dilemma and therefore end up in box 4 competing with each other for consumers' business. In other words, if the sellers weren't in a prisoner's dilemma, consumers would want to put them in one.

Now consider our discussion about the arms race between the United States and the Soviet Union. Just like our two sellers, the two countries are in a prisoner's dilemma. Each country agrees to cooperate with the other (to reduce the arms race between them) but also has an incentive to cheat on any arms agreement. The incentive to cheat (and clearly establish military superiority over the other country) is what gets each country to break the arms agreement. Outcome: Arms race.

It is not clear in this case that there are any obvious beneficiaries (other than perhaps armament producers) to the two countries being stuck in a prisoner's dilemma and ending up in box 4, engaged in an arms race. So this might be an example of a prisoner's dilemma that almost everyone would have preferred did not exist.

! analyzing the scene

If Carl and Amanda both want to end grade inflation, why don't they just do it?

Carl and Amanda are stuck in a prisoner's dilemma game. Think of how you might model the game. Each professor enters into an agreement with every other professor to stop inflating grades. Each professor now has the choice of holding to the agreement or breaking it (continuing to inflate grades). If a professor wants to raise the relative grading standard of his students relative to other students, he may choose to inflate grades—thinking that other professors are not inflating grades. The result? All (or almost all) professors will end up inflating grades.

chapter summary

Monopolistic Competition

- The theory of monopolistic competition is built on three assumptions: (1) There are many sellers and buyers. (2) Each firm in the industry produces and sells a slightly differentiated product. (3) There is easy entry and exit.

- The monopolistic competitor is a price searcher.

- For the monopolistic competitor, $P > MR$, and the marginal revenue curve lies below the demand curve.

- The monopolistic competitor produces the quantity of output at which $MR = MC$. It charges the highest price per unit for this output.

- Unlike the perfectly competitive firm, the monopolistic competitor does not exhibit resource allocative efficiency.

- The monopolistic competitive firm does not earn profits in the long run (because of easy entry into the industry) unless it can successfully differentiate its product (e.g., by brand name) in the minds of buyers.

Excess Capacity Theorem

- The excess capacity theorem states that a monopolistic competitor will, in equilibrium, produce an output smaller than the one at which average total costs (unit costs) are minimized. Thus, the monopolistic competitor is not productive efficient.

Oligopoly Assumptions

- There are many different oligopoly theories. All are built on the following assumptions: (1) There are few sellers and many buyers. (2) Firms produce and sell either homogeneous or differentiated products. (3) There are significant barriers to entry.
- One of the key characteristics of oligopolistic firms is their interdependence.

Oligopoly Theories

- The cartel theory assumes that firms in an oligopolistic industry act in a manner consistent with there being only one firm in the industry.
- Four problems are associated with cartels: (1) the problem of forming the cartel, (2) the problem of formulating policy, (3) the problem of entry into the industry, and (4) the problem of cheating.
- Firms that enter into a cartel agreement are in a prisoner's dilemma situation where individually rational behavior leads to a jointly inefficient outcome.
- The kinked demand curve theory assumes that if a single firm lowers price, other firms will do likewise, but if a single firm raises price, other firms will not follow suit.
- The kinked demand curve theory predicts that an oligopolistic firm will experience price stickiness or rigidity. This is because there is a gap in its marginal revenue curve in which the firm's marginal cost can rise or fall and the firm will still produce the same quantity of output and charge the same price. The evidence in some empirical tests rejects the theory.
- The price leadership theory assumes that the dominant firm in the industry determines price and all other firms take this price as given.

The Theory of Contestable Markets

- A contestable market is one in which the following conditions are met: (1) There is easy entry into the market and costless exit from it. (2) New firms entering the market can produce the product at the same cost as current firms. (3) Firms exiting the market can easily dispose of their fixed assets by selling them elsewhere (less depreciation).
- Compared to orthodox market structure theories, the theory of contestable markets places more emphasis on the issue of entry into and exit from an industry and less emphasis on the number of sellers in an industry.

Game Theory

- Game theory is a mathematical technique used to analyze the behavior of decision makers who (1) try to reach an optimal position through game playing or the use of strategic behavior, (2) are fully aware of the interactive nature of the process at hand, and (3) anticipate the moves of other decision makers.
- The prisoner's dilemma game illustrates a case where individually rational behavior leads to a jointly inefficient outcome.

key terms and concepts

Monopolistic Competition	Oligopoly	Cartel	Price Leadership Theory
Excess Capacity Theorem	Concentration Ratio	Kinked Demand Curve Theory	Game Theory
	Cartel Theory		Contestable Market

questions and problems

1 What, if anything, do all firms in all four market structures have in common?

2 What causes the unusual appearance of the marginal revenue curve in the kinked demand curve theory?

3 Would you expect cartel formation to be more likely in industries comprised of a few firms or in those that include many firms? Explain your answer.

4 Does the theory of contestable markets shed any light on oligopoly pricing theories? Explain your answer.

5 There are 60 types or varieties of product X on the market. Is product X made in a monopolistic competitive market? Explain your answer.

6 Why does interdependence of firms play a major role in oligopoly but not in perfect competition or monopolistic competition?

7   Airline companies sometimes fly airplanes that are one-quarter full between cities. Some people point to this as evidence of economic waste. What do you think? Would it be better to have fewer airline companies and more full planes?

8   Concentration ratios have often been used to note the tightness of an oligopoly market. A high concentration ratio indicates a tight oligopoly market, and a low concentration ratio indicates a loose oligopoly market. Would you expect firms in tight markets to reap higher profits, on average, than firms in loose markets? Would

it matter if the markets were contestable? Explain your answers.

9   Market theories are said to have the happy consequence of getting individuals to think in more focused and analytical ways. Has this happened to you? Give examples to illustrate.

10   Give an example of a prisoner's dilemma situation other than the ones mentioned in this chapter.

11   How are oligopoly and monopolistic competition alike? How are they different?

working with numbers and graphs

1   Diagrammatically identify the quantity of output a monopolistic competitor produces and the price it charges.

2   Diagrammatically identify a monopolistic competitor that is incurring losses.

3   In Exhibit 6, what is the highest dollar amount to which marginal cost can rise without changing price?

4   Total industry sales are $105 million. The top four firms account for sales of $10 million, $9 million, $8 million, and $5 million, respectively. What is the four-firm concentration ratio?

5   According to the kinked demand curve theory, if the firm is considering a price hike, which demand curve in the following figure does it believe it faces and why?

6   Refer to the following figure. Because of a cartel agreement, the firm has been assigned a production quota of q_2 units. The cartel price is P_2. What do the firm's profits equal if it adheres to the cartel agreement? What do the firm's profits equal if it breaks the cartel agreement and produces q_3?

23 Government and Product Markets: Antitrust and Regulation

Setting the Scene

The following conversations took place on a day in December.

9:55 A.M. GOVERNMENT OFFICE, KUALA LUMPUR, MALAYSIA

First person:
> The AIDS problem is getting worse. People are dying because they can't afford treatment. I think we should issue a compulsory license.

Second person:
> To Cipla?

First person:
> Yes.

10:43 A.M. OFFICE OF THE ATTORNEY GENERAL OF TENNESSEE

First person:
> That company is violating antitrust laws, and the Justice Department hasn't filed any action against it. If the federal government isn't going to do its job, then maybe we should.

Second person:
> I think you may be right.

1:00 P.M. A PUB IN ENNIS, IRELAND

First person:
> Remember the days when you could smoke in a pub?

Second person:
> I miss those days.

3:07 P.M. AN APARTMENT IN MANHATTAN

First person:
> Excessive regulation is killing businesses.

Second person:
> I'm not sure you're right. I think that sometimes businesses want to be regulated. Some regulation can keep competition out.

First person:
> At every business club meeting I've ever attended, businesspeople were talking about how government overburdened them with regulations and red tape. They always say that they'd be better off—and the economy would be better off—with fewer regulations.

Second person:
> Well, I think some regulation can stifle business, and perhaps regulation is excessive in some cases. But I remember hearing once that sometimes a business asks government to regulate it. For instance, firms in a particular industry might ask government to set prices so that firms don't continue to compete on price. If one firm lowers price, then another firm has to follow, and so on.

First person:
> You may have a point. Maybe there are different types of regulation—some that hurt businesses and others that help.

? Here are some questions to keep in mind as you read this chapter:

- *What does AIDS have to do with antitrust?*

- *At what level of government are antitrust and regulatory issues best addressed?*

- *What are the arguments for and against outlawing smoking in Irish pubs?*

- *Would businesses ever ask for government regulation?*

See analyzing the scene at the end of this chapter for answers to these questions.

Antitrust

A monopoly (1) produces a smaller output than is produced by a perfectly competitive firm with the same revenue and cost considerations, (2) charges a higher price, and (3) causes a deadweight loss. Some economists argue that based on these facts, government should place certain restrictions on monopolies. In addition, government should restrict the activities of cartels because the objective of a cartel is to behave as if it were a monopoly.

Other economists argue that monopolies do not have as much market power as some people think—witness the competition some monopolies face from broadly defined substitutes and imports. As for cartels, they usually contain the seeds of their own destruction. Therefore, it is only a matter of time (usually short) before they crumble naturally.

We are not concerned here with the debate about whether or not to restrict monopoly power. Instead, we examine the ways government deals with it. Two of the ways include antitrust laws and regulation. We examine antitrust law in this section and regulation in the next.

Antitrust law is legislation passed for the stated purpose of controlling monopoly power and preserving and promoting competition. Let's look at how a few of the major antitrust acts have been used and the effects they have had.

Antitrust Law
Legislation passed for the stated purpose of controlling monopoly power and preserving and promoting competition.

Antitrust Acts

A few key acts that constitute U.S. antitrust policy are the Sherman Act (1890), the Clayton Act (1914), the Federal Trade Commission Act (1914), the Robinson-Patman Act (1936), the Wheeler-Lea Act (1938), and the Celler-Kefauver Antimerger Act (1950).

THE SHERMAN ACT (1890) The Sherman Act was passed when mergers of companies were common. (A merger occurs when two companies combine under single ownership of control.) At that time, the organization that companies formed by combining was called a **trust**; this in turn gave us the word *antitrust*.

The Sherman Act contains two major provisions:

Trust
A combination of firms that come together to act as a monopolist.

1. "Every contract, combination in the form of trust or otherwise, or conspiracy, in restraint of trade or commerce among the several states, or with foreign nations, is hereby declared to be illegal."

2. "Every person who shall monopolize, or attempt to monopolize, or combine or conspire with any other person or persons to monopolize any part of the trade or commerce . . . shall be guilty of a misdemeanor."

Some people have argued that the provisions of the Sherman Act are vague. For example, the act never explains which specific acts constitute "restraint of trade," although it declares such acts illegal.

THE CLAYTON ACT (1914) The Clayton Act makes the following business practices illegal when their effects "may be to substantially lessen competition or tend to create a monopoly":

1. Price discrimination—charging different customers different prices for the same product where the price differences are not related to cost differences.

2. Exclusive dealing—selling to a retailer on the condition that the retailer not carry any rival products.

3. Tying contracts—arrangements whereby the sale of one product is dependent on the purchase of some other product(s).

4. The acquisition of competing companies' stock if the acquisition reduces competition. (Some say a major loophole of the act is that it does not ban the acquisition of competing companies' physical assets and therefore does not prevent anticompetitive mergers as it was designed to do.)

5. Interlocking directorates—an arrangement whereby the directors of one company sit on the board of directors of another company in the same industry. These were made illegal, irrespective of their effects (i.e., interlocking directorates are illegal at all times, not just when their effects "may be to substantially lessen competition . . .").

THE FEDERAL TRADE COMMISSION ACT (1914) The Federal Trade Commission Act contains the broadest and most general language of any antitrust act. It declares illegal "unfair methods of competition in commerce." In essence, this amounts to declaring illegal acts that are judged to be "too aggressive" in competition. The problem is how to decide what is fair and what is unfair, what is aggressive but not too aggressive. This act also set up the Federal Trade Commission (FTC) to deal with "unfair methods of competition."

THE ROBINSON-PATMAN ACT (1936) The Robinson–Patman Act was passed in an attempt to decrease the failure rate of small businesses by protecting them from the competition of large and growing chain stores. The large chain stores were receiving price discounts from suppliers and, in turn, were passing the discounts on to their customers. As a result, small businesses had a difficult time competing, and many of them failed. The Robinson-Patman Act prohibits suppliers from offering special discounts to large chain stores unless they also offer the discounts to everyone else. Many economists believe that, rather than preserving and strengthening competition, the Robinson-Patman Act limits it. The act seems to be more concerned about a certain group of competitors than about the process of competition and the buying public as a whole.

THE WHEELER-LEA ACT (1938) The Wheeler-Lea Act empowers the Federal Trade Commission to deal with false and deceptive acts or practices. Major moves in this area have been against advertising that the FTC has deemed false and deceptive.

THE CELLER-KEFAUVER ANTIMERGER ACT (1950) The Celler-Kefauver Act was designed to close the merger loophole in the Clayton Act (see point 4 of the Clayton Act). It bans anticompetitive mergers that occur as a result of one company acquiring the physical assets of another company.

Unsettled Points in Antitrust Policy

It is not always clear where lines should be drawn in implementing antitrust policy. Which firms should be allowed to enter into a merger, and which firms should be prohibited? What constitutes restraint of trade? Which firms should be termed "monopolists" and broken into smaller firms, and which firms should be left alone?

As you might guess, not everyone answers these questions the same way. In short, some points of antitrust policy are still unsettled. A few of the more important unsettled points are noted here.

DOES THE DEFINITION OF THE MARKET MATTER? Should a market be defined broadly or narrowly? The way the market is defined helps determine whether or not a particular firm is considered a monopoly. For example, in an important antitrust suit in 1945, a court ruled that Alcoa (Aluminum Company of America) was a monopoly because it had 90 percent of the virgin aluminum ingot market. If Alcoa's market had been broadened to include stainless steel, copper, tin, nickel, and zinc (some of the goods competing with aluminum), it is unlikely that Alcoa would have been ruled a monopoly.

Later court rulings have tended to define markets broadly rather than narrowly. For instance, in the DuPont case in 1956, the market relevant to DuPont was ruled to be the flexible wrapping materials market rather than the narrower cellophane market.

CONCENTRATION RATIOS Concentration ratios have often been used to gauge the amount of competition in an industry, but as pointed out in the last chapter, their use presents two major problems. First, concentration ratios do not address the issue of foreign competition. For example, the four-firm concentration ratio may be very high, but the four firms that make up the concentration ratio may still face stiff competition from abroad. Second, a four-firm concentration ratio can remain stable over time even though there is competition among the four major firms in the industry.

In 1982, the Justice Department replaced the four- and eight-firm concentration ratios with the Herfindahl index, although it too is subject to some of the same criticisms as the concentration ratios. The **Herfindahl index** measures the degree of concentration in an industry. It is equal to the sum of the squares of the market shares of each firm in the industry:

$$\text{Herfindahl index} = (S_1)^2 + (S_2)^2 + \ldots + (S_n)^2$$

Herfindahl Index

Measures the degree of concentration in an industry. It is equal to the sum of the squares of the market shares of each firm in the industry.

where S_1 through S_n are the market shares of firms 1 through n. For example, if there are 10 firms in an industry, and each firm has a 10 percent market share, the Herfindahl index is 1,000 ($10^2 + 10^2 + 10^2 + 10^2 + 10^2 + 10^2 + 10^2 + 10^2 + 10^2 + 10^2 = 1,000$).

Exhibit 1 compares the Herfindahl index and the four-firm concentration ratio. When the four-firm concentration ratio is used, the top four firms, A–D, have a 48 percent market share, which generally is thought to describe a concentrated industry. A merger between any of the top four firms and any other firm (e.g., between firm B and firm G in Exhibit 1) would give the newly merged firm a greater market share than any existing firm and usually would incur frowns from the Justice Department.

The Herfindahl index for the industry is 932, however, and the Justice Department generally considers any number less than 1,000 representative of an unconcentrated (or competitive) industry. An index between 1,000 and 1,800 is considered representative of a moderately concentrated industry, and an index greater than 1,800 is representative of a concentrated industry.

Antitrust actions are usually brought by the Justice Department if (1) the index rises by 100 points or more and the (premerger) index is initially in the 1,000 to 1,800 category

exhibit **1**

A Comparison of the Four-Firm Concentration Ratio and the Herfindahl Index

Using the old method (in this case, the four-firm concentration ratio), the top four firms in the industry have a 48 percent market share. The Justice Department would likely frown on a proposed merger between any of the top four firms and any other firm. However, the Herfindahl index of 932 is representative of an unconcentrated industry.

Firms	Market Share
A	15%
B	12
C	11
D	10
E	8
F	7
G	7
H	6
I	6
J	6
K	6
L	6

OLD METHOD: FOUR-FIRM CONCENTRATION RATIO

15% + 12% + 11% + 10% = 48%

NEW METHOD: HERFINDAHL INDEX

Square the market share of each firm and then add:

$(15)^2 + (12)^2 + (11)^2 + (10)^2 + (8)^2 + (7)^2 + (7)^2 + (6)^2 + (6)^2 + (6)^2 + (6)^2 + (6)^2 = 932$

economics 24/7

© CRAIG AURNESS/CORBIS

THOMAS EDISON AND HOLLYWOOD

Thomas Alva Edison was born in 1847 and died in 1931. In his 84 years of life, Edison was granted 1,093 patents. Almost everyone knows the role Edison played in the development of electric light and power, but not everyone knows the role he played in indirectly and unwittingly making Hollywood the film capital of the world.

Our story begins with an Edison invention—a machine called the kinetophonograph. The kinetophonograph showed a moving picture that was synchronized with a phonograph record. Later, Edison invented the kinetoscope, which was a device that allowed users to deposit a coin and watch a short motion picture through a small hole.

After inventing the kinetophonograph and kinetoscope, Edison went on to construct the first building that was used solely to make movies. A hole in the ceiling of the building allowed the sun to shine through and illuminate the stage. The entire building was on a set of tracks so that it could be moved around to follow the sun. The first film that Edison produced was a 15-minute movie called *The Great Train Robbery.* Over the years, he produced more than 2,000 short films.

There is some evidence that Edison and a few other people tried to gain complete control over the movie industry in its early days. Edison played a critical role in putting together the Movie Trust, sometimes called the Edison Trust, a group of ten film producers and distributors. The Movie Trust reportedly tried to eliminate its competition. First, the Movie Trust entered into a contract with Eastman Kodak Company, which manufactured film, to sell film only to it. Second, the Movie Trust refused to lease or sell equipment to certain filmmakers and theater owners.

One of the independent movie producers whom the Movie Trust tried to run out of the industry was Carl Laemmie. Laemmie and some other movie producers decided to leave the East Coast where the Movie Trust had the greatest control over the industry. They went to the West Coast, specifically to southern California, to get away from the stranglehold the Movie Trust had over the industry on the East Coast. Others soon followed. The rush of independent filmmakers to southern California set the stage for the development of Hollywood as the film capital of the world. In 1917, the Movie Trust was dissolved by court order, but by then, the movie industry had a new home. Laemmie, for example, founded Universal Studios in Hollywood in 1912.

Would Hollywood be the film capital of the world had it not been for the Movie Trust? It is doubtful. Without the exclusionary and anticompetitive tactics of the Movie Trust, the film capital of the world would probably be on the East Coast of the United States, very likely in or near New York City.

or (2) the index rises by 50 points or more and the (premerger) index is initially in the greater than 1,800 category.

To illustrate, suppose 2 firms, A and B, want to merge. The market share of firm A is 20 percent, and the market share of firm B is 10 percent; together, these firms account for 30 percent of the market. We assume there are 7 other firms in the industry, and each has a 10 percent market share. The Herfindahl index in this industry is 1,200 ($20^2 + 10^2 + 10^2 + 10^2 + 10^2 + 10^2 + 10^2 + 10^2 + 10^2 = 1,200$).

If the merger is approved, there will be 8, not 9, firms. Moreover, the market share of the merged firm (A and B now form one firm) will be 30 percent. The Herfindahl index after the merger will be 1,600. In other words, there will be an increase of 400 points if the firms merge. With this substantial increase in the index, it is likely the proposed merger would be blocked.

INNOVATION AND CONCENTRATION RATIOS According to the 1999 *Economic Report of the President,* more than half of all productivity gains in the U.S. economy in the previous 50 years, as measured by output per labor hour, came from innovation and technical change. Because innovation and technical change are so important to our economic well-being, some economists argue that concentration ratios should not play so large a role in determining a merger's approval. The merger's effect on innovation should also be taken into account. There is some evidence that antitrust authorities are beginning to accept this line of thinking.

It used to be thought that small firms in highly competitive markets with many rivals had a stronger incentive to innovate than firms in markets where only a few firms existed and each firm had sizable market power. Increasingly, however, it is thought that these small competitive firms often face a greater risk of innovation than firms with substantial market power. And therefore, they innovate less.

To illustrate, consider a market with 100 firms, each of which supplies one-hundredth of the market. Suppose one of these firms invests heavily in research and develops a new product or process. It has to worry about any of its 99 rivals soon developing a similar innovation and therefore reducing the value of its innovation. On the other hand, if a firm is 1 of 4 firms and has substantial market power, it doesn't face as much "innovative risk." It has only 3, not 99, rivals to worry about. And of course, the less likely that competitors can make one's own innovations less valuable, the higher the expected return from innovating.

Today, antitrust authorities say that they consider the benefits of both competition and innovation when ruling on proposed mergers. On the one hand, increased competition lowers prices for consumers. On the other hand, monopoly power may yield more innovation. If it does, then the lower prices brought about through increased competition have to be weighed against the increased innovation that may come about through greater market concentration and monopoly power.

Antitrust and Mergers

There are three basic types of mergers.

1. A **horizontal merger** is a merger between firms that are selling similar products in the same market. For example, suppose both companies *A* and *B* produce cars. If the two companies combined under single ownership of control, it would be a horizontal merger.

2. A **vertical merger** is a merger between companies in the same industry but at different stages of the production process. Stated differently, a vertical merger occurs between companies where one buys (or sells) something from (to) the other. For example, suppose company *C*, which produces cars, buys tires from company *D*. If the two companies combined under single ownership of control, it would be a vertical merger.

3. A **conglomerate merger** is a merger between companies in different industries. For example, if company *E*, in the car industry, and company *F*, in the pharmaceutical industry, combined under single ownership of control, it would be a conglomerate merger.

Of the three types of mergers—vertical, horizontal, and conglomerate—the federal government looks most carefully at proposed horizontal mergers. The reason is that horizontal mergers are more likely (than vertical or conglomerate mergers) to change the degree of concentration, or competition, in an industry. For example, if General Motors

---

Q&A   *Does the Herfindahl index have an advantage over the four- and eight-firm concentration ratios?*

Yes. It provides information about the dispersion of firm size in an industry. For example, the Herfindahl index will distinguish between these two situations: (1) 4 firms together have a 50 percent market share and there are only 4 other firms in the industry and (2) 4 firms together have a 50 percent market share and there are 150 other firms in the industry.

Of course, both the Herfindahl index and the four- and eight-firm concentration ratios have been criticized for implicitly arguing from firm size to market power. Both assume firms that have large market shares have market power that they are likely to be abusing. But of course, size could be a function of efficiency, and a firm with a large market share could be serving the buying public well.

Thinking like AN ECONOMIST   *Suppose we observe that a firm has a large share of the market. The economist will ask, "Is there only one possible explanation for this, or are there many?" If there are many, then the economist will try to find out which one is the correct explanation. Think of an analogy. Suppose someone gets the highest grade in three of three courses. Is there more than one explanation for this? Yes, there is. The person could be studying more than anyone else. Or the person could be innately smarter than anyone else. Or the person could be cheating. The economist knows that there are usually different roads that end up at the same destination. Trying to figure out which road was taken to the destination is part of the task economists set for themselves.*

Horizontal Merger
A merger between firms that are selling similar products in the same market.

Vertical Merger
A merger between companies in the same industry but at different stages of the production process.

Conglomerate Merger
A merger between companies in different industries.

(cars) and Ford Motor Company (cars) horizontally merge, competition in the car industry is likely to decrease by more than if General Motors (cars) and BF Goodrich (tires) vertically merge. In the latter case, it is even possible that the competition among car companies, and among tire companies, will be the same after the merger as it was before. This is not necessarily the case, however, and the government does not always approve vertical mergers; in some notable examples, it has not.

Seven Antitrust Cases and Actions

Most people agree that the stated purpose of the antitrust laws—promoting and strengthening competition—is a worthwhile goal. Often, however, the stated purpose or objective of a policy and its effects turn out to be quite different. Some economists have argued that the antitrust laws have not, in all instances, accomplished their stated objective. The following cases and actions illustrate some of the ways that courts and government policymakers have approached antitrust cases over the years.

CASE 1: VON'S GROCERY In 1966, the U.S. Supreme Court ruled on the legality of a merger between Von's Grocery Co. and Shopping Bag Food Stores, both of Los Angeles. Together, the two grocery chains had a little more than 7 percent of the grocery market in the Los Angeles area. However, the Supreme Court ruled that a merger between the two companies violated the Clayton Act. The Court based its ruling largely on the fact that between 1950 and the early 1960s, the number of small grocery stores in Los Angeles had declined sharply. The Court took this as an indication of increased concentration in the industry.

Economists are quick to point out that the number of firms in an industry might be falling due to technological changes, and when this happens, the average size of an existing firm rises. Justice Potter Stewart, in a dissenting opinion to the 1966 decision, argued that the Court had erroneously assumed that the "degree of competition is invariably proportional to the number of competitors."

CASE 2: UTAH PIE In 1967, the Utah Pie Company, which was based in Salt Lake City, charged that three of its competitors in Los Angeles were practicing price discrimination. Utah Pie charged that these companies were selling pies in Salt Lake City for lower prices than they were selling pies near their plants of operation. The Supreme Court ruled in favor of Utah Pie.

Some economists note, though, that Utah Pie charged lower prices for its pies than did its competitors and that it continued to increase its sales volume and make a profit during the time its competitors were supposedly exhibiting anticompetitive behavior. They suggest that Utah Pie was using the antitrust laws to hinder its competition.

CASE 3: CONTINENTAL AIRLINES In 1978, Continental Airlines set out to acquire National Airlines. The Justice Department opposed the merger of the two companies on the grounds that the merged company would dominate the New Orleans air-traffic market. The Civil Aeronautics Board (CAB) did not oppose the merger because it believed the market under consideration was contestable. Recall that firms in a contestable market that operate inefficiently or that consistently earn positive economic profits will be joined by competing firms. By refusing to oppose the merger, the CAB implied that it believed that statistical measures, such as concentration ratios, mean less than whether the market is contestable.

CASE 4: IBM In 1969, the Justice Department filed antitrust charges against IBM, saying that it had monopolized the "general-purpose computer and peripheral-equipment" industry. IBM argued that the antitrust authorities had interpreted its market too narrowly.

economics 24/7

HIGH-PRICED INK CARTRIDGES AND EXPENSIVE MINI-BARS

You want to buy a printer for your computer. You see one priced at $69. That's a good price you say, so you buy it. Later, you learn that you have to pay $33 for an ink cartridge. The printer wasn't so well-priced after all, you think.

You spend the night at a hotel. Once in your room, you open the mini-bar and look around. You decide to eat a small bag of almonds. You learn later, after looking at your bill, that the small bag of almonds came with the big price of $6.

You sign up with a cell phone company. You decide on a plan; you get a cell phone for free. Later, you learn that for every minute you go over your allotted monthly number of minutes, you pay 33 cents.

Because of these everyday occurrences, some economists today are talking about the "hidden fee" economy—an economy in which many main items for sale (printer, hotel room, cell phone service) have attached to them certain hidden (high) fees—fees you did not expect when you purchased the main item.

So, why the hidden fees? According to two economists, David Laibson and Xavier Gabaix, it is because there are certain benefits (firms reap) through hidden fees. There are certain costs, too, but sometimes the benefits are greater than the costs.

To illustrate why a seller may use hidden fees, consider the following example.[1] Suppose there are two similar hotels, X and Y. Hotel X rents its rooms for $80 a night. It also has some hidden fees: $12 for parking, $6 for a small bag of almonds from the mini-bar, and $3 for a local call.

Hotel Y rents its rooms for $95 a night and it has no hidden high fees. It does not charge for parking nor for a local call and the small bag of almonds comes at the same price one could buy it at a grocery store.

What are the major differences between the two hotels? When it comes to the price of a room, Hotel X is cheaper than Hotel Y. When it comes to hidden and unexpectedly high fees, Hotel X is a culprit and Hotel Y is not.

The natural question that arises is: Why doesn't Hotel Y simply advertise the fact that its competitor, Hotel X, is trying to "dupe its customers" by charging high hidden fees? (The ad might read: "Sure, Hotel X has cheaper rooms, but what about all the hidden fees?") According to Laibon and

Gabaix, it's because that strategy could backfire. It backfires because of one of the two types of customers that frequent Hotel X.

One type of customer is somewhat clueless to the hidden fees and initially responds to the lower room rate of Hotel X. With this customer, the ad campaign by Hotel Y (pointing out the hidden fees of Hotel X) will be successful. But another type of customer is sophisticated when it comes to sellers' tactics. The sophisticated customer realizes that if she doesn't park at Hotel X, doesn't purchase anything from the mini-bar in her room, and makes calls on her cell phone instead of on the hotel telephone, she can then get a lower-priced room at Hotel X than Y. The ad by Hotel Y simply notifies the sophisticated customer that she can get a good deal at the hotel with the hidden fees—assuming she doesn't purchase the goods or services that come with the high hidden fees.

Simply put, Hotel Y gains and loses with its ad pointing out the high hidden fees of Hotel X. It gains the clueless customers ("thanks for telling me about those hidden fees") but it may end up losing some sophisticated customers ("thanks for telling me about the lower-priced rooms your competitor is offering"). If it thinks it will lose more sophisticated customers than it will gain clueless customers, it will not run the ad. Instead, it may simply join the ranks of hotels like Hotel X and lower its room rate and increase the use of high hidden fees.

But there is something else to consider. Barry Nalebuff, a professor of business strategy, has noted that there is a cost to a firm that charges hidden fees. That cost comes in the form of customers getting angry at the hidden fees. And angry customers, Nalebuff says, often turn their backs on sellers they are angry with. In other words, they seek out other (perhaps more up front and straightforward) sellers to buy from.

In the end, it becomes a matter of a seller having to consider both the benefits and the costs of a hidden fees strategy. Perhaps initially the benefits outweigh the costs, but there is no guarantee that in time the costs won't rise above the benefits.

---

[1] The source of the material in this feature (and the example) is "The Hidden Economy" by Christopher Shea, *The Boston Globe*, June 27, 2006.

After 13 years of litigation against IBM, the government decided to drop the suit. During the years of litigation, the computer market had changed. New competitors had entered the broadly defined computer market. Although IBM might have once dominated the mainframe computer industry, there was little evidence that it dominated the minicomputer, word processor, or computer-services markets.

CASE 5: UNIVERSITIES For many years, the upper level administrators of some of the country's top universities—Brown, Columbia, Cornell, Dartmouth, Harvard, MIT, Princeton, the University of Pennsylvania, and Yale—met to discuss such things as tuition, faculty salaries, and financial aid. There seemed to be evidence that these meetings occurred because the universities were trying to align tuition, faculty raises, and financial need. For example, one of the universities once wanted to raise faculty salaries by more than the others wanted and was persuaded not to do so. At these meetings, the administrators also compared lists of applicants to find the names of students who had applied to more than one of their schools (e.g., someone might have applied to Harvard, Yale, and MIT). Then, the administrators adjusted their financial aid packages for that student so that no university was offering more than another.

The Justice Department charged the universities with a conspiracy to fix prices. Eight of the universities settled the case by agreeing to sign a consent decree to cease colluding on tuition, salaries, and financial aid. MIT did not agree to sign the consent decree and pursued the case to the Supreme Court. In 1992, the Supreme Court ruled against MIT, saying that it had violated antitrust laws.

CASE 6: LOCKHEED MARTIN AND NORTHROP GRUMMAN In 1997, Lockheed Martin Corporation proposed to acquire Northrop Grumman Corporation. Both Lockheed and Northrop were leading suppliers of aircraft and electronics systems to the U.S. military. The Justice Department challenged the acquisition, saying that it would give Lockheed a monopoly in fiberoptic-towed decoys and in systems for airborne early warning radar. In this case, the issue of innovation played a major role. The Justice Department noted that both Lockheed and Northrop had invested heavily in the research and development of advanced airborne early warning radar systems. If the two companies merged, research and development activities would decline, and innovation would be hampered. The Justice Department blocked the acquisition of Northrop by Lockheed.

CASE 7: BOEING AND MCDONNELL DOUGLAS In 1997, the Federal Trade Commission approved the merger of Boeing Co. and McDonnell Douglas Corp., the two largest commercial aircraft manufacturers in the United States. Innovation was an issue in the Boeing–McDonnell Douglas case, just as it was in the Lockheed Martin–Northrop Grumman case. However, innovation played a different role in this case. The FTC approved the merger to *increase* innovation. The FTC's analysis showed that McDonnell Douglas had fallen behind technologically and was no longer applying competitive innovative pressure on Boeing. The FTC felt that because McDonnell Douglas was not stimulating innovation in the aircraft manufacturing market, nothing would be lost from the standpoint of innovation in allowing the two firms to merge. In fact, something might be gained. McDonnell Douglas's assets might be put to better use by a technologically advanced company like Boeing.

Network Monopolies

A network connects things. For example, a telephone network connects telephones, the Internet (which is a network of networks) connects computers, and a bank network may connect automated teller machines (ATMs). A **network good** is a good whose value increases as the expected number of units sold increases. A telephone is a network good. You buy a telephone to network with other people. It has little value to you if you expect only 100 people to buy telephones. Its value increases if you expect thousands of people to buy telephones.

Software is also a network good in the sense that if Smith buys software X and Jones also buys software X, they can then easily exchange documents with each other. As new buyers buy a network good, present owners of the good receive greater benefits because the network connects them to more people. For example, if Brown and Thompson also buy software X, Smith and Jones will receive greater benefits because they can exchange documents with two more people.

Let's see how the production and sales of a network good can lead to monopoly. Suppose three companies, A, B, and C, make some version of network good X. Company A makes the most popular version of good X, or has the greatest "network worthiness" linked to its good. Consequently, people who are thinking of buying good X buy it from company A. As more people purchase good X from company A, the "network worthiness" increases even more. This prompts even more people to buy good X from company A rather than to buy it from the other two companies. Eventually, the customers of companies B and C may switch to company A, and at some point, almost everyone buys good X from company A. Company A is a network monopoly.

ANTITRUST POLICY FOR NETWORK MONOPOLIES Currently, the antitrust authorities move against a network monopoly based on how it behaves, not because of what it is. For example, the authorities would not issue a complaint against company A in our example unless it undertook predatory or exclusionary practices to *maintain* its monopoly position.

INNOVATION IN NETWORK MONOPOLIES Recall that economists are still undecided as to whether market share assists or detracts from innovation. For example, it was argued that 1 firm among 4 firms may have less "innovative risk" than 1 firm among 100 firms. Therefore, the firm with a larger market share would innovate more, *ceteris paribus*. Presumably, a network monopoly will have a large market share and therefore should be a major innovator. But actually, the situation may be different for network monopolies because high switching costs sometimes accompany a network monopoly.

To illustrate, suppose firm A produces network good A. Network good A begins to sell quite well. Because it is a network good, its robust sales increase the value of the good to potential customers. Potential customers turn into actual customers, and before long, good A has set the market, or industry, standard.

Because network good A is now the industry standard and because network goods (especially those related to the high-tech industries) are sometimes difficult to learn, it may have a "lock" on the market. Specifically, there is a **lock-in effect** that increases the costs of switching from good A to another good. Because of the (relatively) high switching costs, good A has some staying power in the market. Firm A, the producer of good A, thus has staying power too. This may cause firm A to rest on its laurels, so to speak. Instead of innovating, instead of trying to outcompete its existing and future rivals with better production processes or better products, it may do very little. Firm A will realize that the high switching costs keep customers from changing to a different network good. Some economists suggest that in this environment, the network monopoly may have little reason to innovate.

Network Good
A good whose value increases as the expected number of units sold increases.

Lock-In Effect
Descriptive of the situation where a particular product or technology becomes settled upon as the standard and is difficult or impossible to dislodge as the standard.

Civil Action No. 98-1232

On May 18, 1998, the U.S. Department of Justice joined with 20 states and issued a civil action complaint against Microsoft, Inc. The action claimed basis in Sections 1 and 2 of the Sherman Act. The complaint claimed that Microsoft possessed monopoly power in the market for personal computer operating systems. It stated that (1) Microsoft Windows is used on more than 80 percent of Intel-based PCs, and (2) there are high barriers to entry in the market for PC operating systems essentially because Microsoft Windows is a network good that is the industry standard.

The Justice Department claimed that Microsoft was using its dominance in the personal computer operating systems market not only to maintain monopoly power but also to gain dominance in the Internet browser market. The Justice Department claimed that Microsoft, which packaged its Internet browser with Windows, required computer manufacturers to agree, as a condition for receiving licenses to install Windows on their products, not to remove Microsoft's browser and not to allow a more prominent display of a rival browser. The Justice Department also claimed that Microsoft refused to display the icons of Internet service providers (ISPs) on the main Windows screen unless the ISPs would first agree to withhold information from their customers about non-Microsoft browsers.

In the antitrust case, Microsoft argued that it did not have a monopoly in the operating systems market. It stated that it was part of a cutthroat software industry where today's industry leaders could go out of business tomorrow. It essentially argued that none of its business practices hurt any consumers and that all were necessary to its survival. Microsoft claimed that if it was guilty of anything, it was guilty of charging prices that were too low. It charged nothing, for example, for its Internet browser. Furthermore, Microsoft said that the addition of its browser to Windows was not an attempt to monopolize anything; it was an attempt to provide the buying public with a better product. In short, the browser was simply a new feature of Windows and not an illegal tie-in that violated a consent degree that Microsoft had signed in 1995.

Some economists contended that Microsoft's low pricing strategy made sense. They argued that it approximated marginal cost pricing. After all, software, once written, costs very little for each additional copy. Also, low prices are simply a way to sell a lot of copies. And what is wrong with that?

Critics contended that the low prices to gain customers worked to Microsoft's advantage because its operating system was a network good. Low prices mean more customers, and more customers mean Microsoft would eventually become the industry standard. Once there, it would wield its market power to maintain its current position and would try to establish itself as a monopolist in other markets (such as the browser market).

On Friday, November 4, 1999, Judge Thomas Penfield Jackson, the judge who heard the case against Microsoft, issued his findings of fact. Findings of fact simply present the facts of the case as the judge sees them; it does not constitute a ruling in the case. (The ruling was to come later.) In his findings of fact, Judge Jackson essentially agreed with the case the Justice Department made against Microsoft. He said that Microsoft is not only a monopolist in the operating systems market but also that it used its monopoly power to thwart competition. Specifically, it tied its operating system (Windows) together with its browser (Internet Explorer) not for purposes of efficiency and not to satisfy consumers but to establish a monopoly position in the browser market and to preserve its monopoly position in the operating systems market.

Before issuing his final judgment in the case, Judge Jackson appointed Judge Richard Posner, chief of the 7th U.S. Circuit of Appeals, to try to mediate a settlement between the government and Microsoft. After a few months, mediation talks broke down. There was to be no settlement between the two parties.

On Monday, April 3, 2000, Judge Jackson issued a ruling in the case. He ruled that Microsoft had violated the Sherman Act. The judge wrote that Microsoft was guilty of "unlawfully tying its Web browser" to Windows. He continued by saying that "Microsoft's anticompetitive actions trammeled the competitive process through which the computer software industry generally stimulates innovation."

On July 7, 2000, Judge Jackson issued his final ruling in the case. He ordered that Microsoft be split into two companies: one for operating systems and one for applications. Bill Gates said that Microsoft would appeal the ruling to a higher court.

The U.S. Court of Appeals heard the case months later. On June 28, 2001, the U.S. Court of Appeals reversed Judge Jackson's order to break up Microsoft, but it agreed with some of the judge's findings—specifically, that Microsoft had broken federal antitrust law. The appeals court sent the Microsoft case back to a lower court but this time to a different judge.

The new judge, U.S. District Judge Colleen Kollar-Kotelly, ordered both Microsoft and the Justice Department to set out the key issues in the case and determine how it might proceed. Before Judge Kollar-Kotelly issued a decision in the case, Microsoft and the Justice Department announced on November 2, 2001, that they had reached a settlement that would end the case. Under the settlement, Microsoft would make portions of its Windows software code available to competitors and Microsoft would allow computer manufacturers to choose the products they would load onto their machines without the threat of any retaliation from Microsoft. As of this writing, the plaintiffs in the case and the defendant (Microsoft) periodically file joint status reports on Microsoft's compliance with the final judgment. These reports can be found at the U.S. Department of Justice Web site (http://www.usdoj.gov).

SELF-TEST

(Answers to Self-Test questions are in the Self-Test Appendix.)

1.   Why does it matter whether a market is defined broadly or narrowly for purposes of antitrust policy?

2.   Suppose there are 20 firms in an industry and each firm has a 5 percent market share. What is the four-firm concentration ratio for this industry? What is the Herfindahl index?

3.   What is the advantage of the Herfindahl index over the four- and eight-firm concentration ratios? Explain your answer.

Regulation

This section examines the types of regulation, theories of regulation, the stated objectives of regulatory agencies, and the effects of regulation on natural and other monopolies.

The Case of Natural Monopoly

In an earlier chapter, we noted that if economies of scale are so pronounced or large in an industry that only one firm can survive, that firm is a *natural monopoly*. Firms that supply local electricity, gas, and water service are usually considered natural monopolies.

Let's consider the situation in Exhibit 2. There is one firm in the market, and it produces Q_1 units of output at an average total cost of ATC_1. (Q_1 is the output at which $MR = MC$; to simplify the diagram, the MR curve is not shown.) At Q_1, there is an inefficient allocation of resources. Resource allocative efficiency exists when the marginal benefit to demanders of the resources used in the goods they buy equals the marginal cost to suppliers of the resources used in the production of the goods they sell. In Exhibit 2, resource allocative efficiency exists at Q_2, corresponding to the point where the demand curve intersects the MC curve.

The Natural Monopoly Situation

The only existing firm produces Q_1 at an average total cost of ATC_1. (Q_1 is the output at which $MR = MC$; to simplify the diagram, the MR curve is not shown.) Resource allocative efficiency exists at Q_2. There are two ways to obtain this output level: (1) The only existing firm can increase its production to Q_2, or (2) a new firm can enter the market and produce Q_3, which is the difference between Q_2 and Q_1. The first way minimizes total cost; the second way does not. This, then, is a natural monopoly situation: One firm can supply the entire output demanded at a lower cost than two or more firms can.

In many towns, the local gas company is considered a natural monopoly; local government officials argue that no other firm can successfully compete with it (it can produce gas at a lower average total cost than all other firms, therefore outcompeting them). Furthermore, the government officials prohibit other firms from even **trying** to compete with the gas company.

But why does the government need to prohibit other firms from competing with the local gas company? If the gas company really is a natural monopolist, it can outcompete all newcomers. Why does it need government protection from the competitors it can outcompete?

One answer is that government isn't so much protecting the natural monopolist from competition as it is protecting the public from inefficient entry into the natural monopoly setting. According to this argument, if new firms are permitted to enter a natural monopoly setting to compete against the natural monopolist, they will be outcompeted, leave the industry, and the resources they used to enter the industry will have been wasted. The situation is analogous to preventing a 135-pound weakling from getting into the boxing ring with a 250-pound professional boxer. If you know the 135-pound weakling is going to lose anyway, it may be better (some say) to prevent him from wasting his time trying to do something he can't possibly do.

Other economists do not accept this argument. They point out that we don't protect the public from "inefficient entry" in other market structures, and therefore, we should not do so here. In addition, they sometimes note, it is difficult to know for certain if a particular firm's entry into an industry will turn out to waste resources or not.

There are two ways to reach the higher, efficient quantity of output, Q_2: (1) The firm currently producing Q_1 could increase its output to Q_2. (2) Another firm could enter the market and produce Q_3—the difference between Q_2 and Q_1.

Different costs are associated with each way. If the firm currently in the market increases its production to Q_2, it incurs average total costs of ATC_2. If, instead, a new firm enters the market and produces Q_3, it incurs an average total cost of ATC_3. In this way, both firms together produce Q_2, but the new firm incurs average total costs of ATC_3, while the existing firm incurs average total costs of ATC_1.

As long as the objective is to increase output to the level of resource allocative efficiency, it is cheaper (lower total costs) to have the firm currently in the market increase its output to Q_2 than to have two firms together produce Q_2. So the situation in Exhibit 2 describes a natural monopoly situation. *Natural monopoly* exists when one firm can supply the entire output demanded at lower cost than two or more firms can. It is a natural monopoly because a monopoly situation will naturally evolve over time as the low-cost producer undercuts its competitors.

Will the natural monopolist charge the monopoly price? Some economists say yes. See Exhibit 3, where the natural monopoly firm produces Q_1, at which marginal revenue equals marginal cost, and charges price P_1, which is the highest price per unit consistent with the output it produces.

Profit-maximizing natural monopoly will:

1. Produce Q_1 where $MR = MC$
2. Charge monopoly price, P_1

exhibit 3

The Profit-Maximizing Natural Monopoly

The natural monopoly that seeks to maximize profits will produce the quantity of output at which $MR = MC$ and charge the (monopoly) price, P_1.

Because it charges the monopoly price, some people argue that the natural monopoly firm should be regulated. What form should the regulation take? This question is addressed in the next section.

Regulating the Natural Monopoly

The natural monopoly may be regulated through price, profit, or output regulation.

1. **Price regulation.** Marginal cost pricing is one form of price regulation. The objective is to set a price for the natural monopoly firm that equals its marginal cost at the quantity of output at which demand intersects marginal cost. In Exhibit 4, this price is P_1. At this price, the natural monopoly takes a loss. At Q_1, average total

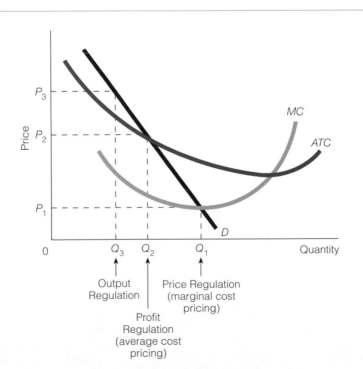

exhibit 4

Regulating a Natural Monopoly

The government can regulate a natural monopoly through (1) price regulation, (2) profit regulation, or (3) output regulation. Price regulation usually means marginal cost pricing, and profit regulation usually means average cost pricing.

cost is greater than price, and thus, total cost is greater than total revenue.[2] Obviously, the natural monopoly would rather go out of business than be subject to this type of regulation unless it receives a subsidy for its operation.

2. **Profit regulation.** Government may want the natural monopoly to earn only zero economic profits. If so, government will require the natural monopoly to charge a price of P_2 (because $P_2 = ATC$) and to supply the quantity demanded at that price (Q_2). This form of regulation is often called *average cost pricing.* Theoretically, this may seem like a good way to proceed, but in practice, it often turns out differently. The problem is that if the natural monopoly is always held to zero economic profits—and is not allowed to fall below or rise above this level—then it has an incentive to let costs rise. Higher costs—in the form of higher salaries or more luxurious offices—simply mean higher prices to cover the higher costs. In this case, it is unlikely that average cost pricing is an efficient way to proceed.

3. **Output regulation.** Government can mandate a quantity of output it wants the natural monopoly to produce. Suppose this is Q_3 in Exhibit 4. Here, there are positive economic profits because price is above average total cost at Q_3. It is possible, however, that the natural monopoly would want even higher profits. At a fixed quantity of output, this can be obtained by lowering costs. The natural monopolist might lower costs by reducing the quality of the good or service it sells, knowing that it faces no direct competition and that it is protected (by government) from competitors.

Regulation of a natural monopoly does not always turn out the way it was intended. Government regulation of a natural monopoly—whether it takes the form of price, profit, or output regulation—can distort the incentives of those who operate the natural monopoly. For example, if profit is regulated to the extent that zero economic profits are guaranteed, then the natural monopoly has little incentive to hold costs down. Furthermore, the owners of the natural monopoly have an incentive to try to influence the government officials or other persons who are regulating the natural monopoly.

In addition, each of the three types of regulation requires information. For example, if the government wishes to set price equal to marginal cost or average total cost for the natural monopoly, it must know the cost conditions of the firm.

Three problems arise in gathering information: (1) The cost information is not easy to determine, even for the natural monopoly itself. (2) The cost information can be rigged (to a degree) by the natural monopoly, and therefore, the regulators will not get a true picture of the firm. (3) The regulators have little incentive to obtain accurate information because they are likely to keep their jobs and prestige even if they work with less-than-accurate information. (This raises a question: Who will ensure that the regulators do a good job?)

Finally, there is the issue of *regulatory lag,* which is indirectly related to information. **Regulatory lag** refers to the time period between when a natural monopoly's costs change and when the regulatory agency adjusts prices for the natural monopoly. For example, suppose the rates your local gas company charges customers are regulated. The gas company's costs rise, and it seeks a rate hike through the local regulatory body. The rate hike is not likely to be approved quickly. The gas company will probably have to submit an application for a rate hike, document its case, have a date set for a hearing, argue its case at the hearing, and then wait for the regulatory agency to decide on the merits of the application. Many months may pass between the beginning of the process and the end. During that time, the regulated firm is operating in ways and under conditions that both the firm and the regulatory body might not have desired.

Regulatory Lag

The time period between when a natural monopoly's costs change and when the regulatory agency adjusts prices for the natural monopoly.

---

[2]Remember that $TC = ATC \times Q$ and $TR = P \times Q$. Here $ATC > P$, so it follows that $TC > TR$.

Regulating Industries That Are Not Natural Monopolies

Some firms are regulated even though they are not natural monopolies. For instance, in the past, government has regulated both the airline and trucking industries. In the trucking industry, the Interstate Commerce Commission (ICC) fixed routes, set minimum freight rates, and erected barriers to entry. In the airline industry, the Civil Aeronautics Board (CAB) did much the same thing. Some economists view the regulation of competitive industries as unnecessary. They see it as evidence that the firms being regulated are controlling the regulation to reduce their competition. We discuss this in greater detail next.

Theories of Regulation

The **capture theory of regulation** holds that no matter what the motive is for the initial regulation and the establishment of the regulatory agency, eventually, the agency will be "captured" (controlled) by the special interests of the industry being regulated. The following are a few of the interrelated points that have been put forth to support this theory:

1. In many cases, persons who have been in the industry are asked to regulate the industry because they know the most about it. Such regulators are likely to feel a bond with people in the industry, see their side of the story more often than not, and thus be inclined to cater to them.

2. At regulatory hearings, members of the industry attend in greater force than do taxpayers and consumers. The industry turns out in force because the regulatory hearing can affect it substantially and directly. In contrast, the effect on individual taxpayers and consumers is usually small and indirect (the effect is spread over millions of people). Thus, regulators are much more likely to hear and respond to the industry's side of the story.

3. Members of the regulated industry make a point of getting to know the members of the regulatory agency. They may talk frequently about business matters; perhaps they socialize. The bond between the two groups grows stronger over time. This may have an impact on regulatory measures.

4. After they either retire or quit their jobs, regulators often go to work for the industries they once regulated.

The capture theory is markedly different from what has come to be called the **public interest theory of regulation**. This theory holds that regulators are seeking to do, and will do through regulation, what is in the best interest of the public or society at large.

An alternative to both theories is the **public choice theory of regulation**. This theory suggests that to understand the decisions of regulatory bodies, we must first understand how the decisions affect the regulators themselves. For example, a regulation that increases the power of the regulators and the size and budget of the regulatory agency should not be viewed the same way as a regulation that decreases the agency's power and size. The theory predicts that the outcomes of the regulatory process will tend to favor the regulators instead of either business interests or the public.

Here, then, are three interesting, different, and at first sight, believable theories of regulation. Economists have directed much effort to testing the three theories. There is no clear consensus yet, but in the area of business regulation, the adherents of the capture and public choice theories have been increasing.

Thinking like **AN ECONOMIST**

The public is perhaps naturally inclined to think that a solution (e.g., regulation) to a problem (e.g., monopoly) is better than no solution at all—that something is better than nothing. The economist has learned, though, that a "solution" can do one of three things: (1) solve a problem, (2) not solve a problem but do no damage, or (3) make the problem worse. Thinking in terms of the entire range of possibilities is natural for an economist, who, after all, understands that solutions come with both costs and benefits.

Capture Theory of Regulation

Holds that no matter what the motive is for the initial regulation and the establishment of the regulatory agency, eventually, the agency will be "captured" (controlled) by the special interests of the industry being regulated.

Public Interest Theory of Regulation

Holds that regulators are seeking to do, and will do through regulation, what is in the best interest of the public or society at large.

Public Choice Theory of Regulation

Holds that regulators are seeking to do, and will do through regulation, what is in their best interest (specifically to enhance their power and the size and budget of their regulatory agencies).

The Costs and Benefits of Regulation

Suppose a business firm is polluting the air with smoke from its factories. The government passes an environmental regulation requiring such firms to purchase antipollution devices that reduce the smoke emitted into the air.

What are the benefits of this kind of regulation? The obvious benefit is cleaner air. But cleaner air can lead to other benefits. For example, people may have fewer medical problems in the future. In some parts of the country, pollution from cars and factories causes people to cough, feel tired, and experience eye discomfort. More important, some people have chronic medical problems from constantly breathing dirty air. Government regulation that reduces the amount of pollution in the air clearly helps these people.

But regulation usually doesn't come with benefits only. It comes with costs too. For example, when a business firm incurs the cost of antipollution devices, its overall costs of production rise. Simply put, it is costlier for the business firm to produce its product after the regulation is imposed. As a result, the business firm may produce fewer units of its product, raising its product price and causing some workers to lose their jobs.

If you are the worker who loses your job, you may view the government's insistence that businesses install antipollution devices differently than if, say, you are the person suffering from chronic lung disease. If you have asthma, less pollution may be the difference between feeling well and feeling sick. If you are a worker for the business firm, less pollution may end up costing you your job. Ideally, you prefer a little less pollution in your neighborhood, but perhaps not at the cost of losing your job.

Are economists for or against government regulation of the type described? The answer is neither. The job of the economist is to make the point that regulation involves both benefits and costs. To the person who sees only the costs, the economist asks: But what about the benefits? And to the person who sees only the benefits, the economist asks: But what about the costs? Then, the economist goes on to outline the benefits and the costs as best she can.

Some Effects of Regulation Are Unintended

Besides outlining the benefits and costs of regulation, the economist tries to point out the unintended effects that can occur with regulation. To illustrate, consider the example concerning fuel standards. Suppose the government requires new cars to get an average of 40 miles per gallon of gasoline instead of, say, 30 miles per gallon. Many people will say that this is a good thing. They will reason that if car companies are made to produce cars that get better mileage, people will not need to buy and burn as much gasoline. When less gasoline is burned, less air pollution will be produced.

There is no guarantee the regulation will have this effect, though. The effects could be quite different. If cars are more fuel efficient, people will buy less gasoline to drive from one place to another—say, from home to college. This means that the (dollar) cost per mile of driving will fall. As a result of lower costs, people might begin to drive more. Leisure driving on the weekend might become more common, people might begin to drive farther on vacations, and so on. If people begin to drive more, then the gasoline saving that resulted from the higher fuel economy standards might be offset or even outweighed. And more gasoline consumption due to more driving will mean more gasoline will be burned and more pollutants will end up in the air.

Thus, a regulation requiring automakers to produce cars that get better fuel mileage may have an unintended effect. The net result might be that people purchase and burn more gasoline and thus produce more air pollution, not less as the government intended.

economics 24/7

"WHY AM I ALWAYS FLYING TO DALLAS?"

The shortest distance between two points is a straight line. Some say that the airline industry doesn't care much about straight lines (or obviously, about short distances). It cares about hubs and spokes.

Suppose you want to go from Phoenix to New York City. The shortest route is the direct route: Phoenix directly to New York. Very likely, however, you won't be able to get a direct flight. Often (but not always), you will be routed through Dallas or Chicago. In other words, you will get on the plane in Phoenix, get off the plane in Dallas, get on another plane in Dallas, fly to New York, and finally get off the plane in New York. This is referred to as the hub-and-spoke delivery system. The hub represents the center of an airline network; the spokes (much like the spokes on a bicycle wheel) represent origin and destination cities and are always linked through the hub.

The hub-and-spoke system has been used more often since airline deregulation. In several instances, airline departures from major hubs (e.g., Dallas and Chicago) have doubled. Most economists believe the increased use of the hub-and-spoke system, which makes average travel time longer, is the result of increased price competition brought on by deregulation.

After deregulation, airlines were under greater pressure to compete on price; thus, it became more important to cut costs. One way to cut costs is to use bigger planes because bigger planes cost less to operate per seat mile. But it takes more people to fill the bigger planes. To accomplish both objectives—flying bigger planes that are more fully occupied—the airlines began to gather passengers at one spot. Then at the hub, they could put more passengers on one plane and fly them to the same destination. For example, instead of flying people in Phoenix and people in Albuquerque directly but separately to New York, both groups of people are flown first to Dallas, and then the combined group is flown to New York.

This system may have benefits that offset the costs of inconvenience and longer travel time. Some people think it is better to pay lower airline ticket prices and reach one's destination a little later than to pay higher prices and get there sooner. They also maintain that increased use of the hub-and-spoke system has given passengers more options to travel on different airlines (in Dallas, numerous airlines can fly you to New York) at more convenient times (numerous flights leave Dallas every hour).

Deregulation

In the early 1970s, many economists, basing their arguments on the capture and public choice theories of regulation, argued that regulation was actually promoting and protecting market power instead of reducing it. They argued for deregulation. And since the late 1970s, many industries have been deregulated, including airlines, trucking, long-distance telephone service, and more.

Consider a few details that relate to the deregulation of the airline industry. The Civil Aeronautics Act, which was passed in 1938, gave the Civil Aeronautics Authority (CAA) the authority to regulate airfares, the number of carriers on interstate routes, and the pattern of routes. The CAA's successor, the Civil Aeronautics Board (CAB), regulated fares in such a way that major air carriers could meet their average costs. An effect of this policy was that fares were raised so high-cost, inefficient air carriers could survive. In addition, the CAB did not allow price competition between air carriers. As a result, air carriers usually competed in a nonprice dimension: They offered more scheduled flights, better meals, more popular in-flight movies, and so forth.

In 1978, under CAB Chairman Alfred Kahn, an economist, the airline industry was deregulated. With deregulation, airlines can compete on fares, initiate service along a new route, or discontinue a route. Empirical research after deregulation showed that passenger miles increased and fares decreased. For example, in 1978, fares fell 20 percent, and between 1979 and 1984, fares fell approximately 14 percent.

Deregulation has also led to a decline in costs in various industries. For example, a recent study by Clifford Winston of the Brookings Institution shows that since deregulation, costs in the airline industry have fallen 24 percent (per unit of output); in trucking, operating costs have fallen 30–35 percent per mile; in railroads, there has been a 50 percent decline in costs per ton–mile and a 141 percent increase in productivity; and in natural gas, there has been a 35 percent decline in operating and maintenance expenses.

SELF-TEST

1.   What is a criticism of average cost pricing?

2.   State the essence of the capture theory of regulation.

3.   What is the difference between the capture theory and the public choice theory of regulation?

4.   Are economists for or against regulation?

A Reader Asks...

Do Auction Houses Engage in Price Fixing?

Not too long ago, I read that the two major auction houses, Sotheby's and Christie's, were engaged in price fixing. What were the details?

Sotheby's (founded in 1744) and Christie's (founded in 1766) are the two biggest auction houses in the world. In 1983, A. Alfred Taubman, a Michigan shopping-mall magnate, bought Sotheby's (some say for his wife as a wedding present). In 1994, Taubman appointed Diana Brooks president and CEO of Sotheby's. In 1997, the U.S. Justice Department began investigating possible collusion between Sotheby's and Christie's to fix the prices people paid to have their items auctioned.

Under American law, accused conspirators are encouraged to confess and to name others involved in the conspiracy. In fact, the first party to do this is given leniency. Christopher Davidge, the president and CEO of Christie's, came forth and turned over papers describing the price-fixing arrangement with Sotheby's.

According to Diana Brooks, who pleaded guilty to the charge, she had been ordered by Taubman to enter into the illegal collusive agreement with Christie's. Taubman claimed that Brooks was lying. Taubman's spokesman declared, "We believe that Mrs. Brooks is lying to save her skin and that she has a clear motivation for doing so."

On April 23, 2002, A. Alfred Taubman was sentenced to a year and a day in prison and fined $7.5 million for leading a 6-year price-fixing scheme with Sotheby's chief competitor, Christie's, that is said to have swindled more than $100 million from their customers. In handing down the sentence, the judge said, "Price fixing is a crime whether it's committed in the grocery store or the halls of a great auction house."

! analyzing the scene

What does AIDS have to do with antitrust?

Differences of opinion often surface in antitrust issues. To illustrate, some people argue that patent laws are necessary to stimulate innovation. Someone might argue that a pharmaceutical company will not spend millions of dollars in research on a new drug unless it will be the only company (for a period of years) permitted to sell the drug. Why spend the money to develop the drug if once it is developed and marketed, another company can copy the drug and sell it?

Now consider that AIDS is a major medical problem in some countries. Many of these are relatively poor countries. This means that many of the individuals in the poor countries who have AIDS will not be able to purchase the best AIDS treatment that exists—which costs approximately $12,000 a year today in the United States. Along comes Cipla, an Indian pharmaceutical company. Cipla has developed a generic for the best AIDS treatment possible, and the company sells its generic for approximately $300 a year. The Malaysian government recently issued a compulsory license to Cipla, which means Cipla can sell its generic AIDS treatment in Malaysia. Some argue that this situation constitutes an antitrust issue. If the original manufacturers of the AIDS treatment (U.S. firms) are not protected from "copycats," then they will no longer have so strong an incentive to spend the money necessary to develop effective drugs—for AIDS or anything else. On the other hand, without the "copycat drugs" (without the generics), no doubt some people will die. One alternative, which is sometimes adopted, is for the country that issues the compulsory license to pay the original manufacturers some royalty rate.

At what level of government are antitrust and regulatory issues best addressed?

In December 2003, the Ford Motor Company paid $52 million to resolve claims that it had misled consumers about the safety of its sports utility vehicles. Instead of settling with federal authorities, it settled with 50 state attorneys general. When Household International paid out $484 million to settle allegations of predatory mortgage lending, it settled with the states. In recent years, the question has been asked: Should antitrust and regulatory issues be dealt with at (1) only the federal level, (2) only the state level, or (3) both the federal

and state levels? State attorneys general often comment that they move in when the federal authorities are negligent. They argue that they fill a void left by federal regulators and politicians who are too often swayed by big business. Critics point out that if both federal and state authorities can launch antitrust and regulatory actions against companies, then the cost of doing business will unnecessarily escalate.

What are the arguments for and against outlawing smoking in Irish pubs?

When issues of regulation are raised, the discussion often turns to who has the right to regulate what. Not long ago, an Irish law was passed that banned smoking in public places, such as restaurants and pubs. Critics of the law often remarked that the restaurant or pub owner is the right person to decide on regulations within his or her environment. If the pub owner wants a smoking pub, then so be it; if he wants a non-smoking pub, so be that too. In the end, customers will go to the pubs they most want to frequent. Others argue differently, saying that no one should have to breathe in cigarette or cigar smoke if he or she doesn't want to. In other words, it is fine to smoke, as long as I am not harmed by your smoke.

Would businesses ever ask for government regulation?

According to the capture theory of regulation, businesses seek to control government regulatory agencies. That is, a business seeks to "pull the strings" of its regulatory agency so that the agency advances the policies that the business wants. Think back to the discussion of cartels in the last chapter. Business firms may want to form a cartel and raise prices, but cheating among them prevents them from doing so. Now suppose the business firms can get a government regulatory agency to do for them what they can't do for themselves. A government regulatory agency has the power to prevent business firms from competing on prices. For example, when airlines in the United States were regulated, the price of an airline ticket from Los Angeles to New York was the same no matter what airline you traveled on. At that time, the airlines were effectively prevented (by government) from competing on price. When the airlines were deregulated, they began to compete on price—and ticket prices fell.

chapter summary

Dealing with Monopoly Power

- A monopoly produces less than a perfectly competitive firm produces (assuming the same revenue and cost conditions), charges a higher price, and causes a dead-weight loss. This is the monopoly power problem, and solving it is usually put forth as a reason for antitrust laws and/or government regulatory actions. Some economists note, though, that government antitrust and regulatory actions do not always have the intended effect. In addition, they are sometimes implemented when there is no monopoly power problem to solve.

Antitrust Laws

- Two major criticisms have been directed at the antitrust acts. First, some argue that the language in the laws is vague; for example, even though the words "restraint of trade" are used in the Sherman Act, the act does not clearly explain what actions constitute a restraint of trade. Second, it has been argued that some antitrust acts appear to hinder, rather than promote, competition; an example is the Robinson-Patman Act.

- There are a few unsettled points in antitrust policy. One centers on the proper definition of a market. Should a market be defined narrowly or broadly? How this question is answered will have an impact on which firms are considered monopolies. In addition, the use of concentration ratios for identifying monopolies or deciding whether to allow two firms to enter into a merger has been called into question. Recently, concentration ratios have been largely replaced (for purposes of implementing antitrust policy) with the Herfindahl index. This index is subject to some of the same criticisms as the concentration ratios. Antitrust authorities are also

beginning to consider the benefits of innovation in ruling on proposed mergers.

Regulation

- Even if we assume that the intent of regulation is to serve the public interest, it does not follow that this will be accomplished. To work as desired, regulation must be based on complete information (e.g., the regulatory body must know the cost conditions of the regulated firm), and it must not distort incentives (e.g., to keep costs down). Many economists are quick to point out that neither condition is likely to be fully met. In itself, this does not mean that regulation should not be implemented but only that regulation may not have the expected effects.

- Government uses three basic types of regulation to regulate natural monopolies: price, profit, or output regulation. Price regulation usually means marginal cost price regulation—that is, setting $P = MC$. Profit regulation usually means zero economic profits. Output regulation specifies a particular quantity of output that the natural monopoly must produce.

- The capture theory of regulation holds that no matter what the motive is for the initial regulation and the establishment of the regulatory agency, eventually, the agency will be "captured" (controlled) by the special interests of the industry being regulated. The public interest theory holds that regulators are seeking to do, and will do through regulation, what is in the best interest of the public or society at large. The public choice theory holds that regulators are seeking to do, and will do through regulation, what is in their best interest (specifically, to enhance their power and the size and budget of their regulatory agencies).

key terms and concepts

Antitrust Law

Trust

Herfindahl Index

Horizontal Merger

Vertical Merger

Conglomerate Merger

Network Good

Lock-In Effect

Regulatory Lag

Capture Theory
of Regulation

Public Interest Theory
of Regulation

Public Choice Theory
of Regulation

questions and problems

1 Why was the Robinson-Patman Act passed? the Wheeler-Lea Act? the Celler-Kefauver Antimerger Act?

2 Explain why defining a market narrowly or broadly can make a difference in how antitrust policy is implemented.

3 What is one difference between the four-firm concentration ratio and the Herfindahl index?

4 How does a vertical merger differ from a horizontal merger? Why would the government look more carefully at one than at the other?

5 What is the implication of saying that regulation is likely to affect incentives?

6 Explain price regulation, profit regulation, and output regulation.

7 Why might profit regulation lead to rising costs for the regulated firm?

8 What is the major difference between the capture theory of regulation and the public interest theory of regulation?

9 George Stigler and Claire Friedland studied both unregulated and regulated electric utilities and found no difference in the rates they charged. One could draw the conclusion that regulation is ineffective when it comes to utility rates. What ideas or hypotheses presented in this chapter might have predicted this result?

10 The courts have ruled that it is a reasonable restraint of trade (and therefore permissible) for the owner of a business to sell his business and sign a contract with the new owner saying he will not compete with her within a vicinity of, say, 100 miles, for a period of, say, 5 years. If this is a reasonable restraint of trade, can you give an example of what you would consider an unreasonable restraint of trade? Explain how you decide what is a reasonable restraint of trade and what isn't.

11 In your opinion, what is the best way to deal with the monopoly power problem? Do you advocate antitrust laws, regulation, or something not discussed in the chapter? Give reasons for your answer.

12 It is usually asserted that public utilities such as electric companies and gas companies are natural monopolies. But an assertion is not proof. How would you go about trying to prove (disprove) that electric companies and the like are (are not) natural monopolies? (Hint: You might consider comparing the average total cost of a public utility that serves many customers with the average total cost of a public utility that serves relatively few customers.)

13 Discuss the advantages and disadvantages of regulation (as you see it).

working with numbers and graphs

1 Calculate the Herfindahl index and the four-firm concentration ratio for the following industry:

Firms	Market Share
A	17%
B	15
C	14
D	14
E	12
F	10
G	9
H	9

Use the following figure to answer Questions 2–4.

2 Is the firm in the figure a natural monopoly? Explain your answer.

3 Will the firm in the figure earn profits if it produces Q_3 and charges P_3? Explain your answer.

4 Which quantity in the figure is consistent with profit regulation? with price regulation? Explain your answers.

Setting the Scene

The following events occurred one day in May.

9:07 A.M.

Marion Smithies owns a small company that produces fans. Currently, she has 35 employees. She is thinking of hiring a few more workers but is unsure of the right number to hire. Are three too few? Are six too many? What is the right number?

1:03 P.M.

Jesse and Sid are having lunch together. Jesse comments, "I don't see how this country can compete any longer. Wages are so much lower in other countries."

"I know," agrees Sid. "What company is going to pay an employee $20 an hour when it can pay $3 an hour?"

Jesse sighs and shakes his head. "I think it's just a matter of time," he says, "until it's impossible to get a decent job here."

3:01 P.M.

Harry Masterson is reading a government report. It states that higher wages are likely to increase the number of hours workers want to work. A thought runs through Harry's mind: This has got to be wrong. I'd want to work fewer at higher wages. After all, at higher wages, I wouldn't need to work as much.

5:45 P.M.

Aaron Lawrence and his 13-year-old son, Damon, are at Yankee Stadium in New York watching the New York Yankees play the Boston Red Sox. The Yankees have two men on base and two outs. Alex Rodriguez, who bats next, is walking up to the plate. Aaron turns to his son and asks, "Do you know how much money Rodriguez is paid to play baseball?" His son says no. Aaron says, "$25 million a year." Then he adds, "That seems like a lot of money just to play baseball, doesn't it?" Damon nods in agreement.

? Here are some questions to keep in mind as you read this chapter:

- *What is the right number of employees to hire?*

- *Will jobs always flow to where wages are the lowest?*

- *Would you work more or less at higher wages?*

- *Is Alex Rodriguez paid too much?*

See analyzing the scene at the end of this chapter for answers to these questions.

© ASSOCIATED PRESS, AP

Factor Markets

Just as there is a demand for and supply of a product, there is a demand for and a supply of a factor, or resource, such as the demand for and supply of labor.

The Demand for a Factor

Why do firms purchase factors? The answer is obvious: to produce products to sell. This is true for all firms, whether they are perfectly competitive firms, oligopolistic firms, or whatever. For example, farmers buy tractors and fertilizer to produce crops to sell. General Motors buys steel to build cars to sell.

Derived Demand

Demand that is the result of some other demand. For example, factor demand is the result of the demand for the products that the factors go to produce.

The demand for factors is a **derived demand**. It is derived from and directly related to the demand for the product that the resources go to produce. If the demand for the product rises, the demand for the factors used to produce the product rises. If the demand for the product falls, the demand for the factors used to produce the product falls. For example, if the demand for a university education falls, so does the demand for university professors. If the demand for computers rises, so does the demand for skilled computer workers.

When the demand for a seller's product rises, the seller needs to decide how much more of a factor it should buy. The concepts of marginal revenue product and marginal factor cost are relevant to this decision.

> ## micro Theme
>
> In an earlier chapter, we discussed a few questions that every business firm has to answer. One of those questions was, "How many units of a resource (or factor) should a firm buy?" That is the question we explicitly address in this chapter.

Marginal Revenue Product: Two Ways to Calculate It

Marginal Revenue Product (MRP)

The additional revenue generated by employing an additional factor unit.

Marginal revenue product (*MRP*) is the additional revenue generated by employing an additional factor unit. For example, if a firm employs one more unit of a factor and its total revenue rises by $20, the *MRP* of the factor equals $20. Marginal revenue product can be calculated in two ways:

$$MRP = \Delta TR / \Delta \text{Quantity of the factor}$$

or

$$MRP = MR \times MPP$$

where TR = total revenue, MR = marginal revenue, and MPP = marginal physical product. In Exhibit 1, we use data for a hypothetical firm to show the two methods for calculating *MRP*.

METHOD 1: *MRP* = $\Delta TR/\Delta$QUANTITY OF THE FACTOR Look at Exhibit 1(a). Column 1 shows the different quantities of factor X. Column 2 shows the quantity of output produced at the different quantities of factor X.

Column 3 lists the price and the marginal revenue of the product that the factor goes to produce. Notice that we have assumed the price of the product (P) equals the product's marginal revenue (MR). So we have assumed the seller in Exhibit 1 is a perfectly competitive firm. Recall that for a perfectly competitive firm, $P = MR$.

In column 4, we calculate the total revenue, or price multiplied by quantity. In column 5, we calculate the marginal revenue product (*MRP*) by dividing the change in total revenue (from column 4) by the change in the quantity of the factor.

(1) Quantity of Factor X	(2) Quantity of Output, Q	(3) Product Price, Marginal Revenue $(P = MR)$	(4) Total Revenue $TR = P \times Q$ $= (3) \times (2)$	(5) Marginal Revenue Product of Factor X $MRP = \Delta TR / \Delta \text{Quantity of factor } X$ $= \Delta(4)/\Delta(1)$
0	10★	$5	$ 50	—
1	19	5	95	$45
2	27	5	135	40
3	34	5	170	35
4	40	5	200	30
5	45	5	225	25

(a)

(1) Quantity of Factor X	(2) Quantity of Output, Q	(3) Marginal Physical Product $MPP = \Delta(2)/\Delta(1)$	(4) Product Price, Marginal Revenue $(P = MR)$	(5) Marginal Revenue Product of Factor X $MRP = MR \times MPP$ $= (4) \times (3)$
0	10★	—	$5	—
1	19	9	5	$45
2	27	8	5	40
3	34	7	5	35
4	40	6	5	30
5	45	5	5	25

(b)

★Because the quantity of output is 10 at 0 units of factor X, other factors (not shown in the exhibit) must also be used to product the good.

exhibit **1**

Calculating Marginal Revenue Product (MRP)

There are two methods of calculating MRP. Part (a) shows one method ($MRP = \Delta TR / \Delta$ Quantity of the factor), and (b) shows the other ($MRP = MR \times MPP$).

METHOD 2: $MRP = MR \times MPP$ Now look at Exhibit 1(b). Columns 1 and 2 are the same as in Exhibit 1(a).

In column 3, we calculate the marginal physical product (MPP) of factor X. Recall (from an earlier chapter) that MPP is the change in the quantity of output divided by the change in the quantity of the factor.

Column 4 lists the price and marginal revenue of the product. Column 4 is the same as column 3 in part (a).

In column 5, we calculate the MRP by multiplying the marginal revenue (in column 4) by MPP (in column 3). The MRP figures in column 5 of (b) are the same as the MRP figures in column 5 of (a), showing that MRP can be calculated in two ways.

The *MRP* Curve Is the Firm's Factor Demand Curve

Look again at column 5 in Exhibit 1, which shows the MRP for factor X. By plotting the data in column 5 against the quantity of the factor (shown in column 1), we derive the MRP curve for factor X. This curve is the same as the firm's demand curve for factor X (or simply, the firm's factor demand curve) (see Exhibit 2).

MRP curve = Factor demand curve

Notice that the MRP curve in Exhibit 2 is downward sloping. You can understand why when you recall that MRP can be calculated as $MRP = MR \times MPP$. What do you know about MPP, the marginal physical product of a factor? According to the law of

Value Marginal Product (VMP)

The price of the good multiplied by the marginal physical product of the factor: $VMP = P \times MPP$.

exhibit **2**

The *MRP* Curve Is the Firm's Factor Demand Curve

The data in columns (1) and (5) in Exhibit 1 are plotted to derive the *MRP* curve. The *MRP* curve shows the various quantities of the factor the firm is willing to buy at different prices, which is what a demand curve shows. The *MRP* curve is the firm's factor demand curve.

Thinking like **AN ECONOMIST**   *As we have stated before, when decisions need to be made, it is customary to compare one thing to another. The decision before the firm is: How much of a factor or resource should it buy or hire? When making this decision, the firm will want to look at the additional benefits of hiring or buying one more unit of the factor against the additional costs of hiring or buying one more unit of the factor.*

Marginal Factor Cost (MFC)

The additional cost incurred by employing an additional factor unit.

Factor Price Taker

A firm that can buy all of a factor it wants at the equilibrium price. It faces a horizontal (flat, perfectly elastic) supply curve of factors.

diminishing marginal returns, eventually, the *MPP* of a factor will diminish. Because *MRP* is equal to $MR \times MPP$ and *MPP* will eventually decline, it follows that *MRP* will eventually decline too.

Value Marginal Product

Value marginal product (*VMP*) is equal to the price of the product multiplied by the marginal physical product of the factor:

$$VMP = P \times MPP$$

For example, if $P = \$10$ and $MPP = 9$ units, then $VMP = \$90$. Think of *VMP* as a measure of the value that each factor unit adds to the firm's product. Or you can think of it simply as "*MPP* measured in dollars."

A firm wants to know the *VMP* of a factor because it helps the firm decide how many units of the factor to hire. To illustrate, put yourself in the shoes of the owner of a firm that produces computers. Suppose one of the factors you need to produce computers is labor. Currently, you are thinking of hiring an additional worker. Whether or not you actually hire the additional worker will depend on (1) how much better off you are—in dollars and cents—with the additional worker than without him or her and (2) what you have to pay to hire the worker. Simply put, you want to know what the worker will do for you and what you will have to pay for the worker. The *VMP* of a factor is a dollar measure of how much an additional unit of the factor will do for you.

An Important Question: Is *MRP* = *VMP*?

In the computations of *MRP* shown in Exhibit 1, price (*P*) was equal to marginal revenue (*MR*) because we assumed the firm was perfectly competitive. Because $P = MR$ for a perfectly competitive firm, does it follow that for a perfectly competitive firm $MRP = VMP$? The answer is yes.

Given that

$$MRP = MR \times MPP$$

and

$$VMP = P \times MPP$$

then because $P = MR$ for a perfectly competitive firm, it follows that

$$MRP = VMP \text{ for a perfectly competitive firm}$$

See Exhibit 3(a).

Although $MRP = VMP$ for perfectly competitive firms, this is not the case for firms that are price searchers: monopoly, monopolistic competitive, and oligopolistic firms. All these firms face downward-sloping demand curves for their products. For all of these firms, $P > MR$, and so *VMP* (which is $P \times MPP$) is greater than *MRP* (which is $MR \times MPP$).[1] See Exhibit 3(b).

Marginal Factor Cost: The Firm's Factor Supply Curve

Marginal factor cost (*MFC*) is the additional cost incurred by employing an additional factor unit. It is calculated as

$$MFC = \Delta TC / \Delta \text{Quantity of the factor}$$

where $TC =$ total costs.

Let's suppose a firm is a **factor price taker**. This means it can buy all it wants of a factor at the equilibrium price. For example, suppose the equilibrium price for factor X

---

[1]An exception is the perfectly price-discriminating monopoly firm. For this firm, $P = MR$.

This is the case for a perfectly competitive firm.

$MRP = MR \times MPP$
$VMP = P \times MPP$

MRP (= factor demand curve)
VMP

Price of Factor

0   Quantity of Factor

(a)

This is the case for a monopolist, a monopolistic competitor, and an oligopolist.

$MRP = MR \times MPP$

$VMP = P \times MPP$

VMP

MRP (= factor demand curve)

Price of Factor

0   Quantity of Factor

(b)

is $5. If a firm is a factor price taker, it can buy any quantity of factor X at $5 per factor unit (see Exhibit 4(a)).

What would the marginal factor cost (MFC) curve (the firm's factor supply curve) look like for this kind of firm? It would be horizontal (flat, or perfectly elastic), as shown in Exhibit 4(b).[2]

How Many Units of a Factor Should a Firm Buy?

Suppose you graduate with a B.A. in economics and go to work for a business firm. The first day on the job, you are involved in a discussion about factor X. Your employer asks you, "How many units of this factor should we buy?" What would you say?

---

[2]Although the MFC, or factor supply curve, for the single factor price taker is horizontal, the market supply curve is upward sloping. This is similar to the situation for the perfectly competitive firm where the firm's demand curve is horizontal but the market (or industry) demand curve is downward sloping. In factor markets, we are simply talking about the supply side of the market instead of the demand side. The firm's supply curve is flat because it can buy additional factor units without driving up the price of the factor; it buys a relatively small portion of the factor. For the industry, however, higher factor prices must be offered to entice factors (e.g., workers) from other industries. The difference in the two supply curves—the firm's and the industry's—is basically a reflection of the different sizes of the firm and the industry.

exhibit **3**

MRP and *VMP* Curves

$MRP = MR \times MPP$ and $VMP = P \times MPP$. (a) The *MRP* (factor demand) curve and *VMP* curve. These are the same for a price taker, or perfectly competitive firm, because $P = MR$. (b) The *MRP* (factor demand) curve and *VMP* curve for a firm that is a price searcher (monopolist, monopolistic competitor, oligopolist). The *MRP* curve lies below the *VMP* curve because for these firms, $P > MR$.

exhibit **4**

Calculating *MFC* and Deriving the *MFC* Curve (the Firm's Factor Supply Curve)

In (a), *MFC* is calculated in column 4. Notice that the firm is a factor price taker because it can buy a quantity of factor X at a given price ($5, as shown in column 2). In (b), the data from columns (1) and (4) are plotted to derive the *MFC* curve, which is the firm's factor supply curve.

(1) Quantity of Factor X	(2) Price of Factor X	(3) Total cost $TC = (2) \times (1)$	(4) $MFC = \Delta TC / \Delta \text{quantity}$ of the factor $= \Delta(3)/\Delta(1)$
0	$5	$ 0	—
1	5	5	$5
2	5	10	5
3	5	15	5
4	5	20	5
5	5	25	5
6	5	30	5

(a)

$5

MFC Curve = Factor Supply Curve

Price of Factor X

0   1   2   3   4   5   6
Quantity of Factor X

(b)

Thinking like
AN ECONOMIST
In the product market, a firm produces that quantity of output at which marginal revenue equals marginal cost, MR = MC. In the factor market, a firm buys the factor quantity at which marginal revenue product equals marginal factor cost, MRP = MFC. The economic principle of equating additional benefits with additional costs holds in both markets.

Recall that economists often make use of marginal analysis. An economist is likely to answer this question by saying, "Continue buying additional units of the factor until the additional revenue generated by employing an additional factor unit is equal to the additional cost incurred by employing an additional factor unit." Simply stated, keep buying additional units of the factor until $MRP = MFC$. In Exhibit 5, MRP equals MFC at a factor quantity of Q_1.

When There Is More Than One Factor, How Much of Each Factor Should the Firm Buy?

Until now, we have only discussed the purchase of one factor. Suppose we have two factors. For example, suppose a firm requires two factors, labor (L) and capital (K), to produce its product. How does it combine these two factors to minimize costs? Does it combine, say, 20 units of labor with 5 units of capital or perhaps 15 units of labor with 8 units of capital?

The firm purchases the two factors until the ratio of MPP to price for one factor equals the ratio of MPP to price for the other factor. In other words,

$$\frac{MPP_L}{P_L} = \frac{MPP_K}{P_K}$$

Least-Cost Rule

Specifies the combination of factors that minimizes costs. This requires that the following condition be met: $MPP_1/P_1 = MPP_2/P_2 = \ldots = MPP_N/P_N$, where the numbers stand for the different factors.

This is the **least-cost rule**. To understand the logic behind it, let's consider an example. Suppose for a firm, (1) the price of labor is $5, (2) the price of capital is $10, (3) an extra unit of labor results in an increase in output of 25 units, and (4) an extra unit of capital results in an increase in output of 25 units.

Notice that MPP_L/P_L is greater than MPP_K/P_K: $25/\$5 > 25/\$10$. Thus, for this firm, $1 spent on labor is more effective at raising output than $1 spent on capital. In fact, it is twice as effective.

Now suppose the firm currently spends an extra $5 on labor and an extra $10 on capital. With this purchase of the two factors, the firm *is not* minimizing costs. It spends an additional $15 ($5 on labor and $10 on capital) and produces 50 additional units of output. If, instead, it spends an additional $10 on labor and spends $0 on capital, it can still produce the 50 additional units of output and will save $5.

To minimize costs, the firm will rearrange its purchases of factors until the least-cost rule is met. To illustrate, if $MPP_L/P_L > MPP_K/P_K$, the firm buys more labor and less capital. As this happens, the MPP of labor falls and the MPP of capital rises, bringing the two ratios closer in line. The firm continues to buy more of the factor whose MPP-to-price ratio is larger. It stops when the two ratios are equal.

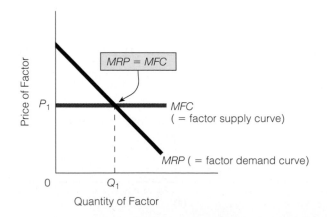

> ### Thinking like AN ECONOMIST
>
> *We can compare a firm's least-cost rule with the way buyers allocate their consumption dollars. A buyer of goods in the product market chooses combinations of goods so that the marginal utility of good A divided by the price of good A is equal to the marginal utility of good B divided by the price of good B; that is, $MU_A/P_A = MU_B/P_B$.*
>
> *A firm buying factors in the factor market chooses combinations of factors so that the marginal physical product of, say, labor divided by the price of labor (the wage rate) is equal to the marginal physical product of capital divided by the price of capital; that is, $MPP_L/P_L = MPP_K/P_K$.*
>
> *Consumers buy goods the same way firms buy factors. This points out something that you may have already sensed. Economic principles are few, but they sometimes seem numerous because we find them in so many different settings.*
>
> *The same economic principle lies behind equating the MU/P ratio for different goods in the product market and equating the MPP/P ratio for different resources in the resource market. In short, there are not two different economic principles at work—one in the product market and another in the factor market—but only one economic principle at work in two markets. That principle simply says that economic actors will, in their attempt to meet their objectives, arrange their purchases in such a way that they receive equal additional benefits per dollar of expenditure.*
>
> *Seeing how a few economic principles operate in many different settings is part of the economic way of thinking.*

SELF-TEST

(Answers to Self-Test questions are in the Self-Test Appendix.)

1. When a perfectly competitive firm employs one worker, it produces 20 units of output, and when it employs two workers, it produces 39 units of output. The firm sells its product for $10 per unit. What is the marginal revenue product connected with hiring the second worker?

2. What is the difference between marginal revenue product (*MRP*) and value marginal product (*VMP*)?

3. What is the distinguishing characteristic of a factor price taker?

4. How much labor should a firm purchase?

The Labor Market

Labor is a factor of special interest because at one time or another, most people find themselves in the labor market. This section first discusses the demand for labor, then the supply of labor, and finally the two together. The discussion focuses on the firm that is a price taker in the product market (i.e., a perfectly competitive firm) and also is a price taker in the factor market.[3] In this setting, the demand for and supply of labor are the forces that determine wage rates.

Shifts in a Firm's *MRP*, or Factor Demand, Curve

As mentioned earlier, a firm's *MRP* curve is its factor demand curve, and marginal revenue product equals marginal revenue multiplied by marginal physical product:

$$MRP = MR \times MPP \qquad (1)$$

---

[3]It is important to keep in mind that the labor market we discuss here is a labor market in which neither buyers nor sellers have any control over wage rates. Because of this, supply and demand are our analytical tools. In the next chapter, we modify this analysis.

economics 24/7

WHY JOBS DON'T ALWAYS MOVE TO THE LOW-WAGE COUNTRY

Are tariffs needed to protect U.S. workers? Some people think so. They argue that without tariffs, U.S. companies will relocate to countries where wages are lower. They will produce their products there and then transport the products to the United States to sell them. Tariffs will make this scenario less likely because the gains the companies receive in lower wages will be offset by the tariffs imposed on their goods.

What this argument overlooks is that U.S. companies are not only interested in what they pay workers; they are also interested in the marginal productivity of the workers.

For example, suppose a U.S. worker earns $10 an hour and a Mexican worker earns $4 an hour. Also suppose the marginal physical product (*MPP*) of the U.S. worker is 10 units of good *X* and the *MPP* of the Mexican worker is 2 units of good *X*. Thus, we have lower wages in Mexico and higher productivity in the United States. Where will the company produce?

To answer this question, we need to compare the output produced per $1 of cost in the two countries.

$$\text{Output produced per \$1 of cost} = \frac{MPP \text{ of the factor}}{\text{Cost of the factor}}$$

In the United States, at an *MPP* of 10 units of good *X* and a wage rate of $10, workers produce 1 unit of good *X* for every $1 they are paid:

$$\frac{MPP \text{ of U.S. labor}}{\text{Wage rate of U.S. labor}} = \frac{10 \text{ units of good } X}{\$10}$$
$$= 1 \text{ unit of good } X \text{ per \$1}$$

In Mexico, at an *MPP* of 2 units and a wage rate of $4, workers produce 1/2 unit of good *X* for every $1 they are paid:

$$\frac{MPP \text{ of Mexican labor}}{\text{Wage rate of Mexican labor}} = \frac{2 \text{ units of good } X}{\$4}$$
$$= 1/2 \text{ unit of good } X \text{ per \$1}$$

Thus, the company gets more output per $1 of cost by using U.S. labor and will produce good *X* in the United States. It is cheaper to produce the good in the United States than it is in Mexico—even though wages are lower in Mexico.

In other words, U.S. companies look at the following ratios:

(1)	(2)
$\dfrac{MPP \text{ of labor in U.S.}}{\text{Wage rate in U.S.}}$	$\dfrac{MPP \text{ of labor in country } X}{\text{Wage rate in country } X}$

If ratio (1) is greater than ratio (2), U.S. companies will hire labor in the United States. As they do this, the *MPP* of labor in the United States will decline. (Remember the law of diminishing marginal returns?) Companies will continue to hire labor in the United States until ratio (1) is equal to ratio (2).

For a perfectly competitive firm, where $P = MR$, we can write equation (1) as

$$MRP = P \times MPP \qquad\qquad (2)$$

Now consider the demand for a specific factor input, labor. What will happen to the factor demand (*MRP*) curve for labor as the price of the product that the labor produces changes?

In Exhibit 6, we start with a product price of $10 and factor demand curve MRP_1. At the wage rate of W_1, the firm hires Q_1 labor.

Suppose product price rises to $12. As we can see from equation (2), *MRP* rises. At each wage rate, the firm wants to hire more labor. For example, at W_1, it wants to hire Q_2 labor instead of Q_1. In short, a rise in product price shifts the firm's *MRP*, or factor demand, curve rightward.

If product price falls from $10 to $8, *MRP* falls. At each wage rate, the firm wants to hire less labor. For example, at W_1, it wants to hire Q_3 labor instead of Q_1. In short, a fall in product price shifts the firm's *MRP*, or factor demand, curve leftward.

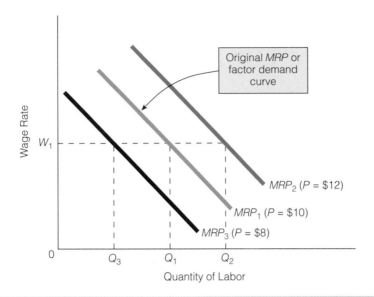

exhibit **6**

Shifts in the Firm's *MRP*, or Factor Demand, Curve

It is always the case that *MRP* = *MR* × *MPP*. For a perfectly competitive firm, where *P* = *MR*, it follows that *MRP* = *P* × *MPP*. If *P* changes, *MRP* will change. For example, if product price rises, *MRP* rises, and the firm's *MRP* curve (factor demand curve) shifts rightward. If product price falls, *MRP* falls, and the firm's *MRP* curve (factor demand curve) shifts leftward. If *MPP* rises (reflected in a shift in the *MPP* curve), *MRP* rises and the firm's *MRP* curve shifts rightward. If *MPP* falls, *MRP* falls and the firm's *MRP* curve shifts leftward.

Changes in the *MPP* of the factor—reflected in a shift in the *MPP* curve—also change the firm's *MRP* curve. As we can see from equation (2), an increase in, say, the *MPP* of labor will increase *MRP* and shift the *MRP*, or factor demand, curve rightward. A decrease in *MPP* will decrease *MRP* and shift the *MRP*, or factor demand, curve leftward.[4]

> ### micro Theme
>
> One of the themes that gets played over and again in microeconomics is this one: (1) Derive a particular curve and then (2) explain what factors will shift it. We first encountered this theme back in Chapter 3 when discussing supply and demand. We derived a demand curve (from a demand schedule) and then discussed the factors that could shift the curve. We are playing that theme again here. We have just derived the firm's demand curve for a factor. Then we identified factors (e.g., a change in the price of the good the factor goes to produce and a change in MPP) that could shift the curve.

Market Demand for Labor

We would expect the market demand curve for labor to be the horizontal "addition" of the firms' demand curves (*MRP* curves) for labor. However, this is not the case, as Exhibit 7 illustrates.

Assume two firms, *A* and *B*, make up the buying side of the factor market. Also assume that the product price for both firms is P_1. Parts (a) and (b) in the exhibit show the *MRP* curves for the two firms based on this product price.

At a wage rate of W_1, firm *A* purchases 100 units of labor. This is the amount of labor at which its marginal revenue product equals marginal factor cost (or the wage). At this same wage rate, firm *B* purchases 150 units of labor. If we horizontally "add" the *MRP* curves of firms *A* and *B*, we get the *MRP* curve in (c) where the two firms together purchase 250 units of labor at W_1.

---

[4]Notice here that we are talking about a change in *MPP* that is reflected in a *shift* in the *MPP* curve; we are not talking about a *movement* along a given *MPP* curve.

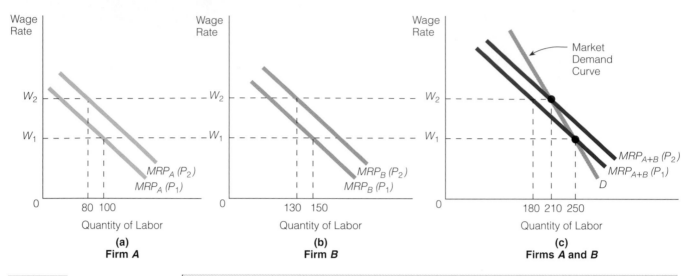

exhibit 7

The Derivation of the Market Demand Curve for Labor Units

Two firms, A and B, make up the buying side of the market for labor. At a wage rate of W_1, firm A purchases 100 units of labor and firm B purchases 150 units. Together, they purchase 250 units, as illustrated in (c). The wage rate rises to W_2, and the amount of labor purchased by both firms initially falls to 180 units, as shown in (c). Higher wage rates translate into higher costs, a fall in product supply, and a rise in product price from P_1 to P_2. Finally, an increased price raises *MRP* and each firm has a new *MRP* curve. The horizontal "addition" of the new *MRP* curves shows they purchase 210 units of labor. Connecting the units of labor purchased by both firms at W_1 and W_2 gives the market demand curve.

Now assume the wage rate increases to W_2. In (c), firms A and B move up the given MRP_{A+B} curve and purchase 180 units of labor. This may seem to be the end of the process, but of course, it is not. But why not? It's because a higher wage rate increases each firm's costs and thus shifts its supply curve leftward. This leads to an increase in product price to P_2.

Recall that the firm's marginal revenue product is equal to marginal revenue (or price, when the firm is perfectly competitive) times marginal physical product: $MRP = MR \times MPP = P \times MPP$. So if price rises (which it has), so does MRP, and therefore, each firm faces a new MRP curve at the wage rate W_2. Parts (a) and (b) in Exhibit 7 illustrate these new MRP curves for firms A and B, and (c) shows the horizontal "addition" of the *new MRP* curves. The firms together now purchase 210 units of labor at W_2.

After all adjustments have been made, connecting the units of labor purchased by both firms at W_1 and W_2 gives the market demand curve in (c).

micro Theme

One of the themes in microeconomics is that if one thing changes, this leads to something else changing, which in turn leads to something else changing, and so on. You have just seen that theme in action. The wage rate increased, which raised the firm's costs, which caused the firm's supply curve (for the good it produces) to shift leftward. But then, a leftward shift in the supply curve ended up raising the price of the good the firm produces and sells, which resulted in the firm's demand for factors rising.

Think of a pebble you throw into a lake. The pebble causes ripples in the lake. It is much the same in economics. If you throw the "pebble" of a "higher wage rate" into a market setting, certain ripples will materialize.

The Elasticity of Demand for Labor

Elasticity of Demand for Labor
The percentage change in the quantity demanded of labor divided by the percentage change in the wage rate.

If the wage rate rises, firms will cut back on the labor they hire. But how much they cut back depends on the elasticity of demand for labor. The **elasticity of demand for labor** is the percentage change in the quantity demanded of labor divided by the percentage change in the price of labor (the wage rate).

$$E_L = \frac{\text{Percentage change in quantity demanded of labor}}{\text{Percentage change in wage rate}}$$

where E_L = coefficient of elasticity of demand for labor, or simply elasticity coefficient.

For example, suppose when the wage rate changes by 20 percent, the quantity demanded of a particular type of labor changes by 40 percent. Then the elasticity of demand for this type of labor is 2 (40 percent/20 percent), and the demand between the old wage rate and the new wage rate is elastic. There are three main determinants of elasticity of demand for labor.

ELASTICITY OF DEMAND FOR THE PRODUCT THAT LABOR PRODUCES If the demand for the product that labor produces is highly elastic, a small percentage increase in price (e.g., owing to a wage increase that shifts the supply curve for the product leftward) will decrease quantity demanded of the product by a relatively large percentage. In turn, this will greatly reduce the quantity of labor needed to produce the product, implying the demand for labor is highly elastic too.

The relationship between the elasticity of demand for the product and the elasticity of demand for labor is as follows:

The higher the elasticity of demand for the product, the higher the elasticity of demand for the labor that produces the product; the lower the elasticity of demand for the product, the lower the elasticity of demand for the labor that produces the product.

RATIO OF LABOR COSTS TO TOTAL COSTS Labor costs are a part of total costs. Consider two situations. In one, labor costs are 90 percent of total costs, and in the other, labor costs are only 5 percent of total costs. Now suppose wages increase by $2 per hour. Total costs are affected more when labor costs are 90 percent of total costs (the $2-per-hour wage increase is being applied to 90 percent of all costs) than when labor costs are only 5 percent of total costs. Thus, price rises by more when labor costs are a larger percentage of total costs. And of course, the more price rises, the more quantity demanded of the product falls. It follows that labor, being a derived demand, is affected more. In short, the decline in the quantity demanded of labor is greater for a $2-per-hour wage increase when labor costs are 90 percent of total costs than when labor costs are 5 percent of total costs.

The relationship between the labor cost–total cost ratio and the elasticity of demand for labor is as follows:

The higher the labor cost–total cost ratio, the higher the elasticity of demand for labor (the greater the cutback in labor for any given wage increase); the lower the labor cost–total cost ratio, the lower the elasticity of demand for labor (the less the cutback in labor for any given wage increase).

NUMBER OF SUBSTITUTE FACTORS The more substitutes there are for labor, the more sensitive buyers of labor will be to a change in the price of labor. This principle was established in the discussion of price elasticity of demand. The more possibilities for substituting other factors for labor, the more likely firms will cut back on their use of labor if the price of labor rises.

The more substitutes for labor, the higher the elasticity of demand for labor; the fewer substitutes for labor, the lower the elasticity of demand for labor.

Market Supply of Labor

As the wage rate rises, the quantity supplied of labor rises, *ceteris paribus*. The upward-sloping labor supply curve in Exhibit 8 illustrates this.

economics 24/7

HOW MAY CRIME, OUTSOURCING, AND MULTITASKING BE RELATED?

Consider three seemingly unrelated images of life in the United States in recent years:

- A lower crime rate. For example, violent crime, property crime, and homicides were all down in the late 1990s and early 2000s.

- More people choosing to multitask—that is, to work on more than one task at a time. For example, if you drive a car at the same time as you talk to your office on your cell phone, you are multitasking.

- Increasingly more professional people outsourcing their routine tasks. They are hiring people to run errands, buy groceries, plan parties, drop off dry cleaning, take pets to the vet, and so on.

Could all three images be the result of the same thing—higher real wages?[5] How might higher real wages affect crime, multitasking, and outsourcing? Let's consider crime first. There are both costs and benefits to committing a crime. As long as the benefits are greater than the costs, crimes will be committed; increase the costs of crime relative to the benefits, and the crime rate will decline. Suppose part of the cost of crime is equal to the probability of being sentenced to jail multiplied by the real wage that would be earned if the person were not in jail.

Part of the cost of crime = Probability of jail sentence
× Real wage

If this is the case, then as the real wage rises, the overall cost of crime rises and fewer crimes will be committed.

How does the real wage relate to individuals outsourcing their routine tasks? To illustrate, suppose John and Mary are married and have two daughters. Currently, Mary works as a physician and John works part time as an accountant. Because John has chosen to work part time, he takes care of many of the routine household tasks. He buys the groceries, runs the errands, and so on. If the real wage rises

for accountants, John may rethink his part-time work. An increase in the real wage is the same as an increase in the reward from working, and so John may choose to work more. In fact, it may be cheaper for him to work full time and pay someone else to run the errands, buy the groceries, and so on.

Finally, what about multitasking? As the real wage rises, one's time becomes more valuable. And as time becomes more valuable, people will want to economize on it. One way to economize on time is to do several things at the same time. Instead of spending 20 minutes driving to work and another 10 minutes talking on the phone, why not "kill two birds with one stone" and talk on the phone while driving to work? Ten minutes are saved this way. Of course, there is a downside to this. (Economists are quick to point out that most activities come with both benefits and costs.) Talking on a cell phone while driving is not only illegal in some states, but it probably makes you and others around you less safe while driving.

If higher real wages can affect the crime rate, the amount of outsourcing, and the degree to which people multitask, it is important to know what can cause real wages to rise. One way real wages can rise is through a technological advance that increases the quality of the capital goods used by labor. To illustrate, consider a technological advance that makes it possible for computers to complete more tasks in less time. As a result, the productivity of labor rises and the demand curve for labor shifts to the right. Higher demand for labor increases the nominal wage rate and, as long as the price level doesn't rise by more than the nominal wage rate, the real wage rises too.

Can a technological advance indirectly lead to a lower crime rate, more outsourcing, and greater multitasking? We think so.

[5]Nominal wages are dollar wages—such as $30 an hour. Real wages are nominal wages adjusted for price changes. Stated differently, real wages measure what nominal wages can actually buy in terms of goods and services. So when real wages rise, people can buy more goods and services.

At a wage rate of W_1, individuals are willing to supply 100 labor units. At the higher wage rate of W_2, individuals are willing to supply 200 labor units. Some individuals who were not willing to work at a wage rate of W_1 are willing to work at a wage rate of W_2, and some individuals who were working at W_1 will be willing to supply more labor units at W_2. At the even higher wage rate of W_3, individuals are willing to supply 280 labor units.

An Individual's Supply of Labor

Exhibit 8 shows an upward-sloping *market* supply curve of labor. Let's consider an individual's supply curve of labor—say, John's supply curve of labor. Is it upward sloping? The answer to this question depends on the relative strengths of the substitution and income effects.

To illustrate, suppose John currently earns $10 an hour and works 40 hours a week. If John's wage rate rises to, say, $15 an hour, he will feel two effects, each pulling him in opposite directions.

One effect, the *substitution effect,* works as follows: As his wage rate rises, John recognizes that the monetary reward from working has increased. As a result, John will want to work more—say, 45 hours a week instead of 40 hours (+5 hours).

The other effect, the *income effect,* works this way: As his wage rate rises, John knows that he can earn $600 a week (40 hours at $15 an hour) instead of $400 a week (40 hours at $10 an hour). If leisure is a normal good (the demand for which increases as income increases), then John will want to consume more leisure as his income rises. But the only way to consume more leisure is to work fewer hours. Let's say John wants to decrease his work hours per week from 40 to 37 hours (–3 hours).

The substitution effect pulls John in one direction (toward working 5 more hours), and the income effect pulls John in the opposite direction (toward working 3 fewer hours). Which effect is stronger? In our numerical example, the substitution effect is stronger, so on net, John wants to work 2 more hours a week as his wage rate rises. This means John's supply curve of labor is upward sloping between a wage rate of $10 and $15.

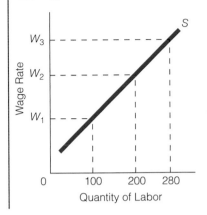

The Market Supply of Labor

A direct relationship exists between the wage rate and the quantity of labor supplied.

Shifts in the Labor Supply Curve

Changes in the wage rate change the quantity supplied of labor units; that is, they cause a *movement* along a given supply curve. But what *shifts* the entire labor supply curve? Two factors of major importance are wage rates in other labor markets and the nonmoney, or nonpecuniary, aspects of a job.

WAGE RATES IN OTHER LABOR MARKETS Deborah currently works as a technician in a television manufacturing plant. She has skills suitable for a number of jobs. One day, she learns that the computer manufacturing plant on the other side of town is offering 33 percent more pay per hour. Deborah is also trained to work as a computer operator, so she decides to leave her current job and apply for work at the computer manufacturing plant. In short, the wage rate offered in other labor markets can bring about a shift of the supply curve in a particular labor market.

NONMONEY, OR NONPECUNIARY, ASPECTS OF A JOB Other things held constant, people prefer to avoid dirty, heavy, dangerous work in cold climates. An increase in the overall "unpleasantness" of a job (e.g., an increased probability of contracting lung cancer working in a coal mine) will cause a decrease in the supply of labor to that firm or industry and a leftward shift in its labor supply curve. An increase in the overall "pleasantness" of a job (e.g., employees are now entitled to a longer lunch break and use of the company gym) will cause an increase in the supply of labor to that firm or industry and a rightward shift in its labor supply curve.

Putting Supply and Demand Together

Exhibit 9 illustrates a particular labor market. The equilibrium wage rate and quantity of labor are established by the forces of supply and demand. At a wage rate of W_2, there is a surplus of labor. Some people who want to work at this wage rate will not be able to find jobs. A subset of this group will begin to offer their services for a lower wage rate. The wage rate will move down until it reaches W_1.

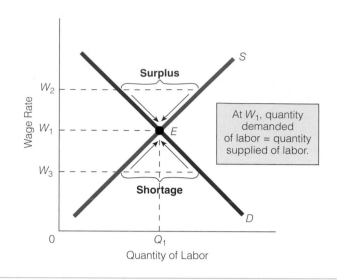

exhibit 9

Equilibrium in a Particular Labor Market

The forces of supply and demand bring about the equilibrium wage rate and quantity of labor. At the equilibrium wage rate, the quantity demanded of labor equals the quantity supplied. At any other wage rate, there is either a surplus or a shortage of labor.

At a wage rate of W_3, there is a shortage of labor. Some demanders of labor will begin to bid up the wage rate until it reaches W_1. At the equilibrium wage rate, W_1, the quantity supplied of labor equals the quantity demanded of labor.

Why Do Wage Rates Differ?

To discover why wage rates differ, we must determine what conditions would be necessary for everyone to receive the same pay. Assume the following conditions hold:

1. The demand for every type of labor is the same. (Throughout our analysis, any wage differentials caused by demand are short-run differentials.)

2. There are no special nonpecuniary aspects to any job.

3. All labor is ultimately homogeneous and can costlessly be trained for different types of employment.

4. All labor is mobile at zero cost.

Given these conditions, there would be no difference in wage rates in the long run. To illustrate, consider Exhibit 10, where two labor markets, A and B, are shown. Initially, the supply conditions are different, with a greater supply of workers in labor market B (represented by S_B) than in labor market A (represented by S_A). Because of the different supply conditions, more labor is employed in labor market B (Q_B) than in labor market A (Q_A), and the equilibrium wage rate in labor market B ($10) is lower than the equilibrium wage rate in labor market A ($30).

The differences in the wage rates between the two labor markets will not last. We have assumed (1) labor can move costlessly from one labor market to another (so why not move from the lower paying job to the higher paying job?), (2) there are no special nonpecuniary aspects to any job (there is no nonpecuniary reason for not moving), (3) labor is ultimately homogeneous (workers who work in labor market B can work in labor market A), and (4) if workers need training to make a move from one labor market to another, they not only are capable of being trained but also can acquire the training costlessly.

As a result, some workers in labor market B will relocate to labor market A, decreasing the supply of workers to S'_B in labor market B and increasing the supply of workers to S'_A in labor market A. The relocation of workers ends when the equilibrium wage rate in both markets is the same—$20. We conclude that wage rates will not differ in the long run if our four conditions hold.

(a)
Labor Market A

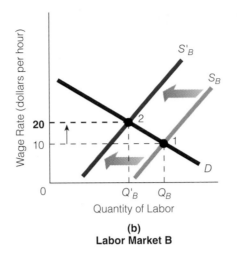

(b)
Labor Market B

exhibit **10**

Wage Rate Equalization Across Labor Markets

Given the four necessary conditions (noted in the text), there will be no wage rate differences across labor markets. We start with a wage rate of $30 in labor market *A* and a wage rate of $10 in labor market *B*. Soon some individuals in *B* relocate to *A*. This increases the supply in one market (*A*), driving down the wage rate, and decreases the supply in the other market (*B*), driving up the wage rate. Equilibrium comes when the same wage rate is paid in both labor markets. This outcome critically depends on the necessary conditions holding.

Because we know the conditions under which wage rates will not differ, we now know why wage rates do differ. Obviously, they differ because demand conditions are not the same in all labor markets (important to explain short-run wage differentials only) and because supply conditions are not the same in all markets: There are nonpecuniary aspects to different jobs, labor is not homogeneous, labor cannot be retrained without cost, and labor is not costlessly mobile.

Why Demand and Supply Differ in Different Labor Markets

Saying that wage rates differ because demand and supply conditions in different labor markets differ raises the question of why this is the case. Let's consider what factors affect the demand for and supply of labor.

DEMAND FOR LABOR The market demand curve for labor is based on the *MRP* curves for labor of the individual firms in the market. So we need to look at what affects the components of *MRP*, namely, *MR* and *MPP*.

Marginal revenue is indirectly affected by product supply and demand conditions because these conditions determine price ($MR = \Delta TR/\Delta Q$ and $TR = P \times Q$). Thus, product demand and supply conditions affect factor demand. In short, because the supply and demand conditions in different product markets are different, it follows that the demand for labor in different labor markets will be different too.

The second factor, the marginal physical product of labor, is affected by individual workers' *own abilities and skills* (both innate and learned), the *degree of effort* they put forth on the job, and the *other factors of production* available to them. With respect to the latter, American workers are more productive than workers in many other countries because they work with many more capital goods and much more technical know-how. If all individuals had the same innate and learned skills and abilities, applied the same degree of effort on the job, and worked with the same amount and quality of other factors of production, wages would differ less than they currently do.

SUPPLY OF LABOR As noted earlier, the supply conditions in different labor markets are different. First, jobs have *different nonpecuniary qualities*. Working as a coal miner in West Virginia is not as attractive a job as working as a tour guide at a lush resort in Hawaii. We would expect this fact to be reflected in the supply of coal miners and tour guides.

economics 24/7

WHAT IS THE WAGE RATE FOR A STREET-LEVEL PUSHER IN A DRUG GANG?

Gangs that deal drugs exist in almost every large city in the United States. It is not uncommon to see a 16- or 17-year-old gang member selling or delivering drugs in Los Angeles, New York, Chicago, Houston, or elsewhere. Often, in a public debate about drugs in one of these cities, someone will say, "No wonder these kids sell drugs; it's the best job they can get. When your alternatives are working at McDonald's earning the minimum wage or selling drugs for big money, you sell drugs. If we want to get kids off the streets and out of gangs and if we want to stop them from selling drugs, we need to have something better for them than the minimum wage."

But we wonder: Do the young gang members who sell and deliver drugs really earn "big money"? Economics would predict that they wouldn't. After all, one would think that the supply of people who can sell or deliver drugs is rather large. In fact, a recent study found that low-level foot soldiers in a drug gang actually earned very low wages.

Steven Levitt, an economist, and Sudhir Venkatesh, a sociologist, analyzed the data set of a drug-selling street gang.[6] They estimated that the average hourly wage rate in the gang was $6 at the time they started the study and $11 at the time they finished.[7] They also noted that the distribution of wages was extremely skewed. Actual street-level dealers (foot soldiers) appeared to earn less than the minimum wage. According to Levitt and Venkatesh, "While these wages are almost too low to be believable, there are both theoretical arguments and corroborating empirical evidence in support of these numbers. From a theoretical perspective, it is hardly surprising that foot-soldier wages would be low given the minimal skill requirements for the job and the presence of a 'reserve army' of potential replacements among the rank and file."

---

[6]Steven Levitt and Sudhir Venkatesh, *An Economic Analysis of a Drug-Selling Gang's Finances,* NBER Working Paper No. W6592 (Cambridge, MA: National Bureau of Economic Research, 1998).
[7]Wage rates are in 1995 dollars.

Second, supply is also a reflection of the *number of persons who can actually do a job.* Williamson may want to be a nuclear physicist but may not have the ability in science and mathematics to become one. Johnson may want to be a basketball player but may not have the ability to become one.

Third, even if individuals have the ability to work at a certain job, they may perceive the *training costs as too high* (relative to the perceived benefits) to train for it. Tyler may have the ability to be a brain surgeon but views the years of schooling required to become one too high a price to pay.

Fourth, sometimes supply in different labor markets reflects a difference in the *cost of moving* across markets. Wage rates might be higher in Alaska than in Alabama for comparable labor because the workers in Alabama find the cost of relocating to Alaska too high relative to the benefits of receiving a higher wage.

In conclusion, because the wage rate is determined by supply-and-demand forces, the factors that affect these forces indirectly affect wage rates. Exhibit 11 summarizes these factors.

Why Did You Choose the Major That You Chose?

Our lives are sometimes influenced by what happens in labor markets. Consider a college student who is trying to decide whether to major in accounting or English. The student believes that English is more fun and interesting but that accounting, on average, will earn her enough additional income to compensate for the lack of fun in accounting. Specif-

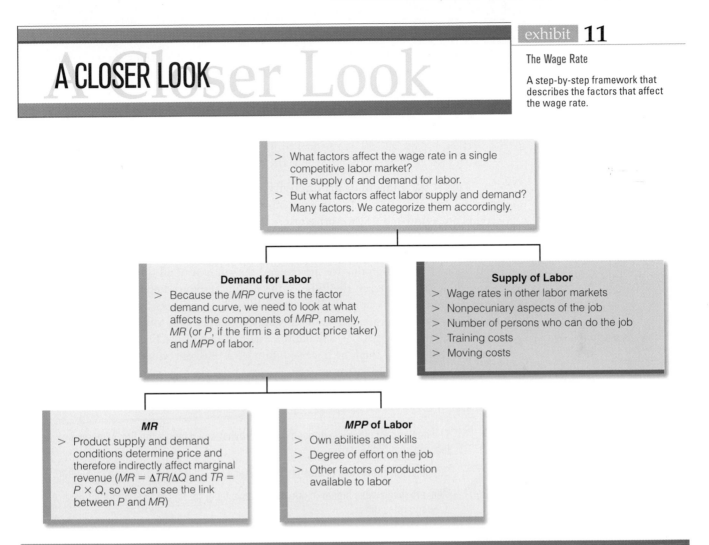

exhibit **11**

The Wage Rate

A step-by-step framework that describes the factors that affect the wage rate.

A CLOSER LOOK

> What factors affect the wage rate in a single competitive labor market?
> The supply of and demand for labor.
> But what factors affect labor supply and demand?
> Many factors. We categorize them accordingly.

Demand for Labor
> Because the *MRP* curve is the factor demand curve, we need to look at what affects the components of *MRP*, namely, *MR* (or *P*, if the firm is a product price taker) and *MPP* of labor.

Supply of Labor
> Wage rates in other labor markets
> Nonpecuniary aspects of the job
> Number of persons who can do the job
> Training costs
> Moving costs

MR
> Product supply and demand conditions determine price and therefore indirectly affect marginal revenue ($MR = \Delta TR/\Delta Q$ and $TR = P \times Q$, so we can see the link between P and MR)

MPP of Labor
> Own abilities and skills
> Degree of effort on the job
> Other factors of production available to labor

ically, at a $55,000 annual salary for accounting and a $39,000 annual salary for English, the student is indifferent between accounting and English. But at a $56,000 annual salary for accounting and a $39,000 annual salary for English, accounting moves ahead.

Of course, what accounting "pays" is determined by the demand for and supply of accountants. When we realize this, we realize that other people influenced the person's decision to become an accountant. To illustrate, suppose Congress passes more intricate tax laws that require more accountants to figure them out. This increases the demand for accountants, which in turn raises the wage rate for accountants. And an increase in the wage rate that accountants receive increases the probability that more people—perhaps you—will major in accounting and not in English, philosophy, or history.

As you can see, economics—in which markets play a major role—helps explain why part of your life is the way it is.

Marginal Productivity Theory

Let's see where an analysis of some of the things we know from this chapter leads us:

1. If a firm is a factor price taker, marginal factor cost is constant and equal to factor price, $MFC = P$. Suppose the factor price taker hires labor. For the firm, $MFC = W$, where W is the wage rate.

2. Firms hire the factor quantity at which $MRP = MFC$.

3. Taking points 1 and 2 together, a factor price taker pays labor a wage equal to its marginal revenue product: $W = MRP$. That is, because $MFC = W$ (point 1) and $MRP = MFC$ (point 2), it follows that $W = MRP$.

4. If a firm is perfectly competitive, $MRP = VMP$.

5. If a firm is both perfectly competitive (a product price taker) and a factor price taker, it pays labor a wage equal to its value marginal product: $W = VMP$. That is, because $W = MRP$ (point 3) and $MRP = VMP$ (point 4), it follows that $W = VMP$.

Marginal Productivity Theory

States that firms in competitive or perfect product and factor markets pay factors their marginal revenue products.

This is the **marginal productivity theory**, which states that if a firm sells its product and purchases its factors in competitive or perfect markets (i.e., it is a perfectly competitive firm and a factor price taker), it pays its factors their MRP or VMP (the two are equal for a product price taker).

The theory holds that under the competitive conditions specified, if a factor unit is withdrawn from the productive process and the amount of all other factors remains the same, then the decrease in the value of the product produced equals the factor payment received by the factor unit. To illustrate, suppose Wilson works for a perfectly competitive firm (firm X) producing good X. One day, he quits his job (but nothing else relevant to the firm changes). As a result, the total revenue of the firm falls by $100. If Wilson was paid $100, then he received his MRP. He was paid a wage equal to his contribution to the productive process.[8]

SELF-TEST

1. The demand for labor is a derived demand. What could cause the firm's demand curve for labor to shift rightward?

2. Suppose the coefficient of elasticity of demand for labor is 3. What does this mean?

3. Why are wage rates higher in one competitive labor market than in another? In short, why do wage rates differ?

4. Workers in labor market X do the same work as workers in labor market Y, but they earn $10 less per hour. Why?

Labor Markets and Information

This section looks at job hiring, employment practices, employment discrimination, and how information, or the lack of it, affects these processes.

Screening Potential Employees

Employers typically do not know exactly how productive a potential employee will be. What the employer wants, but lacks, is complete information about the potential employee's future job performance.

This raises two questions: Why would an employer want complete information about a potential employee's future job performance? What does the employer do because he or she lacks complete information?

The answer to the first question is obvious. Employers have a strong monetary incentive to hire good, stable, quick-learning, responsible, hardworking, punctual

---

[8]Recall that there are two ways to calculate MRP: $MRP = \Delta TR/\Delta$quantity of the factor, and $MRP = MR \times MPP$. In this example, we use the first method. When Wilson quits his job, the change in the denominator is 1 factor unit. If, as a result, TR falls by $100, then the change in the numerator must be $100.

employees. One study found that corporate spending on training employees reached $40 billion annually. Obviously, corporations want to see the highest return possible for their training expenditures, so they try to hire employees who will make the training worthwhile. This is where screening comes in.

Screening is the process used by employers to increase the probability of choosing "good" employees based on certain criteria. For example, an employer might ask a young college graduate searching for a job what his or her GPA was in college. This is a screening mechanism. The employer might know from past experience that persons with high GPAs turn out to be better employees, on average, than persons with low GPAs. Screening is one thing an employer does because he or she lacks complete information.

Screening
The process used by employers to increase the probability of choosing "good" employees based on certain criteria.

Promoting from Within

Sometimes, employers promote from within the company because they have more information about company employees than about potential employees.

Suppose the executive vice president in charge of sales is retiring from Trideck, Inc. The president of the company could hire an outsider to replace the vice president, but often, she will select an insider about whom she has some knowledge. What may look like discrimination to outsiders—"That company discriminates against persons not working for it"—may simply be a reflection of the difference in costs to the employer of acquiring relevant information about employees inside and outside the company.

Is It Discrimination or Is It an Information Problem?

Suppose the world is made up of just two kinds of people: those with characteristic X and those with characteristic Y. We call them X people and Y people, respectively. Over time, we observe that most employers are X people and that they tend to hire and promote proportionally more X than Y people. Are the Y people being discriminated against?

They could be. Nothing we have said so far rules this out. But then, it may be that X people rarely hire or promote Y people because over time X employers have learned that Y people, on average, do not perform as well as X people.

So in this example, we simply state that X people are not discriminating against Y people. Instead, Y people are not being hired and promoted as often as X people because, for whatever reason, Y people, on average, are not as productive as X people.

Suppose in this environment, an extremely productive Y person applies for a job with an X employer. The problem is that the X employer does not know—she lacks complete information—about the full abilities of the Y person. Furthermore, acquiring complete information is costly. She bases her decision to reject the Y person's job application on what she knows about Y people, which is that, on average, they are not as productive as X people. She doesn't do this because she has something against Y people but because it is simply too costly for her to acquire complete information on every potential employee—X or Y.

We do not mean to imply that everything that looks like discrimination is really a problem of the high cost of information. Nonetheless, sometimes, what looks like discrimination ("he doesn't like me; I'm a Y person") is a consequence of living in a world where acquiring complete information is "too costly."

Legislation mandating equal employment opportunities requires employers to absorb some information costs to open labor markets to all. All but the smallest of firms are required to search for qualified Y persons who can perform the job even if the employer believes that the average Y person cannot. Requiring employers to forgo the use of a screening mechanism will likely increase firm costs and raise prices to consumers, but the premise of the legislation is that those costs are more than outweighed by the social benefits of having more Y persons in the mainstream of society.

A Reader Asks...

Does Education Matter to Income?

The greater the demand for my labor and the smaller the supply, the higher the wage I'll be paid. One of the things that can shift the factor demand curve for my labor to the right (and thus bring me a higher wage) is a rise in "my *MPP*." Is this where education plays a role? Does more education lead to a higher *MPP* and higher wages?

Certainly, there are people with little education who earn high salaries, but generally speaking, more education does seem to raise one's productivity. And as a result, it tends to raise one's pay. For example, in 2001, a person with only a high school diploma had average annual earnings of $26,795; a person with a bachelor's degree, $50,623; and a person with a master's degree, $63,592.

Let's also consider Charles, who is 22 years old and has just completed his associate's degree. He is trying to decide whether or not to continue his education. In 2001, a person with an associate's degree (as the highest degree) had average annual earnings of $34,744. Let's look at Charles's lifetime earnings in two cases.

If Charles stops his education with an associate's degree and works until he is 65 years old, he will earn $34,744 each year for 43 years.[9] That is a total of $1,493,992. If, however, Charles goes on to get a master's degree and we assume it takes him 6 more years of schooling to do so, then he will earn $63,592 each year for the next 37 years. That is a total of $2,352,904. The difference in lifetime earnings for a person with an associate's degree and a person with a master's degree is $858,912. Stated differently, Charles's lifetime earnings will be approximately 57 percent higher with a master's degree than with an associate's degree (as the highest degree).

The difference in lifetime earnings is even greater for a person with a doctorate. (In 2001, a person with a doctorate had average annual earnings of $85,675.) If we assume a doctorate requires 2 years of additional schooling beyond a master's degree, then the total lifetime earnings with a doctorate will be $2,998,625. It follows, then, that the difference in lifetime earnings (between an associate's degree and a doctorate) is $1,504,633. This is more than 100 percent more lifetime earnings.

Or we can think of it this way. If going from an associate's degree to a doctorate more than doubles Charles's lifetime earnings, it is as if he produces a clone of his associate-degree self during his 8 more years of schooling. (What do you produce in school? Nothing is the wrong answer. You produce clones of yourself.)

---

[9]We are not adjusting in our example for annual percentage increases in earnings.

! analyzing the scene

What is the right number of employees to hire?

Marion Smithies, the owner of a small company, is undecided as to how many additional employees to hire. The right number of employees is the number at which the *MRP* of an additional employee equals the *MFC* of the additional employee. As long as the additional benefits the employee brings to the firm are greater than the additional costs incurred by hiring the employee, it is best to hire the employee. She should stop hiring when additional benefits equal additional costs.

Will jobs always flow to where wages are the lowest?

People often believe that jobs will flow to where wages are the lowest. But if this is true, then why is there a single job in the United States, a relatively high-wage country? Obviously, wages aren't the only thing considered by firms. Firms also look at the productivity of workers—the marginal physical product of the labor that they hire. For example, suppose John is paid $4 an hour and can produce 1 unit of *X* an hour, and Stephanie is paid $10 an hour and can produce 5 units of X an hour. John receives the relatively lower wage, and Stephanie receives the relatively higher wage, but is John really "cheaper" than Stephanie? The feature "Why Jobs Don't Always Move to the Low-Wage Country" discusses this topic in detail.

Would you work more or less at higher wages?

Whether you would work more or less at higher wages depends on how strong your substitution effect is relative to your income effect. If your substitution effect is stronger than your income effect, you will work more at higher wages. If your income effect is stronger than your substitution effect, you will work less at higher wages. If your substitution effect is equal in strength to your income effect, you will work no more and no less at higher wages than at lower wages.

Keep in mind that at some range of wage rates—say, $10 to $40 an hour—your substitution effect might be stronger than your income effect and at another range of wage rates—say, anything over $40 an hour—your income effect might be stronger than your substitution effect. In other words, as wages rise from $10 to $40, you work more, but then if wages rise over $40, you begin to cut back on how much you work. What would your supply curve of labor look like under these conditions?

Is Alex Rodriguez paid too much?

Before we can accurately answer this question, we need to determine what it means to say a person is worth a certain salary—whether the salary is $25 million or $25,000.

Consider this example. Suppose if a firm hires a person, she will generate $90,000 a year in additional revenue for the firm, but the firm will have to pay her only $75,000 a year. Is she worth $75,000? The obvious answer is yes. The additional benefits of hiring her ($90,000) are greater than the additional costs of hiring her ($75,000). Another way of saying this is that her marginal revenue product (MRP) is greater than her marginal factor cost (MFC). In this setting, a person is worth hiring at a particular salary as long as the person's (annual) MRP is greater than her (annual) salary.

So is Alex Rodriguez worth $25 million a year? There is no way to know for sure without knowing his MRP. If his MRP is greater than $25 million a year, then he is worth $25 million. He might be worth even more. If his MRP is less than $25 million, then he isn't worth $25 million. We can say one thing, though: Certainly, the owner of the New York Yankees expected Alex Rodriguez's MRP to be greater than $25 million a year, or he wouldn't have paid him that amount.

chapter summary

Derived Demand

- The demand for a factor is derived; hence, it is called a *derived demand*. Specifically, it is derived from and directly related to the demand for the product that the factor goes to produce; for example, the demand for auto workers is derived from the demand for autos.

MRP, MFC, VMP

- Marginal revenue product (MRP) is the additional revenue generated by employing an additional factor unit. Marginal factor cost (MFC) is the additional cost incurred by employing an additional factor unit. The profit-maximizing firm buys the factor quantity at which $MRP = MFC$.

- The MRP curve is the firm's factor demand curve; it shows how much of a factor the firm buys at different prices.

- Value marginal product (VMP) is a measure of the value that each factor unit adds to the firm's product. Whereas $MRP = MR \times MPP$, $VMP = P \times MPP$. For a perfectly competitive firm, $P = MR$, so $MRP = VMP$. For a monopolist, a monopolistic competitor, or an oligopolist, $P > MR$, so $VMP > MRP$.

The Least-Cost Rule

- A firm minimizes costs by buying factors in the combination at which the MPP-to-price ratio for each factor is the same. For example, if there are two factors, labor (L) and capital (K), the least-cost rule reads $MPP_L / P_L = MPP_K / P_K$.

Labor and Wages

- A change in the price of the product labor produces or a change in the marginal physical product of labor (reflected in a shift in the MPP curve) will shift the demand curve for labor.

- The higher (lower) the elasticity of demand for the product labor produces, the higher (lower) the elasticity of demand for labor. The higher (lower) the labor cost–total cost ratio, the higher (lower) the elasticity of demand for labor. The more (fewer) substitutes for labor, the higher (lower) the elasticity of demand for labor.

- As the wage rate rises, the quantity supplied of labor rises, *ceteris paribus*.

- At the equilibrium wage rate, the quantity supplied of labor equals the quantity demanded of labor.

Demand for and Supply of Labor

- The demand for labor is affected by (1) marginal revenue and (2) marginal physical product. The supply of labor is affected by (1) wage rates in other labor markets, (2) nonpecuniary aspects of the job, (3) number of persons who can do the job, (4) training costs, and (5) moving costs.

Marginal Productivity Theory

- Marginal productivity theory states that firms in competitive or perfect product and factor markets pay their factors their marginal revenue products.

key terms and concepts

Derived Demand

Marginal Revenue
  Product (*MRP*)

Value Marginal Product
  (*VMP*)

Marginal Factor Cost
  (*MFC*)

Factor Price Taker

Least-Cost Rule

Elasticity of Demand for
  Labor

Marginal Productivity
  Theory

Screening

questions and problems

1 The supply curve is horizontal for a factor price taker; however, the industry supply curve is upward sloping. Explain why this occurs.

2 What forces and factors determine the wage rate for a particular type of labor?

3 What is the relationship between labor productivity and wage rates?

4 What might be one effect of government legislating wage rates?

5 Using the theory developed in this chapter, explain the following: (a) why a worker in Ethiopia is likely to earn much less than a worker in Japan; (b) why the army expects recruitment to rise during economic recessions; (c) why basketball stars earn relatively large incomes; (d) why jobs that carry a health risk offer higher pay than jobs that do not, *ceteris paribus*.

6 Discuss the factors that might prevent the equalization of wage rates for identical or comparable jobs across labor markets.

7 Prepare a list of questions that an interviewer is likely to ask an interviewee in a job interview. Try to identify which of the questions are part of the interviewer's screening process.

8 Explain why the market demand curve for labor is not simply the horizontal "addition" of the firms' demand curves for labor.

9 Discuss the firm's objective, its constraints, and how it makes choices in its role as a buyer of resources.

10 Explain the relationship between each of the following pairs of concepts: (a) the elasticity of demand for a product and the elasticity of demand for the labor that produces the product; (b) the labor cost–total cost ratio and the elasticity of demand for labor; (c) the number of substitutes for labor and the elasticity of demand for labor.

working with numbers and graphs

1   Determine the appropriate numbers for the lettered spaces.

(1) Units of Factor X	(2) Quantity of Output	(3) Marginal Physical Product of X (MPP_X)	(4) Product Price, Marginal Revenue $(P = MR)$	(5) Total Revenue	(6) Marginal Revenue Product of X (MRP_X)
0	15	0	$8	F	L
1	24	A	8	G	M
2	32	B	8	H	N
3	39	C	8	I	O
4	45	D	8	J	P
5	50	E	8	K	Q

2   If the price of a factor is constant at $48, how many units of the factor will the firm buy?

3   On the same diagram, draw the *VMP* curve and the *MRP* curve for an oligopolist. Explain why the curves look the way you drew them.

4   Explain why the factor supply curve is horizontal for a factor price taker.

5   Look at the two factor demand curves in the following figure. Is the price of the product that labor goes to produce higher for MRP_2 than for MRP_1? Explain your answer.

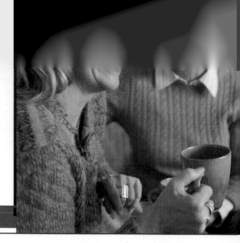

25 Wages, Unions, and Labor

Setting the Scene

The following events occurred one day in November.

8:32 A.M.

The leaders of a union are sitting around a table, discussing what they should do in the current situation. One person says, "I think we should ask for a general wage increase of 7 percent."

"Why not more?" another person asks. "I don't think a 10 percent increase will cause much job loss."

10:04 A.M.

Sophie and Lily are having their morning coffee together at Sophie's house.

"Elliot is going to have to postpone his surgery again," Lily says. "Some union at the hospital is going on strike if the workers don't get a wage increase. The hospital is canceling all elective surgeries. Unions are always causing trouble. Too many workers in this country are members of unions."

"How many workers in the country *are* union members?" Sophie asks. "About half?"

"That would be my guess," answers Lily. "Somewhere around half."

12:46 P.M.

Tom and Carla Jenson have just finished their lunch in their company's cafeteria. They've been discussing their daughter's job prospects.

"I know Debbi has a good job that she likes, but I still think she should join the union," Tom says. "Union workers always get better wages."

"I know that's true in construction because my nephew's a union electrician," Carla replies. "But are you sure union wages are higher than nonunion wages in every industry?"

"I'm sure," replies Tom.

 Here are some questions to keep in mind as you read this chapter:

- *What does the wage increase a union seeks have to do with the number of union members working?*

- *What percentage of U.S. workers are members of unions?*

- *Are union wages always higher than nonunion wages in a given industry?*

See analyzing the scene at the end of this chapter for answers to these questions.

The Facts and Figures of Labor Unions

This section discusses the different types of labor unions and gives some statistics that place unions within the overall labor force.

Types of Unions

Economists often speak of three different types of labor unions: craft (trade) unions, industrial unions, and public employee unions. A **craft** or **trade union** is a union whose membership is made up of individuals who practice the same craft or trade. Examples include the plumbers', electricians', and musicians' unions.

An **industrial union** is a union whose membership is made up of workers who work in the same firm or industry but do not all practice the same craft or trade. Examples include the autoworkers' and the steelworkers' unions. For an industrial union to be successful, it must unionize all firms in an industry. If it does not, union firms will face competition from (possibly lower cost) nonunion firms, which may lead to a decrease in the number of union firms and workers.

A **public employee union** is a union whose membership is made up of workers who work for the local, state, or federal government. Examples include teachers', police, and firefighters' unions.

Besides these three types of unions, some economists hold that employee associations, such as the American Medical Association (AMA), the American Association of University Professors (AAUP), and the American Bar Association (ABA), are a type of union. An **employee association** is an organization whose members belong to a particular profession. Many people would probably not place professional employee associations into the union category. Some economists argue, however, that employee associations often have the same objectives and implement the same practices to meet those objectives as craft, industrial, and public employee unions; consequently, these associations should be considered unions.

Craft (Trade) Union
A union whose membership is made up of individuals who practice the same craft or trade.

Industrial Union
A union whose membership is made up of individuals who work in the same firm or industry but do not all practice the same craft or trade.

Public Employee Union
A union whose membership is made up of individuals who work for the local, state, or federal government.

Employee Association
An organization whose members belong to a particular profession.

Union Membership: The United States and Abroad

Union membership as a percentage of the U.S. labor force (total number of union members divided by total work force) was 5.6 percent in 1910, rising to about 12 percent in 1920. By 1930, it was down to about 7.4 percent, and in 1934, it fell to approximately 5 percent. From the late 1930s until the mid-1950s, union membership as a percentage of the labor force grew. It reached its peak of 25 percent in the mid-1950s. In recent years, union membership has declined. In 1983, it was 20.1 percent; in 1998, it was 13.9 percent; and in 2005, it was 12.5 percent.

Union membership as a percentage of the labor force is much higher in some countries than it is in the United States. For example, in 2001, it was more than 80 percent in Denmark, about 79 percent in Sweden, more than 40 percent in Ireland, about 39 percent in Austria, more than 30 percent in both Italy and Germany, and about 20 percent in Japan.

Objectives of Labor Unions

Labor unions usually seek one of three objectives: (1) to employ all their members, (2) to maximize the total wage bill, or (3) to maximize income for a limited number of union members.

Employment for All Members

One possible objective of a labor union is employment for all its members. To illustrate, suppose the demand curve in Exhibit 1 represents the demand for labor in a given union. Also assume the total membership of the union is Q_1. If the objective of the union is to have its total membership employed, then the wage rate that must exist in the market is W_1. At W_1, firms want to hire the total union membership.

Maximizing the Total Wage Bill

The total wage bill received by the membership of a union is equal to the wage rate multiplied by the number of labor hours worked. One possible objective of a labor union is to maximize this dollar amount—that is, to maximize the number of dollars coming *from* the employer *to* union members.

In Exhibit 1, the wage rate that maximizes the total wage bill is W_2. At W_2, the quantity of labor is Q_2 and the elasticity of demand for labor is equal to 1. Recall that total revenue (or total expenditure) is maximized when price elasticity of demand is equal to 1, or demand has unit elasticity. It follows that the total wage bill is maximized at that point where the demand for labor is unit elastic. Note, however, that less union labor is working at W_2 than at W_1, indicating that there is a tradeoff between higher wages and the employment of union members.

Maximizing Income for a Limited Number of Union Members

Some economists have suggested that a labor union might want neither total employment of its membership nor maximization of the total wage bill. Instead, it might prefer to maximize income for a *limited number* of union members, perhaps those with the most influence or seniority in the union. Suppose this group is represented by Q_3 in Exhibit 1. The highest wage at which this group can be employed is W_3; thus, the union might seek this wage rate instead of any lower wage.

Q&A **Wouldn't a higher wage than W_2 mean that more money was being transferred from the employer to the labor union?**

Think back to our discussion of price elasticity of demand in an earlier chapter. In that chapter, we learned that if demand (for a good) is elastic, raising the price of the good results in lower total revenue instead of greater total revenue. It is the same here with respect to the wage rate. If the demand for labor is elastic, then raising the wage rate will end up lowering the total amount employers spend on labor.

micro Theme

In an earlier chapter, we said that economic agents (firms, individuals, etc.) have objectives. Once we know their objectives, it follows that we can predict their behavior. To illustrate, if the firm's objective is to maximize profit, then it will produce the quantity of output at which $MR = MC$. We also know that different behavior is a result of different objectives. For example, the firm will behave differently if it wants to maximize profit than if it wants to maximize sales.

The same idea holds with respect to labor unions. If the objective of the labor union is to, say, employ all the workers in the union, then it will behave differently from when its objective is to maximize the income for a limited number of individuals. In the first case, the wage rate the union seeks will be lower than in the second case.

Wage-Employment Tradeoff

Exhibit 1 suggests that a union can get higher wage rates, but some of the union members will lose their jobs in the process. Hence, a wage-employment tradeoff exists. This wage-employment tradeoff depends on the *elasticity of demand for labor*.

To illustrate, consider the demand for labor in two unions, *A* and *B*, in Exhibit 2. Suppose both unions bargain for a wage increase from W_1 to W_2. The quantity of labor

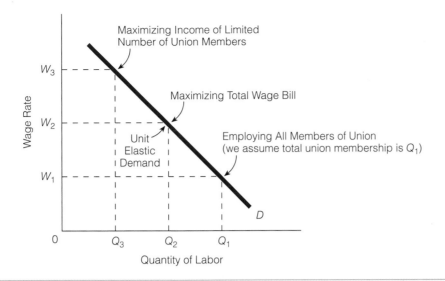

exhibit **1**

Labor Union Objectives

If total membership in the union is Q_1, and the union's objective is employment for all its members, it chooses W_1. If the objective is to maximize the total wage bill, it chooses W_2, where the elasticity of demand for labor equals 1. If the union's objective is to maximize the income of a limited number of union workers (represented by Q_3), it chooses W_3.

drops much more in union *B,* where demand for labor is elastic between the two wage rates, than in union *A,* where the demand for labor is inelastic between the two wage rates. We would expect union *B* to be less likely than union *A* to push for higher wages, *ceteris paribus.* The reason is that the wage-employment tradeoff is more pronounced for union *B* than for union *A.* It is simply costlier (in terms of union members' jobs) for union *B* to push for higher wages than it is for union *A* to do so.

micro
Theme   In an earlier chapter, we said that all economic agents face constraints. Different constraints will often bring about different behavior. For example, in our discussion of labor unions *A* and *B,* we noted that labor union *B* faces a sharper wage-employment tradeoff than labor union *A.* As a result, we predict that labor union *B* would be "less likely to push for higher wages, *ceteris paribus.*"

(a)
Union *A*

The lower the elasticity of demand for labor, the smaller the cutback in labor for a given wage increase.

(b)
Union *B*

exhibit **2**

The Wage-Employment Tradeoff: Two Cases

For union *A,* which has an inelastic demand for its labor between W_1 and $W_2,$ a higher wage rate brings about a smaller cutback in the quantity of labor than for union *B,* which has an elastic demand for its labor between W_1 and $W_2.$ We predict that union *B* will be less likely to push for higher wages than union *A* because its wage-employment tradeoff is more pronounced.

Practices of Labor Unions

This section explains how labor unions try to meet their objectives by influencing one or more of the following factors: the elasticity of demand for labor, the demand for labor, and the supply of labor. We also discuss how unions can directly affect wages.

Affecting Elasticity of Demand for Union Labor

Exhibit 2 shows that the lower the elasticity of demand for labor, the smaller the cutback in labor for any given wage increase. Obviously, the smaller the cutback in labor for a given wage increase, the better it is from the viewpoint of the labor union. Given a choice between losing either 200 jobs or 50 jobs because of a wage rate increase of $2, the labor union prefers to lose the smaller number of jobs. Thus, a labor union looks for ways to lower the elasticity of demand for its labor. It does this mainly by attempting to reduce the availability of substitutes.

AVAILABILITY OF SUBSTITUTE PRODUCTS Consider the autoworkers' union, whose members produce American automobiles. We know that the lower the elasticity of demand for American automobiles, the lower the elasticity of demand for the labor that produces automobiles. We would expect, then, that unions would attempt to reduce the availability of substitutes for the products they produce through such means as import restrictions. The autoworkers' union, for example, has in past years proposed restrictions on the U.S. import of Japanese cars.

AVAILABILITY OF SUBSTITUTE FACTORS The fewer the substitute factors for union labor, the lower the elasticity of demand for union labor. There are two general substitutes for union labor: nonunion labor and certain types of machines. For example, a musical synthesizer (which can sound like many different instruments) is a substitute for a group of musicians playing different instruments. Labor unions have often attempted to reduce the availability of substitute factors—both the nonunion labor variety and the nonhuman variety. Thus, labor unions commonly oppose the relaxation of immigration laws, they usually favor the repatriation of illegal aliens, they generally are in favor of a high minimum wage (which increases the relative price of nonunion labor vis-à-vis union labor), and they usually oppose machines that can be substituted for their labor. Also, in the area of construction, unions usually specify that certain jobs are done by, say, electricians only (thus prohibiting substitute factors from being employed on certain jobs).

Affecting the Demand for Union Labor

Labor unions can try to meet their objectives by increasing the demand for union labor. All other things held constant, this leads to higher wage rates and more union labor employed. How can labor unions increase the demand for their labor? Consider the following possibilities.

INCREASING PRODUCT DEMAND Unions occasionally urge the buying public to buy the products produced by union labor. Union advertisements urge people to "look for the union label" or to look for the label that reads "Made in the U.S.A." As mentioned earlier, they sometimes also support legislation that either keeps out imports altogether or makes them more expensive.

INCREASING SUBSTITUTE FACTOR PRICES If union action leads to a rise in the relative price of factors that are substitutes for union labor, the demand for union labor rises. (Recall that if X and Y are substitutes and the price of X rises, so does the demand for Y.) For this reason, unions have often lobbied for an increase in the minimum wage—the wage received mostly by unskilled labor, which is a substitute for skilled union labor. The first minimum wage legislation was passed when many companies were moving from the unionized North to the nonunionized South. The minimum wage made the nonunionized, relatively unskilled labor in the South more expensive and is said to have slowed the movement of companies to the South.

INCREASING MARGINAL PHYSICAL PRODUCT If unions can increase the productivity of their members, the demand for their labor will rise. With this in mind, unions prefer to add skilled labor to their ranks, and they sometimes undertake training programs for new entrants.

Affecting the Supply of Union Labor

A third way labor unions try to meet their objectives is by decreasing the supply of labor. A decreased supply translates into higher wage rates. How might the labor union decrease the supply of labor from what it might be if the labor union did not exist? One possibility is to control the supply of labor in a market.

Craft unions, in particular, have been moderately successful in getting employers to hire only union labor. In the past, they were successful at turning some businesses into closed shops. A **closed shop** is an organization in which an employee must belong to the union before he or she can work. (In contrast, in an *open shop,* an employer may hire union or nonunion workers.) When unions can determine, or at least control in some way, the supply of labor in a given market, they can decrease it from what it would ordinarily have been. They can do this by restricting membership, by requiring long apprenticeships, or by rigid certification requirements. The closed shop was prohibited in 1947 by the Taft-Hartley Act.

The union shop, however, is legal in many states today. A **union shop** is an organization that does not require individuals to be union members to be hired but does require them to join the union within a certain period of time after becoming employed.

Today, unions typically argue for union shops, against open shops, and against the prohibition of closed shops. They also typically argue against state right-to-work laws (which some, but not all, states have), which make it illegal to require union membership for purposes of employment. (The Taft-Hartley Act allowed states to pass right-to-work laws and thus to override federal legislation that legalized union shops.) In short, the union shop is illegal in right-to-work states.

Affecting Wages Directly: Collective Bargaining

Besides increasing wage rates indirectly by influencing the demand for and supply of their labor, unions can directly affect wage rates through collective bargaining. **Collective bargaining** is the process whereby wage rates are determined by the union bargaining with management on behalf of all its members. In collective bargaining, union members act together as a single unit to increase their bargaining power with management. On the other side of the market, the employers of labor may also band together and act as one unit. Their objective is the same as the union's: to increase their bargaining power.

From the viewpoint of the labor union, collective bargaining is unlikely to be successful unless the union can strike. A **strike** occurs when unionized employees refuse to work at a certain wage or under certain conditions. Exhibit 3 illustrates the effects of successful union collective bargaining.

Closed Shop

An organization in which an employee must belong to the union before he or she can be hired.

Union Shop

An organization in which a worker is not required to be a member of the union to be hired but must become a member within a certain period of time after being employed.

Collective Bargaining

The process whereby wage rates and other issues are determined by a union bargaining with management on behalf of all union members.

Strike

The situation in which union employees refuse to work at a certain wage or under certain conditions.

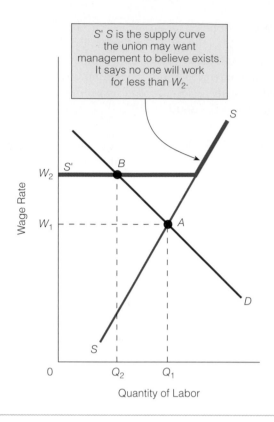

S' S is the supply curve the union may want management to believe exists. It says no one will work for less than W_2.

exhibit 3

Successful Collective Bargaining by the Union

We start at a wage rate of W_1. The union's objective is to increase the wage rate to W_2. This means the union holds that the new supply curve of labor is $S'S$—the heavy supply curve. To convince management that the new supply curve looks as the union says it does, the union will have to either threaten a strike or call one. We assume that the union is successful at raising the wage rate to W_2. As a consequence, the quantity of labor employed is less than it would have been at W_1.

Suppose the initial wage rate that exists in the labor market is the competitive wage rate W_1. This is the wage rate that would exist if each employee were to bargain separately with management. The equilibrium quantity of labor is Q_1.

Management and the union (which represents all labor in this market) now sit down at a collective bargaining session. The union specifies that it wants a wage rate of W_2 and says that *none of its members will work at a lower wage rate*. This means the union holds that the new supply curve is $S'S$—the heavy supply curve in Exhibit 3. In effect, the union is telling management that it cannot hire anyone for a wage rate lower than W_2.

Whether the union can bring about this higher wage rate (W_2) depends on whether it can prevent labor from working at less than this wage. That is, if management does not initially agree to W_2, the union will have to call a strike and show management that it cannot hire any labor for a wage rate lower than W_2. It has to convince management that the new supply curve looks the way the union says it looks. We assume in Exhibit 3 that the strike threat, or actual strike, is successful for the union, and management agrees to the higher wage rate of W_2. As a result, the quantity of labor employed, Q_2, is less than it would have been at W_1. The new equilibrium is at point B instead of point A.

Strikes

The purpose of a strike is to convince management that the supply curve is what the union says it is. Often, this depends on the ability of striking union employees to prevent nonstriking and nonunion employees from working for management at a lower wage rate than the union is seeking through collective bargaining. For example, if management can easily hire individuals at a wage rate lower than W_2 in Exhibit 3, it will not be convinced that the heavy supply curve is the relevant supply curve.

economics 24/7

TECHNOLOGY, THE PRICE OF COMPETING FACTORS, AND DISPLACED WORKERS[1]

For most of the 18th century in England, spinners and weavers worked on hand-operated spinning wheels and looms. Then in the 1770s, a mechanical spinner was invented. This new machine required steam or water power, and so yarn-spinning factories were set up near water mills. The factory workers, working with mechanical spinners, could produce 100 times more yarn in a day than they could produce using hand-operated spinners.

Because of the increased supply of yarn, the price fell and the quantity demanded of yarn increased substantially. In turn, this increased the demand for weavers, who continued to use hand-operated looms. As a result of the increased demand for weavers, their wages increased. In reaction to the higher wages for weavers, entrepreneurs and inventors began to experiment with different kinds of weaving machines. Their experiments began to pay off; in 1787, the power loom was invented, although it was not perfected until the 1820s. By the 1830s, two workers using a power loom could produce in one day 20 times what a weaver could produce on a hand-operated loom.

Soon, the weavers who used hand-operated looms found themselves without jobs. They had been displaced by the introduction of the power loom. Some of the displaced workers showed their frustration and anger at their predicament by burning power looms and factories.

The story of spinners and weavers in 18th-century England helps us realize two important points about technology. First, as long as there are advancements in technology, some workers will be temporarily displaced. Second, an advance in technology often has an identifiable cause; it doesn't simply fall out of the sky. If it had not been for the higher weavers' wages, it is not clear that the power loom would have been invented.

[1]This feature is based on Elizabeth Hoffman, "How Can Displaced Workers Find Better Jobs?" in *Second Thoughts: Myths and Morals of U.S. Economic History*, ed. by Donald McCloskey (Oxford: Oxford University Press, 1993).

SELF-TEST

(Answers to Self-Test questions are in the Self-Test Appendix.)

1. What will lower the demand for union labor?
2. What is the difference between a closed shop and a union shop?
3. What is the objective of a strike?

Effects of Labor Unions

What are the effects of labor unions on wage rates? Are the effects the same in all labor markets? These two questions are addressed in this section.

The Case of Monopsony

A single buyer in a factor market is known as a **monopsony**. Some economists refer to a monopsony as a "buyer's monopoly." A monopoly is a single seller of a product; a monopsony is a single buyer of a factor.

Suppose a firm in a small town is the only buyer of labor because there are no other firms for miles around. This firm would be considered a monopsony. Because it is a monopsony, it cannot buy additional units of a factor without increasing the price it pays

Monopsony
A single buyer in a factor market.

economics 24/7

WHAT ARE COLLEGE PROFESSORS' OBJECTIVES?

Labor unions try to meet their objectives by influencing the elasticity of demand for labor and the demand for labor. To influence these factors, they try to (1) reduce the availability of substitute products, (2) reduce the availability of substitute factors, (3) increase demand for the product they produce, (4) increase substitute factor prices, and (5) increase the *MPP* of their members. Labor unions try to do (1) and (2) because they want the elasticity of demand for their labor to be low (so that any wage increase only slightly reduces the quantity demanded of union labor). They try to do (3), (4), and (5) because they want the demand for their labor to be high (so that they will receive high wages). Thus, labor unions have as overall objectives to reduce the wage-employment tradeoff and to raise their wages. Unionized workers are not the only group of people with these overall objectives.

Consider (classroom) college professors. Do college professors do some of the same things that labor unions do? Do they try to reduce their wage-employment tradeoff and raise their wages? There is some (anecdotal) evidence that they do. This evidence is often found by listening to the way college professors discuss college education. Let's examine the behavior of college professors in terms of three of the five factors mentioned with respect to labor unions: (1) reduce the availability of substitute services, (2) reduce the availability of substitute factors, and (3) increase demand for what they sell.

Reduce the Availability of Substitute Services

Classroom college professors often argue that the college classroom is the best setting in which to learn. In a classroom, lectures can be given, discussions carried out, questions asked and answered, and so on.[2]

Alternatives, such as courses on the Internet, correspondence courses, and other educational settings, cannot take the place of the college classroom experience. This would imply that the classroom experience is unique. And if it is unique, there are no substitutes for it.

Recall that the fewer substitutes there are for a good or service, the lower the price elasticity of demand for that good or service, *ceteris paribus*. And of course, as the elasticity of demand for the service college professors provide decreases, the wage-employment tradeoff diminishes for the professors.

Are college professors simply acting selfishly when they argue this way? Or are they stating the truth? The answer to both questions could be yes. It may be true that the college classroom is the best setting in which to learn, and it may also be true that it is in the best interest of college professors to make sure that students (customers) understand this.

---

[2] The author of this text is a college professor and often finds he argues this way. He is not saying anything about college professors in this feature that may not hold for him too.

---

for the factor (in much the same way that a monopolist in the product market cannot sell an additional unit of its good without lowering price). The reason is that the supply of labor it faces is the market supply of labor.

For the monopsonist, marginal factor cost increases as it buys additional units of a factor, and the supply curve of the factor *is not the same* as the monopsonist's marginal factor cost curve. (In the last chapter, we saw that for a price taker in the factor market, marginal factor cost was constant, and the *MFC* curve was the same as the supply curve for the factor. A monopsonist is not a price taker in the factor market: Marginal factor cost rises as it buys additional units of a factor, and its *MFC* curve and supply curve [for the factor] are not the same.)

As shown in Exhibit 4, marginal factor cost increases as additional units of the factor are purchased. Notice in part (a) that as workers are added, the wage rate rises. For example, for the monopsonist to employ two workers, the wage rate must rise from $6.00 per hour to $6.05. To employ three workers, the monopsonist must offer to pay

Reduce the Availability of Substitute Factors

College professors often argue against large classes (90 students or more). They say that students can get a better education when classes are smaller—ideally, about 30 students. In a smaller class, the professor can give students more individual attention, can discuss things with them that are impossible to discuss in large lecture halls, can give them more writing assignments, which are important to their education, and so on.

All this sounds reasonable, and it may be true. But arguing against large classes is also a way of trying to reduce the availability of substitute factors. To illustrate, suppose there are 10 economics professors at one college, each professor teaches 3 classes a semester, and classes are limited to 30 students each. Thus, there are 30 economics classes offered each semester. Furthermore, suppose students may enroll in any of the 30 economics classes available. In this setting, Professor Jones, say, teaches 3 classes and there are 9 professors who are substitutes for him (who teach a total of 27 substitute courses for his courses).

Then one day, 1 of the 10 economics professors retires from the college. The college mandates that the new professor who replaces her must teach 3 classes each semester and each class must have 90 students. Thus, the new professor teaches 3 times as many students each semester as every other professor.

By raising class size for the new professor, is the university adding only 1 professor or the equivalent of 3 professors?

Look at it from Professor Jones's point of view. He still teaches 3 classes a semester, and there are still only 9 professors who are substitutes for him. But under the 1 class = 30 students rule, the new professor is doing her job and the job of 2 other professors. It is as if the new professor brought 2 other (shadow) professors with her; she walked into the college as 3 people, not as a single person. So

instead of Professor Jones having 9 other professors who are substitutes for him (together teaching 27 substitute classes), he effectively has 11 other professors who are substitutes for him (together teaching 33 substitute classes). In conclusion, when Professor Jones argues against big classes, he effectively argues against substitutes for himself.

Increasing Demand for What Professors Sell

Most college professors argue in favor of subsidies for higher education. [3] Occasionally, a university professor may say that all higher education should be privatized and that government shouldn't use tax dollars to subsidize a person's college education, but this is a rare event. Most college professors are in favor of subsidies for college education, and many of them would like to see these subsidies increased. We do not mean to imply that professors' arguments for subsidizing higher education are fallacious; we only state that they make these arguments. But certainly, subsidies for higher education cause the demand for a college education to be higher than it would be otherwise. And if the demand for a college education is higher, so is the demand for college professors because the demand for college professors is a derived demand.

Conclusion

Many college professors argue that the college classroom is the best setting in which to learn. They also argue against large classes and in favor of subsidies for higher education. They may be honest in the arguments they put forth to support their positions, and moreover, their arguments may be solid and true. Still, these positions, if realized, have the effect of reducing the college professor wage-employment tradeoff and increasing college professors' salaries.

---

[3]For purposes here, think of the subsidy as a dollar rebate for each unit of education purchased. This has the effect of shifting the demand curve upward a vertical distance equal to the subsidy.

$6.10. Comparing column 2 with column 4, we notice that the marginal factor cost for a monopsonist is greater than the wage rate (in the same way that for a monopolist in a product market, price is greater than marginal revenue). Plotting columns 1 and 2 gives the supply curve for the monopsonist (see Exhibit 4(b)); plotting columns 1 and 4 gives the monopsonist's MFC curve. Because $MFC >$ wage rate, it follows that the supply curve lies below the MFC curve.

Exhibit 4(b) shows that the monopsonist chooses to purchase Q_1 units of labor (where $MRP = MFC$) and that it pays a wage rate of W_1. (W_1 is the wage rate necessary to get Q_1 workers to offer their services.)

If the monopsonist were to pay workers what their services were worth to it (as represented by the MRP curve), it would pay a higher wage. Some persons contend that labor unions and collective bargaining are necessary in situations such as this, where labor is paid less than its marginal revenue product. Furthermore, they argue that successful collective bargaining on the part of the labor union in this setting will not be

(1) Workers	(2) Wage Rate	(3) Total Labor Cost (1) × (2)	(4) Marginal Factor Cost $\dfrac{\Delta(3)}{\Delta(1)}$
0	—	—	—
1	$6.00	$6.00	$6.00
2	6.05	12.10	6.10
3	6.10	18.30	6.20
4	6.15	24.60	6.30
5	6.20	31.00	6.40

(a)

(b)

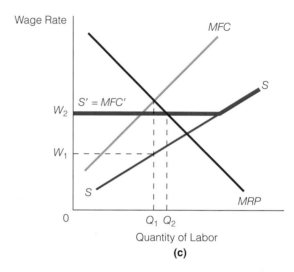

(c)

exhibit **4**

The Labor Union and the Monopsonist

(a) For the monopsonist, MFC >
wage rate. This implies that the supply curve the monopsonist faces lies
below its MFC curve. (b) The monopsonist purchases Q_1 quantity of labor
and pays a wage rate of W_1, which is
less than MRP (labor is being paid
less than its MRP). (c) If the labor
union succeeds in increasing the
wage rate from W_1 to W_2 through
collective bargaining, then the firm
will also hire more labor (Q_2 instead
of Q_1). We conclude that in the case
of monopsony, higher wage rates
(over a range) do not imply fewer
persons working.

subject to the wage-employment tradeoff it encounters in other settings. This is illustrated in Exhibit 4(c).

Successful collective bargaining by the labor union moves the wage rate from W_1 to
W_2 in part (c). The labor union is essentially saying to the monopsonist that it cannot
hire any labor below W_2. This changes the monopsonist's marginal factor cost curve from
MFC to MFC', which corresponds to the new supply curve the monopsonist faces, $S'S$.
The monopsonist once again purchases that quantity of labor at which marginal revenue
product equals marginal factor cost. But now, because the marginal factor cost curve is
MFC', equality is at Q_2 workers and a wage rate of W_2. We conclude that over a range,
there is no wage-employment tradeoff for the labor union when it faces a monopsonist.
It is possible to raise both the wage rate and the number of workers employed.

micro Theme

All economic actors have to make certain decisions. An individual consumer has to decide what combination of goods to buy (how much of
good X and how much of good Y); a firm has to decide what quantity of output
it will produce. A firm that is a monopsonist in a factor market has to make a
decision: It has to decide how much of a factor (e.g., labor) it will hire. It decides
to buy the quantity of a factor at which MRP = MFC.

Unions' Effects on Wages

Most studies show that some unions have increased their members' wages substantially, whereas other unions have not increased their members' wages at all. Work by H. Gregg Lewis concludes that during the period 1920–1979, the average wage of union members was 10 to 15 percent higher than that of comparable nonunion labor. (Keep in mind, though, that the union-nonunion wage differential can differ quite a bit in different years and between industries.) For data on this subject, see Exhibit 5.

THE UNION-NONUNION WAGE GAP Exhibit 6 illustrates the theoretical basis of the observation that higher union wages lead to lower nonunion wages, or to a union-nonunion wage gap. Two sectors of the labor market are shown: the unionized sector in part (a) and the nonunionized sector in part (b). We assume that labor is homogeneous and that the wage rate is $15 an hour in both sectors.

The labor union either collectively bargains to a higher wage rate of $18 an hour or manages to reduce supply so that the higher wage rate comes about (the exhibit shows a decrease in supply). As a consequence, less labor is employed in the unionized sector. If we hold that the persons who now are not working in the unionized sector can work in the nonunionized sector, it follows that the supply of labor in the nonunionized sector increases from S_{NU} to S'_{NU} and the wage rate in the nonunionized sector falls to $12 an hour. We conclude that there are theoretical and empirical reasons for believing that labor unions increase the wages of union employees and decrease the wages of nonunion employees.

Do the higher wages that union employees receive through unionization outweigh the lower wages that nonunion employees receive in terms of the percentage of the national income that goes to labor? It appears not. The percentage of the national income that goes to labor (union plus nonunion labor) has been fairly constant over time. In fact, it was approximately the same when unions were weak and union membership was relatively low as when unions were strong and union membership was relatively high.

WHY DON'T EMPLOYERS PAY? The layperson's view of labor unions is that they obtain higher wages for their members *at the expense of the owners of the firms*, not at the expense of other workers. The preceding section suggests this may not be true. Why don't the higher wages that go to union employees come out of profits?

exhibit **5**

Median Weekly Earnings in the Union and Nonunion Sectors, Selected Industries, 2004

In four of the five (selected) industries shown, union workers earned a higher weekly salary in 2004 than did nonunion workers. Overall in 2004, the median weekly salary was $776 for a union worker and $612 for a nonunion worker (not shown).

Source: Statistical Abstract of the United States, 2006.

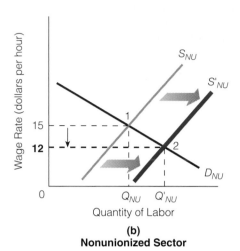

Changes in supply conditions and wage rates in the unionized sector can cause changes in supply and wage rates in the nonunionized sector.

(a)
Unionized Sector

(b)
Nonunionized Sector

exhibit **6**

The Effect of Labor Unions on Union and Nonunion Wages

We begin at a wage rate of $15 in both the unionized sector, (a), and the nonunionized sector, (b). Next, the union manages to increase its wage rate to $18 either through collective bargaining or by decreasing the supply of labor in the unionized sector (shown). Fewer persons now work in the unionized sector, and we assume that those persons who lose their jobs move to the nonunionized sector. The supply of labor in the nonunionized sector rises, and the wage rate falls.

To answer this question, we need to differentiate between the short run and the long run. In the theory of perfect competition, when there are short-run profits, new firms enter the industry, the industry supply curve shifts rightward, prices fall, and profits are competed away. Also, when there are short-run losses, firms exit the industry, the industry supply curve shifts leftward, prices increase, and losses finally disappear. So in the long run, there is zero economic profit in the perfectly competitive market.

Consider a labor union in this market structure that manages to obtain higher wages for its members. It is possible that in the short run, these higher wages will diminish profits—the way any cost increase would diminish profits, *ceteris paribus*—but in the long run, there will be adjustments as firms exit the industry, supply curves shift, and prices change. In the long run, zero economic profit will exist. We conclude that it is possible in the short run for "higher wages to come out of profits," but in the long run, this isn't likely to be the case.

Thinking like
AN ECONOMIST   *Economists make the important distinction between primary and secondary effects, or between what happens in the short run and what happens in the long run. For example, higher wages for union workers may initially come at the expense of profits, but as time passes, this may not continue to be the case.*

Unions' Effects on Prices

One effect of labor unions is that union wages are relatively higher and nonunion wages are relatively lower. The higher union wages mean higher costs for the firms that employ union labor, and higher costs affect supply curves, which in turn affect product prices. We conclude that higher union wages will cause higher prices for the products that the union labor produces. Conversely, lower nonunion wages mean lower costs for the firms that employ nonunion labor and thus lower prices for the products produced by nonunion labor.

Unions' Effects on Productivity and Efficiency: Two Views

There are two major views of the effects labor unions have on productivity and efficiency.

THE TRADITIONAL (OR ORTHODOX) VIEW The traditional view holds that labor unions have a negative impact on productivity and efficiency. Its proponents make the following arguments: (1) Labor unions often have unnecessary staffing requirements and insist that only certain persons be allowed to do certain jobs. Because of this, the economy operates below its potential—that is, inefficiently. (2) Strikes disrupt production and prevent

© PAN AMERICA/JUPITER IMAGES

economics 24/7

"ARE YOU READY FOR SOME FOOTBALL?"

Sometimes, firms that sell a similar good try to form a cartel so they can act as a monopoly. Can this behavior occur when firms buy a factor? Do firms that buy a specific factor sometimes try to form a cartel so they can act as a monopsony? No doubt you know such a "firm." Many universities and colleges have banded together to buy the services of college-bound athletes. In other words, they have entered into a cartel agreement to reduce the monetary competition among themselves for college-bound athletes. The National Collegiate Athletic Association (NCAA) is the cartel or monopsony enforcer. How does all this work?

The NCAA sets certain rules and regulations by which its member universities and colleges must abide or else face punishment and fines. For example, universities and colleges are prohibited from offering salaries to athletes to play on their teams. They are prohibited from "making work" for them at the university or paying them relatively high wage rates for a job that usually pays much less—for example, paying athletes $30 an hour to reshelve books in the university library. Universities and colleges are also prohibited from offering inducements such as cars, clothes, and trips to attract athletes.

The stated objectives of these NCAA regulations are to maintain the amateur standing of college athletes, to prevent the rich schools from getting all the good players, and to enhance the competitiveness of college sports. Some economists suggest that some schools may have other objectives. They note that college athletics can be a revenue-raising activity for schools and that these institutions would rather pay college athletes less than their marginal revenue products (the way a monopsony does) to play sports.

Currently, universities and colleges openly compete for athletes by offering scholarships, free room and board, and school jobs. They also compete in terms of their academic reputations and the reputations of their sports programs (obviously, some find it easier to do this than others). Although it is prohibited, some universities and colleges compete for athletes in ways not sanctioned by the NCAA; that is, they compete "under the table." This is evidence, some economists maintain, that some schools are cheating on the cartel agreement. Such cheating usually benefits the college athletes, who receive a "payment" for their athletic abilities that is closer to their marginal revenue products. For example, it has occasionally been noted that some college athletes, many of whom come from families of modest means, drive flashy, expensive cars in college. Where do they get these cars? Often, they come from community friends of the university or boosters of its sports program. Such payments to college athletes may be prohibited by the NCAA, but as we saw earlier, members of cartels (of the monopoly or monopsony variety) usually find ways of evading the rules.

Not all economists agree that the NCAA is a cartel. Some economists argue that paying college athletes would diminish the reputation of college athletics, which would decrease the public demand for college sports programs. They conclude that the NCAA imposes its rules and regulations—one of which is that college athletes should not be paid to play sports—to keep college sports nonprofessional and in relatively high demand, and not to suppress players' wages.

the economy from realizing its productive potential. (3) Labor unions drive an artificial wedge between the wages of comparable labor in the union and nonunion sectors of the labor market.

This last point warrants elaboration. Look again at Exhibit 6. Remember, we are dealing with homogeneous labor, and we start with the same wage rate in both sectors of the labor market. Union efforts increase the wage rate in the union sector and decrease the wage rate in the nonunion sector.

At this point, the marginal revenue product of persons who work in the union sector is higher than the marginal revenue product of individuals who work in the nonunion sector. (We are farther up the factor demand curve, or *MRP* curve, in the union than in the nonunion sector.) If labor could move from the nonunionized sector to the unionized sector, it would be moving from where it is worth less to where it is worth more. But this cannot happen owing to the supply-restraining efforts of the union. Economists call this a misallocation of labor; not all labor is employed where it is most valuable.

A NEW VIEW: THE LABOR UNION AS A COLLECTIVE VOICE There is evidence that in some industries, union firms have a higher rate of productivity than nonunion firms do. Some economists believe this is a result of the labor union's role as a collective voice mechanism for its members. Without a labor union, workers who are disgruntled with their jobs, who feel taken advantage of by their employers, or who feel unsafe in their work will leave their jobs and seek work elsewhere. This "job exiting" comes at a cost; it raises the turnover rate, results in lengthy job searches during which individuals are not producing goods and services, and raises training costs. Such costs can be reduced, it is argued, when a labor union acts as a collective voice for its members. Instead of individual employees having to discuss ticklish employment matters with their employer, the labor union does it for them. Overall, the labor union makes employees feel more confident, less intimidated, and more secure in their work. Such positive feelings usually mean happier, more productive employees. Some proponents of this view also hold that employees are less likely to quit their jobs. In fact, there is evidence that unionism does indeed reduce job quits.

Critics have contended, though, that the reduced job quits are less a function of the labor union as a collective voice mechanism than of the labor union as an institution capable of increasing its members' wages. It has also been noted that the productivity-increasing aspects of the labor union, which are linked to its role as a collective voice mechanism, are independent of the productivity-decreasing aspects of the labor union in its role as "monopolizer of labor."

SELF-TEST

1. What is a major difference between a monopsonist and a factor price taker?

2. Under what conditions will the minimum wage increase the number of people working?

3. How could a collectively bargained higher wage rate in the unionized sector of the economy lead to a lower wage rate in the nonunionized sector of the economy?

A Reader Asks . . .

What Are the Facts of Labor Unions?

Earlier in the chapter, it's noted that 12.5 percent of the U.S. labor force is comprised of union workers. In what state is union membership the largest percentage of the work force? Is union membership greater in some industries than in others? Is the private sector more or less unionized than the public sector?

The following information about labor unions is from 2002. Some of this information will answer your questions.

- The five states with the highest union membership rates (percentage of workers in unions) were Alaska, Hawaii, New York, New Jersey, and Michigan—all with membership rates over 20 percent. The two states with the lowest membership rates were North Carolina (2.9 percent) and South Carolina (2.3 percent).

- Six states—California, New York, Illinois, Michigan, Ohio, and New Jersey—accounted for 33 percent of all workers but had 50 percent of all union members.

- Workers in the public sector had unionization rates that were four times higher than their counterparts in the private sector.
- The unionization rate of government workers was about 36.5 percent, compared with 7.8 percent among private sector employees.
- Local government workers—a group that includes police officers and firefighters—had the highest unionization rate (41.9 percent) among all occupations.
- The nonagricultural industry with the lowest unionization rate (2.3 percent) was financial activities.
- Union membership rates of government employees have held steady since 1983, while those of private nonagricultural employees have declined.

- Unionization membership rates were higher among men (13.5 percent) than women (11.3 percent).
- African American men had the highest rate of union membership among all major worker groups.
- Workers aged 45 to 54 were more likely to be unionized than either their younger or their older counterparts.
- Full-time workers were more than twice as likely as part-time workers to be members of a union.
- Approximately 1.6 million workers who were not union members were represented by unions at their place of work.
- About 15.7 million workers in the United States were members of a labor union.

! analyzing the scene

What does the wage increase a union seeks have to do with the number of union members working?

One union representative thinks the union should seek a 7 percent increase in wages, and another thinks the union should seek a greater increase. The second representative's statement that a 10 percent increase will not cause much job loss indicates that the union leaders are aware of the wage-employment tradeoff. As long as the demand for labor (any labor) is downward sloping, higher wages come with a reduction in the number of individuals firms will hire. As discussed, the amount of job loss depends on the elasticity of demand for labor in the union.

What percentage of U.S. workers are members of unions?

In 2005, 12.5 percent of U.S. workers were members of unions. This percentage is much less than the 50 percent esti-

mated by Lily and Sophie. People often say things without a basic knowledge of the facts. Economists often argue that people need to identify facts before they draw conclusions.

Are union wages always higher than nonunion wages in a given industry?

Some people are inclined to believe that union wages are always higher than nonunion wages in the same industry. Perhaps this is because they often see union leaders bargaining for higher wages with management, but no one is visibly bargaining for higher wages for nonunion workers. Wouldn't it have to be the case that when someone is arguing for higher wages on your behalf that you'd have to earn more than when no one argues for higher wages on your behalf? Well, as Exhibit 5 shows, the answer is no. Union wages are higher than nonunion wages in construction, but lower in finance, insurance, and real estate.

chapter summary

Types of Unions

- There are three different types of labor unions: craft (or trade) unions, industrial unions, and public employee unions. Some economists hold that employee associations are also a type of union.

Objectives of a Union

- Objectives of a union include (1) employment for all its members, (2) maximization of the total wage bill, and (3) maximization of the income for a limited number of union members. A labor union faces a wage-employment tradeoff; higher wage rates mean less labor union employment. There is an exception, however. When a labor union faces a monopsonist, it is possible for the union to raise both wage rates and employment of its members (over a range). Exhibit 4(c) illustrates this.

Practices of a Labor Union

- To soften the wage-employment tradeoff, a labor union seeks to lower the elasticity of demand for its labor. Ways of doing this include (1) reducing the availability of substitute products and (2) reducing the availability of substitute factors for labor.

- Union wage rates can be increased indirectly by increasing the demand for union labor or by reducing the supply of union labor, or they can be increased directly by collective bargaining. To increase demand for its labor, a union might try to increase (1) the demand for the good it produces, (2) substitute factor prices, or (3) its marginal physical product. To decrease the supply of its labor, a union might argue for closed and union shops and against right-to-work laws.

- In a way, successful collective bargaining on the part of a labor union changes the supply curve of labor that the employer faces. The labor union is successful if, through its collective bargaining efforts, it can prevent the employer from hiring labor at a wage rate below a union-determined level. In this case, the supply curve of labor becomes horizontal at this wage rate (see Exhibit 3).

Monopsony

- For a monopsonist, marginal factor cost rises as it buys additional units of a factor and its supply curve lies below its marginal factor cost curve. The monopsonist buys the factor quantity at which $MRP = MFC$. The price of the factor is less than the monopsonist's marginal factor cost, so the monopsonist pays the factor less than its marginal revenue product.

Effects of Unions

- There is evidence that labor unions generally have the effect of increasing their members' wage rates (over what they would be without the union) and lowering the wage rates of nonunion labor.

- The traditional view of labor unions holds that unions negatively affect productivity and efficiency. They do this by (1) arguing for and often obtaining unnecessary staffing requirements, (2) calling strikes that disrupt production, and (3) driving an artificial wedge between the wages of comparable labor in the union and nonunion sectors.

- The "new" view of labor unions holds that labor unions act as a collective voice mechanism for individual union employees and cause them to feel more confident in their jobs and less intimidated by their employers. This leads to more productive employees, who are less likely to quit and so forth.

key terms and concepts

Craft (Trade) Union	Public Employee Union	Closed Shop	Collective Bargaining
Industrial Union	Employee Association	Union Shop	Strike
			Monopsony

questions and problems

1   What is the difference between a craft (trade) union and an industrial union?

2   What view is a labor union likely to hold on each of the following issues? (a) easing of the immigration laws; (b) a quota on imported products; (c) free trade; (d) a decrease in the minimum wage.

3   Most actions or practices of labor unions are attempts to affect one of three factors. What are these three factors?

4   Explain why the monopsonist pays labor a wage rate less than labor's marginal revenue product.

5   It has been suggested that organizing labor unions is easier in some industries than in others. What industry characteristics make unionization easier?

6   What is the effect of labor unions on nonunion wage rates?

7   Some persons argue that a monopsony firm exploits its workers if it pays them less than their marginal revenue products. Others disagree. They say that as long as the firm pays the workers their opportunity costs (which must be the case or the workers would not stay with the firm), the workers are not being exploited. This suggests that there are two definitions of exploitation:

(a) paying workers below their marginal revenue products (even if wages equal the workers' opportunity costs) and (b) paying workers below their opportunity costs. Keeping in mind that this may be a subjective judgment, which definition of exploitation do you think is more descriptive of the process and why?

8 A discussion of labor unions usually evokes strong feelings. Some people argue vigorously against labor unions; others argue with equal vigor for labor unions. Some people see labor unions as the reason workers in this country enjoy as high a standard of living as they do; others see labor unions as the reason the country is not so well off economically as it might be. Speculate on why the topic of labor unions generates such strong feelings and emotions and often such little analysis.

9 What forces may lead to the breakup of an employer (monopsony) cartel?

working with numbers and graphs

1 Determine the appropriate numbers for the lettered spaces:

(1) Workers	(2) Wage Rate	(3) Total Labor Cost	(4) Marginal Factor Cost
1	_A_	$12.00	$12.00
2	$12.10	24.20	_E_
3	12.20	_C_	_F_
4	_B_	_D_	12.60

2 Which demand curve for labor in the following figure exhibits the most pronounced wage-employment trade-off? Explain your answer.

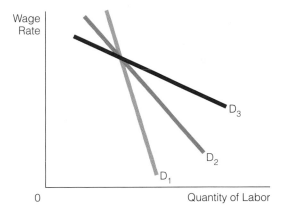

3 Diagrammatically explain how changes in supply conditions and wage rates in the unionized sector can cause changes in supply and wage rates in the nonunionized sector.

The Distribution of Income and Poverty

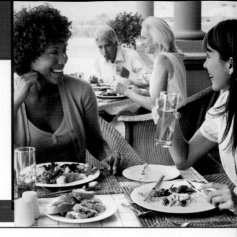

Setting the Scene

Madison and Leslie, who have been friends since high school, are often on different sides of social and political issues. Today, they are discussing a report in the newspaper about the distribution of income in the country.

LESLIE:

The top one-fifth of income earners earned a larger percentage of the total income of the country this year than they did last year. The rich keep getting richer and the poor get poorer.

MADISON:

Just because the rich are getting richer doesn't mean the poor are getting poorer. The poor could be getting more income too.

LESLIE:

That's impossible. The rich have to be getting their larger percentage of income from somewhere—and they always get it from the poor.

MADISON:

Not necessarily. Everyone's income could rise if the national income of the country rises.

LESLIE:

Well, I still think everyone but the rich is worse off when incomes become more unequal.

MADISON:

I'm not sure about that. I seem to recall reading somewhere that whether or not people are better off depends on how many things—like goods and services—they can buy.

LESLIE:

Do you mean that if poor people can buy more things, then they're better off, even if they have a smaller percentage of the total income of the country?

MADISON:

That's exactly what I mean. An unequal income distribution isn't necessarily bad news for the poor.

? Here is a question to keep in mind as you read this chapter:

• *Can everyone become better off as the income distribution becomes more unequal?*

See analyzing the scene at the end of this chapter for an answer to this question.

Some Facts About Income Distribution

In discussing public policy issues, people sometimes talk about a single fact when they should talk about facts. A single fact is usually not as informative as facts are, in much the same way that a single snapshot does not tell as much of a story as a moving picture—a succession of snapshots. This section presents a few facts about the distribution of income.

Who Are the Rich and How Rich Are They?

By many interpretations, the lowest fifth (lowest quintile) of households in the United States is considered poor, the top fifth is considered rich, and the three-fifths in between are considered middle income.[1]

In 2004, the lowest fifth (the poor) in the United States received 3.4 percent of the total money income, the second fifth received 8.9 percent, the third fifth received 14.7 percent, the fourth fifth received 23.0 percent, and the top fifth (the rich) received 50.0 percent (see Exhibit 1).[2]

Has the income distribution become more or less equal over time? Exhibit 2 shows the income shares of households in 1967 and 2004. In 1967, the highest fifth (top) of households accounted for 43.8 percent of all income; in 2004, the percentage had risen to 50.0 percent.

At the other end of the income spectrum, in 1967, the lowest fifth received 4.0 percent of all income; in 2004, the percentage had fallen to 3.4 percent. The middle groups—the three-fifths of income recipients between the lowest fifth and the highest fifth—accounted for 52.3 percent of all income in 1967 and 46.6 percent in 2004.

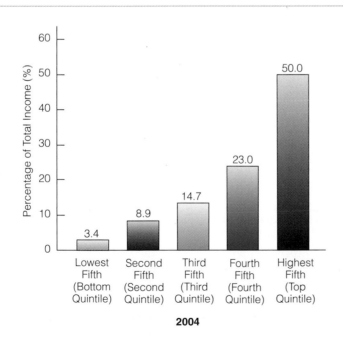

exhibit **1**

Distribution of Household Income Shares, 2004

The annual income shares for different quintiles of households is shown here.

Source: U.S. Bureau of the Census.

---

[1]A household consists of all people who occupy a housing unit. It includes the related family members and all unrelated people.

[2]Percentages in this chapter do not always equal 100 percent due to rounding.

1967

2004

exhibit **2**

Income Distribution, 1967 and 2004

Note that income shares have not been adjusted for such things as taxes and in-kind transfer payments, which are transfer payments made in terms of a specific good or service rather than in cash.

Keep in mind as you look at the data that most persons implicitly assume that the quintiles (the fifths) in income distributions contain equal shares of the population. But the official Bureau of the Census income "quintiles" do not contain equal shares of the population. The Census Bureau quintiles are unequal in size because they are based on a count of households rather than persons. In the United States, high-income households tend to be married couples with many members and earners. Low-income households tend to be single persons with little or no earnings. The average household in the top quintile contains 3.2 persons, and the average household in the bottom quintile contains 1.8 persons.

Some economists have argued that the unequal quintile populations skew the Census's measure of the income distribution. For example, in 2002, the top quintile contained 24.6 percent of the population, and the bottom quintile contained 14.3 percent of the population. Stated differently, there were 69.4 million persons in the highest "fifth" and 40.3 million persons in the lowest "fifth."

If we adjust the income distribution so that each quintile actually contains 20 percent of the population, then we get different results. In 2002, the income share of the lowest fifth rises from 3.5 percent to 9.4 percent, and the income share of the highest fifth falls from 49.7 percent to 39.6 percent.

Sometimes, economists make further adjustments to the income distribution. For example, the persons in each fifth do not all work the same number of hours. In 2002, individuals in the lowest fifth performed 4.3 percent of all work in the U.S. economy, and those in the highest fifth performed 33.9 percent. To be fair, the low levels of paid employment in the lowest fifth reflect the low numbers of working-age population in this group. In 2002, the lowest fifth contained only 11.2 percent of all working-age adults, and the highest fifth contained 27.6 percent. However, when we compare working-age adults in the lowest fifth with working-age adults in the highest fifth, we learn that the average working-age adult in the lowest fifth worked about half as many hours a year as the working-age adult in the highest fifth.

Q&A   *What was the median household income in the United States in 2004?*

It was $44,389. You might also be interested in knowing that between 1967 and 2004, real median household income increased by 30 percent.

The Effect of Age on the Income Distribution

In analyzing the income distribution, it is important to distinguish between people who are poor for long periods of time (sometimes their entire lives) and people who are poor temporarily. Consider Sherri Holmer, who attends college and works part time as a waitress at a nearby restaurant. Currently, her income is so low that she falls into the lowest quintile of income earners. But it isn't likely that this will always be the case. After she graduates from college, Sherri's income will probably rise. If she is like most people, her income will rise during her twenties, thirties, and forties. In her late forties or early fifties, her income will take a slight downturn and then level off.

It is possible, in fact highly likely, that a person in her late twenties, thirties, or forties will have a higher income than a person in his early twenties or a person in her sixties, even though their total lifetime incomes will be identical. If we view each person over time, income equality is greater than if we view each person at a particular point in time (say, when one person is 58 years old and the other is 68 years old).

To illustrate, look at Exhibit 3, which shows the incomes of John and Stephanie in different years. In 2000, John is 18 years old and earning $10,000 per year, and Stephanie is 28 years old and earning $30,000 a year. The income distribution between John and Stephanie is unequal in 2000.

Ten years later, the income distribution is still unequal, with Stephanie earning $45,000 and John earning $35,000. In fact, the income distribution is unequal in every year shown in the exhibit. However, the total income earned by each person is $236,000, giving a perfectly equal income distribution over time.

In the United States, there seems to be quite a bit of upward income mobility over time. The University of Michigan's Panel Survey on Dynamics tracked 50,000 Americans for 17 years. Of the people in the lowest fifth of the income distribution in 1975, only 5.1 percent were still there in 1991—and 29 percent of them were in the highest fifth.

A Simple Equation

Before discussing the possible sources or causes of income inequality, we need to identify the factors that determine a person's income. The following simple equation combines four of these factors: labor income, asset income, transfer payments, and taxes:

Individual income = Labor income + Asset income + Transfer payments − Taxes

Q&A

Are there some data that show that people, once poor, do not always stay poor?

Yes, according to the Bureau of the Census, of households that were in the lowest quintile in 1996, 38 percent were in a higher quintile in 1999. Of households that were in the highest quintile in 1996, 34 percent were in a lower quintile in 1999. Also, 49.5 percent of persons in poverty in 1996 were not in poverty in 1999.

Thinking like **AN ECONOMIST**

Many people believe that poor is poor. This is not the case for the economist. The economist wants to know why the person is poor. Is he poor because he is young and just starting out in life? Would he be poor if we were to consider the **in-kind transfer payments** *or in-kind benefits he receives? Some people argue that when someone is poor, you don't ask questions, you simply try to help him. But the economist knows that not everyone is in the same situation for the same reason. The reason may determine whether or not you proceed with help, and if you do proceed, just how you do so. Both the elderly person with a disability and the young, smart college student may earn the same low income, but you may feel it is more important to help the elderly person with a disability than the college student.*

In-Kind Transfer Payments
Transfer payments, such as food stamps, medical assistance, and subsidized housing, that are made in a specific good or service rather than in cash.

exhibit **3**

Income Distribution at One Point in Time and Over Time

In each year, the income distribution between John and Stephanie is unequal, with Stephanie earning more than John in 2000, 2010, 2020, and 2030 and John earning more than Stephanie in 2040. In the five years specified, however, both John and Stephanie earned the same total income of $236,000, giving a perfectly equal income distribution over time.

Year	John's Age	John's Income	Stephanie's Age	Stephanie's Income
2000	18 years	$10,000	28 years	$30,000
2010	28	35,000	38	45,000
2020	38	52,000	48	60,000
2030	48	64,000	58	75,000
2040	58	75,000	68	26,000
Total		$236,000		$236,000

Labor income is equal to the wage rate an individual receives multiplied by the number of hours he or she works. Asset income consists of such things as the return to saving, the return to capital investment, and the return to land. **Transfer payments** refer to payments to persons that are not made in return for goods and services currently supplied (e.g., Social Security payments and cash welfare assistance are government transfer payments). Finally, from the sum of labor income, asset income, and transfer payments, we subtract taxes to see what an individual is left with (individual income). This equation provides a quick way of focusing on the direct and indirect factors that affect an individual's income and the degree of income inequality. The next section examines the conventional ways that income inequality is measured.

Transfer Payments

Payments to persons that are not made in return for goods and services currently supplied.

SELF-TEST

(Answers to Self-Test questions are in the Self-Test Appendix.)

1. How can government change the distribution of income?

2. Income inequality at one point in time is sometimes consistent with income equality over time. Comment.

3. Smith and Jones have the same income this year, $40,000. Does it follow that their income came from the same sources? Explain your answer.

Lorenz Curve

A graph of the income distribution. It expresses the relationship between cumulative percentage of households and cumulative percentage of income.

Measuring Income Equality

Two commonly used measures of income inequality are the Lorenz curve and the Gini coefficient. We explain and discuss both measures in this section.

The Lorenz Curve

The **Lorenz curve** represents the distribution of income; it expresses the relationship between cumulative percentage of households and *cumulative percentage of income*. Exhibit 4 shows a hypothetical Lorenz curve.

Quintile	Income Share (percent)	Cumulative Income Share (percent)
Lowest fifth	10%	10%
Second fifth	15	25
Third fifth	20	45
Fourth fifth	25	70
Highest fifth	30	100

(a)

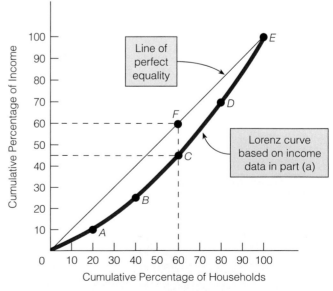

(b)

The data in part (a) are used to plot the Lorenz curve in part (b). According to (a), the lowest fifth of households has an income share of 10 percent, the second fifth has an income share of 15 percent, and so on. The Lorenz curve in (b) is derived by plotting five points. Point *A* represents the cumulative income share of the lowest fifth of households (10 percent of income goes to the lowest fifth of households). Point *B* represents the cumulative income share of the lowest fifth plus the second fifth (25 percent of income goes to two-fifths, or 40 percent, of the income recipients). Point *C* represents the cumulative income share of the lowest fifth plus the second fifth plus the third fifth (45 percent of income goes to three-fifths, or 60 percent, of the income recipients). The same procedure is used for points *D* and *E*. Connecting these points gives the Lorenz curve that represents the data in (a); the Lorenz curve is another way of depicting the income distribution in (a). Exhibit 5 illustrates the Lorenz curve for the United States based on the (money) income shares in Exhibit 1.

What would the Lorenz curve look like if there were perfect income equality among different households? In this case, every household would receive exactly the same percentage of total income, and the Lorenz curve would be the line of perfect income equality illustrated in Exhibit 4(b). At any point on this 45-degree line, the cumulative percentage of income (on the vertical axis) equals the cumulative percentage of households (on the horizontal axis). For example, at point *F,* 60 percent of the households receive 60 percent of the total income.

The Gini Coefficient

The **Gini coefficient** is a measure of the degree of inequality in the income distribution and is used in conjunction with the Lorenz curve. It is equal to the area between the line of perfect income equality (or 45-degree line) and the actual Lorenz curve divided by the entire triangular area under the line of perfect income equality.

Gini Coefficient

A measure of the degree of inequality in the income distribution.

$$\text{Gini Coefficient} = \frac{\text{Area between the line of perfect income equality and actual Lorenz curve}}{\text{Entire triangular area under the line of perfect income equality}}$$

Exhibit 6 illustrates both the line of perfect income equality and an actual Lorenz curve. The Gini coefficient is computed by dividing the shaded area (the area between

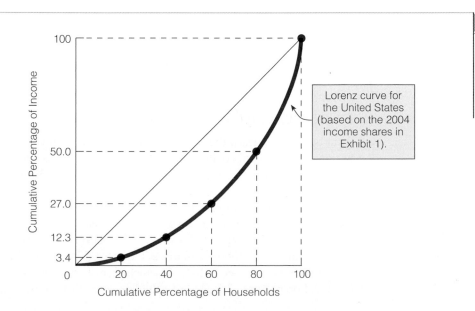

exhibit **5**

Lorenz Curve for the United States, 2004

This Lorenz curve is based on the 2004 income shares for the United States.

Lorenz curve for the United States (based on the 2004 income shares in Exhibit 1).

The Gini Coefficient

The Gini coefficient is a measure of the degree of income inequality. It is equal to the area between the line of perfect income equality and the actual Lorenz curve divided by the entire triangular area under the line of perfect income equality. In the diagram, this is equal to the shaded portion divided by the triangular area 0AB. A Gini coefficient of 0 means perfect income equality; a Gini coefficient of 1 means complete income inequality. The larger the Gini coefficient, the greater the income inequality; the smaller the Gini coefficient, the lower the income inequality

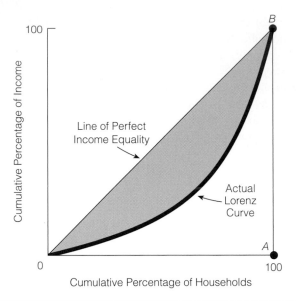

the line of perfect income equality and the actual Lorenz curve) by the area 0AB (the entire triangular area under the line of perfect income equality).

The Gini coefficient is a number between 0 and 1. At one extreme, the Gini coefficient equals 0 if the numerator in the equation is 0. A numerator of 0 means there is no area between the line of perfect income equality and the actual Lorenz curve, implying that they are the same. It follows that a Gini coefficient of 0 means perfect income equality.

At the other extreme, the Gini coefficient equals 1 if the numerator in the equation is equal to the denominator. If this is the case, the actual Lorenz curve is as far away from the line of perfect income equality as is possible. It follows that a Gini coefficient of 1 means complete income inequality. (What would the actual Lorenz curve look like if there were complete income inequality? In this situation, one person would have all the total income, and no one else would have any income. In Exhibit 4, a Lorenz curve representing complete income inequality would lie along the horizontal axis from 0 to A and then move from A to B.)

If a Gini coefficient of 0 represents perfect income equality and a Gini coefficient of 1 represents complete income inequality, then it follows that the larger the Gini coefficient, the higher the degree of income inequality, and the smaller the Gini coefficient, the lower the degree of income inequality. In 2004, the Gini coefficient in the United States was 0.450; in 1947, the Gini coefficient in the United States was 0.376.

A Limitation of the Gini Coefficient

Although we can learn the degree of inequality in the income distribution from the Gini coefficient, we have to be careful not to misinterpret it. For example, suppose the Gini coefficient is 0.33 in country 1 and 0.25 in country 2. We know the income distribution is more equal in country 2 than in country 1. But in which country does the lowest fifth of households receive the larger percentage of income? The natural inclination is to answer in the country with the more equal income distribution—country 2. However, this may not be true.

To see this, consider Exhibit 7, which shows two Lorenz curves. Overall, Lorenz curve 2 is closer to the line of perfect income equal-

Q&A **What is the Gini coefficient of various countries?**

Argentina, 0.52 (in 2001); Brazil, 0.59 (2004); Canada, 0.33 (1998); China, 0.44 (2002); Denmark, 0.23 (2002); France, 0.33 (1995); Iran, 0.43 (1998); Ireland, 0.36 (1996); Israel, 0.34 (2005); Japan, 0.38 (2000); Mexico, 0.55 (2000); Turkey, 0.42 (2003).

exhibit 7

Limitation of the Gini Coefficient

By itself, the Gini coefficient cannot tell us anything about the income share of a particular quintile. Although there is a tendency to believe that the bottom quintile receives a larger percentage of total income the lower the Gini coefficient, this need not be the case. In the diagram, the Gini coefficient for Lorenz curve 2 is lower than the Gini coefficient for Lorenz curve 1. But, the bottom 20 percent of households obtains a smaller percentage of total income in the lower Gini coefficient case.

ity than Lorenz curve 1 is; thus, the Gini coefficient for Lorenz curve 2 is smaller than the Gini coefficient for Lorenz curve 1. But notice that the lowest 20 percent of households has a smaller percentage of total income with Lorenz curve 2 than with Lorenz curve 1.

Our point is that the Gini coefficient cannot tell us what is happening in different quintiles. We should not jump to the conclusion that because the Gini coefficient is lower in country 2 than in country 1, the lowest fifth of households has a greater percentage of total income in country 2 than in country 1.

SELF-TEST

1. Starting with the top fifth of income earners and proceeding to the lowest fifth, suppose the income share of each group is 40 percent, 30 percent, 20 percent, 10 percent, and 5 percent. Can these percentages be right?

2. Country *A* has a Gini coefficient of 0.45. What does this mean?

Why Income Inequality Exists

Why does income inequality exist? This question can be answered by focusing on our simple equation:

Individual income = Labor income + Asset income + Transfer payments − Taxes

Generally, income inequality exists because people do not receive the same labor income, asset income, and transfer payments, or pay the same taxes. But why don't they receive, say, the same labor income and asset income? This section discusses some of the specific reasons for income inequality by focusing on factors that often contribute to differences in labor and asset income. The next section looks at some of the proposed standards of income distribution.

Factors Contributing to Income Inequality

Six factors that contribute to income inequality are innate abilities and attributes, work and leisure, education and other training, risk taking, luck, and wage discrimination.

economics 24/7

WINNER-TAKE-ALL MARKETS[3]

Two economists, Robert Frank and Philip Cook, published a book in 1995 titled *The Winner-Take-All Society.* In the book, they argue that there are more winner-take-all markets today than in the past. A winner-take-all market is one in which the top producer or performer in the market earns appreciably more than others in the market earn. In fact, the top producers earn so much more than others that it is as if they "take it all."

For example, in making major movies, the producer, director, and leading actor may earn much more than anyone else involved in the movie. In the sports market, the sports stars earn more than their fellow players. For example, the last year that Michael Jordan played basketball with the Chicago Bulls, he earned 121 times the salary of the lowest paid player.

Frank and Cook state that there is nothing new about winner-take-all markets in sports and entertainment. What is new, they argue, is that winner-take-all is becoming a common feature of other markets. Winner-take-all is becoming increasingly more descriptive in such fields as law, journalism, design, investment banking, and medicine.

Do the data support what Frank and Cook are saying? Recent statistics show that "within-group" income inequality has been rising. In other words, the "winnings" have come to be concentrated on a smaller percentage of people in an industry. To illustrate, in 1980, major U.S. chief executive officers (CEOs) earned an average of 42 times the amount an average American production worker earned; by 2003, this multiple had jumped to 301.[4] There are other examples that illustrate the same phenomenon, prompting Frank and Cook to comment that we are increasingly coming to live in a winner-take-all society.

What has happened in recent years to bring about more winner-take-all markets and greater within-group income inequality? Frank and Cook identify two things: (1) developments in communications, manufacturing technology, and transportation costs that let top performers serve broader markets (a global marketplace) and (2) implicit and explicit rules that have led to more competition for top performers.

Let's look at the first cause identified by Frank and Cook. In a winner-take-all market, the demand for goods and services is focused on a small number of suppliers. This is not, as some

INNATE ABILITIES AND ATTRIBUTES Individuals are not all born with the same innate abilities and attributes. People vary in the degree of intelligence, good looks, and creativity they possess. Some individuals have more marketable innate abilities and attributes than others have. For example, the man or woman born with exceptionally good looks, the "natural" athlete, or the person who is musically gifted or mathematically adept is more likely to earn a higher income than someone with lesser abilities or attributes.

WORK AND LEISURE There is a tradeoff between work and leisure: More work means less leisure, and less work means more leisure. Some individuals will choose to work more hours (or take a second job) and thus have less leisure. This choice will be reflected in their labor income. They will earn a larger income than persons who choose not to work more, *ceteris paribus.*

EDUCATION AND OTHER TRAINING Economists usually refer to schooling and other types of training as an "investment in human capital." To buy a capital good or to invest in one, a person has to give up present consumption. A person does so in the hope that the capital good will increase his or her future consumption.

Schooling can be looked on as capital. First, one must give up present consumption to obtain it. Second, by providing individuals with certain skills and knowledge, schooling can increase their future consumption over what it would be without the schooling.

may think, because government is limiting our choices. According to Frank and Cook, we are simply focusing on "the best" suppliers to a greater degree than before because of changes in technology, communications, and transportation costs.

For example, consumers today do not have to settle for buying tires, cars, clothes, books, or much of anything else from regional or national producers of these items. They can buy these items from the best producers in the world. As Frank notes, while once a firm that produced a good tire in northern Ohio could be assured of selling tires in its regional market, today it cannot. Consumers buy tires from a handful of the best tire producers in the world.

Let's consider another example, one in which technological development plays an important part. Before there were records, tapes, or CDs, a person had to go to a concert to hear music. After the technology was developed for producing records, tapes, and CDs, this was no longer necessary. The best singers and bands in the world could simply put their music on a record, tape, or CD, and anyone in the world could listen to it. It was no longer necessary for a person living in a small town to go to a local concert to hear music performed by what may have been a very mediocre musician. Now, that person could listen to music performed by the best musicians in the world. His demand for music, and that of others, became focused on a smaller pool of musicians. As a consequence, these top musicians began to witness large increases in their earnings.

Now consider the second cause identified by Frank and Cook for the increase in within-group income inequality.

Frank and Cook argue that greater competition for top performers can be the result of a legal change. For example, consider the deregulation in airline, trucking, banking, brokerage, and other industries. Deregulation may have increased the salary competition for top performers, thus driving up their wages.

But why would this be an effect of deregulation? The answer is because in a deregulated environment, (market) competition comes to play a bigger role in determining outcomes—both "good" and "bad." Specifically, in a deregulated environment, the potential for both profits and losses is greater than in a regulated (less competitive) environment. To capture the higher potential profits and to guard against the increased likelihood of losses, talented professionals become more valuable to a firm.

Also, perhaps as a result of a less regulated, more fiercely competitive product market, the once widely accepted practice of companies promoting from within is today falling by the wayside. Increasingly, companies search for the top talent in other firms and industries and not just the top talent in their company pool. While once a top performer in a soft-drink company could expect only soft-drink companies to compete for his or her services, he or she can now expect to receive offers from soft-drink companies, computer companies, insurance companies, and more.

[3]This feature is based on Robert H. Frank, "Talent and the Winner-Take-All Society," in *The American Prospect*, no. 17 (Spring 1994): 97–107.
[4]The 2003 multiple is from *BusinessWeek*'s 54th Annual Executive Compensation Survey, April 2004.

Schooling, then, is human capital. In general, **human capital** refers to education, the development of skills, and anything else that is particular to the individual and increases his or her productivity.

    Contrast a person who has obtained an education with a person who has not. The educated person is likely to have certain skills, abilities, and knowledge that the uneducated person lacks. Consequently, he or she is likely to be worth more to an employer. Most college students know this; it is part of the reason they attend college.

RISK TAKING Individuals have different attitudes toward risk. Some individuals are more willing to take on risk than others are. Some of the individuals who are willing to take on risk will do well and rise to the top of the income distribution, and others will fall to the bottom. Individuals who prefer to play it safe aren't as likely to reach the top of the income distribution or to hit the bottom.

LUCK When individuals can't explain why something has happened to them, they often say it was the result of good or bad luck. At times, the good or bad luck explanation makes sense; at other times, it is more a rationalization than an explanation.

    Good and bad luck may influence incomes. For example, the college student who studies biology only to find out in her senior year that the bottom has fallen out of the biology market has experienced bad luck. The farmer who hits oil while digging a well

Human Capital
Education, development of skills, and anything else that is particular to the individual and increases his or her productivity.

has experienced good luck. An automobile worker who is unemployed owing to a recession he had no part in causing is experiencing bad luck. A person who trains for a profession in which there is an unexpected increase in demand experiences good luck.

Although luck can and does influence incomes, it is not likely to have (on average) a large or long-run effect. The person who experiences good luck today, and whose income reflects this fact, isn't likely to experience luck-boosting income increases time after time. In the long run, such factors as innate ability and attributes, education, and personal decisions (how much work, how much leisure?) are more likely to have a larger, more sustained effect on income than luck will have.

Wage Discrimination

The situation that exists when individuals of equal ability and productivity (as measured by their contribution to output) are paid different wage rates.

WAGE DISCRIMINATION **Wage discrimination** exists when individuals of equal ability and productivity, as measured by their marginal revenue products, are paid different wage rates by the same employer. It is a fact that in the period as a whole since World War II, the median income of African Americans has been approximately 60 percent that of whites. It is also a fact that since the late 1950s, females working full time have earned approximately 60–70 percent of the male median income. Are these differences between white and black incomes and between male and female incomes due wholly to discrimination? Most empirical studies show that approximately half the differences are due to differences in education, productivity, and job training (although one may ask if discrimination has anything to do with the education, productivity, and job training differences). The remainder of the wage differential is due to other factors, one of which is hypothesized to be discrimination.

Most people agree that discrimination exists, although they differ on the degree to which they think it affects income. We should also note that discrimination is not always directed at employees by employers. For example, consumers may practice discrimination—some white consumers may wish to deal only with white physicians and lawyers; some Asian Americans may wish to deal only with Asian American physicians and lawyers.

Income Differences: Some Are Voluntary, Some Are Not

Even in a world with no discrimination, differences in income would still exist. Other factors, which we have noted, account for this. Some individuals would have more marketable skills than others, some individuals would decide to work harder and longer hours than others, some individuals would take on more risk than others, and some individuals would undertake more schooling and training than others. Thus, some degree of income inequality occurs because individuals are innately different and make different choices. However, some degree of income inequality is also due to factors unrelated to innate ability or choices—such as discrimination or luck.

An interesting debate continues to be waged on the topic of discrimination-based income inequality. The opposing sides weight different factors differently. Some people argue that wage discrimination would be reduced if markets were allowed to be more competitive, more open, and freer. They believe that in an open and competitive market with few barriers to entry and no government protection of privileged groups, discrimination would have a high price. Firms that didn't hire the best and the brightest—regardless of a person's race, religion, or gender—would suffer. They would ultimately pay for their act of discrimination by having higher labor costs and lower profits. Individuals holding this view usually propose that government deregulate, reduce legal barriers to entry, and in general, not hamper the workings of the free market mechanism.

Others contend that even if the government were to follow this script, much wage discrimination would still exist. They think government should play an active legislative role in reducing both wage discrimination and other types of discrimination that they believe ultimately result in wage discrimination. The latter include discrimination in education and discrimination in on-the-job training. Proponents of an active role for government usually believe that such policy programs as affirmative action, equal pay for equal work, and comparable worth (equal pay for comparable work) are beneficial in reducing both the amount of wage discrimination in the economy and the degree of income inequality.

SELF-TEST

1.   Jack and Harry work for the same company, but Jack earns more than Harry. Is this evidence of wage discrimination? Explain your answer.

2.   A person decides to assume a lot of risk in earning an income. How could this affect his or her income?

Normative Standards of Income Distribution

For hundreds of years, economists, political philosophers, and political scientists, among others, have debated what constitutes a proper, just, or fair distribution of income and have proposed different normative standards. This section discusses three of the better known normative standards of income distribution: the marginal productivity normative standard, the absolute (complete) income equality normative standard, and the Rawlsian normative standard.

The Marginal Productivity Normative Standard

The marginal productivity theory of factor prices states that in a competitive setting, people tend to be paid their marginal revenue products.[5] The marginal productivity normative standard of income distribution holds that people *should* be paid their marginal revenue products.

This idea is illustrated in Exhibit 8(a). The first "income pie" in (a) represents the actual income shares of eight individuals, *A–H,* who work in a competitive setting and are paid their respective *MRP*s. The income distribution is unequal because the eight persons do not contribute equally to the productive process. Some individuals are more productive than others.

The second income pie in (a), which is the same as the first, is the income distribution that the proponents of the marginal productivity normative standard believe should exist. In short, individuals should be paid their marginal revenue products.

Proponents of this position argue that it is just for individuals to receive their contribution (high, low, or somewhere in between) to the productive process, no more and no less. In addition, paying people according to their productivity gives them an incentive to become more productive. For example, individuals have an incentive to learn more and to become better trained if they know they will be paid more as a consequence. According to this argument, without such incentives, work effort would decrease, laziness would increase, and in time, the entire society would feel the harmful effects. Critics respond that some persons are innately more productive than others and that rewarding them for innate qualities is unfair.

Keep in mind that this discussion assumes a competitive setting where people are paid their *MRP*s. Suppose a person is in a monopsony setting and is not being paid his or her *MRP.* Would the proponents of the marginal productivity normative standard argue that he or she should be? The answer is yes. People who propose normative standards think the marginal productivity standard should be applied regardless of the current

---

[5]Recall that in a competitive setting, value marginal product (*VMP*) equals marginal revenue product (*MRP*). Thus, the marginal productivity theory holds that in a competitive setting, people tend to be paid their *VMP*s, or *MRP*s.

(a) MARGINAL PRODUCTIVITY NORMATIVE STANDARD

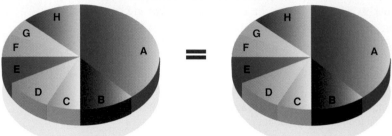

Income Distribution That Is   Income Distribution That Should Be

(b) ABSOLUTE INCOME EQUALITY NORMATIVE STANDARD

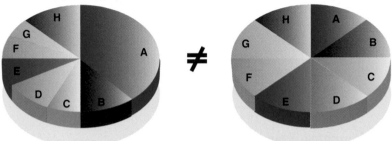

Income Distribution That Is   Income Distribution That Should Be

(c) RAWLSIAN NORMATIVE STANDARD

Income Distribution That Is   Income Distribution Agreed to   Income Distribution That Should Be
                                    Behind the Veil of Ignorance

exhibit **8**

**Different Normative Standards
of Income Distribution**

(a) The marginal productivity, (b) the
absolute, and (c) the Rawlsian normative standards of income distribution. Note that the income pies do
not change as income distribution
changes. In reality, the size of the
income pies might depend on the
income distribution. We are not concerned with this point here, but only
with illustrating what different income
distributions, based on different normative standards, look like at one
point in time.

situation. In other words, it is possible to be a proponent of the marginal productivity
normative standard whether or not you believe people are currently being paid their
marginal revenue products.

The Absolute Income Equality Normative Standard

Exhibit 8(b) illustrates the viewpoint of persons who advocate the absolute income
equality normative standard. The first income pie represents the income distribution that
exists—in which there is income inequality. The second income pie represents the
income distribution that the persons who argue for absolute income equality believe
should exist. Notice that each individual receives an equal percentage of the income pie.
No one has any more or any less than anyone else.

Proponents of this position hold that an equal distribution of income will lead to the maximization of total utility (in society). The argument is as follows: (1) Individuals are alike when it comes to how much satisfaction they receive from an added increase in income. (2) Receiving additional income is subject to the law of diminishing marginal utility; that is, each additional dollar is worth less to the recipient than the dollar that preceded it. (3) From points 1 and 2, it follows that redistributing income from the rich to the poor will raise total utility. The rich will not lose as much utility from the redistribution as the poor will gain. Overall, total utility (of society) will rise through the redistribution of income from the rich to the poor. Total utility will be maximized when all persons receive the same income.

Opponents of this position hold that it is impossible to know if all individuals receive equal utility from an added dollar of income and that a rich person may receive far more utility from an added dollar of income than a poor person receives. If so, then redistributing income until it is equalized would not maximize total utility.

The Rawlsian Normative Standard

In *A Theory of Justice,* philosopher John Rawls states that individuals are less likely to argue for a different income distribution if they know what their position is in the current income distribution than if they don't know what their position is.[6]

To illustrate, Patricia Jevons is thought to be a rich person. Her income is $500,000 per year, so she is in the top 5 percent of income earners. Furthermore, the income distribution in which she occupies this position is largely unequal. There are few rich people and many poor people. Given that Patricia knows her position in the income distribution and considers it a comfortable position to occupy, she is less likely to argue for a more equal income distribution (and the high taxes that will be needed to bring it about) than if she were placed behind John Rawls's fictional *veil of ignorance.*

The **veil of ignorance** is the imaginary veil, or curtain, behind which a person does not know her position in the income distribution; that is, a person does not know whether she will be rich or poor when the veil is removed. Rawls argues that the "average" person would be more likely to vote for a more equal income distribution behind the veil than she would vote for without the veil.

The full power of Rawls's veil of ignorance idea and its impact on income distribution can be seen in the following scenario. On Monday, everyone knows his position in the income distribution. Some people are arguing for more income equality, but a sizable group does not want this. They are satisfied with the status quo income distribution.

On Tuesday, everyone is somehow magically transported behind Rawls's veil of ignorance. Behind it, no one knows his position on the other side of the veil. No one knows whether he is rich or poor, innately talented or not, lucky or unlucky. As a group, the persons behind the veil must decide on the income distribution they wish to have when the veil is removed. Rawls believes that individuals are largely risk avoiders and will not want to take the chance that when the veil is removed, they will be poor. They will opt for an income distribution that will assure them that if they are (relatively) poor, their standard of living is not too low.

The Rawlsian normative standard is illustrated in Exhibit 8(c), which shows three income pies. The first represents the income distribution that currently exists. The second represents the income distribution that individuals behind the veil of ignorance would accept. The third and last income pie, which is the same as the second, represents the income distribution that Rawls holds should exist because it was agreed to in an

Veil of Ignorance
The imaginary veil or curtain behind which a person does not know his or her position in the income distribution.

---

[6] John Rawls, *A Theory of Justice* (Cambridge: Harvard University Press, 1971).

Thinking like
AN ECONOMIST *The income pies in Exhibit 8 are drawn so that their size does not change no matter what the income distribution is. To an economist, the size of the pie is likely to change over time, and how much it changes may be related to the current income distribution. To illustrate, suppose government is determined to make all incomes the same, no matter how much income growth there is in a country. Given this, we would expect that the size of the income pie would not grow much at all. After all, individuals may not work as hard if they know that government is determined to make all incomes the same.*

environment where individuals were, in a sense, equal: No one knew how he or she would fare when the veil was removed.

Critics of the Rawlsian position argue that individuals behind the veil of ignorance might not reach a consensus on the income distribution that should exist and that they might not be risk avoiders to the degree Rawls assumes they will be.

Furthermore, the individuals behind the veil of ignorance will consider the tradeoff between less income inequality and more output. In a world where the income distribution is likely to be unequal due to unequal individual productivities (sharply different marginal revenue products), reducing income inequality requires higher taxes and a lower reward for productive effort. In the end, this will lead to less productive effort being expended and less output for consumption. In short, the size of the income pie might change given different income distributions. Some of Rawls's critics maintain that individuals are likely to consider this information to a greater degree than Rawls assumes they will.

Poverty

This section presents some facts about poverty and examines its causes.

What Is Poverty?

There are principally two views of poverty. One view holds that poverty should be defined in absolute terms; the other holds that poverty should be defined in relative terms.

In absolute terms, poverty might be defined as follows: Poverty exists when the income of a family of four is less than $10,000 per year. In relative terms, poverty might be defined as follows: Poverty exists when the income of a family of four places it in the lowest 10 percent of income recipients.

Viewing poverty in relative terms means that poverty will always exist—unless, of course, there is absolute income equality. Given any unequal income distribution, some persons will always occupy the bottom rung of the income ladder; thus, there will always be poverty. This holds no matter how high the absolute standard of living of the members of the society. For example, in a society of ten persons where nine earn $1 million per year and one earns $400,000 per year, the person earning $400,000 per year is in the bottom 10 percent of the income distribution. If poverty is defined in relative terms, this person is considered to be living in poverty.

Poverty Income Threshold (Poverty Line)

Income level below which people are considered to be living in poverty.

The U.S. government defines poverty in absolute terms. The absolute poverty measure was developed in 1964 by the Social Security Administration based on findings of the Department of Agriculture. Called the **poverty income threshold** or **poverty line**, this measure refers to the income below which people are considered to be living in poverty. Individuals or families with incomes below the poverty income threshold, or poverty line, are considered poor.

In 2004, the poverty income threshold was $19,307 for a family of four. It was $9,827 for an individual under 65 years old. For an individual 65 years and older, it was $9,060.

The poverty threshold is updated yearly to reflect changes in the consumer price index. In 2004, 37 million people (in the United States), or 12.7 percent of the entire population, were living below the poverty line.

Limitations of the Official Poverty Income Statistics

The official poverty income statistics have certain limitations and shortcomings. First, the poverty figures are based solely on money incomes. Many money-poor persons receive in-kind benefits. For example, a family of four with a money income of $19,307 in 2004 was defined as poor, although it might have received in-kind benefits worth, say, $4,000. If the poverty figures are adjusted for in-kind benefits, the percentage of persons living in poverty drops.

Second, poverty figures are not adjusted for unreported income, leading to an overestimate of poverty. Third, poverty figures are not adjusted for regional differences in the cost of living, leading to both overestimates and underestimates of poverty.

Finally, government counters are unable to find some poor persons—such as some of the homeless—which leads to an underestimate of poverty.

What state has the highest poverty rate? the lowest poverty rate? What state has the largest number of people living in poverty?

In 2004, the state with the highest poverty rate (18.6 percent) was Mississippi. The state with the lowest poverty rate (5.4 percent) that year was New Hampshire. In 2004, the state with the most people living in poverty (4.7 million) was California.

Who Are the Poor?

Although the poor are persons of all religions, colors, genders, ages, and ethnic backgrounds, some groups are represented much more prominently in the poverty figures than others. For example, a greater percentage of African Americans and Hispanics than whites are poor. In 2004, 24.7 percent of African Americans, 21.9 percent of Hispanics, and 8.6 percent of whites lived below the poverty line.

A greater percentage of families headed by females than families headed by males are poor, and families with seven or more persons are much more likely to be poor than are families with fewer than seven persons. In addition, a greater percentage of young persons than others are poor, and the uneducated and poorly educated are more likely to be poor than are the educated. Overall, a disproportionate percentage of the poor are African American or Hispanic and live in large families headed by a female who is young and has little education.

If we look at poverty in terms of absolute numbers instead of percentages, then most poor persons are white, largely because there are more whites than other groups in the total population. In 2004, 25 million whites, 9.3 million African Americans, and 9.1 million Hispanics lived below the poverty line.

What Is the Justification for Government Redistributing Income?

Is there some justification for government redistributing income from the rich to the poor? Some individuals say there is no justification for government welfare assistance. In their view, playing Robin Hood is not a proper role of government. Persons who make this argument say they are not against helping the poor (e.g., they are usually in favor of private charitable organizations), but they are against government using its powers to take from some to give to others.

Some persons who believe in government welfare assistance usually present the *public good–free rider* justification or the *social-insurance* justification. Proponents of the public good–free rider position make the following arguments:

1. Most individuals in society would feel better if there were little or no poverty. It is distressing to view the signs of poverty, such as slums, hungry and poorly clothed people, and the homeless. Therefore, there is a demand for reducing or eliminating poverty.

economics 24/7

© ALISON WRIGHT/CORBIS

MONKS, BLESSINGS, AND FREE RIDERS

A chief way to deal with poverty and the inequality of income is through government redistribution programs. In essence, the government can tax people with relatively high incomes and redistribute the funds—either directly or in the form of goods and services—to people with relatively low or no incomes. For example, government may use tax revenue to provide food, shelter, and medical care for the poor.

Almost all countries redistribute income in other ways too. In the United States, for example, there are private (nonreligious) and religious charities. A private organization may collect voluntary donations and use the funds to provide shelter for the homeless. Or a religious organization may collect donations from its members and use the funds to provide food and clothes for the poor.

In Thailand, Buddhist monks often play an important role in redistributing income.[7] By 10 A.M. each day, hundreds of Buddhist believers wait for the Buddhist monk, Luang Poh Koon, to emerge from his residence at the Ban Rai Temple.

When he arrives, the believers raise their right hands, which are holding (paper) money. Luang Poh Koon circulates through the crowd, taking the money from their upraised hands. He keeps one of the bills from each person; the others are returned as good-luck charms. As each person files past him to leave, he taps the person on the head with a wand of rolled-up paper as a blessing.

The believers come to Luang Poh Koon, it is reported, for two reasons. First, they believe that he will use their donations for worthwhile purposes. Luang Poh Koon collects approximately $1,000 a day, and there is strong evidence that he gives away most of the money to help build schools and hospitals. Speaking of the donors, he says, "The way I

see it, they entrust it (their money) to me to do things that are useful for the country." The second reason donors give is to be blessed. Moreover, they believe that the better the person receiving the offering, the more merit they will get.

Other monks in Thailand collect donations from believers too. Not all of them allocate the funds the way Luang Poh Koon does, however. Some of them use the money to enrich their lives. For example, some monks use the donations to purchase expensive cars and to furnish their monastery cells with high-tech audio and video equipment.

Before we conclude, think of how the "monk system" of redistributing income (to benefit the needy) solves the public good–free rider problem. Recall that the reduction or elimination of poverty is a public good; that is, when poverty is reduced or eliminated, everyone can share in the benefits of not having to view and feel the upsetting sights of poverty. But it is the public good aspect of poverty reduction and elimination that produces free riders. If no one can be excluded from experiencing the benefits of poverty reduction, then individuals will not have any incentive to pay for what they can get for free.

How does the "monk system" deal with the public good–free rider problem? If a person doesn't give funds to the monk—funds that are to be used for worthwhile purposes—then the person doesn't receive the monk's blessing. No donation, no blessing. In this way, the monks have tied something that people can receive only if they pay for it—the blessing—to a public good—the reduction or elimination of poverty.

---

[7]This feature is adapted from "Rich Are the Blessed," *Far Eastern Economic Review,* May 4, 1995. As of this writing, Luang Poh Koon is in very poor health, but he still blesses people who come to see him.

2. The reduction or elimination of poverty is a *(nonexcludable) public good*—a good that if consumed by one person can be consumed by other persons to the same degree and the consumption of which cannot be denied to anyone. That is, when poverty is reduced or eliminated, everyone will benefit from no longer viewing the ugly and upsetting sights of poverty, and no one can be excluded from such benefits.

3. If no one can be excluded from experiencing the benefits of poverty reduction, then individuals will not have any incentive to pay for what they can get for free. Thus, they will become free riders. Economist Milton Friedman sums up the force of the argument this way:

I am distressed by the sight of poverty. I am benefited by its alleviation; but I am benefited equally whether I or someone else pays for its alleviation; the benefits of other people's charity therefore partly accrue to me. To put it differently, we might all of us be willing to contribute to the relief of poverty, provided everyone else did it. We might not be willing to contribute the same amount without such assurance.[8]

Accepting the public good–free rider argument means that government is justified in taxing all persons to pay for the welfare assistance of some.

The social-insurance justification is a different type of justification for government welfare assistance. It holds that individuals currently not receiving welfare think they might one day need welfare assistance and thus are willing to take out a form of insurance for themselves by supporting welfare programs (with their tax dollars and votes).

SELF-TEST

1. "Poor people will always exist." Comment.

2. What percentage of the U.S. population was living in poverty in 2004?

3. What is the general description of a disproportionate percentage of the poor?

A Reader Asks...

Are There Degrees of Poverty?

For a family of four, the poverty threshold or poverty line was $19,307 in 2004. This means that if a family of four earned less than $19,307 in 2004, it was living in poverty. But it seems that just setting a dollar figure below which someone is said to be living in poverty doesn't capture the severity or depth of poverty. After all, couldn't two four-person families have earned less than $19,307 in 2004, but still one family have earned much less than the other?

To focus in on the severity or depth of poverty, economists sometimes talk about the ratio of income to poverty.

$$\text{Ratio of income to poverty} = \frac{\text{Family's income}}{\text{Family's poverty income threshold}}$$

For example, consider two four-person families, *A* and *B*. In 2004, family *A* earned $16,000 and family *B* earned $9,000. The ratio of income to poverty for family *A* is:

$16,000/$19,307 = 0.83

The ratio of income to poverty for family *B* is:

$9,000/$19,307 = 0.47

In other words, both families are poor, but family *B* is poorer than family *A*. The depth or severity of family *B*'s poverty is greater than family *A*'s poverty.

Now suppose we consider family *C*, another four-person family, whose income was, say, $21,000 in 2004. The ratio of income to poverty for family *C* is:

$21,000/$19,307 = 1.08

Any time the ratio of income to poverty is greater than 1.00, a family is not considered to be living in poverty. However, if the ratio of income to poverty is between 1.00 and 1.25, the family is considered to be "near poor." Family *C*, therefore, is near poor.

As an aside, data show that one's chances of living in poverty decrease as one's educational level rises. To illustrate, 21.3 percent of the persons who did not have a high school diploma were living in poverty in 2003. This contrasts with 11.3 percent who had a high school diploma but no college, 8.5 percent who had some college but not a bachelor's degree, and 4.7 percent who had completed college and earned a bachelor's degree.

---

[8]Milton Friedman, *Capitalism and Freedom* (Chicago: University of Chicago Press, 1962), p. 191.

! analyzing the scene

Can everyone become better off as the income distribution becomes more unequal?

Let's suppose that the income distribution has become more unequal and that the top one-fifth of all income earners has increased its income relative to all other fifths. Is it possible for everyone to be better off as the income distribution becomes more unequal? The answer is yes. To illustrate, suppose society is made up of five individuals, *A–E*. The yearly income for each individual is as follows: *A* earns $20,000, *B* earns $10,000, *C* earns $5,000, *D* earns $2,500, and *E* earns $1,250. The total yearly income in this society is $38,750, and the distribution of income is certainly unequal. *A* earns 51.61 percent of the income, *B* earns 25.81 percent, *C* earns 12.90 percent, *D* earns 6.45 percent, and *E* earns only 3.23 percent.

Now suppose each person earns additional real income. *A* earns $10,000 more real income for a total of $30,000, *B* earns $3,000 more real income for a total of $13,000,

C earns $2,000 more real income for a total of $7,000, *D* earns $1,000 more real income for a total of $3,500, and *E* earns $200 more real income for a total of $1,450. In terms of real income, each of the five persons is better off. But the income distribution has become even more unequal. For example, *A* (at the top fifth of income earners) now receives 54.60 percent of all income instead of 51.61 percent, and *E* (at the bottom fifth of income earners) now receives 2.64 percent instead of 3.22 percent. A newspaper headline might read, "The rich get richer as the poor get poorer." People reading this headline might naturally think that the poor in society are now worse off. But we know they are not worse off in terms of the goods and services they can purchase. They now have more real income than they had when the income distribution was less unequal. In short, it is possible for everyone to be better off even though the income distribution has become more unequal.

chapter summary

The Distribution of Income

- In 2004, the lowest fifth of households received 3.4 percent of the total money income, the second fifth received 8.9 percent, the third fifth received 14.7 percent, the fourth fifth received 23.0 percent, the top fifth received 50.0 percent.

- The government can change the distribution of income through taxes and transfer payments. Individual income = Labor income + Asset income + Transfer payments − Taxes. Government directly affects transfer payments and taxes.

- The Lorenz curve represents the income distribution. The Gini coefficient is a measure of the degree of inequality in the distribution of income. A Gini coefficient of 0 means perfect income equality; a Gini coefficient of 1 means complete income inequality.

- Income inequality exists because individuals differ in their innate abilities and attributes, their choices of work and leisure, their education and other training, their attitudes about risk taking, the luck they experience, and the amount of wage discrimination directed against them. Some income inequality is the result of voluntary choices, and some is not.

- There are three major normative standards of income distribution: (1) The marginal productivity normative standard holds that the income distribution should be

based on workers being paid their marginal revenue products. (2) The absolute income equality normative standard holds that there should be absolute or complete income equality. (3) The Rawlsian normative standard holds that the income distribution decided on behind the veil of ignorance (where individuals are equal) should exist in the real world.

Poverty

- The income poverty threshold, or poverty line, is the income level below which a family or person is considered poor and living in poverty.

- It is important to be aware of the limitations of poverty income statistics. The statistics are usually not adjusted for (1) in-kind benefits, (2) unreported and illegal income, and (3) regional differences in the cost of living. Furthermore, the statistics do not count the poor who exist but are out of sight, such as some of the homeless.

- People who believe government should redistribute income from the rich to the poor usually base their argument on the public good–free rider justification or the social-insurance justification. The public good–free rider justification holds that many people are in favor of redistributing income from the rich to the poor and that the elimination of poverty is a public good. But unfortunately, it is a public good that individuals cannot "produce" because of the incentive everyone has to free ride on the contributions of others. Consequently, government is justified in taxing all persons to pay for the welfare assistance of some. The social-insurance justification holds that individuals not currently receiving redistributed monies may one day find themselves in a position where they will need to, so they are willing to take out a form of insurance. In essence, they are willing to support redistribution programs today so that these programs exist if they should need them in the future.

key terms and concepts

Transfer Payments	Lorenz Curve	Human Capital	Veil of Ignorance
In-Kind Transfer Payments	Gini Coefficient	Wage Discrimination	Poverty Income Threshold (Poverty Line)

questions and problems

1   The Gini coefficient for country *A* is 0.35, and for country *B*, it is 0.22. From this, it follows that the bottom 10 percent of income recipients in country *B* have a greater percentage of the total income than the bottom 10 percent of the income recipients in country *A*. Do you agree or disagree? Why?

2   Would you expect greater income inequality in country *A*, where there is great disparity in age, or in country *B*, where there is little disparity in age? Explain your answer.

3   Has U.S. income inequality increased or decreased (if we compare the income distribution in 1967 with the income distribution in 2004)? What percentage of total money income did the top fifth of U.S. households receive in 2004?

4   What is a major criticism of the absolute income equality normative standard?

5   In what ways does the Rawlsian technique of hypothesizing individuals behind a veil of ignorance help or not help us decide whether we should have a 65 mph speed limit or a higher one, a larger or smaller welfare system, and higher or lower taxes imposed on the rich?

6   Welfare recipients would rather receive cash benefits than in-kind benefits, but much of the welfare system provides in-kind benefits. Is there any reason for not giving recipients their welfare benefits the way they want to receive them? Would it be better to move to a welfare system that provides benefits only in cash?

7   What is the effect of age on the income distribution?

8   Can more people live in poverty at the same time that a smaller percentage of people live in poverty? Explain your answer.

9   Can luck partly explain income inequality? Explain your answer.

10   How would you determine whether or not the wage difference between two individuals is due to wage discrimination?

working with numbers and graphs

1   The lowest fifth of income earners have a 10 percent income share, the second fifth a 17 percent income share, the third fifth a 22 percent income share, the fourth fifth a 24 percent income share, and the highest fifth a 27 percent income share. Draw the Lorenz curve.

2   In Exhibit 7, using Lorenz curve 2, approximately what percentage of income goes to the second highest 20 percent of households?

3   Is it possible for real income for everyone in society to rise even though the income distribution has become more unequal? Prove your answer with a numerical example.

27 Interest, Rent, and Profit

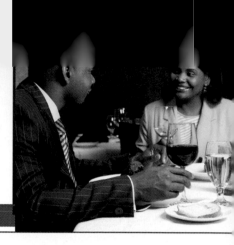

7:54 P.M.

Jake and Becky Townsend, who are spending a few days in New York City, have just finished dinner at a fashionable restaurant on the Upper East Side of Manhattan. Dinner for two: $180.

"Dinner is pretty expensive here," Jake comments. "I wonder why." "I guess it's because of the rent on a place like this," Becky says. "High rent means high prices."

8:09 P.M.

A woman notices the bumper sticker on a car: What if the world were to end next week?

9:14 P.M.

Ellie is at her desk, writing checks for some bills, when her roommate Caro gets home from her workout at the nearby fitness center.

"I can't believe the interest rate I'm paying on my MasterCard," says Ellie.

"High, isn't it? My rate is outrageous," Caro responds.

"I think I'm beginning to agree with the view that usury is sinful." Ellie pauses for a moment and then adds, "In fact, charging interest is sinful."

"At least there should be a cap on how high an interest rate a company can charge," says Caro.

> **?** Here are some questions to keep in mind as you read this chapter:
>
> *Does high rent cause high prices?*
>
> *How would things change today if everyone knew the world would end next week?*
>
> *Is interest sinful?*
>
> See **analyzing the scene** at the end of this chapter for answers to these questions.

Interest

The word *interest* is used in two ways in economics. Sometimes, it refers to the price for credit or **loanable funds**. For example, Lars borrows $100 from Rebecca and, a year later, pays her back $110. The interest is $10.

Interest can also refer to the return earned by capital as an input in the production process. A person who buys a machine (a capital good) for $1,000 and earns $100 a year by using the productive services of the machine is said to earn $100 interest, or a 10 percent interest rate, on the capital.

Economists refer to both the price for loanable funds and the return on capital goods as interest because there is a tendency for the two to become equal, as discussed later in this section.

Loanable Funds

Funds that someone borrows and another person lends, for which the borrower pays an interest rate to the lender.

Loanable Funds: Demand and Supply

The equilibrium interest rate, or the price for loanable funds (or credit), is determined by the demand for and supply of loanable funds (or credit). The demand for loanable funds is composed of the demand for consumption loans, the demand for investment loans, and government's demand for loanable funds. With respect to the latter, the U.S. Treasury may need to finance budget deficits by borrowing (demanding) loanable funds in the loanable funds market. This chapter focuses on the demand for consumption loans and the demand for investment loans.

The supply of loanable funds comes from people's saving and from newly created money. This chapter discusses only people's saving.

In summary, in our discussion in this chapter, the demand for loanable funds is composed of (1) the demand for consumption loans and (2) the demand for investment loans. The supply of loanable funds is composed of people's saving.

Q&A *I've heard that* **interest** *is the price of money. Is this true?*

No, interest is not the price of money. This definition of interest seems to suggest that interest would not exist in a moneyless, or barter, economy. But interest would exist in a barter economy. For example, someone might borrow 2 coconuts today in exchange for 3 coconuts next month. The one extra coconut that the borrower pays (to the lender) is the nonmoney interest or price paid for consuming coconuts now instead of later.

THE SUPPLY OF LOANABLE FUNDS Savers are people who consume less than their current income. Without savers, there would be no supply of loanable funds. Savers receive an interest rate for the use of their funds, and the amount of funds saved and loaned is directly related to the interest rate.[1] Specifically, the supply curve of loanable funds is upward sloping: The higher the interest rate, the greater the quantity supplied of loanable funds; the lower the interest rate, the less the quantity supplied of loanable funds.

THE DEMAND FOR LOANABLE FUNDS: CONSUMPTION LOANS Loanable funds are demanded by consumers because they have a **positive rate of time preference**; that is, consumers prefer earlier availability of goods to later availability. For example, most people would prefer to have a car today than to have a car five years from today.

There is nothing irrational about a positive rate of time preference—most, if not all, people have it. People differ, though, as to the *degree* of their preference for earlier, compared with later, availability. Some people have a high rate of time preference, signifying that they greatly prefer present to future consumption (I must have that new car today).

Positive Rate of Time Preference

Preference for earlier availability of goods over later availability of goods.

---

[1]Because a higher interest rate may have both a substitution effect and an income effect, many economists argue that a higher interest rate can lead to either more saving or less saving depending on which effect is stronger. We will ignore these complications at this level of analysis and hold that the supply curve of loanable funds (from savers) is upward sloping.

Other people have a low rate, signifying that they prefer present to future consumption only slightly. (Who would be more likely to save—that is, postpone consumption—people with a high rate of time preference or people with a low rate? The answer is people with a low rate of time preference. People with a high rate of time preference feel they need to have things now.)

Because consumers have a positive rate of time preference, there is a demand for consumption loans. Consumers borrow today to buy today; they will pay back the borrowed amount plus interest tomorrow. The interest payment is the price consumers–borrowers pay to obtain the earlier availability of goods.

Roundabout Method of Production

The production of capital goods that enhance productive capabilities to ultimately bring about increased consumption.

THE DEMAND FOR LOANABLE FUNDS: INVESTMENT LOANS Investors (or firms) demand loanable funds (or credit) so they can invest in capital goods and finance **roundabout methods of production**. A firm using a roundabout method of production first directs its efforts to producing capital goods and then uses those goods to produce consumer goods.

Let's consider the direct method and the roundabout method for catching fish. In the direct method, a person uses his hands to catch fish. In the roundabout method, the person weaves a net (which is a capital good) and then uses the net to catch fish. Let's suppose that by using the direct method, Charlie can catch 4 fish per day. Using the roundabout method, he can catch 10 fish per day.

Furthermore, let's suppose it takes Charlie 10 days to weave a net. If Charlie does not weave a net and instead catches fish by hand, he can catch 1,460 fish per year (4 fish per day times 365 days). If, however, Charlie spends 10 days weaving a net (during which time he catches no fish), he can catch 3,550 fish the first year (10 fish per day times 355 days). We conclude that the capital-intensive roundabout method of production is highly productive.

Because roundabout methods of production are so productive, investors are willing to borrow funds to finance them. For example, Charlie might reason, "I'm more productive if I use a fishing net, but I'll need to take 10 days off from catching fish and devote all my energies to weaving a net. What will I eat during the 10 days? Perhaps I can borrow some fish from my neighbor. I'll need to borrow 40 fish for the next 10 days. But I must make it worthwhile for my neighbor to enter into this arrangement, so I will promise to pay her back 50 fish at the end of the year. Thus, my neighbor will lend me 40 fish today in exchange for 50 fish at the end of the year. I realize I'm paying an interest rate of 25 percent (the interest payment of 10 fish is 25 percent of the number of fish borrowed, 40), but still it will be worth it." The highly productive nature of the capital-intensive roundabout method of production is what makes it worthwhile.

The reasoning in our fish example is repeated whenever a firm makes a capital investment. Producing computers on an assembly line is a roundabout method of production compared with producing them one by one by hand. Making copies on a copying machine is a roundabout method of production compared with copying by hand. In both cases, firms are willing to borrow now, use the borrowed funds to invest in capital goods to finance roundabout methods of production, and pay back the loan with interest later. If roundabout methods of production were not productive, firms would not be willing to do this.

THE LOANABLE FUNDS MARKET The sum of the demand for consumption loans and the demand for investment loans is the total demand for loanable funds. The demand curve for loanable funds is downward sloping. As interest rates rise, consumers' cost of earlier availability of goods rises, and they curtail their borrowing. Also, as interest rates rise, some investment projects that would be profitable at a lower interest rate will no longer be profitable. We conclude that the interest rate and the quantity demanded of loanable funds are inversely related.

Exhibit 1 illustrates the demand for and supply of loanable funds. The equilibrium interest rate occurs where the quantity demanded of loanable funds equals the quantity supplied of loanable funds.

The Price for Loanable Funds and the Return on Capital Goods Tend to Equality

As mentioned earlier, both the *price for loanable funds* and the *return on capital* are referred to as interest because they tend to equality. To illustrate, suppose the return on capital is 10 percent and the price for loanable funds is 8 percent. In this setting, firms will borrow in the loanable funds market and invest in capital goods. As they do this, the quantity of capital increases, and its return falls (capital is subject to diminishing marginal returns). In short, the return on capital and the price for loanable funds begin to approach each other.

Suppose, instead, that the percentages are reversed, and the price for loanable funds is 10 percent and the return on capital is 8 percent. In this situation, no one will borrow loanable funds at 10 percent to invest at 8 percent. Over time, the capital stock will decrease (capital depreciates over time; it doesn't last forever), its marginal physical product will rise, and the return on capital and the price for loanable funds will eventually equal each other.

Why Do Interest Rates Differ?

The supply-and-demand analysis in Exhibit 1 may suggest that there is only one interest rate in the economy. In reality, there are many. For example, a major business is not likely to pay the same interest rate for an investment loan to purchase new machinery as the person next door pays for a consumption loan to buy a car. Some of the factors that affect interest rates are discussed in the following paragraphs. In each case, the *ceteris paribus* condition holds.

RISK Any time a lender makes a loan, there is a possibility that the borrower will not repay it. Some borrowers are better credit risks than others. A major corporation with a long and established history is probably a better credit risk than a person who has been unemployed three times in the last seven years. The more risk associated with a loan, the higher the interest rate; the less risk associated with a loan, the lower the interest rate.

TERM OF THE LOAN In general, the longer the term of the loan, the higher the interest rate; the shorter the term of the loan, the lower the interest rate. Borrowers are usually more willing to pay higher interest rates for long-term loans because this gives them greater flexibility. Lenders require higher interest rates to part with funds for extended periods.

COST OF MAKING THE LOAN A loan for $1,000 and a loan for $100,000 may require the same amount of recordkeeping, making the larger loan cheaper (per dollar) to process than the smaller loan. In addition, some loans require frequent payments (e.g., payments for a car loan), whereas others do not. This difference is likely to be reflected in higher administrative costs for loans with more frequent payments. We conclude that loans that cost more to process and administer will have higher interest rates than loans that cost less to process and administer.

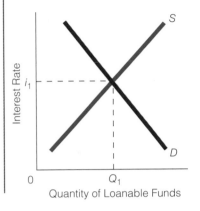

exhibit 1

Loanable Funds Market

The demand curve shows the different quantities of loanable funds demanded at different interest rates. The supply curve shows the different quantities of loanable funds supplied at different interest rates. Through the forces of supply and demand, the equilibrium interest rate and the quantity of loanable funds at that rate are established as i_1 and Q_1.

Thinking like **AN ECONOMIST** *In economics, it is not uncommon for factors to converge. For example, in supply-and-demand analysis, the quantity demanded and the quantity supplied of a good tend to equality (through the equilibrating process). In consumer theory, the marginal utility-price ratios for different goods tend to equality. And as just discussed, the price of loanable funds and the return on capital tend to equality.*

But why do many things tend to equality in economics? It is because equality is often representative of equilibrium. When quantity demanded equals quantity supplied, a market is said to be in equilibrium. When the marginal utility-price ratio for all goods is the same, the consumer is said to be in equilibrium. Inequality, therefore, often signifies disequilibrium. When the price of loanable funds is greater than the return on capital, there is disequilibrium. The next logical question is, "So what happens now?"

The economist, knowing that equality often signifies equilibrium, looks for inequalities and then asks, "So what happens now?"

596   **Part 8**   Factor Markets and Related Issues

Nominal and Real Interest Rates

Nominal Interest Rate

The interest rate determined by the forces of supply and demand in the loanable funds market.

The **nominal interest rate** is the interest rate determined by the forces of supply and demand in the loanable funds market. It is the interest rate in current dollars. The nominal interest rate will change if the demand for or supply of loanable funds changes. Individuals' expectations of inflation are one of the factors that can change both the demand for and supply of loanable funds. Inflation occurs when the money prices of goods, on average, increase over time. To see exactly how this can affect the nominal interest rate, look at Exhibit 2.

We start with an interest rate of 8 percent and an actual and expected inflation rate of zero (actual inflation rate = expected inflation rate = 0 percent). Later, both the demanders and suppliers of loanable funds expect a 4 percent inflation rate. What will this 4 percent expected inflation rate do to the demand for and supply of loanable funds? Borrowers (demanders of loanable funds) will be willing to pay 4 percent more interest for their loans because they expect to be paying back the loans with dollars that have 4 percent less buying power than the dollars they are being lent. (Another way of looking at this is to say that if they wait to buy goods, the prices of the goods they want will have risen by 4 percent. To beat the price increase, they are willing to pay up to 4 percent more to borrow and purchase the goods now.) In effect, the demand for loanable funds curve shifts rightward, so that at Q_1, borrowers are willing to pay a 4 percent higher interest rate.

On the other side of the loanable funds market, the lenders (suppliers of loanable funds) require a 4 percent higher interest rate (i.e., 12 percent) to compensate them for the 4 percent less valuable dollars in which the loan will be repaid. In effect, the supply of loanable funds curve shifts leftward, so that at Q_1, lenders will receive an interest rate of 12 percent.

Thus, an expected inflation rate of 4 percent increases the demand for loanable funds and decreases the supply of loanable funds, so that the interest rate is 4 percent higher than it was when there was a zero expected inflation rate. In this example, 12 percent is the nominal interest rate. It is the interest rate in current dollars, and it includes the expected inflation rate.

If we adjust for the expected inflation rate, we have the **real interest rate**. The real interest rate is the nominal interest rate adjusted for the expected inflation rate; that is, it

Q&A

If a lender charges one borrower a higher interest rate for a $1,000 loan than he or she charges another borrower, isn't this a form of "price discrimination"?

Remember that price discrimination entails charging one customer a higher price than another customer when there is no difference in the cost of providing the good to either customer. This is not the case if a lender charges a higher interest rate to one borrower than to another borrower because the risk of one borrower paying back the loan is higher than the risk of the other borrower paying back the loan.

Real Interest Rate

The nominal interest rate adjusted for expected inflation—that is, the nominal interest rate minus the expected inflation rate.

exhibit 2

Expected Inflation and Interest Rates

We start at an 8 percent interest rate and an actual and expected inflation rate of 0 percent. Later, both borrowers and lenders expect an inflation rate of 4 percent. Borrowers are willing to pay a higher interest rate because they will be paying off their loans with cheaper dollars. Lenders require a higher interest rate because they will be paid back in cheaper dollars. The demand and supply curves shift such that at Q_1, borrowers are willing to pay and lenders require a 4 percent higher interest rate. The nominal interest rate is now 12 percent. The real interest rate is 8 percent (the real interest rate = nominal interest rate − expected inflation rate).

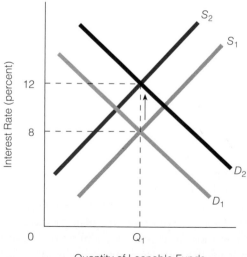

economics 24/7

IS THE CAR WORTH BUYING?

Business firms often compute present values when trying to decide whether or not to buy capital goods. Should consumers do the same when they are thinking about buying a durable good (a good that will last for a few years), such as a car?

Suppose you are thinking about buying a car. The market price of the car is $15,500. You anticipate that you will receive $2,000 worth of services from the car each year for the next 10 years, after which time the car will have to be scrapped and will have no scrap value.

What is the question you should ask yourself? Ask the same question that the business firm asks when it considers buying a capital good. In your case ask: Is the present value of the car more than, less than, or equal to the present market price of the car?

What is the present value of the car in our discussion? A car that yields $2,000 worth of benefits each year for 10 years at a 4 percent interest rate has a present value of approximately $16,223:

$$PV = \$2{,}000/(1 + 0.04)^1 + \$2{,}000/(1 + 0.04)^2 + \ldots$$
$$+ \$2{,}000/(1 + 0.04)^{10} = \$16{,}223 \text{ (approximately)}$$

The market price of the car ($15,500) is less than the present value of the car ($16,223), so it is worthwhile to purchase the car.

What will an increase in the interest rate do to the present value of the car? All other things remaining constant, an increase in the interest rate will lower the present value of the car. For example, at a 7 percent interest rate, the present value of the car is approximately $15,377. Now, the market price of the car ($15,500) is greater than the present value of the car ($15,377); it is not worthwhile to purchase this car. We would expect fewer cars to be sold when the interest rate rises and more cars to be sold when the interest rate falls. Why? A change in the interest rate changes the present value of cars.

---

is the nominal interest rate minus the expected inflation rate. In our example, the real interest rate is 8 percent (real interest rate = nominal interest rate − expected inflation rate).

The real interest rate, not the nominal interest rate, matters to borrowers and lenders. Consider a lender who grants a $1,000 loan to a borrower at a 20 percent nominal interest rate at a time when the actual inflation rate is 15 percent. The amount repaid to the lender is $1,200, but $1,200 with a 15 percent inflation rate does not have the buying power that $1,200 with a zero inflation rate has. The 15 percent inflation rate wipes out much of the gain, and the lender's real return on the loan is not 20 percent, but rather only 5 percent. Thus, the rate lenders receive and borrowers pay (and therefore, the rate they care about) is the real interest rate.

Present Value: What Is Something Tomorrow Worth Today?

Because of people's positive rate of time preference, $100 today is worth more than $100 a year from now. (Don't you prefer $100 today to $100 in a year?) Thus, $100 a year from now must be worth less than $100 today. Can we be more specific and say just *how much* $100 a year from now is worth today?

This question introduces the concept of *present value*. **Present value** refers to the current worth of some future dollar amount (of receipts or income). In our example, present value refers to what $100 a year from now is worth today.

Present value (*PV*) is computed by using the formula:

$$PV = A_n/(1 + i)^n$$

Present Value

The current worth of some future dollar amount of income or receipts.

where A_n is the actual amount of income or receipts in a particular year in the future, i is the interest rate (expressed as a decimal), and n is the number of years in the future. The present value of $100 one year in the future at a 10 percent interest rate is $90.91:

$$PV = \$100/(1 + 0.10)^1$$
$$= \$90.91$$

This means that the right to receive $100 a year from now is worth $90.91 today. Another way to look at this is to realize that if $90.91 is put in a savings account paying a 10 percent interest rate, it would equal $100 in a year.

Now suppose we wanted to know what a particular future income stream was worth today. That is, instead of finding out what a particular future dollar amount is worth today, our objective is to find out what a series of future dollar amounts are worth today. The general formula is:

$$PV = \Sigma A_n/(1 + i)^n$$

where the Greek letter Σ stands for "sum of."

Suppose a firm buys a machine that will earn $100 a year for the next 3 years. What is this future income stream—$100 per year for 3 years—worth today? What is its present value? At a 10 percent interest rate, this income stream has a present value of $248.68:

$$PV = A_1/(1 + 0.10)^1 + A_2/(1 + 0.10)^2 + A_3/(1 + 0.10)^3$$
$$= \$100/1.10 + \$100/1.21 + \$100/1.331$$
$$= \$90.91 + \$82.64 + \$75.13$$
$$= \$248.68$$

Deciding Whether or Not to Purchase a Capital Good

Business firms often compute present values when trying to decide whether or not to buy a capital good. Let's look again at the machine that will earn $100 a year for the next 3 years. Suppose we assume that after the 3-year period, the machine must be scrapped and that it will have no scrap value. The firm will compare the present value of the future income generated by the machine ($248.68) with the cost of the machine. Suppose the cost of the machine is $250. The firm will decide not to buy it because the cost of the machine is greater than the present value of the income stream the machine will generate.

Would the business firm buy the machine if the interest rate had been 4 percent instead of 10 percent? The present value of $100 a year for 3 years at 4 percent interest is $278. Comparing this amount with the cost of the machine ($250), we see that the firm is likely to buy the machine. We conclude that as interest rates decrease, present values increase, and firms will buy more capital goods; as interest rates increase, present values decrease, and firms will buy fewer capital goods, all other things held constant.

SELF-TEST

(Answers to Self-Test questions are in the Self-Test Appendix.)

1. Why does the price for loanable funds tend to equal the return on capital goods?

2. Why does the real interest rate, and not the nominal interest rate, matter to borrowers and lenders?

3. What is the present value of $1,000 two years from today if the interest rate is 5 percent?

4. A business firm is thinking of buying a capital good. The capital good will earn $2,000 a year for the next 4 years, and it will cost $7,000. The interest rate is 8 percent. Should the firm buy the capital good? Explain your answer.

Rent

Mention the word *rent,* and people naturally think of someone living in an apartment who makes monthly payments to a landlord. This is not the type of rent discussed here. To an economist, rent means **economic rent**. Economic rent is a payment in excess of opportunity costs. (We discussed economic rent in the chapter on monopoly.) There is also a subset of economic rent called **pure economic rent**. This is a payment in excess of opportunity costs when opportunity costs are zero. Historically, the term *pure economic rent* was first used to describe the payment to the factor land, which is perfectly inelastic in supply.

In Exhibit 3, the total supply of land is fixed at Q_1 acres; there can be no more and no less than this amount of land. The payment for land is determined by the forces of supply and demand; this payment turns out to be R_1.

Notice that R_1 is more than sufficient to bring Q_1 acres into supply. In fact, we know by looking at the fixed supply of land (the supply curve is perfectly inelastic) that Q_1 acres would have been forthcoming at a payment of zero dollars. In short, this land has zero opportunity costs. Therefore, the full payment, all of R_1, is referred to as pure economic rent.

David Ricardo, the Price of Grain, and Land Rent

In 19th-century England, people were concerned about the rising price of grains, which were a staple in many English diets. Some argued that grain prices were rising because land rents were rising rapidly. People began pointing fingers at the landowners, as they maintained that the high rents the landowners received for their land made it more and more costly for farmers to raise grains. These higher costs, in turn, were passed on to consumers in the form of higher prices. According to this argument, the solution was to lower rents, which would lead to lower costs for farmers and eventually to lower prices for consumers.

English economist David Ricardo thought this reasoning was faulty. He contended that grain prices weren't high because rents were high (as most individuals thought) but rather that rents were high because grain prices were high.

In current economic terminology, his argument was as follows: Land is a factor of production; therefore, the demand for it is derived. Land is also in fixed supply; therefore, the only thing that will change the payment made to land is a change in the demand for land. (The supply curve isn't going to shift, and thus, the only thing that can change price is a shift in the demand curve.) Landowners have no control over the demand for land. Demand comes from other persons who want to use it. In 19th-century England, the demand came from farmers who were raising grains and other foodstuffs. Therefore, landowners could not have pushed up land rents because they had no control over the demand for their land. It follows that if rents were high, this must have been because the demand for land was high, and the demand for land was high because grain prices were high. Economists put it this way: *Land rents are price determined, not price determining.*

The Supply Curve of Land Can Be Upward Sloping

Exhibit 3 depicts the supply of land as fixed. This is the case when the total supply of land is in question. For example, there are only so many acres of land in this country, and that amount is not likely to change.

Most subparcels of land, however, have competing uses. Consider 25 acres of land on the periphery of a major city. It can be used for farmland, a shopping mall, or a road. If a particular parcel of land (as opposed to all land, or the total supply of land) has competing uses (the land can be used one way or another way), it follows that the parcel of land has opportunity costs. Land that is used for farming could have been used for a

Economic Rent

Payment in excess of opportunity costs.

Pure Economic Rent

A category of economic rent where the payment is to a factor that is in fixed supply, implying that it has zero opportunity costs.

exhibit **3**

Pure Economic Rent and the Total Supply of Land

The total supply of land is fixed at Q_1. The payment for the services of this land is determined by the forces of supply and demand. Because the payment is for a factor in fixed supply, it is referred to as pure economic rent.

economics 24/7

LOANS FOR THE POOREST OF THE POOR

The Norwegian Nobel Committee has decided to award the Nobel Peace Prize for 2006, divided into two equal parts, to Muhammad Yunus and Grameen Bank for their efforts to create economic and social development from below. Lasting peace cannot be achieved unless large population groups find ways in which to break out of poverty. Micro-credit is one such means. Development from below also serves to advance democracy and human rights.

—October 13, 2006

On October 13, 2006, Muhammad Yunus and the bank that he founded, Grameen Bank, were jointly awarded the Nobel Peace Prize. Yunus, an economist, thought that giving loans to the poorest of the poor—even if they did not have any collateral—would not only help them, but could be a successful business too. (The Grameen Bank has been profitable in all but three years since it came into existence.) Giving loans to the poorest of the poor goes by different names: micro-finance, micro-credit, micro-loans. Here is how Yunus describes micro-finance in an October 14, 2006 article he wrote for the *Wall Street Journal.*

> *The basic philosophy behind micro-finance is that the poor, although spurned by traditional banks because they can't provide collateral, are actually a great investment: No one works harder than someone who is striving to achieve life's basic necessities, particularly a woman with children to support."[2]*

It was back in 1974 when Muhammad Yunus, then a young economics professor at Chittagong University in Bangladesh, started a conversation with a 21-year-old woman making bamboo stools in a small Bangladeshi village. It turned out that she had borrowed approximately nine cents to buy the materials she needed to make the stools. After she paid back the lender, she would earn only a few cents for her work. Yunus found 43 others in the same situation as the young woman; in total they had borrowed $27. Yunus promised the people he would give them the $27 to pay off their loan if they assumed mutual responsibility (for the $27 loan) and pledged to guarantee repayment. They did, and in a year they had paid back the money. If it worked one time, why not again, Yunus must have thought. Today, the Grameen Bank gives loans to those who might want to start a business, buy a cow or a rickshaw, or buy materials such as cloth or pottery.

One of the interesting things about the repayment plan for the loans is that every person who receives a micro-loan from the Grameen Bank must be part of a five-member group of borrowers. The first two borrowers in the group must begin repaying the loan over a set period of time before the other members of the group can take out loans. Thus, peer pressure gives borrowers an incentive to repay their loans.

According to Yunus, since the Grameen Bank officially opened, it has given out $5.7 billion in loans (97 percent of the loans have gone to women). The average loan is about $100 and the recovery rate on the loans is approximately 99 percent. In many cases, the micro-loans have made the difference between people living in poverty and getting out of poverty. As Muhummad Yunus has stated " . . . very poor people need only a little money to set up a business that can make a dramatic difference in the quality of their lives."[3]

[2]"A Hand Up Doesn't Always Require a Handout," *Wall Street Journal,* October 14, 2006: A6
[3]Ibid.

shopping mall. To reflect the opportunity cost of that land, we draw its supply curve as upward sloping. This implies that if individuals want more land for a specific purpose—say, for a shopping mall—they must bid high enough to attract existing land away from other uses (e.g., farming). This is illustrated in Exhibit 4, where the equilibrium payment to land is R_1. The shaded area indicates the economic rent.

Economic Rent and Other Factors of Production

The concept of economic rent applies to economic factors besides land. For example, it applies to labor. Suppose Hanson works for company X and is paid $40,000 a year. Furthermore, suppose that in his next best alternative job, he would be earning $37,000. Is

Hanson receiving economic rent working for company *X*? Yes, he is receiving a payment in excess of his opportunity costs; thus, he is receiving economic rent.

Or consider the local McDonald's that hires teenagers. It pays all its beginning employees the same wage. But not every beginning employee has the same opportunity costs as every other employee. Suppose two teenagers, Tracy and Paul, sign on to work at McDonald's for $7.00 an hour. Tracy's next best alternative wage is $7.00 an hour working for her mother's business, and Paul's next best alternative wage is $6.25 an hour. Tracy receives no economic rent in her McDonald's job, but Paul receives 75 cents an hour economic rent in the same job.

Over time, teenagers and other beginning employees usually find that their opportunity costs rise (owing to continued schooling and job experience) and that the McDonald's wage no longer covers their opportunity costs. When this happens, they quit their jobs.

Economic Rent and Baseball Players: The Perspective from Which the Factor Is Viewed Matters

Economic rent differs depending on the perspective from which the factor is viewed. Let's look at a baseball star who earns $1 million a year playing baseball. Suppose that if he weren't playing baseball, he would be a coach at a high school. Therefore, the difference between what he is currently paid ($1 million a year) and what he would earn as a coach (say, $40,000 a year) is economic rent. This amounts to $960,000. In this case, economic rent is determined by identifying the alternative to the baseball star playing baseball.

However, a different alternative would be identified by asking: What is the alternative to the baseball star playing baseball for his present team? The answer is that he probably can play baseball for another team. For example, if he weren't playing for the Boston Red Sox, he might be playing for the Pittsburgh Pirates and earning $950,000 a year. His economic rent in this instance is only $50,000.

The baseball player's economic rent as *a player for the Boston Red Sox* is $50,000 a year (his next best alternative is playing for the Pittsburgh Pirates earning $950,000 a year). But his economic rent as *a baseball player* is $960,000 (his next best alternative is being a high school coach earning $40,000 a year).

Competing for Artificial and Real Rents

Individuals and firms will compete for both *artificial rents* and *real rents*. An artificial rent is an economic rent that is artificially contrived by government; it would not exist without government. Suppose government decides to award a monopoly right to one firm to produce good *X*. In so doing, it legally prohibits all other firms from producing good *X*. If the firm with the monopoly right receives a price for good *X* in excess of its opportunity costs, it receives a "rent" or "monopoly profit" because of government's supply restraint. Firms that compete for the monopoly right to produce good *X* expend resources in a socially wasteful manner.[4] They use resources to lobby politicians in the hope of getting the monopoly—resources that (from society's perspective) are better used to produce goods and services.

Competing for real rents is different, however. If the rent is real (it has not been artificially created) and there are no barriers to competing for it, resources are used in a way that is socially productive. For example, suppose firm *Z* currently receives economic rent in the production of good *Z*. Government does not prohibit other firms from competing with firm *Z*, so some do. These other firms also produce good *Z*, thus increasing the supply of the good and lowering its price. The lower price reduces the rent firm *Z*

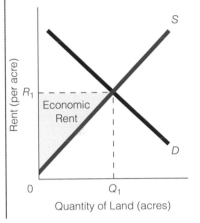

Economic Rent and the Supply of Land (Competing Uses)

A particular parcel of land, as opposed to the total supply of land, has competing uses, or positive opportunity costs. For example, to obtain land to build a shopping mall, the developers must bid high enough to attract existing land away from competing uses. The supply curve is upward-sloping. At a payment of R_1, economic rent is identified as the payment in excess of (positive) opportunity costs.

---

[4]This may sound familiar. The process described here where individuals expend resources lobbying government for a special privilege was described as rent seeking in the chapter about monopoly.

receives in its production of good Z. In the end, firm Z has less rent, and society has more of good Z and pays a lower price for it.

Do People Overestimate Their Worth to Others, or Are They Simply Seeking Economic Rent?

Johnson is an accountant with seven years of experience who is currently earning $95,000 annually. One day, he walks into his employer's office and asks for a raise in salary to $105,000. His employer asks him why he thinks he deserves the $10,000 raise. Johnson says that he is sure he is worth that much. (If he is, he can leave his current company and receive an offer of $105,000 from another company. We don't know whether he can do this or not.)

His employer believes that Johnson is overestimating his worth to others. She thinks, "There is no way Johnson is worth $10,000 more a year. He is simply overestimating his worth."

Is the employer correct? Is Johnson really overestimating his worth to others? Not necessarily. Johnson could believe his worth to others is $95,000—in other words, $95,000 is his opportunity cost—but he could be attempting to receive economic rent ($10,000 more than his opportunity cost) by getting his employer to believe his opportunity cost is really $105,000. Thus, a person who may appear to others to be overestimating his worth may be attempting to obtain economic rent.

SELF-TEST

1. Give an example to illustrate that economic rent differs depending on the perspective from which the factor is viewed.

2. Nick's salary is pure economic rent. What does this imply about Nick's "next best alternative salary"?

3. What are the social consequences of firms competing for artificial rents as opposed to competing for real rents (where there are no barriers to competing for real rents)?

Profit

The "profits" that appear in newspaper headlines are *accounting profits,* not economic profits. Economic profit is the difference between total revenue and total cost, where both explicit and implicit costs are included in total cost.

Economists emphasize economic profit over accounting profit because economic profit determines entry into and exit from an industry. For the most part, this is how economic profit figures in the discussion of market structures in earlier chapters.

In this section, we discuss profit as the payment to a resource. Recall that economists talk about four resources, or factors of production: land, labor, capital, and entrepreneurship. Firms make payments to each of these resources: Wages are the payment to labor, interest is the payment to capital, rent is the payment to land, and profit is the payment to entrepreneurship. We begin with a discussion of the source of profits to find out why economic profit exists.

Theories of Profit

Several different theories address the question of where profit comes from, or the source of profit. One theory holds that profit would not exist in a world of certainty; hence, uncertainty is the source of profit. Another theory holds that profit is the return for alertness to (broadly defined) arbitrage opportunities. A third theory holds that profit is the return to the entrepreneur as innovator.

PROFIT AND UNCERTAINTY Uncertainty exists when a potential occurrence is so unpredictable that a probability cannot be estimated. (For example, what is the probability that the United States will enter a world war in 2020? Who knows?) Risk, which many people mistake for uncertainty, exists when the probability of a given event can be estimated. (For example, there is a 50–50 chance that a coin toss will come up heads.) It follows that risks can be insured against, but uncertainties cannot.

> *Thinking like* **AN ECONOMIST**
>
> *Economists do not only want to identify the returns to various factors—such as wages to labor, interest to capital, and so on. They also want to know why the return exists. In other words, if profit is the return to entrepreneurship, why does profit exist? What exactly is being done by someone to receive profit?*

Anything that can be insured against can be treated as just another cost of doing business. Insurance coverage is an input in the production process. Only uncertain events can cause a firm's revenues to diverge from costs (including insurance costs). The investor–decision maker who is adept at making business decisions under conditions of uncertainty earns a profit. For example, based on experience and some insights, an entrepreneur may believe that 75 percent of college students will buy personal computers next year. This assessment, followed by the act of investing in a chain of retail computer stores near college campuses, will ultimately prove to be right or wrong. The essential point is that the entrepreneur's judgment is not something that can be insured against. If correct, the entrepreneur will earn a profit; if incorrect, a loss.

PROFIT AND ARBITRAGE OPPORTUNITIES The way to make a profit, the advice goes, is to "buy low and sell high." Usually, what is bought (low) and sold (high) is the same item. For example, someone might buy an ounce of gold in New York for $450 and sell the same ounce of gold in London for $470. We might say that the person is alert to where she can buy low and sell high, thereby earning a profit. She is alert to an arbitrage opportunity.

Sometimes, buying low and selling high does not refer to the same item. It can refer to buying factors in one set of markets at the lowest possible prices, combining the factors into a finished product, and then selling the product in another market for the highest possible price. An example of this would be buying oranges and sugar (in the oranges and sugar markets), combining the two, and selling an orange soft drink (in the soft-drink market). If doing this results in profit, we would then say that the person who undertook the act was alert to a (broadly defined) arbitrage opportunity. He saw that oranges and sugar together, in the form of an orange soft drink, would fetch more than the sum of oranges and sugar separately.

PROFIT AND INNOVATION In this theory, profit is the return to the entrepreneur as innovator—the person who creates new profit opportunities by devising a new product, production process, or marketing strategy. Viewed in this way, profit is the return to "innovative genius." People such as Thomas Edison, Henry Ford, and Richard Sears and Alvah Roebuck are said to have had innovative genius.

What Is Entrepreneurship?

An earlier chapter referred to entrepreneurship as "the particular talent that some people have for organizing the resources of land, labor, and capital to produce goods, seek new business opportunities, and develop new ways of doing things." Taking the three profit theories together, we can define entrepreneurship more narrowly: *An entrepreneur bears uncertainty, is alert to arbitrage opportunities, and exhibits innovative behavior.* Most entrepreneurs probably exhibit different degrees of each. For example, Thomas Edison may have been more the innovator-entrepreneur than the arbitrager-entrepreneur.

Notice that entrepreneurship is not like the other factors of production (land, labor, capital) in that it cannot be measured. There are no entrepreneurial units as there are labor, capital, and land units. Furthermore, an entrepreneur receives profit as a residual after the other factors of production have been paid. Thus, the actual dollar amount of profit depends on the payments to the other three factors of production.

What Do a Microwave Oven and an Errand Runner Have in Common?

The answer to this question is: They both economize on your time. Many people today complain that they don't have enough time to do all they want to do. Where these people see a problem, the entrepreneur sees a business opportunity. If people do not have enough time to do what they want, she reasons, then perhaps they will be willing to pay for a product or service that economizes on their time and frees some time for another use. Consider the microwave oven. The microwave oven reduces the time it takes to cook a meal, thus freeing time for other activities such as reading a book, working, sleeping, and so on.

Thinking like AN ECONOMIST

Throughout history, interest, land rent, and profits have often been attacked. For example, Henry George (1839–1897), who wrote the influential book Progress and Poverty, *believed that all land rents were pure economic rents and should be heavily taxed. Landowners benefited simply because they had the good fortune to own land. In George's view, landowners did nothing productive. He maintained that the early owners of land in the American West reaped high land rents not because they had made their land more productive but because individuals from the East began to move West, driving up the price of land. In arguing for a heavy tax on land rents, George said there would be no supply response in land owing to the tax because land was in fixed supply.*

Profits have also frequently come under attack. High profits are somehow thought to be evidence of corruption or manipulation. Those who earn profits are sometimes considered no better than thieves.

The economist thinks of interest, land rent, and profits differently from many laypersons. The economist understands that all are returns to resources, or factors of production. Most people find it easy to understand that labor is a factor of production and that wages are the return to this factor. But understanding that land, capital, and entrepreneurship are also genuine factors of production with returns that flow to them seems more difficult.

Another point that is overlooked is that interest exists largely because individuals naturally have a positive rate of time preference. Those who dislike interest are in fact criticizing individuals because of a natural characteristic. If these critics could change this natural trait and make individuals not weight present consumption higher than future consumption, interest would diminish.

A similar point can be made about profit. Some say profit is the consequence of living in a world of uncertainty. If those who do not like profit could make the world less uncertain, or bring certainty to it, then profit would disappear.

© PATRICK BAZ/AFP/GETTY IMAGES

economics 24/7

INSURING ONESELF AGAINST TERRORISM[5]

Earlier, we said that an entrepreneur is a person who bears uncertainty, is alert to arbitrage opportunities, and exhibits innovative behavior. Meet Abbas Shaheed al-Taiee, an executive at the Iraq Insurance Company in Baghdad, Iraq. Mr. Shaheed is an innovator. He came up with the idea of selling the Iraqi people something he thought they had a demand for: terrorism insurance.

Mr. Shaheed says terrorism insurance is his gift to the Iraqi people. He says, "We have expanded the principles of life insurance to cover everything that happens in Iraq." The terrorism insurance policy looks much like an ordinary life insurance policy, except for a one-page rider that insures a person against (1) explosions caused by weapons of war and car bombs, (2) assassinations, and (3) terrorist attacks.

According to Mr. Shaheed, it doesn't matter who fires the shots or sets off the bombs. The policy pays off no matter who is at fault.

The cost of the policy depends on what your occupation happens to be. If it is one of the safer occupations, the cost is $45 for about $3,500 worth of coverage (which is what an Iraqi policeman earns a year). If you have a relatively unsafe profession (e.g., a policeman or translator for a Western company), the cost is $90 for about $3,500 worth of coverage.

[5]This feature is based on "New Business Blooms in Iraq: Terror Insurance," by Robert F. Worth, *The New York Times*, March 21, 2006.

Consider Stanley Richards, who recently started a business that tries to economize on people's time. Richards started a company called Stan's Mobile Car Service. For $29.95 plus tax, he drives to a customer's car, whether it is at home or at work, and changes the oil, lubricates the chassis, and checks the engine. He says that he expects to do 90 jobs a day after his three vans are in operation.

Or consider the professional errand runner who will pick up the laundry, manage the house, feed the cat, pick up food for a party, and do other such things. In some large cities around the country, professional errand runners will do the things that two-earner families or working single men and women would rather pay someone to do than take the time to do themselves.

Profit and Loss as Signals

Too often, profit and loss are viewed in terms of the benefit or hurt they bring to particular persons. However, profit and loss also signal how a market may be changing.

When a firm earns a profit, entrepreneurs in other industries view this as a signal that the profit-earning firm is producing and selling a good that buyers value more than the factors that go to make the good. (The firm would not earn a profit unless its product had more value than the total of the payments to the other three factors of production.) The profit causes entrepreneurs to move resources into the production of the particular good to which the profit is linked. In short, resources follow profit.

On the other hand, if a firm is taking a loss, this is a signal to the entrepreneur that the firm is producing and selling a good that buyers value less than the factors that go to make the good. The loss causes resources to move out of the production of the particular good to which the loss is linked. Resources turn away from losses.

SELF-TEST

1. What is the difference between risk and uncertainty?

2. Why does profit exist?

3. "Profit is not simply a dollar amount; it is a signal." Comment.

A Reader Asks...

Are There Calculators to Help Me Plan My Life?

Present value is discussed in this chapter, and I know that the World Wide Web has calculators available for finding present value. Are other calculators available— especially ones that will help me plan my life?

People often have questions about the financial aspects of their lives that they would like to answer. For example, you might want to know how much you have to save each month (beginning now) to have $1 million by the time you retire. Or you might want to know what your mortgage payments will be if you put a $50,000 down payment on a house that sells for $200,000. Or perhaps you want to know what $1 million will be worth 10 years from now if the annual inflation rate over this time period is 4 percent.

With this in mind, here are some specific questions (yours may be similar) and their answers, along with the location of the online calculators we used.

1. I plan on taking out a $200,000 mortgage loan to buy a house. The term of the loan will be 30 years and the interest rate will be 7 percent. What will my monthly mortgage payment be? Answer: $1,330.60.

   Go to http://www.bloomberg.com/analysis/calculators/mortgage.html and fill in the information for loan amount, number of years, and interest rate.

2. If I save $200 a month at 5 percent interest (compounded monthly), how much will I have in savings in 30 years? Answer: $166,451.

Go to http://www.planningtips.com/cgi-bin/savings.pl and click "Simple Savings Calculator." Fill in the information requested.

By the way, just adding another $100 a month increases the total to approximately $250,000.

3. I am 20 years old and plan to retire when I am 65. I currently have $5,000 in my savings account. If I reap an annual return of 6 percent, how much do I need to save each year to retire with $1 million? Answer: $4,377.

   Go to http://www.bloomberg.com/analysis/calculators/retire.html and fill in the information.

4. I have a young child who will start college in the year 2020. The college I would like her to attend currently charges $20,000 tuition per year. If tuition inflation is 2 percent, a 5 percent return on savings is reasonable, and I am paying a 28 percent marginal tax rate, what dollar amount must I save each week to pay my child's tuition in the future? Answer: $80.93.

   Go to http://www.bloomberg.com/invest/calculators/mortgage.html and fill in the information.

5. I currently have a $200,000 mortgage loan (30 years) at 8 percent. My monthly payment is $1,467. If I want to pay off the loan in half the time (15 instead of 30 years), what should I increase my monthly mortgage payment to? Answer: $1,916.

   Go to http://www.hughchou.org/calc/duration.cgi and fill in the information.

   If you voluntarily increase your payment by $449 a month, you will pay off your loan 15 years earlier and save approximately $185,195 in interest.

! analyzing the scene

Does high rent cause high prices?

The misperception about high rents and high prices in 19th-century England still exists today. Many people complain that prices in stores, hotels, and restaurants in New York City are high. When they notice that land rents are also high, they reason that prices are high because land rents are high. But as Ricardo pointed out, the reverse is true: Land rents are high because prices are high. If the demand for living, visiting, and shopping in New York City was not as high as it is, prices for goods would not be as high. In turn, the demand for land would not be as high, and therefore, the payments to land would not be as high.

How would things change today if everyone knew the world would end next week? Is interest sinful?

Many things might change if everyone knew the world would end next week. For example, dieters would probably stop dieting. But let's ask a specific question with respect to interest rates: How would the interest rate change today if everyone knew the world would end next week? Interest exists because people have a positive rate of time preference (individuals prefer earlier availability of goods to later availability), so we would expect their positive rate of time preference to increase dramatically if the world were about to end. Everyone would want to borrow today to consume today because next week would be the last. We would expect interest rates to skyrocket.

As to whether or not interest is sinful, keep in mind that interest is a reflection of the fact that individuals have a positive rate of time preference. So the question really is: Is it sinful to have a positive rate of time preference, to prefer the earlier availability of goods to the later availability of goods?

chapter summary

Interest

- Interest refers to (1) the price paid by borrowers for loanable funds and (2) the return on capital in the production process. There is a tendency for these two to become equal.

- The equilibrium interest rate (in terms of the price for loanable funds) is determined by the demand for and supply of loanable funds. The supply of loanable funds comes from savers, people who consume less than their current incomes. The demand for loanable funds comes from the demand for consumption and investment loans.

- Consumers demand loanable funds because they have a positive rate of time preference; they prefer earlier availability of goods to later availability. Investors (or firms) demand loanable funds so they can finance roundabout methods of production.

- The nominal interest rate is the interest rate determined by the forces of supply and demand in the loanable funds market. It is the interest rate in current dollars. The real interest rate is the nominal interest rate adjusted for expected inflation. Specifically, real interest rate = nominal interest rate − expected inflation rate

(which means nominal interest rate = real interest rate + expected inflation rate).

Rent

- Economic rent is a payment in excess of opportunity costs. A subset of this is pure economic rent, which is a payment in excess of opportunity costs when opportunity costs are zero. Historically, the term *pure economic rent* was used to describe the payment to the factor land because land (in total) was assumed to be fixed in supply (perfectly inelastic). Today, the terms *economic rent* and *pure economic rent* are also used when speaking about economic factors other than land.

- David Ricardo argued that high land rents were an effect of high grain prices, not a cause of them (in contrast to many of his contemporaries who thought high rents caused the high grain prices). Land rents are price determined, not price determining.

- The amount of economic rent a factor receives depends on the perspective from which the factor is viewed. For example, a university librarian earning $50,000 a year receives $2,000 economic rent if his next best alternative income at another university is $48,000. The economic rent is $10,000 if his next best alternative is in a nonuniversity (nonlibrarian) position that pays $40,000.

Profit

- Several different theories of profit address the question of the source of profit. One theory holds that profit would not exist in a world of certainty; hence, uncertainty is the source of profit. Another theory holds that profit is the return for alertness to arbitrage opportunities. A third theory holds that profit is the return to the entrepreneur as innovator.

- Taking the three profit theories together, we can say that profit is the return to entrepreneurship, where entrepreneurship entails bearing uncertainty, being alert to arbitrage opportunities, and being innovative.

key terms and concepts

Loanable Funds

Positive Rate of Time
  Preference

Roundabout Method of
  Production

Nominal Interest Rate

Real Interest Rate

Present Value

Economic Rent

Pure Economic Rent

questions and problems

1   What type of person is most willing to pay high interest rates?

2   Some people have argued that in a moneyless (or barter) economy, interest would not exist. Is this true? Explain your answer.

3   In what ways are a baseball star who can do nothing but play baseball and a parcel of land similar?

4   What is the overall economic function of profits?

5   "The more economic rent a person receives in his job, the less likely he is to leave the job and the more content he will be on the job." Do you agree or disagree? Explain your answer.

6   It has been said that a society with a high savings rate is a society with a high standard of living. What is the link (if any) between saving and a relatively high standard of living?

7   Make an attempt to calculate the present value of your future income.

8   Describe the effect of each of the following events on individuals' rate of time preference and thus on interest rates: (a) a technological advance that increases longevity; (b) an increased threat of war; (c) growing older.

9   "As the interest rate falls, firms are more inclined to buy capital goods." Do you agree or disagree? Explain your answer.

working with numbers and graphs

1   Compute the following:
   a   The present value of $25,000 each year for 4 years at a 7 percent interest rate.
   b   The present value of $152,000 each year for 5 years at a 6 percent interest rate.
   c   The present value of $60,000 each year for 10 years at a 6.5 percent interest rate.

2   Bobby is a baseball player who earns $1 million a year playing for team X. If he weren't playing baseball for team X, he would be playing baseball for team Y and earning $800,000 a year. If he weren't playing baseball at all, he would be working as an accountant earning $120,000 a year. What is his economic rent as a baseball player playing for team X? What is his economic rent as a baseball player?

3   Diagrammatically represent pure economic rent.

Market Failure: Externalities, Public Goods, and Asymmetric Information

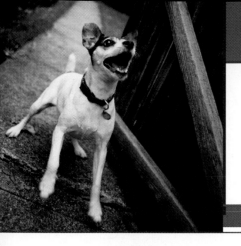

Setting the Scene

The following events occurred on a day in November.

6:32 A.M.

It's Friday and Michael Olson is trying to sleep in because today is the first day of his 3-week vacation. There's only one problem. The dog next door has been barking, on and off, for the last 30 minutes.

9:19 A.M.

A professor in the School of Education is speaking before a group of her colleagues. She states, "It seems to me that we are underpaid for the contribution we make to society. We teach the teachers who teach the students. And when those students learn math, English, or history, they not only benefit themselves, they benefit others too. In the words of the economist, there are positive externalities connected to the production of a person's education. Those positive externalities—those external benefits—should be considered when determining the worth of what we do."

2:05 P.M.

Bob Nelson is walking into a grocery store. Outside the entrance of the store, a man is asking for donations to a local homeless shelter. Bob Nelson doesn't make a donation.

3:33 P.M.

Two college students are talking as they walk across campus.

First student:
I learned today in my economics class that sometimes some pollution is better than no pollution.

Second student:
I've thought all along that economics doesn't make sense. No pollution is always best.

7:45 P.M.

Frank and Marie, two friends, are at a restaurant. Frank's meal is a little spicier than he thought it was going to be. "But I would have still ordered it," he says, "even if I'd known how spicy it was going to be."

? Here are some questions to keep in mind as you read this chapter:

- *Can there be too little as well as too much dog barking?*

- *Why does the professor in the School of Education argue the way she does?*

- *Why doesn't Bob Nelson contribute to the homeless?*

- *Is there a right amount of pollution?*

- *Does it matter if Frank's meal is spicier than he thought it was going to be?*

See analyzing the scene at the end of this chapter for answers to these questions.

Market Failure

Markets are a major topic of this book. We have analyzed how markets work, beginning with the simple supply-and-demand model. We have also examined various market structures: perfect competition, monopoly, and so on. As you know, goods and services are produced in markets. For example, cars are produced in car markets, houses are produced in housing markets, and computers are produced in computer markets. We now ask: Do these markets produce the "right amount" (the optimal or ideal amount) of these various goods, and what does the "right amount" mean? For example, what is the ideal or optimal amount of houses to produce, and does the housing market actually produce this amount?

When a market produces more or less than the ideal or optimal amount of a particular good, economists say there is **market failure**. Economists want to know under what conditions market failure may occur. This chapter presents three topics in which market failure is a prominent part of the discussion: externalities, public goods, and asymmetric information.

Market Failure

A situation in which the market does not provide the ideal or optimal amount of a particular good.

Externalities

Sometimes, when goods are produced and consumed, side effects (spillover or third-party effects) occur that are felt by people who are not directly involved in the market exchanges. In general, these side effects are called **externalities** because the costs or benefits are external to the person(s) who caused them.

In this section, we discuss the various costs and benefits of different activities and describe how and when activities cause externalities. We then explain graphically how externalities can result in market failure.

Externality

A side effect of an action that affects the well-being of third parties.

Costs and Benefits of Activities

Most activities in life have both costs and benefits. For example, when Jimmy sits down to read a book, this activity has some benefits for Jimmy and some costs. These benefits and costs are private to him—they only affect him—hence, we call them *private benefits* and *private costs*.

Can Jimmy undertake some activity that has benefits and costs not only for him but also for others? Suppose Jimmy decides to smoke a cigarette in the general vicinity of Angelica. For Jimmy, there are both benefits and costs to smoking a cigarette—his private benefits and costs. But might Jimmy's smoking also affect Angelica in some way?

Suppose Angelica reacts to cigarette smoke by coughing when she is around it. In this case, Jimmy's smoking might impose a cost on Angelica. Because the cost Jimmy imposes on Angelica is external to him, we call it an *external cost*. Stated differently, we might say that Jimmy's activity imposes a *negative externality* on Angelica for which she incurs an external cost. A **negative externality** exists when a person's or group's actions cause a cost (or adverse side effect) to be felt by others.

Now let's consider a slightly different example. Suppose Jimmy lives across the street from Yvonne and beautifies his front yard (which Yvonne can clearly see from her house) by planting trees, flowers, and a new lawn. Obviously, Jimmy receives some benefits and costs by beautifying his yard, but might Yvonne receive some benefits too? Might Yvonne benefit when Jimmy beautifies his yard? Not only does she have a pretty yard to gaze at (in much the same way that someone might benefit by gazing at a beautiful painting), but Jimmy's beautification efforts may also raise the market value of Yvonne's property.

Because the benefit that Jimmy generates for Yvonne is external to him, we call it an *external benefit*. Stated differently, we might say that Jimmy's activity generates a *positive*

Negative Externality

Exists when a person's or group's actions cause a cost (adverse side effect) to be felt by others.

externality for Yvonne for which she receives an external benefit. A **positive externality** exists when a person's or group's actions cause a benefit (or beneficial side effect) to be felt by others.

Positive Externality

Exists when a person's or group's actions cause a benefit (beneficial side effect) to be felt by others.

Marginal Costs and Benefits of Activities

When considering activities for which there are different degrees or amounts of costs and benefits (Does Jimmy smoke one cigarette an hour or two? Does Jimmy plant three trees or four?), it makes sense to speak in terms of marginal benefits and costs. More specifically, for Jimmy, there are marginal private benefits (*MPB*) and marginal private costs (*MPC*) to various activities. If Jimmy's activities generate external benefits or costs for others, then it makes sense to speak in terms of marginal external benefits (*MEB*) and marginal external costs (*MEC*).

To analyze the effects of an activity, we need to know the total marginal costs and benefits. So we sum the various benefits and sum the various costs.

The sum of marginal private costs (*MPC*) and marginal external costs (*MEC*) is **marginal social costs (*MSC*)**.

$$MSC = MPC + MEC$$

To illustrate, let's return to our example of Jimmy smoking a cigarette and imposing an external cost on Angelica. Suppose Jimmy's *MPC* of smoking a cigarette is $1, and Angelica's *MEC* of Jimmy smoking a cigarette is $2; it follows, then, that the *MSC* of Jimmy smoking a cigarette (taking into account both Jimmy's private costs and Angelica's external costs) is $3.

The sum of marginal private benefits (*MPB*) and marginal external benefits (*MEB*) is **marginal social benefits (*MSB*)**.

$$MSB = MPB + MEB$$

To illustrate, let's return to our example of Jimmy beautifying his yard and causing an external benefit for Yvonne. Suppose Jimmy's *MPB* of beautifying his yard is $5, and Yvonne's *MEB* of Jimmy beautifying his yard is $3; it follows, then, that the *MSB* of Jimmy beautifying his yard (at a given level of beautification) is $8.

Marginal Social Costs (*MSC*)

The sum of marginal private costs (*MPC*) and marginal external costs (*MEC*). *MSC = MPC + MEC.*

Marginal Social Benefits (*MSB*)

The sum of marginal private benefits (*MPB*) and marginal external benefits (*MEB*). *MSB = MPB + MEB.*

> **Q&A**
>
> *Suppose there is an activity for which there are no marginal external benefits (no **MEB**). Does it follow that MSB = MPB?*
>
> *Yes. Because* MSB = MPB + MEB, *if* MEB = 0, *then* MSB = MPB.

Social Optimality, or Efficiency, Conditions

For an economist, there is always a right amount of something. There is a right amount of time to study for a test, a right amount of exercise, and a right number of cars to be produced. The "right amount," for an economist, is the **socially optimal amount (output)**, or the efficient amount (output).

But what is the socially optimal amount, or efficient, amount? It is the amount at which a particular condition is met: *MSB = MSC*. In other words, the right amount of anything is the amount at which the *MSB* (of that thing) equals the *MSC* (of that thing). Later in this section, we illustrate this condition graphically.

Three Categories of Activities

For the person who engages in an activity (whether producing a computer or studying for an exam), there are almost always benefits and costs. It is hard to think of any activities in life in which private benefits and private costs do not exist.

It is not so hard, however, to think of activities in life in which external benefits and external costs do not exist. For example, again consider reading a book. The person reading the book incurs benefits and costs, but probably, no one else does. We can

Socially Optimal Amount (Output)

An amount that takes into account and adjusts for all benefits (external and private) and all costs (external and private). The socially optimal amount is the amount at which *MSB = MSC*. Sometimes, the socially optimal amount is referred to as the efficient amount.

characterize this activity the following way: $MPB > 0$, $MPC > 0$, $MEB = 0$, $MEC = 0$. Both marginal private benefits and costs are positive (greater than zero), but there are no marginal external benefits or costs. Another way of saying this is that there are no positive or negative externalities.

Therefore, activities may be categorized according to whether negative or positive externalities exist, as shown in the following table.[1]

Category	Definition	Meaning in Terms of Marginal Benefits and Costs
1	No negative or positive externality	$MEC = 0$ and $MEB = 0$; it follows that $MSC = MPC$ and $MSB = MPB$
2	Negative externality but no positive externality	$MEC > 0$ and $MEB = 0$; it follows that $MSC > MPC$ and $MSB = MPB$
3	Positive externality but no negative externality	$MEB > 0$ and $MEC = 0$; it follows that $MSB > MPB$ and $MSC = MPC$

Externalities in Consumption and in Production

Externalities can arise because someone *consumes* something that has an external benefit or cost for others or because someone *produces* something that has an external benefit or cost for others. To illustrate, consider two examples. Suppose Barbara plays the radio in her car loudly, adversely affecting drivers around her at the stoplight. In this situation, Barbara is "consuming" music and creating a negative externality for others.

Now consider John, who produces cars in his factory. As a result of the production process, he emits some pollution into the air that adversely affects some people who live downwind from the factory. In this situation, we have a negative externality that is the result of John's producing a good.

Diagram of a Negative Externality

Exhibit 1 shows the downward-sloping demand curve, D, for some good. The demand curve represents the marginal private benefits received by the buyers of the good, so it is the same as the MPB curve. Because there are no positive externalities in this case, it follows that $MPB = MSB$. So the demand curve is also the MSB curve.

The supply curve, S, represents the marginal private costs (MPC) of the producers of the good. Equilibrium in this market setting is at E_1; Q_1 is the output—specifically, the market output.

Now assume negative externalities arise as a result of the production of the good. For example, suppose the good happens to be cars that are produced in a factory, and as a result of producing the cars, some air pollution results.

Because negative externalities exist, there are external costs associated with the production of the good that are not taken into account at the market output. The marginal external costs linked to the negative externalities are taken into account by adding them (as best we can) to the marginal private costs. The result is the marginal social cost (MSC) curve shown in Exhibit 1. If all costs are taken into account (both external costs

---

[1]Theoretically, there is a fourth category—where both a positive externality and a negative externality exist—but one would reasonably assume that this category has little, if any, practical relevance. For example, suppose Jimmy smokes a cigarette, and cigarette smoke is a negative externality for Angelica but a positive externality for Bobby. It is possible that what is a "bad" for Angelica is a "good" for Bobby, but little is added to the discussion (at this time) by reviewing such cases.

economics 24/7

SOFTWARE, SWITCHING COSTS AND BENEFITS, AND MARKET FAILURE

Let's consider a series of events that some economists believe are occurring today. A company produces a good, say, software *X*. It finds that its major costs of producing the software are "up front"—at the research and development stage. After it has produced one copy of the software program, it is relatively cheap to produce each additional copy. The company sells software *X* at a price that is likely to generate a large number of sales. As some people buy the software program, additional people find it worth buying because the good is important in terms of "networking" with others. (For example, if some people use the spreadsheet Excel, you may choose Excel as your spreadsheet.) Because of its "network externalities," good *X* becomes widely used in the industry. At some point, the good simply dominates the market. For example, it may have 90 percent of market sales.

At this point, some economists ask, "Is good *X* the best product, or is it inferior to the substitutes that exist for it?" For example, if software *Y* and *Z* are substitutes for *X*, is *X* superior to both *Y* and *Z* or is either *Y* or *Z* superior to *X*? A real-world example illustrates our point. Both Beta and VHS formats for VCRs came out at about the same time. VHS initially sold better than Beta, although Beta was a strong competitor. At some point, the higher percentage of VHS users in the market (relative to Beta users) seemed to matter to people who were considering buying a VCR. "Why not buy a VHS format?" they thought. "That way, videotapes can be shared with more people." At this point, the sales of VHS began to explode, and before long, very few people were buying Beta. Some of the initial buyers of the Beta format even switched over to the VHS format.

In the race between VHS and Beta, VHS won, not necessarily because it is superior to Beta, but simply because it got an early lead in the race. If network externalities are present, the early lead may be the only lead that is necessary to win the race for customers' dollars.

Some economists conclude that if only the early lead counts and not the quality of the product, then it is possible for an inferior product that gets an early lead to outsell a superior product that doesn't get an early lead. To go back to our software example, if *X* outcompetes *Y* and *Z* not because it is superior but because it gets an early lead in the software market, then there is the possibility that the market has "chosen" the inferior product. Stated differently, there is market failure in the sense that the market has failed to choose a superior product over an inferior product.

But not all economists agree with this analysis. Some economists say that to justify market failure, it is not sufficient to have the market choose an inferior product over a superior product. There must also be net benefits to switching (from the inferior to the superior product) that are not being acted on by market participants. To illustrate, suppose the market has chosen good *X* and that it is inferior to good *Y*. Furthermore, suppose the benefits of switching from *X* to *Y* are $30 and the costs of switching are $45. In this case, even if the market stays with good *X*, there is no market failure because it is not worthwhile switching to the superior product. The market fails, argue these economists, only if the benefits of switching are, say, $30 and the costs are $10 (and therefore there are net benefits to switching)—yet the market doesn't switch. In short, when the benefits and costs of switching are considered, what may initially look like a market failure may turn out not to be.

and private costs), equilibrium is at E_2, where $MSB = MSC$. The quantity produced at E_2—Q_2—is the socially optimal output, or efficient output.

Notice that the market output (Q_1) is greater than the socially optimal output (Q_2) when negative externalities exist. The market is said to "fail" (hence, market failure) because it *overproduces* the good connected with the negative externality. The triangle in Exhibit 1 is the visible manifestation of the market failure. It represents the net social cost of producing the market output (Q_1) instead of the socially optimal output (Q_2), or of moving from the socially optimal output to the market output.

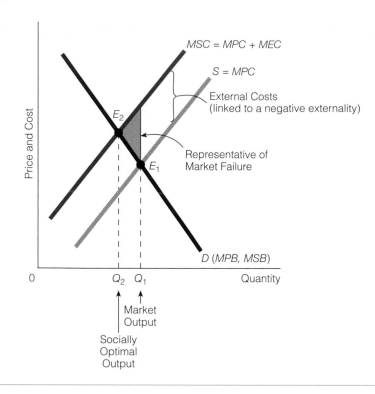

exhibit **1**

The Negative Externality Case

Because of a negative externality, marginal social costs (*MSC*) are greater than marginal private costs (*MPC*) and the market output is greater than the socially optimal output. The market is said to fail in that it overproduces the good.

To understand exactly how the triangle in Exhibit 1 represents the net social cost of moving from the socially optimal output to the market output, look at Exhibit 2, where, as in Exhibit 1, Q_2 is the socially optimal output and Q_1 is the market output. If "society" moves from Q_2 to Q_1, who specifically benefits and how do we represent these benefits? Buyers benefit (they are a part of society) because they will be able to buy more output at prices they are willing to pay. Thus, the area under the demand curve between Q_2 and Q_1 represents the benefits to society of moving from Q_2 to Q_1 (see the shaded area in Window 1 of Exhibit 2).

Next, if society moves from Q_2 to Q_1, how can we illustrate the costs that are incurred? Both sellers and third parties incur costs. Sellers incur private costs, and third parties incur external costs. The area under S (the *MPC* curve) only takes into account part of society—sellers—and ignores third parties. The area under the *MSC* curve between Q_2 and Q_1 represents the full costs to society of moving from Q_2 to Q_1 (see the shaded area in Window 2).

The shaded area in Window 2 is larger than the shaded area in Window 1, so the costs to sellers and third parties of moving from Q_2 to Q_1 outweigh the benefits to buyers of moving from Q_2 to Q_1. The difference between the shaded areas is the triangle shown in the main diagram. Thus, the costs to society outweigh the benefits to society by the triangle. In short, the triangle in this example represents the net social cost of moving from Q_2 to Q_1, or of producing Q_1 instead of Q_2.

Thinking like
AN ECONOMIST *Economists prefer to look at the complete picture instead of only part of it. If there are both private costs and external costs, then economists will consider both, not just one or the other. Similarly, if there are both private benefits and external benefits, economists will consider both.*

Diagram of a Positive Externality

Exhibit 3 shows the downward-sloping demand curve, *D*, for some good. As earlier, the demand curve represents the marginal private benefits received by the buyers of the good, so it is the same as the *MPB* curve.

The supply curve, *S*, represents the marginal private costs (*MPC*) of the producers of the good. The marginal social costs (*MSC*) are the same as the marginal private costs—*MPC* = *MSC*—because

Window 1
Benefits of moving from Q_2 to Q_1

Window 2
Costs of moving from Q_2 to Q_1

exhibit **2**

The Triangle

Q_2 is the socially optimal output; Q_1 is the market output. If society moves from Q_2 to Q_1, buyers benefit by an amount represented by the shaded area in Window 1, but sellers and third parties together incur greater costs, represented by the shaded area in Window 2. The triangle (the difference between the two shaded areas) represents the net social cost to society of moving from Q_2 to Q_1, or of producing Q_1 instead of Q_2.

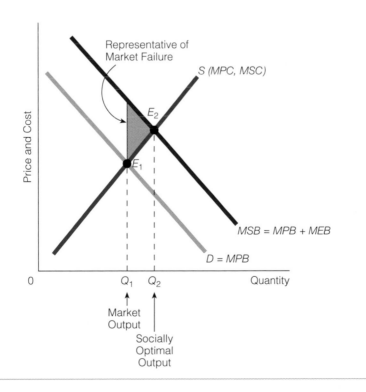

exhibit **3**

The Positive Externality Case

Because of a positive externality, marginal social benefits (*MSB*) are greater than marginal private benefits (*MPB*) and the market output is less than the socially optimal output. The market is said to fail in that it underproduces the good.

there are no negative externalities in this case. Equilibrium in this market setting is at E_1; Q_1 is the output—specifically, the market output.

Now assume positive externalities arise as a result of the production of the good. For example, suppose Erica is a beekeeper who produces honey. Erica lives near an apple orchard, and her bees occasionally fly over to the orchard and pollinate the blossoms, in

Under what condition will the market output and the socially optimal output be the same?

Under the condition that there are neither negative nor positive externalities. In this case, both MEC and MEB equal zero so that MSB = MPB and MSC = MPC. Obviously, the market output (MPB = MPC) is the same here as the socially optimal output (MSB = MSC) because MSB = MPB and MSC = MPC.

Thinking like
AN ECONOMIST *From what we have said so far, it may be natural to conclude that the economist prefers the socially optimal output (where all benefits and costs are taken into account) to the market output (where only private benefits and costs are taken into account). But this is not necessarily true. An economist prefers the socially optimal output to the market output (assuming they are different) only when the benefits of moving from the market output to the socially optimal output are greater than the costs.*

To illustrate, suppose $400 in benefits exists if we move from the market output to the socially optimal output, but the costs of making the move are $1,000. According to an economist, it wouldn't be worthwhile trying to make the adjustment.

the process making the orchard more productive. Doesn't the orchard owner benefit from Erica's bees?

Because positive externalities exist, there are external benefits associated with the production of the good that are not taken into account at the market output. The marginal external benefits linked to the positive externalities are taken into account by adding them (as best we can) to the marginal private benefits. The result is the marginal social benefit (*MSB*) curve shown in Exhibit 3. If all benefits are taken into account (both external benefits and private benefits), equilibrium is at E_2, where $MSB = MSC$. The quantity produced at E_2—Q_2—is the socially optimal output, or efficient output.

Notice that the market output (Q_1) is less than the socially optimal output (Q_2) when positive externalities exist (just the opposite of when negative externalities exist). The market is said to "fail" (hence, market failure) because it *underproduces* the good connected with the positive externality. The triangle in Exhibit 3 is the visible manifestation of the market failure. It represents the net social benefit *that is lost* by producing the market output (Q_1) instead of the socially optimal output (Q_2). Stated differently, at the socially optimal output (Q_2), society realizes greater benefits than at the market output (Q_1). So by being at Q_1, society loses out on some net benefits it could obtain if it were at Q_2.

SELF-TEST

(Answers to Self-Test questions are in the Self-Test Appendix.)

1. What is the major difference between the market output and the socially optimal output?

2. For an economist, is the socially optimal output preferred to the market output?

Internalizing Externalities

Internalizing Externalities

An externality is internalized if the persons or group that generated the externality incorporate into their own private or internal cost-benefit calculations the external benefits (in the case of a positive externality) or the external costs (in the case of a negative externality) that third parties bear.

An externality is **internalized** if the persons or group that generated the externality incorporate into their own private or *internal* cost-benefit calculations the external benefits (in the case of a positive externality) or the external costs (in the case of a negative externality) that third parties bear. Simply put, internalizing externalities is the same as adjusting for externalities. An externality has been internalized or adjusted for *completely* if, as a result, the socially optimal output emerges. A few of the numerous ways to adjust for, or internalize, externalities are presented in this section.

Persuasion

Many negative externalities arise partly because persons or groups do not consider other individuals when they decide to undertake an action. Consider the person who plays his CD player loudly at 3 o'clock in the morning. Perhaps if he considered the external cost his action imposes on his neighbors, he either would not play the CD player at all or would play it at low volume.

Trying to persuade those who impose external costs on us to adjust their behavior to take these costs into account is one way to make the imposers adjust for—or internalize—externalities. In today's world, such slogans as "Don't Drink and Drive" and

"Don't Litter" are attempts to persuade individuals to take into account the fact that their actions affect others. The golden rule of ethical conduct, "Do unto others as you would have them do unto you," makes the same point.

Taxes and Subsidies

Taxes and subsidies are sometimes used as corrective devices for a market failure. A tax adjusts for a negative externality; a subsidy adjusts for a positive externality.

Consider the negative externality case in Exhibit 1. The objective of a corrective tax is to move the supply curve from S to the MSC curve (recall from earlier chapters that a tax can shift a supply curve) and therefore move from the market determined output, Q_1, to the socially optimal output, Q_2.

In the case of a positive externality, illustrated in Exhibit 3, the objective is to subsidize the demand side of the market so that the demand curve moves from D to the MSB curve and output moves from Q_1 to the socially optimal output, Q_2.

However, taxes and subsidies also involve costs and consequences. For example, suppose, as illustrated in Exhibit 4, government misjudges the external costs when it imposes a tax on the supplier of a good. Instead of the supply curve moving from S_1 to S_2 (the MSC curve), it moves from S_1 to S_3. As a result, the output level will be farther away from the socially optimal output than it was before the "corrective" tax was applied.

Assigning Property Rights

Consider the idea that air pollution and ocean pollution—both of which are examples of negative externalities—are the result of the air and oceans being unowned. No one owns the air, no one owns the oceans, and because no one does, many individuals feel free to emit wastes into them. If private property, or ownership, rights in air and oceans

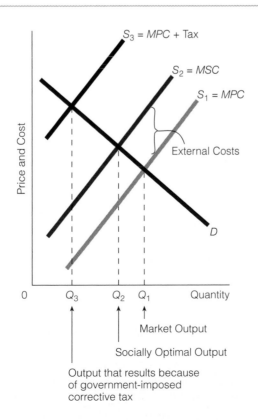

exhibit 4

A Corrective Tax Gone Wrong

Government may miscalculate external costs and impose a tax that moves the supply curve from S_1 to S_3 instead of from S_1 to S_2. As a result, the output level will be farther away from the socially optimal output than before the "corrective" tax was applied. Q_3 is farther away from Q_2 than Q_1 is from Q_2.

Q&A *In the example of grazing lands, assigning private property rights, or establishing ownership rights to unowned land, would have reduced the externality problem. Establishing ownership rights in land is possible, but how can this be done with the air and oceans?*

It is difficult and costly to establish ownership rights in air. Consequently, assigning property rights is not likely to be the method chosen to deal with externalities that arise as a consequence of unowned air or oceans. There are other ways of dealing with the problem, however. One method we have already discussed is taxes. Another method we will shortly discuss is regulation.

could be established, the negative externalities would likely become much less. If someone owns a resource, then actions that damage it have a price; namely, the resource owner can sue for damages.

For example, in the early West, when grazing lands were open and unowned (common property), many cattle ranchers allowed their herds to overgraze. The reason for this was simple. No one owned the land, so no one could stop the overgrazing to preserve the value of the land. Even if one rancher decided not to allow his herd to graze, this simply meant there was more grazing land for other ranchers. As a consequence of overgrazing, a future generation inherited barren, wasted land. From the point of view of future generations, the cattle ranchers who allowed their herds to overgraze were generating negative externalities.

What would have happened if the western lands had been privately owned? In this case, there would not have been any overgrazing because the monetary interests of the owner of the land would not have permitted it. The landowner would have charged ranchers a fee to graze their cattle, and more grazing would have entailed additional fees. There would have been less grazing at a positive fee than at a zero fee (the case when the lands were open and unowned). The externalities would have been internalized.

Voluntary Agreements

Externalities can sometimes be internalized through individual voluntary agreements. Consider two persons, Pete and Sean, living alone on a tiny island. Pete and Sean have agreed between themselves that Pete owns the northern part of the island and Sean owns the southern part. Pete occasionally plays his drums in the morning, and the sound awakens Sean. They have a negative externality problem. Pete wants to be free to play his drums in the morning, and Sean would like to continue to sleep.

Suppose Sean values his sleep in the morning by a maximum of 6 oranges. He would give up 6 oranges to be able to sleep without Pete playing his drums. On the other hand, Pete values drum playing in the morning by 3 oranges. He would give up a maximum of 3 oranges to be able to play his drums in the morning. Because Sean values his sleep by more than Pete values playing his drums, they have an opportunity to strike a deal. Sean can offer Pete some number of oranges greater than 3, but less than 6, to refrain from playing his drums in the morning. The deal will make both Pete and Sean better off.

In this example, the negative externality problem is successfully addressed through the individuals' voluntarily entering into an agreement. The condition for this output is that the *transaction costs,* or costs associated with making and reaching the agreement, must be low relative to the expected benefits of the agreement.

Combining Property Rights Assignments and Voluntary Agreements

The last two ways of internalizing externalities—property rights assignments and voluntary agreements—can be combined, as in the following example.[2] Suppose a rancher's cattle occasionally stray onto the adjacent farm and damage (or eat) some of the farmer's crops. The court assigns liability to the cattle rancher and orders him to

---

[2]See Ronald Coase, "The Problem of Social Cost," *Journal of Law and Economics,* 3 (October 1960): 1–44.

prevent his cattle from straying, so a property rights assignment solves the externality problem. As a result, the rancher puts up a strong fence to prevent his cattle from damaging his neighbor's crops.

But the court's property rights assignment may be undone by the farmer and the cattle rancher if they find it in their mutual interest to do so. Suppose the rancher is willing to pay $100 a month to the farmer for permission to allow his cattle to stray onto the farmer's land, and the farmer is willing to give permission for $70 a month. Assuming trivial or zero transaction costs, the farmer and the rancher will undo the court's property rights assignment. For a payment of $70 or more a month, the farmer will allow the rancher's cattle to stray onto his land.

COASE THEOREM Suppose in our example that the court, instead of assigning liability to the cattle rancher, had given him the property right to allow his cattle to stray. What would the resource allocative outcome have been in this case? With this (opposite) property rights assignment, the cattle would have been allowed to stray (which was exactly the outcome of the previous property rights assignment after the cattle rancher and farmer voluntarily agreed to undo it). We conclude that *in the case of trivial or zero transaction costs, the property rights assignment does not matter to the resource allocative outcome.* In a nutshell, this is the **Coase theorem**.

The Coase theorem can be expressed in other ways, two of which we mention here: (1) In the case of trivial or zero transaction costs, a property rights assignment will be undone (exchanged) if it benefits the relevant parties to undo it. (2) In the case of trivial or zero transaction costs, the resource allocative outcome will be the same no matter who is assigned the property right.

The Coase theorem is significant for two reasons: (1) It shows that under certain conditions, the market can internalize externalities. (2) It provides a benchmark for analyzing externality problems; that is, it shows what will happen if transaction costs are trivial or zero.

PIGOU VERSUS COASE The first editor of the *Journal of Law and Economics* was Aaron Director. In 1959, Director published an article by Ronald Coase entitled "The Federal Communications Commission." In the article, Coase took issue with economist A. C. Pigou, a trailblazer in the area of externalities and market failure, who had argued that government should use taxes and subsidies to adjust for negative and positive externalities, respectively. Coase argued that in the case of negative externalities, it is not clear that the state should tax the person imposing the negative externality. First, Coase stressed the reciprocal nature of externalities, pointing out that it takes two to make a negative externality (it is not always clear who is harming whom). Second, Coase proposed a market solution to externality problems that was not implicit in Pigou's work.

Aaron Director and others believed that Coase was wrong and Pigou was right. Coase, who was teaching at the University of Virginia at the time, was invited to discuss his thesis with Director and a handful of well-known economists. The group included Martin Bailey, Milton Friedman, Arnold Harberger, Reuben Kessel, Gregg Lewis, John McGee, Lloyd Mints, George Stigler, and of course, Director.

The group met at Aaron Director's house one night. Before Coase began to outline his thesis, the group took a vote and found that everyone (with the exception of Coase) sided with Pigou. Then the sparks began to fly. Friedman, it is reported, "opened fire" on Coase. Coase answered the intellectual attacks of his colleagues. At the end of the debate, another vote was taken. Everyone sided with Coase against Pigou. It is reported that as the members of the group left Director's home that night, they said to one another that they had witnessed history in the making. The Coase theorem had taken hold in economics.

Coase Theorem

In the case of trivial or zero transaction costs, the property rights assignment does not matter to the resource allocative outcome.

economics 24/7

TELEMARKETERS AND EFFICIENCY

Effective October 1, 2003, the Federal Trade Commission (FTC) amended its Telemarketing Sales Rule (TSR). The amended rule created a National Do Not Call Registry. Anyone could add his telephone number to the registry if he chose not to be called by telemarketers.

Essentially, we are dealing with two property rights assignments in this situation. Before October 1, 2003, telemarketers had the right to call you on the phone. After October 1, 2003, they did not.

Was the change in the property rights assignment consistent with efficiency? To answer the question, think of what was happening before October 1, 2003. Surely, there were some people who were being called by telemarketers who valued not being called more than the telemarketers valued calling them. For example, suppose Smith valued not being called at $10 a month, and collectively, the telemarketers valued calling him at $8 a month. If Smith were called, a net loss would arise. Perhaps this is why so many individuals got angry over being called by telemarketers (especially around dinner time).

It is likely, though, that not every individual who was called by a telemarketer valued not being called by more than the telemarketer valued calling. Therefore, calling these persons would have been efficient.

What the Do Not Call Registry does, in fact, is act as a means for individuals to register how much they value not being called. Those who value not being called quite a bit will likely be the ones who will place their phone numbers on the Do Not Call Registry. Those who do not place a high value on not being called will not. With the Do Not Call Registry, we are closer to achieving efficiency than we were without it. Telemarketers will call people who place a low value on not being called, and they will not call people who place a high value on not being called.

Some economists have proposed that an even better system to achieve efficiency exists. Instead of simply allowing individuals to register their phone numbers with the Do Not Call Registry, allow them the added advantage of stating the dollar price they value not being called. Things would work like this: Smith is willing to pay $1 not to be called by telemarketers. She registers her phone number with the Do Not Call Registry along with the $1 she is willing to pay not to be called by telemarketers. A telemarketer notices that Smith's phone number is registered and only calls her if he is willing to pay something more than $1 to Smith.

Who will telemarketers call? Who will they not call? They will call persons who value not being called less than the telemarketer values calling; they will not call persons who value not being called more than the telemarketer values calling.

Beyond Internalizing: Setting Regulations

One way to deal with externalities, in particular with negative externalities, is for government to apply regulations directly to the activities that generate the externalities. For example, factories producing goods also produce smoke that rises up through smokestacks. The smoke is often seen as a negative externality. Government may decide that the factory must install pollution-reducing equipment, that it can emit only a certain amount of smoke into the air per day, or that it must move to a less populated area.

Critics of this approach often note that regulations, once instituted, are difficult to remove even if conditions warrant removal. Also, regulations are often applied across the board when circumstances dictate otherwise. For example, factories in relatively pollution-free cities might be required to install the same pollution control equipment as factories in smoggy, pollution-ridden cities.

Finally, regulation entails costs. If government imposes regulations, there must be regulators (whose salaries must be paid), offices (to house the regulators), word processors (to produce the regulations), and more. As previously noted, dealing with externalities successfully may offer benefits, but the costs need to be considered as well.

SELF-TEST

1. What does it mean to *internalize* an externality?

2. Are the transaction costs of buying a house higher or lower than the transaction costs of buying a hamburger at a fast-food restaurant? Explain your answer.

3. Does the property rights assignment a court makes matter to the resource allocative outcome?

4. What condition must be satisfied for a tax to correctly adjust for a negative externality?

Q&A *Is there any one best way of dealing with externalities? It is not clear whether it is better to use persuasion, to use, say, taxes and subsidies, or to use regulation.*

Almost all economists would agree that some methods of dealing with externalities are more effective in some situations than in others. For example, if the smoke from Vincent's neighbor's barbecue comes into his yard and bothers him, it is unlikely that any economist would think this negative externality situation warrants direct government involvement in the form of regulation or taxes. In this case, persuasion may be the best way to proceed. In the case of a firm emitting smoke into the air, however, persuasion might not be effective. Voluntary agreement might not be the best way to proceed because the transaction costs of entering into an agreement would very likely be high. In this case, the inclination to propose taxes or regulations would be strong.

Dealing with a Negative Externality in the Environment

The environment has become a major economic, political, and social issue. Environmental problems are manifold and include acid rain, the greenhouse effect, deforestation (including the destruction of the rain forests), solid waste (garbage) disposal, water pollution, air pollution, and many more. This section mainly discusses air pollution.

Economists make three principal points about pollution. First, it is a negative externality. Second, and perhaps counterintuitively, no pollution is sometimes worse than some pollution. Third, the market can be used to deal with the problem of pollution.

Is No Pollution Worse Than Some Pollution?

When might some pollution be preferred to no pollution? The answer is when all other things are not held constant—in short, most of the time.

Certainly, if all other things are held constant, less pollution is preferred to more pollution, and therefore, no pollution is preferred to some pollution. But the world would be different with no pollution—and not only because it would have cleaner air, rivers, and oceans. Pollution is a by-product of the production of many goods and services. For example, it is unlikely that steel could be produced without some pollution as a by-product. Given the current state of pollution technology, less pollution from steel production means less steel and fewer products made from steel.

Pollution is also a by-product of many of the goods we use daily, including our cars. We could certainly end the pollution caused by cars tomorrow, but to do so, we would have to give up driving cars. Are there any benefits to driving cars? If there are, then perhaps we wouldn't choose zero pollution. In short, zero pollution is not preferable to some positive amount of pollution when we realize that goods and services must be forfeited to have less pollution.

The same conclusion can be reached through Coasian-type analysis. Suppose there are two groups, polluters and nonpolluters. For certain units of pollution, the value of polluting to polluters might be greater than the value of a less polluted environment to nonpolluters. In the presence of trivial or zero transaction costs, a deal will be struck. The outcome will be characterized by some positive amount of pollution.

Two Methods to Reduce Air Pollution

One of the biggest movements of the early 1990s was market environmentalism: the use of market forces to clean up the environment. This was the idea behind the Clean Air Act amendments, which President Bush signed into law in November 1990. The amendments lowered the maximum allowable sulfur dioxide emissions (the major factor in acid rain) for 111 utilities but gave the utilities the right to trade permits for sulfur dioxide emissions. That is, the amendments to the Clean Air Act make it possible for the utilities to buy and sell the right to pollute.

"To buy and sell the right to pollute" may sound odd to people accustomed to thinking about dealing with pollution through government regulations or standards. Let's consider two methods of reducing pollution. In method 1, the government sets pollution standards. In method 2, the government allocates pollution permits and allows them to be traded.

METHOD 1: GOVERNMENT SETS POLLUTION STANDARDS Suppose three firms, $X, Y,$ and $Z,$ are located in the same area. Currently, each firm is spewing 3 units of pollution into the area under consideration, for a total of 9 pollution units. The government wants to reduce the total pollution in the area to 3 units and, to accomplish this objective, sets pollution standards (or regulations) stating that each firm must reduce its pollution by 2 units.

Exhibit 5 shows the respective cost of eliminating each unit of pollution for the three firms. The costs are different because eliminating pollution is more difficult for some kinds of firms than it is for others. For example, the air pollution that an automobile manufacturer produces might be more costly to eliminate than the air pollution a clothing manufacturer produces. Stated differently, we assume that the three firms eliminate pollution by installing antipollution devices in their factories, and the cost of the antipollution devices may be much higher for an automobile manufacturer than for a clothing manufacturer.

The cost to firm X of eliminating its first 2 units is \$125 (\$50 + \$75 = \$125); the cost to firm Y of eliminating its first 2 units is \$155; and the cost to firm Z of eliminating its first 2 units is \$1,500. Thus, the total cost of eliminating 6 units of pollution is \$1,780 (\$125 + \$155 + \$1,500).

Total cost of eliminating 6 units of pollution through standards or regulations = \$1,780

METHOD 2: MARKET ENVIRONMENTALISM AT WORK: GOVERNMENT ALLOCATES POLLUTION PERMITS AND THEN ALLOWS THEM TO BE BOUGHT AND SOLD The objective of the government is still to reduce the pollution in the area of firms $X, Y,$ and Z from 9 units to 3 units, but this time, the government issues one pollution permit (sometimes, these permits are

exhibit **5**

The Cost of Reducing Pollution for Three Firms

These are hypothetical data showing the cost of reducing pollution for three firms. The text shows that it is cheaper to reduce pollution through market environmentalism than through government standards or regulations.

	Firm X	Firm Y	Firm Z
Cost of Eliminating:			
First unit of pollution	\$ 50	\$ 70	\$ 500
Second unit of pollution	75	85	1,000
Third unit of pollution	100	200	2,000

called allowances or credits) to each firm. The government tells each firm that it can emit 1 unit of pollution for each permit it has in its possession. Furthermore, the firms are allowed to buy and sell these permits.

Look at the situation from the perspective of firm *X*. It has one pollution permit in its possession, so it can emit 1 unit of pollution and must eliminate the other 2 units of pollution. But firm *X* does not have to keep its pollution permit and emit 1 unit of pollution. Instead, firm *X* can sell its permit. If it does so, the firm can emit no pollution. Might firm *X* be better off selling the permit and eliminating all 3 units of pollution?

Firm *Y* is in the same situation as firm *X*. This firm also has only one permit and must therefore eliminate 2 units of pollution. Firm *Y* also wonders if it might be better off selling the permit and eliminating 3 units of pollution.

But what about firm *Z*? Exhibit 5 shows that this firm has to pay $500 to eliminate its first unit of pollution and $1,000 to eliminate its second unit. Firm *Z* wonders if it might be better off buying the two permits in the possession of firms *X* and *Y* and not eliminating any pollution at all.

Suppose the owners of the three firms get together. The owner of firm *Z* says to the owners of the other firms, "I have to spend $500 to eliminate my first unit of pollution and $1,000 to eliminate my second unit. If either of you is willing to sell me your pollution permit for less than $500, I'm willing to buy it."

The owners of the three firms agree on a price of $330 for a permit, and both firms *X* and *Y* sell their permits to firm *Z*. This exchange benefits all three parties. Firm *X* receives $330 for its permit and then spends $100 to eliminate its third unit of pollution. Firm *Y* receives $330 for its permit and then spends $200 to eliminate its third unit of pollution. Firm *Z* spends $660 for the two pollution permits instead of spending $1,500 to eliminate its first 2 units of pollution.

Under this scheme, firm *X* and firm *Y* eliminate all their pollution (neither firm has a pollution permit). Firm *X* spends $225 ($50 + $75 + $100) to eliminate all 3 units of its pollution, and firm *Y* spends $355 to do the same. The two firms together spend $580 ($225 + $355) to eliminate 6 units of pollution.

Total cost of eliminating 6 units of pollution through market environmentalism = $580

This cost is lower than the cost incurred by the three firms when government standards simply ordered each firm to eliminate 2 units of pollution (or 6 units for all three firms). The cost in that case was $1,780. In both cases, however, 6 pollution units were eliminated. We conclude that it is less costly for firms to eliminate pollution when the government allocates pollution permits that can be bought and sold than when it simply directs each firm to eliminate so many units of pollution.

Q&A *What about the $660 that firm Z paid to buy the two pollution permits?* **This was not included in the cost of reducing pollution in the second method. Why not?**

Although the $660 is a real cost of doing business for firm Z, it is not a cost to society of eliminating pollution. The $660 was not actually used to eliminate pollution. It was simply a transfer from firm Z to firms X and Y. The distinction is between a resource cost, which signifies an expenditure of resources, and a transfer, which does not.

SELF-TEST

1. The layperson finds it odd that economists often prefer some pollution to no pollution. Explain how the economist reaches this conclusion.

2. Why does reducing pollution cost less by using market environmentalism than by setting standards?

3. Under market environmentalism, the dollar amount firm *Z* has to pay to buy the pollution permits from firms *X* and *Y* is not counted as a cost to society. Why not?

Public Goods: Excludable and Nonexcludable

Many economists maintain that the market fails to produce nonexcludable public goods. We discuss public goods in general and nonexcludable public goods in particular in this section.

Goods

Economists talk about two kinds of goods: private goods and public goods. A *private good* is a good the consumption of which by one person reduces the consumption for another person. For example, a sweater, an apple, and a computer are all private goods. If one person is wearing a sweater, another person cannot wear (consume) the same sweater. If one person takes a bite of an apple, there is that much less apple for someone else to consume. If someone is using a computer, someone else can't use the same computer. A private good is said to be **rivalrous in consumption**.

A **public good**, in contrast, is a good the consumption of which by one person does not reduce the consumption by another person. For example, a movie in a movie theater is a public good. If there are 200 seats in the theater, then 200 people can see the movie at the same time, and no one person's viewing of the movie detracts from another person's viewing of the movie. An economics lecture is also a public good. If there are 30 seats in the classroom, then 30 people can consume the economics lecture at the same time, and one person's consumption does not detract from any other person's consumption. The chief characteristic of a public good is that it is **nonrivalrous in consumption**, which means that its consumption by one person does not reduce its consumption by others.

All public goods are nonrivalrous in consumption, but they are not all the same. Some public goods are excludable and some are nonexcludable. A public good is **excludable** if it is possible, or not prohibitively costly, to exclude someone from obtaining the benefits of the good after it has been produced. For example, a movie in a movie theater is excludable in that persons who do not pay to see the movie can be excluded from seeing it. The same holds for an economics lecture. If someone does not pay the tuition to obtain the lecture, he or she can be excluded from consuming it. We summarize by noting that both movies in movie theaters and economics lectures in classrooms are *excludable public goods*.

A public good is **nonexcludable** if it is impossible, or prohibitively costly, to exclude someone from obtaining the benefits of the good after it has been produced. Consider national defense. First, national defense is a public good in that it is nonrivalrous in consumption. For example, if the U.S. national defense system is protecting people in New Jersey from incoming missiles, then it is automatically protecting people in New York as well. And just as important, protecting people in New Jersey does not reduce the degree of protection for the people in New York. Second, once national defense has been produced, it is impossible (or prohibitively costly) to exclude someone from consuming its services. Thus, national defense is a *nonexcludable public good*. The same holds for flood control or large-scale pest control. After the dam has been built or the pest spray has been sprayed, it is impossible to exclude persons from benefiting from it.

The Free Rider

When a good is excludable (whether it is a private good or a public good), individuals can obtain the benefits of the good only if they pay for it. For example, no one can con-

Rivalrous in Consumption
A good is rivalrous in consumption if its consumption by one person reduces its consumption by others.

Public Good
A good the consumption of which by one person does not reduce the consumption by another person—that is, a public good is characterized by nonrivalry in consumption. There are both excludable and nonexcludable public goods. An excludable public good is a good that while nonrivalrous in consumption can be denied to a person who does not pay for it. A nonexcludable public good is a good that is nonrivalrous in consumption and that cannot be denied to a person who does not pay for it.

Nonrivalrous in Consumption
A good is nonrivalrous in consumption if its consumption by one person does not reduce its consumption by others.

Excludability
A good is excludable if it is possible, or not prohibitively costly, to exclude someone from receiving the benefits of the good after it has been produced.

Nonexcludability
A good is nonexcludable if it is impossible, or prohibitively costly, to exclude someone from receiving the benefits of the good after it has been produced.

sume an apple (a private good) or a movie in a movie theater (a public good) without first paying for the good. This is not the case with a nonexcludable public good, though. Individuals can obtain the benefits of a nonexcludable public good without paying for it. Persons who do so are referred to as **free riders**. Because of the so-called *free rider problem,* most economists hold that the market will fail to produce nonexcludable public goods or at least fail to produce them at a desired level.

> **Free Rider**
>
> Anyone who receives the benefits of a good without paying for it.

To illustrate, consider someone contemplating the production of nonexcludable public good *X,* which because it is a public good, is also nonrivalrous in consumption. After good *X* has been produced and provided to one person, there is no incentive for others to pay for it (even if they demand it) because they can receive all of its benefits without paying. No one is likely to supply a good that people can consume without paying for it. The market, it is argued, will not produce nonexcludable public goods. The door then is opened to government involvement in the production of nonexcludable public goods. It is often stated that if the market will not produce nonexcludable public goods, although they are demanded, then the government must.

The free rider argument is the basis for accepting government (the public or taxpayers) provision of nonexcludable public goods. We need to remind ourselves, though, that a nonexcludable public good is not the same as a government-provided good. A nonexcludable public good is a good that is nonrivalrous in consumption and nonexcludable. A government-provided good is self-defined: It is a good that government provides. In some instances, a government-provided good is a nonexcludable public good, such as when the government furnishes national defense. But it need not be. The government furnishes mail delivery and education, two goods that are also provided privately and are excludable and thus not subject to free riding.

Nonexcludable Versus Nonrivalrous

The market only fails to produce a demanded good when the good is nonexcludable because the free rider problem only arises if the good is nonexcludable. The rivalry versus nonrivalry issue is not relevant to the issue of market failure; that is, a good can be rivalrous in consumption or nonrivalrous in consumption and still be produced by the market. For example, a movie may be nonrivalrous in consumption but be excludable too. And the market has no problem producing movies and movie theaters. The free rider problem occurs only with goods that are nonexcludable.

The "lighthouse in economics" is relevant to this discussion. For a long time, a lighthouse was thought to have the two characteristics of a nonexcludable public good: (1) It is nonrivalrous in consumption—any ship can use the light from the lighthouse, and one ship's use of the light does not detract from another's use. (2) It is nonexcludable—it is difficult to exclude any nonpaying ships from using the light. The lighthouse seemed to be a perfect good for government provision.

However, economist Ronald Coase found that in the 18th and early 19th centuries, many lighthouses were privately owned, which meant that the market had not failed to provide lighthouses. Economists were left to conclude either that the market could provide nonexcludable public goods or that the lighthouse wasn't a nonexcludable public good, as had been thought. Closer examination showed that while the lighthouse was nonrivalrous in consumption (it was a public good), the costs of excluding others from using it were fairly low (so it was an excludable public good). Lighthouse owners knew that usually only one ship was near the lighthouse at a time and that they could turn off the light if a ship did not exhibit the flag of a paying vessel.

economics 24/7

THE RIGHT QUANTITY AND QUALITY OF A NONEXCLUDABLE PUBLIC GOOD

We know this so far: Because of free riders, the market is unlikely to produce nonexcludable public goods. This is the basis for accepting government provision of nonexcludable public goods.

Let's say the particular nonexcludable public good that government will now provide is national defense. A thorny issue immediately arises: What quantity and quality of national defense will government provide? Will it produce a large national defense with many technologically advanced weapons systems? Will it produce a small national defense with very few technologically advanced weapons systems but with a relatively large number of soldiers?

It is one thing to provide a good; it is quite another to provide the number of units of the good and the quality of the good that most people demand.

To illustrate further, some Americans want a national defense that consists of U.S. armed forces present in many different countries around the world. They might argue that the U.S. needs to have a presence in countries such as Saudi Arabia, Iraq, Germany, and so on because it is in the best interests of the safety and security of the United States. Other Americans will vehemently disagree. They will argue that the type of national defense they demand is one where U.S. armed forces "stay home" until and unless the United States is provoked in some way—for example, by an attack on U.S. citizens residing in the United States.

Our point is a simple one: When it comes to nonexcludable public goods, once they are provided, people are likely to argue over how much of the public good is provided and what quality the public good is. Things are noticeably different when it comes to private goods. With private goods, people can consume the particular type of good they demand. For example, if one person wants brown shoes and another person wants black shoes, the person who wants brown shoes buys brown shoes and the person who wants black shoes buys black shoes. There are a wide variety of private goods to choose from. But when it comes to nonexcludable public goods, there is usually one particular nonexcludable public good that everyone consumes. As we hinted at earlier, there is only one U.S. national defense and national defense policy, and everyone in the United States, no matter his or her particular preferences, consumes that same national defense and national defense policy. As a result, people will often argue over, and try to change, the one nonexcludable public good they all have to consume in a way that comes closer to matching their particular preferences.

SELF-TEST

1. Why does the market fail to produce nonexcludable public goods?

2   Identify each of the following goods as a nonexcludable public good, an excludable public good, or a private good: (a) composition notebook used for writing, (b) Shakespearean play performed in a summer theater, (c) apple, (d) telephone in service, (e) sunshine.

3. Give an example, other than a movie in a movie theater or a play in a theater, of a good that is nonrivalrous and excludable.

Asymmetric Information

Market failure is a situation in which the market does not provide the efficient or optimal amount of a particular good. This chapter has shown that both externalities and nonexcludable public goods can lead to market failure. Specifically, when externalities exist, the market output is different from the socially optimal output. In the case of negative externalities, the market produces "too much"; in the case of positive externalities, the market produces "too little." In the case of nonexcludable public goods, some economists maintain that the market "produces" zero output. Assuming that there is a demand for the nonexcludable public good, this is definitely "too little."

This section looks at another possible cause of market failure—asymmetric information. **Asymmetric information** exists when either the buyer or the seller in a market exchange has some information that the other does not have. In other words, some information is "hidden." For example, the seller of a house may have information about the house that the buyer does not have, such as the roof leaks during a heavy rainfall.

The analysis of the effects of asymmetric information is similar to the analysis of externalities—with one important difference. The discussion of externalities considers buyers, sellers, and third parties; this discussion considers only buyers and sellers.

Asymmetric Information

Exists when either the buyer or the seller in a market exchange has some information that the other does not have.

Asymmetric Information in a Product Market

In the discussion of externalities, the demand for a good represents marginal private benefits, and the supply of a good represents marginal private costs. This is also the case for the asymmetric information situation shown in Exhibit 6; that is, the demand curve, D_1, represents marginal private benefits (MPB) and the supply curve, S_1, represents marginal private costs (MPC). In Exhibit 6, D_1 and S_1 are the relevant curves when the seller has some information that the buyer does not have. It follows that Q_1 is the market output when there is asymmetric information.

Now suppose the buyer acquires the information she previously did not have (but which the seller did have). With the new information, buying this particular good does not seem as appealing. The information that the buyer has acquired causes her to lower her demand for the good. The relevant demand curve is now D_2. With symmetric information, the market output will be Q_2, which is less than Q_1.

Let's consider an example. Suppose the good is cigarettes. Furthermore, suppose the suppliers of cigarettes know that cigarette consumption can cause cancer but do not release this information to potential buyers of cigarettes. Under this condition, suppliers of cigarettes have certain information about cigarettes that buyers don't have; there is asymmetric information. Without this information, the demand for cigarettes may be higher than it would be if buyers had the information. In Exhibit 6, demand is D_1

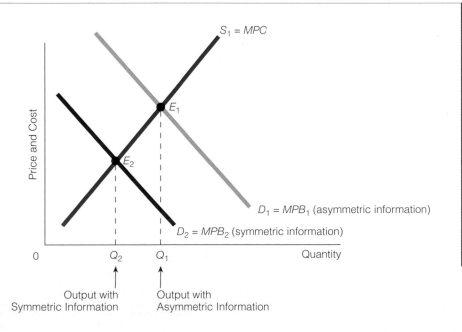

exhibit 6

Asymmetric Information in a Product Market

Initially, the seller has some information that the buyer does not have; there is asymmetric information. As a result, D_1 represents the demand for the good and Q_1 is the equilibrium quantity. Then, the buyer acquires the information that she did not have earlier, and there is symmetric information. The information causes the buyer to lower her demand for the good so that now D_2 is the relevant demand curve and Q_2 is the equilibrium quantity. Conclusion: Fewer units of the good are bought and sold when there is symmetric information than when there is asymmetric information.

instead of D_2. It follows, then, that more cigarettes will be purchased and consumed (Q_1) when there is asymmetric information than when there is symmetric information (Q_2).

Asymmetric Information in a Factor Market

Now consider a resource or factor market, such as the labor market shown in Exhibit 7. In this case, the buyer has information that the seller does not have. Suppose a firm knows that its workers will be using a possibly toxic substance that may cause health problems in 20 to 30 years. Furthermore, suppose the company does not release this information to workers—that is, it is "hidden" from them. Without this information, the supply curve of labor is represented by S_1, and the quantity of labor will be Q_1 at a wage rate of W_1.

With the information, though, not as many people will be willing to work at the firm at the current wage. The supply curve of labor shifts left to S_2. The new equilibrium position shows that the quantity of labor falls to Q_2, and the wage rate rises to W_2.

Is There Market Failure?

Does asymmetric information cause markets to fail? That is, does it cause a situation in which the market does not provide the optimal output of a particular good? Certainly, in our examples, the output level of a good and the quantity of labor were lower when there was symmetric information than when there was asymmetric information. Stated differently, asymmetric information seemingly resulted in "too much" or "too many" of something—either too much of a good being consumed or too many workers for a particular firm.

Some people argue that asymmetric information exists in nearly all exchanges. Rarely do buyers and sellers have the same information; each usually knows something the other doesn't.

This argument misses the point, however. The point is whether or not the asymmetric information fundamentally changes the outcome from what it would be if there were symmetric information. For example, a seller may know something that a buyer doesn't know, but even if the buyer knew what the seller knows, it may not change the outcome.

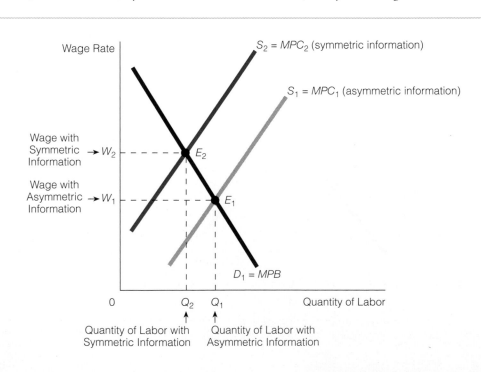

exhibit 7

Asymmetric Information in a Factor Market

Initially, the buyer (of the factor labor), or the firm, has some information that the seller (of the factor) does not have; there is asymmetric information. Consequently, S_1 is the relevant supply curve, W_1 is the equilibrium wage, and Q_1 is the equilibrium quantity of labor. Then, sellers acquire information that they did not have earlier, and there is symmetric information. The information causes the sellers to reduce their supply of the factor so that now S_2 is the relevant supply curve, W_2 is the equilibrium wage, and Q_2 is the equilibrium quantity of labor. Conclusion: Fewer factor units are bought and sold and wages are higher when there is symmetric information than when there is asymmetric information.

To illustrate, suppose a person buys a particular medication to relieve a severe headache. The person does not know that one side effect of the medication is sleepiness. Does asymmetric information matter here? Maybe not. It's possible the buyer would not have changed her behavior even if she had known the medication caused sleepiness. So there is asymmetric information, but it may not change the outcome.

But of course, in another setting, the result may be different. Suppose the seller of a used car knows the car is a "lemon," but the buyer doesn't know this. The person buys the car because he doesn't have the information the seller has. Does asymmetric information matter to the outcome in this situation? It does if the buyer would not have bought the car or would not have bought the car at a given price had he known what the seller knew. In this setting, asymmetric information changes the outcome.

We conclude, then, that the presence of asymmetric information does not guarantee that the market fails. What matters is whether the asymmetric information brings about a different outcome than the outcome that would exist if there were symmetric information. If this occurs, then the case for market failure can be made.

Adverse Selection

Some economists argue that under certain conditions, information problems can eliminate markets *(missing markets)* or change the composition of markets *(incomplete markets)*. To illustrate, let's return to our discussion of used cars.[3]

In the used car market, sellers know more than buyers about the cars they are offering to sell; there is asymmetric information. For example, a seller knows whether or not his car requires a lot of maintenance. Because it is difficult for most buyers to tell the difference between good used cars and "lemons," a single used car price will emerge for a given model-make-year car that is a reflection of both lemons and good cars. Suppose this price is $10,000.

A lemon owner will think this is a good price because she will receive an average price for a below-average car. On the other hand, a person who owns an above-average car will find this price too low; he won't want to sell his above-average car for an average price. As a result of lemon owners liking the price and the owners of good cars not liking it, lemon owners will offer their cars for sale ("great price"), and the owners of good used cars will not ("the price is too low").

This situation is called the problem of adverse selection. **Adverse selection** exists when the parties on one side of the market, who have information not known to others, self-select in a way that adversely affects the parties on the other side of the market. In the example, the owners of lemons offer their cars for sale—they select to sell their cars—because they know, and only they know, that the average price they are being offered for their below-average cars is a "good deal."

Through adverse selection, the supply of lemons on the market will rise, and the supply of high-quality, or good, used cars will fall. The relatively greater number of lemons will lower the average quality of a used car. As a result, there will be a new average price for a given make-model-year used car that is lower than previously. Let's say this new price is $8,000.

The process repeats: People with above-average cars will think the average price of $8,000 is too low, and people with below-average cars will think this is a good price. The people with above-average cars will drop out of the used car market, leaving only those with below-average used cars. Again, this will lead to a decline in the average quality of a used car, and eventually, the average price of a used car will drop.

Adverse Selection
Exists when the parties on one side of the market, who have information not known to others, self-select in a way that adversely affects the parties on the other side of the market.

---

[3]The material here is based on the classic article by George Akerlof, "The Market for Lemons," *Quarterly Journal of Economics* (August 1970): 488–500.

economics 24/7

FINDING ECONOMICS IN COLLEGE LIFE

A series of young children's books titled *Where's Waldo?* present the character Waldo drawn among hundreds of people and things. While the objective, finding Waldo, may seem easy, finding Waldo is roughly similar to finding a needle in a haystack. If you look long and hard, you'll eventually find him; if you simply glance at the page, you won't.

Finding economics is similar to finding Waldo. If you simply glance at your daily life, you'll miss the economics; if you look long and hard, you'll often find it.

With this in mind, consider your life as a college student. On a typical day, you walk into a college classroom, sit down, listen to a lecture and take notes, enter into discussions, ask questions, answer questions, and then leave. Can you find the economics in this daily experience? Here are some places you might find economics lurking.

Arriving Late to Class

Class started five minutes ago. You are sitting at your desk, listening to the professor, and taking notes. The professor is discussing an unusually challenging topic today, and you are listening attentively. Then, the classroom door opens. You

turn at the sound and see two of your classmates arriving late to class. For a few seconds, your attention is diverted from the lecture. When you refocus your attention on the professor, you realize that you have missed an essential point. You are mildly frustrated over this.

The scenario described is a negative externality. Your two classmates undertook an action—they arrived to class late—and you incurred a cost because of their action. Your two classmates considered only their private benefits and costs of arriving to class late. They did not consider your cost—the external cost—of their action.

What can be done to get students to internalize the cost to others of their being late? The professor could try to persuade students not to be late. She could say that lateness imposes a cost on those who arrive at class on time and are attentively listening to the lecture. Alternatively, the professor could impose a "corrective tax" on tardy students. In other words, she could try to set a tax equal to the external cost. The tax could take the form of a one-half to one point deduction from a student's test grade for each time he or she is late.

Thus, asymmetric information leads to adverse selection, which in the used car market example, brings about a steady decline in the quality of used cars offered for sale. Theoretically, the adverse selection problem could lead to the total elimination of the good used car market. In other words, the lemons will "drive out" all the good cars.

What might prevent this outcome? Is there anything implicit in the way markets work that could solve the adverse selection problem? There are several possible solutions for adverse selection in the used car market. For example, a buyer could hire his own mechanic to check the car he is thinking about buying. By doing this, he would acquire almost as much, if not as much, information about the car as the seller has. Thus, there would no longer be asymmetric information.

Or the seller of a high-quality used car could offer a warranty on her car. Essentially, she could offer to fix any problems with the used car for a period of time after she sells it. The warranty offer would likely increase both the demand for the car and its price. (Lemon owners would not be likely to offer warranties, so their cars would sell for less than cars with warranties.)

In some cases, government has played a role in dealing with adverse selection problems. State governments can pass, and in some situations have passed, "lemon laws," stating that car dealers must take back any defective cars. In addition, many states now require car dealers to openly state on used cars whether a warranty is included or a car is offered "as is."

Grading on a Curve

Consider Alex, who is currently taking a sociology course. Ideally, he would like to get an A or a B in the class, but this can't be guaranteed. He believes he is likely to receive a C or a D. Alex's situation is similar to that of a person who would like to be healthy every day for the rest of her life but knows that she probably won't be.

What does a person do when she knows she probably won't be healthy for her entire life? She buys health insurance. And as discussed in this chapter, after a person has purchased health insurance, a moral hazard problem may arise. The person may not have so strong an incentive to remain healthy when she has health insurance as when she doesn't.

Will Alex react the same way if he can buy grade insurance? Suppose his sociology professor promises Alex that he will grade on a curve and that no one in the class will receive a grade lower than a C−. With this assurance from his professor, will Alex have as strong an incentive to work hard to learn sociology? Does a moral hazard problem now arise? An economist is likely to answer the first question no and the second question yes.

Studying Together for the Midterm

Consider two types of colleges: (1) a dormitory-based college in which many of the students live on campus in dormitories and (2) a commuter college in which the entire student body lives off campus.

Students usually study together if they think it will be mutually beneficial to them. That is, when two people agree to

study together (say, for a midterm), they are usually entering into an exchange: I will help you learn more of the material so you can get a better grade if you do the same for me.

It is more common for students to study together on dormitory-based campuses than on commuter campuses. Why? The transaction costs of studying together—of entering into the aforementioned exchange—are relatively lower on a dormitory-based campus. If you live in a dormitory on campus, you incur relatively low transaction costs by studying with someone who also lives on campus (maybe a person living down the hall from you). But if everyone lives off campus, you incur relatively high transaction costs by studying with a fellow student. Do you drive over to that person's house or apartment, or does she drive over to your house or apartment? Do you meet at a local coffee bar?

Moral Hazard

In the used car example illustrating adverse selection, asymmetric information existed *prior* to an exchange. That is, before dollars changed hands, the seller of the used car had information about the car that the potential buyer did not have.

Asymmetric information can also exist *after* a transaction has been made. If it does, it can cause a moral hazard problem. **Moral hazard** occurs when one party to a transaction changes his behavior in a way that is hidden from and costly to the other party. For example, suppose Smith buys a health insurance policy. After she has the insurance, she may be less careful to maintain good health because the cost to her of future health problems is not so high as it would have been without the insurance. We are not implying that Smith sets out to make herself ill so she can collect on the insurance. We are simply saying that her incentive to be as careful about her health and physical well-being is not as strong as it once was.

Consider another example: A person who has automobile collision insurance may be more likely to drive on an icy road in December in Minneapolis than he would if he didn't have the insurance. Or a person who has earthquake insurance may be more likely to "forget" to do a few things that will minimize damage during an earthquake, such as attaching bookcases to the walls. In these examples, the moral hazard problem causes people to take "too few" precautionary actions.

Moral Hazard

Exists when one party to a transaction changes his or her behavior in a way that is hidden from and costly to the other party.

Insurance companies try to control for moral hazard in different ways. One way is by specifying certain precautions that an insured person must take. For example, a company that insures your house from fire may require you to have smoke detectors and a fire extinguisher. The insurance company may also set a deductible so that you must pay part of the loss in case of a fire. This increases your cost of a fire and provides you with an added incentive to be careful.

SELF-TEST

1. Give an example that illustrates how asymmetric information can lead to more of a good being consumed than if there is symmetric information.

2. Adverse selection has the potential to eliminate some markets. How is this possible?

3. Give an example (not discussed in the text) that illustrates moral hazard.

A Reader Asks . . .

Are Houses and Shopping Centers a Sign of "Progress"?

I live in an area that used to have many trees, large parcels of empty land, creeks, and so on, but in the past two years, more and more houses, apartment buildings, and shopping centers have been built. What was once a nice place to live has become filled with people; the natural beauty of the place and the quality of life have suffered. Would an economist call what has happened "progress"?

The economist doesn't have a preconceived notion of the way the world should look—whether an area should have creeks, trees, and birds or houses and shopping centers. The economist wants resources to be allocated in a welfare-maximizing way. To illustrate, let's discuss the area in which you live. To keep things simple, let's suppose we are talking about an area of five square miles that we call area X. Now it sounds like you (and perhaps others) preferred area X the way it was. Let's say that you and others with similar preferences constitute group A. There may be other persons, though, who prefer area X the way it has become. We'll say these other persons constitute group B. In some sense, then, we are talking about two groups of people—A and B—who want to do different things with area X.

Which group should get to do what it wants with area X? Should group A have the right to keep area X the way it wants—an area with few houses and shopping centers and with many trees, empty parcels of land, and so on? Or should group B have the right to change area X to what it wants—an area with many houses and shopping centers and with few trees, empty parcels of land, and so on?

Suppose group A values area X at a maximum of $40 million, and group B values it at a maximum of $50 million. This means that even if group A owned area X, it would sell it to group B. If group B offered $45 million for area X, group A would sell it because area X is only worth a maximum of $40 million to group A. (If the dollar amounts were reversed, group A wouldn't sell area X.)

It is hard to tell how much group A valued area X the way it was. It is certainly possible that group A valued area X more than group B did but that the transaction costs of individuals in this group getting together and bidding the land away from group B were just too high to overcome. In this case, area X may have ended up in the hands of people who value it less than others do.

It may also be the case that because certain things were "not priced," group B was able to buy area X for something less than a price that accounts for full costs. To illustrate, suppose some of the members of group B are developers who bought parcels of area X to put up houses. In building the houses, they create noise and congestion (on the roads) for the nearby residents. As far as the nearby residents are concerned, the noise and congestion are negative externalities. If the price of the land the developers purchased (for the purpose of building houses) did not fully reflect the external costs incurred by nearby residents, then it is very possible that more houses were built in area X than was socially optimal or efficient.

! analyzing the scene

Can there be too little as well as too much dog barking?

From Michael Olson's perspective, there is too much dog barking. The dog's barking is a negative externality, or we can say that the dog's barking inflicts an external cost on Michael. Can there also be too little dog barking? The answer is yes. The socially optimal amount of dog barking is that amount at which the *MSB* of dog barking equals the *MSC* (*MPC* + *MEC*) of dog barking.

Why does the professor in the School of Education argue the way she does?

The professor in the School of Education states that some of the benefits of teachers' education at her school spill over to society at large. The professor argues that those external benefits should be taken into account when determining her salary. Why does she argue this way? Perhaps she genuinely believes that the external benefits (she identifies) exist and that it is only right to pay people for the benefits they create for others. Or perhaps she has simply found an argument she can use to increase her salary. We are not sure why she argues the way she does. We do know, however, that it is sometimes very easy to argue that what you do contributes benefits far beyond the benefits for which you are compensated. Take this textbook, for example. One person wrote it. Certain benefits may accrue to the readers. But are there any benefits that extend beyond the readers? If so, should the author seek payment?

Why doesn't Bob Nelson contribute to the homeless?

Charitable giving appears to be a nonexcludable public good. It is nonrivalrous in consumption and nonexcludable. If a rich entrepreneur builds and staffs a homeless shelter, Bob Nelson receives utility from the gesture as easily as the rich entrepreneur; and it is impossible to exclude him from receiving the utility after the rich entrepreneur's charity has been reported.

Is Bob Nelson a free rider? Is that why he doesn't make a donation for the homeless? Using the following line of reasoning, many persons will argue that he is: (1) The average person's charitable contribution is a tiny percentage of total charitable contributions. (2) Consequently, the average person realizes that even if he does not make a charitable contribution, charitable giving by others will not be much different. (3) A person has an incentive to become a free rider when the person realizes that his or her contribution will not affect total contributions by more than the tiniest amount and that he or she can benefit from the charitable giving of others. We conclude: When a person feels that his contribution is insignificant to the total contribution or that the benefits he receives from a good will not be appreciably different in the absence of his paying for it, then he has a strong incentive to become a free rider.

Is there a right amount of pollution?

The economist often draws raised eyebrows when she says that there is a right amount of everything—even pollution. Eyebrows rise even higher when she adds that the right amount of pollution is probably some positive amount and not zero.

Does it matter if Frank's meal is spicier than he thought it was going to be?

Frank's meal turns out to be spicier than he thought it would be, but he says he would have ordered it anyway even if he had known how spicy it was going to be. Before Frank received his meal, there was asymmetric information: The chef knew more about the meal than Frank knew about it. After the meal was served, Frank knew something about the meal that he didn't know earlier. But he said it didn't matter to him. His behavior would have been the same even if he had known about the spiciness of the meal. In short, asymmetric information doesn't always matter to the outcome.

chapter summary

Externalities

- An externality is a side effect of an action that affects the well-being of third parties. There are two types of externalities: negative and positive. A negative externality exists when an individual's or group's actions cause a cost (adverse side effect) to be felt by others. A positive externality exists when an individual's or group's actions cause a benefit (beneficial side effect) to be felt by others.

- When either negative or positive externalities exist, the market output is different from the socially optimal output. In the case of a negative externality, the market is said to overproduce the good connected with the negative externality (the socially optimal output is less than the market output). In the case of a positive externality, the market is said to underproduce the good connected with the positive externality (the socially optimal output is greater than the market output). See Exhibits 1 and 3.

- Negative and positive externalities can be internalized or adjusted for in a number of different ways, including persuasion, the assignment of property rights, voluntary agreements, and taxes and subsidies. Also, regulations may be used to adjust for externalities directly.

The Coase Theorem

- The Coase theorem holds that in the case of trivial or zero transaction costs, the property rights assignment does not matter to the resource allocative outcome. To put it differently, a property rights assignment will be undone if it benefits the relevant parties to undo it. The Coase theorem is significant for two reasons: (1) It shows that under certain conditions, the market can internalize externalities. (2) It provides a benchmark for analyzing externality problems; that is, it shows what would happen if transaction costs were trivial or zero.

The Environment

- Some pollution is likely to be a better situation than no pollution. The reason is that people derive utility from things that cause pollution, such as cars to drive.
- There is more than one way to tackle environmental problems. For example, both setting standards and selling pollution permits can be used to deal with pollution. The economist is interested in finding the cheapest way to solve environmental problems. Often, this tends to be through some measure of market environmentalism.

Public Goods

- A public good is a good characterized by nonrivalry in consumption. A public good can be excludable or nonexcludable. Excludable public goods are goods that while nonrivalrous in consumption can be denied to people if they do not pay for them. Nonexcludable public goods are goods that are nonrivalrous in consumption and cannot be denied to people who do not pay for them. The market is said to fail in the provision of nonexcludable public goods because of the free rider problem; that is, a supplier of the good would not be able to extract payment for the good because its benefits can be received without making payment.

Asymmetric Information

- Asymmetric information exists when either the buyer or the seller in a market exchange has some information that the other does not have. Outcomes based on asymmetric information may be different from outcomes based on symmetric information.
- Adverse selection exists when the parties on one side of the market, who have information not known to others, self-select in a way that adversely affects the parties on the other side of the market. Adverse selection can lead to missing or incomplete markets.
- Moral hazard occurs when one party to a transaction changes his or her behavior in a way that is hidden from and costly to the other party.

key terms and concepts

Market Failure	Marginal Social Benefits (*MSB*)	Rivalrous in Consumption	Nonexcludability
Externality	Socially Optimal Amount (Output)	Public Good	Free Rider
Negative Externality		Nonrivalrous in Consumption	Asymmetric Information
Positive Externality	Internalizing Externalities		Adverse Selection
Marginal Social Costs (*MSC*)	Coase Theorem	Excludability	Moral Hazard

questions and problems

1 Give an example that illustrates the difference between private costs and social costs.

2 Consider two types of divorce laws. Law *A* allows either the husband or the wife to obtain a divorce without the other person's consent. Law *B* permits a divorce only if both parties agree to the divorce. Will there be more divorces under law *A* or law *B,* or will there be the same number of divorces under both laws? Why?

3 People have a demand for sweaters, and the market provides sweaters. There is evidence that people also have a demand for national defense, yet the market does not provide national defense. What is the reason the market does not provide national defense? Is it because government is providing national defense, and therefore, there is no need for the market to do so, or is it because the market won't provide national defense?

4   Identify three activities that generate negative externalities and three activities that generate positive externalities. Explain why each activity you identified generates the type of externality you specified.

5   Give an example of each of the following: (a) a good rivalrous in consumption and excludable; (b) a good nonrivalrous in consumption and excludable; (c) a good rivalrous in consumption and nonexcludable; (d) a good nonrivalrous in consumption and nonexcludable.

6   Some individuals argue that with increased population growth, negative externalities will become more common, and there will be more instances of market failure and more need for government to solve externality problems. Other individuals believe that as time passes, technological advances will be used to solve negative externality problems. They conclude that over time there will be fewer instances of market failure and less need for government to deal with externality problems. What do you believe will happen? Give reasons to support your position.

7   Name at least five government-provided goods that are not nonexcludable public goods.

8   One view is that life is one big externality. Just about everything that someone does affects someone else either positively or negatively. To permit government to deal with externality problems is to permit government to tamper with everything in life. No clear line divides externalities government should become involved in and those it should not. Do you support this position? Why or why not?

9   Economists sometimes shock noneconomists by stating that they do not favor the complete elimination of pollution. Explain the rationale for this position.

10 Why is it cheaper to reduce, say, air pollution through market environmentalism than through government standards and regulations?

11 Identify each of the following as an adverse selection or a moral hazard problem.

a   A person with car insurance fails to lock his car doors when he shops at a mall.

b   A person with a family history of cancer purchases the most complete health coverage available.

c   A person with health insurance takes more risks on the ski slopes of Aspen than he would otherwise.

d   A college professor receives tenure (assurance of permanent employment) from her employer.

e   A patient pays his surgeon before she performs the surgery.

working with numbers and graphs

1   Graphically portray (a) a negative externality and (b) a positive externality.

2   Graphically represent (a) a corrective tax that achieves the socially optimal output and (b) one that moves the market output further away from the socially optimal output than was the case before the tax was applied.

3   Using the following data, prove that pollution permits that can be bought and sold can reduce pollution from 12 units to 6 units at lower cost than a regulation that specifies each of the three firms must cut its pollution in half.

	Firm X	Firm Y	Firm Z
Cost of eliminating:			
First unit of pollution	$200	$500	$1,000
Second unit of pollution	300	700	2,000
Third unit of pollution	400	800	2,900
Fourth unit of pollution	500	900	3,400

Public Choice: Economic Theory Applied to Politics

Setting the Scene

Every day in the United States, people talk about politics. Listen in on some conversations that occurred one day in October.

A COMMUTER TRAIN TRAVELING INTO CHICAGO

George:

The election is only two weeks away, and I still haven't decided how I'm going to vote. To tell you the truth, I don't see much difference between the two candidates.

Jackie:

I don't see much difference between them either. A couple of months ago, they seemed to be on different sides of some issues. But now, they almost sound alike.

A HOUSE IN A NEW SUBDIVISION IN SACRAMENTO

Sam:

It says in the newspaper that in the last mayoral election here only 30 percent of the eligible voters chose to vote. That's really a low turnout.

Margie:

People just don't seem to care about elections. I was talking to our neighbor Daphne yesterday afternoon and asked her if she was going to vote tomorrow. She said that she wasn't going to bother, that she was really busy tomorrow and wouldn't have time to vote.

Sam:

I think that's just an excuse. Daphne's like a lot of people; she's not interested in politics.

GOVERNMENT CLASS AT A HIGH SCHOOL IN ATLANTA

Teacher:

How many of you know the names of our two U.S. senators?

Two of the 30 students raise their hands.

Teacher:

That's not a very good showing. If you want to be a good citizen, you have to stay informed about what's happening in our government. There's no reason for young men and women your age to not know the names of your U.S. senators.

? Here are some questions to keep in mind as you read this chapter:

- *Why isn't there much difference between the two candidates?*

- *What explains the low voter turnout?*

- *Why don't more students know the names of their U.S. senators?*

See analyzing the scene at the end of this chapter for answers to these questions.

Public Choice Theory

Economics is a powerful analytical tool. As you have already seen in this text, it can be used to analyze how markets and the economy work. In this chapter, we use economics to analyze the behavior of politicians, voters, members of special interest groups, and bureaucrats. Specifically, we analyze **public choice**, the branch of economics that deals with the application of economic principles and tools to public sector decision making. You can think of public choice as economics applied to politics.

Public choice theorists reject the notion that people are like Dr. Jekyll and Mr. Hyde: exhibiting greed and selfishness in their transactions in the private (market) sector and altruism and public spirit in their actions in the public sector. The same people who are the employers, employees, and consumers in the market sector are the politicians, bureaucrats, members of special interest groups, and voters in the public sector. According to public choice theorists, people in the market sector and people in the public sector behave differently not because they have different motives (or are different types of people) but because the two sectors have different institutional arrangements.

Consider a simple example. Erin Bloom currently works for a private, profit-seeking firm that makes radio components. Erin is cost conscious, does her work on time, and generally works hard. She knows that she must exhibit this particular work behavior if she wants to keep her job and be promoted.

Time passes. Erin leaves her job at the radio components company and takes a job with the Department of Health and Human Services (HHS) in Washington, D.C. Is Erin a different person (with different motives) working for HHS than she was when she worked for the radio components company? Public choice theorists would say no.

But simply because Erin is the same person in and out of government, it does not necessarily follow that she will exhibit the same work behavior. The reason is that the costs and benefits of certain actions may be substantially different at HHS than at the radio components company. For example, perhaps the cost of being late for work is less in Erin's new job at HHS than it was at her old job. In her job at the radio components company, she had to work overtime if she came in late; in her new job, her boss doesn't say anything when she comes in late. We predict that Erin is more likely to be late in her new job than she was in her old one. She is simply responding to costs and benefits as they exist in her new work environment.

Public Choice

The branch of economics that deals with the application of economic principles and tools to public sector decision making.

Q&A *Some people talk as if government is made up exclusively of good and giving people who have only the public good in mind. Other people talk as if government is made up exclusively of bad and grabbing people who have only their own welfare at stake. Are public choice theorists saying that both are caricatures of the real people who work in government?*

Yes, they are. One of the first public choice theorists, James Buchanan, said, "If men should cease and desist from their talk about and their search for evil men [and his sentiments include "purely good men" too] and commence to look instead at the institutions manned by ordinary people, wide avenues for genuine social reform might appear."

The Political Market

Economists who practice positive economics want to understand their world. They want to understand not only the production and pricing of goods, unemployment, inflation, and the firm but also political outcomes and political behavior. This section is an introduction to the political market.

Moving Toward the Middle: The Median Voter Model

During political elections, voters often complain that the candidates for office are "too much alike." Some find this frustrating; they say they would prefer to have more choice. However, as the following discussion illustrates, two candidates running for the same office often sound alike because they are competing for votes.

In Exhibit 1, parts (a), (b), and (c) show a distribution of voters in which the political spectrum goes from the "Far Left" to the "Far Right." Note that (relatively) few voters hold positions in either of these two extreme wings. We assume that voters will vote for the candidate who comes closest to matching their ideological or political views. People whose views are in the Far Left of the political spectrum will vote for the candidate closest to the Far Left and so on.

Our election process begins with two candidates, a Democrat and a Republican, occupying the positions D_1 and R_1 in part (a), respectively. If the election were held today, the Republican would receive more votes than his Democrat opponent. The Republican would receive all the votes of the voters who position themselves to the right of R_1, the Democrat would receive all the votes of the voters who position themselves to the left of D_1, and the voters between R_1 and D_1 would divide their votes between the two candidates. The Republican would receive more votes than the Democrat.

If, however, the election were not held today, the Democrat would likely notice (through polls and the like) that her opponent was doing better than she was. To offset this, she would move toward the center, or middle, of the political spectrum to pick up some votes. Part (b) in Exhibit 1 illustrates this move by the Democrat. Relative to her position in part (a), the Democrat is closer to the middle of the political spectrum, and as a result, she picks up votes. Voters to the left of D_2 would vote for the Democrat, voters to the right of R_2 would vote for the Republican, and the voters between the two positions would divide their votes between the two candidates. If the election were held now, the Democrat would win.

In part (c), the candidates, in an attempt to get more votes than their opponent, have moved to positions D_3 and R_3—close to the middle of the political spectrum. At election time, the two candidates are likely to be positioned side by side at the political center, or middle. Notice that in part (c), both candidates have become middle-of-the-roaders in their attempt to pick up votes.

The tendency of political candidates to move to a position at the center of the voter distribution—captured in the **median voter model**—is what causes many voters to complain that there is not much difference between the candidates for political office.

What Does the Theory Predict?

The theory we have just presented explains why politicians running for the same office often sound alike. But what does the median voter model predict? Here are a few of the theory's predictions:

Median Voter Model

Suggests that candidates in a two-person political race will move toward matching the preferences of the median voter (i.e., the person whose preferences are at the center, or in the middle, of the political spectrum).

The Move Toward the Middle

Political candidates tend to move toward the middle of the political spectrum. Starting with (a), the Republican receives more votes than the Democrat and would win the election if it were held today. To offset this, as shown in (b), the Democrat moves inward toward the middle of the political spectrum. The Republican tries to offset the Democrat's movement inward by also moving inward. As a result, both candidates move toward the political middle, getting closer to each other over time.

(a)

(b)

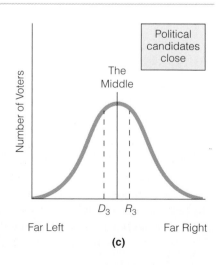

(c)

1. **Candidates will label their opponent as either "too far right" or "too far left."** The candidates know that whoever is closer to the middle of the political spectrum (in a two-person race) will win more votes and thus the election. As noted earlier, to accomplish this feat, they will move toward the political middle. At the same time, they will say that their opponent is a member of the political fringe (i.e., a person far from the center). A Democrat may argue that his Republican opponent is "too conservative"; a Republican may argue that her Democrat opponent is "too liberal."

2. **Candidates will call themselves "middle-of-the-roaders," not right- or left-wingers.** In their move toward the political middle, candidates will try to portray themselves as moderates. In their speeches, they will assert that they represent the majority of voters and that they are practical, not ideological. They will not be likely to refer to themselves as "ultraliberal" or "ultraconservative" or as right- or left-wingers because to do so would send the wrong message to the voters.

3. **Candidates will take polls, and if they are not doing well in the polls and their opponent is, they will modify their positions to become more like their opponent.** Polls tell candidates who the likely winner of the election will be. A candidate who finds out that she would lose the election (she is down in the polls) is not likely to sit back and do nothing. The candidate will change her positions. Often, this means becoming more like the winner of the poll—that is, becoming more like her opponent in the political race.

4. **Candidates will speak in general, instead of specific, terms.** Voters agree more on ends than on the means of accomplishing those ends. For example, voters of the left, right, and middle believe that a strong economy is better than a weak economy. However, they do not all agree on the best way to obtain a strong economy. The person on the right might advocate less government intervention as a way to strengthen the economy, whereas the person on the left might advocate more government intervention. Most political candidates soon learn that addressing the issues specifically requires them to discuss "means" and that doing so increases the probability they will have an extreme-wing label attached to them.

    For example, a candidate who advocates less government intervention in the economy is more likely to be labeled a right-winger than a candidate who simply calls for a stronger national economy without discussing the specific means he would use to bring this about. In the candidate's desire to be perceived as a middle-of-the-roader, he is much more likely to talk about ends, on which voters agree, than about means, on which voters disagree.

© JEFF HAYNES/AFP/GETTY IMAGES

Thinking like
AN ECONOMIST   *An economist thinks about theories and then tests them. She is not content to have a theory—such as the one that says candidates in a two-person political race will gravitate toward the center of the political distribution—simply sound right. The economist asks herself, "If the theory is right, what should I expect to see in the real world? If the theory is wrong, what should I expect to see in the real world?" Such questions direct the economist to look at effects to see whether the theory has explanatory and predictive power. If we actually see the four predictions of the median voter theory occurring in the real world—candidates labeling themselves one way, speaking in general terms, and so on—then we can conclude that the evidence supports the theory. But suppose we see that candidates en masse do not speak in general terms and so on. What then? Then we would know to reject the theory.*

economics 24/7

SIMPLE MAJORITY VOTING RULE: THE CASE OF THE STATUE IN THE PUBLIC SQUARE

Public questions are often decided by the simple majority decision rule. Most people think this is the fair and democratic way to do things. In certain instances, however, a simple majority vote leads to undertaking a project whose costs are greater than its benefits.

Consider a community of ten people. The names of the individuals in the community are listed in column 1 of Exhibit 2. The community is considering whether or not to purchase a statue to put in the center of the public square. The cost of the statue is $1,000, and the community has previously agreed that if the statue is purchased, the ten individuals will share the cost equally—that is, each will pay $100 in taxes (see column 3).

Column 2 shows the dollar value of the benefits each individual will receive from the statue. For example, Applebaum places a dollar value of $150 on the statue, Browning places a dollar value of $140 on the statue, and so on. Column 4

notes the net benefit (+) or net cost (−) of the statue to each individual. There is a net benefit for an individual if the dollar value he or she places on the statue is greater than the tax (cost) he or she must incur. There is a net cost if the reverse holds true. Finally, column 5 indicates how each member of the community would vote. If an individual believes there is a net benefit to the statue, he or she will vote for it. If an individual believes there is a net cost to the statue, he or she will vote against it. Six individuals vote for the statue and four individuals vote against it. The majority rules, and the statue is purchased and placed in the center of the public square.

Notice, though, that the total dollar value of benefits to the community ($812) is less than the total tax cost to the community ($1,000). Using the simple majority decision rule has resulted in the purchase of the statue even though the benefits of the statue to the community are less than the costs of the statue to the community.

This outcome is not surprising when you understand that the simple majority decision rule does not take into account the intensity of individuals' preferences. No matter how strongly a person feels about the issue, he or she simply registers one vote. For example, even though Emerson places a net benefit of $1 on the statue and Isley places a net cost of $90 on the statue, each individual has only one vote. There is no way for Isley to register that he does not want the statue more than Emerson wants it.

exhibit 2

Simple Majority Voting and Inefficiency

The simple majority decision rule sometimes generates inefficient results. Here the statue is purchased even though the total dollar value of the benefits of the statue is less than the total dollar costs.

(1) Individuals	(2) Dollar Value of Benefits to Individual	(3) Tax Levied on Individual	(4) Net Benefit (+) or Net Cost (−)	(5) Vote For or Against
Applebaum	$150	$100	+$50	For
Browning	140	100	+ 40	For
Carson	130	100	+ 30	For
Davidson	110	100	+ 10	For
Emerson	101	100	+ 1	For
Finley	101	100	+ 1	For
Gunter	50	100	− 50	Against
Harris	10	100	− 90	Against
Isley	10	100	− 90	Against
Janowitz	10	100	− 90	Against
Total	$812	$1,000		

Voters and Rational Ignorance

The preceding section explains something about the behavior of politicians, especially near or at election time. We turn now to a discussion of voters.

The Costs and Benefits of Voting

Political commentators often remark that the voter turnout for a particular election was low. They might say, "Only 54 percent of registered voters actually voted." Are voter turnouts low because Americans are apathetic or because they do not care who wins an election? Are they uninterested in political issues? Public choice economists often explain low voter turnouts in terms of the costs and benefits of voting.

Consider Mark Quincy, who is thinking about voting in a presidential election. Mark may receive many benefits from voting. He may feel more involved in public affairs or think that he has met his civic responsibility. He may see himself as more patriotic. Or he may believe he has a greater right to criticize government if he takes an active part in it. In short, he may benefit from seeing himself as a doer instead of a talker. Ultimately, however, he will weigh these positive benefits against the costs of voting, which include driving to the polls, standing in line, and so on. If, in the end, Mark perceives the benefits of voting as greater than the costs, he will vote.

But suppose Mark believes he receives only one benefit from voting—that his vote will have an impact on the election outcome. His benefits-of-voting equation may look like this:

$$\begin{array}{c} \text{Mark's benefits} \\ \text{of voting} \end{array} = \begin{array}{c} \text{Probability of Mark's vote} \\ \text{affecting the outcome} \end{array} \times \begin{array}{c} \text{Additional benefits Mark receives} \\ \text{if his candidate wins} \end{array}$$

Let's analyze this equation. Suppose two candidates, *A* and *B,* are running for office. If Mark votes, he will vote for *A* because he estimates that he benefits $100 if *A* is elected but only $40 if *B* is elected. The difference, $60, represents the additional benefits Mark receives if his candidate wins.

What is the probability of Mark's vote affecting the outcome? When there are many potential voters, such as in a presidential election, the probability that one person's vote will affect the outcome is close to zero. To recognize this fact on an intuitive level, consider any presidential election. Say there are two major candidates, *X* and *Y,* running for office. If you, as an individual voter, vote for *X,* the outcome of the election is likely to be the same as if you had voted for *Y* or as if you had not voted at all. In other words, whether you vote, vote for *X,* or vote for *Y,* the outcome is likely to be the same. In short, the probability of one person's vote changing the outcome of an election is close to zero when there are many potential voters.

In Mark's benefits-of-voting equation, $60 is multiplied by a probability so small that it might as well be zero. So $60 times zero is zero. In short, Mark receives no benefits from voting. But Mark may face certain costs. His costs-of-voting equation may look like this:

$$\begin{array}{c} \text{Mark's cost} \\ \text{of voting} \end{array} = \begin{array}{c} \text{Cost of driving} \\ \text{to the polls} \end{array} + \begin{array}{c} \text{Cost of} \\ \text{standing in line} \end{array} + \begin{array}{c} \text{Cost of filling out} \\ \text{the ballot} \end{array}$$

Obviously, Mark faces some positive costs of voting. Because his benefits of voting are zero and his costs of voting are positive, Mark makes the rational choice if he chooses not to vote.

Will everyone behave the same way Mark behaves and choose not to vote? Obviously not; many people do vote in elections. Probably what separates the Marks in the world from the people who vote is that the people who vote receive some benefits from voting that Mark does not. They might receive benefits from simply being part of the

economics 24/7

ARE YOU RATIONALLY IGNORANT?

Rational ignorance is usually easier to see in others than in ourselves. We understand that most people are not well informed about politics and government, but we often fail to put ourselves into the same category, even when we deserve to be there. We can take a giant leap forward in understanding rational ignorance and special interest legislation if we see ourselves more clearly. With this in mind, try to answer the following questions about politics or government.

1. What is the name of your most recently elected U.S. senator, and what party does he or she belong to?
2. How has your congressional representative voted in any of the last 20 votes in Congress?
3. What is the approximate dollar amount of federal government spending? What is the approximate dollar amount of federal government tax revenues?
4. Which political party controls the House of Representatives?
5. What is the name of your representative in the state legislature?
6. Name just one special interest group and note how much it received in federal monies (within a broad range) in the last federal budget.

7. Explain an issue in the most recent local political controversy that did not have to do with someone's personality or personal life.
8. Approximately how many persons sit in your state's legislature?
9. What political positions (if any) did the governor of your state hold before becoming governor?
10. In what month and year will the next congressional elections in your state be held?

If you know the answers to only a few of the questions, then consider yourself rationally ignorant about politics and government. This is what we would expect.

Now ask yourself why you don't know the answers to the questions. Is it because they are too hard (and almost impossible) to answer or because you have not been interested in answering such questions?

Finally, ask yourself if you will now take the time to find the answers to the questions you couldn't answer. If you do not know the answer to Question 6, for example, are you going to take the time to find the answer? We think not. If we're right, then you should now understand rational ignorance—on a personal level.

excitement of Election Day, from doing what they perceive as their civic duty, or from some other reason.

The point that public choice economists make is that if many individual voters will vote only if they perceive their vote as making a difference, then they probably will not vote because their vote is unlikely to make a difference. The low turnouts that appear to be a result of voter apathy may instead be a result of cost-benefit calculations.

Rational Ignorance

"Democracy would be better served if voters would take more of an interest in and become better informed about politics and government. They don't know much about the issues." How often have you heard this?

The problem is not that voters are too stupid to learn about the issues. Many people who know little about politics and government are quite capable of learning about both, but they choose not to learn.

But why would many voter-citizens choose to be uninformed about politics and government? The answer is perhaps predictable: because the benefits of becoming informed are often outweighed by the costs of becoming informed. In short, many persons believe that becoming informed is simply not worth the effort. Hence, on an individual basis, it makes sense to be uninformed about politics and government, to be in a state of **rational ignorance**.

Consider Shonia Tyler. Shonia has many things she could do with her leisure time. She could read a good novel, watch a television program, or go out with friends. Shonia could also become better informed about the candidates and the issues in the upcoming U.S. Senate race.

Becoming informed, however, has costs. If Shonia stays home and reads about the issues, she can't go out with her friends. If she stays up late to watch a news program, she might be too tired to work efficiently the next day. These costs have to be weighed against the benefits of becoming better informed about the candidates and the issues. For Shonia, as for many people, the benefits are unlikely to be greater than the costs.

Many people see little personal benefit to becoming more knowledgeable about political candidates and issues. As with voting, the decision to remain uninformed may be linked to the small impact any single individual can have in a large–numbers setting.

 Earlier it was said that politicians move toward the middle of the political spectrum to increase the probability that they will win an election. Now it turns out that the voter in the middle of the political spectrum, or any other voter for that matter, isn't likely to be knowledgeable about the issues. Doesn't this imply that politicians are trying to match the political preferences of a group of largely uninformed voters?

Yes, it does. Some people believe this is one of the deficiencies of representative democracy.

Rational Ignorance
The state of not acquiring information because the costs of acquiring the information are greater than the benefits.

SELF-TEST

(Answers to Self-Test questions are in the Self-Test Appendix.)

1. If a politician running for office does not speak in general terms, does not try to move to the middle of the political spectrum, and does not take polls, does it follow that the median voter model is wrong?

2. Voters often criticize politicians running for office who do not speak in specific terms (tell them what spending programs will be cut, whose taxes will be raised, etc.). If voters want politicians running for office to speak in specific terms, then why don't politicians do this?

3. Would bad weather be something that could affect the voter turnout? Explain your answer.

More About Voting

Voting is often the method used to make decisions in the public sector. In this section, we discuss two examples to describe some of the effects (some might say "problems") of voting as a decision-making method.

Example 1: Voting for a Nonexcludable Public Good

Suppose a community of seven persons, A–G, wants to produce or purchase nonexcludable public good X. Each person in the community wants a different number of units of X, as shown in the following table.

Person	Number of Units of X Desired
A	1
B	2
C	3
D	4
E	5
F	6
G	7

If the community of seven persons holds a simple majority vote, then all seven people will vote to produce or purchase at least 1 unit of X. Six people (B–G) will vote for at least 2 units. Five people (C–G) will vote for at least 3 units. Four people (D–G) will vote for at least 4 units. Three people (E–G) will vote for at least 5 units. Two people (F–G) will vote for at least 6 units. Only one person (G) will vote for 7 units.

The largest number of units that receives a simple majority vote (half the total number of voters plus 1, or 4 votes) is 4 units. In other words, the community will vote to produce or purchase 4 units of X.

What is interesting is that 4 units is the most preferred outcome of only one of the seven members of the community, person D, who is the median voter. Half the voters (A, B, and C) preferred fewer than 4 units, and half the voters (E, F, and G) preferred more than 4 units. Thus, our voting process has resulted in only the median voter obtaining his most preferred outcome.

The outcome would have been the same even if the numbers had looked the way they do in the following table.

Person	Number of Units of X Desired
A	0
B	0
C	0
D	4
E	7
F	7
G	7

In this case, four people (D–G) would have voted for at least 4 units and only three people would have voted for anything less than 4 units. Again, 4 units would have been the outcome of the vote, and only the median voter would have obtained his most preferred outcome.

Example 2: Voting and Efficiency

Let's suppose three individuals have the marginal private benefits (MPB) shown in the following table for various units of nonexcludable public good Y.

Person	MPB of First Unit of Y	MPB of Second Unit of Y	MPB of Third Unit of Y
A	$400	$380	$190
B	150	110	90
C	100	90	80

If the cost of providing a unit of good Y is $360, what is the socially optimal, or efficient, amount of good Y? To answer this question, we need to review a few of the relationships from the last chapter:

1. The socially optimal, or efficient, amount of anything is the amount at which the marginal social benefits (MSB) equal the marginal social costs (MSC).

2. The sum of the marginal private benefits and the marginal external benefits equals the marginal social benefits: $MPB + MEB = MSB$.

3. The sum of the marginal private costs and the marginal external costs equals the marginal social costs: $MPC + MEC = MSC$.

In our example, the MSC for each unit is given as $360. We calculate the MSB for each unit by summing the MPB for each unit. For the first unit, the MSB is $650 ($400 + $150 + $100); for the second unit, it is $580; and for the third unit, it is $360. The socially optimal, or efficient, amount of good Y is 3 units because this is the amount at which $MSB = MSC$.

Now will voting give us efficiency? The answer largely depends on what tax each person, A–C, expects to pay. Suppose each person must pay an equal share of the price of a unit of good Y. In other words, the tax for each person is $120 ($360 per unit divided by 3 persons equals $120 per person per unit).

Person A will vote for 3 units because his MPB for each unit is greater than his tax of $120 per unit. Person B will vote for only 1 unit because his MPB for the first unit is greater than his tax of $120 per unit but his MPB is not greater for the second or third unit. Person C will not vote for any units because his MPB for each unit is less than his tax of $120 per unit. The outcome, using a simple majority vote, is only 1 unit. A process of voting where each voter pays an equal tax results in an inefficient outcome.

Now suppose instead of each person paying an equal tax (of $120), each person pays a tax equal to his MPB at the socially optimal, or efficient, outcome. The socially optimal, or efficient, outcome is 3 units of good Y, so person A would pay a tax of $190 (his MPB for the third unit is $190). Person B would pay a tax of $90, and person C would pay a tax of $80. (Keep in mind that the sum of the taxes paid is equal to the cost of the unit, or $360.)

With this different tax structure, will voting generate efficiency? If each person casts a truthful vote, the answer is yes. Each person will vote for 3 units.[1] In other words, if everyone casts a truthful vote and everyone pays a tax equal to his or her MPB at the efficient outcome, then voting will generate efficiency.

Comparing the two tax structures—one where each person paid an equal tax and one where each person paid a tax equal to his MPB—we see that the tax structure makes the difference. In the case of equal tax shares, voting did not lead to efficiency; in the case of unequal tax shares, it did.

SELF-TEST

1. If the MSC in Example 2 had been $580 instead of $360, what would the socially optimal, or efficient, outcome have been?

2. In Example 2 with equal taxes, did the outcome of the vote make anyone worse off? If so, who and by how much?

Special Interest Groups

Special interest groups are subsets of the general population that hold (usually) intense preferences for or against a particular government service, activity, or policy. Often, special interest groups gain from public policies that may not be in accord with the interests of the general public. In recent decades, they have played a major role in government.

Special Interest Groups

Subsets of the general population that hold (usually) intense preferences for or against a particular government service, activity, or policy. Often, special interest groups gain from public policies that may not be in accord with the interests of the general public.

---

[1] Look at the situation for person A: His MPB for the first unit is $400 and his tax is $190, so he votes for the first unit; his MPB for the second unit is $380 and his tax is $190, so he votes for the second unit; his MPB for the third unit is $190 and his tax is $190, so he votes for the third unit. With respect to the last unit for person A, we are assuming that if his MPB is equal to the tax, he will vote in favor of the unit. The same holds for the analysis of voting for persons B and C.

Information and Lobbying Efforts

The general voter is usually uninformed about issues. The same does not hold for members of a special interest group. For example, it is likely that teachers will know a lot about government education policies, farmers will know about government farm policies, and union members will know about government union policies. When it comes to "their" issue, the members of a particular special interest group will know much more than will the general voter. The reason for this is simple: The more directly and intensely issues affect them, the greater the incentive of individuals to become informed about the issues.

Given an electorate composed of uninformed general voters and informed members of a special interest group, we often observe that the special interest group is able to sway politicians in its direction. This occurs even when the general public will be made worse off by such actions (which, of course, is not always the case).

Q&A

Is special interest legislation necessarily bad legislation? Can't legislation proposed and lobbied for by a special interest group benefit not only the special interest group (directly) but also the public interest (perhaps indirectly)?

Special interest legislation is not necessarily bad legislation, and certainly, such legislation can benefit the public interest. What we are saying is the costs and benefits of being informed about particular issues and of lobbying for and against issues are different for the member of the special interest group and for the member of the general public. This can make a difference in the type of legislation that will be proposed, passed, and implemented.

Suppose special interest group *A*, composed of 5,000 individuals, favors a policy that will result in the redistribution of $50 million from 100 million general taxpayers to the group. The dollar benefit for each member of the special interest group is $10,000. Given this substantial dollar amount, it is likely that the members of the special interest group (1) will have sponsored or proposed the legislation and (2) will lobby the politicians who will decide the issue.

But will the politicians also hear from the general voter (general taxpayer)? The general voter-taxpayer will be less informed about the legislation than the members of the special interest group, and even if he or she were informed, each person would have to calculate the benefits and the costs of lobbying against the proposed legislation. If the legislation passes, the average taxpayer will pay approximately 50 cents. The benefits of lobbying against the legislation are probably not greater than 50 cents. Therefore, we can reasonably conclude that even if the general taxpayer were informed about the legislation, he or she would not be likely to argue against it. The benefits just wouldn't be worth the time and effort. We predict that special interest bills have a good chance of being passed in our legislatures.

Congressional Districts as Special Interest Groups

Most people do not ordinarily think of congressional districts as special interest groups. Special interest groups are commonly thought to include the ranks of public school teachers, steel manufacturers, automobile manufacturers, farmers, environmentalists, bankers, truck drivers, doctors, and so on. For some issues, however, a particular congressional district may be a special interest group.

Suppose an air force base is located in a Texas congressional district. Then, a Pentagon study determines that the air force base is not needed and that Congress should close it down. The Pentagon study demonstrates that the cost to the taxpayers of keeping the base open is greater than the benefits to the country of maintaining the base.

But closing the air force base will hurt the pocketbooks of the people in the congressional district that houses the base. Their congressional representative knows as much; she also knows that if she can't keep the base open, she isn't as likely to be reelected to office.

Therefore, she speaks to other members of Congress about the proposed closing. In a way, she is a lobbyist for her congressional district. Will the majority of the members of Congress be willing to go along with the Texas representative? If they do, they know that their constituents will be paying more in taxes than the Pentagon has said is necessary to assure the national security of the country. But if they don't, when they need a vote on one of their own special interest (sometimes the term *pork barrel* is used) projects, the representative from Texas may not be forthcoming. In short, members of Congress sometimes trade votes: my vote on your air force base for your vote on subsidies to dairy farmers in my district. This type of vote trading—the exchange of votes to gain support for legislation—is commonly referred to as **logrolling**.

Logrolling
The exchange of votes to gain support for legislation.

Public Interest Talk, Special Interest Legislation

Special interest legislation usually isn't called by that name by the special interest group lobbying for it. Instead, it is referred to as "legislation in the best interest of the general public." A number of examples, both past and present, come to mind.

In the early 19th century, the British Parliament passed the Factory Acts, which put restrictions on women and children working. Those who lobbied for the restrictions said they did so for humanitarian reasons, such as to protect young children and women from difficult and hazardous work in the cotton mills. There is evidence, however, that the men working in the factories were the main lobbyists for the Factory Acts and that a reduced supply of women and children directly benefited them by raising their wages. The male factory workers appealed to individuals' higher sensibilities instead of letting it be known that they would benefit at the expense of others.

Today, people calling for, say, economic protection from foreign competitors or greater federal subsidies rarely explain that they favor the measure because it will make them better off while someone else pays the bill. Instead, they usually voice the public interest argument. Economic protectionism isn't necessary to protect industry X, but it is necessary to protect American jobs and the domestic economy. The special interest message often is, "Help yourself by helping us."

Sometimes, this message holds true, but other times, it does not. Nevertheless, it is likely to be as forcefully voiced in the latter case as it is in the former.

Special Interest Groups and Rent Seeking

Special interest groups often engage in rent-seeking behavior, which has consequences for society as a whole. Although rent seeking was discussed in earlier chapters, we review the concept here and describe how it relates to special interest groups.

RENT VERSUS PROFIT The term *rent seeking* was first used by Anne Krueger in an article in 1974, but the theory behind rent seeking had already been put forth by Gordon Tullock in a 1969 article. Strictly speaking, the term *rent* refers to the part of the payment to an owner of resources over and above the amount those resources could command in any alternative use. In other words, rent is payment over and above opportunity cost. Everyone would like to receive payment in excess of opportunity cost, so the motive to seek rent is strong.

When rent is the result of entrepreneurial activity designed to either satisfy a new demand or rearrange resources in an increasingly valuable way, then rent is usually called profit. To illustrate, suppose Jack finds a way to rearrange resources X, Y, and Z to produce a new good, A. If Jack receives a price for A that is greater than the cost of the resources, he receives a payment in excess of opportunity cost. Thus, Jack receives some rent; but in this setting, the rent is called profit.

In what setting is rent not referred to as profit? The answer is *in a setting where no new demand is satisfied or no additional value is created.* To illustrate, suppose Vernon lives and works as a taxi driver in a city in the Midwest. The city council licenses taxi drivers as long as they meet certain minimum requirements, such as having a valid driver's license and so on. Currently, Vernon receives a monthly income that is equal to his opportunity

economics 24/7

INHERITANCE, HEIRS, AND WHY THE FIRSTBORN BECAME KING OR QUEEN

Some economists have said that rent-seeking activity often goes on within families, especially when an inheritance is involved. We present their argument in the form of a short story.

An elderly widow with three children has an estate worth $10 million. It is understood that she will leave her $10 million to her children upon her death. But of course, there are different ways to leave $10 million to three adult children. She can split the $10 million into three equal parts, leaving $3.333 million to each. Or she can divide the $10 million unequally, perhaps leaving $9 million to *A*, $500,000 to *B*, and $500,000 to *C*. Furthermore, she can either tell each child how much he or she will inherit, or she can keep the dollar amount secret (until after her death). In other words, the elderly woman has two major decisions to make. The first relates to how much money she will give each child. The second relates to whether or not she will tell each child what he or she will receive upon her death.

If the woman is the type of person who craves attention and wants her children to fawn over her, can she use her inheritance to bring this about? She certainly can. All she has to do is (1) tell her children that she will not divide her estate equally among the three of them and (2) say that she hasn't yet decided on the amount each will receive. If she promises unequal inheritances that are yet to be determined, she almost guarantees that her children will engage in a rent-seeking battle for the bulk of her inheritance. This rent-seeking battle is likely to take the form of each child fawning over the mother to curry favor.

Let's look at the situation from the perspective of any one child, say *A*. He knows there is a fixed inheritance, $10 million, and what goes to one of his siblings will not go to him. For example, if $3 million goes to sibling *B* or to sibling *C*, this is $3 million less for him (*A*). The widow has effectively set up an arrangement where her three children will invest resources (to fawn over her) to effect a pure transfer. This is rent seeking.

The situation is different if the woman tells her children what she plans to leave each and then guarantees that under no circumstances will she change her mind. For

example, if she tells child *A* that he will receive $2 million, child *B* that she will receive $7 million, and child *C* that he will receive $1 million, then there is no reason for any of the children to invest resources in rent seeking. The $10 million has already been split up. Alternatively, the mother can simply tell her children that she plans to divide her inheritance equally and nothing on earth can get her to do differently. Once again, if the children know how things are guaranteed to turn out and that any resources they use to change the results will be wasted, they will decide against trying to change the outcome. No child will seek rents, in other words.

Now, let's consider the concept of rent seeking in a slightly different context. In the days when kings and queens ruled, the firstborn of a king or queen usually inherited the throne. But why the first? Couldn't the third child be a more capable king or queen than the first? Was every first child more capable of being king or queen than every second, third, or fourth child?

Before you answer these questions, consider what might have happened if it was not predetermined that the first child inherited the throne. The king's or queen's children would have engaged in a rent-seeking battle for the throne. In and of itself, the queen or king may not have had anything against this. In fact, they may have liked it.

But they wouldn't have liked it if their children engaged in such an intense rent-seeking battle that each might have tried to kill the others. From the child's perspective, there would be two ways to get the throne. The first would be to have the queen or king choose you from among all your brothers and sisters to ascend to the throne. The second would be to kill your brothers and sisters so that you were the only one left to ascend to the throne. One way to cut down on sibling killings was to simply have a rule stating that the firstborn would become king or queen. This rule didn't eliminate sibling murders completely because it was still possible for the second child to try to kill the first and therefore inherit the throne, but it certainly reduced sibling murders over and above what might happen if any of the many children could ascend to the throne.

cost. In other words, he does not receive any rent. Then, one day, Vernon and the other taxi drivers in the city lobby the city council to stop issuing taxi licenses, and the city council grants this request. Over time, the demand for taxis is likely to rise, but the supply of taxis will not. As a result, the dollar price for a taxi ride will rise. In time, it is possible that Vernon will earn an income over and above his opportunity cost. In other words, he will receive some rent.

In this setting, Vernon and the other taxi drivers have neither satisfied a new demand nor rearranged resources in a way that increases value. They have simply lobbied the city government to bring about a change that results in their receiving higher taxi fares and higher incomes at the expense of the customers who must pay the higher fares. There has been a transfer of income from taxi riders to taxi drivers. Notice that this transfer of income has a cost. Vernon and the other taxi drivers expended resources to bring about this pure transfer, which is referred to as rent seeking. In short, *rent seeking is the expenditure of scarce resources to capture a pure transfer.*

RENT SEEKING IS SOCIALLY WASTEFUL From society's perspective, the resources used in rent seeking are wasted and make society (but not necessarily all individuals in society) poorer as a result. To illustrate, suppose there are only two people in a society, Smith and Brown. The total amount of resources in this society, or the total income, is $10,000. We could (1) give all of the income to Smith, (2) give all of it to Brown, or (3) give some amount to each. Exhibit 3 shows a line, I_1, that represents the possible combinations of income the two persons may receive. Currently, Smith and Brown are located at point A on I_1, where each receives some income.[2]

Smith would prefer to be located at point B, where he would receive more income than he currently does at point A. To this end, Smith lobbies legislators to pass a law that effectively redistributes income from Brown to him. Smith is successful in his lobbying efforts, and the law passes. Do Brown and Smith move from point A to point B as a result? No. This movement doesn't adjust for the resources that were used by Smith when he was rent seeking. If we take these resources into account, there is now less total

[2]The analysis here is based on Chapter 18, "The Rent-Seeking Society" in Richard McKenzie and Gordon Tullock, *The New World of Economics* (New York: McGraw-Hill, 1994).

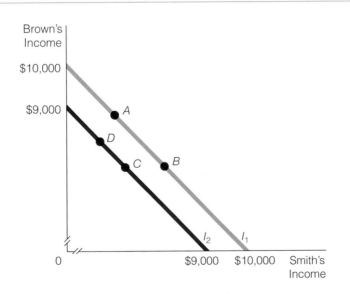

exhibit **3**

Rent Seeking

Brown and Smith are the only two people in a society in which the total amount of resources, or the total income, is $10,000. Currently, Brown and Smith are located at point A on I_1, where each receives some of the $10,000. Smith wants to move to point B, where he would receive more income than he does at point A. To try to bring this outcome about, he lobbies legislators to pass a law that will transfer income away from Brown to him. In other words, he is rent seeking. Because rent-seeking activity uses resources in a socially unproductive way, there are fewer resources, or less total income, to divide between Brown and Smith. Still, Smith may not mind this if he has moved from point A on I_1 to point C on I_2 as a result of his rent-seeking activities. Overall, Brown and Smith are worse off (sharing $9,000 instead of $10,000), but Smith is better off at point C than at point A.

income for Smith and Brown to share. If $1,000 worth of resources were expended in effecting the transfer, income is now $9,000 instead of $10,000. Therefore, I_1 is no longer relevant; I_2 is. The result of Smith's rent seeking is that he and Brown move from point A to point C. At point C, Smith receives more income than he did at point A and Brown receives less.

One effect of Smith's rent seeking is that he is made better off and Brown is made worse off. The other effect is that society as a whole (i.e., the sum of Smith and Brown) is poorer than it was when there was no rent seeking. In short, rent seeking may be rational from an individual's perspective (after all, Smith does make himself better off through rent seeking), but it is harmful to society.

Now consider a slight modification to our analysis. Suppose Brown is aware that Smith is lobbying legislators in an attempt to transfer income from her to him. Brown may try to lobby defensively—that is, to lobby against Smith. Brown's lobbying efforts are not costless; resources are expended in trying to defend the status quo income distribution. Brown may not be seeking rent, but she is using resources to prevent someone else from obtaining rent. The resources she uses are wasted as far as society is concerned because they do not go to build bridges, educate children, or do any number of other things. These resources are used to prevent a pure transfer. In other words, because of Brown's defensive lobbying efforts, society may move from I_1 to I_2. If Brown is successful at preventing Smith from effecting a pure transfer, then Brown and Smith may end up moving from point A to point D. The relative income shares of the two individuals may not be any different at point D than at point A, but both Brown and Smith receive less income at point D than at point A. The combination of offensive lobbying (for rent) by Smith and defensive lobbying (to prevent Smith from getting rent) by Brown results in both individuals being made worse off.

SELF-TEST

1. The "average" farmer is likely to be better informed about federal agricultural policy than the "average" food consumer is. Why?

2. Consider a piece of special interest legislation that will transfer $40 million from group A to group B, where group B includes 10,000 persons. Is this piece of special interest legislation more likely to pass (a) when group A includes 10,000 persons or (b) when group A includes 10 million persons? Explain your answer.

3. Give an example of public interest talk spoken by a special interest group.

4. Why is rent-seeking activity socially wasteful?

Government Bureaucracy

Government Bureaucrat

An unelected person who works in a government bureau and is assigned a special task that relates to a law or program passed by the legislature.

A discussion of politics and government is not complete without mention of the government bureau and bureaucrat. A **government bureaucrat** is an unelected person who works in a government bureau and is assigned a special task that relates to a law or program passed by the legislature.

Let's consider a few facts about government bureaus:

1. A government bureau receives its funding from the legislature. Often, its funding in future years depends on how much it spends carrying out its specified duties in the current year.

2. A government bureau does not maximize profits.

3.   There are no transferable ownership rights in a government bureau. There are no stockholders in a government bureau.

4.   Many government bureaus provide services for which there is no competition. For example, if a person wants a driver's license, there is usually only one place to go—the Department of Motor Vehicles.

5.   If the legislation that established the government bureau in the first place is repealed, there is little need for the government bureau.

These five facts about government bureaus have corresponding consequences. Many economists see these consequences as follows:

1.   Government bureaus are not likely to end the current year with surplus funds. If they do, their funding for the following year is likely to be less than it was for the current year. Their motto is "spend the money, or lose it."

2.   Because a government bureau does not attempt to maximize profits the way a private firm would, it does not watch its costs as carefully. Combining points 1 and 2, we conclude that government bureau costs are likely to remain constant or rise but are not likely to fall.

3.   No one has a monetary incentive to monitor the government bureau because no one "owns" the government bureau and no one can sell an "ownership right" in the bureau. Stockholders in private firms have a monetary incentive to ensure that the managers of the firms do an efficient job. Because there is no analog to stockholders in a government bureau, there is no one to ensure that the bureau manager operates the bureau efficiently.

4.   Government bureaus and bureaucrats are not as likely to try to please the "customer" as private firms are because (in most cases) they have no competition and are not threatened by any in the future. If the lines are long at the Department of Motor Vehicles, the bureaucrats do not care. Customers cannot go anywhere else to get what they need.

5.   Government bureaucrats are likely to lobby for the continued existence and expansion of the programs they administer. To behave differently would go against their best interests. To argue for the repeal of a program, for example, is to argue for the abolition of their jobs.

Q&A *This description makes it sound as if government bureaucrats are petty, selfish people. Aren't many government bureaucrats nice, considerate people who work hard at their jobs?*

The point is not that government bureaucrats are bad people set out to take advantage of the general public. The point is that ordinary people will behave in certain predictable ways in a government bureau that is funded by the legislature, does not maximize profits, has no analog to private sector stockholders, has little (if any) competition, and depends on the continuance of certain legislation for its existence.

A View of Government

The view of government presented in this chapter is perhaps much different from the view presented by your elementary school social studies teacher. He may have described politicians and bureaucrats as people who were kind, charitable, altruistic, generous, and above all, dedicated to serving the public good. He may have described voters as willingly performing their civic responsibility.

No doubt some will say that the view of government in this chapter is cynical and exaggerated. It may very well be. But remember, it is based on a theory, and most theories are not descriptively accurate. The real question is whether the theory of public sector decision making presented here meets the test that any theory must meet. It must explain and predict real-world events. Numerous economists and political scientists have concluded that it does.

A Reader Asks . . .

What Is the Significance of Public Choice?

Public choice hits on some interesting topics—such as the median voter model, special interests, and rational ignorance—but why is it studied in economics? Why isn't it studied in political science?

According to public choice economists, public choice fills a gap that existed in economics. They often say that before public choice came along, too many economists simply assumed that if "markets failed," government would and could step up and fix the problem. For example, if a negative externality caused the market to "fail"—and the market overproduced a good—then government officials could be relied on to set the right tax and correct the problem. If individuals demanded a nonexcludable public good and the market didn't provide it, then government would. In the area of macroeconomics, if the self-regulating properties of the economy were not working and the unemployment rate rose too high, then government would step forward and stimulate the economy in just the right way to reduce the unemployment rate to an acceptable level.

What was assumed, say public choice economists, is that government would work flawlessly to correct the failures of the market. Public choice theory questions whether government works as flawlessly and as unselfishly as many people assume. Just as there is "market failure," say public choice economists, there is "government failure," or "political failure," too.

Here is what James Buchanan, one of the founders of public choice, has to say about the subject:

Lest we forget, it is useful to remind ourselves in the 1990s that the predominant emphasis of the theoretical welfare economics of the 1950s and 1960s was placed on the identification of "market failure," with the accompanying normative argument for politicized correction. In retrospect, it seems naïve in the extreme to advance institutional comparisons between the workings of an observed and idealized alternative. Despite Wicksell's early criticism, however, economists continued to assume, implicitly, that politics would work ideally in the corrective adjustments to market failures that analysis enabled them to identify.

The lasting contribution of public choice theory has been to correct this obvious imbalance in analysis. Any institutional comparison that is worthy of serious considerations must compare relevant alternatives; if market organization is to be replaced by politicized order, or vice versa, the two institutional structures must be evaluated on the basis of predictions as to how they will actually work. Political failure, as well as market failure, must become central to the comprehensive analysis that precedes normative judgment.[3]

---

[3]James M. Buchanan, *Better Than Plowing and Other Personal Essays* (Chicago: University of Chicago Press, 1992), p. 99.

! analyzing the scene

Why isn't there much difference between the two candidates?

According to George and Jackie, the two candidates sound almost alike two weeks before the election. Of course, this is evidence in support of the median voter model. We would expect that two candidates would be very much alike if each is trying to get the vote of the median voter. Even if the two

candidates didn't sound alike, we wouldn't necessarily say that the median voter model has no predictive power. That's because the model simply predicts that the candidate who comes closer to expressing the preferences of the median voter will win the election. The median voter model can still be a good model when two candidates don't sound alike. To illustrate, suppose candidate *A* expresses the preferences of the median voter and candidate B does not. Candidate B, let's say, is to the far right of the median voter because he mistakenly believes that the median voter is further right than he really is. In short, there is nothing about the median voter model that says candidates won't make mistakes on locating the position of the median voter. The model simply predicts that candidates who do not make mistakes in locating the real median voter and come closer to expressing this person's preferences will win the election.

What explains the low voter turnout?

Margie and Sam think people don't care about elections and are uninterested in politics. However, contrary to popular belief, you can be enthusiastic about the outcome of a political election and choose not to vote. If your one vote is unlikely to change the voting outcome, you have an incentive not to vote. Think of it this way. You might want tomorrow to be a sunny and warm day because you are planning an outdoor wedding. You are extremely interested in tomorrow's weather. But of course, there is absolutely nothing that you can do to influence the weather tomorrow. It is much the

same when it comes to the voting outcome. You can be very interested in how the vote turns out and at the same time realize that your one vote has almost no chance of affecting the voting outcome. And so you choose not to vote.

Why don't more students know the names of their U.S. senators?

Only two of the 30 students in the class know the names of their U.S. senators. Shocking, right? Maybe not. What might be more shocking is that even two students knew the names of their U.S. senators. The government teacher who admonishes his students to stay informed and be good citizens overlooks the fact that his students—like him—are rationally ignorant about certain things. Ask the government teacher the dollar amount of federal spending on agriculture in the last year, and he may not know. Why not? Ask the government teacher what percentage of federal income taxes are paid for by the top 10 percent of income earners, and he may not know. Why not? The truth is that rational ignorance—choosing to be uninformed when the costs of becoming informed are greater than the benefits of becoming informed—is common.

chapter summary

Politicians and the Middle: The Median Voter Model

- In a two-person race, candidates for the same office will gravitate toward the middle of the political spectrum to pick up votes. If a candidate does not do this and her opponent does, the opponent will win the election. Candidates do a number of things during campaigns that indicate they understand where they are headed—toward the middle. For example, candidates attempt to label their opponents as either "too far right" or "too far left." Candidates usually pick labels for themselves that represent the middle of the political spectrum, they speak in general terms, and they take polls and adjust their positions accordingly.

Voting and Rational Ignorance

- There are both costs and benefits to voting. Many potential voters will not vote because the costs of voting—in terms of time spent going to the polls and so on—outweigh the benefits of voting, measured as the probability of their single vote affecting the election outcome.
- There is a difference between being unable to learn certain information and choosing not to learn certain

information. Most voters choose not to be informed about political and government issues because the costs of becoming informed outweigh the benefits of becoming informed. They choose to be rationally ignorant.

More About Voting

- In a simple majority vote where there are several options from which to choose, the voting outcome is the same as the most preferred outcome of the median voter.
- Simple majority voting and equal tax shares can generate a different result than simple majority voting and unequal tax shares.

Special Interest Groups

- Special interest groups are usually well informed about their issues. Individuals have a greater incentive to become informed about issues the more directly and intensely the issues affect them.
- Legislation that concentrates the benefits on a few and disperses the costs over many is likely to pass because the beneficiaries will have an incentive to lobby for it,

whereas those who pay the bill will not lobby against it because each of them pays such a small part of the bill.

- Special interest groups often engage in rent seeking, which is the expenditure of scarce resources to capture a pure transfer. Rent seeking is a socially wasteful activity because resources that are used to effect transfers are not used to produce goods and services.

Bureaucracy

- Public choice economists do not believe government bureaucrats are bad people set on taking advantage of the general public. They believe bureaucrats are ordinary people (just like our friends and neighbors) who behave in predictable ways in a government bureau that is funded by the legislature, does not maximize profits, has no analog to private sector stockholders, has little (if any) competition, and depends on the continuance of certain legislation for its existence.

key terms and concepts

Public Choice	Special Interest Groups
Median Voter Model	Logrolling
Rational Ignorance	Government Bureaucrat

questions and problems

1 Some observers maintain that not all politicians move toward the middle of the political spectrum to obtain votes. They often cite Barry Goldwater in the 1964 presidential election and George McGovern in the 1972 presidential election as examples. Goldwater was viewed as occupying the right end of the political spectrum and McGovern the left end. Would this necessarily be evidence that does not support the median voter model? Are the exceptions to the theory explained in this chapter?

2 Would voters have a greater incentive to vote in an election in which there were only a few registered voters or in one in which there were many registered voters? Why?

3 Many individuals learn more about the car they are thinking of buying than about the candidates running for president of the United States. Explain why.

4 If the model of politics and government presented in this chapter is true, what are some of the things we would expect to see?

5 It has often been remarked that Democrat candidates are more liberal in Democrat primaries and Republican candidates are more conservative in Republican primaries than either is in the general election, respectively. Explain why.

6 What are some ways of reducing the cost of voting to voters?

7 Provide a numerical example that shows simple majority voting may be consistent with efficiency. Next, provide a numerical example that shows simple majority voting may be inconsistent with efficiency.

8 What are some ways of making government bureaucrats and bureaus more cost conscious?

9 Some individuals see national defense spending as benefiting special interests—in particular, the defense industry. Others see it as directly benefiting not only the defense industry but the general public as well. Does this same difference in view exist for issues other than national defense? Name a few.

10 Evaluate each of the following proposals for reform in terms of the material discussed in this chapter: (a) linking all spending programs to visible tax hikes; (b) a balanced budget amendment that stipulates that Congress cannot spend more than total tax revenues; (c) a budgetary referenda process whereby the voters actually vote on the distribution of federal dollars to the different categories of spending (X percentage to agriculture, Y percentage to national defense, etc.) instead of the elected representatives deciding.

11 Rent seeking may be rational from the individual's perspective, but it is not rational from society's perspective. Do you agree or disagree? Explain your answer.

working with numbers and graphs

1   Suppose there are three major candidates, *A, B,* and *C,* running for president of the United States, and the distribution of voters is the same as shown in Exhibit 1. Two of the candidates, *A* and *B,* are currently viewed as right of the median, and *C* is viewed as left of the median. Is it possible to predict which candidate is most likely to win?

2   Look back at Exhibit 2. Suppose net benefits and net costs for each person are known a week before Election Day, and it is legal to buy and sell votes. Furthermore, suppose there is no conscience cost to either buying or selling votes. Would the outcome of the election be the same? Explain your answer.

3   In part (a) of the following figure, the distribution of voters is skewed to the left; in part (b), the distribution of voters is skewed neither left nor right; and in part (c), the distribution of voters is skewed right. Assuming a two-person race for each distribution, will the candidate who wins the election in (a) hold different positions from the candidates who win the elections in (b) and (c)? Explain your answer.

(a)

(b)

(c)

International Trade 30

Setting the Scene

The following events happened on a day in February.

9:33 A.M.

Daisy Castle, a reporter for a local newspaper, is in the office of Duncan Carlyle, president of a nearby steel company. Daisy is interviewing the president about his company's future.

"Your company has had some problems recently," comments Daisy. "You've had to lay off some workers because your sales have been down. Do things look better for the months ahead?"

"Much depends on what Congress does in the next few weeks," replies Duncan. "We would be greatly helped—and so would this community—if Congress imposes a tariff on steel imports. That would give us the breathing room we need right now."

"Steel imports have risen dramatically the last six months," says Daisy. "Can U.S. companies compete with foreign producers?"

"Not without the tariff," Duncan answers. "We need to level the playing field."

11:54 A.M.

Jack and Harry, engineers for a large telecommunications company, are sitting at lunch, passing the time.

"What do you think about the president's newest plan on immigration?" Jack asks.

"I think the president should be cutting back on the number of immigrants instead of increasing the numbers," Harry replies. "More immigrants in the country simply lead to lower wages for Americans."

"I guess that's true," comments Jack.

"Of course it's true. It's basic supply and demand," Harry says. "An increased supply of people means more people applying for jobs, and wages have to go down."

2:43 P.M.

A student in a college economics class asks her professor if economics is really nothing more than "good ol' common sense"? In response, the professor begins to talk about comparative advantage.

? Here are some questions to keep in mind as you read this chapter:

- *How will a tariff help the domestic steel company?*

- *Do increased numbers of immigrants lower wages?*

- *Is economics nothing more than "good ol' common sense"?*

See analyzing the scene at the end of this chapter for answers to these questions.

International Trade Theory

International trade exists for the same reasons that trade at any level exists. Individuals trade to make themselves better off. Pat and Zach, both of whom live in Cincinnati, Ohio, trade because they both value something the other has more than they value some of their own possessions. On an international scale, Elaine in the United States trades with Cho in China because Cho has something that Elaine wants and Elaine has something that Cho wants.

Obviously, different countries have different terrains, climates, resources, worker skills, and so on. It follows that some countries will be able to produce some goods that other countries cannot produce or can produce only at extremely high costs.

For example, Hong Kong has no oil, and Saudi Arabia has a large supply. Bananas do not grow easily in the United States, but they flourish in Honduras. Americans could grow bananas if they used hothouses, but it is cheaper for Americans to buy bananas from Hondurans than to produce bananas themselves.

Major U.S. exports include automobiles, computers, aircraft, corn, wheat, soybeans, scientific instruments, coal, and plastic materials. Major imports include petroleum, automobiles, clothing, iron and steel, office machines, footwear, fish, coffee, and diamonds. Some of the countries of the world that are major exporters are the United States, Germany, Japan, France, and the United Kingdom. These same countries are some of the major importers in the world too.

How Do Countries Know What to Trade?

To explain how countries know what to trade, we need to review the concept of *comparative advantage,* an economic concept first discussed in Chapter 2. In this section, we discuss comparative advantage in terms of countries rather than in terms of individuals.

COMPARATIVE ADVANTAGE Assume a two country–two good world. The countries are the United States and Japan, and the goods are food and clothing. Both countries can produce the two goods in the four different combinations listed in Exhibit 1. For example, the United States can produce 90 units of food and 0 units of clothing, 60 units of food and 10 units of clothing, or other combinations. Japan can produce 15 units of food and 0 units of clothing, 10 units of food and 5 units of clothing, or other combinations.

Suppose the United States is producing and consuming the two goods in the combination represented by point *B* on its production possibilities frontier, and Japan is producing and consuming the combination of the two goods represented by point *F* on its production possibilities frontier. In this case, neither of the two countries is specializing in the production of one of the two goods, nor are the two countries trading with each other. We call this the *no specialization–no trade (NS-NT) case* (see column 1 in Exhibit 2).

Now suppose the United States and Japan decide to specialize in the production of a specific good and to trade with each other, called the *specialization–trade (S-T) case.* Will the two countries be better off through specialization and trade? A numerical example will help answer this question. But first, we need to find the answers to two other questions: What good should the United States specialize in producing? What good should Japan specialize in producing?

The general answer to both these questions is the same: *Countries specialize in the production of the good in which they have a comparative advantage.* A country has a **comparative advantage** in the production of a good when it can produce the good at lower opportunity cost than another country can.

For example, in the United States, the opportunity cost of producing 1 unit of clothing is 3 units of food (for every 10 units of clothing it produces, it forfeits 30 units of food). So the opportunity cost of producing 1 unit of food is 1/3 unit of clothing. In

Comparative Advantage
The situation when a country can produce a good at lower opportunity cost than another country can.

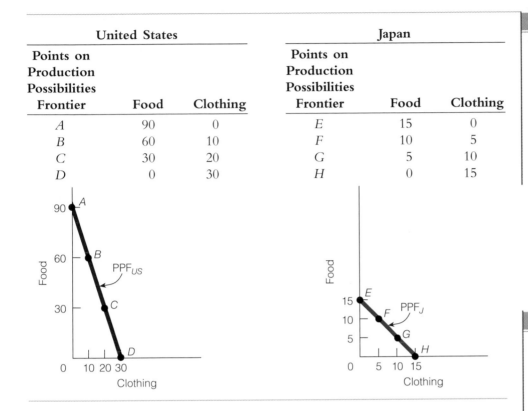

exhibit **1**

Production Possibilities in Two Countries

The United States and Japan can produce the two goods in the combinations shown. Initially, the United States is at point B on its PPF and Japan is at point F on its PPF. Both countries can be made better off by specializing in and trading the good in which each has a comparative advantage.

United States

Points on Production Possibilities Frontier	Food	Clothing
A	90	0
B	60	10
C	30	20
D	0	30

Japan

Points on Production Possibilities Frontier	Food	Clothing
E	15	0
F	10	5
G	5	10
H	0	15

Japan, the opportunity cost of producing 1 unit of clothing is 1 unit of food (for every 5 units of clothing it produces, it forfeits 5 units of food). To recap, in the United States, the situation is $1C = 3F$, or $1F = 1/3C$; in Japan the situation is $1C = 1F$, or $1F = 1C$.

The United States can produce food at a lower opportunity cost ($1/3C$ as opposed to $1C$ in Japan), whereas Japan can produce clothing at a lower opportunity cost ($1F$ as opposed to $3F$ in the United States). Thus, the United States has a comparative advantage in food, and Japan has a comparative advantage in clothing.

Suppose the two countries specialize in the production of the good in which they have a comparative advantage. That is, the United States specializes in the production of food (producing 90 units), and Japan specializes in the production of clothing (producing 15 units). In Exhibit 1, the United States locates at point A on its PPF, and Japan locates at point H on its PPF (see column 2 in Exhibit 2).

exhibit **2**

Both Countries Gain from Specialization and Trade

Column 1: Both the United States and Japan operate independently of each other. The United States produces and consumes 60 units of food and 10 units of clothing. Japan produces and consumes 10 units of food and 5 units of clothing. Column 2: The United States specializes in the production of food; Japan specializes in the production of clothing. Column 3: The United States and Japan agree to the terms of trade of 2 units of food for 1 unit of clothing. They actually trade 20 units of food for 10 units of clothing. Column 4: Overall, the United States consumes 70 units of food and 10 units of clothing. Japan consumes 20 units of food and 5 units of clothing. Column 5: Consumption levels are higher for both the United States and Japan in the *S-T* case than in the *NS-NT* case.

	No Specialization–No Trade (NS-NT) Case	Specialization-Trade (S-T) Case			
Country	(1) Production and Consumption in the NS-NT Case	(2) Production in the S-T Case	(3) Exports (−) Imports (+) Terms of Trade Are 2F = 1C	(4) Consumption in the S-T Case (2) + (3)	(5) Gains from Specialization and Trade (4) − (1)
United States					
Food	60 } Point B in	90 } Point A in	−20	70	10
Clothing	10 } Exhibit 1	0 } Exhibit 1	+10	10	0
Japan					
Food	10 } Point F in	0 } Point H in	+20	20	10
Clothing	5 } Exhibit 1	15 } Exhibit 1	−10	5	0

Q&A   *Specialization and trade appear to allow a country's inhabitants to consume at a level beyond its production possibilities frontier. Is this correct?*

Yes, that is correct. To see this, look at the PPF for the United States in Exhibit 1. In the NS–NT case, the United States consumes 60 units of food and 10 units of clothing—that is, the United States consumes at point B on its PPF. In the S-T case, however, it consumes 70 units of food and 10 units of clothing. A point that represents this combination of the two goods is beyond the country's PPF.

SETTLING ON THE TERMS OF TRADE After they have determined which good to specialize in producing, the two countries must settle on the terms of trade—that is, how much food to trade for how much clothing. The United States faces the following situation: For every 30 units of food it does not produce, it can produce 10 units of clothing, as shown in Exhibit 1. Thus, 3 units of food have an opportunity cost of 1 unit of clothing ($3F = 1C$), or 1 unit of food has a cost of 1/3 unit of clothing ($1F = 1/3C$). Meanwhile, Japan faces the following situation: For every 5 units of food it does not produce, it can produce 5 units of clothing. Thus, 1 unit of food has an opportunity cost of 1 unit of clothing ($1F = 1C$). Recapping, for the United States, $3F = 1C$, and for Japan, $1F = 1C$.

With these cost ratios, it would seem likely that both countries could agree on terms of trade that specify $2F = 1C$. The United States would benefit by giving up 2 units of food instead of 3 units for 1 unit of clothing, whereas Japan would benefit by getting 2 units of food instead of only 1 unit for 1 unit of clothing. Suppose the two countries agree to the terms of trade of $2F = 1C$ and trade, in absolute amounts, 20 units of food for 10 units of clothing (see column 3 in Exhibit 2). Will they make themselves better off? We'll soon see that they do.

RESULTS OF THE SPECIALIZATION-TRADE *(S-T)* CASE

Now the United States produces 90 units of food and trades 20 units to Japan, receiving 10 units of clothing in exchange. It consumes 70 units of food and 10 units of clothing. Japan produces 15 units of clothing and trades 10 to the United States, receiving 20 units of food in exchange. It consumes 5 units of clothing and 20 units of food (see column 4 in Exhibit 2).

Comparing the consumption levels in both countries in the two cases, the United States and Japan each consume 10 more units of food and no less clothing in the specialization–trade case than in the no specialization–no trade case (column 5 in Exhibit 2). We conclude that a country gains by specializing in producing and trading the good in which it has a comparative advantage.

How Do Countries Know When They Have a Comparative Advantage?

Government officials of a country do not analyze pages of cost data to determine what their country should specialize in producing and then trade. Countries do not plot production possibilities frontiers on graph paper or calculate opportunity costs. Instead, it is individuals' desire to earn a dollar, a peso, or a euro that determines the pattern of international trade. The desire to earn a profit determines what a country specializes in and trades.

To illustrate, consider Henri, an enterprising Frenchman who visits the United States. Henri observes that beef is relatively cheap in the United States (compared with the price in France) and perfume is relatively expensive. Noticing the price differences for beef and perfume between his country and the United States, he decides to buy some perfume in France, bring it to the United States, and sell it for the relatively higher U.S. price. With his profits from the perfume transaction, he buys beef in the United States, ships it to France, and sells it for the relatively higher French price. Obviously, Henri is buying low and selling high. He buys a good in the country where it is cheap and sells it in the country where the good is expensive.

What are the consequences of Henri's activities? First, he is earning a profit. The larger the price differences in the two goods

Thinking like **AN ECONOMIST**   *Is the desire to earn profit useful to society at large? In our example of Henri, his desire for profit ended up moving both the United States and France toward specializing in and trading the good in which they had a comparative advantage. And as we showed earlier in the chapter, when countries specialize and trade, they are better off than when they do neither.*

economics 24/7

DIVIDING UP THE WORK

John and Veronica, husband and wife, have divided up their household tasks the following way: John usually does all the lawn work, fixes the cars, and does the dinner dishes, while Veronica cleans the house, cooks the meals, and does the laundry. Why have John and Veronica divided up the household tasks the way they have? Some sociologists might suggest that John and Veronica have divided up the tasks along gender lines: Men have for years done the lawn work, fixed the cars, and so on, and women have for years cleaned the house, cooked the meals, and so on. In other words, John is doing "man's work," and Veronica is doing "woman's work."

Well, maybe, but that leaves unanswered the question of why certain work became "man's work" and other work became "woman's work." Moreover, it doesn't explain why John and Veronica don't split every task evenly. In other words, why doesn't John clean half the house and Veronica clean half the house? Why doesn't Veronica mow the lawn on the second and fourth week of every month and John mow the lawn every first and third week of the month?

The law of comparative advantage may be the answer to all our questions. To illustrate, suppose we consider two tasks: cleaning the house and mowing the lawn. The following table shows how long John and Veronica take to complete the two tasks individually.

	Time to Clean the House	Time to Mow the Lawn
John	120 minutes	50 minutes
Veronica	60 minutes	100 minutes

Here is the opportunity cost of each task for each person.

	Opportunity Cost of Cleaning the House	Opportunity Cost of Mowing the Lawn
John	2.40 mowed lawns	0.42 clean houses
Veronica	0.60 mowed lawns	1.67 clean houses

In other words, John has a comparative advantage in mowing the lawn, and Veronica has a comparative advantage in cleaning the house.

Now let's compare two settings. In setting 1, John and Veronica each do half of each task. In setting 2, John only mows the lawn and Veronica only cleans the house.

In setting 1, John spends 60 minutes cleaning half of the house and 25 minutes mowing half of the lawn for a total of 85 minutes; Veronica spends 30 minutes cleaning half of the house and 50 minutes mowing half of the lawn for a total of 80 minutes. The total time spent by Veronica and John cleaning the house and mowing the lawn is 165 minutes.

In setting 2, John spends 50 minutes mowing the lawn, and Veronica spends 60 minutes cleaning the house. The total time spent by Veronica and John cleaning the house and mowing the lawn is 110 minutes.

In which setting, 1 or 2, are Veronica and John better off? John works 85 minutes in setting 1 and 50 minutes in setting 2, so he is better off in setting 2. Veronica works 80 minutes in setting 1 and 60 minutes in setting 2, so Veronica is better off in setting 2. Together, John and Veronica spend 55 fewer minutes in setting 2 than in setting 1. Getting the job done in 55 fewer minutes is the benefit of specializing in various duties around the house. Given our numbers, we would expect that John will mow the lawn (and nothing else) and Veronica will clean the house (and nothing else).

between the two countries and the more he shuffles goods between countries, the more profit Henri earns.

Second, Henri's activities are moving each country toward its comparative advantage. The United States ends up exporting beef to France, and France ends up exporting perfume to the United States. Just as the pure theory predicts, individuals in the two countries specialize in and trade the good in which they have a comparative advantage. The outcome is brought about spontaneously through the actions of individuals trying to make themselves better off; they are simply trying to gain through trade.

SELF-TEST

(Answers to Self-Test questions are in the Self-Test Appendix.)

1. Suppose the United States can produce 120 units of *X* at an opportunity cost of 20 units of *Y*, and Great Britain can produce 40 units of *X* at an opportunity cost of 80 units of *Y*. Identify favorable terms of trade for the two countries.

2. If a country can produce more of all goods than any other country, would it benefit from specializing and trading? Explain your answer.

3. Do government officials analyze data to determine what their country can produce at a comparative advantage?

Trade Restrictions

International trade theory shows that countries gain from free international trade—that is, from specializing in the production of the goods in which they have a comparative advantage and trading these goods for other goods. In the real world, however, there are numerous types of trade restrictions, which raise the question: If countries gain from international trade, why are there trade restrictions?

The answer to this question requires an analysis of costs and benefits; specifically, we need to determine who benefits and who loses when trade is restricted. But first, we need to discuss some pertinent background information.

The Distributional Effects of International Trade

The previous section explained that specialization and international trade benefit individuals in different countries. But this benefit occurs on net. Every individual person may not gain.

To illustrate, suppose Pam Dickson lives and works in the United States making clock radios. She produces and sells 12,000 clock radios per year at a price of $40 each. As the situation stands, there is no international trade. Individuals in other countries who make clock radios do not sell their clock radios in the United States.

Then one day, the U.S. market is opened to clock radios from China. It appears that the Chinese manufacturers have a comparative advantage in the production of clock radios. They sell their clock radios in the United States for $25 each. Pam realizes that she cannot compete at this price. Her sales drop to such a degree that she goes out of business. Thus, the introduction of international trade in this instance has harmed Pam personally.

The example of Pam Dickson raises the issue of the distributional effects of free trade. The benefits of international trade are not equally distributed to all individuals in the population. The topics of consumers' and producers' surplus are relevant to our analysis.

Consumers' and Producers' Surplus

The concepts of consumers' and producers' surplus were first discussed in Chapter 3. We review them briefly in this section.

Consumers' surplus is the difference between the maximum price a buyer is willing and able to pay for a good or service and the price actually paid.

Consumers' surplus = Maximum buying price − Price paid

Consumers' surplus is a dollar measure of the benefit gained by being able to purchase a unit of a good for less than one is willing to pay for it. For example, if Yakov would have paid $10 to see the movie at the Cinemax but paid only $4, his consumer surplus is $6. Consumers' surplus is the consumers' net gain from trade.

Producers' surplus (or sellers' surplus) is the difference between the price sellers receive for a good and the minimum or lowest price for which they would have sold the good.

Producers' surplus = Price received – Minimum selling price

Producers' surplus is a dollar measure of the benefit gained by being able to sell a unit of output for more than one is willing to sell it. For example, if Joan sold her knit sweaters for $24 each but would have sold them for as low as (but no lower than) $14 each, her producer surplus is $10 per sweater. Producers' surplus is the producers' net gain from trade.

Both consumers' and producers' surplus are represented in Exhibit 3. In part (a), consumers' surplus is represented by the shaded triangle. This triangle includes the area under the demand curve and above the equilibrium price. In part (b), producers' surplus is represented by the shaded triangle. This triangle includes the area above the supply curve and under the equilibrium price.

The Benefits and Costs of Trade Restrictions

There are numerous ways to restrict international trade. Tariffs and quotas are two of the more commonly used methods. We discuss these two methods using the tools of supply and demand. We concentrate on two groups: U.S. consumers and U.S. producers.

TARIFFS A **tariff** is a tax on imports. The primary effect of a tariff is to raise the price of the imported good for the domestic consumer. Exhibit 4 illustrates the effects of a tariff on cars imported into the United States.

The world price for cars is P_W, as shown in Exhibit 4(a). At this price in the domestic (U.S.) market, U.S. consumers buy Q_2 cars, as shown in part (b). They buy Q_1 from U.S. producers and the difference between Q_2 and Q_1 ($Q_2 - Q_1$) from foreign producers. In other words, U.S. imports at P_W are $Q_2 - Q_1$.

What are consumers' and producers' surplus in this situation? Consumers' surplus is the area under the demand curve and above the world price, P_W. This is areas 1 + 2 +

Tariff
A tax on imports.

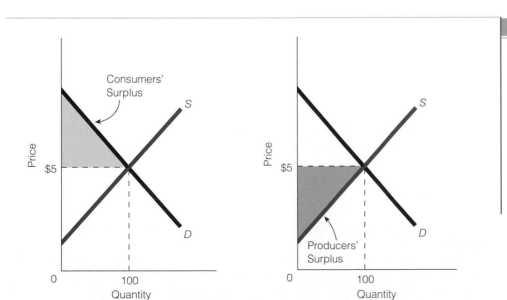

exhibit **3**

Consumers' and Producers' Surplus

(a) Consumers' surplus. As the shaded area indicates, the difference between the maximum or highest amount consumers would be willing to pay and the price they actually pay is consumers' surplus. (b) Producers' surplus. As the shaded area indicates, the difference between the price sellers receive for the good and the minimum or lowest price they would be willing to sell the good for is producers' surplus.

	Consumers' Surplus	Producers' Surplus	Government Tariff Revenue
Free trade (No tariff)	1 + 2 + 3 + 4 + 5 + 6	7	None
Tariff	1 + 2	3 + 7	5
Loss or Gain	− (3 + 4 + 5 + 6)	+3	+5
Result of Tariff = Loss to consumers + Gain to producers + Tariff revenue = − (3 + 4 + 5 + 6) +3 +5 = − (4 + 6)			

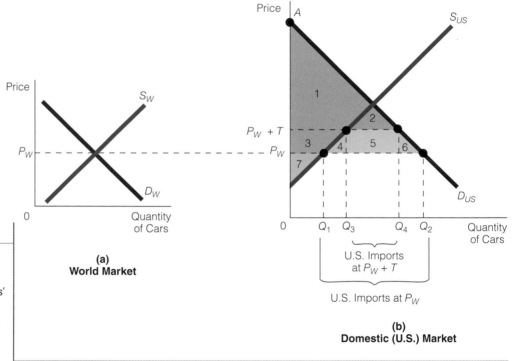

exhibit 4

The Effects of a Tariff

A tariff raises the price of cars from P_W to $P_W + T$, decreases consumers' surplus, increases producers' surplus, and generates tariff revenue. Because consumers lose more than producers and government gain, there is a net loss due to the tariff.

(a)
World Market

(b)
Domestic (U.S.) Market

3 + 4 + 5 + 6. Producers' surplus is the area above the supply curve and below the world price, P_W. This is area 7 (see Exhibit 4(b)).

Now suppose a tariff is imposed. The price for imported cars in the U.S. market rises to $P_W + T$ (the world price plus the tariff). At this price, U.S. consumers buy Q_4 cars: Q_3 from U.S. producers and $Q_4 − Q_3$ from foreign producers. U.S. imports are $Q_4 − Q_3$, which is a smaller number of imports than at the pretariff price. An effect of tariffs, then, is to reduce imports. What are consumers' and producers' surplus equal to after the tariff has been imposed? At price $P_W + T$, consumers' surplus is areas 1 + 2 and producers' surplus is areas 3 + 7.

Notice that consumers receive more consumers' surplus when tariffs do not exist and less when they do exist. In our example, consumers received areas 1 + 2 + 3 + 4 + 5 + 6 in consumers' surplus when the tariff did not exist but only areas 1 + 2 when the tariff did exist. Because of the tariff, consumers' surplus was reduced by an amount equal to areas 3 + 4 + 5 + 6.

Producers, though, receive less producers' surplus when tariffs do not exist and more when they do exist. In our example, producers received producers' surplus equal to area 7 when the tariff did not exist, but they received producers' surplus equal to areas 3 + 7 with the tariff. Because of the tariff, producers' surplus increased by an amount equal to area 3.

The government collects tariff revenue equal to area 5. This area is obtained by multiplying the number of imports $(Q_4 - Q_3)$ by the tariff, which is the difference between $P_W + T$ and P_W.[1]

In conclusion, the effects of the tariff are a decrease in consumers' surplus, an increase in producers' surplus, and tariff revenue for government. Because the loss to consumers (areas $3 + 4 + 5 + 6$) is greater than the gain to producers (area 3) plus the gain to government (area 5), it follows that *a tariff results in a net loss*. The net loss is areas $4 + 6$.

QUOTAS A **quota** is a legal limit on the amount of a good that may be imported. For example, the government may decide to allow no more than 100,000 foreign cars to be imported, or 10 million barrels of OPEC oil, or 30,000 Japanese television sets. A quota reduces the supply of a good and raises the price of imported goods for domestic consumers (Exhibit 5).

Quota

A legal limit on the amount of a good that may be imported.

---

[1]For example, if the tariff is $100 and the number of imports is 50,000, then the tariff revenue is $5 million.

exhibit **5**

The Effects of a Quota

A quota that sets the legal limit of imports at $Q_4 - Q_3$ causes the price of cars to increase from P_W to P_Q. A quota raises price, decreases consumers' surplus, increases producers' surplus, and increases the total revenue importers earn. Because consumers lose more than producers and importers gain, there is a net loss due to the quota.

	Consumers' Surplus	Producers' Surplus	Revenue of Importers
Free trade (No quota)	$1 + 2 + 3 + 4 + 5 + 6$	7	8
Quota	$1 + 2$	$3 + 7$	$5 + 8$
Loss or Gain	$-(3 + 4 + 5 + 6)$	$+3$	$+5$

Result of Quota = Loss to consumers + Gain to producers + Gain to importers
$= -(3 + 4 + 5 + 6)$ $+3$ $+5$
$= -(4 + 6)$

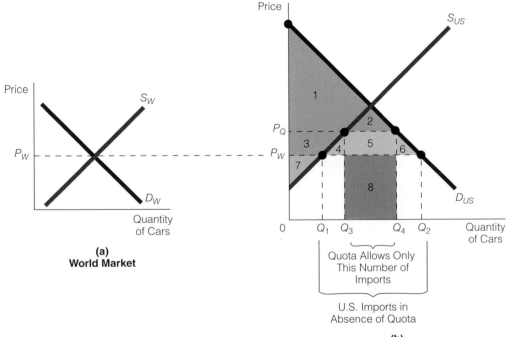

(a)
World Market

(b)
Domestic (U.S.) Market

Quota Allows Only This Number of Imports

U.S. Imports in Absence of Quota

Once again, we consider the situation in the U.S. car market. At a price of P_W (established in the world market for cars), U.S. consumers buy Q_1 cars from U.S. producers and $Q_2 - Q_1$ cars from foreign producers. Consumers' surplus is equal to areas $1 + 2 + 3 + 4 + 5 + 6$. Producers' surplus is equal to area 7.

Suppose now that the U.S. government sets a quota equal to $Q_4 - Q_3$. Because this is the number of foreign cars U.S. consumers imported when the tariff was imposed (see Exhibit 4), the price of cars rises to P_Q in Exhibit 5 (which is equal to $P_W + T$ in Exhibit 4). At P_Q, consumers' surplus is equal to areas $1 + 2$ and producers' surplus is areas $3 + 7$. The decrease in consumers' surplus due to the quota is equal to areas $3 + 4 + 5 + 6$; the increase in producers' surplus is equal to area 3.

But what about area 5? Is this area transferred to government, as was the case when a tariff was imposed? No, it isn't. This area represents the additional revenue earned by the importers (and sellers) of $Q_4 - Q_3$. Look at it this way: Before the quota, importers were importing $Q_2 - Q_1$, but only part of this total amount, or $Q_4 - Q_3$, is relevant here. Only $Q_4 - Q_3$ is relevant because this is the amount of imports now that the quota has been established. So what dollar amount did the importers receive for $Q_4 - Q_3$ before the quota was established? The answer is $P_W \times (Q_4 - Q_3)$, or area 8. Because of the quota, the price rises to P_Q and they now receive $P_Q \times (Q_4 - Q_3)$, or areas $5 + 8$. The difference between the total revenues on $Q_4 - Q_3$ with a quota and without a quota is area 5.

In conclusion, the effects of a quota are a decrease in consumers' surplus, an increase in producers' surplus, and an increase in total revenue for the importers who sell the allowed number of imported units. Because the loss to consumers (areas $3 + 4 + 5 + 6$) is greater than the increase in producers' surplus (area 3) plus the gain to importers (area 5), there is a *net loss as a result of the quota*. The net loss is equal to areas $4 + 6$.[2]

If Free Trade Results in Net Gain, Why Do Nations Sometimes Restrict Trade?

Based on the analysis in this chapter so far, the case for free trade (no tariffs or quotas) appears to be a strong one. The case for free trade has not gone unchallenged, however. Some persons maintain that at certain times, free trade should be restricted or suspended. In almost all cases, they argue that it is in the best interest of the public or country as a whole to do so. In short, they advance a public interest argument. Other persons contend that the public interest argument is only superficial; down deep, they say, it is a special interest argument clothed in pretty words. As you might guess, the debate between the two groups is often heated.

The following sections describe some arguments that have been advanced for trade restrictions.

THE NATIONAL-DEFENSE ARGUMENT It is often stated that certain industries—such as aircraft, petroleum, chemicals, and weapons—are necessary to the national defense. Suppose the United States has a comparative advantage in the production of wheat and country X has a comparative advantage in the production of weapons. Should the United States

---

[2]It is perhaps incorrect to imply that government receives nothing from a quota. Although it receives nothing directly, it may gain indirectly. Economists generally argue that because government officials are likely to be the persons who will decide which importers will get to satisfy the quota, they will naturally be lobbied by importers. Thus, government officials will likely receive something, if only dinner at an expensive restaurant while the lobbyist makes his or her pitch. In short, in the course of the lobbying, resources will be spent by lobbyists as they curry favor with government officials or politicians who have the power to decide who gets to sell the limited number of imported goods. In economics, lobbyists' activities geared toward obtaining a special privilege are referred to as rent seeking.

© STR/AFP/GETTY IMAGES

economics 24/7

OFFSHORE OUTSOURCING, OR OFFSHORING

Outsourcing is the term used to describe work done for a company by another company or by people other than the original company's employees. It entails purchasing a product or process from an outside supplier rather than producing this product or process in house. To illustrate, suppose company X has, in the past, hired employees for personnel, accounting, and payroll services within the company. Currently, though, it has these duties performed by a company in another state. Company X, then, has outsourced certain work activities.

When a company outsources certain work activities to individuals in another country, it is said to be engaged in offshore outsourcing, or *offshoring*. Consider a few examples. A New York securities firm replaces 800 software engineering employees with a team of software engineers in India. A computer company replaces 200 on-call technicians in its headquarters in Texas with 150 on-call technicians in India.

The benefits of offshoring for a U.S. firm are obvious; it pays lower wages to individuals in other countries for the same work that U.S. employees do for higher wages. Benefits also flow to the employees hired in the foreign countries. The costs of offshoring are said to fall on persons who lose their jobs as a result, such as the software engineer in New York or the on-call computer technician in Texas. Some have argued that offshoring will soon become a major political issue and that it could bring with it a wave of protectionism.

There is no doubt that there will be both proponents of and opponents to offshoring. But what are the effects of offshoring on net? Are there more benefits than costs or more costs than benefits? Consider a U.S. company that currently employs Jones as a software engineer, paying her $\$X$ a year. Then, one day, the company tells Jones that it has to let her go; it is replacing her with a software engineer in India who will work for $\$Z$ a year (where $\$Z$ is less than $\$X$).

Now some have asked why Jones doesn't simply say that she will work for $\$Z$. That is, why doesn't she offer to work for the same wage as that agreed to by the Indian software engineer? The obvious answer is because Jones can work elsewhere for some wage between $\$X$ and $\$Z$. Assume this wage is $\$Y$. Thus, while offshoring has moved Jones from earning $\$X$ to earning $\$Y$, $\$Y$ is still more than $\$Z$.

In short, the U.S. company is able to lower its costs from $\$X$ to $\$Z$, and Jones's income falls from $\$X$ to $\$Y$. Notice that the U.S. company lowers its costs more than Jones's income falls. That's because the difference between $\$X$ and $\$Z$ is greater than the difference between $\$X$ and $\$Y$.

If the U.S. company operates within a competitive environment, its lower costs will shift its supply curve to the right and end up lowering prices. In other words, offshoring can end up reducing prices for U.S. consumers. The political fallout from offshoring might, in the end, depend on how visible to the average American the employment effects of offshoring are relative to the price reduction effects.

specialize in the production of wheat and then trade wheat to country X in exchange for weapons? Many Americans would answer no. It is too dangerous, they maintain, to leave weapons production to another country.

The national-defense argument may have some validity. But even valid arguments may be abused. Industries that are not really necessary to the national defense may maintain otherwise. In the past, the national-defense argument has been used by some firms in the following industries: pens, pottery, peanuts, papers, candles, thumbtacks, tuna fishing, and pencils.

THE INFANT-INDUSTRY ARGUMENT Alexander Hamilton, the first U.S. secretary of the treasury, argued that "infant," or new, industries often need protection from older, established foreign competitors until they are mature enough to compete on an equal basis. Today, some persons voice the same argument. The infant-industry argument is clearly an argument for temporary protection. Critics charge, however, that after an industry is protected from foreign competition, removing the protection is almost impossible. The once infant industry will continue to maintain that it isn't old enough to go it alone. Critics of the infant-industry argument say that political realities make it unlikely that a benefit once bestowed will be removed.

Finally, the infant-industry argument, like the national-defense argument, may be abused. It may well be that all new industries, whether they could currently compete successfully with foreign producers or not, would argue for protection on infant-industry grounds.

Dumping

The sale of goods abroad at a price below their cost and below the price charged in the domestic market.

THE ANTIDUMPING ARGUMENT Dumping is the sale of goods abroad at a price below their cost and below the price charged in the domestic market. If a French firm sells wine in the United States for a price below the cost of producing the wine and below the price charged in France, it is said to be dumping wine in the United States. Critics of dumping maintain that it is an unfair trade practice that puts domestic producers of substitute goods at a disadvantage.

In addition, critics charge that dumpers seek only to penetrate a market and drive out domestic competitors; then they will raise prices. However, some economists point to the infeasibility of this strategy. After the dumpers have driven out their competition and raised prices, their competition is likely to return. The dumpers, in turn, would have obtained only a string of losses (owing to their selling below cost) for their efforts. Opponents of the antidumping argument also point out that domestic consumers benefit from dumping because they pay lower prices.

THE FOREIGN-EXPORT-SUBSIDIES ARGUMENT Some governments subsidize the firms that export goods. If a country offers a below-market (interest rate) loan to a company, it is often argued that the government subsidizes the production of the good the firm produces. If, in turn, the firm exports the good to a foreign country, that country's producers of substitute goods call foul. They complain that the foreign firm has been given an unfair advantage that they should be protected against.[3]

Others say that one should not turn one's back on a gift (in the form of lower prices). If foreign governments want to subsidize their exports, and thus give a gift to foreign consumers at the expense of their own taxpayers, then the recipients should not complain. Of course, the recipients are usually not the ones who are complaining. Usually, the ones complaining are the domestic producers who can't sell their goods at as high a price because of the gift domestic consumers are receiving from foreign governments.

THE LOW-FOREIGN-WAGES ARGUMENT It is sometimes argued that American producers can't compete with foreign producers because American producers pay high wages to their workers and foreign producers pay low wages to their workers. The American producers insist that international trade must be restricted or they will be ruined. However, the argument overlooks the reason American wages are high and foreign wages are low in the first place: productivity. High productivity and high wages are usually linked, as are low productivity and low wages. If an American worker, who receives $20 per hour, can produce (on average) 100 units of X per hour, working with numerous capital goods, then the cost per unit may be lower than when a foreign worker, who receives $2 per hour, produces (on average) 5 units of X per hour, working by hand. In short, a coun-

---

[3]Words are important in this debate. For example, domestic producers who claim that foreign governments have subsidized foreign firms say that they are not asking for *economic protectionism,* but only *retaliation,* or *reciprocity,* or simply *tit-for-tat*—words that have less negative connotation than the words their opponents use.

try's high-wage disadvantage may be offset by its productivity advantage; a country's low-wage advantage may be offset by its productivity disadvantage. High wages do not necessarily mean high costs when productivity (and the costs of nonlabor resources) is included.

THE SAVING-DOMESTIC-JOBS ARGUMENT Sometimes, the argument against completely free trade is made in terms of saving domestic jobs. Actually, we have already discussed this argument in its different guises. For example, the low-foreign-wages argument is one form of it. That argument continues along this line: If domestic producers cannot compete with foreign producers because foreign producers pay low wages and domestic producers pay high wages, domestic producers will go out of business and domestic jobs will be lost. The foreign-export-subsidies argument is another form of this argument. Its proponents generally state that if foreign-government subsidies give a competitive edge to foreign producers, not only will domestic producers fail, but as a result of their failure, domestic jobs will be lost. Critics of the saving-domestic-jobs argument (in all its guises) often argue that if a domestic producer is being outcompeted by foreign producers and domestic jobs in a particular industry are being lost as a result, the world market is signaling that those labor resources could be put to better use in an industry in which the country holds a comparative advantage.

The World Trade Organization (WTO)

The international trade organization, the *World Trade Organization (WTO),* came into existence on January 1, 1995. It is the successor to the General Agreement on Tariffs and Trade (GATT), which was set up in 1947. In mid-2006, 149 countries in the world were members of the WTO.

According to the WTO, its "overriding objective is to help trade flow smoothly, freely, fairly, and predictably." It does this by administering trade agreements, acting as a forum for trade negotiations, settling trade disputes, reviewing national trade policies, assisting developing countries in trade policy issues, and cooperating with other international organizations. Perhaps its most useful and controversial role is adjudicating trade disputes. For example, suppose the United States claims that the Canadian government is preventing U.S. producers from openly selling their goods in Canada. The WTO will look at the matter, consult with trade experts, and then decide the issue. A country that is found engaging in unfair trade can either desist from this practice or face appropriate retaliation from the injured country.

In theory, at least, the WTO is supposed to lead to freer international trade, and there is some evidence that it has done just this. The critics of the WTO often say that it has achieved this objective at some cost to a nation's sovereignty. For example, in the past, some of the trade disputes between the United States and other countries have been decided against the United States.

Also, some of the critics of the WTO often argue that the member countries often put trade issues above environmental issues and do not do enough to help the poor in the world. In the past, some of the critics of the WTO have taken to the streets to demonstrate against it. In a few cases, riots have broken out.

Thinking like **AN ECONOMIST** *International trade often becomes a battleground between economics and politics. The simple tools of supply and demand and consumers' and producers' surplus show that there are net gains from free trade. On the whole, tariffs and quotas make living standards lower than they would be if free trade were permitted.*

On the other side, though, are the realities of business and politics. Domestic producers may advocate quotas and tariffs to make themselves better off, giving little thought to the negative effects felt by foreign producers or domestic consumers.

Perhaps the battle over international trade comes down to this: Policies are largely advocated, argued, and lobbied for based more on their distributional effects than on their aggregate or overall effects. On an aggregate level, free trade produces a net gain for society, whereas restricted trade produces a net loss. But economists understand that just because free trade in the aggregate produces a net gain, it does not necessarily follow that every single person benefits more from free trade than from restricted trade. We have just shown how a subset of the population (producers) gains more, in a particular instance, from restricted trade than from free trade. In short, economists realize that the crucial question in determining real-world policies is more often "How does it affect me?" than "How does it affect us?"

SELF-TEST

1. Who benefits and who loses from tariffs? Explain your answer.

2. Identify the directional change in consumers' surplus and producers' surplus when we move from free trade to tariffs. Is the change in consumers' surplus greater than, less than, or equal to the change in producers' surplus?

3. What is a major difference between the effects of a quota and the effects of a tariff?

4. Outline the details of the infant-industry argument for trade restriction.

𝒜 𝓡𝑒𝒶𝒹𝑒𝓇 𝒜𝓈𝓀𝓈 . . .

Why Does the Government Impose Tariffs and Quotas?

If tariffs and quotas result in higher prices for U.S. consumers, then why does the government impose them?

The answer is that government is sometimes more responsive to producer interests than to consumer interests. But then, we have to wonder why. To explain, consider the following example.

Suppose there are 100 U.S. producers of good X and 20 million U.S. consumers of good X. The producers want to protect themselves from foreign competition, so they lobby for and receive a quota on foreign goods that compete with good X. As a result, consumers must pay higher prices. For simplicity's sake, let's say that consumers must pay $40 million more. Thus, producers receive $40 million more for good X than they would have if the quota had not been imposed.

If the $40 million received is divided equally among the 100 producers, each producer receives $400,000 more as a result of the quota. If the additional $40 million paid is divided equally among the 20 million consumers, each customer pays $2 more as a result of the quota.

A producer is likely to think, "I should lobby for the quota because if I'm effective, I'll receive $400,000." A consumer is likely to think, "Why should I lobby against the quota? If I'm effective, I'll only save $2. Saving $2 isn't worth the time and trouble my lobbying would take."

In short, the benefits of quotas are concentrated on relatively few producers, and the costs of quotas are spread out over relatively many consumers. This makes each producer's gain relatively large compared with each consumer's loss. We predict that producers will lobby government to obtain the relatively large gains from quotas but that consumers will not lobby government to keep from paying the small additional cost due to quotas.

Politicians are in the awkward position of hearing from people who want the quotas but not hearing from people who are against them. It is likely the politicians will respond to the vocal interests. Politicians may mistakenly assume that consumers' silence means that the consumers accept the quota policy, when in fact they may not. Consumers may simply not find it worthwhile to do anything to fight the policy.

! analyzing the scene

How will a tariff help the domestic steel company?

The domestic steel company gains producers' surplus from a tariff, government gains tariff revenue, and consumers lose consumers' surplus. More important, consumers lose more than what producers and government gain. It is sometimes thought that private producers are always promarket. Not so. A domestic company is often better off operating in an environment where its foreign competition has been stifled (as is the case through tariffs).

Do increased numbers of immigrants lower wages?

Some residents of the United States argue that increased immigration will cause wages in the United States to decline. Their argument is based on simple supply-and-demand analysis: Increased immigration leads to a greater supply of workers and lower wages.

There is little doubt that increased immigration will affect the supply of labor in the country. But it will affect the demand for labor too. The demand for labor is a derived demand—derived from the demand for the product that labor produces. With increased immigration, there will be more people living in the United States. A larger population translates into higher demand for food, housing, clothes, entertainment services, and so on. A higher demand for these goods translates into a higher demand for the workers who produce these goods.

In summary, increased immigration will affect both the supply of and demand for labor. What will be the effect on wages? It depends on whether the increase in demand is greater than, less than, or equal to the increase in supply.

If demand increases by more than supply, wages will rise; if supply increases by more than demand, wages will fall; if demand rises by the same amount as supply rises, wages will not change.

Is economics nothing more than "good ol' common sense"?

Many people think economics requires only common sense. But common sense often leads us to accept what sounds reasonable and sensible, and much in economics is counterintuitive—that is, it is different from what we might expect. Consider the discussion of comparative advantage. One country—the United States—is better than another country—Japan—at producing both food and clothing. Common sense might lead us to conclude that because the United States is better than Japan at producing both food and clothing, the United States could not gain by specializing and trading with Japan. But our analysis shows differently. For many people, that conclusion is counterintuitive; it goes against what intuition or good ol' common sense indicates.

chapter summary

Specialization and Trade

- A country has a comparative advantage in the production of a good if it can produce the good at a lower opportunity cost than another country can.

- Individuals in countries that specialize and trade have a higher standard of living than would be the case if their countries did not specialize and trade.

- Government officials do not analyze cost data to determine what their country should specialize in and trade. Instead, the desire to earn a dollar, peso, or euro guides individuals' actions and produces the unintended consequence that countries specialize in and trade the good(s) in which they have a comparative advantage. However, trade restrictions can change this outcome.

Tariffs and Quotas

- A tariff is a tax on imports. A quota is a legal limit on the amount of a good that may be imported.

- Both tariffs and quotas raise the price of imports.

- Tariffs lead to a decrease in consumers' surplus, an increase in producers' surplus, and tariff revenue for the government. Consumers lose more through tariffs than producers and government (together) gain.

- Quotas lead to a decrease in consumers' surplus, an increase in producers' surplus, and additional revenue for the importers who sell the amount specified by the

quota. Consumers lose more through quotas than producers and importers (together) gain.

Arguments for Trade Restrictions

- The national-defense argument states that certain goods—such as aircraft, petroleum, chemicals, and weapons—are necessary to the national defense and should be produced domestically whether the country has a comparative advantage in their production or not.

- The infant-industry argument states that "infant," or new, industries should be protected from free (foreign) trade so that they may have time to develop and compete on an equal basis with older, more established foreign industries.

- The antidumping argument states that domestic producers should not have to compete (on an unequal basis) with foreign producers that sell products below cost and below the prices they charge in their domestic markets.

- The foreign-export-subsidies argument states that domestic producers should not have to compete (on an unequal basis) with foreign producers that have been subsidized by their governments.

- The low-foreign-wages argument states that domestic producers cannot compete with foreign producers that pay low wages to their employees when domestic producers pay high wages to their employees. For high-paying domestic firms to survive, limits on free trade are proposed.

- The saving-domestic-jobs argument states that through low foreign wages or government subsidies (or dumping etc.), foreign producers will be able to outcompete domestic producers, and therefore, domestic jobs will be

lost. For domestic firms to survive and domestic jobs not to be lost, limits on free trade are proposed.

- Everyone does not accept the arguments for trade restrictions as valid. Critics often maintain that the arguments can be and are abused and, in most cases, are motivated by self-interest.

key terms and concepts

Comparative Advantage

Tariff

Quota

Dumping

questions and problems

1   Although a production possibilities frontier is usually drawn for a country, one could be drawn for the world. Picture the world's production possibilities frontier. Is the world positioned at a point on the PPF or below it? Give a reason for your answer.

2   "Whatever can be done by a tariff can be done by a quota." Discuss.

3   Consider two groups of domestic producers: those that compete with imports and those that export goods. Suppose the domestic producers that compete with imports convince the legislature to impose a high tariff on imports—so high, in fact, that almost all imports are eliminated. Does this policy in any way adversely affect domestic producers that export goods? If so, how?

4   Suppose the U.S. government wants to curtail imports. Would it be likely to favor a tariff or a quota to accomplish its objective? Why?

5   Suppose the landmass known to you as the United States of America had been composed, since the nation's founding, of separate countries instead of separate states. Would you expect the standard of living of the people who inhabit this landmass to be higher, lower, or equal to what it is today? Why?

6   Even though Jeremy is a better gardener and novelist than Bill is, Jeremy still hires Bill as his gardener. Why?

7   Suppose a constitutional convention was called tomorrow, and you were chosen as one of the delegates from your state. You and the other delegates must decide whether it will be constitutional or unconstitutional for the federal government to impose tariffs and quotas or restrict international trade in any way. What would be your position?

8   Some economists have argued that because domestic consumers gain more from free trade than domestic producers gain from (import) tariffs and quotas, consumers should buy out domestic producers and rid themselves of costly tariffs and quotas. For example, if consumers save $400 million from free trade (through paying lower prices) and producers gain $100 million from tariffs and quotas, consumers can pay producers something more than $100 million but less than $400 million and get producers to favor free trade too. Assuming this scheme were feasible, what do you think of it?

9   If there is a net loss to society from tariffs, why do tariffs exist?

working with numbers and graphs

1   Using the data in the table, answer the following questions: (a) For which good does Canada have a comparative advantage? (b) For which good does Italy have a comparative advantage? (c) What might be a set of favorable terms of trade for the two countries? (d) Prove that both countries would be better off in the specialization–trade case than in the no specialization–no trade case.

Points on Production Possibilities Frontier	Canada		Italy	
	Good *X*	Good *Y*	Good *X*	Good *Y*
A	150	0	90	0
B	100	25	60	60
C	50	50	30	120
D	0	75	0	180

2   In the following figure, P_W is the world price and $P_W + T$ is the world price plus a tariff. Identify the following:

a   The level of imports at P_W
b   The level of imports at $P_W + T$
c   The loss in consumers' surplus as a result of a tariff
d   The gain in producers' surplus as a result of a tariff
e   The tariff revenue as the result of a tariff
f   The net loss to society as a result of a tariff
g   The net benefit to society of moving from a tariff situation to a no-tariff situation

International Finance

Setting the Scene

The following events occurred on a day in December.

12:01 P.M.

Karen Sullivan is packing for a trip. Tomorrow, at 7:05 A.M., she'll be on a plane headed for London. She'll spend five days in London and then go to Oxford, where she'll spend two days. Then she'll board a train for Scotland and spend four days in Edinburgh. After Edinburgh, she'll head back down to England and spend a day in Harrogate, two days in Birmingham, and finally, two days in Cambridge. She's been saving for this trip for three years, and even though the dollar has been falling relative to the pound, she's still going on the trip.

1:56 P.M.

Robert Ivans owns a furniture business in North Carolina. In a given year, he exports 25 percent of the furniture he produces. This year, he expects his export business will boom because the U.S. dollar is falling in value. In fact, in four minutes, he'll begin to interview individuals for two new positions in his company.

3:06 P.M.

Winona Murphy-Collins, a business columnist for a local newspaper, just wrote the following headline: U.S. Balance of Payments at Record High.

6:11 P.M.

The president of the United States is speaking with one of his economic advisors. The advisor is telling the president that the recent run of big budget deficits is likely to affect interest rates, the value of the dollar, exports and imports, and the merchandise trade balance. The president looks at the economic advisor for a few seconds and then says, "I didn't realize things were so interconnected when it comes to the economy."

? Here are some questions to keep in mind as you read this chapter:

- *What does the value of the dollar have to do with Karen's trip?*

- *What does the value of the dollar have to do with Robert Ivans's business?*

- *Is anything wrong with the headline that the business columnist wrote?*

- *Do big budget deficits really affect as many things as the president's economic advisor indicates?*

See analyzing the scene at the end of this chapter for answers to these questions.

The Balance of Payments

Countries keep track of their domestic level of production by calculating their gross domestic product (GDP). Similarly, they keep track of the flow of their international trade (receipts and expenditures) by calculating their balance of payments.

The **balance of payments** is a periodic statement (usually annual) of the money value of all transactions between residents of one country and residents of all other countries. The balance of payments provides information about a nation's imports and exports, domestic residents' earnings on assets located abroad, foreign earnings on domestic assets, gifts to and from foreign countries (including foreign aid), and official transactions by governments and central banks.

Balance of payments accounts record both debits and credits. A debit is indicated by a minus (–) sign, and a credit is indicated by a plus (+) sign. *Any transaction that supplies the country's currency in the foreign exchange market is recorded as a* **debit**. (The **foreign exchange market** is the market in which currencies of different countries are exchanged.) For example, suppose a U.S. retailer wants to buy Japanese television sets so that he can sell them in his stores in the United States. To buy the TV sets from the Japanese, the retailer first has to supply U.S. dollars (in the foreign exchange market) in return for Japanese yen. Then he will turn over the yen to the Japanese in exchange for the television sets.

Any transaction that creates a demand for the country's currency in the foreign exchange market is recorded as a **credit**. For example, suppose a Russian retailer wants to buy computers from U.S. computer producers. Can she pay the U.S. producers in Russian rubles? Probably not; U.S. producers want U.S. dollars. So the Russian retailer must supply rubles (in the foreign exchange market) in return for dollars. Then she will turn over the dollars to the U.S. producers in exchange for the computers. Exhibit 1 presents a summary of debits and credits.

The international transactions that occur, and that are summarized in the balance of payments, can be grouped into three categories, or three accounts—the current account, the capital account, and the official reserve account—and a statistical discrepancy. Exhibit 2 illustrates a U.S. balance of payments account for year Z. The data in the exhibit are hypothetical (to make the calculations simpler) but not unrealistic. In this section, we describe and explain each of the items in the balance of payments using the data in Exhibit 2 for our calculations.

Balance of Payments

A periodic statement (usually annual) of the money value of all transactions between residents of one country and residents of all other countries.

Debit

In the balance of payments, any transaction that supplies the country's currency in the foreign exchange market.

Foreign Exchange Market

The market in which currencies of different countries are exchanged.

Credit

In the balance of payments, any transaction that creates a demand for the country's currency in the foreign exchange market.

Q&A

When Americans buy Japanese goods, they supply dollars and demand yen. When the Japanese buy American goods, they supply yen and demand dollars. Thus, the first transaction is recorded as a debit (it supplies U.S. currency), and the second transaction is recorded as a credit (it increases demand for U.S. currency) in the U.S. balance of payments. Is this correct?

Yes, that is correct.

exhibit **1**

Debits and Credits

Item	Definition	Example
Debit (−)	Any transaction that supplies the country's currency.	Jim, an American, supplies dollars in exchange for yen so that he can use the yen to buy Japanese goods.
Credit (+)	Any transaction that creates a demand for the country's currency.	Svetlana, who is Russian and living in Russia, supplies rubles in order to demand dollars so that she can use the dollars to buy U.S. goods.

CURRENT ACCOUNT

1. EXPORTS OF GOODS AND SERVICES   +340
   a. Merchandise exports (including military sales)   +220
   b. Services   +30
   c. Income from U.S. assets abroad   +90

2. IMPORTS OF GOODS AND SERVICES   −390
   a. Merchandise imports (including military purchases)   −300
   b. Services   −40
   c. Income from foreign assets in U.S.   −50

Merchandise Trade Balance
Difference between value of merchandise exports (item 1a)
and value of merchandise imports (item 2a): +220 − 300 = −80

3. NET UNILATERAL TRANSFERS ABROAD   −11

Current Account Balance
Items 1, 2, 3: +340 − 390 − 11 =   −61

CAPITAL ACCOUNT

4. OUTFLOW OF U.S. CAPITAL   −16
5. INFLOW OF FOREIGN CAPITAL   +60

Capital Account Balance
Items 4 and 5: −16 + 60 =   +44

OFFICIAL RESERVE ACCOUNT

6. INCREASE (−) IN U.S. OFFICIAL RESERVE ASSETS   −4
7. INCREASE (+) IN FOREIGN OFFICIAL ASSETS IN U.S.   +3

Official Reserve Balance
Items 6 and 7: −4 + 3 =   −1

STATISTICAL DISCREPANCY   +18

TOTAL $0 $0
(always zero)

BALANCE OF PAYMENTS =

Summary statistic of all ◇ items (items 1–7 and the statistical discrepancy)

+$340 − $390 − $11 − $16 + $60 − $4 + $3 + $18 = $0

or

Summary statistic of all ▪ items (current account balance, capital account balance, official reserve balance, and the statistical discrepancy)

−$61 + $44 − $1 + $18 = $0

Note: The pluses (+) and the minuses (−) in the exhibit serve two purposes. First, they distinguish between credits and debits. A plus is always placed before a credit, and a minus is always placed before a debit. Second, in terms of the calculations, the pluses and minuses are viewed as operational signs. In other words, if a number has a plus in front of it, it is added to the total. If a number has a minus in front of it, it is subtracted from the total.

exhibit **2**

U.S. Balance of Payments, Year Z

The data in this exhibit are hypothetical, but not unrealistic. All numbers are in billions of dollars. The plus and minus signs in the exhibit should be viewed as operational signs.

Current Account

Current Account

Includes all payments related to the purchase and sale of goods and services. Components of the account include exports, imports, and net unilateral transfers abroad.

The **current account** includes all payments related to the purchase and sale of goods and services. The current account has three major components: exports of goods and services, imports of goods and services, and net unilateral transfers abroad.

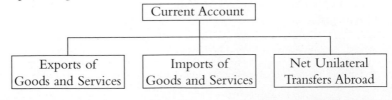

1. **Exports of goods and services.** Americans export goods (e.g., cars), they export services (e.g., insurance, banking, transportation, and tourism), and they receive income on assets they own abroad. All three activities increase the demand for U.S. dollars at the same time that they increase the supply of foreign currencies in the foreign exchange market; thus, they are recorded as credits (+). For example, if a foreigner buys a U.S. computer, payment must ultimately be made in U.S. dollars. Thus, she is required to supply her country's currency when she demands U.S. dollars. (We use foreigner in this chapter to refer to a resident of a foreign country.)

2. **Imports of goods and services.** Americans import goods and services, and foreigners receive income on assets they own in the United States. These activities increase the demand for foreign currencies at the same time that they increase the supply of U.S. dollars to the foreign exchange market; thus, they are recorded as debits (–). For example, if an American buys a Japanese car, payment must ultimately be made in Japanese yen. Thus, he is required to supply U.S. dollars when he demands Japanese yen.

   In Exhibit 2, exports of goods and services total +$340 billion in year *Z,* and imports of goods and services total –$390 billion.[1] Before discussing the third component of the current account—net unilateral transfers abroad—we define some important relationships between exports and imports.

   Look at the difference between the *value of merchandise exports* (1a in Exhibit 2) and the *value of merchandise imports* (2a in the exhibit). This difference is the merchandise trade balance or the balance of trade. Specifically, the **merchandise trade balance** is the difference between the value of merchandise exports and the value of merchandise imports. In year *Z,* the merchandise trade balance is $220 billion − $300 billion = −$80 billion.

   > Merchandise trade balance = Value of merchandise exports
   >   − Value of merchandise imports

   Merchandise Trade Balance
   The difference between the value of merchandise exports and the value of merchandise imports.

   If the value of a country's merchandise exports is less than the value of its merchandise imports, it is said to have a **merchandise trade deficit.**

   > Merchandise trade deficit: Value of merchandise exports
   >   < Value of merchandise imports

   Merchandise Trade Deficit
   The situation where the value of merchandise exports is less than the value of merchandise imports.

   If the value of a country's merchandise exports is greater than the value of its merchandise imports, it is said to have a **merchandise trade surplus**.

   > Merchandise trade surplus: Value of merchandise exports
   >   > Value of merchandise imports

   Merchandise Trade Surplus
   The situation where the value of merchandise exports is greater than the value of merchandise imports.

   Exhibit 3 shows the U.S. merchandise trade balance from 1990 to 2005. Notice that there has been a merchandise trade deficit in each of these years.

3. **Net unilateral transfers abroad.** Unilateral transfers are one-way money payments. They can go from Americans or the U.S. government to foreigners or foreign governments. If an American sends money to a relative in a foreign country, if the U.S. government gives money to a foreign country as a gift or grant, or if an American retires in a foreign country and receives a Social Security check there, all these transactions are referred to as unilateral transfers. If an American or the U.S. government makes a unilateral transfer abroad, this gives rise to a demand for foreign currency and a supply of U.S. dollars; thus, it is entered as a debit item in the U.S. balance of payments accounts.

---

[1] In everyday language, people do not say, "Exports are a positive $X billion and imports are a negative $Y billion." Placing a plus sign (+) in front of exports and a minus sign (–) in front of imports simply reinforces the essential point that exports are credits and imports are debits. This will be useful later when we calculate certain account balances.

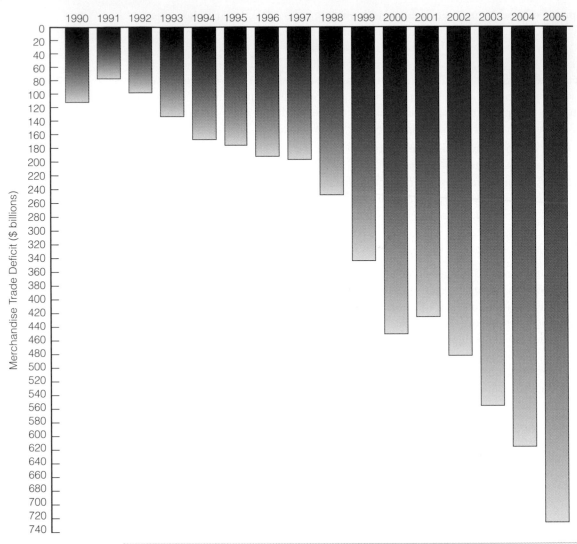

Merchandise Trade Deficit ($ billions)

exhibit 3

U.S. Merchandise Trade Balance

In each of the years shown, 1990–2005, a merchandise trade deficit has existed.

Source: U.S. Department of Commerce, Bureau of Economic Analysis.

Current Account Balance

The summary statistic for exports of goods and services, imports of goods and services, and net unilateral transfers abroad.

Unilateral transfers can also go from foreigners or foreign governments to Americans or to the U.S. government. If a foreign citizen sends money to a relative living in the United States, this is a unilateral transfer. If a foreigner makes a unilateral transfer to an American, this gives rise to a supply of foreign currency and a demand for U.S. dollars; thus, it is entered as a credit item in the U.S. balance of payments accounts.

Net unilateral transfers abroad include both types of transfers—from the United States to foreign countries and from foreign countries to the United States. The dollar amount of net unilateral transfers is negative if U.S. transfers are greater than foreign transfers. It is positive if foreign transfers are greater than U.S. transfers.

For year Z in Exhibit 2, we have assumed that unilateral transfers made by Americans to foreign citizens are greater than unilateral transfers made by foreign citizens to Americans. Thus, there is a *negative* net dollar amount, −$11 billion, in this case.

Items 1, 2, and 3 in Exhibit 2—exports of goods and services, imports of goods and services, and net unilateral transfers abroad—comprise the current account. The **current account balance** is the summary statistic for these three items. In year Z, it is −$61 billion. The news media sometimes call the current account balance the balance of payments. To an economist, this is incorrect; the balance of payments includes several more items.

Capital Account

The **capital account** includes all payments related to the purchase and sale of assets and to borrowing and lending activities. Its major components are outflow of U.S. capital and inflow of foreign capital.

1. **Outflow of U.S. capital.** American purchases of foreign assets and U.S. loans to foreigners are outflows of U.S. capital. As such, they give rise to a demand for foreign currency and a supply of U.S. dollars on the foreign exchange market. Hence, they are considered a debit. For example, if an American wants to buy land in Japan, U.S. dollars must be supplied to purchase (demand) Japanese yen.

2. **Inflow of foreign capital.** Foreign purchases of U.S. assets and foreign loans to Americans are inflows of foreign capital. As such, they give rise to a demand for U.S. dollars and to a supply of foreign currency on the foreign exchange market. Hence, they are considered a credit. For example, if a Japanese citizen buys a U.S. Treasury bill, Japanese yen must be supplied to purchase (demand) U.S. dollars.

Items 4 and 5 in Exhibit 2—outflow of U.S. capital and inflow of foreign capital—comprise the capital account. The **capital account balance** is the summary statistic for these two items. It is equal to the difference between the outflow of U.S. capital and the inflow of foreign capital. In year Z, it is $44 billion.

Official Reserve Account

A government possesses official reserve balances in the form of foreign currencies, gold, its reserve position in the **International Monetary Fund**, and **special drawing rights (SDRs)**. Countries that have a deficit in their combined current and capital accounts can draw on their reserves. For example, if the United States has a deficit in its combined current and capital accounts of $5 billion, it can draw down its official reserves to meet this deficit.

Item 6 in Exhibit 2 shows that the United States increased its reserve assets by $4 billion in year Z. This is a debit item because if the United States acquires official reserves (say, through the purchase of a foreign currency), it has increased the demand for the foreign currency and supplied dollars. Thus, an increase in official reserves is like an outflow of capital in the capital account and appears as a payment with a negative sign. It follows that an increase in foreign official assets in the United States is a credit item.

Statistical Discrepancy

If someone buys a U.S. dollar with, say, Japanese yen, someone must sell a U.S. dollar. Thus, dollars purchased equal dollars sold.

In all the transactions discussed earlier—exporting goods, importing goods, sending money to relatives in foreign countries, buying land in foreign countries—dollars were bought and sold. The total number of dollars sold must always equal the total number of dollars purchased. However, balance of payments accountants do not have complete information; they can record only credits and debits that they observe. There may be more debits or credits than those observed in a given year.

Suppose in year Z, all debits are observed and recorded, but not all credits are observed and recorded—perhaps because of smuggling activities, secret bank accounts,

Capital Account

Includes all payments related to the purchase and sale of assets and to borrowing and lending activities. Components include outflow of U.S. capital and inflow of foreign capital.

Capital Account Balance

The summary statistic for the outflow of U.S. capital. It is equal to the difference between the outflow of U.S. capital and the inflow of foreign capital.

International Monetary Fund (IMF)

An international organization created to oversee the international monetary system. The IMF does not control the world's money supply, but it does hold currency reserves for member nations and make loans to central banks.

Special Drawing Right (SDR)

An international money, created by the IMF, in the form of bookkeeping entries; like gold and currencies, that can be used by nations to settle international accounts.

people living in more than one country, and so on. To adjust for this, balance of payments accountants use the *statistical discrepancy,* which is the part of the balance of payments that adjusts for missing information. In Exhibit 2, the statistical discrepancy is +$18 billion. This means that $18 billion worth of credits (+) went unobserved in year Z. There may have been some hidden exports and unrecorded capital inflows that year.

What the Balance of Payments Equals

The balance of payments is the summary statistic for the following:

- Exports of goods and services (item 1 in Exhibit 2)
- Imports of goods and services (item 2)
- Net unilateral transfers abroad (item 3)
- Outflow of U.S. capital (item 4)
- Inflow of foreign capital (item 5)
- Increase in U.S. official reserve assets (item 6)
- Increase in foreign official assets in the United States (item 7)
- Statistical discrepancy

Calculating the balance of payments in year Z using these items, we have (in billions of dollars) $+340 - 390 - 11 - 16 + 60 - 4 + 3 + 18 = 0$.

Alternatively, the balance of payments is the summary statistic for the following:

- Current account balance
- Capital account balance
- Official reserve balance
- Statistical discrepancy

Calculating the balance of payments in year Z using these items, we have (in billions of dollars) $-61 + 44 - 1 + 18 = 0$. The balance of payments for the United States in year Z equals zero.

Q&A

Why does the balance of payments always equal zero?

The reason the balance of payments always equals zero is that the three accounts that comprise the balance of payments, when taken together, plus the statistical discrepancy, include all of the sources *and all of the* uses *of dollars in international transactions. And because every dollar used must have a source, adding the sources (+) to the uses (−) necessarily gives us zero.*

SELF-TEST

(Answers to Self-Test questions are in the Self-Test Appendix.)

1. If an American retailer buys Japanese cars from a Japanese manufacturer, is this transaction recorded as a debit or a credit? Explain your answer.

2. Exports of goods and services equal $200 billion and imports of goods and services equal $300 billion. What is the merchandise trade balance?

3. What is the difference between the merchandise trade balance and the current account balance?

The Foreign Exchange Market

If a U.S. buyer wants to purchase a good from a U.S. seller, the buyer simply gives the required number of U.S. dollars to the seller. If, however, a U.S. buyer wants to purchase a good from a seller in Mexico, the U.S. buyer must first exchange her U.S. dollars for Mexican pesos. Then, with the pesos, she buys the good from the Mexican seller.

As mentioned earlier, the market in which currencies of different countries are exchanged is the foreign exchange market. In the foreign exchange market, currencies are bought and sold for a price; an **exchange rate** exists. For instance, it might take 96 cents to buy a euro, 10 cents to buy a Mexican peso, and 13 cents to buy a Danish krone.

Exchange Rate
The price of one currency in terms of another currency.

In this section, we explain why currencies are demanded and supplied in the foreign exchange market. Then we discuss how the exchange rate expresses the relationship between the demand for and supply of currencies.

The Demand for Goods

To simplify our analysis, we assume that there are only two countries in the world, the United States and Mexico. This, then, means there are only two currencies in the world, the U.S. dollar (USD) and the Mexican peso (MXN). We want to answer the following two questions:

1. What creates the demand for and supply of dollars on the foreign exchange market?
2. What creates the demand for and supply of pesos on the foreign exchange market?

Suppose an American wants to buy a couch from a Mexican producer. Before he can purchase the couch, the American must buy Mexican pesos; hence, Mexican pesos are demanded. But the American buys Mexican pesos with U.S. dollars; that is, he supplies U.S. dollars to the foreign exchange market to demand Mexican pesos. We conclude that *the U.S. demand for Mexican goods leads to (1) a demand for Mexican pesos and (2) a supply of U.S. dollars on the foreign exchange market* (see Exhibit 4(a)). Thus, the demand for pesos and the supply of dollars are linked:

Demand for pesos ↔ Supply of dollars

The result is similar for a Mexican who wants to buy a computer from a U.S. producer. Before she can purchase the computer, the Mexican must buy U.S. dollars; hence, U.S. dollars are demanded. The Mexican buys the U.S. dollars with Mexican pesos. We conclude that *the Mexican demand for U.S. goods leads to (1) a demand for U.S. dollars and (2) a supply of Mexican pesos on the foreign exchange market* (see Exhibit 4(b)). Thus, the demand for dollars and the supply of pesos are linked:

Demand for dollars ↔ Supply of pesos

The Demand for and Supply of Currencies

Now let's look at Exhibit 5, which shows the markets for pesos and dollars. Part (a) shows the market for Mexican pesos. The quantity of pesos is on the horizontal axis, and the exchange rate—stated in terms of the dollar price per peso—is on the vertical axis. Exhibit 5(b) shows the market for U.S. dollars, which mirrors what is happening in the market for Mexican pesos. Notice that the exchange rates in (a) and (b) are reciprocals of each other. If 0.10 USD = 1 MXN, then 10 MXN = 1 USD.

exhibit **4**

The Demand for Goods and the Supply of Currencies

In Exhibit 5(a), the demand curve for pesos is downward sloping, indicating that as the dollar price per peso increases, Americans buy fewer pesos, and as the dollar price per peso decreases, Americans buy more pesos.

Dollar price per peso ↑   Americans buy fewer pesos
Dollar price per peso ↓   Americans buy more pesos

For example, if it takes 0.10 dollars to buy a peso, Americans will buy more pesos than they would if it takes 0.20 dollars to buy a peso. (It is analogous to buyers purchasing more soft drinks at $3 a six-pack than at $5 a six-pack.) Simply put, the higher the dollar price per peso, the more expensive Mexican goods are for Americans and the fewer Mexican goods Americans will buy. Thus, a smaller quantity of pesos is demanded.

The supply curve for pesos in Exhibit 5(a) is upward sloping. It is easy to understand why when we recall that the supply of Mexican pesos is linked to the Mexican demand for U.S. goods and U.S. dollars. Consider a price of 0.20 dollars for 1 peso compared with a price of 0.10 dollars for 1 peso. At 0.10 USD = 1 MXN, a Mexican buyer gives up 1 peso and receives 10 cents in return. But at 0.20 USD = 1 MXN, a Mexican buyer gives up 1 peso and receives 20 cents in return. At which exchange rate are U.S. goods cheaper for Mexicans? The answer is at the exchange rate of 0.20 USD = 1 MXN.

To illustrate, suppose a U.S. computer has a price tag of $1,000. At an exchange rate of 0.20 USD = 1 MXN, a Mexican will have to pay 5,000 pesos to buy the American computer; but at an exchange rate of 0.10 USD = 1 MXN, a Mexican will have to pay 10,000 pesos for the computer:

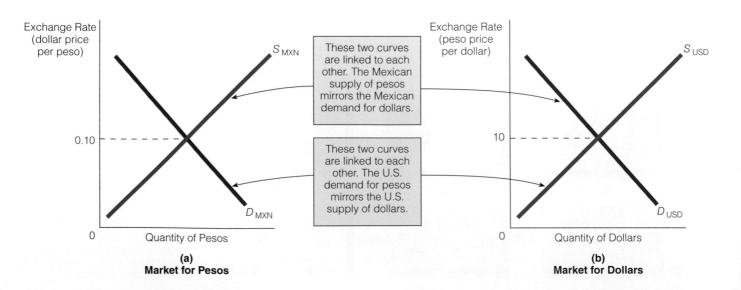

exhibit 5

Translating U.S. Demand for Pesos into U.S. Supply of Dollars and Mexican Demand for Dollars into Mexican Supply of Pesos

(a) The market for pesos. (b) The market for dollars. The demand for pesos in (a) is linked to the supply of dollars in (b): When Americans demand pesos, they supply dollars. The supply of pesos in (a) is linked to the demand for dollars in (b): When Mexicans demand dollars, they supply pesos. In (a), the exchange rate is 0.10 USD = 1 MXN, which is equal to 10 MXN = 1 USD in (b). Exchange rates are reciprocals of each other.

0.20 USD = 1 MXN	0.10 USD = 1 MXN
1 USD = (1/0.20) MXN	1 USD = (1/0.10) MXN
1,000 USD = (1,000/0.20) MXN	1,000 USD = (1,000/0.10) MXN
= 5,000 MXN	= 10,000 MXN

To a Mexican buyer, the American computer is cheaper at the exchange rate of 0.20 dollars per peso than at 0.10 dollars per peso.

Exchange Rate	Dollar Price	Peso Price
0.20 USD = 1 MXN	1,000 USD	5,000 MXN [(1,000/0.20) MXN]
0.10 USD = 1 MXN	1,000 USD	10,000 MXN [(1,000/0.10) MXN]

THE NOBEL PRIZE IN ECONOMICS AND FOREIGN EXCHANGE MARKETS

Do winners of the Nobel Prize in Economics care what is happening on foreign exchange markets? Because the prize money they win is paid in Swedish kronor, should they care?[2]

Consider the case of Robert Mundell, the 1999 winner of the prize. Mundell received a prize of 7.9 million Swedish kronor. In mid-October, when he was informed that he had won the prize, the prize money was worth nearly $1 million. Mundell, however, decided not to take the prize money in kronor and then exchange it for dollars. Instead, he asked the Nobel Foundation to deposit the funds in his bank account in euros because he expected that over the next few months, the euro would appreciate relative to the dollar.

Gary Becker was the 1992 winner of the Nobel Prize in Economics. Like all winners, he was notified of his winning the coveted prize in mid-October. He would not actually collect the prize money, however, until late December. In mid-October, the prize money (at current exchange rates)

was worth $1.2 million. Becker thought that the Swedish kronor was likely to depreciate in the near future, and so intended to buy dollars on the futures market. He never got around to doing so, though. Two weeks after he had been notified that he had won the Nobel Prize, there was a currency crisis in Sweden. As a result, his prize money shrank to $900,000.

Ronald Coase, who won the Nobel Prize in Economics in 1991, was to be paid his prize money at the end of 1991. Coase suspected that the kronor was about to appreciate in value relative to the dollar, so he asked the foundation to pay him part of his prize money in January 1992, to which the foundation agreed. In January, the kronor appreciated in value, giving Coase more dollars per kronor.

[2]This feature is based on Sylvia Nasar, "Nobel Economics: Spending the Check," *The New York Times*, December 5, 1999.

It follows, then, that the higher the dollar price per peso, the greater the quantity demanded of dollars by Mexicans (because U.S. goods will be cheaper), and therefore, the greater the quantity supplied of pesos to the foreign exchange market. The upward-sloping supply curve for pesos illustrates this.

Flexible Exchange Rates

In this section, we discuss how exchange rates are determined in the foreign exchange market when the forces of supply and demand are allowed to rule. Economists refer to this as a **flexible exchange rate system**. In the next section, we discuss how exchange rates are determined under a fixed exchange rate system.

The Equilibrium Exchange Rate

In a completely flexible exchange rate system, the exchange rate is determined by the forces of supply and demand. In our two country–two currency world, suppose the equilibrium exchange rate (dollar price per peso) is 0.10 USD = 1 MXN, as shown in Exhibit 6. At this dollar price per peso, the quantity demanded of pesos equals the quantity supplied of pesos. There are no shortages or surpluses of pesos. At any other exchange rate, however, either an excess demand for pesos or an excess supply of pesos exists.

Thinking like **AN ECONOMIST**

The demand for dollars is linked to the supply of pesos, and the demand for pesos is linked to the supply of dollars. Economists often think in terms of one activity being linked to another because economics, after all, is about exchange. In an exchange, one gives (supply) and gets (demand): John "supplies" $25 to demand the new book from the shopkeeper; the shopkeeper supplies the new book so that he may "demand" the $25. In such a transaction, we usually diagrammatically represent the demand for and supply of the new book—but we could also diagrammatically represent the demand for and supply of money. Of course, in international exchange, where monies are bought and sold before goods are bought and sold, this is exactly what we do.

Flexible Exchange Rate System
The system whereby exchange rates are determined by the forces of supply and demand for a currency.

exhibit 6

A Flexible Exchange Rate System

The demand curve for pesos is downward-sloping. The higher the dollar price for pesos, the fewer pesos will be demanded; the lower the dollar price for pesos, the more pesos will be demanded. At 0.12 USD = 1 MXN, there is a surplus of pesos, placing downward pressure on the exchange rate. At 0.08 USD = 1 MXN, there is a shortage of pesos, placing upward pressure on the exchange rate. At the equilibrium exchange rate, 0.10 USD = 1 MXN, the quantity demanded of pesos equals the quantity supplied of pesos.

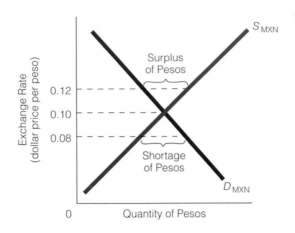

Q&A

Are the demand and supply curves in Exhibit 6 related to the U.S. balance of payments in Exhibit 2?

Yes, they are. For example, U.S. exports represent a demand for U.S. dollars by foreigners (and therefore constitute the supply of foreign currencies), while U.S. imports represent the U.S. demand for foreign currencies (and therefore constitute the supply of U.S. dollars). In fact, any dollar amount with a plus sign (+) in front of it in Exhibit 2 represents a demand for U.S. dollars and a supply of foreign currencies, and any dollar amount with a minus sign (–) in front of it represents a demand for foreign currencies and a supply of U.S. dollars.

Appreciation

An increase in the value of one currency relative to other currencies.

Depreciation

A decrease in the value of one currency relative to other currencies.

At the exchange rate of 0.12 USD = 1 MXN, a surplus of pesos exists. As a result, downward pressure will be placed on the dollar price of a peso (just as downward pressure will be placed on the dollar price of an apple if there is a surplus of apples). At the exchange rate of 0.08 USD = 1 MXN, there is a shortage of pesos, and upward pressure will be placed on the dollar price of a peso.

Changes in the Equilibrium Exchange Rate

Chapter 3 explains that a change in the demand for a good, in the supply of a good, or in both will change the equilibrium price of the good. The same holds true for the price of currencies. A change in the demand for pesos, in the supply of pesos, or in both will change the equilibrium dollar price per peso. If the dollar price per peso rises—say, from 0.10 USD = 1 MXN to 0.12 USD = 1 MXN—the peso is said to have **appreciated** and the dollar to have **depreciated**.

A currency has appreciated in value if it takes more of a foreign currency to buy it. A currency has depreciated in value if it takes more of it to buy a foreign currency. For example, a movement in the exchange rate from 0.10 USD = 1 MXN to 0.12 USD = 1 MXN means that it now takes 12 cents instead of 10 cents to buy a peso, so the dollar has depreciated. The other side of the "coin," so to speak, is that it takes fewer pesos to buy a dollar, so the peso has appreciated. That is, at an exchange rate of 0.10 USD = 1 MXN, it takes 10 pesos to buy $1, but at an exchange rate of 0.12 USD = 1 MXN, it takes only 8.33 pesos to buy $1.

Factors That Affect the Equilibrium Exchange Rate

If the equilibrium exchange rate can change owing to a change in the demand for and supply of a currency, then it is important to understand what factors can change the demand for and supply of a currency. Three are presented in this section.

A DIFFERENCE IN INCOME GROWTH RATES An increase in a nation's income will usually cause the nation's residents to buy more of both domestic and foreign goods. The increased demand for imports will result in an increased demand for foreign currency.

Suppose U.S. residents experience an increase in income, but Mexican residents do not. As a result, the demand curve for pesos shifts rightward, as illustrated in Exhibit 7.

economics 24/7

BACK TO THE FUTURES

Meet (the fictional) Bill Whatley, owner of a Toyota dealership in Tulsa, Oklahoma. It is currently May, and Bill is thinking about a shipment of Toyotas he plans to buy in August. He knows that he must buy the Toyotas from Japan with yen, but he has a problem. At the present time, the price of 1 yen is 0.008 dollars. Bill wonders what the dollar price of a yen will be in August when he plans to make his purchase. Suppose the price of 1 yen rises to 0.010 dollars. If this happens, then instead of paying $20,000 for a Toyota priced at 2.5 million yen, he would have to pay $25,000.[3] This difference of $5,000 may be enough to erase his profit on the sale of the Toyotas.

What is Bill to do? He could purchase a futures contract today for the needed quantity of yen in August. A futures contract is a contract in which the seller agrees to provide a particular good (in this example, a particular currency) to the buyer on a specified future date at an agreed-on price. In short, Bill can buy yen today at a specified dollar price and take delivery of the yen at a later date (in August).

But suppose the price of 1 yen falls to 0.007 dollars in August. If this happens, Bill would have to pay only $17,500 (instead of $20,000) for a Toyota priced at 2.5 million yen. Although he could increase his profit in this case, Bill, like other car dealers, might not be interested in assuming the risk associated with changes in exchange rates. He may prefer to lock in a sure thing.

Who would sell yen to Bill? The answer is someone who is willing to assume the risk of changes in the value of currencies—for example, Julie Jackson. Julie thinks to herself, "I think the dollar price of a yen will go down between now and August. Therefore, I'll enter into a contract with Bill stating that I'll give him 2.5 million yen in August for $20,000—the exchange rate specified in the contract being 1 JPY = 0.008 USD. If I'm right, and the actual exchange rate in August is 1 JPY = 0.007 USD, then I can purchase the 2.5 million yen for $17,500 and fulfill my contract with Bill by turning the yen over to him for $20,000. I walk away with $2,500 in profit."

Many economists argue that futures contracts offer people a way of dealing with the risk associated with a flexible exchange rate system. If a person doesn't know what next month's exchange rate will be and doesn't want to take the risk of waiting to see, then he or she can enter into a futures contract and effectively shift the risk to someone who voluntarily assumes it.

---

[3]If 1 yen equals 0.008 dollars, then a Toyota with a price of 2.5 million yen costs $20,000 because 2.5 million × 0.008 dollars = $20,000. If 1 yen equals 0.010 dollars, then a Toyota with a price of 2.5 million yen costs $25,000 dollars because 2.5 million × 0.010 dollars equals $25,000.

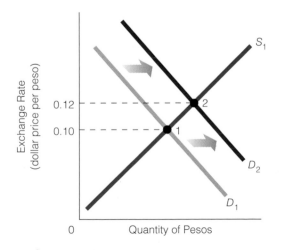

Exchange Rate (dollar price per peso) — 0.12, 0.10

0   Quantity of Pesos

S_1, D_2, D_1, 1, 2

exhibit 7

The Growth Rate of Income and the Exchange Rate

If U.S. residents experience a growth in income but Mexican residents do not, U.S. demand for Mexican goods will increase, and with it, the demand for pesos. As a result, the exchange rate will change; the dollar price of pesos will rise. The dollar depreciates, the peso appreciates.

This causes the equilibrium exchange rate to rise from 0.10 USD = 1 MXN to 0.12 USD = 1 MXN. *Ceteris paribus,* if one nation's income grows and another's lags behind, the currency of the higher-growth-rate country *depreciates,* and the currency of the lower-growth-rate country *appreciates.* To many persons, this seems paradoxical; nevertheless, it is true.

DIFFERENCES IN RELATIVE INFLATION RATES Suppose the U.S. price level rises 10 percent at a time when Mexico experiences stable prices. An increase in the U.S. price level will make Mexican goods relatively less expensive for Americans and U.S. goods relatively more expensive for Mexicans. As a result, the U.S. demand for Mexican goods will increase, and the Mexican demand for U.S. goods will decrease.

How will this affect the demand for and supply of Mexican pesos? As shown in Exhibit 8, the demand for Mexican pesos will increase (Mexican goods are relatively cheaper than they were before the U.S. price level rose), and the supply of Mexican pesos will decrease (American goods are relatively more expensive, so Mexicans will buy fewer American goods; thus, they demand fewer U.S. dollars and supply fewer Mexican pesos).

As Exhibit 8 shows, the result of an increase in the demand for Mexican pesos and a decrease in the supply of Mexican pesos is an *appreciation* in the peso and a *depreciation* in the dollar. It takes 11 cents instead of 10 cents to buy 1 peso (dollar depreciation); it takes 9.09 pesos instead of 10 pesos to buy $1 (peso appreciation).

An important question is: How much will the U.S. dollar depreciate as a result of the rise in the U.S. price level? (Recall that there is no change in Mexico's price level.) The **purchasing power parity (PPP) theory** predicts that the U.S. dollar will depreciate by 10 percent as a result of the 10 percent rise in the U.S. price level. This requires the dollar price of a peso to rise to 11 cents (10 percent of 10 cents is 1 cent, and 10 cents + 1 cent = 11 cents). A 10 percent depreciation in the dollar restores the *original relative prices of American goods to Mexican customers.*

Consider a U.S. car with a price tag of $20,000. If the exchange rate is 0.10 USD = 1 MXN, a Mexican buyer of the car will pay 200,000 pesos. If the car price increases by 10 percent to $22,000 and the dollar depreciates 10 percent (to 0.11 USD = 1 MXN), the Mexican buyer of the car will still pay only 200,000 pesos.

Purchasing Power Parity (PPP) Theory

States that exchange rates between any two currencies will adjust to reflect changes in the relative price levels of the two countries.

---

exhibit **8**

Inflation, Exchange Rates, and Purchasing Power Parity (PPP)

If the price level in the United States increases by 10 percent while the price level in Mexico remains constant, then the U.S. demand for Mexican goods (and therefore pesos) will increase and the supply of pesos will decrease. As a result, the exchange rate will change; the dollar price of pesos will rise. The dollar depreciates, and the peso appreciates. PPP theory predicts that the dollar will depreciate in the foreign exchange market until the original price (in pesos) of American goods to Mexican customers is restored. In this example, this requires the dollar to depreciate 10 percent.

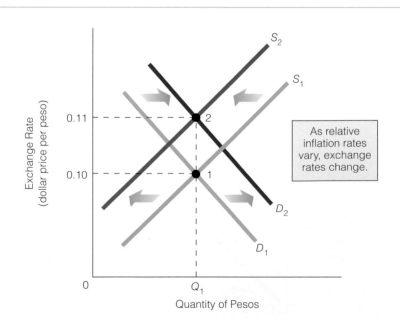

As relative inflation rates vary, exchange rates change.

Exchange Rate (dollar price per peso)

0.11

0.10

Q_1

Quantity of Pesos

Exchange Rate	Dollar Price	Peso Price
0.10 USD = 1 MXN	20,000 USD	200,000 MXN [(20,000/0.10) MXN]
0.11 USD = 1 MXN	22,000 USD	200,000 MXN [(22,000/0.11) MXN]

In short, the PPP theory predicts that *changes in the relative price levels of two countries will affect the exchange rate in such a way that 1 unit of a country's currency will continue to buy the same amount of foreign goods* as it did before the change in the relative price levels. In our example, the higher U.S. inflation rate causes a change in the equilibrium exchange rate and leads to a depreciated dollar, but 1 peso continues to have the same purchasing power it previously did.

On some occasions, the PPP theory of exchange rates has predicted accurately, but on others, it has not. Many economists suggest that the theory does not always predict accurately because the demand for and supply of a currency are affected *by more than the difference in inflation rates between countries.* For example, we have already noted that different income growth rates affect the demand for a currency and therefore the exchange rate. In the *long run,* however, and in particular, when there is a *large difference in inflation rates across countries,* the PPP theory does predict exchange rates accurately.

CHANGES IN REAL INTEREST RATES As shown in the U.S. balance of payments in Exhibit 2, more than goods flow between countries. Financial capital also moves between countries. The flow of financial capital depends on different countries' *real interest rates*—interest rates adjusted for inflation.

To illustrate, suppose initially that the real interest rate is 3 percent in both the United States and Mexico. Then the real interest rate in the United States increases to 4.5 percent. What will happen? Mexicans will want to purchase financial assets in the United States that pay a higher real interest rate than financial assets in Mexico. The Mexican demand for dollars will increase, and therefore, Mexicans will supply more pesos. As the supply of pesos increases on the foreign exchange market, the exchange rate (dollar price per peso) will change; fewer dollars will be needed to buy pesos. In short, the dollar will appreciate, and the peso will depreciate.

SELF-TEST

1. In the foreign exchange market, how is the demand for dollars linked to the supply of pesos?

2. What could cause the U.S. dollar to appreciate against the Mexican peso on the foreign exchange market?

3. Suppose the U.S. economy grows while the Swiss economy does not. How will this affect the exchange rate between the dollar and the Swiss franc? Why?

4. What does the purchasing power parity theory say? Give an example to illustrate your answer.

Fixed Exchange Rates

The major alternative to the flexible exchange rate system is the **fixed exchange rate system**. This system works the way it sounds. Exchange rates are fixed; they are not allowed to fluctuate freely in response to the forces of supply and demand. Central banks buy and sell currencies to maintain agreed-on exchange rates. The workings of the fixed exchange rate system are described in this section.

Fixed Exchange Rate System

The system where a nation's currency is set at a fixed rate relative to all other currencies, and central banks intervene in the foreign exchange market to maintain the fixed rate.

Fixed Exchange Rates and Overvalued/Undervalued Currency

Once again, we assume a two country–two currency world. Suppose this time, the United States and Mexico agree to fix the exchange rate of their currencies. Instead of letting the dollar depreciate or appreciate relative to the peso, the two countries agree to set the price of 1 peso at 0.12 dollars; that is, they agree to the exchange rate of 0.12 USD = 1 MXN. Generally, we call this the fixed exchange rate or the *official price* of a peso.[4] We will deal with more than one official price in our discussion, so we refer to 0.12 USD = 1 MXN as official price 1 (Exhibit 9).

     If the dollar price of pesos is above its equilibrium level (which is the case at official price 1), a surplus of pesos exists, and the peso is said to be **overvalued**. This means that the peso is fetching more dollars than it would at equilibrium. For example, if in equilibrium, 1 peso trades for 0.10 dollars, but at the official exchange rate, 1 peso trades for 0.12 dollars, then the peso is said to be overvalued.

     It follows that if the peso is overvalued, the dollar is undervalued, which means it is fetching fewer pesos than it would at equilibrium. For example, if in equilibrium, $1 trades for 10 pesos, but at the official exchange rate, $1 trades for 8.33 pesos, then the dollar is undervalued.

     Similarly, if the dollar price of pesos is below its equilibrium level (which is the case at official price 2 in Exhibit 9), a shortage of pesos exists, and the peso is **undervalued**. This means that the peso is not fetching as many dollars as it would at equilibrium. It follows that if the peso is undervalued, the dollar must be overvalued.

Overvalued peso ↔ Undervalued dollar
Undervalued peso ↔ Overvalued dollar

Overvaluation

A currency is overvalued if its price in terms of other currencies is above the equilibrium price.

Undervaluation

A currency is undervalued if its price in terms of other currencies is below the equilibrium price.

exhibit **9**

A Fixed Exchange Rate System

In a fixed exchange rate system, the exchange rate is fixed—and it may not be fixed at the equilibrium exchange rate. The exhibit shows two cases. (1) If the exchange rate is fixed at official price 1, the peso is overvalued, the dollar is undervalued, and a surplus of pesos exists. (2) If the exchange rate is fixed at official price 2, the peso is undervalued, the dollar is overvalued, and a shortage of pesos exists.

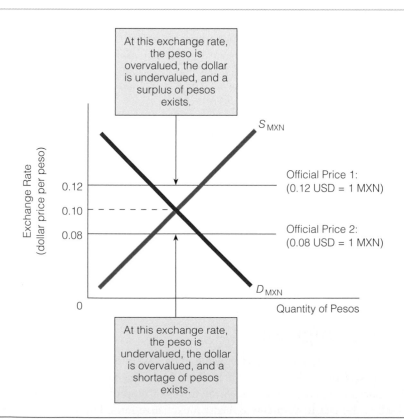

[4]If the price of 1 peso is 0.12 dollars, it follows that the price of $1 is approximately 8.33 pesos. Thus, setting the official price of a peso in terms of dollars automatically sets the official price of a dollar in terms of pesos.

What Is So Bad About an Overvalued Dollar?

Suppose you read in the newspaper that the dollar is overvalued. You also read that economists are concerned about the overvalued dollar. "But why are economists concerned?" you ask.

Economists are concerned because the exchange rate—and hence, the value of the dollar in terms of other currencies—affects the amount of U.S. exports and imports. Because it affects exports and imports, it naturally affects the merchandise trade balance.

To illustrate, suppose the demand for and supply of pesos are represented by D_1 and S_1 in Exhibit 10. With this demand curve and supply curve, the equilibrium exchange rate is 0.10 USD = 1 MXN. Let's also suppose the exchange rate is fixed at this exchange rate. In other words, the equilibrium exchange rate and the fixed exchange rate are initially the same.

Time passes and eventually the demand curve for pesos shifts to the right, from D_1 to D_2. Under a flexible exchange rate system, the exchange rate would rise to 0.12 USD = 1 MXN. But a flexible exchange rate is not operating here—a fixed one is. Therefore, the exchange rate stays fixed at 0.10 USD = 1 MXN. This means the fixed exchange rate (0.10 USD = 1 MXN) is below the new equilibrium exchange rate (0.12 USD = 1 MXN).

Recall that if the dollar price per peso is below its equilibrium level (which is the case here), the peso is undervalued and the dollar is overvalued. At equilibrium (point 2 in Exhibit 10), 1 peso would trade for 0.12 dollars, but at its fixed rate (point 1), it trades for only 0.10 dollars—so the peso is undervalued. At equilibrium (point 2), $1 would trade for 8.33 pesos, but at its fixed rate (point 1), it trades for 10 pesos—so the dollar is overvalued.

But what is so bad about an overvalued dollar? The answer is that it makes U.S. goods more expensive (for foreigners to buy), which in turn can affect the U.S. merchandise trade balance.

For example, suppose a U.S. good costs $100. At the equilibrium exchange rate (0.12 USD = 1 MXN), a Mexican would pay 833 pesos for the good; but at the fixed exchange rate (0.10 USD = 1 MXN), he will pay 1,000 pesos.

Exchange Rate	Dollar Price	Peso Price
0.12 USD = 1 MXN (equilibrium)	100 USD	833 MXN [(100/0.12) MXN]
0.10 USD = 1 MXN (fixed)	100 USD	1,000 MXN [(100/0.10) MXN]

The higher the prices of U.S. goods (exports), the fewer of those goods Mexicans will buy, and as just shown, an overvalued dollar makes U.S. export goods higher in price.

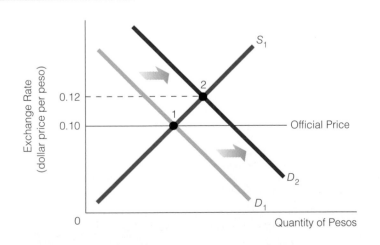

exhibit **10**

Fixed Exchange Rates and an Overvalued Dollar

Initially, the demand for and supply of pesos are represented by D_1 and S_1, respectively. The equilibrium exchange rate is 0.10 USD = 1 MXN, which also happens to be the official (fixed) exchange rate. In time, the demand for pesos rises to D_2, and the equilibrium exchange rate rises to 0.12 USD = 1 MXN. The official exchange rate is fixed, however, so the dollar will be overvalued. As explained in the text, this can lead to a trade deficit.

Ultimately, an overvalued dollar can affect the U.S. merchandise trade balance. As U.S. exports become more expensive for Mexicans, they buy fewer U.S. exports. If exports fall below imports, the result is a U.S. trade deficit.[5]

Government Involvement in a Fixed Exchange Rate System

Look back at Exhibit 9. Suppose the governments of Mexico and the United States agree to fix the exchange rate at 0.12 USD = 1 MXN. At this exchange rate, a surplus of pesos exists. What becomes of the surplus of pesos?

To maintain the exchange rate at 0.12 USD = 1 MXN, the Federal Reserve System (the Fed) could buy the surplus of pesos. But what would it use to buy the pesos? The Fed would buy the surplus of pesos with dollars. Consequently, the demand for pesos will increase and the demand curve will shift to the right, ideally, by enough to raise the equilibrium rate to the current fixed exchange rate.

Alternatively, instead of the Fed buying pesos (to mop up the excess supply of pesos), the Banco de Mexico (the central bank of Mexico) could buy pesos with some of its reserve dollars. (Why doesn't it buy pesos with pesos? Using pesos would not reduce the surplus of pesos on the market.) This action by the Banco de Mexico will also increase the demand for pesos and raise the equilibrium rate.

Finally, the two actions could be combined; that is, both the Fed and the Banco de Mexico could buy pesos.

> **Q&A**
>
> **Why does the Fed play a much larger role under a fixed exchange rate system than under a flexible exchange rate system?**
>
> *To support or maintain a fixed exchange rate, someone or something has to do the support or the maintenance. Central banks play this role. Under a flexible exchange rate system, there is no exchange rate to support or maintain; exchange rates simply respond to the forces of supply and demand.*

Options Under a Fixed Exchange Rate System

Suppose there is a surplus of pesos in the foreign exchange market—indicating that the peso is overvalued and the dollar is undervalued. The Fed and the Banco de Mexico each attempt to rectify this situation by buying pesos. But suppose this combined action is not successful. The surplus of pesos persists for weeks, along with an overvalued peso and an undervalued dollar. What is left to do? There are a few options.

DEVALUATION AND REVALUATION Mexico and the United States could agree to reset the official price of the dollar and the peso. This entails *devaluation* and *revaluation*.

Devaluation

A government act that changes the exchange rate by lowering the official price of a currency.

Revaluation

A government act that changes the exchange rate by raising the official price of a currency.

A **devaluation** occurs when the official price of a currency is lowered. A **revaluation** occurs when the official price of a currency is raised. For example, suppose the first official price of a peso is 0.10 USD = 1 MXN. It follows that the first official price of $1 is 10 pesos.

Now suppose Mexico and the United States agree to change the official price of their currencies. The second official price is 0.12 USD = 1 MXN. This means that the second official price of $1 is 8.33 pesos.

Moving from the first official price to the second, the peso has been revalued. That's because it takes *more dollars to buy a peso* (12 cents instead of 10 cents). Of course, moving from the first official price to the second means the dollar has been devalued. That's because it takes *fewer pesos to buy a dollar* (8.33 pesos instead of 10 pesos).

---

[5]The other side of the coin, so to speak, is that if the dollar is overvalued, the peso must be undervalued. An undervalued peso makes Mexican goods cheaper for Americans. So while the overvalued dollar is causing Mexicans to buy fewer U.S. exports, the undervalued peso is causing Americans to import more goods from Mexico. In conclusion, U.S. exports fall, U.S. imports rise, and we move closer to a trade deficit, or if one already exists, it becomes larger.

© CHARLES PERTWEE/BLOOMBERG NEWS/LANDOV

economics 24/7

BIG MACS AND EXCHANGE RATES

In an earlier chapter, we explained why goods that can be easily transported from one location to another usually sell for the same price in all locations. For example, if a candy bar can be moved from Atlanta to Seattle, then we would expect the candy bar to sell for the same price in both locations. Why? Because if the candy bar is priced higher in Seattle than Atlanta, people will move candy bars from Atlanta (where the price is relatively low) to Seattle to fetch the higher price. In other words, the supply of candy bars will rise in Seattle and fall in Atlanta. These changes in supply in the two locations affect the price of the candy bars in the two locations. In Seattle, the price will fall, and in Atlanta, the price will rise. This price movement will stop when the price of a candy bar is the same in the two locations.

Now consider a good that is sold all over the world, McDonald's Big Mac. Suppose the exchange rate between the dollar and the yen is $1 = ¥100 and the price of a Big Mac in New York City is $3 and ¥400 in Tokyo. Given the exchange rate, is a Big Mac selling for the same price in the two cities? The answer is no. In New York, it is $3, but in Tokyo it is $4 (the price in Tokyo is ¥400, and $1 = ¥100). Stated differently, in New York, $1 buys one-third of a Big Mac, but in Tokyo, $1 buys only one-fourth of a Big Mac.

Will Big Macs be shipped from New York to Tokyo to fetch the higher price? No. The exchange rate is likely to adjust in such a way that the price of a Big Mac is the same in both cities.

Now ask yourself what the exchange rate has to be between the dollar and yen before the Big Mac is the same dollar price in New York and Tokyo. Here are three different exchange rates. Pick the correct one.

(a) $1 = ¥133.33
(b) $1 = ¥150.00
(c) $1 = ¥89.00

The answer is (a), $1 = ¥133.33. At this exchange rate, a Big Mac in New York is $3 (as we stated earlier), and a Big Mac in Tokyo that is ¥400 is $3 (once we have computed its price in dollars). Here are the steps: (1) The exchange rate is $1 = ¥133.33; (2) 1 yen is equal to $0.0075; (3) $0.0075 × 400 yen is $3.

The *purchasing power parity theory* in economics predicts that the exchange rate between two currencies will adjust so that, in the end, $1 buys the same amount of a given good in all places around the world. Thus, if the exchange rate is initially $1 = ¥100 when a Big Mac is $3 in New York and ¥400 in Tokyo, it will change to become $1 = ¥133.33. That is, the dollar will soon appreciate relative to the yen.

The Economist, a well-known economics magazine, publishes what it calls the "Big Mac index" each year. It shows what exchange rates currently are, and it shows what a Big Mac costs in different countries (just as we did here). Then it predicts which currencies will appreciate and depreciate based on this information. *The Economist* does not always predict accurately, but it does do so in many cases.

If you want to predict whether the euro, pound, or peso is going to appreciate or depreciate in the next few months, looking at exchange rates in terms of the price of Big Mac will be a useful source of information.

Might one country want to devalue its currency but another country not want to revalue its currency? For example, suppose Mexico wants to devalue its currency relative to the U.S. dollar. Would U.S. authorities always willingly comply? Not necessarily.

To see why, we have to understand that the United States will not sell as many goods to Mexico if the dollar is revalued. That's because, as we stated earlier, revaluing the dollar means Mexicans have to pay more for it—instead of paying, say, 8.33 pesos for $1, Mexicans might have to pay 10 pesos. At a revalued dollar (higher peso price for a dollar), Mexicans will find U.S. goods more expensive and not want to buy as many.

Americans who produce goods to sell to Mexico may see that a revalued dollar will hurt their pocketbooks, and so they will argue against it.

PROTECTIONIST TRADE POLICY (QUOTAS AND TARIFFS) Recall that an overvalued dollar can bring on or widen a trade deficit. How can a country deal with both the trade deficit and the overvalued dollar at once? Some say it can impose quotas and tariffs to reduce domestic consumption of foreign goods. (The previous chapter explains how both tariffs and quotas meet this objective.) A drop in the domestic consumption of foreign goods goes hand in hand with a decrease in the demand for foreign currencies. In turn, this can affect the value of the country's currency on the foreign exchange market. In this case, it can get rid of an overvalued dollar.

Economists are quick to point out, though, that trade deficits and overvalued currencies are sometimes used as an excuse to promote trade restrictions—many of which simply benefit special interests (e.g., U.S. producers that compete for sales with foreign producers in the U.S. market).

CHANGES IN MONETARY POLICY Sometimes, a nation can use monetary policy to support the exchange rate or the official price of its currency. Suppose the United States is continually running a merchandise trade deficit; year after year, imports are outstripping exports. To remedy this, the United States might enact a tight monetary policy to retard inflation and drive up interest rates (at least in the short run). The tight monetary policy will reduce the U.S. rate of inflation and thereby lower U.S. prices relative to prices in other nations. This will make U.S. goods relatively cheaper than they were before (assuming other nations didn't also enact a tight monetary policy) and promote U.S. exports and discourage foreign imports. It will also generate a flow of investment funds into the United States in search of higher real interest rates.

Some economists argue against fixed exchange rates because they think it unwise for a nation to adopt a particular monetary policy simply to maintain an international exchange rate. Instead, they believe domestic monetary policies should be used to meet domestic economic goals—such as price stability, low unemployment, low and stable interest rates, and so forth.

The Gold Standard

If nations adopt the gold standard, they *automatically fix* their exchange rates. Suppose the United States defines a dollar as equal to 1/10 of an ounce of gold and Mexico defines a peso as equal to 1/100 of an ounce of gold. This means that 1 ounce of gold could be bought with either 10 dollars or 100 pesos. What, then, is the exchange rate between dollars and pesos? It is 10 MXN = 1 USD or 0.10 USD = 1 MXN. This is the fixed exchange rate between dollars and pesos.

To have an international gold standard, countries must do the following:

1. Define their currencies in terms of gold.
2. Stand ready and willing to convert gold into paper money and paper money into gold at the rate specified (e.g., the United States would buy and sell gold at $10 an ounce).
3. Link their money supplies to their holdings of gold.

With this last point in mind, consider how a gold standard would work. Let's again look at Mexico and the United States and initially assume that the gold-standard (fixed) exchange rate of 0.10 USD = 1 MXN is the equilibrium exchange rate. Then, a change occurs: Inflation in Mexico raises prices there by 100 percent. A Mexican table that was priced at 2,000 pesos before the inflation is now priced at 4,000 pesos. At the gold-standard (fixed) exchange rate, Americans now have to pay $400 (4,000 pesos/10 pesos per dollar) to buy the table, whereas before the inflation Americans had to pay only $200 (2,000 pesos/10 pesos per dollar) for the table. As a result, Americans buy fewer Mexican tables; Americans import less from Mexico.

At the same time, Mexicans import more from the United States because American prices are now relatively lower than before inflation hit Mexico. A quick example illustrates our point. Suppose that before inflation hit Mexico, an American pair of shoes cost $200, and as before, a Mexican table cost 2,000 pesos. At 0.10 USD = 1 MXN, the $200 American shoes cost 2,000 pesos and the 2,000-peso Mexican table cost $200. In other words, 1 pair of American shoes traded for (or equaled) 1 Mexican table.

Now look at things after inflation has raised the price of the Mexican table to 4,000 pesos, or $400. Because the American shoes are still $200 (there has been no inflation in the United States) and the exchange rate is still fixed at 0.10 USD = 1 MXN, 1 pair of American shoes no longer equals 1 Mexican table; instead, it equals 1/2 of a Mexican table. In short, the inflation in Mexico has made U.S. goods *relatively cheaper* for Mexicans. As a result, Mexicans buy more U.S. goods; Mexicans import more from the United States.

To summarize: The inflation in Mexico has caused Americans to buy fewer goods from Mexico and Mexicans to buy more goods from the United States. What does this mean in terms of the merchandise trade balance for each country? In the United States, imports decline (Americans are buying less from Mexico) and exports rise (Mexicans are buying more from the United States), so the U.S. trade balance is likely to move into surplus. Contrarily, in Mexico, exports decline (Americans are buying less from Mexico) and imports rise (Mexicans are buying more from the United States), so Mexico's trade balance is likely to move into deficit.

On a gold standard, Mexicans have to pay for the difference between their imports and exports with gold. Gold is therefore shipped to the United States. An increase in the supply of gold in the United States expands the U.S. money supply. A decrease in the supply of gold in Mexico contracts the Mexican money supply. Prices are affected in both countries. In the United States, prices begin to rise; in Mexico, prices begin to fall.

As U.S. prices go up and Mexican prices go down, the earlier situation begins to reverse itself. American goods look more expensive to Mexicans, and they begin to buy less, whereas Mexican goods look cheaper to Americans, and they begin to buy more. Consequently, American imports begin to rise and exports begin to fall; Mexican imports begin to fall and exports begin to rise. Thus, by changing domestic money supplies and price levels, the gold standard begins to correct the initial trade balance disequilibrium.

The change in the money supply that the gold standard sometimes requires has prompted some economists to voice the same argument against the gold standard that is often heard against the fixed exchange rate system; that is, it subjects domestic monetary policy to international instead of domestic considerations. In fact, many economists cite this as part of the reason many nations abandoned the gold standard in the 1930s. At a time when unemployment was unusually high, many nations with trade deficits felt that matters would only get worse if they contracted their money supplies to live by the edicts of the gold standard.

SELF-TEST

1. Under a fixed exchange rate system, if one currency is overvalued, then another currency must be undervalued. Explain why this is true.

2. How does an overvalued dollar affect U.S. exports and imports?

3. In each case, identify whether the U.S. dollar is overvalued or undervalued.

    a. The fixed exchange rate is $2 = 1 pound and the equilibrium exchange rate is $3 = 1 pound.
    b. The fixed exchange rate is $1.25 = 1 euro and the equilibrium exchange rate is $1.10 = 1 euro.
    c. The fixed exchange rate is $1 = 10 pesos and the equilibrium exchange rate is $1 = 14 pesos.

4. Under a fixed exchange rate system, why might the United States want to devalue its currency?

Fixed Exchange Rates Versus Flexible Exchange Rates

As is the case in many economic situations, there are both costs and benefits to any exchange rate system. This section discusses some of the arguments and issues surrounding fixed exchange rates and flexible exchange rates.

Promoting International Trade

Which are better at promoting international trade, fixed or flexible exchange rates? This section presents the case for each.

THE CASE FOR FIXED EXCHANGE RATES Proponents of a fixed exchange rate system often argue that fixed exchange rates promote international trade, whereas flexible exchange rates stifle it. A major advantage of fixed exchange rates is certainty. Individuals in different countries know from day to day the value of their nation's currency. With flexible exchange rates, individuals are less likely to engage in international trade because of the added risk of not knowing from one day to the next how many dollars, euros, or yen they will have to trade for other currencies. Certainty is a necessary ingredient in international trade; flexible exchange rates promote uncertainty, which hampers international trade.

Economist Charles Kindleberger, a proponent of fixed exchange rates, believes that having fixed exchange rates is analogous to having a single currency for the entire United States instead of having a different currency for each of the 50 states. One currency in the United States promotes trade, whereas 50 different currencies would hamper it. In Kindleberger's view:

> The main case against flexible exchange rates is that they break up the world market. . . . Imagine trying to conduct interstate trade in the USA if there were fifty different state monies, none of which was dominant. This is akin to barter, the inefficiency of which is explained time and again by textbooks.[6]

THE CASE FOR FLEXIBLE EXCHANGE RATES Advocates of flexible exchange rates, as we have noted, maintain that it is better for a nation to adopt policies to meet domestic economic goals than to sacrifice domestic economic goals to maintain an exchange rate. They also say that there is too great a chance that the fixed exchange rate will diverge greatly from the equilibrium exchange rate, creating persistent balance of trade problems. This leads deficit nations to impose trade restrictions (tariffs and quotas) that hinder international trade.

---

[6]Charles Kindleberger, *International Money* (London: Allen and Unwin, 1981), p. 174.

Optimal Currency Areas

As of 2006, the European Union (EU) consists of 25 member states. According to the European Union, its ultimate goal is "an ever closer union among the peoples of Europe, in which decisions are taken as closely as possible to the citizen." As part of meeting this goal, the EU established its own currency—the euro—on January 1, 1999.[7] Although euro notes and coins were not issued until January 1, 2002, certain business transactions were made in euros beginning January 1, 1999.

The European Union and the euro are relevant to a discussion of an *optimal currency area*. An **optimal currency area** is a geographic area in which exchange rates can be fixed or a *common currency* used without sacrificing domestic economic goals, such as low unemployment. The concept of an optimal currency area originated in the debate over whether fixed or flexible exchange rates are better. Most of the pioneering work on optimal currency areas was done by Robert Mundell, the winner of the 1999 Nobel Prize in Economics.

Before discussing an optimal currency area, we need to look at the relationships among labor mobility, trade, and exchange rates. Labor mobility means that it is easy for the residents of one country to move to another country.

TRADE AND LABOR MOBILITY Suppose there are only two countries, the United States and Canada. The United States produces calculators and soft drinks, and Canada produces bread and muffins. Currently, the two countries trade with each other, and there is complete labor mobility between the two countries.

One day, the residents of both countries reduce their demand for bread and muffins and increase their demand for calculators and soft drinks. In other words, there is a change in relative demand. Demand increases for U.S. goods and falls for Canadian goods. Business firms in Canada lay off employees because their sales have plummeted. Incomes in Canada begin to fall, and the unemployment rate begins to rise. In the United States, prices initially rise because of the increased demand for calculators and soft drinks. In response to the higher demand for their products, U.S. business firms begin to hire more workers and increase their production. Their efforts to hire more workers drive wages up and reduce the unemployment rate.

Because labor is mobile, some of the newly unemployed Canadian workers move to the United States to find work. This will ease the economic situation in both countries. It will reduce some of the unemployment problems in Canada, and with more workers in the United States, more output will be produced, thus dampening upward price pressures on calculators and soft drinks. Thus, changes in relative demand pose no major economic problems for either country if labor is mobile.

TRADE AND LABOR IMMOBILITY Now let's change things. Suppose that relative demand has changed, but this time, labor is not mobile between the United States and Canada (labor immobility). There are either political or cultural barriers to people moving between the two countries. What happens in the economies of the two countries if people cannot move? The answer depends largely on whether exchange rates are fixed or flexible.

If exchange rates are flexible, the value of U.S. currency changes vis-à-vis Canadian currency. If Canadians want to buy more U.S. goods, they will have to exchange their domestic currency for U.S. currency. This increases the demand for U.S. currency on the foreign exchange market at the same time that it increases the supply of Canadian currency. Consequently, U.S. currency appreciates and Canadian currency depreciates. Because Canadian currency depreciates, U.S. goods become relatively more expensive for Canadians, so they buy fewer. And because U.S. currency appreciates, Canadian goods become relatively cheaper for Americans, so they buy more. Canadian business firms

---

Optimal Currency Area

A geographic area in which exchange rates can be fixed or a common currency used without sacrificing domestic economic goals, such as low unemployment.

---

[7]So far, 12 of the 25 member states have adopted the euro as their official currency.

begin to sell more goods, so they hire more workers, the unemployment rate drops, and the bad economic times in Canada begin to disappear.

If exchange rates are fixed, however, U.S. goods will not become relatively more expensive for Canadians, and Canadian goods will not become relatively cheaper for Americans. Consequently, the bad economic times in Canada (high unemployment) might last for a long time indeed instead of beginning to reverse. Thus, if labor is immobile, changes in relative demand may pose major economic problems when exchange rates are fixed but not when they are flexible.

COSTS, BENEFITS, AND OPTIMAL CURRENCY AREAS There are both costs and benefits to flexible exchange rates. The benefits we have just discussed. The costs include the cost of exchanging one currency for another (there is a charge to exchange, say, U.S. dollars for Canadian dollars or U.S. dollars for Japanese yen) and the added risk of not knowing what the value of one's currency will be on the foreign exchange market on any given day. For many countries, the benefits outweigh the costs, and so they have flexible exchange rate systems.

Suppose some of the costs of flexible exchange rates could be eliminated, while the benefits were maintained. Under what conditions could two countries have a fixed exchange rate or adopt a common currency and retain the benefits of flexible exchange rates? The answer is when labor is mobile between the two countries. Then, there is no reason to have separate currencies that float against each other because resources (labor) can move easily and quickly in response to changes in relative demand. There is no reason the two countries cannot fix exchange rates or adopt the same currency.

When labor in countries within a certain geographic area is mobile enough to move easily and quickly in response to changes in relative demand, the countries are said to constitute an *optimal currency area*. Countries in an optimal currency area can either fix their currencies or adopt the same currency and thus keep all the benefits of flexible exchange rates without any of the costs.

It is commonly argued that the states within the United States constitute an optimal currency area. Labor can move easily and quickly between, say, North Carolina and South Carolina in response to relative demand changes. Some economists argue that the countries that compose the European Union are within an optimal currency area and that adopting a common currency—the euro—will benefit these countries. Other economists disagree. They argue that while labor is somewhat more mobile in Europe today than in the past, there are still certain language and cultural differences that make labor mobility less than sufficient to truly constitute an optimal currency area.

The Current International Monetary System

Managed Float

A managed flexible exchange rate system, under which nations now and then intervene to adjust their official reserve holdings to moderate major swings in exchange rates.

Today's international monetary system is best described as a managed flexible exchange rate system, sometimes referred to more casually as a **managed float**. In a way, this system is a rough compromise between the fixed and flexible exchange rate systems. The current system operates under flexible exchange rates, but not completely. Nations now and then intervene to adjust their official reserve holdings to moderate major swings in exchange rates.

Proponents of the managed float system stress the following advantages:

1. **It allows nations to pursue independent monetary policies.** Under a (strictly) fixed exchange rate system, fixed either by agreement or by gold, a nation with a merchandise trade deficit might have to enact a tight monetary policy to retard inflation and promote its exports. This would not be the case with the managed float. Its proponents argue that it is better to solve trade imbalances by adjusting one price—the exchange rate—than by adjusting the price level.

2. **It solves trade problems without trade restrictions.** As stated earlier, under a fixed exchange rate system, nations sometimes impose tariffs and quotas to solve trade imbalances. For example, a deficit nation might impose import quotas so that exports and imports of goods will be more in line. Under the current system, trade imbalances are usually solved through changes in exchange rates.

3. **It is flexible and therefore can easily adjust to shocks.** In 1973–1974, the OPEC nations dramatically raised the price of oil, which resulted in many oil-importing nations running trade deficits. A fixed exchange rate system would have had a hard time accommodating such a major change in oil prices. The current system had little trouble, however. Exchange rates took much of the shock (there were large changes in exchange rates) and thus allowed most nations' economies to weather the storm with a minimum of difficulty.

Opponents of the current international monetary system stress the following disadvantages:

1. **It promotes exchange rate volatility and uncertainty and results in less international trade than would be the case under fixed exchange rates.** Under a flexible exchange rate system, volatile exchange rates make it riskier for importers and exporters to conduct business. As a result, there is less international trade than there would be under a fixed exchange rate system. Proponents respond that the futures market in currencies allows importers and exporters to shift the risk of fluctuations in exchange rates to others. For example, if an American company wants to buy a certain quantity of a good from a Japanese company three months from today, it can contract today for the desired quantity of yen it will need at a specified price. It will not have to worry about a change in the dollar price of yen during the next three months. There is, of course, a cost to purchasing a futures contract, but it is usually modest.

2. **It promotes inflation.** As we have seen, the monetary policies of different nations are not independent of one another under a fixed exchange rate system. For example, a nation with a merchandise trade deficit is somewhat restrained from inflating its currency because this will worsen the deficit problem. It will make the nation's goods more expensive relative to foreign goods and promote the purchase of imports. In its attempt to maintain the exchange rate, a nation with a merchandise trade deficit would have to enact a tight monetary policy.

   Under the current system, a nation with a merchandise trade deficit does not have to maintain exchange rates or try to solve its deficit problem through changes in its money supply. Opponents of the current system argue that this frees nations to inflate. They predict more inflation will result than would occur under a fixed exchange rate system.

3. **Changes in exchange rates alter trade balances in the desired direction only after a long time; in the short run, a depreciation in a currency can make the situation worse instead of better.** It is often argued that soon after a depreciation in a trade-deficit nation's currency, the trade deficit will increase (not decrease, as was hoped). The reason is that import demand is inelastic in the short run: Imports are not very responsive to a change in price. For example, suppose Mexico is running a trade deficit with the United States at the present exchange rate of 0.12 USD = 1 MXN. At this exchange rate, the peso is overvalued. Mexico buys 2,000 television sets from the United States, each with a price tag of $500. Assume Mexico therefore spends 8.33 million pesos on imports of American television sets. Now suppose the overvalued peso begins to depreciate, say, to 0.11 USD = 1 MXN. Furthermore, in the short run, Mexican customers buy only 100 fewer American television sets; that is, they import 1,900 television sets. At a price of $500

each and an exchange rate of 0.11 USD = 1 MXN, Mexicans now spend 8.63 million pesos on imports of American television sets. In the short run, then, a depreciation in the peso has widened the trade deficit because imports fell by only 5 percent while the price of imports (in terms of pesos) increased by 9.09 percent. As time passes, imports will fall off more (it takes time for Mexican buyers to shift from higher priced American goods to lower priced Mexican goods), and the deficit will shrink.

SELF-TEST

1. What is an optimal currency area?

2. Country 1 produces good X and country 2 produces good Y. People in both countries begin to demand more of good X and less of good Y. Assume there is no labor mobility between the two countries and that a flexible exchange rate system exists. What will happen to the unemployment rate in country 2? Explain your answer.

3. How important is labor mobility in determining whether or not an area is an optimal currency area?

A Reader Asks...

How Do I Convert Currencies?

I plan to travel to several different countries during the summer. How do I convert prices of products in other countries into dollars?

Here is the general formula you would use:

Price of the product in dollars = Price of the product in foreign currency × Price of the foreign currency in dollars

For example, suppose you travel to Mexico and see something priced at 100 pesos. You'd change the general formula into a specific one:

Price of the product in dollars = Price of the product in pesos × Price of a peso in dollars

If the dollar price of a peso is, say, 0.12 dollars, then the dollar price of the product is $12. Here is the calculation:

Price of the product in dollars = 100 × 0.12 = 12

Or suppose you are in Tokyo and you see a product for 10,000 yen. What is the price in dollars? At the exchange rate of 0.008 USD = 1 JPY, it is $80.

Price of the product in dollars = 10,000 × 0.008 = 80

Now let's suppose you are in Russia and you don't know what the exchange rate is between dollars and rubles. You pick up a newspaper to find out (often, exchange rates are quoted in the newspaper). But instead of finding the exchange rate quoted in terms of the dollar price of a ruble (e.g., 0.0318 dollars for 1 ruble), you find the ruble price of a dollar (31.4190 rubles for 1 dollar). What do you do now?

Perhaps the easiest thing to do is first convert rubles per dollar into dollars per ruble and then use the earlier formula to find the price of the Russian product in dollars. Recall that exchange rates are reciprocals, so:

$$\text{Dollars per ruble} = \frac{1}{\text{Rubles per dollar}}$$

To illustrate, if it takes 31.4190 rubles to purchase $1, then it takes 0.0318 dollars to buy 1 ruble. Here is the computation:

$$\text{Dollars per ruble} = \frac{1}{31.41990} = 0.0318$$

Now, because you know that 0.0318 dollars = 1 ruble, it follows that, say, a Russian coat that costs 10,000 rubles costs $318:

Price of the product in dollars = 10,000 × 0.0318 = 318

! analyzing the scene

What does the value of the dollar have to do with Karen's trip? What does the value of the dollar have to do with Robert Ivans's business?

These questions show two sides of how a fall in the value of the dollar affects people's lives. In Karen's case, the dollar is falling relative to the pound. So the dollar is depreciating and the pound is appreciating. Karen will now have to pay more in dollars and cents to buy a pound, so everything she buys on her trip (denominated in pounds) will be more expensive for her.

For Robert Ivans, if the dollar is depreciating, then some other currency is appreciating—say, the pound. An appreciating pound makes it cheaper for the British to buy U.S. goods, such as Robert Ivans's goods. If the British demand for U.S. goods is elastic, we can expect the British to spend more on U.S. goods as their currency appreciates.

Is anything wrong with the headline that the business columnist wrote?

The business columnist could not have been referring to the balance of payments because the balance of payments *always* equals zero. The reason the balance of payments always equals zero is that the three accounts that comprise the balance of

payments, when taken together, plus the statistical discrepancy, include all of the *sources* and all of the *uses* of dollars in international transactions. And because every dollar used must have a source, adding the sources (+) to the uses (–) necessarily gives us zero. The columnist probably meant that the merchandise trade deficit was at a record high. Often, the news media erroneously use the term *balance of payments* to refer to the current account balance or the merchandise trade balance.

Do big budget deficits really affect as many things as the president's economic advisor indicates?

When the economic advisor tells the president that the recent run of big budget deficits is likely to affect interest rates, the value of the dollar, exports and imports, and the merchandise trade balance, he is probably thinking that big budget deficits will mean the federal government will have to borrow more funds, which will increase the demand for credit. This will push up the interest rate. As the U.S. interest rate rises relative to interest rates in other countries, foreigners will want to purchase financial assets in the United States that pay a higher return. This will increase the demand for dollars, the dollar will appreciate, and foreign currencies will depreciate. In turn, this will affect both import and export spending, and therefore, it will affect the merchandise trade balance.

chapter summary

Balance of Payments

- The balance of payments provides information about a nation's imports and exports, domestic residents' earnings on assets located abroad, foreign earnings on domestic assets, gifts to and from foreign countries, and official transactions by governments and central banks.

- In a nation's balance of payments, any transaction that supplies the country's currency in the foreign exchange market is recorded as a debit (–). Any transaction that creates a demand for the country's currency is recorded as a credit (+).

- The three main accounts of the balance of payments are the current account, the capital account, and the official reserve account.

- The current account includes all payments related to the purchase and sale of goods and services. The three major components of the account are exports of goods and services, imports of goods and services, and net unilateral transfers abroad.

- The capital account includes all payments related to the purchase and sale of assets and to borrowing and lending activities. The major components are outflow of U.S. capital and inflow of foreign capital.

- The official reserve account includes transactions by the central banks of various countries.

- The merchandise trade balance is the difference between the value of merchandise exports and the value of merchandise imports. If exports are greater than imports, a nation has a trade surplus; if imports are greater than exports, a nation has a trade deficit.

- The balance of payments equals current account balance + capital account balance + official reserve balance + statistical discrepancy.

The Foreign Exchange Market

- The market in which currencies of different countries are exchanged is called the foreign exchange market. In this market, currencies are bought and sold for a price; an exchange rate exists.

- If Americans demand Mexican goods, they also demand Mexican pesos and supply U.S. dollars. If Mexicans demand American goods, they also demand U.S. dollars and supply Mexican pesos. When the residents of a nation demand a foreign currency, they must supply their own currency.

Flexible Exchange Rates

- Under flexible exchange rates, the foreign exchange market will equilibrate at the exchange rate where the quantity demanded of a currency equals the quantity supplied of the currency; for example, the quantity demanded of U.S. dollars equals the quantity supplied of U.S. dollars.

- If the price of a nation's currency increases relative to a foreign currency, the nation's currency is said to have appreciated. For example, if the price of a peso rises from 0.10 USD = 1 MXN to 0.15 USD = 1 MXN, the peso has appreciated. If the price of a nation's currency decreases relative to a foreign currency, the nation's currency is said to have depreciated. For example, if the price of a dollar falls from 10 MXN = 1 USD to 8 MXN = 1 USD, the dollar has depreciated.

- Under a flexible exchange rate system, the equilibrium exchange rate is affected by a difference in income growth rates between countries, a difference in inflation rates between countries, and a change in (real) interest rates between countries.

Fixed Exchange Rates

- Under a fixed exchange rate system, countries agree to fix the price of their currencies. The central banks of the countries must then buy and sell currencies to maintain the agreed-on exchange rate.

- If a persistent deficit or surplus in a nation's combined current and capital account exists at a fixed exchange rate, the nation has a few options to deal with the problem: devalue or revalue its currency, enact protectionist trade policies (in the case of a deficit), or change its monetary policy.

- A gold standard automatically fixes exchange rates. To have an international gold standard, nations must do the following: (1) define their currencies in terms of gold; (2) stand ready and willing to convert gold into paper money and paper money into gold at a specified rate; and (3) link their money supplies to their holdings of gold. The change in the money supply that the gold standard sometimes requires has prompted some economists to voice the same argument against the gold standard that is often heard against the fixed exchange rate system: It subjects domestic monetary policy to international instead of domestic considerations.

The Current International Monetary System

- Today's international monetary system is described as a managed flexible exchange rate system, or managed float. For the most part, the exchange rate system is flexible, although nations do periodically intervene in the foreign exchange market to adjust exchange rates. Because it is a managed float system, it is difficult to tell if nations will emphasize the "float" part or the "managed" part in the future.

- Proponents of the managed flexible exchange rate system believe it offers several advantages: (1) It allows nations to pursue independent monetary policies. (2) It solves trade problems without trade restrictions. (3) It is flexible and therefore can easily adjust to shocks. Opponents of the managed flexible exchange rate system believe it has several disadvantages: (1) It promotes exchange rate volatility and uncertainty and results in less international trade than would be the case under fixed exchange rates. (2) It promotes inflation. (3) It corrects trade deficits only a long time after a depreciation in the currency; in the interim, it can make matters worse.

key terms and concepts

Balance of Payments	Merchandise Trade Surplus	Exchange Rate	Overvaluation
Debit		Flexible Exchange Rate System	Undervaluation
Foreign Exchange Market	Current Account Balance		Devaluation
Credit	Capital Account	Appreciation	Revaluation
Current Account	Capital Account Balance	Depreciation	Optimal Currency Area
Merchandise Trade Balance	International Monetary Fund (IMF)	Purchasing Power Parity (PPP) Theory	Managed Float
Merchandise Trade Deficit	Special Drawing Right (SDR)	Fixed Exchange Rate System	

questions and problems

1 Suppose the United States and Japan have a flexible exchange rate system. Explain whether each of the following events will lead to an appreciation or depreciation in the U.S. dollar and Japanese yen. (a) U.S. real interest rates rise above Japanese real interest rates. (b) The Japanese inflation rate rises relative to the U.S. inflation rate. (c) Japan imposes a quota on imports of American radios.

2 Give an example that illustrates how a change in the exchange rate changes the relative price of domestic goods in terms of foreign goods.

3 Suppose the media report that the United States has a deficit in its current account. What does this imply about the U.S. capital account balance and official reserve account balance?

4 Suppose Canada has a merchandise trade deficit and Mexico has a merchandise trade surplus. The two countries have a flexible exchange rate system, so the Mexican peso appreciates and the Canadian dollar depreciates. It is noticed, however, that soon after the depreciation of the Canadian dollar, Canada's trade deficit grows instead of shrinks. Why might this occur?

5 What are the strong and weak points of the flexible exchange rate system? What are the strong and weak points of the fixed exchange rate system?

6 Individuals do not keep a written account of their balance of trade with other individuals. For example, John doesn't keep an account of how much he sells to Alice and how much he buys from her. In addition, neither cities nor any of the 50 states calculate their balance of trade with all other cities and states. However, nations do calculate their merchandise trade balance with other nations. If nations do it, should individuals, cities, and states do it? Why or why not?

7 Every nation's balance of payments equals zero. Does it follow that each nation is on an equal footing in international trade and finance with every other nation? Explain your answer.

8 Suppose your objective is to predict whether the euro (the currency of the European Union) and the U.S. dollar will appreciate or depreciate on the foreign exchange market in the next two months. What information would you need to help make your prediction? Specifically, how would this information help you predict the direction of the foreign exchange value of the euro and dollar? Next, explain how a person who could accurately predict exchange rates could become extremely rich in a short time.

9 Suppose the price of a Big Mac always rises by the percentage rise in the price level of the country in which it is sold. According to the purchasing power parity (PPP) theory, we would expect the price of a Big Mac to be the same everywhere in the world. Why?

10 If everyone in the world spoke the same language, would the world be closer to or further from being an optimal currency area? Explain your answer.

working with numbers and graphs

1 The following foreign exchange information appeared in a newspaper:

	U.S. Dollar Equivalent		Currency per U.S. Dollar	
	THURS.	FRI.	THURS.	FRI.
Russia (ruble)	0.0318	0.0317	31.4190	31.5290
Brazil (real)	0.3569	0.3623	2.8020	2.7601
India (rupee)	0.0204	0.0208	48.9100	47.8521

a Between Thursday and Friday, did the U.S. dollar appreciate or depreciate against the Russian ruble?
b Between Thursday and Friday, did the U.S. dollar appreciate or depreciate against the Brazilian real?
c Between Thursday and Friday, did the U.S. dollar appreciate or depreciate against the Indian rupee?

2 If $1 equals 0.0093 yen, then what does 1 yen equal?

3 If $1 equals 7.7 krone (Danish), then what does 1 krone equal?

4 If $1 equals 31 rubles, then what does 1 ruble equal?

5 If the current account is −$45 billion, the capital account is +$55 billion, and the official reserve balance is −$1 billion, what does the statistical discrepancy equal?

6 Why does the balance of payments always equal zero?

Globalization

Setting the Scene

The following events occurred one day in September.

10:13 A.M.

The leaders of some of the richest countries in the world were gathering for a meeting in a small town in Switzerland. The topic for discussion was economic globalization. Outside the meeting, hundreds of people from all over the world screamed slogans and held up signs. One of the most common signs read, "Globalization hurts the poor." One of the chants heard there was, "Hey, Hey, Ho, Ho. Globalization has got to go!"

6:14 P.M.

Ken works as a software engineer for a large firm in New York City. He just walked into his house after a hard day at work. His wife, Alexis, who usually gets home about 7:00, is already home. She says to Ken, "What's got you so down? You look as if you lost your job today." "I did," says Ken. "The company is sending my job out of the country."

7:45 P.M.

Diane is watching a television news show. Here is what the TV news reporter is currently saying: "People are somewhat afraid that with globalization, their jobs and their livelihoods will be determined by forces outside their control, perhaps by forces emanating from halfway around in the world. This is the scary side of globalization. But on the other hand, some people look upon this new and global economy with optimism. They say that with globalization come opportunities— opportunities to end poverty and to turn a turbulent and hostile world into a peaceful one. We'll just have to wait and see. For WTYX News, this is Tabitha Sherman."

11:54 P.M.

Elizabeth lives in Kentucky. Last week, she bought a computer online from a U.S. company. She is having a little trouble with the computer, so she calls the customer service number. It is a 1-800 number. A voice on the other end of the line asks for her service tag number. She gives it to the person. The person she is speaking with is in India.

? Here are some questions to keep in mind as you read this chapter:

- *What is globalization and does it hurt the poor?*

- *Will globalization lead to some people losing jobs?*

- *Does everyone agree as to what the benefits and costs of globalization are?*

- *Why does Elizabeth's customer service call connect to a person in India?*

See **analyzing the scene** at the end of this chapter for answers to these questions.

What Is Globalization?

What is this thing called **globalization**? Many economists define it as (1) a phenomenon by which individuals and businesses in any part of the world are much more affected by events elsewhere in the world than before. Globalization can also be defined as (2) the growing integration of the national economies of the world to the degree that we may be witnessing the emergence and operation of a single worldwide economy. These factors—people and businesses across the world having greater impact on each other, creating a smaller world, and the movement toward a worldwide economy—are repeated in the many different definitions of globalization. Let's take a closer look at these key features of globalization.

Globalization
A phenomenon by which economic agents in any given part of the world are more affected by events elsewhere in the world than before; the growing integration of the national economies of the world to the degree that we may be witnessing the emergence and operation of a single worldwide economy.

A Smaller World

The first definition emphasizes that economic agents in any given part of the world are affected by events elsewhere in the world. If you live in the United States, you are not only affected by what happens in the United States but also by what happens in Brazil, Russia, and China. For example, in 2005, the Chinese government was taking much of the money it earned in trade with the United States and buying bonds issued by the U.S. government. As a result of Chinese purchases of U.S. bonds, interest rates in the United States ended up being lower than they would have been. Because of lower interest rates, some people took out mortgage loans to buy a house who otherwise would not have. Some people took out car loans to buy a car who otherwise would not have.

But can you see how, in a sense, globalization makes the world smaller? China hasn't moved physically; it isn't any closer to the United States (in terms of distance) than it was 100 years ago. Still, what happens in distant China today, because of globalization, has an effect on you as, in the past, what happened between locations only 10 miles or 100 miles away. For all practical purposes, we live in a "smaller world" today than people did 100 years ago.

A World Economy

Globalization is closely aligned with a movement toward more free enterprise, freer markets, and more freedom of movement for people and goods. Thomas Friedman, author of several books on globalization, states that "globalization means the spread of free-market capitalism in the world." Economic globalization is essentially a free enterprise activity, and to the degree that many countries are "globalizing," they are moving toward greater free enterprise practices. Much of this globalization, and much of the movement toward freer markets, is occurring in the world today.

With globalization, the world is moving from hundreds of national economies toward *one large world economy*. In this world economy, it does not make as much sense to speak of *different* economic systems as it once did. It makes sense to speak of "the" economic system for that one world economy. And as we said, the economic system that best describes what is happening in the world economy is free enterprise or capitalism.

Q&A *I've heard that globalization is bad for U.S. workers. After all, can't globalization lead to a lot of Americans losing their jobs to people in other countries?*

You will learn more about this later in the chapter, but for now, keep two points in mind: (1) Yes, globalization can lead to some American workers losing jobs, but (2) during a relatively intense period of globalization in the United States (during the 1990s and early 2000s), the U.S. unemployment rate was at historic lows. If globalization necessarily led to large numbers of Americans losing their jobs and staying unemployed, we would expect the unemployment rate in the country to be much higher than it was during the period of, say, 1990 to 2006. Instead, we find that for this period in the United States, globalization and lower unemployment rates seem to have gone together.

Two Ways to "See" Globalization

Sometimes, a definition is not as good as a picture to describe and explain something. Let's try to create two mental pictures that should give you a good idea of what globalization is about. The first picture is of a world without any barriers to trade, where the cost of dealing with anyone in the world is essentially the same.

No Barriers

Suppose land was not divided into nation states—no United States, no China, no Russia. Also suppose physical, economic, or political barriers to trade did not exist. Essentially, then, you could trade with whomever you wanted to trade with, no matter where in the world this person lived. You could trade with a person living 5,000 miles away as easily as you could trade with your next-door neighbor.

In this pretend world, businesses could hire workers and set up factories anywhere in the world. People could open savings accounts in banks 7,000 miles away or buy stock in companies located on the other side of the globe.

Now, in a sense, our world—the world that we live in today—is moving in the direction of this pretend world just described. As this movement proceeds, a nation's economy (e.g., the U.S. economy) becomes more and more a part of the world economy. As this process continues, it becomes more and more relevant to speak of a world or global economy rather than the Russian, U.S., or Chinese economies.

A Union of States

The second way to see globalization is familiar to people who reside in the United States. We know that the United States is made up of 50 states. Today, it is easy to move goods and services between these states. If a person wants to, he can produce goods in, say, North Carolina and then transport those goods (with only a few exceptions) for sale to every state in the country. In addition, a person living anywhere in the United States can move to any state and work, save, purchase, sell, and so on. In other words, within the United States, free movement of people and goods is possible.

Some people will argue today that economic globalization is, in a way, similar to changing countries (of the world) into states of one country. It is similar to taking independent countries such as the United States, Russia, China, Brazil, and Japan and turning them into the United States of the World.

Globalization Facts

How do we know globalization is occurring? What do you need to see happening in the world before you could say that globalization was taking place?

You would see countries in the world opening up to more trade with each other. You would see people in one country investing some of their money in other countries. You would see companies in one country hiring people in other countries. Essentially, you would see people in the world acting more like they once acted only within their individual countries. Some evidence suggests that all these things are happening.

Q&A   *What specifically is the difference between a national economy and a global economy?*

Think of an invisible string connecting you and everyone you have an economic relationship with. If you buy something from someone, a string connects the two of you; if you work for someone, a string connects you. Now, perhaps the best way to think of a national economy is to think of strings only linking people who reside in the same country. In a world or global economy, however, strings link individuals with people in their own country and in other countries too. Their economic relationships extend beyond the nation's borders. In the past, a few strings extended outside country borders, but only a few, and for a long time, the strings only went to certain countries. With globalization, more and more strings, a seemingly unlimited number of strings, are being connected across borders. And these strings are being connected between people in more and more countries.

International Trade

The average **tariff** rate in the United States was 40 percent in 1946. According to the 2006 *Economic Report of the President,* the average tariff today is about 1.4 percent. You may also be interested in knowing that federal government revenue from tariffs in the early 1900s accounted for half of all federal government revenues, whereas today they account for less than 2 percent. Exhibit 1 presents average tariff rates in the United States during the period 1930–2005.

What has been occurring in the United States (a decline in tariff rates) has also been happening in countries such as India, China, Brazil, and many others. For example, in 2000, the average tariff rate in China was 18.7 percent; one year later, it was 12.8 percent. In 2000, the average tariff rate in India was 30.2 percent; one year later, it was 21 percent. Furthermore, both India and China are trading more with other countries. For example, 15 years ago, China did not trade much with the countries of Europe. Today, for most European countries, China is one of their top five trading partners.

As further evidence of globalization, between 1973 and 2006, countries exported and imported more goods. Exports became a larger percentage of a country's total output. To explain these changes, think of an analogy. Suppose you produce computers. Last year, all the computers you produced were purchased by residents of the country in which you live. This year, half the computers you produced are purchased by residents of the country in which you live, and the other half are purchased by persons who live in foreign countries. In 2006, U.S. exports and imports were more like the second scenario; in 1973, things were closer to the first scenario.

Foreign Exchange Trading

When people of one country want to trade with people of another country or invest in a foreign company, they have to buy the currency used in the other country. So if globalization occurred, we would expect a lot more currency exchanges to take place. In economics, *foreign exchange trading* is a term that means "buying and selling foreign currencies." In 1995, daily foreign exchange trading was 60 times higher than it was in 1977. In 1992, daily foreign exchange trading amounted to $820 billion. In 1998, this amount had risen to $1.5 trillion, close to doubling in just 6 years.

Foreign Direct Investment

If a U.S. company wants to invest in a company in, say, Russia, it undertakes what is called *foreign direct investment.* The more foreign direct investment there is, the more likely

Tariff
A tax on imports.

exhibit **1**

Average U.S. Tariff Rates, 1930–2005

economics 24/7

HOW HARD WILL IT BE TO GET INTO HARVARD IN 2025?

The Indian Institute of Technology (in India) is one of the hardest universities in the world to be admitted to, largely because of its reputation. It has been compared to putting Harvard, MIT (Massachusetts Institute of Technology), and Princeton together.

In an average year, about 178,000 high school seniors in India take the exam necessary to apply to the Indian Institute of Technology. Just over 3,500 students (only 1.96 percent of all applicants) are admitted. In comparison, the admission rate of Harvard University is nearly 10 percent. Often, students from India who are admitted to MIT, Princeton, and Cal Tech (all of which are listed in the top 10 of U.S. colleges and universities) cannot gain admission to the Indian Institute of Technology.

Now consider some highly prestigious U.S. universities and colleges, such as Brown, Columbia, Cornell, Dartmouth, Harvard, the University of Pennsylvania, Princeton, Yale, Stanford, Northwestern, and Duke. These schools have some of the most selective admission criteria of all colleges and universities in the country. Each year, students who have the grade point average and standardized test scores to (potentially) be admitted to these universities are turned away.

This phenomenon has been occurring at the same time that college tuition has been increasing rapidly. For example, during the period 1990 to 2003, college tuition went up by 130 percent, considerably more than medical care costs, the price of housing, food, gasoline, cars, and so on.

If we look around the world at other prestigious institutions of higher learning, we see the same theme: The admission rate is usually low, and the cost is usually high.

Consider how grades (one major admissions criterion) and money actually function in this situation: They are rationing devices. We know that because of scarcity, some mechanism has to ration the available resources, goods, and services. Still we have to ask: Why have these two rationing

devices—grades and money—become stiffer when it comes to being admitted to the top universities in the world? Why ever higher grades and ever more money? The answer is twofold.

First, the population of the world increased at the same time that the number of Harvards did not. Harvard cannot clone itself, nor can Yale, the Indian Institute of Technology, or MIT. To a large degree, the world has only one Harvard, Oxford (in the United Kingdom), and Indian Institute of Technology. We can produce more computers, houses, and dining room chairs as the population of the world increases, but it seems much more difficult to produce more Harvards. So, what happens over time is a heightened scarcity of top-notch, one-of-a-kind educational institutions. As a result, the rationing devices for such institutions must do more work to ration, which essentially means that it will become harder and more expensive to get admitted to such places.

The second reason involves globalization. One of things that pays a high dividend in a global economy is education. "Brains" seem to matter more than "brawn," which will increase the overall demand for a college education—and not just at Harvard but at all levels of higher education (from community colleges to 4-year state and private universities). So, will the premium placed on education in a global economy cause the demand at the most prestigious educational establishments to rise at a faster rate than at other colleges? It would be similar to asking: If the premium for playing music were to rise, would the demand to be at Juilliard (one of the premier music institutions in the world) rise faster than the demand to study with the local piano teacher down the street? The likely answer is yes. With a growing world population, and with the global economy paying a high premium to those who are educated (compared to those who are not), we can expect it to get increasingly more difficult and more expensive to be admitted to the world's best institutions of higher learning.

the process of globalization is at work. In 1975, foreign direct investment amounted to $23 billion. In 1997, it had risen to $644 billion, a 30-fold increase. In 1980, 6.2 percent of the U.S. population was foreign born; in 2005, it was 12 percent. Between 1984 and 2003, U.S. investment holdings in foreign companies tripled while foreign investment in the U.S. increased six-fold.

Personal Investments

Many people in the United States own stocks. If you own a number of stocks, you are said to have a stock portfolio. In 1980, these stock portfolios were comprised of no more than 2 percent of foreign stocks. Today, it is 14 percent. Thus, Americans are increasingly buying stock in foreign companies.

The World Trade Organization

The World Trade Organization (sometimes called the WTO) is an international organization whose mission is to promote international free trade (trade between countries). In 1948, only 23 countries of the world chose to be members of the precursor to the WTO, GATT (General Agreement on Tariffs and Trade); in mid-2006, that number had risen to 149 countries.

Business Practices

It is becoming increasingly common for Americans to work for foreign companies that have offices in the United States. For example, the number of Americans working for foreign companies (with offices in the United States) grew from 4.9 million in 1991 to 6.5 million in 2001, an increase of 1.6 million.

Movement Toward Globalization

How did we come to live in a global economy? Did someone push a button years ago and start the process of globalization? No, things don't happen that way.

Globalization did not just appear on the world stage two decades ago. The world has gone through different globalization periods. For example, during the period from the mid-1800s to the late-1920s, globalization was occurring. Some people today refer to it as the First Era of globalization. In some ways, that world was a freer world when it came to the movement of people than the world today, as evidenced by the fact that many people moved from country to country without a passport, which was not required.

This early era of globalization was largely ended by the two world wars (World War I and World War II) and the Great Depression. Even though the Great Depression and both world wars were over by 1945, globalization did not start anew. The Cold War essentially divided the world into different camps (free vs. unfree, capitalist vs. communist), which led to relatively high political and economic barriers. The visible symbol of these barriers—the Berlin Wall—separated not only East from West Germany but one group of countries living under one political and economic system from another group of countries living under a different political and economic system.

The more recent period of globalization that we speak about today has several causal factors. Not everyone agrees as to what all the factors are, and not everyone agrees as to the weight one assigns to each of the factors. For example, some people will argue that one factor means more to globalization than another factor. Still, it is important that you are aware of the causal factors of globalization most often mentioned.

The End of the Cold War

The Cold War intensified after World War II and, most agree, ended with the visible fall of the Berlin Wall in 1989. This event, while historic in and of itself, occurred at the time when the Soviet empire was beginning to crumble and many of the communist East European countries were breaking away from the Soviet Union. As some explain it, the end of the Cold War resulted in turning two different worlds (the capitalist and communist worlds) into one world. It resulted in a thawing of not only political but economic relations between former enemies. You might not trade with your enemy, but once that person or country is no longer your enemy, you don't feel the same need to cut him or it out of your political and economic life.

At the beginning of this section, we asked you to imagine a world where no barriers affected your trading with anyone in the world. The barriers might be distance, culture, politics, or anything else. The Cold War acted as a political barrier between certain groups of countries; once it ended, one barrier standing in the way of trade was no longer there.

One way to view the current period of economic liberalization (freer markets, lower tariffs) and globalization is to ask whether it would be occurring as it is today if the United States and the Soviet Union were still engaged in the Cold War. This is doubtful. Even though the end of the Cold War might not be the full and only cause for the current period of globalization, it is probably true that if the Cold War had not ended, globalization would not be accelerating at the pace it is today.

Advancing Technology

In the past, innovations such as the internal combustion engine, steamship, telephone, and telegraph led to increased trade between people in different countries. All of these inventions led to lower transportation or communication costs, and lower costs mean fewer barriers to trade. What technology often does is lower the hindrances (of physical distance) that act as stumbling blocks to trade. For example, the cost of a 3-minute telephone call from New York to London in 1930 was $250. In 1960, it was $60.42; in 1980, it was $6.32; and in 2000, it was 40 cents. Today, the cost is even less. As the costs of communicating continue to fall, in some sense, the hindrance of physical distance (to trade) is overcome. Businesspeople in the United States, for example, can more cheaply talk with businesspeople in China.

Now consider the price of a computer in various years. What was the cost of a computer in 1960, one comparable to the desktop computer that many people today have on their desk at home? The answer is $1.8 million. That computer was $199,983 in 1970, $27,938 in 1980, $7,275 in 1990, and only $1,000 in 2000. People today not only use computers for their work, but they communicate with others via the Internet. This computer and Internet technology makes it possible for people to communicate with others over long distances, thus increasing the probability that people will trade with each other.

Today, even farmers in poor developing countries can have access to people and information they didn't have access to only a few years ago. A farmer in the Ivory Coast can check agricultural prices in the world with a cell phone—something that was unheard of a decade ago. Or consider such innovations as online banking. Years ago, it was common to have "your bank" just down the road from you. Today, it is possible to open up an account with an online bank, many of which are located nowhere near you.

Policy Changes

Governments have the power to slow down the process of globalization if they want. Suppose two countries, A and B, have free economic relations with each other. Neither country imposes tariffs on the goods of the other country. Neither country prevents its citizens from going to the other country to live and work. Neither country hampers its citizens from investing in the other country. Then, one day, for whatever reason, the government of country A decides to impose tariffs on the goods of country B and limit its citizens from traveling to and investing in country B. In other words, the government of country A decides to close its political and economic doors.

Well, just as a government of one country can close the door on another country, it can open that door too. It can open that door a little, more than a little, or a lot. In

economics 24/7

WILL GLOBALIZATION CHANGE THE SOUND OF MUSIC?

Suppose you had only 100 people to whom you could sell some good. Given this small number, if you want to sell something, you had better sell something that some of these 100 people want to buy. For example, if these 100 people don't like fruit salad, then you better not produce and offer to sell fruit salad; if some of these 100 people like bread, then perhaps you should produce and offer to sell bread.

Now increase the number of people from 100 to 1 million. Is it more or less likely that some people in a group of 1 million will like fruit salad than in a group of 100? The answer is that as the size of the potential customer base increases, the number of things you can sell increases too. In a world of 100 people, you can only sell bread, but in a world of 1 million people, you can sell fruit salad or bread.

Now suppose you are a musician. As a musician, you can play different styles of music: jazz, pop, classical, hard rock, metal, hip hop, and so on. If you are limited to selling your music to the people of a single state of the United States, you would have fewer styles of music you could offer to sell than if you could sell your music to the people who reside throughout the United States.

Our general point is a simple one: The larger the size of the potential customer base (simply put, the more people you can possibly sell to), the greater is the variety of goods we are likely to see.

Globalization is, to a large degree, expanding everyone's ability to potentially sell to more people. American companies aren't limited to selling only to Americans; they can sell to others in the world too. Chinese firms aren't limited to selling only to Chinese; they can sell to others in the world too.

As an example, consider some musician in the United States who is experimenting with a new style of music. With a population of only the United States as a potential customer base (the population of the U.S. is 300 million), the musician might not yet have enough actual customers to make it worth producing and offering to sell this particular, unique, and narrowly defined music. However, if the musician can draw on the population of the world (population: 6.4 billion), then the musician might then be able to find enough people who are willing to buy this particular new type of music.

As we move toward a world economy, we see a greater variety of goods within almost every category of goods you can think of: a greater variety of music to listen to, books to read, types of television shows to watch, and so on. Today, the greater variety of goods you see in your world is an effect of globalization.

recent decades, governments of many countries have been opening their doors to other countries. China has opened its door, India has opened its door, and Russia has opened its door.

The driving forces of this most recent period of globalization have been (1) the end of the Cold War, (2) technological changes that lower the costs of transporting goods and communicating with people, and (3) government policy changes that express an openness toward freer markets and long-distance trade.

SELF-TEST

(Answers to Self-Test questions are in the Self-Test Appendix.)

1. Some have said that the end of the Cold War has led to greater globalization. Explain the reasoning here.

2. What is globalization?

3. How might advancing technology lead to increased globalization?

Benefits and Costs of Globalization

Some people believe that globalization is, in general, a good thing and that its benefits outweigh its costs. Other people take the opposite view and believe that the costs of globalization are greater than the benefits. Let's look at what those who favor globalization say are its benefits and what those who oppose it say are its costs. As you read, you will probably begin to form your own opinion.

The Benefits

TRADE To say that the world is undergoing the process of globalization is really no more than saying that people are trading with more people, at greater distances, than they once did. They are trading different things: money for goods, their labor services for money, their savings for expected returns, and so on. Expanding trade—which is what globalization is about—is no more than extending the benefits of trading to people one might not have traded with earlier.

Economist David Friedman compared free international trade to a technology. He says that you can produce, say, cars in two ways. You can set up factories in Detroit, Michigan, and produce cars. Or you can harvest wheat in the Midwest, load it on ships and send it to Japan, and then wait for the ships to return with cars.

Looking at things the second way sometimes brings out the "magic" of trade. After all, with free trade across countries, wheat gets turned into cars, an accomplishment that really is magical. The lesson Friedman is trying to communicate is that we all think a technological improvement is a good thing because it often leads to a higher standard of living. Well, then, trading with people across the world really is nothing more than a technology of sorts; it is a way to turn wheat into cars. The more we trade with others, the more magic we witness.

INCOME PER PERSON Now let's consider the benefits of globalization in a slightly more concrete way. As both India and China opened up their economies to globalization in recent decades, they experienced increases in income per person. For example, between 1980 and 2000, income per person doubled in India. Between 1940 and 2000, income per person increased by 400 percent in China, much of this increase coming in recent years. According to the International Monetary Fund, these dramatic increases in income per person accompanied the expansion of free international trade (which is a key component of globalization).

Q&A *Isn't it the case that prices can fall even if they are not traded between countries? If so, how do we identify whether a good's price has fallen because of, say, technology or because it is a good that is traded between countries?*

One way is to compare prices between more and less traded goods. According to the 2006 Economic Report *of the President, "a clear divergence in price trends emerges when products are split this way. Internationally traded products tend to experience lower inflation rates—even real price declines—while nontraded goods tend to experience price increases."*

PRICES Numerous studies have established a link between lower prices and the degree of international trade and globalization. Simply put, international trade (a key component of globalization) lowers prices. For example, in Exhibit 2, we show the CPI (consumer price index) and an import price index for the period 1990–2004. You will notice that the CPI (which contains domestic goods and imported goods) has risen faster than the import price index (which contains only imported goods). Also, between 1977 and 2004, the inflation-adjusted prices for an array of goods traded between countries fell while the inflation-adjusted prices for an array of goods not traded between countries actually increased. Some of the traded goods whose prices fell include audio equipment (−26 percent), TV sets (−51 percent), toys (−34 percent), and clothing (−9 percent); some of the nontraded goods whose prices increased include whole milk (+28 percent), butter (+23 percent), ice cream (+18 percent), peanut butter (+9 percent).

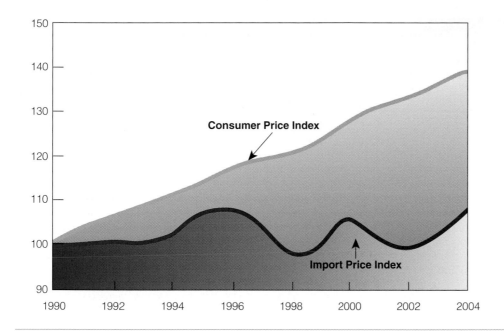

exhibit **2**

CPI and Import Price Index, 1990–2004

The CPI increased at a faster rate during the period 1990–2004 than the import price index (which both increased and decreased during the period).

Source: Bureau of Labor Statistics.

PRODUCTIVITY AND INNOVATION Firms that face global competition are often pushed to increase their productivity and to innovate more. According to the 2006 *Economic Report of the President,* "Studies show that firms exposed to the world's best practices demonstrate higher productivity through many channels, such as learning from these best practices, and also creating new products and processes in response to this exposure." For example, one study from the United Kingdom showed that almost 3 times as many firms that faced global competition reported product or process innovations than firms that did not face global competition.

Or consider an extreme case, North and South Korea. The two countries share a people and a culture, but North Korea avoided the process of globalization during the period in which South Korea embraced it. What we observe is that South Koreans enjoy a much higher standard of living than North Koreans.

Q&A *How do we know that the benefits you say are a result of globalization are, in fact, caused by globalization? Couldn't they be caused by something else?*

Economists are fairly sure that globalization leads to an increased standard of living based on their comparisons of countries with similar characteristics, except for the fact that one set of countries is globalizing while the other set is not. For example, take a look at Exhibit 3, which shows that the annual percentage change during the 1990s in output per person (a measure of material standard of living) is positive in globalized developing countries but negative in less globalized countries.

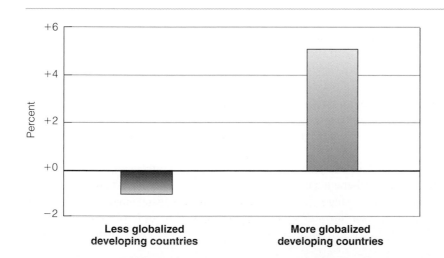

exhibit **3**

Annual Average Percentage Change in Output per Person in the 1990s

economics 24/7

SHOULD YOU LEAVE A TIP?

In the United States, tipping in restaurants amounts to $16 billion a year. Even though tipping in the United States is common today, 24 percent of the individuals in one study said that they thought tipping was unfair to customers. In the past, some states prohibited tipping. For example, in the early 1900s, Arkansas, Mississippi, Iowa, South Carolina, Tennessee, and Washington passed laws to prohibit tipping.

What about the rest of the world? Do people around the world have the same tipping practices as Americans? Some do, but certainly not all. For example, it is increasingly more customary in European restaurants to have an automatic service charge added to a restaurant bill than to tip the server. Little tipping of any sort goes on in Argentina and Vietnam. Much less tipping occurs (fewer service providers expect tips) in Australia, New Zealand, and Italy than in the United States, and more tipping goes on in Mexico and Egypt than in the United States.

In several studies, researchers looked at the number of different service providers (out of a total of 33) for which tipping is customary in a given country. The more service providers it was customary to tip in a country, the higher the country's "prevalence of tipping." For example, if it was customary to tip 31 different service providers in country A but only 15 in country B, then country A would have a higher prevalence of tipping than country B.

The conclusion of these studies is that countries where success and materialism were highly valued had a higher prevalence to tip than countries where caring and personal relationships were highly valued. In addition, the prevalence of tipping increased as the national need for achievement and recognition rose. In one study, tipping was more prevalent in countries with lower taxes than in countries with higher taxes.

If it becomes increasingly relevant to speak of a world economy instead of hundreds of national economies, will tipping practices around the world become more common? If they do become more common, toward what degree of tipping will they gravitate?

We do not know the answer to these questions, so you might then wonder: Why ask? The answer is twofold. First, it gets us to think about what *changes* we are likely to see in our everyday lives as globalization continues forward and whether those changes will only be in the strictly economic realm (e.g., we can buy more clothes from China) or will disperse outward into the social and cultural realms too. Second, it forces us to separate into categories things that are so deeply embedded in the character of a people (and therefore unlikely to change) from things that are somewhat superficial (and therefore more likely to change). Which is a rock (incapable of absorbing), and which is a sponge (capable of absorbing)?

The Costs

INCREASED INCOME INEQUALITY Globalization's critics often point out that globalization seems to go hand in hand with increased income inequality in the world. Has income inequality increased? Yes it has. For example, 100 years ago, people in rich countries had about 10 times more income than people in poor countries. Today, they have about 75 times more income. Without a doubt, globalization and income inequality (between rich and poor countries) are strongly correlated. The question, though, is whether globalization causes the income inequality. The critics of globalization say it does, whereas the supporters say it does not.

The supporters of globalization argue that it is much like a train. Economic systems that get on the train will benefit (and reach their economic destinies faster), but those that don't will get left increasingly farther behind. In other words, it may not be globalization that delivers greater income inequality but a combination of some countries globalizing while others are not. (If everyone is walking, some faster than others, then some will always be in front of others. If those who are walking fast start to run while the others continue their slow walking pace, the gap between the ones in front and the ones in back will grow.)

Of course, it is not only a matter of choosing to get on the train of globalization. Sometimes, a "conductor" on the train doesn't let some people on. Some rich countries work against some poor countries when it comes to the poor countries' globalization efforts. For example, tariffs on goods imported from the poor, developing world are 30 percent above the global average for all tariffs.

LOSING AMERICAN JOBS Many critics of globalization argue that globalization can result in Americans losing certain jobs. Suppose a U.S. company hires engineers in India to do jobs that once were done by Americans. This practice of hiring people in other countries is often called **offshoring**.

It is true that some Americans may lose their jobs to workers in other countries due to globalization. It has already happened. Over the past few years, a major New York securities firm replaced its team of 800 American software engineers, who earned about $150,000 per year, with an equally competent team in India earning an average of about $20,000 a year. Additionally, the number of radiologists in the United States is expected to fall significantly because it is now possible to send the data (that U.S. radiologists analyze) over the Internet to Asian radiologists who can analyze the data at a fraction of the cost.

Keep in mind, though, that offshoring is a two-way street: The United States might offshore certain jobs to, say, India or China, but foreign countries around the world offshore jobs to the United States too. Although some Americans do lose jobs due to globalization efforts, we also need to keep in mind that jobs are always being lost (and found) in a dynamic economy that is responding to market changes. Even if the degree of offshoring in the United States was zero, people would still be losing old jobs and getting new jobs every day.

MORE POWER TO BIG CORPORATIONS Many critics of globalization argue that the process will simply "turn over" the world (and especially the developing countries of the world) to large Western corporations (corporations headquartered in the United States, the United Kingdom, Canada, and etc.). In fact, in the minds of many people, globalization is not what we have defined it as in this chapter, but rather, it is the process of *corporatizing* the world. Instead of governments deciding what will and will not be done, large corporations will assume the responsibility.

The proponents of globalization often point out a major difference between a corporation and a government. First, a government can force people to do certain things (pay taxes, join the military). No corporation can do the same; instead, corporations can simply produce goods that they hope customers will buy. Additionally, the proponents of globalization often argue that the critics overestimate the influence and reach of large transnational companies. For example, in 2000, the top 100 transnational companies produced only 4.3 percent of the entire world's output, which is about as much as what one country, the United Kingdom, produced in 2000.

The Continuing Globalization Debate

Many (but certainly not all) economists argue that the worldwide benefits of globalization are likely to be greater than the worldwide costs. Of course, it doesn't mean that everyone is going to see the beneficial side of globalization. To a large degree, whether one supports or criticizes globalization seems to depend on where "one is sitting." Globalization doesn't affect everyone in the same way, and often, *how* it affects *you* determines how you feel about it. For example, suppose Sanders, an American worker residing in

Offshoring
Work done for a company by persons other than the original company's employees in a country other than the one in which the company is located.

New York, loses his job to an Indian worker in New Delhi, India, who will do Sanders's job for less pay. In this case, Sanders incurs real costs, but what about Sanders's company and the company's customers? For the company, this change means lower costs and higher profits. For the company's customers, prices for the company's products may go down. So in this case, Sanders is probably a strong opponent of offshoring, while his company and its customers are probably supporters.

When it comes to globalization, it is often much more difficult to see the benefits than it is to see the costs. For example, the supporters of globalization argue that it brings greater economic wealth, lower prices (than would otherwise exist), more innovation, less poverty, and so on. Yet sometimes, it is difficult for us to see all these benefits. When you buy cheaper goods or different goods because of globalization, you probably never say, "Wow, I can't believe all the benefits I get from globalization!" In fact, you might not even connect the lower priced goods with globalization at all. The benefits of globalization tend to be difficult to see, partly because they are so widely dispersed.

The costs of globalization, in contrast, are more visible, often because they are so concentrated. A person who loses a job because of freer international trade in the world knows exactly what is to blame for the predicament he or she is in. This person surely could receive some benefits from globalization (in the role of a consumer), but this person also could, for a time, incur some rather high costs from globalization (in the role of a worker). It is likely that this person will know of the costs but be unaware of the benefits.

In the end, things may stack up this way: The people who receive only benefits from globalization might not be able to see the benefits or to connect them with globalization. The people who receive benefits and costs from globalization may only be aware of the costs. This one-sided view could create strong antiglobalization sentiment in a country.

More or Less Globalization: A Tug of War?

Is increased globalization inevitable? Will the day come when all countries in the world are similar to all 50 states in the United States—part of one global economy with easy movement of people, resources, financial capital, goods, and services among the countries? Or will the conditions that prevented globalization reappear and reverse the recent trend?

Think of this struggle as a tug of war. We have the forces of globalization pulling in one direction, and we have the forces of antiglobalization pulling in the other direction. As of today, the forces of globalization are moving things in their direction. Will this trend continue uninterrupted? Well, maybe not, some say. Surely, at any time, the forces of antiglobalization could get a burst of energy and make an extra strong tug on the rope.

To answer the question, let's go back to what we stated were the driving forces of the most recent era of globalization: the end of the Cold War, changes in technology (which lowered the costs of transportation and communication), and policy changes that opened up countries' economies to each other.

Less Globalization

INCREASED POLITICAL TENSION The end of the Cold War is a historical fact that we cannot "undo." We could, however, enter a period when political tensions among countries, or among groups of countries, emerge. We are not suggesting that such a period of tension will happen, only that it could. If it did, it could slow down globalization or, depending on the severity of the tension, even reverse it.

Terrorism. Another inhibiting factor to globalization is global terrorism. Global terrorism tends to motivate certain countries into closing borders and into being much more careful about the people and goods that cross their borders.

Technology. We cannot undo our technology. We cannot go from a world with the Internet to one without it. So it is unlikely that anything on the technological front will slow down or reverse globalization.

Government Policies. However, we can witness policy changes that will slow down or reverse globalization. Governments of countries that opened up their economies to others could reverse their course; doors that opened to others can be closed. We cannot say whether this sort of isolationism will happen in the future.

More Globalization

Still, some will argue that even with the forces of antiglobalization looming on the horizon, the forces of globalization are stronger. In the end, these individuals say, the forces of globalization will win the tug of war. They believe that in the long run, economics is what influences politics rather than the other way around. To give some proof to what they are saying, they often point to the former Soviet Union and to China. Both were strongly communist countries. Both countries saw, in the end, that they were worse off by holding themselves outside the orbit of free market forces. You might say that they found themselves "out of step" with the economic forces that were loudly playing on the world stage.

Thomas Friedman states that "globalization is not just some economic fad, and it is not a passing trend." He also argues that the "relevant market today is planet Earth." The basic globalization force that will probably not be overcome—no matter how strong the political forces may be against it—is the human inclination that the founder of modern economics, Adam Smith, noticed more than 200 years ago. Smith said that human beings want to trade with each other. In fact, it is the desire to trade that separates us from all other species, he says. In his words, "Man is an animal that makes bargains: no other animal does this—no dog exchanges bones with another."

We want to trade with people: our next-door neighbor, the person down the street, the person on the other side of town, the person in the next state, the person on the other side of the country, and finally, the person on the other side of the world. Some economists go on to suggest that this "trading" inclination we possess is a good thing in that, when we trade with people, we not only tolerate them but we have much less reason to fight with them. Robert Wright, a visiting scholar at the University of Pennsylvania, argues that it is not a coincidence that religious toleration is high in the United States, a country that is open to trade and globalization. What we often see, he argues, is that people who live in countries that trade with other people, people who live in countries that are open to other people, end up being countries that tolerate different types of people.

In a similar vein, Thomas Friedman advanced his "Golden Arches theory of conflict prevention," which says that "no two countries that both had McDonald's had fought a war against each other since each got its McDonald's." The United States will not fight Germany since both countries have McDonald's. France won't fight Mexico since both countries have McDonald's. Certainly, it is not the sheer presence of a McDonald's in a country that prevents people from fighting with other people. It's because McDonald's is symbolic of certain things being present in the country. For Friedman, it is a symbol for a certain degree of economic globalization and a level of economic development sufficient enough to support a large middle class.

SELF-TEST

1. Identify some of the benefits of globalization.

2. Identify some of the costs of globalization.

$\mathscr{A}\ \mathscr{R}\ e\ a\ d\ e\ r\ \ \mathscr{A}\ s\ k\ s\ .\ .\ .$

Will My Job Be Sent Overseas?

One hears much these days about outsourcing or offshoring jobs. Are some jobs more likely to be sent overseas than others?

When it comes to some jobs, location matters. But when it comes to other jobs, location does not seem to matter. First, let's look at some jobs where location matters.

If you are sick and need a doctor, you prefer to have a doctor close to you. If you live in Ithaca, New York, you will probably want a doctor who works in Ithaca, New York, not in Bangkok, 8,553 miles away.

If you need a plumber, you will probably want a plumber close by, not one on the other side of the world. If you want to go out to eat, you will most likely go to a restaurant near where you live, not one on the other side of the world.

Now when it comes to buying a book, location may not matter: It may not matter to you where the bookseller resides, as long as you can get the book fairly quickly. When it comes to someone answering your technical computer questions, it may not matter where the technician lives. As long as the technician speaks your language, listens well, and gives clear and concise instructions, you probably don't care where he or she is located.

In short, when a provider's (supplier's, worker's) location is important to you, you can be fairly sure that the kind of job the provider performs will not be off-shored to another country. When a provider's location is not important to you, the probability of the provider's job being offshored rises.

In 2004, *Forbes* magazine ran a story titled "Ten Professions Not Likely to Be Outsourced." Here is the list:

- Chief Executive Officer
- Physician and Surgeon
- Pilot, Copilot, and Flight Engineer
- Lawyer
- Computer and Information Systems Manager
- Sales Manager
- Pharmacist
- Chiropractor
- Physician's Assistant
- Education Administrator, Elementary and Secondary School

! analyzing the scene

What is globalization and does it hurt the poor?

Globalization is a phenomenon by which economic agents in any given part of the world are affected by events elsewhere in the world; it represents the growing integration of the national economies of the world to the degree that we may be witnessing the emergence and operation of a single worldwide economy. So far, most of the evidence shows that globalization does not hurt the poor. For example, output per person (a measure of one's material standard of living) grew at positive rates during the 1990s in more globalized developing countries but declined in less globalized countries (see Exhibit 3). Also both India and China, countries that have been opening up their economies to globalization, have seen their income per person increase in recent decades. According to the International Monetary Fund, in the past 30 years, hunger and child labor have been cut in half and life expectancy has increased in developing countries. Work done by economists Gary Hufbauer and Paul L. E. Grieco shows that globalization increases U.S. income by roughly $1 trillion a year, or $10,000 per household.

Will globalization lead to some people losing jobs?

Yes. Globalization is not a static process in which everything stays the same from day to day. Globalization will cause some people to lose jobs, but even without globalization, some people will lose jobs. Even in a country without any trade with other countries, people's preferences would change for goods and services, and some people would lose their jobs as a consequence.

Does everyone agree as to what the benefits and costs of globalization are?

No, but this chapter tries to give you some idea of the nature of the debate over globalization.

Why does Elizabeth's customer service call connect to a person in India?

It could be because the U.S. company found it cheaper to hire the person in India than to hire a person in, say, the United States, the United Kingdom, or some other country to answer customers' calls.

chapter summary

What Is Globalization?

- Globalization is a phenomenon by which individuals and businesses in any part of the world are much more affected by events elsewhere in the world than before; it is the growing integration of national economies of the world to the degree that we may be witnessing the emergence and operation of a single worldwide economy.

- There are certain facts that provide evidence that globalization is occurring. Some of these facts are (1) lower tariff rates in many countries; (2) many countries exporting and importing more goods than in the past; (3) greater foreign exchange trading; (4) more foreign direct investment; (5) many more people own foreign stocks; (6) many more countries have joined the WTO in recent years; (7) a greater number of Americans working for foreign companies that have offices in the United States.

Movement Toward Globalization

- What has caused this most recent push toward globalization? In the chapter we identified (1) the end of the Cold War, (2) advancing technology, and (3) policy changes as causal factors.

Benefits and Costs of Globalization

- Some of the benefits of globalization include (1) benefits from increased international trade, (2) greater income per person, (3) lower prices for goods, (4) greater product variety, and (5) increased productivity and innovation.

- Some of the costs of globalization include (1) increased income inequality (although there is some debate here), (2) offshoring, and (3) increased economic power for large corporations (although there is some debate here too).

- When it comes to globalization, it is often much more difficult to see the benefits than the costs. The benefits are largely dispersed over a large population while the costs (e.g., offshoring) might be concentrated on relatively few.

The Future of Globalization

- There is a debate over the future of globalization. Some persons argue that globalization will continue; others say it will stall and (perhaps) backtrack.

key terms and concepts

Globalization

Tariff

Offshoring

questions and problems

1   Why might it be easier to recognize the costs of globalization than the benefits?

2   If globalization continues over the next few decades, how might your life be different?

3   How might governments impact globalization?

4   Identify and explain two of the benefits and two of the costs of globalization.

5   What effect might advancing technology have on globalization?

6   Some have argued that the end of the Cold War acted as a catalyst toward greater globalization. How so?

7   What is Thomas Friedman's "Golden Arches theory of conflict prevention"?

8   David Friedman said that free (international) trade is a technology. Explain what he means.

9   Will globalization lead to some people losing jobs? Explain your answer.

10   How do tariff rates in the United States today compare with 1946?

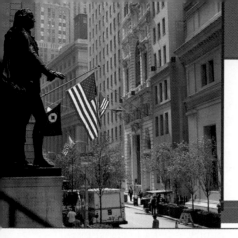

Stocks, Bonds, Futures, and Options

Setting the Scene

The following events occurred one day in August.

7:13 A.M.

Priscilla is having breakfast with her husband, Paul. She says, "I think we should put a little money into the stock market. I heard that the Dow went up by 279 points yesterday." "Is that good?" her husband asks. "I think it is," said Priscilla.

8:34 A.M.

Jack lives in Kansas. He is a wheat farmer, his father was a wheat farmer, and his grandfather was a wheat farmer. Things haven't been going well for Jack in the last year or so. He has been losing money. He will be harvesting a big wheat crop in the next few months and is afraid that wheat prices may drop before he takes his wheat to market.

10:56 A.M.

Karen is at home watching the financial news. Someone on television just said, "If he times his purchases correctly, he can make millions." Karen wonders if the investment types on television know something she doesn't know. How can you make millions, she wonders, just by timing purchases (what purchases?) correctly?

5:42 P.M.

Wilson is on a commuter train headed home after a busy day at work. The person in the seat next to him is reading *The Wall Street Journal*. Wilson turns to him and says, "What do you think about what the market did today?" "That was quite unusual," came the response.

? Here are some questions to keep in mind as you read this chapter:

- *What is the Dow?*

- *Is there any way that Jack can protect himself from a drop in the price of wheat?*

- *Does timing matter?*

- *What does "the market" refer to?*

See analyzing the scene at the end of this chapter for answers to these questions.

Financial Markets

Everyone has heard of stocks and bonds. Everyone knows that stocks and bonds can be sold and purchased, but not everyone knows the economic purpose served by stocks and bonds.

Buying and selling stocks and bonds occur in a financial market. Financial markets serve the purpose of channeling money from some people to other people. Suppose Jones saved $10,000 over two years, and Smith is just starting a new company. Smith needs some money to get the new company up and running. On the other hand, Jones would like to invest the savings and receive a return. Jones and Smith may not know each other; in fact, they may live on opposite ends of the country. What a financial market does, though, is bring these two people together. It allows Jones either to invest in Smith's company or to lend Smith some money. For example, Jones might buy stock in Smith's company or perhaps buy a bond that Smith's company is issuing. In this chapter, we discuss more about the ways in which people like Smith and Jones help each other through use of a financial market. Specifically, in this section, we discuss stocks, and in the next section, we discuss bonds.

Q&A

If I buy shares of stock, do I have to hold on to them for any set period of time? Also, where can I buy shares of stock?

No. You can buy shares of stock at 10:12 in the morning and sell those shares 5 minutes later if you want. As for buying stock, you can buy stock through a stockbroker—in person, over the phone, or online. For example, many people today buy stocks from an online broker. They simply go online, open an account with an online broker, deposit funds into that account, and then buy and sell stock.

Stock

A claim on the assets of a corporation that gives the purchaser a share of the corporation.

Stocks

What does it mean when someone tells you that she owns 100 shares of a particular stock? For example, suppose Jane owns 100 shares of Yahoo! stock. It means that she is a part owner in Yahoo!, Inc., which is a global Internet media company that offers a network of World Wide Web programming. A **stock** is a claim on the assets of a corporation that gives the purchaser a share in the corporation.

In our example, Jane is not an owner in the sense that she can walk into Yahoo! headquarters (in Santa Clara, California) and start issuing orders. She cannot hire or fire anyone, and she cannot decide what the company will or will not do over the next few months or years. But still, she is an owner. And as an owner she can, if she wants, sell her ownership rights in Yahoo!. All she has to do is find a buyer for her 100 shares of stock. Most likely, she could do so in a matter of minutes, if not seconds.

Where Are Stocks Bought and Sold?

You know where groceries are bought and sold—at the grocery store. You know where clothes are bought and sold—at the clothing store. But where are stocks bought and sold?

Let's go back in time to help answer the question. In 1792, twenty-four men met under a buttonwood tree on what is now Wall Street in New York City. They essentially bought and sold stock (for themselves and their customers) at this location. Someone might have said, "I want to sell 20 shares in company *X*. Are you willing to buy these shares for $2 a share?"

From this humble beginning came the New York Stock Exchange (NYSE). Every weekday (excluding holidays), men and women meet at the NYSE in New York City and buy and sell stock.

Suppose you own 100 shares of a stock that is listed on the NYSE. Do you have to go to the NYSE in New York to sell it? Not at all. You would simply contact a stockbroker (either over the phone, in person, or online), and he or she would convey your wishes to sell the stock to a person at the NYSE itself. That person at the NYSE would then execute your order.

economics 24/7

IS THERE GENIUS WHEN IT COMES TO PICKING STOCKS?

Warren Buffett is the second richest person in the world. In 2005, he had $46 billion. He was born in Omaha, Nebraska, in 1930. He is one of the few billionaires who has amassed his fortune by investing in stocks. If you had invested $10,000 in Buffett's investment company (Berkshire Hathaway) in 1969, you would have had $50 million in 2003.

Buffett's ability at picking winning companies and their stocks is without parallel. Does Buffett know something the rest of us don't know? Is he a financial genius or just one of the luckiest people in the world?

Before we answer those questions, think of the following game. We start with 1 million people; we then match them up in pairs. Now there are 500,000 pairs of people. We ask each pair of people to pick a number between 1 and 10. The person who is closer to the number chosen (by a third party) wins.

After the first round, 250,000 people are winners and 250,000 people are losers. The losers are excused and the 250,000 winners are paired off. Now we have 125,000 pairs. We play our game again. We are now down to 62,500 winners, which we pair off again.

How many rounds pass before we are down to only one pair (two people)? The answer is eighteen. In the eighteenth round, we are down to two people. Obviously, there will be a winner and a loser in this ninth, and last, round.

The single winner can say that he or she has won over 999,999 people. He has won every one of nine rounds.

How did he win, though? Was he more intelligent than the rest? Braver? Better looking? It is, of course, none of these things. He was simply luckier than everyone else (in much the same way that the person who wins the lottery is luckier than anyone else who played the lottery).

Our point is a simple one: A person can defeat many other people, and win round after round, by just being lucky.

So does this explain Warren Buffett? Has it been luck that explains his winning round after round in the stock market? Is he simply the winner of the stock market lottery in much the same way a person might win a real lottery? We think the answer is probably not. So why explain the game? Why show that luck can explain a shocking outcome?

For two reasons. The first reason is to show that sometimes what we think is brilliance or intelligence can be luck.

The second reason is to show the difference between the game (as we played it out) and the stock market. In our game, there had to be a final winner. When we first started playing the game with 500,000 pairs of people, we knew that after so many rounds there would be only one winner. (It is sort of like the television show *American Idol*. We know that no matter how many contestants try out for the show, at the end of the season, there will be only one winner.)

The stock market is different, though. A consistent winner is not necessarily in the cards. We don't have to be left with one winner after 20 or 30 years of buying and selling stock. And that is why we believe that what Warren Buffett brings to his stock picking is probably something more than luck. It is probably some "sense of genius" that most of us do not have (in much the same way that few of us are music or math prodigies).

Will Buffett's uncanny ability to pick stocks be with him for the rest of his life? We don't know. What we do know is that sometimes by noticing the "genius" among us, we come to get a better sense of ourselves. For the person who thinks that picking successful stocks is easy, let him or her recognize that for every one Warren Buffett there are literally millions of people who can't do what he does. But to think otherwise, and to go softly into that dark night thinking you can, often ends in disaster.

Now just as there is a NYSE where stocks are bought and sold, there are other stock exchanges and markets where stocks and bonds are sold too. For example, there is the American Stock Exchange (AMEX) and the NASDAQ stock market (NASDAQ is pronounced "NAS-dak" and stands for National Association of Securities Dealers Automated Quotations). Buying and selling stock on the NASDAQ do not take place the same way they take place on the NYSE. Instead of the buying and selling in one central location, the NASDAQ is an electronic stock market with trades executed through a sophisticated computer and telecommunications network. The NYSE might in fact change to this kind of market in the near future; instead of people meeting in one location to buy and sell stock, they could do it electronically.

Increasingly, Americans are not only buying and selling stocks on the U.S. stock exchanges and markets but in foreign stock exchanges and markets too. For example, an American might buy a stock listed on the German Stock Exchange, the Montreal Stock Exchange, or the Swiss Exchange.

The Dow Jones Industrial Average (DJIA)

Dow Jones Industrial Average (DJIA)

The most popular, widely cited indicator of day-to-day stock market activity. The DJIA is a weighted average of 30 widely traded stocks on the New York Stock Exchange.

You may have heard news commentators say, "The Dow fell 302 points on heavy trading." They are talking about the Dow Jones Industrial Average. The **Dow Jones Industrial Average (DJIA)** first appeared on the scene more than 100 years ago, on May 26, 1896. It was devised by Charles H. Dow. Dow took 11 stocks, summed their prices on a particular day, and then divided by 11. The "average price" was the DJIA. (Some of the original companies included American Cotton Oil, Chicago Gas, National Lead, and U.S. Rubber.)

When Charles Dow first computed the DJIA, the stock market was not highly regarded in the United States. Prudent investors bought bonds, not stocks. Stocks were thought to be the area in which speculators and conniving Wall Street operators plied their trade. It was thought back then that Wall Streeters managed stock prices to make themselves better off at the expense of others. There was a lot of gossip about what was and was not happening in the stock market.

Dow devised the DJIA to convey some information about what was happening in the stock market. Before the DJIA, people had a hard time figuring out whether the stock market, on average, was rising or falling. Instead, they only knew that a particular stock went up or down by so many cents or dollars. Dow decided to find an average price of a certain number of stocks (11) that he thought would largely mirror what was happening in the stock market as a whole. With this number, people could then have some sense of what the stock market was doing on any given day.

Today, the DJIA consists of 30 stocks, which are widely held by individuals and institutional investors (see Exhibit 1). This list can and does change from time to time, as determined by the editors of *The Wall Street Journal*.

---

exhibit 1

The 30 Stocks of the Dow Jones Industrial Average (DJIA)

Here are the 30 stocks that comprise the Dow Jones Industrial Average.

3M Co.	Home Depot Inc.
Alcoa Inc.	Honeywell International Inc.
Altria Group Inc.	Intel Corp.
American Express Co.	International Business Machines Corp.
American International Group Inc.	Johnson & Johnson
AT&T Inc.	JPMorgan Chase & Co.
Boeing Co.	McDonald's Corp.
Caterpillar Inc.	Merck & Co. Inc.
Citigroup Inc.	Microsoft Corp.
Coca-Cola Co.	Pfizer Inc.
E.I. DuPont de Nemours & Co.	Procter & Gamble Co.
Exxon Mobile Corp.	United Technologies Corp.
General Electric Co.	Verizon Communications Inc.
General Motors Corp.	Wal-Mart Stores Inc.
Hewlett-Packard Co.	Walt Disney Co.

You may think that the DJIA is computed by summing the prices of stocks and dividing by 30, but it is not quite that simple today. A special divisor is used to avoid distortions that can occur, such as companies splitting their stock shares. Exhibit 2 shows the Dow Jones Industrial Average during the period of January 1, 2002–October 30, 2006.

In addition to the DJIA, other prominent stock indexes (besides the Dow) are cited in the United States. A few include the NASDAQ Composite, the Standard & Poor's 500, the Russell 2000, and the Wilshire 5000. There are also prominent stock indexes around the world, including the Hang Seng (in Hong Kong), the Bovespa (Brazil), IPC (Mexico), BSE 30 (India), CAC 40 (France), and so on.

Different economic consulting firms have attempted to find out what influences the Dow. What causes it to go up? What causes it to go down?

According to many economists, the Dow is closely connected to changes in such things as consumer credit, business expectations, exports and imports, personal income, and the money supply. For example, increases in consumer credit are expected to push up the Dow, the thought being that when consumer credit rises, people will buy more goods and services, and this is good for the companies that sell goods and services. When consumer credit falls, the reverse happens.

 If the DJIA goes up or down, does this affect me if I do not own any of the stocks that make up the DJIA?

It doesn't affect you if we are looking at daily changes in the DJIA, but if we are talking about a long decline in the DJIA or a long rise in the DJIA, then it indirectly affects you. Many economists say that what happens in the stock market—or to the DJIA—is a forerunner of future economic events. So if the DJIA goes down over time, it is indicating that the economic future is somewhat depressed; if it goes up over time, it is indicating that the economic future looks good. The economic future—good or bad—is something that does affect you. It affects what prices you pay, how easy or hard it is to get a job, how large or small a raise in income you get, and so on.

How the Stock Market Works

Suppose a company wants to raise money so that it can invest in a new product or a new manufacturing technique. It can do one of three things to get the money. First, it can go to a bank and borrow the money. Second, it can borrow the money by issuing a bond (a promise to repay the borrowed money with interest; you will learn more about bonds later in the chapter). Third, it can sell or issue stock in the company, or put another way, it sells part of the company. Stocks are also called *equity* because the buyer of the stock has part ownership of the company.

exhibit **2**

DJIA, January 1, 2002– October 30, 2006

Here we show the ups and downs of the DJIA from January 1, 2002 to October 30, 2006.

economics 24/7

ARE SOME ECONOMISTS POOR INVESTORS?

You might think that economists would do pretty well in the stock market compared to the average person. After all, their job is to understand how markets work and to study key economic indicators.

So how do you explain a May 11, 2005, article in the *Los Angeles Times* titled "Experts Are at a Loss on Investing"? The article looked at the investments of four economists—all Nobel Prize winners in economics. Not one of them said that he invests the way he should invest, and none of them seemed to be getting rich through their investments. Often, it appears there is a big difference between knowing what to do and doing it.

Harry M. Markowitz won the Nobel Prize in Economics in 1990. He won the prize for his work in financial economics; he is known as the father of "modern portfolio theory," the main idea being that people should diversify their investments.

Did Markowitz follow his own advice? Not really. Most of his life, he put half of his money in a stock fund and the other half in a conservative, low-interest investment. Markowitz, age 77 at the time, says, "In retrospect, it would have been better to have been more in stocks when I was younger."

George Akerlof, who won the Nobel Prize in Economics in 2001, had invested most of his money in money market accounts, which tend to have relatively low interest rate returns but are safe. Akerlof, when confronted with this fact, said, "I know it's utterly stupid."

Clive Granger, who won the Nobel Prize in Economics in 2003, was asked about his investments. He said, "I would rather spend my time enjoying my income than bothering about investments."

Daniel Kahneman, who won the Nobel Prize in Economics in 2002, had this to say about his investments: "I think very little about my retirement savings, because I know that thinking could make me poorer or more miserable or both."

Keep in mind what we said in an earlier chapter: Almost every activity comes with both benefits and costs. There are certainly benefits to investing wisely, but there are costs too. It takes time to find out about various investments, to research them, and to keep informed on how they are doing.

The actions of our four Nobel Prize winners also point out something else. As we said once before, many people think that economics is simply about money and money matters. But it is not. It is about utility and happiness and making oneself better off. Each of our four Nobel Prize winners might not have been doing the best thing for his wallet, but certainly, each knew this and continued on the same path anyway. Each was willing to sacrifice some money to live a preferred lifestyle.

What is the lesson for you? Should you care nothing about your investments and hope that your financial future will take care of itself? Or should you spend time regularly watching, researching, and evaluating various investments that either you have made or plan to make? Neither extreme is too sensible. But then, it is not a matter of *either* one *or* the other. It is possible to learn enough about investments to protect yourself from the financial uncertainties of the future but not spend so much time worrying about the future that you don't enjoy the present.

When a company is initially formed, the owners set up a certain amount of stock, which is worth very little. The owners of the company try to find people (usually friends and associates) who would be willing to buy the stock (in the hopes that one day it will be worth something). It would be nearly impossible in these early days of the company for anyone who owned stock to sell it. For example, if Jones owned 100 shares of some new company that almost no one had heard of, hardly anyone would be willing to pay any money to buy the stock.

As the company grows and needs more money, it may decide to offer its stock on the open market. In other words, it offers its stock to anyone who wants to buy it. By this time, the company may be known well enough that there are people who are willing to buy it. The company makes what is called an **initial public offering (IPO)** of its stock. The process is quite simple. Usually, an **investment bank** sells the stock for the company for an initial price – say, $10 a share. How do you find out about an IPO? They are announced in *The Wall Street Journal*.

Once there is an IPO for a stock, it is usually traded on a stock exchange or in an electronic stock market. Sometimes, the stock that initially sold for $10 will rise in price, and sometimes, it will fall like a rock. It all depends on what people in the stock market think the company that initially issued the stock will do in the future If they think the company is destined for big earnings, the stock will likely rise in price. If they think the company is destined for losses, or only marginal earnings, the stock will likely fall in price.

In a way, you can think of trading stock in much the same way you think about trading baseball cards, paintings, or anything else. The price depends on the forces of supply and demand. If demand rises and supply is constant, then the price of the stock will rise. If demand falls and supply is constant, then the price of the stock will fall.

Sometimes, people buy certain stocks because they hear that other people are buying the stock and because they think the stock is "hot." In other words, it is very popular and everyone wants it. In the 1990s, some of the Internet stocks fit this description. Stocks such as Yahoo!, Amazon.com, and eBay were bought because people thought the Internet was the wave of the future and almost anything connected with the Internet was destined for great profit.

More often, though, people buy a particular stock if they think the earnings of the company that initially issued the stock are likely to rise. After all, remember that a share of stock represents ownership in a company. The more profitable that company is expected to be, the more likely people are going to want to own that company, and therefore, the greater the demand for the stock of that company. For example, suppose William Welch started a company in 1895. Through the years, the company has been passed down to family members. In 2007, the family members running the company want to expand it—to two, three, or four times its current size. Where might they get the money to do this? One way is by selling shares in the company—that is, by issuing stock in the company. Once they have issued shares in the company to the public, the company is no longer solely family owned. Now many of the public own part of it too.

Why Do People Buy Stock?

Millions of people in the United States, and in countries all over the world, buy stock every day. Why do they do it? There are a couple reasons. Some people buy stocks for the **dividends**, which are payments made to stockholders based on a company's profits. For example, suppose company *X* has issued one million shares of stock that are owned by different people. Each year, the company tabulates its profit and loss, and if there is a profit, it divides up much of the profit among the owners of the company as dividends. This year's dividend might be $1 for each share of stock a person owns. So if Jones owns 50,000 shares of stock, she will receive a dividend check for $50,000.

The other reason to buy stock is for the expected gain in its price. Stockholders can make money if they buy shares at a lower price and sell at a higher price. For example, Smith buys 100 shares of Microsoft stock today. He thinks that the company is going to do well and that a year from now he can sell it for as much as $50 more a share than he purchased it. In other words, he hopes to earn $5,000 on his stock purchase.

Initial Public Offering (IPO)

A company's first offering of stock to the public.

Investment Bank

Firm that acts as an intermediary between the company that issues the stock and the public that wishes to buy the stock.

Dividend

A share of the profits of a corporation distributed to stockholders.

Q&A *Suppose I buy 100 shares of stock at a price of $40 a share. The stock goes down in price to $32. Shouldn't I wait until the share price rises to $40 or higher before I sell it?*

When it comes to stock, what goes down is not guaranteed to go up. Even if the stock's price has gone down by $8, it might go down more. You want to always look forward to the future (not backward to the past) when deciding whether or not to sell a stock. If you think there is a reason for the price to fall even farther, it is better to sell at $32 (and take an $8 per share loss) than to sell at $25 and take a bigger loss. If you think there is a reason for the price to rise, then you would want to hold on to the stock.

People also sell stock for many reasons. Smith might sell his 100 shares of IBM because he currently needs the money to help his son pay for college. Or he might sell his stock to help put together a down payment for a house. Another common reason for selling stock is that the stockholder thinks the stock is likely to go down in price soon. It is better today to sell at $25 a share than to sell one week from now at $18 a share.

How to Buy and Sell Stock

Buying and selling stock are relatively easy. You can buy or sell stock through a full-service stockbrokerage firm, a discount broker, or an online broker. With all varieties of brokers, you usually open an account by depositing a certain dollar amount into it, most commonly between $1,000 and $2,500. Once you have opened an account, you can begin to trade (buy and sell stock).

With a full-service broker, you may call up on the phone and ask your broker to recommend some good stock. Your broker, usually called an *account representative,* might say that you should buy *X, Y,* or *Z* stock. You may ask why these are good stocks to buy. He may say that the research department in the firm has looked closely at these stocks and believes they are headed for good times based on the current economic situation in the country, the level of exports, the new technology that is coming to market, and so on.

If you do not require help with selecting stocks, you can go either to a discount broker or to an online broker. You can call up a discount broker the same way you called up a full-service broker and tell the broker that you want to buy or sell so many shares of a given stock. The broker will execute the trade to you. He or she is not there to offer any advice.

The same process can be undertaken online. You go to your broker's Web site, log in, enter your username and password, and then buy or sell stock. You may submit an order to buy 100 shares of stock *X.* Your online broker will register your buy request and then note when it has been executed. Your account, easily visible online, will show how much cash you have in it, how many shares of a particular stock you hold, and so on.

Buying Stocks or Buying the Market

You can use various methods to decide which stocks to purchase. The first way is to buy shares of stock that you think are going to rise in price. So you might buy 50 shares of Microsoft, 100 shares of General Electric, and 500 shares of Amazon.com.

Another way is to invest in a stock mutual fund, which is a collection of stocks. The fund is managed by a fund manager who works for a mutual fund company. For example, Smith may operate Mutual Fund *Z* at Mutual Fund Company *Z.* If you put, say, $10,000 in Mutual Fund *Z,* you are in effect buying the stocks in that fund. Let's say that fund consists of stocks *A, B, C, W,* and *X* at the current time. The fund manager may, on any given day, buy more of *A* and sell some of *B* or sell all of *C* and add stock *D* to the fund portfolio.

It is up to the fund manager to do what he or she thinks is best to maximize the overall returns from the fund. As a buyer of the fund, you put your money in the fund manager's hands to do what he or she thinks will be the best.

Mutual fund companies often advertise the records of their fund managers. They might say, "Our fund managers have the best record on Wall Street. Invest with us and get the highest returns you can." You may be prompted to put your money in the hands of the "experts" because you feel they know better than you which stocks to buy and sell and when to do each.

You could use another strategy, though, and buy the stocks that make up a stock index. Earlier, we discussed the DJIA. The DJIA is a stock index. It gives us information

economics 24/7

$1.3 QUADRILLION

At the close of the 20th century, the editors of the financial magazine *The Economist* identified the highest returning investments for each year, beginning in 1900 and ending in 1999. For example, the highest returning investment in 1974 was gold, in 1902 it was U.S. Treasury bills, and in 1979 it was silver.

The editors then asked how much income a person would have earned at the end of 1999, if she had invested $1 in the highest returning investment in 1900, and then taken the returns from that investment and invested it in the highest returning investment in 1901 and so on for each year during the century. After taxes and dealer costs, she would have earned $1.3 quadrillion. (Quadrillion comes after trillion. In 2004, Bill Gates, the richest person in the world, had $47 billion, so $1.3 quadrillion is 27,659 times what Bill Gates has.) What is the lesson? With perfect foresight (or with a crystal ball that always correctly tells you what the highest returning investment of the year will be), one would be rich beyond his or her imagination.

After the editors ran their experiment, they changed it. They went back and asked themselves what one would have earned over the 20th century if, instead of investing in the highest returning investment in a given year, she invested in it one year late. That is, if *X* is the best investment in 1956, then invest in it in 1957.

Why did the editors choose to proceed this way? Because they believed that many people only invest in a "hot" investment when it is too late. They invest in it after they have heard about it, but investing in it after they have heard about it is usually too late. (Think of an investment as a mountain and going up the mountain is comparable to increasing returns on the investment and going down the mountain is comparable to decreasing returns. It's only when the investment is near its peak that many people hear about it. But then it's too late. There is no place to go but down.)

To put this into context, while the person with the crystal ball, or with perfect foresight, would have invested in the Polish stock market in 1993, when no one was talking about it, and reaped a 754 percent gain, the typical investor would have invested in it one year later, in 1994, when everyone was talking about it. The problem is that the Polish stock market fell by 55 percent in 1994.

So, what would the person who is always one year late have earned over the 20th century? After taxes and dealer costs, $290.

What are the economic lessons here? First, the best investments are often the ones that you don't hear about until it is too late. Second, ignoring the first lesson, and thinking that a popular investment is necessarily a good investment, is often the way to low returns.

---

on the performance of the 30 stocks that make up the Dow. There are other indexes too. For example, there is the Standard & Poor's 500 index. This index is a broad index of stock market activity because it is made up of 500 of the largest U.S. companies. Another broad-based stock index is the Wilshire 5000, which consists of the stocks of about 6,500 firms. (Yes, even though the index consists of more than 5,000 firms, it is still called the Wilshire 5000.) You can today buy stock index funds. That is, instead of buying a mutual fund that consists of various stocks picked by the so-called experts, you can buy a mutual fund that consists of the stocks that make up a particular index.

A particularly easy way to do this is to buy what are called "Spyders." The term *Spyders,* or SPDRs, stands for "Standard & Poor's Depository Receipts." They are securities representing ownership in the SPDR Trust. The SPDR Trust buys the stocks that make up the Standard & Poor's (S&P) 500 index. Spyders are traded under the symbol SPY. When this was being written, Spyders were selling for about $120 a share. Spyders cost one-tenth of the S&P index (total of the share prices of the stocks in the S&P). For example, if the S&P index is 1,200, then a Spyder will sell for $120.

Q&A

Is it a good idea to buy stock?

A lot depends on such factors as your age (are you at the beginning of your work career or near the end), your income, and how much you can afford to invest in the stock market. There is no guarantee that the stock you buy will go up in price. For example, consider what happened to the DJIA over the 1930s. In the beginning of 1930, the Dow stood around 250, but at the end of 1939, it was around 150. Over the decade of the 1930s, the Dow went down by 40 percent.

However, having said this, it is generally the case that stock prices have gone up over the long run. For example, suppose we look at the S&P Index during the period 1926–2004. The data here show that you would have had a 70 percent likelihood of earning a positive investment return over a 1-year period, but that would have risen to 86.5 percent chance of a positive investment return if you had held the stocks in the index over a 5-year period. The probability of a positive return goes up to 97.1 percent if you had held the stocks for 10 years. The longer you hold stocks in the stock market, the more likely you will earn a positive return.

When you buy Spyders, you are buying the stock of 500 companies. Since you are buying the stock of so many companies, you are said to be "buying the market." For example, suppose Jack decides to "buy the market" instead of buying a few individual stocks. He opens an account with an online broker. This is a matter of going online, opening up an account with an online broker, and sending the broker a check so that he can start trading (buying and selling stock). He then checks (at the online broker Web site) on the current price of Spyders. He's sees the current price is $120.16 per share. He decides to buy 100 shares, for a total price of $12,016. (His online broker charges him a small commission for this stock purchase.) In a minute or less, he sees that he has purchased the 100 shares of Spyders. That is all there is to it.

How to Read the Stock Market Page

Suppose you have purchased some stock and now you want to find out how it is doing. Is it rising or falling in price? Is it paying a dividend? How many shares were traded today?

One of the places you can go to find the answers to these questions and more is the newspaper. Turn to the stock market page in the newspaper. (Keep in mind that many newspapers are online.) You will see something similar to what you see in Exhibit 3. We will discuss what each item in each column of the bottom line stands for.

52W high. This stands for the high price of the stock during the past 52 weeks. For this stock, you see the number 51.25, which is $51.25.

52W low. This stands for the low price of the stock during the past 52 weeks. For this stock, you see the number 27.69, which is $27.69.

Stock. In this column, you see Rockwell. This is either an abbreviation of the name or the full name of the company whose stock we are investigating. The company here is Rockwell Automation Incorporated.

exhibit 3

How to Read the Stock Market Page of a Newspaper

We show here part of the stock market page of a newspaper. We explain how to read the page in the text.

(1)	(2)	(3)	(4)	(5)	(6)	(7)	(8)	(9)	(10)	(11)	(12)
52W high	52W low	Stock	Ticker	Div	Yield %	P/E	Vol 00s	High	Low	Close	Net chg
45.39	19.75	ResMed	RMD			57.5	3831	42.00	39.51	41.50	-1.90
11.63	3.55	Revlon A	REV				162	6.09	5.90	6.09	+0.12
77.25	55.13	RioTinto	RTP	2.30	3.2		168	72.75	71.84	72.74	+0.03
31.31	16.63	RitchieBr	RBA			20.9	15	24.49	24.29	24.49	-0.01
8.44	1.75	RiteAid	RAD				31028	4.50	4.20	4.31	+0.21
38.63	18.81	RobtHall	RHI			26.5	6517	27.15	26.50	26.50	+0.14
51.25	**27.69**	**Rockwell**	**ROK**	**1.02**	**2.1**	**14.5**	**6412**	**47.99**	**47.00**	**47.54**	**+0.24**

Ticker. In this column, you see ROK, which is the stock or ticker symbol for Rockwell Automation Incorporated.

Div. This stands for dividend. You see the number 1.02, which means that the last annual dividend per share of stock was $1.02. For example, a person who owned 5,000 shares of Rockwell Automation stock would have received $1.02 per share or $5,100 in dividends. (If this space is blank, it means the company does not currently pay out dividends.)

Yield %. The yield of a stock is the dividend divided by the closing price.

$$\text{Yield} = \frac{\text{Dividend per share}}{\text{Closing price per share}}$$

The closing price of the stock (shown in the one of the later columns) is 47.54, which is $47.54. If we divide the dividend ($1.02) by the closing price ($47.54), we get a yield of 2.1 percent. The higher the yield, the better, all other things being the same. For example, a stock that yields 5 percent is better than a stock that yields 3 percent, if all other things between the two stocks are the same.

P/E. This stands for P-E ratio, or price-earnings ratio. The number here is 14.5. This number is obtained by taking the latest closing price per share and dividing it by the latest available net earnings per share.

$$\text{P-E} = \frac{\text{Closing price per share}}{\text{Net earnings per share}}$$

A stock with a P-E ratio of 14.5 means that the stock is selling for a share price that is 14.5 times its earnings per share.

Now suppose that most stocks have a P-E ratio of 14.5. This means that most stocks sell for a share price that is 14.5 times their earnings per share. In comparison, let's look at stock X that has a P-E ratio of, say, 50. What would make stock X have a P-E ratio so much higher than most stocks? Obviously, the people buying stock X expect that its future earnings will somehow warrant the higher prices they are paying for the stock today. In other words, a high P-E ratio usually indicates that people believe there will be higher than average growth in earnings. Whether or not they are right remains to be seen.

Vol 00s. This stands for volume in the hundreds. The number is 6412, which translates to 641,200. It means that 641,200 shares of this stock were traded (bought and sold) on this particular day.

High. This stands for the high price the stock traded for on this particular day. The number is 47.99, which translates to $47.99.

Low. This stands for the low price the stock traded for on this particular day. The number is 47.00, which translates to $47.00.

Close. This is the share price of the stock when trading stopped on this particular day. The number here is 47.54, which translates to $47.54.

Net chg. This stands for net change. The number here is +0.24, which translates to $0.24. This means that the price of the stock on this particular day closed 24 cents higher than it did the day before.

SELF-TEST

(Answers to Self-Test questions are in the Self-Test Appendix.)

1. How many stocks does the DJIA consist of?
2. Why do people buy stocks?
3. What does the yield of a stock equal?
4. A stock's P-E ratio is currently 23. What does this mean?

Bonds

Bond
An IOU, or promise to pay.

Suppose a company in St. Louis wants to build a new factory. How can it get the money to build the factory? You will recall that companies use three principal ways to raise money. First, they can go to banks and take out loans. Second, they can issue stock, or sell ownership rights in the company. Third, they can issue bonds. A **bond** is simply an IOU, or a promise to pay. Typically, bonds are issued by companies, governments, or government agencies. In each case, the purpose of issuing a bond is to borrow money. The issuer of a bond is a borrower. The person who buys the bond is a lender.

The Components of a Bond

There are three major components of a bond: face (par) value, maturity date, and coupon rate.

Face Value (Par Value)
Dollar amount specified on a bond. The total amount the issuer of the bond will repay to the buyer of the bond.

FACE VALUE The **face value**, or **par value**, of a bond is the total amount the issuer of the bond will repay to the buyer of the bond. For example, suppose Smith buys a bond from Company Z, and the face value of the bond is $10,000. It follows that Company Z promises to pay Smith $10,000 at some point in the future.

MATURITY DATE The maturity date is the day when the issuer of the bond must pay the buyer of the bond the face value of the bond. For example, suppose Smith buys a bond with a face value of $10,000 that matures on December 31, 2015. This means that on December 31, 2015, he receives $10,000 from the issuer of the bond.

COUPON RATE The coupon rate is the percentage of the face value that the bondholder receives each year until the bond matures. For example, suppose Smith buys a bond with a face value of $10,000 that matures in 5 years and has a coupon rate of 10 percent. This means he receives a coupon payment of $1,000 each year for 5 years.

To illustrate the concepts of face value, maturity date, and coupon rate, suppose Jack buys a bond with a face value of $100,000 and a coupon rate of 7 percent. The maturity date of the bond is 10 years from today. Each year, for the next 10 years, Jack receives 7 percent of $100,000 from the issuer of the bond. This amounts to $7,000 a year for each of 10 years. In the 10th year, he also receives $100,000 from the bond issuer. With respect to this bond, the maturity date is 10 years, the coupon rate is 7 percent, and the face value is $100,000.

Bond Ratings

Bonds are rated or evaluated. The more likely the bond issuer will pay the face value of the bond at maturity and will meet all scheduled coupon payments, the higher the bond's rating. Two of the best known ratings are Standard & Poor's and Moody's. If a bond gets a

Q&A

I don't quite understand how a person that buys something (like a bond) can be called a lender. I thought when you lend money, you just turn over money to the borrower and he or she pays you back later.

Suppose a friend asks to borrow $10 and tells you that he will pay you back $11 next month if you lend him the $10 today. You say okay and hand over $10. Now suppose your friend takes out a piece of paper and writes the following on it: "I owe the person who returns this piece of paper one month from today a total of $11." Then he signs his name, writes the date, and gives the piece of paper to you. For all practical purposes, that piece of paper is a bond (an IOU statement), and you, by purchasing the IOU, have become a lender.

rating of AAA from Standard & Poor's or a rating of Aaa from Moody's, it has received the highest rating possible. You can be sure that it is one of the securest bonds you can buy; there is little doubt that the bond issuer will pay the face value of the bond at maturity and meet all scheduled coupon payments.

Bonds rated in the B to D category are lower quality bonds than those rated in the A category. In fact, if a bond is in the C category, it may be in default (the issuer of the bond cannot pay off the bond), and if it is in the D category, it is definitely in default.

Bond Prices and Yields (or Interest Rates)

The price that a person pays for a bond depends on market conditions. The greater the demand for the bond relative to the supply, the higher the price. The price is important because it determines the yield or interest rate that the bondholder receives on the bond.

Let's suppose that Smith is currently the owner of a bond with a face value of $1,000 and a coupon rate of 5 percent. He decides to sell this bond to Jones for $950. Now we know that the coupon payment on this bond will be 5 percent of $1,000 each year, or $50, so Jones can expect to receive $50 each year. But the **yield** on the bond is the coupon payment divided by the price paid for the bond. (As an aside, sometimes in everyday language, the yield on the bond is referred to as the interest rate on the bond. For example, someone might ask: What interest rate is that bond paying? We could easily substitute the term *yield* for the term *interest rate* here and give an answer of something like "5.26 percent.")

$$\text{Yield (or interest rate)} = \frac{\text{Annual coupon payment}}{\text{Price paid for the bond}}$$

In this example, it is $50/$950, or 5.26 percent. For the bond buyer, the higher the yield, the better.

Now suppose Jones had paid $1,100 for the bond instead of $950. In this case, the yield would be $50/$1100, or 4.54 percent. In other words, as the price paid for the bond rises, the yield declines.

When are the coupon rate and yield the same? Obviously, they are the same when the price paid for the bond equals the face value. For example, consider a bond with a face value of $1,000 and a coupon rate of 5 percent. If the bond is purchased for $1,000, then the yield ($50/$1,000), which is 5 percent, is equal to the coupon rate.

To illustrate, suppose Robin buys a bond with the face value of $10,000 for $9,000. The coupon rate on the bond is 4 percent. Because the coupon rate is 4 percent, Robin receives 4 percent of $10,000 (the face value of the bond) each year through the time the bond matures. This is $400 a year. Because Robin bought the bond for a price lower than the face value, her yield will be higher than the coupon rate. To find the yield, we divide the annual coupon payment of $400 by the price of the bond ($9,000). This gives Robin a yield of 4.4 percent.

Types of Bonds

As stated earlier, bonds are typically issued by companies, governments, and government agencies. This section briefly describes some of the many types of bonds that these entities issue.

Q&A   *Suppose I want to buy a bond issued by some corporation. Would I buy the bond from the corporation itself or from someone else (e.g., from a person who had purchased a bond from the corporation at an early time)?*

If the corporation is currently issuing (selling) bonds, you could buy the bond from the corporation. (You would do this through a broker who is finding buyers for the bonds the corporation wants to sell.) But if the corporation is not currently issuing bonds, you could buy the bond from someone who purchased and still holds the bond he or she bought from the corporation at an earlier date.

The terminology here is primary and secondary markets. If you are buying a bond, say, that is newly issued, you are buying it in the primary market; if you are buying a bond from someone that currently owns the bond, you are buying it in the secondary market.

As an aside, the same thing that we have said here for bonds holds for stocks too. If you buy the stock that is newly issued by the corporation, you are buying it in the primary market; if you buy the stock from someone who owns the stock, you are buying it in the secondary market.

By far, most of your bond and stock purchases are going to be in the secondary market.

Yield
Equal to the annual coupon payment divided by the price paid for the bond.

Q&A

Can a bond issuer set the coupon rate at anything he or she wants? If so, why wouldn't the bond issuer always set the coupon rate at something like 1 percent?

The answer has to do with competition. Suppose company A needs to borrow $1 million and decides to issue $10,000 bonds. The only way anyone would be willing to buy one of these bonds (lend the company $10,000) would be if the company promised the buyers a rate of return comparable to the interest rate they could get if they simply put the money in a savings account. The company has to set the coupon rate in such a way that it can attract people to its bonds. If people are earning, say, 5 percent on their savings accounts, they will not lend money to the company unless the company pays a coupon rate of at least 5 percent. In short, the coupon rate is set at a competitive level—not just any level the company wants to set it at.

CORPORATE BONDS A corporate bond is issued by a private corporation. It is typical to find a corporate bond with a $10,000 face value. Corporate bonds may sell for a price above or below face value depending on current supply-and-demand conditions for the bond. The interest that corporate bonds pay is fully taxable.

MUNICIPAL BONDS Municipal bonds are issued by state and local governments. States may issue bonds to help pay for a new highway. Local governments may issue bonds to finance a civic auditorium or a sports stadium. Many people purchase municipal bonds because the interest paid on the bonds is not subject to federal taxes.

TREASURY BILLS, NOTES, AND BONDS When the federal government wants to borrow funds, it can issue Treasury bills (T-bills), notes, or bonds. The only difference between bills, notes, and bonds is the time to maturity. Although called by different names, all are bonds. Treasury bills mature in 13, 26, or 52 weeks. Treasury notes mature in 2 to 10 years, and Treasury bonds mature (come due) in more than 10 to 30 years. Treasury bills, notes, and bonds are considered very safe investments because it is unlikely the federal government will default on its bond obligations. After all, the federal government has the power to tax to pay off bondholders.

INFLATION-INDEXED TREASURY BONDS In 1997, the federal government began to issue inflation-indexed bonds. The first indexed Treasury bonds that were issued matured in 10 years and were available at face values as small as $1,000.

What is the difference between an inflation-indexed Treasury bond and a Treasury bond that is not indexed? An inflation-indexed Treasury bond guarantees the purchaser a certain real rate of return, but a nonindexed Treasury bond does not. For example, suppose you purchase an inflation-indexed, 10-year, $1,000 bond that pays 4 percent coupon rate. If there is no inflation, the annual interest payment will be $40. But if the inflation rate is, say, 3 percent, the government will "mark up" the value of the bond by 3 percent—from $1,000 to $1,030. Then it will pay 4 percent on this higher dollar amount. So instead of paying $40 each year, it pays $41.20. By increasing the monetary value of the security by the rate of inflation, the government guarantees the bondholder a real return of 4 percent.

How to Read the Bond Market Page

If you turn to the bond market page of the newspaper, you can find information about the different types of bonds. Here we discuss how to read the information that relates to both corporate bonds and Treasury bonds. First, let's look at corporate bonds.

CORPORATE BONDS Not all publications will present corporate bond information in exactly the same format. The format we show you here is common, though.

(1) Bonds	(2) Cur Yld	(3) Vol	(4) Close	(5) Net Chg
AT&T 6 5/8 34	6.7	115	99 1/2	−3/4

Bonds. This column presents three pieces of information. The first is the abbreviation for the company that issued the bond. Here you see AT&T, which is a telecommunications company. Next to that you see 6 5/8. This is the coupon rate of the bond. Next you see 34, which stands for the year the bond matures. In this case, it is 2034.

Cur Yld. In this column, you find the current yield. (We showed how to compute the yield on a bond earlier.) This current yield bond means that if the bond is purchased today (hence the word *current*), it will provide a yield of 6.7 percent.

Vol. In this column, you find the volume. The number here is 115, so the dollar volume today is $115,000.

Close. In this column, you find the closing price for the bond on this particular day. This number is 99 1/2. Bond prices are quoted in points and fractions; each point is $10. Thus, 99 1/2 is $999.50 (99.5 × 10 = $999.50).

Net Chg. In this column, you find the net change for the day. Here, it is −3/4, which means the price on this day was $7.50 lower than it was the previous day.

TREASURY BONDS Not all publications will present Treasury bond information in exactly the same format. The format we show you here is common, though.

(1) Rate	(2) Maturity	(3) Bid	(4) Ask	(5) Chg	(6) Yield
7 3/4	Feb. 09	105:12	105:14	−1	5.50

Rate. In this column, you find the coupon rate of the bond. This Treasury bond pays 7 3/4 percent of the face value of the bond in annual interest payments.

Maturity. In this column, you find when the bond matures. This Treasury bond matures in February 2009.

Bid. In this column, you find how much the buyer is willing to pay for the bond. (Another way to look at it is that this is the price you will receive if you sell the bond.) The number here is 105:12. The number after the colon stands for 32nds of $10. Therefore, 105:12 is $1,053.75. (First multiply 105 × $10, which gives you $1,050. Then turn 12/32 into 0.375, which you will now multiply by $10, giving you $3.75. If we add the $3.75 to $1,050, we get $1,053.75.)

Ask. In this column, you find how much the seller is asking for to sell the bond. This is the price you will pay if you buy the bond, which is $1,054.37.

Chg. In this column, you find the change in the price of the bond from the previous trading day. The change is in 32nds. It follows, then, that −1 means that the price of the bond fell by 1/32nd of $10, or approximately 32 cents from the previous day.

Yield. In this column, you find the yield, which is based on the ask price. What it means is that if a person buys the bond today (at the ask price) and holds it to maturity, he or she will reap a return of 5.50 percent.

Risk and Return

We discussed stocks in the first section of this chapter and bonds in the second. The common denominator between both these sections is that people buy stocks or bonds for the return. Simply stated, they buy stocks and bonds in the hope that they will "make money."

We need to keep in mind that stocks and bonds often come with different risk and return factors. For example, it might be much riskier to buy stock in a new company than it is to buy a Treasury bond issued by the U.S. Treasury. You can be fairly sure that the U.S. Treasury is going to pay off that bond; after all, the U.S. government has the ability to tax people.

But you can't be so sure you'll have a positive return on the stock you buy in the new company. You might buy the stock for $10 one day, and three days later, it falls to $1 and stays at that price (or thereabouts) for 10 years.

Back in Chapter 1, we said there was a well-known principle in economics: There is no such thing as a free lunch. Applied to stocks and bonds (or any investment), it means that you never get something for nothing. In short, higher returns come with higher risks, and lower returns come with lower risks. Treasury bonds, for example, will often pay (relatively) low returns because they are so safe (risk-free).

SELF-TEST

1. What is a bond?

2. If the coupon payment on a bond is $400 a year and the coupon rate is 7 percent, then what is the face value of the bond?

3. If the annual coupon payment for a bond is $1,000 and the price paid for the bond was $9,500, then what is the yield or interest rate?

4. What is the difference between a municipal bond and a Treasury bond?

Futures and Options

In this section, we discuss both futures and options.

Futures

Myers is a miller. He buys wheat from the wheat farmer, turns the wheat into flour, and then sells the flour to the baker. Obviously, he wants to earn a profit for what he does. But how much, if any, profit he earns depends on the price at which he can buy the wheat and the price at which he can sell the flour.

Now suppose Myers enters into a contract with a baker. Myers promises to deliver to the baker 1,000 pounds of flour in six months. At the current wheat price, $3 a bushel, Myers knows he can earn a profit on his deal with the baker. But Myers doesn't need the wheat now; he needs it in about six months. What will the price of wheat be then? If it is, say, $2 a bushel, then Myers will earn more profit on the deal with the baker. But if it is, say, $4 a bushel, then he will lose money on the deal. Myers's problem is that he doesn't know what a bushel of wheat will sell for in six months.

Futures Contract

Agreement to buy or sell a specific amount of something (commodity, currency, financial instrument) at a particular price on a stipulated future date.

Myers decides to buy a futures contract in wheat. A **futures contract** is a contract in which the seller agrees to provide a particular good (in this case, wheat) to the buyer on a specified future date at an agreed-upon price. For example, Myers might buy bushels of wheat now, for a price of $3 a bushel, to be delivered to him in six months.

But who would sell him the futures contract? A likely possibility would be a speculator, someone who buys and sells commodities to profit from changes in the market. A speculator assumes risk in the hope of making a gain.

Suppose Smith, a speculator, believes that the price of wheat six months from now is going to be lower than it is today. She may look at things this way: "The price of wheat today is $3 a bushel. I think the price of wheat in six months will be close to $2 a bushel. Why not promise the miller that I will deliver him as much wheat as he wants in six months if, in return, he agrees today to pay me $3 a bushel for it. Then, in six months, I will buy the wheat for $2 a bushel, sell it to the miller for $3 a bushel, and earn myself $1 profit per bushel."

Myers, the miller, and Smith, the speculator, enter into a futures contract. Myers buys 200 bushels of wheat for delivery in six months; Smith sells 200 bushels of wheat for delivery in six months.

What does each person get out of the deal? Myers, the miller, gets peace of mind. He knows that he will be able to buy the wheat at a price that will let him earn a profit on his deal with the baker. Smith takes a chance, which she is willing to take, for the chance of earning a profit.

Now let's consider another example to show how all of this works. Wilson is a farmer who grows primarily corn. The current price of corn is $2.34 a bushel. Wilson doesn't have any corn to sell right now, but he will in two months. He hopes that between now and two months, the price of corn won't fall—say, to something under $2. He decides to enter into a futures contract in corn. He promises to deliver 5,000 bushels of corn two months from now for $2.34 a bushel. Johnson, a speculator in corn, decides that this is a good deal for him because he believes that in two months the price of a bushel of corn will have risen to $3.14. So Wilson and Johnson enter into a futures contract. Two months pass and the price of corn has dropped to $2.10. Johnson turned out to be wrong about the price rising. So Farmer Wilson delivers 5,000 bushels of corn to Speculator Johnson, for which Johnson pays Wilson $2.34 a bushel (total: $11,700) as agreed. Then Johnson turns around and sells the corn for $2.10 a bushel (receiving $10,500). Johnson has lost $1,200 on the deal.

In the example, the price of corn went down. It could have gone up, though. In this case, would Wilson, the farmer, have lost money?

Let's suppose the price of corn rose to $4.00. In this case, Wilson would have delivered 5,000 bushels of corn to Speculator Johnson for $2.34 a bushel, and then Johnson would have turned around and sold the corn for $4 a bushel. In this case, Speculator Johnson would have earned the difference between $4 and $2.34—or $1.66—for every one of the 5,000 bushels. This amounts to $8,300.

Did Wilson, the farmer, lose this $8,300? In a way, he did. He didn't lose it in the sense that it was once in his pocket, but now it isn't. He lost it in the sense that it could have been in his pocket (if he hadn't entered into the futures contract with Johnson), but now it isn't.

But this might be okay with Wilson. Wilson, remember, may not want to be in the speculating business. He might want to only be worried about growing and selling corn and nothing else. Maybe he doesn't want to be involved in speculating on the price of corn. Maybe he is willing to "give up" $8,300 now and then so that he can sleep soundly at night and not worry constantly about possible price declines.

CURRENCY FUTURES   A futures contract can be written for wheat, as we have seen, or for a currency, a stock index, or even bonds. Here is how a currency futures contract works.

Suppose you check the dollar price of a euro today and find that it is 83 cents. Thus, for every 83 cents, you get 1 euro in return. Let's say that you believe that in three months, you will have to pay $1.10 to buy a euro. With this in mind, you enter into a futures contract: Essentially, you say that you are willing to buy $10 million worth of euros three months from now for 83 cents a euro. Who might be willing to enter into this contract with you? Anyone who thinks the dollar price of a euro will be lower (not higher) in three months. Suppose you and this other person enter a contract. You promise to buy $10 million worth of euros in three months (at 83 cents a euro), and this other person promises to sell you $10 million worth of euros in three months (at 83 cents a euro).

Three months pass, and we learn that it takes 97 cents to buy a euro (not 83 cents and not $1.10). What happens now? The person who entered into a contract with you has to buy $10 million worth of euros at an exchange rate of 97 cents = 1 euro. This means for $10 million, he gets 10,309,278 euros. He then turns these euros over to you and gets 83 cents for every euro, which gives him $8,556,701. Obviously, this person has taken a loss; he spent $10 million to get $8,556,701 in return. That's a loss of $1,443,299.

But what about you? You now have 10,309,278 euros for which you paid $8,556,701. How many dollars will you get if you sell all those euros? Well, since you get 97 cents for every euro, you will get approximately $10 million. Are you better off or worse off now? You are better off by $1,443,299.

Options

Option

Contract that gives the owner the right, but not the obligation, to buy or sell shares of a stock at a specified price on or before a specified date.

An **option** is a contract that gives the owner of the option the right, but not the obligation, to buy or sell shares of a stock at a specified price on or before a specified date. There are two types of options: calls and puts.

CALL OPTION Call options give the owner of the option the right to buy shares of a stock at a specified price within the time limits of the contract. The specified price at which the buyer can buy shares of a stock is called the *strike price*. For example, suppose Brown buys a call option for $20. The call option specifies that he can buy 100 shares of IBM stock at a strike price of $150 within the next month. If the price of IBM stocks falls below $150, Brown doesn't exercise his call option. He simply tears it up and accepts the fact that he has lost $20. If he still wants to buy IBM stock, he can do so through his stockbroker as he normally does and pay the going price, which is lower than $150. But if the price rises above $150, he exercises his call option. He buys the stock at $150 a share and then turns around and sells it for the higher market price. He has made a profit.

If Brown buys a call option, then there has to be someone who sells it to him. Who would sell him a call option? Any person who thought the option wouldn't be exercised by the buyer. For example, if Jones believed that the price of IBM was going to fall below $150, then he would gladly sell a call option to Brown for $20, thinking that the option would never be exercised. That's $20 in his pocket.

Q&A

I've heard about some people working today who get part of their pay in the form of stock options. What are these?

Stock options are something an employer may give an employee. These stock options give the employee the right to buy a specific number of shares of the company's stock during a time and at a price that is specified by the employer. Sometimes, employers give their employees stock options because they want them to feel that they are a part owner of the company, and sometimes, they give them as a form of compensation. Also, a new company that is just starting out may prefer to give employees stock options instead of as much pay because the company wants to use what cash it has to add to the business.

Let's go back to one major point. We said that the stock option gives the employee the right to buy a specific number of shares of stock at a price specified by the employer. The "price" specified by the employer is often the current market price of the stock when the stock option is issued. The hope for the employee is that the market price will rise over time. To illustrate, suppose the stock option specifies the price of $10 a share. This means the employee has the right to buy the stock at $10. Now suppose time passes, and the market price of the stock rises to $40. What can the employee do now? He or she can buy the stock for $10 a share and then turn around and sell it for $40 a share.

PUT OPTIONS Put options give the owner the right, but not the obligation, to *sell* (rather than buy, as in a call option) shares of a stock at a strike price during some period of time. For example, suppose Martin buys a put option to sell 100 shares of IBM stock at $130 during the next month. If the share price rises above $130, Martin will not exercise his put option. He will simply tear it up and sell the stock for more than $130. On the other hand, if the price drops below $130, then he will exercise his option to sell the stock for $130 a share. Who buys put options? People who think the price of the stock is going to decline.

Who sells put options? Obviously, the people who think the price of the stock is going to rise. Why not sell a put option for, say, $20, if you believe that the price of the stock is going to rise and the buyer of the put option is not going to exercise the option.

HOW YOU CAN USE CALL AND PUT OPTIONS Suppose there is a stock that you think is going to rise in price during the next few months. Currently, the stock sells for $250 a share. You don't have enough money to buy many shares of stock, but you would like to benefit from what you expect will be a rise in the price of the stock. What can you do? You can buy a call option. A call option will sell for a fraction of the cost of the stock. So with limited resources, you decide to buy the call option, which gives you the right to buy, say, 100 shares of the stock at $250 anytime during the next three months.

But wait a minute, someone says. If you don't have the money to buy the stock at $250 a share now, why does anyone think you will have the money to buy the stock at $250 in a few months? But you don't have to buy the stock. If you are right that the price of the stock will rise, then the call option you are holding will become worth more to people. In other words, if you bought the option when the price of the stock was $250 and the stock rises to $300, then your call option has become more valuable. You can sell it and benefit from the uptick in the price of the stock.

Alternatively, let's say you expect the price of the stock to fall. Then you can buy a put option. In other words, you buy the right to sell the stock for $250 anytime during the next three months. If the price does fall, then your option becomes more valuable. In fact, the further the price falls, the more valuable your put option becomes. People who have the stock and want to sell it for a price higher than it currently fetches on the market will be willing to buy your put option from you for some price higher than the price you paid.

To illustrate what we are saying, suppose the current price of a call option for AT&T stock is $10, while the current price of the AT&T stock is $100. Ginny decides to buy a call option for $10. This call option gives her the right to buy AT&T at a price of $100. Five months pass and the price of AT&T shares has risen to $150. If Ginny wants, she can exercise her call option to buy AT&T stock at $100 (which is $50 less than the current price of $150). In other words, she can spend $100 to buy a share of stock, which she can turn around and immediately sell for $150, making a profit of $50 per share.

SELF-TEST

1. What is a futures contract?

2. There is a stock that you think will rise in the next few months, but you do not have enough money to buy many shares of the stock. What can you do instead?

3. What is a put option?

A Reader Asks...

Is There a Financial Language All Its Own?

Sometimes, when I watch the financial news, I hear people using terms I am unfamiliar with. Some of the terms they use seem to be particular to their field of financial expertise. What are some of these terms and what do they mean?

Here are some of the terms, followed by what they mean.

After the Bell
This means "after the close of the stock market."

Air Pocket Stock
This refers to a stock that plunges fast and furiously, much like an airplane that hits an air pocket.

Big Board
This is a nickname for the New York Stock Exchange.

Bo Derek
Named after the movie actress who starred in the 1979 movie *10*. This is slang for a perfect stock or investment.

Bull and Bear Markets
A bull market is one in which prices are expected to rise. A bear market is one in which prices are expected to fall. The use of the terms *bull* and *bear* comes from the way these animals attack their opponents. The bull puts its horns up in the air, and a bear moves its paws down (across its opponent).

Casino Finance
An investment strategy that is considered extremely risky.

Deer Market

A flat market where not much is happening and investors are usually timid. It is neither a bull nor a bear market.

Eat Well, Sleep Well

When it comes to investing, no one gets anything for nothing. If you want a high return, you usually have to assume some risk. If you don't want to take on much risk, then you will likely have a low return. In short, high risk comes with high return, and low risk comes with low return. "Eat well, sleep well" captures the idea here. Do you want a risky investment that may end up feeding you well, or do you want a safe investment that lets you sleep at night?

Falling Knife

This is a stock whose price has fallen significantly in a short time. Someone might say, "Don't try to catch a falling knife" (because you can hurt yourself).

Goldilocks Economy

An economy that is not too hot or too cold but is just right. People often referred to the economy in the mid- to late 1990s in the United States as the Goldilocks economy.

Lemon

A disappointing investment.

Love Money

Money given by family or friends to a person to start a business.

Nervous Nellie

An investor who isn't comfortable with investing, mainly because of the risks.

Sandwich Generation

Refers to people usually of middle age who are "sandwiched" between their children and their parents. They are said to have to take care of two groups of people, one on either side of them.

Santa Claus Rally

A jump in the price of stocks that often occurs the week between Christmas and New Year.

Short Selling

This is a technique used by investors who are trying to benefit from a falling stock price. To illustrate, suppose Brian believes that stock X will soon fall in price. He borrows the stock from someone who currently owns it and promises to return the stock later. He then sells the stock, hoping to buy it back later at a lower price.

War Babies

This is the name given to stocks issued by companies that produce military hardware (e.g., tanks, airplanes, etc.).

! analyzing the scene

What is the Dow?

The Dow is the Dow Jones Industrial Average (DJIA). The DJIA is popular, widely cited indicator of day-to-day stock market activity. The DJIA is a weighted average of 30 widely traded stocks on the New York Stock Exchange.

Is there any way that Jack can protect himself from a drop in the price of wheat?

Jack could enter into a futures contract, promising to deliver so many bushels of wheat in the future for a predetermined set price.

Does timing matter?

Yes, it can matter a lot. Ideally, when investing in stocks, bonds, real estate, or whatever, one wants to "buy low" and "sell high." Buying and selling activities should be timed just right so that buying corresponds to "low price" and selling corresponds to "high price." There is one place it doesn't seem to matter much, though. For example, during the period of 1926–2004, there was not much difference in the return earned by a person who bought stocks on the best days and a person who bought stock on the worst days—as long as both persons held the stocks for 10 years. Specifically, the one who bought on the best days earned a return of 8.89 percent per year while the one who bought on the worst days earned a return of 7.28 percent per year.

What does "the market" refer to?

When someone refers to "the market" in the context of financial issues, one is usually talking about a stock index, such as the Dow, or DJIA. When the Dow goes down, someone might say, "The market is down today." Sometimes "the market" refers to a stock index like the Standard & Poor's 500.

chapter summary

Stocks

- A stock is a claim on the assets of a corporation that gives the purchaser a share (ownership) in the corporation. Stocks are sometimes called equity because the buyer of the stock has part ownership of the company (that initially issued the stock).

- Stocks are bought and sold on exchanges and markets such as the New York Stock Exchange.

- Some people buy stocks for the dividends, which are payments made to stockholders based on a company's profits, or to make money by buying shares at a lower price and selling at a higher price.

- Today, 30 stocks make up the Dow Jones Industrial Average (DJIA). The DJIA was devised by Charles Dow to convey some information about what was happening in the stock market.

- A stock index fund consists of the stocks that make up a particular index.

- The yield (or interest rate) of a stock is equal to the dividend divided by the closing price of the stock.

- The P-E ratio for a stock is equal to the closing price per share (of the stock) divided by the net earnings per share. A stock with a P-E ratio of, say, 15 means that the stock is selling for a share price that is 15 times its earnings per share.

Bonds

- A bond is simply an IOU, or a promise to pay, typically issued by companies, governments, or government agencies.

- The three major components of a bond are face or par value, maturity date, and coupon rate.

- The price that a person pays for a bond depends on market conditions: The greater the demand for the bond relative to the supply, the higher the price.

- The yield on the bond is the coupon payment divided by the price paid for the bond.

- Bonds are rated or evaluated. The more likely the bond issuer will pay the face value of the bond at maturity and will meet all scheduled coupon payments, the higher the bond's rating.

- The price of a bond and its yield (or interest rate) are inversely related.

Futures and Options

- In a futures contract, a seller agrees to provide a particular good to the buyer on a specified future date at an agreed-upon price.

- An option is a contract giving the owner the right, but not the obligation, to buy or sell a particular good at a specified price on or before a specified date.

key terms and concepts

Stock	Initial Public Offering (IPO)	Dividend	Yield
Dow Jones Industrial Average (DJIA)	Investment Bank	Bond	Futures Contract
		Face Value (Par Value)	Option

questions and problems

1 What is the purpose of financial markets?

2 What does it mean if the Dow Jones Industrial Average rises by, say, 100 points in a day?

3 What does it mean to "buy the market"?

4 What does it mean if someone invests in a mutual fund? in a stock market fund?

5 Suppose the share price of each of 500 stocks rises on Monday. Does everyone in the stock market believe that stocks are headed even higher, since no one would buy a stock if he or she thought share prices were headed lower?

6 Which of the two stocks has a bigger gap between its closing price and net earnings per share: Stock A with a P-E ratio of 15 or Stock B with a P-E ratio of 44? Explain your answer.

7 "An issuer of a bond is a borrower." Do you agree or disagree? Explain your answer.

8 If the face value of a bond is $10,900 and the annual coupon payment is $600, then what is the coupon rate?

9 Why might a person purchase an inflation-indexed Treasury bond?

10 "If you can predict interest rates, then you can earn a fortune buying and selling bonds." Do you agree or disagree? Explain your answer.

11 Why might a person buy a futures contract?

12 Why might a person buy a call option?

13 "The currency speculator who sells futures contracts assumes the risk that someone else doesn't want to assume." Do you agree or disagree? Explain your answer.

14 If you thought the share price of a stock was going to fall, would you buy a call option or a put option?

working with numbers and graphs

1 You own 1,250 shares of stock X. You read in the newspaper that the dividend for the stock is 3.88. What did you earn in dividends?

2 The closing price of a stock is 90.25 and the dividend is 3.50. What is the yield of the stock?

3 The closing price of the stock is $66.40 and the net earnings per share are $2.50. What is the stock's P-E ratio?

4 The face value of a bond is $10,000 and the annual coupon payment is $850. What is the coupon rate?

5 A person buys a bond that matures in 10 years and pays a coupon rate of 10 percent. The face value of the bond is $10,000. How much money will the bondholder receive in the tenth year?

Self-Test Appendix

Chapter 1

CHAPTER 1, PAGE 5

1 False. It takes two things for scarcity to exist: finite resources and infinite wants. If people's wants were equal to or less than the finite resources available to satisfy their wants, there would be no scarcity. Scarcity exists only because people's wants are greater than the resources available to satisfy their wants. Scarcity is the condition of infinite wants clashing with finite resources.

2 Because of scarcity, there is a need for a rationing device. People will compete for the rationing device. For example, if dollar price is the rationing device, people will compete for dollars.

3 Because our unlimited wants are greater than our limited resources—that is, because scarcity exists—some wants must go unsatisfied. We must choose which wants we will satisfy and which we will not.

CHAPTER 1, PAGE 12

1 Every time a person is late to history class, the instructor subtracts one-tenth of a point from the person's final grade. If the instructor raised the opportunity cost of being late to class—by subtracting one point from the person's final grade—economists predict there would be fewer persons late to class. In summary, the higher the opportunity cost of being late to class, the less likely people will be late to class.

2 Yes. To illustrate, suppose the marginal benefits and marginal costs (in dollars) are as follows for various hours of studying.

Hours	Marginal Benefits	Marginal Costs
First hour	$20.00	$10.00
Second hour	$14.00	$11.00
Third hour	$13.00	$12.00
Fourth hour	$12.10	$12.09
Fifth hour	$11.00	$13.00

Clearly, you will study the first hour because the marginal benefits are greater than the marginal costs. Stated differently, there is a net benefit of $10 (the difference between the marginal benefits of $20 and the marginal costs of $10) for studying the first hour. If you stop studying after the first hour and do not proceed to the second, then you will forfeit the net benefit of $3 for the second hour. To maximize your net benefits of studying, you must proceed until the marginal benefits and the marginal costs are as close to equal as possible. (In the extreme, this is an epsilon away from equality. However, economists simply speak of "equality" between the two for convenience.) In this case, you will study through the fourth hour. You will not study the fifth hour because it is not worth it; the marginal benefits of studying the fifth hour are less than the marginal costs. In short, there is a net cost to studying the fifth hour.

3 You might feel sleepy the next day, you might be less alert while driving, and so on.

Chapter 2

CHAPTER 2, PAGE 38

1 A straight-line PPF represents constant opportunity costs between two goods. For example, for every unit of X produced, one unit of Y is forfeited. A bowed-outward PPF represents increasing opportunity costs. For example, we may have to forfeit one unit of X to produce the eleventh unit of Y, but we have to forfeit two units of X to produce the one hundredth unit of Y.

2 A bowed-outward PPF is representative of increasing costs. In short, the PPF would not be bowed outward if increasing costs did not exist. To prove this, look back at Exhibits 1 and 2. In Exhibit 1, costs are constant (not increasing), and the PPF is a straight line. In Exhibit 2, costs are increasing, and the PPF is bowed outward.

3 The first condition is that the economy is currently operating *below* its PPF. It is possible to move from a point below the PPF to a point on the PPF and get more of all goods. The second condition is that the economy's PPF shifts outward.

4 False. Take a look at Exhibit 5. There are numerous productive efficient points, all of which lie on the PPF.

CHAPTER 2, PAGE 42

1 Transaction costs are the costs associated with the time and effort needed to search out, negotiate, and consummate a trade. The transaction costs are likely to be higher for buying a house than for buying a car because buying a house is a more detailed and complex process.

2 Under certain conditions, Smith will buy good X from Jones. For example, suppose Smith and Jones agree on a price of, say, $260, and neither person incurs transaction costs greater than $40. If transaction costs are zero for each person, then each person benefits $40 from the trade. Specifically, Smith buys the good for $40 less than his maximum price, and Jones sells the good for $40 more than his minimum price. But suppose each person incurs a transaction cost of, say, $50. Smith would be unwilling to pay $260 to Jones and $50 in transaction costs (for a total of $310) when he is only willing to pay a maximum price of $300 for good X. Similarly, Jones would be unwilling to sell good X for $260 and incur $50 in transaction costs (leaving him with only $210, or $10 less than his minimum selling price).

3 Answers will vary. Sample answer: John buys a magazine and reads it. There is no third-party effect. Sally asks a rock band to play at a party. Sally's next-door neighbor (a third party) is disturbed by the loud music.

CHAPTER 2, PAGE 46

1 If George goes from producing 5X to 10X, he gives up 5Y. This means the opportunity cost of 5 more X is 5 fewer Y. It follows that the opportunity cost of 1X is 1Y. Conclusion: The opportunity cost of 1X is 1Y.

2 If Harriet produces 10 more X she gives up 15Y. It follows that the opportunity cost of 1X is 1.5Y, and the opportunity cost of 1Y is 0.67X. If Bill produces 10 more X, he gives up 20Y. It follows that the opportunity cost of 1X is 2Y, and the opportunity cost of 1Y is 0.5X. Harriet is the lower cost producer of X, and Bill is the lower cost producer of Y. In short, Harriet has the comparative advantage in the production of X; Bill has the comparative advantage in the production of Y.

Chapter 3

CHAPTER 3, PAGE 60

1 Popcorn is a normal good for Sandi. Prepaid telephone cards are an inferior good for Mark.

2 Asking why demand curves are downward sloping is the same as asking why price and quantity demanded are inversely related (as one rises, the other falls). There are two reasons mentioned in this section: (1) As price rises, people substitute lower priced goods for higher priced goods. (2) Because individuals receive less utility from an additional unit of a good they consume, they are only willing to pay less for the additional unit. The second reason is a reflection of the law of diminishing marginal utility.

3 Suppose only two people, Bob and Alice, have a demand for good X. At a price of $7, Bob buys 10 units and Alice buys 3 units; at a price of $6, Bob buys 12 units and Alice buys 5 units. One point on the market demand curve represents a price of $7 and a quantity demanded of 13 units; another point represents $6 and 17 units. A market demand curve is derived by adding the quantities demanded at each price.

4 A change in income, preferences, prices of related goods, number of buyers, and expectations of future price can change demand. A change in the price of the good changes the quantity demanded of the good. For example, a change in *income* can change the *demand* for oranges, but only a change in the *price* of oranges can directly change the *quantity demanded* of oranges.

CHAPTER 3, PAGE 65

1 It would be difficult to increase the quantity supplied of houses over the next ten hours, so the supply curve in (a) is vertical, as in Exhibit 7. It is possible to increase the quantity supplied of houses over the next 3 months, however, so the supply curve in (b) is upward sloping.

2 **a** The supply curve shifts to the left.

b The supply curve shifts to the left.

c The supply curve shifts to the right.

3 False. If the price of apples rises, the *quantity supplied* of apples will rise—not the *supply* of apples. We are talking about a *movement* from one point on a supply curve to a point higher up on the supply curve and not about a shift in the supply curve.

CHAPTER 3, PAGE 73

1 Disagree. In the text, we plainly saw how supply and demand work at an auction. Supply and demand are at work in the grocery store, too, although no auctioneer is present. The essence of the auction example is the auctioneer raising the price when there was a shortage and lowering the price when there was a surplus. The same thing happens at the grocery store. For example, if there is a surplus of corn flakes, the manager of the store is likely to have a sale (lower prices) on corn flakes. Many markets without auctioneers act *as if* there are auctioneers raising and lowering prices in response to shortages and surpluses.

2 No. It could be the result of a higher supply of computers. Either a decrease in demand or an increase in supply will lower price.

3 **a** Lower price and quantity

b Lower price and higher quantity

c Higher price and lower quantity

d Lower price and quantity

4 At equilibrium quantity, the maximum buying price and the minimum selling price are the same. For example, in Exhibit 14, both prices are $40 at the equilibrium quantity 4. Equilibrium quantity is the only quantity at which the maximum buying price and the minimum selling price are the same.

5 $46; $34.

CHAPTER 3, PAGE 77

1 Yes, if nothing else changes—that is, yes, *ceteris paribus*. If some other things change, though, they may not. For example, if the government imposes an effective price ceiling on gasoline, Jamie may pay lower gas prices at the pump but have to wait in line to buy the gas (due to first come, first served trying to ration the shortage). It is not clear if Jamie is better off paying a higher price and not waiting in line or paying a lower price and waiting in line. The point, however, is that buyers don't necessarily prefer lower prices to higher prices unless everything else (quality, wait, service, etc.) stays the same.

2 Disagree. Both long-lasting shortages and long lines are caused by price ceilings. First, the price ceiling is imposed, creating the shortage; then, the rationing device first come, first served emerges because price isn't permitted to fully ration the good. There are shortages every day that don't cause long lines to form. Instead, buyers bid up price, output and price move to equilibrium, and there is no shortage.

3 Buyers might argue for price ceilings on the goods they buy—especially if they don't know that price ceilings have some effects they may not like (e.g., fewer exchanges, FCFS used as a rationing device, etc.). Sellers might argue for price floors on the goods they sell—especially if they expect their profits to rise. Employees might argue for a wage floor on the labor services they sell—especially if they don't know that they may lose their jobs or have their hours cut back as a result.

Chapter 4

CHAPTER 4, PAGE 83

1 If supply and tuition are constant and demand rises, the shortage of openings at the university will become greater. The university will continue to use its nonprice rationing devices (GPA, SAT scores, ACT scores) but will have to raise the standards of admission. Instead of requiring a GPA of, say, 3.5 for admission, it may raise the requirement to 3.8.

2 Not likely. A university that didn't make admission easier in the face of a surplus of openings might not be around much longer. When tuition cannot be adjusted directly—in other words, when the rationing device of price cannot be adjusted—it is likely that the nonprice rationing device (standards) will be.

CHAPTER 4, PAGE 84

1 Price will fall.

2 Quantity will rise.

CHAPTER 4, PAGE 86

1 The recording industry is trying to raise the "price" of downloading music.

2 The recording industry has to consider the costs and expected benefits of various actions. It will follow the path that it thinks will have the biggest bang for the buck. The industry likely believes that trying to lower demand will have fewer positive results than either trying to reduce supply or trying to raise price.

CHAPTER 4, PAGE 86

1 A higher expected price for houses would likely raise the (current) demand for houses. The reasoning: Buy now before the price rises.

2 A lower expected price for cars would likely lower the (current) demand for cars. The reasoning: Buy later when the price is lower.

CHAPTER 4, PAGE 88

1 Yes. At the equilibrium wage rate, the quantity demanded of labor equals the quantity supplied. At a higher wage (the minimum wage), the quantity supplied stays constant (given the vertical supply curve), but the quantity demanded falls. Thus, a surplus results.

2 The person is assuming that the labor demand curve is vertical (no matter what the wage rate is, the quantity demanded of labor is always the same).

CHAPTER 4, PAGE 91

1 Agree. At any price below equilibrium price, a shortage exists: The quantity demanded of kidneys is greater than the quantity supplied of kidneys. As price rises toward its equilibrium level, quantity supplied rises and quantity demanded falls until the two are equal.

2 It depends on whether or not $0 is the equilibrium price of kidneys. If it is—that is, if the kidney demand and supply curves intersect at $0—then there is no shortage of kidneys. But if, at $0, the quantity demanded of kidneys is greater than the quantity supplied, then a shortage exists.

CHAPTER 4, PAGE 92

1 Moving from a system where patients cannot sue their HMOs to one where they can gives patients something they didn't have before (the right to sue) at a higher price (higher charges for healthcare coverage). The "free lunch"—the right to sue—isn't free after all.

2 If the students get the extra week and nothing else changes, then the students will probably say they are better off. In other words, more of one thing (time) and no less of anything else makes one better off. But if because of the extra week, the professor grades their papers harder than she would have otherwise, then some or all of the students may say that they weren't made better off by the extra week.

CHAPTER 4, PAGE 93

1 A demand curve exists, and it is downward sloping, if the law of demand holds. If the law of demand holds for using foul language, then there is a downward-sloping demand curve for using foul language.

2 There probably is not a downward-sloping demand curve for sneezing because sneezing is an automatic response. In other words, it is hard to control your sneezing in such a way that you sneeze less when the price of sneezing rises.

CHAPTER 4, PAGE 94

1   The answer can be either the shifting supply of gold or the attempt to earn profit. Consider the first answer. If the price of gold is higher in one location than another, the supply of gold shifts from the lower priced location to the higher priced location. In the process, the gold prices in the two locations converge. Now, if we want to know what causes the shifting supply of gold, the answer is the attempt to earn profit. Specifically, the attempt to earn profit prompts people to buy gold in the lower priced location and sell it in the higher priced location.

2   You can move a Honda Pilot from one place to another in response to a rising price. What holds for gold holds for Honda Pilots too.

CHAPTER 4, PAGE 94

1   One possible answer is: There are two cities, one with clean air and the other with dirty air. The demand to live in the clean-air city is higher than the demand to live in the dirty-air city. As a result, housing prices are higher in the clean-air city than in the dirty-air city.

2   Ultimately, the person who owns the land in the good-weather city receives the payment. Look at it this way: People have a higher demand for houses in good-weather cities than they do for houses in bad-weather cities. As a result, house builders receive higher prices for houses built and sold in good-weather cities. Because of the higher house prices in good-weather cities, house builders have a higher demand for land in good-weather cities. In the end, higher demand for land translates into higher land prices or land rents for landowners.

CHAPTER 4, PAGE 96

1   The shortage is greater in computer science. If (1) supply in each field is the same, (2) the wage rate is the same, and (3) demand is greater in computer science than in biology, then the horizontal difference (which measures the degree of shortage) between the demand curve and supply curve is greater in computer science than in biology. Draw this and see.

2   Under the condition that demand and supply are the same in all fields. Stated differently, under the condition that the equilibrium wage in each field is the same.

CHAPTER 4, PAGE 97

1   Look at the demand curve and the supply curve between Q_2 and Q_1. Notice that the demand curve lies *above* the supply curve in this area. This means that buyers are willing to pay more for each of the units between Q_2 and Q_1 (more, say, for the $Q_2 + 1$ unit) than sellers need to receive for them to place these units on the market. In short, moving from an equilibrium price to a price floor lowers the number of mutually beneficial trades that will be made. As discussed in Chapter 3, price floors lead to fewer exchanges.

2   It is likely that producers care more about how a change affects them than how it affects society. At the price floor, they receive more producers' surplus than they receive at the equilibrium price, even though consumers lose, in terms of consumers' surplus, more than producers gain. Look at it like this: Producers gain $10 and consumers lose $12. The sum of positive $10 and negative $12 is negative $2. Producers may not care about the sum (–$2); they care about their $10 gain.

CHAPTER 4, PAGE 99

1   Suppose University X gives a full scholarship to every one of its football players (all of whom are superathletes). In addition, suppose that the full scholarship (translated into wages) is far below the equilibrium wage of each of the football players. (Think of it this way: Each football player gets a wage, or full scholarship, of $10,000 a year, when his equilibrium wage is $40,000 a year.) Paying lower than the equilibrium wage will end up transferring dollars and other benefits from the football players to the university to the new field house and track and perhaps to you if you use the track for exercise.

2   If paying student athletes (a wage above the full scholarship) lowers consumers' demand for college athletics, then the equilibrium wage for college athletes is not as high as shown in Exhibit 7.

CHAPTER 4, PAGE 100

1   Any price above 70 cents.

2   Assuming that tolls are not used, freeway congestion will worsen. An increase in driving population simply shifts the demand curve for driving to the right.

CHAPTER 4, PAGE 101

1   A person's time is worth something. For example, if a person spends one hour doing something instead of working and has a wage rate of $10 an hour, then one hour of her time is worth $10. When we know a person's wage rate, we can convert "time spent" into "dollars forfeited."

2   If demand rises more than supply and price is held constant, there will be a shortage of parking. Some non-price rationing device will emerge to allocate parking spaces along with dollar price. It will probably be first come, first served (whoever gets to an empty parking spot first gets to park).

CHAPTER 4, PAGE 103

1   Answers will vary. Students sometimes say that it is "fairer" if everyone is charged the same price. Is it unfair then that moviegoers pay less if they go to the 2 P.M. movie than if they go to the 8 P.M. movie?

2 In the application dealing with the kidney market, there was a price ceiling that resulted in a shortage of kidneys. In the application dealing with the 10:00 A.M. class, the university charged a below-equilibrium price for the 10:00 A.M. class, leading to a shortage of such classes.

CHAPTER 4, PAGE 104

1 It is not necessarily the case that if government places a tax on the seller of a good that the seller of the good will end up paying the full tax. The key word here is *full* tax. In other words, some of the tax may be paid for by the buyer of the good. We showed this explicitly in Exhibit 10. Government placed the $1 tax fully on the seller. This resulted in the supply curve shifting upward and leftward. As a result, there was a new equilibrium price that was, in our example, 50 cents higher than the old equilibrium price. Conclusion: Although the tax was placed fully on the seller of the good, the buyer of the good ended up paying a part of the tax in terms of a higher price for the good.

2 What matters to sellers is how much they keep for each DVD sold, not how much buyers pay. If sellers are keeping $15 per DVD for Q_1 DVDs before the tax is imposed, then they want to keep $15 per DVD for Q_1 DVDs after the tax is imposed. But if the tax is $1, the only way they can keep $15 per DVD for Q_1 DVDs is to receive $16 per DVD. They receive $16 per DVD from buyers, turn over $1 to the government, and keep $15. In other words, each quantity on the new supply curve, S_2, corresponds to a $1 higher price than it did on the old supply curve, S_1.

Chapter 5

CHAPTER 5, PAGE 120

1 The CPI is calculated as follows: (1) Define a market basket. (2) Determine how much it would cost to purchase the market basket in the current year and in the base year. (3) Divide the dollar cost of purchasing the market basket in the current year by the dollar cost of purchasing the market basket in the base year. (4) Multiply the quotient by 100. For a review of this process, see Exhibit 2.

2 It is a year that is used for comparison purposes with other years.

3 Annual (nominal) income has risen by 13.85 percent while prices have risen by 4.94 percent. We conclude that because (nominal) income has risen more than prices, real income has increased. Alternatively, you can look at it this way: Real income in year 1 is $31,337, and real income in year 2 is $33,996.

CHAPTER 5, PAGE 127

1 The frictionally unemployed person has readily transferable skills, and the structurally unemployed person does not.

2 It implies that the (actual, measured) unemployment rate in the economy is greater than the natural unemployment rate. For example, if the unemployment rate is 8 percent and the natural unemployment rate is 6 percent, the cyclical unemployment rate is 2 percent.

Chapter 6

CHAPTER 6, PAGE 135

1 The three approaches are expenditure, income, and value-added. In the expenditure approach, we add the amount of money spent by buyers on final goods and services. In the income approach, we sum the payments to the resources of production. In our example in the text, income consisted of the returns to labor (wages) and entrepreneurship (profits). In the value-added approach, we sum the dollar value contribution over all stages of production.

2 No. GDP doesn't account for all productive activity (e.g., it omits the production of nonmarket goods and services). Even if GDP is $0, it doesn't necessarily follow that there was no production in the country.

CHAPTER 6, PAGE 144

1 In the expenditure approach, GDP is computed by finding the sum of consumption, investment, government purchases, and net exports. (Net exports are equal to exports minus imports.)

2 Yes. To illustrate, suppose consumption is $200, investment is $80, and government purchases are $70. The sum of these three spending components of GDP is $350. Now suppose exports are $0 but imports are $100, which means that net exports are –$100. Since GDP = $C + I + G + (EX - IM)$, it follows that GDP is $250.

3 No. Each individual would have $40,000 worth of goods and services only if the entire GDP were equally distributed across the country. There is no indication that this is the case. The $40,000 (per capita GDP) says that the "average" person in the country has access to $40,000 worth of goods and services, but in reality, there may not be any "average" person. For example, if Smith earns $10,000 and Jones earns $20,000, then the average person earns $15,000. But neither Smith nor Jones earns $15,000, so neither is average.

CHAPTER 6, PAGE 148

1 We can't know for sure; we can say what might have caused the rise in GDP. It could be (a) a rise in prices, no change in output, (b) a rise in output, no change in prices, (c) rises in both prices and output, or (d) a percentage increase in prices that is greater than the percentage decrease in output, or some other situation.

2 More output was produced in year 2 than in year 1.

3 Yes. Business cycles—ups and downs in Real GDP—don't prevent Real GDP from growing over time. Exhibit 8 shows Real GDP higher at the second peak than at the first even though there is a business cycle between the peaks.

Chapter 7

CHAPTER 7, PAGE 162

1 Real balance effect: a rise (fall) in the price level causes purchasing power to fall (rise), which decreases (increases) a person's monetary wealth. As people become less (more) wealthy, the quantity demanded of Real GDP falls (rises).

2 If the dollar appreciates, it takes more foreign currency to buy a dollar and fewer dollars to buy foreign currency. This makes U.S. goods (denominated in dollars) more expensive for foreigners and foreign goods cheaper for Americans. In turn, foreigners buy fewer U.S. exports, and Americans buy more foreign imports. As exports fall and imports rise, net exports fall. If net exports fall, total expenditures fall, *ceteris paribus*. As total expenditures fall, the *AD* curve shifts to the left.

3 If personal income taxes decline, disposable incomes rise. As disposable incomes rise, consumption rises. As consumption rises, total expenditures rise, *ceteris paribus*. As total expenditures rise, the *AD* curve shifts to the right.

CHAPTER 7, PAGE 165

1 As wage rates decline, the cost per unit of production falls. In the short run (assuming prices are constant), profit per unit rises. Higher profit causes producers to produce more units of their goods and services. In short, the *SRAS* curve shifts to the right.

2 Last year, 10 workers produced 100 units of good X in 1 hour. This year, 10 workers produced 120 units of good X in 1 hour.

3 Workers initially misperceive the change in their real wage due to a change in the price level. For example, suppose the nominal wage is $30 and the price level is 1.50; it follows that the real wage is $20. Now suppose the nominal wage falls to $25 and the price level falls to 1.10. The real wage is now $22.72. But suppose workers misperceive the decline in the price level and mistakenly believe it has fallen to 1.40. They will now perceive their real wage as $17.85 ($25/1.40). In other words, they will misperceive their real wage as falling when it has actually increased. How will workers react if they believe their real wage has fallen? They will cut back on the quantity supplied of labor, which will end up reducing output (or Real GDP). This process is consistent with an upward-sloping *SRAS* curve: A decline in the price level leads to a reduction in output.

CHAPTER 7, PAGE 173

1 In long-run equilibrium, the economy is producing Natural Real GDP. In short-run equilibrium, the economy is not producing Natural Real GDP, although the quantity demanded of Real GDP equals the quantity supplied of Real GDP.

2 The diagram should show the price level in the economy at P_1 and Real GDP at Q_1 but the intersection of the *AD* curve and the *SRAS* curve at some point other than (P_1, Q_1). In addition, the *LRAS* curve should not be at Q_1 or at the intersection of the *AD* and *SRAS* curves.

Chapter 8

CHAPTER 8, PAGE 181

1 Say's law states that supply creates its own demand. In a barter economy, Jones supplies good X only so that he can use it to demand some other good (e.g., good Y). The act of supplying is motivated by the desire to demand. Supply and demand are opposite sides of the same coin.

2 No, total spending will not decrease. For classical economists, an increase in saving (reflected in a decrease in consumption) will lower the interest rate and stimulate investment spending. So, one spending component goes down (consumption), and another spending component goes up (investment). Moreover, according to classical economists, the decrease in one spending component will be completely offset by an increase in another spending component so that overall spending does not change.

3 They are flexible; they move up and down in response to market conditions.

CHAPTER 8, PAGE 185

1 A recessionary gap exists if the economy is producing a Real GDP level that is less than Natural Real GDP. An inflationary gap exists if the economy is producing a Real GDP level that is more than Natural Real GDP.

2 There is a surplus in the labor market when the economy is in a recessionary gap. There is a shortage in the labor market when the economy is in an inflationary gap.

3 The economy is somewhere above the institutional PPF and below the physical PPF.

CHAPTER 8, PAGE 191

1 In a recessionary gap, the existing unemployment rate is greater than the natural unemployment rate. This implies that unemployment is relatively high. When old wage contracts expire, business firms negotiate contracts that pay workers lower wage rates. As a result, the *SRAS* curve shifts rightward. As this happens, the price level begins to fall. The economy moves down the *AD* curve—eventually moving to the point where it intersects the *LRAS* curve. At this point, the economy is in long-run equilibrium.

2   In an inflationary gap, the existing unemployment rate is less than the natural unemployment rate. This implies that unemployment is relatively low. When old wage contracts expire, business firms negotiate contracts that pay workers higher wage rates. As a result, the *SRAS* curve shifts leftward. As this happens, the price level begins to rise. The economy moves up the *AD* curve—eventually moving to the point where it intersects the *LRAS* curve. At this point, the economy is in long-run equilibrium.

3   Any changes in aggregate demand will affect—in the long run—only the price level and not the Real GDP level or the unemployment rate. Stated differently, changes in *AD* in an economy will have no long-run effect on the Real GDP that a country produces or on its unemployment rate; changes in *AD* will only change the price level in the long run.

Chapter 9

CHAPTER 9, PAGE 201

1   They mean that an economy may not self-regulate at Natural Real GDP (Q_N). Instead, an economy can get stuck in a recessionary gap.

2   To say that the economy is self-regulating is the same as saying that prices and wages are flexible and adjust quickly. They are just two ways of describing the same thing.

3   The main reason is because Say's law may not hold in a money economy. This raises the question: Why *doesn't* Say's law hold in a money economy? Keynes argued that an increase in saving (which leads to a decline in demand) does not necessarily bring about an equal amount of additional investment (which would lead to an increase in demand) because neither saving nor investment is exclusively affected by changes in the interest rate. See Exhibit 1 for the way Keynes might have used numbers to explain his position.

CHAPTER 9, PAGE 206

1   Autonomous consumption is one of the components of overall consumption. To illustrate, look at the consumption function: $C = C_0 + (MPC)(Y_d)$. The part of overall consumption (*C*) that is autonomous is C_0. This part of consumption does not depend on disposable income. The part of consumption that does depend on disposable income (i.e., changes as disposable income changes) is the $(MPC)(Y_d)$ part. For example, assume the *MPC* =

0.80. If Y_d rises by \$1,000, then consumption goes up by \$800.

2   $1/1 - 0.70 = 1/0.30 = 3.33$

3   The multiplier falls. For example, if *MPC* = 0.20, then the multiplier is 1.25, but if *MPC* = 0.80, then the multiplier is 5.

CHAPTER 9, PAGE 210

1   Keynes believed that the economy may not always self-regulate itself at Natural Real GDP. In other words, households and businesses (the private sector of the economy) are not always capable of generating enough aggregate demand in the economy so that the economy equilibrates at Natural Real GDP.

2   The increase in autonomous spending will lead to a greater increase in total spending and to a shift rightward in the *AD* curve. If the economy is operating in the horizontal section of the Keynesian *AS* curve, Real GDP will rise and there will be no change in prices.

3   Agree. The economist who believes the economy is inherently unstable sees a role for government. Government is supposed to stabilize the economy at Natural Real GDP. The economist who believes the economy is self-regulating (capable of moving itself to Natural Real GDP) sees little if any role for government in the economy because the economy is already doing the job government would supposedly do.

CHAPTER 9, PAGE 217

1   When *TP* > *TE*, firms are producing and offering for sale more units of goods and services than households and government want to buy. As a result, business inventories rise above optimal levels. In reaction, firms cut back on their production of goods and services. This leads to a decline in Real GDP. Real GDP stops falling when *TP* = *TE*.

2   When *TE* > *TP*, households and businesses want to buy more than firms are producing and offering for sale. As a result, business inventories fall below optimal levels. In reaction, firms increase the production of goods and services. This leads in a rise in Real GDP. Real GDP stops rising when *TP* = *TE*.

Chapter 10

CHAPTER 10, PAGE 226

1   With a proportional income tax, the tax rate is constant as one's income rises. With a progressive income tax, the tax rate rises as one's income rises (up to some point). With a regressive income tax, the tax rate falls as one's income rises.

2   In 2005, the top 5 percent of income earners received 31 percent of all income and paid 54.1 percent of all income taxes.

3   Individual income tax, corporate income tax, and Social Security taxes.

4   The cyclical budget deficit is that part of the budget deficit that is the result of a downturn in economic activity.

CHAPTER 10, PAGE 233

1   If there is no crowding out, expansionary fiscal policy is predicted to increase aggregate demand and, if the economy is in a recessionary gap, either reduce or eliminate the gap. However, if there is, say, complete crowding out, expansionary fiscal policy will not meet its objective. The following example illustrates complete crowding out: If government purchases rise by $100 million, private spending will decrease by $100 million so that there is no net effect on aggregate demand.

2   Suppose the economy is currently in a recessionary gap at time period 1. Expansionary fiscal policy is needed to remove the economy from its recessionary gap, but the fiscal policy lags (data lag, wait-and-see lag, etc.) may be so long that by the time the fiscal policy is implemented, the economy has moved itself out of the recessionary gap, making the expansionary fiscal policy not only unnecessary but potentially capable of moving the economy into an inflationary gap. Exhibit 5 describes the process.

3   The federal government spends more on some particular program. As a result, the budget deficit grows and the federal government increases its demand for loanable funds (or credit) to finance the larger deficit. Because of the greater demand for loanable funds, the interest rate rises in response to the higher interest rate, and business firms cut back on investment. An increase in government spending has indirectly led to a decline in investment spending.

CHAPTER 10, PAGE 237

1   Let's suppose that a person's taxable income rises by $1,000 to $45,000 and that her taxes rise from $10,000 to $10,390 as a result. Her marginal tax rate—the percentage of her additional taxable income she pays in taxes—is 39 percent. Her average tax rate—the percentage of her (total) income she pays in taxes—is 23 percent.

2   Not necessarily. It depends on whether the percentage rise in tax rates is greater than or less than the percentage fall in the tax base. Here's a simple example: Suppose the average tax rate is 10 percent and the tax base is $100. Tax revenues then equal $10. If the tax rate rises to 12 percent (a 20 percent rise) and the tax base falls to $90 (a 10 percent fall), tax revenues rise to $10.80. In other words, if the tax rate rises by a greater percentage than the tax base falls, tax revenues rise. But then, let's suppose that the tax base falls to $70 (a 30 percent fall) instead of to $90. Now tax revenues are $8.40. In other words, if the tax rate rises by a smaller percentage than the tax base falls, tax revenues fall.

Chapter 11

CHAPTER 11, PAGE 248

1   Money evolved because individuals wanted to make trading easier (less time-consuming). This motivated individuals to accept the good (in a barter economy) that had relatively greater acceptability than all other goods. In time, the effect snowballed, and finally, the good that (initially) had relatively greater acceptability emerged into a good that was widely accepted for purposes of exchange. At this point, the good became money.

2   No. M1 will fall, but M2 will not rise—it will remain constant. To illustrate, suppose M1 = $400 and M2 = $600. If people remove $100 from checkable deposits, M1 will decline to $300. For purposes of illustration, think of M2 as equal to M1 + money market accounts. The M1 component of M2 falls by $100, but the money market accounts component rises by $100, so there is no net effect on M2. In conclusion, M1 falls and M2 remains constant.

3   In a barter (moneyless) economy, a double coincidence of wants will not occur for every transaction. When it does not occur, the cost of the transaction increases because more time must be spent to complete the trade. In a money economy, money is acceptable for every transaction, so a double coincidence of wants is not necessary. All buyers offer money for what they want to buy, and all sellers accept money for what they want to sell.

CHAPTER 11, PAGE 257

1   $55 million

2   $6 billion

3   $0. Bank *A* was required to hold only $1 million in reserves but held $1.2 million instead. Therefore, its loss of $200,000 in reserves does not cause it to be reserve deficient.

Chapter 12

CHAPTER 11, PAGE 264

1   Federal Reserve Bank of New York.

2   Control the money supply.

3   It means the Fed stands ready to lend funds to banks that are suffering cash management, or liquidity, problems.

CHAPTER 12, PAGE 269

1   a Money supply falls.
    b Money supply rises.
    c Money supply falls.

2   The federal funds rate is the interest rate one bank charges another bank for a loan. The discount rate is the interest rate the Fed charges a bank for a loan.

3 Reserves in bank *A* rise; reserves in the banking system remain the same (bank *B* lost the reserves that bank *A* borrowed).

4. Reserves in bank *A* rise; reserves in the banking system rise because there is no offset in reserves for any other bank.

Chapter 13

CHAPTER 13, PAGE 278

1 If *M* times *V* increases, total expenditures increase. In other words, people spend more. For example, instead of spending $3 billion on goods and services, they spend $4 billion on goods and services. But if there is more spending (greater total expenditures), it follows that there must be greater total sales. *P* times *Q* represents this total dollar value of sales.

2 The equation of exchange is a truism: *MV* necessarily equals *PQ*. This is similar to saying that 2 + 2 necessarily equals 4. It cannot be otherwise. The simple quantity theory of money, which is built on the equation of exchange, can be tested against real-world events. That is, the simple quantity theory of money assumes that both velocity and Real GDP are constant and then, based on these assumptions, predicts that changes in the money supply will be strictly proportional to changes in the price level. This prediction can be measured against real-world data, so the simple quantity theory of money may offer insights into the way the economy works. The equation of exchange does not do this.

3 **a** *AD* curve shifts rightward.

b *AD* curve shifts leftward.

c *AD* curve shifts rightward.

d *AD* curve shifts leftward.

CHAPTER 13, PAGE 281

1 **a** As velocity rises, the *AD* curve shifts to the right. In the short run, *P* rises and *Q* rises. In the long run, *Q* will return to its original level, and *P* will be higher than it was in the short run.

b As velocity falls, the *AD* curve shifts to the left. In the short run, *P* falls and *Q* falls. In the long run, *Q* will return to its original level, and *P* will be lower than it was in the short run.

c As the money supply rises, the *AD* curve shifts to the right. In the short run, *P* rises and *Q* rises. In the long run, *Q* will return to its original level, and *P* will be higher than it was in the short run.

d As the money supply falls, the *AD* curve shifts to the left. In the short run, *P* falls and *Q* falls. In the long run, *Q* will return to its original level, and *P* will be lower than it was in the short run.

2 Yes, a change in velocity can offset a change in the money supply (on aggregate demand). Suppose that the money supply rises and velocity falls. A rise in the money supply shifts the *AD* curve to the right, and a fall in velocity shifts the *AD* curve to the left. If the strength of each change is the same, there is no change in *AD*.

CHAPTER 13, PAGE 287

1 We cannot answer this question based on the information given. We know only that three prices have gone up; we don't know if other prices (in the economy) have gone up, if other prices have gone down, or if some have gone up and others have gone down. To determine whether inflation has occurred, we have to know what has happened to the price level, not simply to three prices.

2 No. For continued inflation (continued increases in the price level) to be the result of continued decreases in *SRAS,* workers would have to continually ask for and receive higher wages while output was dropping and the unemployment rate rising. This is not likely.

3 Continued inflation.

CHAPTER 13, PAGE 293

1 3 percent.

2 Yes, it is possible. This would occur if the expectations effect immediately set in and outweighed the liquidity effect.

3 Certainly, the Fed directly affects the supply of loanable funds and the interest rate through an open market operation. But it works as a catalyst to indirectly affect the loanable funds market and the interest rate via the changes in Real GDP, the price level, and the expected inflation rate. We can say this: The Fed directly affects the interest rate via the liquidity effect, and it indirectly affects the interest rate via the income, price-level, and expectations effects.

Chapter 14

CHAPTER 14, PAGE 306

1 Smith buys a bond for a face value of $10,000 that promises to pay a 10 percent interest rate each year for 10 years. In one year, though, bonds are offered for a face value of $10,000 that pay an 11 percent interest rate each year for 10 years. If Smith wants to sell his bond, he won't be able to sell it for $10,000 because no one today will pay $10,000 for a bond that pays a 10 percent interest rate when he or she can pay $10,000 for a bond that pays an 11 percent interest rate. Smith will have to lower the price of his bond if he wants to sell it. Thus, as interest rates rise, bond prices decrease (for old or existing bonds).

2 We disagree for two reasons. First, if the money market is in the liquidity trap, a rise in the money supply will not affect interest rates and therefore will not affect investment or the goods and services market. Second, even if the money market is not in the liquidity trap, a rise in the money supply does not affect the goods and services market directly. It affects it indirectly: The rise in the money supply lowers the interest rate, causing investment to rise (assuming investment is not interest insensitive). As investment rises, the *AD* curve shifts rightward, affecting the goods and services market. In other words, there is an important intermediate market between the money market and the goods and services market in the Keynesian transmission mechanism. Thus, the money market can affect the goods and services market only indirectly.

3   A rise in the money supply brings about an excess supply of money in the money market that flows to the goods and services market, stimulating aggregate demand.

CHAPTER 14, PAGE 312

1   Because they believe that prices and wages are inflexible downward but not upward. They believe it is more likely that natural forces will move an economy out of an inflationary gap than out of a recessionary gap.

2   Suppose the economy is regulating itself out of a recessionary gap, but this is not known to Fed officials. Thinking that the economy is stuck in a recessionary gap, the Fed increases the money supply. When the money supply is felt in the goods and services market, the *AD* curve intersects the *SRAS* curve (that has been moving rightward, unbeknownst to officials) at a point that represents an inflationary gap. In other words, the Fed has moved the economy from a recessionary gap to an inflationary gap instead of from a recessionary gap to long-run equilibrium at the Natural Real GDP level.

3   It makes it stronger, *ceteris paribus*. If the economy can't get itself out of a recessionary gap, then the case is stronger that the Fed should. This does not mean to imply that expansionary monetary policy will work ideally. There may still be problems with the correct implementation of the policy.

CHAPTER 14, PAGE 315

1   This is an open-ended question, and the answer depends on many factors. First, the answer depends on what the rule specifies because not all rules are alike. Second, it depends on the stability and predictability of velocity. For example, suppose the rule specifies that each year the money supply will rise by the average annual growth rate in Real GDP. If velocity is constant, this will produce price stability. But suppose velocity is extremely volatile. In this case, changes in velocity might offset changes in the money supply, leading to deflation instead of price stability. (For example, suppose Real GDP rises by 3 percent and the money supply increases by 3 percent, but velocity decreases by 3 percent. The change in velocity offsets the change in the money supply, leaving a net effect of a 3 percent rise in

Real GDP. This, then, would lead to a 3 percent decline in the price level.)

2   The inflation gap is the difference between the actual inflation rate and the target for inflation. The output gap is the percentage difference between actual Real GDP and its full-employment or natural level.

Chapter 15

CHAPTER 15, PAGE 326

1   A given Phillips curve identifies different combinations of inflation and unemployment; for example, 4 percent inflation with 5 percent unemployment and 2 percent inflation with 7 percent unemployment. For these combinations of inflation and unemployment to be permanent, there must be only one (downward-sloping) Phillips curve that never changes.

2   Sometimes there is and sometimes there isn't. Look at Exhibit 3. Unemployment is higher and inflation is lower in 1964 than in 1965, so there is a tradeoff between these two years. But both unemployment and inflation are higher in 1980 than in 1979—that is, between these two years, there is not a tradeoff between inflation and unemployment.

3   Workers are fooled into thinking that the inflation rate is lower than it is. In other words, they underestimate the inflation rate and, therefore, overestimate the purchasing power of their wages.

CHAPTER 15, PAGE 332

1   No. PIP says that, under certain conditions, neither expansionary fiscal policy nor expansionary monetary policy will be able to increase Real GDP and lower the unemployment rate in the short run. The conditions are that the policy change is anticipated correctly, individuals form their expectations rationally, and wages and prices are flexible.

2   None. When there is an unanticipated increase in aggregate demand, the economy moves from point 1 to 2 (in Exhibit 6(a)) in the short run and then to point 3. This occurs whether people are holding rational or adaptive expectations.

3   Yes. To illustrate, suppose the economy is initially in long-run equilibrium at point 1 in Exhibit 6(a). As a result of an unanticipated rise in aggregate demand, the economy will move from point 1 to point 2 and then to point 3. If there is a correctly anticipated rise in aggregate demand, the economy will simply move from point 1 to point 2, as in Exhibit 6(b). If there is an incorrectly anticipated rise in aggregate demand—and furthermore, the anticipated rise overestimates the actual rise—then the economy will move from point 1 to point 2′ in Exhibit 7. In conclusion, Real GDP may initially increase, may remain constant, or may decline depending on whether the rise in aggregate demand is

unanticipated, anticipated correctly, or anticipated incorrectly (overestimated in our example), respectively.

CHAPTER 15, PAGE 334

1 Both. The relevant question is: Was the decline in the money supply caused by a change on the supply side of the economy? If the answer is no, then the decline in the money supply is consistent with a demand-induced business cycle. If the answer is yes, then it is consistent with a supply-induced (real) business cycle.

2 New Keynesians believe that prices and wages are somewhat inflexible; new classical economists believe that prices and wages are flexible.

Chapter 16

CHAPTER 16, PAGE 350

1 An increase in GDP does not constitute economic growth because GDP can rise from one year to the next if prices rise and output stays constant. Economic growth refers to an increase either in Real GDP or in per capita Real GDP. The emphasis here is on "real" as opposed to nominal (or money) GDP.

2 If the *AD* curve remains constant, a shift rightward in the *LRAS* curve (which is indicative of economic growth) will bring about falling prices. If the *AD* curve shifts to the right by the same amount that the *LRAS* curve shifts rightward, prices will remain stable. Only if the *AD* curve shifts to the right by more than the *LRAS* curve shifts to the right could we witness economic growth and rising prices.

3 Labor is more productive when there are more capital goods. Furthermore, a rise in labor productivity promotes economic growth (an increase in labor productivity is defined as an increase in output relative to total labor hours). So increases in capital investment can lead to increases in labor productivity and, therefore, to economic growth.

CHAPTER 16, PAGE 353

1 One worry concerns the costs of economic growth. Some persons argue that with more economic growth come more "bads"—such as pollution, crowded cities, greater emphasis on material goods, more psychological problems, and so on. The other worry concerns the relationship between economic growth and the future availability of resources. Specifically, some persons argue that continued economic (and population) growth threatens the survival of the human race because this growth will hasten the time when the world runs out of resources. Both these worries (and the arguments put forth relevant to these worries) have their critics.

2 If technology is endogenous, then we can promote advances in technology. Technology does not simply "fall out of the sky"; we can promote technology, not simply wait for it to "rain down" on us. This means we can actively promote economic growth (because advances in technology can promote economic growth).

3 In new growth theory, ideas are important to economic growth. Countries that discover how to encourage and develop new and better ideas will likely grow faster than those that do not. New growth theory, in essence, places greater emphasis on the intangibles (e.g., ideas) in the growth process than on the tangibles (e.g., natural resources, capital, etc.).

Chapter 17

CHAPTER 17, PAGE 367

1 $E_d = 1.44$

2 It means that if there is a change in price, quantity demanded will change (in the opposite direction) by 0.39 times the percentage change in price. For example, if price rises 10 percent, then quantity demanded will fall 3.9 percent. If price rises 20 percent, then quantity demanded will fall 7.8 percent.

3 **a** Total revenue falls.

b Total revenue falls.

c Total revenue remains constant.

d Total revenue rises.

e Total revenue rises.

4 Alexi is implicitly assuming that demand is inelastic. If, however, she is wrong and demand is elastic, then a rise in price will actually lower total revenue.

CHAPTER 17, PAGE 371

1 No. Moving from 7 to 9 substitutes doesn't necessarily change demand from being inelastic to elastic. It simply leads to a rise in price elasticity of demand, *ceteris paribus*. For example, if price elasticity of demand is 0.45 when there are 7 substitutes, it will be higher than this when there are 9 substitutes, *ceteris paribus*. Higher could be 0.67. If this is the case, demand is still inelastic (but less so than before).

2 **a** Dell computers

b Heinz ketchup

c Perrier water

In all three cases, the good with the higher price elasticity of demand is the more specific of the two goods; therefore, it has more substitutes.

CHAPTER 17, PAGE 375

1 It means that the good (in question) is a normal good and that it is income elastic—that is, as income rises, the quantity demanded rises by a greater percentage. In this case, quantity demanded rises by 1.33 times the percentage

change in income. If income rises by 10 percent, the quantity demanded of the good will rise by 13.3 percent.

2   A change in price does not change quantity supplied.

Chapter 18

CHAPTER 18, PAGE 385

1   The paradox is that water, which is essential to life, is cheap, and diamonds, which are not essential to life, are expensive. The solution to the paradox depends on knowing the difference between total and marginal utility and the law of diminishing marginal utility. By saying that water is essential to life and diamonds are not essential to life, we signify that water gives us high total utility relative to diamonds. But then someone asks, "Well, if water gives us greater total utility than diamonds do, why isn't the price of water greater than the price of diamonds?" The answer is, "Price isn't a reflection of total utility; it is a reflection of marginal utility. The marginal utility of water is less than the marginal utility of diamonds." This answer raises another question, "How can the total utility of water be greater than the total utility of diamonds, but the marginal utility of water be less than the marginal utility of diamonds?" The answer is based on the fact that water is plentiful and diamonds are not and on the law of diminishing marginal utility. There is so much more water relative to diamonds that the next (additional) unit of water gives us less utility (lower marginal utility) than the next unit of diamonds.

2   If total utility declines, marginal utility must be negative. For example, if total utility is 30 utils when Lydia consumes 3 apples and 25 utils when she consumes 4 apples, it must be because the fourth apple had a marginal utility of minus 5 utils. Chapter 1 explains that something that takes utility away from us (or gives us disutility) is called a *bad*. For Lydia, the fourth apple is a bad, not a good.

3   The total and marginal utility of a good are the same for the first unit of the good consumed. For example, before Tomas eats his first apple, he receives no utility or disutility from apples. Eating the first apple, he receives 15 utils. So the total utility (*TU*) for 1 apple is 15 utils, and the marginal utility (*MU*) for the first apple is 15 utils. Exhibit 1 shows that *TU* and *MU* are the same for the first unit of good *X*.

CHAPTER 18, PAGE 388

1   Alesandro is not in consumer equilibrium because the marginal utility per dollar of *X* is 16 utils and the marginal utility per dollar of *Y* is 13.14 utils. To be in equilibrium, a consumer has to receive the same marginal utility per dollar for each good consumed.

2   It means the marginal utility-price ratio for one of the goods is higher than the ratio for the other good.

CHAPTER 18, PAGE 392

1   Yes, Brandon is compartmentalizing. He is treating $100 that comes from his grandmother differently from $100 that comes from his father.

2   The endowment effect relates to individuals valuing *X* more highly when they possess it than when they don't have it but are thinking of acquiring it. Friedman argues that if we go back in time to a hunter-gatherer society when there were no well-established property rights (no rules as to what is "mine" and "thine"), individuals who would fight hard to keep what they possessed, but wouldn't fight as hard to acquire what they did not possess, would have a higher probability of surviving than individuals who would fight hard at both times. Thus, those who would fight hard only to keep what they possessed would have a higher probability of reproductive success. The characteristic of "holding on to what you have" has been passed down from generation to generation, and although it may not be as important today as it was in a hunter-gatherer society, it still influences behavior.

Chapter 19

CHAPTER 19, PAGE 411

1   No. Individuals will only form teams or firms when the sum of what they can produce as a team (or firm) is greater than the sum of what they can produce working alone.

2   The person earning the low salary has lower implicit costs and so is more likely to start his or her own business. He or she gives up less to start a business.

3   Accounting profit is larger. Only explicit costs are subtracted from total revenue in computing accounting profit, but both explicit and implicit costs are subtracted from total revenue in computing economic profit. If implicit costs are zero, then accounting profit and economic profit are the same. Economic profit is never greater than accounting profit.

4   When he is earning (positive) accounting profit but his total revenue does not cover the sum of his explicit and implicit costs. For example, suppose Brad earns total revenue of $100,000 and has explicit costs of $40,000 and implicit costs of $70,000. His accounting profit is $60,000, but his total revenue of $100,000 is not large enough to cover the sum of his explicit and implicit costs ($110,000). Brad's economic profit is a negative $10,000. In other words, while Brad earns an accounting profit, he takes an economic loss.

CHAPTER 19, PAGE 416

1   No. The short run and the long run are not "lengths of time." The short run is that period of time when some inputs are fixed, and therefore, the firm has fixed costs. The long run is that period of time when no inputs are

fixed (i.e., all inputs are variable), and thus, all costs are variable costs. It's possible for the short run to be, say, 6 months and the long run to be a much shorter period of time. In other words, the time period when there are no fixed inputs can be shorter than the time period when there are fixed inputs.

2 The law of diminishing marginal returns holds only when we add more of one input to a given (fixed) quantity of another input. The statement does not identify one input as fixed (it says that both increase), and so the law of diminishing marginal returns is not relevant in this situation.

3 When MC is declining, MPP is rising; when MC is constant, MPP is constant; and when MC is rising, MPP is falling.

CHAPTER 19, PAGE 426

1 $ATC = TC/Q$ and $ATC = AFC + AVC$

2 Yes. Suppose a business incurs a cost of $10 to produce a product. Before it can sell the product, though, the demand for the product falls and moves the market price from $15 to $6. Does the owner of the business say, "I can't sell the product for $6 because I'd be taking a loss"? If she does, she chooses to let a sunk cost affect her current decision. Instead, she should ask herself, "Do I think the market price of the product will rise or fall?" If she thinks it will fall, she should sell the product today for $6.

3 Unit costs are another name for average total costs (ATC), so the question is: What happens to ATC as MC rises? You might be inclined to say that as MC rises, so does ATC—but this is not necessarily so (see Region 1 in Exhibit 5(b)). What matters is whether or not MC is greater than ATC. If it is, then ATC will rise. If it is not, then ATC will decline. This is a trick question of sorts. There is a tendency to misinterpret the average-marginal rule and to believe that as marginal cost rises, average total cost rises; and as marginal cost falls, average total cost falls. But this is not what the average-marginal rule says. The rule says that when MC is above ATC, ATC rises; and when MC is below ATC, ATC falls.

4 Yes. As marginal physical product (MPP) rises, marginal cost (MC) falls. If MC falls enough to move below unit cost (which is the same as average total cost), then unit cost declines. Similarly, as MPP falls, MC rises. If MC rises enough to move above unit cost, then unit cost rises.

CHAPTER 19, PAGE 429

1 It currently takes 10 units of X and 10 units of Y to produce 50 units of good Z. Let both X and Y double to 20 units each. As a result, the output of Z more than doubles—say, to 150 units. When inputs are increased by some percentage and output increases by a greater percentage, then economies of scale are said to exist. When economies of scale exist, unit costs fall. And another name for unit costs is average total costs.

2 The $LRATC$ curve would be horizontal. When there are constant returns to scale, output doubles if inputs double. If this happens, unit costs stay constant. In other words, they don't rise and they don't fall, so the $LRATC$ curve is horizontal.

3 Unit costs must have been lower when it produced 200 units than when it produced 100 units. That is, there were economies of scale between 100 units and 200 units. To explain further: Profit per unit is the difference between price per unit and cost per unit (or unit costs): Profit per unit = Price per unit − Cost per unit. Suppose the unit cost is $3 when the price is $4—giving a profit per unit of $1. Next, there are economies of scale as the firm raises output from 100 units to 200 units. It follows that unit costs fall—let's say to $2 per unit. If price is $3, then there is still a $1 per-unit profit.

Chapter 20

CHAPTER 20, PAGE 441

1 It means the firm cannot change the price of the product it sells by its actions. For example, if firm A cuts back on the supply of what it produces and the price of its product does not change, then we'd say that firm A cannot control the price of the product it sells. In other words, if price is independent of a firm's actions, that firm does not have any control over price.

2 The easy, and incomplete, answer is that a perfectly competitive firm is a price taker because it is in a market where it cannot control the price of the product it sells. But this simply leads to the question: Why can't it control the price of the product it sells? The answer is because it is in a market where its supply is small relative to the total market supply, it sells a homogeneous good, and all buyers and sellers have all relevant information.

3 If a perfectly competitive firm tries to charge a price higher than equilibrium price, all buyers will know this (assumption 3). These buyers will then simply buy from another firm that sells the same (homogeneous) product (assumption 2).

4 No. A market doesn't have to perfectly match all assumptions of the theory of perfect competition for it to be labeled a perfectly competitive market. What is important is whether or not it acts *as if* it is perfectly competitive. You know the old saying, "If it walks like a duck and it quacks like a duck, it's a duck." Well, if it acts like a perfectly competitive market, it's a perfectly competitive market.

CHAPTER 20, PAGE 447

1 No. Whether a firm earns profits or not depends on the relationship between price (P) and average total cost (ATC). If $P > ATC$, then the firm earns profits. To understand this, remember that profits exist when total

revenue (TR) minus total cost (TC) is a positive number. Total revenue is simply price times quantity ($TR = P \times Q$), and total cost is average total cost times quantity ($TC = ATC \times Q$). Because quantity (Q) is common to both TR and TC, if $P > ATC$, then $TR > TC$, and the firm earns profits.

2   In the short run, whether or not a firm should shut down operations depends on the relationship between price and average variable cost (AVC), not between price and ATC. It depends on whether price is greater than or less than average variable cost. If $P > AVC$, the firm should continue to produce; if $P < AVC$, it should shut down.

3   As long as $MR > MC$—for example, $MR = \$6$ and $MC = \$4$—the firm should produce and sell additional units of a good because this adds more to TR than it does to TC. It's adding $6 to TR and $4 to TC. Whenever you add more to TR than you do to TC, the gap between the two becomes larger.

4   We start with the upward-sloping market supply curve and work backward. First, market supply curves are upward sloping because they are the "addition" of individual firms' supply curves—which are upward sloping. Second, individual firms' supply curves are upward sloping because they are that portion of their marginal cost curves above their average variable cost curves, and this portion of the MC curve is upward sloping. Third, marginal cost curves have upward-sloping portions because of the law of diminishing marginal returns. In conclusion, market supply curves are upward sloping because of the law of diminishing marginal returns.

CHAPTER 20, PAGE 455

1   According to the theory of perfect competition, the profits will draw new firms into the market. As these new firms enter the market, the market supply curve will shift to the right. As a result of a larger supply, price will fall. As price declines, profit will decline until firms in the market are earning (only) normal (or zero economic) profit. When there is zero economic profit, there is no longer an incentive for firms to enter the market.

2   No. The market is only in long-run competitive equilibrium when (1) there is no incentive for firms to enter or exit the industry, (2) there is no incentive for firms to produce more or less output, and (3) there is no incentive for firms to change their plant size. If any of these conditions is not met, then the market is not in long-run equilibrium.

3   Initially, price will rise. Recall from Chapter 3 that when demand increases, *ceteris paribus,* price rises. In time, though, price will drop because new firms will enter the industry due to the positive economic profits generated by the higher price. How far the price drops depends on whether the firms are in a constant-cost, an increasing-cost, or a decreasing-cost industry. In a constant-cost industry, price will return to its original level; in an increasing-cost industry, price will return to a level above its original level; and in a decreasing-cost industry, price will return to a level below its original level.

4   Maybe initially, but probably not after certain adjustments are made. If firm A really has a genius on its payroll and, as a result, earns higher profits than firm B, then firm B might try to hire the genius away from firm A by offering the genius a higher income. To keep the genius, firm A will have to match the offer. As a result, the costs of firm A will rise, and if nothing else changes, its profits will decline.

CHAPTER 20, PAGE 456

1   It depends on how many firms in the market witness higher costs. If it is only one, then it is doubtful that the market supply curve will shift enough to bring about a higher price. If, however, many firms in the market witness higher costs, then the market supply curve will shift left, and price will rise.

2   No. Perfectly competitive firms that sell homogeneous products won't advertise individually, but this doesn't mean that the industry won't advertise in the hope of pushing the market (industry) demand curve (for their product) to the right.

Chapter 21

CHAPTER 21, PAGE 464

1   Let's assume that John is right when he says that there are always some close substitutes for the product a firm sells. The question, however, is: How close does the substitute have to be before the theory of monopoly is not useful? For example, a "slightly close" substitute for a seller's product may not be close enough to matter. The theory of monopoly may still be useful in predicting a firm's behavior.

2   Economies of scale exist when a firm doubles inputs and its output more than doubles, lowering its unit costs (average total costs) in the process. If economies of scale exist only when a firm produces a large quantity of output and one firm is already producing this output, then new firms (that start off producing less output) will have higher unit costs than those of the established firm. Some economists argue that this will make the new firms uncompetitive when compared to the established firm. In other words, economies of scale will act as a barrier to entry, effectively preventing firms from entering the industry and competing with the established firm.

3   In a monopoly, there is a single seller of a good for which there are no close substitutes, and there are extremely high barriers to competing with the single seller. If a movie superstar has so much talent that the moviegoing public puts her in a class by herself, she might be considered a monopolist. Can anyone compete with her? They can try, but she may have such great talent (relative to everyone else) that no one will be able to effectively compete with her. Her immense talent acts as a barrier to entry in the sense that even if someone does try to compete with her, they won't be a close substitute for her.

CHAPTER 21, PAGE 470

1 The single-price monopolist has to lower price to sell an additional unit of its good (this is what a downward-sloping demand curve necessitates). As long as it has to lower price to sell an additional unit, its marginal revenue will be below its price. A demand curve plots price (P) and quantity (Q), and a marginal revenue curve plots marginal revenue (MR) and quantity (Q). Because $P > MR$ for a monopolist, its demand curve will lie above its marginal revenue curve.

2 No. Profit depends on whether or not price is greater than average total cost. It is possible for a monopolist to produce the quantity of output at which $MR = MC$, charge the highest price per unit possible for the output, and still have its unit costs (ATC) greater than price. If this is the case, the monopolist incurs losses; it does not earn profits.

3 No. The last chapter explains that a firm is resource allocative efficient when it charges a price equal to its marginal cost ($P = MC$). The monopolist does not do this; it charges a price above marginal cost. Profit maximization ($MR = MC$) does not lead to resource allocative efficiency ($P = MC$) because for the monopolist, $P > MR$. This is not the case for the perfectly competitive firm, where $P = MR$.

4 A monopolist is searching for the highest price at which it can sell its product. In contrast, the perfectly competitive firm doesn't have to search; it simply takes the equilibrium price established in the market. For example, suppose Nancy is a wheat farmer. She gets up one morning and wants to know at what price she should sell her wheat. She simply turns on the radio, listens to the farm report, and finds out that the equilibrium price per bushel of wheat is, say, $5. Being a price taker, she knows she can't sell her wheat for a penny more than this ($5 is the highest price), and she won't want to sell her wheat for a penny less than this. The monopoly firm doesn't know what the highest price is for the product it sells. It has to search for it; it has to experiment with different prices before it finds the "highest" price.

CHAPTER 21, PAGE 477

1 There are three in particular:

a A monopoly firm produces too little output relative to a perfectly competitive firm; this causes the deadweight loss of monopoly.

b The profits of the monopoly are sometimes subject to rent-seeking behavior. Rent seeking, while rational for an individual firm, wastes society's resources. What good does society receive if one firm expends resources to take over the monopoly position of another firm? Answer: none. Resources that could have been used to produce goods (e.g., computers, software, shoes, houses, etc.) are instead used to transfer profits from one firm to another.

c A monopolist may not produce its products at the lowest possible cost. Again, this wastes society's resources.

2 An example helps to illustrate this concept. Suppose a perfectly competitive firm would produce 100 units of good X, but a monopoly firm would produce only 70 units of good X. This is a difference of 30 units. Buyers value these 30 units by more than it would cost the monopoly firm to produce them, yet the monopoly firm chooses not to produce the units. The net benefit (benefits to buyers minus costs to the monopolist) of producing these 30 units is said to be the deadweight loss of monopoly. It represents how much buyers lose because the monopolist chooses to produce less than the perfectly competitive firm.

3 If a seller is not a price searcher, then he is a price taker. A price taker can sell his product at only one price, the market equilibrium price.

Chapter 22

CHAPTER 22, PAGE 487

1 It is like a monopolist in that it faces a downward-sloping demand curve; it is a price searcher, $P > MR$; and it is not resource allocative efficient. It is like a perfect competitor in that it sells to many buyers and competes with many sellers, and there is easy entry into and exit from the market.

2 Essentially, because they face downward-sloping demand curves. Because the demand curve is downward sloping, it cannot be tangent to the lowest point on a U-shaped ATC curve (see Exhibit 3).

CHAPTER 22, PAGE 494

1 The incentive in both cases is the same: profit. Firms have an incentive to form a cartel to increase their profits. After the cartel is formed, however, each firm has an incentive to break the cartel to increase its profits even further. This is illustrated in Exhibit 5. If there is no cartel agreement, the firm is earning zero profits by producing q_1. After the cartel is formed, it earns CP_CAB in profits by producing q_C. But it can earn even higher profits (FP_CDE) by cheating on the cartel and producing q_{CC}.

2 There is a kink because the demand curve for an oligopolist is more elastic above the kink than it is below the kink. The difference in elasticity is based on the assumption that rival (oligopoly) firms will not match a price hike but will match a price decline. Thus, if a given oligopolist raises product price, it is assumed that its quantity demanded will fall a lot, but if it lowers price, its quantity demanded will not rise much.

3 The dominant firm tries to figure out the price that would exist if it were not in the market. Suppose this price is $10. Then it figures out how much it would supply at this price (the answer is zero) and at all prices less than this. For example, suppose the firm supplies 0 units at $10, 20 units at $9, and 30 units at $8. These, then, are three points on the dominant firm's demand curve—sometimes called the residual demand curve. Next, the dominant firm produces the level of output at which $MR = MC$ and charges the highest price per unit consistent with this output.

Chapter 23

CHAPTER 23, PAGE 519

1   The way a market is defined will help determine whether or not a particular firm is considered a monopoly. If a market is defined broadly, it will include more substitute goods, and so the firm is less likely to be considered a monopolist. If a market is defined narrowly, it will include fewer substitute goods, and so the firm is more likely to be considered a monopolist.

2   The four-firm concentration ratio is 20 percent; the Herfindahl index is 500. The formulas in Exhibit 1 show how each is computed.

3   The Herfindahl index provides information about the dispersion of firm size in an industry. For example, suppose the top four firms in an industry have 15 percent, 10 percent, 9 percent, and 8 percent market shares. The four-firm concentration ratio will be the same for an industry with 15 firms as it is for an industry with 150 firms. The Herfindahl index will be different in the two situations.

CHAPTER 23, PAGE 526

1   Average cost pricing is the same as profit regulation. The regulators state that the natural monopolist must charge a price equal to its average total costs ($P = ATC$). Under this pricing policy, there is no incentive for the natural monopolist to keep costs down. In fact, there may be an incentive to deliberately push costs up. Higher costs—in the form of higher salaries or more luxurious offices—simply mean higher prices to cover the higher costs.

2   No matter what the motive for initially regulating an industry, eventually, the regulating agency will be "captured" by the special interests (the firms) in the industry. In the end, the regulatory body will not so much regulate the industry as serve the interests of the firms in the industry.

3   According to the capture theory, the outcomes of the regulatory process will favor the regulated firms. According to the public choice theory, the outcomes of the regulatory process will favor the regulators.

4   Sometimes, they favor regulation, and at other times, they do not. Economists make the point that regulation involves both costs and benefits, and whether the particular regulation in question is worthwhile depends on whether the costs are greater than or less than the benefits.

Chapter 24

CHAPTER 24, PAGE 537

1   $MRP = MR \times MPP$. For a perfectly competitive firm, $MR = P$, so MR is $10. MPP in this case is 19 units. It follows that $MRP = 190.

2   There is no difference between MRP and VMP if the firm is perfectly competitive. In this situation, $P = MR$, and because $MRP = MR \times MPP$ and $VMP = P \times MPP$, the two are the same. If the firm is a price searcher—monopolist, monopolistic competitor, or oligopolist—$P > MR$; therefore, $VMP > MRP$.

3   It can buy all it wants of a factor at the equilibrium price, and it will not cause factor price to rise. For example, if firm X is a factor price taker in the labor market, it can buy all the labor it wants at the equilibrium wage, and it will not cause this wage to rise.

4   It should buy that quantity at which MRP of labor = MFC of labor.

CHAPTER 24, PAGE 548

1   The MRP curve is the firm's factor demand curve. $MRP = P \times MPP$ for a perfectly competitive firm, so if either the price of the product that labor produces rises or the MPP of labor rises (reflected in a shift in the MPP curve), the factor demand curve shifts rightward.

2   It means that for every 1 percent change in the wage rate, the quantity demanded of labor changes by 3 times this percentage. For example, if wage rates rise 10 percent, then the quantity demanded of labor falls 30 percent.

3   The short answer is because supply-and-demand conditions differ among markets. But this raises the question: Why do supply-and-demand conditions differ? This question is answered in Exhibit 11.

4   We can't answer this question specifically without more information. We know that under four conditions, wage rates would not differ. These conditions are: (1) the demand for every type of labor is the same; (2) there are no special nonpecuniary aspects to any job; (3) all labor is ultimately homogeneous and can costlessly be trained for different types of employment; and (4) all labor is mobile at zero cost. For wage rates to differ, one or more of these conditions is not being met. For example, perhaps labor is not mobile at zero cost.

Chapter 25

CHAPTER 25, PAGE 561

1   The demand for union labor is lowered by (a) a decline in the demand for the product union labor produces, (b) a decline in the price of substitute factors, and (c) a decline in the marginal physical product of union labor.

2   A closed shop requires an employee to be a member of the union before he or she can be hired; a union shop does not. The union shop does require employees to join the union within a certain period of time after becoming employed.

3   To prove to management that union members will not work for a wage rate that is lower than the rate specified

by the union. In terms of Exhibit 3, it is to prove that union members will not work for less than W_2.

CHAPTER 25, PAGE 568

1 A monopsonist cannot buy additional units of a factor without increasing the price it pays for the factor. A factor price taker can.

2 Under the following conditions: (1) The firm hiring the labor is a monopsonist and (2) the minimum wage is above the wage it is already paying and below the wage that corresponds to the point where $MFC = MRP$. To understand this completely, look at Exhibit 4(c). Suppose the firm is currently purchasing Q_1 labor and paying W_1. Then, W_2 becomes the minimum wage the monopsonist can pay to workers. Now it hires Q_2 workers. Notice, however, that if the monopsonist had to pay a wage higher than the wage that equates MFC and MRP, it would employ fewer workers than Q_1.

3 If the higher wage rate reduces the number of people working in the unionized sector and the people who lose their jobs in the unionized sector move to the nonunionized sector, then the supply of labor will increase in the nonunionized sector and wage rates will fall. This is illustrated in Exhibit 6.

Chapter 26

CHAPTER 26, PAGE 576

1 It can change the distribution of income through transfer payments and taxes. Look at this equation: Individual income = Labor income + Asset income + Transfer payments − Taxes. By increasing one person's taxes and increasing another person's transfer payments, government can change people's incomes.

2 The statement is true. For example, two people can have unequal incomes at any one point in time and still earn the same incomes over time. For example, in year 1, Patrick earns $40,000 and Francine earns $20,000. In year 2, Francine earns $40,000 and Patrick earns $20,000. In each year, there is income inequality, but over the 2 years, Patrick and Francine earn the same income ($60,000).

3 No. Individual income = Labor income + Asset income + Transfer payments − Taxes. It is possible for Smith's income to come entirely from labor income and Jones's income to come entirely from asset income. The same dollar income does not necessitate the same source of income.

CHAPTER 26, PAGE 579

1 No. The income shares total 105 percent.

2 A Gini coefficient of 0 represents perfect income equality and a Gini coefficient of 1 represents complete income inequality, so we are sure that country A has

neither perfect income equality nor complete income inequality. Beyond this, it is difficult to say anything. Usually, the Gini coefficient is used as a comparative measure. For example, if country A's Gini coefficient is 0.45 and country B's is 0.60, we could then conclude that country A has a more equal (less unequal) distribution of income than country B has.

CHAPTER 26, PAGE 583

1 The simple fact that Jack earns more than Harry is not evidence of wage discrimination. We lack the information necessary to know whether wage discrimination exists. For example, we don't know if Jack and Harry work the same job, we don't know how productive each person is, and so on.

2 It could affect it negatively or positively. There is a higher probability of both higher and lower income if a person assumes a lot of risk than if a person simply plays it safe. To illustrate, suppose Nancy has decided she wants to be an actress, although her parents want her to be an accountant. The chances of her being successful in acting are small, but if she is successful, she will earn a much higher income than if she had been an accountant (a top actress earns more than a top accountant). Of course, if she isn't successful, she will earn less income as an actress than she would have as an accountant (the average actress earns less than the average accountant).

CHAPTER 26, PAGE 589

1 Whether poor people always exist or not depends on how we define poor. If we define poor in relative terms and we assume that there is not absolute income equality, then there must be some people who fall into, say, the lowest 10 percent of income earners. We could refer to these persons as poor. Remember, though, these persons are relatively poor—they earn less than a large percentage of the income earners in the country—but we do not know anything about their absolute incomes. In a world of multimillion-dollar income earners, a person who earns $100,000 might be considered poor.

2 12.7 percent

3 An African American or Hispanic female who is the head of a large family and who is young and has little education.

Chapter 27

CHAPTER 27, PAGE 598

1 Because there is a monetary incentive for them to be equal. To illustrate, suppose the return on capital is 12 percent, and the price for loanable funds is 10 percent. In this case, a person could borrow loanable funds at 10 percent and invest in capital goods to earn the 12 percent return. As this happens, though, the amount of capital increases and its return falls. If the interest rates are

reversed and the return on capital is lower than the price for a loanable fund, no one will borrow to invest in capital goods. Over time, then, the stock of capital will diminish and its return will rise.

2   Because the real interest rate is the rate paid by borrowers and received by lenders. For example, if a person borrows funds at a 12 percent interest rate and the inflation rate is 4 percent, he will be paying only an 8 percent (real) interest rate to the lender. Stated differently, the lender has 8 percent, not 12 percent, more buying power because he made the loan.

3   $907.03. The formula is $PV = \$1,000/(1 + 0.05)^2$.

4   No. The present value of $2,000 a year for 4 years at an 8 percent interest rate is $6,624.25. $[PV = \$2,000/(1 + 0.08)^1 + \$2,000/(1 + 0.08)^2 + \$2,000/(1 + 0.08)^3 + \$2,000/(1 + 0.08)^4]$. The present value is less than the cost of the capital good, so it is not worth purchasing.

CHAPTER 27, PAGE 602

1   Jones earns $2 million a year as a news anchor for KNBC. His next best alternative in the news industry is earning $1.9 million a year as a news anchor for KABC. If Jones were not working in the news industry, his next best alternative would be as a journalism professor earning $100,000 a year. Within the news industry, Jones earns $100,000 economic rent (which is the difference between $2 million and $1.9 million). If we move beyond the news industry, Jones earns $1.9 million economic rent (which is the difference between $2 million and $100,000).

2   It is zero dollars.

3   When a firm competes for artificial rents, it expends resources to simply transfer economic rent from another firm to itself. In other words, resources are used to bring about a transfer only. There are no additional goods and services produced as a part of the process. But when a firm competes for real rents, resources are used to produce additional goods and services.

CHAPTER 27, PAGE 606

1   A probability cannot be assigned to uncertainty; a probability can be assigned to risk.

2   There are many different theories that purport to explain profit. One theory states that profit exists because uncertainty exists. No uncertainty, no profit. Another theory states that profit exists because arbitrage opportunities exist (the opportunities to buy low and sell high), and some people are alert to these opportunities. Still another theory states that profit exists because some people (called entrepreneurs) are capable of creating profit opportunities by devising a new product, production process, or marketing strategy.

3   Profit can be a signal, especially if the profit is earned in a competitive market. Specifically, profit signals that buyers value a good (as evidenced by the price they are willing and able to pay for the good) by more than the factors that go to make the good.

Chapter 28

CHAPTER 28, PAGE 616

1   The market output does not reflect or adjust for either external costs (in the case of a negative externality) or external benefits (in the case of a positive externality). The socially optimal output does.

2   Certainly, if there are no costs incurred by moving from the market output to the socially optimal output, the answer is yes. But this isn't likely to be the case. The economist considers whether the benefits of moving to the socially optimal output are greater than or less than the costs of moving to the socially optimal output. If the benefits are greater than the costs, then yes; if the benefits are less than the costs, then no.

CHAPTER 28, PAGE 621

1   It means to adjust the private cost by the external cost. To illustrate, suppose someone's private cost is $10 and the external cost is $2. If the person internalizes the externality, the external cost becomes his cost, which is now $12.

2   Transaction costs are associated with the time and effort needed to search out, negotiate, and consummate an exchange. These costs are higher for buying a house than they are for buying a hamburger. It takes more time and effort to search out a house to buy, negotiate a price, and consummate the deal than it takes to search out and buy a hamburger.

3   Under certain conditions, no. Specifically, if transaction costs are zero or trivial, the property rights assignment that a court makes is irrelevant to the resource allocative outcome. Of course, if transaction costs are not zero or trivial, then the property rights assignment a court makes does matter.

4   If there is a negative externality, there is a marginal external cost. The marginal external cost (MEC) plus the marginal private cost (MPC) equals the marginal social cost (MSC): $MSC = MPC + MEC$. If a corrective tax (t) is to correctly adjust for the marginal external cost associated with the negative externality, it must be equal to the marginal external cost—in other words, tax $= MEC$. With this condition fulfilled, MPC + tax $= MSC = MPC + MEC$.

CHAPTER 28, PAGE 623

1   All other things held constant, less pollution is preferable to more pollution. Zero pollution is the least amount of pollution possible; therefore, zero pollution is best. But in reality, all other things are not held constant. Sometimes, when we reduce pollution, we also eliminate some of the things we want. The economist wants to eliminate pollution as long as the benefits of eliminating pollution are greater than the costs. When the benefits equal the costs, the economist would stop eliminating pollution. If society has eliminated so much pol-

lution that the costs of eliminating it are greater than the benefits, then society has gone too far. It has eliminated too much pollution. Some units of pollution were simply not worth eliminating.

2 Under market environmentalism, the entities that can eliminate pollution at least cost are the ones that eliminate the pollution. This is not the case under standards, where both the low-cost and high-cost eliminators of pollution must reduce pollution.

3 The dollar price of the pollution permits is a cost for firm Z, but it is not a cost to society. As far as society is concerned, firm Z simply paid $660 to firms X and Y. Firm Z ended up with $660 less, and firms X and Y ended up with $660 more; the amounts offset. Only when resources are used in eliminating pollution is the dollar cost of those resources counted as a cost to society of eliminating pollution.

CHAPTER 28, PAGE 626

1 Because after a nonexcludable public good is produced, the individual or firm that produced it wouldn't be able to collect payment for it. When a nonexcludable public good is provided to one person, it is provided to everyone. Because an individual can consume the good without paying for it, he is likely to take a free ride. Another way of answering this question is simply to say, "The market fails to produce nonexcludable public goods because of the free rider problem."

2 (a) A composition notebook is a private good. It is rivalrous in consumption; if one person is using it, someone else cannot. (b) A Shakespearean play performed in a summer theater is an excludable public good. It is nonrivalrous in consumption (everyone in the theater can see the play) but excludable (a person must pay to get into the theater). (c) An apple is a private good. It is rivalrous in consumption; if one person eats it, someone else cannot. (d) A telephone in service is a private good. One person using the phone (e.g., in your house) prevents someone else from using it. (e) Sunshine is a nonexcludable public good. It is nonrivalrous in consumption (one person's consumption of it doesn't reduce its consumption by others) and nonexcludable (it is impossible to exclude free people from consuming the sunshine).

3 A concert is an example. If one person consumes the concert, this does not take away from others consuming it to the same degree. However, people can be excluded from consuming it.

CHAPTER 28, PAGE 632

1 Consider a fictional product, X. The sellers of X know that the good could, under certain conditions, cause health problems, but they do not release this information to the buyers. Consequently, the demand for good X is likely to be greater than it would be if there were symmetric information. The quantity consumed of good X is likely to be higher when there is asymmetric information than when there is symmetric information.

2 To illustrate, consider again the used car market discussed in the text. If there are two types of used cars—good used cars and "lemons"—and asymmetric information, the market price for a used car may understate the value of a good used car and overstate the value of a lemon. This will induce sellers of lemons to enter the market and sellers of good cars to leave it. (The owners of good used cars will not want to sell their cars for less than their cars are worth.) In theory, the used car market may consist of nothing but lemons. In other words, a used car market for good cars does not exist.

3 A college professor tells her students that she does not believe in giving grades of D or F. As a result, her students do not take as many "precautionary" measures to guard against receiving low grades. Does your example have the characteristic of this example—namely, one person's assurance affects another person's incentive?

Chapter 29

CHAPTER 29, PAGE 643

1 No. The model doesn't say every politician has to do these things; it simply predicts that politicians who do these things have an increased chance of winning the election in a two-person race.

2 Voters may want more information from politicians, but supplying that information is not always in the best interests of politicians. When they speak in specific terms, politicians are often labeled as being at one end or the other of the political spectrum. But politicians don't win elections by being in the right wing or left wing; they win elections by being in the middle.

3 Yes. In the cost equation of voting, we included (1) the cost of driving to the polls, (2) the cost of standing in line, and (3) the cost of filling out the ballot. Bad weather (heavy rain, snow, ice) would likely raise the cost of driving to the polls and the cost of standing in line, therefore raising the cost of voting. The higher the cost of voting, the less likely people will vote, *ceteris paribus*.

CHAPTER 29, PAGE 645

1 2 units

2 In Example 2 with equal taxes, 1 unit received a simple majority of the votes. Person C was made worse off because his *MPB* for the first unit of good Y was $100, but he ended up paying a tax of $120 and was worse off by $20.

CHAPTER 29, PAGE 650

1 Both farmers and consumers are affected by federal agricultural policy—but not in the same way and not to the same degree. Federal agricultural policy directly affects farmers' incomes, usually by a large amount. It indirectly affects consumers' costs, but not as much as it affects farmers' incomes. Simply put, farmers have more at stake than consumers when it comes to federal

agricultural policy. People tend to be better informed about matters that mean more to them.

2   The legislation is more likely to pass when group *A* includes 10 million persons because the wider the dispersal of the costs of the legislation, the greater the likelihood of passage. When costs are widely dispersed, the cost to any one individual is so small that she or he is unlikely to lobby against the legislation.

3   Examples include teachers saying that more money for education will help the country compete in the global marketplace; domestic car manufacturers saying that tariffs on foreign imports will save American jobs and U.S. manufacturing; farmers saying that subsidies to farmers will preserve the "American" farm and a way of life that Americans cherish. Whether any of these groups is right or wrong is not the point. The point is that special interest groups are likely to advance their arguments (good or bad) with public interest talk.

4   Rent seeking is socially wasteful because the resources that are used to seek rent could instead be used to produce goods and services.

Chapter 30

CHAPTER 30, PAGE 662

1   For the United States, $1X = 1/6Y$ or $1Y = 6X$. For England, $1X = 2Y$ or $1Y = 1/2X$. Let's focus on the opportunity cost of $1X$ in each country. In the United States, $1X = 1/6Y$, and in Great Britain, $1X = 2Y$. Terms of trade that are between these two endpoints would be favorable for the two countries. For example, suppose we choose $1X = 1Y$. This is good for the United States because it would prefer to give up $1X$ and get $1Y$ in trade than to give up $1X$ and only get $1/6Y$ (without trade). Similarly, Great Britain would prefer to give up $1Y$ and get $1X$ in trade than to give up $1Y$ and get only $1/2X$ (without trade). Any terms of trade between $1X = 1/6Y$ and $1X = 2Y$ will be favorable to the two countries.

2   Yes; this is what the theory of comparative advantage shows. Exhibit 1 shows that the United States could produce more of both food and clothing than Japan. Still, the United States benefits from specialization and trade, as shown in Exhibit 2. In column 5 of this exhibit, the United States can consume 10 more units of food by specializing and trading.

3   No. It is the desire to buy low and sell high (earn a profit) that pushes countries into producing and trading at a comparative advantage. Government officials do not collect cost data and then issue orders to firms in the country to produce X, Y, or Z. We have not drawn the PPFs in this chapter and identified the cost differences between countries to show what countries actually do in the real world. We described things technically to simply show how countries benefit from specialization and trade.

CHAPTER 30, PAGE 670

1   Domestic producers benefit because producers' surplus rises; domestic consumers lose because consumers' surplus falls. Also, government benefits in that it receives the tariff revenue. Moreover, consumers lose more than producers and government gain, so that there is a net loss resulting from tariffs.

2   Consumers' surplus falls by more than producers' surplus rises.

3   With a tariff, the government receives tariff revenue. With a quota, it does not. In the latter case, the revenue that would have gone to government goes, instead, to the importers who get to satisfy the quota.

4   Infant or new domestic industries need to be protected from older, more established competitors until they are mature enough to compete on an equal basis. Tariffs and quotas provide these infant industries the time they need.

Chapter 31

CHAPTER 31, PAGE 680

1   A debit. When an American enters into a transaction in which he has to supply U.S. dollars in the foreign exchange market (to demand a foreign currency), the transaction is recorded as a debit.

2   We do not have enough information to answer this question. The merchandise trade balance is the difference between the value of *merchandise* exports and *merchandise* imports. The question gives only the value of exports and imports. *Exports* is a more inclusive term than merchandise exports. Exports include (a) merchandise exports, (b) services, and (c) income from U.S. assets abroad (see Exhibit 2). Similarly, *imports* is a more inclusive term than merchandise imports. It includes (a) merchandise imports, (b) services, and (c) income from foreign assets in the United States.

3   The merchandise trade balance includes fewer transactions than are included in the current account balance. The merchandise trade balance is the summary statistic for merchandise exports and merchandise imports. The current account balance is the summary statistic for exports of goods and services (which include merchandise exports), imports of goods and services (which include merchandise imports), and net unilateral transfers abroad (see Exhibit 2).

CHAPTER 31, PAGE 687

1   As the demand for dollars increases, the supply of pesos increases. For example, suppose someone in Mexico wants to buy something produced in the United States. The American wants to be paid in dollars, but the Mexican doesn't have any dollars—she has pesos. So she has to buy dollars with pesos; in other words, she has to supply pesos to buy dollars. Thus, as she demands more dollars, she will necessarily have to supply more pesos.

2 The dollar is said to have appreciated (against the peso) when it takes more pesos to buy a dollar and fewer dollars to buy a peso. For this to occur, either the demand for dollars must increase (which means the supply of pesos increases) or the supply of dollars must decrease (which means the demand for pesos decreases). To see this graphically, look at Exhibit 5(b). The only way for the peso price per dollar to rise (on the vertical axis) is for either the demand curve for dollars to shift to the right or the supply curve of dollars to shift to the left. Each of these occurrences is mirrored in the market for pesos in part (a) of the exhibit.

3 *Ceteris paribus,* the dollar will depreciate relative to the franc. As incomes for Americans rise, the demand for Swiss goods rises. This increases the demand for francs and the supply of dollars on the foreign exchange market. In turn, this leads to a depreciated dollar and an appreciated franc.

4 The theory states that the exchange rate between any two currencies will adjust to reflect changes in the relative price levels of the two countries. For example, suppose the U.S. price level rises 5 percent and Mexico's price level remains constant. According to the PPP theory, the U.S. dollar will depreciate 5 percent relative to the Mexican peso.

CHAPTER 31, PAGE 693

1 The terms *overvalued* and *undervalued* refer to the equilibrium exchange rate: the exchange rate at which the quantity demanded and quantity supplied of a currency are the same in the foreign exchange market. Let's suppose the equilibrium exchange rate is 0.10 USD = 1 MXN. This is the same as saying that 10 pesos = $1 If the exchange rate is fixed at 0.12 USD = 1 MXN (which is the same as 8.33 pesos = $1), the peso is overvalued and the dollar is undervalued. Specifically, a currency is overvalued if 1 unit of it fetches more of another currency than it would in equilibrium; a currency is undervalued if 1 unit of it fetches less of another currency than it would in equilibrium. In equilibrium, 1 peso would fetch 0.10 dollars and at the current exchange rate it fetches 0.12 dollars—so the peso is overvalued. In equilibrium, $1 would fetch 10 pesos, and at the current exchange rate, it fetches only 8.33 pesos—so the dollar is undervalued.

2 An overvalued dollar means some other currency is undervalued—let's say it is the Japanese yen. An overvalued dollar makes U.S. goods more expensive for the Japanese, so they buy fewer U.S. goods. This reduces U.S. exports. On the other hand, an undervalued yen makes Japanese goods cheaper for Americans, so they buy more Japanese goods; the U.S. imports more. Thus, an overvalued dollar reduces U.S. exports and raises U.S. imports.

3 **a** Dollar is overvalued.

    b Dollar is undervalued.

    c Dollar is undervalued.

4 When a country devalues its currency, it makes it cheaper for foreigners to buy its products.

CHAPTER 31, PAGE 698

1 An optimal currency area is a geographic area in which exchange rates can be fixed or a common currency used without sacrificing any domestic economic goals.

2 As the demand for good Y falls, the unemployment rate in country 2 will rise. This increase in the unemployment rate is likely to be temporary, though. The increased demand for good X (produced by country 1) will increase the demand for country 1's currency, leading to an appreciation in country 1's currency and a depreciation in country 2's currency. Country 1's good (good X) will become more expensive for the residents of country 2, and they will buy less. Country 2's good (good Y) will become less expensive for the residents of country 1, and they will buy more. As a result of the additional purchases of good Y, country 2's unemployment rate will begin to decline.

3 Labor mobility is very important to determining whether or not an area is an optimal currency area. If there is little or no labor mobility, an area is not likely to be an optimal currency area. If there is labor mobility, an area is likely to be an optimal currency area.

Chapter 32

CHAPTER 32, PAGE 709

1 As some explain it, the end of the Cold War resulted in turning two different worlds (the capitalist and communist worlds) into one world. It resulted in a thawing of not only political but economic relations between former enemies. You might not trade with your enemy, but once that person or country is no longer your enemy, you don't feel the same need to cut him or it out of your political and economic life.

2 Globalization is the phenomenon by which individuals and businesses in any part of the world are much more affected by events elsewhere in the world than before; it is the growing integration of the national economies of the world to the degree that we may be witnessing the emergence and operation of a single worldwide economy.

3 Advancing technology can reduce both transportation and communication costs, thus making it less costly to trade with people around the world.

CHAPTER 32, PAGE 715

1 Benefits identified in the section include (a) benefits from increased international trade, (b) greater income per person, (c) lower prices for goods, (d) greater product variety, and (e) increased productivity and innovation.

2 Costs identified in the section include (a) increased income inequality, (b) offshoring, and (c) more power for big corporations.

Chapter 33

CHAPTER 33, PAGE 730

1 30

2 Stocks are purchased either for the dividends that the stocks may pay, the expected gain in price (of the stock), or both.

3 The dividend per share (of the stock) divided by the closing price per share.

4 It means that the stock is selling for a share price that is 23 times its earnings per share.

CHAPTER 33, PAGE 734

1 A bond is an IOU or a promise to pay. The issuer of a bond is borrowing funds and promising to pay back those funds (with interest) at a later date.

2 $0.07X = \$400$, so $X = \$400/0.07$, or $\$5,714.29$.

3 $\$1,000/\$9,500 = 10.53$ percent

4 Municipal bonds are issued by state and local governments, and a Treasury bond is issued by the federal government.

CHAPTER 33, PAGE 737

1 A futures contract is a contract in which the seller agrees to provide a good to the buyer on a specified future date at an agreed-upon price.

2 You can buy a call option, which sells for a fraction of the cost of the stock. A call option gives the owner of the option the right to buy shares of a stock at a specified price within the time limits of the contract.

3 A put option gives the owner the right, but not the obligation, to *sell* (rather than buy, as in a call option) shares of a stock at a strike price during some period of time.

Web Chapter 34

CHAPTER 34, PAGE 745

1 She does so through the futures market. Specifically, she enters into a futures contract with someone who will guarantee to take delivery of her foodstuff (in the future) for a stated price. Then, if the price goes up or down between the present and the future, the farmer does not have to worry. She has locked in the price of her foodstuff.

2 If the farmer faces an inelastic demand curve, the order of preference would be (b)-(a)-(c). That is, he prefers (b) to (a) and he prefers (a) to (c). If all farmers except himself have bad weather (b), then the market supply curve of the individual farmer's product shifts to the left. This brings about a higher price. But the individual farmer's supply curve doesn't shift to the left; it stays where it is. Thus, the individual farmer sells the same amount of output at the higher price. Consequently, his total revenue rises. In (a), both the market supply curve and the individual farmer's supply curve shift left, so the farmer has less to sell at a higher price. Again, if the demand is inelastic, the individual farmer will increase his total revenue but not as much as in (b) where the individual farmer's output did not fall. Finally, in (c), the market supply curve shifts to the right, lowering price. If demand is inelastic, this lowers total revenue.

3 Increased productivity will lead to higher total revenue when demand is elastic. To illustrate, increased productivity shifts the supply curve to the right. This lowers price. If demand is elastic, then the percentage rise in quantity sold is greater than the percentage fall in price; therefore, total revenue rises. In summary, increased productivity leads to higher total revenue when demand is elastic.

CHAPTER 34, PAGE 750

1 Because the deficiency payment is the difference between the target price and the market price, the answer depends on what the market price is. If the market price is, say, $4, and the target price is $7, then the deficiency payment is $3.

2 A farmer pledges a certain number of bushels of foodstuff to obtain a loan—say, 500 bushels. He receives a loan equal to the number of bushels times the designated loan rate per bushel. For example, if the loan rate is $2 per bushel and 500 bushels are pledged, then the loan is $1,000. The farmer ends up paying back the loan with interest or keeping the loan and forfeiting the bushels of the crop. Which course of action the farmer takes depends on the market price of the crop. If the market price of the crop is higher than the loan rate, he or she pays back the loan and sells the crop. If the market price is less than the loan rate, he or she forfeits the crop. A nonrecourse loan guarantees that the farmer will not receive less than the loan rate for each bushel of his crop.

3 The effects of a price support are (a) a surplus, (b) fewer exchanges (less bought by private citizens), (c) higher prices paid by consumers of the crop (on which the support exists) and (d) government purchase and storage of the surplus crop (for which taxpayers pay).

Web Chapter 35

CHAPTER 35, PAGE 756

1 In country *A,* there is an economic expansion, and real income in the country rises. As a result, residents of the country buy more imports from country *B.* In country *B,* exports rise relative to imports, thus increasing net exports. As net exports in country *B* rise, the *AD* curve for country *B* shifts to the right, increasing Real GDP.

2 If the dollar appreciates, the Japanese yen depreciates. U.S. products become more expensive for the Japanese, and Japanese products become cheaper for Americans. U.S. imports will rise, U.S. exports will fall, and consequently, U.S. net exports will fall. As a result, the *AD* curve in the United States will shift leftward, pushing down Real GDP.

CHAPTER 35, PAGE 759

1   Foreign input prices can change directly as a result of supply conditions in the foreign country, or they can change indirectly as a result of a change in the exchange rate. In either case, as foreign input prices rise—either directly or as a result of a depreciated dollar—the U.S. *SRAS* curve shifts leftward. If foreign input prices fall—either directly or as a result of an appreciated dollar—the *SRAS* curve shifts rightward.

2   The higher real interest rates in the United States attract capital to the United States. This increases the demand for the dollar. As a result, the dollar appreciates and the yen depreciates. An appreciated dollar shifts the U.S. *AD* curve leftward and the U.S. *SRAS* curve rightward. The *AD* curve shifts leftward by more than the *SRAS* curve shifts rightward, so the price level falls.

CHAPTER 35, PAGE 763

1   When the money supply is raised, the *AD* curve shifts rightward, pushing up Real GDP. Also, as a result of the increased money supply, interest rates may decline in the short run. This promotes U.S. capital outflow and a depreciated dollar. As a result of the depreciated dollar, imports become more expensive for Americans, and U.S. exports become cheaper for foreigners. Imports fall and exports rise, thereby increasing net exports and *again* shifting the *AD* curve to the right. Real GDP rises.

2   Expansionary fiscal policy pushes the *AD* curve rightward and (under certain conditions) raises Real GDP. If the expansionary fiscal policy causes a deficit, then the government will have to borrow to finance the deficit, and interest rates will be pushed upward. As a result of the higher interest rates, there will be increased foreign capital inflows and dollar appreciation, thus pushing the *AD* curve leftward and the *SRAS* curve rightward.

A

Absolute (Money) Price   The price of a good in money terms.

Absolute Real Economic Growth   An increase in Real GDP from one period to the next.

Accounting Profit   The difference between total revenue and explicit costs.

Activists   Persons who argue that monetary and fiscal policies should be deliberately used to smooth out the business cycle.

Adaptive Expectations   Expectations that individuals form from past experience and modify slowly as the present and the future become the past (as time passes).

Adverse Selection   Exists when the parties on one side of the market, who have information not known to others, self-select in a way that adversely affects the parties on the other side of the market.

Aggregate Demand   The quantity demanded of all goods and services (Real GDP) at different price levels, *ceteris paribus.*

Aggregate Demand (AD) Curve   A curve that shows the quantity demanded of all goods and services (Real GDP) at different price levels, *ceteris paribus.*

Aggregate Supply   The quantity supplied of all goods and services (Real GDP) at different price levels, *ceteris paribus.*

Antitrust Law   Legislation passed for the stated purpose of controlling monopoly power and preserving and promoting competition.

Appreciation   An increase in the value of one currency relative to other currencies.

Arbitrage   Buying a good at a low price and selling the good for a higher price.

Asymmetric Information   Exists when either the buyer or the seller in a market exchange has some information that the other does not have.

Automatic Fiscal Policy   Changes in government expenditures and/or taxes that occur automatically without (additional) congressional action.

Autonomous Consumption   The part of consumption that is independent of disposable income.

Average Fixed Cost (AFC)   Total fixed cost divided by quantity of output: $AFC = TFC / Q.$

Average Total Cost (ATC), or Unit Cost   Total cost divided by quantity of output: $ATC = TC / Q.$

Average Variable Cost (AVC)   Total variable cost divided by quantity of output: $AVC = TVC / Q.$

Average–Marginal Rule   When the marginal magnitude is above the average magnitude, the average magnitude rises; when the marginal magnitude is below the average magnitude, the average magnitude falls.

B

Bad   Anything from which individuals receive disutility or dissatisfaction.

Balance of Payments   A periodic statement (usually annual) of the money value of all transactions between residents of one country and residents of all other countries.

Balanced Budget   Government expenditures equal to tax revenues.

Barter   Exchanging goods and services for other goods and services without the use of money.

Base Year   The year chosen as a point of reference or basis of comparison for prices in other years; a benchmark year.

Board of Governors   The governing body of the Federal Reserve System.

Bond   An IOU, or promise to pay.

Budget Constraint   All the combinations or bundles of two goods a person can purchase given a certain money income and prices for the two goods.

Budget Deficit   Government expenditures greater than tax revenues.

Budget Surplus   Tax revenues greater than government expenditures.

Business Cycle   Recurrent swings (up and down) in Real GDP.

Business Firm   An entity that employs factors of production (resources) to produce goods and services to be sold to consumers, other firms, or the government.

C

Capital   Produced goods that can be used as inputs for further production, such as factories, machinery, tools, computers, and buildings.

Capital Account   Includes all payments related to the purchase and sale of assets and to borrowing and lending activities. Components include outflow of U.S. capital and inflow of foreign capital.

Capital Account Balance   The summary statistic for the outflow of U.S. capital. It is equal to the difference between the outflow of U.S. capital and the inflow of foreign capital.

Capital Consumption Allowance (Depreciation)   The estimated amount of capital goods used up in production through natural wear, obsolescence, and accidental destruction.

Capture Theory of Regulation   Holds that no matter what the motive is for the initial regulation and the establishment of the regulatory agency, eventually, the agency will be "captured" (controlled) by the special interests of the industry being regulated.

Cartel   An organization of firms that reduces output and increases price in an effort to increase joint profits.

Cartel Theory   In this theory of oligopoly, oligopolistic firms act as if there were only one firm in the industry.

Cash Leakage   Occurs when funds are held as currency instead of deposited into a checking account.

Ceteris Paribus   A Latin term meaning "all other things constant" or "nothing else changes."

Checkable Deposits   Deposits on which checks can be written.

Closed Economy   An economy that does not trade goods and services with other countries.

Closed Shop   An organization in which an employee must belong to the union before he or she can be hired.

Coase Theorem   In the case of trivial or zero transaction costs, the property rights assignment does not matter to the resource allocative outcome.

Collective Bargaining   The process whereby wage rates and other issues are determined by a union bargaining with management on behalf of all union members.

Comparative Advantage   The situation when a person or country can produce a good at lower opportunity cost than another person or country can.

Complements   Two goods that are used jointly in consumption. If two goods are complements, the demand for one rises as the price of the other falls (or the demand for one falls as the price of the other rises).

Complete Crowding Out   A decrease in one or more components of private spending completely offsets the increase in government spending.

Concentration Ratio   The percentage of industry sales (or assets, output, labor force, or some other factor) accounted for by x number of firms in the industry.

Conglomerate Merger   A merger between companies in different industries.

Constant Returns to Scale   Exist when inputs are increased by some percentage and output increases by an equal percentage, causing unit costs to remain constant.

Constant-Cost Industry   An industry in which average total costs do not change as (industry) output increases or decreases when firms enter or exit the industry, respectively.

Consumer Equilibrium   Occurs when the consumer has spent all income and the marginal utilities per dollar spent on each good purchased are equal: $MU_A/P_A = MU_B/P_B = \ldots = MU_Z/P_Z$, where the letters A–Z represent all the goods a person buys.

Consumer Price Index (CPI)   A widely cited index number for the price level; the weighted average of prices of a specific set of goods and services purchased by a typical household.

Consumers' Surplus (CS)   The difference between the maximum price a buyer is willing and able to pay for a good or service and the price actually paid. $CS = $ Maximum buying price – Price paid.

Consumption   The sum of spending on durable goods, nondurable goods, and services.

Consumption Function   The relationship between consumption and disposable income. In the consumption function used here, consumption is directly related to disposable income and is positive even at zero disposable income: $C = C_0 + (MPC)(Y_d)$.

Contestable Market   A market in which entry is easy and exit is costless, new firms can produce the product at the same cost as current firms, and exiting firms can easily dispose of their fixed assets by selling them.

Continued Inflation   A continued increase in the price level.

Contractionary Fiscal Policy   Decreases in government expenditures and/or increases in taxes to achieve particular economic goals.

Contractionary Monetary Policy   The Fed decreases the money supply.

Craft (Trade) Union   A union whose membership is made up of individuals who practice the same craft or trade.

Credit   In the balance of payments, any transaction that creates a demand for the country's currency in the foreign exchange market.

Cross Elasticity of Demand   Measures the responsiveness in quantity demanded of one good to changes in the price of another good.

Crowding Out   The decrease in private expenditures that occurs as a consequence of increased government spending or the financing needs of a budget deficit.

Currency   Coins and paper money.

Current Account   Includes all payments related to the purchase and sale of goods and services. Components of the account include exports, imports, and net unilateral transfers abroad.

Current Account Balance   The summary statistic for exports of goods and services, imports of goods and services, and net unilateral transfers abroad.

Cyclical Deficit   The part of the budget deficit that is a result of a downturn in economic activity.

Cyclical Unemployment Rate   The difference between the unemployment rate and the natural unemployment rate.

D

Deadweight Loss   The loss to society of not producing the competitive, or supply-and-demand-determined, level of output.

Deadweight Loss of Monopoly   The net value (value to buyers over and above costs to suppliers) of the difference between the monopoly quantity of output (where $P > MC$) and the competitive quantity of output (where $P = MC$). The loss of not producing the competitive quantity of output.

Debit   In the balance of payments, any transaction that supplies the country's currency in the foreign exchange market.

Decisions at the Margin   Decision making characterized by weighing the additional (marginal) benefits of a change against the additional (marginal) costs of a change with respect to current conditions.

Decreasing-Cost Industry   An industry in which average total costs decrease as output increases and increase as output decreases when firms enter and exit the industry, respectively.

Demand   The willingness and ability of buyers to purchase different quantities of a good at different prices during a specific time period.

Demand for Money (Balances)   Represents the inverse relationship between the quantity demanded of money balances and the price of holding money balances.

Demand Schedule   The numerical tabulation of the quantity demanded of a good at different prices. A demand schedule is the numerical representation of the law of demand.

Depreciation   A decrease in the value of one currency relative to other currencies.

Derived Demand   Demand that is the result of some other demand. For example, factor demand is the result of the demand for the products that the factors go to produce.

Devaluation A government act that changes the exchange rate by lowering the official price of a currency.

Diamond–Water Paradox The observation that things that have the greatest value in use sometimes have little value in exchange and things that have little value in use sometimes have the greatest value in exchange.

Directly Related Two variables are directly related if they change in the same way.

Discount Rate The interest rate the Fed charges depository institutions that borrow reserves from it.

Discretionary Fiscal Policy Deliberate changes of government expenditures and/or taxes to achieve particular economic goals.

Diseconomies of Scale Exist when inputs are increased by some percentage and output increases by a smaller percentage, causing unit costs to rise.

Disequilibrium A state of either surplus or shortage in a market.

Disequilibrium Price A price other than equilibrium price. A price at which quantity demanded does not equal quantity supplied.

Disposable Income The portion of personal income that can be used for consumption or saving. It is equal to personal income minus personal taxes (especially income taxes).

Disutility The dissatisfaction one receives from a bad.

Dividend A share of the profits of a corporation distributed to stockholders.

Double Coincidence of Wants In a barter economy, a requirement that must be met before a trade can be made. It specifies that a trader must find another trader who is willing to trade what the first trader wants and at the same time wants what the first trader has.

Double Counting Counting a good more than once when computing GDP.

Dow Jones Industrial Average (DJIA) The most popular, widely cited indicator of day-to-day stock market activity. The DJIA is a weighted average of 30 widely traded stocks on the New York Stock Exchange.

(Downward-Sloping) Demand Curve The graphical representation of the law of demand.

Dumping The sale of goods abroad at a price below their cost and below the price charged in the domestic market.

E

Economic Growth Increases in Real GDP.

Economic Profit The difference between total revenue and total cost, including both explicit and implicit costs.

Economic Rent Payment in excess of opportunity costs.

Economics The science of scarcity; the science of how individuals and societies deal with the fact that wants are greater than the limited resources available to satisfy those wants.

Economies of Scale Exist when inputs are increased by some percentage and output increases by a greater percentage, causing unit costs to fall.

Efficiency Exists when marginal benefits equal marginal costs.

Efficiency Wage Models These models hold that it is sometimes in the best interest of business firms to pay their employees higher-than-equilibrium wage rates.

Elastic Demand The percentage change in quantity demanded is greater than the percentage change in price. Quantity demanded changes proportionately more than price changes.

Elasticity of Demand for Labor The percentage change in the quantity demanded of labor divided by the percentage change in the wage rate.

Employee Association An organization whose members belong to a particular profession.

Employment Rate The percentage of the civilian noninstitutional population that is employed: Employment rate = Number of employed persons / Civilian noninstitutional population.

Entrepreneurship The particular talent that some people have for organizing the resources of land, labor, and capital to produce goods, seek new business opportunities, and develop new ways of doing things.

Equation of Exchange An identity stating that the money supply times velocity must be equal to the price level times Real GDP.

Equilibrium Equilibrium means "at rest." Equilibrium in a market is the price-quantity combination from which there is no tendency for buyers or sellers to move away. Graphically, equilibrium is the intersection point of the supply and demand curves.

Equilibrium Price (Market-Clearing Price) The price at which quantity demanded of the good equals quantity supplied.

Equilibrium Quantity The quantity that corresponds to equilibrium price. The quantity at which the amount of the good that buyers are willing and able to buy equals the amount that sellers are willing and able to sell, and both equal the amount actually bought and sold.

Ex Ante Phrase that means "before," as in before a trade.

Ex Post Phrase that means "after," as in after a trade.

Excess Capacity Theorem States that a monopolistic competitor in equilibrium produces an output smaller than the one that would minimize its costs of production.

Excess Reserves Any reserves held beyond the required amount. The difference between (total) reserves and required reserves.

Exchange (Trade) The process of giving up one thing for something else.

Exchange Rate The price of one currency in terms of another currency.

Excludability A good is excludable if it is possible, or not prohibitively costly, to exclude someone from receiving the benefits of the good after it has been produced.

Expansionary Fiscal Policy Increases in government expenditures and/or decreases in taxes to achieve particular economic goals.

Expansionary Monetary Policy The Fed increases the money supply.

Expectations Effect The change in the interest rate due to a change in the expected inflation rate.

Explicit Cost A cost incurred when an actual (monetary) payment is made.

Exports Total foreign spending on domestic (U.S.) goods.

Externality A side effect of an action that affects the well-being of third parties.

F

Face Value   Dollar amount specified on a bond. The total amount the issuer of the bond will repay to the buyer of the bond.

Factor Price Taker   A firm that can buy all of a factor it wants at the equilibrium price. It faces a horizontal (flat, perfectly elastic) supply curve of factors.

Federal Funds Market   A market where banks lend reserves to one another, usually for short periods.

Federal Funds Rate   The interest rate in the federal funds market; the interest rate banks charge one another to borrow reserves.

Federal Open Market Committee (FOMC)   The 12-member policymaking group within the Fed. The committee has the authority to conduct open market operations.

Federal Reserve Notes   Paper money issued by the Fed.

Federal Reserve System (the Fed)   The central bank of the United States.

Final Good   A good in the hands of its final user.

Fine-tuning   The (usually frequent) use of monetary and fiscal policies to counteract even small undesirable movements in economic activity.

Fiscal Policy   Changes in government expenditures and/or taxes to achieve particular economic goals, such as low unemployment, stable prices, and economic growth.

Fixed Costs   Costs that do not vary with output; the costs associated with fixed inputs.

Fixed Exchange Rate System   The system where a nation's currency is set at a fixed rate relative to all other currencies, and central banks intervene in the foreign exchange market to maintain the fixed rate.

Fixed Input   An input whose quantity cannot be changed as output changes.

Fixed Investment   Business purchases of capital goods, such as machinery and factories, and purchases of new residential housing.

Flexible Exchange Rate System   The system whereby exchange rates are determined by the forces of supply and demand for a currency.

Foreign Exchange Market   The market in which currencies of different countries are exchanged.

Fractional Reserve Banking   A banking arrangement that allows banks to hold reserves equal to only a fraction of their deposit liabilities.

Free Rider   Anyone who receives the benefits of a good without paying for it.

Frictional Unemployment   Unemployment due to the natural "frictions" of the economy, which is caused by changing market conditions and is represented by qualified individuals with transferable skills who change jobs.

Friedman Natural Rate Theory   The idea that in the long run, unemployment is at its natural rate. Within the Phillips curve framework, the natural rate theory specifies that there is a long-run Phillips curve, which is vertical at the natural rate of unemployment.

Full Employment   The condition that exists when the unemployment rate is equal to the natural unemployment rate.

Futures Contract   Agreement to buy or sell a specific amount of something (commodity, currency, financial instrument) at a particular price on a stipulated future date.

G

Game Theory   A mathematical technique used to analyze the behavior of decision makers who try to reach an optimal position for themselves through game playing or the use of strategic behavior, are fully aware of the interactive nature of the process at hand, and anticipate the moves of other decision makers.

Gini Coefficient   A measure of the degree of inequality in the income distribution.

Globalization   A phenomenon by which economic agents in any given part of the world are more affected by events elsewhere in the world than before; the growing integration of the national economies of the world to the degree that we may be witnessing the emergence and operation of a single worldwide economy.

Good   Anything from which individuals receive utility or satisfaction.

Government Bureaucrat   An unelected person who works in a government bureau and is assigned a special task that relates to a law or program passed by the legislature.

Government Purchases   Federal, state, and local government purchases of goods and services and gross investment in highways, bridges, and so on.

Government Transfer Payments   Payments to persons that are not made in return for goods and services currently supplied.

Gross Domestic Product (GDP)   The total market value of all final goods and services produced annually within a country's borders.

H

Herfindahl Index   Measures the degree of concentration in an industry. It is equal to the sum of the squares of the market shares of each firm in the industry.

Horizontal Merger   A merger between firms that are selling similar products in the same market.

Human Capital   Education, development of skills, and anything else that is particular to the individual and increases his or her productivity.

I

Implicit Cost   A cost that represents the value of resources used in production for which no actual (monetary) payment is made.

Imports   Total domestic (U.S.) spending on foreign goods.

Income Effect   The change in the interest rate due to a change in Real GDP.

Income Elastic   The percentage change in quantity demanded of a good is greater than the percentage change in income.

Income Elasticity of Demand   Measures the responsiveness of quantity demanded to changes in income.

Income Inelastic   The percentage change in quantity demanded of a good is less than the percentage change in income.

Income Unit Elastic   The percentage change in quantity demanded of a good is equal to the percentage change in income.

Incomplete Crowding Out   The decrease in one or more components of private spending only partially offsets the increase in government spending.

Increasing-Cost Industry   An industry in which average total costs increase as output increases and decrease as output decreases when firms enter and exit the industry, respectively.

Independent   Two variables are independent if as one changes, the other does not.

Indifference Curve   Represents an indifference set. A curve that shows all the bundles of two goods that give an individual equal total utility.

Indifference Curve Map   Represents a number of indifference curves for a given individual with reference to two goods.

Indifference Set   Group of bundles of two goods that give an individual equal total utility.

Industrial Policy   A deliberate policy by which government "waters the green spots," or aids industries that are most likely to be successful in the world marketplace.

Industrial Union   A union whose membership is made up of individuals who work in the same firm or industry but do not all practice the same craft or trade.

Inelastic Demand   The percentage change in quantity demanded is less than the percentage change in price. Quantity demanded changes proportionately less than price changes.

Inferior Good   A good the demand for which falls (rises) as income rises (falls).

Inflation   An increase in the price level.

Inflation Targeting   This requires the Fed to try to keep the inflation rate near a predetermined level.

Inflationary Gap   The condition where the Real GDP the economy is producing is greater than the Natural Real GDP and the unemployment rate is less than the natural unemployment rate.

Initial Public Offering (IPO)   A company's first offering of stock to the public.

In-Kind Transfer Payments   Transfer payments, such as food stamps, medical assistance, and subsidized housing, that are made in a specific good or service rather than in cash.

Interest Rate Effect   The changes in household and business buying as the interest rate changes (which, in turn, is a reflection of a change in the demand for or supply of credit brought on by price level changes).

Intermediate Good   A good that is an input in the production of a final good.

Internalizing Externalities   An externality is internalized if the persons or group that generated the externality incorporate into their own private or internal cost-benefit calculations the external benefits (in the case of a positive externality) or the external costs (in the case of a negative externality) that third parties bear.

International Monetary Fund (IMF)   An international organization created to oversee the international monetary system. The IMF does not control the world's money supply, but it does hold currency reserves for member nations and make loans to central banks.

International Trade Effect   The change in foreign sector spending as the price level changes.

Interpersonal Utility Comparison   Comparing the utility one person receives from a good, service, or activity with the utility another person receives from the same good, service, or activity.

Inventory Investment   Changes in the stock of unsold goods.

Inversely Related   Two variables are inversely related if they change in opposite ways.

Investment   The sum of all purchases of newly produced capital goods, changes in business inventories, and purchases of new residential housing.

Investment Bank   Firm that acts as an intermediary between the company that issues the stock and the public that wishes to buy the stock.

J

J-Curve   The curve that shows a short-run worsening in net exports after a currency depreciation, followed later by an improvement.

K

Kinked Demand Curve Theory   A theory of oligopoly that assumes that if a single firm in the industry cuts prices, other firms will do likewise, but if it raises price, other firms will not follow suit. The theory predicts price stickiness or rigidity.

L

Labor   The physical and mental talents people contribute to the production process.

Labor Force Participation Rate   The percentage of the civilian noninstitutional population that is in the civilian labor force. Labor force participation rate = Civilian labor force/Civilian noninstitutional population.

Laffer Curve   The curve, named after Arthur Laffer, that shows the relationship between tax rates and tax revenues. According to the Laffer curve, as tax rates rise from zero, tax revenues rise, reach a maximum at some point, and then fall with further increases in tax rates.

Laissez-faire   A public policy of not interfering with market activities in the economy.

Land   All natural resources, such as minerals, forests, water, and unimproved land.

Law of Demand   As the price of a good rises, the quantity demanded of the good falls, and as the price of a good falls, the quantity demanded of the good rises, *ceteris paribus.*

Law of Diminishing Marginal Returns   As ever-larger amounts of a variable input are combined with fixed inputs, eventually, the marginal physical product of the variable input will decline.

Law of Diminishing Marginal Utility   The marginal utility gained by consuming equal successive units of a good will decline as the amount consumed increases.

Law of Increasing Opportunity Costs   As more of a good is produced, the opportunity costs of producing that good increase.

Law of Supply   As the price of a good rises, the quantity supplied of the good rises, and as the price of a good falls, the quantity supplied of the good falls, *ceteris paribus.*

Least-Cost Rule   Specifies the combination of factors that minimizes costs. This requires that the following condition be met: $MPP_1/P_1 = MPP_2/P_2 = \ldots = MPP_N/P_N$, where the numbers stand for the different factors.

Liquidity Effect   The change in the interest rate due to a change in the supply of loanable funds.

Liquidity Trap   The horizontal portion of the demand curve for money.

Loanable Funds   Funds that someone borrows and another person lends, for which the borrower pays an interest rate to the lender.

Lock-In Effect   Descriptive of the situation where a particular product or technology becomes settled upon as the standard and is difficult or impossible to dislodge as the standard.

Logrolling   The exchange of votes to gain support for legislation.

Long Run   A period of time in which all inputs in the production process can be varied (no inputs are fixed).

Long-Run Aggregate Supply (LRAS) Curve   The *LRAS* curve is a vertical line at the level of Natural Real GDP. It represents the output the economy produces when wages and prices have adjusted to their (final) equilibrium levels and neither producers nor workers have any relevant misperceptions.

Long-Run Average Total Cost (LRATC) Curve   A curve that shows the lowest (unit) cost at which the firm can produce any given level of output.

Long-Run Competitive Equilibrium   The condition where $P = MC = SRATC = LRATC$. There are zero economic profits, firms are producing the quantity of output at which price is equal to marginal cost, and no firm has an incentive to change its plant size.

Long-Run Equilibrium   The condition that exists in the economy when wages and prices have adjusted to their (final) equilibrium levels and neither producers nor workers have any relevant misperceptions. Graphically, long-run equilibrium occurs at the intersection of the *AD* and *LRAS* curves.

Long-Run (Industry) Supply (LRS) Curve   Graphic representation of the quantities of output that the industry is prepared to supply at different prices after the entry and exit of firms are completed.

Lorenz Curve   A graph of the income distribution. It expresses the relationship between cumulative percentage of households and cumulative percentage of income.

M

M1   Includes currency held outside banks + checkable deposits + traveler's checks.

M2   Includes M1 + savings deposits (including money market deposit accounts) + small-denomination time deposits + money market mutual funds (retail).

Macroeconomics   The branch of economics that deals with human behavior and choices as they relate to highly aggregate markets (e.g., the goods and services market) or the entire economy.

Managed Float   A managed flexible exchange rate system, under which nations now and then intervene to adjust their official reserve holdings to moderate major swings in exchange rates.

Managerial Coordination   The process in which managers direct employees to perform certain tasks.

Marginal Benefits   Additional benefits. The benefits connected to consuming an additional unit of a good or undertaking one more unit of an activity.

Marginal Cost (MC)   The change in total cost that results from a change in output: $MC = \Delta TC/\Delta Q$.

Marginal Costs   Additional costs. The costs connected to consuming an additional unit of a good or undertaking one more unit of an activity.

Marginal Factor Cost (MFC)   The additional cost incurred by employing an additional factor unit.

Marginal (Income) Tax Rate   The change in a person's tax payment divided by the change in the person's taxable income: ΔTax payment/ΔTaxable income.

Marginal Physical Product (MPP)   The change in output that results from changing the variable input by one unit, holding all other inputs fixed.

Marginal Productivity Theory   States that firms in competitive or perfect product and factor markets pay their factors their marginal revenue products.

Marginal Propensity to Consume (MPC)   The ratio of the change in consumption to the change in disposable income: $MPC = \Delta C/\Delta Y_d$.

Marginal Propensity to Save (MPS)   The ratio of the change in saving to the change in disposable income: $MPS = \Delta S/\Delta Y_d$.

Marginal Rate of Substitution   The amount of one good an individual is willing to give up to obtain an additional unit of another good and maintain equal total utility.

Marginal Revenue (MR)   The change in total revenue that results from selling one additional unit of output.

Marginal Revenue Product (MRP)   The additional revenue generated by employing an additional factor unit.

Marginal Social Benefits (MSB)   The sum of marginal private benefits (*MPB*) and marginal external benefits (*MEB*): $MSB = MPB + MEB$.

Marginal Social Costs (MSC)   The sum of marginal private costs (*MPC*) and marginal external costs (*MEC*): $MSC = MPC + MEC$.

Marginal Utility   The additional utility a person receives from consuming an additional unit of a particular good.

Market   Any place people come together to trade.

Market Coordination   The process in which individuals perform tasks, such as producing certain quantities of goods, based on changes in market forces, such as supply, demand, and price.

Market Failure   A situation in which the market does not provide the ideal or optimal amount of a particular good.

Market Structure   The particular environment of a firm, the characteristics of which influence the firm's pricing and output decisions.

Median Voter Model   Suggests that candidates in a two-person political race will move toward matching the preferences of the median voter (i.e., the person whose preferences are at the center, or in the middle, of the political spectrum).

Medium of Exchange   Anything that is generally acceptable in exchange for goods and services. A function of money.

Merchandise Trade Balance The difference between the value of merchandise exports and the value of merchandise imports.

Merchandise Trade Deficit The situation where the value of merchandise exports is less than the value of merchandise imports.

Merchandise Trade Surplus The situation where the value of merchandise exports is greater than the value of merchandise imports.

Microeconomics The branch of economics that deals with human behavior and choices as they relate to relatively small units—an individual, a firm, an industry, a single market.

Minimum Efficient Scale The lowest output level at which average total costs are minimized.

Monetary Policy Changes in the money supply, or the rate of growth of the money supply, to achieve particular macroeconomic goals.

Monetary Wealth The value of a person's monetary assets. Wealth, as distinguished from monetary wealth, refers to the value of all assets owned, both monetary and nonmonetary. In short, a person's wealth equals his or her monetary wealth (e.g., $1,000 cash) plus nonmonetary wealth (e.g., a car or a house).

Money Any good that is widely accepted for purposes of exchange and in the repayment of debt.

Money Market Deposit Account An interest-earning account at a bank or thrift institution. Usually, a minimum balance is required for an MMDA. Most MMDAs offer limited check-writing privileges.

Money Market Mutual Fund An interest-earning account at a mutual fund company. Usually, a minimum balance is required for an MMMF account. Most MMMF accounts offer limited check-writing privileges. Only retail MMMFs are part of M2.

Monitor Person in a business firm who coordinates team production and reduces shirking.

Monopolistic Competition A theory of market structure based on three assumptions: many sellers and buyers, firms producing and selling slightly differentiated products, and easy entry and exit.

Monopoly A theory of market structure based on three assumptions: There is one seller, it sells a product for which no close substitutes exist, and there are extremely high barriers to entry.

Monopsony A single buyer in a factor market.

Moral Hazard Exists when one party to a transaction changes his or her behavior in a way that is hidden from and costly to the other party.

Multiplier The number that is multiplied by the change in autonomous spending to obtain the overall change in total spending. The multiplier (m) is equal to $1/(1 - MPC)$. If the economy is operating below Natural Real GDP, then the multiplier turns out to be the number that is multiplied by the change in autonomous spending to obtain the change in Real GDP.

N

National Income Total income earned by U.S. citizens and businesses, no matter where they reside or are located. National income is the sum of the payments to resources (land, labor, capital, and entrepreneurship). National income = compensation of employees + proprietors' income + corporate profits + rental income of persons + net interest.

Natural Monopoly The condition where economies of scale are so pronounced that only one firm can survive.

Natural Real GDP The Real GDP that is produced at the natural unemployment rate. The Real GDP that is produced when the economy is in long-run equilibrium.

Natural Unemployment Unemployment caused by frictional and structural factors in the economy. Natural unemployment rate = Frictional unemployment rate + Structural unemployment rate.

Negative Externality Exists when a person's or group's actions cause a cost (adverse side effect) to be felt by others.

Net Domestic Product (NDP) GDP minus the capital consumption allowance.

Net Exports Exports minus imports.

Network Good A good whose value increases as the expected number of units sold increases.

Neutral Good A good the demand for which does not change as income rises or falls.

Nominal Income The current-dollar amount of a person's income.

Nominal Interest Rate The interest rate actually charged (or paid) in the market; the market interest rate. The nominal interest rate = Real interest rate + Expected inflation rate.

Nonactivists Persons who argue against the deliberate use of discretionary fiscal and monetary policies. They believe in a permanent, stable, rule-oriented monetary and fiscal framework.

Nonexcludability A good is nonexcludable if it is impossible, or prohibitively costly, to exclude someone from receiving the benefits of the good after it has been produced.

Nonrivalrous in Consumption A good is nonrivalrous in consumption if its consumption by one person does not reduce its consumption by others.

Normal Good A good the demand for which rises (falls) as income rises (falls).

Normal Profit Zero economic profit. A firm that earns normal profit is earning revenue equal to its total costs (explicit plus implicit costs). This is the level of profit necessary to keep resources employed in that particular firm.

Normative Economics The study of "what should be" in economic matters.

O

Offshoring Work done for a company by persons other than the original company's employees in a country other than the one in which the company is located.

Oligopoly A theory of market structure based on three assumptions: few sellers and many buyers, firms producing either homogeneous or differentiated products, and significant barriers to entry.

One-Shot Inflation A one-time increase in the price level. An increase in the price level that does not continue.

Open Economy An economy that trades goods and services with other countries.

Open Market Operations The buying and selling of government securities by the Fed.

Open Market Purchase   The buying of government securities by the Fed.

Open Market Sale   The selling of government securities by the Fed.

Opportunity Cost   The most highly valued opportunity or alternative forfeited when a choice is made.

Optimal Currency Area   A geographic area in which exchange rates can be fixed or a common currency used without sacrificing domestic economic goals, such as low unemployment.

Option   Contract that gives the owner the right, but not the obligation, to buy or sell shares of a stock at a specified price on or before a specified date.

Overvaluation   A currency is overvalued if its price in terms of other currencies is above the equilibrium price.

Own Price   The price of a good. For example, if the price of oranges is $1, this is (its) own price.

P

Per Capita Real Economic Growth An increase from one period to the next in per capita Real GDP, which is Real GDP divided by population.

Perfect Competition   A theory of market structure based on four assumptions: There are many sellers and buyers, sellers sell a homogeneous good, buyers and sellers have all relevant information, and there is easy entry and exit from the market.

Perfect Price Discrimination   Occurs when the seller charges the highest price each consumer would be willing to pay for the product rather than go without it.

Perfectly Elastic Demand   A small percentage change in price causes an extremely large percentage change in quantity demanded (from buying all to buying nothing).

Perfectly Inelastic Demand   Quantity demanded does not change as price changes.

Personal Income   The amount of income that individuals actually receive. It is equal to national income minus undistributed corporate profits, social insurance taxes, and corporate profits taxes, plus transfer payments.

Phillips Curve   A curve that originally showed the relationship between wage inflation and unemployment. Now it more often shows the relationship between price inflation and unemployment.

Policy Ineffectiveness Proposition (PIP)   If (1) a policy change is correctly anticipated, (2) individuals form their expectations rationally, and (3) wages and prices are flexible, then neither fiscal policy nor monetary policy is effective at meeting macroeconomic goals.

Positive Economics   The study of "what is" in economic matters.

Positive Externality   Exists when a person's or group's actions cause a benefit (beneficial side effect) to be felt by others.

Positive Rate of Time Preference Preference for earlier availability of goods over later availability of goods.

Poverty Income Threshold (Poverty Line)   Income level below which people are considered to be living in poverty.

Present Value   The current worth of some future dollar amount of income or receipts.

Price Ceiling   A government-mandated maximum price above which legal trades cannot be made.

Price Discrimination   Occurs when the seller charges different prices for the product it sells and the price differences do not reflect cost differences.

Price Elasticity of Demand   A measure of the responsiveness of quantity demanded to changes in price.

Price Elasticity of Supply   Measures the responsiveness of quantity supplied to changes in price.

Price Floor   A government-mandated minimum price below which legal trades cannot be made.

Price Index   A measure of the price level.

Price Leadership Theory   In this theory of oligopoly, the dominant firm in the industry determines price, and all other firms take their price as given.

Price Level   A weighted average of the prices of all good and services.

Price Searcher   A seller that has the ability to control to some degree the price of the product it sells.

Price Support   A government-mandated minimum price for agricultural products; an example of a price floor.

Price Taker   A seller that does not have the ability to control the price of the product it sells; it takes the price determined in the market.

Price-Level Effect   The change in the interest rate due to a change in the price level.

Producers' (Sellers') Surplus (PS) The difference between the price sellers receive for a good and the minimum or lowest price for which they would have sold the good. $PS = $ Price received $-$ Minimum selling price.

Production Possibilities Frontier (PPF)   Represents the possible combinations of the two goods that can be produced in a certain period of time under the conditions of a given state of technology and fully employed resources.

(Production) Subsidy   A monetary payment by government to a producer of a good or service.

Productive Efficiency   The condition where the maximum output is produced with given resources and technology; The situation that exists when a firm produces its output at the lowest possible per-unit cost (lowest ATC).

Productive Inefficiency   The condition where less than the maximum output is produced with given resources and technology. Productive inefficiency implies that more of one good can be produced without any less of another good being produced.

Profit   The difference between total revenue and total cost.

Profit-Maximization Rule   Profit is maximized by producing the quantity of output at which $MR = MC$.

Progressive Income Tax   An income tax system in which one's tax rate rises as one's taxable income rises (up to some point).

Proportional Income Tax   An income tax system in which one's tax rate is the same no matter what one's taxable income is.

Public Choice   The branch of economics that deals with the application of economic principles and tools to public sector decision making.

Public Choice Theory of Regulation Holds that regulators are seeking to do, and will do through regulation, what is in their best interest (specifically to enhance their power and the size and budget of their regulatory agencies).

Public Debt The total amount the federal government owes its creditors.

Public Employee Union A union whose membership is made up of individuals who work for the local, state, or federal government.

Public Franchise A right granted to a firm by government that permits the firm to provide a particular good or service and excludes all others from doing the same.

Public Good A good the consumption of which by one person does not reduce the consumption by another person—that is, a public good is characterized by nonrivalry in consumption. There are both excludable and nonexcludable public goods. An excludable public good is a good that while nonrivalrous in consumption can be denied to a person who does not pay for it. A nonexcludable public good is a good that is nonrivalrous in consumption and that cannot be denied to a person who does not pay for it.

Public Interest Theory of Regulation Holds that regulators are seeking to do, and will do through regulation, what is in the best interest of the public or society at large.

Purchasing Power The quantity of goods and services that can be purchased with a unit of money. Purchasing power and the price level are inversely related: As the price level goes up (down), purchasing power goes down (up).

Purchasing Power Parity (PPP) Theory States that exchange rates between any two currencies will adjust to reflect changes in the relative price levels of the two countries.

Pure Economic Rent A category of economic rent where the payment is to a factor that is in fixed supply, implying that it has zero opportunity costs.

Q

Quota A legal limit on the amount of a good that may be imported.

R

Rational Expectations Expectations that individuals form based on past experience and also on their predictions about the effects of present and future policy actions and events.

Rational Ignorance The state of not acquiring information because the costs of acquiring the information are greater than the benefits.

Rationing Device A means for deciding who gets what of available resources and goods.

Real Balance Effect The change in the purchasing power of dollar-denominated assets that results from a change in the price level.

Real GDP The value of the entire output produced annually within a country's borders, adjusted for price changes.

Real Income Nominal income adjusted for price changes.

Real Interest Rate The nominal interest rate minus the expected inflation rate. When the expected inflation rate is zero, the real interest rate equals the nominal interest rate.

Recessionary Gap The condition where the Real GDP the economy is producing is less than the Natural Real GDP and the unemployment rate is greater than the natural unemployment rate.

Regressive Income Tax An income tax system in which one's tax rate declines as one's taxable income rises.

Regulatory Lag The time period between when a natural monopoly's costs change and when the regulatory agency adjusts prices for the natural monopoly.

Relative Price The price of a good in terms of another good.

Rent Seeking Actions of individuals and groups who spend resources to influence public policy in the hope of redistributing (transferring) income to themselves from others.

Required Reserve Ratio (r) A percentage of each dollar deposited that must be held on reserve (at the Fed or in the bank's vault).

Required Reserves The minimum amount of reserves a bank must hold against its checkable deposits as mandated by the Fed.

Reserve Requirement The rule that specifies the amount of reserves a bank must hold to back up deposits.

Reserves The sum of bank deposits at the Fed and vault cash.

Residual claimant Persons who share in the profits of a business firm.

Resource Allocative Efficiency The situation that exists when firms produce the quantity of output at which price equals marginal cost: $P = MC$.

Revaluation A government act that changes the exchange rate by raising the official price of a currency.

Rivalrous in Consumption A good is rivalrous in consumption if its consumption by one person reduces its consumption by others.

Roundabout Method of Production The production of capital goods that enhance productive capabilities to ultimately bring about increased consumption.

S

Savings Deposit An interest-earning account at a commercial bank or thrift institution. Normally, checks cannot be written on savings deposits, and the funds in a savings deposit can be withdrawn (at any time) without a penalty payment.

Say's Law Supply creates its own demand. Production creates demand sufficient to purchase all goods and services produced.

Scarcity The condition in which our wants are greater than the limited resources available to satisfy those wants.

Screening The process used by employers to increase the probability of choosing "good" employees based on certain criteria.

Second-Degree Price Discrimination Occurs when the seller charges a uniform price per unit for one specific quantity, a lower price for an additional quantity, and so on.

Shirking The behavior of a worker who is putting forth less than the agreed-to effort.

Short Run A period of time in which some inputs in the production process are fixed.

Short-Run Aggregate Supply (SRAS) Curve A curve that shows the quantity supplied of all goods and services (Real GDP) at different price levels, *ceteris paribus*.

Short-Run Equilibrium The condition that exists in the economy when the quantity demanded of Real GDP equals the (short-run) quantity supplied of Real GDP. This condition is met where the aggregate demand curve intersects the short-run aggregate supply curve.

Short-Run (Firm) Supply Curve The portion of the firm's marginal cost curve that lies above the average variable cost curve.

Short-Run Market (Industry) Supply Curve The horizontal "addition" of all existing firms' short-run supply curves.

Shortage (Excess Demand) A condition in which quantity demanded is greater than quantity supplied. Shortages occur only at prices below equilibrium price.

Simple Deposit Multiplier The reciprocal of the required reserve ratio, $1/r$.

Simple Quantity Theory of Money The theory that assumes that velocity (V) and Real GDP (Q) are constant and predicts that changes in the money supply (M) lead to strictly proportional changes in the price level (P).

Slope The ratio of the change in the variable on the vertical axis to the change in the variable on the horizontal axis.

Socially Optimal Amount (Output) An amount that takes into account and adjusts for all benefits (external and private) and all costs (external and private). The socially optimal amount is the amount at which $MSB = MSC$. Sometimes, the socially optimal amount is referred to as the efficient amount.

Special Drawing Right (SDR) An international money, created by the IMF, in the form of bookkeeping entries; like gold and currencies, that can be used by nations to settle international accounts.

Special Interest Groups Subsets of the general population that hold (usually) intense preferences for or against a particular government service, activity, or policy. Often, special interest groups gain from public policies that may not be in accord with the interests of the general public.

Stagflation The simultaneous occurrence of high rates of inflation and unemployment.

Stock A claim on the assets of a corporation that gives the purchaser a share of the corporation.

Store of Value The ability of an item to hold value over time. A function of money.

Strike The situation in which union employees refuse to work at a certain wage or under certain conditions.

Structural Deficit The part of the budget deficit that would exist even if the economy were operating at full employment.

Structural Unemployment Unemployment due to structural changes in the economy that eliminate some jobs and create other jobs for which the unemployed are unqualified.

Substitutes Two goods that satisfy similar needs or desires. If two goods are substitutes, the demand for one rises as the price of the other rises (or the demand for one falls as the price of the other falls).

Sunk Cost A cost incurred in the past that cannot be changed by current decisions and therefore cannot be recovered.

Supply The willingness and ability of sellers to produce and offer to sell different quantities of a good at different prices during a specific time period.

Supply Schedule The numerical tabulation of the quantity supplied of a good at different prices. A supply schedule is the numerical representation of the law of supply.

Surplus (Excess Supply) A condition in which quantity supplied is greater than quantity demanded. Surpluses occur only at prices above equilibrium price.

T

T-Account A simplified balance sheet that shows the changes in a bank's assets and liabilities.

Target Price A guaranteed price; if the market price is below the target price, the farmer receives a deficiency payment equal to the difference between the market price and the target price.

Tariff A tax on imports

Tax Base When referring to income taxes, the total amount of taxable income. Tax revenue = Tax base × (average) Tax rate.

Technology The body of skills and knowledge concerning the use of resources in production. An advance in technology commonly refers to the ability to produce more output with a fixed amount of resources or the ability to produce the same output with fewer resources.

Terms of Trade How much of one thing is given up for how much of something else.

Theory An abstract representation of the real world designed with the intent to better understand the world.

Third-Degree Price Discrimination Occurs when the seller charges different prices in different markets or charges a different price to different segments of the buying population.

Tie-in Sale A sale whereby one good can be purchased only if another good is also purchased.

Time Deposit An interest-earning deposit with a specified maturity date. Time deposits are subject to penalties for early withdrawal. Small-denomination time deposits are deposits of less than $100,000.

Total Cost (TC) The sum of fixed costs and variable costs.

Total Revenue (TR) Price times quantity sold.

Total Surplus (TS) The sum of consumers' surplus and producers' surplus. $TS = CS + PS$

Total Utility The total satisfaction a person receives from consuming a particular quantity of a good.

Transaction Costs The costs associated with the time and effort needed to search out, negotiate, and consummate an exchange.

Transfer Payment A payment to a person that is not made in return for goods and services currently supplied.

Transitivity The principle whereby if A is preferred to B, and B is preferred to C, then A is preferred to C.

Transmission Mechanism The routes, or channels, that ripple effects created in the money market travel to affect the goods and services market (represented by the aggregate demand and aggregate supply curves in the *AD-AS* framework).

Trust A combination of firms that come together to act as a monopolist.

Undervaluation A currency is undervalued if its price in terms of other currencies is below the equilibrium price.

Unemployment Rate The percentage of the civilian force that is unemployed: Unemployment rate = Number of unemployed persons/Civilian labor force.

Union Shop An organization in which a worker is not required to be a member of the union to be hired but must become a member within a certain period of time after being employed.

Unit Elastic Demand The percentage change in quantity demanded is equal to the percentage change in price. Quantity demanded changes proportionately to price changes.

Unit of Account A common measure in which relative values are expressed. A function of money.

(Upward–Sloping) Supply Curve The graphical representation of the law of supply.

U.S. Treasury Securities Bonds and bondlike securities issued by the U.S. Treasury when it borrows.

Util An artificial construct used to measure utility.

Utility The satisfaction one receives from a good.

Value Added The dollar value contributed to a final good at each stage of production.

Value Marginal Product (VMP) The price of the good multiplied by the marginal physical product of the factor: $VMP = P \times MPP$.

Variable Costs Costs that vary with output; the costs associated with variable inputs.

Variable Input An input whose quantity can be changed as output changes.

Veil of Ignorance The imaginary veil or curtain behind which a person does not know his or her position in the income distribution.

Velocity The average number of times a dollar is spent to buy final goods and services in a year.

Vertical Merger A merger between companies in the same industry but at different stages of the production process.

"Voluntary" Export Restraint (VER) An agreement between two countries in which the exporting country "voluntarily" agrees to limit its exports to the importing country.

Wage Discrimination The situation that exists when individuals of equal ability and productivity (as measured by their contribution to output) are paid different wage rates.

Wealth The value of all assets owned, both monetary and nonmonetary.

X-Inefficiency The increase in costs and organizational slack in a monopoly resulting from the lack of competitive pressure to push costs down to their lowest possible level.

Y

Yield Equal to the annual coupon payment divided by the price paid for the bond.

A

multiplier and, 205
 Natural Real GDP, 171, 181–182
real income, 117
real interest rate, 292–293, 596–597, 687
real rents, 602
recession
 expectations theory and, 330–332
 Real GDP and, 147
recessionary gap, 114, 181
 fiscal policy and, 228
 Keynes on, 208–209, 214–216
 labor market and, 183
 monetary policy and, 306–308
 self-regulating economy and, 185–186
recording industry, supply and demand, 85–86
recovery, of business cycle, 147
reentrants, 123
regressive income tax, 224
regulation. *see also* antitrust issues
 airline industry example, 525
 auction houses example, 526
 capture theory of, 523
 of competitive industries, 523
 costs and benefits of, 524
 deregulation, 525–526
 externalities and, 620–621
 Irish pubs example, 508, 527
 natural monopoly and, 519–522
 public choice theory of, 523
 public interest theory of, 523
 unintended effects of, 524
regulatory lag, 522
"Relation Between Unemployment and the Rate of
 Change of Money Wages in the United Kingdom,
 1861—1957, The" (Phillips), 320
relative prices, 53
religion
 competition and, 439
 economic growth and, 347
 redistribution of income and, 588
rent, 592, 599–603, 607–608. *see also* interest; profit
 economic rent, 599–603
 land, supply curve, 601
 land and grains, 599–601
 rent seeking, 471–472, 647–650
 supply and demand, 91–92
rental income (of persons), 141
required reserve ratio, 250, 267
required reserves, 250
reserve requirement, 267

reserves, 250. *see also* Federal Reserve System (the Fed)
residual claimant, 407
resource allocative efficiency, 442
restaurant noise volume, supply and demand, 88–89
restaurant tipping practice, 712
revaluation, 690–692
Ricardo, David, 354, 599–601
rich population, 573–574. *see also* income distribution
rivalrous in consumption, 624
Rivlin, Alice, 27
Robinson-Patman Act (1936), 510
Romer, Christina, 169
Romer, Paul, 350–352
roundabout method of production, 594
Royal Economic Society, 29
royalty, rent seeking, 648
rules-based monetary policy, 309–312

S

salaries
 baseball salaries and economic rent, 601–602
 converting dollars from one year to another, 111, 118,
 119, 128
 of economists, 30
 of mathematicians, 127
 perfect competition and, 435, 457
 of professors, 94–96
 of U.S. presidents, 118
Samuelson, Paul, 320–321
"sandwich generation," 738
"Santa Claus rally," 738
Sargent, Thomas, 326
saving-domestic-jobs argument, trade restrictions and, 669
savings
 consumption and, 203
 real estate and, 208
savings deposit, 247
Say's Law, 177, 178, 180, 192, 196–198
scarcity, 2–5
 defined, 2
 PPF and, 35–37
Scrabble (game), 169
screening, 549
second-degree price discrimination, 473
Seinfeld, 44
self-regulating-economic instability category, 114
self-regulating economy, 177–194
 classical economics and, 178–181
 defined, 185